S0-CAR-523

# *THE TRADITION OF PHILOSOPHY*

*Harrison Hall*
*University of Delaware*

*Norman E. Bowie*
*University of Delaware*

Wadsworth Publishing Company
Belmont, California
A Division of Wadsworth, Inc.

*Philosophy Editor:* Kenneth King
*Production Editor:* Jane Townsend
*Managing Designer:* MaryEllen Podgorski
*Text and Cover Designer:* Adriane Bosworth
*Print Buyer:* Barbara Britton
*Copy Editor:* Toni Haskell



Printed in the United States of America
1 2 3 4 5 6 7 8 9 10---90 89 88 87 86

ISBN 0-534-05322-X

Library of Congress Cataloging-in-Publication Data
Main entry under title:

The Tradition of philosophy.

1. Philosophy--Introductions. 2. Philosophy--Addresses, essays, lectures. I. Hall, Harrison, 1945– . II. Bowie, Norman E., 1942–
BD21.T67 1986 100 85-17880
ISBN 0-534-05322-X

For Gerardo and Priscilla Joffe

# CONTENTS

# PREFACE

Editors of introduction to philosophy anthologies have not had an easy time in the last twenty-five years. Instructors would like to introduce bright, eager, well-trained young men and women to the traditional problems of philosophy through a combination of the best classical and contemporary sources. But in the 1960s and the early 1970s, nearly every instructor was pressured to prove that philosophy was "relevant." The traditional texts wouldn't do. Learned discussions of the analytic-synthetic distinction, for example, seemed dry and lifeless to students actively engaged in civil rights, anti-war, and other movements. Hence a new generation of introductory texts arose that attempted to speak to the spirit of the times. No sooner had the textbook market responded than student attitudes shifted again. Suddenly students were more interested in jobs than in protest. However, a return to the standard introductory texts of earlier years was impossible. Vocation-oriented students again raised the relevancy issue, albeit in a new way. Undergraduates of the late 1970s and 1980s seemed either unwilling or unable to understand and appreciate the best classical and contemporary philosophers. Yet instructors were understandably reluctant to "water down" the discipline being introduced. The ideal introductory text needed to be accessible to undergraduates without excessively diluting the subject. This was our goal in organizing, editing, and introducing the material in this text. We believe that the average introductory student, although unlikely to fully appreciate a typical unedited professional journal article, can be introduced to the best of philosophy and philosophers in an intellectually challenging way.

If students are to read original works, classical and contemporary texts have to be edited—carefully and extensively. Antiquated expressions, Latin phrases, the host of qualifications and references to other philosophers which typically characterize articles taken from professional journals—all need to go, and we have edited them out. In addition, we have provided extensive introductory material, including an entire introductory part and introductions to each subsection and individual selection in the text. Each part and subsection introduction provides an overview of the topic under discussion. We lay out a number of the relevant philosophical issues and questions and provide a brief explanation of some of the more important attempts to grapple with those issues and respond to those questions. But all of our remarks are introductory in nature. We have tried to provide some of the information and motivation that students will need as they approach these readings for the first time. Our aim has been to help the student *begin* the process of understanding by indicating what the general problem areas are and how specific selections fit into those areas. We have not tried to provide a substitute for the kind of lecture material that will enable students' understanding to advance beyond the beginning stages. We leave that task entirely to the instructor in keeping with our firm conviction that there is *no* substitute for competent instruction. Similarly, none of the introductions to specific selections contains even a complete summary of the essay it introduces. We have not tried to provide students with an alternative to reading the original works collected in this text. What we have tried to furnish is the kind of introductory material that will make it possible for students to read the selection with some understanding and appreciation. Real understanding will require reading and frequently re-reading of the selections in addition to careful attention to the material presented in class.

The prevalent myth is that introductory courses and texts must begin with ethics, political philosophy, or philosophy of religion in order to engage student interest. Our experience is that an introductory course that begins this way often suffers pedagogically as a result. Philosophy is a new discipline for the vast majority of students—one of few or perhaps the only entirely new subject they encounter in college. To start with ethics, contemporary moral problems, or an examination of religious beliefs can give them a false sense that they already know what philosophy is and what counts as a philosophical question or view. Confusion, disillusion and frustration follow when students reach the sections of course and text devoted to epistemology and philosophy of mind. Although the order of topics in a text certainly does not *dictate* the order followed in the course, we have structured this book in accordance with our most successful teaching experiences introducing large numbers of students to philosophy. The first part of the book introduces the discipline as a whole rather than introducing a single area of its application in which students are very *non-philosophically* interested, and the next parts of the text grapple with those central philosophical issues with which introductory students are less familiar. The benefits are as follows. First, the general level of natural interest in the topics rises as the course progresses. Second, and more important, student response to later parts dealing with morality, politics, and religion is much more sophisticated. Students encounter philosophical theories of value and obligation after they have had a chance to grasp the nature of philosophical theories as such and after they have developed the ability to recognize and set aside a host of interesting but philosophically irrelevant considerations. And they examine religious belief and experience having already had substantial practice in the philosophical assessment and criticism of beliefs, belief systems, and the relation of experience to belief and knowledge in more mundane contexts.

Within each part and subsection we have arranged the selections in a natural order or progression and have explained that arrangement in our introductory remarks. No section of the text consists of just a random collection of readings, and students should not find themselves at a loss to know why a selection is included or why it is located in a particular place in the section. Within each division of the readings we have taken up problems and solutions in either their historical order of development or in order of increasing complexity and difficulty, as appropriate. Both within each of its parts and in the text as a whole, we have attempted to tell a coherent story about the nature of the philosophic enterprise, and to fit the very best historical and contemporary essays into that story in a way that addresses the real needs of students in introductory courses. If we have achieved even partial success in this endeavor our time will not have been wasted.

*Acknowledgments*

In preparing this book we have been assisted by a host of people who deserve our thanks. They include Ken King, Jane Townsend, and MaryEllen Podgorski, all of Wadsworth Publishing Company; Toni Haskell, copy editor; and Mary Imperatore, secretary of the philosophy department at the University of Delaware. In addition, we thank the publisher's reviewers: James W. Cox, West Georgia College; Charles E. Hornbeck, Keene State University; Virginia H. Ringer, California State University, Long Beach; Stewart Shapiro, Ohio State University at Newark; Steven A. Smith, Claremont McKenna College; Craig Staudenbauer, Michigan State University; George L. Stengren, Central Michigan University; William F. Williamson, William Rainey Harper College; and especially Kenneth C. Kennard, Illinois State University, for his lengthy review and many helpful comments. Special thanks go to Sandy Manno, secretary of the Center for the Study of Values at the University of Delaware, who assisted with permissions, proofreading, editing, and manuscript preparation, and who, in the course of keeping to a difficult schedule, has consistently shown grace under pressure.

# *THE TRADITION OF PHILOSOPHY*

# 1

# SCOPE AND METHOD

Philosophy is a unique discipline, importantly different from virtually all others with which you are familiar. And that uniqueness is not easy to identify and explain. The question "What is philosophy?" is a natural question for you to raise at this point in your education, whereas "What is biology?" or "psychology?" or "sociology?" may not be. Part of the reason is that you probably know the answers to most of the latter questions, but not the former. And part of the reason is that the question about the nature of philosophy cannot be answered in the same way that the others can. Answers to each of the others can be given by identifying the subject matter of the discipline in question. Biology is the study of living organisms, psychology the study of the mind, sociology the study of social institutions and relations, and so on for other fields of study. In one sense, philosophy has no such subject matter. In another sense it seems to have every possible subject matter, intruding in one way or another in the domain of every other discipline. There is philosophy of biology, philosophy of psychology, philosophy of social science, and so on. The point is that philosophy must be defined not in terms of its subject matter but in terms of its unique approach or method. And the task of doing that, especially before you have encountered any examples of philosophical thinking, is a difficult one. Some introductory texts raise this question only at the end. And most of us who have taught introductory courses have felt the temptation to put the question off until students have read a number of philosophical essays, and then look back and just say that that's what philosophy is, and other things like that.

But you should have an answer to the question now, since your successful introduction to the discipline may well depend on your having some idea of what to look for as you begin your reading of the following selections. We will suggest two answers to the question "What is philosophy?" which, although they tend to come to the same thing, may make it easier for you to see the point. One way to characterize the activity of philosophy is to think of it as the attempt to analyze or understand our concepts or ideas. Philosophy involves conceptual analysis. In each of the other disciplines, and in the course of daily life as well, we use concepts all the time. But they are, in a sense, taken for granted. We pay attention to what we are thinking about, not to the concepts employed in our thinking. As philosophers we stand back from that activity and examine the concepts themselves rather than the things to which we apply them. So, for example, in daily life we make moral judgments or decisions, think about what we ought or ought not to do, evaluate others or ourselves as moral agents. In moral philosophy we try to reach an understanding of the concepts used and, hence, a deeper or clearer understanding of the activity of using them, by raising questions about the meaning of the concepts employed. What is it for something to be morally right or obligatory? What do we mean by rights or duties? Similarly, in each of the empirical sciences we gather evidence and form theories about the behavior of the subject matter under investigation. In philosophy of science we examine the concepts used in that enterprise. What is evidence? What is the relation between evidence and theory? Is that relation the same in the natural and social sciences? If not, is there anything about our conceptions of natural and social reality that will explain or illuminate the differences?

Another way to identify philosophy is in terms of the level of thinking involved. Philosophy has been characterized as "thinking about thinking" or second-order thought. In the other disciplines we think about living organisms, social institutions, human minds, and any number of other things. Philosophy of these disciplines doesn't really duplicate that effort. It thinks about the thinking involved in the other disciplines—or the thinking involved in daily life and its ordinary activities. The thinking of the other disciplines and of daily life is, in that sense, first-order or first-level thinking, aimed at the appropriate subject matter. Philosophy involves a kind of second-order or second-level thinking, aimed not at the object of the first-level thought but at the thinking itself. For example, in daily life we frequently think that it is wrong to do something. In philosophical thinking we think about what is involved in, or required by, thinking that something is morally wrong. Since such thinking requires the utilization of concepts, these two ways of identifying the method of philosophy really come to much the same thing.

One last preview of what is involved in philosophy is suggested by a tendency that every small child exhibits at some point and that philosophers are unique in being unable to outgrow. A child can ask "Why?" beyond the limit of almost any parent's patience. "Why can't I do that?" "Because I said you couldn't." "Why?" "Because I don't want you to do it." "Why?" "Because it's wrong." "Why?" . . . Now curiosity is the force behind the pursuit of knowledge in every area, and no one should outgrow it completely. But the above series of "why's" equals or exceeds the normal adult quota of that commodity. However, the last "Why?" above is the first one of real interest to the philosopher. It is the only one of the series that requires an answer in terms of some moral principle or theory that can provide at least a partial understanding of what the concept "morally wrong" means. The philosopher is the last *adult* to stop asking "Why?"

To say that the method of philosophy is conceptual analysis, the attempt to provide an understanding of important practical and theoretical concepts, may be sufficient to distinguish its method from that of other disciplines, but does not indicate its true scope. Philosophers are not, for the most part, interested in the understanding of concepts for its own sake. Philosophical interest in understanding concepts is typically motivated by the need for clarification or rational justification of our beliefs and practices. It is when our uncritical use of concepts raises questions that we can't answer, leads to conclusions that seem strange or puzzling, or commits us to conflicting claims or paradoxes that philosophical analysis and understanding become especially important. It is because it is not at all clear to us how we know many of the things we think we know that the philosopher is motivated to clarify our concepts of belief, knowledge, evidence, and justification. It is because there are no quick and obviously correct answers to the following questions:

1. Is the human mind anything over and above some part(s) of the human body?
2. Could a computing machine have a mind?
3. Do we have obligations to future generations?
4. If we do have obligations to future generations, how do we weigh the rights of those generations against the rights of people living now when these conflict?

that philosophers are interested in a deeper understanding of the concepts involved—mind, body, machine, rights and duties. And it is the apparent conflict between the following claims:

1. Everything that happens is a necessary product of the events preceding it, present circumstances, and universal laws of nature.
2. Human beings are responsible for their voluntary acts.

(the first of which seems to be essential to science and the second of which seems to be essential to the legal institution of punishment as well as to the whole of morality) that focuses philosophical attention on the issue of freedom of the will and the associated concepts of cause and effect, necessary connection, universal law, freedom and responsibility, and voluntary behavior.

Philosophical interest, then, is not directed at concepts in isolation, but rather at concepts as they figure in the questions, puzzles, paradoxes, and confusion that motivate philosophical inquiry. The philosopher hopes to achieve an understanding of our beliefs and practices that is free of conceptual confusion and will allow us to answer questions, solve puzzles, and resolve paradoxes like those above. This broader interest in meaning — in making sense of beliefs and practices as well as the individual concepts associated with them — is at the same time an interest in the relations that hold among beliefs, between beliefs and practices, or between beliefs and those features of reality that the beliefs are about. That is, it is an interest in **logic** or logical relations in a very broad sense. In this very broad sense of logic it is the apparent logical gap between experience and belief or between evidence and theory that gives rise to the philosophical problems associated with our everyday and scientific knowledge of the world. And it is the apparent logical conflict between two of our beliefs, or the logical incompatibility of the practices that rest on those beliefs, that produces the philosophical problem of freedom of the will.

There is a popular misconception of philosophy that is a near enough miss to be instructive, although it makes many of us involved in the discipline cringe because it blurs the distinction between philosopher and guru. It is the notion that philosophy is the search for the meaning of life. It conjures up the image of an old man with white hair and beard, wearing a loincloth and sitting on a mountaintop, looking out over the world and pondering the point of it all — succeeding when he can capture the wisdom of the ages in a single deep and clever saying that no one else will ever fully understand. Now although the actual practice of philosophy shares little with that image, the connection drawn between philosophy and the meaning of life is a legitimate one when properly understood. Philosophy is certainly involved in the search for meaning, as we have said above, and, in a sense, the ultimate goal *is* to understand the meaning of life. Human life is, at least in part, a network of beliefs, practices, goals, and values. The aim of philosophy is to clarify the concepts involved in that network so as to make those beliefs, practices, goals, and values — and their interrelations — intelligible. The result of that enterprise, even if we imagine it magically completed, is unlikely to be a catchy one-liner — but it will certainly be relevant, if not equivalent, to understanding the "point of it all."

Philosophers differ as to which parts of the enterprise described above are most important. Some feel that our moral beliefs and practices are the most urgently in need of study since they directly affect the way we live and not just the way we think about life. Others feel that the investigation of the structure of human knowledge and the nature of reality is of fundamental importance, since the study of our beliefs and practices in any area may be largely a waste of time if we are not first clear about what there is to know and what is required in order for us to come to know it. And there are even philosophers who have maintained that no single area of human life can be singled out for first or exclusive investigation, but that we need instead to come initially to some general understanding of reality as a whole — that we really do need first and foremost a sense of the "point of it all." The idea behind this approach is that the parts of reality and the individual areas of human life can be properly understood only in terms of their place in the entire system and their contribution to the whole.

So philosophers, like practitioners in other fields, differ in their priorities and in their approaches to the study of their discipline. But there is fairly general agreement on the nature and importance of philosophical understanding. Most would still echo the words of Socrates spoken nearly twenty-four centuries ago: "The unexamined life is not worth living." The business of philosophy is to critically examine the basic beliefs that guide human life, both individually and collectively — to find the reasons for those beliefs and provide us with the logical and conceptual resources to assess those reasons and to weigh those beliefs against alternatives. Philosophy seeks to replace irrational prejudice and uninformed opinion with rational understanding and justified belief. That enterprise may never succeed entirely, but the attempt itself tends to produce a life that is understood rather than just undergone. To refuse even to make that attempt is to settle for a life that is something less than fully human.

The following selections include a fourth century B.C. dialogue by Plato and a number of fairly brief excerpts from the writings of twentieth century philosophers that try to explain what philosophy is and why it is worth pursuing. *Euthyphro* is one of Plato's earliest and shortest dialogues. Each of Plato's dialogues is devoted to the understanding of a particular concept. For example, one of Plato's longest and best-known dialogues, the *Republic,* is devoted to answering the question "What is justice?" *Euthyphro,* in ostensibly attempting to answer the question "What is piety?", takes the form of a conversation between Euthyphro and Socrates. Euthyphro regards himself as an authority on religious matters, and Socrates is about to be put on trial for "introducing religious reforms." So Socrates has the motive, and Euthyphro provides the opportunity, for trying to find out just what is and isn't pious and why — that is, for investigating the concept of piety. In fact, the investigation doesn't get very far. No satisfactory answer to the question of the dialogue is reached. And that's probably just as well, since differences between ancient Greek religion and religion in our times would make the Greek conception of piety somewhat different from ours and primarily of historical interest anyway. What makes the dialogue important in spite of its age and inconclusiveness are the mistakes that Euthyphro makes along the way in trying to analyze or define the concept of piety, and the attempts by Socrates to identify those mistakes and to put Euthyphro on the right track.

The dialogue stands as the first published lesson in the practice of philosophy, and much of that lesson is as important today as it was twenty-four centuries ago. Plato rejects the voice of authority as a source of philosophical wisdom. Any proposed analysis of the meaning of a concept must be subjected to careful scrutiny and must stand up under rational criticism. For this reason, our usual nonphilosophical source of information about meaning, the dictionary, won't answer the philosophical request for the analysis or definition of a concept either. The dictionary is just one more supposed authority and leaves open the question of whether or not its proposed meaning is in fact the correct one. Examples, things to which the concept applies (pious acts in the case of the concept of piety), are also rejected. The philosopher wants to know why a purported example really is an example (why a particular act is pious), and no example by itself can answer that question. Finally, Plato draws a distinction between essential and accidental features of a thing, rejecting accidental features as relevant to the philosophical understanding of a concept. In terms of any particular concept, the **essential** features of a thing are those features that make the concept apply, the features that make the thing that kind of thing. **Accidental** features are any other features the thing may possess, but which are not necessary to the thing's being the kind of thing it is. So, for example, relative to being a chair, being a piece of furniture and being made to be sat upon are essential features; being brown and made of wood are accidental features. Being brown or wooden does not make a thing a chair. A chair could equally well be gray and made of metal. It could not equally well not be a piece of furniture and not be for sitting upon. The essential features of a thing are so called because they are essential to its being a particular kind of thing, to its having a particular concept apply to it. Plato argues that questions of the form "What is ____________?" where the blank is filled in by a concept call for all and only the essential features that would make that concept apply to something. Plato has Socrates suggest that the essential features included in the definition of a concept will take the genus-species form. Piety is a part (or a species) of justice (the larger concept or genus)—namely, that part of justice having to do with the relations between men and gods (the distinguishing characteristic that separates it from other species of justice). But Euthyphro isn't able to explain clearly what constitutes a just or pious relation between gods and humans, and so the suggestion is not developed.

If we cannot simply trust what some person or text says, the obvious question is "Where do we go for the answers to philosophical questions?" According to Plato we find such answers by engaging in **dialectic,** a process of cooperative inquiry involving discussion with others. We try out an answer, subject it to criticism, improve the initial answer in light of the weaknesses that criticism reveals, and continue this process until we reach the correct answer. But what is it we are finding by this process? How can we know that any answer we reach is the correct one? R. M. Hare, in the brief selection following *Euthyphro,* suggests an answer to these questions. He compares the process of philosophical discussion to the actions of a group of dancers trying to find out exactly how a particular dance, the eightsome reel, is danced. Unable to say exactly what sequence of steps is required at a given point, they dance the dance to see. They know the dance in the sense of being able to do it, but not in the sense of being able to say precisely how it is done. In the same way, Hare argues, we know how to use concepts but may not be able to say exactly what is involved. Philosophical discussion, like dancing the dance, serves to make this implicit understanding explicit. We recognize the correct answer because we already possess it implicitly. And making it explicit may extend our knowledge of how to use it from familiar contexts to some of the unfamiliar circumstances that cause philosophical puzzlement or confusion.

The remaining essays in this chapter provide accounts of the nature and value of philosophy. C. D. Broad divides philosophy in terms of two distinguishable functions, criticism and speculation. The critical task of philosophy involves the examination and clarification of concepts and the identification and assessment of basic assumptions underlying our beliefs and practices. The speculative task of philosophy is to come to some understanding of the nature of reality as a whole and the ways in which human beings and their experience fit into this whole. A. C. Ewing argues that philosophy is of value both because of the importance of its results as the basis for or as supplemental to the sciences and because of the beneficial side effects of the philosophical point of view for all human endeavors. Finally, Brand Blanshard presents a clear and eloquent account of the nature and value of "the philosophic enterprise" which needs no introduction. We will leave it to speak for itself.

Part I is introductory in nature, providing a minimal sample of philosophical thinking and some idea of what philosophy is all about. Your real introduction to the discipline will occur only after you move on to subsequent parts of this book and examine in depth several of the basic problem areas of philosophy in light of some of the most famous attempts to solve them.

## *Plato (427–347 B.C.)*

Although there had been a number of Greek philosophers before Plato, most notably Socrates, Plato is the first to have systematically treated virtually all of the major problem areas of the western philosophical tradition. Although many of the answers he proposed would be generally rejected today, most of the questions and issues he raised have endured. It is for this reason that Plutarch wrote "Plato is philosophy, and philosophy is Plato." And Whitehead once characterized all of western philosophy as "a series of footnotes to Plato." Plato wrote more than twenty dialogues, ranging in length from little more than a dozen pages to several hundred pages. Most of the dialogues bear the name of the principal person with whom Socrates converses. It is a matter of scholarly controversy as to how closely the Socrates of Plato's dialogues resembles the historical Socrates. The historical Socrates spent most of his life engaging in critical conversation with the citizens of Athens but did not write his own account of these conversations or of his philosophical views. Plato's dialogues represent only one of a number of different pictures left us by Socrates' contemporaries. Suffice it to say that Socrates was the major influence on Plato's philosophical development. He emerges from the dialogues as a philosophical hero, a seeker of the truth at all costs, a tireless critic of error and defender of right in thinking and in acting. Plato's Socrates is a kind of philosophical Perry Mason, winning case after case by the depth of his insight and his skill in constructing arguments and conducting debate. Nevertheless, from around the edges of Plato's admiration for Socrates we catch an occasional glimpse of an almost ruthless willingness to embarrass or humiliate his opponents, which helps to explain how Socrates could have made sufficient enemies to account for his prosecution and conviction (see *Euthyphro* below) as soon as a barely plausible charge could be found. Plato's account of Socrates' trial, imprisonment, and death can be found in the following three dialogues: *Apology, Crito,* and *Phaedo.*

# Euthyphro

## *Plato*

CHARACTERS: Socrates, Euthyphro

SCENE: The Hall of the King

*Euthyphro.* What in the world are you doing here in the king's hall,* Socrates? Why have you left your haunts in the Lyceum? You surely cannot have a suit before him, as I have.

*Socrates.* The Athenians, Euthyphro, call it an indictment, not a suit.

*Euth.* What? Do you mean that someone is prosecuting you? I cannot believe that you are prosecuting anyone yourself.

*Socr.* Certainly I am not.

*Euth.* Then is someone prosecuting you?

*Socr.* Yes.

*Euth.* Who is he?

*Socr.* I scarcely know him myself, Euthyphro; I think he must be some unknown young man. His name, however, is Meletus, and his district Pitthis, if you can call to mind any Meletus of that district — a hook-nosed man with lanky hair and rather a scanty beard.

*Euth.* I don't know him, Socrates. But tell me, what is he prosecuting you for?

*Socr.* What for? Not on trivial grounds, I think. It is no small thing for so young a man to have formed an opinion on such an important matter. For he, he says, knows how the young are corrupted, and who are their corrupters. He must be a wise man who, observing my ignorance, is going to accuse me to the state, as his mother, of corrupting his friends. I think that he is the only one who begins at the right point in his political reforms; for his first care is to make the young men as good as possible, just as a good farmer will take care of his young plants first, and, after he has done that, of the others. And so Meletus, I suppose, is first clearing us away who, as he says, corrupt the young men growing up; and then, when he has done that, of course he will turn his attention to the older men, and so become a very great public benefactor. Indeed, that is only what you would expect when he goes to work in this way.

*Euth.* I hope it may be so, Socrates, but I fear the opposite. It seems to me that in trying to injure you, he is really setting to work by striking a blow at the foundation of the state. But how, tell me, does he say that you corrupt the youth?

*Socr.* In a way which sounds absurd at first, my friend. He says that I am a maker of gods; and so he is prosecuting me, he says, for inventing new gods and for not believing in the old ones.

*Euth.* I understand, Socrates. It is because you say that you always have a divine guide. So he is prosecuting you for introducing religious reforms; and he is going into court to arouse prejudice against you, knowing that the multitude are easily prejudiced about such matters. Why, they laugh even at me, as if I were out of my mind, when I talk about divine things in the assembly and tell them what is going to happen; and yet I have never foretold anything which has

* The anachronistic title "king" was retained by the magistrate who had jurisdiction over crimes affecting the state religion. — Ed.

Plato, *Euthyphro, Apology, Crito,* translated by F. J. Church; translation revised by Robert D. Cumming (New York: The Liberal Arts Press, Inc., a division of the Bobbs-Merrill Co., Inc., 1948). 2d rev. ed., 1956. 

not come true. But they are resentful of all people like us. We must not worry about them; we must meet them boldly.

*Socr.* My dear Euthyphro, their ridicule is not a very serious matter. The Athenians, it seems to me, may think a man to be clever without paying him much attention, so long as they do not think that he teaches his wisdom to others. But as soon as they think that he makes other people clever, they get angry, whether it be from resentment, as you say, or for some other reason.

*Euth.* I am not very anxious to test their attitude toward me in this matter.

*Socr.* No, perhaps they think that you are reserved, and that you are not anxious to teach your wisdom to others. But I fear that they may think that I am; for my love of men makes me talk to everyone whom I meet quite freely and unreservedly, and without payment. Indeed, if I could I would gladly pay people myself to listen to me. If then, as I said just now, they were only going to laugh at me, as you say they do at you, it would not be at all an unpleasant way of spending the day—to spend it in court, joking and laughing. But if they are going to be in earnest, then only prophets like you can tell where the matter will end.

*Euth.* Well, Socrates, I dare say that nothing will come of it. Very likely you will be successful in your trial, and I think that I shall be in mine.

*Socr.* And what is this suit of yours, Euthyphro? Are you suing, or being sued?

*Euth.* I am suing.

*Socr.* Whom?

*Euth.* A man whom people think I must be mad to prosecute.

*Socr.* What? Has he wings to fly away with?

*Euth.* He is far enough from flying; he is a very old man.

*Socr.* Who is he?

*Euth.* He is my father.

*Socr.* Your father, my good man?

*Euth.* He is indeed.

*Socr.* What are you prosecuting him for? What is the accusation?

*Euth.* Murder, Socrates.

*Socr.* Good heavens, Euthyphro! Surely the multitude are ignorant of what is right. I take it that it is not everyone who could rightly do what you are doing; only a man who was already well advanced in wisdom.

*Euth.* That is quite true, Socrates.

*Socr.* Was the man whom your father killed a relative of yours? But, of course, he was. You would never have prosecuted your father for the murder of a stranger?

*Euth.* You amuse me, Socrates. What difference does it make whether the murdered man were a relative or a stranger? The only question that you have to ask is, did the murderer kill justly or not? If justly, you must let him alone; if unjustly, you must indict him for murder, even though he share your hearth and sit at your table. The pollution is the same if you associate with such a man, knowing what he has done, without purifying yourself, and him too, by bringing him to justice. In the present case the murdered man was a poor laborer of mine, who worked for us on our farm in Naxos. While drunk he got angry with one of our slaves and killed him. My father therefore bound the man hand and foot and threw him into a ditch, while he sent to Athens to ask the priest what he should do. While the messenger was gone, he entirely neglected the man, thinking that he was a murderer, and that it would be no great matter, even if he were to die. And that was exactly what happened; hunger and cold and his bonds killed him before the messenger returned. And now my father and the rest of my family are indignant with me because I am prosecuting my father for the murder of this murderer. They assert that he did not kill the man at all; and they say that, even if he had killed him over and over again, the man himself was a murderer, and that I ought not to concern myself about such a person because it is impious for a son to prosecute his father for murder. So little, Socrates, do they know the divine law of piety and impiety.

*Socr.* And do you mean to say, Euthyphro, that you think that you understand divine things and piety and impiety so accurately that, in such a case as you have stated, you can bring your father to justice without fear that you yourself may be doing something impious?

*Euth.* If I did not understand all these matters accurately, Socrates, I should not be worth much — Euthyphro would not be any better than other men.

*Socr.* Then, my dear Euthyphro, I cannot do better than become your pupil and challenge Meletus on this very point before the trial begins. I should say that I had always thought it very important to have knowledge about divine things; and that now, when he says that I offend by speaking carelessly about them, and by introducing reforms, I have become your pupil. And I should say, "Meletus, if you acknowledge Euthyphro to be wise in these matters and to hold the correct belief, then think the same of me and do not put me on trial; but if you do not, then bring a suit, not against me, but against my master, for corrupting his elders — namely, myself whom he corrupts by his teaching, and his own father whom he corrupts by admonishing and punishing him." And if I did not succeed in persuading him to release me from the suit or to indict you in my place, then I could repeat my challenge in court.

*Euth.* Yes, by Zeus! Socrates, I think I should find out his weak points if he were to try to indict me. I should have a good deal to say about him in court long before I spoke about myself.

*Socr.* Yes, my dear friend, and knowing this I am anxious to become your pupil. I see that Meletus here, and others too, seem not to notice you at all, but he sees through me without difficulty and at once prosecutes me for impiety. Now, therefore, please explain to me what you were so confident just now that you knew. Tell me what are righteousness and sacrilege with respect to murder and everything else. I suppose that piety is the same in all actions, and that impiety is always the opposite of piety, and retains its identity, and that, as impiety, it always has the same character, which will be found in whatever is impious.

*Euth.* Certainly, Socrates, I suppose so.

*Socr.* Tell me, then, what is piety and what is impiety?

*Euth.* Well, then, I say that piety means prosecuting the unjust individual who has committed murder or sacrilege, or any other such crime, as I am doing now, whether he is your father or your mother or whoever he is; and I say that impiety means not prosecuting him. And observe, Socrates, I will give you a clear proof, which I have already given to others, that it is so, and that doing right means not letting off unpunished the sacrilegious man, whosoever he may be. Men hold Zeus to be the best and the most just of the gods; and they admit that Zeus bound his own father, Cronos, for wrongfully devouring his children; and that Cronos, in his turn, castrated his father for similar reasons. And yet these same men are incensed with me because I proceed against my father for doing wrong. So, you see, they say one thing in the case of the gods and quite another in mine.

*Socr.* Is not that why I am being prosecuted, Euthyphro? I mean, because I find it hard to accept such stories people tell about the gods? I expect that I shall be found at fault because I doubt those stories. Now if you who understand all these matters so well agree in holding all those tales true, then I suppose that I must yield to your authority. What could I say when I admit myself that I know nothing about them? But tell me, in the name of friendship, do you really believe that these things have actually happened?

*Euth.* Yes, and more amazing things, too, Socrates, which the multitude do not know of.

*Socr.* Then you really believe that there is war among the gods, and bitter hatreds, and battles, such as the poets tell of, and which the great painters have depicted in our temples, notably in the pictures which cover the robe that is carried up to the Acropolis at the great Panathenaic festival? Are we to say that these things are true, Euthyphro?

*Euth.* Yes, Socrates, and more besides. As I was saying, I will report to you many other stories about divine matters, if you like, which I am sure will astonish you when you hear them.

*Socr.* I dare say. You shall report them to me at your leisure another time. At present please try to give a more definite answer to the question which I asked you just now. What I asked you, my friend, was, What is piety? and you have not explained it to me to my satisfaction. You only tell me that what you are doing now, namely, prosecuting your father for murder, is a pious act.

*Euth.* Well, that is true, Socrates.

*Socr.* Very likely. But many other actions are pious, are they not, Euthyphro?

*Euth.* Certainly.

*Socr.* Remember, then, I did not ask you to tell me one or two of all the many pious actions that there are; I want to know what is characteristic of piety which makes all pious actions pious. You said, I think, that there is one characteristic which makes all pious actions pious, and another characteristic which makes all impious actions impious. Do you not remember?

*Euth.* I do.

*Socr.* Well, then, explain to me what is this characteristic, that I may have it to turn to, and to use as a standard whereby to judge your actions and those of other men, and be able to say that whatever action resembles it is pious, and whatever does not, is not pious.

*Euth.* Yes, I will tell you that if you wish, Socrates.

*Socr.* Certainly I do.

*Euth.* Well, then, what is pleasing to the gods is pious, and what is not pleasing to them is impious.

*Socr.* Fine, Euthyphro. Now you have given me the answer that I wanted. Whether what you say is true, I do not know yet. But, of course, you will go on to prove that it is true.

*Euth.* Certainly.

*Socr.* Come, then, let us examine our statement. The things and the men that are pleasing to the gods are pious, and the things and the men that are displeasing to the gods are impious. But piety and impiety are not the same; they are as opposite as possible—was not that what we said?

*Euth.* Certainly.

*Socr.* And it seems the appropriate statement?

*Euth.* Yes, Socrates, certainly.

*Socr.* Have we not also said, Euthyphro, that there are quarrels and disagreements and hatreds among the gods?

*Euth.* We have.

*Socr.* But what kind of disagreement, my friend, causes hatred and anger? Let us look at the matter thus. If you and I were to disagree as to whether one number were more than another, would that make us angry and enemies? Should we not settle such a dispute at once by counting?

*Euth.* Of course.

*Socr.* And if we were to disagree as to the relative size of two things, we should measure them and put an end to the disagreement at once, should we not?

*Euth.* Yes.

*Socr.* And should we not settle a question about the relative weight of two things by weighing them?

*Euth.* Of course.

*Socr.* Then what is the question which would make us angry and enemies if we disagreed about it, and could not come to a settlement? Perhaps you have not an answer ready; but listen to mine. Is it not the question of the just and unjust, of the honorable and the dishonorable, of the good and the bad? Is it not questions about these matters which make you and me and everyone else quarrel, when we do quarrel, if we differ about them and can reach no satisfactory agreement?

*Euth.* Yes, Socrates, it is disagreements about these matters.

*Socr.* Well, Euthyphro, the gods will quarrel over these things if they quarrel at all, will they not?

*Euth.* Necessarily.

*Socr.* Then, my good Euthyphro, you say that some of the gods think one thing just, the others another; and that what some of them hold to be honorable or good, others hold to be dishonorable or evil. For there would not have been quarrels among them if they had not disagreed on these points, would there?

*Euth.* You are right.

*Socr.* And each of them loves what he thinks honorable, and good, and just; and hates the opposite, does he not?

*Euth.* Certainly.

*Socr.* But you say that the same action is

held by some of them to be just, and by others to be unjust; and that then they dispute about it, and so quarrel and fight among themselves. Is it not so?

*Euth.* Yes.

*Socr.* Then the same thing is hated by the gods and loved by them; and the same thing will be displeasing and pleasing to them.

*Euth.* Apparently.

*Socr.* Then, according to your account, the same thing will be pious and impious.

*Euth.* So it seems.

*Socr.* Then, my good friend, you have not answered my question. I did not ask you to tell me what action is both pious and impious; but it seems that whatever is pleasing to the gods is also displeasing to them. And so, Euthyphro, I should not be surprised if what you are doing now in punishing your father is an action well pleasing to Zeus, but hateful to Cronos and Uranus, and acceptable to Hephaestus, but hateful to Hera; and if any of the other gods disagree about it, pleasing to some of them and displeasing to others.

*Euth.* But on this point, Socrates, I think that there is no difference of opinion among the gods: they all hold that if one man kills another unjustly, he must be punished.

*Socr.* What, Euthyphro? Among mankind, have you never heard disputes whether a man ought to be punished for killing another man unjustly, or for doing some other unjust deed?

*Euth.* Indeed, they never cease from these disputes, especially in courts of justice. They do all manner of unjust things; and then there is nothing which they will not do and say to avoid punishment.

*Socr.* Do they admit that they have done something unjust, and at the same time deny that they ought to be punished, Euthyphro?

*Euth.* No, indeed, that they do not.

*Socr.* Then it is not the case that there is nothing which they will not do and say. I take it, they do not dare to say or argue that they must not be punished if they have done something unjust. What they say is that they have not done anything unjust, is it not so?

*Euth.* That is true.

*Socr.* Then they do not disagree over the question that the unjust individual must be punished. They disagree over the question, who is unjust, and what was done and when, do they not?

*Euth.* That is true.

*Socr.* Well, is not exactly the same thing true of the gods if they quarrel about justice and injustice, as you say they do? Do not some of them say that the others are doing something unjust, while the others deny it? No one, I suppose, my dear friend, whether god or man, dares to say that a person who has done something unjust must not be punished.

*Euth.* No, Socrates, that is true, by and large.

*Socr.* I take it, Euthyphro, that the disputants, whether men or gods, if the gods do disagree, disagree over each separate act. When they quarrel about any act, some of them say that it was just, and others that it was unjust. Is it not so?

*Euth.* Yes.

*Socr.* Come, then, my dear Euthyphro, please enlighten me on this point. What proof have you that all the gods think that a laborer who has been imprisoned for murder by the master of the man whom he has murdered, and who dies from his imprisonment before the master has had time to learn from the religious authorities what he should do, dies unjustly? How do you know that it is just for a son to indict his father and to prosecute him for the murder of such a man? Come, see if you can make it clear to me that the gods necessarily agree in thinking that this action of yours is just; and if you satisfy me, I will never cease singing your praises for wisdom.

*Euth.* I could make that clear enough to you, Socrates; but I am afraid that it would be a long business.

*Socr.* I see you think that I am duller than the judges. To them, of course, you will make it clear that your father has committed an unjust action, and that all the gods agree in hating such actions.

*Euth.* I will indeed, Socrates, if they will only listen to me.

*Socr.* They will listen if they think that you are a good speaker. But while you were talking, it occurred to me to ask myself this question: suppose that Euthyphro were to prove to me as clearly as possible that all the gods think such a death unjust, how has he brought me any nearer to understanding what piety and impiety are? This particular act, perhaps, may be displeasing to the gods, but then we have just seen that piety and impiety cannot be defined in that way; for we have seen that what is displeasing to the gods is also pleasing to them. So I will let you off on this point, Euthyphro; and all the gods shall agree in thinking your father's action wrong and in hating it, if you like. But shall we correct our definition and say that whatever all the gods hate is impious, and whatever they all love is pious; while whatever some of them love, and others hate, is either both or neither? Do you wish us now to define piety and impiety in this manner?

*Euth.* Why not, Socrates?

*Socr.* There is no reason why I should not, Euthyphro. It is for you to consider whether that definition will help you to teach me what you promised.

*Euth.* Well, I should say that piety is what all the gods love, and that impiety is what they all hate.

*Socr.* Are we to examine this definition, Euthyphro, and see if it is a good one? Or are we to be content to accept the bare statements of other men or of ourselves without asking any questions? Or must we examine the statements?

*Euth.* We must examine them. But for my part I think that the definition is right this time.

*Socr.* We shall know that better in a little while, my good friend. Now consider this question. Do the gods love piety because it is pious, or is it pious because they love it?

*Euth.* I do not understand you, Socrates.

*Socr.* I will try to explain myself: we speak of a thing being carried and carrying, and being led and leading, and being seen and seeing; and you understand that all such expressions mean different things, and what the difference is.

*Euth.* Yes, I think I understand.

*Socr.* And we talk of a thing being loved, of a thing loving, and the two are different?

*Euth.* Of course.

*Socr.* Now tell me, is a thing which is being carried in a state of being carried because it is carried, or for some other reason?

*Euth.* No, because it is carried.

*Socr.* And a thing is in a state of being led because it is led, and of being seen because it is seen?

*Euth.* Certainly.

*Socr.* Then a thing is not seen because it is in a state of being seen: it is in a state of being seen because it is seen; and a thing is not led because it is in a state of being led: it is in a state of being led because it is led; and a thing is not carried because it is in a state of being carried: it is in a state of being carried because it is carried. Is my meaning clear now, Euthyphro? I mean this: if anything becomes or is affected, it does not become because it is in a state of becoming: it is in a state of becoming because it becomes; and it is not affected because it is in a state of being affected: it is in a state of being affected because it is affected. Do you not agree?

*Euth.* I do.

*Socr.* Is not that which is being loved in a state either of becoming or of being affected in some way by something?

*Euth.* Certainly.

*Socr.* Then the same is true here as in the former cases. A thing is not loved by those who love it because it is in a state of being loved; it is in a state of being loved because they love it.

*Euth.* Necessarily.

*Socr.* Well, then, Euthyphro, what do we say about piety? Is it not loved by all the gods, according to your definition?

*Euth.* Yes.

*Socr.* Because it is pious, or for some other reason?

*Euth.* No, because it is pious.

*Socr.* Then it is loved by the gods because it is pious; it is not pious because it is loved by them?

*Euth.* It seems so.

*Socr.* But, then, what is pleasing to the gods is pleasing to them, and is in a state of being loved by them, because they love it?

*Euth.* Of course.

*Socr.* Then piety is not what is pleasing to the gods, and what is pleasing to the gods is not pious, as you say, Euthyphro. They are different things.

*Euth.* And why, Socrates?

*Socr.* Because we are agreed that the gods love piety because it is pious, and that it is not pious because they love it. Is not this so?

*Euth.* Yes.

*Socr.* And that what is pleasing to the gods because they love it, is pleasing to them by reason of this same love, and that they do not love it because it is pleasing to them.

*Euth.* True.

*Socr.* Then, my dear Euthyphro, piety and what is pleasing to the gods are different things. If the gods had loved piety because it is pious, they would also have loved what is pleasing to them because it is pleasing to them; but if what is pleasing to them had been pleasing to them because they loved it, then piety, too, would have been piety because they loved it. But now you see that they are opposite things, and wholly different from each other. For the one is of a sort to be loved because it is loved, while the other is loved because it is of a sort to be loved. My question, Euthyphro, was, What is piety? But it turns out that you have not explained to me the **essential** character of piety; you have been content to mention an effect which belongs to it — namely, that all the gods love it. You have not yet told me what its essential character is. Do not, if you please, keep from me what piety is; begin again and tell me that. Never mind whether the gods love it, or whether it has other effects: we shall not differ on that point. Do your best to make clear to me what is piety and what is impiety.

*Euth.* But, Socrates, I really don't know how to explain to you what is in my mind. Whatever statement we put forward always somehow moves round in a circle, and will not stay where we put it.

*Socr.* I think that your statements, Euthyphro, are worthy of my ancestor Daedalus.* If they had been mine and I had set them down, I dare say you would have made fun of me, and said that it was the consequence of my descent from Daedalus that the statements which I construct run away, as his statues used to, and will not stay where they are put. But, as it is, the statements are yours, and the joke would have no point. You yourself see that they will not stay still.

*Euth.* Nay, Socrates, I think that the joke is very much in point. It is not my fault that the statement moves round in a circle and will not stay still. But you are the Daedalus, I think; as far as I am concerned, my statements would have stayed put.

*Socr.* Then, my friend, I must be a more skillful artist than Daedalus; he only used to make his own works move, while I, you see, can make other people's works move, too. And the beauty of it is that I am wise against my will. I would rather that our statements had remained firm and immovable than have all the wisdom of Daedalus and all the riches of Tantalus to boot. But enough of this. I will do my best to help you to explain to me what piety is, for I think that you are lazy. Don't give in yet. Tell me, do you not think that all piety must be just?

*Euth.* I do.

*Socr.* Well, then, is all justice pious, too? Or, while all piety is just, is a part only of justice pious, and the rest of it something else?

*Euth.* I do not follow you, Socrates.

*Socr.* Yet you have the advantage over me in your youth no less than your wisdom. But, as I say, the wealth of your wisdom makes you complacent. Exert yourself, my good friend: I am not asking you a difficult question. I mean the opposite of what the poet† said, when he wrote:

> "You shall not name Zeus the creator, who made all things: for where there is fear there also is reverence."

* Daedalus' statues were reputed to have been so lifelike that they came alive. — Ed.

† Stasinus.

Now I disagree with the poet. Shall I tell you why?

*Euth.* Yes.

*Socr.* I do not think it true to say that where there is fear, there also is reverence. Many people who fear sickness and poverty and other such evils seem to me to have fear, but no reverence for what they fear. Do you not think so?

*Euth.* I do.

*Socr.* But I think that where there is reverence there also is fear. Does any man feel reverence and a sense of shame about anything, without at the same time dreading and fearing the reputation of wickedness?

*Euth.* No, certainly not.

*Socr.* Then, though there is fear wherever there is reverence, it is not correct to say that where there is fear there also is reverence. Reverence does not always accompany fear; for fear, I take it, is wider than reverence. It is a part of fear, just as the odd is a part of number, so that where you have the odd you must also have number, though where you have number you do not necessarily have the odd. Now I think you follow me?

*Euth.* I do.

*Socr.* Well, then, this is what I meant by the question which I asked you. Is there always piety where there is justice? Or, though there is always justice where there is piety, yet there is not always piety where there is justice, because piety is only a part of justice? Shall we say this, or do you differ?

*Euth.* No, I agree. I think that you are right.

*Socr.* Now observe the next point. If piety is a part of justice, we must find out, I suppose, what part of justice it is? Now, if you had asked me just now, for instance, what part of number is the odd, and what number is an odd number, I should have said that whatever number is not even is an odd number. Is it not so?

*Euth.* Yes.

*Socr.* Then see if you can explain to me what part of justice is piety, that I may tell Meletus that now that I have been adequately instructed by you as to what actions are righteous and pious, and what are not, he must give up prosecuting me unjustly for impiety.

*Euth.* Well, then, Socrates, I should say that righteousness and piety are that part of justice which has to do with the careful attention which ought to be paid to the gods; and that what has to do with the careful attention which ought to be paid to men is the remaining part of justice.

*Socr.* And I think that your answer is a good one, Euthyphro. But there is one little point about which I still want to hear more. I do not yet understand what the careful attention is to which you refer. I suppose you do not mean that the attention which we pay to the gods is like the attention which we pay to other things. We say, for instance, do we not, that not everyone knows how to take care of horses, but only the trainer of horses?

*Euth.* Certainly.

*Socr.* For I suppose that the skill that is concerned with horses is the art of taking care of horses.

*Euth.* Yes.

*Socr.* And not everyone understands the care of dogs, but only the huntsman.

*Euth.* True.

*Socr.* For I suppose that the huntsman's skill is the art of taking care of dogs.

*Euth.* Yes.

*Socr.* And the herdsman's skill is the art of taking care of cattle.

*Euth.* Certainly.

*Socr.* And you say that piety and righteousness are taking care of the gods, Euthyphro?

*Euth.* I do.

*Socr.* Well, then, has not all care the same object? Is it not for the good and benefit of that on which it is bestowed? For instance, you see that horses are benefited and improved when they are cared for by the art which is concerned with them. Is it not so?

*Euth.* Yes, I think so.

*Socr.* And dogs are benefited and improved by the huntsman's art, and cattle by the herdsman's, are they not? And the same is always true. Or do you think care is ever meant to harm that which is cared for?

*Euth.* No, indeed; certainly not.

*Socr.* But to benefit it?

*Euth.* Of course.

*Socr.* Then is piety, which is our care for the gods, intended to benefit the gods, or to improve them? Should you allow that you make any of the gods better when you do a pious action?

*Euth.* No indeed; certainly not.

*Socr.* No, I am quite sure that that is not your meaning, Euthyphro. It was for that reason that I asked you what you meant by the careful attention which ought to be paid to the gods. I thought that you did not mean that.

*Euth.* You were right, Socrates. I do not mean that.

*Socr.* Good. Then what sort of attention to the gods will piety be?

*Euth.* The sort of attention, Socrates, slaves pay to their masters.

*Socr.* I understand; then it is a kind of service to the gods?

*Euth.* Certainly.

*Socr.* Can you tell me what result the art which serves a doctor serves to produce? Is it not health?

*Euth.* Yes.

*Socr.* And what result does the art which serves a shipwright serve to produce?

*Euth.* A ship, of course, Socrates.

*Socr.* The result of the art which serves a builder is a house, is it not?

*Euth.* Yes.

*Socr.* Then tell me, my good friend: What result will the art which serves the gods serve to produce? You must know, seeing that you say that you know more about divine things than any other man.

*Euth.* Well, that is true, Socrates.

*Socr.* Then tell me, I beg you, what is that grand result which the gods use our services to produce?

*Euth.* There are many notable results, Socrates.

*Socr.* So are those, my friend, which a general produces. Yet it is easy to see that the crowning result of them all is victory in war, is it not?

*Euth.* Of course.

*Socr.* And, I take it, the farmer produces many notable results; yet the principal result of them all is that he makes the earth produce food.

*Euth.* Certainly.

*Socr.* Well, then, what is the principal result of the many notable results which the gods produce?

*Euth.* I told you just now, Socrates, that accurate knowledge of all these matters is not easily obtained. However, broadly I say this: if any man knows that his words and actions in prayer and sacrifice are acceptable to the gods, that is what is pious; and it preserves the state, as it does private families. But the opposite of what is acceptable to the gods is sacrilegious, and this it is that undermines and destroys everything.

*Socr.* Certainly, Euthyphro, if you had wished, you could have answered my main question in far fewer words. But you are evidently not anxious to teach me. Just now, when you were on the very point of telling me what I want to know, you stopped short. If you had gone on then, I should have learned from you clearly enough by this time what piety is. But now I am asking you questions, and must follow wherever you lead me; so tell me, what is it that you mean by piety and impiety? Do you not mean a science of prayer and sacrifice?

*Euth.* I do.

*Socr.* To sacrifice is to give to the gods, and to pray is to ask of them, is it not?

*Euth.* It is, Socrates.

*Socr.* Then you say that piety is the science of asking of the gods and giving to them?

*Euth.* You understand my meaning exactly, Socrates.

*Socr.* Yes, for I am eager to share your wisdom, Euthyphro, and so I am all attention; nothing that you say will fall to the ground. But tell me, what is this service of the gods? You say it is to ask of them, and to give to them?

*Euth.* I do.

*Socr.* Then, to ask rightly will be to ask of them what we stand in need of from them, will it not?

*Euth.* Naturally.

*Socr.* And to give rightly will be to give back to them what they stand in need of from us? It would not be very skillful to make a present to a man of something that he has no need of.

*Euth.* True, Socrates.

*Socr.* Then piety, Euthyphro, will be the art of carrying on business between gods and men?

*Euth.* Yes, if you like to call it so.

*Soc.* But I like nothing except what is true. But tell me, how are the gods benefited by the gifts which they receive from us? What they give is plain enough. Every good thing that we have is their gift. But how are they benefited by what we give them? Have we the advantage over them in these business transactions to such an extent that we receive from them all the good things we possess, and give them nothing in return?

*Euth.* But do you suppose, Socrates, that the gods are benefited by the gifts which they receive from us?

*Socr.* But what *are* these gifts, Euthyphro, that we give the gods?

*Euth.* What do you think but honor and praise, and, as I have said, what is acceptable to them.

*Socr.* Then piety, Euthyphro, is acceptable to the gods, but it is not profitable to them nor loved by them?

*Euth.* I think that nothing is more loved by them.

*Socr.* Then I see that piety means that which is loved by the gods.

*Euth.* Most certainly.

*Socr.* After that, shall you be surprised to find that your statements move about instead of staying where you put them? Shall you accuse me of being the Daedalus that makes them move, when you yourself are far more skillful than Daedalus was, and make them go round in a circle? Do you not see that our statement has come round to where it was before? Surely you remember that we have already seen that piety and what is pleasing to the gods are quite different things. Do you not remember?

*Euth.* I do.

*Socr.* And now do you not see that you say that what the gods love is pious? But does not what the gods love come to the same thing as what is pleasing to the gods?

*Euth.* Certainly.

*Socr.* Then either our former conclusion was wrong or, if it was right, we are wrong now.

*Euth.* So it seems.

*Socr.* Then we must begin again and inquire what piety is. I do not mean to give in until I have found out. Do not regard me as unworthy; give your whole mind to the question, and this time tell me the truth. For if anyone knows it, it is you; and you are a Proteus whom I must not let go until you have told me. It cannot be that you would ever have undertaken to prosecute your aged father for the murder of a laboring man unless you had known exactly what piety and impiety are. You would have feared to risk the anger of the gods, in case you should be doing wrong, and you would have been afraid of what men would say. But now I am sure that you think that you know exactly what is pious and what is not; so tell me, my good Euthyphro, and do not conceal from me what you think.

*Euth.* Another time, then, Socrates. I am in a hurry now, and it is time for me to be off.

*Socr.* What are you doing, my friend! Will you go away and destroy all my hopes of learning from you what is pious and what is not, and so of escaping Meletus? I meant to explain to him that now Euthyphro has made me wise about divine things, and that I no longer in my ignorance speak carelessly about them or introduce reforms. And then I was going to promise him to live a better life for the future.

## R. M. Hare (b. 1919)

R. M. Hare is one of the most influential philosophers of the last half of the twentieth century. He is most famous for his work in ethical theory and is the author of several important works in that area, including *The Language of Morals* (1952), *Freedom and Reason* (1963), and *Moral Thinking: Its Levels, Methods and Point* (1982). Hare is also the author of numerous articles in ethical theory and its applications, in philosophy of religion, and in several other areas.

# Philosophical Discoveries

## *R. M. Hare*

. . . Meno, in the Platonic dialogue named after him, is asked by Socrates what goodness is (a question much more closely akin than is commonly allowed to the question, How and for what purposes is the word "good" used?). Being a young man of a sophistical turn of mind, Meno says "But Socrates, how are you going to look for something, when you don't in the least know what it is? . . . Or even if you do hit upon it, how are you going to know that this is *it*, without having previous knowledge of what *it* is?" In more modern terms, if we do not already know the use of the word "good" (or, in slightly less fashionable language, its analysis), how, when some account of its use (some analysis) is suggested, shall we know whether it is the correct account? Yet (as Socrates goes on to point out) if we knew already, we should not have asked the question in the first place. So philosophy either cannot begin, or cannot reach a conclusion.

It will be noticed that my dancers could be put in the same paradoxical position. If they know already how the dance is danced, what can they be arguing about? But if they do not know already, how will they know, when they have danced the dance, whether they have danced it correctly? The solution to the paradox lies in distinguishing between knowing how to dance a dance and being able to say how it is danced. Before the enquiry begins, they are able to do the former, but not the latter; after the enquiry is over they can do the latter, and they know that they are right because all along they could do the former. And it is the same with the analysis of concepts. We know how to use a certain expression, but are unable to say how it is used (*λογὸν διδοναι*, give an analysis or definition, formulate in words the use of the expression). Then we try to do the latter; and we know we have succeeded when we have found an analysis which is in accordance with our hitherto unformulated knowledge of how to use the word. And finding out whether it *is* in accordance involves talking **(dialectic),** just as finding out whether the account of the dance is right involves dancing.

Dialectic, like dancing, is typically a cooperative activity. It consists in trying out the proposed account of the use of a word by using the word in accordance with it, and seeing what happens. It is an experiment with words, though not, as we

Abridged from *Mind,* Vol. 69, No. 274, April 1960. Edited by Gilbert Ryle. (Thomas Nelson & Sons, Ltd., 1960). Reprinted by permission of R. M. Hare.

have seen, an altogether empirical experiment. In the same way, we might dance the dance according to someone's account of how it is danced, and see if we can say afterwards whether what we have danced is the dance that we were arguing about (e.g. the eightsome reel) or at least a dance, or whether it is no dance at all. There is no space here to give many examples of dialectic; but I will give the most famous one of all. It is a destructive use of the technique, resulting in the *rejection* of a suggested analysis. An account of the use of the word "right" is being tried out which says that "right" means the same as "consisting in speaking the truth and giving back anything that one has received from anyone." The analysis is tried out by "dancing" a certain statement, *viz.* "It is always right to give a madman back his weapons which he entrusted to us when sane." But the dance has clearly gone wrong; for this statement is certainly not (as the proposed definition would make it) **analytic,** since to deny it, as most people would, is not to contradict oneself. So the analysis has to be rejected.

Plato was right in implying that in recognizing that such a proposition is not analytic we are relying on our memories. It is an example of the perceptive genius of that great logician, that in spite of being altogether at sea concerning the *source* of our philosophical knowledge; and in spite of the fact that his use of the material mode of speech misled him as to the *status* of the analyses he was looking for—that in spite of all this he spotted the very close logical analogies between philosophical discoveries and remembering. He was wrong in supposing that we are remembering something that we learnt in a former life—just as more recent mythologists have been wrong in thinking that we are discerning the structure of some entities called "facts." What we are actually remembering is what we learnt on our mothers' knees, and cannot remember learning.

Provisionally, then, we might agree . . . that philosophy has to contain statements which are neither empirical statements about the way words are actually used, nor yet expressions of decisions about how they are to be used; but we should refuse to infer from this that these statements are about some nonempirical order of being. The philosopher elucidates (not by mere observation) the nature of something which exists before the elucidation begins (for example, there is such an operation as negation before the philosopher investigates it; the philosopher no more invents negation than Aristotle made man rational). He neither creates the objects of his enquiry, nor receives them as mere data of experience; yet for all that, to say that there is such an operation as **negation** is no more mysterious than to say that there is such a dance as the eightsome reel. But even that is quite mysterious enough.

## C. D. Broad (1887–1972)

C. D. Broad was one of the best-known British philosophers of the twentieth century. He made influential contributions in **epistemology,** metaphysics, and moral philosophy, and developed an interest in parapsychology in the latter part of his career. His major works include *Perception, Physics, and Reality* (1913), *Scientific Thought* (1923), *The Mind and Its Place in Nature* (1925), *Five Types of Ethical Theory* (1930), *An Examination of McTaggart's Philosophy* (1933), *Ethics and the History of Philosophy* (1952), *Religion, Philosophy, and Psychical Research* (1953), and *Lectures on Psychical Research* (1962).

# Critical and Speculative Philosophy

*C. D. Broad*

It seems to me that under the name of "Philosophy" two very different subjects are included. They are pursued by different methods, and can expect to reach quite different degrees of certainty. I am wont to call them *Critical* and *Speculative* Philosophy. I do not assert that either can be wholly separated from the other. The second quite certainly presupposes the first, and it is probable that in the first we tacitly assume some things that belong to the second. But they certainly can be separated to a considerable extent, and it will be best to begin by explaining and illustrating what I mean by each in turn.

## CRITICAL PHILOSOPHY

In ordinary life and in the special sciences we constantly make use of certain very general concepts, such as number, thing, quality, change, cause, etc. Now, although we constantly *use* them and apply them with fair consistency, it cannot be said that we have any very clear ideas as to their proper analysis or their precise relations. And it is not the business of any of the special sciences to clear up these obscurities. Chemistry, e.g., tells us a great deal about particular substances, such as gold and *aqua regia,* and about their qualities and relations; but we should not go to a chemistry book for a discussion on substance, quality, and relation. Chemistry simply assumes these general concepts as fully understood and concerns itself with particular instances of them.

Now it is certain that our ideas about such general concepts are highly confused, and this shows itself as soon as we try to apply them to cases which are a little out of the ordinary. We think we know what we mean by "place" and "person," for instance; and we do no doubt agree in the main in applying and withholding these terms. But suppose we are asked: "In what place is the mirror image of a pin? And is it in this place in the same sense in which the pin itself is in *its* place?" Or suppose we are asked: "Was Sally Beauchamp a person?" We find ourselves puzzled by such questions, and this puzzlement is certainly due in part to the fact that we are not clear as to what we mean by "being in a place" or "being a person." Similar difficulties could be raised about all the fundamental concepts which we constantly use. Thus there is both need and room for a science which shall try to analyze and define the concepts which are used in daily life and in the special sciences. There is need for it, because these concepts really are obscure, and because their obscurity really does lead to difficulties. And there is room for it, because, whilst all the special sciences *use* these concepts, none of them is *about* these concepts as such. I regard Critical Philosophy as the science which has this for its most fundamental task.

It seems to me that such a science is perfectly possible, and that it actually exists, and has made a good deal of progress. I will illustrate this with some examples. Since the time of Berkeley and Descartes philosophers have devoted much attention to the problem of the "Reality of the External World." I do not pretend that there is any agreed answer to the question among them, but their inquiries have been most valuable in clearing up the meanings of such terms as

Abridged from *Contemporary British Philosophy.* Edited by J. H. Muirhead, First Series. (London: George Allen & Unwin, Ltd., 1924), Secs. 4–18, pp. 82–100. Reprinted by permission of the publisher.

"matter," "sensible appearance," "sensation," "perception," "independence," etc. Any competent philosopher nowadays, whether he asserts or denies the independent existence of matter, is asserting or denying something far more subtle and far better analyzed than anything which Berkeley or Descartes would have understood by the same form of words. Again, we are not agreed on the right analysis of "cause"; but any view we may reach should be far subtler and clearer than that which could have been held before Hume wrote his classical criticism of this category. . . .

Now Critical Philosophy has another and closely connected task. We do not merely use unanalyzed concepts in daily life and in science. We also assume uncritically a number of very fundamental propositions. In all our arguments we assume the truth of certain principles of reasoning. Again, we always assume that every change has a cause. And in **induction** we certainly assume something—it is hard to say what—about the fundamental "make-up" of the existent world. Now the second task of Critical Philosophy is to take these propositions which we uncritically assume in science and daily life and to subject them to criticism. . . . [S]ometimes it is quite certain that propositions of *some* kind are being assumed, and yet it is by no means easy to say exactly what these propositions are. In such cases the first business of Critical Philosophy is to find these assumptions and to state them clearly. This is one of the main difficulties of the theory of induction. Nearly every one was agreed that something, which they called the "Uniformity of Nature," was presupposed in all inductions. But *(a)* no one stated clearly what they meant by this; and *(b)* most writers seemed to think that nothing further was needed except the ordinary principles of deductive logic. It has therefore been an important task of Critical Philosophy to show *(a)* that inductive arguments can only be valid if they state their conclusions in terms of probability, and that they therefore use the principles of probability; and *(b)* that, if they do not *also* use some premise about nature, they will be unable to give any finite probability to their conclusions. The way is then clear for seeking the assumptions about nature which would suffice to give a reasonably high probability to the conclusions of generally accepted inductive arguments. It is easy to show that something more concrete than the Law of Causation is needed, and that the assumption of something like Natural Kinds at least is necessary. Finally, we are in a position to estimate the kind and degree of evidence which there is for such assumptions. . . .

## SPECULATIVE PHILOSOPHY

It is quite evident that what I have been describing under the name of *Critical Philosophy* does not include all that is understood by philosophy. It is certainly held to be the function of a philosopher to discuss the nature of Reality as a whole, and to consider the position and prospects of men in it. In a sense Critical Philosophy presupposes a certain view on this question. It assumes that our minds are so far in accord with the rest of Reality that by using them carefully and critically we approach nearer to the truth. But it is still clearer that Speculative Philosophy presupposes a considerable amount of Critical Philosophy. Its business is to take over all aspects of human experience, to reflect upon them, and to try to think out a view of Reality as a whole which shall do justice to all of them. Now it is perfectly useless to take over the scientific, social, ethical, aesthetic, and religious experiences of mankind in their crude, unanalyzed form. We do not know what they mean or what weight to attach to various parts of the whole mass till we have submitted them to a critical analytic investigation. . . .

It seems to me that the main value of Speculative Philosophy lies . . . in the collateral effects which it has, or ought to have, on the persons who pursue it. The speculative philosopher is forced to look at the world synoptically, and anyone who does not do this at some time in his life is bound to hold a very narrow and inadequate idea of Reality. This is a danger to which the natural scientist is peculiarly liable. The extraordinary success of physics and chemistry within their own sphere tempts men to think that the world is simply a physico-chemical system. These sciences, quite rightly for their own purposes, ignore the existence of minds; and scientists are liable to forget that somehow minds have grown up in a world of matter, and that it is by means of their activities that matter and its laws have become known. If a man referred to his brother or his cat as "an ingenious mechanism" we should know that he was either a fool or a physiologist. No one in practice treats himself or his fellow-men or his pet animals as machines, but scientists who have never made a study of Speculative Philosophy seem often to think it their duty to hold in theory what no one outside a lunatic asylum would accept in practice. If we remember that physics and chemistry are simply constructed to unify the correlations which we find among a selection of the sensa of three or four senses, the idea that these sciences give a complete account of the structure of all Reality becomes ludicrous. Thus our inability to explain the facts of life and mind in purely physico-chemical terms is not a paradox to be explained away, but is what might reasonably have been expected from the outset.

On the other hand, the man who starts from the side of mind is equally liable to fail to do justice to the facts. The properties with which physics and chemistry deal *are* very pervasive, and we *do* know them more accurately and thoroughly than we know anything else. And minds *are* very closely bound up with certain bits of matter, viz., our brains and nervous systems, and they *do* seem to have gradually developed in a world which once contained nothing but matter. The characteristic fault of Idealism is to be unable to see the trees for the wood, and the characteristic fault of Realism is to be unable to see the wood for the trees.The great merit of Idealism is that it really has tried to do justice to the social, ethical, aesthetic, and religious facts of the world. The great merit of Realism is that it really has tried to face in a patient and detailed way the problem of matter and of our perception of it. But neither of these activities is a substitute for the other; and a genuine Speculative Philosophy must combine the detailed study of the lower categories with the due recognition of the higher categories, and must try to reconcile the pervasiveness of the former with the apparently growing importance of the latter.

There is one thing which Speculative Philosophy must take into most serious consideration, and that is the religious and mystical experiences of mankind. These form a vast mass of facts which obviously deserve at least as careful attention as the sensations of mankind. They are of course less uniform than our sensations; many people, of whom I am one, are practically without these experiences. But probably most people have them to some extent, and there is a considerable amount of agreement between those people of all nations and ages, who have them to a marked degree. Of course the theoretical interpretations which have been put upon them are very varied, and it is obvious that they depend largely on the traditions of the time, place, and society in which the experient lives. I have compared the experiences themselves with sensations; we might compare the common features in the interpretations which have been put upon them with our ordinary common-sense beliefs about matter; and elaborate systems of theology might be compared with big scientific theories, like the wave theory of light. Obviously there remains a further step to be taken, comparable with the philosophic criticism and interpretation of scientific theories about matter. It seems reasonable to suppose at the outset that the whole mass of mystical and religious experience brings us into contact with an aspect of Reality which is not revealed in ordinary sense-perception, and that any system of Speculative Philosophy which ignores it will be extremely one-sided. In fact it cannot safely be ignored. If we count all such experiences as purely delusive, we must explain how such a widespread and comparatively coherent mass of illusion arose. And, if we find it impossible to take this view, we must try to understand and criticize these experiences; to sift away those factors in them which are of merely local and temporary interest; and to see what the residuum has to tell us about the probable nature of Reality. The great practical difficulty here is that those who have the experiences most vividly are seldom well fitted for the task of philosophical criticism and construction; whilst those who are fitted for the latter task are not often mystics or persons of religious genius. It is alleged, and it may well be true, that the capacity for such experiences can be cultivated by a suitable mode of life and a suitable system of training and meditation. In so far as this can be done without detriment to the critical faculties it deserves the serious attention of philosophers; for theories which are built on experiences known only by description are always unsatisfactory.

## A. C. Ewing (1899–1974)

A. C. Ewing is the author of numerous articles and books in metaphysics, moral theory and its applications, and philosophy of religion. Among his works are *The Morality of Punishment* (1929), *Idealism: A Critical Survey* (1934), *The Individual, the State and World Government* (1947), *The Definition of Good* (1947), and *Second Thoughts on Moral Philosophy* (1959).

# What Philosophy Is and Why It Is Worth Studying

### A. C. Ewing

A precise definition of the term "philosophy" is not practicable and to attempt it, at least at the beginning, would be misleading. A sarcastic person might define it as "everything and/or nothing." That is, it differs from the special sciences in that it attempts to give a picture of human thought as a whole, and even of Reality in so far as it is held that this can be done. . . . The term "philosopher" originally meant "lover of wisdom," and took its origin from a famous retort which Pythagoras made when he was called "wise." He said that his wisdom only consisted in knowing that he was ignorant, and that he should therefore not be called "wise," but "a lover of wisdom." "Wisdom" here is not restricted to any particular part of thought, and "philosophy" used to be understood as including what we now call the "sciences." This usage still survives in such phrases as "Chair of Natural Philosophy." As a great mass of specialized knowledge came to be acquired in a given field, the study of that field broke off from philosophy and came to be an independent discipline. The last sciences to do that have been Psychology and Sociology. Thus there is a tendency for the sphere of philosophy to contract as knowledge advances. We refuse to regard as philosophical those questions the answer to which can be given empirically. But this does not mean that philosophy will eventually shrink to nothing. The fundamental concepts of the sciences and the general picture of human experience, and of reality in so far as we

Abridged from *The Fundamental Questions of Philosophy,* by A. C. Ewing. (London: Routledge & Kegan Paul PLC, 1962), pp. 13–18. Reprinted by permission of the publisher.

form justified beliefs about it, remain within the purview of philosophy, since they cannot from the nature of the case be determined by the methods of any of the special sciences. It is discouraging that philosophers have not succeeded in attaining more agreement in regard to these matters, but we must not conclude that, where there is no agreed result, the effort has been wasted. Two philosophers who disagree may well each be contributing something of great value, though they are not yet in a position to disentangle it completely from error, and their rival accounts may be taken as supplementing each other. The fact that different philosophers are thus needed to supplement each other brings out the point that philosophizing is not only an individual but a social process. One of the cases of useful division of labor is the emphasis by different people of different sides of a question. Very much philosophy is, however, concerned rather with the way we know things than with the things known, and this is another reason why it may seem lacking in content. But discussions as to the ultimate criteria of truth may eventually determine in their application which propositions we decide in practice to be true. Philosophical discussions of the theory of knowledge have had indirectly an important effect on the sciences. . . .

Whitehead, one of the greatest and most respected thinkers of modern times, describes the gifts of philosophy as "insight and foresight, and a sense of the worth of life, in short, that sense of importance which nerves all civilized effort."* He adds "that when civilization culminates, the absence of a co-ordinating philosophy of life, spread throughout the community, spells decadence, boredom, and the slackening of effort." The importance of philosophy is based for him on the fact that it is "an attempt to clarify those fundamental beliefs which finally determine the emphasis of attention that lies at the basis of character." However that may be, it is certain that the character of a civilization is greatly influenced by its general view of life and reality. This till recently has been provided for most people by religious teaching, but religious views themselves have been greatly influenced by philosophic thought. Further, experience shows that religious views are apt to end in folly unless subject to constant review by reason. As for those who discard all religious views, they should be all the more concerned to work out a new view, if they can, to take the place of religious belief, and to work out such a new view is to engage in philosophy.

Science cannot take the place of philosophy, but itself raises philosophical problems. For science itself cannot possibly tell us what place in the whole scheme of things is held by the realm of facts with which it deals or even how they are related to the human minds which observe them. It cannot even demonstrate, though it must assume, the existence of the physical world, or the legitimacy of using the ordinary principles of **induction** to predict what will probably happen or to pass in any way beyond what has actually been observed. No scientific laboratory can demonstrate in what sense human beings have souls, whether or not the universe has a purpose, whether and in what sense we are free, and so on. I do not say that philosophy can solve these problems, but if it cannot nothing else can do so, and it is certainly worthwhile at least trying to see whether they are soluble. Science itself, as we shall see, is all the while presupposing concepts which fall within the subject matter of philosophy. And, while we cannot even start science without tacitly assuming answers to some philosophical questions, we certainly cannot make adequate mental use of it for our intellectual development without having a more or less coherent world-view. The successes of modern science would themselves have probably never been achieved if the scientist had not taken from great original philosophers certain assumptions on which he based his whole procedure. The "mechanistic" view of the universe characteristic of science during the last three centuries is derived chiefly from the philosopher Descartes. This mechanistic scheme has achieved such

*Adventures of Ideas,* p. 125.

wonderful results that it must be partly true, but it is also partly breaking down, and the scientist may have to look to the philosopher to help him build up a new one in its place.

Another very valuable service of philosophy (this time especially "critical philosophy") lies in the habit it forms of attempting an impartial judgment of all sides and the idea it gives of what evidence is and what one should look for and expect in a proof. This should be an important check on emotional bias and hasty conclusions and is specially needed and often specially lacking in political controversies. If both sides looked at political questions in the philosophical spirit, it is difficult to see how there could ever be a war between them. The success of democracy depends very much on the ability of the citizen to distinguish good and bad arguments and not to be misled by confusions. Critical philosophy sets up an ideal of good thinking and trains one in removing confusions. This is perhaps why Whitehead . . . says that "there can be no successful democratic society till general education conveys a philosophic outlook." . . .

## *Brand Blanshard (b. 1892)*

Brand Blanshard is one of the most distinguished twentieth century American philosophers and perhaps the most eloquent defender of a philosophical point of view which he labels "rationalism" and which is described in the essay below. He is most famous for his contributions in epistemology and metaphysics, but he has also worked in the areas of moral theory, philosophy of mind, and philosophy of religion. His major works are *The Nature of Thought* (1939), *Reason and Goodness* (1961), and *Reason and Analysis* (1962).

# The Philosophic Enterprise

## *Brand Blanshard*

### I

Philosophy is best understood, I think, as part of an older and wider enterprise, the enterprise of understanding the world. We may well look first at this understanding in the large. I shall ask, to begin with, what is its goal, then what are its chief stages, then what are the ways in which philosophy enters into it.

The enterprise, we have just said, is that of understanding the world. What do we mean by understanding—understanding anything at all? We mean, I suppose, explaining it to ourselves. Very well; what does explaining anything mean? We stumble upon some fact or event that is unintelligible to us; what would make it intelligible? The first step in the answer is, seeing it as an instance of some rule. You suffer some evening

Note: This paper is a revised form of a Mahlon Powell Lecture delivered at the University of Indiana in 1961. Abridged from *The Owl of Minerva: Philosophers on Philosophy*. Edited by C. J. Bontempo and S. Jack Odell (New York: McGraw-Hill Book Company, 1975). Reprinted by permission of C. J. Bontempo and S. Jack Odell.

from an excruciating headache and despondently wonder why. You remember that you just ate two large pieces of chocolate cake and that you are allergic to chocolate; the headache seems then to be explained. It is no longer a mere demonic visitor intruding on you from nowhere; you have domesticated it, assimilated it to your knowledge, by bringing it under a known rule.

What sort of rules are these that serve to render facts intelligible? They are always rules of connection, rules relating the fact to be explained to something else. You explain the headache by bringing it under a law relating it *causally* to something else. In like manner, you explain the fact that a figure on the board has angles equal to two right angles by relating it *logically* to something else; by pointing out that it is a triangle, and that it belongs to the triangles as such to have this property.

Such bringing of a case under a rule explains admirably so far as it goes. But suppose someone asks for a further explanation. When you explain your headache by reference to the chocolate or the angle sum of the figure by referring to its triangularity, he says: "Yes, yes, I know this, but what I don't understand is why the rule itself holds. How do you explain *that?*" We can only give the same answer as before. To explain a rule is to connect it with some other rule from which it follows, just as to explain a fact or event is to connect it with some other fact or event. When you can so connect it, you can explain it; when you cannot, you can't. You can explain why a triangle should have angles equal to a straight line because you can show that this must be true if certain other propositions are true that you normally accept without question. Can you show similarly that the rule about chocolate producing headaches follows from some further rule? No doubt an expert allergist could. He would show that in trying to assimilate the protein molecules of the chocolate, certain of your body cells break down; and the rule that eating chocolate produces a headache follows from the further and more precise rule that a certain kind of cell deterioration produces a certain kind of headache. But then why should *this* hold? Why should a change in body cells produce a conscious ache? All explanations so far offered here run into a stone wall. We can see that certain changes in the body are in fact followed by changes in consciousness; we have not the slightest idea why.

At this point two courses are open to one who is trying to explain his world. He has come — or if he has not, he soon will — to a generalization that he cannot now explain by bringing it under anything more general. Is he to continue in his attempt or not? The likelihood of his doing so may well depend on what he takes the ideal of explanation to be. Present-day **empiricists** are quite content to end their inquiries with rules or laws that are merely statements of general **conjunction.** Certain changes in the body are always accompanied by certain changes in consciousness. Why? That is a foolish question. If they are always in fact so connected, what more could a sensible person ask? One explains a falling snowflake or raindrop or meteor by bringing it under the law of gravitation, and if that law has been made precise, if one can show that the earth and the snowflake are so connected that each pulls the other with a force varying directly with its mass and inversely with the square of its distance, what more could one want? One might, to be sure, find some still wider generalization from which the law of gravitation itself followed; this was a leading interest of Einstein's toward the end of his life, and it made sense. But if further explanation means more than this, the empiricist holds, it is a will-o'-the-wisp. Every explanation of fact must come sooner or later to a dead end. It must halt somewhere with a generalization that is a pure statement of ***de facto*** togetherness, itself opaque to reason.

But there is another ideal of explanation open to us, that of the rationalists, of whom I am one. They hold that when you end with any law whatever that is a mere statement of conjunction, your explanation is incomplete and you are bound to *try* at least to go beyond it. What leads them to say this? It is their sense of the goal that understanding is seeking, of what would bring the attempt to explain finally to rest. When you ask the question "Why?" you are seeking an answer of some kind; but of what kind? We can see with regard to some answers that we can raise the same question again, of others that we cannot because we have already reached the end of the line. Suppose you remark that two straight lines do not enclose a space, or that whatever is colored is extended, or that a thing cannot at once have a property and not have it, and suppose now some bright skeptic asks you why. Could you give him an answer? I do not think you could, not because there is an answer that you don't know, but because anyone who understood your remark would know the answer already and would be asking a silly question. When you have a law that connects things by a self-evident necessity, the question "Why?" has no point, for the kind of insight you have is just the kind you are asking for. If you see that, being what it is, A *must* be B, the further question "Why?" is meaningless.

*What understanding is seeking, then, what would bring the search to rest, is seen necessity.* Where it is present, we have what we wanted; where it is absent, we have not yet fully understood.

Now a rationalist is a person who assumes that behind every *is* there is a *must,* that if snow is white or fire burns or John has a cold, the question "Why?" has an answer, and that this answer would disclose a necessity. You may protest: "Can you prove this? Do you really think that because we are seeking necessity, it must be there to be found, that things must be intelligible because it would be so satisfactory to us if they were?" The answer, of course, is "No." The philosopher who takes something to be true because he wants it to be true betrays his calling. But unless the philosopher could assume that there was some answer to his questions, he would have no motive for pressing them. For the critical rationalist the intelligibility of things is neither a necessary conclusion nor an arbitrary assumption, but a postulate, that is, a proposition which for practical purposes he must assume and which experience progressively confirms, but which is incapable of present proof.

Thus the rationalist is, if you will, a man of faith. His faith is that there is to be found in the universe the kind of intelligibility that would satisfy his intellect, that there is a coincidence between reality and his intellectual ideal, that at every point there is an answer to his question "Why?" This faith is the mainspring of his endeavor. He is ready to discard it if he has to, but not until he has to; and he will regard an apparent defeat as only a temporary setback if he can. After all, if there is no answer, why seek it? One may say indeed with George Saintsbury that "the end of all things is bafflement, but it is good not to be baffled too soon." But if we expect nature at any moment to set a roadblock to our reason, we shall almost surely be baffled too soon. . . .

## II

Now the career of reason, of which philosophy is one part, is a slow persistent climb toward the vision of [the world as a whole]. On its way it passes through four levels—those of infancy, common sense, science, and philosophy. We shall see more clearly the part of philosophy in this enterprise if we briefly retrace our steps through the earlier levels.

For each of us the adventure of the mind begins in a swamp so far below where we now stand that we cannot see it or clearly imagine it. We begin with sensation, "a booming, buzzing confusion" of sensations, signifying nothing. What takes us out of the primitive swamp is the formation of solid little islands in the swamp, nodules of qualities that stick together and behave in settled ways. It is a triumph of tender reason when the child can grasp one stable cluster of qualities as a bottle and another as a rattle. He is breaking through to the level of common sense where we chiefly live.

By the commonsense world I mean the world of things and persons. The transition into this world the child makes in those years that Bertrand Russell called the most decisive in one's life, the years from one to two. About this most familiar of all realms I want to make two observations, first that it is an intellectual construction, and second that it is no permanent home.

First, it is a construction. Things as a whole are never given in sensation; when we perceive a red ball, what we see must be pieced out by interpretation based on our past experience of its having another side. Common sense believes that some of the things I see moving about are persons with feelings and ideas like my own, though this is a metaphysical flight that it can never directly verify. Further, it believes that when you and I look at the ball, we are seeing the same thing—a daring and highly dubious theory. Indeed the head of the plain man is full of theories about men, women, foreigners, artists, and communists, and his religious beliefs are brimming over with **metaphysics.**

The second remark to be made is that much of this theory is bad theory. The plain man's theory of knowledge, his religious beliefs, and his generalizations about things and people, recorded often in his proverbs, are riddled with inconsistencies. "Be not pennywise," he says, and adds, "Take care of the pence and the pounds will take care of themselves." He accepts both quite serenely.

In the commonsense world, then, reason can find no permanent home or halting place. It must move forward into science. This advance is not an abrupt leap into a new order or dimension. Science, as T. H. Huxley said, *is* common sense refined and organized. The commonsense world is a theoretical construction that has been built up by roughly fifty thousand centuries of trial and error, and much of it comes as a legacy acquired without effort. The scientific order is a superstructure most of which has been built in the last three centuries. But the two structures are continuous, and the newly built upper story will perhaps be occupied by our descendants as effortlessly as we have acquired the lower ones. To pass from the lower to the higher, however, requires the ascent of two flights of stairs, the first of which takes us to a new level of abstraction and the second to a new level of exactness.

First, abstraction. The physicist as a man may have much interest in Jane Doe as a person, but as a scientist he has little or none. He breaks her up into a set of properties and studies these singly. In point of mass, she is indiscriminable from a sack of potatoes, and if dropped from the leaning tower, she would accelerate at the same rate. For science, the interest held by a law is proportioned to its generality, and the more general it is, the more abstract are the qualities that are related by its laws.

Secondly, exactness. The scientist is never satisfied until the characters he correlates are measured and their variations can be stated as functions of each other. Anyone may notice an apple falling from a tree or the increasing pressure in the pot when it boils, but it takes a Newton with his law of the inverse squares to describe exactly what the apple is doing, and Boyle with his inverse variation of volume and pressure to describe exactly what is happening in the kettle.

## III

The passage from common sense to science is not a passage to a new kind of thinking, but a refining of processes already at work. So is the passage from science to philosophy. It is a grave mistake to set up science and philosophy as rivals of each other; they are continuous with each other. A philosophy that ignores science will probably build castles in the air, and a science that ignores philosophy will be dogmatic or myopic or both. Philosophy, as I view it, is so bound up with science, so integral a part of the same enterprise, that I have here insisted on winding into it through the avenue of science.

Is there any need for going further? Many people in these days say no. "What is knowledge is science," Russell remarked, "and what is not science is not knowledge." It used to be said that to the English had been given the realm of the sea, to the French the domain of the land, and to the Germans the kingdom of the air; this meant of course the stratosphere, where philosophers are supposed to live, and indeed have been living ever since Thales wandered abroad with his head in the clouds and fell into a well. With these critics I must confess that I have much sympathy. The philosopher who pontificates about being and nonbeing in a prose that follows Dr. Johnson's alleged rule of never using a word of one syllable if he could find one of six seems to me rather worse than a bore. He is supposed to be a specialist in clear thinking and therefore clear speaking, and if he appears in public in a state of logical and linguistic unbuttonedness, groping for words for what are themselves mere gropings for ideas, he does neither philosophy nor education any good. But that is not philosophy as practiced by those who have known their craft — by McTaggart and Moore, by Broad and Price and Lovejoy. Surely no one who has understood these philosophers could regard as anything but important what they were trying to do. Well, what have they been trying to do?

They have tried to supplement the work of science in at least two respects. In both of these respects science has to be extended if our thirst for understanding is to be satisfied, but in neither of them do scientists take much interest. The fact is that, logically speaking, philosophy begins before science does, and goes on after science has completed its work. In the broad spectrum of knowledge, science occupies the central band. But we know that there is more to the spectrum than this conspicuous part. On one side, beyond the red end of the spectrum, there is a broad band of infrared rays; and on the other side, beyond the violet end, are the ultraviolet rays. Philosophy deals with the infrareds and the ultraviolets of science, continuous with the central band but more delicate and difficult of discernment.

Take the red end first. Consider the sense in which philosophy comes before science. Many of the concepts the scientist uses and many of his working assumptions he prefers to take for granted. He can examine them if he wishes, and some scientists do. Most do not, because if they waited till they were clear on these difficult basic ideas, they might never get to what most interests them at all. But it would be absurd to leave these basic ideas unexamined altogether. This somewhat thankless preliminary work is the task of the philosopher.

We referred to these unexamined ideas as concepts and assumptions. Let us illustrate the concepts first.

Common sense and science are constantly using certain little words of one syllable that seem too familiar and perhaps unimportant to call for definition. We say, "What time is it?" "There is less space in a compact car," "There was no cause for his taking offense," "He must be out of his mind," "I think these strikes are unjust to the public." Consider the words we have used: "time," "space," "cause," "good," "truth," "mind," "just," "I." If someone said to us, "What do you mean, *I*?" or, when we asked what time it was, "What do you mean by 'time'?" we should probably say, "Oh, don't be an idiot," or perhaps with St. Augustine, "I know perfectly well what time means until you ask me, and then I don't know." I suspect this last is the sound answer regarding all these words. We know what they mean well enough for everyday purposes, but to think about them is to reveal depth after depth of unsuspected meaning. This fact suggests both the strength and the weakness of present-day linguistic philosophy. It is surely true, as this school contends, that a main business of philosophy is to define words. The first great outburst of philosophy in the talk of Socrates was largely an attempt at defining certain key words of the practical life — "justice," "piety," "temperance," "courage." But their meanings proved bafflingly elusive; he chased the ghost of justice through ten books of the *Republic* and barely got his hands on it in the end. Socrates saw that to grasp the meaning even of these simple and common terms would solve many of the deepest problems in ethics and metaphysics. But we must add that Socrates was no ordinary language philosopher. He was not an Athenian Noah Webster, collecting the shopworn coins that were current in the marketplace; on the contrary, he took special pleasure in showing that at the level of ordinary usage our meanings were muddled and incoherent. Only by refining and revising them could we arrive at meanings that would stand.

Now the scientist who is trying to find the truth about the cause of flu cannot discontinue his experiments till he has reached clearness on the nature of truth or the concept of causality. The political scientist who holds that democracy is in certain respects better than communism cannot remain dumb till all his colleagues have agreed as to the definition of "good." These people must get on with their work, and they are right not to stop and moon about ultimates. But these ideas are ultimates after all; we must use them hourly in our thinking; and it would be absurd if, while researchers were trying to be clear about relatively unimportant matters, no one tried to get clear about the most important things of all. And the right persons to make that effort are surely the philosophers. A philosopher friend of mine sat down in a railway car beside a salesman who, recognizing a kindred spirit, poured out a stream of talk about his line. "And what's your line?" he concluded. "Notions," replied the philosopher. That seemed all right to the salesman, and it should be so to us. Notions are the line of the philosopher, such key notions as truth, validity, value, knowledge, without which scientific thought could not get under way, but which the scientist himself has neither the time nor the inclination to examine.

We suggested that it is not only his ultimate concepts but also his ultimate assumptions that the scientist prefers to turn over to others for inspection. Let me list a few and ask whether there is any natural scientist who does not take them for granted. That we can learn the facts of the physical order through perception. That the laws of our logic are valid of this physical order. That there is a public space and a public time in which things happen and to which we all have access. That every event has a cause. That under like conditions the same sort of thing has always happened, and always will. That we ought to adjust the degree of our assent to any proposition to the strength of the evidence for it. These are all propositions of vast importance, which the scientist makes use of every day of his life. If any one of them were false, his entire program would be jeopardized. But they are not scientific propositions. They are assumed by all sciences equally; they are continuous with the thought of all; yet they are the property of none. It would be absurd to leave these unexamined, for some or all of them may be untrue. But the scientist would be aghast if, before he used a microscope or a telescope, he had to settle the question whether knowledge was possible through perception, or whether there could be a logic without **ontology.** Scientists have at times discussed these matters, and their views are always welcome, but they generally and sensibly prefer to turn them over to specialists. And the specialists in these problems are philosophers.

I have now, I hope, made clear what was meant by saying that philosophy comes before science. It comes before it in the sense of taking for examination the main concepts and assumptions with which scientists begin their work. Science is logically dependent on philosophy. If philosophy succeeded in showing, as Hume and Carnap thought it had, that any reference to a nonsensible existent was meaningless, the physics that talks of electrons and photons would either have to go out of business or revise its meanings radically. If philosophy succeeded, as James, Schiller, and Freud thought it had, in showing that our thinking is inescapably chained to our impulses and emotions, then the scientific enterprise, as an attempt at impartial and objective truth, would be defeated before it started. Philosophy does not merely put a bit of filigree on the mansion of science; it provides its foundation stones.

## IV

If philosophy begins before science does, it also continues after the scientist has finished his work. Each science may be conceived as a prolonged effort to answer one large question. Physics asks, "What are the laws of matter in motion?" Biology asks, "What kinds of structure and behavior are exhibited by living things?" Each science takes a field of nature for its own and tries to keep within its own fences. But nature has no fences; the movement of electrons is somehow continuous with the writing of *Hamlet* and the rise of Lenin. Who is to study this continuity? Who is to reflect on whether the physicist, burrowing industriously in his hole, can break a tunnel through to the theologian, mining anxiously in his? Surely here again is a task that only the philosopher can perform. One way of performing it, which I do not say is the right way, is suggested by the definition of philosophy as the search by a blind man in a dark room for a black hat that isn't there, with the addendum that if he finds it, that is theology. It may be thought that since no two true propositions can contradict each other, the results of independent scientific search could not conflict, and that there is no problem in harmonizing them. On the contrary, when we examine even the most general results of the several sciences, we see that they clash scandalously and that the task of harmonizing them is gigantic. Indeed the most acute and fascinating of metaphysical problems arise in the attempt to reconcile the results of major disciplines with each other.

How are you to reconcile physics with psychology, for example? The physicist holds that every physical event has a physical cause, which seems innocent enough. To say that a material thing could start moving, or, once started, could have its motion accelerated or changed in direction without any physical cause, would seem absurd. If you say that a motion occurs with no cause at all, that is to the physicist irresponsible; if you say that it represents interference from outside the spatial order, it is superstitious. Now is not the psychologist committed to saying that this interference in fact occurs daily? If my lips and vocal cords now move as they do, it is because I am thinking certain thoughts and want to communicate them to you. And the only way in which a thought or desire can produce such results is through affecting the physical motions of waves or particles in my head. It will not do to say that only the nervous correlates of my thought are involved in producing these results, for those physical changes are not my thoughts, and if my thoughts themselves can make no difference to what I do, then rational living becomes a mummery. My action is never in fact guided by conscious choice, nor anything I say determined by what I think or feel. Common sense would not accept that, nor can a sane psychology afford to; the evidence against it is too massive. And what this evidence shows is that conscious choice, which is not a physical event at all, does make a difference to the behavior of tongue and lips, of arms and legs. Behavior may be consciously guided. But how are you to put that together with the physicist's conviction that all such behavior is caused physically? That is the lively philosophical problem of body and mind.

Conflicts of this kind may occur not only between natural sciences but between a natural and a normative science. Take physics and ethics. For the physicist all events—at least all macroscopic events—are caused; that is, they follow in accordance with some law from events immediately preceding them. This too seems innocent enough. But now apply the principle in ethics. A choice of yours is an event, even if not a physical event, and thus falls under the rule that all events are caused. That means that every choice you make follows in accordance with law from some event or events just preceding it. But if so, given the events that just preceded any of my choices, I had to do what I did do; I could not have done otherwise. But if that is true, does it not make nonsense to say in any case that I ought to have done otherwise, since I did the only thing that I could have done? But then what becomes of ethics as ordinarily conceived? If the scientific principle is true, one will have to rethink the ethical ground for remorse and reward and punishment and praise and blame. This is the ancient problem of free will, which was discussed with fascination by Milton's angels while off duty from their trumpets, and is discussed with equal fascination by undergraduates today.

To be sure, there are people nowadays who say that these old metaphysical issues are really only linguistic and disappear with a due regard to common usage. Thus when we see a man making something happen and know that he is not acting under coercion or some special inducement, we say he is acting freely; that is standard usage and hence correct usage; hence when we say that the man is acting freely, we are speaking correctly; hence we *are* acting freely; and hence there is no problem. I am not convinced. No doubt the man *is* acting freely in the sense chosen. Unfortunately this sense is irrelevant to the metaphysical issue. For what the determinist is saying is that even when we are *not* under any sort of coercion in the ordinary sense, our choices still follow from causes; and whether *that* is true is not to be settled by studying the plain man's language, for the chances are that he has never thought about it; nor would he necessarily be right if he had.

There are many other conflicts like the two we have mentioned. They fall in no one of the disciplines, but between them, and they must be arbitrated by an agency committed to nonpartisanship. The only plausible nominee for this post is philosophy. Philosophy is the interdepartmental conciliation agency, the National Labor Relations Board, or if you prefer, the World Court, of the intellectual community. Like these other agencies, it has no means of enforcing its verdicts. Its reliance is on the reasonableness of its decisions.

We are now in a position to see the place of philosophy in the intellectual enterprise as a whole. Intelligence has shown from the beginning a drive to understand. To understand anything means to grasp it in the light of other things or events that make it intelligible. The first great breakthrough of this drive was the system of common sense, which was molded into form by millennia of trial and error. This system is being superseded by science, whose network of explanation is far more precise and comprehensive. Philosophy is the continuation of this enterprise into regions that science leaves unexplored. It is an attempt to carry understanding to its furthest possible limits. It brings into the picture the foundations on which science builds and the arches and vaultings that hold its structures together. Philosophy is at once the criticism and the completion of science. That, as I understand it, is what all the great philosophers have been engaged upon, from Plato to Whitehead.

They may never wholly succeed. It is quite possible that men will use such understanding as they have achieved to blow themselves and their enterprise off the planet. But while they do allow themselves further life, the enterprise is bound to go on. For the effort to understand is not a passing whim or foible; it is no game for a leisure hour or "lyric cry in the midst of business." It is central to the very nature and existence of man; it is what has carried him from somewhere in the slime to the lofty but precarious perch where he now rests. The drive of his intelligence has constructed his world for him and slowly modified it into conformity with the mysterious world without. To anyone who sees this, philosophy needs no defense. It may help in practical ways, and of course it does. But that is not the prime reason why men philosophize. They philosophize because they cannot help it, because the enterprise of understanding, ancient as man himself, has made him what he is, and alone can make him what he might be.

# Part 1 — Glossary

**Accidental** A property of a thing is accidental if it is not necessary to make the thing what it is. For example, relative to the concept "triangular," having sides of equal length is an accidental property. It is not even part of what makes something triangular, whereas having exactly three sides is essential or nonaccidental. It *is* part of what makes a thing triangular. See also **essential,** below.

**Analytic** A proposition or statement is analytic if its truth depends only on the meanings of the terms it contains, and not on any facts about the rest of reality. Analytic propositions are definitional truths. For example, the proposition "All triangles have exactly three sides" is analytic. Three-sidedness is part of the definition of the term "triangle." One need only know the definition of a triangle (closed, three-sided, rectilinear plane figure) to know that the proposition is true.

**Conjunction** Conjunction refers to the coming together of two or more things or the occurring together of two or more events. The laws of science are typically laws of constant conjunction. For example, that metals expand when heated is a law of physical science that expresses (at least) the constant conjunction of two events, the heating of a metal and the expanding of that metal. See the selection by Hume in Part 2 for the view that the real relationship between causes and effects consists of a constant conjunction of events in our past experience and nothing more.

**De facto** This phrase is Latin and can be loosely translated "as a matter of fact." The usual opposition is between de facto and de jure, between the occurrence of something as a matter of fact that could have been otherwise (de facto) and the occurrence of something as a matter of law or principle that could not have been otherwise (de jure).

**Dialectic** Dialectic is a process of conversation through which individuals try to answer a question by talking with each other. Any answer will serve as a starting point. The proposed answer is then subjected to criticism by the participants, and a better answer produced in light of the weaknesses of the initial answer that criticism reveals. This second answer undergoes the same process, and so on. The idea is that each stage profits from the previous one so that the answers approach nearer and nearer to the correct answer, the one that will have no further weaknesses for critical inquiry to reveal. See the discussion of *Euthyphro* in the introduction to this part, "Scope and Method."

**Empiricist** An empiricist is a philosopher who believes that all of our ideas come to us through sense experience and that all of our knowledge of the world is a matter of observations and generalizations from those observations.

**Epistemology** Epistemology is the branch of philosophy devoted to the theory of knowledge. It studies such things as the nature and limits of human knowledge, the relation between knowledge and experience, and the justification of various kinds of beliefs or belief systems.

**Essential** A property of a thing is essential if it is necessary to make the thing what it is. See also **accidental,** above.

**Induction** Induction is the process of reasoning from observed facts to facts about things or events that have not been observed — for example, from facts about the past and present to conclusions about the future or from facts about observed objects of a certain kind to conclusions about all objects of that kind.

**Logic** Logic is the study of the relations among propositions, especially the relation that holds between the premises (propositions offered in support of another proposition) and conclusion (the proposition supported) of an argument. An argument in this sense is any group of propositions consisting of one or more premises and a conclusion.

**Metaphysics** Metaphysics is the branch of philosophy devoted to the study of reality. It examines the various categories or kinds of things that reality includes and relations between these categories.

**Negation** Negation refers both to the logical operation that transforms a proposition into its opposite and the product of such an operation. The negation of the proposition "All men are mortal" would be the proposition "Not all men are mortal" or equivalently "At least one man is immortal."

**Ontology** Ontology is the study of the nature or essence of things. The distinction between ontology and metaphysics is both complicated and controversial. At this point in your study of philosophy, it would be best to treat them as equivalent. See also **metaphysics,** above.

# *Part 1—Study Questions*

1. Euthyphro's first response to the question "What is piety?" is that prosecuting one's father for murder is, and that failing to do so would be impiety. Even if Euthyphro is correct that the former is pious and the latter impious, this still won't answer Socrates' question. Why not?
2. Socrates is willing to suppose, just for the sake of the argument, that the gods love all pious acts and only pious acts, and yet rejects Euthyphro's claim that "pious" means "loved by the gods." Socrates is right. Here is an analogous (having the same structure or form) case. Suppose that George's favorite shape is that of a triangle. Then all and only those things that are George's favorite shape are triangles. Nonetheless, "triangular" does not mean "having George's favorite shape." Why not? That is, explain why Socrates is right.
3. How does pointing out that justice is a particular "part" of piety help to define it? What more would be needed to complete the understanding of the concept? Give an analogous definition of some other concept.

# 2

# EXPERIENCE AND KNOWLEDGE

Interest in the relation between experience and knowledge, in whether or how experience of something gives us knowledge about it, is almost as old as philosophy itself. So is sceptical doubt, the sweeping suggestion that our experience is always or almost always unequal to the task of giving us knowledge about reality. What is unique about the period referred to as "modern philosophy" (the seventeenth and eighteenth centuries) is that **epistemology** or theory of knowledge became central to philosophy, and that a particular way of looking at sceptical doubt and responding to it gave the entire tradition a new direction whose influence is still felt today. The French philosopher Descartes is given credit for turning philosophy from the scholasticism of the Middle Ages and putting it upon its modern course. Although we associate sceptical doubt with Descartes, it was certainly not a novel discovery of his. Not only does **scepticism** of much the same scope go back to the Greek and Roman sceptics of the late fourth and early third centuries B.C., but Descartes himself grew up in the sceptical milieu of early seventeenth century France, which included such famous sceptical philosophers as Montaigne and Gassendi. Descartes' scepticism was exceptionally thorough, but what was unique was his claim to have discovered through sceptical doubt an access to certainty and knowledge. Some of the details of this discovery will be discussed in the introduction to the first section of this part that follows. For now we will describe briefly the shape that Descartes gave to the philosophical discussion of human knowledge, since the model that emerges from his investigation of knowledge and its limitations has not yet lost all of its grip on the discipline.

For Descartes, the problems associated with human knowledge have a common form. Our knowledge is typically about things or objects. Our experience contains only the ideas or representations of those things or objects, not the things themselves. And so in order to know anything about the way things really are, we need some guarantee that our ideas represent things correctly, that the world outside us really is the way it appears to be inside our experience. The problem is that such a guarantee seems to be beyond our reach. We cannot break out of our experience to check the relation of its contents to reality, and real objects, as opposed to their mental representations, cannot break into our experience to give us a way to check that relation from inside. This gap between experience and reality is the common thread running through epistemological discussions from Descartes to the present. Philosophers who find scepticism attractive or unavoidable argue that the gap cannot be successfully bridged. Philosophers unsympathetic to the sceptical point of view argue either that it can be bridged or that it isn't wide enough to create the serious difficulties the sceptic claims it does. But the problem is understood by sceptics and nonsceptics alike along the lines sketched by Descartes, and the battles are fought, for the most part, entirely on Cartesian terms. It is because of this influence that Descartes is referred to as "the father of modern philosophy" and remains to this day one of our most important philosophical ancestors.

Sceptical doubt can be understood in terms of a particular analysis of the concept of knowledge. What exactly is required before we are entitled to apply the concept, to make a claim to know? I believe that the next president of this country will be a democrat, but I wouldn't claim to *know* that she will be. I believe that you are capable of understanding everything I have written in this part introduction, but I don't think I *know* that either. On the other hand, I know what my name is and that I am wearing shoes right now, and in neither case would I be inclined to say that I merely believe it. So the question becomes: What more is required to change mere belief into knowledge? And a natural answer is that the difference is a matter of certainty. When I am certain—as with my having shoes on and my own identity—I am entitled to claim to know. Whereas when I fall short of certainty—as with the next president and your ability to comprehend what I write—I may have beliefs, perhaps strongly held ones, but I fall short of being able to say with confidence that I *know* these things. So this tiny exploration seems to yield the following partial analysis of knowledge. There may be much more to the concept than we have considered, but one requirement is that we be certain that something is the case before we claim to know it. Knowledge requires certainty. What then does certainty require? What must be the case in order for us to be certain?

Suppose we consider the following case. I am standing in front of a large lecture hall which looks to be little more than half full. I glance up quite briefly for the first time since entering the room and then announce that there are 143 persons in the lecture hall, not counting myself. Do I know that? Of course not, I just guessed. And it is possible, to say the least, that I guessed wrong. So now I carefully count the people in the room and report that there are actually 127 people present, not counting myself. Do I know this time? Well, just as it was possible that I guessed wrong the first time, isn't it possible that I counted wrong this time, in spite of trying to be careful? It is a large room and the seats are close together, and there are a number of ways I could have missed someone or counted someone twice. And once I realize this I see that I am not yet certain and shouldn't claim to know. So I count carefully twice more and ask a student in the first row to do likewise (but to include himself)—and the result of all three checks on my initial count is the same as that count was: 127 people in the lecture hall, not counting me. Finally I can claim to know that there are 127 persons present in addition to myself. I do so. Then a young man in the front of the room raises his hand and, when I ask him what he wants, explains that he and a number of other members of the class are pledging the same fraternity. It seems that one of the pranks the pledges must participate in consists of one of them bringing a very lifelike mannequin to each of his large lecture classes each day and propping it up in the seat next to him to look just like a regular member of the class. The young man turns around and scans the class and sure enough spots a fellow pledge in the back of the room with the dummy sitting next to him. When I look more closely I can see that it is just a mannequin. I now go back over the entire class checking not just the number but enough of the nature of each occupant of a seat to make sure each is a person rather than a dummy (no pun intended). The already discovered mannequin was the only one of its kind present, and at last I come to know that there are 126 persons in the lecture hall in addition to myself. We can leave the story at this point. If a sceptic were telling it, it would continue indefinitely, of course, since the sceptic's point is that we never do and never can complete the process of making certain of the truth of claims like the one in our story, claims about the way things really are in the world.

The story above gives us a way to see what is involved in certainty with respect to claims to know. We seem to have to check so as to eliminate or rule out the various things that stand in the way of our being certain. In our story we had to rule out misguessing, miscounting, and misidentifying the things counted. Let's call such things counterpossibilities to the knowledge claim in question. To be a counterpossibility, something must be both possible and counter to what we claim to know. If we claim to know that some belief is true (in the story above, the belief that there are 143 persons in the lecture hall, not counting me with the number changed to 127 and finally to 126), we seem to need to rule out every state of affairs that is possible and that would, if actual, mean that we were not in a position to be certain the belief is true. So knowledge seems to require certainty and certainty seems to require the elimination of counterpossibilities (Descartes uses the term *doubts* for what we have referred to as counterpossibilities).

Scepticism is the view that, because we cannot rule out all the counterpossibilities for most of the things we claim to know, we cannot be certain of their truth and, hence, do not really know them at all. Sometimes this view is put forward on the basis of there being an indefinite number of counterpossibilities and so more of them than we can ever check and eliminate. More often the view is based on one or more special counterpossibilities, sometimes referred to as sceptical doubts, which by themselves make it impossible for us to be certain of the truth of most of the things we ordinarily claim to know. The most famous of these is Descartes' suggestion that we might be dreaming. Is that a legitimate counterpossibility to most of our knowledge claims? Well it does seem to be just barely possible that I might now be dreaming. I have mistaken dreams for waking experiences on occasion. That's what nightmares are, after all. So although it doesn't seem at all likely to me that I am dreaming right now and it would be an incredible waste of potential fantasy time if I were, it does seem that it is just possible. If I were actually dreaming, would that be counter to most of my knowledge claims? Absolutely. Not just claims about the number of people in the classroom, but also such apparently clear-cut cases of knowledge as that I have shoes on right now and that my name is what I think it is. If I am dreaming right now I might well be in bed with nothing on my feet and I might well wake up and suddenly realize that I had only been dreaming that I was Harry Hall. So the counterpossibility does seem to be legitimate, and this means that I will need to rule it out before I can claim to know much of anything. So I pinch myself and it hurts, or I ask others to verify that I'm really awake, or, perhaps, to my amazement I actually have the experience of waking up. Would any of these things allow me to be certain that I am not now dreaming? Well, they would if I could tell whether I had actually pinched myself and felt the pain or only dreamed that I had pinched myself and felt the pain—or that I had really checked with others and verified that I was awake as opposed to only dreaming that I had checked and dreaming that I had received such verification—or, again, that I had really awakened rather than simply dreamt that I had, since people have had the experience of a dream within a dream. And suddenly the point of the sceptical doubt starts to hit us. What is special about this counterpossibility is that once we admit that there's even the remotest possibility that it might be actual, we seem to be unable to make certain that it isn't. Once we grant that we just might be "inside" such a possibility, there doesn't seem to be any way to find out that we are ever "outside" of it. And once we see this we should realize that dreams represent just one such counterpossibility or doubt. Hallucinations, the control of our experience by some mad scientist or powerful alien, all share the same crucial features. They don't seem to be absolutely impossible and, granting that, there doesn't seem to be any experience that could show conclusively that they aren't actually the case right now. And each has the power to render uncertain any claim that depends upon our experience of the reality outside our own minds, which seems to place incredible limitations on the scope of human knowledge.

For Descartes, sceptical doubt was not an end in itself, not a goal to be achieved, but rather the means used to discover those things of which we could be absolutely certain. Methodical doubt revealed certain truths to be immune to sceptical assault, and these provided the secure foundation on which the structure of human knowledge was to be erected. The introduction to the first section of this part describes the building blocks and plan for that structure as Descartes envisioned it. Few philosophers today would agree to his blueprint for that building, but the view of what kinds of things are most certain and able to be known, along with the sceptical challenge that led Descartes to that view, has survived. What is most certain and able to be known is the existence and content of the mind itself, experience rather than its objects. As we try to move outward, the gap between experience and reality opens and sceptical doubt finds room to work. Much of the philosophical effort of the three centuries since Descartes has been devoted to attempts to close that gap and defenses of our beliefs against the sceptical challenge.

The classical **empiricists** responded to the challenge in a number of ways. Locke argued that our belief in the reality of the objects of perception was so basic and instinctive that it could not really be doubted. One could try to imagine it all a dream as an intellectual exercise, but in the end nature would win out and return us to our instinctive faith in sense experience almost in spite of ourselves. Of course, if knowledge requires certainty, the fact that our beliefs are natural, unavoidable, or the best we can do doesn't seem to be enough to qualify them as knowledge. Berkeley argued that there wasn't any physical reality outside experience to be known and accounted for the regularity and stability of the apparently material things in our experience by interpreting them as ideas in the mind of God. Reid argued that the most basic beliefs of common sense require no justification and should be accepted without question. In most cases Descartes and his basic problem of knowledge were not met head on.

But there was, in Locke and in Hume as well, the beginnings of a continuing effort to change the question from "How do we know?" to "Why do we believe?" Locke and Hume argued, in effect, that the dilemma between absolute certainty and the notion that there's nothing worthy of belief was a false one. After all, we may have good reasons for holding many of the beliefs that we do even when we fall short of having absolute certainty of their truth. A number of such reasons have been proposed—among them, that the practice of trusting experience and instinctive belief has been necessary for our survival and successful coping with life, that the kind of evidence we do have is just the sort appropriate to this kind of belief, and that the system of beliefs produced by this practice fits together with the whole of our experience.

In the twentieth century a group of philosophers did attempt to meet the Cartesian challenge to our ordinary knowledge claims directly. Austin, Moore, Malcolm, and others argued that we *do* know we aren't dreaming, at least most of the time, and that we *are* as certain of a number of perfectly ordinary claims about things in the real world as we are about anything—and that such certainty is enough to qualify such claims as knowledge in the strictest sense of the term. Frequently such views are accompanied by a diagnosis of the mistake made by the sceptical philosopher that leads to the strange denial of our ordinary knowledge claims. Some of these diagnoses are that the sceptical philosopher has ignored the ordinary context in which the knowledge claims are made, changed the meaning of "know" so as to place unreasonable demands upon our ordinary use of the concept, or misused language in the assault upon common sense so that the sceptical claims are just meaningless or nonsense.

As evidenced by the final selection in the first section of this part, scepticism is still alive in spite of all the attempts to defend common sense and uphold our ordinary claims to know. That doesn't mean that scepticism is correct, but rather that it is still viable, able to be argued for or defended by competent contemporary philosophers. One of the positive side effects of twentieth century scepticism is a renewed emphasis in the direction of the rationality of belief rather than the certainty of knowledge.

This leads naturally to a philosophical interest in the beliefs that make up **empirical** science. Empirical science is a rational enterprise. Scientists believe that certain theories are true for good reasons, not just as a matter of arbitrary whim or personal taste. Of course the best reason for believing a theory to be true would be that one is absolutely certain of it, that it couldn't possibly be false given the evidence provided by experience. And some scientists have actually suggested this to be the case. But the sceptical point of view and the constant succession of theories in natural science, the replacement of theories as well established and firmly accepted as Newton's mechanics by alternatives as novel and initially inconceivable as Einstein's relativity theory, make it almost impossible to believe any longer in the ability of experience to guarantee the truth of our beliefs, practical or theoretical. But if experience cannot prove a theory to be true, how can it justify belief in the theory or the rejection of competing beliefs? The second section of this part suggests some answers to that question in terms of twentieth century philosophy of science. An overview of those accounts is provided in the introduction to that section of the readings. In addition to furnishing criteria for preferring one scientific theory to another, the readings attempt to explain what makes a theory scientific in the first place—what it is that makes certain theories or views legitimate candidates for rational belief rather than cleverly contrived frauds or hoaxes, suitable only for irrational acceptance.

# *Doubt and Certainty*

Two major schools of philosophical thinking emerged during the modern period of the history of philosophy (seventeenth and eighteenth centuries)—the **rationalists** and the **empiricists.** These two groups of philosophers differed in terms of their approaches to philosophy, their views on philosophic method. The basic difference was over the question of priority with respect to the two major sources of human understanding or knowledge, namely, reason and experience. The rationalists put the emphasis on reason—on rational intuition and necessary principles of reason as the most important sources of truth and understanding. The empiricists put the emphasis on experience—on concrete sensory awareness of the world and probable inferences from that awareness as the most important sources of truth and understanding. The rationalists believed in the existence of innate ideas, that there are some mental contents that are in the human mind from the beginning and not put there by experience. In the following selection by Descartes you will find mention of at least two such ideas. The empiricists believed that all ideas or mental contents originate in sense experience, that without any experience the mind would be completely blank. The first part of the selection by Hume in this section argues for the truth of that claim. Another way to look at the difference between rationalism and empiricism is in terms of two different kinds of science, mathematical and natural. The rationalists took the former and the empiricists the latter as the model for human understanding. So the rationalists thought primarily in terms of self-evident first principles and absolutely certain **deductions** from them. The empiricists, on the other hand, looked for observational evidence, reliable inferences from that evidence, and further observational tests of those inferences.

Descartes, the first major figure in the rationalist tradition, was a mathematician as well as a philosopher. Cartesian coordinates in geometry are so called because of him. From geometry he had a very definite idea about what the structure of human knowledge had to be like if it was to be a system of absolutely certain truths. The structure had to be foundational, with absolutely certain beginnings and a method for building from those beginnings that preserved the same certainty at every higher level of the structure. Just as Euclid's geometry begins with self-evident axioms and derives its theorems in such a way that the truth of the axioms guarantees the truth of the theorems, so human knowledge as a whole must rest on some absolutely certain and self-evident truth or truths and the rest of knowledge be built upon that foundation in such a way that the certainty of the foundation extends throughout the rest of the system.

Descartes uses sceptical doubt as a tool in the search for foundational truth. The way to discover absolutely certain truths is to subject every candidate to the full range of conceivable doubts and see what, if anything, survives this process. Descartes discovers that any beliefs we have that are based upon sense experience fail this test, as do beliefs that rest upon mental calculation or computation. Sense experience can be deceptive, as in the case of optical illusions and other forms of misperception. And if sense experience can be the source of inaccurate information, it can provide knowledge on any particular occasion only if its accuracy on that occasion can be established beyond doubt. At this point the true sceptical counterpossibilities, discussed in the general introduction to this part, are brought in to put such guaranteed accuracy indefinitely beyond our reach on all occasions. Beliefs based upon mental calculation or computation, such as the belief that two plus two equals four, fall before the sceptical possibility of an unknown controller of our mental processes. Such an "evil genius" could interfere with the mental calculation so that we always miscalculated with no way to detect or correct it.

That is, for all we know, our entire system of arithmetic may be a system of systematic error produced by an unknown deceiver.

After dismissing in the first meditation virtually all of what we would ordinarily claim to know as doubtful, Descartes searches in the early part of the second meditation for something that can be known with absolute certainty even if any or all of the sceptical possibilities should be actual. He finds one such truth that we will leave you to discover along with him in your reading. Armed with this truth and the sceptical doubts of the first meditation he goes on to prove that our bodies are, at most, an accidental or nonessential feature of us and, finally, that they are not even required as a means to any real or essential knowledge we might have of ordinary physical objects, should it turn out that such objects really exist.*

In spite of the demonstrated truths of the second meditation, Descartes enters the third meditation still knowing very little. If the edifice of human knowledge is going to get more than barely off the ground, Descartes must make some major additions. The addition he proposes is the certain knowledge of God's existence. Descartes argues that the fact that he has a certain idea in his mind demonstrates conclusively that God exists. The argument is a cosmological argument (see Part 6), although a very idiosyncratic one, claiming that God's actual existence is necessary in order to account for a certain feature of the world, namely, the presence of a particular idea in the mind of Descartes. This one piece of knowledge, assuming Descartes has succeeded, is supposed to pay tremendous dividends. God would not allow us to be systematically deceived with no means of detecting and correcting our errors. The existence of an all-powerful nondeceiver gives us a guarantee against the sceptical doubts of the first meditation. We may still make errors, but we cannot be so constructed that error is the best we can do on the basis of our experience. God would not have made us that way or allowed any outside influence to have altered things so as to produce that effect. So we get back a great deal of the knowledge that was lost as a result of the first meditation.

On the other hand, this makes virtually all of our knowledge of the real world depend upon this proof of God's existence. If the proof is not entirely conclusive, and few philosophers today would grant that it is, the result of the *Meditations* as a whole is scepticism with respect to our knowledge of anything beyond the contents of our own experience.

Locke, a philosopher in the empiricist tradition, argues that we ought to count as knowledge at least some of the beliefs that scepticism seems to undermine, namely those beliefs that are about objects we are perceiving right now. It is not that the sceptical possibilities are shown to be impossible. It is rather that the evidence of the senses while the object is right there in front of us is so compelling that we cannot help but believe. Locke goes on to suggest a number of features of such experience which support such belief, including finally the fact that we cannot do any better and don't need to for practical purposes anyway. Still, memory is ruled out as a source of knowledge because the beliefs to which it gives rise are merely probable and not certain. It is not entirely clear how the considerations Locke gives in support of perceptual belief render such belief certain as opposed to highly probable.

Hume defends the basic empiricist thesis that all of our ideas or conceptions originate in sense experience. Sense experience supplies us with impressions, both simple and complex. Ideas are either the mental copies of these impressions or constructed out of the pieces of such copies by means of one or more of the four capacities the mind possesses for making new ideas out of old. Hume gives two kinds of argument in support of this view, both of which are contained in the first part of the selection we have provided and worthy

*Most of these conclusions conflict sharply with common sense. Don't just take them lying down. Follow the arguments carefully and make sure Descartes has really proven the truth of their conclusions before you throw in the towel. You may find it helpful at this point to look at the appendix in the back of this text on constructing and evaluating arguments.

of careful study. One thing that is fairly clear is that none of this argument aims to establish Hume's thesis with absolute certainty or beyond conceivable doubt. The movement away from the absolute certainty of knowledge toward the relative rationality of belief as the crucial philosophical issue which began with Locke is completed in Hume's writing. Certainty is restricted to a narrow and well-defined area consisting of analytic truths and the demonstrable propositions of mathematics (Hume calls these *relations of ideas*). For the rest, including all of our claims about the experienced world (Hume calls such claims *matters of fact*), the question is one of probable rather than certain truth, of whether or not it is rational to hold the belief in question, of how such a belief might be rationally justified and not how it might be conclusively demonstrated.

In spite of this, however, Hume arrives at conclusions about the rational justification of many of our ordinary beliefs which he labels "sceptical" and which conflict with common sense at least as sharply as Descartes' sceptical doubts. He finds that all of our beliefs about the world that go beyond what we observe or remember depend on the relationship of cause and effect. And this includes all of the beliefs of natural science and most of the beliefs that make up practical wisdom or common sense. The obvious thing to do is to explain why we are justified in believing in the existence of causal connections between events. Since all ideas come from the impressions provided by sense experience, the justification should consist of locating the source of the impression of causal connection in our sense experience of the events we think of as so connected in the real world. The shocking result of Hume's search for this impression is that there is none of the sort that would clearly constitute a rational justification for our beliefs about causal relations. Hume can find a psychological explanation for such beliefs and can point to the practical utility of our having had such beliefs in the past, and some philosophers have suggested that this is enough; but he can produce nothing more in the way of a rational justification for our continuing the practice of forming and holding such beliefs.

Russell, whose selection in this section places him squarely within the empiricist tradition of Locke and Hume, points to the instinctive nature of our basic beliefs in the existence of the world of objects which experience seems to present to us, and seeks to find a justification for holding such beliefs rather than a way to rule out every doubt that can be conceived with respect to them. Russell does not find sceptical doubt unreasonable. What he tries to argue is that most of the beliefs of science and common sense are more reasonable, and hence that we are justified in holding them. One of the important things that Russell does in this essay is to draw sharply the distinction between appearance and reality without the aid of sceptical doubt. His goal is not to show that we know nothing about reality, but rather that any knowledge we do have of real objects must be indirect, the result of inferences based upon the appearances with which experience puts us in direct contact. We see appearances and infer or judge that those appearances are caused by the existence of stable and enduring physical objects having roughly the properties they appear to have. Russell claims that our beliefs that result from such inferences are justified by the following considerations. The appearances we experience directly provide us with data that need to be explained. Why do we experience just the systems of appearances we do when, for example, we seem to walk around a table? Russell argues that the best explanation available, given the data, is that there really is a table there that has the properties required to produce the changes in experienced appearances as we move relative to it. Sometimes this kind of justification of belief is referred to as "inference to the best explanation."

There is a kind of progression of problems and positions that is worth noting here. Descartes' sceptical doubts in the first meditation rule out our knowing anything even about something that seems to be right before our eyes. If we imagine this problem somehow solved, we could still have Locke's worries about knowledge based upon memory of things no longer before our eyes. The solution of this problem would still leave Hume's worries about justified belief in causal relations untouched. And even if we imagine all of these problems solved, we might still be able to make Russell's distinction between appearance and reality and still need a justification of the inference from appearance to reality in our knowledge of or beliefs about the material world.

Austin and Malcolm refuse to grant the opening moves of any of the examinations of our ordinary knowledge that we have discussed so far. Both claim that the best of our ordinary beliefs are, in fact, absolutely certain and immune to doubt of any kind. In the paradigm case where we are in familiar surroundings and confronting an ordinary object face-to-face, we can just see that it is there and that is the end of it. There isn't any evidence to collect or inference to be made or tested. We can in such a situation know that we aren't dreaming, know that there is a pig right in front of us, or know that there is an ink bottle on our desk. The philosophers who have thought otherwise have either failed to see the force and appropriateness of our ordinary claims because they have ignored, or uprooted them from, their ordinary practical contexts; or they have introduced senses of the word *know* which have no use in such contexts; or, again, they have produced doubts about our ordinary beliefs which are just "plain nonsense."

Lehrer defends scepticism against such allegations. The important question, he says, is not whether scepticism is compelling at the level of practical life. Even Hume noted that his sceptical worries seemed to vanish as soon as he left his study and returned to the activities of daily life. But scepticism isn't proposed as appropriate to our ordinary practical interests, but as the appropriate response to the philosophical question: Are any of the things we take to be certain and beyond doubt in ordinary practical life really certain and indubitable? Pointing out that we do take them to be so ordinarily and couldn't be made to do otherwise in practical contexts hardly seems to answer that question. It seems rather to miss the point or change the subject. Once we see this, the defense of commonsense knowledge on the basis of what we would ordinarily do or say when not engaged in philosophical inquiry begins to look more like dogmatic assertion than rational argument. Of course, in ordinary situations we can still say with Austin's "plain man," "Well, if that's not seeing a real chair then I don't know what is." But that's just the sceptic's point. We *can't* know with *complete certainty* that any experience is seeing a real chair, even those experiences that are the closest we can imagine coming to the ideal of certainty that knowledge requires.

## René Descartes (1596–1650)

René Descartes is regarded as the founder of modern philosophy. His best-known philosophical works are the *Discourse on Method* (1637), the *Meditations on First Philosophy* (1641), from which the selection below is taken, and the *Rules for the Direction of the Mind* (1701). In addition to his contributions to the philosophical study of knowledge, which have had a lasting impact on this area of philosophy, he made major contributions in other fields as well. He is the inventor of analytic geometry, almost stumbled on calculus a century before its actual discovery by others, and produced a brief physics (just by thinking about how matter ought to be in order for the material world to be a rational or intelligible system), which bears some interesting structural resemblance to Einstein's relativity theory. He also wrote a number of essays in physiology.

Descartes' philosophy is concerned almost entirely with the nature of human knowledge and the kinds of things that can be known. He had no interest in moral philosophy, believing that its questions were beyond our power to answer with certainty. His only moral advice is that we should go along with the received social opinion on moral questions so as not to cause trouble and encourage others to disturb the solitude we require for genuine philosophical meditation. The search for truth for Descartes was primarily a solitary enterprise, not a social activity. Others tended to hinder rather than help in this search. One knows, according to Descartes, only those things that one has made self-evident to oneself or demonstrated to oneself to be absolutely certain.

Descartes sought to turn the entirety of human knowledge into a single system of absolutely certain truths. He used the method of doubt to search for truths that could be completely certain or beyond all doubt. With such truth(s) at the foundation, he sought to build the rest of the things that could be known upon the foundational level in such a way as to preserve and guarantee truth and certainty throughout the entire structure. The following selection traces the beginning of that process.

# Sceptical Doubt and the Foundations of Human Knowledge

***René Descartes***

## MEDITATION I
## OF THE THINGS WHICH MAY BE BROUGHT WITHIN THE SPHERE OF THE DOUBTFUL

It is now some years since I detected how many were the false beliefs that I had from my earliest youth admitted as true, and how doubtful was everything I had since constructed on this basis; and from that time I was convinced that I must once for all seriously undertake to rid myself of all the opinions which I had formerly accepted, and commence to build anew from the foundation, if I wanted to establish any firm and permanent structure in the sciences. But as this enterprise appeared to be a very great one, I waited until I had attained an age so mature that I could not hope that at any later date I should be better fitted to execute my design. This reason caused me to delay so long that I should feel that I was doing wrong were I to occupy in deliberation the time that yet remains to me for action. Today, then, since very opportunely for the plan I have in view I have delivered my mind from every care [and am happily agitated by no passions] and since I have procured for myself an assured leisure in a peaceable retirement, I shall at last seriously and freely address myself to the general upheaval of all my former opinions.

Now for this object, it is not necessary that I should show that all of these are false — I shall perhaps never arrive at this end. But inasmuch as reason already persuades me that I ought no less carefully to withhold my assent from matters which are not entirely certain and indubitable than from those which appear to me manifestly to be false, if I am able to find in each one some reason to doubt, this will suffice to justify my rejecting the whole. And for that end it will not be requisite that I should examine each in particular,

From *The Philosophical Works of Descartes.* Translated by Elizabeth S. Haldane and G. R. T. Ross, Vol. I. (Cambridge University Press, 1972), pp. 141–71. Reprinted by permission of Cambridge University Press.

which would be an endless undertaking; for owing to the fact that the destruction of the foundations of necessity brings with it the downfall of the rest of the edifice, I shall only in the first place attack those principles upon which all my former opinions rested.

All that up to the present time I have accepted as most true and certain I have learned either from the senses or through the senses; but it is sometimes proved to me that these senses are deceptive, and it is wiser not to trust entirely to any thing by which we have once been deceived.

But it may be that although the senses sometimes deceive us concerning things which are hardly perceptible, or very far away, there are yet many others to be met with as to which we cannot reasonably have any doubt, although we recognize them by their means. For example, there is the fact that I am here, seated by the fire, attired in a dressing gown, having this paper in my hands and other similar matters. And how could I deny that these hands and this body are mine, were it not perhaps that I compare myself to certain persons, devoid of sense, whose cerebella are so troubled and clouded by the violent vapors of black bile, that they constantly assure us that they think they are kings when they are really quite poor, or that they are clothed in purple when they are really without covering, or who imagine that they have an earthenware head or are nothing but pumpkins or are made of glass. But they are mad, and I should not be any the less insane were I to follow examples so extravagant.

At the same time I must remember that I am a man, and that consequently I am in the habit of sleeping, and in my dreams representing to myself the same things or sometimes even less probable things, than do those who are insane in their waking moments. How often has it happened to me that in the night I dreamt that I found myself in this particular place, that I was dressed and seated near the fire, whilst in reality I was lying undressed in bed! At this moment it does indeed seem to me that it is with eyes awake that I am looking at this paper; that this head which I move is not asleep, that it is deliberately and of set purpose that I extend my hand and perceive it; what happens in sleep does not appear so clear nor so distinct as does all this. But in thinking over this I remind myself that on many occasions I have in sleep been deceived by similar illusions, and in dwelling carefully on this reflection I see so manifestly that there are no certain indications by which we may clearly distinguish wakefulness from sleep that I am lost in astonishment. And my astonishment is such that it is almost capable of persuading me that I now dream.

Now let us assume that we are asleep and that all these particulars, e.g. that we open our eyes, shake our head, extend our hands, and so on, are but false delusions; and let us reflect that possibly neither our hands nor our whole body are such as they appear to us to be. At the same time we must at least confess that the things which are represented to us in sleep are like painted representations which can only have been formed as the counterparts of something real and true, and that in this way those general things at least, i.e. eyes, a head, hands, and a whole body, are not imaginary things, but things really existent. For, as a matter of fact, painters, even when they study with the greatest skill to represent sirens and satyrs by forms the most strange and extraordinary, cannot give them natures which are entirely new, but merely make a certain medley of the members of different animals; or if their imagination is extravagant enough to invent something so novel that nothing similar has ever before been seen, and that then their work represents a thing purely fictitious and absolutely false, it is certain all the same that the colors of which this is composed are necessarily real. And for the same reason, although these general things, to wit, [a body], eyes, a head, hands, and such like, may be imaginary, we are bound at the same time to confess that there are at least some other objects yet more simple and more universal, which are real and true; and of these just in the same way as with certain real colors, all these images of things which dwell in our thoughts, whether true and real or false and fantastic, are formed.

To such a class of things pertains corporeal nature in general, and its extension, the figure of extended things, their quantity or magnitude and number, as also the place in which they are, the time which measures their duration, and so on.

That is possibly why our reasoning is not unjust when we conclude from this that Physics, Astronomy, Medicine and all other sciences which have as their end the consideration of composite things, are very dubious and uncertain; but that Arithmetic, Geometry and other sciences of that kind which only treat of things that are very simple and very general, without taking great trouble to ascertain whether they are actually existent or not, contain some measure of certainty and an element of the indubitable. For whether I am awake or asleep, two and three together always form five, and the square can never have more than four sides, and it does not seem possible that truths so clear and apparent can be suspected of any falsity [or uncertainty].

Nevertheless I have long had fixed in my mind the belief that an all-powerful God existed by whom I have been created such as I am. But how do I know that He has not brought it to pass that there is no earth, no heaven, no extended body, no magnitude, no place, and that nevertheless [I possess the perceptions of all these things and that] they seem to me to exist just exactly as I now see them? And, besides, as I sometimes imagine that others deceive themselves in the things which they think they know best, how do I know that I am not deceived every time that I add two and three, or count the sides of a square, or judge of things yet simpler, if anything simpler can be imagined? But possibly God has not desired that I should be thus deceived, for He is said to be supremely good. If, however, it is contrary to His goodness to have made me such that I constantly deceive myself, it would also appear to be contrary to His goodness to permit me to be sometimes deceived, and nevertheless I cannot doubt that He does permit this.

There may indeed be those who would prefer to deny the existence of a God so powerful, rather than believe that all other things are uncertain. But let us not oppose them for the present, and grant that all that is here said of a God is a fable; nevertheless in whatever way they suppose that I have arrived at the state of being that I have reached — whether they attribute it to fate or to accident, or make out that it is by a continual succession of antecedents, or by some other method — since to err and deceive oneself is a defect, it is clear that the greater will be the probability of my being so imperfect as to deceive myself ever, as is the Author to whom they assign my origin the less powerful. To these reasons I have certainly nothing to reply, but at the end I feel constrained to confess that there is nothing in all that I formerly believed to be true, of which I cannot in some measure doubt, and that not merely through want of thought or through levity, but for reasons which are very powerful and maturely considered; so that henceforth I ought not the less carefully to refrain from giving credence to these opinions than to that which is manifestly false, if I desire to arrive at any certainty [in the sciences].

But it is not sufficient to have made these remarks, we must also be careful to keep them in mind. For these ancient and commonly held opinions still revert frequently to my mind, long and familiar custom having given them the right to occupy my mind against my inclination and rendered them almost masters of my belief; nor will I ever lose the habit of deferring to them or of placing my confidence in them, so long as I consider them as they really are, i.e. opinions in some measure doubtful, as I have just shown, and at the same time highly probable, so that there is much more reason to believe in than to deny them. That is why I consider that I shall not be acting amiss, if, taking of set purpose a contrary belief, I allow myself to be deceived, and for a certain time pretend that all these opinions are entirely false and imaginary, until at last, having thus balanced my former prejudices with my latter [so that they cannot divert my opinions more to one side than to the other], my judgment will no longer be dominated by bad usage or turned away from the right knowledge of the truth. For I am assured that there can be neither peril nor error in this course, and that I cannot at present yield too much to distrust, since I am not considering the question of action, but only of knowledge.

I shall then suppose, not that God who is supremely good and the fountain of truth, but some evil genius not less powerful than deceitful, has employed his whole energies in deceiving me; I shall consider that the heavens, the earth, colors, figures, sound, and all other external things are nought but the illusions and dreams of which this genius has availed himself in order to lay traps for my credulity; I shall consider myself as having no hands, no eyes, no flesh, no blood, nor any senses, yet falsely believing myself to possess all these things; I shall remain obstinately attached to this idea, and if by this means it is not in my power to arrive at the knowledge of any truth, I may at least do what is in my power [i.e. suspend my judgment], and with firm purpose avoid giving credence to any false thing, or being imposed upon by this arch deceiver, however powerful and deceptive he may be. But this task is a laborious one, and insensibly a certain lassitude leads me into the course of my ordinary life. And just as a captive who in sleep enjoys an imaginary liberty, when he begins to suspect that his liberty is but a dream, fears to awaken, and conspires with these agreeable illusions that the deception may be prolonged, so insensibly of my own accord I fall back into my former opinions, and I dread awakening from this slumber, lest the laborious wakefulness which would follow the tranquillity of this repose should have to be spent not in daylight, but in the excessive darkness of the difficulties which have just been discussed.

## MEDITATION II
## OF THE NATURE OF THE HUMAN MIND; AND THAT IT IS MORE EASILY KNOWN THAN THE BODY

The Meditation of yesterday filled my mind with so many doubts that it is no longer in my power to forget them. And yet I do not see in what manner I can resolve them; and, just as if I had all of a sudden fallen into very deep water, I am so disconcerted that I can neither make certain of setting my feet on the bottom, nor can I swim and so support myself on the surface. I shall nevertheless make an effort and follow anew the same path as that on which I yesterday entered, i.e. I shall proceed by setting aside all that in which the least doubt could be supposed to exist, just as if I had discovered that it was absolutely false; and I shall ever follow in this road until I have met with something which is certain, or at least, if I can do nothing else, until I have learned for certain that there is nothing in the world that is certain. Archimedes, in order that he might draw the terrestrial globe out of its place, and transport it elsewhere, demanded only that one point should be fixed and immoveable; in the same way I shall have the right to conceive high hopes if I am happy enough to discover one thing only which is certain and indubitable.

I suppose, then, that all the things that I see are false; I persuade myself that nothing has ever existed of all that my fallacious memory represents to me. I consider that I possess no senses; I imagine that body, figure, extension, movement and place are but the fictions of my mind. What, then, can be esteemed as true? Perhaps nothing at all, unless that there is nothing in the world that is certain.

But how can I know there is not something different from those things that I have just considered, of which one cannot have the slightest doubt? Is there not some God, or some other being by whatever name we call it, who puts these reflections into my mind? That is not necessary, for is it not possible that I am capable of producing them myself? I myself, am I not at least something? But I have already denied that I had senses and body. Yet I hesitate, for what follows from that? Am I so dependent on body and senses that I cannot exist without these? But I was persuaded that there was nothing in all the world, that there was no heaven, no earth, that there were no minds, nor any bodies: was I not then likewise persuaded that I did not exist? Not at all; of a surety I myself did exist since I persuaded myself of something [or merely because I thought of something]. But there is some deceiver or other, very powerful and very cunning, who ever employs his ingenuity in deceiving me. Then without doubt I exist also if he deceives me, and let him deceive me as much as he will, he can never cause me to be nothing so long as I think that I am something. So that after having reflected well and carefully examined all things, we must come to the definite conclusion that this proposition: I am, I exist, is necessarily true each time that I pronounce it, or that I mentally conceive it.

But I do not yet know clearly enough what I am, I who am certain that I am; and hence I must be careful to see that I do not imprudently take some other object in place of myself, and thus that I do not go astray in respect of this knowledge that I hold to be the most certain and most evident of all that I have formerly learned. That is why I shall now consider anew what I believed myself to be before I embarked upon these last reflections; and of my former opinions I shall withdraw all that might even in a small degree be invalidated by the reasons which I have just brought forward, in order that there may be nothing at all left beyond what is absolutely certain and indubitable.

What then did I formerly believe myself to be? Undoubtedly I believed myself to be a man. But what is a man? Shall I say a reasonable animal? Certainly not; for then I should have to inquire what an animal is, and what is reasonable; and thus from a single question I should insensibly fall into an infinitude of others more difficult; and I should not wish to waste the little time and leisure remaining to me in trying to unravel subtleties like these. But I shall rather stop here to consider the thoughts which of themselves spring up in my mind, and which were not inspired by anything beyond my own nature alone when I applied myself to the consideration of my being. In the first place, then, I considered myself as having a face, hands, arms, and all that system of members composed of bones and flesh as seen in a corpse which I designated by the name of body. In addition to this I considered that I was nourished, that I walked, that I felt, and that I thought, and I referred all these actions to the soul: but I did not stop to consider what the soul was, or if I did stop, I imagined that it was something extremely rare and subtle like a wind, a flame, or an ether, which was spread throughout my grosser parts. As to body I had no manner of doubt about its nature, but thought I had a very clear knowledge of it; and if I had desired to explain it according to the notions that I had then formed of it, I should have described it thus: By the body I understand all that which can be defined by a certain figure: something which can be confined in a certain place, and which can fill a given space in such a way that every other body will be excluded from it; which can be perceived either by touch, or by sight, or by hearing, or by taste, or by smell: which can be moved in many ways not, in truth, by itself, but by something which is foreign to it, by which it is touched [and from which it receives impressions]: for to have the power of self-movement, as also of feeling or of thinking, I did not consider to appertain to the nature of body: on the contrary, I was rather astonished to find that faculties similar to them existed in some bodies.

But what am I, now that I suppose that there is a certain genius which is extremely powerful, and, if I may say so, malicious, who employs all his powers in deceiving me? Can I affirm that I possess the least of all those things which I have just said pertain to the nature of body? I pause to consider, I revolve all these things in my mind, and I find none of which I can say that it pertains to me. It would be tedious to stop to enumerate them. Let us pass to the attributes of soul and see if there is any one which is in me? What of nutrition or walking [the first mentioned]? But if it is so that I have no body it is also true that I can neither walk nor take nourishment. Another attribute is sensation. But one cannot feel without body, and besides I have thought I perceived many things during sleep that I recognized in my waking moments as not having been experienced at all. What of thinking? I find here that thought is an attribute that belongs to me; it alone cannot be separated from me. I am, I exist, that is certain. But how often? Just when I think; for it might possibly be the case if I ceased entirely to think, that I should likewise cease altogether to exist. I do not now admit anything which is not necessarily true: to speak accurately I am not more than a thing which thinks, that is to say a mind or a soul, or an understanding, or a reason, which are terms whose significance was formerly unknown to me. I am, however, a real thing and really exist; but what thing? I have answered: a thing which thinks.

And what more? I shall exercise my imagination [in order to see if I am not something more]. I am not a collection of members which we call the human body: I am not a subtle air distributed through these members, I am not a wind, a fire, a vapor, a breath, nor anything at all which I can imagine or conceive; because I have assumed that all these were nothing. Without changing that supposition I find that I only leave myself certain of the fact that I am somewhat. But perhaps it is true that these same things which I supposed were non-existent because they are unknown to me, are really not different from the self which I know. I am not sure about this, I shall not dispute about it now; I can only give judgment on things that are known to me. I know that I exist, and I inquire what I am, I whom I know to exist. But it is very certain that the knowledge of my existence taken in its precise significance does not depend on things whose existence is not yet known to me; consequently it does not depend on those which I can feign in imagination. And indeed the very term *feign* in imagination proves to me my error, for I really do this if I image myself a something, since to imagine is nothing else than to contemplate the figure or image of a corporeal thing. But I already know for certain that I am, and that it may be that all these images, and, speaking generally, all things that relate to the nature of body are nothing but dreams [and chimeras]. For this reason I see clearly that I have as little reason to say, "I shall stimulate my imagination in order to know more distinctly what I am," than if I were to say, "I am now awake, and I perceive somewhat that is real and true: but because I do not yet perceive it distinctly enough, I shall go to sleep of express purpose, so that my dreams may represent the perception with greatest truth and evidence." And, thus, I know for certain that nothing of all that I can understand by means of my imagination belongs to this knowledge which I have of myself, and that it is necessary to recall the mind from this mode of thought with the utmost diligence in order that it may be able to know its own nature with perfect distinctness.

But what then am I? A thing which thinks. What is a thing which thinks? It is a thing which doubts, understands, [conceives], affirms, denies, wills, refuses, which also imagines and feels.

Certainly it is no small matter if all these things pertain to my nature. But why should they not so pertain? Am I not that being who now doubts nearly everything, who nevertheless understands certain things, who affirms that one only is true, who denies all the others, who desires to know more, is averse from being deceived, who imagines many things, sometimes indeed despite his will, and who perceives many likewise, as by the intervention of the bodily organs? Is there nothing in all this which is as true as it is certain that I exist, even though I should always sleep and though he who has given me being employed all his ingenuity in deceiving me? Is there likewise any one of these attributes which can be distinguished from my thought, or which might be said to be separated from myself? For it is so evident of itself that it is I who doubts, who understands, and who desires, that there is no reason here to add anything to explain it. And I have certainly the power of imagining likewise; for although it may happen (as I formerly supposed) that none of the things which I imagine are true, nevertheless this power of imagining does not cease to be really in use, and it forms part of my thought. Finally, I am the same who feels, that is to say, who perceives certain things, as by the organs of sense, since in truth I see light, I hear noise, I feel heat. But it will be said that these phenomena are false and that I am dreaming. Let it be so; still it is at least quite certain that it seems to me that I see light, that I hear noise and that I feel heat. That cannot be false; properly speaking it is what is in me called feeling; and used in this precise sense that is no other thing than thinking.

From this time I begin to know what I am with a little more clearness and distinction than before; but nevertheless it still seems to me, and I cannot prevent myself from thinking, that corporeal things, whose images are framed by thought, which are tested by the senses, are much more distinctly known than that obscure part of me which does not come under the imagination. Although really it is very strange to say that I know and understand more distinctly these things whose existence seems to me dubious, which are unknown to me, and which do not belong to me, than others of the truth of which I am convinced, which are known to me and which pertain to my real nature, in a word, than myself. But I see clearly how the case stands: my mind loves to wander, and cannot yet suffer itself to be retained within the just limits of truth. Very good, let us once more give it the freest rein, so that, when afterwards we seize the proper occasion for pulling up, it may the more easily be regulated and controlled.

Let us begin by considering the commonest matters, those which we believe to be the most distinctly comprehended, to wit, the bodies which we touch and see; not indeed bodies in general, for these general ideas are usually a little more confused, but let us consider one body in particular. Let us take, for example, this piece of wax: it has been taken quite freshly from the hive, and it has not yet lost the sweetness of the honey which it contains; it still retains somewhat of the odor of the flowers from which it has been culled; its color, its figure, its size are apparent; it is hard, cold, easily handled, and if you strike it with the finger, it will emit a sound. Finally all the things which are requisite to cause us distinctly to recognize a body, are met with in it. But notice that while I speak and approach the fire what remained of the taste is exhaled, the smell evaporates, the color alters, the figure is destroyed, the size increases, it becomes liquid, it heats, scarcely can one handle it, and when one strikes it, no sound is emitted. Does the same wax remain after this change? We must confess that it remains; none would judge otherwise. What then did I know so distinctly in this piece of wax? It could certainly be nothing of all that the senses brought to my notice, since all these things which fall under taste, smell, sight, touch, and hearing, are found to be changed, and yet the same wax remains.

Perhaps it was what I now think, viz. that this wax was not that sweetness of honey, nor that agreeable scent of flowers, nor that particular whiteness, nor that figure, nor that sound, but simply a body which a little while before appeared to me as perceptible under these forms, and which is now perceptible under others. But what, precisely, is it that I imagine when I form such conceptions? Let us attentively consider this, and, abstracting from all that does not belong to the wax, let us see what remains. Certainly nothing remains excepting a certain extended thing which is flexible and movable. But what is the meaning of flexible and movable? Is it not that I imagine that this piece of wax being round is capable of becoming square and of passing from a square to a triangular figure? No, certainly it is not that, since I imagine it admits of an infinitude of similar changes, and I nevertheless do not know how to compass the infinitude by my imagination, and consequently this conception which I have of the wax is not brought about by the faculty of imagination. What now is this extension? Is it not also unknown? For it becomes greater when the wax is melted, greater when it is boiled, and greater still when the heat increases; and I should not conceive [clearly] according to truth what wax is, if I did not think that even this piece that we are considering is capable of receiving more variations in extension than I have ever imagined. We must then grant that I could not even understand through the imagination what this piece of wax is, and that it is my mind alone which perceives it. I say this piece of wax in particular, for as to wax in general it is yet clearer. But what is this piece of wax which cannot be understood excepting by the [understanding or] mind? It is certainly the same that I see, touch, imagine, and finally it is the same which I have always believed it to be from the beginning. But what must particularly be observed is that its perception is neither an act of vision, nor of touch, nor of imagination, and has never been such although it may have appeared formerly to be so, but only an intuition of the mind, which may be imperfect and confused as it was formerly, or clear and distinct as it is at present, according as my attention is more or less directed to the elements which are found in it, and of which it is composed.

Yet in the meantime I am greatly astonished when I consider [the great feebleness of mind] and its proneness to fall [insensibly] into error; for although without giving expression to my thoughts I consider all this in my own mind, words often impede me and I am almost deceived by the terms of ordinary language. For we say that we see the same wax, if it is present, and not that we simply judge that it is the same from its having the same color and figure. From this I should conclude that I knew the wax by means of vision and not simply by the intuition of the mind; unless by chance I remember that, when looking from a window and saying I see men who pass in the street, I really do not see them, but infer that what I see is men, just as I say that I see wax. And yet what do I see from the window but hats and coats which may cover automatic machines? Yet I judge these to be men. And similarly solely by the faculty of judgment which rests in my mind, I comprehend that which I believed I saw with my eyes.

A man who makes it his aim to raise his knowledge above the common should be ashamed to derive the occasion for doubting from the forms of speech invented by the vulgar; I prefer to pass on and consider whether I had a more evident and perfect conception of what the wax was when I first perceived it, and when I believed I knew it by means of the external senses or at least by the common sense as it is called, that is to say by the imaginative faculty, or whether my present conception is clearer now that I have most carefully examined what it is, and in what way it can be known. It would certainly be absurd to doubt as to this. For what was there in this first perception which was distinct? What was there which might not as well have been perceived by any of the animals? But when I distinguish the wax from its external forms, and when, just as if I had taken from it its vestments, I consider it quite naked, it is certain that although some error may still be found in my judgment, I can nevertheless not perceive it thus without a human mind.

But finally what shall I say of this mind, that is, of myself, for up to this point I do not admit in myself anything but mind? What then, I who seem to perceive this piece of wax so distinctly, do I not know myself, not only with much more truth and certainty, but also with much more distinctness and clearness? For if I judge that the wax is or exists from the fact that I see it, it certainly follows much more clearly that I am or that I exist myself from the fact that I see it. For it may be that what I see is not really wax, it may also be that I do not possess eyes with which to see anything; but it cannot be that when I see, or (for I no longer take account of the distinction) when I think I see, that I myself who think am nought. So if I judge that the wax exists from the fact that I touch it, the same thing will follow, to wit, that I am; and if I judge that my imagination, or some other cause, whatever it is, persuades me that the wax exists, I shall still conclude the same. And what I have here remarked of wax may be applied to all other things which are external to me [and which are met with outside of me]. And further, if the [notion or] perception of wax has seemed to me clearer and more distinct, not only after the sight or the touch, but also after many other causes have rendered it quite manifest to me, with how much more [evidence] and distinctness must it be said that I now know myself, since all the reasons which contribute to the knowledge of wax, or any other body whatever, are yet better proofs of the nature of my mind! And there are so many other things in the mind itself which may contribute to the elucidation of its nature, that those which depend on body such as these just mentioned, hardly merit being taken into account.

But finally here I am, having insensibly reverted to the point I desired, for, since it is now manifest to me that even bodies are not properly speaking known by the senses or by the faculty of imagination, but by the understanding only, and since they are not known from the fact that they are seen or touched, but only because they are understood, I see clearly that there is nothing which is easier for me to know than my mind. But because it is difficult to rid oneself so promptly of an opinion to which one was accustomed for so long, it will be well that I should halt a little at this point, so that by the length of my meditation I may more deeply imprint on my memory this new knowledge.

## MEDITATION III
## OF GOD: THAT HE EXISTS

I shall now close my eyes, I shall stop my ears, I shall call away all my senses, I shall efface even from my thoughts all the images of corporeal things, or at least (for that is hardly possible) I shall esteem them as vain and false; and thus holding converse only with myself and considering my own nature, I shall try little by little to reach a better knowledge of and a more familiar acquaintanceship with myself. I am a thing that thinks, that is to say, that doubts, affirms, denies, that knows a few things, that is ignorant of many [that loves, that hates], that wills, that desires, that also imagines and perceives; for as I remarked before, although the things which I perceive and imagine are perhaps nothing at all apart from me and in themselves, I am nevertheless assured that these modes of thought that I call perceptions and imaginations, inasmuch only as they are modes of thought, certainly reside [and are met with] in me.

And in the little that I have just said, I think I have summed up all that I really know, or at least all that hitherto I was aware that I knew. In order to try to extend my knowledge further, I shall now look around more carefully and see whether I cannot still discover in myself some other things which I have not hitherto perceived. I am certain that I am a thing which thinks; but do I not then likewise know what is requisite to render me certain of a truth? Certainly in this first knowledge there is nothing that assures me of its truth, excepting the clear and distinct perception of that which I state, which would not indeed suffice to assure me that what I say is true, if it could ever happen that a thing which I conceived so clearly and distinctly could be false; and accordingly it seems to me that already I can establish as a general rule that all things which I perceive very clearly and very distinctly are true.

At the same time I have before received and admitted many things to be very certain and manifest, which yet I afterwards recognized as being dubious. What then were these things? They were the earth, sky, stars and all other objects which I apprehended by means of the senses. But what did I clearly [and distinctly] perceive in them? Nothing more than that the ideas or thoughts of these things were presented to my mind. And not even now do I deny that these ideas are met with in me. But there was yet another thing which I affirmed, and which, owing to the habit which I had formed of believing it, I thought I perceived very clearly, although in truth I did not perceive it at all, to wit, that there were objects outside of me from which these ideas proceeded, and to which they were entirely similar. And it was in this that I erred, or, if perchance my judgment was correct, this was not due to any knowledge arising from my perception.

But when I took anything very simple and easy in the sphere of arithmetic or geometry into consideration, e.g. that two and three together made five, and other things of the sort, were not these present to my mind so clearly as to enable me to affirm that they were true? Certainly if I judged that since such matters could be doubted, this would not have been so for any other reason than that it came into my mind that perhaps a God might have endowed me with such a nature that I may have been deceived even concerning things which seemed to me most manifest. But every time that this preconceived opinion of the sovereign power of a God presents itself to my thought, I am constrained to confess that it is easy to Him, if He wishes it, to cause me to err, even in matters in which I believe myself to have the best evidence. And, on the other hand, always when I direct my attention to things which I believe myself to perceive very clearly, I am so persuaded of their truth that I let myself break out into words such as these: Let who will deceive me, He can never cause me to be nothing while I think that I am, or some day cause it to be true to say that I have never been, it being true now to say that I am, or that two and three make more or less than five, or any such thing in which I see a manifest contradiction. And, certainly, since I have no reason to believe that there is a God who is a deceiver, and as I have not yet satisfied myself that there is a God at all, the reason for doubt which depends on this opinion alone is very slight, and so to speak metaphysical. But in order to be able altogether to remove it, I must inquire whether there is a God as soon as the occasion presents itself; and if I find that there is a God, I must also inquire whether He may be a deceiver; for without a knowledge of these two truths I do not see that I can ever be certain of anything. . . .

Now as to what concerns ideas, if we consider them only in themselves and do not relate them to anything else beyond themselves, they cannot properly speaking be false; for whether I imagine a goat or a chimera, it is not less true that I imagine the one than the other. We must not fear likewise that falsity can enter into will and into affections, for although I may desire evil things, or even things that never existed, it is not the less true that I desire them. Thus there remains no more than the judgments which we make, in which I must take the greatest care not to deceive myself. But the principal error and the commonest which we may meet with in them, consists in my judging that the ideas which are in me are similar or conformable to the things which are outside me; for without doubt if I considered the ideas only as certain modes of my thoughts, without trying to relate them to anything beyond, they could scarcely give me material for error. . . .

If ideas are only taken as certain modes of thought, I recognize amongst them no difference or inequality, and all appear to proceed from me in the same manner; but when we consider them as images, one representing one thing and the other another, it is clear that they are very different one from the other. There is no doubt that those which represent to me substances are something more, and contain so to speak more objective reality within them [that is to say, by representation participate in a higher degree of being or perfection] than those that simply represent modes or accidents; and that idea again by which I understand a supreme God, eternal, infinite, [immutable], omniscient, omnipotent, and Creator of all things which are outside of Himself, has certainly more objective reality in itself than those ideas by which finite substances are represented.

Now it is manifest by the natural light that there must at least be as much reality in the efficient and total cause as in its effect. For, pray, whence can the effect derive its reality, if not from its cause? And in what way can this cause communicate this reality to it, unless it possessed it in itself? And from this it follows, not only that something cannot proceed from nothing, but likewise that what is more perfect—that is to say, which has more reality within itself—cannot proceed from the less perfect. And this is not only evidently true of those effects which possess actual or **formal reality,** but also of the ideas in which we consider merely what is termed **objective reality.** To take an example, the stone which has not yet existed not only cannot now commence to be unless it has been produced by something which possesses within itself, either formally or eminently, all that enters into the composition of the stone [i.e. it must possess the same things or other more excellent things than those which exist in the stone] and heat can only be produced in a subject in which it did not previously exist by a cause that is of an order [degree or kind] at least as perfect as heat, and so in all other cases. But further, the idea of heat, or of a stone, cannot exist in me unless it has been placed within me by some cause which possesses within it at least as much reality as that which I conceive to exist in the heat or the stone. For although this cause does not transmit anything of its actual or formal reality to my idea, we must not for that reason imagine that it is necessarily a less real cause; we must remember that [since every idea is a work of the mind] its nature is such that it demands of itself no other formal reality than that which it borrows from my thought, of which it is only a mode [i.e. a manner or way of thinking]. But in order that an idea should contain some one certain objective reality rather than another, it must without doubt derive it from some cause in which there is at least as much formal reality as this idea contains of objective reality. For if we imagine that something is found in an idea which is not found in the cause, it must then have been derived from nought; but however imperfect may be this mode of being by which a thing is objectively [or by representation] in the understanding by its idea, we cannot certainly say that this mode of being is nothing, nor, consequently, that the idea derives its origin from nothing.

Nor must I imagine that, since the reality that I consider in these ideas is only objective, it is not essential that this reality should be formally in the causes of my ideas, but that it is sufficient that it should be found objectively. For just as this mode of objective existence pertains to ideas by their proper nature, so does the mode of formal existence pertain to the causes of those ideas (this is at least true of the first and principal) by the nature peculiar to them. And although it may be the case that one idea gives birth to another idea, that cannot continue to be so indefinitely; for in the end we must reach an idea whose cause shall be so to speak an archetype, in which the whole reality [or perfection] which is so to speak objectively [or by representation] in these ideas is contained formally [and really]. Thus the light of nature causes me to know clearly that the ideas in me are like [pictures or] images which can, in truth, easily fall short of the perfection of the objects from which they have been derived, but which can never contain anything greater or more perfect.

And the longer and the more carefully that I investigate these matters, the more clearly and distinctly do I recognize their truth. But what am I to conclude from it all in the end? It is this, that if the objective reality of any one of my ideas is of such a nature as clearly to make me recognize that it is not in me either formally or eminently, and that consequently I cannot myself be the cause of it, it follows of necessity that I am not alone in the world, but that there is another being which exists, or which is the cause of this idea. On the other hand, had no such an idea existed in me, I should have had no sufficient argument to convince me of the existence of any being beyond myself; for I have made very careful investigation everywhere and up to the present time have been able to find no other ground.

But of my ideas, beyond that which represents me to myself, as to which there can here be no difficulty, there is another which represents a God, and there are others representing corporeal and inanimate things, others angels, others animals, and others again which represent to me men similar to myself.

As regards the ideas which represent to me other men or animals, or angels, I can however easily conceive that they might be formed by an admixture of the other ideas which I have of myself, of corporeal things, and of God, even although there were apart from me neither men nor animals, nor angels, in all the world.

And in regard to the ideas of corporeal objects, I do not recognize in them anything so great or so excellent that they might not have possibly proceeded from myself; for if I consider them more closely, and examine them individually, as I yesterday examined the idea of wax, I find that there is very little in them which I perceive clearly and distinctly. Magnitude or extension in length, breadth, or depth, I do so perceive; also figure which results from a termination of this extension, the situation which bodies of different figure preserve in relation to one another, and movement or change of situation; to which we may also add substance, duration and number. As to other things such as light, colors, sounds, scents, tastes, heat, cold and the other tactile qualities, they are thought by me with so much obscurity and confusion that I do not even know if they are true or false, i.e. whether the ideas which I form of these qualities are actually the ideas of real objects or not [or whether they only represent chimeras which cannot exist in fact]. For although I have before remarked that it is only in judgments that falsity, properly speaking, or formal falsity, can be met with, a certain material falsity may nevertheless be found in ideas, i.e. when these ideas represent what is nothing as though it were something. For example, the ideas which I have of cold and heat are so far from clear and distinct that by their means I cannot tell whether cold is merely a privation of heat, or heat a privation of cold, or whether both are real qualities, or are not such. And inasmuch as [since ideas resemble images] there cannot be any ideas which do not appear to represent some things, if it is correct to say that cold is merely a privation of heat, the idea which represents it to me as something real and positive will not be improperly termed false, and the same holds good of other similar ideas.

To these it is certainly not necessary that I should attribute any author other than myself. For if they are false, i.e. if they represent things which do not exist, the light of nature shows me that they issue from nought, that is to say, that they are only in me in so far as something is lacking to the perfection of my nature. But if they are true, nevertheless because they exhibit so little reality to me that I cannot even clearly distinguish the thing represented from non-being, I do not see any reason why they should not be produced by myself.

As to the clear and distinct idea which I have of corporeal things, some of them seem as though I might have derived them from the idea which I possess of myself, as those which I have of substance, duration, number, and such like. For [even] when I think that a stone is a substance, or at least a thing capable of existing of itself, and that I am a substance also, although I conceive that I am a thing that thinks and not one that is extended, and that the stone on the other hand is an extended thing which does not think, and that thus there is a notable difference between the two conceptions — they seem, nevertheless, to agree in this, that both represent substances. In the same way, when I perceive that I now exist and further recollect that I have in former times existed, and when I remember that I have various thoughts of which I can recognize the number, I acquire ideas of duration and number which I can afterwards transfer to any object that I please. But as to all the other qualities of which the ideas of corporeal things are composed, to wit, extension, figure, situation and motion, it is true that they are not formally in me, since I am only a thing that thinks; but because they are merely certain modes of substance [and so to speak the vestments under which corporeal substance appears to us] and because I myself am also a substance, it would seem that they might be contained in me eminently.

Hence there remains only the idea of God, concerning which we must consider whether it is something which cannot have proceeded from me myself. By the name God I understand a substance that is infinite [eternal, immutable], independent, all-knowing, all-powerful, and by which I myself and everything else, if anything else does exist, have been created. Now all these characteristics are such that the more diligently I attend to them, the less do they appear capable of proceeding from me alone; hence, from what has been already said, we must conclude that God necessarily exists.

For although the idea of substance is within me owing to the fact that I am substance, nevertheless I should not have the idea of an infinite substance — since I am finite — if it had not proceeded from some substance which was veritably infinite.

Nor should I imagine that I do not perceive the infinite by a true idea, but only by the negation of the finite, just as I perceive repose and darkness by the negation of movement and of light; for, on the contrary, I see that there is manifestly more reality in infinite substance than in finite, and therefore that in some way I have in me the notion of the infinite earlier than the finite — to wit, the notion of God before that of myself. For how would it be possible that I should know that I doubt and desire, that is to say, that something is lacking to me, and that I am not quite perfect, unless I had within me some idea of a Being more perfect than myself, in comparison with which I should recognize the deficiencies of my nature?

And we cannot say that this idea of God is perhaps materially false and that consequently I can derive it from nought [i.e. that possibly it exists in me because I am imperfect], as I have just said is the case with ideas of heat, cold and other such things; for, on the contrary, as this idea is very clear and distinct and contains within it more objective reality than any other, there can be none which is of itself more true, nor any in which there can be less suspicion of falsehood. The idea, I say, of this Being who is absolutely perfect and infinite, is entirely true; for although, perhaps, we can imagine that such a Being does not exist, we cannot nevertheless imagine that His idea represents nothing real to me, as I have said of the idea of cold. This idea is also very clear and distinct; since all that I conceive clearly and distinctly of the real and the true, and of what conveys some perfection, is in its entirety contained in this idea. And this does not cease to be true although I do not comprehend the infinite, or though in God there is an infinitude of things which I cannot comprehend, nor possibly even reach in any way by thought; for it is of the nature of the infinite that my nature, which is finite and limited, should not comprehend it; and it is sufficient that I should understand this, and that I should judge that all things which I clearly perceive and in which I know that there is some perfection, and possibly likewise an infinitude of properties of which I am ignorant, are in God formally or eminently, so that the idea which I have of Him may become the most true, most clear, and most distinct of all the ideas that are in my mind.

But possibly I am something more than I suppose myself to be, and perhaps all those perfections which I attribute to God are in some way potentially in me, although they do not yet disclose themselves, or issue in action. As a matter of fact I am already sensible that my knowledge increases [and perfects itself] little by little, and I see nothing which can prevent it from increasing more and more into infinitude; nor do I see, after it has thus been increased [or perfected], anything to prevent my being able to acquire by its means all the other perfections of the Divine nature; nor finally why the power I have of acquiring these perfections, if it really exists in me, shall not suffice to produce the ideas of them.

At the same time I recognize that this cannot be. For, in the first place, although it were true that every day my knowledge acquired new degrees of perfection, and that there were in my nature many things potentially which are not yet there actually, nevertheless these excellences do not pertain to [or make the smallest approach to] the idea which I have of God in whom there is nothing merely potential [but in whom all is present really and actually]; for it is an infallible token of imperfection in my knowledge that it increases little by little. And further, although my knowledge grows more and more, nevertheless I do not for that reason believe that it can ever be actually infinite, since it can never reach a point so high that it will be unable to attain to any greater increase. But I understand God to be actually infinite, so that He can add nothing to His supreme perfection. And finally I perceive that the objective being of an idea cannot be produced by a being that exists potentially only, which properly speaking is nothing, but only by a being which is formal or actual.

To speak the truth, I see nothing in all that I have just said which by the light of nature is not manifest to anyone who desires to think attentively on the subject; but when I slightly relax my attention, my mind, finding its vision somewhat obscured and so to speak blinded by the images of sensible objects, I do not easily recollect the reason why the idea that I possess of a being more perfect than I, must necessarily have been placed in me by a being which is really more perfect; and this is why I wish here to go on to inquire whether I, who have this idea, can exist if no such being exists.

And I ask, from whom do I then derive my existence? Perhaps from myself or from my parents, or from some other source less perfect than God; for we can imagine nothing more perfect than God, or even as perfect as He is.

But [were I independent of every other and] were I myself the author of my being, I should doubt nothing and I should desire nothing, and finally no perfection would be lacking to me; for I should have bestowed on myself every perfection of which I possessed any idea and should thus be God. And it must not be imagined that those things that are lacking to me are perhaps more difficult of attainment than those which I already possess; for, on the contrary, it is quite evident that it was a matter of much greater difficulty to bring to pass that I, that is to say, a thing or a substance that thinks, should emerge out of nothing, than it would be to attain to the knowledge of many things of which I am ignorant, and which are only the accidents of this thinking substance. But it is clear that if I had of myself possessed this greater perfection of which I have just spoken [that is to say, if I had been the author of my own existence], I should not at least have denied myself the things which are the more easy to acquire [to wit, many branches of knowledge of which my nature is destitute]; nor should I have deprived myself of any of the things contained in the idea which I form of God, because there are none of them which seem to me specially difficult to acquire: and if there were any that were more difficult to acquire, they would certainly appear to me to be such (supposing I myself were the origin of the other things which I possess) since I should discover in them that my powers were limited.

But though I assume that perhaps I have always existed just as I am at present, neither can I escape the force of this reasoning, and imagine that the conclusion to be drawn from this is, that I need not seek for any author of my existence. For all the course of my life may be divided into an infinite number of parts, none of which is in any way dependent on the other; and thus from the fact that I was in existence a short time ago it does not follow that I must be in existence now, unless some cause at this instant, so to speak, produces me anew, that is to say, conserves me. It is as a matter of fact perfectly clear and evident to all those who consider with attention the nature of time, that, in order to be conserved in each moment in which it endures, a substance has need of the same power and action as would be necessary to produce and create it anew, supposing it did not yet exist, so that the light of nature shows us clearly that the distinction between creation and conservation is solely a distinction of the reason.

All that I thus require here is that I should interrogate myself, if I wish to know whether I possess a power which is capable of bringing it to pass that I who now am shall still be in the future; for since I am nothing but a thinking thing, or at least since thus far it is only this portion of myself which is precisely in question at present, if such a power did reside in me, I should certainly be conscious of it. But I am conscious of nothing of the kind, and by this I know clearly that I depend on some being different from myself.

Possibly, however, this being on which I depend is not that which I call God, and I am created either by my parents or by some other cause less perfect than God. This cannot be, because, as I have just said, it is perfectly evident that there must be at least as much reality in the cause as in the effect; and thus since I am a thinking thing, and possess an idea of God within me, whatever in the end be the cause assigned to my existence, it must be allowed that it is likewise a thinking thing and that it possesses in itself the idea of all the perfections which I attribute to God. We may again inquire whether this cause derives its origin from itself or from some other thing. For if from itself, it follows by the reasons before brought forward, that this cause must itself be God; for since it possesses the virtue of self-existence, it must also without doubt have the power of actually possessing all the perfections of which it has the idea, that is, all those which I conceive as existing in God. But if it derives its existence from some other cause than itself, we shall again ask, for the same reason, whether this second cause exists by itself or through another, until from one step to another, we finally arrive at an ultimate cause, which will be God.

And it is perfectly manifest that in this there can be no regression into infinity, since what is in question is not so much the cause which formerly created me, as that which conserves me at the present time.

Nor can we suppose that several causes may have concurred in my production, and that from one I have received the idea of one of the perfections which I attribute to God, and from another the idea of some other, so that all these perfections indeed exist somewhere in the universe, but not as complete in one unity which is God. On the contrary, the unity, the simplicity or the inseparability of all things which are in God is one of the principal perfections which I conceive to be in Him. And certainly the idea of this unity of all Divine perfections cannot have been placed in me by any cause from which I have not likewise received the ideas of all the other perfections; for this cause could not make me able to comprehend them as joined together in an inseparable unity without having at the same time caused me in some measure to know what they are [and in some way to recognize each one of them].

Finally, so far as my parents [from whom it appears I have sprung] are concerned, although all that I have ever been able to believe of them were true, that does not make it follow that it is they who conserve me, nor are they even the authors of my being in any sense, in so far as I am a thinking being; since what they did was merely to implant certain dispositions in that matter in which the self—i.e. the mind, which alone I at present identify with myself—is by me deemed to exist. And thus there can be no difficulty in their regard, but we must of necessity conclude from the fact alone that I exist, or that the idea of a Being supremely perfect—that is of God—is in me, that the proof of God's existence is grounded on the highest evidence.

It only remains to me to examine into the manner in which I have acquired this idea from God; for I have not received it through the senses, and it is never presented to me unexpectedly, as is usual with the ideas of sensible things when these things present themselves, or seem to present themselves, to the external organs of my senses; nor is it likewise a fiction of my mind, for it is not in my power to take from or to add anything to it; and consequently the only alternative is that it is innate in me, just as the idea of myself is innate in me.

And one certainly ought not to find it strange that God, in creating me, placed this idea within me to be like the mark of the workman imprinted on his work; and it is likewise not essential that the mark shall be something different from the work itself. For from the sole fact that God created me it is most probable that in some way he has placed his image and similitude upon me, and that I perceive this similitude (in which the idea of God is contained) by means of the same faculty by which I perceive myself—that is to say, when I reflect on myself I not only know that I am something [imperfect], incomplete and dependent on another, which incessantly aspires after something which is better and greater than myself, but I also know that He on whom I depend possesses in Himself all the great things towards which I aspire [and the ideas of which I find within myself], and that not indefinitely or potentially alone, but really, actually and infinitely; and that thus He is God. And the whole strength of the argument which I have here made use of to prove the existence of God consists in this, that I recognize that it is not possible that my nature should be what it is, and indeed that I should have in myself the idea of a God, if God did not veritably exist—a God, I say, whose idea is in me, i.e. who possesses all those supreme perfections of which our mind may indeed have some idea but without understanding them all, who is liable to no errors or defect [and who has none of all those marks which denote imperfection]. From this it is manifest that He cannot be a deceiver, since the light of nature teaches us that fraud and deception necessarily proceed from some defect. . . .

## *John Locke (1632–1704)*

John Locke's *Essay Concerning Human Understanding* (1690), from which the following selection is taken, is a classic statement of empiricism, the view that all knowledge about the world originates in, and is justified by, sense experience. Locke is also famous for his political theory based upon natural rights, which is contained in his *Treatises on Government* (1685).

The selection below, while granting that our beliefs about the physical world are not indubitable, argues that we have good reasons for some of these beliefs and that we should count them as knowledge in spite of the sceptical possibilities. The beliefs about the world that should be so counted are those about objects actually present to the senses. When our beliefs go beyond the content of present perception, as in the case of those based upon the memory of past perceptions, Locke believes that we lack the certainty required for knowledge.

# Perception and Knowledge

## *John Locke*

### SENSITIVE KNOWLEDGE OF PARTICULAR EXISTENCE

These two, *viz.*, intuition and demonstration, are the degrees of our knowledge; whatever comes short of one of these, with what assurance soever embraced, is but faith or opinion, but not knowledge, at least in all general truths. There is, indeed, another perception of the mind employed about the particular existence of finite beings without us; which, going beyond bare probability, and yet not reaching perfectly to either of the foregoing degrees of certainty, passes under the name of "knowledge." There can be nothing more certain, than that the idea we receive from an external object is in our minds; this is intuitive knowledge. But whether there be anything more than barely that idea in our minds, whether we can thence certainly infer the existence of anything without us which corresponds to that idea, is that whereof some men think there may be a question made; because men may have such ideas in their minds when no such thing exists, no such object affects their senses. But yet here, I think, we are provided with an evidence that puts us past doubting; for I ask any one, whether he be not invincibly conscious to himself of a different perception when he looks on the sun by day, and thinks on it by night; when he actually tastes wormwood, or smells a rose, or only thinks on that savour or odor? We as plainly find the difference there is between any idea revived in our minds by our own memory, and actually coming into our minds by our senses, as we do between any two distinct ideas. If any one say, "A dream may do the same thing, and all these ideas may be produced in us without any external objects;" he may please to dream that I make him this answer: (1) That it is no great matter whether I remove his scruple or no; where all is but dream, reasoning and arguments are of no use, truth and knowledge nothing. (2) That I believe he will allow a very manifest difference between dreaming of being in the fire, and being actually in it. But yet if he be resolved to appear so sceptical as to maintain, that what I call "being

Abridged from *Essay Concerning Human Understanding*, by John Locke. (Chicago: Open Court, 1917), pp. 282–338. Reprinted by permission of Open Court Publishing Co.

actually in the fire" is nothing but a dream; and that we cannot thereby certainly know that any such thing as fire actually exists without us; I answer, that we certainly finding that pleasure or pain follows upon the application of certain objects to us, whose existence we perceive, or dream that we perceive, by our senses; this certainty is as great as our happiness or misery, beyond which we have no concernment to know or to be. So that, I think, we may add to the two former sorts of knowledge this also, of the existence of particular external objects by that perception and consciousness we have of the actual entrance of ideas from them, and allow these three degrees of knowledge, viz., intuitive, demonstrative, and sensitive: in each of which there are different degrees and ways of evidence and certainty. . . .

## OF OUR KNOWLEDGE OF THE EXISTENCE OF OTHER THINGS

1. *It is to be had only by sensation.* The knowledge of our own being we have by intuition. The existence of a God reason clearly makes known to us, as has been shown.

The knowledge of the existence of any other thing, we can have only by sensation: for, there being no necessary connection of real existence with any idea a man hath in his memory, nor of any other existence but that of God with the existence of any particular man, no particular man can know the existence of any other being, but only when by actual operating upon him it makes itself perceived by him. For, the having the idea of any thing in our mind no more proves the existence of that thing than the picture of a man evidences his being in the world, or the visions of a dream make thereby a true history.

2. *Instance whiteness of this paper.* It is therefore the actual receiving of ideas from without that gives us notice of the existence of other things, and makes us know that something doth exist at that time without us which causes that idea in us, though perhaps we neither know nor consider how it does it: for it takes not from the certainty of our senses, and the ideas we receive by them, that we know not the manner wherein they are produced; e.g., whilst I write this, I have, by the paper affecting my eyes, that idea produced in my mind which whatever object causes, I call "white"; by which I know that that quality or accident (*i.e.*, whose appearance before my eyes always causes that idea) doth really exist and hath a being without me. And of this the greatest assurance I can possibly have, and to which my faculties can attain, is the testimony of my eyes, which are the proper and sole judges of this thing; whose testimony I have reason to rely on as so certain that I can no more doubt, whilst I write this, that I see white and black, and that something really exists that causes that sensation in me, than that I write or move my hand; which is a certainty as great as human nature is capable of concerning the existence of any thing but a man's self alone and of God.

3. *This, though not so certain as demonstration, yet may be called "knowledge," and proves the existence of things without us.* The notice we have by our senses of the existing of things without us, though it be not altogether so certain as our intuitive knowledge, or the deductions of our reason employed about the clear abstract ideas of our own minds; yet it is an assurance that deserves the name of knowledge. If we persuade ourselves that our faculties act and inform us right concerning the existence of those objects that affect them, it cannot pass for an ill-grounded confidence: for I think nobody can, in earnest, be so sceptical as to be uncertain of the existence of those things which he sees and feels. At least, he that can doubt so far (whatever he may have with his own thoughts), will never have any controversy with me: since he can never be sure I say any thing contrary to his own opinion. As to myself, I think God has given me assurance enough of the existence of things without me; since, by their different application, I can produce in myself both pleasure and pain, which is one great concernment of my present state. This is certain, the confidence that our faculties do not herein deceive us is the greatest assurance

we are capable of concerning the existence of material beings. For we cannot act any thing but by our faculties, nor talk of knowledge itself but by the help of those faculties which are fitted to apprehend even what knowledge is. But, besides the assurance we have from our senses themselves, that they do not err in the information they give us of the existence of things without us, when they are affected by them, we are farther confirmed in this assurance by other concurrent reasons.

4. *First, because we cannot have them but by the inlet of the senses.* First, it is plain those perceptions are produced in us by exterior causes affecting our senses, because those that want the organs of any sense never can have the ideas belonging to that sense produced in their minds. This is too evident to be doubted: and therefore we cannot but be assured that they come in by the organs of that sense, and no other way. The organs themselves, it is plain, do not produce them; for then the eyes of a man in the dark would produce colors, and his nose smell roses in the winter: but we see nobody gets the relish of a pineapple till he goes to the Indies where it is, and tastes it.

5. *Secondly, because an idea from actual sensation and another from memory are very distinct perceptions.* Secondly, because sometimes I find that I cannot avoid the having those ideas produced in my mind: for though when my eyes are shut, or windows fast, I can at pleasure recall to my mind the ideas of light or the sun, which former sensations had lodged in my memory; so I can at pleasure lay by that idea, and take into my view that of the smell of a rose, or taste of sugar. But if I turn my eyes at noon towards the sun, I cannot avoid the ideas which the light or sun then produces in me. So that there is a manifest difference between the ideas laid up in my memory (over which, if they were there only, I should have constantly the same power to dispose of them, and lay them by at pleasure), and those which force themselves upon me and I cannot avoid having. And therefore it must needs be some exterior cause, and the brisk acting of some objects without me, whose efficacy I cannot resist, that produces those ideas in my mind, whether I will or no. Besides, there is nobody who doth not perceive the difference in himself between contemplating the sun as he hath the idea of it in his memory, and actually looking upon it: of which two his perception is so distinct, that few of his ideas are more distinguishable one from another: and therefore he hath certain knowledge that they are not both memory, or the actions of his mind and fancies only within him; but that actual seeing hath a cause without.

6. *Thirdly, pleasure or pain, which accompanies actual sensation, accompanies not the returning of those ideas without the external objects.* Thirdly, add to this, that many of those ideas are produced in us with pain, which afterwards we remember without the least offence. Thus the pain of heat or cold, when the idea of it is revived in our minds, gives us no disturbance; which, when felt, was very troublesome, and is again when actually repeated: which is occasioned by the disorder the external object causes in our bodies when applied to them. And we remember the pain of hunger, thirst, or the headache, without any pain at all; which would either never disturb us, or else constantly do it as often as we thought of it, were there nothing more but ideas floating in our minds, and appearances entertaining our fancies, without the real existence of things affecting us from abroad. The same may be said of pleasure accompanying several actual sensations; and, though mathematical demonstration depends not upon sense, yet the examining them by diagrams gives great credit to the evidence of our sight, and seems to give it a certainty approaching to that of demonstration itself. For it would be very strange that a man should allow it for an undeniable truth, that two angles of a figure which he measures by lines and angles of a diagram, should be bigger one than the other, and yet doubt of the existence of those lines and angles which, by looking on, he makes use of to measure that by.

7. *Fourthly, our senses assist one another's testimony of the existence of outward things.* Fourthly, our senses, in many cases, bear witness to the truth of each other's report concerning the

existence of sensible things without us. He that sees a fire may, if he doubt whether it be any thing more than a bare fancy, feel it too, and be convinced by putting his hand in it; which certainly could never be put into such exquisite pain by a bare idea or phantom, unless that the pain be a fancy too: which yet he cannot, when the burn is well, by raising the idea of it, bring upon himself again.

Thus I see, whilst I write this, I can change the appearance of the paper; and, by designing the letters, tell beforehand what new idea it shall exhibit the very next moment, by barely drawing my pen over it; which will neither appear (let me fancy as much as I will) if my hand stand still, or though I move my pen, if my eyes be shut; nor, when those characters are once made on the paper, can I choose afterwards but see them as they are; that is, have the ideas of such letters as I have made. Whence it is manifest that they are not barely the sport and play of my own imagination, when I find that the characters that were made at the pleasure of my own thoughts do not obey them; nor yet cease to be, whenever I shall fancy it, but continue to affect my senses constantly and regularly, according to the figures I made then. To which if we will add, that the sight of those shall, from another man, draw such sounds as I beforehand design they shall stand for, there will be little reason left to doubt that those words I write do really exist without me, when they cause a long series of regular sounds to affect my ears, which could not be the effect of my imagination, nor could my memory retain them in that order.

8. *This certainty is as great as our condition needs.* But yet, if after all this any one will be so sceptical as to distrust his senses, and to affirm that all we see and hear, feel and taste, think and do, during our whole being, is but the series and deluding appearances of a long dream whereof there is no reality, and therefore will question the existence of all things or our knowledge of any thing; I must desire him to consider, that if all be a dream, then he doth but dream that he makes the question; and so it is not much matter that a waking man should answer him. But yet, if he pleases, he may dream that I make him this answer, that the certainty of things existing in *rerum natura,* when we have the testimony of our senses for it, is not only as great as our frame can attain to, but as our condition needs. For, our faculties being suited not to the full extent of being, nor to a perfect, clear, comprehensive knowledge of things free from all doubt and scruple, but to the preservation of us, in whom they are, and accommodated to the use of life, they serve to our purpose well enough, if they will but give us certain notice of those things which are convenient or inconvenient to us. For he that sees a candle burning, and hath experimented the force of its flame by putting his finger in it, will little doubt that this is something existing without him, which does him harm and puts him to great pain; which is assurance enough, when no man requires greater certainty to govern his actions by than what is as certain as his actions themselves. And if our dreamer pleases to try whether the glowing heat of a glass furnace be barely a wandering imagination in a drowsy man's fancy, by putting his hand into it, he may, perhaps, be awakened into a certainty, greater than he could wish, that it is something more than bare imagination. So that this evidence is as great as we can desire, being as certain to us as our pleasure or pain, *i.e.,* happiness or misery; beyond which we have no concernment either of knowing or being. Such an assurance of the existence of things without us, is sufficient to direct us in the attaining the good and avoiding the evil which is caused by them, which is the important concernment we have of being made acquainted with them.

9. *But reaches no farther than actual sensation.* In fine, then, when our senses do actually convey into our understandings any idea, we cannot but be satisfied that there doth something at that time really exist without us which doth affect our senses, and by them give notice of itself to our apprehensive faculties, and actually produce that idea which we then perceive: and we cannot so far distrust their testimony as to

doubt that such collections of simple ideas as we have observed by our senses to be united together, do really exist together. But this knowledge extends as far as the present testimony of our senses, employed about particular objects that do then affect them, and no farther. For if I saw such a collection of simple ideas as is wont to be called "man" existing together one minute since, and am now alone; I cannot be certain that the same man exists now, since there is no necessary connection of his existence a minute since with his existence now: by a thousand ways he may cease to be, since I had the testimony of my senses for his existence. And if I cannot be certain that the man I saw last today is now in being, I can less be certain that he is so who hath been longer removed from my senses, and I have not seen since yesterday, or since the last year; and much less can I be certain of the existence of men that I never saw. And therefore, though it be highly probable that millions of men do now exist, yet, whilst I am alone writing this, I have not that certainty of it which we strictly call "knowledge"; though the great likelihood of it puts me past doubt, and it be reasonable for me to do several things upon the confidence that there are men (and men also of my acquaintance, with whom I have to do) now in the world: but this is but probability, not knowledge.

10. *Folly to expect demonstration in every thing.* Whereby yet we may observe how foolish and vain a thing it is for a man of a narrow knowledge, who having reason given him to judge of the different evidence and probability of things, and to be swayed accordingly; how vain, I say, it is to expect demonstration and certainty in things not capable of it, and refuse assent to very rational propositions, and act contrary to very plain and clear truths, because they cannot be made out so evident as to surmount every the least (I will not say reason, but) pretence of doubting. He that in the ordinary affairs of life would admit of nothing but direct plain demonstration, would be sure of nothing in this world but of perishing quickly. The wholesomeness of his meat or drink would not give him reason to venture on it: and I would fain know what it is he could do upon such grounds as were capable of no doubt, no objection. . . .

## David Hume (1711–1776)

David Hume is probably the most influential of the British empiricists. His major philosophical work is the *Treatise of Human Nature* (1739). *An Inquiry Concerning Human Understanding* (1748), from which the following selection is taken, and *An Inquiry Concerning the Principles of Morals* (1751) are briefer and more popular restatements of most of the theories contained in the *Treatise.* Hume wrote one of the most famous works in the philosophy of religion, *Dialogues Concerning Natural Religion* (1779). He was also a noted historian, author of the very lengthy *History of England* (1755).

The selection below begins with arguments for the empiricist thesis that all ideas originate in sense experience. Hume takes this thesis, once established, to indicate the correct form that philosophical analysis should take. Since ideas come from the simple impressions of sense, analysis should break them down to those simple components. Since no one could endlessly dispute over simple sense impressions, all of the age-old problems of philosophy can be resolved by tracing the concepts that give rise to them back to their simple sense impression components. This method, however, yields a surprising result when the idea of causal connection is analyzed in an attempt to rationally justify our beliefs about matters of fact that are not just products of present perception or memory. Hume finds that there is no impression of the sort that would clearly give us good reasons for holding such beliefs. The impression he does find seems, at most, to explain psychologically why we nonetheless hold them.

# Scepticism About Causal Reasoning

***David Hume***

## OF THE ORIGIN OF IDEAS

Every one will readily allow, that there is a considerable difference between the perceptions of the mind, when a man feels the pain of excessive heat, or the pleasure of moderate warmth, and when he afterwards recalls to his memory this sensation, or anticipates it by his imagination. These faculties may mimic or copy the perceptions of the senses; but they never can entirely reach the force and vivacity of the original sentiment. The utmost we say of them, even when they operate with greatest vigor, is, that they represent their object in so lively a manner, that we could *almost* say we feel or see it: But, except the mind be disordered by disease or madness, they never can arrive at such a pitch of vivacity, as to render these perceptions altogether undistinguishable. All the colors of poetry, however splendid, can never paint natural objects in such a manner as to make the description be taken for a real landscape. The most lively thought is still inferior to the dullest sensation.

We may observe a like distinction to run through all the other perceptions of the mind. A man in a fit of anger, is actuated in a very different manner from one who only thinks of that emotion. If you tell me, that any person is in love, I easily understand your meaning, and form a just conception of his situation; but never can mistake that conception for the real disorders and agitations of the passion. When we reflect on our past sentiments and affections, our thought is a faithful mirror, and copies its objects truly; but the colors which it employs are faint and dull, in comparison of those in which our original perceptions were clothed. It requires no nice discernment or metaphysical head to mark the distinction between them.

Here therefore we may divide all the perceptions of the mind into two classes or species, which are distinguished by their different degrees of force and vivacity. The less forcible and lively are commonly denominated *Thoughts* or *Ideas.* The other species want a name in our language, and in most others; I suppose, because it was not requisite for any, but philosophical purposes, to rank them under a general term or appellation. Let us, therefore, use a little freedom, and call them *Impressions;* employing that word in a sense somewhat different from the usual. By the term *impression,* then, I mean all our more lively perceptions, when we hear, or see, or feel, or love, or hate, or desire, or will. And impres-

Abridged from *An Enquiry Concerning Human Understanding,* by David Hume. (Chicago: Open Court, 1912), pp. 14–56. Reprinted by permission of Open Court Publishing Company.

sions are distinguished from ideas, which are the less lively perceptions, of which we are conscious, when we reflect on any of those sensations or movements above mentioned.

Nothing, at first view, may seem more unbounded than the thought of man, which not only escapes all human power and authority, but is not even restrained within the limits of nature and reality. To form monsters, and join incongruous shapes and appearances, costs the imagination no more trouble than to conceive the most natural and familiar objects. And while the body is confined to one planet, along which it creeps with pain and difficulty; the thought can in an instant transport us into the most distant regions of the universe; or even beyond the universe, into the unbounded chaos, where nature is supposed to lie in total confusion. What never was seen, or heard of, may yet be conceived; nor is any thing beyond the power of thought, except what implies an absolute contradiction.

But though our thought seems to possess this unbounded liberty, we shall find, upon a nearer examination, that it is really confined within very narrow limits, and that all this creative power of the mind amounts to no more than the faculty of compounding, transposing, augmenting, or diminishing the materials afforded us by the senses and experience. When we think of a golden mountain, we only join two consistent ideas, *gold,* and *mountain,* with which we were formerly acquainted. A virtuous horse we can conceive; because, from our own feeling, we can conceive virtue; and this we may unite to the figure and shape of a horse, which is an animal familiar to us. In short, all the materials of thinking are derived either from our outward or inward sentiment: the mixture and composition of these belongs alone to the mind and will. Or, to express myself in philosophical language, all our ideas or more feeble perceptions are copies of our impressions or more lively ones.

To prove this, the two following arguments will, I hope, be sufficient. First, when we analyze our thoughts or ideas, however compounded or sublime, we always find that they resolve themselves into such simple ideas as were copied from a precedent feeling or sentiment. Even those ideas, which, at first view, seem the most wide of this origin, are found, upon a nearer scrutiny, to be derived from it. The idea of God, as meaning an infinitely intelligent, wise, and good Being, arises from reflecting on the operations of our own mind, and augmenting, without limit, those qualities of goodness and wisdom. We may prosecute this enquiry to what length we please; where we shall always find, that every idea which we examine is copied from a similar impression. Those who would assert that this position is not universally true nor without exception, have only one, and that an easy method of refuting it; by producing that idea, which, in their opinion, is not derived from this source. It will then be incumbent on us, if we would maintain our doctrine, to produce the impression, or lively perception, which corresponds to it.

Secondly. If it happen, from a defect of the organ, that a man is not susceptible of any species of sensation, we always find that he is as little susceptible of the correspondent ideas. A blind man can form no notion of colors; a deaf man of sounds. Restore either of them that sense in which he is deficient; by opening this new inlet for his sensations, you also open an inlet for the ideas; and he finds no difficulty in conceiving these objects. . . .

Here, therefore, is a proposition, which not only seems, in itself, simple and intelligible; but, if a proper use were made of it, might render every dispute equally intelligible, and banish all that jargon, which has so long taken possession of metaphysical reasonings, and drawn disgrace upon them. All ideas, especially abstract ones, are naturally faint and obscure: the mind has but a slender hold of them: they are apt to be confounded with other resembling ideas; and when we have often employed any term, though without a distinct meaning, we are apt to imagine it has a determinate idea annexed to it. On the contrary, all impressions, that is, all sensations, either outward or inward, are strong and vivid: the limits between them are more exactly determined: nor is it easy to fall into any error or mistake with regard to them. When we entertain, therefore, any suspicion that a philosophical term is employed without any meaning or idea (as is but too frequent), we need but enquire, *from what impression is that supposed idea derived?* And if it be impossible to assign any, this will serve to confirm our suspicion. By bringing ideas into so clear a light we may reasonably hope to remove all dispute, which may arise, concerning their nature and reality.

## SCEPTICAL DOUBTS CONCERNING THE OPERATIONS OF THE UNDERSTANDING

### Part I

All the objects of human reason or enquiry may naturally be divided into two kinds, to wit, *Relations of Ideas,* and *Matters of Fact.* Of the first kind are the sciences of Geometry, Algebra, and Arithmetic; and in short, every affirmation which is either intuitively or demonstratively certain. *That the square of the hypotenuse is equal to the squares of the two sides,* is a proposition which expresses a relation between these figures. *That three times five is equal to the half of thirty,* expresses a relation between these numbers. Propositions of this kind are discoverable by the mere operation of thought, without dependence on what is anywhere existent in the universe. Though there never were a circle or triangle in nature, the truths demonstrated by Euclid would for ever retain their certainty and evidence.

Matters of fact, which are the second objects of human reason, are not ascertained in the same manner; nor is our evidence of their truth, however great, of a like nature with the foregoing. The contrary of every matter of fact is still possible; because it can never imply a contradiction, and is conceived by the mind with the same facility and distinctness, as if ever so conformable to reality. *That the sun will not rise tomorrow* is no less intelligible a proposition, and implies no more contradiction than the affirmation, *that it will rise.* We should in vain, therefore, attempt to demonstrate its falsehood. Were it demonstratively false, it would imply a contradiction, and could never be distinctly conceived by the mind.

It may, therefore, be a subject worthy of curiosity, to enquire what is the nature of that evidence which assures us of any real existence and matter of fact, beyond the present testimony of our senses, or the records of our memory. This part of philosophy, it is observable, has been little cultivated, either by the ancients or moderns; and therefore our doubts and errors, in the prosecution of so important an enquiry, may be the more excusable; while we march through such difficult paths without any guide or direction. They may even prove useful, by exciting curiosity, and destroying that implicit faith and security, which is the bane of all reasoning and free enquiry. The discovery of defects in the common philosophy, if any such there be, will not, I presume, be a discouragement, but rather an incitement, as is usual, to attempt something more full and satisfactory than has yet been proposed to the public.

All reasonings concerning matter of fact seem to be founded on the relation of *Cause and Effect.* By means of that relation alone we can go beyond the evidence of our memory and senses. If you were to ask a man, why he believes any matter of fact, which is absent; for instance, that his friend is in the country, or in France; he would give you a reason; and this reason would be some other fact; as a letter received from him, or the knowledge of his former resolutions and promises. A man finding a watch or any other machine in a desert island, would conclude that there had once been men in that island. All our reasonings concerning fact are of the same nature. And here it is constantly supposed that there is a connection between the present fact and that which is inferred from it. Were there nothing to bind them together, the inference would be entirely precarious. The hearing of an articulate voice and rational discourse in the dark assures us of the presence of some person: Why? because these are the effects of the human make and fabric, and closely connected with it. If we anatomize all the other reasonings of this nature, we shall find that they are founded on the relation of cause and effect, and that this relation is either near or remote, direct or collateral. Heat and light are collateral effects of fire, and the one effect may justly be inferred from the other.

If we would satisfy ourselves, therefore, concerning the nature of that evidence, which assures us of matters of fact, we must enquire how we arrive at the knowledge of cause and effect. . . .

This proposition, *that causes and effects are discoverable, not by reason but by experience,* will readily be admitted with regard to such objects, as we remember to have once been altogether unknown to us; since we must be conscious of the utter inability, which we then lay under, of foretelling what would arise from them. Present two smooth pieces of marble to a man who has no tincture of natural philosophy; he will never discover that they will adhere together in such a manner as to require great force to separate them in a direct line, while they make so small a resistance to a lateral pressure. Such events, as bear little analogy to the common course of nature, are also readily confessed to be known only by experience; nor does any man imagine that the explosion of gunpowder, or the attraction of a loadstone, could ever be discovered by arguments ***a priori.*** In like manner, when an effect is supposed to depend upon an intricate machinery or secret structure of parts, we make no difficulty in attributing all our knowledge of it to experience. Who will assert that he can give the ultimate reason, why milk or bread is proper nourishment for a man, not for a lion or a tiger?

But the same truth may not appear, at first sight, to have the same evidence with regard to events, which have become familiar to us from our first appearance in the world, which bear a close analogy to the whole course of nature, and which are supposed to depend on the simple qualities of objects, without any secret structure of parts. We are apt to imagine that we could discover these effects by the mere operation of our reason, without experience. We fancy, that were we brought on a sudden into this world, we could at first have inferred that one Billiard-ball would communicate motion to another upon impulse; and that we needed not to have waited for the event, in order to pronounce with certainty concerning it. Such is the influence of custom, that, where it is strongest, it not only covers our natural ignorance, but even conceals itself, and seems not to take place, merely because it is found in the highest degree.

But to convince us that all the laws of nature, and all the operations of bodies without exception, are known only by experience, the following reflections may, perhaps, suffice. Were any object presented to us, and were we required to pronounce concerning the effect, which will result from it, without consulting past observation; after what manner, I beseech you, must the mind proceed in this operation? It must invent or imagine some event, which it ascribes to the object as its effect; and it is plain that this invention must be entirely arbitrary. The mind can never possibly find the effect in the supposed cause, by the most accurate scrutiny and examination. For the effect is totally different from the cause, and consequently can never be discovered in it. Motion in the second Billiard-ball is a quite distinct event from motion in the first; nor is there anything in the one to suggest the smallest hint of the other. A stone or piece of metal raised into the air, and left without any support, immediately falls: but to consider the matter *a priori,* is there anything we discover in this situation which can beget the idea of a downward, rather than an upward, or any other motion, in the stone or metal?

And as the first imagination or invention of a particular effect, in all natural operations, is arbitrary, where we consult not experience; so must we also esteem the supposed tie or connection between the cause and effect, which binds them together, and renders it impossible that any other effect could result from the operation of that cause. When I see, for instance, a Billiard-ball moving in a straight line towards another; even suppose motion in the second ball should by accident be suggested to me, as the result of their contact or impulse; may I not conceive, that a hundred different events might as well follow from that cause? May not both these balls remain at absolute rest? May not the first ball return in a straight line, or leap off from the second in any line or direction? All these suppositions are consistent and conceivable. Why then should we give the preference to one, which is no more consistent or conceivable than the rest? All our reasonings *a priori* will never be able to show us any foundation for this preference.

In a word, then, every effect is a distinct event from its cause. It could not, therefore, be discovered in the cause, and the first invention or conception of it, *a priori,* must be entirely arbitrary. And even after it is suggested, the conjunction of it with the cause must appear equally arbitrary; since there are always many other effects, which, to reason, must seem fully as consistent and natural. In vain, therefore, should we pretend to determine any single event, or infer any cause or effect, without the assistance of observation and experience. . . .

### Part II

But we have not yet attained any tolerable satisfaction with regard to the question first proposed. Each solution still gives rise to a new question as difficult as the foregoing, and leads us on to farther enquiries. When it is asked, *What is the nature of all our reasonings concerning matter of fact?* the proper answer seems to be, that they are founded on the relation of cause and effect. When again it is asked, *What is the foundation of all our reasonings and conclusions concerning that relation?* it may be replied in one word, Experience. But if we still carry on our sifting humor, and ask, *What is the foundation of all conclusions from experience?* this implies a new question, which may be of more difficult solution and explication. Philosophers, that give themselves airs of superior wisdom and sufficiency, have a hard task when they encounter persons of inquisitive dispositions, who push them from every corner to which they retreat, and who are sure at last to bring them to some dangerous dilemma. The best expedient to prevent this confusion, is to be modest in our pretensions; and even to discover the difficulty ourselves before it is objected to us. By this means, we may make a kind of merit of our very ignorance.

I shall content myself, in this section, with an easy task, and shall pretend only to give a negative answer to the question here proposed. I say then, that, even after we have experience of the operations of cause and effect, our conclusions from that experience are *not* founded on reasoning, or any process of the understanding. This answer we must endeavor both to explain and to defend. . . .

In reality, all arguments from experience are founded on the similarity which we discover among natural objects, and by which we are induced to expect effects similar to those which we have found to follow from such objects. And though none but a fool or madman will ever pretend to dispute the authority of experience, or to reject that great guide of human life, it may surely be allowed a philosopher to have so much curiosity at least as to examine the principle of human nature, which gives this mighty authority to experience, and makes us draw advantage from that similarity which nature has placed among different objects. From causes which appear *similar* we expect similar effects. This is the sum of all our experimental conclusions. Now it seems evident that, if this conclusion were formed by reason, it would be as perfect at first, and upon one instance, as after ever so long a course of experience. But the case is far otherwise. Nothing so like as eggs; yet no one, on account of this appearing similarity, expects the same taste and relish in all of them. It is only after a long course of uniform experiments in any kind, that we attain a firm reliance and security with regard to a particular event. Now where is that process of reasoning which, from one instance, draws a conclusion, so different from that which it infers from a hundred instances that are nowise different from that single one? This question I propose as much for the sake of information, as with an intention of raising difficulties. I cannot find, I cannot imagine any such reasoning. But I keep my mind still open to instruction, if any one will vouchsafe to bestow it on me.

Should it be said that, from a number of uniform experiments, we *infer* a connection between the sensible qualities and the secret powers; this, I must confess, seems the same difficulty, couched in different terms. The question still recurs, on what process of argument this *inference* is founded? Where is the medium, the interposing ideas, which join propositions so very wide of each other? It is confessed that the color, consistence, and other sensible qualities of bread appear not, of themselves, to have any connection with the secret powers of nourishment and support. For otherwise we could infer these secret powers from the first appearance of these sensible qualities, without the aid of experience; contrary to the sentiment of all philosophers, and contrary to plain matter of fact. Here, then, is our natural state of ignorance with regard to the powers and influence of all objects. How is this remedied by experience? It only shows us a number of uniform effects, resulting from certain objects, and teaches us that those particular objects, at that particular time, were endowed with such powers and forces. When a new object, endowed with similar sensible qualities, is produced, we expect similar powers and forces, and look for a like effect. From a body of like color and consistence with bread we expect like nourishment and support. But this surely is a step or progress of the mind, which wants to be explained. When a man says, *I have found, in all past instances, such sensible qualities conjoined with such secret powers:* And when he says, *Similar sensible qualities will always be conjoined with similar secret powers,* he is not guilty of a tautology, nor are these propositions in any respect the same. You say that the one proposition is an inference from the other. But you must confess that the inference is not intuitive; neither is it demonstrative: Of what nature is it, then? To say it is experimental, is begging the question. For all inferences from experience suppose, as their foundation, that the future will resemble the past, and that similar powers will be conjoined with similar sensible qualities. If there be any suspicion that the course of nature may change, and that the past may be no rule for the future, all experience becomes useless, and can give rise to no inference or conclusion. It is impossible, therefore, that any arguments from experience can prove this resemblance of the past to the future; since all these arguments are founded on the supposition of that resemblance. Let the course of things be allowed hitherto ever so regular; that alone, without some new argument or inference, proves not that, for the future, it will continue so. In vain do you pretend to have learned the nature of bodies from your past experience. Their secret nature, and consequently all their effects and influence, may change, without any change in their sensible qualities. This happens sometimes, and with regard to some objects: Why may it [not] happen always, and with regard to all objects? What logic, what process of argument secures you against this supposition? My practice, you say, refutes my doubts. But you mistake the purport of my question. As an agent, I am quite satisfied in the point; but as a philosopher, who has some share of curiosity, I will not say **scepticism,** I want to learn the foundation of this inference. No reading, no enquiry has yet been able to remove my difficulty, or give me satisfaction in a matter of such importance. Can I do better than propose the difficulty to the public, even though, perhaps, I have small hopes of obtaining a solution? We shall, at least, by this means, be sensible of our ignorance, if we do not augment our knowledge.

I must confess that a man is guilty of unpardonable arrogance who concludes, because an argument has escaped his own investigation, that therefore it does not really exist. I must also confess that, though all the learned, for several ages, should have employed themselves in fruitless search upon any subject, it may still, perhaps, be rash to conclude positively that the subject must, therefore, pass all human comprehension. Even though we examine all the sources of our knowledge, and conclude them unfit for such a subject, there may still remain a suspicion, that the enumeration is not complete, or the examination not accurate. But with regard to the present subject, there are some considerations which seem to remove all this accusation of arrogance or suspicion of mistake.

It is certain that the most ignorant and stupid peasants — nay infants, nay even brute beasts — improve by experience, and learn the qualities of natural objects, by observing the effects which result from them. When a child has felt the sensation of pain from touching the flame of a candle, he will be careful not to put his hand near any candle; but will expect a similar effect from a cause which is similar in its sensible qualities and appearance. If you assert, therefore, that the understanding of the child is led into this conclusion by any process of argument or ratiocination, I may justly require you to produce that argument; nor have you any pretense to refuse so equitable a demand. You cannot say that the argument is abtruse, and may possibly escape your enquiry; since you confess that it is obvious to the capacity of a mere infant. If you hesitate, therefore, a moment, or if, after reflection, you produce any intricate or profound argument, you, in a manner, give up the question, and confess that it is not reasoning which engages us to suppose the past resembling the future, and to expect similar effects from causes which are, to appearance, similar. This is the proposition which I intended to enforce in the present section. If I be right, I pretend not to have made any mighty discovery. And if I be wrong, I must acknowledge myself to be indeed a very backward scholar; since I cannot now discover an argument which, it seems, was perfectly familiar to me long before I was out of my cradle.

## SCEPTICAL SOLUTION OF THESE DOUBTS

### Part I

. . . Nature will always maintain her rights, and prevail in the end over any abstract reasoning whatsoever. Though we should conclude, for instance, as in the foregoing section, that, in all reasonings from experience, there is a step taken by the mind which is not supported by any argument or process of the understanding; there is no danger that these reasonings, on which almost all knowledge depends, will ever be affected by such a discovery. If the mind be not engaged by argument to make this step, it must be induced by some other principle of equal weight and authority; and that principle will preserve its influence as long as human nature remains the same. What that principle is may well be worth the pains of enquiry.

Suppose a person, though endowed with the strongest faculties of reason and reflection, to be brought on a sudden into this world; he would, indeed, immediately observe a continual succession of objects, and one event following another; but he would not be able to discover anything farther. He would not, at first, by any reasoning, be able to reach the idea of cause and effect; since the particular powers, by which all natural operations are performed, never appear to the senses; nor is it reasonable to conclude, merely because one event, in one instance, precedes another, that therefore the one is the cause, the other the effect. Their conjunction may be arbitrary and casual. There may be no reason to infer the existence of one from the appearance of the other. And in a word, such a person, without more experience, could never employ his conjecture or reasoning concerning any matter of fact, or be assured of anything beyond what was immediately present to his memory and senses.

Suppose, again, that he has acquired more experience, and has lived so long in the world as to have observed familiar objects or events to be constantly conjoined together; what is the consequence of this experience? He immediately infers the existence of one object from the appearance of the other. Yet he has not, by all his experience, acquired any idea or knowledge of the secret power by which the one object produces the other; nor is it, by any process of reasoning, he is engaged to draw this inference. But still he finds himself determined to draw it: And though he should be convinced that his understanding has no part in the operation, he would nevertheless continue in the same course of thinking. There is some other principle which determines him to form such a conclusion.

This principle is Custom or Habit. For wherever the repetition of any particular act or operation produces a propensity to renew the same act or operation, without being impelled by any reasoning or process of the understanding, we always say, that this propensity is the effect of *Custom*. By employing that word, we pretend not to have given the ultimate reason of such a propensity. We only point out a principle of human nature, which is universally acknowledged, and which is well known by its effects. Perhaps we can push our enquiries no farther, or pretend to give the cause of this cause; but must rest contented with it as the ultimate principle, which we can assign, of all our conclusions from experience. It is sufficient satisfaction, that we can go so far, without repining at the narrowness of our faculties because they will carry us no farther. And it is certain we here advance a very intelligible proposition at least, if not a true one, when we assert that, after the constant conjunction of two objects — heat and flame, for instance, weight and solidity — we are determined by custom alone to expect the one from the appearance of the other. This hypothesis seems even the only one which explains the difficulty, why we draw, from a thousand instances, an inference which we are not able to draw from one instance, that is, in no respect, different from them. Reason is incapable of any such variation. The conclusions which it draws from considering one circle are the same which it would form upon surveying all the circles in the universe. But no man, having seen only one body move after being impelled by another, could infer that every other body will move after a like impulse. All inferences from experience, therefore, are effects of custom, not of reasoning.

Custom, then, is the great guide of human life. It is that principle alone which renders our experience useful to us, and makes us expect, for the future, a similar train of events with those which have appeared in the past. Without the influence of custom, we should be entirely ignorant of every matter of fact beyond what is immediately present to the memory and senses. We should never know how to adjust means to ends, or to employ our natural powers in the production of any effect. There would be an end at once of all action, as well as of the chief part of speculation.

But here it may be proper to remark, that though our conclusions from experience carry us beyond our memory and senses, and assure us of matters of fact which happened in the most distant places and most remote ages, yet some fact must always be present to the senses or memory, from which we may first proceed in drawing these conclusions. A man, who should find in a desert country the remains of pompous buildings, would conclude that the country had, in ancient times, been cultivated by civilized inhabitants; but did nothing of this nature occur to him, he could never form such an inference. We learn the events of former ages from history; but then we must peruse the volumes in which this instruction is contained, and thence carry up our inferences from one testimony to another, till we arrive at the eyewitnesses and spectators of these distant events. In a word, if we proceed not upon some fact, present to the memory or senses, our reasonings would be merely hypothetical; and however the particular links might be connected with each other, the whole chain of inferences would have nothing to support it, nor could we ever, by its means, arrive at the knowledge of any real existence. If I ask why you believe any particular matter of fact, which you relate, you must tell me some reason; and this reason will be some other fact, connected with it. But as you cannot proceed after this manner, *in infinitum,* you must at last terminate in some fact, which is present to your memory or senses; or must allow that your belief is entirely without foundation.

What, then, is the conclusion of the whole matter? A simple one; though, it must be confessed, pretty remote from the common theories of philosophy. All belief of matter of fact or real existence is derived merely from some object, present to the memory or senses, and a customary conjunction between that and some other object. Or in other words; having found in many instances, that any two kinds of objects—flame and heat, snow and cold—have always been conjoined together; if flame or snow be presented anew to the senses, the mind is carried by custom to expect heat or cold, and to *believe* that such a quality does exist, and will discover itself upon a nearer approach. This belief is the necessary result of placing the mind in such circumstances. It is an operation of the soul, when we are so situated, as unavoidable as to feel the passion of love, when we receive benefits; or hatred, when we meet with injuries. All these operations are a species of natural instincts, which no reasoning or process of the thought and understanding is able either to produce or to prevent. . . .

## Part II

Nothing is more free than the imagination of man; and though it cannot exceed that original stock of ideas furnished by the internal and external senses, it has unlimited power of mixing, compounding, separating, and dividing these ideas, in all the varieties of fiction and vision. It can feign a train of events, with all the appearance of reality, ascribe to them a particular time and place, conceive them as existent, and paint them out to itself with every circumstance, that belongs to any historical fact, which it believes with the greatest certainty. Wherein, therefore, consists the difference between such a fiction and belief? It lies not merely in any peculiar idea, which is annexed to such a conception as commands our assent, and which is wanting to every known fiction. For as the mind has authority over all its ideas, it could voluntarily annex this particular idea to any fiction, and consequently be able to believe whatever it pleases; contrary to what we find by daily experience. We can, in our conception, join the head of a man to the body of a horse; but it is not in our power to believe that such an animal has ever really existed.

It follows, therefore, that the difference between *fiction* and *belief* lies in some sentiment or feeling, which is annexed to the latter, not to the former, and which depends not on the will, nor can be commanded at pleasure. It must be excited by nature, like all other sentiments; and must arise from the particular situation, in which the mind is placed at any particular juncture. Whenever any object is presented to the memory or senses, it immediately, by the force of custom, carries the imagination to conceive that object, which is usually conjoined to it; and this conception is attended with a feeling or sentiment, different from the loose reveries of the fancy. In this consists the whole nature of belief. For as there is no matter of fact which we believe so firmly that we cannot conceive the contrary, there would be no difference between the conception assented to and that which is rejected, were it not for some sentiment which distinguishes the one from the other. If I see a Billiard-ball moving towards another, on a smooth table, I can easily conceive it to stop upon contact. This conception implies no contradiction; but still it feels very differently from that conception by which I represent to myself the impulse and the communication of motion from one ball to another.

Were we to attempt a *definition* of this sentiment, we should, perhaps, find it a very difficult, if not an impossible task; in the same manner as if we should endeavor to define the feeling of cold or passion of anger, to a creature who never had any experience of these sentiments. Belief is the true and proper name of this feeling; and no one is ever at a loss to know the meaning of that term; because every man is every moment conscious of the sentiment represented by it. It may not, however, be improper to attempt a *description* of this sentiment; in hopes we may, by that means, arrive at some analogies, which may afford a more perfect explication of it. I say, then, that belief is nothing but a more vivid, lively, forcible, firm, steady conception of an object, than what the imagination alone is ever able to attain. This variety of terms, which may seem so unphilosophical, is intended only to express that act of the mind, which renders realities, or what is taken for such, more present to us than fictions, causes them to weigh more in the thought, and gives them a superior influence on the passions and imagination. Provided we agree about the thing, it is needless to dispute about the terms. The imagination has the command over all its ideas, and can join and mix and vary them, in all the ways possible. It may conceive fictitious objects with all the circumstances of place and time. It may set them, in a manner, before our eyes, in their true colors, just as they might have existed. But as it is impossible that this faculty of imagination can ever, of itself, reach belief, it is evident that belief consists not in the peculiar nature or order of ideas, but in the *manner* of their conception, and in their *feeling* to the mind. I confess, that it is impossible perfectly to explain this feeling or manner of conception. We may make use of words which express something near it. But its true and proper name, as we observed before, is *belief;* which is a term that every one sufficiently understands in common life. And in philosophy, we can go no farther than assert, that *belief* is something felt by the mind, which distinguishes the ideas of the judgment from the fictions of the imagination. It gives them more weight and influence; makes them appear of greater importance; enforces them in the mind; and renders them the governing principle of our actions. I hear at present, for instance, a person's voice, with whom I am acquainted; and the sound comes as from the next room. This impression of my senses immediately conveys my thought to the person, together with all the surrounding objects. I paint them out to myself as existing at present, with the same qualities and relations, of which I formerly knew them possessed. These ideas take faster hold of my mind than ideas of an enchanted castle. They are very different to the feeling, and have a much greater influence of every kind, either to give pleasure or pain, joy or sorrow.

Let us, then, take in the whole compass of this doctrine, and allow, that the sentiment of belief is nothing but a conception more intense and steady than what attends the mere fictions of the imagination, and that this *manner* of conception arises from a customary conjunction of the object with something present to the memory or senses: I believe that it will not be difficult, upon these suppositions, to find other operations of the mind analogous to it, and to trace up these phenomena to principles still more general.

We have already observed that nature has established connections among particular ideas, and that no sooner one idea occurs to our thoughts than it introduces its correlative, and carries our attention towards it, by a gentle and insensible movement. These principles of connection or association we have reduced to three, namely, *Resemblance, Contiguity* and *Causation;* which are the only bonds that unite our thoughts together, and beget that regular train of reflection or discourse, which, in a greater or less degree, takes place among mankind. Now here arises a question, on which the solution of the present difficulty will depend. Does it happen, in all these relations, that, when one of the objects is presented to the senses or memory, the mind is not only carried to the conception of the correlative, but reaches a steadier and stronger conception of it than what otherwise it would have been able to attain? This seems to be the case with that belief which arises from the relation of cause and effect. And if the case be the same with the other relations or principles of associations, this may be established as a general law, which takes place in all the operations of the mind.

We may, therefore, observe, as the first experiment to our present purpose, that, upon the appearance of the picture of an absent friend, our idea of him is evidently enlivened by the *resemblance,* and that every passion, which that idea occasions, whether of joy or sorrow, acquires new force and vigor. In producing this effect, there concur both a relation and a present impression. Where the picture bears him no resemblance, at least was not intended for him, it never so much as conveys our thought to him: And where it is absent, as well as the person, though the mind may pass from the thought of the one to that of the other, it feels its idea to be rather weakened than enlivened by that transition. We take a pleasure in viewing the picture of a friend, when it is set before us; but when it is removed, rather choose to consider him directly than by reflection in an image, which is equally distant and obscure. . . .

We may add force to these experiments by others of a different kind, in considering the effects of *contiguity* as well as of *resemblance*. It is certain that distance diminishes the force of every idea, and that, upon our approach to any object; though it does not discover itself to our senses; it operates upon the mind with an influence, which imitates an immediate impression. The thinking on any object readily transports the mind to what is contiguous; but it is only the actual presence of an object, that transports it with a superior vivacity. When I am a few miles from home, whatever relates to it touches me more nearly than when I am two hundred leagues distant; though even at that distance the reflecting on any thing in the neighborhood of my friends or family naturally produces an idea of them. But as in this latter case, both the objects of the mind are ideas; notwithstanding there is an easy transition between them; that transition alone is not able to give a superior vivacity to any of the ideas, for want of some immediate impression. . . .

We may observe, that, in these phenomena, the belief of the correlative object is always presupposed; without which the relation could have no effect. The influence of the picture supposes, that we *believe* our friend to have once existed. Contiguity to home can never excite our ideas of home, unless we *believe* that it really exists. Now I assert, that this belief, where it reaches beyond the memory or senses, is of a similar nature, and arises from similar causes, with the transition of thought and vivacity of conception here explained. When I throw a piece of dry wood into a fire, my mind is immediately carried to conceive, that it augments, not extinguishes the flame. This transition of thought from the cause to the effect proceeds not from reason. It derives its origin altogether from custom and experience. And as it first begins from an object, present to the senses, it renders the idea or conception of flame more strong and lively than any loose, floating reverie of the imagination. That idea arises immediately. The thought moves instantly towards it, and conveys to it all that force of conception, which is derived from the impression present to the senses. When a sword is levelled at my breast, does not the idea of wound and pain strike me more strongly, than when a glass of wine is presented to me, even though by accident this idea should occur after the appearance of the latter object? But what is there in this whole matter to cause such a strong conception, except only a present object and a customary transition to the idea of another object, which we have been accustomed to conjoin with the former? This is the whole operation of the mind, in all our conclusions concerning matter of fact and existence; and it is a satisfaction to find some analogies, by which it may be explained. The transition from a present object does in all cases give strength and solidity to the related idea.

Here, then, is a kind of pre-established harmony between the course of nature and the succession of our ideas; and though the powers and forces, by which the former is governed, be wholly unknown to us; yet our thoughts and conceptions have still, we find, gone on in the same train with the other works of nature. Custom is that principle, by which this correspondence has been effected; so necessary to the subsistence of our species, and the regulation of our conduct, in every circumstance and occurrence of human life. Had not the presence of an object, instantly excited the idea of those objects, commonly conjoined with it, all our knowledge must have been limited to the narrow sphere of our memory and senses; and we should never have been able to adjust means to ends, or employ our natural powers, either to the producing of good, or avoiding of evil. Those, who delight in the discovery and contemplation of *final causes,* have here ample subject to employ their wonder and admiration.

I shall add, for a further confirmation of the foregoing theory, that, as this operation of the mind, by which we infer like effects from like causes, and *vice versa,* is so essential to the subsistence of all human creatures, it is not probable, that it could be trusted to the fallacious deductions of our reason, which is slow in its operations; appears not, in any degree, during the first years of infancy; and at best is, in every age and period of human life, extremely liable to error and mistake. It is more conformable to the ordinary wisdom of nature to secure so necessary an act of the mind, by some instinct or mechanical tendency, which may be infallible in its operations, may discover itself at the first appearance of life and thought, and may be independent of all the labored deductions of the understanding. As nature has taught us the use of our limbs, without giving us the knowledge of the muscles and nerves, by which they are actuated; so has she implanted in us an instinct, which carries forward the thought in a correspondent course to that which she has established among external objects; though we are ignorant of those powers and forces, on which this regular course and succession of objects totally depends.

## *Bertrand Russell (1872–1970)*

Bertrand Russell was one of the greatest thinkers of the twentieth century. He wrote more than a dozen books in philosophy as well as books and essays on education, politics, and morals. He made major contributions to the foundations of mathematics, philosophical logic, epistemology, and metaphysics. For his ardent pacifism and radical social and moral views he was imprisoned, dismissed from a university position in England, and barred from accepting a position in America, all during the first half of the century. The value of his work has been clearly recognized, however, and he has received numerous awards including the Nobel Prize for Literature.

The selection below is taken from the opening chapters of Russell's *Problems of Philosophy* (1912), which was written as an introductory text for those just beginning the study of philosophy. Russell believes that the problems of philosophy emerge as soon as we examine very carefully our ordinary beliefs. In this selection he draws the distinction between appearance and reality and argues that all of our beliefs about material objects must be understood as indirect or involving inference as well as perception.

# Appearance and Reality

## *Bertrand Russell*

Is there any knowledge in the world which is so certain that no reasonable man could doubt it? This question, which at first sight might not seem difficult, is really one of the most difficult that can be asked. When we have realized the obstacles in the way of a straightforward and confident answer, we shall be well launched on the study of philosophy—for philosophy is merely the attempt to answer such ultimate questions, not carelessly and dogmatically, as we do in ordinary life and even in the sciences, but critically, after exploring all that makes such questions puzzling,

Abridged from *The Problems of Philosophy*, by Bertrand Russell, 1912. Reprinted by permission of Oxford University Press.

and after realizing all the vagueness and confusion that underlie our ordinary ideas.

In daily life, we assume as certain many things which, on a closer scrutiny, are found to be so full of apparent contradictions that only a great amount of thought enables us to know what it is that we really may believe. In the search for certainty, it is natural to begin with our present experiences, and in some sense, no doubt, knowledge is to be derived from them. But any statement as to what it is that our immediate experiences make us know is very likely to be wrong. It seems to me that I am now sitting in a chair, at a table of a certain shape, on which I see sheets of paper with writing or print. By turning my head I see out of the window buildings and clouds and the sun. I believe that the sun is about ninety-three million miles from the earth; that it is a hot globe many times bigger than the earth; that, owing to the earth's rotation, it rises every morning, and will continue to do so for an indefinite time in the future. I believe that, if any other normal person comes into my room, he will see the same chairs and tables and books and papers as I see, and that the table which I see is the same as the table which I feel pressing against my arm. All this seems to be so evident as to be hardly worth stating, except in answer to a man who doubts whether I know anything. Yet all this may be reasonably doubted, and all of it requires much careful discussion before we can be sure that we have stated it in a form that is wholly true.

To make our difficulties plain, let us concentrate attention on the table. To the eye it is oblong, brown and shiny, to the touch it is smooth and cool and hard; when I tap it, it gives out a wooden sound. Any one else who sees and feels and hears the table will agree with this description, so that it might seem as if no difficulty would arise; but as soon as we try to be more precise our troubles begin. Although I believe that the table is "really" of the same color all over, the parts that reflect the light look much brighter than the other parts, and some parts look white because of reflected light. I know that, if I move, the parts that reflect the light will be different, so that the apparent distribution of colors on the table will change. It follows that if several people are looking at the table at the same moment, no two of them will see exactly the same distribution of colors, because no two can see it from exactly the same point of view, and any change in the point of view makes some change in the way the light is reflected.

For most practical purposes these differences are unimportant, but to the painter they are all-important: the painter has to unlearn the habit of thinking that things seem to have the color which common sense says they "really" have, and to learn the habit of seeing things as they appear. Here we have already the beginning of one of the distinctions that cause most trouble in philosophy—the distinction between "appearance" and "reality," between what things seem to be and what they are. The painter wants to know what things seem to be, the practical man and the philosopher want to know what they are; but the philosopher's wish to know this is stronger than the practical man's, and is more troubled by knowledge as to the difficulties of answering the question.

To return to the table. It is evident from what we have found, that there is no color which pre-eminently appears to be *the* color of the table, or even of any one particular part of the table—it appears to be of different colors from different points of view, and there is no reason for regarding some of these as more really its color than others. And we know that even from a given point of view the color will seem different by artificial light, or to a color-blind man, or to a man wearing blue spectacles, while in the dark there will be no color at all, though to touch and hearing the table will be unchanged. This color is not something which is inherent in the table, but something depending upon the table and the spectator and the way the light falls on the table. When, in ordinary life, we speak of *the* color of the table, we only mean the sort of color which it will seem to have to a normal spectator from an ordinary point of view under usual conditions of light. But the other colors which appear under other conditions have just as good a right to be considered real; and therefore, to avoid favoritism, we are compelled to deny that, in itself, the table has any one particular color.

The same thing applies to the texture. With the naked eye one can see the grain, but otherwise the table looks smooth and even. If we looked at it through a microscope, we should see roughnesses and hills and valleys, and all sorts of differences that are imperceptible to the naked eye. Which of these is the "real" table? We are naturally tempted to say that what we see through the microscope is more real, but that in turn would be changed by a still more powerful microscope. If, then, we cannot trust what we see with the naked eye, why should we trust what we see through a microscope? Thus, again, the confidence in our senses with which we began deserts us.

The *shape* of the table is no better. We are all in the habit of judging as to the "real" shapes of things, and we do this so unreflectingly that we come to think we actually see the real shapes. But, in fact, as we all have to learn if we try to draw, a given thing looks different in shape from every different point of view. If our table is "really" rectangular, it will look, from almost all points of view, as if it had two acute angles and two obtuse angles. If opposite sides are parallel, they will look as if they converged to a point away from the spectator; if they are of equal length, they will look as if the nearer side were longer. All these things are not commonly noticed in looking at a table, because experience has taught us to construct the "real" shape from the apparent shape, and the "real" shape is what interests us as practical men. But the "real" shape is not what we see; it is something inferred from what we see. And what we see is constantly changing in shape as we move about the room; so that here again the senses seem not to give us the truth about the table itself, but only about the appearance of the table.

Similar difficulties arise when we consider the sense of touch. It is true that the table always gives us a sensation of hardness, and we feel that it resists pressure. But the sensation we obtain depends upon how hard we press the table and also upon what part of the body we press with; thus the various sensations due to various pressures or various parts of the body cannot be supposed to reveal *directly* any definite property of the table, but at most to be *signs* of some property which perhaps *causes* all the sensations, but is not actually apparent in any of them. And the same applies still more obviously to the sounds which can be elicited by rapping the table.

Thus it becomes evident that the real table, if there is one, is not the same as what we immediately experience by sight or touch or hearing. The real table, if there is one, is not *immediately* known to us at all, but must be an inference from what is immediately known. . . .

Before we go farther it will be well to consider for a moment what it is that we have discovered so far. It has appeared that, if we take any common object of the sort that is supposed to be known by the senses, what the senses *immediately* tell us is not the truth about the object as it is apart from us, but only the truth about certain . . . [appearances] which, so far as we can see, depend upon the relations between us and the object. Thus what we directly see and feel is merely "appearance," which we believe to be a sign of some "reality" behind. But if the reality is not what appears, have we any means of knowing whether there is any reality at all? And if so, have we any means of finding out what it is like?

Such questions are bewildering, and it is difficult to know that even the strangest hypotheses may not be true. Thus our familiar table, which has roused but the slightest thoughts in us hitherto, has become a problem full of surprising possibilities. The one thing we know about it is that it is not what it seems. Beyond this modest result, so far, we have the most complete liberty of conjecture. Leibniz tells us it is a community of souls: Berkeley tells us it is an idea in the mind of God; sober science, scarcely less wonderful, tells us it is a vast collection of electric charges in violent motion.

Among these surprising possibilities, doubt suggests that perhaps there is no table at all. Philosophy, if it cannot *answer* so many questions as we could wish, has at least the power of *asking* questions which increase the interest of the world, and show the strangeness and wonder lying just below the surface even in the commonest things of daily life.

. . . Is there a table which has a certain intrinsic nature, and continues to exist when I am not looking, or is the table merely a product of my imagination, a dream-table in a very prolonged dream? This question is of the greatest importance. For if we cannot be sure of the independent existence of objects, we cannot be sure of the independent existence of other people's bodies, and therefore still less of other people's minds, since we have no grounds for believing in their minds except such as are derived from observing their bodies. Thus if we cannot be sure of the independent existence of objects, we shall be left alone in a desert—it may be that the whole outer world is nothing but a dream, and that we alone exist. This is an uncomfortable possibility; but although it cannot be strictly *proved* to be false, there is not the slightest reason to suppose that it is true. [. . .] We have to see why this is the case.

Before we embark upon doubtful matters, let us try to find some more or less fixed point from which to start. Although we are doubting the physical existence of the table, we are not doubting the existence of the . . . [appearances] which made us think there was a table; we are not doubting that, while we look, a certain color and shape appear to us, and while we press, a certain sensation of hardness is experienced by us. All this, which is psychological, we are not calling in question. In fact, whatever else may be doubtful, some at least of our immediate experiences seem absolutely certain.

Descartes (1596–1650), the founder of modern philosophy, invented a method which may still be used with profit—the method of systematic doubt. He determined that he would believe nothing which he did not see quite clearly and distinctly to be true. Whatever he could bring himself to doubt, he would doubt, until he saw reason for not doubting it. By applying this method he gradually became convinced that the only existence of which he could be *quite* certain was his own. He imagined a deceitful demon, who presented unreal things to his senses in a perpetual phantasmagoria; it might be very improbable that such a demon existed, but still it was possible, and therefore doubt concerning things perceived by the senses was possible.

But doubt concerning his own existence was not possible, for if he did not exist, no demon could deceive him. If he doubted, he must exist; if he had any experiences whatever, he must exist. Thus his own existence was an absolute certainty to him. "I think, therefore I am," he said *(Cogito, ergo sum);* and on the basis of this certainty he set to work to build up again the world of knowledge which his doubt had laid in ruins. By inventing the method of doubt, and by showing that subjective things are the most certain, Descartes performed a great service to philosophy, and one which makes him still useful to all students of the subject.

But some care is needed in using Descartes' argument. "*I* think, therefore *I* am" says rather more than is strictly certain. It might seem as though we were quite sure of being the same person today as we were yesterday, and this is no doubt true in some sense. But the real Self is as hard to arrive at as the real table, and does not seem to have that absolute, convincing certainty that belongs to particular experiences. When I look at my table and see a certain brown color, what is quite certain at once is not "*I* am seeing a brown color," but rather, "a brown color is being seen." This of course involves something (or somebody) which (or who) sees the brown color; but it does not of itself involve that more or less permanent person whom we call "I." So far as immediate certainty goes, it might be that the something which sees the brown color is quite momentary, and not the same as the something which has some different experience the next moment.

Thus it is our particular thoughts and feelings that have primitive certainty. And this applies to dreams and hallucinations as well as to normal perceptions: when we dream or see a ghost, we certainly do have the sensations we think we have, but for various reasons it is held that no physical object corresponds to these sensations.

Thus the certainty of our knowledge of our own experiences does not have to be limited in any way to allow for exceptional cases. Here, therefore, we have, for what it is worth, a solid basis from which to begin our pursuit of knowledge.

The problem we have to consider is this: Granted that we are certain of [the internal content of] our own . . . [experiences], have we any reason for regarding them as signs of the existence of something else, which we can call the physical object? When we have enumerated all the . . . [appearances] which we should naturally regard as connected with the table, have we said all there is to say about the table, or is there still something else—something not a[n . . . appearance], something which persists when we go out of the room? Common sense unhesitatingly answers that there is. What can be bought and sold and pushed about and have a cloth laid on it, and so on, cannot be a *mere* collection of . . . [appearances]. If the cloth completely hides the table, we shall derive no . . . [appearances] from the table, and therefore, if the table were merely . . . [appearances], it would have ceased to exist, and the cloth would be suspended in empty air, resting, by a miracle, in the place where the table formerly was. This seems plainly absurd; but whoever wishes to become a philosopher must learn not to be frightened by absurdities.

One great reason why it is felt that we must secure a physical object in addition to the . . . [appearances], is that we want the *same* object for different people. When ten people are sitting round a dinner-table, it seems preposterous to maintain that they are not seeing the same tablecloth, the same knives and forks and spoons and glasses. But the . . . [appearances] are private to each separate person; what is immediately present to the sight of one is not immediately present to the sight of another: they all see things from slightly different points of view, and therefore see them slightly differently. Thus, if there are to be public neutral objects, which can be in some sense known to many different people, there must be something over and above the private and particular . . . [appearances] which appear to various people. What reason, then, have we for believing that there are such public neutral objects?

The first answer that naturally occurs to one is that, although different people may see the table slightly differently, still they all see more or less similar things when they look at the table, and the variations in what they see follow the laws of perspective and reflection of light, so that it is easy to arrive at a permanent object underlying all the different people's . . . [appearances]. I bought my table from the former occupant of my room; I could not buy *his* . . . [appearances], which died when he went away, but I could and did buy the confident expectation of more or less similar . . . [appearances]. Thus it is the fact that different people have similar . . . [experiences], and that one person in a given place at different times has similar . . . [experiences], which makes us suppose that over and above the . . . [appearances] there is a permanent public object which underlies or causes the . . . [experiences] of various people at various times.

Now in so far as the above considerations depend upon supposing that there are other people besides ourselves, they beg the very question at issue. Other people are represented to me by certain . . . [appearances], such as the sight of them or the sound of their voices, and if I had no reason to believe that there were physical objects independent of my . . . [experiences], I should have no reason to believe that other people exist except as part of my dream. Thus, when we are trying to show that there must be objects independent of our own . . . [experiences], we cannot appeal to the testimony of other people, since this testimony itself consists of . . . [appearances], and does not reveal other people's experiences unless our own . . . [appearances] are signs of things existing independently of us. We must therefore, if possible, find, in our own purely private experiences, characteristics which show, or tend to show, that there are in the world things other than ourselves and our private experiences.

In one sense it must be admitted that we can

never *prove* the existence of things other than ourselves and our experiences. No logical absurdity results from the hypothesis that the world consists of myself and my thoughts and feelings and sensations, and that everything else is mere fancy. In dreams a very complicated world may seem to be present, and yet on waking we find it was a delusion; that is to say, we find that the . . . [contents of our experiences] in the dream do not appear to have corresponded with such physical objects as we should naturally infer from our . . . [appearances]. (It is true that, when the physical world is assumed, it is possible to find physical causes for the . . . [appearances] in dreams: a door banging, for instance, may cause us to dream of a naval engagement. But although, in this case, there is a physical *cause* for the . . . [appearances], there is not a physical object *corresponding* to the . . . [appearances] in the way in which an actual naval battle would correspond.) There is no logical impossibility in the supposition that the whole of life is a dream, in which we ourselves create all the objects that come before us. But although this is not logically impossible, there is no reason whatever to suppose that it is true; and it is, in fact, a less simple hypothesis, viewed as a means of accounting for the facts of our own life, than the common-sense hypothesis that there really are objects independent of us, whose action on us causes our sensations.

The way in which simplicity comes in from supposing that there really are physical objects is easily seen. If the cat appears at one moment in one part of the room, and at another in another part, it is natural to suppose that it has moved from the one to the other, passing over a series of intermediate positions. But if it is merely a set of . . . [appearances], it cannot have ever been in any place where I did not see it; thus we shall have to suppose that it did not exist at all while I was not looking, but suddenly sprang into being in a new place. If the cat exists whether I see it or not, we can understand from our own experience how it gets hungry between one meal and the next; but if it does not exist when I am not seeing it, it seems odd that appetite should grow during non-existence as fast as during existence. And if the cat consists only of . . . [appearances], it cannot be *hungry,* since no hunger but my own can be a . . . [content of experience for] me. Thus the behavior of the . . . [appearances] which represent the cat to me, though it seems quite natural when regarded as an expression of hunger, becomes utterly inexplicable when regarded as mere movements and changes of patches of color, which are as incapable of hunger as a triangle is of playing football.

But the difficulty in the case of the cat is nothing compared to the difficulty in the case of human beings. When human beings speak—that is, when we hear certain noises which we associate with ideas, and simultaneously see certain motions of lips and expressions of face—it is very difficult to suppose that what we hear is not the expression of a thought, as we know it would be if we emitted the same sounds. Of course similar things happen in dreams, where we are mistaken as to the existence of other people. But dreams are more or less suggested by what we call waking life, and are capable of being more or less accounted for on scientific principles if we assume that there really is a physical world. Thus every principle of simplicity urges us to adopt the natural view, that there really are objects other than ourselves and our . . . [appearances] which have an existence not dependent upon our perceiving them.

Of course it is not by argument that we originally come by our belief in an independent external world. We find this belief ready in ourselves as soon as we begin to reflect: it is what may be called an *instinctive* belief. We should never have been led to question this belief but for the fact that, at any rate in the case of sight, it seems as if the . . . [appearance] itself were instinctively believed to be the independent object, whereas argument shows that the object cannot be identical with the . . . [appearance]. This discovery, however—which is not at all paradoxical in the case of taste and smell and sound, and only slightly so in the case of touch—leaves undiminished our instinctive belief that there *are* objects *corresponding* to our . . . [appearances]. Since this belief does not lead to any difficulties, but on the contrary tends to simplify and systematize our account of our experiences, there seems no good reason for rejecting it. We may therefore admit—though with a slight doubt derived from dreams—that the external world does really exist, and is not wholly dependent for its existence upon our continuing to perceive it.

The argument which has led us to this conclusion is doubtless less strong than we could wish, but it is typical of many philosophical arguments, and it is therefore worth while to consider briefly its general character and validity. All knowledge, we find, must be built up upon our instinctive beliefs, and if these are rejected, nothing is left. But among our instinctive beliefs some are much stronger than others, while many have, by habit and association, become entangled with other beliefs, not really instinctive, but falsely supposed to be part of what is believed instinctively.

Philosophy should show us the hierarchy of our instinctive beliefs, beginning with those we hold most strongly, and presenting each as much isolated and as free from irrelevant additions as possible. It should take care to show that, in the form in which they are finally set forth, our instinctive beliefs do not clash, but form a harmonious system. There can never be any reason for rejecting one instinctive belief except that it clashes with others; thus, if they are found to harmonize, the whole system becomes worthy of acceptance.

It is of course *possible* that all or any of our beliefs may be mistaken, and therefore all ought to be held with at least some slight element of doubt. But we cannot have *reason* to reject a belief except on the ground of some other belief. Hence, by organizing our instinctive beliefs and their consequences, by considering which among them is most possible, if necessary, to modify or abandon, we can arrive, on the basis of accepting as our sole data what we instinctively believe, at an orderly systematic organization of our knowledge, in which, though the *possibility* of error remains, its likelihood is diminished by the interrelation of the parts and by the critical scrutiny which has preceded acquiescence.

This function, at least, philosophy can perform. Most philosophers, rightly or wrongly, believe that philosophy can do much more than this—that it can give us knowledge, not otherwise attainable, concerning the universe as a whole, and concerning the nature of ultimate reality. Whether this be the case or not, the more modest function we have spoken of can certainly be performed by philosophy, and certainly suffices, for those who have once begun to doubt the adequacy of common sense, to justify the arduous and difficult labors that philosophical problems involve.

## *J. L. Austin (1911–1960)*

J. L. Austin is famous for a number of very influential papers, many of which were given as lectures but not published until after his death. He made contributions in several areas of philosophy, but he is best known for his views on philosophic method and the subsequent influence of those views, particularly in the philosophy of language. His lectures and papers have appeared in three book-length volumes: *Sense and Sensibilia* (1962), from which the excerpts below were taken, *How to Do Things with Words* (1962), and *Philosophical Papers* (1961).

Austin is one of a group of philosophers who were described as "ordinary language" philosophers. Although Austin did not believe that philosophy consisted only of examining the way that language is actually used ("what we would say when . . ."), he did believe that the actual use of language in ordinary contexts was an appropriate place for philosophical investigation to begin. He tried in his writing to show how attention to the nuances and richness of natural language in use was frequently sufficient to throw light on deeper or grander-looking philosophical problems and puzzles. In the following selection he points out how poorly a number of sceptical attacks on our ordinary beliefs would fare if we tried to conduct them within the context of ordinary life, that is, within the context in which the beliefs being examined are actually "at home." Whether taking the perspective of the "plain man" in this way really counters the sceptical doubts is of course open to debate, but it at least forces us to look more closely at just what the sceptic is doing and why scepticism seems to work in one's philosophical study but not in the real world.

# Ordinary Knowledge and Philosophical Doubt

## *J. L. Austin*

. . . [The sceptical attack on our ordinary knowledge typically begins with the assumption] that there is [always] *room* for doubt and suspicion, whether or not the plain man feels any. [It is suggested] that when, for instance, I look at a chair a few yards in front of me in broad daylight, my view is that I have *(only)* as much certainty as I need and can get that there is a chair and that I see it. But in fact the plain man would regard doubt in such a case, not as far-fetched or over-refined or somehow unpractical, but as plain *nonsense;* he would say, quite correctly, "Well, if that's not seeing a real chair then *I don't know what is.*" . . .

Is it the case that "delusive and veridical experiences" are not "qualitatively different"? Well, at least it seems perfectly extraordinary to say so in this sweeping way. Consider a few examples. I may have the experience (dubbed "delusive" presumably) of dreaming that I am being presented to the Pope. Could it be seriously suggested that having this dream is "qualitatively indistinguishable" from *actually being* presented to the Pope? Quite obviously not. After all, we have the phrase "a dream-like quality"; some waking experiences are said to have this dream-like quality, and some artists and writers occasionally try to impart it, usually with scant success, to their works. But of course, if the fact here alleged *were* a fact, the phrase would be perfectly meaningless, because applicable to everything. If dreams were not "qualitatively" different from waking experiences, then *every* waking experience would be like a dream; the dream-like quality would be, not difficult to capture, but impossible to avoid.[1] . . .

. . . If, when I make some statement, it is true that nothing whatever could in fact be produced as a cogent ground for retracting it, this can only be because I am in, have got myself into, the very best possible position for making that statement—I have, and am entitled to have, *complete* confidence in it when I make it. . . . Whether this is so or not is . . . [a matter] of what *the circumstances are* in which I make it. . . . If I watch for some time an animal a few feet in front of me, in a good light, if I prod it perhaps, sniff, and take note of the noises it makes, I may say, "That's a pig"; and this . . . will be "incorrigible," nothing could be produced that would show that I had made a mistake. . . .

It is not the case . . . that whenever a "material-object" statement is made, the speaker must have or could produce evidence for it. This may sound plausible enough; but it involves a gross misuse of the notion of "evidence." The situation in which I would properly be said to have *evidence* for the statement that some animal is a pig is that, for example, in which the beast itself is not actually on view, but I can see plenty of pig-like marks on the ground outside its retreat. If I find a few buckets of pig-food, that's a bit more evidence, and the noises and the smell may provide better evidence still. But if the animal then emerges and stands there plainly in view, there is no longer any question of collecting evidence; its coming into view doesn't provide me with more *evidence* that it's a pig, I can now just *see* that it is, the question is settled. And of course I might, in different circumstances, have just seen this in the first place, and not had to bother with collecting evidence at all. . . .

Ayer's doctrine is that "the notion of certainty does not apply to propositions . . . [about material objects]." And his ground for saying this is that, in order to verify a proposition of this kind conclusively, we should have to perform the self-contradictory feat of completing "an infinite series of verifications"; however many tests we may carry out with favorable results, we can never complete all the possible tests, for these are infinite in number; but nothing *less* than all the possible tests would be *enough*.

Now why does Ayer (and not he alone) put forward this very extraordinary doctrine? It is, of course, not true in general that statements about "material things," as such, *need* to be "verified." If, for instance, someone remarks in casual conversation, "As a matter of fact I live in Oxford," the other party to the conversation may, if he finds it worth doing, verify this assertion; but the *speaker*, of course, has no need to do this — he knows it to be true (or, if he is lying, false). Strictly speaking, indeed, it is not just that he has no *need* to verify his statement; the case is rather that, since he already knows it to be true, nothing whatever that he might do could *count* as his "verifying" it. Nor need it be true that he is in this position by virtue of having verified his assertion at some previous stage; for of how many people really, who know quite well where they live, could it be said that they have at any time *verified* that they live there? When could they be supposed to have done this? In what way? And why? What we have here, in fact, is an erroneous doctrine which is a kind of mirror-image of the erroneous doctrine about evidence we discussed just now; the idea that statements about "material things" *as such* need to be verified is just as wrong as, and wrong in just the same way as, the idea that statements about "material things" *as such* must be based on evidence. And both ideas go astray, at bottom, through the pervasive error of neglecting *the circumstances in which* things are said — of supposing that *the words alone* can be discussed, in a quite general way.

But even if we agree to confine ourselves to situations in which statements can be, and do need to be, verified, the case still looks desperate. Why on earth should one think that such verification can't ever be conclusive? If, for instance, you tell me there's a telephone in the next room, and (feeling mistrustful) I decide to verify this, how could it be thought *impossible* for me to do this conclusively? I go into the next room, and certainly there's something there that looks exactly like a telephone. But is it a case perhaps of *trompe l'oeil* painting? I can soon settle that. Is it just a dummy perhaps, not really connected up and with no proper works? Well, I can take it to pieces a bit and find out, or actually use it for ringing somebody up — and perhaps get them to ring me up too, just to make sure. And of course, if I do all these things, I *do* make sure; what more could possibly be required? This object has already stood up to amply enough tests to establish that it really is a telephone; and it isn't just that, for everyday or practical or ordinary purposes, enough is *as good as* a telephone; what meets all these tests just *is* a telephone, no doubt about it. . . .

Of the many objectionable elements in [the] doctrine [that statements about material objects entail an infinite number of propositions and hence cannot be conclusively verified], in some ways the strangest is the use made of the notion of entailment. What does the sentence, "That is a pig," *entail?* Well, perhaps there is somewhere, recorded by some zoological authority, a statement of the necessary and sufficient conditions for belonging to the species *pig*. And so perhaps, if we use the word "pig" strictly in that sense, to say of an animal that it's a pig will entail that it satisfies those conditions, whatever they may be. But clearly it isn't this sort of entailment that Ayer has in mind; nor, for that matter, is it particularly relevant to the use that non-experts make of the word "pig."[2] But what other kind of entailment is there? We have a pretty rough idea what pigs look like, what they smell and sound like, and how they normally behave; and no doubt, if something didn't look at all right for a pig, behave as pigs do, or make pig-like noises and smells, we'd say that it wasn't a pig. But are there—do there *have* to be—*statements* of the form, "It looks . . . ," "It sounds . . . ," "It smells . . . ," of which we could say straight off that "That is a pig" entails them? Plainly not. We learn the word "pig," as we learn the vast majority of words for ordinary things, ostensively—by being told, in the presence of the animal, "*That* is a pig"; and thus, though certainly we learn what sort of thing it is to which the word "pig" can and can't be properly applied, we don't go through any kind of intermediate stage of relating the word "pig" to a lot of *statements* about the way things look, or sound, or smell. The word is just not introduced into our vocabulary in this way. Thus, though of course we come to have certain expectations as to what will and won't be the case when a pig is in the offing, it is wholly artificial to represent these expectations in the guise of *statements entailed by* "That is a pig." And for just this reason it is, at best, wholly artificial to speak as if *verifying* that some animal is a pig consists in checking up on the statements entailed by "That is a pig." If we do think of verification in this way, certainly difficulties abound; we don't know quite where to begin, how to go on, or where to stop. But what this shows is, not that "That is a pig" is very difficult to verify or incapable of being conclusively verified, but that this is an impossible travesty of verification. If the procedure of verification were rightly described in this way, then indeed we couldn't say just what would constitute conclusive verification that some animal was a pig. But this doesn't show that there is actually any difficulty at all, usually, in verifying that an animal is a pig, if we have occasion to do so; it shows only that what verification *is* has been completely misrepresented.

We may add to this the rather different but related point that, though certainly we have more or less definite views as to what objects of particular kinds will and won't do, and of how they will and won't react in one situation or another, it would again be grossly artificial to represent these in the guise of definite entailments. There are vast numbers of things which I take it for granted that a telephone won't do, and doubtless an infinite number of things which it never enters my head to consider the possibility that it might do; but surely it would be perfectly absurd to say that "This is a telephone" *entails* the whole galaxy of statements to the effect that it doesn't and won't do these things, and to conclude that I haven't *really* established that anything is a telephone until, *per impossibile,* I have confirmed the whole infinite class of these supposed entailments. Does "This is a telephone" *entail* "You couldn't eat it"? Must I try to eat it, and fail, in the course of making sure that it's a telephone?[3] . . .

## NOTES

1. This is part, no doubt *only* part, of the absurdity in Descartes' toying with the notion that the whole of our experience might be a dream.

2. Anyway, the official definition won't cover *everything*—freaks, for instance. If I'm shown a five-legged pig at a fair, I can't get my money back on the plea that being a pig entails having only four legs.
3. Philosophers, I think, have taken too little notice of the fact that most words in ordinary use are defined ostensively. For example, it has often been thought to be a puzzle why A *can't* be B, if being A doesn't *entail* being not-B. But it is often just that 'A' and 'B' are brought in as, ostensively defined as, words for *different things*. Why can't a Jack of Hearts be a Queen of Spades? Perhaps we need a new term, "ostensively analytic."

## *Norman Malcolm (b. 1911)*

Norman Malcolm is perhaps best known as an interpreter of Wittgenstein's later philosophy. He is the author of a number of books, including *Ludwig Wittgenstein: A Memoir* (1958), *Dreaming* (1959), and *Knowledge and Certainty* (1963), from which the following selection is taken. Several volumes of collected papers of his have also been published. Malcolm's philosophical work shows the influence of Wittgenstein's *Philosophical Investigations* as well as the emphasis on commonsense certainty deriving from J. L. Austin and G. E. Moore.

In the selection below Malcolm addresses the question of whether or not all of our ordinary or commonsense beliefs, even the most certain, really could turn out to be false as the sceptic suggests. He finds, as Austin seemed to in the preceding selection, that in the case of beliefs about ordinary objects right in front of us, it is the sceptic's doubts that would give way rather than our ordinary beliefs, even in the face of the wildest experiences imaginable. It seems, then, that some of our beliefs about the world are in fact incorrigible, and that we do not need to allow the sceptical philosopher even the conceivable dubitability of such beliefs; that is, we can simply refuse the opening gambit of the sceptic and play the game strictly on commonsense terms.

# Knowledge and Belief

## *Norman Malcolm*

. . . Descartes said that we have a "moral assurance" of the truth of some . . . [empirical] propositions but that we lack a "metaphysical certainty."[1] Locke said that the perception of the existence of physical things is not "so certain as our intuitive knowledge, or the deductions of our reason" although "it is an assurance that deserves the name of knowledge."[2] Some philosophers have held that when we make judgments of perception such as that there are peonies in the garden, cows in the field, or dishes in the cupboard, we are "taking for granted" that the peonies, cows, and dishes exist, but not knowing it in the "strict" sense. Others have held that all empirical propositions, including judgments of perception, are merely hypotheses.[3] The thought behind this exaggerated mode of expression is that any empirical proposition

Abridged from *Knowledge and Certainty*, by Norman Malcolm. (Englewood Cliffs, N. J.: Prentice-Hall, Inc., 1963), pp. 64–72. Reprinted by permission of Norman Malcolm. Footnotes renumbered.

whatever *could* be refuted by future experience—that is, it *could* turn out to be false. Are these philosophers right?

Consider the following propositions:

1. The sun is about ninety million miles from the earth.
2. There is a heart in my body.
3. Here is an ink-bottle.

In various circumstances I should be willing to assert of each of these propositions that I know it to be true. Yet they differ strikingly. This I see when, with each, I try to imagine the possibility that it is false.

1. If in ordinary conversation someone said to me "The sun is about twenty million miles from the earth, isn't it?" I should reply "No, it is about ninety million miles from us." If he said "I think that you are confusing the sun with Polaris," I should reply, "I *know* that ninety million miles is roughly the sun's distance from the earth." I might invite him to verify the figure in an encyclopedia. A third person who overheard our conversation could quite correctly report that I knew the distance to the sun, whereas the other man did not. But this knowledge of mine is little better than hearsay. I have seen that figure mentioned in a few books. I know nothing about the observations and calculations that led astronomers to accept it. If tomorrow a group of eminent astronomers announced that a great error had been made and that the correct figure is twenty million miles, I should not insist that they were wrong. It would surprise me that such an enormous mistake could have been made. But I should no longer be willing to say that I *know* that ninety million is the correct figure. Although I should *now* claim that I know the distance to be about ninety million miles, it is easy for me to envisage the possibility that some future investigation will prove this to be false.

2. Suppose that after a routine medical examination the excited doctor reports to me that the X-ray photographs show that I have no heart. I should tell him to get a new machine. I should be inclined to say that the fact that I have a heart is one of the few things that I can count on as absolutely certain. I can feel it beat. I know it's there. Furthermore, how could my blood circulate if I didn't have one? Suppose that later on I suffer a chest injury and undergo a surgical operation. Afterwards the astonished surgeons solemnly declare that they searched my chest cavity and found no heart, and that they made incisions and looked about in other likely places but found it not. They are convinced that I am without a heart. They are unable to understand how circulation can occur or what accounts for the thumping in my chest. But they are in agreement and obviously sincere, and they have clear photographs of my interior spaces. What would be my attitude? Would it be to insist that they were all mistaken? I think not. I believe that I should eventually accept their testimony and the evidence of the photographs. I should consider to be false what I now regard as an absolute certainty.

3. Suppose that as I write this paper someone in the next room were to call out to me "I can't find an ink-bottle; is there one in the house?" I should reply "Here is an ink-bottle." If he said in a doubtful tone "Are you sure? I looked there before," I should reply "Yes, I know there is; come and get it."

Now could it turn out to be false that there is an ink-bottle directly in front of me on this desk? Many philosophers have thought so. They would say that many things could happen of such a nature that if they did happen it would be proved that I am deceived. I agree that many extraordinary things could happen, in the sense that there is no logical absurdity in the supposition. It could happen that when I next reach for this ink-bottle my hand should seem to pass *through* it and I should not feel the contact of any object. It could happen that in the next moment the ink-bottle will suddenly vanish from sight; or that I should find myself under a tree in the garden with no ink-bottle about; or that one or more persons should enter this room and declare with apparent sincerity that they see no ink-bottle on this desk; or that a photograph taken now of the top of the desk should clearly show all of the objects on it except the ink-bottle. Having admitted that these things *could happen*,[4] am I compelled to admit that if they did happen then it would be proved that there is no ink-bottle here *now?* Not at all! I could say that when my hand seemed to pass through the ink-bottle I should *then* be suffering from hallucination; that if the ink-bottle suddenly vanished it would have miraculously ceased to exist; that the other persons were conspiring to drive me mad, or were themselves victims of remarkable concurrent hallucinations; that the camera possessed some strange flaw or that there was trickery in developing the negative. I admit that in the next moment I could find myself under a tree or in the bathtub. But this is not to admit that it could be revealed in the next moment that I am now dreaming. For what I admit is that I might be instantaneously transported to the garden, but not that in the next moment I might *wake up* in the garden. There is nothing that could happen to me in the next moment that I should call "waking up"; and therefore nothing that could happen to me in the next moment would be accepted by me now as proof that I now dream.

Not only do I not *have* to admit that those extraordinary occurrences would be evidence that there is no ink-bottle here; the fact is that I *do not* admit it. There is nothing whatever that could happen in the next moment or the next year that would by me be called *evidence* that there is not an ink-bottle here now. No future experience or investigation could prove to me that I am mistaken. . . .

## NOTES

1. Descartes, *Discourse on the Method,* Part IV.
2. Locke, *Essay,* Book IV, ch. 11, sec. 3.
3. E.g., ". . . no proposition, other than a tautology, can possibly be anything more than a probable hypothesis." A. J. Ayer, *Language, Truth and Logic,* 2d ed. (New York: Dover Publications, Inc., 1951), p. 38.
4. My viewpoint is somewhat different here from what it is in "The Verification Argument." There I am concerned with bringing out the different ways in which such a remark as "these things *could* happen" can be taken. I wish to show, furthermore, that from none of the senses in which the remark is *true* does it follow that it is *not certain* that the things in question will *not* happen. Finally, I hold there, that it is perfectly certain that they will not happen. Here, I am not disagreeing with any of those points, but I am adding the further point that my admission that, in some sense, the things *could happen,* does not require me to admit that *if* they were to happen, that would be evidence that there is no ink-bottle here now.

## *Keith Lehrer (b. 1936)*

Keith Lehrer is a contemporary philosopher who has made many contributions in the areas of epistemology, philosophy of mind, inductive logic and probability, and philosophy of science. Among his major works are an introductory text (with James Cornman) *Philosophical Problems and Arguments* (1968), *Knowledge* (1974), and (with Carl Wagner) *Rational Concensus in Science and Society* (1982). A volume of his articles and addresses has recently been published. He has edited several collections of philosophical essays and is currently the editor of a well-known journal, *Philosophical Studies.*

In the essay below Lehrer argues that the empirical beliefs of science and common sense are never absolutely certain—and that the sceptic is entirely within her rights to point this out to us. In considering various arguments against scepticism, Lehrer finds that they either depend, at bottom, on the dogmatic refusal to take the sceptic seriously and give his or her arguments a reasonable hearing, or else they leave scepticism as a live option in the end. And scepticism, unlike its commonsense denial, need only be a live option in order to win the day.

# Why Not Scepticism?*

***Keith Lehrer***

. . . You may have your doubts about whether **scepticism** makes any sense at all. There are familiar lingering doubts about the intelligibility of such matters which we have inherited from Wittgenstein and his followers. Let us put these doubts on the therapeutic couch. The sceptic says, "No one knows anything." Appalled you reply, "I know many things, that I see this paper for example." The sceptic says you do not know. Now if we imagine an ordinary situation, which this is not, where a man denies that you know that you see this paper, you would not understand. His speech act would not make sense to you. Notice, however, that this does not imply that you would not understand what he has said, or that he would have said nothing. On the contrary, you would understand what he has said, but you would not understand his saying it. You cannot understand why he said it. When a man denies that we know what we see right before our eyes, ordinarily we do not understand his behavior. But this is the *ordinary* case. In the extraordinary case in which men are not about their humdrum practical affairs but are engaged in intellectual speculation, we may well understand a man denying that we know things. We understand why he said it. He said it because he is a sceptic showing his . . . goods.

From these considerations one can appreciate that we must avoid the trap of refuting the sceptic by intentionally misunderstanding his behavior. If we treat his speech acts like those of a man with more ordinary and less intellectual interests, we are guilty of bad manners and bad philosophy. We know why he utters the words he does, he utters them to affirm his [scepticism] and to deny that we know what we say we know. Thus we can understand his behavior, it does make sense, but a doubt still lingers. Does what he says really make sense?

Very intelligent philosophers have held widely divergent views on this matter. Some have thought that what he said is meaningless. If this contention has no more content than to imply that what the sceptic says is nonsense, then perhaps it is correct, *if* the sceptic is mistaken. There is a sense of "nonsense" in which it is nonsense to say what is obviously false. If a man says what is obviously false, we say, "Nonsense!" and that is well said. However, this sort of remark is a compliment that may be returned. When we say we know, the sceptic may retort, "Nonsense!" and then we shall have both relieved our frustrations without any notable philosophical illumination. However, those who have maintained that what the sceptic says is meaningless have implied that he utters words with the intent of affirming or asserting the truth of something, but, in fact, he has not succeeded in asserting or affirming the truth of anything! Negatively put, he intended to deny something by uttering the words he did, namely, that we know the things we think we know, but he has failed because the words he utters are without meaning.

The sceptic may surely regard it as a peculiar matter that words should go about losing their meaning in this way. You say you know, the sceptic says you do not know, and according to the dogmatist, the words the sceptic utters suddenly have no meaning. But this is implausible.

*An earlier version of this paper was presented at the Pacific Coast Division Meetings of the American Philosophical Association in Los Angeles on May 28, 1971. Support by N.S.F. of related projects on inductive inference enabled me to find time to appreciate the merits of scepticism. So many philosophers have written about scepticism that to cite them all would result in more footnotes than content. Instead, I only footnote sources that are unfamiliar or specifically discussed. However, I should like to cite "A Defense of Scepticism" in *The Philosophical Review,* April 1971, by Peter Unger as an interesting bit of recent sceptical philosophy.

Abridged from *The Philosophical Forum,* Vol. II, No. 3, Spring 1971. (Boston: Dept. of Philosophy, Boston University.) Reprinted by permission. Footnotes renumbered.

We do understand what the sceptic says precisely because we can tell that he has denied what we have affirmed. No matter how hard one tries not to understand, one cannot fail to understand that much. Thus, because you understand what you affirm, you must understand what the sceptic denies. You might still think the sceptic is talking nonsense—but it is meaningful. Even a dogmatist must concede that the sceptic speaks meaningful nonsense.

A related attempt to demolish the sceptic semantically is to aver that the systematic difference from ordinary practice in the use of the word "know" by the sceptic shows that he means something different by that term than we do. Here we have shifted from the position that he does not mean anything to the thesis that he means something different. The model for this argument is the foreigner who calls all and only blue things "red" and so we conclude that he means by the term "red" what we mean by the term "blue." The best explanation of the use that the foreigner makes of the word "red" is that what he means by "red" is what we mean by the word "blue," but a similar conclusion would be quite inappropriate in the case of the sceptic. We can easily explain why the sceptic uses the word "know" as he does without supposing that he means something different by the term. The way in which he uses the term is most readily and simply explained by supposing that he believes something different from the rest of us. This contrasts with the case of the foreigner, where the way in which he uses the word "red" is most readily and simply explained by supposing that he means something different by that term than we do. Thus, the correct conclusion to draw is that the sceptic means what we mean by the word "know," and the reason he says what he does is that he believes that nobody knows anything. What could be simpler?

. . . I have argued . . . that the words of the sceptic may be understood as having meaning. He denies what we assert and there is nothing inconsistent or semantically unacceptable in so doing. Language allows for such radical disagreement as that between the sceptic and his detractors. It is this resource of language that provides for the possibility of speculation and innovation. Thus, the question to which we must now turn is this—if the position of scepticism is neither meaningless nor contradictory, then why not scepticism?

The most common answer stems from Thomas Reid. It is based on the assumption that some beliefs are completely justified, because they are beliefs of a special kind which are justified without any supporting justificatory argument.[1] Beliefs of this kind are *basic* beliefs. Thus, if a man believes *that p,* where this is a basic belief of kind K, then he is completely justified in believing *that p* without argument unless there is some good reason for believing *p* to be false. The kind K of basic beliefs may be specified differently by philosophers of different epistemic biases, which already offers succor to the sceptic, but dogmatists have generally agreed that at least some kinds of perceptual beliefs, memory beliefs, and beliefs concerning our conscious states are among them.

Now it is not at all difficult to conceive of some hypothesis that would yield the conclusion that beliefs of the kind in question are not justified, indeed, which if true would justify us in concluding that the beliefs in question were more often false than true. The sceptical hypothesis might run as follows. There are a group of creatures in another galaxy, call them Googols, whose intellectual capacity is $10^{100}$ that of men, and who amuse themselves by sending out a peculiar kind of wave that affects our brain in such a way that our beliefs about the world are mostly incorrect. This form of error infects beliefs of every kind, but most of our beliefs, though erroneous, are nevertheless very nearly correct. This allows us to survive and manipulate our environment. However, whether any belief of any man is correct or even nearly correct depends entirely on the whimsy of some Googol rather than on the capacities and faculties of the man. If you are inclined to wonder why the Googols do not know anything, it is because there is another group of men, call them Googolplexes, whose intellectual capacity is $10^{100}$ that of the Googols, and who amuse themselves by sending out a peculiar wave that affects the brains of Googols in such a way that . . . I think you can see how the story goes from here. I shall refer to this hypothesis as the *sceptical hypothesis.* On such a hypothesis our beliefs about our conscious states, what we perceive by our senses, or recall from memory, are more often erroneous than correct. Such a sceptical hypothesis as this would, the sceptic argues, entail that the beliefs in question are not completely justified.

The reply of the dogmatist to such imaginings might be that we are not only justified in those basic beliefs, we are also justified in rejecting any hypothesis, such as the sceptical one, which conflicts with those beliefs. But the sceptic may surely intercede long enough to protest that he has been ruled out by fiat. The beliefs of common sense are said to be basic and thus completely justified without any justificatory arguments. But why, the sceptic may query, should the dogmatists' beliefs be considered completely justified without argument and his hypothesis be rejected without argument? Dogmatists affirm that the beliefs of common sense are innocent until proven guilty, but why, the sceptic might inquire, should his hypothesis not receive comparable treatment before the bar of evidence? Why not regard the sceptical hypothesis as innocent until proven guilty. Indeed, the sceptic might continue, why not regard all belief as innocent until proven guilty? And, he might add, where all is innocence, nothing is justified or unjustified, which is precisely . . . scepticism.

Some opponents of scepticism have been willing to concede that unless we hold some beliefs to be justified without argument, then we must surely accept the conclusion of scepticism. But, when replying to the sceptic, it will not do to say that we must regard the beliefs of common sense as justified or else we shall wind up on the road to scepticism. For that is precisely the route the sceptic would have us travel.

Let me clarify the preceding argument. In one passage, Bishop Berkeley replies to a dogmatist by appeal to the . . . precept that the burden of proof always lies with the affirmative.[2] The precept could be doubted, and generally arguments about where the burden of proof lies are unproductive. It is more reasonable to suppose that such questions are best left to courts of law where they have suitable application. In philosophy a different principle . . . is appropriate, to wit, that no hypothesis should be rejected as unjustified without argument against it. Consequently, if the sceptic puts forth a hypothesis inconsistent with the hypotheses of common sense, then there is no burden of proof on either side, but neither may one side to the dispute be judged unjustified in believing his hypothesis unless an argument is produced to show that this is so. If contradictory hypotheses are put forth without reason being given to show that one side is correct and the other in error, then neither party may be fairly stigmatized as unjustified. However, if a belief is completely justified, then those with which it conflicts are unjustified. Therefore, if neither of the conflicting hypotheses is shown to be unjustified, then we must refrain from concluding that belief in one of the hypotheses is completely justified.

We have here an argument that does not prejudicially presuppose that the burden of proof rests on one side or the other but instead takes an impartial view of the matter and refuses to side with either party until some argument has been given. Thomas Reid was wont to argue that the beliefs of common sense had a right of ancient possession and were justified until shown to be unjustified.[3] But such **epistemology** favors the sentiments of conservative defenders of the status quo in both philosophy and politics. And the principle that, what is, is justified, is not a better principle of epistemology than of politics or morals. It should be supplanted by the . . . principle of impartiality. Thus, before scepticism may be rejected as unjustified, some argument must be given to show that the infamous hypotheses employed by sceptics are incorrect and the beliefs of common sense have the truth on their side. If this is not done, then the beliefs of common sense are not completely justified, because conflicting sceptical hypotheses have not been shown to be unjustified. From this premise it follows in a single step that we do not know those beliefs to be true because they are not completely justified. And then the sceptic wins the day.

The preceding . . . argument can be extended to defeat a whole range of alleged refutations of scepticism. For example, some philosophers have rejected scepticism on the grounds that the sceptic is denying our standards of evidence or our criteria of justification or something of the sort. Now, of course, this may be trivially true; obviously the sceptic is denying that we are completely justified in certain beliefs which we consider to be completely justified, and if that constitutes rejecting our ordinary standards or criteria of evidence, then the sceptic is indeed denying them. But that is no argument against the sceptic; it is a restatement of his position. Unless we can show that the sceptical hypothesis is false, we cannot justly conclude that it is unjustified. In that case our beliefs, which contradict the sceptical hypotheses, are not completely justified. So much the worse for our standards or criteria of evidence.

Next, there are arguments claiming that the sceptic is making proposals which undermine our conceptual framework and change the very concepts we use to formulate our beliefs. The reply is twofold. Sometimes talking about changing concepts is a disguised way of talking about changing meaning of words. I have already argued that scepticism does not have that consequence. So I discount that contention. Other than that, the change of concepts implied by scepticism seems to me, to amount to no more than a change of belief, perhaps of very fundamental beliefs. The reply to this objection is that first, the [scepticism] of the sceptic allows him to embrace most of the same beliefs we do. He need not *believe* the sceptical hypothesis to argue that if the sceptical hypothesis is true, then our more familiar beliefs are more often false than true. By thus employing the hypothesis, he has placed us in a position of either showing the hypothesis to be false, or else conceding that our beliefs are not completely justified. Thus the sceptic need not advocate ceasing to believe those fundamental hypotheses which constitute the assumptions, presuppositions, or what not of our conceptual framework. He only denies that we know those beliefs to be true.

Thus appeals to ancient rights, standards of evidence, and conceptual frameworks are all equally ineffective against the basic challenge of scepticism, to wit—either show that the sceptical hypothesis is false and unjustified or concede that beliefs inconsistent with that hypothesis are not completely justified!

We must now turn to a rather different sort of maneuver against the sceptic. It might be conceded that we cannot show that our beliefs are true and the sceptical hypothesis false, but contended that we can show that our beliefs are completely justified, not perhaps for the purpose of arriving at the truth, but for other epistemic ends. Thus it has been proposed that we believe whatever will facilitate explanation and increase our information. If a person is seeking to have beliefs which facilitate explanation and increase information, then he is completely justified in adopting beliefs contributing to those objectives. This argument against scepticism is, I believe, the very strongest that can be offered. For, even if we can offer no argument to show that our beliefs are true and the sceptical hypothesis false, still we may [be] completely justified in our beliefs in terms of objectives other than truth.

Finally, the move has an intuitive appeal. For, the sceptical hypothesis according to which most of our beliefs arise because of the deception of Googols yields results that would make it difficult to explain in a satisfactory manner what we believe to be the case and, it would make it even more difficult for us to increase our information about the world. Many generalizations about the world, and theories as well, would turn out to be incorrect on that hypothesis, thus making explanation difficult and complicated. Moreover, we would, by hypothesis, have no way of telling when our beliefs give us information about the world and when we are simply being misled by the Googols. All in all the sceptical hypothesis is quite unsatisfactory from the standpoint of explaining things and increasing our information; so unsatisfactory that anyone seeking to explain as much as possible and to increase his information as much as possible would be completely justified in rejecting it.

Is there any reply to this line of argument? The sceptic might reply that he is under no obligation to accept the ends of facilitating explanation and increasing information. But this will not refute the claim that we who do accept such ends are completely justified in believing what we do for the sake of obtaining those objectives. There is a better line of reply available to the sceptic, namely, that our disregard for truth will, in the final accounting, destroy our assets. For [scepticism] shows that such pragmatic justification of belief ultimately depends on the assumption that the beliefs are true. Suppose we adopt those beliefs that are most full of explanatory power and informative content, and those admirable beliefs turn out to be false. In that case, by adopting those beliefs we shall have correctly explained nothing and increased our genuine information not at all. For any belief to correctly explain or genuinely inform it must first be true. Only what correctly explains or genuinely informs can constitute knowledge. Therefore, we must be completely justified in believing what we do simply because by so doing we shall obtain true beliefs, or else our beliefs are not completely justified in the manner requisite for knowledge.

The preceding line of argument leads to an inevitable conclusion. To meet the . . . challenge of scepticism, we must provide some argument to show that the sceptical hypothesis is false and that the beliefs of common sense are correct. And this leads to a second equally inescapable conclusion. The challenge cannot be met. Many reasons may be given for not *believing* the sceptical hypothesis. Indeed, a sceptic himself need not believe the sceptical hypothesis, and he might agree that there are practical disadvantages in believing such a hypothesis. But he might justifiably insist that we are not completely justified in concluding that the hypothesis is *false*. The hypothesis might seem silly, it might interfere with the attempt to explain things, and it might make it very difficult to arrive at any sensible set of beliefs for conducting practical affairs and scientific investigations. There are perfectly cogent practical considerations, the sceptic might concede, for not believing the hypothesis. However, . . . he rejects the premise contending that inconvenient hypotheses are false. To suppose that would be to trip back into the clutches of a simplistic pragmatism from which we have been rescued all too recently.

The principal argument offered to show that sceptical hypotheses are false is simply that they conflict with our dogmatic beliefs. Since it is precisely the justification of the latter that is in question, this conflict cannot be taken to adjudicate against the sceptical hypothesis. We are not completely justified in rejecting the sceptical hypothesis, and thus we are not completely justified in believing the others. We do not know that the sceptical hypothesis is false, and thus we do not know that anything else is true. That is . . . [what] sustains scepticism.

In conclusion, let me remark that we need not mourn the passing of knowledge as a great loss. The assumption of dogmatists that some beliefs are completely justified and that they are true, is not a great asset in scientific inquiry where all contentions should be subject to question and must be defended on demand. . . .

I would contend that just as we can give an analysis of rational decision in terms of probabilities and practical values, so we can give an analysis of rational belief on the basis of probabilities and epistemic values. In the first case we maximize practical utilities and in the second case we maximize epistemic ones. Neither analysis requires the assumption that we know anything. We can instead regard practical action and scientific inquiry as aiming at the satisfaction of objectives appropriate to each sphere. We change our beliefs to better satisfy those objectives. Thus, we may, while remaining sceptics, contend that our beliefs and actions are rational even though we agree that such beliefs are not so completely justified as to constitute knowledge. As such, all beliefs, even those we consider rational, are subject to critical review. None can be exempted from evaluation on the grounds that it is known to be true without need of supporting argument. Such are the fruits of [scepticism].

## NOTES

1. Thomas Reid, *The Works of Thomas Reid, D.D.* (Edinburgh: Maclaugh and Steward, 1863), p. 234.
2. George Berkeley, *Dialogues 1* in *Principles, Dialogues and Correspondence.* C. M. Turbayne, ed. (New York: Bobbs-Merrill, 1965), p. 146.
3. *Ibid.,* p. 617.

# *Justified Belief and Scientific Method*

Philosophy of science attempts to understand, in terms of scientific method and practice, just what a scientific theory is and what justifies belief in it. A simple understanding of these issues might be the following. A theory is scientific if it is based on observation or experiment, and we are justified in believing it if observation and experiment prove it to be true. The problem with these definitions is that they are both too broad and too narrow. The definitions are too broad because almost anything could qualify as scientific. For example, the theory that the earth is resting on the back of an elephant which in turn is standing on the back of a turtle could be based upon the observation that we don't feel as if we are falling through space. And the definitions are too narrow because they rule out justified belief in any theory. No single theory can be demonstrated to be true on the basis of observation and experiment. There will always be an open and indefinite range of possible theoretical explanations for any collection of observational or experimental evidence. For example, the heliocentered astronomy of Copernicus did not succeed the geocentered astronomy of Ptolemy because Copernicus's system corresponded to experience and Ptolemy's didn't. With sufficient epicycles Ptolemy's system could be made to correspond to our observations. Ptolemy's system was rejected because it was too complex. So the relation between scientific theories that we are justified in believing and the experience that somehow both gives rise to and confirms them is not a simple matter. Experience does not simply require a particular theory and then go on to demonstrate its truth. What, then, is the relation between experience (observation and experiment) and scientific theory?

In the first selection of this section, Popper argues that what makes a theory scientific is its falsifiability. To say that a theory is falsifiable is not to say that it actually has been falsified, but that it could be falsified. There must be events or discoveries that would clearly show that the theory is false. Theories that are compatible with virtually any event that might occur are not scientific theories at all. Experience confirms a scientific theory and tends to justify belief in it only if that experience is the result of an unsuccessful attempt to falsify the theory. The greater risk a theory runs of being shown false, and the more times attempts to take advantage of such risks prove unsuccessful, the better the scientific theory and the more justified our belief in it.

Lakatos argues that Popper's notion of simple falsification, though an improvement on the idea that observation confirms a theory by proving it true once and for all, is still naive. Only in textbooks do theories fall before a single crucial negative experiment or observation. In the real world of science, theories are embedded in systems of auxiliary hypotheses and problem-solving strategies ("research programs") which, if generally successful in dealing with observations and experimental results, serve to insulate the theory from quick and easy refutation. Problems for the theory are recognized as **anomalies,** but do not, by themselves, result in its abandonment. Theories, or better, the research programs in which they are embedded, are abandoned only after they have become degenerating (pseudoscientific) programs and progressive (scientific) ones arisen to take their place. A research program is degenerating when it predicts no novel facts that can be independently tested and when it adds auxiliary **(ad hoc)** hypothesis after auxiliary hypothesis to explain already existent anomalies that have no predictive power beyond the cases they are brought in to explain. A research program is progressive when it explains novel facts, facts that everyone would have expected to be otherwise in terms of previous or rival programs.

Quine and Ullian approach the same issue in terms of the notion of "hypothesis" and provide a set of virtues scientific hypotheses should have that is more extensive than, but consistent with, the requirements Lakatos places on scientific theories. The point of a scientific hypothesis is to explain the past and predict the future. Hypotheses are more likely to serve those purposes if they have more of the five virtues Quine and Ullian discuss: conservatism, modesty, simplicity, generality, and refutability. Possession of greater degrees of these virtues—and Quine and Ullian argue that each of them is a matter of degree, even refutability (as Lakatos argued)—explains why we prefer one hypothesis to another.

Kitcher uses a currently popular pseudoscience, creationism, and its opposition to modern evolutionary biology to illustrate some of the differences between good science, bad science, and pseudoscience. In the process he demonstrates that typical creationists have misunderstood the central issues in philosophy of science as well as the important features of Darwinian biology. The general picture of scientific method Kitcher presents resembles the one sketched briefly by Lakatos, and the three characteristics of successful science, which he finds clearly present in Darwinian biology and in Newtonian mechanics, are closely akin to several of the virtues of scientific hypotheses described by Quine and Ullian. A good or flourishing scientific theory will clearly show all three characteristics: *independent testability* of its auxiliary hypotheses, *unification* of the science by the successful application of a small set of problem-solving strategies to a broad range of problems in the science, and *fecundity*, the ability to raise new and interesting questions and open up new areas of fruitful investigation. As these characteristics begin to be lost, a scientific theory begins to wither and becomes bad science, ripe for replacement by a better theory. And if a theory fails badly enough in terms of these characteristics, it isn't a scientific theory at all.

## *Karl Popper (b. 1902)*

Karl Popper was a leading figure in the overthrow of the traditional model of scientific method that marked the revolution in mid-twentieth century philosophy of science. He is the author of a number of books in the philosophy of science including *The Logic of Scientific Discovery* (1959), *Conjectures and Refutations* (1962), from which the selection below is taken, and *Objective Knowledge* (1972).

In this selection Popper argues that it is falsifiability alone that makes a theory scientific. Only those tests of a theory that involve real risk and the frustrated expectation of failure give us good reason to accept a scientific theory. Popper illustrates his contention by comparing scientific and pseudoscientific theories in terms of this criterion.

# Science: Conjectures and Refutations*

***Karl Popper***

*Mr. Turnbull had predicted evil consequences, . . . and was now doing the best in his power to bring about the verification of his own prophecies.*

ANTHONY TROLLOPE

## I

When I received the list of participants in this course and realized that I had been asked to speak to philosophical colleagues I thought, after some hesitation and consultation, that you would probably prefer me to speak about those problems which interest me most, and about those developments with which I am most intimately acquainted. I therefore decided to do what I have never done before: to give you a report on my own work in the philosophy of science, since the autumn of 1919 when I first began to grapple with the problem, *"When should a theory be ranked as scientific?"* or *"Is there a criterion for the scientific character or status of a theory?"*

The problem which troubled me at the time was neither, "When is a theory true?" nor, "When is a theory acceptable?" My problem was different. I *wished to distinguish between science and pseudo-science;* knowing very well that science often errs, and that pseudo-science may happen to stumble on the truth.

I knew, of course, the most widely accepted answer to my problem: that science is distinguished from pseudo-science—or from **"metaphysics"**—by its ***empirical*** method, which is essentially ***inductive,*** proceeding from observation or experiment. But this did not satisfy me. On the contrary, I often formulated my problem as one of distinguishing between a genuinely empirical method and a non-empirical or even a pseudo-empirical method—that is to say, a method which, although it appeals to observation and experiment, nevertheless does not come up to scientific standards. The latter method may be exemplified by astrology, with its stupendous mass of empirical evidence based on observation—on horoscopes and on biographies.

But as it was not the example of astrology which led me to my problem I should perhaps briefly describe the atmosphere in which my problem arose and the examples by which it was stimulated. After the collapse of the Austrian Empire there had been a revolution in Austria: the air was full of revolutionary slogans and ideas, and new and often wild theories. Among the theories which interested me Einstein's theory of relativity was no doubt by far the most important. Three others were Marx's theory of history, Freud's psychoanalysis, and Alfred Adler's so-called "individual psychology."

There was a lot of popular nonsense talked about these theories, and especially about relativity (as still happens even today), but I was fortunate in those who introduced me to the study of this theory. We all—the small circle of students to which I belonged—were thrilled with the result of Eddington's eclipse observations which in 1919 brought the first important confirmation of Einstein's theory of gravitation. It was a great experience for us, and one which had a lasting influence on my intellectual development.

*A lecture given at Peterhouse, Cambridge, in Summer 1953, as part of a course on developments and trends in contemporary British philosophy, organized by the British Council; originally published under the title "Philosophy of Science: A Personal Report" in *British Philosophy in Mid-Century,* ed. C. A. Mace, 1957.

Reprinted by permission. From *Conjectures and Refutations,* Karl Popper. (Harper & Row, 1968. Basic Books, 1962).

The three other theories I have mentioned were also widely discussed among students at that time. I myself happened to come into personal contact with Alfred Adler, and even to cooperate with him in his social work among the children and young people in the working-class districts of Vienna where he had established social guidance clinics.

It was during the summer of 1919 that I began to feel more and more dissatisfied with these three theories—the Marxist theory of history, psychoanalysis, and individual psychology; and I began to feel dubious about their claims to scientific status. My problem perhaps first took the simple form, "What is wrong with Marxism, psychoanalysis, and individual psychology? Why are they so different from physical theories, from Newton's theory, and especially from the theory of relativity?"

To make this contrast clear I should explain that few of us at the time would have said that we believed in the *truth* of Einstein's theory of gravitation. This shows that it was not my doubting the *truth* of those other three theories which bothered me, but something else. Yet neither was it that I merely felt mathematical physics to be more *exact* than the sociological or psychological type of theory. Thus what worried me was neither the problem of truth, at that stage at least, nor the problem of exactness or measurability. It was rather that I felt that these other three theories, though posing as sciences, had in fact more in common with primitive myths than with science; that they resembled astrology rather than astronomy.

I found that those of my friends who were admirers of Marx, Freud, and Adler, were impressed by a number of points common to these theories, and especially by their apparent *explanatory power.* These theories appeared to be able to explain practically everything that happened within the fields to which they referred. The study of any of them seemed to have the effect of an intellectual conversion or revelation, opening your eyes to a new truth hidden from those not yet initiated. Once your eyes were thus opened you saw confirming instances everywhere: the world was full of *verifications* of the theory. Whatever happened always confirmed it. Thus its truth appeared manifest; and unbelievers were clearly people who did not want to see the manifest truth; who refused to see it, either because it was against their class interest, or because of their repressions which were still "unanalyzed" and crying aloud for treatment.

The most characteristic element in this situation seemed to me the incessant stream of confirmations, of observations which "verified" the theories in question; and this point was constantly emphasized by their adherents. A Marxist could not open a newspaper without finding on every page confirming evidence for his interpretation of history; not only in the news, but also in its presentation—which revealed the class bias of the paper—and especially of course in what the paper did *not* say. The Freudian analysts emphasized that their theories were constantly verified by their "clinical observations." As for Adler, I was much impressed by a personal experience. Once, in 1919, I reported to him a case which to me did not seem particularly Adlerian, but which he found no difficulty in analyzing in terms of his theory of inferiority feelings, although he had not even seen the child. Slightly shocked, I asked him how he could be so sure. "Because of my thousandfold experience," he replied; whereupon I could not help saying: "And with this new case, I suppose, your experience has become thousand-and-one-fold."

What I had in mind was that his previous observations may not have been much sounder than this new one; that each in its turn had been interpreted in the light of "previous experience," and at the same time counted as additional confirmation. What, I asked myself, did it confirm? No more than that a case could be interpreted in the light of the theory. But this meant very little, I reflected, since every conceivable case could be interpreted in the light of Adler's theory, or equally of Freud's. I may illustrate this by two very different examples of human behavior: that of a man who pushes a child into the water with the intention of drowning it; and that of a man who sacrifices his life in an attempt to save the child. Each of these two cases can be explained with equal ease in Freudian and in Adlerian terms. According to Freud the first man suffered from repression (say, of some component of his Oedipus complex), while the second man had achieved sublimation. According to Adler the first man suffered from feelings of inferiority (producing perhaps the need to prove to himself that he dared to commit some crime), and so did the second man (whose need was to prove to himself that he dared to rescue the child). I could not think of any human behavior which could not be interpreted in terms of either theory. It was precisely this fact—that they always fitted, that they were always confirmed—which in the eyes of their admirers constituted the strongest argument in favor of these theories. It began to dawn on me that this apparent strength was in fact their weakness.

With Einstein's theory the situation was strikingly different. Take one typical instance—Einstein's prediction, just then confirmed by the findings of Eddington's expedition. Einstein's gravitational theory had led to the result that light must be attracted by heavy bodies (such as the sun), precisely as material bodies were attracted. As a consequence it could be calculated that light from a distant fixed star whose apparent position was close to the sun would reach the earth from such a direction that the star would seem to be slightly shifted away from the sun; or, in other words, that stars close to the sun would look as if they had moved a little away from the sun, and from one another. This is a thing which cannot normally be observed since such stars are rendered invisible in daytime by the sun's overwhelming brightness; but during an eclipse it is possible to take photographs of them. If the same constellation is photographed at night one can measure the distances on the two photographs, and check the predicted effect.

Now the impressive thing about this case is the *risk* involved in a prediction of this kind. If observation shows that the predicted effect is definitely absent, then the theory is simply refuted. The theory is *incompatible with certain possible results of observation*—in fact with results which everybody before Einstein would have expected.[1] This is quite different from the situation I have previously described, when it turned out that the theories in question were compatible with the most divergent human behavior, so that it was practically impossible to describe any human behavior that might not be claimed to be a verification of these theories.

These considerations led me in the winter of 1919–20 to conclusions which I may now reformulate as follows.

1. It is easy to obtain confirmations, or verifications, for nearly every theory—if we look for confirmations.

2. Confirmations should count only if they are the result of *risky predictions;* that is to say, if, unenlightened by the theory in question, we should have expected an event which was incompatible with the theory—an event which would have refuted the theory.

3. Every "good" scientific theory is a prohibition: it forbids certain things to happen. The more a theory forbids, the better it is.

4. A theory which is not refutable by any conceivable event is nonscientific. Irrefutability is not a virtue of a theory (as people often think) but a vice.

5. Every genuine *test* of a theory is an attempt to falsify it, or to refute it. Testability is falsifiability; but there are degrees of testability: some theories are more testable, more exposed to refutation, than others; they take, as it were, greater risks.

6. Confirming evidence should not count except *when it is the result of a genuine test of the theory;* and this means that it can be presented as a serious but unsuccessful attempt to falsify the theory. (I now speak in such cases of "corroborating evidence.")

7. Some genuinely testable theories, when found to be false, are still upheld by their admirers—for example by introducing ***ad hoc*** some auxiliary assumption, or by reinterpreting the theory *ad hoc* in such a way that it escapes refutation. Such a procedure is always possible, but it rescues the theory from refutation only at the price of destroying, or at least lowering, its

scientific status. (I later described such a rescuing operation as a *"conventionalist twist"* or a *"conventionalist stratagem."*)

One can sum up all this by saying that *the criterion of the scientific status of a theory is its falsifiability, or refutability, or testability.*

## II

I may perhaps exemplify this with the help of the various theories so far mentioned. Einstein's theory of gravitation clearly satisfied the criterion of falsifiability. Even if our measuring instruments at the time did not allow us to pronounce on the results of the tests with complete assurance, there was clearly a possibility of refuting the theory.

Astrology did not pass the test. Astrologers were greatly impressed, and misled, by what they believed to be confirming evidence—so much so that they were quite unimpressed by any unfavorable evidence. Moreover, by making their interpretations and prophecies sufficiently vague they were able to explain away anything that might have been a refutation of the theory had the theory and the prophecies been more precise. In order to escape falsification they destroyed the testability of their theory. It is a typical soothsayer's trick to predict things so vaguely that the predictions can hardly fail: that they become irrefutable.

The Marxist theory of history, in spite of the serious efforts of some of its founders and followers, ultimately adopted this soothsaying practice. In some of its earlier formulations (for example in Marx's analysis of the character of the "coming social revolution") their predictions were testable, and in fact falsified.[2] Yet instead of accepting the refutations the followers of Marx reinterpreted both the theory and the evidence in order to make them agree. In this way they rescued the theory from refutation; but they did so at the price of adopting a device which made it irrefutable. They thus gave a "conventionalist twist" to the theory; and by this stratagem they destroyed its much advertised claim to scientific status.

The two psychoanalytic theories were in a different class. They were simply non-testable, irrefutable. There was no conceivable human behavior which could contradict them. This does not mean that Freud and Adler were not seeing certain things correctly: I personally do not doubt that much of what they say is of considerable importance, and may well play its part one day in a psychological science which is testable. But it does mean that those "clinical observations" which analysts naively believe confirm their theory cannot do this any more than the daily confirmations which astrologers find in their practice.[3] And as for Freud's epic of the Ego, the Super-ego, and the Id, no substantially stronger claim to scientific status can be made for it than for Homer's collected stories from Olympus. These theories describe some facts, but in the manner of myths. They contain most interesting psychological suggestions, but not in a testable form.

At the same time I realized that such myths may be developed, and become testable; that historically speaking all—or very nearly all—scientific theories originate from myths, and that a myth may contain important anticipations of scientific theories. Examples are Empedocles' theory of evolution by trial and error, or Parmenides' myth of the unchanging block universe in which nothing ever happens and which, if we add another dimension, becomes Einstein's block universe (in which, too, nothing ever happens, since everything is, four-dimensionally speaking, determined and laid down from the beginning). I thus felt that if a theory is found to be non-scientific, . . . it is not thereby found to be unimportant, or insignificant, or "meaningless," or "nonsensical."[4] But it cannot claim to be backed by empirical evidence in the scientific sense—although it may easily be, in some genetic sense, the "result of observation."

(There were a great many other theories of this pre-scientific or pseudoscientific character, some of them, unfortunately, as influential as the Marxist interpretation of history; for example, the racialist interpretation of history—another of those impressive and all-explanatory theories which act upon weak minds like revelations.)

Thus the problem which I tried to solve by proposing the criterion of falsifiability was neither a problem of meaningfulness or significance, nor a problem of truth or acceptability. It was the problem of drawing a line (as well as this can be done) between the statements, or systems of statements, of the empirical sciences, and all other statements. . . . Years later—it must have been in 1928 or 1929—I called this first problem of mine the *"problem of demarcation."* The criterion of falsifiability is a solution to this problem of demarcation, for it says that statements or systems of statements, in order to be ranked as scientific, must be capable of conflicting with possible, or conceivable, observations. . . .

## NOTES

1. This is a slight oversimplification, for about half of the Einstein effect may be derived from the classical theory, provided we assume a ballistic theory of light.
2. See, for example, my *Open Society and Its Enemies,* ch. 15, section iii, and notes 13–14.
3. "Clinical observations," like all other observations, are *interpretations in the light of theories;* and for this reason alone they are apt to seem to support those theories in the light of which they were interpreted. But real support can be obtained only from observations undertaken as tests (by "attempted refutations"); and for this purpose *criteria of refutation* have to be laid down beforehand: it must be agreed which observable situations, if actually observed, mean that the theory is refuted. But what kind of clinical responses would refute to the satisfaction of the analyst not merely a particular analytic diagnosis but psychoanalysis itself? And have such criteria ever been discussed or agreed upon by analysts? Is there not, on the contrary, a whole family of analytic concepts, such as "ambivalence" (I do not suggest that there is no such thing as ambivalence), which would make it difficult, if not impossible, to agree upon such criteria? Moreover, how much headway has been made in investigating the question of the extent to which the (conscious or unconscious) expectations and theories held by the analyst influence the "clinical responses" of the patient? (To say nothing about the conscious attempts to influence the patient by proposing interpretations to him, etc.) Years ago I introduced the term *"Oedipus effect"* to describe the influence of a theory or expectation or prediction *upon the event which it predicts* or describes: it will be remembered that the causal chain leading to Oedipus' parricide was started by the oracle's prediction of this event. This is a characteristic and recurrent theme of such myths, but one which seems to have failed to attract the interest of the analysts, perhaps not accidentally. (The problem of confirmatory dreams suggested by the analyst is discussed by Freud, for example in *Gesammelte Schriften,* III, 1925, where he says on p. 314: "If anybody asserts that most of the dreams which can be utilized in an analysis . . . owe their origin to the analyst's suggestion, then no objection can be made from the point of view of analytic theory. Yet there is nothing in this fact," he surprisingly adds, "which would detract from the reliability of our results.")
4. The case of astrology, nowadays a typical pseudoscience, may illustrate this point. It was attacked, by Aristotelians and other rationalists, down to Newton's day, for the wrong reason—for its now accepted assertion that the planets had an "influence" upon terrestrial ("sublunar") events. In fact Newton's theory of gravity, and especially the lunar theory of the tides, was historically speaking an offspring of astrological lore. Newton, it seems, was most reluctant to adopt a theory which came from the same stable as for example the theory that "influenza" epidemics are due to an astral "influence." And Galileo, no doubt for the same reason, actually rejected the lunar theory of the tides; and his misgivings about Kepler may easily be explained by his misgivings about astrology.

## *Imre Lakatos (1922–1974)*

Imre Lakatos was a major figure in the recent revolution in twentieth century philosophy of science. He argued that the failure of both the traditional model of scientific change and Popper's falsificationism did not require that we think of theory change in terms of irrational shifts of allegiance in the scientific community. Lakatos thought that viewing theories in their broader context, in terms of the larger research programs that contained them, would allow us to make rational, objective sense of the actual process of scientific change.

Lakatos is the author of numerous books and articles in the philosophy of mathematics and philosophy of science, including *Proofs and Refutations: The Logic of Mathematical Discovery* (1976), *The Methodology of Scientific Research Programmes* (1977), from which the selection below was taken, and *Mathematics, Science and Epistemology* (1978). In the following selection Lakatos suggests criteria for assessing the quality of research programs, in terms of which we can understand why one program eventually replaces another.

# Science and Pseudoscience*

## *Imre Lakatos*

Man's respect for knowledge is one of his most peculiar characteristics. Knowledge in Latin is *scientia,* and science came to be the name of the most respectable kind of knowledge. But what distinguishes knowledge from superstition, ideology or pseudoscience? The Catholic Church excommunicated Copernicans, the Communist Party persecuted Mendelians on the ground that their doctrines were pseudoscientific. The demarcation between science and pseudoscience is not merely a problem of armchair philosophy: it is of vital social and political relevance.

Many philosophers have tried to solve the problem of demarcation in the following terms: a statement constitutes knowledge if sufficiently many people believe it sufficiently strongly. But the history of thought shows us that many people were totally committed to absurd beliefs. If the strength of beliefs were a hallmark of knowledge, we should have to rank some tales about demons, angels, devils, and of heaven and hell as knowledge. Scientists, on the other hand, are very sceptical even of their best theories. Newton's is the most powerful theory science has yet produced, but Newton himself never believed that bodies attract each other at a distance. So no degree of commitment to beliefs makes them knowledge. Indeed, the hallmark of scientific behavior is a certain scepticism even towards one's most cherished theories. Blind commitment to a theory is not an intellectual virtue: it is an intellectual crime.

Thus a statement may be pseudoscientific even if it is eminently "plausible" and everybody believes in it, and it may be scientifically valuable even if it is unbelievable and nobody believes in it. A theory may even be of supreme scientific value even if no one understands it, let alone believes it.

*This paper was written in early 1973 and was originally delivered as a radio lecture. It was broadcast by the Open University on 30 June 1973. *(Eds.)*

From "The Methodology of Scientific Research," *Philosophical Papers,* Vol. 1, Imre Lakatos. (New York: Cambridge University Press, copyright 1977), pp. 1–7. Reprinted by permission of Cambridge University Press.

The cognitive value of a theory has nothing to do with its psychological influence on people's minds. Belief, commitment, understanding are states of the human mind. But the objective, scientific value of a theory is independent of the human mind which creates it or understands it. Its scientific value depends only on what objective support these conjectures have in facts. As Hume said:

> If we take in our hand any volume; of divinity, or school metaphysics, for instance; let us ask, does it contain any abstract reasoning concerning quantity or number? No. Does it contain any experimental reasoning concerning matter of fact and existence? No. Commit it then to the flames. For it can contain nothing but sophistry and illusion.

But what is "experimental" reasoning? If we look at the vast seventeenth-century literature on witchcraft, it is full of reports of careful observations and sworn evidence — even of experiments. Glanvill, the house philosopher of the early Royal Society, regarded witchcraft as the paradigm of experimental reasoning. We have to define experimental reasoning before we start Humean book burning.

In scientific reasoning, theories are confronted with facts; and one of the central conditions of scientific reasoning is that theories must be supported by facts. Now how exactly can facts support theory?

Several different answers have been proposed. Newton himself thought that he proved his laws from facts. He was proud of not uttering mere hypotheses: he only published theories proven from facts. In particular, he claimed that he deduced his laws from the "phenomena" provided by Kepler. But his boast was nonsense, since according to Kepler, planets move in ellipses, but according to Newton's theory, planets would move in ellipses only if the planets did not disturb each other in their motion. But they do. This is why Newton had to devise a perturbation theory from which it follows that no planet moves in an ellipse.

One can today easily demonstrate that there can be no valid derivation of a law of nature from any finite number of facts; but we still keep reading about scientific theories being proved from facts. Why this stubborn resistance to elementary logic?

There is a very plausible explanation. Scientists want to make their theories respectable, deserving of the title "science," that is, genuine knowledge. Now the most relevant knowledge in the seventeenth century, when science was born, concerned God, the Devil, Heaven and Hell. If one got one's conjectures about matters of divinity wrong, the consequence of one's mistake was eternal damnation. Theological knowledge cannot be fallible: it must be beyond doubt. Now the Enlightenment thought that we were fallible and ignorant about matters theological. There is no scientific theology and, therefore, no theological knowledge. Knowledge can only be about Nature, but this new type of knowledge had to be judged by the standards they took over straight from theology: it had to be proven beyond doubt. Science had to achieve the very certainty which had escaped theology. A scientist, worthy of the name, was not allowed to guess: he had to prove each sentence he uttered from facts. This was the criterion of scientific honesty. Theories unproven from facts were regarded as sinful pseudoscience, heresy in the scientific community.

It was only the downfall of Newtonian theory in this century which made scientists realize that their standards of honesty had been utopian. Before Einstein most scientists thought that Newton had deciphered God's ultimate laws by proving them from the facts. Ampère, in the early nineteenth century, felt he had to call his book on his speculations concerning electromagnetism: *Mathematical Theory of Electrodynamic Phenomena Unequivocally Deduced from Experiment*. But at the end of the volume he casually confesses that some of the experiments were never performed and even that the necessary instruments had not been constructed!

If all scientific theories are equally unprovable, what distinguishes scientific knowledge from ignorance, science from pseudoscience?

One answer to this question was provided in the twentieth century by "**inductive** logicians."

Inductive logic set out to define the probabilities of different theories according to the available total evidence. If the mathematical probability of a theory is high, it qualifies as scientific; if it is low or even zero, it is not scientific. Thus the hallmark of scientific honesty would be never to say anything that is not at least highly probable. **Probabilism** has an attractive feature: instead of simply providing a black-and-white distinction between science and pseudoscience, it provides a continuous scale from poor theories with low probability to good theories with high probability. But, in 1934, Karl Popper, one of the most influential philosophers of our time, argued that the mathematical probability of all theories, scientific or pseudoscientific, given *any* amount of evidence is zero. If Popper is right, scientific theories are not only equally unprovable but also equally improbable. A new demarcation criterion was needed and Popper proposed a rather stunning one. A theory may be scientific even if there is not a shred of evidence in its favor, and it may be pseudoscientific even if all the available evidence is in its favor. That is, the scientific or nonscientific character of a theory can be determined independently of the facts. A theory is "scientific" if one is prepared to specify in advance a crucial experiment (or observation) which can falsify it, and it is pseudoscientific if one refuses to specify such a "potential falsifier." But if so, we do not demarcate scientific theories from pseudoscientific ones, but rather scientific method from non-scientific method. Marxism, for a Popperian, is scientific if the Marxists are prepared to specify facts which, if observed, make them give up Marxism. If they refuse to do so, Marxism becomes a pseudoscience. It is always interesting to ask a Marxist, what conceivable event would make him abandon his Marxism. If he is committed to Marxism, he is bound to find it immoral to specify a state of affairs which can falsify it. Thus a proposition may petrify into pseudoscientific dogma or become genuine knowledge, depending on whether we are prepared to state observable conditions which would refute it.

Is, then, Popper's falsifiability criterion the solution to the problem of demarcating science from pseudoscience? No. For Popper's criterion ignores the remarkable tenacity of scientific theories. Scientists have thick skins. They do not abandon a theory merely because facts contradict it. They normally either invent some rescue hypothesis to explain what they then call a mere **anomaly** or, if they cannot explain the anomaly, they ignore it, and direct their attention to other problems. Note that scientists talk about anomalies, recalcitrant instances, not refutations. History of science, of course, is full of accounts of how crucial experiments allegedly killed theories. But such accounts are fabricated long after the theory had been abandoned. Had Popper ever asked a Newtonian scientist under what experimental conditions he would abandon Newtonian theory, some Newtonian scientists would have been exactly as nonplussed as are some Marxists.

What, then, is the hallmark of science? Do we have to capitulate and agree that a scientific revolution is just an irrational change in commitment, that it is a religious conversion? Tom Kuhn, a distinguished American philosopher of science, arrived at this conclusion after discovering the naïvety of Popper's falsificationism. But if Kuhn is right, then there is no explicit demarcation between science and pseudoscience, no distinction between scientific progress and intellectual decay, there is no objective standard of honesty. But what criteria can he then offer to demarcate scientific progress from intellectual degeneration?

In the last few years I have been advocating a methodology of scientific research programs, which solves some of the problems which both Popper and Kuhn failed to solve.

First, I claim that the typical descriptive unit of great scientific achievements is not an isolated hypothesis but rather a research program. Science is not simply trial and error, a series of conjectures and refutations. "All swans are white" may be falsified by the discovery of one black swan. But such trivial trial and error does not rank as science. Newtonian science, for instance, is not simply a set of four conjectures—

the three laws of mechanics and the law of gravitation. These four laws constitute only the "hard core" of the Newtonian program. But this hard core is tenaciously protected from refutation by a vast "protective belt" of auxiliary hypotheses. And, even more importantly, the research program also has a "heuristic," that is, a powerful problem-solving machinery, which, with the help of sophisticated mathematical techniques, digests anomalies and even turns them into positive evidence. For instance, if a planet does not move exactly as it should, the Newtonian scientist checks his conjectures concerning atmospheric refraction, concerning propagation of light in magnetic storms, and hundreds of other conjectures which are all part of the program. He may even invent a hitherto unknown planet and calculate its position, mass and velocity in order to explain the anomaly.

Now, Newton's theory of gravitation, Einstein's relativity theory, quantum mechanics, Marxism, Freudianism, are all research programs, each with a characteristic hard core stubbornly defended, each with its more flexible protective belt and each with its elaborate problem-solving machinery. Each of them, at any stage of its development, has unsolved problems and undigested anomalies. All theories, in this sense, are born refuted and die refuted. But are they equally good? Until now I have been describing what research programs are like. But how can one distinguish a scientific or progressive program from a pseudoscientific or degenerating one?

Contrary to Popper, the difference cannot be that some are still unrefuted, while others are already refuted. When Newton published his *Principia,* it was common knowledge that it could not properly explain even the motion of the moon; in fact, lunar motion refuted Newton. Kaufmann, a distinguished physicist, refuted Einstein's relativity theory in the very year it was published. But all the research programs I admire have one characteristic in common. They all predict novel facts, facts which had been either undreamt of, or have indeed been contradicted by previous or rival programs. In 1686, when Newton published his theory of gravitation, there were, for instance, two current theories concerning comets. The more popular one regarded comets as a signal from an angry God warning that He will strike and bring disaster. A little known theory of Kepler's held that comets were celestial bodies moving along straight lines. Now according to Newtonian theory, some of them moved in hyperbolas or parabolas never to return; others moved in ordinary ellipses. Halley, working in Newton's program, calculated on the basis of observing a brief stretch of a comet's path that it would return in seventy-two years' time; he calculated to the minute when it would be seen again at a well-defined point of the sky. This was incredible. But seventy-two years later, when both Newton and Halley were long dead, Halley's comet returned exactly as Halley predicted. Similarly, Newtonian scientists predicted the existence and exact motion of small planets which had never been observed before. Or let us take Einstein's program. This program made the stunning prediction that if one measures the distance between two stars in the night and if one measures the distance between them during the day (when they are visible during an eclipse of the sun), the two measurements will be different. Nobody had thought to make such an observation before Einstein's program. Thus, in a progressive research program, theory leads to the discovery of hitherto unknown novel facts. In degenerating programs, however, theories are fabricated only in order to accommodate known facts. Has, for instance, Marxism ever predicted a stunning novel fact successfully? Never! It has some famous unsuccessful predictions. It predicted the absolute impoverishment of the working class. It predicted that the first socialist revolution would take place in the industrially most developed society. It predicted that socialist societies would be free of revolutions. It predicted that there will be no conflict of interests between socialist countries. Thus the early predictions of Marxism were bold and stunning but they failed. Marxists explained all their failures: they explained the rising living standards of the working class by devising a theory of imperialism; they even explained why the first socialist revolution occurred in industrially backward Russia. They "explained" Berlin 1953, Budapest 1956, Prague 1968. They "explained" the Russian–Chinese conflict. But their auxiliary hypotheses were all cooked up after the event to protect Marxian theory from the facts. The Newtonian program led to novel facts; the Marxian lagged behind the facts and has been running fast to catch up with them.

To sum up. The hallmark of empirical progress is not trivial verifications: Popper is right that there are millions of them. It is no success for Newtonian theory that stones, when dropped, fall towards the earth, no matter how often this is repeated. But so-called "refutations" are not the hallmark of empirical failure, as Popper has preached, since all programs grow in a permanent ocean of anomalies. What really count are dramatic, unexpected, stunning predictions: a few of them are enough to tilt the balance; where theory lags behind the facts, we are dealing with miserable degenerating research programs.

Now, how do scientific revolutions come about? If we have two rival research programs, and one is progressing while the other is degenerating, scientists tend to join the progressive program. This is the rationale of scientific revolutions. But while it is a matter of intellectual honesty to keep the record public, it is not dishonest to stick to a degenerating program and try to turn it into a progressive one.

As opposed to Popper the methodology of scientific research programs does not offer instant rationality. One must treat budding programs leniently: programs may take decades before they get off the ground and become empirically progressive. Criticism is not a Popperian quick kill, by refutation. Important criticism is always constructive: there is no refutation without a better theory. Kuhn is wrong in thinking that scientific revolutions are sudden, irrational changes in vision. The history of science refutes both Popper and Kuhn: on close inspection both Popperian crucial experiments and Kuhnian revolutions turn out to be myths: what normally happens is that progressive research programs replace degenerating ones.

The problem of demarcation between science and pseudoscience has grave implications also for the institutionalization of criticism. Copernicus's theory was banned by the Catholic Church in 1616 because it was said to be pseudoscientific. It was taken off the index in 1820 because by that time the Church deemed that facts had proved it and therefore it became scientific. The Central Committee of the Soviet Communist Party in 1949 declared Mendelian genetics pseudoscientific and had its advocates, like Academician Vavilov, killed in concentration camps; after Vavilov's murder Mendelian genetics was rehabilitated; but the Party's right to decide what is science and publishable and what is pseudoscience and punishable was upheld. The new liberal Establishment of the West also exercises the right to deny freedom of speech to what it regards as pseudoscience, as we have seen in the case of the debate concerning race and intelligence. All these judgments were inevitably based on some sort of demarcation criterion. This is why the problem of demarcation between science and pseudoscience is not a pseudo-problem of armchair philosophers: it has grave ethical and political implications.

## W. V. Quine (b. 1908)

W. V. Quine is probably the best-known and most influential living American philosopher. He has been a dominant force in contemporary epistemology, metaphysics, logic, philosophy of science, and philosophy of language. Among his fourteen books are *From A Logical Point of View* (1953), *Word and Object* (1960), *Set Theory and Its Logic* (1963), *Ontological Relativity and Other Essays* (1969), *Philosophy of Logic* (1970), and *The Roots of Reference* (1974).

## J. S. Ullian (b. 1930)

J. S. Ullian has written a number of articles in logic and philosophy of language and made important contributions in computer science as well. He is the coauthor (with W. V. Quine) of an introductory philosophy text, *The Web of Belief* (1970). The selection below is taken from the second edition (1982) of that text.

In the following, Quine and Ullian describe the virtues that a scientific hypothesis should possess if it is to be successful at performing its proper functions, namely, explaining the past and predicting the future. None of these virtues is an all-or-nothing affair, the possession of each is a matter of degree. Sometimes trade-offs are necessary, the sacrifice of some degree of one of the virtues being required as a means to enormous gains in terms of one of the others. It is in terms of all five virtues that we can understand why one hypothesis is to be preferred to another.

# Hypothesis

## W. V. Quine and J. S. Ullian

Some philosophers once held that whatever was true could in principle be proved from self-evident beginnings by self-evident steps. The trait of absolute demonstrability, which we attributed to the truths of logic in a narrow sense and to relatively little else, was believed by those philosophers to pervade all truth. They thought that but for our intellectual limitations we could find proofs for any truths, and so, in particular, predict the future to any desired extent. These philosophers were the **rationalists.** Other philosophers, a little less sanguine, had it that whatever was true could be proved by self-evident steps from two-fold beginnings: self-evident truths and observations. Philosophers of both schools, the rationalists and the somewhat less sanguine ones as well, strained toward their ideals by construing self-evidence every bit as broadly as they in conscience might, or somewhat more so.

Actually even the truths of elementary number theory are presumably not in general derivable, we noted, by self-evident steps from self-evident truths. We owe this insight to Godel's theorem, which was not known to the old-time philosophers.

What then of the truths of nature? Might these be derivable still by self-evident steps from self-evident truths together with observations? Surely not. Take the humblest generalization from observation: that giraffes are mute, that sea water tastes of salt. We infer these from our observations of giraffes and sea water because we expect instinctively that what is true of all observed samples is true of the rest. The principle involved here, far from being self-evident, does not always lead to true generalizations. It worked for the giraffes and the sea water, but it would have let us down if we had inferred from a hundred observations of swans that all swans are white.

Such generalizations already exceed what can be proved from observations and self-evident truths by self-evident steps. Yet such generalizations are still only a small part of natural science. Theories of molecules and atoms are not related to any observations in the direct way in which the generalizations about giraffes and sea water are related to observations of mute giraffes and salty sea water.

It is now recognized that deduction from self-evident truths and observation is not the sole avenue to truth nor even to reasonable belief. A dominant further factor, in solid science as in daily life, is *hypothesis*. In a word, hypothesis is guesswork; but it can be enlightened guesswork.

It is the part of scientific rigor to recognize hypothesis as hypothesis and then to make the most of it. Having accepted the fact that our observations and our self-evident truths do not together suffice to predict the future, we frame hypotheses to make up the shortage.

Calling a belief a hypothesis says nothing as to what the belief is about, how firmly it is held, or how well founded it is. Calling it a hypothesis suggests rather what sort of reason we have for adopting or entertaining it. People adopt or entertain a hypothesis because it would explain, if it were true, some things that they already believe. Its evidence is seen in its consequences. . . .

Hypothesis, where successful, is a two-way street, extending back to explain the past and forward to predict the future. What we try to do in framing hypotheses is to explain some otherwise unexplained happenings by inventing a plausible story, a plausible description or history of relevant portions of the world. What counts in favor of a hypothesis is a question not to be lightly answered. We may note five virtues that a hypothesis may enjoy in varying degrees.

Virtue I is *conservatism*. In order to explain the happenings that we are inventing it to explain, the hypothesis may have to conflict with some of our previous beliefs; but the fewer the better. Acceptance of a hypothesis is of course like acceptance of any belief in that it demands rejection of whatever conflicts with it. The less rejection of prior beliefs required, the more plausible the hypothesis — other things being equal.

Often some hypothesis is available that conflicts with no prior beliefs. Thus we may attribute a click at the door to arrival of mail through the slot. Conservatism usually prevails in such a case; one is not apt to be tempted by a hypothesis that upsets prior beliefs when there is no need to resort to one. When the virtue of conservatism deserves notice, rather, is when something happens that cannot evidently be reconciled with our prior beliefs.

There could be such a case when our friend the amateur magician tells us what card we have drawn. How did he do it? Perhaps by luck, one chance in fifty-two; but this conflicts with our reasonable belief, if all unstated, that he would not have volunteered a performance that depended on that kind of luck. Perhaps the cards were marked; but this conflicts with our belief that he had had no access to them, they being ours. Perhaps he peeked or pushed, with help of a sleight-of-hand; but this conflicts with our belief in our perceptiveness. Perhaps he resorted to telepathy or clairvoyance; but this would wreak havoc with our whole web of belief. The counsel of conservatism is the sleight-of-hand.

Conservatism is rather effortless on the whole, having inertia in its favor. But it is sound strategy too, since at each step it sacrifices as little as possible of the evidential support, whatever that may have been, that our overall system of beliefs has hitherto been enjoying. The truth may indeed be radically remote from our present system of beliefs, so that we may need a long series of conservative steps to attain what might have been attained in one rash leap. The longer the leap, however, the more serious an angular error in the direction. For a leap in the dark the likelihood of a happy landing is severely limited. Conservatism holds out the advantages of limited liability and a maximum of live options for each next move.

Virtue II, closely akin to conservatism, is *modesty*. One hypothesis is more modest than another if it is weaker in a logical sense: if it is implied by the other, without implying it. A hypothesis *A* is more modest than *A* and *B* as a joint hypothesis. Also, one hypothesis is more modest than another if it is more humdrum: that is, if the events that it assumes to have happened are of a more usual and familiar sort, hence more to be expected.

Thus suppose a man rings our telephone and ends by apologizing for dialing the wrong number. We will guess that he slipped, rather than that he was a burglar checking to see if anyone was home. It is the more modest of the two hypotheses, butterfingers being rife. We could be wrong, for crime is rife too. But still the butterfingers hypothesis scores better on modesty than the burglar hypothesis, butterfingers being rifer.

We habitually practice modesty, all unawares, when we identify recurrent objects. Unhesitatingly we recognize our car off there where we parked it, though it may have been towed away and another car of the same model may have happened to pull in at that spot. Ours is the more modest hypothesis, because staying put is a more usual and familiar phenomenon than the alternative combination.

It tends to be the counsel of modesty that the lazy world is the likely world. We are to assume as little activity as will suffice to account for appearances. This is not all there is to modesty. It does not apply to the preferred hypothesis in the telephone example, since Mr. Butterfingers is not assumed to be a less active man than one who might have plotted burglary. Modesty figured there merely in keeping the assumptions down, rather than in actually assuming inactivity. In the example of the parked car, however, the modest hypothesis does expressly assume there to be less activity than otherwise. This is a policy that guides science as well as common sense. It is even erected into an explicit principle of mechanics under the name of the law of least action.

Between modesty and conservatism there is no call to draw a sharp line. But by Virtue I we meant conservatism only in a literal sense—conservation of past beliefs. Thus there remain grades of modesty still to choose among even when Virtue I—compatibility with previous beliefs—is achieved to perfection; for both a slight hypothesis and an extravagant one might be compatible with all previous beliefs.

Modesty grades off in turn into Virtue III, *simplicity*. Where simplicity considerations become especially vivid is in drawing curves through plotted points on a graph. Consider the familiar practice of plotting measurements. Distance up the page represents altitude above sea level, for instance, and distance across represents the temperature of boiling water. We plot our measurements on the graph, one dot for each pair. However many points we plot, there remain infinitely many curves that may be drawn through them. Whatever curve we draw represents our generalization from the data, our prediction of what boiling temperatures would be found at altitudes as yet untested. And the curve we will choose to draw is the simplest curve that passes through or reasonably close to all the plotted points.

There is a premium on simplicity in any hypothesis, but the highest premium is on simplicity in the giant joint hypothesis that is science, or the particular science, as a whole. We cheerfully sacrifice simplicity of a part for greater simplicity of the whole when we see a way of doing so. Thus consider gravity. Heavy objects tend downward: here is an exceedingly simple hypothesis, or even a mere definition. However, we complicate matters by accepting rather the hypothesis that the heavy objects around us are slightly attracted also by one another, and by the neighboring mountains, and by the moon, and that all these competing forces detract slightly from the downward one. Newton propounded this more complicated hypothesis even though, aside from tidal effects of the moon, he had no means of detecting the competing forces; for it meant a great gain in the simplicity of physics as a whole. His hypothesis of universal gravitation, which has each body attracting each in proportion to mass and inversely as the square of the distance, was what enabled him to make a single neat system of celestial and terrestrial mechanics.

A modest hypothesis that was long supported both by theoretical considerations and by observation is that the trajectory of a projectile is a parabola. A contrary hypothesis is that the trajectory deviates imperceptibly from a parabola, constituting rather one end of an ellipse whose other end extends beyond the center of the earth. This hypothesis is less modest, but again it conduces to a higher simplicity: Newton's laws of motion and, again, of gravitation. The trajectories are brought into harmony with Kepler's law of the elliptical orbits of the planets.

Another famous triumph of this kind was achieved by Count Rumford and later physicists when they showed how the relation of gas pressure to temperature could be accounted for by the impact of oscillating particles, for in this way they reduced the theory of gases to the general laws of motion. Such was the kinetic theory of gases. In order to achieve it they had to add the hypothesis, by no means a modest one, that gas consists of oscillating particles or molecules; but the addition is made up for, and much more, by the gain in simplicity accruing to physics as a whole.

What is simplicity? For curves we can make good sense of it in geometrical terms. A simple curve is continuous, and among continuous curves the simplest are perhaps those whose curvature changes most gradually from point to point. When scientific laws are expressed in equations, as they so often are, we can make good sense of simplicity in terms of what mathematicians call the degree of an equation, or the order of a differential equation. This line was taken by Sir Harold Jeffreys. The lower the degree, the lower the order, and the fewer the terms, the simpler the equation. Such simplicity ratings of equations agree with the simplicity ratings of curves when the equations are plotted as in analytical geometry.

Simplicity is harder to define when we turn away from curves and equations. Sometimes in such cases it is not to be distinguished from modesty. Commonly a hypothesis *A* will count as simpler than *A* and *B* together; thus far simplicity and modesty coincide. On the other hand the simplicity gained by Newton's hypothesis of universal gravitation was not modesty, in the sense that we have assigned to that term; for the hypothesis was not logically implied by its predecessors, nor was it more humdrum in respect of the events that it assumed. Newton's hypothesis was simpler than its predecessors in that it covered in a brief unified story what had previously been covered only by two unrelated accounts. Similar remarks apply to the kinetic theory of gases.

In the notion of simplicity there is a nagging subjectivity. What makes for a brief unified story depends on the structure of our language, after all, and on our available vocabulary, which need not reflect the structure of nature. This subjectivity of simplicity is puzzling, if simplicity in hypotheses is to make for plausibility. Why should the subjectively simpler of two hypotheses stand a better chance of predicting objective events? Why should we expect nature to submit to our subjective standards of simplicity?

That would be too much to expect. Physicists and others are continually finding that they have to complicate their theories to accommodate new data. At each stage, however, when choosing a hypothesis subject to subsequent correction, it is still best to choose the simplest that is not yet excluded. This strategy recommends itself on much the same grounds as the strategies of conservatism and modesty. The longer the leap, we reflected, the more and wilder ways of going wrong. But likewise, the more complex the hypothesis, the more and wilder ways of going wrong; for how can we tell which complexities to adopt? Simplicity, like conservatism and modesty, limits liability. Conservatism can be good strategy even though one's present theory be ever so far from the truth, and simplicity can be good strategy even though the world be ever so complicated. Our steps toward the complicated truth can usually be laid out most dependably if the simplest hypothesis that is still tenable is chosen at each step. It has even been argued that this policy will lead us at least asymptotically toward a theory that is true.

There is more, however, to be said for simplicity: the simplest hypothesis often just is the likeliest, apparently, quite apart from questions of cagy strategy. Why should this be? There is a partial explanation in our ways of keeping score on predictions. The predictions based on the simpler hypotheses tend to be scored more leniently. Thus consider curves, where simplicity comparisons are so clear. If a curve is kinky and complex, and if some measurement predicted from the curve turns out to miss the mark by a distance as sizable as some of the kinks of the curve itself, we will count the prediction a failure. We will feel that so kinky a curve, if correct, would have had a kink to catch this wayward point. On the other hand, a miss of the same magnitude might be excused if the curve were smooth and simple. It might be excused as due to inaccuracy of measurement or to some unexplained local interference. This cynical doctrine of selective leniency is very plausible in the case of the curves. And we may reasonably expect a somewhat similar but less easily pictured selectivity to be at work in the interest of the simple hypotheses where curves are not concerned.

Considering how subjective our standards of simplicity are, we wondered why we should expect nature to submit to them. Our first answer was that we need not expect it; the strategy of favoring the simple at each step is good anyway. Now we have noted further that some of nature's seeming simplicity is an effect of our bookkeeping. Are we to conclude that the favoring of simplicity is entirely our doing, and that nature is neutral in the matter? Not quite. Darwin's theory of natural selection offers a causal connection between subjective simplicity and objective truth in the following way. Innate subjective standards of simplicity that make people prefer some hypotheses to others will have survival value insofar as they favor successful prediction. Those who predict best are likeliest to survive and reproduce their kind, in a state of nature anyway, and so their innate standards of simplicity are handed down. Such standards will also change in the light of experience, becoming still better adapted to the growing body of science in the course of the individual's lifetime. (But these improvements do not get handed down genetically.)

Virtue IV is *generality*. The wider the range of application of a hypothesis, the more general it is. When we find electricity conducted by a piece of copper wire, we leap to the hypothesis that all copper, not just long thin copper, conducts electricity.

The plausibility of a hypothesis depends largely on how compatible the hypothesis is with our being observers placed at random in the world. Funny coincidences often occur, but they are not the stuff that plausible hypotheses are made of. The more general the hypothesis is by which we account for our present observation, the less of a coincidence it is that our present observation should fall under it. Hence, in part, the power of Virtue IV to confer plausibility.

The possibility of testing a hypothesis by repeatable experiment presupposes that the hypothesis has at least some share of Virtue IV. For in a repetition of an experiment the test situation can never be exactly what it was for the earlier run of the experiment; and so, if both runs are to be relevant to the hypothesis, the hypothesis must be at least general enough to apply to both test situations.* One would of course like to have it much more general still.

Virtues I, II, and III made for plausibility. So does Virtue IV to some degree, we see, but that is

*We are indebted to Nell E. Scroggins for suggesting this point.

not its main claim; indeed generality conflicts with modesty. But generality is desirable in that it makes a hypothesis interesting and important if true.

We lately noted a celebrated example of generality in Newton's hypothesis of universal gravitation, and another in the kinetic theory of gases. It is no accident that the same illustrations should serve for both simplicity and generality. Generality without simplicity is cold comfort. Thus take celestial mechanics with its elliptical orbits, and take also terrestrial mechanics with its parabolic trajectories, just take them in tandem as a bipartite theory of motion. If the two together cover everything covered by Newton's unified laws of motion, then generality is no ground for preferring Newton's theory to the two taken together. But Virtue III, simplicity, is. When a way is seen of gaining great generality with little loss of simplicity, or great simplicity with no loss of generality, then conservatism and modesty give way to scientific revolution.

The aftermath of the famous Michelson-Morley experiment of 1887 is a case in point. The purpose of this delicate and ingenious experiment was to measure the speed with which the earth travels through the ether. For two centuries, from Newton onward, it had been a well entrenched tenet that something called the ether pervaded all of what we think of as empty space. The great physicist Lorentz (1853–1928) had hypothesized that the ether itself was stationary. What the experiment revealed was that the method that was expected to enable measurement of the earth's speed through the ether was totally inadequate to that task. Supplementary hypotheses multiplied in an attempt to explain the failure without seriously disrupting the accepted physics. Lorentz, in an effort to save the hypothesis of stationary ether, shifted to a new and more complicated set of formulas in his mathematical physics. Einstein soon cut through all this, propounding what is called the special theory of relativity.

This was a simplification of physical theory. Not that Einstein's theory is as simple as Newton's had been; but Newton's physics had been shown untenable by the Michelson-Morley experiment. The point is that Einstein's theory is simpler than Newton's as corrected and supplemented and complicated by Lorentz and others. It was a glorious case of gaining simplicity at the sacrifice of conservatism; for the time-honored ether went by the board, and far older and more fundamental tenets went by the board too. Drastic changes were made in our conception of the very structure of space and time. . . .

Yet let the glory not blind us to Virtue I. When our estrangement from the past is excessive, the imagination boggles; genius is needed to devise the new theory, and high talent is needed to find one's way about in it. Even Einstein's revolution, moreover, had its conservative strain; Virtue I was not wholly sacrificed. The old physics of Newton's classical mechanics is, in a way, preserved after all. For the situations in which the old and the new theories would predict contrary observations are situations that we are not apt to encounter without sophisticated experiment—because of their dependence on exorbitant velocities or exorbitant distances. This is why classical mechanics held the field so long. Whenever, even having switched to Einstein's relativity theory, we dismiss those exorbitant velocities and distances for the purpose of some practical problem, promptly the discrepancy between Einstein's theory and Newton's becomes too small to matter. Looked at from this angle, Einstein's theory takes on the aspect not of a simplification but a generalization. We might say that the sphere of applicability of Newtonian mechanics in its original simplicity was shown, by the Michelson-Morley experiment and related results, to be less than universal; and then Einstein's theory comes as a generalization, presumed to hold universally. Within its newly limited sphere, Newtonian mechanics retains its old utility. What is more, the evidence of past centuries for Newtonian mechanics even carries over, within these limits, as evidence for Einstein's physics; for, as far as it goes, it fits both.

What is thus illustrated by Einstein's relativity is more modestly exemplified elsewhere, and generally aspired to: the retention, in some sense, of old theories in new ones. If the new theory can be so fashioned as to diverge from the old only in ways that are undetectable in most ordinary circumstances, then it inherits the evidence of the old theory rather than having to overcome it. Such is the force of conservatism even in the context of revolution.

Virtues I through IV may be further illustrated by considering Neptune. That Neptune is among the planets is readily checked by anyone with reference material; indeed it passes as common knowledge, and there is for most of us no need to check it. But only through extensive application of optics and geometry was it possible to determine, in the first instance, that the body we call Neptune exists, and that it revolves around the sun. This required not only much accumulated science and mathematics, but also powerful telescopes and cooperation among scientists.

In fact it happens that Neptune's existence and planethood were strongly suspected even before that planet was observed. Physical theory made possible the calculation of what the orbit of the planet Uranus should be, but Uranus' path differed measurably from its calculated course. Now the theory on which the calculations were based was, like all theories, open to revision or refutation. But here conservatism operates: one is loath to revise extensively a well established set of beliefs, especially a set so deeply entrenched as a basic portion of physics. And one is even more loath to abandon as spurious immense numbers of observation reports made by serious scientists. Given that Uranus had been observed to be as much as two minutes of arc from its calculated position, what was sought was a discovery that would render this deviation explicable within the framework of accepted theory. Then the theory and its generality would be unimpaired, and the new complexity would be minimal.

It would have been possible in principle to speculate that some special characteristic of Uranus exempted that planet from the physical laws that are followed by other planets. If such a hypothesis had been resorted to, Neptune would not have been discovered; not then, at any rate. There was a reason, however, for not resorting to such a hypothesis. It would have been what is called an ***ad hoc*** *hypothesis,* and ad hoc hypotheses are bad air; for they are wanting in Virtues III and IV. Ad hoc hypotheses are hypotheses that purport to account for some particular observations by supposing some very special forces to be at work in the particular cases at hand, and not generalizing sufficiently beyond those cases. The vice of an ad hoc hypothesis admits of degrees. The extreme case is where the hypothesis covers only the observations it was invented to account for, so that it is totally useless in prediction. Then also it is insusceptible of confirmation, which would come of our verifying its predictions.

Another example that has something of the implausibility of an ad hoc hypothesis is the water-diviner's belief that a willow wand held above the ground can be attracted by underground water. The force alleged is too special. One feels, most decidedly, the lack of an intelligible mechanism to explain the attraction. And what counts as intelligible mechanism? A hypothesis strikes us as giving an intelligible mechanism when the hypothesis rates well in familiarity, generality, simplicity. We attain the ultimate in intelligibility of mechanism, no doubt, when we see how to explain something in terms of physical impact, or the familiar and general laws of motion.

There is an especially notorious sort of hypothesis which, whether or not properly classified also as ad hoc, shares the traits of insusceptibility of confirmation and uselessness in prediction. This is the sort of hypothesis that seeks to save some other hypothesis from refutation by systematically excusing the failures of its predictions. When the Voice from Beyond is silent despite the incantations of the medium, we may be urged to suppose that "someone in the room is interfering with the communication." In an effort to save the prior hypothesis that certain incantations will summon forth the Voice, the auxiliary hypothesis that untoward thoughts can thwart audible signals is advanced. This auxiliary hypothesis is no wilder than the hypothesis that it was invoked to save, and thus an uncritical person may find the newly wrinkled theory no harder to accept than its predecessor had been. On the other hand the critical observer sees that evidence has ceased altogether to figure. Experimental failure is being milked to fatten up theory.

These reflections bring a fifth virtue to the fore: *refutability,* Virtue V. It seems faint praise of a hypothesis to call it refutable. But the point, we have now seen, is approximately this: some imaginable event, recognizable if it occurs, must suffice to refute the hypothesis. Otherwise the hypothesis predicts nothing, is confirmed by nothing, and confers upon us no earthly good beyond perhaps a mistaken peace of mind.

This is too simple a statement of the matter. Just about any hypothesis, after all, can be held unrefuted no matter what, by making enough adjustments in other beliefs—though sometimes doing so requires madness. We think loosely of a hypothesis as implying predictions when, strictly speaking, the implying is done by the hypothesis together with a supporting chorus of ill-distinguished background beliefs. It is done by the whole relevant theory taken together.

Properly viewed, therefore, Virtue V is a matter of degree, as are its four predecessors. The degree to which a hypothesis partakes of Virtue V is measured by the cost of retaining the hypothesis in the face of imaginable events. The degree is measured by how dearly we cherish the previous beliefs that would have to be sacrificed to save the hypothesis. The greater the sacrifice, the more refutable the hypothesis.

A prime example of deficiency in respect of Virtue V is astrology. Astrologers can so hedge their predictions that they are devoid of genuine content. We may be told that a person will "tend to be creative" or "tend to be outgoing," where the evasiveness of a verb and the fuzziness of adjectives serve to insulate the claim from repudiation. But even if a prediction should be regarded as a failure, astrological devotees can go on believing that the stars rule our destinies; for there is always some item of information, perhaps as to a planet's location at a long gone time, that may be alleged to have been overlooked. Conflict with other beliefs thus need not arise.

All our contemplating of special virtues of hypotheses will not, we trust, becloud the fact that the heart of the matter is observation. Virtues I through V are guides to the framing of hypotheses that, besides conforming to past observations, may plausibly be expected to conform to future ones. When they fail on the latter score, questions are reopened. Thus it was that the Michelson-Morley experiment led to modifications, however inelegant, of Newton's physics at the hands of Lorentz. When Einstein came out with a simpler way of accommodating past observations, moreover, his theory was no mere reformulation of the Newton-Lorentz system; it was yet a third theory, different in some of its predicted observations and answerable to them. Its superior simplicity brought plausibility to its distinctive consequences.

Hypotheses were to serve two purposes: to explain the past and predict the future. Roughly and elliptically speaking, the hypothesis serves these purposes by implying the past events that it was supposed to explain, and by implying future ones. More accurately speaking, as we saw, what does the implying is the whole relevant theory taken together, as newly revised by adoption of the hypothesis in question. Moreover, the predictions that are implied are mostly not just simple predictions of future observations or other events; more often they are conditional predictions. The hypothesis will imply that we will make these further observations if we look in such and such a place, or take other feasible steps. If the predictions come out right, we can win bets or gain other practical advantages. Also, when they come out right, we gain confirmatory evidence for our hypotheses. When they come out wrong, we go back and tinker with our hypotheses and try to make them better. . . .

We talk of framing hypotheses. Actually we inherit the main ones, growing up as we do in a going culture. The continuity of belief is due to the retention, at each particular time, of most beliefs. In this retentiveness science even at its most progressive is notably conservative. Virtue I looms large. A reasonable person will look upon some of his or her retained beliefs as self-evident, on others as common knowledge though not self-evident, on others as vouched for by authority in varying degree, and on others as hypotheses that have worked all right so far.

But the going culture goes on, and each of us participates in adding and dropping hypotheses. Continuity makes the changes manageable. Disruptions that are at all sizable are the work of scientists, but we all modify the fabric in our small way, as when we conclude on indirect evidence that the schools will be closed and the planes grounded or that an umbrella thought to have been forgotten by one person was really forgotten by another.

## *Philip Kitcher (b. 1947)*

Philip Kitcher is a contemporary philosopher of science. He has written *The Nature of Mathematical Knowledge* (1983) and *Abusing Science: The Case Against Creationism* (1982), from which the following selection was taken.

*Abusing Science* consists of a long and careful argument against the creationist claim that creationism is at least as respectable a scientific view as is evolutionary biology. In the chapter excerpted below, Kitcher considers the creationist challenge that Darwinian biology is not really a science at all. In later parts of the book he demolishes various forms of the claim that creationism is a science.

In the process of demonstrating that Darwinian theory is scientific, Kitcher explains what is required in general to make a theory a legitimate candidate for rational scientific belief. First, a theory should be able to be tested by novel or previously unexpected facts it predicts, and not just by the previously known facts it is produced to explain. Second, a theory should unify a range of problems and facts previously seen as unrelated. And, third, a theory should open up new areas of investigation and raise new questions which further inquiry will eventually answer in ways consistent with the theory. How good a scientific theory is depends on how well it measures up when tested in terms of these three characteristics. If it fails badly enough, it does not deserve to be called scientific at all.

# Believing Where We Cannot Prove

### *Philip Kitcher*

. . . When all the distortions have been removed, all the attempts to flaunt credentials examined, all the misleading quotations returned to their contexts, all the fallacies laid bare, we shall see Creation "science" for what it is—an abuse of science. One important theme that I shall emphasize is that, although the Creationist campaign is advertised as an assault on evolutionary

Abridged from "Believing Where We Cannot Prove," *Abusing Science,* by Philip Kitcher. (Cambridge, Mass: MIT Press, 1982), pp. 4–5, 30–54. In-text source references have been deleted. Reprinted by permission of Philip Kitcher.

theory, it really constitutes an attack on the whole of science. Evolutionary biology is intertwined with other sciences, ranging from nuclear physics and astronomy to molecular biology and geology. If evolutionary biology is to be dismissed, then the fundamental principles of other sciences will have to be excised. All other major fields of science will have to be trimmed—or, more exactly, mutilated—to fit the Creationists' bill. Moreover, in attacking the methods of evolutionary biology, Creationists are actually criticizing methods that are used throughout science. As I shall argue extensively, there is no basis for separating the procedures and practices of evolutionary biology from those that are fundamental to all sciences. If we let the Creationists have their way, we may as well go whole hog. Let us reintroduce the flat-earth theory, the chemistry of the four elements, and mediaeval astrology. For these outworn doctrines have just as much claim to rival current scientific views as Creationism does to challenge evolutionary biology. . . .

By training, I am a philosopher of science, a person whose business consists in trying to understand what science is and how it works. Ironically, philosophers of science owe the Creationists a debt. For the "scientific" Creationists have constructed a glorious fake, which we can use to illustrate the differences between science and pseudoscience. . . .

## OPENING MOVES

Simple distinctions come all too easily. Frequently we open the way for later puzzlement by restricting the options we take to be available. So, for example, in contrasting science and religion, we often operate with a simple pair of categories. On one side there is science, proof, and certainty; on the other, religion, conjecture, and faith.

The opening lines of Tennyson's *In Memoriam* offer an eloquent statement of the contrast:

Strong Son of God, immortal love,
Whom we, that have not seen Thy face,
By faith, and faith alone, embrace,
Believing where we cannot prove.

A principal theme of Tennyson's great poem is his struggle to maintain faith in the face of what seems to be powerful scientific evidence. Tennyson had read a popular work by Robert Chambers, *Vestiges of the Natural History of Creation,* and he was greatly troubled by the account of the course of life on earth that the book contains. *In Memoriam* reveals a man trying to believe where he cannot prove, a man haunted by the thought that the proofs may be against him.

Like Tennyson, contemporary Creationists accept the traditional contrast between science and religion. But where Tennyson agonized, they attack. While they are less eloquent, they are supremely confident of their own solution. They open their onslaught on evolutionary theory by denying that it is a science. In *The Troubled Waters of Evolution,* Henry Morris characterizes evolutionary theory as maintaining that large amounts of time are required for evolution to produce "new kinds." As a result, we should not expect to see such "new kinds" emerging. Morris comments, "Creationists in turn insist that this belief is not scientific evidence but only a statement of faith. The evolutionist seems to be saying, Of course, we cannot really *prove* evolution, since this requires ages of time, and so, therefore, you should accept it as a proved fact of science! Creationists regard this as an odd type of logic, which would be entirely unacceptable in any other field of science." David Watson makes a similar point in comparing Darwin with Galileo: "So here is the difference between Darwin and Galileo: Galileo set a demonstrable *fact* against a few words of Bible poetry which the Church at that time had understood in an obviously naive way; Darwin set an unprovable *theory* against eleven chapters of straightforward history which cannot be reinterpreted in any satisfactory way."

The idea that evolution is conjecture, faith, or "philosophy" pervades Creationist writings. It is absolutely crucial to their case for equal time for "scientific" Creationism. This ploy has succeeded in winning important adherents to the Creationist cause. As he prepared to defend Arkansas law 590, Attorney General Steven Clark echoed the Creationist judgment. "Evolution," he said, "is just a theory." Similar words have been heard in Congress. William Dannemeyer, a congressman from California, introduced a bill to limit funding to the Smithsonian with the following words: "If the theory of evolution is just that —a theory—and if that theory can be regarded as a religion . . . then it occurs to this Member that other Members might prefer it not to be given exclusive or top billing in our Nation's most famous museum but equal billing or perhaps no billing at all."

In their attempt to show that evolution is not science, Creationists receive help from the least likely sources. Great scientists sometimes claim that certain facts about the past evolution of organisms are "demonstrated" or "indubitable." But Creationists also can (and do) quote scientists who characterize evolution as "dogma" and contend that there is no conclusive proof of evolutionary theory. Evolution is not part of science because, as evolutionary biologists themselves concede, science demands proof, and, as other biologists point out, proof of evolution is not forthcoming.

The rest of the Creationist argument flows easily. We educate our children in evolutionary theory as if it were a proven fact. We subscribe officially, in our school system, to one faith—an atheistic, materialistic faith—ignoring rival beliefs. Antireligious educators deform the minds of children, warping them to accept as gospel a doctrine that has no more scientific support than the true Gospel. The very least that should be done is to allow for both alternatives to be presented.

We should reject the Creationists' gambit. Eminent scientists notwithstanding, science is not a body of demonstrated truths. Virtually all of science is an exercise in believing where we cannot prove. Yet, scientific conclusions are not embraced by faith alone. Tennyson's dichotomy was too simple.

## INCONCLUSIVE EVIDENCE

Sometimes we seem to have conclusive reasons for accepting a statement as true. It is hard to doubt that $2+2=4$. If, unlike Lord Kelvin's ideal mathematician, we do not find it obvious that

$$\int_{-\infty}^{+\infty} e^{-x^2}\,dx = \sqrt{\pi},$$

at least the elementary parts of mathematics appear to command our agreement. The direct evidence of our senses seems equally compelling. If I see the pen with which I am writing, holding it firmly in my unclouded view, how can I doubt that it exists? The talented mathematician who has proved a theorem and the keen-eyed witness of an episode furnish our ideals of certainty in knowledge. What they tell us can be engraved in stone, for there is no cause for worry that it will need to be modified.

Yet, in another mood, one that seems "deeper" or more "philosophical," skeptical doubts begin to creep in. Is there really anything of which we are so certain that later evidence could not give us reason to change our minds? Even when we think about mathematical proof, can we not imagine that new discoveries may cast doubt on the cogency of our reasoning? (The history of mathematics reveals that sometimes what seems for all the world like a proof may have a false conclusion.) Is it not possible that the most careful observer may have missed something? Or that the witness brought preconceptions to the observation that subtly biased what was reported? Are we not *always* fallible?

I am mildly sympathetic to the skeptic's worries. Complete certainty is best seen as an ideal toward which we strive and that is rarely, if ever, attained. Conclusive evidence always eludes us. Yet even if we ignore skeptical complaints and imagine that we are sometimes lucky enough to have conclusive reasons for accepting a claim as true, we should not include scientific reasoning among our paradigms of proof. Fallibility is the hallmark of science.

This point should not be so surprising. The

trouble is that we frequently forget it in discussing contemporary science. When we turn to the history of science, however, our fallibility stares us in the face. The history of the natural sciences is strewn with the corpses of intricately organized theories, each of which had, in its day, considerable evidence in its favor. When we look at the confident defenders of those theories we should see anticipations of ourselves. The eighteenth-century scientists who believed that heat is a "subtle fluid," the atomic theorists who maintained that water molecules are compounded out of one atom of hydrogen and one of oxygen, the biochemists who identified protein as the genetic material, and the geologists who thought that continents cannot move were neither unintelligent nor ill informed. Given the evidence available to them, they were eminently reasonable in drawing their conclusions. History proved them wrong. It did not show that they were unjustified.

Why is science fallible? Scientific investigation aims to disclose the general principles that govern the workings of the universe. These principles are not intended merely to summarize what some select groups of humans have witnessed. Natural science is not just natural history. It is vastly more ambitious. Science offers us laws that are supposed to hold universally, and it advances claims about things that are beyond our power to observe. The nuclear physicist who sets down the law governing a particular type of radioactive decay is attempting to state a truth that holds throughout the entire cosmos and also to describe the behavior of things that we cannot even see. Yet, of necessity, the physicist's ultimate evidence is highly restricted. Like the rest of us, scientists are confined to a relatively small region of space and time and equipped with limited and imperfect senses.

How is science possible at all? How are we able to have any confidence about the distant regions of the cosmos and the invisible realm that lies behind the surfaces of ordinary things? The answer is complicated. Natural science follows intricate and ingenious procedures for fathoming the secrets of the universe. Scientists devise ways of obtaining especially revealing evidence. They single out some of the things we are able to see as crucial clues to the way that nature works. These clues are used to answer questions that cannot be addressed by direct observation. Scientific theories, even those that are most respected and most successful, rest on indirect arguments from the observational evidence. New discoveries can always call those arguments into question, showing scientists that the observed data should be understood in a different way, that they have misread their evidence.

But scientists often forget the fallibility of their enterprise. This is not just absentmindedness or wishful thinking. During the heyday of a scientific theory, so much evidence may support the theory, so many observational clues may seem to attest to its truth, that the idea that it could be overthrown appears ludicrous. In addition, the theory may provide ways of identifying quickly what is inaccessible to our unaided senses. Electron microscopes and cloud chambers are obvious examples of those extensions of our perceptual system that theories can inspire. Trained biochemists will talk quite naturally of seeing large molecules, and it is easy to overlook the fact that they are presupposing a massive body of theory in describing what they "see." If that theory were to be amended, even in subtle ways, then the descriptions of the "observed characteristics" of large molecules might have to be given up. Nor should we pride ourselves that the enormous successes of contemporary science secure us against future amendments. No theory in the history of science enjoyed a more spectacular career than Newton's mechanics. Yet Newton's ideas had to give way to Einstein's.

When practicing scientists are reminded of these straightforward points, they frequently adopt what the philosopher George Berkeley called a "forlorn skepticism." From the idea of science as certain and infallible, they jump to a cynical description of their endeavors. Science is sometimes held to be a game played with arbitrary rules, an irrational acceptance of dogma, an enterprise based ultimately on faith. Once we have appreciated the fallibility of natural science and recognized its sources, we can move beyond the simple opposition of proof and faith. Between these extremes lies the vast field of cases in which we believe something on the basis of good — even excellent — but inconclusive evidence.

If we want to emphasize the fact that what scientists believe today may have to be revised in the light of observations made tomorrow, then we can describe all our science as "theory." But the description should not confuse us. To concede that evolutionary biology is a theory is not to suppose that there are alternatives to it that are equally worthy of a place in our curriculum. All theories are revisable, but not all theories are equal. Even though our present evidence does not *prove* that evolutionary biology — or quantum physics, or plate tectonics, or any other theory — is true, evolutionary biologists will maintain that the present evidence is overwhelmingly in favor of their theory and overwhelmingly against its supposed rivals. Their enthusiastic assertions that evolution is a proven fact can be charitably understood as claims that the (admittedly inconclusive) evidence we have for evolutionary theory is as good as we ever obtain for any theory in any field of science.

Hence the Creationist try for a quick Fools' Mate can easily be avoided. Creationists attempt to draw a line between evolutionary biology and the rest of science by remarking that large-scale evolution cannot be observed. This tactic fails. Large-scale evolution is no more inaccessible to observation than nuclear reactions or the molecular composition of water. For the Creationists to succeed in divorcing evolutionary biology from the rest of science, they need to argue that evolutionary theory is less well supported by the evidence than are theories in, for example, physics and chemistry. It will come as no surprise to learn that they try to do this. To assess the merits of their arguments we need a deeper understanding of the logic of inconclusive justification. We shall begin with a simple and popular idea: Scientific theories earn our acceptance by making successful predictions.

## PREDICTIVE SUCCESS

Imagine that somebody puts forward a new theory about the origins of hay fever. The theory makes a number of startling predictions concerning connections that we would not have thought worth investigating. For example, it tells us that people who develop hay fever invariably secrete a particular substance in certain fatty tissues and that anyone who eats rhubarb as a child never develops hay fever. The theory predicts things that initially appear fantastic. Suppose that we check up on these predictions and find that they are borne out by clinical tests. Would we not begin to believe — and believe reasonably — that the theory was *at least* on the right track?

This example illustrates a pattern of reasoning that is familiar in the history of science. Theories win support by producing claims about what can be observed, claims that would not have seemed plausible prior to the advancement of the theory, but that are in fact found to be true when we make the appropriate observations. A classic (real) example is Pascal's confirmation of Torricelli's hypothesis that we live at the bottom of an ocean of air that presses down upon us. Pascal reasoned that if Torricelli's hypothesis were true, then air pressure should decrease at higher altitudes (because at higher altitudes we are closer to the "surface" of the atmosphere, so that the length of the column of air that presses down is shorter). Accordingly, he sent his brother-in-law to the top of a mountain to make some barometric measurements. Pascal's clever working out of the observational predictions of Torricelli's theory led to a dramatic predictive success for the theory.

The idea of predictive success has encouraged a popular picture of science. (We shall see later that this picture, while popular, is not terribly accurate.) Philosophers sometimes regard a theory as a collection of claims or statements. Some of these statements offer generalizations about the features of particular, recondite things (genes, atoms, gravitational force, quasars, and the like). These statements are used to infer statements whose truth or falsity can be decided by observation. (This appears to be just what Pascal did.) Statements belonging to this second group are called the **observational consequences** of the theory. Theories are supported when we find that their observational consequences (those that we have checked) are true. The credentials of a theory are damaged if we discover that some of its observational consequences are false.

We can make the idea more precise by being clearer about the inferences involved. Those who talk of inferring observational predictions from our theories think that we can *deduce* from the statements of the theory, and from those statements alone, some predictions whose accuracy we can check by direct observation. Deductive inference is well understood. The fundamental idea of deductive inference is this: We say that a statement *S* is a valid deductive consequence of a group of statements if and only if it is *impossible* that all the statements in the group should be true and that *S* should be false; alternatively, *S* is a valid deductive consequence (or, more simply, a valid consequence) of a group of statements if and only if it would be self-contradictory to assert all the statements in the group and to deny *S*.

It will be helpful to make the idea of valid consequence more familiar with some examples. Consider the statements "All lovers of baseball dislike George Steinbrenner" and "George Steinbrenner loves baseball." The statement "George Steinbrenner dislikes himself" is a deductively valid consequence of these two statements. For it is impossible that the first two should be true and the third false. However, in claiming that this is a case of deductively valid consequence, we do not commit ourselves to maintaining that *any* of the statements is true. (Perhaps there are some ardent baseball fans who admire Steinbrenner. Perhaps Steinbrenner himself has no time for the game.) What **deductive validity** means is that the truth of the first two statements would guarantee the truth of the third; that is, *if* the first two *were* true, then the third would have to be true.

Another example will help rule out other misunderstandings. Here are two statements: "Shortly after noon on January 1, 1982, in the Oval Office, a jelly bean was released from rest more than two feet above any surface"; "Shortly after noon on January 1, 1982, in the Oval Office, a jelly bean fell." Is the second statement a deductively valid consequence of the first? You might think that it is, on the grounds that it would have been impossible for the unfortunate object to have been released and not to have fallen. In one sense this is correct, but that is not the sense of impossibility that deductive logicians have in mind. Strictly speaking, it is not *impossible* for the jellybean to have been released without falling; we can imagine, for example, that the law of gravity might suddenly cease to operate. We do not *contradict* ourselves when we assert that the jellybean was released but deny that it fell; we simply refuse to accept the law of gravity (or some other relevant physical fact).

Thus, *S* is a deductively valid consequence of a group of statements if and only if there is *absolutely no possibility* that all the statements in the group should be true and *S* should be false. This conception allows us to state the popular view of theory and prediction more precisely. Theories are collections of statements. The observational consequences of a theory are statements that have to be true if the statements belonging to the theory are all true. These observational consequences also have to be statements whose truth or falsity can be ascertained by direct observation.

My initial discussion of predictive success presented the rough idea that, when we find the observational consequences of a theory to be true, our findings bring credit to the theory. Conversely, discovery that some observational consequences of a theory are false was viewed as damaging. We can now make the second point much more precise. Any theory that has a false observational consequence must contain some false statement (or statements). For if all the statements in the theory were true, then, according to the standard definitions of *deductive validity* and *observational consequence,* any observational consequence would also have to be true. Hence, if a theory is found to have a false observational consequence, we must conclude that one or more statements of the theory is false.

This means that theories can be conclusively falsified, through the discovery that they have false observational consequences. Some philosophers, most notably Sir Karl Popper, have taken this point to have enormous significance for our understanding of science. According to Popper, the essence of a scientific theory is that it should be *falsifiable.* That is, if the theory is false, then it must be possible to show that it is false. Now, if a theory has utterly no observational consequences, it would be extraordinarily difficult to unmask that theory as false. So, to be a genuine scientific theory, a group of statements must have observational consequences. It is important to realize that Popper is not suggesting that every good theory must be false. The difference between being falsifiable and being false is like the difference between being vulnerable and actually being hurt. A good scientific theory should not be false. Rather, it must have observational consequences that could reveal the theory as mistaken if the experiments give the wrong results.

While these ideas about theory testing may seem strange in their formal attire, they emerge quite frequently in discussions of science. They also find their way into the creation-evolution debate.

## PREDICTIVE FAILURE

From the beginning, evolutionary theory has been charged with just about every possible type of predictive failure. Critics of the theory have argued that (a) the theory makes no predictions (it is unfalsifiable and so fails Popper's criterion for science), (b) the theory makes false predictions (it is falsified), (c) the theory does not make the kinds of predictions it ought to make (the observations and experiments that evolutionary theorists undertake have no bearing on the theory). Many critics, including several Creationists, manage to advance all these objections in the same work. This is somewhat surprising, since points (a) and (b) are, of course, mutually contradictory.

The first objection is vitally important to the Creationist cause. Their opponents frequently insist that Creationism fails the crucial test for a scientific theory. The hypothesis that all kinds of organisms were separately fashioned by some "originator" is unfalsifiable. Creationists retort that they can play the same game equally well. *Any* hypothesis about the origins of life, including that advanced by evolutionary theory, is not subject to falsification. Hence we cannot justify a decision to teach evolutionary theory and not to teach Creationism by appealing to the Popperian criterion for genuine science.

The allegation that evolutionary theory fails to make any predictions is a completely predictable episode in any Creationist discussion of evolution. Often the point is made by appeal to the authority of Popper. Here are two sample passages:

> The outstanding philosopher of science, Karl Popper, though himself an evolutionist, pointed out cogently that evolution, no less than creation, is untestable and thus unprovable.

> Thus, for a theory to qualify as a scientific theory, it must be supported by events, processes or properties which can be observed, and the theory must be useful in predicting the outcome of future natural phenomena or laboratory experiments. An additional limitation usually imposed is that the theory must be capable of falsification. That is, it must be possible to conceive some experiment, the failure of which would disprove the theory.
>
> It is on the basis of such criteria that most evolutionists insist that creation be refused consideration as a possible explanation for origins. Creation has not been witnessed by human observers, it cannot be tested experimentally, and as a theory it is non-falsifiable.
>
> The general theory of evolution also fails to meet all three of these criteria, however.

These passages, and many others, draw on the picture of science sketched above. It is not clear that the Creationists really understand the philosophical views that they attempt to apply. Gish presents the most articulate discussion of the falsifiability criterion. Yet he muddles the issue by describing falsifiability as an "additional limitation" beyond predictive power. (The previous section shows that theories that make predictions are automatically falsifiable.) Nevertheless, the Creationist challenge is a serious one, and, if it could not be met, evolutionary theory would be in trouble.

Creationists buttress their charge of unfalsifiability with further objections. They are aware that biologists frequently look as though they are engaged in observations and experiments. Creationists would allow that researchers in biology sometimes make discoveries. What they deny is that the discoveries support evolutionary theory. They claim that laboratory manipulations fail to teach us about evolution in nature: "Even if modern scientists should ever actually achieve the artificial creation of life from non-life, or of higher kinds from lower kinds, in the laboratory, this would not *prove* in any way that such changes did, or even could, take place in the past by random natural processes." The standards of evidence to be applied to evolutionary biology have suddenly been raised. In this area of inquiry, it is not sufficient that a theory yield observational consequences whose truth or falsity can be decided in the laboratory. Creationists demand special kinds of predictions, and will dismiss as irrelevant any laboratory evidence that evolutionary theorists produce. [In this way, they try to defend point (c).]

Oddly enough, however, the most popular supplement to the charge that evolutionary theory is unfalsifiable is a determined effort to falsify it [point (b)]. Creationists cannot resist arguing that the theory is actually falsified. Some of them, Morris and Gish, for example, recognize the tension between the two objections. They try to paper over the problem by claiming that evolutionary theory and the Creationist account are both "models." Each "model" would "naturally" incline us to expect certain observational results. A favorite Creationist ploy is to draw up tables in which these "predictions" are compared. When we look at the tables we find that the evolutionary expectations are confounded. By contrast, the Creationist "model" leads us to anticipate features of the world that are actually there. Faced with such adverse results, the benighted evolutionary biologist is portrayed as struggling to "explain away" the findings by whatever means he can invent.

Morris's own practice of this form of evolution baiting can serve as an example. Morris constructs a table (see following page) whose function is to indicate "the predictions that would probably be made in several important categories." Morris admits magnanimously that "these primary models may be modified by secondary [additional] assumptions to fit certain conditions. For example, the basic evolution model may be extended to include harmful, as well as beneficial, mutations, but this is not a natural prediction of the basic concept of evolution." The idea that the "natural predictions" of the evolution "model" are at odds with the phenomena is used to suggest that evolutionary biologists are forced to desperate measures to protect their "faith." As Morris triumphantly concludes, "The data must be *explained* by the evolutionist, but they are *predicted* by the creationist."

The careful reader ought to be puzzled. If Morris really thinks that evolutionary theory has been falsified, why does he not say so? Of course, he would have to admit that the theory is falsifiable. Seemingly, however, a staunch Creationist should be delighted to abandon a relatively abstruse point about unfalsifiability in favor of a clear-cut refutation. The truth of the matter is that the alleged refutations fail. No evolutionary theorist will grant that (for example) the theory predicts that the fossil record should show "innumerable transitions." Instead, paleontologists will point out that we can deduce conclusions about what we should find in the rocks only if we make assumptions about the fossilization process. Morris makes highly dubious assumptions, hails them as "natural," and then announces that the "natural predictions" of the theory have been defeated.

To make a serious assessment of these broad

| Category | Evolution Model | Creation Model |
|---|---|---|
| Structure of Natural Law | Constantly changing | Invariable |
| Galactic Universe | Galaxies changing | Galaxies constant |
| Structure of Stars | Stars changing into other types | Stars unchanged |
| Other Heavenly Bodies | Building up | Breaking down |
| Types of Rock Formations | Different in different "Ages" | Similar in all "Ages" |
| Appearance of Life | Life evolving from non-life | Life only from life |
| Array of Organisms | Continuum of Organisms | Distinct Kinds of Organisms |
| Appearance of Kinds of Life | New Kinds Appearing | No New Kinds Appearing |
| Mutations in Organisms | Beneficial | Harmful |
| Natural Selection | Creative Process | Conservative Process |
| Age of Earth | Extremely Old | Probably Young |
| Fossil Record | Innumerable Transitions | Systematic Gaps |
| Appearance of Man | Ape-Human Intermediates | No Ape-Human Intermediates |
| Nature of Man | Quantitatively Superior to Animals | Qualitatively Distinct from Animals |
| Origin of Civilization | Slow and Gradual | Contemporaneous with Man |

Creationist charges, we must begin by asking some basic methodological questions. We cannot decide whether evolutionary biologists are guilty of trying to save their theory by using **ad hoc** assumptions (new and implausible claims dreamed up for the sole purpose of protecting some cherished ideas) unless we have some way of deciding when a proposal is ad hoc. Similarly, we cannot make a reasoned response to the charge that laboratory experiments are irrelevant, or to the fundamental objection that evolutionary theory is unfalsifiable, unless we have a firmer grasp of the relation between theory and evidence.

## NAIVE FALSIFICATIONISM

The time has come to tell a dreadful secret. While the picture of scientific testing sketched above continues to be influential among scientists, it has been shown to be seriously incorrect. (To give my profession its due, historians and philosophers of science have been trying to let this particular cat out of the bag for at least thirty years.) Important work in the history of science has made it increasingly clear that no major scientific theory has ever exemplified the relation between theory and evidence that the traditional model presents.

What is wrong with the old picture? Answer: Either it debars most of what we take to be science from counting as science or it allows virtually anything to count. On the traditional view of "theory," textbook cases of scientific theories turn out to be unfalsifiable. Suppose we identify Newtonian mechanics with Newton's three laws of motion plus the law of gravitation. What observational consequences can we deduce from these four statements? You might think that we could deduce that if, as the (undoubtedly apocryphal) story alleges, an apple became detached from a branch above where Newton was sitting, the apple would have fallen on his head. But this does not follow at all. To see why not, it is only necessary to recognize that the failure of this alleged prediction would not force us to deny any of the four statements of the theory. All we need do is assume that some other forces were at work that overcame the force of gravity and caused the apple to depart from its usual trajectory. So, given this simple way of applying Popper's criterion, Newtonian mechanics would be unfalsifiable. The same would go for any other scientific theory. Hence none of what we normally take to be science would count as science. (I might note that Popper is aware of this problem and has suggestions of his own as to how it should be overcome. However, what concerns me here are the *applications* of Popper's ideas, that are made by Creationists, as well as by scientists in their professional debates.)

The example of the last paragraph suggests an obvious remedy. Instead of thinking about theories in the simple way just illustrated, we might take them to be far more elaborate. Newton's laws (the three laws of motion and the law of gravitation) are *embedded* in Newtonian mechanics. They form the core of the theory, but do not constitute the whole of it. Newtonian mechanics also contains supplementary assumptions, telling us, for example, that for certain special systems the effects of forces other than gravity are negligible. This more elaborate collection of statements *does* have observational consequences and *is* falsifiable.

But the remedy fails. Imagine that we attempt to expose some self-styled spiritual teacher as an overpaid fraud. We try to point out that the teacher's central message—"Quietness is wholeness in the center of stillness"—is unfalsifiable. The teacher cheerfully admits that, taken by itself, this profound doctrine yields no observational consequences. He then points out that, by themselves, the central statements of scientific theories are also incapable of generating observational consequences. Alas, if all that is demanded is that a doctrine be embedded in a group of statements with observational consequences, our imagined guru will easily slither off the hook. He replies, "You have forgotten that my doctrine has many other claims. For example, I believe that if quietness is wholeness in the center of stillness, then flowers bloom in the spring, bees gather pollen, and blinkered defenders of so-called science raise futile objections to the world's spiritual benefactors. You will see that these three predictions are borne out by experience. Of course, there are countless others. Perhaps when you see how my central message yields so much evident truth, you will recognize the wealth of evidence behind my claim. Quietness is wholeness in the center of stillness."

More formally, the trouble is that *any* statement can be coupled with other statements to produce observational consequences. Given any doctrine *D,* and any statement *O* that records the result of an observation, we can enable *D* to "predict" *O* by adding the extra assumption, "If *D,* then *O.*" (In the example, *D* is "Quietness is wholeness in the center of stillness"; examples of *O* would be statements describing the blooming of particular flowers in the spring, the pollen gathering of specific bees, and so forth.)

The falsifiability criterion adopted from Popper—which I shall call the *naive falsificationist* criterion—is hopelessly flawed. It runs aground on a fundamental fact about the relation between theory and prediction: On their own, individual scientific laws, or the small groups of laws that are often identified as theories, do not have observational consequences. This crucial point about theories was first understood by the great historian and philosopher of science Pierre Duhem. Duhem saw clearly that individual scientific claims do not, and cannot, confront the evidence one by one. Rather, in his picturesque phrase, "Hypotheses are tested in bundles." Besides ruling out the possibility of testing an individual scientific theory (read, small group of laws), Duhem's insight has another startling consequence. We can only test relatively large bundles of claims. What this means is that when our experiments go awry we are not logically compelled to select any particular claim as the culprit. We can always save a cherished hypothesis from refutation by rejecting (however implausibly) one of the other members of the bundle. Of course, this is exactly what I did in the illustration of Newton and the apple above. Faced with disappointing results, I suggested that we could abandon the (tacit) additional claim that no large forces besides gravity were operating on the apple.

Creationists wheel out the ancient warhorse of naive falsificationism so that they can bolster their charge that evolutionary theory is not a science. The (very) brief course in deductive logic plus the whirlwind tour through naive falsificationism and its pitfalls enable us to see what is at the bottom of this seemingly important criticism. Creationists can appeal to naive falsificationism to show that evolution is not a science. But, given the traditional picture of theory and evidence I have sketched, one can appeal to naive falsificationism to show that *any* science is not a science. So, as with the charge that evolutionary change is unobservable, Creationists have again failed to find some "fault" of evolution not shared with every other science. (And, as we shall see, Creationists like some sciences, especially thermodynamics.) Consistent application of naive falsificationism can show that anybody's favorite science (whether it be quantum physics, molecular biology, or whatever) is not science. Of course, what this shows is that the naive falsificationist criterion is a very poor test of genuine science. To be fair, this point can cut both ways. Scientists who charge that "scientific" Creationism is unfalsifiable are not insulting the theory as much as they think.

## SUCCESSFUL SCIENCE

Despite the inadequacies of naive falsificationism, there is surely something right in the idea that a science can succeed only if it can fail. An invulnerable "science" would not be science at all. To achieve a more adequate understanding of how a science can succeed and how it runs the risk of failure, let us look at one of the most successful sciences and at a famous episode in its development.

Newtonian celestial mechanics is one of the star turns in the history of science. Among its numerous achievements were convincing explanations of the orbits of most of the known planets. Newton and his successors viewed the solar system as a collection of bodies subject only to gravitational interactions; they used the law of gravitation and the laws of motion to compute the orbits. (Bodies whose effects were negligible in any particular case would be disregarded. For example, the gravitational attraction due to Mercury would not be considered in working out the orbit of Saturn.) The results usually tallied beautifully with astronomical observations. But one case proved difficult. The outermost known planet, Uranus, stubbornly followed an orbit that diverged from the best computations. By the early nineteenth century it was clear that something was wrong. Either astronomers erred in treating the solar system as a Newtonian gravitational system or there was some particular difficulty in applying the general method to Uranus.

Perhaps the most naive of falsificationists would have recommended that the central claim of Newtonian mechanics — the claim that the solar system is a Newtonian gravitational system — be abandoned. But there was obviously a more sensible strategy. Astronomers faced one problematical planet, and they asked themselves what made Uranus so difficult. Two of them, John Adams and Urbain Leverrier, came up with an answer. They proposed (independently) that there was a hitherto unobserved planet beyond Uranus. They computed the orbit of the postulated planet and demonstrated that the **anomalies** of the motion of Uranus could be explained if a planet followed this path. There was a straightforward way to test their proposal. Astronomers began to look for the new planet. Within a few years, the planet — Neptune — was found.

I will extract several morals from this success story. The first concerns an issue we originally encountered in Morris's "table of natural predictions:" What is the proper use of auxiliary hypotheses? Adams and Leverrier saved the central claim of Newtonian celestial mechanics by offering an auxiliary hypothesis. They maintained that there were more things in the heavens than had been dreamed of in previous natural philosophy. The anomalies in the orbit of Uranus could be explained on the assumption of an extra planet. Adams and Leverrier worked out the exact orbit of that planet so that they could provide a detailed account of the perturbations — and so that they could tell their fellow astronomers where to look for Neptune. Thus, their auxiliary hypothesis was *independently testable*. The evidence for Neptune's existence was not just the anomalous motion of Uranus. The hypothesis could be checked independently of any assumptions about Uranus or about the correctness of Newtonian celestial mechanics — by making telescopic observations.

Since hypotheses are always tested in bundles, this method of checking presupposed other assumptions, in particular, the optical principles that justify the use of telescopes. The crucial point is that, while hypotheses are always tested in bundles, they can be tested in *different* bundles. An auxiliary hypothesis ought to be testable independently of the particular problem it is introduced to solve, independently of the theory it is designed to save.

While it is obvious in retrospect — indeed it was obvious at the time — that the problem with Uranus should not be construed as "falsifying" celestial mechanics, it is worth asking explicitly why scientists should have clung to Newton's theory in the face of this difficulty. The answer is not just that nothing succeeds like success, and that Newton's theory had been strikingly successful in calculating the orbits of the other planets. The crucial point concerns the way in which Newton's successes had been achieved. Newton was no opportunist, using one batch of assumptions to cope with Mercury, and then moving on to new devices to handle Venus. Celestial mechanics was a remarkably *unified* theory. It solved problems by invoking the same pattern of reasoning, or *problem-solving strategy,* again and again: From a specification of the positions of the bodies under study, use the law of gravitation to calculate the forces acting; from a statement of the forces acting, use the laws of dynamics to compute the equations of motion; solve the equations of motion to obtain the motions of the bodies. This single pattern of reasoning was applied in case after case to yield conclusions that were independently found to be correct.

At a higher level, celestial mechanics was itself contained in a broader theory. Newtonian physics, as a whole, was remarkably unified. It offered a strategy for solving a diverse collection of problems. Faced with *any* question about motion, the Newtonian suggestion was the same: Find the forces acting, from the forces and the laws of dynamics work out the equations of motion, and solve the equations of motion. The method was employed in a broad range of cases. The revolutions of planets, the motions of projectiles, tidal cycles and pendulum oscillations — all fell to the same problem-solving strategy.

We can draw a second moral. A science should be *unified.* A thriving science is not a gerrymandered patchwork but a coherent whole. Good theories consist of just one problem-solving strategy, or a small family of problem-solving strategies, that can be applied to a wide range of problems. The theory succeeds as it is able to encompass more and more problem areas. Failure looms when the basic problem-solving strategy (or strategies) can resolve almost none of the problems in its intended domain without the "aid" of untestable auxiliary hypotheses.

Despite the vast successes of his theory, Newton hoped for more. He envisaged a time when scientists would recognize other force laws, akin to the law of gravitation, so that other branches of physics could model themselves after celestial mechanics. In addition, he suggested that many physical questions that are not ostensibly about motion — questions about heat and about chemical combination, for example — could be reduced to problems of motion. *Principia,* Newton's masterpiece, not only offered a theory; it also advertised a program:

> I wish we could derive the rest of the phenomena of Nature by the same kind of reasoning from mechanical principles, for I am induced by many reasons to suspect that they may all depend upon certain forces by which the particles of bodies, by some causes hitherto unknown, are either mutually impelled towards one another, and cohere in regular figures, or are repelled and recede from one another. These forces being unknown, philosophers have hitherto attempted the search of Nature in vain; but I hope the principles here laid down will afford some light either to this or some truer method of philosophy.

Newton's message was clear. His own work only began the task of applying an immensely fruitful, unifying idea.

Newton's successors were moved, quite

justifiably, to extend the theory he had offered. They attempted to show how Newton's main problem-solving strategy could be applied to a broader range of physical phenomena. During the eighteenth and nineteenth centuries, the search for understanding of the forces of nature was carried into hydrodynamics, optics, chemistry, and the studies of heat, elasticity, electricity, and magnetism. Not all of these endeavors were equally successful. Nevertheless, Newton's directive fostered the rise of some important new sciences.

The final moral I want to draw from this brief look at Newtonian physics concerns *fecundity*. A great scientific theory, like Newton's, opens up new areas of research. Celestial mechanics led to the discovery of a previously unknown planet. Newtonian physics as a whole led to the development of previously unknown sciences. Because a theory presents a new way of looking at the world, it can lead us to ask new questions, and so to embark on new and fruitful lines of inquiry. Of the many flaws with the earlier picture of theories as sets of statements, none is more important than the misleading presentation of sciences as static and insular. Typically, a flourishing science is incomplete. At any time, it raises more questions than it can currently answer. But incompleteness is no vice. On the contrary, incompleteness is the mother of fecundity. Unresolved problems present challenges that enable a theory to flower in unanticipated ways. They also make the theory hostage to future developments. A good theory should be productive; it should raise new questions and presume that those questions can be answered without giving up its problem-solving strategies.

I have highlighted three characteristics of successful science. *Independent testability* is achieved when it is possible to test auxiliary hypotheses independently of the particular cases for which they are introduced. *Unification* is the result of applying a small family of problem-solving strategies to a broad class of cases. *Fecundity* grows out of incompleteness when a theory opens up new and profitable lines of investigation. Given these marks of successful science, it is easy to see how sciences can fall short, and how some doctrines can do so badly that they fail to count as science at all. A scientific theory begins to wither if some of its auxiliary assumptions can be saved from refutation only by rendering them untestable; or if its problem-solving strategies become a hodgepodge, a collection of unrelated methods, each designed for a separate recalcitrant case; or if the promise of the theory just fizzles, the few questions it raises leading only to dead ends.

When does a doctrine fail to be a science? If a doctrine fails sufficiently abjectly as a science, then it fails to be a science. Where bad science becomes egregious enough, pseudoscience begins. The example of Newtonian physics shows us how to replace the simple (and incorrect) naive falsificationist criterion with a battery of tests. Do the doctrine's problem-solving strategies encounter recurrent difficulties in a significant range of cases? Are the problem-solving strategies an opportunistic collection of unmotivated and unrelated methods? Does the doctrine have too cozy a relationship with auxiliary hypotheses, applying its strategies with claims that can be "tested" only in their applications? Does the doctrine refuse to follow up on unresolved problems, airily dismissing them as "exceptional cases"? Does the doctrine restrict the domain of its methods, forswearing excursions into new areas of investigation where embarrassing questions might arise? If all, or many, of these tests are positive, then the doctrine is not a poor scientific theory. It is not a scientific theory at all.

The account of successful science that I have given not only enables us to replace the naive falsificationist criterion with something better. It also provides a deeper understanding of how theories are justified. Predictive success is one important way in which a theory can win our acceptance. But it is not the only way. In general, theories earn their laurels by solving problems—providing answers that can be independently recognized as correct—and by their fruitfulness. Making a prediction is answering a special kind of question. The astronomers who used celestial mechanics to predict the motion of Mars were answering the question of where Mars would be found. Yet, very frequently, our questions do not concern *what* occurs, but *why* it occurs. We already know that something happens and we want an explanation. Science offers us explanations by setting the phenomena within a unified framework. Using a widely applicable problem-solving strategy, together with independently confirmed auxiliary hypotheses, scientists show that what happened was to be expected. It was known before Newton that the orbits of the planets are approximately elliptical. One of the great achievements of Newton's celestial mechanics was to apply its problem-solving strategy to deduce that the orbit of any planet will be approximately elliptical, thereby explaining the shape of the orbits. In general, science is at least as concerned with reducing the number of unexplained phenomena as it is with generating correct predictions.

The most global Creationist attack on evolutionary theory is the claim that evolution is not a science. If this claim were correct, then the dispute about what to teach in high school science classes would be over. In earlier parts of this chapter, we saw how Creationists were able to launch their broad criticisms. If one accepts the idea that science requires proof, or if one adopts the naive falsificationist criterion, then the theory of evolution — and every other scientific theory — will turn out not to be a part of science. So Creationist standards for science imply that there is no science to be taught.

However, we have seen that Creationist standards rest on a very poor understanding of science. In light of a clearer picture of the scientific enterprise, I have provided a more realistic group of tests for good science, bad science, and pseudoscience. Using this more sophisticated approach, I now want to address seriously the global Creationist questions about the theory of evolution. Is it a pseudoscience? Is it a poor science? Or is it a great science? These are very important questions, for the appropriateness of granting equal time to Creation "science" depends, in part, on whether it can be regarded as the equal of the theory of evolution.

## DARWIN'S DARING

The heart of Darwinian evolutionary theory is a family of problem-solving strategies, related by their common employment of a particular style of historical narrative. A *Darwinian history* is a piece of reasoning of the following general form. The first step consists in a description of an ancestral population of organisms. The reasoning proceeds by tracing the modification of the population through subsequent generations, showing how characteristics were selected, inherited, and became prevalent. ( . . . Natural selection is taken to be the primary — but not the only — force of evolutionary change.)

Reasoning like this can be used to answer a host of biological questions. Suppose that we want to know why a contemporary species manifests a particular trait. We can answer that question by supplying a Darwinian history that describes the emergence of that trait. Equally, we can use Darwinian histories to answer questions about relationships among groups of organisms. One way to explain why two species share a common feature is to trace their descent from a common ancestor. Questions of biogeography can be addressed in a similar way. We can explain why we find contemporary organisms where we do by following the course of their historical modifications and migrations. Finally, we can tackle problems about extinction by showing how characteristics that had enabled organisms to thrive were no longer advantageous when the environment (or the competition) changed. In all these cases, we find related strategies for solving problems. The history of the development of populations, understood in terms of variation, competition, selection, and inheritance, is used to shed light on broad classes of biological phenomena.

The questions that evolutionary theory has addressed are so numerous that any sample is bound to omit important types. The following short selection undoubtedly reflects the idiosyncrasy of my interests: Why do orchids have such intricate internal structures? Why are male birds of paradise so brightly colored? Why do some reptilian precursors of mammals have enormous "sails" on their backs? Why do bats typically roost upside down? Why are the hemoglobins of humans and apes so similar? Why are there no marsupial analogues of seals and whales? Why is the mammalian fauna of Madagascar so distinctive? Why did the large, carnivorous ground birds of South America become extinct? Why is the sex ratio in most species one to one (although it is markedly different in some species of insects)? Answers to these questions, employing Darwinian histories, can be found in works written by contemporary Darwinian biologists. Those works contain answers to a myriad of other questions of the same general types. Darwinian histories are constructed again and again to illuminate the characteristics of contemporary organisms, to account for the similarities and differences among species, to explain why the forms preserved in the fossil record emerged and became extinct, to cast light on the geographical distribution of animals and plants.

We can see the theory in action by taking a brief look at one of these examples. The island of Madagascar, off the east coast of Africa, supports a peculiar group of mammals. Many of these mammals are endemic. Among them is a group of relatively small insectivorous mammals, the *tenrecs*. All tenrecs share certain features that mark them out as relatively primitive mammals. They have very poor vision, their excretory system is rudimentary, the testes in the male are carried within the body, their capacity for regulating their body temperature is poor compared with that of most mammals. Yet, on their simple and rudimentary body plan, specialized characteristics have often been imposed. Some tenrecs have the hedgehog's method of defense. Others have the forelimbs characteristic of moles. There are climbing tenrecs that resemble the shrews, and there are tenrecs that defend themselves by attempting to stick their quills into a would-be predator. Hedgehogs, moles, tree shrews, and porcupines do not inhabit Madagascar. But they seem to have their imitators. (These are examples of convergent evolution, cases in which unrelated organisms take on some of the same characteristics.) Why are these peculiar animals found on Madagascar, and nowhere else?

A straightforward evolutionary story makes sense of what we observe. In the late Mesozoic or early Cenozoic, small, primitive, insectivorous mammals rafted across the Mozambique channel and colonized Madagascar. Later the channel widened and Madagascar became inaccessible to the more advanced mammals that evolved on the mainland. Hence the early colonists developed without competition from advanced mainland forms and without pressure from many of the normal predators who make life difficult for small mammals. The tenrecs have been relatively protected. In the absence of rigorous competition, they have preserved their simple body plan, and they have exploited unoccupied niches, which are filled elsewhere by more advanced creatures. Tenrecs have gone up the trees and burrowed in the ground because those are good ways to make a living and because they have had nobody but one another to contend with.

The same kind of story can be told again and again to answer all sorts of questions about all sorts of living things. Evolutionary theory is unified because so many diverse questions—questions as various as those I listed—can be addressed by advancing Darwinian histories. Moreover, these narratives constantly make claims that are subject to independent check. Here are four examples from the case of the triumphant tenrecs. (1) The explanation presupposes that Madagascar has drifted away from the east coast of Africa. That is something that can be checked by using geological criteria for the movement of landmasses, criteria that are independent of biology. (2) The account claims that the tenrecs would have been able to raft across the Mozambique channel, but that the present channel constitutes a barrier to more advanced mammals (small rodents). These claims could be tested by looking to see whether the animals in question can disperse across channels of the appropriate sizes. (3) The narrative assumes that the specialized methods of defense offered advantages against the predators that were present in Madagascar. Studies of animal interactions can test whether the particular defenses are effective against local predators. (4) Central to the explanatory account is the thesis that the tenrecs are related. If this is so, then studies of the minute details of tenrec anatomy should reveal many common features, and the structures of proteins ought to be similar. In particular, the tenrecs ought to be much more like one another than they are like hedgehogs, shrews, or moles.

Looking at one example, or even at a small number of examples, does not really convey the strength of evolutionary theory. The same patterns of reasoning can be applied again and again, in book after book, monograph after monograph, article after article. Yet the particular successes in dealing with details of natural history, numerous though they are, do not exhaust the accomplishments of the theory. Darwin's original theory — the problem-solving strategies advanced in the *Origin,* which are, in essence, those just described — gave rise to important new areas of scientific investigation. Evolutionary theory has been remarkably fruitful.

Darwin not only provided a scheme for unifying the diversity of life. He also gave a structure to our ignorance. After Darwin, it was important to resolve general issues about the presuppositions of Darwinian histories. The way in which biology should proceed had been made admirably plain, and it was clear that biologists had to tackle questions for which they had, as yet, no answers. How do new characteristics arise in populations? What are the mechanisms of inheritance? How do characteristics become fixed in populations? What criteria decide when a characteristic confers some advantage on its possessor? What interactions among populations of organisms affect the adaptive value of characteristics? With respect to all of these questions, Darwin was forced to confess ignorance. By raising them, his theory pointed the way to its further articulation.

Since Darwin's day, biologists have contributed parts of evolutionary theory that help to answer these important questions. Geneticists have advanced our understanding of the transmission of characteristics between generations and have enabled us to see how new characteristics can arise. Population geneticists have analyzed the variation present in populations of organisms; they have suggested how that variation is maintained and have specified ways in which characteristics can be fixed or eliminated. Workers in morphology and physiology have helped us to see how variations of particular kinds might yield advantages in particular environments. Ecologists have studied the ways in which interactions among populations can affect survival and fecundity.

The moral is obvious. Darwin gambled. He trusted that the questions he left open would be answered by independent biological sciences and that the deliverances of these sciences would be consistent with the presuppositions of Darwinian histories. Because of the breadth of his vision, Darwin made his theory vulnerable from a number of different directions. To take just one example, it could have turned out the mechanisms of heredity would have made it impossible for advantageous variations to be preserved and to spread. Indeed, earlier in this century, many biologists felt that the emerging views about inheritance did not fit into Darwin's picture, and the fortunes of Darwinian evolutionary theory were on the wane.

When we look at the last 120 years of the history of biology, it is impossible to ignore the fecundity of Darwin's ideas. Not only have inquiries into the presuppositions of Darwinian histories yielded new theoretical disciplines (like population genetics), but the problem-solving strategies have been extended to cover phenomena that initially appeared troublesome. One recent triumph has been the development of explanations for social interactions among animals. Behavior involving one animal's promotion of the good of others seems initially to pose a problem for evolutionary theory. How can we construct Darwinian histories for the emergence of such behavior? W. D. Hamilton's concept of inclusive fitness, and the deployment of game-theoretic ideas by R. L. Trivers and John Maynard Smith, revealed how the difficulty could be resolved by a clever extension of traditional Darwinian concepts.

Yet puzzles remain. One problem is the existence of sex. When an organism forms gametes (sperm cells or egg cells) there is a meiotic division, so that in sexual reproduction only half of an organism's genes are transmitted to each of its progeny. Because of this "cost of meiosis," it is hard to see how genotypes for sexual reproduction might have become prevalent. (Apparently, they will spread only half as fast as their asexual rivals.) So why is there sex? We do not have a compelling answer to the question. Despite some ingenious suggestions by orthodox Darwinians, there is no convincing Darwinian history for the emergence of sexual reproduction. However, evolutionary theorists believe that the problem will be solved without abandoning the main Darwinian insights—just as early nineteenth-century astronomers believed that the problem of the motion of Uranus could be overcome without major modification of Newton's celestial mechanics.

The comparison is apt. Like Newton's physics in 1800, evolutionary theory today rests on a huge record of successes. In both cases, we find a unified theory whose problem-solving strategies are applied to illuminate a host of diverse phenomena. Both theories offer problem solutions that can be subjected to rigorous independent checks. Both open up new lines of inquiry and have a history of surmounting apparent obstacles. The virtues of successful science are clearly displayed in both.

There is a simple way to put the point. Darwin is the Newton of biology. Evolutionary theory is not simply an area of science that has had some success at solving problems. It has unified biology and it has inspired important biological disciplines. Darwin himself appreciated the unification achieved by his theory and its promise of further development. Over a century later, at the beginning of his authoritative account of current views of species and their origins, Ernst Mayr explained how that promise had been fulfilled: "The theory of evolution is quite rightly called the greatest unifying theory in biology. The diversity of organisms, similarities and differences between kinds of organisms, patterns of distribution and behavior, adaptation and interaction, all this was merely a bewildering chaos of facts until given meaning by the evolutionary theory." Dobzhansky put the point even more concisely: "Nothing in biology makes sense except in the light of evolution."

# Part 2 — Glossary

**A priori** Reasoning or knowledge based upon it is a priori if it is logically independent of (logically "prior" to) experience. It is usually opposed to a posteriori, which applies to reasoning or knowledge whose basis is our experience of the world. Hume draws the a priori–a posteriori distinction in terms of "relations of ideas" versus "matters of fact." For Hume, a priori (relations of ideas) reasoning is limited to the demonstration of **analytic** propositions (see Part 1 glossary) and the propositions of mathematics.

**Ad hoc** An addition to or adjustment of a theory or hypothesis is ad hoc if it is done just to take care of a particular problem the theory or hypothesis is unable to deal with and if it has no independent support or verification.

**Anomaly** An anomaly is an experimental result or observation that is not in accordance with theoretical predictions. The point of calling such data anomalous or recalcitrant is to indicate that it is insufficient to overthrow the theory and is treated by practicing scientists as a problem to be eventually solved within the existing theoretical framework.

**Deduction** Philosophers use the term *deduction* to refer to an argument that possesses deductive validity (see entry below). It is usually opposed to **induction** (see Part 1 glossary).

**Deductive validity** An argument (or piece of reasoning) possesses deductive validity if the following is true of it: If all of its premises (or statements used to support the reasoning) were true, the truth of its conclusion (the statement supported by the reasoning) would be guaranteed. That is, the truth of the premises of a valid deductive argument makes it logically impossible for the conclusion to be false — truth of premises and falsity of conclusion are contradictory.

**Empirical** A proposition or knowledge claim is empirical if it is about the experienced world or if its truth depends upon facts about the world that could be otherwise without changing the meanings of any of our concepts. It is frequently opposed to **a priori** (see earlier entry in this glossary).

**Empiricist** See Part 1 glossary.

**Epistemology** See Part 1 glossary.

**Formal reality** Descartes uses the term *formal reality* to characterize, roughly, the actual reality that must be in a cause in order to account for its effects. When contrasted with *eminent* the distinction is between reality that is actual and apparent (eminent) as opposed to actual but obscure or hidden (formal). Descartes argues that there must be as much actual reality (formally or eminently present) in the cause of an idea as there is **objective reality** (see **objective reality** in this glossary) in the idea itself.

**Inductive** Argument or reasoning is inductive when it has this property: If its premises were all true, the truth of its conclusion would be likely or probable but would not be guaranteed. In an inductive argument, the truth of the premises supports, but does not guarantee, the truth of the conclusion. **Inductive** is contrasted with **deductive** (see **deductive validity** in this glossary).

**Metaphysics** See Part 1 glossary.

**Objective reality** Descartes uses the term *objective reality* to characterize the kind of reality that belongs to an idea by virtue of the kind of object it is an idea of. He claims that there must be at least as much **formal reality** (see earlier entry in this glossary) in the cause of an idea as there is objective reality in the idea itself.

**Observational consequence** A particular observable event or experimental finding is an observational consequence of a theory if it can be deduced from that theory and other known facts. (See **deduction** and **deductive validity** in this glossary.)

**Probabilism** Probabilism is the view that observations and experimental evidence support scientific theories not by demonstrating their truth but by making their truth probable. The more supporting evidence there is, the higher is the probability that the supported theory is true.

**Rationalist** A rationalist is a philosopher who believes that there are truths about the world that can be known by reason alone, without the intervention of sense experience. The classical rationalists believed in the existence of innate ideas and maintained that absolute certainty was the hallmark of knowledge. (See the introduction to the first section of this part, "Doubt and Certainty.") Rationalists are contrasted with empiricists (see Part 1 glossary).

**Scepticism** Scepticism is the radical view that, contrary to common sense, we know nothing or almost nothing. (See the general introduction to this part for a detailed discussion.)

# *Part 2 — Study Questions*

## *DOUBT AND CERTAINTY*

1. If Descartes is correct, we cannot know anything about the real world without a divine guarantee against scepticism. Locke, Hume, and Russell provide various empiricist responses to that challenge. Compare and contrast their responses. Do any of them show that Descartes was incorrect? Why or why not?
2. Descartes argues that we could not have produced the idea of God from our own mental resources. Hume finds no difficulty in doing so and argues that all ideas can be produced by mental operations on the resources put into the mind by the senses. Descartes and Hume can't both be right. Has Hume really done what Descartes said was impossible? If not, why not? If so, why do you think Descartes thought something that gave Hume so little trouble was not just difficult but impossible?
3. Descartes says that for all we know we might be dreaming right now. Austin and Malcolm claim that that's plainly false. Are they arguing about the same thing? Who is right and why do you think so?
4. Russell argues that we can't see or touch things like tables and chairs—in fact, that none of our senses put us in contact with ordinary material objects. Try to construct the argument for one of the senses Russell doesn't consider carefully: hearing, taste, or smell. Does the argument really work? Why does Russell nonetheless think that we can know things about material objects and the real world on the basis of sense experience?
5. Lehrer argues that Cartesian scepticism emerges victorious from all the philosophical attempts to refute it. Explain exactly how the strategies used by Austin and Malcolm fail to refute the sceptic, according to Lehrer.

## *JUSTIFIED BELIEF AND SCIENTIFIC METHOD*

1. Neither Popper nor Lakatos believes that observing a number of stones dropped from a tower and measuring the accelerations, velocities, and times involved provide much in the way of confirmation for Newtonian mechanics. Explain why in each case. What would serve to confirm the theory for Popper? for Lakatos?
2. Popper, Lakatos, and Kitcher each explain

what would make a theory pseudoscientific. Compare and contrast the three explanations.

3. Quine and Ullian give five criteria for successful scientific hypotheses. Kitcher gives three. How do the two sets of criteria fit together? That is, do Quine and Ullian place any requirements on hypotheses or theories that Kitcher does not, or do some of Kitcher's criteria include more than one of the criteria suggested by Quine and Ullian?

# Part 2 — Suggestions for Further Reading

Some of these readings may be too difficult for many introductory students. Consult your instructor for assistance in selecting from this list or for further suggestions to make sure that additional material is well suited to your interests and abilities.

## *DOUBT AND CERTAINTY*

1. Armstrong, D. M., *Perception and the Physical World* (Humanities Press, 1961).
2. Ayer, A. J., *The Problem of Knowledge* (Penguin Books, 1956).
3. Berkeley, George, *Berkeley: Principles, Dialogues and Correspondence* (Bobbs-Merrill, 1965).
4. Chisholm, R. M., *Theory of Knowledge* (Prentice-Hall, 1966).
5. Lehrer, Keith, *Knowledge* (Oxford U. Press, 1979).
6. Lewis, C. I., *Mind and the World Order* (Dover Books, 1956).
7. Malcolm, Norman, *Knowledge and Certainty* (Prentice-Hall, 1963).
8. Moore, G. E., *Philosophical Papers* (Collier Books, 1962).
9. Russell, Bertrand, *The Problems of Philosophy* (Oxford U. Press, 1959).
10. Unger, Peter, *Ignorance* (Oxford U. Press, 1975).

## *JUSTIFIED BELIEF AND SCIENTIFIC METHOD*

11. Feyerabend, Paul, *Against Method* (Schocken, 1978).
12. Hanson, N. R., *Patterns of Discovery* (Cambridge U. Press, 1958).
13. Hempel, Carl, *Philosophy of Natural Science* (Prentice-Hall, 1966).
14. Kuhn, Thomas, *The Structure of Scientific Revolutions* (Univ. of Chicago Press, 1970).
15. Lakatos, Imre, *The Methodology of Scientific Research Programmes* (Cambridge Univ. Press, 1977).
16. Popper, Karl, *Conjectures and Refutations* (Basic Books, 1962).
17. Quine, W. V. O. and Ullian, J. S., *The Web of Belief* (Random House, 1978).
18. Scheffler, Israel, *The Anatomy of Inquiry* (Knopf, 1963).

# PERSONS AND COMPUTERS

3

Both Parts 3 and 4 deal with topics included in philosophy of mind and involve an important shift from Part 2 in the kinds of issues raised and questions asked. It will be useful for you to keep this shift in mind. The shift is from epistemology to metaphysics, that is, from questions about what we can know and how we can know it to questions about the nature of things and how things behave or function. Human beings or persons are the focus of these two parts. In this part we will investigate the apparently dual nature of human beings, and the extent to which human mental functioning is similar to the functioning of digital computers. In Part 4 we will raise the question of whether or not human behavior is ever free or voluntary, and look at some of the implications of various answers to that question.

The nature of human beings certainly appears to be of two kinds. On the one hand we can be correctly described as thinking about the Pythagorean theorem, wondering whether Chicago will ever win another pennant, or hoping that there will be snow on the ground for Christmas. On the other hand we can equally well be described as taller than our parents, ten pounds overweight, or within three miles of Cincinnati. These latter descriptions are just the sort that typically apply to material objects, things that occupy space—height, weight, and spatial location. But the former descriptions seem to be quite different in kind. They typically apply to beings that are conscious, beings that have experiences—thinking, wondering, and hoping. So it seems to be natural to think of ourselves as composed of two different kinds of things: a material body whose nature is to occupy space and an immaterial mind whose nature is to be conscious.

This view that we are a composite of immaterial mind or soul and material body is as old as philosophy. In *Crito,* Plato has Socrates, who is about to die, giving thanks to the gods that he is about to be free of the physical part of himself. Most religious beliefs in immortality rest on the notion of an immaterial conscious self that survives the death of the body. For Descartes it was perfectly clear that persons consist of two different things or substances: the mind whose essential nature is to be conscious (''thinking'') and immaterial (''nonextended''), and the body whose essential nature is to be material (''extended'') and nonconscious. If we could drop the matter at this point, it looks as though everything would be in order. Common sense seems to lead us to the two natures view of human beings and this coincides with religious and (some) philosophical opinion on the matter. As you know from the introduction to Part 1 and your reading thus far, however, philosophers almost never just let the matter drop. And as soon as we start to think carefully about what is involved in being composed of two entirely different, in fact opposite, sorts of things, a number of very difficult questions arise. How are the two parts of us connected? Do they interact with each other? If so, how is such interaction conceivable? Is the notion of an immaterial thing even a coherent notion? Do we need an immaterial mind in order to account adequately for the mental facts of human life? Are there really any mental facts of human life? Are there really any mental facts of life to account for in the first place? All together, such questions make up what philosophers refer to as "the mind-body problem." And somewhere in the history of philosophy, almost every answer conceivable has been suggested as the appropriate response to each of the questions above.

The first five subsections of this part are devoted to the mind-body problem and represent five different approaches to its solution. In fact, several of them are further divided into two different subapproaches. Even so, this collection by no means exhausts the ways in which the problem has been approached. We have tried to represent the most popular and most important views on the mind-body problem. What follows is a brief overview of the approaches illustrated in the readings. A more detailed account is provided in the individual introductions to the five subsections.

Let's suppose that Descartes and a lot of other people were at least approximately correct about our natural makeup, that we are part mental and part physical. How are the parts connected? When we burn some part of our body, we immediately have the conscious experience of pain. When we stand facing a sunset with eyes open we are conscious of beautiful colors. When we make the conscious decision to raise our arms, our arms usually go up. When we have the experience of extreme fear or terror our legs begin to tremble and our palms perspire. We don't think of any of these pairs of events as coincidences. The natural interpretation is that each pair is a case of cause and effect. Burning the body causes the experience of pain. Light striking the retinas causes visual experience. The intention to raise the arm causes it to go up. Terror makes our legs tremble and our palms perspire. So the verdict of common sense seems to be that, of course, mind and body are connected—they are causally connected. Things that happen to the body cause mental states and processes to occur. And certain mental states and processes give rise to changes in or movements of our bodies.

Descartes was inclined to accept this verdict. He was also inclined to view such causal interaction as rationally incomprehensible, not an easy view for a rationalist. How can we conceive of things essentially opposite in nature, that is, with absolutely nothing in common, as causally connected? We know what sorts of things typically cause material objects to change from motionless to moving or to suddenly change direction. These changes are accomplished by physically pushing or pulling, by sudden impact with another object, or by removing physical support. But what would it be like to accomplish the same effect by means of an immaterial object? How does an immaterial object push, pull, strike, or otherwise affect a material object so as to make it move? Or, from the other side, how can doing something to a material object cause changes in an immaterial object that is somehow associated with it? These are some of the questions that have to be answered if one explains human behavior and experience in terms of two distinct and essentially separate substances—mind and body. Any theory of human nature that is committed to this dual substance view of persons is a version of dualism. There are several different versions of dualism, each involving a different answer to the question of just how the two substances are related to each other. These are discussed in some detail in the introduction to the subsection on dualism.

The questions of the preceding paragraph do not exhaust the difficult or potentially embarrassing questions a dualist must try to answer. They are, however, enough to give you a good idea of the strong motivation philosophers have felt to explain human nature in nondualistic terms. The most obvious alternative to dualism has been to try to avoid the most troublesome of the two substances, namely, the mind. Theories that maintain that all there really is to a person is a material body with its complicated organization and its material (physiological) states and processes are versions of materialism. Materialism has a number of immediate advantages. Because all the states and processes of a human being are viewed as physical, their nature and the existence of causal relations between them are no more mysterious than the rest of physical science (physics, chemistry, biology, physiology). Because materialism seems to make possible a unified physical science of the entire universe as opposed to dualism, which requires both the physical and mental sciences, it makes scientific theory as a whole simpler and, therefore, preferable to dualism (according to the methodological criterion of theoretical simplicity). In addition, materialism makes sense of some of our ordinary or common sense intuitions about the mental that dualism seems to miss. As Descartes noted, our minds seem to be more intimately related to our bodies than even a captain is to his or her ship. The captain is *in* the ship. But the mind is not in space at all; it is just not that kind of thing according to dualism. So it couldn't literally be in the body according to the two substances view. Materialism, on the other hand, can capture a relation more intimate even than spatial inclusion and causal connection. Since all of a person is physical, the conscious part is not just causally connected to and in the body; it is literally part of the body, and perhaps not even a distinct or distinguishable part.

So materialism has a number of advantages over dualism, and is held in some form by many philosophers today. But there are also some serious difficulties for this view of human beings. The materialist must give a plausible account of all of the introspective evidence for the existence of mental states and processes that do not appear to have anything in common with the states and processes the physiologist studies. The anger we feel, the visual images we can examine in great detail as conscious subjects, the thoughts and decisions that seem to us to guide much of our voluntary behavior—all of these are data that the materialist must either account for or explain away in strictly material terms. Plausible explanations of the required kind have not proven easy to come by. In addition, the less radical version of materialism has been alleged to be so conceptually flawed as to make it an untenable theory, and the more radical version alleged to be so counterintuitive as to make it an implausible theory at best. The two versions of materialism, along with their strengths and weaknesses, are discussed at some length in the introduction to the subsection on materialism.

Some philosophers have proposed a double aspect account of human beings as an alternative both to double substance or dualistic accounts and to materialism. They claim that we are not just material bodies with the illusory belief that we possess immaterial minds or souls, nor are we material bodies and immaterial minds or souls somehow connected. We are, instead, unique substances, unlike material objects not because we are part immaterial objects, but rather because we are a different sort of thing altogether. To be a person is to be a unique kind of thing, namely, the kind of thing that can have both mental and physical aspects or properties. This theory seems to avoid all of the difficulties of the previous views. There is no mystery about the relation of the mental and the physical; they are both properties of a single substance, a person. And the fact that persons can have radically different aspects or properties is not so troublesome. We are familiar with many things that have properties of radically different kinds. For example, there are cars that have the properties of weighing less than two tons, carrying five people comfortably, and being my favorite color—and those properties don't seem to have much in common. So we shouldn't be concerned to find that persons can support aspects or properties of very different kinds. The theory also avoids the difficulties of materialism. Mental states and processes are real and mental, but they aren't states or processes of immaterial minds, they are states and processes of persons.

One of the main reasons for dissatisfaction with double aspect theories is their **ad hoc** character. They are produced solely in response to particular problems and have little in the way of independent evidence in their favor. This is at least a reason to be suspicious. Such theories also have some more specific flaws that are discussed in the introduction to the subsection on double aspect theories.

Behaviorism suggests a way around the problems of dualism which is somewhat different from materialism as discussed above. Behaviorists argue that talk of mental states and processes can be eliminated, not in favor of talk about physiological states and processes, but rather in favor of causal correlations between environmental stimuli and behavioral responses or dispositions to respond. The idea, from the point of view of science, is that as long as there is a rigid causal sequence of stimulus, internal event, and response, the internal event, whether physiological or psychical, can be ignored. Since it isn't available for scientific observation and doesn't make any difference, it simply shouldn't count in the scientific story of human behavior. From a logical point of view, we can draw much the same conclusion. Since we learn the meanings of the mental concepts through exposure to environmental situations and behavioral responses to those situations, there can't be anything in the meaning or use of such concepts that requires us to think of them as picking out unobservable states or processes of an immaterial entity. So, from the logical as from the scientific point of view, talk of mental entities seems to reduce to talk of circumstances and behavior or behavioral dispositions. Of course the thrust of behaviorism is in the direction of materialism. It wouldn't be important to show that we can do justice to all of the mental facts of human life while avoiding reference to immaterial minds and mental states and processes, unless we thought there was a clear advantage to being committed to the existence of a material world of things, organisms and their behavior, and nothing more—that is, a world of material things that differed one from another only in degree of complexity and not in terms of their substantial basis.

As a methodology in the science of psychology, behaviorism was a dominant force in this country for many years. It has, however, lost its hold on psychology and been replaced by a different set of working assumptions. Briefly, it seems to be the case that the regularities of human behavior depend, not upon the physical qualities of the environmental stimulus, but upon the environment as mentally interpreted by human beings. And, correlatively, the behavioral responses that need to be treated as similar by the psychologist seem to be grouped, not by their physical properties but by their role in the intentions and purposes of the human beings whose behavior they are. And so psychology has been forced to reintroduce into its theoretical framework those mental states and processes that behaviorism had eliminated.

Behaviorism as a theory about the meanings of mental concepts also lost popularity for two basic but connected reasons. First, there were some mental concepts that seemed to resist analysis in terms of behavior and behavioral dispositions. For example, thinking of the Pythagorean theorem does not seem to involve a cause from the environment, another mental event, or even typical behavioral dispositions. Secondly, the functional approach associated with a new psychological paradigm based on computer information processing seemed to leave no need for the behaviorist approach—as we shall see.

Functionalism appears to be an almost magical way out of the mind-body problem. It claims to give us a way to understand the mental which is compatible with some form of each view on the mind-body problem discussed thus far except behaviorism. Functionalism arose from developments in psychology and a number of related areas that are now collectively known as "cognitive science." The central idea is that types of mental states and processes are to be identified in terms of their causal role in the mental life of an organism. Unlike behaviorism, the theory is not reductive. Mental states and processes do not drop out of scientific or philosophical accounts that are functionalist in nature. In fact the causal role of any type of mental state is likely to involve causal connections with other mental states as well as with environmental causes and behavioral effects. What makes functionalism independent of, and hence compatible with, both dualism and materialism is that its characterization of the mental states and processes of anything is independent of the stuff out of which the thing is made.

For example, the belief that my car is green is to be characterized functionally in terms of its causal connections to certain stimuli, certain types of behavior, and other beliefs. It is the sort of mental state that would typically be produced by things like seeing my car under conditions that vividly brought out its color. It is the sort of mental state that would cause me to say "That's not my car" when the parking attendant brings me a car that looks identical to mine except for its color. It is also a state that would give rise to the belief that some cars are green. And it is a state that could be produced by the beliefs that my car is in the driveway and that the car in the driveway is green. Of course these are just a few of the connections that would tend to identify the functional role of that particular belief. But the point is that a state which played that causal role would be that same mental state regardless of what it was a state of. So Martians or robots could have that mental state as long as some state of them had the same functional role or causal connections in their ongoing activities. And, by the same token, my mental state could, from the functional standpoint, equally well turn out to be a state of an immaterial mind or a state of the central nervous system of a body. At the level of abstraction of functionalism and current cognitive science, the underlying stuff drops out as irrelevant. Mental states and processes are understood and explained in terms of their functional roles, and the medium in which those states and processes are realized just has no part to play.

As a matter of fact, most functionalists suspect that central state materialism will turn out to be correct, that is, that only states of the brain will turn out to have the functional properties that define mental states. But the tremendous advantage of functionalism is that, given its understanding of mental states, the truth of materialism won't make mental states any less real and won't reduce psychology to physical science.

Artificial intelligence (AI for short) is the name given to the branch of cognitive science that attempts to program digital computers to produce intelligent behavior. Developments in this field have produced heated debate among both philosophers and scientists over the actual and potential mentality of computing machines. Some of that debate is illustrated in the readings for the second section of this part. To understand what all the excitement is about, we will need to take a closer look at cognitive science.

In the discussion of functionalism above we said that cognitive science consisted of psychology and a number of related disciplines. Those related disciplines include philosophy, computer science, and linguistics. But we should be much more precise. Cognitive science includes only a part of what has been included in each of these disciplines; in particular, it includes those parts that study mental states and processes under two methodological constraints or assumptions. The first of these is that mental states are **representational**—that is, that mental states consist in part of representations of the states of affairs they "contain." For example, under this assumption, the mental state that is the belief that my car is green will contain a representation of my car as green. This mental state will have something in common with the wish that my car were green; namely, they will have the same representational content. They will differ in terms of the relation I bear to that representation, believing in one case, wishing in the other. And the belief that my car is green will differ from the belief that my car is red or that your car is green by virtue of the different state of affairs represented in each case, that is, by differences in representational content. The second constraint or assumption of cognitive science is that mental processes are **computational** processes on representations with access to only the formal properties of the representations. A process is computational, roughly speaking, if it consists of discrete, rule-governed changes in the state of a system. The formal properties of a representation are those properties that are independent of its interpretation. Formal in this sense is roughly equivalent to nonsemantic. The formal properties of a representation are those it has just as a symbol or system of symbols and independent of its symbolizing anything. So what the representation means or represents or refers to and whether or not it represents accurately—that is, the semantic notions of meaning, reference, and truth—are completely irrelevant from the formal standpoint.

An example of a process that would satisfy all the conditions of this second constraint or assumption would be that of putting a collection of words into alphabetical order. This could be accomplished by putting twenty-six numbered bins in numerical order, treating the words as strings of symbols, and performing the following operations upon them. First, using a rule that associates *a* with 1, *b* with 2, *c* with 3, and so on, put each symbol string into the appropriate bin by checking the first symbol of the string only. Then for each of the twenty-six bins, arrange twenty-six additional bins in the same way and treat the symbol strings in the initial bin exactly as all the strings were initially treated, except that this time only the second symbol of each string will be used. Repeat the same entire process for each of these new bins with newer bins and the third symbol of each string, and so on. When the point is reached at which each of the bins—and there could be very many of them given a large collection of words of the right sort at the start of the process—contains at most one symbol string, all of the words will be in alphabetical order. The important thing is that this operation can be correctly performed just in terms of the shapes of the symbols (their formal properties) and does not involve any use of the facts that the symbol strings can be interpreted as English words; that the individual symbols are letters of the alphabet; that some of the strings are associated with particular concepts, used to refer to certain objects, used to produce true or false propositions, or anything of the kind. The semantic properties of the representations are irrelevant, only the formal properties figure in the process in any way.

There is a large group of entities whose states are defined in terms of the formal properties of symbolic representations and whose processes are computational operations on those symbols—namely, digital computers. The fundamental thesis of cognitive science is that human mentality shares these same features. Or, to put the same point another way, cognition is the same thing everywhere, namely, representational and computational. It differs from human to machine to alien being or whatever only in terms of the material or stuff in which the formally defined states and processes are realized.

If this thesis is correct, there are important implications. For one thing, it means that the project to which the field of artificial intelligence is dedicated is not only possible but an incredibly powerful research opportunity for the cognitive sciences as a whole. Our scientific understanding of human cognitive functions based largely on introspective reports of the processes involved in reasoning, understanding, and so on hasn't gotten very far. The mysteries of the mental seem to resist introspection. This was one of the major attractions of scientific behaviorism—it allowed those mysteries to be ignored entirely. Unfortunately it also failed to capture most of the real connections between intelligent behavior and its environmental causes, and was abandoned as a result. But if the mental can be duplicated by a digital computer, our understanding of how the computer functions suddenly begins to look like the key to solving the mysteries of human cognition. If we can program the computer to match the input and output of human intelligence, then what goes on computationally between the two in the computer will provide at least a working hypothesis for understanding the cognitive processes of human beings. And if we could produce not just the simulation but the functional equivalent of intelligent behavior in a digital computer, the program of the computer would be virtually a psychological theory of the human cognitive process.

For another thing, it looks as though AI provides a way finally to lay the traditional mind-body problem to rest. If the digital computer possesses mentality by virtue of nothing more immaterial than program-directed manipulations of a physical symbol system, it would mean that human mental life could be explained in terms of the manipulation of a physical symbol system in the brain in much the same fashion. The mind-body problem for humans would thus reduce to the software-hardware problem for digital computers, and that just doesn't seem terribly problematic.

Of course, the above preview of the possible payoffs of complete success in artificial intelligence research is very brief and superficial. But it should give you some idea of how high the stakes are both scientifically and philosophically. The introduction to the second section of this part furnishes additional details. The readings illustrate the basic positions of the parties to the current debate over AI's prospects for success. Some feel that it's just too soon to say how things will turn out. Others are quite sure that it's already possible to read the handwriting on the wall. As the selections in this section indicate, however, there are strong differences of opinion about what that handwriting says.

# Minds and Bodies

## Dualism

Dualism is the name given to any theory which holds that human beings are composed of two distinct substances, mind and body. Versions of dualism differ in the relations they claim to exist between the two substances. The two versions illustrated by the readings in this subsection hold that the relation must be causal in nature. These are the two most widely held versions of dualism, **interactionism** and **epiphenomenalism.** But there have been versions of dualism that allowed no causal relations between mind and body. Such theories hold that the fact that states of our bodies and states of our minds seem to coincide—for example stepping on a tack and experiencing pain —is not due to a relation of cause and effect, but is to be explained as either a remarkable coincidence, an elaborate **preestablished harmony** between the careers of separate minds and bodies set up at the beginning, or else as the result of constant acts of God to keep us mentally informed of the physical goings on in our bodies. Although theories of each kind have been held at some point by some philosopher, none of these is considered a viable theory today. They serve, rather, to show how difficult it is to make sense of causal relations between immaterial minds and material bodies and the lengths to which thinkers have been driven by frustrated attempts to do so.

The most common form of dualism is that which holds that minds act causally on bodies and that bodies act causally on minds. This is the causal interaction form of dualism and is sometimes referred to simply as *interactionism.* It captures such common sense beliefs as that injury to the body causes the experience of pain and that the mental intention to move the body, at least in the absence of physical or physiological obstruction, usually achieves the intended result. Common sense isn't entirely on the side of dualism in this or any other form, however. If the mind is really not the sort of thing that can be located in space, then it isn't anywhere at all. But we feel as though we are consciously present as subjects of experience, right here in this building or this room for example, occupying the unique perspective from which our experience opens on the world in or through our bodies, not separated from our bodies or outside of the space we inhabit through them. This common sense of having a location, of being right here and not anywhere else mentally as well as physically, is lost by the dualistic account of mind and body. Lost also is any explanation, spatial or otherwise, of the intimate relation between our minds and bodies. If the only connection between the two substances is causal, and dualism countenances no other bond, then we are no more closely related to our bodies than we are to the lights we cause to turn on or off, to the football we cause to fly through the air, or to anything else to which our only relation is one of cause and effect. So the testimony of common sense is divided with respect to the truth of the causal interaction form of dualism. The theory captures some of our intuitions about the mental and the physical, but misses others.

Descartes' worries about the conceivability of causal interaction between minds and bodies also must be dealt with by interactionism. A philosopher who holds the causal interaction form of dualism must explain how it is conceivable that an immaterial mind can move a material body and how events that occur in a material body can cause changes of state or initiate processes in an immaterial mind. In the selection by Broad in this section, some models are suggested for thinking about this sort of interaction without thinking of the mind as literally pulling or shoving the body around. Whether or not these really make causal interaction conceivable, they are at least a step toward dealing with the difficult questions raised by Descartes and others about such processes.

There is another very important general issue raised in Broad's essay which has to do with conceivability. It is beginning to look as though physical science will eventually be able to account for every movement of the human body in terms of causes that are strictly physical or physiological. If that is so, then it doesn't look as though there will be anything left for mental events to be the causes of. So in addition to the problem of conceiving of mental causes of bodily behavior, we seem to have the problem of conceiving of mental causes of bodily behavior that would have occurred even if the mental cause had been entirely absent. Broad suggests a way to conceive of something for the mental causes to account for even if they aren't needed to account for the fact that certain movements of the body occur. Broad also considers problems produced by the apparent conflict between physical science and interactionism.

Huxley's essay represents an alternative to interactionism which is usually referred to as *epiphenomenalism.* It suggests that the relation between mind and body is causal, but that the causation goes in one direction only. There is causal action, but no causal *inter*action. Things that occur in the body, typically in the central nervous system, give rise to conscious states, but conscious states exert no causal influence over the human body. The idea, as Huxley puts it, is that we are conscious automata. Our bodies work like automatic machines according to the laws of physical science. Our minds simply register some of the "side effects" or epiphenomena of this physical functioning. Mental states and processes are not full-fledged phenomena; they have no causal power of their own. This theory obviously avoids some of the problems of interactionism. Since there is no causal action of minds on bodies, there is no need to explain how something immaterial can move something material. On the other hand, a number of common sense intuitions are lost by the theory. Our sense that we are in conscious control of the movements of our bodies becomes a kind of illusion. The distinction between voluntary action and involuntary or reflex behavior, or at least our ordinary sense of that distinction, seems to be lost on this view of the nature of consciousness. And, contrary to what Descartes thought he had demonstrated beyond doubt, the mind is less real than the body and its true nature less accessible to intuition and hence less easily known, if epiphenomenalism is correct.

There is at least one serious problem for dualism in any form, with or without causal relations between mind and body. The very notion of a distinct immaterial thing raises a difficult conceptual problem. It has been alleged that our most basic idea of what it is to be a thing or entity of any sort is so closely tied to the conception of material reality that the idea of an immaterial thing turns out to be incoherent upon close inspection. The argument for that position is as follows. The very least that is required in order to have a thing or entity is that it be able to be individuated. If we point somewhere in the middle of a large and perfectly homogeneous patch of color, we don't pick out a thing at all. We could indicate a particular small area by outlining it and treat that as a thing, but that's a different matter. The outlining serves to individuate and hence to make the circumscribed area count as a thing. But if we couldn't individuate something at all, couldn't separate it from its surroundings and from other things, we wouldn't have a thing at all. So the next question is, how do we individuate something? What are the minimal requirements for being able to do so? Well, qualitative differences don't seem to be necessary. Even if we had two identical looking apples we would have no trouble individuating them, that is, telling that we were dealing with two apples instead of one. Simple numerical difference seems to be the key. We can tell we have two things because, even if qualitatively identical, they are numerically individuated by the fact that they are in two different places at the same time. Now the problem for minds is that they are not in any place at any time, they aren't spatially located at all according to dualism. And so if there were two (or three or four or . . . ) qualitatively identical minds there would be no way to individuate them or even to think of them as separate individuals. There seems to be no difference between one, two, or any number of qualitatively identical minds. With respect to minds, there is no such thing as simple numerical difference, no way for such a notion to be given meaning at all. But that means that our most basic notion of individuation does not apply to minds, and hence that the notion of such an immaterial thing is not a coherent one. To be a thing is necessarily to be numerically individual, but to be immaterial is to defy numerical individuation in principle.

## *René Descartes (1596–1650)*

For more information about the work of Descartes, see the first selection in Part 2. Like that selection, this one is also taken from the *Meditations*. In the second meditation (see Part 2) Descartes demonstrates that the mind and body (mind and matter of any sort) are independent of each other and entirely different in their essential natures. At that stage of his inquiry, however, he is not even certain that his body exists, and so there is no point in explaining the apparent relation between the two. Having proven in the third meditation that God exists and provides a guarantee against systematic error and deception, he is in a much better position at this point to raise the question of the relation between mind and body. In the following selection Descartes argues that we can know that we have a body, since virtually all of our ordinary experience attests to it, and God would not allow experience to so completely mislead us. And we can know that the body is distinct and different in nature from the mind. Further, we have reason to believe that the body affects the mind causally and that the mind directs the body's voluntary actions. These two together make the apparent relation between mind and body even closer than that of the captain to his or her ship.

But Descartes offers no suggestion as to how this relation can be clearly understood. Instead he argues that the purpose of the body's somehow giving rise to ideas and of our seeming ability to direct our body's movements is the avoidance of things that would be harmful to us as complete and composite beings. Since clear and certain knowledge of things experienced through the body is not essential for this purpose, there is no reason to think we should have the knowledge required to understand the precise nature of the relation of mind and body.

# The Distinction Between the Mind and Body of Man

## *René Descartes*

. . . There is no doubt that in all things which nature teaches me there is some truth contained; for by nature, considered in general, I now understand no other thing than either God Himself or else the order and disposition which God has established in created things; and by my nature in

Abridged from *The Philosophical Works of Descartes*. Translated by Elizabeth S. Haldane and G. R. T. Ross (London: Cambridge University Press, 1972). Reprinted by permission of Cambridge University Press.

particular I understand no other thing than the complexus of all the things which God has given me.

But there is nothing which this nature teaches me more expressly [nor more sensibly] than that I have a body which is adversely affected when I feel pain, which has need of food or drink when I experience the feelings of hunger and thirst, and so on; nor can I doubt there being some truth in all this.

Nature also teaches me by these sensations of pain, hunger, thirst, etc., that I am not only lodged in my body as a pilot in a vessel, but that I am very closely united to it, and so to speak so intermingled with it that I seem to compose with it one whole. For if that were not the case, when my body is hurt, I, who am merely a thinking thing, should not feel pain, for I should perceive this wound by the understanding only, just as the sailor perceives by sight when something is damaged in his vessel; and when my body has need of drink or food, I should clearly understand the fact without being warned of it by confused feelings of hunger and thirst. For all these sensations of hunger, thirst, pain, etc. are in truth none other than certain confused modes of thought which are produced by the union and apparent intermingling of mind and body.

Moreover, nature teaches me that many other bodies exist around mine, of which some are to be avoided, and others sought after. And certainly from the fact that I am sensible of different sorts of colors, sounds, scents, tastes, heat, hardness, etc., I very easily conclude that there are in the bodies from which all these diverse sense-perceptions proceed certain variations which answer to them, although possibly these are not really at all similar to them. And also from the fact that amongst these different sense-perceptions some are very agreeable to me and others disagreeable, it is quite certain that my body (or rather myself in my entirety, inasmuch as I am formed of body and soul) may receive different impressions agreeable and disagreeable from the other bodies which surround it.

But there are many other things which nature seems to have taught me, but which at the same time I have never really received from her, but which have been brought about in my mind by a certain habit which I have of forming inconsiderate judgments on things; and thus it may easily happen that these judgments contain some error. Take, for example, the opinion which I hold that all space in which there is nothing that affects [or makes an impression on] my senses is void; that in a body which is warm there is something entirely similar to the idea of heat which is in me; that in a white or green body there is the same whiteness or greenness that I perceive; that in a bitter or sweet body there is the same taste, and so on in other instances; that the stars, the towers, and all other distant bodies are of the same figure and size as they appear from far off to our eyes, etc. But in order that in this there should be nothing which I do not conceive distinctly, I should define exactly what I really understand when I say that I am taught somewhat by nature. For here I take nature in a more limited signification than when I term it the sum of all the things given me by God, since in this sum many things are comprehended which only pertain to mind (and to these I do not refer in speaking of nature) such as the notion which I have of the fact that what has once been done cannot ever be undone and an infinitude of such things which I know by the light of nature [without the help of the body]; and seeing that it comprehends many other matters besides which only pertain to body, and are no longer here contained under the name of nature, such as the quality of weight which it possesses and the like, with which I also do not deal; for in talking of nature I only treat of those things given by God to me as a being composed of mind and body. But the nature here described truly teaches me to flee from things which cause the sensation of pain, and seek after the things which communicate to me the sentiment of pleasure and so forth; but I do not see that beyond this it teaches me that from those diverse sense-perceptions we should ever form any conclusion regarding things outside of us, without having [carefully and maturely] mentally examined them beforehand. For it seems to me that it is mind alone, and not mind and body in conjunction, that is requisite to a knowledge of the truth in regard to such things. Thus, although a star makes no larger an impression on my eye than the flame of a little candle there is yet in me no real or positive propensity impelling me to believe that it is not greater than that flame; but I have judged it to be so from my earliest years, without any rational foundation. And although in approaching fire I feel heat, and in approaching it a little too near I even feel pain, there is at the same time no reason in this which could persuade me that there is in the fire something resembling this heat any more than there is in it something resembling the pain; all that I have any reason to believe from this is, that there is something in it, whatever it may be, which excites in me these sensations of heat or of pain. So also, although there are spaces in which I find nothing which excites my senses, I must not from that conclude that these spaces contain no body; for I see in this, as in other similar things, that I have been in the habit of perverting the order of nature, because these perceptions of sense having been placed within me by nature merely for the purpose of signifying to my mind what things are beneficial or hurtful to the composite whole of which it forms a part, and being up to that point sufficiently clear and distinct, I yet avail myself of them as though they were absolute rules by which I might immediately determine the essence of the bodies which are outside me, as to which, in fact, they can teach me nothing but what is most obscure and confused. . . .

. . . There is a great difference between mind and body, inasmuch as body is by nature always divisible, and the mind is entirely indivisible. For, as a matter of fact, when I consider the mind, that is to say, myself inasmuch as I am only a thinking thing, I cannot distinguish in myself any parts, but apprehend myself to be clearly one and entire; and although the whole mind seems to be united to the whole body, yet if a foot, or an arm, or some other part, is separated from my body, I am aware that nothing has been taken away from my mind. And the faculties of willing, feeling, conceiving, etc. cannot be properly speaking said to be its parts, for it is one and the same mind which employs itself in willing and in feeling and understanding. But it is quite otherwise with corporeal or extended objects, for there is not one of these imaginable by me which my mind cannot easily divide into parts, and which consequently I do not recognize as being divisible; this would be sufficient to teach me that the mind or soul of man is entirely different from the body, if I had not already learned it from other sources.

I further notice that the mind does not receive the impressions from all parts of the body immediately, but only from the brain, or perhaps even from one of its smallest parts, to wit, from that in which the common sense is said to reside, which, whenever it is disposed in the same particular way, conveys the same thing to the mind, although meanwhile the other portions of the body may be differently disposed, as is testified by innumerable experiments which it is unnecessary here to recount.

I notice, also, that the nature of body is such that none of its parts can be moved by another part a little way off which cannot also be moved in the same way by each one of the parts which are between the two, although this more remote part does not act at all. As, for example, in the cord *ABCD* [which is in tension] if we pull the last part *D*, the first part *A* will not be moved in any way differently from what would be the case if one of the intervening parts *B* or *C* were pulled, and the last part *D* were to remain unmoved. And in the same way, when I feel pain in my foot, my knowledge of physics teaches me that this sensation is communicated by means of nerves dispersed through the foot, which, being extended like cords from there to the brain, when they are contracted in the foot, at the same time contract the inmost portions of the brain which is their extremity and place of origin, and then excite a certain movement which nature has established in order to cause the mind to be affected by a sensation of pain represented as existing in the foot. But because these nerves must pass through the tibia, the thigh, the loins, the back and the neck, in order to reach from the leg to the brain, it may happen that although their extremities which are in the foot are not affected, but only certain ones of their intervening parts [which pass by the loins or the neck], this action will excite the same movement in the brain that might have been excited there by a hurt received in the foot, in consequence of which the mind will necessarily feel in the foot the same pain as if it had received a hurt. And the same holds good of all the other perceptions of our senses.

I notice finally that since each of the movements which are in the portion of the brain by which the mind is immediately affected brings about one particular sensation only, we cannot under the circumstances imagine anything more likely than that this movement, amongst all the sensations which it is capable of impressing on it, causes mind to be affected by that one which is best fitted and most generally useful for the conservation of the human body when it is in health. But experience makes us aware that all the feelings with which nature inspires us are such as I have just spoken of; and there is therefore nothing in them which does not give testimony to the power and goodness of the God [who has produced them]. Thus, for example, when the nerves which are in the feet are violently or more than usually moved, their movement, passing through the medulla of the spine to the inmost parts of the brain, gives a sign to the mind which makes it feel somewhat, to wit, pain, as though in the foot, by which the mind is excited to do its utmost to remove the cause of the evil as dangerous and hurtful to the foot. It is true that God could have constituted the nature of man in such a way that this same movement in the brain would have conveyed something quite different to the mind; for example, it might have produced consciousness of itself either in so far as it is in the brain, or as it is in the foot, or as it is in some other place between the foot and the brain, or it might finally have produced consciousness of anything else whatsoever; but none of all this would have contributed so well to the conservation of the body. Similarly, when we desire to drink, a certain dryness of the throat is produced which moves its nerves, and by their means the internal portions of the brain; and this movement causes in the mind the sensation of thirst, because in this case there is nothing more useful to us than to become aware that we have need to drink for the conservation of our health; and the same holds good in other instances. . . .

## *C. D. Broad (1887–1972)*

For information about Broad's contributions to philosophy, see the third selection in Part 1. The selection that follows is taken from *The Mind and Its Place in Nature* (1925). In it Broad defends the classical dualist position on the mind-body problem against a number of objections. The thrust of Broad's argument is that dualism has enormous evidence in support of it from our common sense understanding of the cooperative workings of our bodies and minds. Experience provides us with the means to distinguish between minds and bodies, and gives us daily evidence of causal interactions between the two. So the burden of proof rests not with the dualist, but with the proponents of alternative theories. It will require very strong objections to justify a preference for any other theory in face of the massive support for dualism that common sense provides. Broad argues that none of the philosophical or scientific objections to dualism are that strong.

# The Traditional Problem of Body and Mind

## *C. D. Broad*

. . . There is a question which has been argued about for some centuries now under the name of "Interaction"; this is the question whether minds really do act on the organisms which they animate, and whether organisms really do act on the minds which animate them. (I must point out at once that I imply no particular theory of mind or body by the word "to animate." I use it as a perfectly neutral name to express the fact that a certain mind is connected in some peculiarly intimate way with a certain body, and, under normal conditions with no other body. . . .

The problem of Interaction is generally discussed at the level of enlightened common-sense; where it is assumed that we know pretty well what we mean by "mind," by "matter" and by "causation." Obviously no solution which is reached at that level can claim to be ultimate. If what we call "matter" should turn out to be a collection of spirits of low intelligence, as Leibniz thought, the argument that mind and body are so unlike that their interaction is impossible would become irrelevant. Again, if causation be nothing but regular sequence and concomitance, as some philosophers have held, it is ridiculous to regard **psycho-neural parallelism** and interaction as mutually exclusive alternatives. For interaction will mean no more than parallelism, and parallelism will mean no less than interaction. Nevertheless I am going to discuss the arguments here at the common-sense level, because they are so incredibly bad and yet have imposed upon so many learned men.

We start then by assuming a developed mind and a developed organism as two distinct things, and by admitting that the two are now intimately connected in some way or other which I express by saying that "this mind *animates* this organism." We assume that bodies are very much as enlightened common-sense believes them to be; and that, even if we cannot define "causation," we have some means of recognizing when it is present and when it is absent. The question then is: "Does a mind ever act on the body which it animates, and does a body ever act on the mind which animates it?" The answer which common-sense would give to both questions is: "Yes, certainly." On the face of it my body acts on my mind whenever a pin is stuck into the former and a painful sensation thereupon arises in the latter. And, on the face of it, my mind acts on my body whenever a desire to move my arm arises in the former and is followed by this movement in the latter. Let us call this common-sense view "Two-sided Interaction." Although it seems so obvious it has been denied by probably a majority of philosophers and a majority of physiologists. So the question is: "Why should so many distinguished men, who have studied the subject, have denied the apparently obvious fact of Two-sided Interaction?"

The arguments against Two-sided Interaction fall into two sets: — Philosophical and Scientific. We will take the philosophical arguments first; for we shall find that the professedly scientific arguments come back in the end to the principles or prejudices which are made explicit in the philosophical arguments.

### PHILOSOPHICAL ARGUMENTS AGAINST TWO-SIDED INTERACTION

No one can deny that there is a close correlation between certain bodily events and certain mental events, and conversely. Therefore anyone

Abridged from *The Mind and Its Place in Nature,* by C. D. Broad (New York: Harcourt Brace and Company, 1925), pp. 95–115. Reprinted by permission of Harcourt Brace Jovanovich, Inc.

who denies that there is action of mind on body and of body on mind must presumably hold *(a)* that concomitant variation is not an adequate criterion of causal connection, and *(b)* that the other feature which is essential for causal connection is absent in the case of body and mind. Now the common philosophical argument is that minds and mental states are so extremely unlike bodies and bodily states that it is inconceivable that the two should be causally connected. It is certainly true that, if minds and mental events are just what they seem to be to introspection and nothing more, and if bodies and bodily events are just what enlightened common-sense thinks them to be and nothing more, the two *are* extremely unlike. And this fact is supposed to show that, however closely correlated certain pairs of events in mind and body respectively may be, they cannot be causally connected.

Evidently the assumption at the back of this argument is that concomitant variation, together with a high enough degree of likeness, is an adequate test for causation; but that no amount of concomitant variation can establish causation in the absence of a high enough degree of likeness. Now I am inclined to admit part of this assumption. I think it is practically certain that causation does not simply *mean* concomitant variation. Hence the existence of the latter is not a proof of the presence of the former. Again, I think it is almost certain that concomitant variation between A and B is not in fact a sufficient sign of the presence of a *direct* causal relation between the two. (I think it may perhaps be a sufficient sign of *either* a direct causal relation between A and B *or* of several causal relations which indirectly unite A and B through the medium of other terms C, D, etc.) So far I agree with the assumptions of the argument. But I cannot see the least reason to think that the other characteristic, which must be added to concomitant variation before we can be sure that A and B are causally connected, is a high degree of likeness between the two. One would like to know just how unlike two events may be before it becomes impossible to admit the existence of a causal relation between them. No one hesitates to hold that draughts and colds in the head are causally connected, although the two are extremely unlike each other. If the unlikeness of draughts and colds in the head does not prevent one from admitting a causal connection between the two, why should the unlikeness of volitions and voluntary movements prevent one from holding that they are causally connected? To sum up. I am willing to admit that an adequate criterion of causal connection needs some other relation between a pair of events beside concomitant variation; but I do not believe for a moment that this other relation is that of qualitative likeness.

This brings us to a rather more refined form of the argument against Interaction. It is said that, whenever we admit the existence of a causal relation between two events, these two events (to put it crudely) must also form parts of a single substantial whole. *E.g.,* all physical events are spatially related and form one great extended whole. And the mental events which would commonly be admitted to be causally connected are always events in a single mind. A mind is a substantial whole of a peculiar kind too. Now it is said that between bodily events and mental events there are no relations such as those which unite physical events in different parts of the same Space or mental events in the history of the same mind. In the absence of such relations, binding mind and body into a single substantial whole, we cannot admit that bodily and mental events can be causally connected with each other, no matter how closely correlated their variations may be.

This is a much better argument than the argument about qualitative likeness and unlikeness. If we accept the premise that causal relations can subsist only between terms which form parts of a single substantial whole must we deny that mental and bodily events can be causally connected? I do not think that we need.

1. It is of course perfectly true that an organism and the mind which animates it do not form a physical whole, and that they do not form a mental whole; and these, no doubt, are the two kinds of substantial whole with which we are most familiar. But it does not follow that a mind

and its organism do not form a substantial whole of *some* kind. There, plainly, is the extraordinary intimate union between the two which I have called "animation" of the one by the other. Even if the mind be just what it seems to introspection, and the body be just what it seems to perception aided by the more precise methods of science, this seems to me to be enough to make a mind and its body a substantial whole. Even so extreme a dualist about Mind and Matter as Descartes occasionally suggests that a mind and its body together form a quasi-substance; and, although we may quarrel with the language of the very numerous philosophers who have said that the mind is "the form" of its body, we must admit that such language would never have seemed plausible unless a mind and its body together had formed something very much like a single substantial whole.

2. We must, moreover, admit the possibility that minds and mental events have properties and relations which do not reveal themselves to introspection, and that bodies and bodily events may have properties and relations which do not reveal themselves to perception or to physical and chemical experiment. In virtue of these properties and relations the two together may well form a single substantial whole of the kind which is alleged to be needed for causal interaction. Thus, if we accept the premise of the argument, we have no right to assert that mind and body *cannot* interact; but only the much more modest proposition that introspection and perception do not suffice to assure us that mind and body are so interrelated that they *can* interact.

3. We must further remember that the Two-sided Interactionist is under no obligation to hold that the *complete* conditions of any mental event are bodily or that the complete conditions of any bodily event are mental. He needs only to assert that some mental events include certain bodily events among their necessary conditions, and that some bodily events include certain mental events among their necessary conditions. If I am paralyzed my volition may not move my arm; and, if I am hypnotized or intensely interested or frightened, a wound may not produce a painful sensation. Now, if the complete cause and the complete effect in all interaction include both a bodily and a mental factor, the two wholes will be related by the fact that the mental constituents belong to a single mind, that the bodily constituents belong to a single body, and that this mind animates this body. This amount of connection should surely be enough to allow of causal interaction.

This will be the most appropriate place to deal with the contention that, in voluntary action, and there only, we are immediately acquainted with an instance of causal connection. If this be true the controversy is of course settled at once in favor of the Interactionist. It is generally supposed that this view was refuted once and for all by Mr. Hume in his *Enquiry concerning Human Understanding* (Sect. VII, Part I). I should not care to assert that the doctrine in question is true; but I do think that it is plausible, and I am quite sure that Mr. Hume's arguments do not refute it. Mr. Hume uses three closely connected arguments. (1) The connection between a successful volition and the resulting bodily movement is as mysterious and as little self-evident as the connection between any other event and its effect. (2) We have to learn from experience which of our volitions will be effective and which will not. *E.g.*, we do not know, until we have tried, that we can voluntarily move our arms and cannot voluntarily move our livers. And again, if a man were suddenly paralyzed, he would still expect to be able to move his arm voluntarily, and would be surprised when he found that it kept still in spite of his volition. (3) We have discovered that the immediate consequence of a volition is a change in our nerves and muscles, which most people know nothing about; and is not the movement of a limb, which most people believe to be its immediate and necessary consequence.

The second and third arguments are valid only against the contention that we know immediately that a volition to make a certain movement is the *sufficient* condition for the happening of that movement. They are quite irrelevant to the contention that we know immediately that the volition is a *necessary* condition for the happening of just that movement at just that time. No doubt many other conditions are also necessary, *e.g.*, that our nerves and muscles shall be in the right state; and these other necessary conditions can be discovered only by special investigation. Since our volitions to move our limbs are in fact followed in the vast majority of cases by the willed movement, and since the other necessary conditions are not very obvious, it is natural enough that we should think that we know immediately that our volition is the ***sufficient* condition** of the movement of our limbs. If we think so, we are certainly wrong; and Mr. Hume's arguments prove that we are. But they prove nothing else. It does not follow that we are wrong in thinking that we know, without having to wait for the result, that the volition is a ***necessary* condition** of the movement.

It remains to consider the first argument. Is the connection between cause and effect as mysterious and as little self-evident in the case of the voluntary production of bodily movement as in all other cases? If so, we must hold that the first time a baby wills to move its hand it is just as much surprised to find its hand moving as it would be to find its leg moving or its nurse bursting into flames. I do not profess to know anything about the infant mind; but it seems to me that this is a wildly paradoxical consequence, for which there is no evidence or likelihood. But there is no need to leave the matter there. It is perfectly plain that, in the case of volition and voluntary movement, there *is* a connection between the cause and the effect which is not present in other cases of causation, and which does make it plausible to hold that in this one case the nature of the effect can be foreseen by merely reflecting on the nature of the cause. The peculiarity of a volition as a cause-factor is that it involves as an essential part of it the idea of the effect. To say that a person has a volition to move his arm involves saying that he has an idea of his arm (and not of his leg or his liver) and an idea of the position in which he wants his arm to be. It is simply silly in view of this fact to say that there is no closer connection between the desire to move my arm and the movement of my arm than there is between this desire and the movement of my leg or my liver. We cannot detect any analogous connection between cause and effect in causal transactions which we view wholly from outside, such as the movement of a billiard-ball by a cue. It is therefore by no means unreasonable to suggest that, in the one case of our own voluntary movements, we can see without waiting for the result that such and such a volition is a necessary condition of such and such a bodily movement.

It seems to me then that Mr. Hume's arguments on this point are absolutely irrelevant, and that it may very well be true that in volition we positively know that our desire for such and such a bodily movement is a necessary (though not a sufficient) condition of the happening of just that movement at just that time. On the whole then I conclude that the philosophical arguments certainly do not disprove Two-sided Interaction, and that they do not even raise any strong presumption against it. And, while I am not prepared definitely to commit myself to the view that, in voluntary movement, we positively *know* that the mind acts on the body, I do think that this opinion is quite plausible when properly stated and that the arguments which have been brought against it are worthless. I pass therefore to the scientific arguments.

## SCIENTIFIC ARGUMENTS AGAINST TWO-SIDED INTERACTION

There are, so far as I know, two of these. One is supposed to be based on the physical principle of the Conservation of Energy, and on certain experiments which have been made on human bodies. The other is based on the close analogy which is said to exist between the structures of the physiological mechanism of reflex action and that of voluntary action. I will take them in turn.

### 1. The Argument from Energy

It will first be needful to state clearly what is asserted by the principle of the Conservation of Energy. It is found that, if we take certain material systems, *e.g.*, a gun, a cartridge, and a bullet, there is a certain magnitude which keeps approximately constant throughout all their changes. This is called "Energy." When the gun has not been fired it and the bullet have no motion, but the explosive in the cartridge has great chemical energy. When it has been fired the bullet is moving very fast and has great energy of movement. The gun, though not moving fast in its recoil, has also great energy of movement because it is very massive. The gases produced by the explosion have some energy of movement and some heat-energy, but much less chemical energy than the unexploded charge had. These various kinds of energy can be measured in common units according to certain conventions. To an innocent mind there seems to be a good deal of "cooking" at this stage, *i.e.*, the conventions seem to be chosen and various kinds and amounts of concealed energy seem to be postulated in order to make the principle come out right at the end. I do not propose to go into this in detail, for two reasons. In the first place, I think that the conventions adopted and the postulates made, though somewhat suggestive of the fraudulent company-promoter, can be justified by their coherence with certain experimental facts, and that they are not simply made ***ad hoc.*** Secondly, I shall show that the Conservation of Energy is absolutely irrelevant to the question at issue, so that it would be [a] waste of time to treat it too seriously in the present connection. Now it is found that the total energy of all kinds in this system, when measured according to these conventions, is approximately the same in amount though very differently distributed after the explosion and before it. If we had confined our attention to a part of this system and *its* energy this would not have been true. The bullet, *e.g.*, had no energy at all before the explosion and a great deal afterwards. A system like the bullet, the gun, and the charge, is called a "Conservative System"; the bullet alone, or the gun and the charge, would be called "Non-conservative Systems." A conservative system might therefore be defined as one whose total energy is redistributed, but not altered in amount, by changes that happen within it. Of course a given system might be conservative for some kinds of change and not for others.

So far we have merely defined a "Conservative System," and admitted that there are systems which, for some kinds of change at any rate, answer approximately to our definition. We can now state the Principle of the Conservation of Energy in terms of the conceptions just defined. The principle asserts that every material system is either itself conservative, or, if not, is part of a larger material system which is conservative. We may take it that there is good inductive evidence for this proposition.

The next thing to consider is the experiments on the human body. These tend to prove that a living body, with the air that it breathes and the food that it eats, forms a conservative system to a high degree of approximation. We can measure the chemical energy of the food given to a man, and that which enters his body in the form of Oxygen breathed in. We can also, with suitable apparatus, collect, measure and analyze the air breathed out, and thus find its chemical energy. Similarly, we can find the energy given out in bodily movement, in heat, and in excretion. It is alleged that, on the average, whatever the man may do, the energy of his bodily movements is exactly accounted for by the energy given to him in the form of food and of Oxygen. If you take the energy put in in food and Oxygen, and subtract the energy given out in waste-products, the balance is almost exactly equal to the energy put out in bodily movements. Such slight differences as are found are as often on one side as on the other, and are therefore probably due to unavoidable experimental errors. I do not propose to criticize the interpretation of these experiments in detail, because, as I shall show soon, they are completely irrelevant to the problem of whether mind and body interact. But there is just one point that I will make before passing on. It is perfectly clear that such experiments can tell us only what happens on the average over a long time. To know whether the balance was accurately kept at every moment we should have to kill the patient at each moment and analyze his body so as to find out the energy present then in the form of stored-up products. Obviously we cannot keep on killing the patient in order to analyze him, and then reviving him in order to go on with the experiment. Thus it would seem that the results of the experiment are perfectly compatible with the presence of quite large excesses or defects in the total bodily energy at certain moments, provided that these average out over longer periods. However, I do not want to press this criticism; I am quite ready to accept for our present purpose the traditional interpretation which has been put on the experiments.

We now understand the physical principle and the experimental facts. The two together are generally supposed to prove that mind and body cannot interact. What precisely is the argument, and is it valid? I imagine that the argument, when fully stated, would run somewhat as follows: "I will to move my arm, and it moves. If the volition has anything to do with causing the movement we might expect energy to flow from my mind to my body. Thus the energy of my body ought to receive a measurable increase, not accounted for by the food that I eat and the Oxygen that I breathe. But no such physically unaccountable increases of bodily energy are found. Again, I tread on a tin-tack, and a painful sensation arises in my mind. If treading on the tack has anything to do with causing the sensation we might expect energy to flow from my body to my mind. Such energy would cease to be measurable. Thus there ought to be a noticeable decrease in my bodily energy, not balanced by increases anywhere in the physical system. But such unbalanced decreases of bodily energy are not found." So it is concluded that the volition has nothing to do with causing my arm to move, and that treading on the tack has nothing to do with causing the painful sensation.

Is this argument valid? In the first place it is important to notice that the conclusion does not follow from the Conservation of Energy and the experimental facts alone. The real premise is a tacitly assumed proposition about causation; viz., that, if a change in A has anything to do with causing a change in B, energy must leave A and flow into B. This is neither asserted nor entailed by the Conservation of Energy. What *it* says is that, *if* energy leaves A, it must appear in something else, say B; so that A and B together form a conservative system. Since the Conservation of Energy is not itself the premise for the argument against Interaction, and since it does not entail that premise, the evidence for the Conservation of Energy is not evidence against Interaction. Is there any independent evidence for the premise? We may admit that it *is* true of many, though not of all, transactions within the physical realm. But there are cases where it is not true even of purely physical transactions; and, even if it were always true in the physical realm, it would not follow that it must also be true of transphysical causation. Take the case of a weight swinging at the end of a string hung from a fixed point. The total energy of the weight is the same at all positions in its course. It is thus a conservative system. But at every moment the direction and velocity of the weight's motion are different, and the proportion between its kinetic and its potential energy is constantly changing. These changes are caused by the pull of the string, which acts in a different direction at each different moment. The string makes no difference to the total energy of the weight; but it makes all the difference in the world to the particular way in which the weight moves and the particular way in which the energy is distributed between the potential and the kinetic forms. This is evident when we remember that the weight would begin to move in an utterly different course if at any moment the string were cut.

Here, then, we have a clear case even in the physical realm where a system is conservative but is continually acted on by something which affects its movement and the distribution of its total energy. Why should not the mind act on the body in this way? If you say that you can see how a string can affect the movement of a weight, but cannot see how a volition could affect the movement of a material particle, you have deserted the scientific argument and have gone back to one of the philosophical arguments. Your real difficulty is either that volitions are so very unlike movements, or that the volition is in your mind whilst the movement belongs to the physical realm. And we have seen how little weight can be attached to these objections. . . . Nevertheless, the facts brought forward by the argument from energy do throw some light on the *nature* of the interaction between mind and body, assuming this to happen. They do suggest that all the energy of our bodily actions comes out of and goes back into the physical world, and that minds neither add energy to nor abstract it from the latter. What they do, if they do anything, is to determine that at a given moment so much energy shall change from the chemical form to the form of bodily movement; and they determine this, so far as we can see, without altering the total amount of energy in the physical world.

## 2. The Argument from the Structure of the Nervous System

There are purely reflex actions, like sneezing and blinking, in which there is no reason to suppose that the mind plays any essential part. Now we know the nervous structure which is used in such acts as these. A stimulus is given to the outer end of an efferent nerve; some change or other runs up this nerve, crosses a synapsis between this and an afferent nerve, travels down the latter to a muscle, causes the muscle to contract, and so produces a bodily movement. There seems no reason to believe that the mind plays any essential part in this process. The process may be irreducibly vital, and not merely physico-chemical; but there seems no need to assume anything more than this. Now it is said that the whole nervous system is simply an immense complication of interconnected nervous arcs. The result is that a change which travels inwards has an immense number of alternative paths by which it may travel outwards. Thus the reaction to a given stimulus is no longer one definite movement, as in the simple reflex. Almost any movement may follow any stimulus according to the path which the afferent disturbance happens to take. This path will depend on the relative resistance of the various synapses at the time. Now a variable response to the same stimulus is characteristic of deliberate as opposed to reflex action.

These are the facts. The argument based on them runs as follows. It is admitted that the mind has nothing to do with the causation of purely reflex actions. But the nervous structure and the nervous processes involved in deliberate action do not differ in kind from those involved in reflex action; they differ only in degree of complexity. The variability which characterizes deliberate action is fully explained by the variety of alternative paths and the variable resistances of the synapses. So it is unreasonable to suppose that the mind has any more to do with causing deliberate actions than it has to do with causing reflex actions.

I think that this argument is invalid. In the first place I am pretty sure that the persons who use it have before their imagination a kind of picture of how mind and body must interact if they interact at all. They find that the facts do not answer to this picture, and so they conclude that there is no interaction. The picture is of the following kind. They think of the mind as sitting somewhere in a hole in the brain, surrounded by telephones. And they think of the efferent disturbance as coming to an end at one of these telephones and there affecting the mind. The mind is then supposed to respond by sending an efferent impulse down another of these telephones. As no such hole, with efferent nerves stopping at its walls and afferent nerves starting from them, can be found, they conclude that the mind can play no part in the transaction. But another alternative is that this picture of how the mind must act if it acts at all is wrong. To put it shortly, the mistake is to confuse a gap in an explanation with a spatio-temporal gap, and to argue from the absence of the latter to the absence of the former.

The Interactionist's contention is simply that there is a gap in any purely physiological explanation of deliberate action; *i.e.*, that all such explanations fail to account completely for the facts because they leave out one necessary condition. It does not follow in the least that there must be a spatio-temporal breach of continuity in the physiological conditions, and that the missing condition must fill this gap in the way in which the movement of a wire fills the spatio-temporal interval between the pulling of a bell-handle and the ringing of a distant bell. To assume this is to make the mind a kind of physical object, and to make its action a kind of mechanical action. Really, the mind and its actions are not literally in Space at all, and the time which is occupied by the mental event is no doubt *also* occupied by some part of the physiological process. Thus I am inclined to think that much of the force which this argument actually exercises on many people is simply due to the presupposition about the *modus operandi* of interaction, and that it is greatly weakened when this presupposition is shown to be a mere prejudice due to our limited power of envisaging unfamiliar alternative possibilities.

We can, however, make more detailed objections to the argument than this. There is a clear introspective difference between the mental accompaniment of voluntary action and that of reflex action. What goes on in our minds when we decide with difficulty to get out of a hot bath on a cold morning is obviously extremely different from what goes on in our minds when we sniff pepper and sneeze. And the difference is qualitative; it is not a mere difference of complexity. This difference has to be explained somehow; and the theory under discussion gives no plausible explanation of it. The ordinary view that, in the latter case, the mind is not acting on the body at all; whilst, in the former, it is acting on the body in a specific way, does at least make the introspective difference between the two intelligible.

Again, whilst it is true that deliberate action differs from reflex action in its greater variability of response to the same stimulus, this is certainly not the whole or the most important part of the difference between them. The really important difference is that, in deliberate action, the response is varied *appropriately* to meet the special circumstances which are supposed to exist at the time or are expected to arise later; whilst reflex action is not varied in this way, but is blind and almost mechanical. The complexity of the nervous system explains the *possibility* of variation; it does not in the least explain why the alternative which actually takes place should as a rule be appropriate and not merely haphazard. And so again it seems as if some factor were in operation in deliberate action which is not present in reflex action; and it is reasonable to suppose that this factor is the volition in the mind.

It seems to me that this second scientific argument has no tendency to disprove interaction; but that the facts which it brings forward do tend to suggest the particular form which interaction probably takes if it happens at all. They suggest that what the mind does to the body in voluntary action, if it does anything, is to lower the resistance of certain synapses and to raise that of others. The result is that the nervous current follows such a course as to produce the particular movement which the mind judges to be appropriate at the time. On such a view the difference between reflex, habitual, and deliberate actions for the present purpose becomes fairly plain. In pure reflexes the mind cannot voluntarily affect the resistance of the synapses concerned, and so the action takes place in spite of it. In habitual action it deliberately refrains from interfering with the resistance of the synapses, and so the action goes on like a complicated reflex. But it *can* affect these resistances if it wishes, though often only with difficulty; and it is ready to do so if it judges this to be expedient. Finally, it may lose the power altogether. This would be what happens when a person becomes a slave to some habit, such as drug-taking.

I conclude that, at the level of enlightened common-sense at which the ordinary discussion of Interaction moves, no good reason has been produced for doubting that the mind acts on the body in volition, and that the body acts on the mind in sensation. The philosophic arguments are quite inconclusive; and the scientific arguments, when properly understood, are quite compatible with Two-sided Interaction. At most they suggest certain conclusions as to the form which interaction probably takes if it happens at all.

## DIFFICULTIES IN THE DENIAL OF INTERACTION

I propose now to consider some of the difficulties which would attend the denial of Interaction, still keeping the discussion at the same common-sense level. If a man denies the action of body on mind he is at once in trouble over the causation of new sensations. Suppose that I suddenly tread on an unsuspected tin-tack. A new sensation suddenly comes into my mind. This is an event, and it presumably has some cause. Now, however carefully I introspect and retrospect, I can find no other mental event which is adequate to account for the fact that just that sensation has arisen at just that moment. If I reject the common-sense view that treading on the tack is an essential part of the cause of the sensation, I must suppose either that it is uncaused, or that it is caused by other events in my mind which I cannot discover by introspection or retrospection, or that it is caused telepathically by other finite minds or by God. Now enquiry of my neighbors would show that it is not caused telepathically by any event in their minds which they can introspect or remember. Thus anyone who denies the action of body on mind, and admits that sensations have causes, must postulate either *(a)* immense numbers of unobservable states in his own mind; or *(b)* as many unobservable states in his neighbors' minds, together with telepathic action; or *(c)* some non-human spirit together with telepathic action. I must confess that the difficulties which have been alleged against the action of body on mind seem to be mild compared with those of the alternative hypotheses which are involved in the denial of such action.

The difficulties which are involved in the denial of the action of mind on body are at first sight equally great; but I do not think that they turn out to be so serious as those which are involved in denying the action of body on mind. The ***prima facie*** difficulty is this. The world contains many obviously artificial objects, such as books, bridges, clothes, etc. We know that, if we go far enough back in the history of their production, we always do in fact come on the actions of some human body. And the minds connected with these bodies did design the objects in question, did will to produce them, and did believe that they were initiating and guiding the physical process by means of these designs and volitions. If it be true that the mind does not act on the body, it follows that the designs and volitions in the agents' minds did not in fact play any part in the production of books, bridges, clothes, etc. This appears highly paradoxical. And it is an easy step from it to say that anyone who denies the action of mind on body must admit that books, bridges, and other such objects *could* have been produced even though there had been no minds, no thought of these objects and no desire for them. This consequence seems manifestly absurd to common-sense, and it might be argued that it reflects its absurdity back on the theory which entails it. . . .

## *Thomas H. Huxley (1825–1895)*

T. H. Huxley is best known as a defender of Darwinian evolutionary theory. He made important biological discoveries of his own as well in the areas of anatomy and physiology. Huxley was quite interested in philosophy and wrote a book on Hume and a number of essays in philosophy of mind and other areas. The selection below is taken from an essay originally published in 1874 and reprinted in a collection of his essays titled *Methods and Results* (1917). Among his most important works are *Man's Place in Nature* (1863), *The Physical Basis of Life* (1868), and *Evolution and Ethics* (1893).

In the following selection Huxley argues that although it is possible to maintain Descartes' hypothesis that animals are unconscious automata, there is good reason to prefer the hypothesis that they are in fact conscious automata. That is, animal functioning is entirely a matter of biological mechanisms, but these mechanisms give rise to conscious experience — pain, pleasure, fear, and so on — as well as to physical behavior. By extension, it is natural to use the same hypothesis with respect to human animals or persons. This is a version of **epiphenomenalism,** the view that some physical events cause mental events to occur, but that mental events themselves have no causal power whatsoever over physical or other mental events.

## Animals as Conscious Automata

### *Thomas H. Huxley*

. . . Thus far, the prepositions respecting the physiology of the nervous system which are stated by Descartes have simply been more clearly defined, more fully illustrated, and, for the most part, demonstrated, by modern physiological research. But there remains a doctrine to which Descartes attached great weight, so that full acceptance of it became a sort of note of a thoroughgoing Cartesian, but which, nevertheless, is so opposed to ordinary prepossessions that it attained more general notoriety, and gave rise to more discussion, than almost any other Cartesian hypothesis. It is the doctrine that brute animals are mere machines or automata, devoid not only of reason, but of any kind of consciousness. . . .

Descartes' line of argument is perfectly clear. He starts from reflex action in man, from the unquestionable fact that, in ourselves, coordinate, purposive, actions may take place, without the intervention of consciousness or volition, or even contrary to the latter. As actions of a certain degree of complexity are brought about by mere mechanism, why may not actions of still greater complexity be the result of a more refined mechanism? What proof is there that brutes are other than a superior race of marionettes, which eat without pleasure, cry without pain, desire nothing, know nothing, and only simulate intelligence as a bee simulates a mathematician? . . .

It must be premised, that it is wholly impossible absolutely to prove the presence or absence of consciousness in anything but one's own brain, though, by analogy, we are justified in assuming its existence in other men. Now if, by some accident, a man's spinal cord is divided, his limbs are paralyzed, so far as his volition is concerned, below the point of injury; and he is incapable of experiencing all those states of consciousness which, in his uninjured state, would be excited by irritation of those nerves which come off below the injury. If the spinal cord is divided in the middle of the back, for example, the skin of the feet may be cut, or pinched, or

Abridged from *Methods and Results, Essays by Thomas H. Huxley* (1917, D. Appleton & Co.) (New York: Greenwood Press Publishers, 1968), pp. 216–45.

burned, or wetted with vitriol, without any sensation of touch, or of pain, arising in consciousness. So far as the man is concerned, therefore, the part of the central nervous system which lies beyond the injury is cut off from consciousness. It must indeed be admitted, that, if any one think fit to maintain that the spinal cord below the injury is conscious, but that it is cut off from any means of making its consciousness known to the other consciousness in the brain, there is no means of driving him from his position by logic. But assuredly there is no way of proving it. . . . However near the brain the spinal cord is injured, consciousness remains intact, except that the irritation of parts below the injury is no longer represented by sensation. On the other hand, pressure upon the anterior division of the brain, or extensive injuries to it, abolish consciousness. Hence, it is a highly probable conclusion, that consciousness in man depends upon the integrity of the anterior division of the brain, while the middle and hinder divisions of the brain, and the rest of the nervous centers, have nothing to do with it. And it is further highly probable, that what is true for man is true for other vertebrated animals.

We may assume, then, that in a living vertebrated animal, any segment of the cerebro-spinal axis (or spinal cord and brain) separated from that anterior division of the brain which is the organ of consciousness, is as completely incapable of giving rise to consciousness as we know it to be incapable of carrying out volitions. Nevertheless, this separated segment of the spinal cord is not passive and inert. On the contrary, it is the seat of extremely remarkable powers. In our imaginary case of injury, the man would, as we have seen, be devoid of sensation in his legs, and would have not the least power of moving them. But, if the soles of his feet were tickled, the legs would be drawn up just as vigorously as they would have been before the injury. We know exactly what happens when the soles of the feet are tickled; a molecular change takes place in the sensory nerves of the skin, and is propagated along them and through the posterior roots of the spinal nerves, which are constituted by them, to the gray matter of the spinal cord. Through that gray matter the molecular motion is reflected into the anterior roots of the same nerves, constituted by the filaments which supply the muscles of the legs, and, travelling along these motor filaments, reaches the muscles, which at once contract, and cause the limbs to be drawn up.

In order to move the legs in this way, a definite coordination of muscular contractions is necessary; the muscles must contract in a certain order and with duly proportioned force; and moreover, as the feet are drawn away from the source of irritation, it may be said that the action has a final cause, or is purposive.

Thus it follows, that the gray matter of the segment of the man's spinal cord, though it is devoid of consciousness, nevertheless responds to a simple stimulus by giving rise to a complex set of muscular contractions, coordinated towards a definite end, and serving an obvious purpose.

If the spinal cord of a frog is cut across, so as to provide us with a segment separated from the brain, we shall have a subject parallel to the injured man, on which experiments can be made without remorse; as we have a right to conclude that a frog's spinal cord is not likely to be conscious, when a man's is not.

Now the frog behaves just as the man did. The legs are utterly paralyzed, so far as voluntary movement is concerned; but they are vigorously drawn up to the body when any irritant is applied to the foot. But let us study our frog a little farther. Touch the skin of the side of the body with a little acetic acid, which gives rise to all the signs of great pain in an uninjured frog. In this case, there can be no pain, because the application is made to a part of the skin supplied with nerves which come off from the cord below the point of section; nevertheless, the frog lifts up the limb of the same side, and applies the foot to rub off the acetic acid; and, what is still more remarkable, if the limb be held so that the frog cannot use it, it will, by and by, move the limb of the other side, turn it across the body, and use it for the same rubbing process. It is impossible that the frog, if it were in its entirety and could reason, should perform actions more purposive than these: and yet we have most complete assurance that, in this case, the frog is not acting from purpose, has no consciousness, and is a mere insensible machine.

But now suppose that, instead of making a section of the cord in the middle of the body, it had been made in such a manner as to separate the hindermost division of the brain from the rest of the organ, and suppose the foremost two-thirds of the brain entirely taken away. The frog is then absolutely devoid of any spontaneity; it sits upright in the attitude which a frog habitually assumes; and it will not stir unless it is touched; but it differs from the frog which I have just described in this, that, if it be thrown into the water, it begins to swim, and swims just as well as the perfect frog does. But swimming requires the combination and successive coordination of a great number of muscular actions. And we are forced to conclude, that the impression made upon the sensory nerves of the skin of the frog by the contact with the water into which it is thrown, causes the transmission to the central nervous apparatus of an impulse which sets going a certain machinery by which all the muscles of swimming are brought into play in due coordination. If the frog be stimulated by some irritating body, it jumps or walks as well as the complete frog can do. The simple sensory impression, acting through the machinery of the cord, gives rise to these complex combined movements.

It is possible to go a step farther. Suppose that only the anterior division of the brain — so much of it as lies in front of the "optic lobes" — is removed. If that operation is performed quickly and skillfully, the frog may be kept in a state of full bodily vigor for months, or it may be for years; but it will sit unmoved. It sees nothing: it hears nothing. It will starve sooner than feed itself, although food put into its mouth is swallowed. On irritation, it jumps or walks; if thrown into the water it swims. If it be put on the hand, it sits there, crouched, perfectly quiet, and would sit there forever. If the hand be inclined very gently and slowly, so that the frog would naturally tend to slip off, the creature's fore paws are shifted on to the edge of the hand, until he can just prevent himself from falling. If the turning of the hand be slowly continued, he mounts up with great care and deliberation, putting first one leg forward and then another, until he balances himself with perfect precision upon the edge; and if the turning of the hand is continued, he goes through the needful set of muscular operations, until he comes to be seated in security, upon the back of the hand. The doing of all this requires a delicacy of coordination, and a precision of adjustment of the muscular apparatus of the body, which are only comparable to those of a rope-dancer. To the ordinary influences of light, the frog, deprived of its cerebral hemispheres, appears to be blind. Nevertheless, if the animal be put upon a table, with a book at some little distance between it and the light, and the skin of the hinder part of its body is then irritated, it will jump forward, avoiding the book by passing to the right or left of it. Therefore, although the frog appears to have no sensation of light, visible objects act through its brain upon the motor mechanism of its body.

It is obvious, that had Descartes been acquainted with these remarkable results of modern research, they would have furnished him with far more powerful arguments than he possessed in favor of his view of the automatism of brutes. The habits of a frog, leading its natural life, involve such simple adaptations to surrounding conditions, that the machinery which is competent to do so much without the intervention of consciousness, might well do all. And this argument is vastly strengthened by what has been learned in recent times of the marvellously complex operations which are performed mechanically, and to all appearance without consciousness, by men, when, in consequence of injury or disease, they are reduced to a condition more or less comparable to that of a frog, in which the anterior part of the brain has been removed. A case has recently been published by an eminent French physician, Dr. Mesnet, which illustrates this condition so remarkably, that I make no apology for dwelling upon it at considerable length.

A sergeant of the French army, F——, twenty-seven years of age, was wounded during the battle of Bazeilles, by a ball which fractured his left parietal bone. He ran his bayonet through the Prussian soldier who wounded him, but almost immediately his right arm became paralyzed; after walking about two hundred yards, his right leg became similarly affected, and he lost his senses. When he recovered them, three weeks afterwards, in hospital at Mayence, the right half of the body was completely paralyzed, and remained in this condition for a year. At present, the only trace of the paralysis which remains is a slight weakness of the right half of the body. Three or four months after the wound was inflicted, periodical disturbances of the functions of the brain made their appearance, and have continued ever since. The disturbances last from fifteen to thirty hours; the intervals at which they occur being from fifteen to thirty days.

For four years, therefore, the life of this man has been divided into alternating phases — short abnormal states intervening between long normal states.

In the periods of normal life, the ex-sergeant's health is perfect; he is intelligent and kindly, and performs, satisfactorily, the duties of a hospital attendant. The commencement of the abnormal state is ushered in by uneasiness and a sense of weight about the forehead, which the patient compares to the constriction of a circle of iron; and, after its termination, he complains, for some hours, of dullness and heaviness of the head. But the transition from the normal to the abnormal state takes place in a few minutes, without convulsions or cries, and without anything to indicate the change to a bystander. His movements remain free and his expression calm, except for a contraction of the brow, an incessant movement of the eyeballs, and a chewing motion of the jaws. The eyes are wide open, and their pupils dilated. If the man happens to be in a place to which he is accustomed, he walks about as usual; but, if he is in a new place, or if obstacles are intentionally placed in his way, he stumbles gently against them, stops, and then, feeling over the objects with his hands, passes on one side of them. He offers no resistance to any change of direction which may be impressed upon him, or to the forcible acceleration or retardation of his movements. He eats, drinks, smokes, walks about, dresses and undresses himself, rises and goes to bed at the accustomed hours. Nevertheless, pins may be run into his body, or strong electric shocks sent through it, without causing the least indication of pain; no odorous substance, pleasant or unpleasant, makes the least impression; he eats and drinks with avidity whatever is offered, and takes asafoetida, or vinegar, or quinine, as readily as water; no noise affects him; and light influences him only under certain conditions. Dr. Mesnet remarks, that the sense of touch alone seems to persist, and indeed to be more acute and delicate than in the normal state: and it is by means of the nerves of touch, almost exclusively, that his organism is brought into relation with the external world. Here a difficulty arises. It is clear from the facts detailed, that the nervous apparatus by which, in the normal state, sensations of touch are excited, is that by which external influences determine the movements of the body, in the abnormal state. But does the state of consciousness, which we term a tactile sensation, accompany the operation of this nervous apparatus in the abnormal state? or is consciousness utterly absent, the man being reduced to an insensible mechanism? . . .

The ex-sergeant has a good voice, and had, at one time, been employed as a singer at a café. In one of his abnormal states he was observed to begin humming a tune. He then went to his room, dressed himself carefully, and took up some parts of a periodical novel, which lay on his bed, as if he were trying to find something. Dr. Mesnet, suspecting that he was seeking his music, made up one of these into a roll and put it into his hand. He appeared satisfied, took his cane and went downstairs to the door. Here Dr. Mesnet turned him round, and he walked quite contentedly, in the opposite direction, towards the room of the concierge. The light of the sun shining through a window now happened to fall upon him, and seemed to suggest the footlights of the stage on which he was accustomed to make his appearance. He stopped, opened his roll of imaginary music, put himself into the attitude of a singer, and sang, with perfect execution, three songs, one after the other. After which he wiped his face with his handkerchief and drank, without a grimace, a tumbler of strong vinegar and water which was put into his hand.

An experiment which may be performed upon the frog deprived of the fore part of its brain, well known as Göltz's "Quak-versuch," affords a parallel to this performance. If the skin of a certain part of the back of such a frog is gently stroked with the finger, it immediately croaks. It never croaks unless it is so stroked, and the croak always follows the stroke, just as the sound of a repeater follows the touching of the spring. In the frog, this "song" is innate—so to speak *à priori*—and depends upon a mechanism in the brain governing the vocal apparatus, which is set at work by the molecular change set up in the sensory nerves of the skin of the back by the contact of a foreign body.

In man there is also a vocal mechanism, and the cry of an infant is in the same sense innate and *à priori,* inasmuch as it depends on an organic relation between its sensory nerves and the nervous mechanism which governs the vocal apparatus. Learning to speak, and learning to sing, are processes by which the vocal mechanism is set to new tunes. A song which has been learned has its molecular equivalent, which potentially represents it in the brain, just as a musical box, wound up, potentially represents an overture. Touch the stop and the overture begins; send a molecular impulse along the proper afferent nerve and the singer begins his song. . . .

As I have pointed out, it is impossible to prove that F—— is absolutely unconscious in his abnormal state, but it is no less impossible to prove the contrary; and the case of the frog goes a long way to justify the assumption that, in the abnormal state, the man is a mere insensible machine.

If such facts as these had come under the knowledge of Descartes, would they not have formed an apt commentary upon that remarkable passage in the "Traité de l'Homme," which I have quoted elsewhere, but which is worth repetition?—

> All the functions which I have attributed to this machine (the body), as the digestion of food, the pulsation of the heart and of the arteries; the nutrition and the growth of the limbs; respiration, wakefulness, and sleep; the reception of light, sounds, odors, flavors, heat, and such like qualities, in the organs of the external senses; the impression of the ideas of these in the organ of common sensation and in the imagination; the retention or the impression of these ideas on the memory; the internal movements of the appetites and the passions; and lastly the external movements of all the limbs, which follow so aptly, as well the action of the objects which are presented to the senses, as the impressions which meet in the memory, that they imitate as nearly as possible those of a real man; I desire, I say, that you should consider that these functions in the machine naturally proceed from the mere arrangement of its organs, neither more nor less than do the movements of a clock, or other automaton, from that of its weights and its wheels; so that, so far as these are concerned, it is not necessary to conceive any other vegetative or sensitive soul, nor any other principle of motion or of life, than the blood and the spirits agitated by the fire which burns continually in the heart, and which is no wise essentially different from all the fires which exist in inanimate bodies.

And would Descartes not have been justified in asking why we need deny that animals are machines, when men, in a state of unconsciousness, perform, mechanically, actions as complicated and as seemingly rational as those of any animals?

But though I do not think that Descartes' hypothesis can be positively refuted, I am not disposed to accept it. The doctrine of continuity is too well established for it to be permissible to me to suppose that any complex natural phenomenon comes into existence suddenly, and without being preceded by simpler modifications; and very strong arguments would be needed to prove that such complex phenomena as those of consciousness, first make their appearance in man. We know that, in the individual man, consciousness grows from a dim glimmer to its full light, whether we consider the infant advancing in years, or the adult emerging from slumber and swoon. We know, further, that the lower animals possess, though less developed, that part of the brain which we have every reason to believe to be the organ of consciousness in man; and as, in other cases, function and organ are proportional, so we have a right to conclude it is with the brain;

and that the brutes, though they may not possess our intensity of consciousness, and though, from the absence of language, they can have no trains of thoughts, but only trains of feelings, yet have a consciousness which, more or less distinctly, foreshadows our own.

I confess that, in view of the struggle for existence which goes on in the animal world, and of the frightful quantity of pain with which it must be accompanied, I should be glad if the probabilities were in favor of Descartes' hypothesis; but, on the other hand, considering the terrible practical consequences to domestic animals which might ensue from any error on our part, it is as well to err on the right side, if we err at all, and deal with them as weaker brethren, who are bound, like the rest of us, to pay their toll for living, and suffer what is needful for the general good. As Hartley finely says, "We seem to be in the place of God to them;" and we may justly follow the precedents He sets in nature in our dealings with them.

But though we may see reason to disagree with Descartes' hypothesis that brutes are unconscious machines, it does not follow that he was wrong in regarding them as automata. They may be more or less conscious, sensitive, automata; and the view that they are such conscious machines is that which is implicitly, or explicitly, adopted by most persons. When we speak of the actions of the lower animals being guided by instinct and not by reason, what we really mean is that, though they feel as we do, yet their actions are the results of their physical organization. We believe, in short, that they are machines, one part of which (the nervous system) not only sets the rest in motion, and coordinates its movements in relation with changes in surrounding bodies, but is provided with special apparatus, the function of which is the calling into existence of those states of consciousness which are termed sensations, emotions, and ideas. I believe that this generally accepted view is the best expression of the facts at present known.

It is experimentally demonstrable — any one who cares to run a pin into himself may perform a sufficient demonstration of the fact — that a mode of motion of the nervous system is the immediate antecedent of a state of consciousness. All but the adherents of **"Occasionalism,"** or of the doctrine of **"Pre-established Harmony"** (if any such now exist), must admit that we have as much reason for regarding the mode of motion of the nervous system as the cause of the state of consciousness, as we have for regarding any event as the cause of another. How the one phenomenon causes the other we know, as much or as little, as in any other case of causation; but we have as much right to believe that the sensation is an effect of the molecular change, as we have to believe that motion is an effect of impact; and there is as much propriety in saying that the brain evolves sensation, as there is in saying that an iron rod, when hammered, evolves heat.

As I have endeavored to show, we are justified in supposing that something analogous to what happens in ourselves takes place in the brutes, and that the affections of their sensory nerves give rise to molecular changes in the brain, which again give rise to, or evolve, the corresponding states of consciousness. Nor can there be any reasonable doubt that the emotions of brutes, and such ideas as they possess, are similarly dependent upon molecular brain changes. Each sensory impression leaves behind a record in the structure of the brain — an "ideagenous" molecule, so to speak, which is competent, under certain conditions, to reproduce, in a fainter condition, the state of consciousness which corresponds with that sensory impression; and it is these "ideagenous molecules" which are the physical basis of memory.

It may be assumed, then, that molecular changes in the brain are the causes of all the states of consciousness of brutes. Is there any evidence that these states of consciousness may, conversely, cause those molecular changes which give rise to muscular motion? I see no such evidence. The frog walks, hops, swims, and goes through his gymnastic performances quite as well without consciousness, and consequently without volition, as with it; and, if a frog, in his natural state, possesses anything corresponding with what we call volition, there is no reason to think that it is anything but a concomitant of the molecular changes in the brain which form part of the series involved in the production of motion.

The consciousness of brutes would appear to be related to the mechanism of their body simply as a collateral product of its working, and to be as completely without any power of modifying that working as the steam-whistle which accompanies the work of a locomotive engine is without influence upon its machinery. Their volition, if they have any, is an emotion indicative of physical changes, not a cause of such changes.

This conception of the relations of states of consciousness with molecular changes in the brain—of [psychic processes] with [neural processes]—does not prevent us from ascribing free will to brutes. For an agent is free when there is nothing to prevent him from doing that which he desires to do. If a greyhound chases a hare, he is a free agent, because his action is in entire accordance with his strong desire to catch the hare; while so long as he is held back by the leash he is not free, being prevented by external force from following his inclination. And the ascription of freedom to the greyhound under the former circumstances is by no means inconsistent with the other aspect of the facts of the case—that he is a machine impelled to the chase, and caused, at the same time, to have the desire to catch the game by the impression which the rays of light proceeding from the hare make upon his eyes, and through them upon his brain.

Much ingenious argument has at various times been bestowed upon the question: How is it possible to imagine that volition, which is a state of consciousness, and, as such, has not the slightest community of nature with matter in motion, can act upon the moving matter of which the body is composed, as it is assumed to do in voluntary acts? But if, as is here suggested, the voluntary acts of brutes—or, in other words, the acts which they desire to perform—are as purely mechanical as the rest of their actions, and are simply accompanied by the state of consciousness called volition, the inquiry, so far as they are concerned, becomes superfluous. Their volitions do not enter into the chain of causation of their actions at all.

The hypothesis that brutes are conscious automata is perfectly consistent with any view that may be held respecting the often discussed and curious question whether they have souls or not; and, if they have souls, whether those souls are immortal or not. It is obviously harmonious with the most literal adherence to the text of Scripture concerning "the beast that perisheth"; but it is not inconsistent with the amiable conviction ascribed by Pope to his "untutored savage," that when he passes to the happy hunting-grounds in the sky, "his faithful dog shall bear him company." If the brutes have consciousness and no souls, then it is clear that, in them, consciousness is a direct function of material changes; while, if they possess immaterial subjects of consciousness, or souls, then, as consciousness is brought into existence only as the consequence of molecular motion of the brain, it follows that it is an indirect product of material changes. The soul stands related to the body as the bell of a clock to the works, and consciousness answers to the sound which the bell gives out when it is struck. . . .

It will be said, that I mean that the conclusions deduced from the study of the brutes are applicable to man, and that the logical consequences of such application are fatalism, materialism, and atheism—whereupon the drums will beat the *pas de charge.*

One does not do battle with drummers; but I venture to offer a few remarks for the calm consideration of thoughtful persons, untrammelled by foregone conclusions, unpledged to shore-up tottering dogmas, and anxious only to know the true bearings of the case.

It is quite true that, to the best of my judgment, the argumentation which applies to brutes holds equally good of men; and, therefore, that all states of consciousness in us, as in them, are immediately caused by molecular changes of the brain-substance. It seems to me that in men, as in brutes, there is no proof that any state of consciousness is the cause of change in the motion of the matter of the organism. If these positions are well based, it follows that our mental conditions are simply the symbols in consciousness of the changes which take place automatically in the organism; and that, to take an extreme illustration, the feeling we call volition is not the cause of a voluntary act, but the symbol of that state of the brain which is the immediate cause of that act. We are conscious automata, endowed with free will in the only intelligible sense of that much-abused term — inasmuch as in many respects we are able to do as we like — but none the less parts of the great series of causes and effects which, in unbroken continuity, composes that which is, and has been, and shall be — the sum of existence.

As to the logical consequences of this conviction of mine, I may be permitted to remark that logical consequences are the scarecrows of fools and the beacons of wise men. The only question which any wise man can ask himself, and which any honest man will ask himself, is whether a doctrine is true or false. Consequences will take care of themselves; at most their importance can only justify us in testing with extra care the reasoning process from which they result.

So that if the view I have taken did really and logically lead to fatalism, materialism, and atheism, I should profess myself a fatalist, materialist, and atheist; and I should look upon those who, while they believed in my honesty of purpose and intellectual competency, should raise a hue and cry against me, as people who by their own admission preferred lying to truth, and whose opinions therefore were unworthy of the smallest attention.

But, as I have endeavored to explain on other occasions, I really have no claim to rank myself among fatalistic, materialistic, or atheistic philosophers. Not among fatalists, for I take the conception of necessity to have a logical, and not a physical foundation; not among materialists, for I am utterly incapable of conceiving the existence of matter if there is no mind in which to picture that existence; not among atheists, for the problem of the ultimate cause of existence is one which seems to me to be hopelessly out of reach of my poor powers. Of all the senseless babble I have ever had occasion to read, the demonstrations of these philosophers who undertake to tell us all about the nature of God would be the worst, if they were not surpassed by the still greater absurdities of the philosophers who try to prove that there is no God.

# *Materialism*

Materialism is the label given to any theory that explicitly asserts that human beings consist of physical bodies and nothing else, that persons are entirely material. As Armstrong notes in the first essay of this subsection, this view is no longer in clear opposition to common sense. We use the concepts of mind and brain almost interchangeably in ordinary conversation. "Use your brain." "Where were you when God handed out brains?" "George hasn't got a brain in his head." "John was brainwashed." All these uses of "brain" refer roughly to mental processes (thought, reasoning) or mental capacities (intelligence, common sense). In the little more than a decade and a half since Armstrong's essay was published, the philosophical point of view that could then be described as "admittedly paradoxical" has become almost commonplace, even among philosophers. Frequently one of the most difficult tasks for an instructor in an introductory lecture on the mind-body problem is to convince a general student audience that it is even possible to distinguish between mind and brain.

All the commonsense evidence for causal interaction is equally evidence for a version of materialism. Of course, stepping on a tack causes pain and intentions cause movements. The relations in each case are between peripheral bodily states and processes (sensory or motor) and states and processes of the central nervous system, and the causal mechanisms are fairly well understood and routinely studied in physiology courses.

The matter is not quite so easily settled, however. The thesis of materialism, while widely held to be true in some form, is not trivially true. We *can* distinguish minds from brains, and once we do materialism requires reasoned support against some fairly strong objections.

There is no difficulty in explaining what the term *brain* refers to. It refers to the organ inside our heads—a convoluted mass of nerve cells, axons, dendrites, and synapses arranged in distinguishable regions and undergoing electrochemical reactions of various sorts. We've seen pictures of brains in medical and scientific literature, and replicas of them in science fiction movies for quite some time. What does the term *mind* refer to? It is that to which we have special access as conscious subjects of experience. We experience our own thoughts, wishes, desires, reasoning, visual and auditory images. Whatever the true nature of these mental events and processes may turn out to be, we certainly have through introspection a first-person perspective on them that does not reveal them in terms of nerve cells and electrochemical states and changes of state. The discovery that the target of such introspective experience is nothing over and above the objects that neuroscience studies would be just that, a discovery. It would not be the simple recognition of an obvious fact.

At this point it becomes important to distinguish clearly the two main versions of materialism, since the reasons for holding each version and the kinds of objections that must be taken seriously are different in each case. The most straightforward and least radical form of materialism is reductive materialism, sometimes referred to as the *identity theory.* It holds that mental states and processes are literally identical to states and processes of the central nervous system—that what we think of as a mind is one and the same thing as what we think of as a brain. Such theories are reductive because the identities reduce references to the mental to references to the physical. Or, equivalently, psychology and physical science reduce to physical science alone. Reductive materialism of this form holds that for each state or process that we currently refer to by means of a mental description (thinking of the Pythagorean theorem, experiencing a particular visual image, and so on) there is a neurophysiological state or process that can be described in strictly physical terms that is identical to it. That is, it will turn out that there is only one thing—a state or process of the central nervous system—picked out in two different ways, introspectively by the conscious subject of experience and physiologically by the appropriate neuroscientist. Of course, neuroscience is not yet complete, and so we do not have all of the identical pairs of descriptions at this point. But the reductive materialist thinks that we have some of the pairs from already successful neuroscientific research and is betting that we will eventually have the complete set, at which time there will no longer be any theoretical use for the introspective descriptions and their misleading and problematic mentalistic vocabulary.

There are two types of identity that are sometimes confused, and that confusion leads to a critical misunderstanding of reductive materialism. *Bachelors* and *unmarried males* are identical in meaning. The two terms necessarily refer to the same things because they are different ways of expressing the same concept. *Morning star* and *evening star* do *not* have the same meaning. They refer to the same object only contingently, not necessarily. It happens that the two terms pick out the same thing as a matter of fact, not as a matter of meaning or conceptual necessity. The latter kind of identity has to be discovered. Astronomers were somewhat surprised when they first learned that the object that is at times the last bright light in the sky at dawn and the object that at other times is the first bright light visible in the evening sky were one and the same. It is this last kind of identity, contingent and discoverable rather than necessary and conceptual, that figures in reductive materialism. So the meanings of the neuroscientists' terms may differ any amount from the meanings of the mentalistic terms we use to introspectively pick out certain inner states and processes. Nonetheless, the identity theorist claims we will discover as a matter of fact that only one set of states and processes is picked out by both sets of terms, and that these are states and processes of the central nervous system rather than states and processes of an immaterial mind.

It is frequently thought that recent advances in the scientific study of the brain demonstrate the truth of reductive materialism. But just as our intuitions about causal relations between conscious experiences and bodily circumstances and events are neutral with respect to the distinction between dualism and materialism, so are the findings of scientific research. The scientist discovers in increasing detail which regions of the brain and which kinds of events in those regions are associated with particular conscious experiences. This is typically accomplished by matching certain electrical and chemical data with the introspective reports of the experimental subject. What the scientist cannot do in this manner is discover any more than rigid correspondence between the objects of the two descriptions or reports. There is no crucial experiment of the sort which could show that these objects were identical rather than that they were distinct but tied together by rigid causal laws. Both dualism and reductive materialism would predict just the sorts of constant correspondence which the scientist discovers.

However, there are two kinds of very strong support for reductive materialism. The first and most obvious is that it avoids all of the really serious difficulties that dualistic theories encounter. The second kind of support comes from a general criterion that applies to all theories and was discussed under the topic of scientific method in Part 2. One of the most important considerations in choosing between competing theories is simplicity. And a theory that can explain all the relevant data in strictly physical terms will be much simpler than a theory that explains the same data in physical and mental terms and that must further explain the relations between the two sets of objects to which the terms refer. So reductive materialism need only be as plausible as dualism to be clearly preferable on methodological grounds. That is, other things being approximately equal, materialism wins and dualism loses on the basis of theoretical simplicity.

Both the Armstrong and Churchland essays deal with a number of objections to reductive materialism and responses that can be made to those objections on behalf of the theory. There is a general difficulty for the theory in addition to the specific problems discussed in the readings that follow. If we think about the kinds of identities that science has discovered, they seem to be importantly unlike the identity of the mental and the physical proposed by reductive materialism. Science has discovered, for example, that lightning is identical to a certain massive electrical discharge, that heat is just the energy of motion of molecules, that the morning star, the evening star, and the planet Venus are all one and the same heavenly body. In each of these identities, the crucial discovery was a matter of finding that the apparently different things occupied exactly the same place at the same time. And when two material objects occupy exactly the same space at one time they are really one and not two at all. But the equivalent discovery in the case of conscious phenomena and brain states or processes doesn't seem possible. The conscious phenomena and the physiological events can certainly occur at the same time, but that's not enough to yield identity. Pushing the button and the ringing of the doorbell occur at the same time, but they are distinct and causally related, not identical. And thinking of the conscious phenomena available to introspection as occurring in some place doesn't seem to make sense. We certainly can't tell by introspection of our experiences that they are occurring at the points of the central nervous system indicated by current neuroscience. Furthermore, how can something that doesn't seem to be located at a specific place (for example, my awareness of Pike's Peak) be identical to a brain process that most certainly *is* located at a specific place?

By far the most serious threat to reductive materialism is posed not by difficulties the theory must overcome but by the more radical form of materialism, eliminative materialism. Eliminative materialism holds that persons are strictly material, but does not hold that mind is identical to brain. The eliminative materialist believes that there is no reason to think that the mental part of our conceptual scheme, with its confused and incoherent notions of immaterial things and powers, correctly picks out anything that will be important in the complete scientific account of human behavior and its causes. Mental concepts will suffer the same fate as the parts of our conceptual scheme that once referred to the ether in which the earth moved, the phlogiston which explained combustion, or the witches that accounted for various events at Salem and elsewhere. None of these concepts designate any single sort of thing and our present scheme has nothing that is identical to them in reference or function. So our beliefs in minds and their states and processes will eventually come to look like such interesting blunders or ignorant superstitions, and a complete conceptual scheme, with no room for such items or their equivalents, will come to be seen as quite adequate in its entirety. Mental concepts will simply be eliminated. But rather than finding material concepts to do the same job, we will discover that there is simply no such job to be done.

This radical form of materialism was once thought to be too counterintuitive to be plausible. But this is no longer the case. We now know that our culture's "folk wisdom" in virtually every other area of science suffered this fate. The concepts of "folk physics," "folk astronomy," and "folk biology" have all been eliminated in this way from our current scientific conceptualization of reality. It would, in fact, be strange if our original or **"folk psychology"** and its concepts should be the one area of science that we had gotten right from the start, the one whose basic concepts or their equivalents should have survived intact. And this form of materialism has the advantage over reductive materialism of not having to make sense of identifying the mental and the physical. It requires no simple translation of one set of terms into the other as a necessary condition of its acceptability. The essays by Ziff and Churchland explain these advantages in some detail. The primary difficulty for eliminative materialism is the apparent success of contemporary psychology in using the concepts of folk psychology to identify law-like regularities in at least some areas of human behavior. The section on artificial intelligence provides detailed support for the view that many such concepts will have to be preserved rather than eliminated by the cognitive sciences.

## *D. M. Armstrong (b. 1926)*

D. M. Armstrong has made numerous contributions in epistemology, especially to the understanding of perception, in addition to those in the philosophy of mind. His major works are *Perception and the Physical World* (1961), *A Materialist Theory of the Mind* (1968), from which the selection below was taken, and *Belief, Truth and Knowledge* (1973).

In the following essay, Armstrong argues for a version of reductive materialism, identifying mental states and processes with states and processes of the central nervous system yet to be specified by science. He argues that we can at present pick out mental states and processes in terms of their typical behavioral effects without knowing what their true nature is, just as biologists once picked out genes by their effects on the development of an organism without knowing anything about the true nature of the gene. And just as biologists discovered that the gene was identical to DNA, so neuroscientists will discover that particular mental states and processes are identical to particular states of the brain and particular neurological processes.

# Central-State Materialism

## *D. M. Armstrong*

. . . We must examine the . . . form of Materialism . . . which identifies mental states with purely physical states of the central nervous system. If the mind is thought of as "that which has mental states," then we can say that, on this theory, the mind is simply the central nervous system, or, less accurately but more epigrammatically, the mind is simply the brain.

Many philosophers still regard this theory of mind as a very extraordinary one. In 1962, for instance, A. G. N. Flew wrote:

> In the face of the powerful and resolute advocacy now offered *this admittedly paradoxical view* can no longer be dismissed in such short order. (*Philosophical Review,* Vol. LXXI, 1962, p. 403, my italics)

At the risk of seeming ungrateful to Professor Flew, it is interesting to notice that, even while conceding that the theory merits serious discussion, he calls it "admittedly paradoxical." I think his attitude is shared by many philosophers. Certainly I myself found the theory paradoxical when I first heard it expounded.

But it is important to realize that this opinion that the Central-state theory is paradoxical, is confined almost exclusively to philosophers. They are usually taught as first-year University students that the mind cannot possibly be the brain, and as a result they are inclined to regard the falsity of the Central-state theory as self-evident. But this opinion is not widely shared. Outside philosophy, the Central-state doctrine enjoys wide support. . . .

Let us measure the theory against the various demands that a satisfactory theory of mind must meet, . . . beginning with the demands that create no difficulty.

1. It is clear that this theory accounts very simply for the unity of mind and body. The brain is physically inside the body. It is the pilot in the vessel. This fits in remarkably well with ordinary talk about the mind. It is completely natural to speak of the mind as "in" the body, and to speak of mental processes as "inner" processes. Now "in" is primarily a spatial word. The naturalness of this way of speaking is strikingly, and the more strikingly because quite unconsciously, brought out by Hume. For in the course of putting forward a theory of mind according to which it is not in physical space, he says:

> Suppose we could see clearly into the *breast* of another and observe that succession of perceptions which constitutes his mind or thinking principle . . . (*Treatise,* Bk. I, Pt. IV, Sect. 6, p. 260, ed. Selby-Bigge, my italics)

Hume's way of talking here, indefensible on his own theory, seems to us *all* to be a natural way of talking, although we might now say "head," not "breast." But a Dualist must say that the mind is not in the body in any gross material sense of the word "in." What his own refined sense of the word is, is a mystery.

2. Central-state Materialism can provide a simple principle of numerical difference for minds, viz., difference of place, just as the Attribute and the Behaviorist theory can.

3. Central-state Materialism can explain very simply the interaction of mind and body. Brain and body interact, so mind and body interact.

4. Central-state Materialism allows us to say that the mind comes into being in a gradual way, and that there is no sharp break between not having a mind and having one. For in the evolution of the species, and in the development of

Abridged from *A Materialist Theory of the Mind,* by D. M. Armstrong (London: Routledge & Kegan Paul, 1968), pp. 73–90. Reprinted by permission of Routledge & Kegan Paul, PLC.

the individual, the brain comes into being in a gradual way. The simplification of our world-picture that results is the especial advantage of Materialist theories (including Behaviorism).

5. But unlike Behaviorism, a Central-state theory does not deny the existence of inner mental states. On the contrary, it asserts their existence: they are physical states of the brain.

Nevertheless, a Central-state theory seems to face some serious objections.

1. . . . Any satisfactory theory of mind ought to allow for the logical possibility of disembodied minds. If the mind is the brain, it might seem that a mind logically cannot exist in a disembodied state in any but the crudest sense, that is to say, as a brain without a body. This is not what we mean by a disembodied mind. . . .

2. It is not clear what account a Central-state theory can give of the **"intentionality"** or "pointing" nature of mental processes. It is true that no theory we have examined has cast any particular light on this problem so far. But . . . Materialist theories are at a special disadvantage in dealing with "intentionality," because they cannot treat it as an irreducible, unanalyzable, feature of mental processes on pain of contradicting their Materialism.

3. . . . Behavior and dispositions to behave do enter into the concept of mind in some way. It is not clear how a Central-state theory does justice to this feature of the mental.

But the difficulties considered in the previous section pale before one powerful line of argument that may seem to be a conclusive reason for denying that the mind is the brain. Take the statement "The mind is the brain." ("Mental processes are brain-processes" may be substituted if preferred.) Does the statement purport to be a logically necessary truth, or is it simply claimed to be contingently true? Does a defender of the Central-state theory want to assimilate the statement to "An oculist *is* an eye-doctor" or "7 + 5 *is* 12," on the one hand, or to "The morning star *is* the evening star" or "The gene *is* the DNA molecule," on the other?

It is perfectly clear which way the cat must jump here. If there is anything certain in philosophy, it is certain that "The mind is the brain" is not a **logically necessary** truth. When Aristotle said that the brain was nothing but an organ for keeping the body cool, he was certainly not guilty of denying a necessary truth. His mistake was an empirical one. So if it is true that the mind is the brain, a model must be found among contingent statements of identity. We must compare the statement to "The morning star is the evening star" or "The gene is the DNA molecule," or some other contingent assertion of identity. (The statement "The gene is the DNA molecule" is not a very exact one from the biological point of view. But it will prove to be a useful example in the development of the argument, and it is accurate enough for our purposes here.)

But if "The mind is the brain" is a **contingent** statement, then it follows that it must be possible to give logically independent explanations (or, alternatively, "ostensive definitions") of the meaning of the two words "mind" and "brain." For consider. "The morning star is the evening star" is a contingent statement. We can explain the meaning of the phrase "the morning star" thus: it is the very bright star seen in the sky on certain mornings of the year. We can explain the meaning of the phrase "the evening star" thus: it is the very bright star seen in the sky on certain evenings of the year. We can give logically independent explanations of the meanings of the two phrases. "The gene is the DNA molecule" is a contingent statement. We can explain the meaning of the word "gene" thus: it is that thing or principle within us that is responsible for the transmission of hereditary characteristics, such as color of eyes. We can explain the meaning of the phrase "DNA molecule" along the following lines: it is a molecule of a certain very complex chemical constitution which forms the nucleus of the cell. We can give logically independent explanations of the word "gene" and the phrase "DNA molecule."

Now if it is meaningful to say that "The mind is the brain" it must be possible to treat the words "mind" and "brain" in the same way.

The word "brain" gives no trouble. Clearly it is possible to explain its meaning in a quasi-ostensive way. The problem is posed by the word "mind." What verbal explanation or "ostensive definition" can we give of the meaning of this word without implying a departure from a physicalist view of the world? This seems to be the great problem, or, at any rate, one great problem, faced by a Central-state theory.

The object that we call a "brain" is called a brain in virtue of certain physical characteristics: it is a certain sort of physical object found inside people's skulls. Yet if we say that this object is also the mind, then, since the word "mind" does not mean the same as the word "brain," it seems that the brain can only be the mind in virtue of some *further* characteristic that the brain has. But what can this characteristic be? We seem on the verge of being forced back into an **Attribute theory.**

Put the problem another way. Central-state Materialism holds that when we are *aware* of our mental states what we are aware of are mere physical states of our brain. But we are certainly not aware of the mental states *as* states of the brain. What then are we aware of mental states as? Are we not aware of them as states of a quite peculiar, mental, sort?

The problem has so daunted one physicalist, Paul Feyerabend, that he has suggested that the materialist ought simply to recognize that his world-view does not allow statements that assert or imply the existence of minds. A true **physicalism** will simply talk about the operation of the central nervous system, and will write off talk about the mind as an intellectual loss. (See his "Mental events and the Brain," *The Journal of Philosophy,* Vol. LX, 1963.)

I think that if the situation is as desperate as this it is desperate indeed. It is at least our first duty to see if we can give an explanation of the word "mind" which will meet the demands that have just been outlined. In order to do this, let us turn to a way of thinking about man that has been popularized by psychology. Psychologists very often present us with the following picture. Man is an object continually acted upon by certain physical stimuli. These stimuli elicit from him certain behavior, that is to say, a certain physical response. In the causal chain between the stimulus and the response, falls the mind. The mind is that which causally mediates our response to stimuli. Now the Cental-state theory wants to say that between the stimulus and the response fall physical processes in the central nervous system, and nothing else at all, not even something "epiphenomenal." At the same time the theory cannot mention the central nervous system in its account of the concept of mind. If we now think of the psychologist's picture, the outline of a solution is in our hands. As a first approximation we can say that what we mean when we talk about the mind, or about particular mental processes, is nothing but the effect within a man of certain stimuli, and the cause within a man of certain responses. The intrinsic nature of these effects and causes is not something that is involved in the concept of mind or the particular mental concepts. The concept of a mental state is the concept of that, whatever it may turn out to be, which is brought about in a man by certain stimuli and which in turn brings about certain responses. What it is in its own nature is something for science to discover. Modern science declares that this mediator between stimulus and response is in fact the central nervous system, or more crudely and inaccurately, but more simply, the brain.

If we now consider the two papers that are already "classical" expositions of Central-state Materialism: U. T. Place's "Is Consciousness a Brain Process?" (*British Journal of Psychology,* Vol. XLVII, 1956, pp. 44–50) and J. J. C. Smart's "Sensations and Brain Processes" (*Philosophical Review,* Vol. LXVIII, 1959, pp. 141–56), we find that they give the problem we grappled with in the previous section only very brief consideration. So far as they do consider it, they come down on the side of the stimulus, not the response. Smart wrote:

> When a person says, "I see a yellowish-orange after-image," he is saying something like this: *"There is something going on which is like what is going on when* I have my eyes open, am awake, and there is an orange illuminated in good light in front of me, that is, when I really see an orange."

Here the having of an orange after-image is explicated in terms of the stimulus: an orange acting on a person in suitable conditions. Place took a similar line.

Now if we consider some other mental processes it is at once clear that this sort of analysis solely in terms of the effects of a stimulus can have no hope of success. Suppose I form the intention to go out and get a drink. There may well be no typical physical situations which have the effect of creating this state in me. The account of intentions must clearly proceed instead in terms of the behavior that such an intention initiates. The intention is an inner cause of a certain sort of response, not the inner effect of a certain sort of stimulus. Of course, the intention *is* an effect of certain causes, but it cannot be *defined* in terms of these causes.

In fact, however, the point just made about intentions would constitute no criticism of Place's and Smart's position as put forward in these articles. For with respect to things like intentions they are not Central-state Materialists, but Behaviorists. Place wrote:

> In the case of cognitive concepts like "knowing," "believing," "understanding," "remembering," and volitional concepts like "wanting" and "intending," there can be little doubt, I think, that an analysis in terms of dispositions to behave is fundamentally sound. On the other hand, there would seem to be an intractable residue of concepts clustering around the notions of consciousness, experience, sensation, and mental imagery, where some sort of inner process story is unavoidable.

Smart took the same view.

Against Place and Smart, however, I wish to defend a Central-state account of *all* the mental concepts. We do naturally distinguish between the thought or belief, and its expression in words or action, between the emotion and its expression in action, between the aim or intention and its expression in action. Taking the word literally, something is "expressed" when it is squeezed out, as oil is expressed from olives. Applied to the mind, this yields the picture of an inner state bringing about outward behavior. Surely some strong reason (as opposed to mere current prejudice) must be advanced if this picture is to be rejected? In default of such a reason it should be accepted.

It may be said that all we are ever aware of in introspection are sense-impressions, sensations and mental images. Now it may perhaps be granted that they are the most obtrusive sort of inner item, but it is far from clear that we are not sometimes aware of thoughts and intentions, for example, without accompanying imagery and sensations. Putting the matter at its lowest, it certainly seems to make sense to say "I was aware of thoughts going through my mind. An inner event occurred, but no relevant images went through my mind, nor did I have any relevant sense-impressions or sensations." Perhaps such statements are never true, but, again, perhaps they sometimes are. I think, indeed, that Place's and Smart's position is a mere hang-over from the Sensationalism of the British Empiricists which attempts to reduce all actual mental items to impressions, images and sensations. But once we have accepted any sort of inner mental item, strong arguments should be needed to exclude what are, ***prima facie,*** also items.

Smart has in fact changed his view on this matter. He now accepts a Central-state account of all the mental concepts. His original position was in fact, I think, an interesting example of a quite false spirit of economy. The motive was clear: if we have to admit inner items, let us admit as few as possible. But in fact once one has admitted the necessity for a certain sort of entity in one's theoretical scheme then it will often lead to a more economical theory if this sort of entity is postulated to explain the widest possible range of phenomena. Theoretical economy about entities is not like being economical with money. To be economical with money is to spend as little quantity of money as is consistent with one's purposes. But theoretical economy about entities is a matter of postulating the smallest number of *sorts* of entity that will explain the phenomena. Its analogue with respect to money would be a coinage that had the minimum number of *types* of coin consistent with all the sorts of financial operation that had to be undertaken. So once one admits inner mental states at all it is actually a theoretical economy to give a Central-state account of all the mental concepts.

But even if we confine ourselves to the ground originally chosen by Place and Smart, it is clear that their account of such things as perceptions in terms of the characteristic effects of certain stimuli is inadequate. I am not denying that what they say is part of the truth. . . . It *is* part of our notion of seeing or seeming to see something yellow that it is the sort of inner event characteristically produced in us by the action of a yellow physical object. But a full account of the visual experience involves more than this. To show us that he can perceive, a man must show us that he can do certain things: that he can systematically discriminate in his behavior between certain classes of objects. As Anthony Kenny remarks in his *Action, Emotion and Will* (Routledge, 1963, p. 59) we pick a man's lack of perceptual powers by a certain inefficiency in conduct. So, even in such a case as perception, reference to certain sorts of *responses* for which the perception gives us a capacity is at least as important for elucidating the concept as reference to certain sorts of stimuli.

The difficulties in Place's and Smart's position incline me to look to the response rather than the stimulus in seeking a general account of the mental concepts. The concept of a mental state is primarily the concept of *a state of the person apt for bringing about a certain sort of behavior.* Sacrificing all accuracy for brevity we can say that, although mind is not behavior, it is the *cause* of behavior. In the case of some mental states only they are also *states of the person apt for being brought about by a certain sort of stimulus.* But this latter formula is a secondary one.

It will be advisable to dwell rather carefully on this first formula: state of the person apt for bringing about a certain sort of behavior.

In the first place, I attach no special importance to the word "state." For instance, it is not meant to rule out "process" or "event." I think that in fact useful distinctions can be made between states, processes and events, and that mental "items," to use a neutral term, can be variously classified under these quite separate heads. . . .

In the second place, I call attention to the word "apt." Here there are two points to be made: *(a)* By saying only that mental states are states *apt* for bringing about behavior we allow for some mental states being actual occurrences, even although they result in no behavior. *(b)* The formula is intended to cover more than one sort of relationship between mental state and behavior. If we consider intentions, for instance, then they are naturally construed . . . as causes within our minds that tend to initiate and sustain certain courses of behavior. But it is most implausible to say that perceptions, for instance, are causes tending to initiate certain courses of behavior. Suppose I see a magpie on the lawn. It may well be that magpies are things which I can take or leave, and that no impulse to do anything at all is involved in the perception. What must be said about perception . . . is that it is a matter of acquiring capacities to make systematic physical discriminations within our environment *if we should be so impelled.* (If intentions are like pressures on a door, perceptions are like acquiring a key to the door. You can put the key in your pocket, and never do anything with it.) Other mental states will turn out to stand in still different causal relations to the behavior which constitutes their "expression." In some cases, indeed, it will emerge that certain sorts of mental states can only be described in terms of their *resemblance* to other mental states that stand in causal relations to behavior. Here the relation to behavior is very indirect indeed.

A closely connected point is that, in many cases, an account of mental states involves not only their causal relation to behavior, but their causal relation to other mental states. It may even be that an account of certain mental states will proceed solely in terms of the other mental states they are apt for bringing about. An intention to work out a sum "in one's head" would be a case in point. The intention is a mental cause apt for bringing about the thoughts that are the successive steps in the calculation. So all that is demanded is that our analysis must *ultimately* reach mental states that are describable in terms of the behavior they are apt for.

In the third place, the "bringing about" involved is the "bringing about" of ordinary, efficient, causality. It is no different in principle from the "bringing about" involved when the impact of one billiard-ball brings about the motion of another ball. But the mention of Hume's paradigm should not mislead. I do not wish to commit myself for or against a Humean or semi-Humean analysis of the nature of the causal relation. I am simply saying that causality in the mental sphere is no different from causality in the physical sphere. . . .

In the fourth place, the word "behavior" is ambiguous. We may distinguish between "physical behavior," which refers to any merely physical action or passion of the body, and "behavior proper," which implies relationship to the mind. "Behavior proper" entails "physical behavior," but not all "physical behavior" is "behavior proper," for the latter springs from the mind in a certain particular way. A reflex knee jerk is "physical behavior," but it is not "behavior proper." Now if in our formula "behavior" were to mean "behavior proper," then we would be giving an account of mental concepts in terms of a concept that already presupposes mentality, which would be circular. So it is clear that in our formula "behavior" must mean "physical behavior." (And it is clear also that this is going to make our projected account of the mental concepts that much more difficult to carry through.)

It will be seen that our formula "state of the person apt for bringing about a certain sort of behavior" is something that must be handled with care. Perhaps it is best conceived of as a slogan or catch-phrase which indicates the general lines along which accounts of the individual mental concepts are to be sought, but does no more than this.

This leads on to a final point to be made about the formula. It should not be regarded as a guide to the producing of *translations* of mental statements. It may well be that it is not possible to translate mental statements into statements that mention nothing but physical happenings, in any but the roughest way. It may be still true, nevertheless, that we can give a satisfactory and complete account of the situations covered by the mental concepts in purely physical and topic-neutral terms.

I think the situation is as follows. We apply certain concepts, the mental concepts, to human beings. That is to say, we attribute mental states to them. Then the question arises whether it is possible to do full justice to the nature of these mental states by means of purely physical or neutral concepts. We therefore try to sketch an account of typical mental states in purely physical or neutral terms. The account might fall indefinitely short of giving translations of mental statements, yet it might still be plausible to say that the account had done justice to the phenomena.

Of course, this does leave us with the question how, lacking the test of translation, we can ever know that we have succeeded in our enterprise. But this is just one instance of the perennial problem of finding a decision-procedure for philosophical problems. I think in fact that all we can do is this: we produce an account of a certain range of phenomena in terms of a favored set of concepts; we then try to test this account by looking for actual and possible situations falling within this range of phenomena which seem to defy complete description in terms of the favored concepts. If we can deal successfully with all the difficult cases, we have done all that we can do. But there is unlikely to be any way of *proving* to the general satisfaction that our enterprise has been successful. If there was, philosophy would be easier.

I turn to a question that may be worrying some readers. Now that I have given an account of the concept of a mental state, does it not appear that I am a Behaviorist in disguise? Admittedly, there is one great divergence from Behaviorism: the mind is not to be identified with behavior, but only with the inner principle of behavior. But, in elucidating our formula, there has been talk about tendencies to initiate, and capacities for, behavior. And are not these perilously close to the Behaviorist's dispositions?

There is some force in this. In talking about

dispositions to behave Behaviorism did come quite close to the version of the Central-state theory being defended here, far closer than it came when it talked about behavior itself. But Behaviorism and the Central-state theory still remain deeply at odds about *the way dispositions are to be conceived.*

Speaking of dispositional properties in *The Concept of Mind* Ryle wrote (p. 43):

> To possess a dispositional property *is not to be in a particular state, or to undergo a particular change;* it is to be bound or liable to be in a particular state, or to undergo a particular change, when a particular condition is realized. (My italics)

. . . To this we may oppose what may be called a **Realist** account of dispositions. According to the Realist view, to speak of an object's having a dispositional property entails that the object is in some non-dispositional state or that it has some property . . . which is responsible for the object manifesting certain behavior in certain circumstances, manifestations whose nature makes the dispositional property the particular dispositional property it is. It is true that we may not know anything of the nature of the nondispositional state. But, the Realist view asserts, in asserting that a certain piece of glass is brittle, for instance, we are . . . asserting that it is in a certain non-dispositional state which disposes it to shatter and fly apart in a wide variety of circumstances. Ignorance of the nature of the state does not affect the issue. . . .

I will now present an *a priori* argument which purports to prove the truth of the Realist account of dispositions. Let us consider the following case. Suppose that, on a number of occasions, a certain rubber band has the same force, *F*, applied to it, and that on each occasion it stretches one inch. We can then attribute a disposition to the band. It is disposed to stretch one inch under force *F*.

Now one essential thing about dispositions is that we can attribute them to objects even at times when the circumstances in which the object manifests its dispositions do not obtain. Suppose, now, that I say of the band that, if it had been subjected to force *F* at $T_1$, a time when it was not so subjected, it would have stretched one inch. What warrant have I for my statement? Consider first the answer that a Realist about dispositions will give. He will say that there is every reason to believe that the . . . state of the band which is responsible for its stretching one inch under force *F* obtains at $T_1$. Given that it does obtain at $T_1$, then, as a matter of physical necessity, the band must stretch one inch under force *F*.

But what answer can the **Phenomenalist** about dispositions give? For him, a disposition does not entail the existence of a . . . state. The only reason he can give for saying that the band would have stretched one inch under force *F* at $T_1$ is that numerically the same band behaved in this way on other occasions. But now we may ask the Phenomenalist "What is the magic in numerical identity?" A thing can change its properties over a period of time. Why should it not change its dispositional properties? How does the Phenomenalist know what the band's dispositional properties are at $T_1$? He may reply "We have every reason to think that the relevant [non-dispositional] properties of the object are unchanged at $T_1$, so we have every reason to think that the dispositional properties are unchanged." But since he has asserted that the connection between [non-dispositional] and dispositional [properties] is not a necessary one, he can only be arguing that there is a *contingent* connection between . . . [them] at $T_1$. But how could one ever establish a contingent connection between [non-dispositional] properties and unfulfilled possibilities? It is not as if one could observe the unfulfilled possibilities independently, in order to see how they are correlated with the [non-dispositional] properties! It seems that the Phenomenalist about dispositions will be reduced to utter scepticism about dispositions, except on occasions that they are actually manifested. . . . We must be Realists, not Phenomenalists, about dispositions.

All this is of central importance to the philosophy of mind. Thus, if belief, for instance, is a disposition, then it is entailed that while I believe *p* my mind is in a certain non-dispositional state, a state which in suitable circumstances gives rise to "manifestations of belief that *p*." The fact that we may not know the concrete nature of this state is irrelevant.

The tremendous difference between this and the "Phenomenalist" account of disposition emerges when we consider that, on this "Realist" view of dispositions, we can think of them as *causes* or *causal factors*. On the Phenomenalist view, dispositions cannot be causes. To say the glass breaks because it is brittle is only to say that it breaks because it is the sort of thing that does break easily in the circumstances it is in. But if brittleness can be identified with an actual *state* of the glass, then we can think of it as a cause, or, more vaguely, a causal factor, in the process that brings about breaking. Dispositions are seen to be states that actually *stand behind* their manifestations. It is simply that the states are *identified* in terms of their manifestations in suitable conditions, rather than in terms of their intrinsic nature.

Our argument for a "Realist" account of dispositions can equally be applied to capacities and powers. They, too, must be conceived of as states of the object that has the capacity or power.

It will now be seen that a Behaviorist must reject this account of mental predicates involving dispositions, capacities or powers. For if he subscribed to it he would be admitting that, in talking about the mind, we were committed to talking about inner states of the person. But to make this admission would be to contradict his Behaviorism. . . . Behaviorism concentrates on the case of other minds, and there it substitutes the evidence that we have for the existence of other minds — behavior — for the mental states themselves. To admit dispositions as states lying behind, and in suitable circumstances giving rise to, behavior is to contradict the whole program. If, however, the reader still wishes to call my view a form of Behaviorism, this is no more than a matter of verbal concern. For it remains a "Behaviorism" that permits the contingent identification of mind and brain.

Suppose now we accept for argument's sake the view that in talking about mental states we are simply talking about states of the person apt for the bringing about of behavior of a certain sort. . . . The question then arises "What in fact is the nature of these inner states? What are these inner causes like?" And here no logical analysis can help us. It is a matter of high-level scientific speculation.

At this point we have one of those exciting turn-arounds where old theories appear in a quite new light. We suddenly get a new view of Dualism and of the Attribute theories, not to mention any wilder views that may be proposed. They are not, as we have insisted upon treating them up to this point, accounts of the *concept* of mind at all. Given that the concept of a mental state is the concept of a state of the person apt for bringing about certain sorts of (physical) behavior, then we should view the different accounts of the mind that have been advanced through the ages as different *scientific* answers to the question of the intrinsic nature of these states.

Take the primitive view that the mind or spirit is breath. Consider the difference between a living man and a corpse. A living man behaves in a quite different, and far more complex, way than any other sort of thing, but a corpse is little different from any other material object. What is the inner principle of the living man's behavior? One obvious difference is that the living man breathes, the corpse does not. So it is a plausible preliminary hypothesis that the inner principle of man's unique behavior — his spirit or mind — is breath or air.

Again, it is a meaningful suggestion that the mind is a flame in the body, or a collection of specially smooth and mobile atoms dispersed throughout the members. It is a meaningful suggestion that it is a spiritual substance, or a set of special properties of the body or central nervous system which are not reducible to the physico-chemical properties of matter. Or perhaps, as Central-state Materialism maintains, it is the physico-chemical workings of the central nervous system. . . .

At this point we see that the statement "The gene is the DNA molecule" provides a very good model for many features of the statement "The mind is the brain." (I am greatly indebted to Brian Medlin for this very important model.) The concept of the gene, when it was introduced into biology as a result of Mendel's work, was the concept of a factor in the person or animal apt for the production of certain characteristics in that person or animal. The question then arose what in fact the gene was. All sorts of answers were possible. For instance, the gene might have been an immaterial principle which somehow brought it about that my eyes are the color they are. In fact, however, biologists have concluded that there is sufficient evidence to identify that which is apt for the production of hereditary characteristics as the substance to be found at the center of cells: deoxyribo-nucleic acid. This identification is a theoretical one. Nobody has directly observed, or could ever hope to observe in practice, the details of the causal chain from DNA molecule to the coloring of the eye. But the identification is sufficiently certain.

It may now be asserted that, once it be granted that the concept of a mental state is the concept of a state of the person apt for the production of certain sorts of behavior, the identification of these states with physico-chemical states of the brain is, in the present state of knowledge, nearly as good a bet as the identification of the gene with the DNA molecule. . . .

## *Paul Ziff (b. 1920)*

Paul Ziff is a contemporary philosopher who has produced influential work in philosophy of language, philosophy of art, and philosophy of mind. His major works include *Semantic Analysis* (1960), *Philosophic Turnings* (1966) in which the essay below appears, *Understanding Understanding* (1972), *Epistemic Analysis* (1984), and *Antiaesthetics* (1985).

The following selection is part of a longer essay on the problem of other minds (the problem of how we can know that others have minds or have certain thoughts or feelings on any particular occasion). In it Ziff argues that the relation between the mental and physical is not one of simple identity. Reductive materialism is an inadequate account of the mental, not because there is something immaterial in human beings, but rather because the relation between what we pick out by using mental concepts and what the scientist picks out by using neurophysiological concepts is much more complex than the reductive materialist envisions. The failure of the identity theory, however, does not require that we abandon materialism and "multiply substances." Persons are entirely material in nature. It is just that the mental part of our present conceptual scheme is so confused and incoherent that it will eventually give way to a conceptual scheme that has no terms that are its present terms' exact equivalents.

# Materialism Without Identity

## *Paul Ziff*

. . . 11. In offering a defense of **"physicalism,"** Quine has claimed that

> If there is a case for mental events and mental states, it must be just that the positing of them, like the positing of molecules, has some indirect systematic efficacy in the development of theory. But if a certain organization of theory is achieved by thus positing distinctive mental states and events behind physical behavior, surely as much organization could be achieved by positing merely certain correlative physiological states and events instead.[1]

This ploy is worth considering, though readily countered, for it serves to underline the distinctiveness of mental states and events. But first the riposte: one might as poorly argue that if the positing of molecules has some indirect systematic efficacy in the development of theory, surely as much organization could be achieved by positing merely certain correlative little objects instead. Quine adds: "The bodily states exist anyway; why add the others?" (264) Little objects exist anyway; why add mysterious little configurations?

For of course if there is a case for mental states and events then no doubt, in some sense and as Quine claims, it must be that the positing of them, like the positing of molecules, has some systematic efficacy in the development of theory. But it doesn't follow that the positing of states and events of another kind and character need be similarly efficacious. Obviously, the positing of little objects of essentially the same kind and character as macro-objects would not only not contribute to the organization of quantum theory but would render it utterly incoherent.

What is the case for mental states and events? A minute part of it certainly is this: our psychological concepts are important explanatory devices; one can explain someone's tendency to group certain physiologically unlike stimulations together by saying that in each case he experiences the same feeling, in each case the same mental event occurs. By so saying one can avoid saying, what anyway presently appears to be positively untrue, that in each case the same physiological event occurs.

12. Consider a particular mental event, say that which occurs when one is stung by a bee: one experiences a sudden sharp pain, perhaps of relatively short duration, say one or two seconds. Can this particular mental event be identified with a particular cerebral event? Cerebral events are measured in milliseconds.

> One of the big gaps in our knowledge, not filled either by physiology or by psychology, is an accurate time-space description of central nervous system electrical activity and behavior in the very short time-intervals. Psychologists tend to deal with long cumulative phenomena, the results of many billions of short-term events. The classical learning-motivation-drive studies illustrate the point; even perceptual-discrimination-motor-response experiments involve a long-term, complex, spatial-temporal sequence of stimuli of unending variety from one millisecond to the next.[2]

If, instead of particular cerebral events, one were to attempt to identify mental events with particular collections of cerebral events, the move would be somewhat more plausible but still impossible. Consider a repeatable event, say the feeling of a feather touching one's arm: one first has that feeling at one time and then again at another time, each time the very same feeling. There is no reason to suppose that exactly the same collection of cerebral events recurred.

For first, it is nowadays reasonably clear that there is little reason to suppose that any sort of

From an article entitled "The Simplicity of Other Minds," which appeared in *The Journal of Philosophy*, vol. 62, no. 20, Oct. 21, 1965. Reprinted by permission of *The Journal of Philosophy* and Paul Ziff.

point-to-point relationship exists between the spot touched by the feather and a particular spot on the brain. "Stimulation of the skin at a specific spot will evoke responses in a much larger portion of the somatosensory cortex than the fraction of skin stimulated would lead one to expect on any simple point-to-point relationship."[3] Secondly, as ablation studies have shown over and over again, considerable portions of the brain may be excised without the loss of specific functions. Thus, in connection with patients who have undergone hemispherectomy, it is found that "Language, praxia and higher motor-sensory activities are usually preserved, whichever hemisphere is removed."[4] To suppose that exactly the same cerebral events recur if the same mental events recur subsequent to the hemispherectomy would seem to be a completely unwarranted supposition. More generally, any attempted identification of particular mental events with particular cerebral events or with particular collections of cerebral events or with particular collections of collections of cerebral events and so forth runs afoul of the well-known facts of **functional plasticity:** whether these be accounted for in terms of Lashley's "mass action" theory[5] or in terms of some current version of the standard Sherringtonian picture of central nervous integration,[6] they seem effectively to exclude from serious consideration all identity theories of mind-brain relationship.

13. Mental events cannot be identified with cerebral events. But to abandon an oversimple identity theory is not *ipso facto* to manufacture mysteries or substances. By the denial of identification we are not therewith saddled with multiple entities, double events. This duplicity of **ontology** is simply eliminable.

Any apple has of course a molecular constitution. So it has been said that:

> The atomic theory is all-encompassing in the physical world; it leaves no room for micro-objects *and* correlated macro-objects; the whole point is that a macro-object is a complex micro-structure and nothing more.[7]

Brandt adds that "There is not similar compulsion to identify stabbing pains with states of the brain" (69). On the contrary: the compulsion is quite the same and to be resisted in either case.

I hold an apple in my hand; this apple is not identical with, is not one and the same thing as, a particular collection of molecules. That cannot possibly be so: I do not lose and acquire a new apple each time I toss it in air; yet the molecular constitution of my apple fluctuates from toss to toss: the collection constituting the apple at one toss is not identical with the collection constituting the apple at another toss. Unless the **transitivity of identity** is to be called into question, this is not a case of identity.

Then is my apple to be identified with a particular class of spatiotemporally ordered collections of molecules? But which collections? (Exactly how many hairs can a bald man have? Is water $H_2O$? A glass of lake water is not a glass of $H_2O$. Isn't lake water water? And one can bite an apple, but could one bite that class of spatiotemporally ordered collections of molecules? Or cut it in half? (Alternatively it is sometimes suggested that the apple is identical not with a particular collection of molecules but with a particular configuration of molecules. The switch from "collection" to "configuration" accomplishes nothing; the same problems remain: radically different principles of individuation are still involved.)

14. Apples can no more be identified with collections of molecules than mental events can be identified with cerebral events. But that does not mean that apples must be spiritual concomitants of collections of molecules. If there is no collection of molecules sporting in the neighborhood of a branch then there is no apple dangling there.

To class something an apple is to employ a particular form of conceptualization; to class something a collection of molecules is to employ another. These two forms of conceptualization are two, not one, but they are not totally unrelated: in each case that which is conceived of is an entity of a sort. These two entities, so conceived, are neither one and the same entity nor yet exactly two different entities.

One of the simplest relations one could hope to find between entities would be that of identity: the entity conceived of as an alpha proves to be identical with, one and the same as, that conceived as a beta. Another simple relation would be that of difference: the entities conceived of are not only the same, but the existence of one is wholly independent, directly or indirectly, of the existence of the other. Between these two extremes there are innumerable cases, and there one finds apples and collections of molecules, minds and brains.

15. Psychophysiology is that relatively new branch of science concerned with determining the specific relations obtaining between mind and brain. Its task is to find and state dyadic translation functions, functions that take as arguments ordered pairs, one member of which ranges over psychological matters, the other over physiological matters.[8] The function of a psychophysiological dyadic translation function is to coordinate psychological and physiological descriptions, referential expressions, and so forth, and so bridge the conceptual gap between these different forms of conceptualization.

An identity relation is a simple translation function serving to coordinate different descriptions at the same conceptual level. It is of no utility in connection with expressions exemplifying radically different forms of conceptualization. There is no reason to suppose that an identity function can be of any utility in psychophysiology: the forms of conceptualization employed there are too markedly different to allow any such easy interrelation.

16. There is a translation function that serves to coordinate our talk about apples with talk about collections and configurations of molecules. It is not a simple identity function.[9] It is complex and difficult to state. For, from the point of view of macro-entities, talk about micro-entities is inevitably excessively definite, exact, precise. A particular apple is not a particular class of spatiotemporally ordered collections of molecules, and even if it were, to bite an apple would not be to bite the class but rather to segment some member(s) of the class; but of course the members of such a class, namely collections of molecules, are not specifiable.[10]

Adequate translation functions are hard to come by in psychophysiology; in fact none are known. The reasons for this remarkable lack of knowledge are largely but not exclusively technological. Ablation and stimulation are the major methods of cerebral and neurophysiological research. The presently insuperable problems posed by such techniques should be obvious: think of attempting to determine the functions of the various parts of a full-scale computer by examining the computer's output after removing bits of its mechanism or tampering with its input; and this greatly understates the problem. But the present state of technology is not the only significant difficulty in providing plausible psychophysiological translation functions.

17. Without peering overmuch, one can make out an unfortunate mentalistic conceptual scheme generally accepted today. One can discern an internally structured, albeit incoherent, set of concepts. There appears to be no end to tiresome talk of intentions, of motives, of direct awareness. It is this scheme that gives rise to the disembodied spirit, the death survivor, the telepath, the sufferer of ghostly agonies in the fireless flames of hell. Disembodied spirits not being choice physiological subjects, it need not be a source of astonishment that adequate translation functions are not at once available for all mentalistic concepts.

But fortunately conceptual decay is the order of the day. The current mentalistic scheme is gradually giving up the ghost. Our intellectual concepts, thinking, planning, experimenting, all are tottering; intelligence looks to be not importantly different from a trait of mechanical morons with lightninglike access to prodigious memories, computers. But no doubt pain and other plain concepts are likely to survive. And possibly in time, if the race lingers on, adequate translation functions will be found for the survivors.

## NOTES

1. W. V. O. Quine, *Word and Object* (New York: Wiley, 1960), p. 264.

2. John C. Lilly, "Correlations between Neurophysiological Activity in the Cortex and Short-term Behavior in the Monkey," in Harry F. Harlow and Clinton N. Woolsey, eds., *Biological and Biochemical Bases of Behavior* (Madison: Univ. of Wisconsin Press, 1958), p. 84.
3. Clinton N. Woolsey, "Cortical Localization as Defined by Evoked Potential and Electrical Stimulation Studies," in Georges Schaltenbrand and Clinton N. Woolsey, eds., *Cerebral Localization and Organization* (Madison: Univ. of Wisconsin Press, 1964), p. 17.
4. Sixto Obrador, "Nervous Integration after Hemispherectomy in Man," in Schaltenbrand and Woolsey, *op. cit.*, pp. 144–145.
5. See Lashley, *op. cit.*
6. See R. W. Sperry, "Physiological Plasticity," in Harlow and Woolsey, *op. cit.*, pp. 401–424.
7. Richard B. Brandt, "Doubts about the Identity Theory," in Sidney Hook, ed., *Dimensions of Mind* (New York: Collier, 1961), p. 69.
8. See Albert F. Ax, "Psychophysiological Methodology for the Study of Schizophrenia," in Roessler and Greenfield, *op. cit.*, pp. 29–44.
9. See H. Putnam, "Minds and Machines," in Hook, *op. cit.*, p. 155 ff. Putnam's "theoretical identification" is, I believe, best thought of as a relatively complex translation function.
10. See M. Black, *Problems of Analysis,* (Ithaca: Cornell Univ. Press, 1954), p. 27 ff., in connection with the nonexistence of rigidly demarcated classes.

## *Paul M. Churchland (b. 1942)*

Paul M. Churchland has written a number of essays in philosophy of psychology and philosophy of mind. His major works are *Scientific Realism and the Plasticity of Mind* (1979) and *Matter and Consciousness* (1984) from which the selection below was taken.

In the following essay Churchland suggests ways in which both reductive and eliminative materialism can be defended against standard criticisms. He suggests that the alternatives of either reduction or elimination of the mental part of our present conceptual scheme may not be exhaustive. Perhaps we should view these as the ends of a continuum on which there is a range of intermediate possibilities involving the reduction of some mental concepts to physical concepts and the elimination of others. Even if this is the case, however, Churchland believes that the truth will be located toward the eliminative end of the scale.

# Reductive and Eliminative Materialism

## *Paul M. Churchland*

### REDUCTIVE MATERIALISM (THE IDENTITY THEORY)

*Reductive materialism,* more commonly known as *the identity theory,* is the most straightforward of the several materialist theories of mind. Its central claim is simplicity itself: Mental states *are* physical states of the brain. That is, each type of mental state or process is *numerically identical*

Abridged from *Matter and Consciousness,* by Paul M. Churchland. (Cambridge, Mass: The MIT Press, 1984), pp. 26–34, 43–49. Reprinted by permission of MIT Press.

*with* (is one and the very same thing as) some type of physical state or process within the brain or central nervous system. At present we do not know enough about the intricate functionings of the brain actually to state the relevant identities, but the identity theory is committed to the idea that brain research will eventually reveal them. . . .

As the identity theorist sees it, the result here predicted has familiar parallels elsewhere in our scientific history. Consider sound. We now know that sound is just a train of compression waves traveling through the air, and that the property of being high pitched is identical with the property of having a high oscillatory frequency. We have learned that light is just electromagnetic waves, and our best current theory says that the color of an object is identical with a triplet of reflectance efficiencies the object has, rather like a musical chord that it strikes, though the "notes" are struck in electromagnetic waves instead of in sound waves. We now appreciate that the warmth or coolness of a body is just the energy of motion of the molecules that make it up: warmth is identical with high average molecular kinetic energy, and coolness is identical with low average molecular kinetic energy. We know that lightning is identical with a sudden large-scale discharge of electrons between clouds, or between the atmosphere and the ground. What we now think of as "mental states," argues the identity theorist, are identical with brain states in exactly the same way.

These illustrative parallels are all cases of successful *intertheoretic* **reduction.** That is, they are all cases where a new and very powerful theory turns out to entail a set of propositions and principles that mirror perfectly (or almost perfectly) the propositions and principles of some older theory or conceptual framework. The relevant principles entailed by the new theory have the same structure as the corresponding principles of the old framework, and they apply in exactly the same cases. The only difference is that where the old principles contained (for example) the notions of "heat," "is hot," and "is cold," the new principles contain instead the notions of "total molecular kinetic energy," "has a high mean molecular kinetic energy," and "has a low mean molecular kinetic energy."

If the new framework is far better than the old at explaining and predicting phenomena, then we have excellent reason for believing that the theoretical terms of the *new* framework are the terms that describe reality correctly. But if the old framework worked adequately, so far as it went, and if it parallels a portion of the new theory in the systematic way described, then we may properly conclude that the old terms and the new terms refer to the very same things, or express the very same properties. We conclude that we have apprehended the very same reality that is incompletely described by the old framework, but with a new and more penetrating conceptual framework. And we announce what philosophers of science call "intertheoretic identities": light *is* electromagnetic waves, temperature *is* mean molecular kinetic energy, and so forth.

The examples of the preceding two paragraphs share one more important feature in common. They are all cases where the things or properties on the receiving end of the reduction are *observable* things and properties within our *common-sense* conceptual framework. They show that intertheoretic reduction occurs not only between conceptual frameworks in the theoretical stratosphere: common-sense observables can also be reduced. There would therefore be nothing particularly surprising about a reduction of our familiar introspectible mental states to physical states of the brain. All that would be required would be that an explanatorily successful neuroscience develop to the point where it entails a suitable "mirror image" of the assumptions and principles that constitute our common-sense conceptual framework for mental states, an image where brain-state terms occupy the positions held by mental-state terms in the assumptions and principles of common sense. If this (rather demanding) condition were indeed met, then, as in the historical cases cited, we would be justified in announcing a reduction, and in asserting the identity of mental states with brain states.

What reasons does the identity theorist have for believing that neuroscience will eventually achieve the strong conditions necessary for the reduction of our **"folk" psychology?** There are at least four reasons, all directed at the conclusion that the correct account of human-behavior-and-its-causes must reside in the physical neurosciences.

We can point first to the purely physical origins and ostensibly physical constitution of each individual human. One begins as a genetically programmed monocellular organization of molecules (a fertilized ovum), and one develops from there by the accretion of further molecules whose structure and integration is controlled by the information coded in the DNA molecules of the cell nucleus. The result of such a process would be a purely physical system whose behavior arises from its internal operations and its interactions with the rest of the physical world. And those behavior-controlling internal operations are precisely what the neurosciences are about.

This argument coheres with a second argument. The origins of each *type* of animal also appear exhaustively physical in nature. The argument from evolutionary history . . . lends further support to the identity theorist's claim, since evolutionary theory provides the only serious explanation we have for the behavior-controlling capacities of the brain and central nervous system. Those systems were selected for because of the many advantages (ultimately, the reproductive advantage) held by creatures whose behavior was thus controlled. Again our behavior appears to have its basic causes in neural activity.

The identity theorist finds further support in the argument . . . from the neural dependence of all known mental phenomena. . . . This is precisely what one should expect, if the identity theory is true. Of course, systematic neural dependence is also a consequence of property dualism, but here the identity theorist will appeal to considerations of simplicity. Why admit two radically different classes of properties and operations if the explanatory job can be done by one?

A final argument derives from the growing success of the neurosciences in unraveling the nervous systems of many creatures and in explaining their behavioral capacities and deficits in terms of the structures discovered. The preceding arguments all suggest that neuroscience should be successful in this endeavor, and the fact is that the continuing history of neuroscience bears them out. Especially in the case of very simple creatures (as one would expect), progress has been rapid. And progress has also been made with humans, though for obvious moral reasons exploration must be more cautious and circumspect. In sum, the neurosciences have a long way to go, but progress to date provides substantial encouragement to the identity theorist.

Even so, these arguments are far from decisive in favor of the identity theory. No doubt they do provide an overwhelming case for the idea that the causes of human and animal behavior are essentially physical in nature, but the identity theory claims more than just this. It claims that neuroscience will discover a taxonomy of neural states that stand in a one-to-one correspondence with the mental states of our common-sense taxonomy. Claims for intertheoretic identity will be justified only if such a match-up can be found. But nothing in the preceding arguments guarantees that the old and new frameworks will match up in this way, even if the new framework is a roaring success at explaining and predicting our behavior. Furthermore, there are arguments from other positions within the materialist camp to the effect that such convenient match-ups are rather unlikely. Before exploring those, however, let us look at some more traditional objections to the identity theory.

We may begin with the argument from introspection. . . . Introspection reveals a domain of thoughts, sensations, and emotions, not a domain of electrochemical impulses in a neural network. Mental states and properties, as revealed in introspection, appear radically different from any neurophysiological states and properties. How could they possibly be the very same things?

The answer, as we have already seen, is, "Easily." In discriminating red from blue, sweet from sour, and hot from cold, our external senses are actually discriminating between subtle differences in intricate electromagnetic, stereochemical, and micromechanical properties of physical objects. But our senses are not sufficiently penetrating to reveal on their own the detailed nature of those intricate properties. That requires theoretical research and experimental exploration with specially designed instruments. The same is presumably true of our "inner" sense: introspection. It may discriminate efficiently between a great variety of neural states, without being able to reveal on its own the detailed nature of the states being discriminated. Indeed, it would be faintly miraculous if it did reveal them, just as miraculous as if unaided sight were to reveal the existence of interacting electric and magnetic fields whizzing by with an oscillatory frequency of a million billion hertz and a wavelength of less than a millionth of a meter. For despite "appearances," that is what light is. The argument from introspection, therefore, is quite without force.

The next objection argues that the identification of mental states with brain states would commit us to statements that are literally unintelligible, to what philosophers have called "category errors," and that the identification is therefore a case of sheer conceptual confusion. We may begin the discussion by noting a most important law concerning numerical identity. Leibniz' Law states that two items are numerically identical just in case any property had by either one of them is also had by the other: in logical notation,

$$(x)(y)[(x = y) \equiv (F)(Fx \equiv Fy)].$$

This law suggests a way of refuting the identity theory: find some property that is true of brain states, but not of mental states (or vice versa), and the theory would be exploded.

Spatial properties were often cited to this end. Brain states and processes must of course have some specific spatial location: in the brain as a whole, or in some part of it. And if mental states are identical with brain states, then they must have the very same spatial location. But it is literally meaningless, runs the argument, to say that my feeling-of-pain is located in my ventral thalamus, or that my belief-that-the-sun-is-a-star is located in the temporal lobe of my left cerebral hemisphere. Such claims are as meaningless as the claim that the number 5 is green, or that love weighs twenty grams.

Trying the same move from the other direction, some have argued that it is senseless to ascribe the various **semantic** properties to brain states. Our thoughts and beliefs, for example, have a meaning, a specific propositional content; they are either true or false; and they can enjoy relations such as consistency and entailment. If thoughts and beliefs were brain states, then all these semantic properties would have to be true of brain states. But it is senseless, runs the argument, to say that some resonance in my association cortex is true, or logically entails some other resonance close by, or has the meaning that *P*.

Neither of these moves has the same bite it did twenty years ago, since familiarity with the identity theory and growing awareness of the brain's role have tended to reduce the feelings of semantic oddity produced by the claims at issue. But even if they still struck all of us as semantically confused, this would carry little weight. The claim that sound has a wavelength, or that light has a frequency, must have seemed equally unintelligible in advance of the conviction that both sound and light are wave phenomena. (See, for example, Bishop Berkeley's eighteenth-century dismissal of the idea that sound is a vibratory motion of the air, in Dialogue I of his *Three Dialogues*. The objections are voiced by Philonous.) The claim that warmth is measured in kilogram·meters²/seconds² would have seemed semantically perverse before we understood that temperature is mean molecular kinetic energy. And Copernicus' sixteenth-century claim that the earth *moves* also struck people as absurd to the point of perversity. It is not difficult to appreciate why. Consider the following argument.

Copernicus' claim that the earth moves is sheer conceptual confusion. For consider what it *means* to say that something moves: "x moves" means "x changes position relative to the earth." Thus, to say that earth moves is to say that the earth changes position relative to itself! Which is absurd. Copernicus' position is therefore an abuse of language.

The *meaning analysis* here invoked might well have been correct, but all that would have meant is that the speaker should have set about changing his meanings. The fact is, any language involves a rich network of assumptions about the structure of the world, and if a sentence *S* provokes intuitions of semantic oddness, that is usually because *S* violates one or more of those background assumptions. But one cannot always reject *S* for that reason alone, since the overthrow of those background assumptions may be precisely what the facts require. The "abuse" of accepted modes of speech is often an essential feature of real scientific progress! Perhaps we shall just have to get used to the idea that mental states have anatomical locations and brain states have semantic properties.

While the charge of sheer senselessness can be put aside, the identity theorist does owe us some account of exactly how physical brain states can have semantic properties. The account currently being explored can be outlined as follows. Let us begin by asking how it is that a particular *sentence* (= utterance type) has the specific propositional content it has: the sentence "La pomme est rouge," for example. Note first that a sentence is always an integrated part of an entire system of sentences: a language. Any given sentence enjoys many relations with countless other sentences: it entails many sentences, is entailed by many others, is consistent with some, is inconsistent with others, provides confirming evidence for yet others, and so forth. And speakers who use that sentence within that language draw inferences in accordance with those relations. Evidently, each sentence (or each set of equivalent sentences) enjoys a unique pattern of such entailment relations: it plays a distinct inferential role in a complex linguistic economy. Accordingly, we say that the sentence "La pomme est rouge" has the propositional content, *the apple is red,* because the sentence "La pomme est rouge" plays *the same role* in French that the sentence "The apple is red" plays in English. To have the relevant propositional content is just to play the relevant inferential role in a cognitive economy.

Returning now to types of brain states, there is no problem in principle in assuming that one's brain is the seat of a complex inferential economy in which types of brain states are the role-playing elements. According to the theory of meaning just sketched, such states would then have propositional content, since having content is not a matter of whether the contentful item is a pattern of sound, a pattern of letters on paper, a set of raised Braille bumps, or a pattern of neural activity. What matters is the inferential role the item plays. Propositional content, therefore, seems within the reach of brain states after all.

[Earlier we presented] . . . an argument against materialism that appealed to the qualitative *nature* of our mental states, as revealed in introspection. The next argument appeals to the simple fact that they are introspectible at all.

1. My mental states are introspectively known by me as states of my conscious self.
2. My brain states are *not* introspectively known by me as states of my conscious self.

Therefore, by Leibniz' Law (that numerically identical things must have exactly the same properties),

3. My mental states are not identical with my brain states.

This, in my experience, is the most beguiling form of the argument from introspection, seductive of freshmen and faculty alike. But it is a straightforward instance of a well-known fallacy, which is clearly illustrated in the following parallel arguments:

1. Muhammad Ali is widely known as a heavyweight champion.
2. Cassius Clay is *not* widely known as a heavyweight champion.

Therefore, by Leibniz' Law,

3. Muhammad Ali is not identical with Cassius Clay.

or,

1. Aspirin is recognized by John to be a pain reliever.
2. Acetylsalicylic acid is *not* recognized by John to be a pain reliever.

Therefore, by Leibniz' Law,

3. Aspirin is not identical with acetylsalicylic acid.

Despite the truth of the relevant premises, both conclusions are false: the identities are wholly genuine. Which means that both arguments are invalid. The problem is that the "property" ascribed in premise (1), and withheld in premise (2), consists only in the subject item's being *recognized, perceived,* or *known* as something-or-other. But such apprehension is not a genuine property of the item itself, fit for divining identities, since one and the same subject may be successfully recognized under one name or description, and yet fail to be recognized under another (accurate, coreferential) description. Bluntly, Leibniz' Law is not valid for these bogus "properties." The attempt to use them as above commits what logicians call an *intensional* fallacy. The premises may reflect, not the failure of certain objective identities, but only our continuing failure to appreciate them.

A different version of the preceding argument must also be considered, since it may be urged that one's brain states are more than merely not (yet) known by introspection: they are not know*able* by introspection under any circumstances. Thus,

1. My mental states are knowable by introspection.
2. My brain states are *not* knowable by introspection.

Therefore, by Leibniz' Law,

3. My mental states are not identical with my brain states.

Here the critic will insist that being know*able* by introspection *is* a genuine property of a thing, and that this modified version of the argument is free of the "intensional fallacy" discussed above.

And so it is. But now the materialist is in a position to insist that the argument contains a false premise — premise (2). For if mental states are indeed brain states, then it is really brain states we have been introspecting all along, though without fully appreciating what they are. And if we can learn to think of and recognize those states under mentalistic descriptions, as we all have, then we can certainly learn to think of and recognize them under their more penetrating neurophysiological descriptions. At the very least, premise (2) simply begs the question against the identity theorist. The mistake is amply illustrated in the following parallel argument:

1. Temperature is knowable by feeling.
2. Mean molecular kinetic energy is *not* knowable by feeling.

Therefore, by Leibniz' Law,

3. Temperature is not identical with mean molecular kinetic energy.

This identity, at least, is long established, and this argument is certainly unsound: premise (2) is false. Just as one can learn to feel that the summer air is about 70°F, or 21°C, so one can learn to feel that the mean KE of its molecules is about $6.2 \times 10^{-21}$ joules, for whether we realize it or not, that is what our discriminatory mechanisms are keyed to. Perhaps our brain states are similarly accessible. . . .

Consider now a final argument, again based on the introspectible qualities of our sensations. Imagine a future neuroscientist who comes to know everything there is to know about the physical structure and activity of the brain and its visual system, of its actual and possible states. If for some reason she has never actually *had* a sensation-of-red (because of color blindness, say, or an unusual environment), then there will remain something she does *not* know about certain sensations: *what it is like to have a sensation-of-red.* Therefore, complete knowledge of the physical facts of visual perception and its related brain activity still leaves something out. Accordingly, materialism cannot give an adequate account of all mental phenomena, and the identity theory must be false.

The identity theorist can reply that this argument exploits an unwitting equivocation on the term "know." Concerning our neuroscientist's utopian knowledge of the brain, "knows" means something like "has mastered the relevant set of neuroscientific propositions." Concerning her (missing) knowledge of what it is like to have a sensation-of-red, "knows" means something like "has a prelinguistic representation of redness in her mechanisms for noninferential discrimination." It is true that one might have the former without the latter, but the materialist is not committed to the idea that having knowledge in the former sense automatically constitutes having knowledge in the second sense. The identity theorist can admit a duality, or even a plurality, of different *types of knowledge* without thereby committing himself to a duality in *types of things known*. The difference between a person who knows all about the visual cortex but has never enjoyed the sensation-of-red, and a person who knows no neuroscience but knows well the sensation-of-red, may reside not in *what* is respectively known by each (brain states by the former, nonphysical *qualia* by the latter), but rather in the different *type*, or *medium*, or *level* of representation each has of exactly the same thing: brain states.

In sum, there are pretty clearly more ways of "having knowledge" than just having mastered a set of sentences, and the materialist can freely admit that one has "knowledge" of one's sensations in a way that is independent of the neuroscience one may have learned. Animals, including humans, presumably have a prelinguistic mode of sensory representation. This does not mean that sensations are beyond the reach of physical science. *It just means that the brain uses more modes and media of representation than the mere storage of sentences.* All the identity theorist needs to claim is that those other modes of representation will also yield to neuroscientific explanation.

The identity theory has proved to be very resilient in the face of these predominantly antimaterialist objections. But further objections, rooted in competing forms of materialism, constitute a much more serious threat. . . .

## ELIMINATIVE MATERIALISM

The identity theory was called into doubt not because the prospects for a materialist account of our mental capacities were thought to be poor, but because it seemed unlikely that the arrival of an adequate materialist theory would bring with it the nice one-to-one match-ups, between the concepts of folk psychology and the concepts of theoretical neuroscience, that intertheoretic reduction requires. The reason for that doubt was the great variety of quite different physical systems that could instantiate the required functional organization. *Eliminative materialism* also doubts that the correct neuroscientific account of human capacities will produce a neat reduction of our common-sense framework, but here the doubts arise from a quite different source.

As the eliminative materialists see it, the one-to-one match-ups will not be found, and our common-sense psychological framework will not enjoy an intertheoretic reduction, *because our common-sense psychological framework is a false and radically misleading conception of the causes of human behavior and the nature of cognitive activity.* On this view, folk psychology is not just an incomplete representation of our inner natures; it is an outright *mis*representation of our internal states and activities. Consequently, we cannot expect a truly adequate neuroscientific account of our inner lives to provide theoretical categories that match up nicely with the categories of our common-sense framework. Accordingly, we must expect that the older framework will simply be eliminated, rather than be reduced, by a matured neuroscience.

As the identity theorist can point to historical cases of successful intertheoretic reduction, so the eliminative materialist can point to historical cases of the outright elimination of the **ontology** of an older theory in favor of the ontology of a new and superior theory. For most of the eighteenth and nineteenth centuries, learned people believed that heat was a subtle *fluid* held in bodies, much in the way water is held in a sponge. A fair body of moderately successful theory described the way this fluid substance—called "caloric"—flowed within a body, or from one body to another, and how it produced thermal expansion, melting, boiling, and so forth. But by the end of the last century it had become abundantly clear that heat was not a substance at all, but just the energy of motion of the trillions of jostling molecules that make up the heated body itself. The new theory—the "corpuscular/kinetic theory of matter and heat"—was much more successful than the old in explaining and predicting the thermal behavior of bodies. And since we were unable to *identify* caloric fluid with kinetic energy (according to the old theory, caloric is a material *substance;* according to the new theory, kinetic energy is a form of *motion*), it was finally agreed that there is *no such thing* as caloric. Caloric was simply eliminated from our accepted ontology.

A second example. It used to be thought that when a piece of wood burns, or a piece of metal rusts, a spiritlike substance called "phlogiston" was being released: briskly, in the former case, slowly in the latter. Once gone, that "noble" substance left only a base pile of ash or rust. It later came to be appreciated that both processes involve, not the loss of something, but the *gaining* of a substance taken from the atmosphere: oxygen. Phlogiston emerged, not as an incomplete description of what was going on, but as a radical misdescription. Phlogiston was therefore not suitable for reduction to or identification with some notion from within the new oxygen chemistry, and it was simply eliminated from science.

Admittedly, both of these examples concern the elimination of something nonobservable, but our history also includes the elimination of certain widely accepted "observables." Before Copernicus' views became available, almost any human who ventured out at night could look up at *the starry sphere of the heavens,* and if he stayed for more than a few minutes he could also see that it *turned,* around an axis through Polaris. What the sphere was made of (crystal?) and what made it turn (the gods?) were theoretical questions that exercised us for over two millennia. But hardly anyone doubted the existence of what everyone could observe with their own eyes. In the end, however, we learned to reinterpret our visual experience of the night sky within a very different conceptual framework, and the turning sphere evaporated.

Witches provide another example. Psychosis is a fairly common affliction among humans, and in earlier centuries its victims were standardly seen as cases of demonic possession, as instances of Satan's spirit itself, glaring malevolently out at us from behind the victims' eyes. That witches exist was not a matter of any controversy. One would occasionally see them, in any city or hamlet, engaged in incoherent, paranoid, or even murderous behavior. But observable or not, we eventually decided that witches simply do not exist. We concluded that the concept of a witch is an element in a conceptual framework that misrepresents so badly the phenomena to which it was standardly applied that literal application of the notion should be permanently withdrawn. Modern theories of mental dysfunction led to the elimination of witches from our serious ontology.

The concepts of folk psychology—belief, desire, fear, sensation, pain, joy, and so on—await a similar fate, according to the view at issue. And when neuroscience has matured to the point where the poverty of our current conceptions is apparent to everyone, and the superiority of the new framework is established, we shall then be able to set about *re*conceiving our internal states and activities, within a truly adequate conceptual framework at last. Our explanations of one another's behavior will appeal to such things as our neuropharmacological states, the neural activity in specialized anatomical areas, and whatever other states are deemed relevant by the new theory. Our private introspection will also be transformed, and may be profoundly enhanced by reason of the more accurate and penetrating framework it will have to work with—just as the astronomer's perception of the night sky is much enhanced by the detailed knowledge of modern astronomical theory that he or she possesses.

The magnitude of the conceptual revolution here suggested should not be minimized: it would be enormous. And the benefits to humanity might be equally great. If each of us possessed an accurate neuroscientific understanding of (what we now conceive dimly as) the varieties and causes of mental illness, the factors involved in learning, the neural basis of emotions, intelligence, and socialization, then the sum total of human misery might be much reduced. The simple increase in mutual understanding that the new framework made possible could contribute substantially toward a more peaceful and humane society. Of course, there would be dangers as well: increased knowledge means increased power, and power can always be misused.

The arguments for eliminative materialism are diffuse and less than decisive, but they are stronger than is widely supposed. The distinguishing feature of this position is its denial that a smooth intertheoretic reduction is to be expected—even a species-specific reduction—of the framework of folk psychology to the framework of a matured neuroscience. The reason for this denial is the eliminative materialist's conviction that folk psychology is a hopelessly primitive and deeply confused conception of our internal activities. But why this low opinion of our common-sense conceptions?

There are at least three reasons. First, the eliminative materialist will point to the widespread explanatory, predictive, and manipulative failures of folk psychology. So much of what is central and familiar to us remains a complete mystery from within folk psychology. We do not know what *sleep* is, or why we have to have it, despite spending a full third of our lives in that condition. (The answer, "For rest," is mistaken. Even if people are allowed to rest continuously, their need for sleep is undiminished. Apparently, sleep serves some deeper functions, but we do not yet know what they are.) We do not understand how *learning* transforms each of us from a gaping infant to a cunning adult, or how differences in *intelligence* are grounded. We have not the slightest idea how *memory* works, or how we manage to retrieve relevant bits of information instantly from the awesome mass we have stored. We do not know what *mental illness* is, nor how to cure it.

In sum, the most central things about us remain almost entirely mysterious from within folk psychology. And the defects noted cannot be blamed on inadequate time allowed for their correction, for folk psychology has enjoyed no significant changes or advances in well over 2,000 years, despite its manifest failures. Truly successful theories may be expected to reduce, but significantly unsuccessful theories merit no such expectation.

This argument from explanatory poverty has a further aspect. So long as one sticks to normal brains, the poverty of folk psychology is perhaps not strikingly evident. But as soon as one examines the many perplexing behavioral and cognitive deficits suffered by people with *damaged* brains, one's descriptive and explanatory resources start to claw the air. . . . As with other humble theories asked to operate successfully in unexplored extensions of their old domain (for example, Newtonian mechanics in the domain of velocities close to the velocity of light, and the classical gas law in the domain of high pressures or temperatures), the descriptive and explanatory inadequacies of folk psychology become starkly evident.

The second argument tries to draw an inductive lesson from our conceptual history. Our early folk theories of motion were profoundly confused, and were eventually displaced entirely by more sophisticated theories. Our early folk theories of the structure and activity of the heavens were wildly off the mark, and survive only as historical lessons in how wrong we can be. Our folk theories of the nature of fire, and the nature of life, were similarly cockeyed. And one could go on, since the vast majority of our past folk conceptions have been similarly exploded. All except folk psychology, which survives to this day and has only recently begun to feel pressure. But the phenomenon of conscious intelligence is surely a more complex and difficult phenomenon than any of those just listed. So far as accurate understanding is concerned, it would be a *miracle* if we had got *that* one right the very first time, when we fell down so badly on all the others. Folk psychology has survived for so very long, presumably, not because it is basically correct in its representations, but because the phenomena addressed are so surpassingly difficult that any useful handle on them, no matter how feeble, is unlikely to be displaced in a hurry.

A third argument attempts to find an a priori advantage for eliminative materialism over the identity theory. . . . It attempts to counter the common intuition that eliminative materialism is distantly possible, perhaps, but is much less probable than . . . the identity theory. . . . The focus again is on whether the concepts of folk psychology will find vindicating match-ups in a matured neuroscience. The eliminativist bets no; the [identity theorist] . . . bet[s] yes. . . .

The eliminativist will point out that the requirements on a reduction are rather demanding. The new theory must entail a set of principles and embedded concepts that mirrors very closely the specific conceptual structure to be reduced. And the fact is, there are vastly many more ways of being an explanatorily successful neuroscience while *not* mirroring the structure of folk psychology, than there are ways of being an explanatorily successful neuroscience while also *mirroring* the very specific structure of folk psychology. Accordingly, the a priori probability of eliminative materialism is not lower, but substantially *higher* than that of . . . its competitors. One's initial intuitions here are simply mistaken.

Granted, this initial a priori advantage could be reduced if there were a very strong presumption in favor of the truth of folk psychology—true theories are better bets to win reduction. But according to the first two arguments, the presumptions on this point should run in precisely the opposite direction.

The initial plausibility of this rather radical view is low for almost everyone, since it denies deeply entrenched assumptions. That is at best a question-begging complaint, of course, since those assumptions are precisely what is at issue. But the following line of thought does attempt to mount a real argument.

Eliminative materialism is false, runs the argument, because one's introspection reveals directly the existence of pains, beliefs, desires, fears, and so forth. Their existence is as obvious as anything could be.

The eliminative materialist will reply that this argument makes the same mistake that an ancient or medieval person would be making if he insisted that he could just see with his own eyes that the heavens form a turning sphere, or that witches exist. The fact is, all observation occurs within some system of concepts, and our observation judgments are only as good as the conceptual framework in which they are expressed. In all three cases—the starry sphere, witches, and the familiar mental states—precisely what is challenged is the integrity of the background conceptual frameworks in which the observation judgments are expressed. To insist on the validity of one's experiences, *traditionally interpreted,* is therefore to beg the very question at issue. For in all three cases, the question is whether we should *re*conceive the nature of some familiar observational domain.

A second criticism attempts to find an incoherence in the eliminative materialist's position. The bald statement of eliminative materialism is that the familiar mental states do not really exist. But that statement is meaningful, runs the argument, only if it is the expression of a certain *belief,* and an *intention* to communicate, and a *knowledge* of the language, and so forth. But if the statement is true, then no such mental states exist, and the statement is therefore a meaningless string of marks or noises, and cannot be true. Evidently, the assumption that eliminative materialism is true entails that it cannot be true.

The hole in this argument is the premise concerning the conditions necessary for a statement to be meaningful. It begs the question. If eliminative materialism is true, then meaningfulness must have some different source. To insist on the "old" source is to insist on the validity of the very framework at issue. Again, an historical parallel may be helpful here. Consider the medieval theory that being biologically *alive* is a matter of being ensouled by an immaterial *vital spirit*. And consider the following response to someone who has expressed disbelief in that theory.

> My learned friend has stated that there is no such thing as vital spirit. But this statement is incoherent. For if it is true, then my friend does not have vital spirit, and must therefore be *dead*. But if he is dead, then his statement is just a string of noises, devoid of meaning or truth. Evidently, the assumption that antivitalism is true entails that it cannot be true! Q.E.D.

This second argument is now a joke, but the first argument begs the question in exactly the same way.

A final criticism draws a much weaker conclusion, but makes a rather stronger case. Eliminative materialism, it has been said, is making mountains out of molehills. It exaggerates the defects in folk psychology, and underplays its real successes. Perhaps the arrival of a matured neuroscience will require the elimination of the occasional folk-psychological concept, continues the criticism, and a minor adjustment in certain folk-psychological principles may have to be endured. But the large-scale elimination forecast by the eliminative materialist is just an alarmist worry or a romantic enthusiasm.

Perhaps this complaint is correct. And perhaps it is merely complacent. Whichever, it does bring out the important point that we do not confront two simple and mutually exclusive possibilities here: pure reduction versus pure elimination. Rather, these are the end points of a smooth spectrum of possible outcomes, between which there are mixed cases of partial elimination and partial reduction. Only empirical research . . . can tell us where on that spectrum our own case will fall. Perhaps we should speak here, more liberally, of "revisionary materialism," instead of concentrating on the more radical possibility of an across-the-board elimination. Perhaps we should. But it has been my aim . . . to make it at least intelligible to you that our collective conceptual destiny lies substantially toward the revolutionary end of the spectrum.

# Double Aspect Theories

Double aspect theories hold that persons are neither composites of body and mind nor reducible to bodies alone. The best known modern version of the theory was introduced by Strawson to avoid these alternatives—Cartesian dualism and reductive materialism—which were thought at the time to be the only plausible options available. Strawson maintains that the concept of a person is the most basic or fundamental concept that applies to us. We are not to be thought of as composed of something more basic into which persons can be divided or reduced, but rather as that unique and undivided kind of thing that has both mental and physical properties or aspects. Part of the support for Strawson's position is provided by the following considerations. If we think of ourselves as strictly material, there is no way to explain how we can have those aspects to which mental terms refer and which ordinary material things lack entirely. If we think of ourselves as a subject of mental aspects joined to a subject of material aspects, there is no explanation for the apparent unity of the person and the ability of a person to refer to him/herself under all aspects by the singular expression "I." So there must be a single kind of thing that a person is and that is sufficient to designate the subject under all of his or her possible aspects. That is what Strawson uses the term *person* to do. Further explanation, as well as criticism, of Strawson's view is provided in Shaffer's essay.

Most of the strength of the double aspect

theory lies in its ability to avoid the difficulties of dualism and reductive materialism. But the source of its strength is also a source of one of its major weaknesses. That source is the sharp distinction between persons and minds or bodies. Persons are not, even in part, immaterial minds or physical bodies. But if a person's physical aspects do not constitute a physical body, then it looks as though the laws of physical science, the laws that apply to physical bodies, should not apply to persons at all, which is absurd. It also looks as though at death persons do not just cease to function, but undergo a substantial change from person substance to physical substance when what were just physical aspects become a physical thing, a corpse. So the separation of persons from the two substances of dualistic theories ends up making human bodies and their relation to ordinary material objects mysterious and problematic. In addition, the dualism of substances reappears in the person theory, not within persons, but between persons and every other thing in the universe. And the relations between persons and the entirely different sort of substance of which the rest of reality is composed are no less troublesome than the mind-body interactions the theory was designed to avoid.

## *P. F. Strawson (b. 1919)*

P. F. Strawson is famous for his criticism of Russell's theory of denotation in an article titled "On Referring" (1950) as well as other contributions in philosophy of language. He is also well known for his work in philosophy of logic and metaphysics. His book-length publications include *An Introduction to Logical Theory* (1952), *Individuals* (1959), in which the essay below appears, and *The Bounds of Sense* (1966).

In the selection below Strawson argues that persons should not be identified with bodies, with minds, or with some composite of the two. The concept of a person enjoys a logical priority over the concepts of body and mind and should be thought of as self-sufficient rather than derivative. What it is to be a person must be specified in terms of the unique properties that make persons fit in a different category than other kinds of things — namely, the ability to be the subjects of both mental and physical properties or attributes. But there is no reason, Strawson contends, for thinking that this characteristic requires that we be two kinds of things rather than one. And there are good independent reasons for not thinking of us in terms of two substances.

# Persons

## *P. F. Strawson*

. . . What we have to acknowledge . . . is the primitiveness of the concept of a person. What I mean by the concept of a person is the concept of a type of entity such that *both* predicates ascribing states of consciousness *and* predicates ascribing corporeal characteristics, a physical situa-

Abridged from *Individuals,* by P. F. Strawson (London: Methuen & Co. Ltd., © 1959). Reprinted by permission.

tion etc. are equally applicable to a single individual of that single type. What I mean by saying that this concept is primitive can be put in a number of ways. One way is to return to those two questions I asked earlier: viz. (1) why are states of consciousness ascribed to anything at all? and (2) why are they ascribed to the very same thing as certain corporeal characteristics, a certain physical situation etc.? [It is] . . . not to be supposed that the answers to these questions were independent of each other. Now I shall say that they are connected in this way: that a necessary condition of states of consciousness being ascribed at all is that they should be ascribed to the *very same things* as certain corporeal characteristics, a certain physical situation etc. That is to say, states of consciousness could not be ascribed at all *unless* they were ascribed to persons, in the sense I have claimed for this word. We are tempted to think of a person as a sort of compound of two kinds of subjects: a subject of experiences (a pure consciousness, an ego) on the one hand, and a subject of corporeal attributes on the other. Many questions arise when we think in this way. But, in particular, when we ask ourselves how we come to frame, to get a use for, the concept of this compound of two subjects, the picture—if we are honest and careful—is apt to change from the picture of two subjects to the picture of one subject and one non-subject. For it becomes impossible to see how we could come by the idea of different, distinguishable, identifiable subjects of experiences—different consciousnesses—*if this idea is thought of as logically primitive,* as a logical ingredient in the compound-idea of a person, the latter being composed of two subjects. For there could never be any question of assigning an experience, as such, to any subject other than oneself; and therefore never any question of assigning it to oneself either, never any question of ascribing it to a subject at all. So the concept of the pure individual consciousness—the pure ego—is a concept that cannot exist; or, at least, cannot exist as a primary concept in terms of which the concept of a person can be explained or analyzed. It can exist only, if at all, as a secondary, non-primitive concept, which itself is to be explained, analyzed, in terms of the concept of a person. It was the entity corresponding to this illusory primary concept of the pure consciousness, the ego-substance, for which Hume was seeking, or ironically pretending to seek, when he looked into himself, and complained that he could never discover himself without a perception and could never discover anything but the perception. More seriously—and this time there was no irony, but a confusion, a Nemesis of confusion for Hume—it was this entity of which Hume vainly sought for the principle of unity, confessing himself perplexed and defeated; sought vainly because there is no principle of unity where there is no principle of differentiation. It was this, too, to which Kant, more perspicacious here than Hume, accorded a purely formal ("analytic") unity: the unity of the "I think" that accompanies all my perceptions and therefore might just as well accompany none. Finally it is this, perhaps, of which Wittgenstein spoke, when he said of the subject, first that there is no such thing, and then that it is not a part of the world, but its limits.

So, then, the word "I" never refers to this, the pure subject. But this does not mean . . . that "I" in some cases does not refer at all. It refers; because I am a person among others; and the predicates which would, *per impossibile* belong to the pure subject if it could be referred to, belong properly to the person to which "I" does refer.

The concept of a person is logically prior to that of an individual consciousness. The concept of a person is not to be analyzed as that of an animated body or of an embodied anima. This is not to say that the concept of a pure individual consciousness might not have a logically secondary existence, if one thinks, or finds, it desirable. We speak of a dead person—a body—and in the same secondary way we might at least think of a disembodied person. A person is not an embodied ego, but an ego might be a disembodied person, retaining the logical benefit of individuality from having been a person.

It is important to realize the full extent of the

acknowledgement one is making in acknowledging the logical primitiveness of the concept of a person. Let me rehearse briefly the stages of the argument. There would be no question of ascribing one's own states of consciousness, or experiences, to anything, unless one also ascribed, or were ready and able to ascribe, states of consciousness, or experiences, to other individual entities of the same logical type as that thing to which one ascribes one's own states of consciousness. The condition of reckoning oneself as a subject of such predicates is that one should also reckon others as subjects of such predicates. The condition, in turn, of this being possible, is that one should be able to distinguish from one another, to pick out or identify, different subjects of such predicates, i.e. different individuals of the type concerned. The condition, in turn, of this being possible is that the individuals concerned, including oneself, should be of a certain unique type: of a type, namely, such that to each individual of that type there must be ascribed, or ascribable, *both* states of consciousness *and* corporeal characteristics. But this characterization of the type is still very opaque and does not at all clearly bring out what is involved. To bring this out, I must make a rough division, into two, of the kinds of predicates properly applied to individuals of this type. The first kind of predicate consists of those which are also properly applied to material bodies to which we would not dream of applying predicates ascribing states of consciousness. . . . They include things like "weighs 10 stone," "is in the drawing-room" and so on. The second kind consists of all the other predicates we apply to persons. These . . . will be very various. They will include things like "is smiling," "is going for a walk," as well as things like "is in pain," "is thinking hard," "believes in God," and so on.

So far I have said that the concept of a person is to be understood as the concept of a type of entity such that *both* predicates ascribing states of consciousness *and* predicates ascribing corporeal characteristics, a physical situation etc. are equally applicable to an individual entity of that type. All I have said about the meaning of saying that this concept is primitive is that it is not to be analyzed in a certain way or ways. We are not, for example, to think of it as a secondary kind of entity in relation to two primary kinds, viz. a particular consciousness and a particular human body. I implied also that the Cartesian error is just a special case of the more general error . . . of thinking of the designations, or apparent designations, of persons as *not* denoting precisely the same thing or entity for all kinds of predicate ascribed to the entity designated. . . .

## Jerome Shaffer (b. 1929)

Jerome Shaffer is the author of numerous essays in philosophy of mind as well as a well-known text, *Philosophy of Mind* (1968) from which the selection below was taken.

In this essay, Shaffer tries to translate Strawson's logical thesis about the concept of a person into a metaphysical thesis about the substance of a person that could support the logical theory. The result is that we seem to be composed of a unique and undivided kind of substance, similar to minds in terms of some of the properties we have and to bodies in terms of others, but composed of neither. The result, Shaffer argues, is that the gains of the theory in avoiding the difficulties associated with other solutions to the mind-body problem are more than offset by its inability to give any satisfactory account of the nature of a person's body or of the relation between persons and their bodies.

# The Person Theory and Its Difficulties

## *Jerome Shaffer*

. . . The person theory . . . is the view that mental events happen neither to purely immaterial substances nor to purely material substances, but to some thing which is *neither immaterial nor material;* let us call them persons. Mental events happen to *persons,* and persons are subject to *both* mental *and* material happenings.

The historical ancestor of the person theorist is Spinoza, the Dutch philosopher of the seventeenth century. Confronted on the one side by the English materialist Hobbes and on the other side by the French dualist Descartes, Spinoza said, in effect, a plague on both your houses. The mental and the physical are both of them simply aspects of something which in itself is neither mental nor physical. A man can equally well be considered as an extended, physical thing or as a thinking thing, although each of these characterizations only brings out one aspect of the man. The analogy has been proposed of an undulating line which at a given moment may be concave from one point of view and convex from the other. The line itself is not completely described by either term, but only by the use of both terms. Yet it is not that there are two different things, one concave and the other convex. There is only one thing which is, from one point of view, concave and, from another point of view, convex. So with man. He is both a thinking thing and an extended, physical thing — not that he is two things but rather that he is one thing with these two aspects. Such a view is traditionally known as a double aspect view. It is like some versions of the identity theory, but, at least in Spinoza's case, differs with respect to the conception of the thing that has the two aspects. For Spinoza what has the two aspects is not material (nor is it mental either), whereas for the identity theory . . . what has the two aspects is material.

Although we cannot examine the details of Spinoza's theory, we might note that Spinoza believed *everything* which existed had these two aspects. This view is called panpsychism. It is the view that consciousness occurs wherever anything exists and thus that every tree, rock, cloud, and even every atom is conscious to some degree. To be sure, Spinoza did not believe that all things had so fully developed a consciousness as man has; presumably a rock's mind is so crude and inferior that it is only barely conscious at all. Still, for Spinoza, it is conscious to some degree.

For a double aspect theory, there are two issues of crucial importance — what is the nature of the underlying stuff which has the aspects, and what exactly are "aspects"? Unfortunately in Spinoza's theory both of these are left in deep obscurity. Each man, and, in fact, everything else that exists, is just a particular instance or specimen of what Spinoza calls "Substance" and also calls "God" or "Nature." But it is very difficult to understand what this stuff is. An indication of the difficulty is that since Spinoza's time there has been an unending controversy whether Spinoza was an atheist or what one commentator called "a God-intoxicated man." If an issue so general as that cannot be settled, then it is unlikely that we can hope for much clarification about the nature of this underlying stuff. The second question, What is an "aspect"?, is equally important to answer, for we do not know what it means to say that the mental and the physical are "aspects" of the same thing until we know what an "aspect" is. Again, Spinoza is not of much help. In his theory, the mental and the physical are both

Abridged from *Philosophy of Mind,* by Jerome A. Shaffer, ©1968, pp. 50–57. Reprinted by permission of Prentice-Hall, Inc., Englewood Cliffs, N.J. Footnotes omitted.

basic attributes of the underlying stuff but he never says how they are related or, indeed, how one and the same thing could have such *different* attributes. . . . It is very difficult to explain with any precision in what sense the mental and the physical are "aspects." The suggestion, by analogy with perception, is that they are different appearances of the thing, the thing as seen from different points of view, but when we try to replace the analogy with a literal characterization, we find ourselves unable to say very much.

In recent philosophy, a modified version of the double aspect theory which we will call the person theory has been presented by P. F. Strawson. It is the view that the mental and the physical are both of them attributes of *persons;* the person is the underlying entity which has both mental and physical attributes. Thus we could say of the *person* that he is six feet tall, weighs one hundred and seventy-five pounds, is moving at the rate of three miles an hour (all physical attributes), and we could also say of the very same entity, that person, that he is now thinking about a paper he is writing, feels a pang of anxiety about that paper, and then wishes it were already over and done with (all mental attributes). We have here neither attributions to two different subjects, a mind and a body (dualism), nor attributions to a body (materialism), but attributions to a person. We may say that the person has a mind and a body, but all that means is that both mental and physical attributes are applicable to him.

Why does Strawson reject materialism and hold that mental states must be attributed to a *person* rather than to a body? His argument is very difficult to grasp but it appears to be as follows. . . . We must admit that we often do ascribe states of consciousness to things; e.g., we say of some particular subject that the subject had a headache. Now Strawson wishes to argue that the notion of attributing a state of consciousness to a subject cannot be analyzed as the notion of attributing a state of consciousness to a body. Consider the epiphenomenalist, who claims that to say "Subject A has a headache" is synonymous with saying "Body *a* is producing a headache." Now the epiphenomenalist would grant that this contention — that all of subject A's headaches are produced by body *a* — is *controversial,* and that some argumentation is needed. But what exactly is the contention? It is not that *all* headaches are produced by body *a*. That is obviously false. Only subject A's headaches are produced by body *a*. But if "Subject A has a headache" is synonymous with "Body *a* is producing a headache," then to say "All subject A's headaches are produced by body *a*" is simply to say "All the headaches produced by body *a* are produced by body *a*." And that is a claim about which controversy would be impossible, since it is an utter tautology. Exactly the same reasoning would be directed by Strawson against the kind of materialism which holds that "Subject A has a headache" means "Body *a* has a headache."

Strawson's point, if we are interpreting him properly, is that in order for materialists and epiphenomenalists even to formulate their claim, they must have a concept of a subject of mental states which is different from the concept of a material body. For they wish to single out sets of mental states and go on to make the nontrivial claim about each of those sets that it is dependent upon some particular body. So they cannot use the body to single out the sets. Hence, their notion of a subject of states of consciousness must be different from their notion of a material body. Otherwise their claim degenerates into the triviality that all those states of consciousness dependent upon a body are dependent upon that body, a claim too empty to be worth asserting.

I believe that this argument is sound. But it is important to note what it does and does not establish. It establishes the *logical* distinctness of subjects of consciousness and bodies. That is to say, it establishes that expressions referring to the one cannot *mean* the same as expressions referring to the other; they cannot be synonymous; the one cannot be analyzed in terms of the other. But the argument does not rule out some form of the identity theory, i.e., the claim that the *entities* which exemplify the one set of expressions are one and the same as the entities which exemplify the other. Even if the expression "subject of consciousness" does not *mean* a body of a certain sort, it still might turn out that whatever is a subject of consciousness is identical with a body of a certain sort. We shall return to this issue shortly.

In rejecting the logical identity of persons (i.e., subjects of consciousness) and bodies, Strawson might be suspected of accepting dualism. But this would be a mistake. Strawson also rejects dualism, at least in the Cartesian form . . . ; he rejects the view that the subject of states of consciousness is a wholly immaterial, nonphysical thing, a thing to which nothing but states of consciousness can be ascribed. His argument is as follows. If someone has the concept of a subject of consciousness, then he must be willing to allow that there could be other subjects than himself, i.e., that he might be only one self among many. To have the concept of other subjects of consciousness is to be able to distinguish one from another, pick out or identify different subjects, be able to say on some occasions at least that here is one subject rather than another. (If one had no idea how to distinguish one subject from another, then one would not have the concept of *different* subjects.) Now if other subjects of consciousness were wholly immaterial, then there would be no way of distinguishing one subject from another—how could we possibly tell how many such subjects were around us right now or which subject was which? And if there was no way of distinguishing one subject from another, then, as was just pointed out, one would not have the concept of other subjects. And therefore, as was pointed out at the beginning of this argument, one would not have the concept of a subject of consciousness at all. So the Cartesian concept of the subject as wholly immaterial is without meaning.

Therefore, if we do have a concept of a subject of consciousness, as we surely do, then it can be neither merely the concept of a body (as materialism holds) nor merely the concept of an immaterial thing (as the dualist holds). It must be the concept of an entity to which both physical and mental attributions can be made. That is to say, this subject must be not only conscious but physical as well. Strawson calls entities which admit of both mental and physical attributes *persons*.

The person theory has very attractive features. It gives full weight to the distinction between mental and physical attributes, allowing them to be attributes of basically different natures. Yet it also does justice to the fact that they seem to be attributes of one and the same subject; we say, "As he fell through space, he wondered if the parachute would ever open," not "As his body fell through space, his mind wondered if the parachute would ever open." Nor do we seem committed to that curious entity, the immaterial, extensionless thinking substance of Descartes' dualism.

And yet, alas, there are difficulties with the person theory. These begin to emerge when we begin probing deeper into the concept of the *person* which is involved here. Strawson defines "person" very simply, as "a type of entity such that *both* predicates ascribing states of consciousness *and* predicates ascribing corporeal characteristics, a physical situation, etc. are equally applicable to a single individual of that single type." But such a definition does not help us very much. That it does not comes out when we ask how the person theory differs from the identity theory.

Identity theorists wish to say that mental attributes are attributes of bodies. Furthermore, most of them wish to say that in some sense the mental attributes are reducible to physical attributes. . . . Now Strawson would certainly reject the contention that mental attributes are reducible in any sense to physical attributes. But would he reject the claim that they are attributes of bodies? Does he wish to say that persons are bodies of a certain sort, namely bodies which have mental attributes as well?

It is clear that Strawson holds persons to be things which have bodily attributes. But that does not make them bodies any more than the fact that something has red in it makes it red. For, unlike ordinary bodies, persons are things which have mental attributes as well. Furthermore, for Strawson it is not the case that persons are things which just happen to have bodily attributes (but might not have had them), nor is it the case that they are things which just happen to have mental attributes (but might not have had them). It is essential to persons, on Strawson's conception of them, that they be entities which necessarily have *both* mental and bodily attributes. And that means that they are things which differ essentially from bodies (which have only bodily attributes necessarily). They are different types of stuffs or substances or entities. And therefore the person theory is fundamentally different from materialism of any sort. It is dualistic in holding that there are two different types of subjects in the natural world, physical bodies and persons. Physical bodies necessarily have solely the physical dimension; persons necessarily have two dimensions, a physical and a mental dimension. It is the latter contention which distinguishes it from Spinoza's double aspect theory; for Spinoza, everything which exists in the world is, in Strawson's sense, a person, i.e., a thing which necessarily has both a mental and a physical dimension.

If we cannot say, on the person theory, that a person *is* a body, perhaps we can say that a person is, *in part,* a body (in the way that a thing which has red in it may be in part red). But this will not do either, for it inevitably raises the question what the rest of it is. That is, it suggests that a person is some sort of an amalgam, a compound of a body and something else (perhaps a soul?). Such suggestions are precisely what the person theory attempts to combat.

Can we even say that a person *has* a body? I suppose that Strawson would want to be able to say that. But what would it mean on the person theory? Doubtless it means that persons have bodily attributes. But does it mean any more? Is it to say anything about a relation between a person and a *body?* Not on the person theory. For a *body* is something which necessarily has solely bodily attributes and such a thing has nothing to do with persons, which, as we saw, are things which necessarily have both bodily and mental attributes.

Does very much hang on this question of the relation (on the person theory) between persons and bodies? A good deal. For example, consider the laws of nature which hold for bodies, the laws of physics, chemistry, biology. Surely we would want to be able to say that these laws are true for human bodies as well as other bodies. If it is true, in its Newtonian formulation, that "a *body* continues its state of rest or steady motion unless . . . ," we would want this to hold for the bodies of persons as well as for all other bodies. Yet if we cannot even say that a person's "body" is a *body* in the same sense that rocks and trees are bodies, then these laws of nature, which apply to *bodies,* cannot be applied to the "bodies" of persons. And that would be so great an inconvenience, to say nothing of its absurdity, as to count against the person theory.

To be sure, the term "body" is used in many ways besides the Newtonian one cited above, some of which tie better with the person theory. For example, consider the old song "Gin a body meet a body comin' thro the rye." Here of course we are not envisioning a collision of solids but an encounter between persons. In this context, the term "body" is simply used to mean a person. (Sometimes the reverse is the case. When we say "They searched his person," we are using "person" to mean a body.)

There is another use which comes even closer to the Strawsonian conception of a body. If someone said "They found a body in the lake today," we would be very surprised if he meant a rock, or a tree trunk, or an old, sunken boat, or a fish, although all of these are, in the Newtonian sense, bodies. Here "body" means "corpse," i.e., a dead human being (a dead *animal* is called a carcass rather than a corpse). A corpse or "body" in this sense is what is left when a person dies, although it is not a *part* of a living person or something which he *has* while he is alive (he does have the right to say what is to be done with it after he dies). This concept of the body becomes gruesomely explicit when we refer to it as "the remains."

It is this conception of the body which comes closest to that found in the person theory. For, in that theory, as we have seen, a body is not a person, nor is it a part of a person, nor is it something a person has. At most it is the person insofar as he is thought of as the subject of bodily attributes. It is then an abstraction, an intellectual construction, rather than a reality. But it becomes a reality at death. It materializes into that thing we call a corpse. On the person theory, a human body is what would be the person's corpse if he died; the only way we can talk about a person's body is if we consider him as if he were dead.

It is, then, one of the paradoxical implications of the person theory that the body which a person has cannot be conceived of as a physical object subject to the laws of the physical world. In its attempt to establish the unity of the person (contra dualism) without sacrificing the thesis that persons are conscious (contra materialism), the person theory seems to end with the absurdity that a person's body is not a *physical* thing.

# Behaviorism

Behaviorism arose as a method in psychology and the social sciences. In its original form it was not really a metaphysical claim about human nature. It was rather a claim about what kinds of things are legitimate objects of the sciences of human behavior. Since the method of science is to find the causal laws that relate observable or experimentally accessible data, certain kinds of psychological explanation are obviously preferable to others. In particular, unobservable inner mental events and unverifiable social forces have no place in legitimate explanations of behavior. In both cases, the entities are inferred rather than observed to exist. Psychological explanation can simply ignore or bypass such inferred entities in favor of the observable phenomena on which the inferences are based. In the case of the inner mental entities, this amounts to the following. There will be observable circumstances that are taken to produce the unobservable mental state, disposition, or process, which will in turn give rise to appropriate observable behavior. Since the experimentally inaccessible inner item is tied causally to its observable environmental causes and behavioral effects, the science that seeks to predict and control human behavior can simply ignore this mysterious intermediary and produce a complete theory of the causal connections between the environmental stimulus and behavioral response. This is the crucial insight of stimulus-response psychology or behaviorism. Unobservable inner mental entities cannot alter the causal connections between observable stimuli and behavioral responses. So from the standpoint of scientific theory they serve no function and should not be given theoretical existence. Entities not needed to account for any observable phenomena should not be inferred into existence, since such inferences violate the criterion of simplicity for scientific theories in general.

Although scientific behaviorism is not explicitly materialistic, the exclusion of unobservable psychic states and processes in favor of observable stimuli and responses has a definite bias in favor of materialism. If we can and should produce a complete account of human behavior and its causes in strictly physical (observable) terms, then we have good reason to think that there is nothing being left out of such accounts, that human beings are material through and through.

The major difficulty for scientific behaviorism was the apparent regularity of human behavior under descriptions that violated the methodological constraints of the theory. Behaviorism worked fairly well for some lower animals, for reflex and automatic behavior in humans, and in artificial and carefully controlled laboratory situations. But for a wide range of human behavior, the limitations of the theory seemed to prohibit access to the real causes of human behavior and the real behavioral responses of human subjects to those causes. People respond not to the physical properties of things in their environment, but to what they take the things in their environment to be. This "taking to be" is already an inner process, and it frequently depends in turn on such unobservable inner states as beliefs and desires. We respond to the environment in terms of its meaning for us, not in terms of a strictly physical description of it. Similarly, what makes a number of very different physical behaviors the same response is frequently their intended goal rather than their strictly physical characteristics. But intentions are just the sort of thing that behaviorism excludes from psychological explanation. The result is that such simple laws as "that people will try to get help when faced with emergencies they are not equipped to handle" are beyond the scope of behaviorist psychology. Whether or not something is perceived as an emergency is not just a matter of the physical characteristics of the stimulus. The same stimulus would be perceived as an emergency if the person thought herself to be on a city street, but not as an emergency if she thought herself to be on a movie set during rehearsal. And whether or not the emergency is taken to require outside help will depend upon the beliefs of the person regarding her competence to deal with it. Finally, there are an indefinite range of physical behaviors that are instances of "trying to get help"—grouped not as physical movements but in terms of the intentions of the person who engages in them. Accounts of these and other problems that behavioristic psychology proved unable to handle are contained in the essay by Fodor in the subsection on functionalism which immediately follows this subsection, and in the essay by Pylyshyn in the artificial intelligence section in this part.

Logical behaviorism is essentially a theory about the meaning and use of the mentalistic vocabulary. It consists of the claim that all references to immaterial states and processes can be replaced by references to behavior or behavioral dispositions. For example, to say that a person is angry is not, according to logical behaviorism, to say that the immaterial part of that person is in the state called *anger.* It is simply to say that she is behaving or disposed to behave in certain ways—clenching her fists, reddening in the face, raising her voice, engaging in violence with very little (additional) provocation, saying things like "I'm so angry I could scream," and so on. The list of actual and potential behavior (dispositions to behave in specified ways if certain situations should arise) may be indefinitely long, but the important idea is that the list exhausts the meaning of the mental term involved without residue. If this were the case, then all mental terms could be completely and correctly analyzed without recourse to anything immaterial whatsoever.

Part of the support for this view comes from thinking about the ways in which typical mental terms are learned. We do not learn how to use the term *anger,* for example, by having someone point to an inner state and name it for us. We learn the meaning of the term and how it is to be used by observing people in situations that typically evoke angry behavior, and by observing that behavior when it occurs. We learn to use the term to designate typical patterns of behavior and behavioral dispositions. Logical behaviorists conclude that the meaning and reference of the term are determined by such practices and limited to the things that figure in such practices.

Logical behaviorism involves no explicit metaphysical thesis about the nature of persons, but, like behaviorism in the human sciences, is materialistic in its motivation. The aim of logical behaviorism is to avoid the difficulties that result from interpreting mental terms in the manner suggested by Cartesian dualism. After all, the advantages of eliminating talk about inner mental states don't come to much if dualism is in fact the correct metaphysical account of the nature of human beings. If dualism were true, mental states would have to be dealt with.

Logical behaviorism encountered at least two specific kinds of difficulty. The first is that a number of emotional states—for example, anger, grief, and regret—seem to have an introspectable content that is not captured by behavior or behavioral dispositions. Surely part of what the term *anger* picks out is the inner feeling that we are aware of, even if behavior and behavioral tendencies are also involved. In addition to the behavior we exhibit when angry or grief-stricken—clenching our fists, tightening stomach or jaw muscles, shaking or sobbing uncontrollably—there is what we feel subjectively—the feeling of rage or disgust welling up inside of us, the feeling of emptiness or loss—which are as much a part of the emotion as the behavior to which they give rise. So the behaviorist account seems to be missing something that should be included in the analysis of terms that designate feelings or emotional states.

The second kind of difficulty is the existence of mental states and processes that don't seem to have any essential connection to typical behavior of any kind. Ordinary perception is a good example. There is no typical behavior produced by most of our seeing, hearing, and so on. Only when perception is part of some other activity or provides something surprising or unexpected does it give rise to specific behavior. Frequently we just see and hear things without altering our behavior as a result. So there appear to be mental states and processes that don't connect up with patterned or standard forms of behavior in a way that would allow them to be defined in terms of such behavior.

By far the most important factor in the declining popularity of logical behaviorism was the appearance of alternative theories that avoided the "ghost in the machine" of dualism without the difficulties involved in translating mental terms into either material or behavioristic ones. These alternative theories were eliminative materialism, already discussed in the subsection on materialism, and functionalism, which will be discussed in the next subsection.

## *B. F. Skinner (b. 1904)*

B. F. Skinner is perhaps the best-known advocate of the behaviorist approach to the sciences of human behavior which dominated psychology and related disciplines for a number of years. His interests and writings are not limited to those sciences, but extend to the social, political, and philosophical implications of behaviorism. His books include *The Behavior of Organisms* (1938), *Walden Two* (1948), *Science and Human Behavior* (1955), from which the selection below was taken, *Beyond Freedom and Dignity* (1971), and *About Behaviorism* (1976).

In this selection Skinner describes and defends behaviorism as the appropriate method in explanations of behavior. Behaviorism requires that we explain behavior without recourse to unobservable and uncontrollable inner states and processes of any kind. Behavior must be explained solely in terms of its (physical) environmental causes (or stimuli) and its (physical) behavioral effects (or responses). Skinner argues that the behaviorist constraints preclude nothing of explanatory value in psychology and that without them psychology and related disciplines would not be *sciences* of human behavior at all.

# Scientific Behaviorism

*B. F. Skinner*

## Psychic Inner Causes

A . . . common practice is to explain behavior in terms of an inner agent which lacks physical dimensions and is called "mental" or "psychic." The purest form of the psychic explanation is seen in the animism of primitive peoples. From the immobility of the body after death it is inferred that a spirit responsible for movement has departed. The *enthusiastic* person is, as the etymology of the word implies, energized by a "god within." It is only a modest refinement to attribute every feature of the behavior of the physical organism to a corresponding feature of the "mind" or of some inner "personality." The inner man is regarded as driving the body very much as the man at the steering wheel drives a car. The inner man wills an action, the outer executes it. The inner loses his appetite, the outer stops eating. The inner man wants and the outer gets. The inner has the impulse which the outer obeys.

It is not the layman alone who resorts to these practices, for many reputable psychologists use a similar system of explanation. The inner man is sometimes personified clearly, as when delinquent behavior is attributed to a "disordered personality," or he may be dealt with in fragments, as when behavior is attributed to mental processes, faculties, and traits. Since the inner man does not occupy space, he may be multiplied at will. It has been argued that a single physical organism is controlled by several psychic agents and that its behavior is the resultant of their several wills. The Freudian concepts of the ego, superego, and id are often used in this way. They are frequently regarded as nonsubstantial creatures, often in violent conflict, whose defeats or victories lead to the adjusted or maladjusted behavior of the physical organism in which they reside.

Direct observation of the mind comparable with the observation of the nervous system has not proved feasible. It is true that many people believe that they observe their "mental states" just as the physiologist observes neural events, but another interpretation of what they observe is possible. . . . Introspective psychology no longer pretends to supply direct information about events which are the causal antecedents, rather than the mere accompaniments, of behavior. It defines its "subjective" events in ways which strip them of any usefulness in a causal analysis. The events appealed to in early mentalistic explanations of behavior have remained beyond the reach of observation. Freud insisted upon this by emphasizing the role of the unconscious—a frank recognition that important mental processes are not directly observable. The Freudian literature supplies many examples of behavior from which unconscious wishes, impulses, instincts, and emotions are inferred. Unconscious thought-processes have also been used to explain intellectual achievements. Though the mathematician may feel that he knows "how he thinks," he is often unable to give a coherent account of the mental processes leading to the solution of a specific problem. But any mental event which is unconscious is necessarily inferential, and the explanation is therefore not based upon independent observations of a valid cause.

The fictional nature of this form of inner cause is shown by the ease with which the men-

---

Abridged from *Science and Human Behavior,* by B. F. Skinner (Copyright © 1955 by Macmillan Publishing Co., renewed 1983 by B. F. Skinner), pp. 29–36. Reprinted by permission of Macmillan Publishing Company, Inc.

tal process is discovered to have just the properties needed to account for the behavior. When a professor turns up in the wrong classroom or gives the wrong lecture, it is because his *mind* is, at least for the moment, *absent.* If he forgets to give a reading assignment, it is because it has slipped his *mind* (a hint from the class may re*mind* him of it). He begins to tell an old joke but pauses for a moment, and it is evident to everyone that he is trying to make up his *mind* whether or not he has already used the joke that term. His lectures grow more tedious with the years, and questions from the class confuse him more and more, because his *mind* is failing. What he says is often disorganized because his *ideas* are confused. He is occasionally unnecessarily emphatic because of the force of his *ideas.* When he repeats himself, it is because he has an *idée fixe;* and when he repeats what others have said, it is because he borrows his *ideas.* Upon occasion there is nothing in what he says because he lacks *ideas.* In all this it is obvious that the mind and the ideas, together with their special characteristics, are being invented on the spot to provide spurious explanations. A science of behavior can hope to gain very little from so cavalier a practice. Since mental or psychic events are asserted to lack the dimensions of physical science, we have an additional reason for rejecting them.

### Conceptual Inner Causes

The commonest inner causes have no specific dimensions at all, either neurological or psychic. When we say that a man eats *because* he is hungry, smokes a great deal *because* he has the tobacco habit, fights *because* of the instinct of pugnacity, behaves brilliantly *because* of his intelligence, or plays the piano well *because* of his musical ability, we seem to be referring to causes. But on analysis these phrases prove to be merely redundant descriptions. A single set of facts is described by the two statements: "He eats" and "He is hungry." A single set of facts is described by the two statements: "He smokes a great deal" and "He has the smoking habit." A single set of facts is described by the two statements: "He plays well" and "He has musical ability." The practice of explaining one statement in terms of the other is dangerous because it suggests that we have found the cause and therefore need search no further. Moreover, such terms as "hunger," "habit," and "intelligence" convert what are essentially the properties of a process or relation into what appear to be things. Thus we are unprepared for the properties eventually to be discovered in the behavior itself and continue to look for something which may not exist.

## THE VARIABLES OF WHICH BEHAVIOR IS A FUNCTION

The practice of looking inside the organism for an explanation of behavior has tended to obscure the variables which are immediately available for a scientific analysis. These variables lie outside the organism, in its immediate environment and in its environmental history. They have a physical status to which the usual techniques of science are adapted, and they make it possible to explain behavior as other subjects are explained in science. These independent variables are of many sorts and their relations to behavior are often subtle and complex, but we cannot hope to give an adequate account of behavior without analyzing them.

Consider the act of drinking a glass of water. This is not likely to be an important bit of behavior in anyone's life, but it supplies a convenient example. We may describe the topography of the behavior in such a way that a given instance may be identified quite accurately by any qualified observer. Suppose now we bring someone into a room and place a glass of water before him. Will he drink? There appear to be only two possibilities: either he will or he will not. But we speak of the *chances* that he will drink, and this notion may be refined for scientific use. What we want to evaluate is the *probability* that he will drink. This may range from virtual certainty that drinking will occur to virtual certainty that it will not. The very considerable problem of how to measure such a probability will be discussed later. For the moment, we are interested in how the probability may be increased or decreased.

Everyday experience suggests several possibilities, and laboratory and clinical observations have added others. It is decidedly not true that a horse may be led to water but cannot be made to drink. By arranging a history of severe deprivation we could be "absolutely sure" that drinking would occur. In the same way we may be sure that the glass of water in our experiment will be drunk. Although we are not likely to arrange them experimentally, deprivations of the necessary magnitude sometimes occur outside the laboratory. We may obtain an effect similar to that of deprivation by speeding up the excretion of water. For example, we may induce sweating by raising the temperature of the room or by forcing heavy exercise, or we may increase the excretion of urine by mixing salt or urea in food taken prior to the experiment. It is also well known that loss of blood, as on a battlefield, sharply increases the probability of drinking. On the other hand, we may set the probability at virtually zero by inducing or forcing our subject to drink a large quantity of water before the experiment.

If we are to predict whether or not our subject will drink, we must know as much as possible about these variables. If we are to induce him to drink, we must be able to manipulate them. In both cases, moreover, either for accurate prediction or control, we must investigate the effect of each variable quantitatively with the methods and techniques of a laboratory science.

Other variables may, of course, affect the result. Our subject may be "afraid" that something has been added to the water as a practical joke or for experimental purposes. He may even "suspect" that the water has been poisoned. He may have grown up in a culture in which water is drunk only when no one is watching. He may refuse to drink simply to prove that we cannot predict or control his behavior. These possibilities do not disprove the relations between drinking and the variables listed in the preceding paragraphs; they simply remind us that other variables may have to be taken into account. We must know the history of our subject with respect to the behavior of drinking water, and if we cannot eliminate social factors from the situation, then we must know the history of his personal relations to people resembling the experimenter. Adequate prediction in any science requires information about all relevant variables, and the control of a subject matter for practical purposes makes the same demands.

Other types of "explanation" do not permit us to dispense with these requirements or to fulfill them in any easier way. It is of no help to be told that our subject will drink provided he was born under a particular sign of the zodiac which shows a preoccupation with water or provided he is the lean and thirsty type or was, in short, "born thirsty." Explanations in terms of inner states or agents, however, may require some further comment. To what extent is it helpful to be told, "He drinks because he is thirsty"? If to be thirsty means nothing more than to have a tendency to drink, this is mere redundancy. If it means that he drinks because of a state of thirst, an inner causal event is invoked. If this state is purely inferential—if no dimensions are assigned to it which would make direct observation possible—it cannot serve as an explanation. But if it has physiological or psychic properties, what role can it play in a science of behavior?

The physiologist may point out that several ways of raising the probability of drinking have a common effect: they increase the concentration of solutions in the body. Through some mechanism not yet well understood, this may bring about a corresponding change in the nervous system which in turn makes drinking more probable. In the same way, it may be argued that all these operations make the organism "feel thirsty" or "want a drink" and that such a psychic state also acts upon the nervous system in some unexplained way to induce drinking. In each case we have a causal chain consisting of three links: (1) an operation performed upon the organism from without—for example, water deprivation; (2) an inner condition—for example, physiological or psychic thirst; and (3) a kind of behavior—for example, drinking. Independent information about the second link would obviously permit us to predict the third without recourse to the first. It would be a preferred type of variable because it would be nonhistoric; the first link may lie in the past history of the organism, but the second is a current condition. Direct information about the second link is, however, seldom, if ever, available. Sometimes we infer the second link from the third: an animal is judged to be thirsty if it drinks. In that case, the explanation is spurious. Sometimes we infer the second link from the first: an animal is said to be thirsty if it has not drunk for a long time. In that case, we obviously cannot dispense with the prior history.

The second link is useless in the *control* of behavior unless we can manipulate it. At the moment, we have no way of directly altering neural processes at appropriate moments in the life of a behaving organism, nor has any way been discovered to alter a psychic process. We usually set up the second link through the first: we make an animal thirsty, in either the physiological or the psychic sense, by depriving it of water, feeding it salt, and so on. In that case, the second link obviously does not permit us to dispense with the first. Even if some new technical discovery were to enable us to set up or change the second link directly, we should still have to deal with those enormous areas in which human behavior is controlled through manipulation of the first link. A technique of operating upon the second link would increase our control of behavior, but the techniques which have already been developed would still remain to be analyzed.

The most objectionable practice is to follow the causal sequence back only as far as a hypothetical second link. This is a serious handicap both in a theoretical science and in the practical control of behavior. It is no help to be told that to get an organism to drink we are simply to "make it thirsty" unless we are also told how this is to be done. When we have obtained the necessary prescription for thirst, the whole proposal is more complex than it need be. Similarly, when an example of maladjusted behavior is explained by saying that the individual is "suffering from anxiety," we have still to be told the cause of the anxiety. But the external conditions which are then invoked could have been directly related to the maladjusted behavior. Again, when we are told that a man stole a loaf of bread because "he was hungry," we have still to learn of the external conditions responsible for the "hunger." These conditions would have sufficed to explain the theft.

The objection to inner states is not that they do not exist, but that they are not relevant in a functional analysis. We cannot account for the behavior of any system while staying wholly inside it; eventually we must turn to forces operating upon the organism from without. Unless there is a weak spot in our causal chain so that the second link is not lawfully determined by the first, or the third by the second, then the first and third links must be lawfully related. If we must always go back beyond the second link for prediction and control, we may avoid many tiresome and exhausting digressions by examining the third link as a function of the first. Valid information about the second link may throw light upon this relationship but can in no way alter it.

## A FUNCTIONAL ANALYSIS

The external variables of which behavior is a function provide for what may be called a causal or **functional analysis.** We undertake to predict and control the behavior of the individual organism. This is our "dependent variable"—the effect for which we are to find the cause. Our "independent variables"—the causes of behavior—are the external conditions of which behavior is a function. Relations between the two —the "cause-and-effect relationships" in behavior—are the laws of a science. A synthesis of these laws expressed in quantitative terms yields a comprehensive picture of the organism as a behaving system.

This must be done within the bounds of a natural science. We cannot assume that behavior has any peculiar properties which require unique methods or special kinds of knowledge. It is often argued that an act is not so important as the "intent" which lies behind it, or that it can be described only in terms of what it "means" to the behaving individual or to others whom it may affect. If statements of this sort are useful for scientific purposes, they must be based upon observable events, and we may confine ourselves to such events exclusively in a functional analysis. We shall see later that although such terms as "meaning" and "intent" appear to refer to properties of behavior, they usually conceal references to independent variables. This is also true of "aggressive," "friendly," "disorganized," "intelligent," and other terms which appear to describe properties of behavior but in reality refer to its controlling relations.

The independent variables must also be described in physical terms. An effort is often made to avoid the labor of analyzing a physical situation by guessing what it "means" to an organism or by distinguishing between the physical world and a psychological world of "experience." This practice also reflects a confusion between dependent and independent variables. The events affecting an organism must be capable of description in the language of physical science. It is sometimes argued that certain "social forces" or the "influences" of culture or tradition are exceptions. But we cannot appeal to entities of this sort without explaining how they can affect both the scientist and the individual under observation. The physical events which must then be appealed to in such an explanation will supply us with alternative material suitable for a physical analysis.

By confining ourselves to these observable events, we gain a considerable advantage, not only in theory, but in practice. A "social force" is no more useful in manipulating behavior than an inner state of hunger, anxiety, or skepticism. Just as we must trace these inner events to the manipulable variables of which they are said to be functions before we may put them to practical use, so we must identify the physical events through which a "social force" is said to affect the organism before we can manipulate it for purposes of control. In dealing with the directly observable data we need not refer to either the inner state or the outer force. . . .

## *Gilbert Ryle (1900–1976)*

Gilbert Ryle was a famous British philosopher who made important contributions to philosophy of mind and philosophy of language. His technique for dealing with philosophical problems was to identify them as products of linguistic confusion of various sorts. He is perhaps best known for his criticism of Cartesian dualism which is illustrated in the selection below. Ryle's major works are *Philosophical Arguments* (1945), *The Concept of Mind* (1949), from which the latter part of the selection below was taken, and *Dilemmas* (1954). He was also the editor of *Mind* which was for many years the leading English philosophical journal.

In the following selection Ryle uses a story which he takes to be analogous to the Cartesian story in order to persuade us that dualism is just a philosophical myth. He then rejects the treatment of scientific behaviorism (which he calls simply "behaviorism") as a metaphysical view about what humans are instead of just a view about scientific method. Behaviorism as metaphysics would view humans as simple behaving mechanisms. But the dualist alternative that we are simple behaving mechanisms plus simple behaving (immaterial) paramechanisms is not much better. To categorize human behavior adequately we will need to analyze our mental concepts in such a way that they accurately reflect the differences between human behavior and simple mechanical behavior. But these differences are differences in behavior and behavioral dispositions and provide no reason to think that mental concepts refer to an immaterial or "ghostly" mind once we have seen through the Cartesian myth.

# Logical Behaviorism

## *Gilbert Ryle*

The story is told of some peasants who were terrified at the sight of their first railway-train. Their pastor therefore gave them a lecture explaining how a steam-engine works. One of the peasants then said, "Yes, pastor, we quite understand what you say about the steam-engine. But there is really a horse inside, isn't there?" So used were they to horse-drawn carts that they could not take in the idea that some vehicles propel themselves.

We might invent a sequel. The peasants examined the engine and peeped into every crevice of it. They then said, "Certainly we cannot see, feel, or hear a horse there. We are foiled. But we know there is a horse there, so it must be a ghost-horse which, like the fairies, hides from mortal eyes."

The pastor objected, "But, after all, horses themselves are made of moving parts, just as the steam-engine is made of moving parts. You know what their muscles, joints, and blood-vessels do. So why is there a mystery in the self-propulsion of a steam-engine, if there is none in that of a horse? What do you think makes the horse's hooves go to and fro?" After a pause a peasant replied, "What makes the horse's hooves go is four extra little ghost-horses inside."

Poor simple-minded peasants! Yet just such a story has been the official theory of the mind for the last three very scientific centuries. . . . For the general terms in which the scientists have set their problem of mind and body, we philosophers have been chiefly to blame, though we have been obsessed, not by the rustic idea of horses, but by the newer idea of mechanical contrivances. The legend that we have told and sold runs like this. A person consists of two theatres, one bodily and one non-bodily. In his Theatre A go on the incidents which we can explore by eye and instrument. But a person also incorporates a second theatre, Theatre B. Here there go on incidents which are totally unlike, though synchronized with those that go on in Theatre A. These Theatre B episodes are changes in the states, not of bits of flesh, but of something called "consciousness," which occupies no space. Only the proprietor of Theatre B has first-hand knowledge of what goes on in it. It is a secret theatre. The experimentalist tries to open its doors, but it has no doors. He tries to peep through its windows, but it has no windows. He is foiled.

We tend nowadays to treat it as obvious that a person, unlike a newt, lives the two lives, life "A" and life "B," each completely unlike, though mysteriously geared to the other. Ingrained hypotheses do feel obvious, however redundant they may be. The peasants in my story correctly thought that a steam-engine was hugely different from a cart and automatically but incorrectly explained the difference by postulating a ghost-horse inside. So most of us, correctly thinking that there are huge differences between a clock and a person, automatically but incorrectly explain these differences by postulating an extra set of ghost-works inside. We correctly say that people are not like clocks, since people meditate, calculate, and invent things; they make plans, dream dreams, and shirk their obligations; they get angry, feel depressed, scan the heavens, and have likes and dislikes; they work, play, and idle; they are sane, crazy, or imbecile; they are skillful at some things and bunglers at others. Where we go wrong is in explaining these familiar actions and conditions as the operations of a secondary set of secret works.

Everybody knows quite well when to describe someone as acting absent-mindedly or with heed, as babbling deliriously or reasoning

---

Abridged from a selection by Gilbert Ryle in *A Modern Introduction to Philosophy,* 3d ed. Edited by Paul Edwards and Arthur Pap (New York: Free Press, 1973). Reprinted by permission of Basil Blackwell.

coherently, as feeling angry but not showing it, as wanting one thing but pretending to want another, as being ambitious, patriotic, or miserly. We often get our accounts and estimates of other people and of ourselves wrong; but we more often get them right. We did not need to learn the legend of the two theatres before we were able to talk sense about people and to deal effectively with them. Nor has this fairly new-fangled legend helped us to do it better.

When we read novels, biographies, and reminiscences, we do not find the chapters partitioned into Section "A," covering the hero's "bodily" doings, and Section "B," covering his "mental" doings. We find unpartitioned accounts of what he did and thought and felt, of what he said to others and to himself, of the mountains he tried to climb and the problems he tried to solve. Should an examiner mark the paper written by the candidate's hand but refuse to assess the candidate's wits? Theorists themselves, when actually describing people, sensibly forget Theatre A and Theatre B. Sir Charles Sherrington paid a well-deserved compliment to Professor Adrian, but he did not pay one cool compliment to Professor Adrian "A" and another warmer compliment to Professor Adrian "B."*

In saying that a person is not to be described as a mind coupled with a body I am not saying, with some truculent thinkers, that people are just machines. Nor are engines just wagons or live bodies just corpses. What is wrong with the story of the two theatres is not that it reports differences which are not there but that it misrepresents differences which are there. It is a story with the right characters but the wrong plot. It is an attempt to explain a genuine difference—or rather a galaxy of differences—but its effect, like that of the peasants' theory, is merely to reduplicate the thing to be explained. It says, "The difference between a machine like a human body on the one hand and a human being on the other is that in a human being, besides the organs which we do see, there is a counterpart set of organs which we do not see; besides the causes and effects which we can witness, there is a counterpart series of causes and effects which we cannot witness." So now we ask, "But what explains the differences between what goes on in the Theatre B of a sane man and what goes on in that of a lunatic? A third theatre, Theatre C?"

No, what prevents us from examining Theatre B is not that it has no doors or windows, but that there is no such theatre. What prevented the peasants from finding the horse was not that it was a ghost-horse, but that there was no horse. Nonetheless, the engine *was* different from a wagon and ordinary people *are* different not only from machines, but also from animals, imbeciles, infants, and corpses. They also differ in countless important ways from one another. I have not begun to show how we should grade these differences. I have only shown how we should not grade them.

One last word. In ordinary life (save when we want to sound knowing) we seldom use the noun "Mind" or the adjective "mental" at all. What we do is to talk of people, of people calculating, conjuring, hoping, resolving, tasting, bluffing, fretting, and so on. Nor, in ordinary life, do we talk of "Matter" or of things being "material." What we do is to talk of steel, granite, and water; of wood, moss, and grain; of flesh, bone, and sinew. The umbrella-titles "Mind" and "Matter" obliterate the very differences that ought to interest us. Theorists should drop both these words. "Mind" and "Matter" are echoes from the hustings of philosophy and prejudice the solutions of all problems posed in terms of them.

. . . . . . . . . . . . . . . . . . . . . . . . . . . . . . . . . . . .

* The reference here is to Sir Charles Sherrington and E. D. Adrian, who had given earlier talks in the same series in which Ryle originally gave this talk. (Eds.)

# The Concept of Mind

The general trend of *[The Concept of Mind]* will undoubtedly, and harmlessly be stigmatized as "behaviorist." So it is pertinent to say something about Behaviorism. Behaviorism was, in the beginning, a theory about the proper methods of scientific psychology. It held that the example of the other progressive sciences ought to be followed, as it had not previously been followed, by psychologists; their theories should be based upon repeatable and publicly checkable observations and experiments. But the reputed deliverances of consciousness and introspection are not publicly checkable. Only people's overt behavior can be observed by several witnesses, measured and mechanically recorded. The early adherents of this methodological program seem to have been in two minds whether to assert that the data of consciousness and introspection were myths, or to assert merely that they were insusceptible of scientific examination. It was not clear whether they were espousing a not very sophisticated mechanistic doctrine, like that of Hobbes and Gassendi, or whether they were still cleaving to the Cartesian para-mechanical theory, but restricting their research procedures to those that we have inherited from Galileo; whether, for example, they held that thinking just consists in making certain complex noises and movements or whether they held that though these movements and noises were connected with "inner life" processes, the movements and noises alone were laboratory phenomena.

However it does not matter whether the early Behaviorists accepted a mechanist or a para-mechanist theory. They were in error in either case. The important thing is that the practice of describing specifically human doings according to the recommended methodology quickly made it apparent to psychologists how shadowy were the supposed "inner-life" occurrences which the Behaviorists were at first reproached for ignoring or denying. Psychological theories which made no mention of the deliverances of "inner perception" were at first likened to "Hamlet" without the Prince of Denmark. But the extruded hero soon came to seem so bloodless and spineless a being that even the opponents of these theories began to feel shy of imposing heavy theoretical burdens upon his spectral shoulders.

Novelists, dramatists and biographers had always been satisfied to exhibit people's motives, thoughts, perturbations and habits by describing their doings, sayings, and imaginings, their grimaces, gestures and tones of voice. In concentrating on what Jane Austen concentrated on, psychologists began to find that these were, after all, the stuff and not the mere trappings of their subjects. They have, of course, continued to suffer unnecessary qualms of anxiety, lest this diversion of psychology from the task of describing the ghostly might not commit it to tasks of describing the merely mechanical. But the influence of the bogy of mechanism has for a century been dwindling because, among other reasons, during this period the biological sciences have established their title of "sciences." The Newtonian system is no longer the sole paradigm of natural science. Man need not be degraded to a machine by being denied to be a ghost in a machine. He might, after all, be a sort of animal, namely, a higher mammal. There has yet to be ventured the hazardous leap to the hypothesis that perhaps he is a man.

The Behaviorists' methodological program has been of revolutionary importance to the program of psychology. But more, it has been one of the main sources of the philosophical suspicion that the two-worlds story is a myth. It is a matter of relatively slight importance that the champions of this methodological principle have tended to espouse as well a kind of Hobbist

---

Abridged from *The Concept of Mind,* by G. Ryle, 1949. Permission granted by Barnes & Noble Books, Totowa, N.J.

theory, and even to imagine that the truth of mechanism is entailed by the truth of their theory of scientific research method in psychology.

It is not for me to say to what extent the concrete research procedures of practising psychologists have been affected by their long adherence to the two-worlds story, or to what extent the Behaviorist revolt has led to modifications of their methods. For all that I know, the ill effects of the myth may, on balance, have been outweighed by the good, and the Behaviorist revolt against it may have led to reforms more nominal than real. Myths are not always detrimental to the progress of theories. Indeed, in their youth they are often of inestimable value. Pioneers are, at the start, fortified by the dream that the New World is, behind its alien appearances, a sort of duplicate of the Old World, and the child is not so much baffled by a strange house if, wherever they may actually lead him, its bannisters feel to his hand like those he knew at home.

But it has not been a part of [my] object . . . to advance the methodology of psychology or to canvass the special hypotheses of this or that science. [My] object has been to show that the two-worlds story is a philosophers' myth, though not a fable, and, by showing this, to begin to repair the damage that this myth has for some time been doing inside philosophy. I have tried to establish this point, not by adducing evidence from the troubles of psychologists, but by arguing that the cardinal mental concepts have been credited by philosophers themselves with the wrong sorts of logical behavior. If my arguments have any force, then these concepts have been misallocated in the same general way, though in opposing particular ways, by both mechanists and para-mechanists, by Hobbes and by Descartes.

If, in conclusion, we try to compare the theoretical fruitfulness of the Hobbes-Gassendi story of the mind with that of the Cartesians, we must undoubtedly grant that the Cartesian story has been the more productive. We might describe their opposition in this picture. One company of a country's defenders installs itself in a fortress. The soldiers of the second company notice that the moat is dry, the gates are missing and the walls are in collapse. Scorning the protection of such a rickety fort, yet still ridden by the idea that only from forts like this can the country be defended, they take up their stand in the most fort-like thing they can see, namely, the shadow of the decrepit fort. Neither position is defensible; and obviously the shadow-stronghold has all the vulnerability of the stone fort, with some extra vulnerabilities of its own. Yet in one respect the occupants of the shadow-fort have shown themselves the better soldiers, since they have seen the weaknesses of the stone fort, even if they are silly to fancy themselves secure in a fort made of no stones at all. The omens are not good for their victory, but they have given some evidence of teachability. They have exercised some vicarious strategic sense; they have realized that a stone fort whose walls are broken is not a stronghold. That the shadow of such a fort is not a stronghold either is the next lesson that they may come to learn.

We may apply this picture to one of our own central issues. Thinking, on the one view, is identical with saying. The holders of the rival view rightly reject this identification, but they make this rejection, naturally but wrongly, in the form that saying is doing one thing and thinking is doing another. Thinking operations are numerically different from verbal operations, and they control these verbal operations from another place than the place in which these verbal operations occur. This, however, will not do either, and for the very same reasons as those which showed the vulnerability of the identification of thinking with mere saying. Just as undisciplined and heedless saying is not thinking but babbling, so, whatever shadow-operations may be postulated as occurring in the other place, these too might go on there in an undisciplined and heedless manner; and then they in their turn would not be thinking. But to offer even an erroneous description of what distinguishes heedless and undisciplined chattering from thinking is to recognize a cardinal distinction. The Cartesian myth does indeed repair the defects of the Hobbist myth only by duplicating it. But even doctrinal homeopathy involves the recognition of disorders.

## *Paul Ziff (b. 1920)*

For a listing of Ziff's major works, see the fifth selection in this part.

The essay below appears in *Philosophical Turnings* (1966). In it, Ziff defends logical behaviorism (he refers to it as *philosophical behaviorism*) against two criticisms which he regards as superficial and ineffective. The first is that mental terms cannot have behavioral meanings because if they did we would find out whether or not they were true of a person by finding out whether or not the person was behaving in the appropriate way. But when we are the persons involved this doesn't work. We can find out how we are behaving, but we can't and don't find out about our own mental states at all. We have some very different relation to our own mental states, so behavior and mental states cannot be logically equivalent. The second criticism is this. If behavior and mental states were equivalent, others could (at least in principle) always know of our mental states because they could (at least in principle) always find out about our behavior. Since others cannot (even in principle) always know of our mental states, those states cannot be logically equivalent to behavior.

# About Behaviorism

## *Paul Ziff*

"One behaviorist meeting another on the street said 'You feel fine! How do I feel?'." This bad joke embodies two bad arguments against behaviorism. I want to explain why they are bad arguments.

1. I say "I am angry." My statement is true if and only if a certain organism is behaving in certain ways. If I say "George is angry," my statement is true if and only if a certain organism, viz. George, is behaving in certain ways. The only way I can tell whether or not George is angry is by observing George's behavior, verbal or otherwise. (There is nothing else to tell.) But I do not find out whether or not I am angry by observing my own behavior because I do not find out whether or not I am angry. (That I sometimes suddenly realize that I am or that I have become angry is essentially irrelevant here.) To talk of my finding out whether or not I am angry is generally odd: it would not be odd only in peculiar cases.

2. The first bad argument is not particularly interesting. It is this: if my being angry were a matter of my behaving in certain ways then I should be able to find out whether or not I am angry for I can find out whether or not I am behaving in certain ways. Since it is generally odd to speak of my finding out whether or not I am angry, my being angry cannot be a matter of my behaving in certain ways. (Thus: "How do I feel?")

The mistake here is in the assumption that I can find out whether or not I am behaving in the relevant ways. A behaviorist maintains that to be angry is to behave in certain ways. I shall accordingly speak of "anger behavior" and of "anger behaving."

It is generally odd to speak of my finding out whether or not I am angry: it is neither more nor less odd to speak of my finding out whether or not I am anger behaving.

3. It is not always odd to speak of my finding out whether or not I am behaving in a certain

This essay first appeared in *Analysis*. Edited by Bernard Mayo. Vol. XVII, No. 1, Oct. 1956, (New York: Barnes & Noble, copyright 1967). Reprinted by permission of Barnes & Noble Books.

way. Suppose I have my hands behind my back, my fingers intermeshed. I am asked to move the third finger of my left hand. I may not know whether or not I am in fact moving that finger. I may have to look in a mirror to find out. So it is not in every case odd to speak of my finding out whether or not I am behaving in a certain way. It does not follow that it is not sometimes odd.

I am at this moment talking, hence behaving in a certain way. It would be odd to speak of my finding out whether or not I am talking at this moment. No doubt one can think up cases in which it would not be odd to speak of my finding out whether or not I am talking. That is irrelevant. I am not talking about those cases: I am talking about this case, here and now, and here and now I cannot doubt that I am talking. (More can be said about this point, but I shall not try to say it here.)

It would generally be odd to speak of my finding out whether or not I am anger behaving, e.g. gnashing my teeth.

4. The second bad argument is more serious. It is this: if my being angry were a matter of my behaving in certain ways then you should be able to find out whether or not I am angry for you can find out whether or not I am behaving in certain ways. But sometimes you cannot find out whether or not I am angry. Since you can, in principle at least, always find out whether or not I am behaving in certain ways, my being angry cannot be a matter of my behaving in certain ways. (Thus: "You feel fine!")

The mistake here is in the assumption that there is a difference between your finding out whether or not I am anger behaving and your finding out whether or not I am angry. There is no difference.

5. You cannot in fact always find out whether or not I am angry. I may be artful at concealing my anger and I may refuse to tell you. Neither can you in fact always find out whether or not I am behaving in certain ways. You cannot in fact find out whether or not I am flexing my abdominal muscles. I will not tell you and no one else can.

So what you can or cannot in fact find out is beside the point. What is not beside the point?

6. "You can in principle if not in fact always find out whether or not I am behaving in certain ways. But you cannot even in principle always find out whether or not I am angry." This contention will not bear scrutiny.

(I will not cavil over the locution "you can in principle find out." I consider it an instrument of obfuscation. Even so, I shall let it pass: I believe I can more or less grasp what is intended.)

You can in principle always find out whether or not I am angry because I can tell you. Hence you need attend only to my verbal behavior. (I assume that it would generally be odd to speak of my being mistaken about whether or not I am angry.) To suppose that you cannot in principle find out whether or not I am angry would be to suppose that I cannot in principle tell you whether or not I am angry. I find such a supposition unintelligible.

7. The preceding contention can be reformulated as follows: "You can in principle if not in fact always find out whether or not I am behaving in certain ways. In some cases at least, being angry does not involve verbal behavior. Let us restrict our attention to such cases. Then apart from my subsequent verbal behavior, you cannot even in principle always find out whether or not I am angry."

As I said before, I more or less grasp what is intended by the location, "you can in principle find out": I would not pretend I have a firm grasp. (One cannot have a firm grip on a jellyfish.) In so far as I can grasp what is intended, I am inclined to agree that apart from my subsequent verbal behavior you cannot even in principle always find out whether or not I am angry. But I deny that apart from my subsequent verbal behavior you can in principle always find out whether or not I am anger behaving.

8. Let us suppose that in a certain case my anger behavior consists, amongst other things, in my gnashing my teeth. If we are to suppose that apart from my subsequent verbal behavior you can in principle always find out whether or not I am anger behaving then we must suppose that apart from my subsequent verbal behavior you can in principle always find out whether or not I am gnashing my teeth.

There is a difference between my gnashing

my teeth and the gnashing of my teeth. It is conceivable that by supplying the appropriate stimuli directly to the appropriate muscles one could effect the gnashing of my teeth. In the kind of case I envisage, I could not truly say "I was gnashing my teeth" though I could truly say "My teeth were gnashing" and perhaps add "It felt queer."

I would not deny that apart from my subsequent verbal behavior you can in principle always find out whether or not my teeth are gnashing. But I deny that apart from my subsequent verbal behavior you can in principle always find out whether or not I am gnashing my teeth.

9. Can a behaviorist make a distinction between my gnashing my teeth and the gnashing of my teeth? I see no reason why not.

It is true that my teeth are gnashing if and only if it is true that certain teeth and jaws are moving in certain ways. But it is true that I am gnashing my teeth if and only if it is true that a certain organism is behaving in certain ways. If a certain organism is behaving in certain ways then it may be the case that certain teeth and jaws are moving in certain ways. But the converse need not hold: it does not follow that if certain teeth and jaws are moving in certain ways then a certain organism is behaving in certain ways.

10. There is a difference between someone gnashing his teeth and the gnashing of someone's teeth. But the difference is not a difference in behavior: only the former is an instance of behavior; the latter may be a component of behavior.

If George is gnashing his teeth then George's teeth are gnashing. But whether or not a case in which his teeth are gnashing can rightly be characterized as a case in which he is gnashing his teeth depends (not on whether or not the gnashing of his teeth is accompanied by "a movement of the soul" but simply) on contextual and relational matters.

11. I said that whether or not a case in which George's teeth are gnashing can rightly be characterized as a case in which George is gnashing his teeth depends on contextual and relational matters. I am not saying "Whether or not a case in which my teeth are gnashing can rightly be characterized by me as a case in which I am gnashing my teeth depends on contextual and relational matters": that would be odd. It would indicate that I could in general answer the following generally odd question: "Given that your teeth are gnashing, what entitles you to say not merely that your teeth are gnashing but that you are gnashing your teeth, that you are doing it?" (I believe that Wittgenstein once said, "The first mistake is to ask the question": the second is to answer it.)

What is in question here is what entitles you to say that I am gnashing my teeth and not merely that my teeth are gnashing. The question whether I am gnashing my teeth or whether my teeth are merely gnashing is a question for you, not for me. It would generally be odd for me to ask "Am I gnashing my teeth or are they merely gnashing?"

12. Whether or not a case in which my teeth are gnashing can rightly be characterized by you as a case in which I am gnashing my teeth depends on contextual and relational matters.

The teeth of a corpse may be gnashing but the corpse cannot (without oddity) be said to be gnashing its teeth. So I must be alive, I must behave in characteristic ways. What more is required? Primarily this: my subsequent behavior, both verbal and otherwise, must be consonant with the claim that I was in fact gnashing my teeth. This is not to say that if I assert "I was not gnashing my teeth," then I was not gnashing my teeth: I may be lying, or forgetful, or confused, etc. But my subsequent behavior, both verbal and otherwise, is clearly relevant.

Therefore I deny that apart from my subsequent verbal behavior you can in principle always find out whether or not I am gnashing my teeth. And in consequence I deny that there is a difference between finding out whether or not I am behaving in certain ways and finding out whether or not I am angry.

Philosophical behaviorism is not a metaphysical theory: it is the denial of a metaphysical theory. Consequently, it asserts nothing.

# *Functionalism*

Functionalism is the theory that defines mental states and processes by their causal (functional) roles. It differs from behaviorism, which also gives a causal or functional account of the mental, in two important respects. First it does not attempt to eliminate inner and typically unobservable entities from scientific explanations of human behavior. The functionalist is not bothered by the fact that functionally defined mental states may reside inside of a person's head or even "inside" an immaterial mind. Second, functionalism does not define mental states and processes solely in terms of their causal connections to environmental stimuli and behavioral responses. Part of the essential functional role of a mental state or process will be its causal relations to other mental states and processes. The functionalist can recognize the fact that mental states give rise to and are produced by other mental states, that their causal connections are not limited to environmental causes and behavioral effects.

Functionalism arose as a result of developments in psychology and the other sciences of cognition, and philosophical reflection on those developments. The important and central insight of functionalism is that theories of the mental, of intelligent behavior and its causes, belong naturally at a much higher level of abstraction than had previously been recognized. Even if all of reality is material, physical science is not pitched at the appropriate level to reveal the regularities of intelligent behavior. And once we see why this is so we will understand that adding immaterial stuff to the material stuff doesn't change the level or help provide the appropriate explanatory resources. Roughly speaking, intelligent behavior and its causal regularities can best be captured at the level of abstract meaning or representation, not at the level of material or immaterial stuff and its causal action or interaction. Intelligent behavior responds causally not to the physical nature of the environment but to its interpreted meaning or represented significance. If we think we are in the presence of something dangerous or terrifying, we will react accordingly, even if there is nothing physically present in the environment that constitutes a serious physical threat to us. And the reactions caused by such an experience—for example, turning and running, jumping into an automobile and driving off under full power, or speeding up the rate at which we are pedalling a bicycle—are equivalent not because they involve the same physical motions, but because they are all intended by the person involved as an escape from danger. The point is that psychological generalizations seem to belong naturally at this level of meaning and representation—reality as represented in our perceptions and beliefs, and behavior as purposive action, directed toward intended future goals.

So the guiding idea behind functionalism is that there are different levels of description for behavior. And the appropriate level of description for intelligent behavior is the level of meanings and intentions at which the subject of behavior is affected by representations of her real environment and the resulting behavior is a function of her beliefs and intentions. Whether the underlying stuff of which the subject is composed is material, immaterial, or whatever simply doesn't matter because that level of description will not reveal the causal connections in which the subject is involved *as an intelligently behaving* subject. This means that theories of mentality or cognition will not be theories about the stuff of which the subject is composed. And this is what makes functionalist explanations of the mental neutral with respect to most metaphysical solutions to the mind-body problem. Functionalism is perfectly compatible with the metaphysics of dualism, reductive materialism, and double aspect theories. It is incompatible only with eliminative materialism and behaviorism which deny the existence and/or the explanatory value of the functionally defined states and processes.

Although functionalist explanations of the mental are not explicitly concerned with the stuff of which intelligent entities are composed, there are some requirements about what must occur at the lower levels of description in order for the functionalist theory to provide a real explanation. In particular, the lower levels of description must be free of meanings, intentions and the like, that is, must be free of the states and processes to be explained. The reason for this is as follows. Functional or causal definition of mental processes permits "explanation" of a sort that sheds no light whatsoever on the process to be explained. Suppose we want to know how Smith understands some fact. We can explain Smith's understanding functionally in terms of a little mental "understander" in Smith which does the understanding for him. But this just moves the problem inside; it doesn't make it any less problematic. We now need to know how the mental "understander" in Smith understands, and producing further "understanders" won't help at all. We want to know what the mechanism is whose operation could produce, and hence causally explain, understanding. Trying to explain understanding in terms of more understanding simply begs the question. So the restriction that must be put on the functional explanation is that it be mechanistic and that the mechanism not contain the same mystery it is invoked to dispel. The way that functionalists have honored this requirement is by use of the computer model.

Digital computers perform mechanical operations upon symbolic codes that can be described in terms of at least two different levels. At the level of meaning or representation we can describe the computer's operation in terms of what its symbols mean or represent, that is, in terms of what they symbolize. But at another level of description we can describe the operation of the computer as purely formal manipulations of the symbols themselves which have nothing to do with what or whether they symbolize. (See the discussion of artificial intelligence at the end of the general introduction to this part.) If we restrict explanations of mental processes to operations on symbolic representations that could be duplicated by a digital computer (in practice, by a particular subset of universal computing machines called **Turing machines**), we guarantee the existence of mechanisms that can account for the processes to be explained without simply begging the question.

The use of the computer model leaves psychological explanation at the appropriate level. The symbols to be mechanically manipulated and the machine that does the manipulation can be made of any stuff with the appropriate causal powers. The evidence seems strongly to favor the human brain as the machine and electrochemical patterns as the physical instantiation of the symbol system in the case of human mentality, but there is nothing in the functionalist theory that requires this. What is required is that the representational content of mental states be realized in something, that mechanical (computational) operations on those realizations be capable of explaining what goes on at the level of intelligent behavior, and that the something in which the states and processes are realized have the appropriate causal powers to make the mechanical operations possible. For further discussion of the computer model of mentality and its appropriateness, see the artificial intelligence section in this part.

## *Jerry A. Fodor (b. 1935)*

Jerry A. Fodor is one of the leading philosophical proponents of the approach to human mentality implicit in contemporary cognitive science. He has made important contributions in philosophy of language, philosophy of mind, and philosophy of science. His major works include *Psychological Explanation* (1968), *The Language of Thought* (1975), *Representations* (1980), and *The Modularity of Mind* (1983).

In the selection below Fodor argues that functionalism is the appropriate theory for understanding mental concepts. Functionalism understands mental states and processes in terms of their causal or functional roles, but without the methodological constraints imposed by behaviorism. Fodor believes that the functionalist approach, implicit in cognitive science and artificial intelligence research, preserves the positive features of previous unsuccessful solutions to the mind-body problem without the serious drawbacks. Functionalism does have difficulties of its own, however, which are discussed at the end of the essay.

# The Mind-Body Problem

## *Jerry A. Fodor*

Modern philosophy of science has been devoted largely to the formal and systematic description of the successful practices of working scientists. The philosopher does not try to dictate how scientific inquiry and argument ought to be conducted. Instead he tries to enumerate the principles and practices that have contributed to good science. The philosopher has devoted the most attention to analyzing the methodological peculiarities of the physical sciences. The analysis has helped to clarify the nature of confirmation, the logical structure of scientific theories, the formal properties of statements that express laws and the question of whether theoretical entities actually exist.

It is only rather recently that philosophers have become seriously interested in the methodological tenets of psychology. Psychological explanations of behavior refer liberally to the mind and to states, operations and processes of the mind. The philosophical difficulty comes in stating in unambiguous language what such references imply.

Traditional philosophies of mind can be divided into two broad categories: dualist theories and materialist theories. In the dualist approach the mind is a nonphysical substance. In materialist theories the mental is not distinct from the physical; indeed, all mental states, properties, processes and operations are in principle identical with physical states, properties, processes and operations. Some materialists, known as behaviorists, maintain that all talk of mental causes can be eliminated from the language of psychology in favor of talk of environmental stimuli and behavioral responses. Other materialists, the identity theorists, contend that there are mental causes and that they are identical with neurophysiological events in the brain.

In the past 15 years a philosophy of mind called functionalism that is neither dualist nor materialist has emerged from philosophical reflection on developments in artificial intelligence, computational theory, linguistics, cybernetics and psychology. All these fields, which are collectively known as the cognitive sciences, have in common a certain level of abstraction and a concern with systems that process information. Functionalism, which seeks to provide a philosophical account of this level of abstraction, recognizes the possibility that systems as diverse as human beings, calculating machines and disembodied spirits could all have mental states. In the functionalist view the psychology of a system depends not on the stuff it is made of (living cells, metal or spiritual energy) but on how the stuff is put together. Functionalism is a difficult concept, and one way of coming to grips with it is to review the deficiencies of the dualist and materialist philosophies of mind it aims to displace.

The chief drawback of dualism is its failure to account adequately for mental causation. If the mind is nonphysical, it has no position in physical space. How, then, can a mental cause give rise to a behavioral effect that has a position in space? To put it another way, how can the nonphysical give rise to the physical without violating the laws of the conservation of mass, of energy and of momentum?

The dualist might respond that the problem of how an immaterial substance can cause physical events is not much obscurer than the problem of how one physical event can cause another. Yet there is an important difference: there are many clear cases of physical causation but not one clear case of nonphysical causation. Physical interaction is something philosophers, like all other people, have to live with. Nonphysical interaction, however, may be no more than an artifact of the immaterialist construal of the mental. Most philosophers now agree that no argument has successfully demonstrated why mind-body causation should not be regarded as a species of physical causation.

Dualism is also incompatible with the practices of working psychologists. The psychologist frequently applies the experimental methods of the physical sciences to the study of the mind. If mental processes were different in kind from physical processes, there would be no reason to expect these methods to work in the realm of the mental. In order to justify their experimental methods many psychologists urgently sought an alternative to dualism.

In the 1920's John B. Watson of Johns Hopkins University made the radical suggestion that behavior does not have mental causes. He regarded the behavior of an organism as its observable responses to stimuli, which he took to be the causes of its behavior. Over the next 30 years psychologists such as B. F. Skinner of Harvard University developed Watson's ideas into an elaborate world view in which the role of psychology was to catalogue the laws that determine causal relations between stimuli and responses. In this "radical behaviorist" view the problem of explaining the nature of the mind-body interaction vanishes; there is no such interaction.

Radical behaviorism has always worn an air of paradox. For better or worse, the idea of mental causation is deeply ingrained in our everyday language and in our ways of understanding our fellow men and ourselves. For example, people commonly attribute behavior to beliefs, to knowledge and to expectations. Brown puts gas in his tank because he believes the car will not run without it. Jones writes not "acheive" but "achieve" because he knows the rule about putting *i* before e. Even when a behavioral response is closely tied to an environmental stimulus, mental processes often intervene. Smith carries an umbrella because the sky is cloudy, but the weather is only part of the story. There are apparently also mental links in the causal chain: observation and expectation. The clouds affect Smith's behavior only because he observes them and because they induce in him an expectation of rain.

The radical behaviorist is unmoved by appeals to such cases. He is prepared to dismiss references to mental causes, however plausible they may seem, as the residue of outworn creeds. The radical behaviorist predicts that as psychologists come to understand more about the relations between stimuli and responses they will find it increasingly possible to explain behavior without postulating mental causes.

The strongest argument against behaviorism is that psychology has not turned out this way; the opposite has happened. As psychology has matured, the framework of mental states and processes that is apparently needed to account for experimental observations has grown all the more elaborate. Particularly in the case of human behavior psychological theories satisfying the methodological tenets of radical behaviorism have proved largely sterile, as would be expected if the postulated mental processes are real and causally effective.

Nevertheless, many philosophers were initially drawn to radical behaviorism because, paradoxes and all, it seemed better than dualism. Since a psychology committed to immaterial substances was unacceptable, philosophers turned to radical behaviorism because it seemed to be the only alternative materialist philosophy of mind. The choice, as they saw it, was between radical behaviorism and ghosts.

By the early 1960's philosophers began to

have doubts that dualism and radical behaviorism exhausted the possible approaches to the philosophy of mind. Since the two theories seemed unattractive, the right strategy might be to develop a materialist philosophy of mind that nonetheless allowed for mental causes. Two such philosophies emerged, one called logical behaviorism and the other called the central-state identity theory.

Logical behaviorism is a semantic theory about what mental terms mean. The basic idea is that attributing a mental state (say thirst) to an organism is the same as saying that the organism is disposed to behave in a particular way (for example to drink if there is water available). On this view every mental ascription is equivalent in meaning to an if-then statement (called a behavioral hypothetical) that expresses a behavioral disposition. For example, "Smith is thirsty" might be taken to be equivalent to the dispositional statement "If there were water available, then Smith would drink some." By definition a behavioral hypothetical includes no mental terms. The if-clause of the hypothetical speaks only of stimuli and the then-clause speaks only of behavioral responses. Since stimuli and responses are physical events, logical behaviorism is a species of materialism.

The strength of logical behaviorism is that by translating mental language into the language of stimuli and responses it provides an interpretation of psychological explanations in which behavioral effects are attributed to mental causes. Mental causation is simply the manifestation of a behavioral disposition. More precisely, mental causation is what happens when an organism has a behavioral disposition and the if-clause of the behavioral hypothetical expressing the disposition happens to be true. For example, the causal statement "Smith drank some water because he was thirsty" might be taken to mean "If there were water available, then Smith would drink some, and there was water available."

I have somewhat oversimplified logical behaviorism by assuming that each mental ascription can be translated by a unique behavioral hypothetical. Actually the logical behaviorist often maintains that it takes an open-ended set (perhaps an infinite set) of behavioral hypotheticals to spell out the behavioral disposition expressed by a mental term. The mental ascription "Smith is thirsty" might also be satisfied by the hypothetical "If there were orange juice available, then Smith would drink some" and by a host of other hypotheticals. In any event the logical behaviorist does not usually maintain he can actually enumerate all the hypotheticals that correspond to a behavioral disposition expressing a given mental term. He only insists that in principle the meaning of any mental term can be conveyed by behavioral hypotheticals.

The way the logical behaviorist has interpreted a mental term such as thirsty is modeled after the way many philosophers have interpreted a physical disposition such as fragility. The physical disposition "The glass is fragile" is often taken to mean something like "If the glass were struck, then it would break." By the same token the logical behaviorist's analysis of mental causation is similar to the received analysis of one kind of physical causation. The causal statement "The glass broke because it was fragile" is taken to mean something like "If the glass were struck, then it would break, and the glass was struck."

By equating mental terms with behavioral dispositions the logical behaviorist has put mental terms on a par with the nonbehavioral dispositions of the physical sciences. That is a promising move, because the analysis of nonbehavioral dispositions is on relatively solid philosophical ground. An explanation attributing the breaking of a glass to its fragility is surely something even the staunchest materialist can accept. By arguing that mental terms are synonymous with dispositional terms, the logical behaviorist has provided something the radical behaviorist could not: a materialist account of mental causation.

Nevertheless, the analogy between mental causation as construed by the logical behaviorist and physical causation goes only so far. The logical behaviorist treats the manifestation of a disposition as the sole form of mental causation, whereas the physical sciences recognize additional kinds of causation. There is the kind of causation where one physical event causes another, as when the breaking of a glass is attributed to its having been struck. In fact, explanations that involve event-event causation are presumably more basic than dispositional explanations, because the manifestation of a disposition (the breaking of a fragile glass) always involves event-event causation and not vice versa. In the realm of the mental many examples of event-event causation involve one mental state's causing another, and for this kind of causation logical behaviorism provides no analysis. As a result the logical behaviorist is committed to the tacit and implausible assumption that psychology requires a less robust notion of causation than the physical sciences require.

Event-event causation actually seems to be quite common in the realm of the mental. Mental causes typically give rise to behavioral effects by virtue of their interaction with other mental causes. For example, having a headache causes a disposition to take aspirin only if one also has the desire to get rid of the headache, the belief that aspirin exists, the belief that taking aspirin reduces headaches and so on. Since mental states interact in generating behavior, it will be necessary to find a construal of psychological explanations that posits mental processes: causal sequences of mental events. It is this construal that logical behaviorism fails to provide.

Such considerations bring out a fundamental way in which logical behaviorism is quite similar to radical behaviorism. It is true that the logical behaviorist, unlike the radical behaviorist, acknowledges the existence of mental states. Yet since the underlying tenet of logical behaviorism is that references to mental states can be translated out of psychological explanations by employing behavioral hypotheticals, all talk of mental states and processes is in a sense **heuristic.** The only facts to which the behaviorist is actually committed are facts about relations between stimuli and responses. In this respect logical behaviorism is just radical behaviorism in a **semantic** form. Although the former theory offers a construal of mental causation, the construal is Pickwickian. What does not really exist cannot cause anything, and the logical behaviorist, like the radical behaviorist, believes deep down that mental causes do not exist.

An alternative materialist theory of the mind to logical behaviorism is the central-state identity theory. According to this theory, mental events, states and processes are identical with neurophysiological events in the brain, and the property of being in a certain mental state (such as having a headache or believing it will rain) is identical with the property of being in a certain neurophysiological state. On this basis it is easy to make sense of the idea that a behavioral effect might sometimes have a chain of mental causes; that will be the case whenever a behavioral effect is **contingent** on the appropriate sequence of neurophysiological events.

The central-state identity theory acknowledges that it is possible for mental causes to interact causally without ever giving rise to any behavioral effect, as when a person thinks for a while about what he ought to do and then decides to do nothing. If mental processes are neurophysiological, they must have the causal properties of neurophysiological processes. Since neurophysiological processes are presumably physical processes, the central-state identity theory ensures that the concept of mental causation is as rich as the concept of physical causation.

The central-state identity theory provides a satisfactory account of what the mental terms in psychological explanations refer to, and so it is favored by psychologists who are dissatisfied with behaviorism. The behaviorist maintains that mental terms refer to nothing or that they refer to the parameters of stimulus-response relations. Either way the existence of mental entities is only illusory. The identity theorist, on the other hand, argues that mental terms refer to neurophysiological states. Thus he can take seriously the project of explaining behavior by appealing to its mental causes.

The chief advantage of the identity theory is that it takes the explanatory constructs of psychology at face value, which is surely something a philosophy of mind ought to do if it can. The identity theory shows how the mentalistic explanations of psychology could be not mere heuristics but literal accounts of the causal history of behavior. Moreover, since the identity theory is not a semantic thesis, it is immune to many arguments that cast in doubt logical behaviorism. A drawback of logical behaviorism is that the observation "John has a headache" does not seem to mean the same thing as a statement of the form "John is disposed to behave in such and such a way." The identity theorist, however, can live with the fact that "John has a headache" and "John is in such and such a brain state" are not synonymous. The assertion of the identity theorist is not that these sentences mean the same thing but only that they are rendered true (or false) by the same neurophysiological phenomena.

The identity theory can be held either as a doctrine about mental particulars (John's current pain or Bill's fear of animals) or as a doctrine about mental universals, or properties (having a pain or being afraid of animals). The two doctrines, called respectively token **physicalism** and type physicalism, differ in strength and plausibility. **Token** physicalism maintains only that all the mental particulars that happen to exist are neurophysiological, whereas type physicalism makes the more sweeping assertion that all the mental particulars there could possibly be are neurophysiological. Token physicalism does not rule out the logical possibility of machines and disembodied spirits having mental properties. Type physicalism dismisses this possibility because neither machines nor disembodied spirits have neurons.

**Type** physicalism is not a plausible doctrine about mental properties even if token physicalism is right about mental particulars. The problem with type physicalism is that the psychological constitution of a system seems to depend not on its hardware, or physical composition, but on its software, or program. Why should the philosopher dismiss the possibility that silicon-based Martians have pains, assuming that the silicon is properly organized? And why should the philosopher rule out the possibility of machines having beliefs, assuming that the machines are correctly programmed? If it is logically possible that Martians and machines could have mental properties, then mental properties and neurophysiological processes cannot be identical, however much they may prove to be coextensive.

What it all comes down to is that there seems to be a level of abstraction at which the generalizations of psychology are most naturally pitched. This level of abstraction cuts across differences in the physical composition of the systems to which psychological generalizations apply. In the cognitive sciences, at least, the natural domain for psychological theorizing seems to be all systems that process information. The problem with type physicalism is that there are possible information-processing systems with the same psychological constitution as human beings but not the same physical organization. In principle all kinds of physically different things could have human software.

This situation calls for a relational account of mental properties that abstracts them from the physical structure of their bearers. In spite of the objections to logical behaviorism that I presented above, logical behaviorism was at least on the right track in offering a relational interpretation of mental properties: to have a headache is to be disposed to exhibit a certain pattern of relations between the stimuli one encounters and the responses one exhibits. If that is what having a headache is, however, there is no reason in principle why only heads that are physically similar to ours can ache. Indeed, according to logical behaviorism, it is a necessary truth that any system that has our stimulus-response contingencies also has our headaches.

All of this emerged 10 or 15 years ago as a nasty dilemma for the materialist program in the philosophy of mind. On the one hand the identity theorist (and not the logical behaviorist) had got right the causal character of the interactions of mind and body. On the other the logical behaviorist (and not the identity theorist) had got right the relational character of mental properties. Functionalism has apparently been able to resolve the dilemma. By stressing the distinction computer science draws between hardware and software the functionalist can make sense of both the causal and the relational character of the mental.

The intuition underlying functionalism is that what determines the psychological type to which a mental particular belongs is the causal role of the particular in the mental life of the organism. Functional individuation is differentiation with respect to causal role. A headache, for example, is identified with the type of mental state that among other things causes a disposition for taking aspirin in people who believe aspirin relieves a headache, causes a desire to rid oneself of the pain one is feeling, often causes someone who speaks English to say such things as "I have a headache" and is brought on by overwork, eyestrain and tension. This list is presumably not complete. More will be known about the nature of a headache as psychological and physiological research discovers more about its causal role.

Functionalism construes the concept of causal role in such a way that a mental state can be defined by its causal relations to other mental states. In this respect functionalism is completely different from logical behaviorism. Another major difference is that functionalism is not a reductionist thesis. It does not foresee, even in principle, the elimination of mentalistic concepts from the explanatory apparatus of psychological theories.

The difference between functionalism and logical behaviorism is brought out by the fact that functionalism is fully compatible with token physicalism. The functionalist would not be disturbed if brain events turn out to be the only things with the functional properties that define mental states. Indeed, most functionalists fully expect it will turn out that way.

Since functionalism recognizes that mental particulars may be physical, it is compatible with the idea that mental causation is a species of physical causation. In other words, functionalism tolerates the materialist solution to the mind-body problem provided by the central-state identity theory. It is possible for the functionalist to assert both that mental properties are typically defined in terms of their relations and that interactions of mind and body are typically causal in however robust a notion of causality is required by psychological explanations. The logical behaviorist can endorse only the first assertion and the type physicalist only the second. As a result functionalism seems to capture the best features of the materialist alternatives to dualism. It is no wonder that functionalism has become increasingly popular.

Machines provide good examples of two concepts that are central to functionalism: the concept that mental states are interdefined and the concept that they can be realized by many systems. . . . [We might imagine] a behavioristic Coke machine and a mentalistic one. Both machines dispense a Coke for 10 cents. [One of the machines accepts dimes only. The other machine accepts dimes and nickels in any order.] (The price has not been affected by inflation.) The states of the machines are defined by reference to their causal roles, but only the machine . . . [which takes only dimes] would satisfy the behaviorist. Its single state *(S0)* is completely specified in terms of stimuli and responses. *S0* is the state a machine is in if, and only if, given a dime as the input, it dispenses a Coke as the output.

The [mentalistic] machine . . . has interdefined states (*S1* and *S2*), which are characteristic of functionalism. *S1* is the state a machine is in if, and only if, (1) given a nickel, it dispenses nothing and proceeds to *S2*, and (2) given a dime, it dispenses a Coke and stays in *S1*. *S2* is the state a machine is in if, and only if, (1) given a nickel, it dispenses a Coke and proceeds to *S1*, and (2) given a dime, it dispenses a Coke and a nickel and proceeds to *S1*. What *S1* and *S2* jointly amount to is the machine's dispensing a Coke if it is given a dime, dispensing a Coke and a nickel if it is given a dime and a nickel and waiting to be given a second nickel if it has been given a first one.

Since *S1* and *S2* are each defined by hypothetical statements, they can be viewed as dispositions. Nevertheless, they are not behavioral dispositions because the consequences an input has for a machine in *S1* or *S2* are not specified solely in terms of the output of the machine. Rather, the consequences also involve the machine's internal states.

Nothing about the way I have described the behavioristic and mentalistic Coke machines puts constraints on what they could be made of. Any system whose states bore the proper relations to inputs, outputs and other states could be one of these machines. No doubt it is reasonable to expect such a system to be constructed out of such things as wheels, levers and diodes (token physicalism for Coke machines). Similarly, it is reasonable to expect that our minds may prove to be neurophysiological (token physicalism for human beings).

Nevertheless, the software description of a Coke machine does not logically require wheels, levers and diodes for its concrete realization. By the same token, the software description of the mind does not logically require neurons. As far as functionalism is concerned a Coke machine with states *S1* and *S2* could be made of ectoplasm, if there is such stuff and if its states have the right causal properties. Functionalism allows for the possibility of disembodied Coke machines in exactly the same way and to the same extent that it allows for the possibility of disembodied minds.

To say that *S1* and *S2* are interdefined and realizable by different kinds of hardware is not, of course, to say that a Coke machine has a mind. Although interdefinition and functional specification are typical features of mental states, they are clearly not sufficient for mentality. What more is required is a question to which I shall return below.

Some philosophers are suspicious of functionalism because it seems too easy. Since functionalism licenses the individuation of states by reference to their causal role, it appears to allow a trivial explanation of any observed event *E*; that is, it appears to postulate an *E*-causer. For example, what makes the valves in a machine open? Why, the operation of a valve opener. And what is a valve opener? Why, anything that has the functionally defined property of causing valves to open.

In psychology this kind of question-begging often takes the form of theories that in effect postulate **homunculi** with the selfsame intellectual capacities the theorist set out to explain. Such is the case when visual perception is explained by simply postulating psychological mechanisms that process visual information. The behaviorist has often charged the mentalist, sometimes justifiably, of mongering this kind of question-begging pseudo explanation. The charge will have to be met if functionally defined mental states are to have a serious role in psychological theories.

The burden of the accusation is not untruth but triviality. There can be no doubt that it is a valve opener that opens valves, and it is likely that visual perception is mediated by the processing of visual information. The charge is that such putative functional explanations are mere platitudes. The functionalist can meet this objection by allowing functionally defined theoretical constructs only where mechanisms exist that can carry out the function and only where he has some notion of what such mechanisms might be like. One way of imposing this requirement is to identify the mental processes that psychology postulates with the operations of the restricted class of possible computers called Turing machines.

A **Turing machine** can be informally characterized as a mechanism with a finite number of program states. The inputs and outputs of the machine are written on a tape that is divided into squares each of which includes a symbol from a finite alphabet. The machine scans the tape one square at a time. It can erase the symbol on a scanned square and print a new one in its place. The machine can execute only the elementary mechanical operations of scanning, erasing, printing, moving the tape and changing state.

The program states of the Turing machine are defined solely in terms of the input symbols on the tape, the output symbols on the tape, the elementary operations and the other states of the program. Each program state is therefore functionally defined by the part it plays in the overall operation of the machine. Since the functional role of a state depends on the relation of the state to other states as well as to inputs and outputs, the relational character of the mental is captured by the Turing-machine version of functionalism. Since the definition of a program state never refers to the physical structure of the system running the program, the Turing-machine version of functionalism also captures the idea that the character of a mental state is independent of its physical realization. A human being, a roomful of people, a computer and a disembodied spirit would all be a Turing machine if they operated according to a Turing-machine program.

The proposal is to restrict the functional definition of psychological states to those that can be expressed in terms of the program states of Turing machines. If this restriction can be enforced, it provides a guarantee that psychological theories will be compatible with the demands of mechanism. Since Turing machines are very simple devices, they are in principle quite easy to build. Consequently by formulating a psychological explanation as a Turing-machine program the psychologist ensures that the explanation is mechanistic, even though the hardware realizing the mechanism is left open.

There are many kinds of computational mechanisms other than Turing machines, and so the formulation of a functionalist psychological theory in Turing-machine notation provides only a sufficient condition for the theory's being mechanically realizable. What makes the condition interesting, however, is that the simple Turing machine can perform many complex tasks. Although the elementary operations of the Turing machine are restricted, iterations of the operations enable the machine to carry out any well-defined computation on discrete symbols.

An important tendency in the cognitive sciences is to treat the mind chiefly as a device that manipulates symbols. If a mental process can be functionally defined as an operation on symbols, there is a Turing machine capable of carrying out the computation and a variety of mechanisms for realizing the Turing machine. Where the manipulation of symbols is important the Turing machine provides a connection between functional explanation and mechanistic explanation.

The reduction of a psychological theory to a program for a Turing machine is a way of exorcising the homunculi. The reduction ensures that no operations have been postulated except those that could be performed by a familiar mechanism. Of course, the working psychologist usually cannot specify the reduction for each functionally individuated process in every theory he is prepared to take seriously. In practice the argument usually goes in the opposite direction; if the postulation of a mental operation is essential to some cherished psychological explanation, the theorist tends to assume that there must be a program for a Turing machine that will carry out that operation.

The "black boxes" that are common in flow charts drawn by psychologists often serve to indicate postulated mental processes for which Turing reductions are wanting. Even so, the possibility in principle of such reductions serves as a methodological constraint on psychological theorizing by determining what functional definitions are to be allowed and what it would be like to know that everything has been explained that could possibly need explanation.

Such is the origin, the provenance and the promise of contemporary functionalism. How much has it actually paid off? This question is not easy to answer because much of what is now happening in the philosophy of mind and the cognitive sciences is directed at exploring the scope and limits of the functionalist explanations of behavior. I shall, however, give a brief overview.

An obvious objection to functionalism as a theory of the mind is that the functionalist definition is not limited to mental states and processes. Catalysts, Coke machines, valve openers, pencil sharpeners, mousetraps and ministers of finance are all in one way or another concepts that are functionally defined, but none is a mental concept such as pain, belief and desire. What, then characterizes the mental? And can it be captured in a functionalist framework?

The traditional view in the philosophy of

mind has it that mental states are distinguished by their having what are called either qualitative content or intentional content. I shall discuss qualitative content first.

It is not easy to say what qualitative content is; indeed, according to some theories, it is not even possible to say what it is because it can be known not by description but only by direct experience. I shall nonetheless attempt to describe it. Try to imagine looking at a blank wall through a red filter. Now change the filter to a green one and leave everything else exactly the way it was. Something about the character of your experience changes when the filter does, and it is this kind of thing that philosophers call qualitative content. I am not entirely comfortable about introducing qualitative content in this way, but it is a subject with which many philosophers are not comfortable.

The reason qualitative content is a problem for functionalism is straightforward. Functionalism is committed to defining mental states in terms of their causes and effects. It seems, however, as if two mental states could have all the same causal relations and yet could differ in their qualitative content. Let me illustrate this with the classic puzzle of the inverted spectrum.

It seems possible to imagine two observers who are alike in all relevant psychological respects except that experiences having the qualitative content of red for one observer would have the qualitative content of green for the other. Nothing about their behavior need reveal the difference because both of them see ripe tomatoes and flaming sunsets as being similar in color and both of them call that color "red." Moreover, the causal connection between their (qualitatively distinct) experiences and their other mental states could also be identical. Perhaps they both think of Little Red Riding Hood when they see ripe tomatoes, feel depressed when they see the color green and so on. It seems as if anything that could be packed into the notion of the causal role of their experiences could be shared by them, and yet the qualitative content of the experiences could be as different as you like. If this is possible, then the functionalist account does not work for mental states that have qualitative content. If one person is having a green experience while another person is having a red one, then surely they must be in different mental states.

The example of the inverted spectrum is more than a verbal puzzle. Having qualitative content is supposed to be a chief factor in what makes a mental state conscious. Many psychologists who are inclined to accept the functionalist framework are nonetheless worried about the failure of functionalism to reveal much about the nature of consciousness. Functionalists have made a few ingenious attempts to talk themselves and their colleagues out of this worry, but they have not, in my view, done so with much success. (For example, perhaps one is wrong in thinking one can imagine what an inverted spectrum would be like.) As matters stand, the problem of qualitative content poses a serious threat to the assertion that functionalism can provide a general theory of the mental.

Functionalism has fared much better with the intentional content of mental states. Indeed, it is here that the major achievements of recent cognitive science are found. To say that a mental state has intentional content is to say that it has certain semantic properties. For example, for Enrico to believe Galileo was Italian apparently involves a three-way relation between Enrico, a belief and a proposition that is the content of the belief (namely the proposition that Galileo was Italian). In particular it is an essential property of Enrico's belief that it is about Galileo (and not about, say, Newton) and that it is true if, and only if, Galileo was indeed Italian. Philosophers are divided on how these considerations fit together, but it is widely agreed that beliefs involve semantic properties such as expressing a proposition, being true or false and being about one thing rather than another.

It is important to understand the semantic properties of beliefs because theories in the cognitive sciences are largely about the beliefs organisms have. Theories of learning and perception, for example, are chiefly accounts of how the host of beliefs an organism has are determined by the character of its experiences and its genetic endowment. The functionalist account of mental states does not by itself provide the required insights. Mousetraps are functionally defined, yet mousetraps do not express propositions and they are not true or false.

There is at least one kind of thing other than a mental state that has intentional content: a symbol. Like thoughts, symbols seem to be about things. If someone says "Galileo was Italian," his utterance, like Enrico's belief, expresses a proposition about Galileo that is true or false depending on Galileo's homeland. This parallel between the symbolic and the mental underlies the traditional quest for a unified treatment of language and mind. Cognitive science is now trying to provide such a treatment.

The basic concept is simple but striking. Assume that there are such things as mental symbols (mental representations) and that mental symbols have semantic properties. On this view having a belief involves being related to a mental symbol, and the belief inherits its semantic properties from the mental symbol that figures in the relation. Mental processes (thinking, perceiving, learning and so on) involve causal interactions among relational states such as having a belief. The semantic properties of the words and sentences we utter are in turn inherited from the semantic properties of the mental states that language expresses.

Associating the semantic properties of mental states with those of mental symbols is fully compatible with the computer metaphor, because it is natural to think of the computer as a mechanism that manipulates symbols. A computation is a causal chain of computer states and the links in the chain are operations on semantically interpreted formulas in a machine code. To think of a system (such as the nervous system) as a computer is to raise questions about the nature of the code in which it computes and the semantic properties of the symbols in the code. In fact, the analogy between minds and computers actually implies the postulation of mental symbols. There is no computation without representation.

The representational account of the mind, however, predates considerably the invention of the computing machine. It is a throwback to classical epistemology, which is a tradition that includes philosophers as diverse as John Locke, David Hume, George Berkeley, René Descartes, Immanuel Kant, John Stuart Mill and William James.

Hume, for one, developed a representational theory of the mind that included five points. First, there exist "Ideas," which are a species of mental symbol. Second, having a belief involves entertaining an Idea. Third, mental processes are causal associations of Ideas. Fourth, Ideas are like pictures. And fifth, Ideas have their semantic properties by virtue of what they resemble: the Idea of John is about John because it looks like him.

Contemporary cognitive psychologists do not accept the details of Hume's theory, although they endorse much of its spirit. Theories of computation provide a far richer account of mental processes than the mere association of Ideas. And only a few psychologists still think that imagery is the chief vehicle of mental representation. Nevertheless, the most significant break with Hume's theory lies in the abandoning of resemblance as an explanation of the semantic properties of mental representations.

Many philosophers, starting with Berkeley, have argued that there is something seriously wrong with the suggestion that the semantic relation between a thought and what the thought is about could be one of resemblance. Consider the thought that John is tall. Clearly the thought is true only of the state of affairs consisting of John's being tall. A theory of the semantic properties of a thought should therefore explain how this particular thought is related to this particular state of affairs. According to the resemblance theory, entertaining the thought involves having a mental image that shows John to be tall. To put it another way, the relation between the thought that John is tall and his being tall is like the relation between a tall man and his portrait.

The difficulty with the resemblance theory is that any portrait showing John to be tall must also show him to be many other things: clothed or naked, lying, standing or sitting, having a head or not having one, and so on. A portrait of a tall man who is sitting down resembles a man's being seated as much as it resembles a man's being tall. On the resemblance theory it is not clear what distinguishes thoughts about John's height from thoughts about his posture.

The resemblance theory turns out to encounter paradoxes at every turn. The possibility of construing beliefs as involving relations to semantically interpreted mental representations clearly depends on having an acceptable account of where the semantic properties of the mental representations come from. If resemblance will not provide this account, what will?

The current idea is that the semantic properties of a mental representation are determined by aspects of its functional role. In other words, a sufficient condition for having semantic properties can be specified in causal terms. This is the connection between functionalism and the representational theory of the mind. Modern cognitive psychology rests largely on the hope that these two doctrines can be made to support each other.

No philosopher is now prepared to say exactly how the functional role of a mental representation determines its semantic properties. Nevertheless, the functionalist recognizes three types of causal relation among psychological states involving mental representations, and they might serve to fix the semantic properties of mental representations. The three types are causal relations among mental states and stimuli, mental states and responses and some mental states and other ones.

Consider the belief that John is tall. Presumably the following facts, which correspond respectively to the three types of causal relation, are relevant to determining the semantic properties of the mental representation involved in the belief. First, the belief is a normal effect of certain stimulations, such as seeing John in circumstances that reveal his height. Second, the belief is the normal cause of certain behavioral effects, such as uttering "John is tall." Third, the belief is a normal cause of certain other beliefs and a normal effect of certain other beliefs. For example, anyone who believes John is tall is very likely also to believe someone is tall. Having the first belief is normally causally sufficient for having the second belief. And anyone who believes everyone in the room is tall and also believes John is in the room will very likely believe John is tall. The third belief is a normal effect of the first two. In short, the functionalist maintains that the proposition expressed by a given mental representation depends on the causal properties of the mental states in which that mental representation figures.

The concept that the semantic properties of mental representations are determined by aspects of their functional role is at the center of current work in the cognitive sciences. Nevertheless, the concept may not be true. Many philosophers who are unsympathetic to the cognitive turn in modern psychology doubt its truth, and many psychologists would probably reject it in the bald and unelaborated way that I have sketched it. Yet even in its skeletal form, there is this much to be said in its favor: It legitimizes the notion of mental representation, which has become increasingly important to theorizing in every branch of the cognitive sciences. Recent advances in formulating and testing hypotheses about the character of mental representations in fields ranging from phonetics to computer vision suggest that the concept of mental representation is fundamental to empirical theories of the mind.

The behaviorist has rejected the appeal to mental representation because it runs counter to his view of the explanatory mechanisms that can figure in psychological theories. Nevertheless, the science of mental representation is now flourishing. The history of science reveals that when a successful theory comes into conflict with a methodological scruple, it is generally the scruple that gives way. Accordingly the functionalist has relaxed the behaviorist constraints on psychological explanations. There is probably no better way to decide what is methodologically permissible in science than by investigating what successful science requires.

# *Artificial Intelligence and Human Mentality*

The readings for this section of Part 3 are of three different kinds. The first two selections, by Minsky and McDermott, are primarily introductory in nature. Minsky's essay appeared in *Scientific American* in 1966 when artificial intelligence (AI for short) was no more than ten years old as an organized research field. It shows the excitement and incredibly optimistic outlook typical of the field in its early stages. The rapidly growing capabilities of the digital computer and the partial successes of early attempts to use it to simulate small bits of human intelligent behavior led most researchers to think that intelligent machines, equal or perhaps even far superior to their human programmers, were just around the corner. McDermott's essay, written for the benefit and amusement of fellow AI researchers a decade later, provides a sobering antidote to the early intoxication of Minsky and others. In the decade following Minsky's article, the only thing that had grown at anything like the predicted pace was the availability of raw computing power, that is, storage capacity and processing speed. The simulation of intelligent behavior lagged far behind all of the optimistic forecasts. In fact, Samuel's checker playing program, one of the early successes described by Minsky, is still beaten consistently by human experts today, in spite of thirty-five years of improvements to the program and massive increases in the computing power of the machines on which the program is run.

Computers still cannot duplicate anything close to ordinary human language comprehension, pattern recognition, or common sense understanding and competence. Partial successes in limited domains of each of these skills seem to have depended on strategies that cannot be generalized beyond those artificial domains, and no alternative strategies have given cause for the high hope of immanent future success with which AI began. This is not to say that the project of AI is a hopeless failure at this point. The field is still fairly young and the final verdict may not be in for some time. McDermott is still optimistic, but the optimism is no longer unbridled. It is time to look carefully and soberly at the progress and lack of it in various areas of AI research, to see what has really been accomplished in the attempt to turn digital computers into intelligent beings, and to ask what the outlook is for the future of the enterprise.

The four remaining essays in this section are contemporary appraisals of work in AI and assessments of its future prospects. The first two are by proponents of AI, Pylyshyn and Dennett. They contend that human intelligence appears to be compatible with the basic working assumptions of AI and of the broader field of cognitive science that contains it, and that research in AI has already paid some important dividends in psychology and philosophy of mind. Pylyshyn argues that there are good reasons to believe that mental processes in human beings are computational operations on physical symbols or codes — in particular, on representations physically encoded in the brain. If this is the case, there is no reason in principle why the right program and code should not be capable of producing mental processes in a computing machine. This approach to human mentality is not unique to AI. We encountered it in the discussion of functionalism in the previous section and it is definitive of every branch of what is now referred to as *cognitive science.* It views intelligent systems, whatever they are made of, as information processors and rests on the foundational assumption that information processing is essentially formal and computational in nature. (See the discussion of AI at the end of the general introduction to this part for an explanation of what is involved in that assumption.)

Dennett argues that research in AI has already solved one of the most difficult theoretical problems in psychology and philosophy of mind. The problem is that of explaining how internal mental representations or ideas can be used to explain mental processes like understanding without placing something inside us with the ability to understand what the representations or ideas mean, that is, something with exactly the same mysterious power that needed to be explained in the first place. According to Dennett, AI has shown how tasks like understanding could be broken down into such minimal subtasks that nothing like human understanding would be required to perform them at the bottom level. The power and speed of the computer have made it plausible that such massive decomposition of functions, with millions of simple or basic operations being performed and the results then recomposed, could actually be the correct account of human mental activity which appears to be simple and almost instantaneous. From this perspective the outlook for finally understanding how the mechanical processes of nonconscious material could produce consciousness, that is, for understanding the working relationship between body and mind, is bright indeed.

The last two essays in this section are written by opponents of AI, Dreyfus and Searle. Although they are in agreement about the bottom line—both believe that digital computers will never be capable of anything very like human mental processes—their strategies for reaching that conclusion are very different. Dreyfus argues that once we understand the important differences between human understanding and competence on the one hand, and the functioning of digital computers on the other, we will see that restrictions on the kinds of input the computer can handle and the way that input is processed by the machine make it impossible for the digital computer even to simulate or duplicate the correlations between input and output characteristic of human intelligent behavior. If Dreyfus is correct, the issue is at least in part an empirical one. Computers will never even seem to be intelligent in the way that humans are, and AI research is approaching its natural limits. No major breakthroughs will be possible within the natural limitations of the field.

Searle's approach is quite different and the issue, from his point of view, is not an empirical one at all. Searle argues that even if digital computers did simulate the input-output behavior of intelligent human beings, they still would not possess understanding, beliefs, knowledge, or any other human mental state or process. The argument involves an interesting thought experiment in which we imagine ourselves simulating the behavior associated with understanding a foreign language in the way a computer might, but without understanding anything at all in the process. If Searle's argument is sound, it would mean that even if AI researchers succeeded in doing all the things Dreyfus thinks they cannot do, they would still not have given mental states to the computer or produced any mental processes, and hence would have shed no light whatsoever on human intelligence and provided no answers to any of the interesting psychological and philosophical questions about the nature or workings of the human mind.

## Marvin L. Minsky (b. 1927)

Marvin L. Minsky is a mathematician and computer scientist who has been one of the leaders in the field of artificial intelligence since its inception. In addition to his direction of and contributions to various projects in the AI Lab at M.I.T., he served as a consultant in connection with HAL, the fictional but highly intelligent computer in the movie *2001: A Space Odyssey*. He is the author of a number of important articles and technical reports in artificial intelligence. His book-length works include *Computation: Finite and Infinite Machines* (1967), *Perceptrons* (with S.

Papert, 1969), *Artificial Intelligence* (with S. Papert, 1974), and an edited volume, *Semantic Information Processing* (1968).

In the following article, written in 1966, Minsky describes a number of the early successes in artificial intelligence research. He contends that computers have already exhibited intelligence in a number of areas: playing games such as checkers, solving problems in algebra and geometry including word problems in ordinary English, and recognizing patterns and discovering analogies. The only limitations Minsky sees on the ability to program digital computers to display the full range of human intelligence and more are the (then current) limitations on computing speed and capacity, and the limited research time and funds invested in the enterprise. (It should be added that these limitations have long since disappeared.)

# Artificial Intelligence

## *Marvin L. Minsky*

At first the idea of an intelligent machine seems implausible. Can a computer really be intelligent? In this article I shall describe some programs that enable a computer to behave in ways that probably everyone would agree seem to show intelligence.

The machine achievements discussed here are remarkable in themselves, but even more interesting and significant than what the programs do accomplish are the methods they involve. They set up goals, make plans, consider hypotheses, recognize analogies and carry out various other intellectual activities. As I shall show by example, a profound change has taken place with the discovery that descriptions of thought processes can be turned into prescriptions for the design of machines or, what is the same thing, the design of programs.

The turning point came sharply in 1943 with the publication of three theoretical papers on what is now called cybernetics. Norbert Wiener, Arturo Rosenblueth and Julian H. Bigelow of the Massachusetts Institute of Technology suggested ways to build goals and purposes into machines; Warren S. McCulloch of the University of Illinois College of Medicine and Walter H. Pitts of M.I.T. showed how machines might use concepts of logic and abstraction, and K. J. W. Craik of the University of Cambridge proposed that machines could use models and analogies to solve problems. With these new foundations the use of psychological language for describing machines became a constructive and powerful tool. Such ideas remained in the realm of theoretical speculation, however, until the mid-1950's. By that time computers had reached a level of capacity and flexibility to permit the programming of processes with the required complexity.

In the summer of 1956 a group of investigators met at Dartmouth College to discuss the possibility of constructing genuinely intelligent machines. Among others, the group included Arthur L. Samuel of the International Business Machines Corporation, who had already written a program that played a good game of checkers and incorporated several techniques to improve its own play. Allen Newell, Clifford Shaw and Herbert A. Simon of the Rand Corporation had constructed a theorem-proving program and were well along in work on a "General Problem Solver," a program that administers a hierarchy of goal-seeking subprograms.

John McCarthy was working on a system to do "commonsense reasoning" and I was working on plans for a program to prove theorems in plane geometry. (I was hoping eventually to have the computer use analogical reasoning on diagrams.) After the conference the workers continued in a number of independent investigations. Newell and Simon built up a research group at the Carnegie Institute of Technology with the goal of developing models of human behavior. McCarthy and I built up a group at M.I.T. to make machines intelligent without particular concern with human behavior. (McCarthy is now at Stanford University.) Although the approaches of the various groups were different, it is significant that their studies have resulted in closely parallel results.

Work in this field of intelligent machines and the number of investigators increased rapidly; by 1963 the bibliography of relevant publications had grown to some 900 papers and books. I shall try to give the reader an impression of the state of the field by presenting some examples of what has been happening recently.

The general approach to creating a program that can solve difficult problems will first be illustrated by considering the game of checkers. This game exemplifies the fact that many problems can in principle be solved by trying all possibilities—in this case exploring all possible moves, all the opponent's possible replies, all the player's possible replies to the opponent's replies and so on. If this could be done, the player could see which move has the best chance of winning. In practice, however, this approach is out of the question, even for a computer; the tracking down of every possible line of play would involve some $10^{40}$ different board positions. (A similiar analysis for the game of chess would call for some $10^{120}$ positions.) Most interesting problems present far too many possibilities for complete trial-and-error analysis. Hence one must discover rules that will try the most likely routes to a solution as early as possible.

Samuel's checker-playing program explores thousands of board positions but not millions. Instead of tracking down every possible line of play the program uses a partial analysis (a "static evaluation") of a relatively small number of carefully selected features of a board position—how many men there are on each side, how advanced they are and certain other simple relations. This incomplete analysis is not in itself adequate for choosing the best move for a player in a current position. By combining the partial analysis with a limited search for some of the consequences of the possible moves from the current position, however, the program selects its moves as if on the basis of a much deeper analysis. The program contains a collection of rules for deciding when to continue the search and when to stop. When it stops, it assesses the merits of the "terminal" position in terms of the static evaluation. If the computer finds by this search that a given move leads to an advantage for the player in all the likely positions that may occur a few moves later, whatever the opponent does, it can select this move with confidence.

What is interesting and significant about such a program is not simply that it can use trial and error to solve problems. What makes for intelligent behavior is the collection of methods and techniques that select what is to be tried next, that size up the situation and choose a plausible (if not always good) move and use information gained in previous attempts to steer subsequent analysis in better directions. To be sure, the programs described below do use search, but in the examples we present the solutions were found among the first few attempts rather than after millions of attempts.

A program that makes such judgments about what is best to try next is termed **heuristic.** Our examples of heuristic programs demonstrate some capabilities similar in principle to those of the checkers program, and others that may be even more clearly recognized as ways of "thinking."

In developing a heuristic program one usually begins by programming some methods and techniques that can solve comparatively uncomplicated problems. To solve harder problems one might work directly to improve these basic methods, but it is much more profitable to try to extend the problem solver's general ability to bring a harder problem within reach by breaking it down into subproblems. The machine is provided with a program for a three-step process: (1) break down the problems into subproblems, keeping a record of the relations between these parts as part of the total problem, (2) solve the subproblems and (3) combine the results to form a solution to the problem as a whole. If a subproblem is still too hard, apply the procedure again. It has been found that the key to success in such a procedure often lies in finding a form of description for the problem situation (a descriptive "language") that makes it easy to break the problem down in a useful way.

Our next example of a heuristic program illustrates how descriptive languages can be used to enable a computer to employ analogical reasoning. The program was developed by Thomas Evans, a graduate student at M.I.T., as the basis for his doctoral thesis, and is the best example so far both of the use of descriptions and of how to handle analogies in a computer program.

The problem selected was the recognition of analogies between geometric figures. It was taken from a well-known test widely used for college-admission examinations because its level of difficulty is considered to require considerable intelligence. The general format is familiar: Given two figures bearing a certain relation to each other, find a similar relation between a third figure and one of five choices offered. The problem is usually written: "*A* is to *B* as *C* is to ($D_1$, $D_2$, $D_3$, $D_4$ or $D_5$?)." The particularly attractive feature of this kind of problem as a test of machine intelligence is that it has no uniquely "correct" answer. Indeed, performance on such tests is not graded by any known rule but is judged on the basis of the selections of highly intelligent people on whom the test is tried.

Now, there is a common superstition that "a computer can solve a problem only when every step in the solution is clearly specified by the programmer." In a superficial sense the statement is true, but it is dangerously misleading if it is taken literally. Here we understood the basic concepts Evans wrote into the program, but until the program was completed and tested we had no idea of how the machine's level of performance would compare to the test scores of human subjects.

Evans began his work on the problem of comparing geometric figures by proposing a theory of the steps or processes the human brain might use in dealing with such a situation. His theory suggested a program of four steps that can be described in psychological terms. First, in comparing the features of the figures *A* and *B* one must select from various possibilities some way in which a description of *A* can be transformed into a description of *B*. This transformation defines certain relations between *A* and *B*. . . . There may be several such explanations "plausible" enough to be considered. Second, one looks for items or parts in *C* that correspond to parts in *A*. There may be several such "matches" worthy of consideration. Third, in each of the five figures offering answer choices one searches for features that may relate the figure to *C* in a way similar to the way in which the corresponding features in *B* are related to those in *A*. Wherever the correspondence, if any, is not perfect, one can make it more so by "weakening" the relation, which means accepting a modified, less detailed version of the relation. Fourth and last, one can select as the best answer the figure that required the least modification of relations in order to relate it to *C* as *B* is related to *A*.

This set of hypotheses became the framework of Evans' program. (I feel sure that rules or procedures of the same general character are involved in any kind of analogical reasoning.) His next problem was to translate this rather complex sketch of mental processes into a detailed program for the computer. To do so he had to develop what is certainly one of the most complex programs ever written. The technical device that made the translation possible was the LISP ("list-processor") programming language McCarthy had developed on the basis of earlier work by Newell, Simon and Shaw. This system provides many automatic services for manipulating expressions and complicated data structures. In particular it is a most convenient method of handling descriptions consisting of lists of items. And it makes it easy to write interlocked programs that can, for example, use one another as subprograms.

The input for a specific problem in Evans' program is in the form of lists of vertices, lines and curves describing the geometric figures. A subprogram analyzes this information, identifies the separate parts of the figure and reconstructs them in terms of points on a graph and the connecting lines. . . . The program takes the following course: After receiving the descriptions of the figures (*A*, *B*, *C* and the five answer choices) it searches out topological and geometric relations between the parts in each picture (such as that one object is inside or to the left of or above another). It then identifies and lists similarities between pairs of pictures (*A* and *B*, *A* and *C*, *C* and $D_1$ and so on). The program proceeds to discover all the ways in which the parts of *A* and *B* can be matched up, and on the basis of this examination it develops a hypothesis about the relation of *A* to *B* (what was removed, added, moved or otherwise changed to transform one picture into the other). Next it considers correspondences between the parts of *A* and the parts of *C*. It goes on to look for matchings of the *A*-to-*B* kind between the parts in *C* and each of the *D* figures (the answer choices). When it finds something approaching a match that is consistent with its hypothesis of the relation between *A* and *B*, it proceeds to measure the degree of divergence of the *C*-to-*D* relation from the *A*-to-*B* relation by stripping away the details of the *A*-to-*B* transformation one by one until both relations (*A*-to-*B* and *C*-to-*D*) are essentially alike. In this way it eventually identifies the *D* figure that seems to come closest to a relation to *C* analogous to the *A* and *B* relation.

Evans' program is capable of solving problems considerably more complex or subtle than the one we have considered step by step. Among other things, in making decisions about the details of a picture it can take into account deductions from the situation as a whole. . . . No one has taken the trouble to make a detailed comparison of the machine's performance with that of human subjects on the same problems, but Evans' evidence suggests that the present program can score at about the 10th-grade level, and with certain improvements of the program that have already been proposed it should do even better. Evans' work on his program had to stop when he reached the limitations of the computer machinery available to him. His program could no longer fit in one piece into the core memory of the computer, and mainly for this reason it took several minutes to run each problem in the machine. With the very large memory just installed at M.I.T.'s Project MAC the program could be run in a few seconds. The new capacity will make possible further research on more sophisticated versions of such programs.

The Evans program is of course a single-minded affair: it can deal only with problems in geometrical analogy. Although its ability in this respect compares favorably with the ability of humans, in no other respect can it pretend to approach the scope or versatility of human intelligence. Yet in its limited way it does display qualities we usually think of as requiring "intuition," "taste" or other subjective operations of the mind. With his analysis of such operations and his clarification of their components in terms precise enough to express them symbolically and make them available for use by a machine, Evans laid a foundation for the further development (with less effort) of programs employing analogical reasoning.

Moreover, it is becoming clear that analogical reasoning itself can be an important tool for expanding artificial intelligence. I believe it will eventually be possible for programs, by resorting to analogical reasoning, to apply the experience they have gained from solving one kind of problem to the solution of quite different problems. Consider a situation in which a machine is presented with a problem that is too complicated for solution by any method it knows. Ordinarily to cope with such contingencies the computer would be programmed to split the problem into subproblems or subgoals, so that by solving these it can arrive at a solution to the main problem. In a difficult case, however, the machine may be unable to break the problem down or may become lost in a growing maze of irrelevant subgoals. If a machine is to be able to deal, then, with very hard problems, it must have some kind of planning ability—an ability to find a suitable strategy.

What does the rather imprecise word "planning" mean in this context? We can think of a definition in terms of machine operations that might be useful: (1) Replace the given problem by a similar but simpler one; (2) solve this analogous problem and remember the steps in its solution; (3) try to adapt the steps of the solution to solve the original problem. Newell and Simon have actually completed an experiment embodying a simple version of such a program. It seems to me that this area is one of the most important for research on making machine intelligence more versatile.

I should now like to give a third example of a program exhibiting intelligence. This program has to do with the handling of information written in the English language.

Since the beginnings of the evolution of modern computers it has been obvious that a computer could be a superb file clerk that would provide instant access to any of its information—provided that the files were totally and neatly organized and that the kinds of questions the computer was called on to answer could be completely programmed. But what if, as in real life, the information is scattered through the files and is expressed in various forms of human discourse? It is widely supposed that the handling of information of this informal character is beyond the capability of any machine.

Daniel Bobrow, for his doctoral research at M.I.T., attacked this problem directly: How could a computer be programmed to understand a limited range of ordinary English? For subject matter he chose statements of problems in high school algebra. The purely mathematical solution of these problems would be child's play for the computer, but Bobrow's main concern was to provide the computer with the ability to read the informal verbal statement of a problem and derive from that language the equations required to solve the problem. (This, and not solution of the equations, is what is hard for students too.)

The basic strategy of the program (which is named "Student") is this: The machine "reads in" the statement of the problem and tries to rewrite it as a number of simple sentences. Then it tries to convert each simple sentence into an equation. Finally it tries to solve the set of equations and present the required answer (converted back to a simple English sentence). Each of these steps in interpreting the meaning is done with the help of a library (stored in the core memory) that includes a dictionary, a variety of factual statements and several special-purpose programs for solving particular kinds of problems. To write the program for the machine Bobrow used the LISP programming language with some new extensions of his own and incorporated techniques that had been developed by Victor H. Yngve in earlier work on language at M.I.T.

The problems the machine has to face in interpreting the English statements are sometimes quite difficult. It may have to figure out the antecedent of a pronoun, recognize that two different phrases have the same meaning or discover that a necessary piece of information is missing. Bobrow's program is a model of informality. Its filing system is so loosely organized (although it is readily accessible) that new information can be added to the dictionary by dumping it in anywhere. Perhaps the program's most interesting technical aspect is the way it cuts across the linguist's formal distinction between syntax and semantics, thus avoiding problems that, it seems to me, have more hindered than helped most studies of language.

. . . The remarkable thing about Student is not so much that it understands English as that it shows a basic capacity for understanding anything at all. When it runs into difficulty, it asks usually pertinent questions. Sometimes it has to ask the person operating the computer, but often it resolves the difficulty by referring to the knowledge in its files. When, for instance, it meets a statement such as "Mary is twice as old as Ann was when Mary was as old as Ann is now," the program knows how to make the meaning of "was when" more precise by rewriting the statement as two simple sentences: "Mary is twice as old as Ann was *X* years ago. *X* years ago Mary was as old as Ann is now."

Bobrow's program can handle only a small part of the grammar of the English language, and its semantic dictionaries are quite limited. Yet even though it can make many kinds of mistakes within its linguistic limitations, it probably surpasses the average person in its ability to handle algebra problems stated verbally. Bobrow believes that, given a larger computer memory, he could make Student understand most of the problems that are presented in high school first-algebra textbooks.

As an example of another kind of intelligence programmed into a machine, a program developed by Lawrence C. Roberts as a doctoral thesis at M.I.T. endows a computer with some ability to analyze three-dimensional objects. In a single two-dimensional photograph of a solid object the program detects a number of the object's geometrical features. It uses these to form a description in terms of lines and then tries to analyze the figure as a composite of simpler building blocks (rectangular forms and prisms). Once the program has performed this analysis it can reconstruct the figure from any requested point of view, drawing in lines that were originally hidden and suppressing lines that should not appear in the new picture. The program employs some rather abstract symbolic reasoning.

The exploration of machine intelligence has hardly begun. There have been about 30 experiments at the general level of those described here. Each investigator has had time to try out a few ideas; each program works only in a narrow problem area. How can we make the programs more versatile? It cannot be done simply by putting together a collection of old programs; they differ so much in their representation of objects and concepts that there could be no effective communication among them.

If we ask, "Why are the programs not more intelligent than they are?" a simple answer is that until recently resources—in people, time and computer capacity—have been quite limited. A number of the more careful and serious attempts have come close to their goal (usually after two or three years of work); others have been limited by core-memory capacity; still others encountered programming difficulties. A few projects have not progressed nearly as much as was hoped, notably projects in language translation and mathematical theorem-proving. Both cases, I think, represent premature attempts to handle complex formalisms without also somehow representing their meaning.

The problem of combining programs is more serious. Partly because of the very brief history of the field there is a shortage of well-developed ideas about systems for the communication of partial results between different programs, and for modifying programs already written to meet new conditions. Until this situation is improved it will remain hard to combine the results of separate research projects. Warren Teitelman of our laboratory has recently developed a programming system that may help in this regard; he has demonstrated it by re-creating in a matter of hours the results of some earlier programs that took weeks to write.

The questions people most often ask are: Can the programs learn through experience and thus improve themselves? Is this not the obvious path to making them intelligent? The answer to each is both yes and no. Even at this early stage the programs use many kinds of processes that might be called learning; they remember and use the methods that solved other problems; they adjust some of their internal characteristics for the best performance; they "associate" symbols that have been correlated in the past. No program today, however, can work any genuinely important change in its own basic structure. (A number of early experiments on "self-organizing" programs failed because of excessive reliance on random trial and error. A somewhat later attempt by the Carnegie Institute group to get their General Problem Solver to improve its descriptive ability was based on much sounder ideas; this project was left unfinished when it encountered difficulties in communication between programs, but it probably could be completed with the programming tools now available.)

In order for a program to improve itself substantially it would have to have at least a rudimentary understanding of its own problem-solving process and some ability to recognize an improvement when it found one. There is no inherent reason why this should be impossible for a machine. Given a model of its own workings, it could use its problem-solving power to work on the problem of self-improvement. The present programs are not quite smart enough for this purpose; they can only deal with the improvement of programs much simpler than themselves.

Once we have devised programs with a genuine capacity for self-improvement a rapid evolutionary process will begin. As the machine improves both itself and its model of itself, we shall begin to see all the phenomena associated with the terms "consciousness," "intuition" and "intelligence" itself. It is hard to say how close we are to this threshold, but once it is crossed the world will not be the same.

It is reasonable, I suppose, to be unconvinced by our examples and to be skeptical about whether machines will ever be intelligent. It is unreasonable, however, to think machines could become *nearly* as intelligent as we are and then stop, or to suppose we will always be able to compete with them in wit or wisdom. Whether or not we could retain some sort of control of the machines, assuming that we would want to, the nature of our activities and aspirations would be changed utterly by the presence on earth of intellectually superior beings.

## *Drew McDermott (b. 1949)*

Drew McDermott is a computer scientist whose research area is artificial intelligence. He has written numerous articles and technical reports in artificial intelligence, especially in the area of natural language understanding and the computer logics required to automatically update belief systems in light of ongoing experience and behavior. He is the editor (with E. Charniak and C. Riesbeck) of *Artificial Intelligence Programming* (1980).

In the essay below McDermott has some fun at the expense of himself and his colleagues in the field of artificial intelligence. Underneath the humor, however, lies a serious message. Artificial intelligence as a research field needs to practice the same critical self-evaluation essential to every branch of science. Overestimating results and proclaiming success in advance of achieving it are not conducive to scientific progress and obscure the real, if limited, accomplishments of AI research.

# Artificial Intelligence Meets Natural Stupidity

***Drew McDermott***

As a field, artificial intelligence has always been on the border of respectability, and therefore on the border of crackpottery. Many critics have urged that we are over the border. We have been very defensive toward this charge, drawing ourselves up with dignity when it is made and folding the cloak of Science about us. On the other hand, in private we have been justifiably proud of our willingness to explore weird ideas, because pursuing them is the only way to make progress.

Unfortunately, the necessity for speculation has combined with the culture of the hacker in computer science to cripple our self-discipline. In a young field, self-discipline is not necessarily a virtue, but we are not getting any younger. In the past few years, our tolerance of sloppy thinking has led us to repeat many mistakes over and over. If we are to retain any credibility, this should stop.

This paper is an effort to ridicule some of these mistakes. Almost everyone I know should find himself the target at some point or other; if you don't, you are encouraged to write up your own favorite fault. The three described here I suffer from myself. I hope self-ridicule will be a complete catharsis, but I doubt it. Bad tendencies can be very deep-rooted. Remember, though, if we can't criticize ourselves, someone else will save us the trouble.

## WISHFUL MNEMONICS

A major source of simple-mindedness in AI programs is the use of **mnemonics** like "UNDERSTAND" or "GOAL" to refer to programs and data structures. This practice has been inherited from more traditional programming applications, in which it is liberating and enlightening to be able to refer to program structures by their purposes. Indeed, part of the thrust of the structured programming movement is to program entirely in terms of purposes at one level before implementing them by the most convenient of the (presumably many) alternative lower-level constructs.

However, in AI our programs to a great degree are problems rather than solutions. If a researcher tries to write an "understanding" program, it isn't because he has thought of a better way of implementing this well-understood task, but because he thinks he can come closer to writing the *first* implementation. If he calls the main loop of his program "UNDERSTAND," he is (until proven innocent) merely begging the question. He may mislead a lot of people, most prominently himself, and enrage a lot of others.

What he should do instead is refer to this main loop as "G0034," and see if he can *convince* himself or anyone else that G0034 implements some part of understanding. Or he could give it a name that reveals its intrinsic properties, like NODE-NET-INTERSECTION-FINDER, it being the substance of his theory that finding intersections in networks of nodes constitutes understanding. If Quillian had called his program the "Teachable Language Node Net Intersection Finder," he would have saved us some reading (except for those of us fanatic about finding the part on teachability).

Many instructive examples of wishful mnemonics by AI researchers come to mind once you

Abridged from *Mind Design,* Edited by John Haugeland. (Bradford Books, 1981, a division of MIT Press. Originally published in SIGART [Special Interest Group on Artificial Intelligence of the Association for Computing Machinery]. Newsletter No. 57 [4/76]). Reprinted by permission of MIT Press.

see the point. Remember GPS? By now, "GPS" is a colorless term denoting a particularly stupid program to solve puzzles. But it originally meant "General Problem Solver," which caused everybody a lot of needless excitement and distraction. It should have been called LFGNS—"Local-Feature-Guided Network Searcher."

Compare the mnemonics in Planner with those in Conniver:

| *Planner* | *Conniver* |
|---|---|
| GOAL | FETCH & TRY-NEXT |
| CONSEQUENT | IF-NEEDED |
| ANTECEDENT | IF-ADDED |
| THEOREM | METHOD |
| ASSERT | ADD |

It is so much harder to write programs using the terms on the right! When you say (GOAL . . . ), you can just feel the enormous power at your fingertips. It is, of course, an illusion.

Of course, Conniver has some glaring wishful primitives, too. Calling "multiple data bases" CONTEXTS was dumb. It implies that, say, sentence understanding in context is really easy in this system. . . .

As AI progresses (at least in terms of money spent), this malady gets worse. We have lived so long with the conviction that robots are possible, even just around the corner, that we can't help hastening their arrival with magic incantations. Winograd explored some of the complexity of language in sophisticated detail; and now everyone takes "natural-language interfaces" for granted, though none has been written. Charniak pointed out some approaches to understanding stories, and now the OWL interpreter includes a "story-understanding module." (And, God help us, a top-level "ego loop"). . . .

Concepts borrowed from human language must shake off a lot of surface-structure dust before they become clear. (See [below]. . . .) "Is" is a complicated word, syntactically obscure. We use it with great facility, but we don't understand it well enough to appeal to it for clarification of anything. If we want to call attention to the "property inheritance" use, why not just *say* INHERITS-INDICATORS? Then, if we wish, we can prove from a completed system that this captures a large part of what "is a" means.

Another error is the temptation to write networks like this:

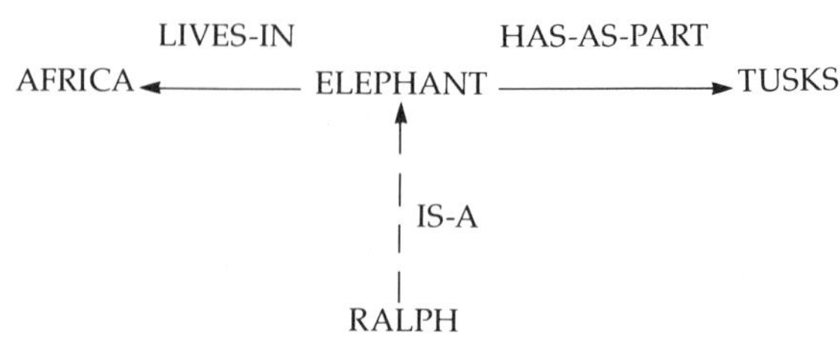


which people do all the time. It is clear to them that Ralph lives in Africa, the same Africa as all the other elephants, but his tusks are his own. But the network doesn't say this. Woods discusses errors like this in detail.

People reason circularly about concepts like IS-A. Even if originally they were fully aware they were just naming INHERITS-INDICATORS with a short, friendly mnemonic, they later use the mnemonic to conclude things about "is a." For example, it has been proposed that a first cut at representing "Nixon is a Hitler" is:

It worked for Ralph and Elephant, didn't it? But we just can't take stuff out of the IS-A concept that we never put in. I find this diagram worse than useless.

Lest this all seem merely amusing, meditate on the fate of those who have tampered with words before. The behaviorists ruined words like "behavior," "response," and, especially, "learning." They now play happily in a dream world, internally consistent but lost to science. And think about this: if "mechanical translation" had been called "word-by-word text manipulation," the people doing it might still be getting government money. . . .

## UNNATURAL LANGUAGE

In discourse, a speaker will introduce a hand and easily refer to "the finger." Frame theorists and other notation-developers find it marvelous that their system practically gives them "the finger" automatically as a piece of the data structure for "hand." As far as I can see, doing this automatically is the worst way of doing it. First, of course, there are four or five fingers, each with its own name, so "the finger" will be ambiguous. Second, a phrase like "the finger" can be used in so many ways that an automatic evaluation to FINGER 109 will be wasteful at best. There are idioms to worry about, as in, "He raised his hand and gave me the finger." (Are we to conclude that the "default finger in the hand frame" is the middle finger?) But even ignoring them, there are many contexts where "the" just doesn't mean what we would like it to. For example, "He removed his glove and I saw the finger was missing." This is like, "The barn burned to the ground five years ago and was completely rebuilt." There are logics in which the same BARN 1051 can have different denotations in different time periods, but do we really want this clumsiness in the heart of our internal representation?

It seems much smarter to put knowledge about translation from natural language to internal representation in the natural language processor, not in the internal representation. I am using "in" loosely; my intent is to condemn an approach that translates language very superficially (using a little syntax and morphology) and hands it to the data base in that form. Instead, the language routine must draw on knowledge about all parts of the sentence in translating "the finger." Its output must be a directly useful internal representation, probably as remote as possible from being "English-like."

These problems stem from a picture of a program constructed of cooperating modules that "talk to" each other. While this may be a reasonable metaphor in some ways, anyone who has actually written such a program knows that "talking" is a very poor model of the communication. Yet many researchers find English to be the ideal notation in which to encode messages. They are aware that message-passing channels are the most frustrating bottleneck through which intelligence must pass, so they wish their way into the solution: let the modules speak in human tongues! Let them use metaphor, allusion, hints, polite requests, pleading, flattery, bribes, and patriotic exhortations to their fellow modules!

It is hard to say where they have gone wronger, in underestimating language or overestimating computer programs. Language is only occasionally a medium of communication of information; even when it is, the ratio of information to packaging is low. The problem of a language speaker is to get the directed attention of an unprepared hearer and slide some information into his mind in a very short time. Since the major time sink is moving his mouth, the language sacrifices everything else to brevity, forcing the hearer to do much quick thinking to compensate. Furthermore, since the speaker doesn't quite know the organization of his hearer's mind, his phrasing of information and packaging must, except for the most stereotyped conversations, be an artwork of suggestiveness and insight.

Communication between computer programs is under completely different constraints. At the current stage of research, it is ridiculous to focus on anything but raw communication of information; we are unable to identify where more devious, Freudian intercourse might occur. Packaging and encoding of the information are usually already done. Ambiguity is avoidable. Even brevity is unimportant (at least for speed), since a huge structure can be transmitted by passing an internal name or pointer to it shared by sender and receiver. Instead, the whole problem is getting the hearer to notice what it has been told. (Not "understand," but "notice." To appeal to understanding at this low level will doom us to tail-chasing failure.) The new structure handed to the receiver should give it "permission" to make progress on its problem. If the sender could give more detailed instructions, it could just execute them itself. Unfortunately, the latitude this leaves the receiver is wasted if it is too "narrow-minded" to see what it has received.

Everyone who has written a large AI program will know what I am talking about. In this communication effort, the naming problem can be irritating, since the sender must make sure the receiver understands its terms. But there are so many approaches to solving the problem (for example, by passing translation tables around), which are not open to conversing humans, that it recedes quickly into the background. The frustrations lie elsewhere.

Reference is not the only "unnatural language" problem. A related one is the feeble analysis of concepts like "the" and "a" by most AI researchers. There is a natural inclination to let "the" flag a definite description and "a" an existential quantifier (or occasionally a description). Except for *Dick, Jane, and Sally,* and some of Bertrand Russell's work, this approach is not even an approximation.

First the typical noun phrase is not directly translated into the internal representation at all, and does not wind up as an object name. For example, "Despite the peripatetic nature of American students and their families . . . there remain wide gaps and serious misconceptions in our understanding of other peoples and cultures." Translating this sentence (whose meaning is transparent) is problematic in the extreme. The author means to allude to the fact that Americans travel a lot, as a way of getting around to the claim that they don't travel enough or well enough. Why? We don't know yet why people talk this way. But translation methods that worked on "the big red block" will never succeed on "the . . . nature of American students."

Second, the difference between "the" and "a" is not the difference between "definite" and "indefinite," except vacuously. For example, what is the difference in meaning between

Due to the decrease in the American birthrate in the 1960's, our schools are underutilized.

Due to a decrease in the American birthrate in the 1960's, our schools are underutilized.

In most respects, they "mean" exactly the same thing, since there can have been only one decrease in the birthrate in the 1960's, and each sentence presupposes that it occurred. But in one the author is assuming we know it already; in the other, he is more casual about whether we do or not. We have no theory at all about what difference this difference makes.

It is unfortunate that a logical back seepage has caused people to see words like "the," "a," "all," "or," "and," etc. as being embellished or ambiguous versions of "iota," "∃," "∀," "∨," and "∧." To cure yourself of this, try examining two pages of a book for ten-year olds, translating the story as you go into an internal representation. If you can do this without difficulty, your case is hopeless.

The obsession with natural language seems to have caused the feeling that the human use of language is a royal road to the cognitive psyche. I find this analogous to preoccupation with imagery as a way of studying vision. Most AI researchers react with amusement to proposals to explain vision in terms of stored images, reducing the physical eye to the mind's eye. But many of the same people notice themselves talking to themselves in English, and conclude that English is very close to the language of thought.

Clearly, there must be some other notation, different in principle from natural language, or we will have done for the ear what imagery theory does for the eye. No matter how fascinating the structure of consciousness is, it is dangerous to gaze too long into its depths. The puzzles we find there can be solved only by sneaking up on them from behind. As of now, we have no idea at all why people experience their thoughts the way they do, in pictures and words. It will probably turn out to be quite different, even simpler, than what we think now, once we understand why and how people experience their thoughts at all. . . .

In this section I have been harsh toward AI's tendency to oversimplify or overglorify natural language, but don't think that my opinion is that research in this area is futile. Indeed, probably because I am an academic verbalizer, I feel that understanding natural language is the most fascinating and important research goal we have in the long run. But it deserves more attention from a theoretical point of view before we rush off and throw together "natural-language" interfaces to programs with inadequate depth. We should do more studies of what language is for, and we should develop complex programs with a need to talk, before we put the two together.

## "**ONLY A PRELIMINARY VERSION OF THE PROGRAM WAS ACTUALLY IMPLEMENTED"

A common idiocy in AI research is to suppose that having identified the shortcomings of Version I of a program is equivalent to having written Version II. Naturally, the sincere researcher doesn't think of his actions this way. From my own experience, the course of a piece of research is like this:

Having identified a problem, the ambitious researcher stumbles one day upon a really good idea that neatly solves several related subproblems of it at once. (Sometimes the solution actually comes before the problem is identified.) The idea is formally pretty and seems to mesh smoothly with the way a rational program ought to think. Let us call it "sidetracking control structure" for concreteness. The researcher immediately implements an elegant program embodying automatic sidetracking, with an eye toward applying it to his original problem. As always, implementation takes much longer than expected, but matters are basically tidy.

However, as he develops and debugs this piece of code, he becomes aware that there are several theoretical holes in his design and that it doesn't work. It doesn't work for good and respectable reasons, most of them depending on the fact that the solution to the problem requires more than one good idea. But, having got a framework, he becomes more and more convinced that those small but numerous holes are where the good ideas are to fit. He may even be right.

Here, however, he begins to lose his grip. Implementing Version I, whose shortcomings are all too obvious, was exhausting; it made him feel grubby for nothing. (Not at all like the TECO macros he took time out for along the way!) He feels as though he's paid his dues; now he can join the theoreticians. What's more, he *should.* Implementation details will make his thesis dull. The people want *epistemology*.

Simultaneously, he enjoys the contradictory feeling that the implementation of Version II would be easy. He has reams of notes on the holes in Version I and how to fill them. When he surveys them, he feels their master. Though a stranger to the trees, he can talk with confidence about the forest. Indeed, that is precisely what he does in his final document. It is full of allusions to a program he seems to be claiming to have written. Only in a cautious footnote does he say, "the program was never actually finished," or, "a preliminary version of the program was actually written."

This final report can have interesting quirks. It is likely to be titled *A Side-Tracking Control Structure Approach to Pornographic Question-Answering,* because the author's fondness for sidetracking never quite left him. However, sidetracking is the only part of the solution he really understands, so he is likely to be quite diffident about it. He feels much better about the multitude of patch mechanisms which he describes. He designed them as solutions, not problems; he wisely avoided implementing them and spoiling the illusion, so he can talk at length about how each one neatly ties up a loose end of sidetracking.

The final report usually pleases most people (more people than it should), impressing them but leaving them a little hungover. They are likely to be taken with sidetracking, especially if a theorem about it is proved, but the overall approach to the real problem lacks definition. Performance and promise run together like the colors of a sunset. The happy feeling is kindled in the reader that indefinite progress has already started. On the other hand, they usually know the author's approach won't solve everything; he avoids claiming this. So the document fails to stimulate or challenge; it merely feeds the addict's desire for reassurance that AI is not standing still, and raises his tolerance a little.

This muddle finally hurts those following in the researcher's path. Long after he has his Ph.D. or his tenure, inquiring students will be put off by the document he has left behind. He seems to have solved everything already, so the report says, yet there is no tangible evidence of it besides the report itself. No one really wants to take up the problem again, even though the original research is essentially a partial success or even a failure! If a student decides sidetracking is a good idea, and wants to study it, people will assume he is "merely implementing" an already fully designed program. (No Ph.D. for that!) He would be willing or even eager to start from a smoothly running Version II and write Version III, incorporating a new theoretical idea like Syntactic Network Data Bases, but there is no Version II. Even a Version I would help, but it isn't really working very well and its author has no desire for it to be publicized.

Of course, the student can turn his back on sidetracking, and develop an entirely new approach to Pornographic Question-Answering. But this will only antagonize people. They thought they understood sidetracking; they had convinced themselves it could be made to work. Disagreeing will only confuse them. Besides, it probably could have been made to work. If only its inventor had left it an open question!

This inflationary spiral can't go on forever. After five theses have been written, each promising with fuzzy grandeur a different solution to a problem, people will begin to doubt that the problem has any solution at all. Five theses, each building on the previous one, might have been enough to solve it completely.

The solution is obvious: insist that people report on Version I (or possibly "I½"). If a thorough report on a mere actual implementation were required, or even *allowed,* as a Ph.D. thesis, progress would appear slower, but it would be real.

Furthermore, the program should be user-engineered enough and debugged enough so that it can be run by people besides its author. What people want to know about such a program is how far they can diverge from the examples given in the thesis before it fails. Think of their awe when they discover that the hardest cases it handles weren't even mentioned! (Nowadays, the cases mentioned are, at the very best, the *only* ones the program handles.)

When a program does fail, it should tell the explorer why it failed by behavior more illuminating than, e.g., going into an infinite loop. Often a program will begin to degrade in time or accuracy before it fails. The program should print out statistics showing its opinion of how hard it had to work ("90,265 sidetracks"), so the user will not have to guess from page faults or console time. If he wishes to investigate further, a clearly written, up-to-date source program should be available for him to run interpretively, trace, etc. (More documentation should not be necessary.) In any other branch of computer science, these things are taken for granted.

My proposal is that thesis research, or any other two-year effort, should be organized as follows:

As before, a new problem, or *old problem with partial solution,* should be chosen. The part of the problem where most progress could be made (a conceptual "inner loop") should be thought about hardest. Good ideas developed here should appear in a research proposal.

The first half of the time allotted thereafter should be applied to writing Version $n+1$, where $n$ is the version number you started with (0 for virgin problems). (Substantial rewriting of Version $n$ should be anticipated.) The second half should be devoted to writing the report and improving Version $n+1$ with enough breadth, clean code, and new user features to make it useful to the next person that needs it.

The research report will then describe the improvements made to Version $n$, good ideas implemented, and total progress made in solving the original problem. Suggestions for further improvements should be included, in the future subjunctive tense.

The standard for such research should be a partial success, but AI as a field is starving for a few carefully documented failures. Anyone can think of several theses that could be improved stylistically and substantively by being rephrased as reports on failures. I can learn more by just being told why a technique won't work than by being made to read between the lines.

## BENEDICTION

This paper has focussed on three methodological and substantive issues over which we have stumbled. Anyone can think of more. I chose these because I am more guilty of them than other mistakes, which I am prone to lose my sense of humor about, such as:

1. The insistence of AI people that an action is a change of state of the world or a world model, and that thinking about actions amounts to stringing state changes together to accomplish a big state change. This seems to me not an oversimplification, but a false start. How many of your actions can be characterized as state changes, or are even performed to effect state changes? How many of a program's actions in problem solving? (Not the actions it strings together, but the actions it *takes,* like "trying short strings first," or "assuming the block is where it's supposed to be.")

2. The notion that a semantic network is a network. In lucid moments, network hackers realize that lines drawn between nodes stand for pointers, that almost everything in an AI program is a pointer, and that any list structure could be drawn as a network, the choice of what to call node and what to call link being arbitrary. Their lucid moments are few.

3. The notion that a semantic network is semantic.

4. Any indulgence in the "procedural-declarative" controversy. Anyone who hasn't figured this "controversy" out yet should be considered to have missed his chance, and be banned from talking about it. Notice that at Carnegie-Mellon they haven't worried too much about this dispute, and haven't suffered at all.

5. The idea that because *you* can see your way through a problem space, your program can: the "wishful control structure" problem.

In this paper I have criticized AI researchers very harshly. Let me express my faith that people in other fields would, on inspection, be found to suffer from equally bad faults. Most AI workers are responsible people who are aware of the pitfalls of a difficult field and produce good work in spite of them. However, to say anything good about anyone is beyond the scope of this paper.

*Acknowledgment:* I thank the AI Lab Playroom crowd for constructive play.

---

## *Zenon W. Pylyshyn (b. 1937)*

Zenon Pylyshyn is a psychologist and computer scientist who has written numerous articles in cognitive science and in various areas of artificial intelligence. He is the author of an important book on the foundations of cognitive science titled *Computation and Cognition* (1984). The essay below bears the same title and is an earlier statement of many of the central themes of that book.

Pylyshyn argues that the basic assumptions of cognitive science, equally basic to the field of artificial intelligence, are at the very least plausible. Those assumptions are that human behavior is governed by representations of goals, of objects of belief, and of the perceived environment, and that mental processes are computational operations on such representations. If these assumptions are correct, then the science of the mental will not be reducible to physical science even though the machine that performs the computational operations (brain or computer) is entirely physical. This also means that a programmed computer whose operations are equivalent (in Pylyshyn's "strong" sense, explained in the essay below) to human mental operations, will in fact be capable of mental processes and will in fact provide an explanation of those mental processes.

# Computation and Cognition

## *Zenon W. Pylyshyn*

### 1. INTRODUCTION AND SUMMARY

The view that cognition can be understood as computation is ubiquitous in modern cognitive theorizing, even among those who do not use computer programs to express models of cognitive processes. One of the basic assumptions behind this approach, sometimes referred to as "information processing psychology," is that cognitive processes can be understood in terms of **formal operations** carried out on symbol structures. It thus represents a formalist approach to theoretical explanation. In practice, tokens of symbol structures may be depicted as expressions written in some lexicographic notation (as is usual in linguistics or mathematics), or they may be physically instantiated in a computer as a data structure or an executable program.

The "information processing" idiom has been with us for about two decades and represents a substantial intellectual commitment among students of cognition. The fields that share this view (notably, segments of linguistics, philosophy of mind, psychology, artificial intelligence, cultural anthropology, and others) have been increasingly looking toward some convergence as the "cognitive sciences." . . . There remains, however, considerable uncertainty regarding precisely what constitutes the core of the approach and what constraints it imposes on theory construction.

In this essay I shall present what I consider some of the crucial characteristics of the computational view of mind and defend them as appropriate for the task of explaining cognition. . . .

### 2. THE COGNITIVE VOCABULARY AND FOLK PSYCHOLOGY

Most people implicitly hold a sophisticated and highly successful cognitive theory; that is, they can systematize, make sense of, and correctly predict an enormous range of human behavior. Although textbook authors are fond of pointing

Abridged from "Computation and Cognition: Issues in the Foundations of Cognitive Science" in *The Behavioral and Brain Sciences,* 1980, pp. 111–21. Reprinted by permission of Cambridge University Press. Paragraphs renumbered.

out the errors in **folk psychology,** it nonetheless far surpasses any current scientific psychology in scope and general accuracy. What is significant about this is the mentalistic vocabulary, or level of description, of folk psychology, and its corresponding taxonomy of things, behaviors, events and so on.

Whatever the shortcomings of folk psychology (and there are plenty, to be sure), the level of abstractness of its concepts (relative to those of physics), and particularly its appeal to the way situations are *represented in the mind* (i.e., its appeal to what human agents think, believe, infer, want, and so on, as opposed to the way they actually are), seems precisely suited to capturing just the kinds of generalizations that concern cognitive psychology — e.g., the nature of our intellectual abilities, the mechanisms underlying intellectual performances, and the causal and rational antecedents of our actions.

It seems overwhelmingly likely that explanations of cognitive phenomena will have to appeal to [beliefs], intentions, and the like, because it appears that certain regularities in human behavior can only be captured in such terms and at that level of abstraction. For example, when a person perceives danger, he will generally set about to remove himself from the source of that danger. Now, this generalization has an unlimited variety of instances. Thus, generally, if a person *knows* how to get out of a building, and *believes* the building to be on fire, then generally he will set himself the *goal* of being out of the building, and use his knowledge to determine a series of actions to satisfy this goal. The point is that even so simple a regularity could not be captured without descriptions that use the italicized mentalistic terms (or very similar ones), because there is an infinite variety of specific ways of "knowing how to get out of the building," of coming to "believe that the building is on fire," and of satisfying the goal of being out of the building. For each combination of these, *an entirely different causal chain* would result if the situation were described in physical or strictly behavioral terms. Consequently the psychologically relevant generalization would be lost in the diversity of possible causal connections. This generalization can only be stated in terms of the agent's *internal representation* of the situation (i.e. in mentalistic terms). For a different example, the laws of color mixture are properly stated over *perceived color,* or what are called "metameric" equivalence classes of colors, rather than over physically specifiable properties of light, since they hold regardless of how the particular color is produced by the environment — e.g., whether, say, the perceived yellow is produced by radiation of (roughly) 580 nm, a mixture of approximately equal energy of radiations of 530 nm and 650 nm, by a mixture of any complex radiations that metamerically match the latter two wavelengths, or even by direct electrical or chemical stimulation of the visual system. We might never be able to specify all the possible physical stimuli that produce a particular perceived color, and yet the laws of color mixture shall hold if stated over perceived color. Hochberg presents a variety of such examples, showing that the regularities of perception must be stated over *perceived* properties — i.e., over internal representations.

Similarly, when a particular event can be given more than one interpretation, then what determines behavioral regularities is not its physical properties, or even some abstract function thereof, but rather each agent's particular *interpretation.* The classical illustrations are ambiguous stimuli, such as the Necker cube, the duck-rabbit or the profiles-vase illusions, or ambiguous sentences. Clearly, what people do (e.g., when asked what they see or hear) depends upon which reading of the ambiguity they take. But all physical events are intrinsically ambiguous, in the sense that they are subject to various interpretations; so psychological regularities will always have to be stated relative to particular readings of stimuli (i.e., how they are internally represented).

Finally, if we include *goals* as well as beliefs among the types of representations, it becomes possible to give an account of a wide range of additional regularities. Behavior that is goal-directed is characterized by such properties as equifinality (i.e., its termination can only be characterized in terms of the terminating state, rather than in terms of the path by which the system arrived at that state.

It is no accident that the systematicity of human behavior is captured in a vocabulary that refers to internal representations, for these are the terms in which we conceptualize and plan our actions in the first place. For example, as I write this paper, I produce certain movements of my fingers and hand. But I do that under control of certain higher level goals, or, as some people prefer to put it, I execute the behaviors under a certain "intended interpretation." I *intend* to make certain *statements* by my behavior. I do not intend to make marks on paper, although clearly I am doing that too. Although this hierarchical aspect of the behavioral description is part of my conceptualization of it, rather than an intrinsic part of the behavior itself, yet it is critical to how the behavior must be treated theoretically if the theory is to capture the systematicity of my actions. A theory that took my behavior to be an instance of finger-movement could not account for why, when my typewriter broke, I proceeded to make quite different movements using pencil and paper. This is an instance of the "equifinality" property associated with goal-directed behavior.

Of course, to say that folk psychology has nonfortuitously settled on some of the appropriate terms for describing our cognitive activity is not to say that it is good scientific theory. It may be that this set of terms needs to be augmented or pruned, that many of the beliefs expressed in folk psychology are either false or empirically empty, and that many of its explanations are either incomplete or circular. But its most serious shortcoming, from the point of view of the scientific enterprise, is that the collection of loose generalizations that makes up this informal body of knowledge is not tied together into an explicit system. The way in which sets of generalizations are tied together in developed sciences is through a theory that shows how the generalizations are derivable in some appropriate idealization from a smaller set of deeper universal principles (or axioms). The categories of the deeper principles are typically quite different from those found in the broader generalization (e.g. pressure and temperature are reduced to aspects of kinetic energy in molecular theory.)

## 3. REPRESENTATION AND COMPUTATION

There are many characteristics that recommend computation as the appropriate form in which to cast models of cognitive processes. For example, the hierarchical character of programs and the abstraction represented by the "information processing" level of analysis make it the ideal vehicle for expressing *functional* models of all kinds. These were the aspects of computation that led Miller, Galanter, and Pribram to propose the basic iterative loop (TOTE, or Test-Operate-Test-Exit) as the fundamental building block for psychological theory — to replace the reflex arc and even the cybernetic energy feedback loop.

What I wish to focus on here is what I take to be the most fundamental reason why cognition ought to be viewed as computation. That reason rests on the fact that computation is the only worked-out view of *process* that is both compatible with a materialist view of how a process is realized and that attributes the behavior of the process to the operation of rules upon representations. In other words, what makes it possible to view computation and cognition as processes of fundamentally the same type is the fact that both are physically realized and both are governed by rules and representations. . . . Furthermore, they both exhibit the same sort of dual character with respect to providing explanations of how they work — and for the same reason.

As a physical device, the operation of a computer can be described in terms of the causal structure of its physical properties. The states of a computer, viewed as a physical device, are individuated in terms of the identity of physical descriptions, and its state transitions are therefore connected by physical laws. By abstracting over these physical properties, it is possible to give a *functional* description of the device. This is a description of the systematic relations that hold over certain (typically very complex) classes of physical properties — such as the ones that correspond to computationally relevant states of the device. While the transitions over states defined in this way are no longer instances of physical laws (i.e., there is no *law* relating state *n* and state *m* of an IBM machine, even though it is wired up so that state *m* always follows state *n*), they are nonetheless reducible to some complex function of various physical laws and of the physical properties of states *n* and *m*. Such a functional description of the device might, for example, be summarized as a finite state transition diagram of the sort familiar in automata theory. We shall see below, however, that this is not an adequate functional description from the point of view of understanding the device as a computer.

On the other hand, if we wish to explain the computation that the device is carrying out, or the regularities exhibited by some particular *programmed* computer, we must refer to objects in a domain that is the *intended interpretation* or the subject matter of the computations, such as, for example, the abstract domain of numbers. Thus, in order to explain why the machine prints out the symbol "5" when it is provided with the expression "(PLUS 2 3)," we must refer to the meaning of the symbols in the expression and in the printout. These meanings are the referents of the symbols in the domain of numbers. The explanation of why the particular symbol "5" is printed out then follows from these semantic definitions (i.e., it prints out "5" because that symbol represents the number five, "PLUS" represents the addition operator applied to the referents of the other two symbols, etc, and five is indeed the sum of two and three). In other words, from the definition of the symbols (numerals) as representations of numbers, and from the definition of the "PLUS" as representing a certain abstract mathematical operation, it follows that some state of the machine after reading the expression will correspond to a state that represents the value of the function and (because of a further definition of the implicit printout function) causes the printout of the appropriate answer.

This is true of computation generally. We explain why the machine does something by referring to certain interpretations of its symbols in some intended domain. This is, of course, precisely what we do in describing how (and why) people do what they do. In explaining why a chess player moves some piece onto a certain square, we refer to the type of piece it is in terms of its role in chess, to the player's immediate goal, and to the rules of chess. As I suggested earlier, this way of describing the situation is not merely a way of speaking or an informal shorthand reference to a more precise functional description. Furthermore, it is not, like the functional description referred to earlier, an abstraction over a set of physical properties. There is a fundamental difference between a description of a computer's operation cast in terms of its states (i.e., equivalence classes of physical descriptions) and one cast in terms of what it is *about,* such as in the illustrative example above. The fundamental difference is that the former refers to intrinsic properties of the *device,* while the latter refers to aspects of some entirely different domain, such as chess. The former can be viewed as a syntactic description, while the latter is semantic, since it refers to the represented domain.

This dual nature of mental functioning (referred to traditionally as the functional or causal, and the intentional) has been a source of profound philosophical puzzlement for a long time. The puzzle arises because, while we believe that people do things because of their goals and beliefs, we nonetheless also assume, for the sake of unity of science and to avoid the extravagance of dualism, that this process is actually carried out by causal sequences of events that can respond only to the intrinsic physical properties of the brain. But how can the process depend both on properties of brain tissue and on some other quite different domain, such as chess or mathematics? The parallel question can of course equally be asked of computers: How can the state transitions in our example depend both on physical laws and on the abstract properties of numbers? The simple answer is that this happens because both numbers and rules relating numbers are *represented* in the machine as symbolic expressions and programs, and that it is the physical realization of these representations that determines the machine's behavior. More precisely, the abstract numbers and rules (e.g. Peano's axioms) are first expressed in terms of **syntactic** operations over symbolic expressions or some notation for the number system, and then these expressions are "interpreted" by the built-in functional properties of the physical device. Of course, the machine does not interpret the symbols as numbers, but only as formal patterns that cause the machine to function in some particular way.

Because a computational process has no access to the actual represented domain itself (e.g., a computer has no way of distinguishing whether a symbol represents a number or letter or someone's name), it is mandatory, if the rules are to continue to be semantically interpretable (say as rules of arithmetic), that all relevant **semantic** distinctions be mirrored by syntactic distinctions—i.e., by features intrinsic to the representation itself. Such features must in turn be reflected in functional differences in the operation of the device. That is what we mean when we say that a device *represents* something. Simply put, all and only syntactically encoded aspects of the represented domain can affect the way a process behaves. This rather obvious assertion is the cornerstone of the formalist approach to understanding the notion of *process.* Haugeland has made the same point, though in a slightly different way. It is also implicit in Newell's "physical symbol system" hypothesis. Many of the consequences of this characteristic of computation and of this way of looking at cognition are far-reaching, however, and not widely acknowledged. . . .

By separating the semantic and syntactic aspects of cognition, we reduce the problem of accounting for meaningful action to the problem of specifying a mechanism that operates upon meaningless symbol tokens and in doing so carries out the meaningful process being modelled (e.g. arithmetic). This, in turn, represents an important breakthrough because, while one can see how the formal process can be realized by causally connected sequences of events (as in a computer), no one has the slightest notion of how carrying out semantically interpreted rules could even be viewed as compatible with natural law. . . . That is, as far as we can see there could be no natural law which says, for example, that when (and only when) a device is in a state that represents the number *five,* and applies the operation that represents the successor function, it will go into the state that represents the number *six.* Whatever the functional states that are being invoked, there is nothing to prevent anyone from consistently and correctly interpreting the same states and the same function as representing something quite different—say, producing the name of the next person on a list, or the location of an adjacent cell in a matrix, or any other consistent interpretation. Indeed, the very same physical state recurs in computers under circumstances in which very different processes, operating in quite different domains of interpretation, are being executed. In other words, the machine's functioning is completely independent of how its states are interpreted (though it is far from clear whether this would still remain so if it were wired up through transducers to a natural environment). For that reason we can never specify the behavior of a computer unequivocally in terms of a semantically interpreted rule such as the one cited above (which referred to the domain of numbers). This is what people like Fodor, Searle, or Dreyfus mean when they say that a computer does not know what it is doing.

The formalist view requires that we take the syntactic properties of representations quite literally. It is literally true of a computer that it contains, in some functionally discernable form (which could even conceivably be a typewritten form, if someone wanted to go through the trouble of arranging the hardware that way), what could be referred to as a code or an inscription of a symbolic expression, whose formal features mirror (in the sense of bearing a one-to-one correspondence with) semantic characteristics of some represented domain, and which causes the machine to behave in a certain way. Because of the requirement that the syntactic structure of representations reflect all relevant semantic distinctions, the state transition diagram description of an automaton is an inadequate means of expressing the functional properties of a computational system. Individual states must be shown as factored into component parts rather than as being distinct atomic or holistic entities. Some functionally distinguishable aspects of the states must correspond to individual terms of the representing symbol structure, while other aspects must correspond to such additional properties as the control state of the device (which determines which operation will be carried out next) and the system's relation to the representation (e.g., whether the representation corresponds to a belief or a goal). Components of the syntactic expressions must be functionally factorable, otherwise we could not account for such regularities as that several distinct representational states may be followed by the same subsequent state, or that rules tend to be invoked in certain systematic ways in relation to one another. Indeed, one could not represent individual *rules* in the state transition notation, since individual rules affect a large (and in principle unbounded) set of different states. For example, the rule that specifies that one remove oneself from danger must be potentially evokable by every belief state a part of whose representational content corresponds to danger. By representing this regularity once for each such state, one misses the generalization corresponding to that one rule. In addition, of course, the fact that there are an unbounded number of possible thoughts and representational states makes it mandatory that the symbolic encoding of these thoughts or states be combinatoric—i.e., that they have a recursive syntactic structure. I mention all this only because there have been some who have proposed that we not view the content of states in terms of some articulation of what they represent—i.e., that we avoid postulating an internal syntax for representations, or a "mentalese."

The syntactic, representation-governed nature of computation thus lends itself to describing cognitive processes in such a way that their relation to causal laws is bridgeable, at least in principle. But beyond that, the exact nature of the device that instantiates the process is no more a direct concern to the task of discovering and explaining cognitive regularities than it is in computation—though in both cases specifying the fixed functional architecture of the underlying system is an essential component of understanding the process itself. Given that computation and cognition can be viewed in these common abstract terms, there is no reason why computation ought to be treated as merely a metaphor for cognition, as opposed to a hypothesis about the literal nature of cognition. . . .

## 4. COGNITIVE SIMULATION AND STRONG EQUIVALENCE

There is a systematic ambiguity in the use of the term "computer simulation" that occasionally causes confusion. Computers are said to simulate economic cycles, traffic flow, chemical reactions, and the motion of celestial bodies. They are also said to simulate aspects of human behavior as well as cognition. It is important, however, to understand the essential difference between the latter sense of simulation (as a psychological model) and the former. When we simulate, say, the motion of planets, the only empirical claim we make is that the coordinate values listed on the printout correspond to the ones that will actually be observed under the specified conditions. Which **algorithm** is used to compute these values is irrelevant to the veridicality of the simulation. In other words, for this purpose we do not distinguish among algorithms that compute the same input-output function. We will refer to such algorithms as being *weakly equivalent.*

The case of cognitive simulation, however, is quite different. . . . Weak equivalence is not a sufficient condition for validity of a model. Intuitively, we require that the algorithm correspond in much greater detail to the one the person actually uses. The difficulty is, of course, that we cannot directly observe this algorithm, so we must discriminate among weakly equivalent processes on the basis of other considerations. . . . Observations such as reaction time can be used as evidence for deciding among weakly equivalent algorithms. Such criteria help us to select a set of what I have referred to as complexity-equivalent processes. Other criteria, such as those that provide evidence for intermediate states and for factorable subcomponents of the process . . . define a sense of equivalence I have referred to . . . as *strong [equivalence].*

There is an important reason why strong equivalence is relevant to cognitive models, though not to other uses of computer simulation, such as those mentioned earlier. The reason was hinted at when we spoke of modelling the algorithm that the person "actually uses." The idea is that the appropriate way to functionally characterize the mental activities that determine a person's behavior is to provide an initial representational state — interpreted as representing beliefs, tacit knowledge, goals and desires, and so on — and a sequence of operations that transform this initial state, through a series of intermediate states, into the commands that are finally sent to the output transducers. All the intermediate states, on this view, are also representations which, in the model, take the form of expressions or data structures. Each of these has psychological significance: it must be interpretable as a mental representation. Thus all intermediate states of the model constitute claims about the cognitive process. . . .

Another closely related reason why strong equivalence is demanded of cognitive models, but not of models of physical processes, is that the former are assumed to be governed by rules acting upon symbolic representations. While we do not assume that planets have a symbolic representation of their orbits (or of the laws governing their trajectory), we *do* claim that the appropriate explanation of cognitive processes must appeal to the organism's use of rules and explicit symbolic representations. The distinction between behavior being governed by symbolic representations and behavior being merely exhibited by a device in virtue of the causal structure of that device is one of the most fundamental distinctions in cognitive science. We shall therefore devote the next section to examining that distinction.

## 5. REPRESENTATION-GOVERNED BEHAVIOR

The question of whether we should explain the behavior of a certain organism or device by ascribing to it certain explicit symbolic *rules and representations,* or whether we should simply describe its *dispositions to respond* (i.e. its intrinsic input-output function) in any way we find convenient (including appealing to exactly the same rules, but without the assumption that they are represented anywhere other than in the theorist's notebook, and consequently without any concern for strong equivalence), is a central philosophical issue in the foundations of cognitive science. To some extent the issue is a conceptual one and relates to the question of whether psychology has a special (and less than objective) status among the sciences. . . . In addition to this more general question, however, there is also a straightforward empirical side to this issue, to which I now turn.

Elsewhere I have sketched some general conditions under which it would be reasonable to speak of behavior as being governed by rules and representations. The general position is that whenever behavior is sufficiently plastic and stimulus-independent, we can at least assume that it is somehow mediated by internal functional states. Such states may be further viewed as representational, or epistemic, if certain other empirical conditions hold. For example, we would describe the behavior as being governed by representations and rules if the relation between environmental events and subsequent behavior, or the relations among functional states themselves, could be shown to be, among other things, a) arbitrary with respect to natural laws, b) informationally plastic, or c) functionally transparent. We elaborate briefly on these conditions below.

The relation between an event and the ensuing behavior would be said to be arbitrary if there were no *necessary* intrinsic connection between them. More precisely, a relation between an environmental event, viewed in a certain way, and a behavioral act, is said to be arbitrary if, *under that particular description of the event and the behavior,* the relation does not instantiate a natural law. For example, there can be no nomological law relating what someone says to you and what you will do, since the latter depends on such things as what you believe, what inferences you draw, what your goals are (which might include obeying totally arbitrary conventions), and, perhaps even more important, how you perceive the event (what you take it to be an instance of). Since all physical events are intrinsically ambiguous, in the sense that they can be seen in very many different ways, each of which could lead to very different behavior, the nonlawfulness of the link between these events and subsequent behavior seems clear. Systematic but nonlawlike relations among functional states are generally attributed to the operation of *rules* rather than natural laws.

The condition that I referred to as informational plasticity . . . I introduce . . . to suggest that epistemic mediation is implicated whenever the relation between environmental events and behavior can be radically, yet systematically, varied by a wide range of conditions that need have no more in common than that they provide certain information, or that they allow the organism to infer that a certain state of affairs holds—perhaps one which, if it were actually perceived, would also produce the same behavior. For example, seeing that the building you are in is on fire, smelling smoke coming in through the ventilation duct, or being told by telephone that the building is on fire, can all lead to similar behavior, and this behavior might be radically different if you believed yourself to be performing in a play at the time.

The third condition, that of transparency of relations among representations, is, in a sense, the converse of the second condition. Whereas informational plasticity reflects the susceptibility of the process between stimulus and response to cognitive influences, the transparency condition reflects the multiple availability of rules governing relations among representational states. Wherever quite different processes appear to use the same set of rules, we have a ***prima facie*** reason for believing that there is a single explicit representation of the rules, or at least a common shared subprocess, rather than independent identical multiple processes. The case can be made even stronger, however, if it is found that whenever the rules appear to change in the context of one process, the other processes also appear to change in a predictable way. In that case we would say (borrowing a term from computer science) that the rules were being used in an "interpretive" or transparent, rather than a "compiled" or opaque mode.

Such seems to be the case with grammatical rules, since we appear to have multiple access to these rules. We appeal to them to account for production, for comprehension, and for linguistic judgments. Since these three functions must be rather thoroughly coordinated (e.g., a rule first available only in comprehension soon becomes effective in the other two functions), it seems a reasonable view that they are explicitly represented and available as a symbolic code. In other words, there are cases, such as grammar, in which rules can be used not only within some specific function, but in some circumstances they can even be referred to or *mentioned* by other parts of the system. These cases argue even more strongly that the system could not simply be behaving *as if* it used rules, but must in fact have access to a symbolic encoding of the rules.

To summarize, then, a *cognitive process* is distinguished from a process in general inasmuch as it models mental events, rather than merely simulating some behavior. This means that the states of the process are representational, and that this representational content is hypothesized to be the same as the content of the mental states (i.e. tacit knowledge, goals, beliefs) being modelled. Thus the computational states do not *represent* biological states, unless by this we mean to suggest that the person being modelled is thinking about biology. The process is, however, realized or carried out by the fixed functional capacities provided by the biological substrate. These functional capacities are called the functional architecture. The decision as to whether or not a particular function should be explained by positing a cognitive process — i.e., by appeal to rules and representations — rests on certain empirical considerations. One sufficient (though not necessary) condition for a function being determined by representations is that it be influencible by beliefs and goals — i.e., that it be cognitively penetrable. Hence only cognitively impenetrable functions constitute the fixed functional capacities, or the functional architecture, out of which cognitive processes are composed. . . .

## Daniel C. Dennett (b. 1942)

Daniel C. Dennett is a contemporary philosopher of mind who has made numerous contributions to the study of cognitive science. His major works include *Content and Consciousness* (1969), *Brainstorms* (1978), and *Elbow Room* (1984).

In the following selection Dennett argues that philosophers of mind and workers in artificial intelligence have much to gain from a cooperative study of each other's disciplines. From philosophy, workers in AI can learn to free their imaginations from some overrestrictive assumptions about human cognition built into the language of computer science. They can also profit from some of the conceptual problems in philosophy of mind that have already been solved or partially solved by philosophers. On the other hand, philosophers of mind can learn to restrict their imaginations by some of the useful constraints of AI. Philosophical thought experiments are more likely to avoid mere wishful thinking if they are in contact with machines that actually put speculations into practice and show what it would be like for a mind to function in the proposed manner. In addition, there is at least one philosophical problem that Dennett believes AI has already solved, namely, how to use representations or ideas to explain mentality without generating an infinite regress of minds to interpret them and further representations and ideas to be interpreted.

Of course all of these gains presuppose that human minds are information processors in roughly the same sense that computers are, that is, that the working assumptions of contemporary cognitive science, including AI, are correct.

# Artificial Intelligence as Philosophy and as Psychology

*Daniel C. Dennett*

Philosophers of mind have been interested in computers since their arrival a generation ago, but for the most part they have been interested only in the most abstract questions of principle, and have kept actual machines at arm's length and actual programs in soft focus. Had they chosen to take a closer look at the details I do not think they would have found much of philosophic interest until fairly recently. But recent work in Artificial Intelligence, or AI, promises to have a much more variegated impact on philosophy, and so, quite appropriately, philosophers have begun responding with interest to the bold manifestos of the Artificial Intelligentsia.[1] My goal in this paper is to provide a sort of travel guide to philosophers pursuing this interest. It is well known that amateur travellers in strange lands often ludicrously misconstrue what they see, and enthusiastically report wonders and monstrosities that later investigations prove never to have existed, while overlooking genuine novelties of the greatest importance. Having myself fallen prey to a variety of misconceptions about AI, and wasted a good deal of time and energy pursuing chimaeras, I would like to alert other philosophers to some of these pitfalls of interpretation. Since I am still acutely conscious of my own amateur status as an observer of AI, I must acknowledge at the outset that my vision of what is going on in AI, what is important and why, is almost certainly still somewhat untrustworthy. There is much in AI that I have not read, and much that I have read but not understood. So traveller beware; take along any other maps you can find, and listen critically to the natives.

The interest of philosophers of mind in Artificial Intelligence comes as no surprise to many tough-minded experimental psychologists, for from their point of view the two fields look very much alike: there are the same broad generalizations and bold extrapolations, the same blithe indifference to the hard-won data of the experimentalist, the same appeal to the deliverances of casual introspection and conceptual analysis, the aprioristic reasonings about what is impossible in principle or what must be the case in psychology. The only apparent difference between the two fields, such a psychologist might say, is that the AI worker pulls his armchair up to a console. I will argue that this observation is largely justified, but should not in most regards be viewed as a criticism. There is much work for the armchair psychologist to do, and a computer console has proven a useful tool in this work.

Psychology turns out to be very difficult. The task of psychology is to explain human perception, learning, cognition, and so forth in terms that ultimately will unite psychological theory to physiology in one way or another. And there are two broad strategies one could adopt: a "bottom-up" strategy that starts with some basic and well-defined unit or theoretical atom for psychology and builds these atoms into molecules and larger aggregates that can account for the complex phenomena we all observe, or a "top-down" strategy that begins with a more abstract decomposition of the highest levels of psychological organization, and hopes to analyze these into more and more detailed smaller systems or processes until finally one arrives at elements familiar to the biologists. It is a commonplace that both endeavors could and should proceed simultaneously, but there is now abundant evidence that the bottom-up strategy in psychology is un-

Abridged from *Philosophical Perspectives in Artificial Intelligence*. Edited by Martin Ringle (Humanities Press, 1979). Reprinted by permission.

likely to prove very fruitful. The two best developed attempts at bottom-up psychology are stimulus-response behaviorism and what we might call "neuron signal physiological psychology," and both are now widely regarded as stymied, the former because stimuli and responses prove not to be perspicuously chosen atoms, the latter because even if synapses and impulse trains are perfectly good atoms, there are just too many of them, and their interactions are too complex to study once one abandons the afferent and efferent peripheries and tries to make sense of the crucial center.[2] Bottom-up strategies have not proved notably fruitful in the early development of other sciences, in chemistry and biology for instance, and so psychologists are only following the lead of "mature" sciences if they turn to the top-down approach. Within that broad strategy there are a variety of starting points that can be ordered in an array. Faced with the practical impossibility of answering the empirical questions of psychology by brute inspection (how *in fact* does the nervous system accomplish X or Y or Z?), psychologists ask themselves an easier preliminary question:

(1) How could any system (with features A, B, C, . . . ) possibly accomplish X?[3]

This sort of question is easier because it is "less empirical"; it is an *engineering* question, a quest for a solution (*any* solution) rather than a discovery. Seeking an answer to such a question can sometimes lead to the discovery of general constraints on all solutions (including of course nature's as yet unknown solution) and therein lies the value of this style of **aprioristic** theorizing. Once one decides to do psychology this way, one can choose a degree of empirical difficulty for one's question by filling in the blanks in the question schema (1).[4] The more empirical constraints one puts on the description of the system, or on the description of the requisite behavior, the greater the claim to "psychological reality" one's answer must make. For instance, one can ask how any neuronal network with such-and-such physical features could possibly accomplish human color discriminations, or we can ask how any finite system could possibly subserve the acquisition of a natural language. Or, one can ask how human memory could possibly be so organized as to make it so relatively easy for us to answer questions like "have you ever ridden an antelope?" and so relatively hard to answer "what did you have for breakfast last Tuesday?" Or, one can ask, with Kant, how anything at all could possibly experience or know anything at all. Pure epistemology thus viewed, for instance, is simply the limiting case of the psychologists' quest, and is ***prima facie*** no less valuable to *psychology* for being so neutral with regard to empirical details. Some such questions are of course better designed to yield good answers than others, but properly carried out, any such investigation can yield constraints that bind all more-data-enriched investigations.

AI workers can pitch their investigations at any level of empirical difficulty they wish; at Carnegie Mellon University, for instance, much is made of paying careful attention to experimental data on human performance and attempting to model human performance closely. Other workers in AI are less concerned with that degree of psychological reality and have engaged in a more abstract version of AI. There is much that is of value and interest to psychology at the empirical end of the spectrum but I want to claim that AI is better viewed as sharing with traditional epistemology the status of being a most general, most abstract asking of the top-down question: how is knowledge possible?[5] It has seemed to some philosophers that AI cannot be plausibly so construed because it takes on an additional burden: it restricts itself to *mechanistic* solutions, and hence its domain is not the Kantian domain of all possible modes of intelligence, but just all possible mechanistically realizable modes of intelligence. This, it is claimed, would beg the question against vitalists, dualists and other anti-mechanists. But as I have argued elsewhere, the mechanism requirement of AI is not an additional constraint of any moment. For, if psychology is possible at all, and if Church's thesis is true, the constraint of mechanism is no more severe than the constraint against begging the question in psychology, and who would wish to evade that?[6]

So I am claiming that AI shares with philosophy (in particular, with epistemology and philosophy of mind) the status of most abstract investigation of the principles of psychology. But it shares with psychology in distinction from philosophy a typical tactic in answering its questions. In AI or cognitive psychology the typical attempt to answer a *general* top-down question consists in designing a *particular* system that does, or appears to do, the relevant job, and then considering which of its features are necessary not just to one's particular system but to any such system. Philosophers have generally shunned such elaborate system-designing in favor of more doggedly general inquiry. This is perhaps the major difference between AI and "pure" philosophical approaches to the same questions, and it is one of my purposes here to exhibit some of the relative strengths and weaknesses of the two approaches.

The system-design approach that is common to AI and other styles of top-down psychology is beset by a variety of dangers of which these four are perhaps the chief:

A. designing a system with component subsystems whose stipulated capacities are miraculous given the constraints one is accepting. (e.g., positing more information-processing in a component than the relevant time and matter will allow, or, at a more abstract level of engineering incoherence, positing a subsystem whose duties would require it to be more "intelligent" or "knowledgeable" than the supersystem of which it is to be a part.)

B. mistaking conditional necessities of one's particular solution for completely general constraints: a trivial example would be proclaiming that brains use LISP; less trivial examples require careful elucidation.

C. restricting oneself artificially to the design of a subsystem, such as a depth perceiver or sentence parser, and concocting a solution that is systematically incapable of being grafted on to the other subsystems of a whole cognitive creature.

D. restricting the performance of one's system to an artificially small part of the "natural" domain of that system and providing no efficient or plausible way for the system to be enlarged.

These dangers are altogether familiar to AI, but are just as common, *if harder to diagnose conclusively,* in other approaches to psychology. Consider danger (A): both Freud's ego subsystem and J. J. Gibson's invariance-sensitive perceptual "tuning forks" have been *charged* with miraculous capacities. Danger (B): behaviorists have *been charged* with illicitly extrapolating from pigeon-necessities to people-necessities, and it is often claimed that what the frog's eye tells the frog's brain is not at all what the person's eye tells the person's brain. Danger (C): it is notoriously hard to see how Chomsky's early syntax-driven system could interact with semantical components to produce or comprehend purposeful speech. Danger (D): it is hard to see how some models of nonsense-syllable rote memorization could be enlarged to handle similar but more sophisticated memory tasks. It is one of the great strengths of AI that when one of its products succumbs to any of these dangers this can usually be quite conclusively demonstrated.

I now have triangulated AI with respect to both philosophy and psychology, as my title suggested I would: AI can be, and should often be taken to be, as abstract and "unempirical" as philosophy in the questions it attempts to answer. But at the same time, it should be as explicit and particularistic in its models as psychology at its best. Thus one might learn as much of value to psychology or epistemology from a particular but highly unrealistic AI model as one could learn from a detailed psychology of, say, Martians. A good psychology of Martians, however unlike us they might be, would certainly yield general principles of psychology or epistemology applicable to human beings. Now, before turning to the all important question: "What, so conceived, has AI accomplished?" I want to consider briefly some misinterpretations of AI that my sketch of it so far does not protect us from.

Since we are viewing AI as a species of top-down cognitive psychology, it is tempting to suppose that the decomposition of function in a computer is intended by AI to be somehow isomorphic to the decomposition of function in a brain. One learns of vast programs made up of literally billions of basic computer events and somehow so organized as to produce a simulacrum of human intelligence, and it is altogether natural to suppose that since the brain is known to be composed of billions of tiny functioning parts, and since there is a gap of ignorance between our understanding of intelligent human behavior and our understanding of those tiny parts, the ultimate, millenial goal of AI must be to provide a hierarchical breakdown of parts in the computer that will mirror or be isomorphic to some hard-to-discover hierarchical breakdown of brain-event parts. The familiar theme of "organs made of tissues made of cells made of molecules made of atoms" is to be matched, one might suppose, in electronic hardware terms. In the thrall of this picture one might be discouraged to learn that some functional parts of the nervous system do not seem to function in the digital way the atomic functioning parts in computers do. The standard response to this worry would be that one had looked too deep in the computer. This is sometimes called the "grain problem." The computer is a digital device at bottom, but a digital device can simulate an "analogue" device to any degree of continuity you desire, and at a higher level of aggregation in the computer one may find the analogue elements that are mapable onto the non-digital brain parts. As many writers have observed,[7] we cannot gauge the psychological reality of a model until we are given the commentary on the model that tells us which features of the model are intended to mirror real saliencies in nature and which are either backstage expediters of the modelling or sheer inadvertent detail. In the eighteenth century, scientists built beautiful brass clockwork models of the solar system called orreries. The *gears* of an orrery are not intended to represent anything real in the firmament, nor are the reflections of one brass globe in another. When one looks at AI programs in detail one sees mountains of digital calculation or "number crunching"; if this looks disappointingly unbiological, this is to be excused, since that part of the model's structure is to be viewed as backstage, not part of the model we are supposed to compare with nature.

This story is fine in principle, I think, and the day may come when this imagined isomorphism down to the neuronal level (but not backstage) is proclaimed. But in fact we see nothing remotely like this in current AI work. We see instead models that diverge from nature very early on the downward path. AI programs typically model relatively high-level cognitive features, such as concept learning or revision of goals or beliefs, and it does indeed often take millions of basic computer events to simulate just a handful of these intended model features. But no one really knows or cares what these basic events are, for no one supposes that any of the saliencies in the mass of activity that subserves the intended features are to be taken seriously as psychology or physiology. The psychological reality of an AI program is thus usually only intended to be skin deep; only the highest levels of program description and commentary are to be counted as the model.

The thinness of the psychological reality of AI models is obscured for the uninitiated by a particularly misleading feature of most of the AI programs that get into the limelight. What especially attracts audiences and evokes wonder is the marvelous verisimilitude of some of the programs. Consider this excerpt of conversation, minus the programmer's excellent commentary, between Terry Winograd's SHRDLU and its interlocutor. (SHRDLU is a program that lives in an imaginary "block world" where it can manipulate colored blocks on a table in response to commands and answer questions about its life in this world). Computer responses are capitalized.

> Had you touched any pyramid before you put the green one on the little cube?
> YES, THE GREEN ONE.
> When did you pick it up?
> WHILE I WAS STACKING UP THE RED CUBE, A LARGE RED BLOCK AND A LARGE GREEN CUBE.
> Why?
> TO GET RID OF IT.

Why did you do that?
TO CLEAR OFF THE RED CUBE.
Why did you clear off that cube?
TO PUT IT ON A LARGE GREEN CUBE.
Why did you do that?
BECAUSE YOU ASKED ME TO.[8]

When SHRDLU replies to the last question with "Because you asked me to," one can hardly help being struck by the apparent humanity of the response — "SHRDLU *is one of us!*" it is tempting to exclaim. If one is naive, one will be awestruck; if one is not, one will still be titillated by the illusion, for that is largely what it is. SHRDLU's response, though perfectly appropriate to the occasion, and not by coincidence, is "canned." Winograd has simply given SHRDLU this whole sentence to print at times like these. If a child gave SHRDLU's response we would naturally expect its behavior to manifest a general capacity which might also reveal itself by producing the response: "because you told me to," or "because that's what I was asked to do" or, on another occasion, "because I felt like it" or "because your assistant told me to." But these are dimensions of subtlety beyond SHRDLU.[9] Its behavior is remarkably versatile, but it does not reveal a rich knowledge of interpersonal relations, of the difference between requests and orders, of being cooperative with other people under appropriate circumstances. It should be added that Winograd's paper makes it very explicit where and to what extent he is canning SHRDLU's responses, so anyone who feels cheated by SHRDLU has simply not read Winograd. Other natural language programs do not rely on canned responses, or rely on them to a minimal extent.

The fact remains, however, that much of the antagonism to AI is due to resentment and distrust engendered by such legerdemain. Why do AI people use these tricks? For many reasons. First, they need to get some tell-tale response back from the program and it is as easy to can a **mnemonically** vivid and "natural" response as something more sober, technical and understated, such as, "REASON: PRIOR COMMAND TO DO THAT." Second, in Winograd's case he was attempting to reveal the minimal conditions for correct analysis of certain linguistic forms (note all the "problems" of pronominal antecedents in the sentences displayed), so "natural" language output to reveal correct analysis of natural language input was entirely appropriate. Third, AI people put canned responses in their programs because it is fun. It is fun to amuse one's colleagues, who are not fooled of course, and it is especially fun to bamboozle the outsiders. As an outsider one must learn to be properly unimpressed by AI verisimilitude, as one is of the chemist's dazzling forest of glass tubing, or the angry mouths full of teeth painted on World War II fighter planes. Joseph Weizenbaum's famous ELIZA program,[10] the computer "psychotherapist" who apparently listens so wisely and sympathetically to one's problems, is intended in part as an antidote to the enthusiasm generated by AI verisimilitude. It is almost all clever canning, and is not a psychologically realistic model of anything, but rather a demonstration of how easily one can be gulled into attributing too much to a program. It exploits **syntactic** landmarks in one's input with nothing approaching genuine understanding, but it makes a good show of comprehension nevertheless. One might say it was a plausible model of a Wernicke's aphasic, who can babble on with well-formed and even **semantically** appropriate responses to his interlocutor, sometimes sustaining the illusion of comprehension for quite a while.

The AI community pays a price for this misleading if fascinating fun, not only by contributing to the image of AI people as tricksters and hackers, but by fueling more serious misconceptions of the point of AI research. For instance, Winograd's real contribution in SHRDLU is not that he has produced an English speaker and understander that is psychologically realistic at many different levels of analysis, though that is what the verisimilitude strongly suggests, and what a lot of the fanfare — for which Winograd is not responsible — has assumed, but that he has explored some of the deepest demands on any system that can take direction, in a natural language, plan, change the world, and keep track of the changes wrought or contemplated. And in the course of this exploration he has clarified the problems and proposed ingenious and plausible partial solutions to them. The real contribution in Winograd's work stands quite unimpeached by the perfectly true but irrelevant charge that SHRDLU doesn't have a rich or human understanding of most of the words in its very restricted vocabulary, or is extremely slow.

In fact, paying so much attention to the performance of SHRDLU, and similar systems, reveals a failure to recognize that AI programs are not *empirical* experiments, but *thought*-experiments, prosthetically regulated by computers. Some AI people have recently become fond of describing their discipline as "experimental epistemology." This unfortunate term should make a philosopher's blood boil, but if AI called itself thought-experimental epistemology (or even better: *Gedanken*-experimental epistemology) philosophers ought to be reassured. The questions asked and answered by the thought experiments of AI are about whether or not one can obtain certain sorts of information processing, recognition, inference, control of various sorts, for instance, from certain sorts of designs. Often the answer is no. The process of elimination looms large in AI. Relatively plausible schemes are explored far enough to make it clear that they are utterly incapable of delivering the requisite behavior, and learning this is important progress even if it doesn't result in a mind-boggling robot.

The hardware realizations of AI are almost gratuitous. Like dropping the cannonballs off the Leaning Tower of Pisa, they are demonstrations that are superfluous to those who have understood the argument, however persuasive they are to the rest. Are computers then irrelevant to AI? "In principle" they are irrelevant, in the same sense as diagrams on the blackboard are "in principle" unnecessary to teaching geometry, but in practice they are not. I described them earlier as "prosthetic regulators" of thought-experiments. What I mean is this: it is notoriously difficult to keep wishful thinking out of one's thought-experiments; computer simulation forces one to recognize all the costs of one's imagined design. As Pylyshyn observes, "What is needed is . . . a technical language with which to discipline one's imagination."[11] The discipline provided by computers is undeniable, and especially palpable to the beginning programmer. It is both a good thing—for the reasons just stated—and a bad thing. Perhaps you have known a person so steeped in, say, playing bridge, that his entire life becomes, in his eyes, a series of finesses, end-plays and cross-ruffs. Every morning he draws life's trumps and whenever he can see the end of a project he views it as a lay-down. Computer languages seem to have a similar effect on people who become fluent in them. Although I won't try to prove it by citing examples, I think it is quite obvious that the "technical language" Pylyshyn speaks of can cripple an imagination in the process of disciplining it.[12]

It has been said so often that computers have huge effects on their users' imaginations that one can easily lose sight of one of the most obvious, but still underrated, ways in which computers achieve this effect, and that is the sheer speed of computers. Before computers came along the theoretician was strongly constrained to ignore the possibility of truly massive and complex processes in psychology because it was hard to see how such processes could fail to *appear* at worst mechanical and cumbersome, at best vegetatively slow, and of course a hallmark of mentality is its swiftness. One might say that the speed of thought defines the upper bound of subjective "fast," the way the speed of light defines the upper bound of objective "fast.". . . The grace in operation of AI programs may be mere illusion. Perhaps nature is graceful *all the way down,* but for better or for worse, computer speed has liberated the imagination of theoreticians by opening up the possibility and plausibility of very complex interactive information processes playing a role in the production of cognitive events so swift as to be atomic to introspection.

At last I turn to the important question. Suppose that AI is viewed as I recommend, as a most abstract inquiry into the possibility of intelligence or knowledge. Has it solved any very general problems or discovered any very important constraints or principles? I think the answer is a qualified yes. In particular, I think AI has broken the back of an argument that has bedeviled philosophers and psychologists for over two hundred years. Here is a skeletal version of it: First, the only psychology that could possibly succeed in explaining the complexities of human activity must posit internal representations. This premise has been deemed obvious by just about everyone except the radical behaviorists (both in psychology and philosophy—both Watson and Skinner, and Ryle and Malcolm). Descartes doubted almost everything but this. For the British Empiricists, the internal representations were called ideas, sensations, impressions; more recently psychologists have talked of hypotheses, maps, schemas, images, propositions, engrams, neural signals, even holograms and whole innate theories. So the first premise is quite invulnerable, or at any rate it has an impressive mandate.[13] But, second, nothing is intrinsically a representation of anything; something is a representation only *for* or *to* someone; any representation or system of representations thus requires at least one user or interpreter of the representation who is external to it. Any such interpreter must have a variety of psychological or intentional traits[14]: it must be capable of a variety of *comprehension,* and must have beliefs and goals, so that it can use the representation to inform itself and thus assist it in achieving its goals. Such an interpreter is then a sort of **homunculus.**

Therefore, psychology *without* homunculi is impossible. But psychology *with* homunculi is doomed to circularity or infinite regress, so psychology is impossible.

The argument given is a relatively abstract version of a familiar group of problems. For instance, it seems to many that we cannot account for perception unless we suppose it provides us with an internal image or model or map of the external world. And yet what good would that image do us unless we have an inner eye to perceive it, and how are we to explain *its* capacity of perception? It also seems to many that understanding a heard sentence must be somehow translating it into some internal message. But how will this message in turn be understood, by translating it into something else? The problem is an old one. Let's call it Hume's Problem, for while he did not state it explicitly, he appreciated its force and strove mightily to escape its clutches. Hume's internal representations were impressions and ideas, and he wisely shunned the notion of an inner self that would intelligently manipulate these items. But this left him with the necessity of getting the ideas and impressions to "think for themselves." The result was his theory of the self as a "bundle" of nothing but impressions and ideas. He attempted to set these impressions and ideas into dynamic interaction by positing various associationistic links, so that each succeeding idea in the stream of consciousness dragged its successor onto the stage according to one or another principle, all without benefit of intelligent *supervision.* It didn't work, of course. It couldn't conceivably work, and Hume's failure is plausibly viewed as the harbinger of doom for any remotely analogous enterprise. On the one hand how could any theory of psychology make sense of representations that understand themselves, and on the other how could any theory of psychology avoid regress or circularity if it posits at least one representation-understander in addition to the representations?

Now no doubt some philosophers and psychologists who have appealed to internal representations over the years have believed in their hearts that somehow the force of this argument could be blunted, that Hume's problem could be solved. But I am sure no one had the slightest idea how to do this until AI and the notion of data-structures came along. Data-structures may or may not be biologically or psychologically realistic representations, but they are, if not living, breathing examples, at least clanking, functioning examples of representations that can be said in the requisite sense to understand themselves.[15]

How this is accomplished can be metaphorically described (and any talk about internal representations is bound to have a large element of metaphor in it) by elaborating our description of AI as a top-down theoretical inquiry.[16] One starts, in AI, with a specification of a whole person or cognitive organism—what I call, more neutrally, an intentional system[17]—or some artificial segment of that person's abilities, such as chess-playing, or answering questions about baseball, and then breaks that largest intentional system into an organization of subsystems, each of which could itself be viewed as an intentional system, with its own specialized beliefs and desires, and hence as formally a homunculus. In fact homunculus talk is ubiquitous in AI, and is almost always illuminating. AI homunculi talk to each other, wrest control from each other, volunteer, sub-contract, supervise and even kill. There seems no better way of describing what is going on.[18] Homunculi are bogeymen only if they duplicate entire the talents they are rung in to explain, a special case of danger (A). If one can get a team or committee of relatively ignorant, narrow-minded, blind homunculi to produce the intelligent behavior of the whole, this is progress. A flow chart is typically the organizational chart of a committee of homunculi (investigators, librarians, accountants, executives); each box specifies a homunculus by prescribing a function without saying how it is to be accomplished. One says, in effect, put a little man in there to do the job. If we then look closer at the individual boxes, we see that the function of each is accomplished by subdividing it, via another flow chart, into still smaller, more stupid homunculi. Eventually this nesting of boxes within boxes lands you with homunculi so stupid (all they have to do is remember whether to say yes or no when asked) that they can be, as one says, "replaced by a machine." One discharges fancy homunculi from one's scheme by organizing armies of such idiots to do the work.

When homunculi at a level interact, they do so by sending messages, and each homunculus has representations which it uses to execute its functions. Thus typical AI discussions do draw a distinction between representation and representation-user.[19] They take the first step of the threatened infinite regress. But as many writers in AI have observed,[20] it has gradually emerged from the tinkerings of AI that there is a trade-off between sophistication in the representation and sophistication in the user. The more raw and uninterpreted the representation—like the mosaic of retinal stimulation at an instant—the more sophisticated the interpreter or user of the representation. The more interpreted a representation—the more procedural information is embodied in it, for instance—the less fancy the interpreter need be. It is this fact that permits one to get away with lesser homunculi at high levels, by getting their earlier or lower brethren to do some of the work. One never quite gets completely self-understanding representations, unless one stands back and views all representation in the system from a global vantage point, but all homunculi are ultimately discharged. One gets the advantage of the tradeoff only by sacrificing versatility and universality in one's subsystems and their representations,[21] so one's homunculi cannot be too versatile nor can the messages they send and receive have the full flavor of normal human linguistic interaction. We've seen an example of how homuncular communications may fall short in SHRDLU's remark "because you asked me to." The context of production and the function of the utterance makes clear that this is a sophisticated communication and the product of a sophisticated representation, but it is not a fully-fledged Gricean speech act. If it were, it would require too fancy a homunculus to use it.

There are two ways a philosopher might view AI data structures. One could grant that they are indeed self-understanding representations or one could cite the various disanalogies between them and prototypical or real representations, such as human statements, paintings, or maps, and conclude that data-structures are not really internal representations at all. But if one takes the latter line, the modest successes of AI simply serve to undercut our first premise: it is no longer obvious that psychology needs internal representations; internal pseudo-representations may do just as well.

It is certainly tempting to argue that since AI has provided us with the only known way of solving Hume's Problem, albeit for very restrictive systems, it must be on the right track, and its categories must be psychologically real, but one might well be falling into danger (B) if one did. We can all be relieved and encouraged to learn that there is a way of solving Hume's Problem, but it has yet to be shown that AI's way is the only way it can be done.

AI has made a major contribution to philosophy and psychology by revealing a particular way in which simple cases of Hume's Problem can be solved. What else has it accomplished of interest to philosophers? I will close by drawing attention to the two main areas where I think the AI approach is of particular relevance to philosophy.

For many years philosophers and psychologists have debated, with scant interdisciplinary communication, about the existence and nature of mental images. These discussions have been relatively fruitless, largely, I think, because neither side had any idea of how to come to grips with Hume's Problem. Recent work in AI, however, has recast the issues in a more perspicuous and powerful framework, and anyone hoping to resolve this ancient issue will find help in the AI discussions.[22]

The second main area of philosophical interest, in my view, is the so-called frame problem.[23] The frame problem is an abstract epistemological problem that was in effect discovered by AI thought-experimentation. When a cognitive creature, an entity with many beliefs about the world, performs an act, the world changes and many of the creature's beliefs must be revised or updated. How? It cannot be that we perceive and notice all the changes. For one thing, many of the changes we know to occur do not occur in our perceptual fields, and hence it cannot be that we rely entirely on perceptual input to revise our beliefs. So we must have internal ways of up-dating our beliefs that will fill in the gaps and keep our internal model, the totality of our beliefs, roughly faithful to the world.

If one supposes, as philosophers traditionally have, that one's beliefs are a set of propositions, and reasoning is inference or deduction from members of the set, one is in for trouble, for it is quite clear, though still controversial, that systems relying only on such processes get swamped by combinatorial explosions in the updating effort. It seems that our entire conception of belief and reasoning must be radically revised if we are to explain the undeniable capacity of human beings to keep their beliefs roughly consonant with the reality they live in.

I think one can find an appreciation of the frame problem in Kant (we might call the frame problem Kant's Problem) but unless one disciplines one's thought-experiments in the AI manner, philosophical proposals of solutions to the problem, including Kant's of course, can be viewed as at best suggestive, at worst mere wishful thinking.

I do not want to suggest that philosophers abandon traditional philosophical method and retrain themselves as AI workers. There is plenty of work to do through thought-experimentation and argumentation disciplined by the canons of philosophical method and informed by the philosophical tradition. Some of the most influential recent work in AI—Minsky's papers on "Frames" is a good example—is loaded with recognizably philosophical speculations of a relatively unsophisticated nature. Philosophers, I have said, should study AI. Should AI workers study philosophy? Yes, unless they are content to reinvent the wheel every few days. When AI reinvents a wheel, it is typically square, or at best hexagonal, and can only make a few hundred revolutions before it stops. Philosophers' wheels, on the other hand, are perfect circles, require in principle no lubrication, and can go in at least two directions at once. Clearly a meeting of minds is in order.[24]

## NOTES AND REFERENCES

1. J. Weizenbaum, *Computer power and human reason* (1976) p. 179, credits Louis Fein with this term.
2. Cf. My *Content and consciousness* (1969) ch. IV and "Why the law of effect will not go away," *Journal of the Theory of Social Behavior* (Oct. 1975).
3. George Smith and Barbara Klein have pointed out to me that this question can be viewed as several ways ambiguous, and hence a variety of quite dif-

ferent responses might be held to answer such a question. Much of what I say below about different tactics for answering a question of this form can be construed to be about tactics for answering different, but related, questions. Philosophers who intend a question of this sort rhetorically can occasionally be embarrassed to receive in a reply a detailed answer of one variety or another.

4. Cf. Zenon Pylyshyn, "Complexity and the study of artificial and human intelligence," for a particularly good elaboration of the top-down strategy, a familiar theme in AI and Cognitive Psychology. Moore and Newell's "How Can MERLIN Understand?" in Lee W. Gregg, *Knowledge and Cognition,* NY (1974), is the most clear and self-conscious employment of this strategy I have found. Cf. also my "Why the law of effect will not go away."
5. This question, and attempts to answer it, constitutes one main branch of epistemology; the other main branch has dealt with the problem of skepticism, and its constitutive question might be "is knowledge possible?"
6. "Why the law of effect will not go away." In summary, the argument is that psychology is impossible if it cannot discharge all its homunculi, but, if it can, then its ultimate non-homuncular constituents will have capacities requiring no intelligence and hence these constituents can be viewed as computing functions that are intuitively "effective," hence mechanistically realizable if Church's thesis is true, as there seems no reason to doubt. See also Judson Webb, "Gödel's theorem and Church's thesis: A prologue to mechanism," *Boston Studies in the Philosophy of Science,* Vol. 31 (1976) Reidel.
7. See esp. Wilfrid Sellars, *Science, Perception and Reality,* (1963) 182 ff.
8. Terry Winograd, *Understanding natural language,* NY (Academic Press, 1972) 12 ff.
9. Cf. Correspondence between Weizenbaum, *et al.* in *Communications of the Association for Computing Machinery;* Weizenbaum, CACM, Vol. 17, no. 7 (July, 1974) 425; Arbib, CACM 17:9 (Sept, 1974) 543; McLeod, CACM 18:9 (Sept, 1975) 546; Wilks, CACM 19:2 (Feb, 1976) 108; Weizenbaum and McLeod, CACM 19:6 (June, 1976) 362.
10. J. Weizenbaum, "Contextual understanding by computers," CACM 10:8 (1967) 474-480; also *Computer power and human reason.*
11. Cf. Pylyshyn, op cit.
12. Cf. Weizenbaum, *Computer power and human reason,* for a detailed support of this claim.
13. Cf. Jerry Fodor, *The language of thought* (1975) and my Critical Notice, *Mind* (April, 1977).
14. Cf. my "Intentional systems," *Journal of Philosophy* (1971).
15. Joseph Weizenbaum has pointed out to me that Turing saw from the very beginning that computers could, in principle, break the threatened regress of Hume's Problem, and George Smith has drawn my attention to similar early wisdom in Von Neumann. It has taken a generation of development for their profound insights to be, after a fashion, confirmed by detailed models. It is one thing—far from negligible—to proclaim a possibility in principle, and another to reveal how the possibility might be made actual in detail. Before the relatively recent inventions of AI, the belief that Hume's Problem could be dissolved somehow by the conceptual advances of computer science provided encouragement but scant guidance to psychologists and philosophers.
16. What follows is an elaboration of my discussion in "Why the law of effect will not go away."
17. Cf. "Intentional systems," loc. cit.
18. Cf. Jerry Fodor, "The appeal to tacit knowledge in psychological explanation," *J. Phil* (1968); F. Attneave, "In defense of homunculi," in W. Rosenblith, (ed) *Sensory communication,* Cambridge, Mass (MIT Press, 1960); R. deSousa, "Rational Homunculi," in A. Rorty, (ed) *The Identities of Persons* (1976); Elliot Sober, "Mental representations," *Synthese,* 33 (1976).
19. See e.g. Daniel Bobrow, "Dimensions of representation," in D. Bobrow and A. Collins (eds) *Representation and understanding,* (Academic Press, 1975).
20. W. A. Woods, "What's in a link?" in Bobrow and Collins, op. cit.; Z. Pylyshyn, "Imagery and artificial intelligence," in C. Wade Savage (ed) *Minnesota Studies in the Philosophy of Science,* Vol IX; and Pylyshyn, "Complexity and the study of human and artificial intelligence." M. Minsky, "A framework for representing knowledge," in P. Winston (ed) *The Psychology of Computer Vision,* New York (Prentice-Hall, 1975).
21. Cf. Winograd on the costs and benefits of declarative representations in Bobrow and Collins, op. cit. p. 188.
22. See, e.g. Winston, op. cit. and Pylyshyn, "Imagery and artificial intelligence," op. cit., "What the mind's eye tells the mind's brain," *Psychological Bulletin,* (1972) and the literature referenced in these papers.
23. See, e.g. Pylyshyn's paper in this volume; Winograd in Bobrow and Collins, op. cit., Moore and Newell, op. cit., Minsky, op. cit.
24. I am indebted to Margaret Boden for valuable advice on an early draft of this paper. Her book, *Artificial Intelligence and Natural Man,* (Harvester, 1978), provides an excellent introduction to the field of AI for philosophers.

## *Hubert L. Dreyfus (b. 1929)*

Hubert L. Dreyfus is a contemporary philosopher who has written extensively in phenomenology and existential philosophy in addition to his philosophical criticisms of the field of artificial intelligence. He is the editor of *Husserl, Intentionality and Cognitive Science* (with H. Hall, 1982) and the author of *What Computers Can't Do* (1979), *Michel Foucault: Beyond Structuralism and Hermeneutics* (1983), *Mind over Machine* (with S. Dreyfus, 1986), and *Being-in-the-World: A Commentary on Heidegger's Being and Time* (1986).

In the essay below Dreyfus argues that digital computers will never display ordinary commonsense understanding or intuitive expertise, and that these are the hallmarks of intelligent human behavior. Digital computers can only possess information in the form of representations, all of whose possibly relevant features must be explicit. And the only processes of which the computer is capable are explicit feature-determined and rule-guided operations on these representations. Dreyfus argues that ordinary human knowledge does not consist of such information, and that intuitive expertise in all areas, from the exercise of common sense to the employment of highly technical skills, is not guided by explicit rules of this sort at all. If these claims are correct, it means that the attempt by AI researchers to represent human knowledge and duplicate intelligent human behavior with digital computers is fundamentally misguided.

# Misrepresenting Human Intelligence

### *Hubert L. Dreyfus*

In *What Computers Can't Do*[1] I argued that research in artificial intelligence (AI for short) was based upon mistaken assumptions about the nature of human knowledge and understanding. In the first part of this essay I will review that argument briefly. In spite of the noisy protestations from AI researchers, most of my critical claims and negative predictions have not only been borne out by subsequent research and developments in the field, but have even come to be acknowledged as accurate indications of major problems by AI workers themselves. In the years since the revised edition of my book was published, what I have come to see is not only that my early pessimism was well-founded, but also that some of my assessments for the future of AI were overly optimistic. In the second part of this essay I will explain why I now believe that even the cautious and guarded optimism which I once had with respect to certain isolated areas of AI research was unjustified and, ultimately, mistaken.

## I

The early stages of AI research were characterized by overly ambitious goals, wishful rhetoric and outlandish predictions. The goal, in general, was to equal or exceed the capacities of human beings in every area of intelligent behavior. The rhetoric turned failure after failure into partial and promising success. And the predictions had computers doing everything an intelligent human being could do within a decade or so at most. The terms on these predictions have all expired with none of the miraculous feats accomplished, and most researchers have begun to face the hard facts about the real limits of artificial intelligence.

The basic project of AI research is to produce genuine intelligence by means of a programmed digital computer. This requires, in effect, that human knowledge and understanding be reconstructed out of bits of isolated and meaningless data and sequences of rule-governed operations. The problems facing this approach can be put quite simply. Human knowledge and understanding do not consist of such data, rules and operations; and nothing which does consist essentially of these things will ever duplicate any interesting range of intelligent human behavior.

Early research projects in artificial intelligence tried to meet head on the task of duplicating human mentality. Major areas of emphasis included natural language understanding, pattern recognition and general problem solving. Problems in each of these areas were seen initially as problems of size — organizing and using a very large quantity of data. In order to understand even a small and ordinary sample of natural language, for example, a very large mass of background facts seemed to be required, and this massive collection of facts seemed in turn to require some kind of organization in terms of relevance so that not every fact required explicit consideration in every exercise of linguistic understanding. Pattern recognition research ran into similar problems. The number of possibly relevant features was immense and rules for separating those features actually relevant to recognition of a given shape or figure from all the others proved incredibly difficult to formulate. More general problem solving faced exactly the same difficulties, only several orders of magnitude larger due to the increased generality of the task.

In the first edition of *What Computers Can't Do* I argued that the problems encountered by AI workers in these research areas were not just a matter of size, and would not succumb to more efficient programs and programming languages or to dramatic increases in computing speed and storage capacity. None of the available empirical evidence suggested that human beings function in the manner required by then current AI models, and much of the evidence suggested an entirely different and incompatible view of human mentality — but this view emerges only after some long-standing psychological and philosophical assumptions are discarded. Those assumptions lie at the very heart of the information processing model of the mind. Put generally, there is only one assumption — that human mental processes are essentially identical to those of a digital computer. Put more specifically, the crucial assumptions are these: 1) that mental processes are sequences of rule-governed operations and 2) that these operations are carried out on determinate bits of data (symbols) which represent features of or facts about the world (information, but only in a technical sense of that term). I can best explain why those specific assumptions are implausible by looking at the problems encountered in each area of AI research.

The main problem for programs whose aim was to understand natural language was the need to do so either without any context to determine or disambiguate meaning, or else with a context completely spelled out in terms of explicit facts, features, and rules for relating them. Even the meanings of individual terms are context- or situation-determined. Whether the word "pen" refers to a writing implement, a place for infants to play, a place in which pigs or other animals are kept, the area of a baseball field in which pitchers warm up or a place for confining criminals is determined by the context in which the term appears within a story or conversation. It is even clearer that context determines the meaning of whole sentences. "The book is in the pen" could mean that the child's storybook is in the playpen, that the pigs' enclosure is where the paperback fell out of the farmer's pocket, that the microfilm of the diary is cleverly concealed in the compartment containing the ink cartridge, and so on. We human beings don't seem to need to explicitly consider all the alternatives; and, in fact, it's not even clear that there could be an exhaustive list of all the alternative meanings for typical samples of natural language. We are always involved in a situation or context which seems to restrict the range of possible meanings without requiring explicit or exhaustive consideration of the range of context-free alternatives.

The obvious solution from the standpoint of AI would be to give the computer the situation. The attempt to do this in a general way has been unsuccessful, and begs some important questions. The most important question begged is whether or not our command of the situation is just a matter of a number of facts which we accept, that is, a system of beliefs which could be made explicit. If it is, then it could, at least in principle, be given to a computer, and the only problems would be practical, problems of size and structure for the belief system. If our command of the situation cannot be represented as such a belief system, however, then there will be no way to get the computer into the situation or the situation into the computer so as to duplicate general human understanding. I believe that this is the real impasse which AI faces.

Influenced by philosophers such as Heidegger and Merleau-Ponty, I believe the evidence points toward the following picture of the relation between facts and situations. Our sense of the situation we are in determines how we interpret things, what significance we place on the facts, and even what counts as facts for us at any given time. But our sense of the situation we are in is not just our belief in a set of facts, nor is it a product of independent facts or context-free features of our environment. The aspects of our surroundings which somehow give us our sense of our current situation are themselves products of a situation we were already in, so that situations grow out of situations without recourse to situation-neutral facts and features at any point. We never get into a situation from outside any situation whatsoever, nor do we do so by means of context-free data. But the computer has only such data to work with and must start completely unsituated. From the standpoint of the programmer, our natural situatedness consists of an indefinite regress of situations with no way to break in from the outside, no way to start from nothing. And this is only part of the problem for AI. Not only can the situation not be constructed out of context-free facts and features, but in fact the situation as it figures in intelligent human behavior is not primarily a matter of facts and features of any kind. It is much more like an implicit and very general sense of appropriateness, and seems to be triggered by global similarities to previously experienced situations rather than by any number of individual facts and features. I will try to make clear just how I think this works in the second part of this essay. Here I will simply observe that, lacking access to anything very like the human situation, it is not surprising that digital computers also lack access to anything very like human understanding.

Pattern recognition programs encountered similarly instructive difficulties. Whether it is a matter of recognizing perceived figures and shapes or the similarity of board positions or sequences of moves in a game of chess, the context seems to guide human pattern recognition in ways that cannot be duplicated by the computer using context-free features and precise rules for relating them. Our sense of our situation seems to allow us to zero in on just those features that are relevant to the task at hand and to virtually ignore an indefinite number of further features. Moreover, a great deal of human pattern recognition seems to be based on the perception of global similarity and not to involve any feature by feature comparison at all.

The expert chess player sees the board in terms of fields of force rather than precise positions of each of the individual pieces, recognizes intuitively the similarity to situations encountered in previous games even though none of the individual positions of pieces and few of the objective relations among individual pieces are the same, and selects a move after explicitly examining relatively few alternatives. The computer, on the other hand, analyzes the board in terms of the position of each of the pieces and then either has recourse to heuristic rules which connect that information to precise moves or else uses brute computing force to examine every possible course of action to as great a depth as time will allow. The latter strategy has been more successful, but the moves selected by this technique are still inferior to those chosen by the human expert in spite of the fact that the computer examines thousands of times as many future positions in its selection process. I will explain exactly why this is so in the second part of the essay.

Humans also recognize people they know or familiar surroundings without noticing, much less carefully comparing, the individual features of the persons or things recognized. Duplicating this kind of ordinary recognition has proven impossible for AI. The reason, I think, is the same as in the case of the expert chess player, but more on this later.

Programs designed to duplicate the general human ability to solve problems achieved results only by restricting the task in such a way that general human problem solving was never at issue. Programs typically solved word puzzles which were restricted so as to include only relevant information and which contained explicit cues to invoke the correct heuristic rule as needed. The human ability to identify the kind of problem faced, to sort information in terms of relevance, and to find the correct method of solution on the basis of similarity to previously solved problems—that is, full-fledged human problem solving—was simply bypassed, supplied, in effect, by the human 'processing' of the problems to be 'solved'.

In the late sixties and early seventies, the difficulties described above were taken seriously by workers in AI. Instead of trying to duplicate in one giant step general human understanding of the world, attention turned to producing understanding in very restricted 'worlds'. These artificially restricted domains were called 'micro-worlds'. Impressive micro-world successes included Terry Winograd's SHRDLU, Thomas Evans's Analogy Problem Program, David Waltz's Scene Analysis Program and Patrick Winston's program for learning concepts from examples. The micro-worlds were constrained in such a way that the problems of context-restricted relevance and context-determined meaning seemed to be manageable. The hope was that micro-world techniques could be extended to more general domains, the micro-worlds made increasingly more realistic and combined to eventually produce the everyday world, and the computer's capacity to cope with these micro-worlds thereby transformed into genuine artificial intelligence.

The subsequent failure of every attempt to generalize micro-world techniques beyond the artificially restricted domains for which they were invented has put an end to the hopes inspired by early micro-world successes and brought AI to a virtual standstill. Some researchers, including Winograd, have given up on AI entirely. The micro-world strategy failures have been instructive, however, focussing attention in the direction I had argued was crucial for more than a decade, namely, toward the nature of everyday human understanding and know-how. The problem encountered in the attempt to move from micro-worlds to any aspect of the everyday world is that micro-worlds aren't worlds at all, or, from the other side, domains within the everyday world aren't anything like micro-worlds. This insight emerged in the attempt to program children's story understanding. It was soon discovered that the 'world' of even a single child's story, unlike a micro-world, is not a self-contained domain and cannot be treated independently of the larger everyday world onto which it opens. Everyday understanding is presupposed in every real domain, no matter how small. The everyday world is not composed of smaller independent worlds at all, is not like a building which can be built up of tiny bricks—but is rather a whole somehow present in each of its parts. Once this was realized, micro-world research and its successes were recognized for what they really were, not small steps toward the programming of everyday or common-sense know-how and understanding, but clever evasions of the real need to program such general competence and understanding. And the prospects for programming a digital computer to display our everyday understanding of the world were looking less bright all the time. Cognitive scientists were discovering the importance of images and prototypes in human understanding. Gradually most researchers were becoming convinced that humans form images and compare them by means of holistic processes very different from the logical operations which computers perform on symbolic descriptions.[2]

A recent *Scientific American* article echoed my earlier assessment of AI:

> Probably the most telling criticism of current work in artificial intelligence is that it has not yet been successful in modeling what is called common sense. . . . [S]ubstantially better models of human cognition must be developed before systems can be designed that will carry out even simplified versions of common-sense tasks.[3]

## II

For the reasons discussed in the preceding section, I concluded in 1979[4] that AI would remain at a standstill in areas that required common-sense understanding of the everyday world, that there would be no major breakthroughs in interpreting ordinary samples of natural language, in recognizing ordinary objects or patterns in everyday contexts, or in everyday problem solving of any kind within a natural rather than artificially constrained setting. The evidence to date indicates that I was correct in my assessment of AI's prospects in these areas. However I also predicted success for AI in certain isolated tasks, cut off from the everyday world and seemingly self-contained, tasks such as medical diagnosis and spectrograph analysis. It appeared to me at the time that ordinary common sense played no role in such tasks and that the computer, with its massive data storage capacity and ability to perform large numbers of inferences almost instantaneously and with unerring accuracy, might well equal or exceed the performance of human experts. It has turned out that I was mistaken about this. In a book that we have just finished,[5] my brother, Stuart, and I attempt to explain this surprising result. Here I can give only a brief account of that explanation.

The attempt to give computers human expertise in these special domains has come to be referred to as "expert systems" research. It works as follows. Human experts in the domain are interviewed to ascertain the rules or principles which they employ. These are then programmed into the computer. The idea seems simple and uncontroversial. Human experts and computers work from the same facts with the same inference rules. Since the computer can't forget or overlook any of the facts, can't make any faulty inferences, and can make correct inferences much more swiftly than the human expert, the expertise of the computer should be superior. And yet in study after study the computer proves inferior to the human experts who provide its working principles. To understand how this is possible, we need to look closely at the process by which humans acquire expertise.

The following model of the stages of skill acquisition emerged from our study of that process among airplane pilots, chess players, automobile drivers, and adult learners of a second language. We later found that our model fit almost perfectly data which had been gathered independently on the acquisition of nursing skills.[6] The model consists of five stages of increasing skill which I will summarize briefly in terms of the chess players. For more mundane skills such as automobile driving, you may be able to check much of the model against your own past experience.

### Stage 1 — Novice

During this first stage of skill acquisition through instruction, the novice is taught to recognize various objective facts and features relevant to the skill, and acquires rules for determining what to do based upon these facts and features. Relevant elements of the situation are defined so clearly and objectively for the novice that recognition of them requires no reference to the overall situation in which they occur. Such elements are, in this sense, context-free. The novice's rules are also context-free in the sense that they are simply to be applied to these context-free elements regardless of anything else that may be going on in the overall situation. For example, the novice chess player is given a formula for assigning point values to pieces independent of their position, and the rule, "always exchange your pieces for the opponent's if the total value of pieces captured exceeds that of pieces lost." The novice is generally not taught that there are situations in which this rule should be violated.

The novice typically lacks a coherent sense of his overall task and judges his performance primarily in terms of how well he has followed the rules he has learned. After he acquires more than just a few such rules, the exercise of this skill requires such concentration that his capacity to talk or listen to advice becomes very limited.

The mental processes of the novice are easily imitated by the digital computer. Since it can use more rules and consider more context-free elements in a given amount of time, the computer typically outperforms the novice.

### Stage 2 — Advanced Beginner

Performance reaches a barely acceptable level only after the novice has considerable experience in coping with real situations. In addition to the ability to handle more context-free facts and more sophisticated rules for dealing with them, this experience has the more important effect of enlarging the learner's conception of the world of the skill. Through practical experience in concrete situations with meaningful elements which neither instructor nor learner can define in terms of objectively recognizable context-free features, the advanced beginner learns to recognize when these elements are present. This recognition is based entirely on perceived similarity to previously experienced examples. These new features are situational rather than context-free. Rules for acting may now refer to situational as well as context-free elements. For example, the advanced chess beginner learns to recognize and avoid over-extended positions, and to respond to such situational aspects of board positions as a weakened king's side or a strong pawn structure even though he lacks precise objective definitional rules for their identification.

Because the advanced beginner has no context-free rules for identifying situational elements, he can communicate this ability to others only by the use of examples. Thus the capacity to identify such features, as well as the ability to use rules which refer to them, is beyond the reach of the computer. The use of concrete examples and the ability to learn context-determined features from them, easy for human beings but impossible for the computer, represents a severe limitation on computer intelligence.

### Stage 3 — Competence

As a result of increased experience, the number of recognizable elements present in concrete situations, both context-free and situational, eventually becomes overwhelming. To cope with this the competent performer learns or is taught to view the process of decision making in a hierarchical manner. By choosing a plan and examining only the relatively small number of facts and features which are most important, given the choice of plan, he can both simplify and improve his performance. A competent chess player,* for example, may decide, after studying his position and weighing alternatives, that he can attack his opponent's king. He would then ignore certain weaknesses in his own position and personal losses created by his attack, and the removal of pieces defending the enemy king would become salient.

The choice of a plan, although necessary, is no simple matter for the competent performer. It is not governed by an objective procedure like the context-free feature recognition of the novice. But performance at this level requires the choice of an organizing plan. And this choice rad-

* Such a player would have a rating of approximately Class A, which would rank him in the top 20 percent of tournament players.

ically alters the relation between the performer and his environment. For the novice and the advanced beginner, performance is entirely a matter of recognizing learned facts and features and then applying learned rules and procedures for dealing with them. Success and failure can be viewed as products of these learned elements and principles, of their adequacy or inadequacy. But the competent performer, after wrestling with the choice of a plan, feels personally responsible for, and thus emotionally involved in, the outcome of that choice. While he both understands his initial situation and decides upon a particular plan in a detached manner, he finds himself deeply involved in what transpires thereafter. A successful outcome will be very satisfying and leave a vivid memory of the chosen plan and the situation as organized in terms of that plan. Failure, also, will not be easily forgotten.

### Stage 4 — Proficiency

The novice and advanced beginner simply follow rules. The competent performer makes conscious choices of goals and plans for achieving them after reflecting upon various alternatives. This actual decision making is detached and deliberative in nature, even though the competent performer may agonize over the selection because of his involvement in its outcome.

The proficient performer is usually very involved in his task and experiences it from a particular perspective as a result of recent previous events. As a result of having this perspective, certain features of the situation will stand out as salient and others will recede into the background and be ignored. As further events modify these salient features, there will be a gradual change in plans, expectations, and even which features stand out as salient or important. No detached choice or deliberation is involved in this process. It seems to just happen, presumably because the proficient performer has been in similar situations in the past and memory of them triggers plans similar to those which worked in the past and expectations of further events similar to those which occurred previously.

The proficient performer's understanding and organizing of his task is intuitive, triggered naturally and without explicit thought by his prior experience. But he will still find himself thinking analytically about what to do. During this reasoning, elements that present themselves as salient due to the performer's intuitive understanding will be evaluated and combined by rule to yield decisions about the best way to manipulate the environment. The spell of involvement in the world of the skill is temporarily broken by this detached and rule-governed thinking. For example, the proficient chess player* can recognize a very large repertoire of types of positions. Recognizing almost immediately, and without conscious effort, the sense of a position, he sets about calculating a move that best achieves his intuitively recognized plan. He may, for example, know that he should attack, but he must deliberate about how best to do so.

### Stage 5 — Expertise

The expert performer knows how to proceed without any detached deliberation about his situation or actions, and without any conscious contemplation of alternatives. While deeply involved in coping with his environment, he does not see problems in a detached way, does not work at solving them, and does not worry about the future or devise plans. The expert's skill has become so much a part of him that he need be no more aware of it than he is of his own body in ordinary motor activity. In fact tools or instruments become like extensions of the expert's body. Chess grandmasters,† for example, when engrossed in a game, can lose entirely the awareness that they are manipulating pieces on a board, and see themselves instead as involved participants in a world of opportunities, threats,

---

* Such players are termed masters; the roughly 400 American masters rank in the top 1 percent of all serious players.

† There are about two dozen players holding this rank in the U.S. and they, as well as about four dozen slightly less strong players called International Masters, qualify as what we call experts.

strengths, weaknesses, hopes and fears. When playing rapidly they sidestep dangers in the same automatic way that a child, himself an expert, avoids missiles in a familiar video game. In general, experts neither solve problems nor make decisions; they simply do what works. The performance of the expert is fluid and his involvement in his task unbroken by detached deliberation or analysis.

The fluid performance of the expert is a natural extension of the skill of the proficient performer. The proficient performer, as a result of concrete experience, develops an intuitive understanding of a large number of situations. The expert recognizes an even larger number along with the associated successful tactic or decision. When a situation is recognized, the associated course of action simultaneously presents itself to the mind of the expert performer. It has been estimated that a master chess player can distinguish roughly 50,000 types of positions. We doubtless store far more typical situations in our memories than words in our vocabularies. Consequently these reference situations, unlike the situational elements learned by the advanced beginner, bear no names and defy complete verbal description.

The grandmaster chess player recognizes a vast repertoire of types of positions for which the desirable tactic or move becomes immediately obvious. Excellent chess players can play at a rate of speed at which they must depend almost entirely on intuition and hardly at all upon analysis and the comparison of alternatives, without any serious degradation in their performance. In a recent experiment International Master Julio Kaplan was required rapidly to add numbers presented to him audibly at the rate of about one number per second, while at the same time playing five-second-a-move chess against a slightly weaker, but master level, player. Even with his analytical mind completely occupied with the addition, Kaplan more than held his own against the master in a series of games. Deprived of the time necessary to see problems or construct plans, Kaplan still produced fluid and coordinated play.

What emerges from this model of human skill acquisition is a progression from the analytic, rule-governed behavior of a detached subject who consciously breaks down his environment into recognizable elements, to the skilled behavior of an involved subject based on an accumulation of concrete experiences and the unconscious recognition of new situations as similar to remembered ones. The innate human ability to recognize whole current situations as similar to past ones facilitates our acquisition of high levels of skill and separates us dramatically from the artificially intelligent digital computer endowed only with context-free fact and feature recognition devices and with inference-making power.

This model provided Stuart and me with an explanation of the failure of the expert systems approach which also connects it with the failure of previous work in AI. When the interviewer elicits rules and principles from the human expert, he forces him, in effect, to revert to a much lower skill level at which rules were actually operative in determining his actions and decisions. This is why experts frequently have a great deal of trouble 'recalling' the rules they use even when pressed by the interviewer. They seem more naturally to think of their field of expertise as a huge set of special cases.[7] It is no wonder that systems based on principles abstracted from experts do not capture those experts' expertise and hence do not perform as well as the experts themselves.

In terms of skill level, the computer is stuck somewhere between the novice and advanced beginner level and, if our model of skill acquisition is accurate, has no way of advancing beyond this stage. What has obscured this fact for so long is the tremendous memory of the computer, in terms of numbers of facts and features which can be stored, and the tremendous number of rules and principles which it can utilize with superhuman speed and accuracy. Although its skill is of a kind which would place it below the level of the advanced beginner, its computing power makes its performance vastly superior to that of a human being at the same skill level. But power of this kind alone is not sufficient to duplicate the ability, the intuitive expertise, of the human expert.

This model of human skill levels also explains the failure of AI researchers to duplicate human language understanding, pattern recognition, and problem solving. In each of these areas we are, for the most part, experts. We are expert perceivers, expert speakers, hearers and readers of our native language, and expert problem solvers in most areas of everyday life. That doesn't mean that we don't make mistakes, but it does mean that our performance is entirely different in kind from that of the programmed digital computer. In each of these areas the computer is, at best, a very powerful and sophisticated beginner, competent in artificial micro-worlds where situational understanding and intuitive expertise have no part to play, but incompetent in the real world of human expertise.

I still believe, as I did in 1965,* that computers may someday be intelligent. Real computer intelligence will be achieved, however, only after researchers abandon the idea of finding a symbolic representation of the everyday world and a rule-governed equivalent of common-sense know-how, and turn to something like a neural-net modeling of the brain instead. If such modeling turns out to be the direction that AI should follow, it will be aided by the massively parallel computing machines on the horizon—not because parallel machines can make millions of inferences per second—but because faster, more parallel architecture can better implement the kind of pattern processing that does not use representations of rules and features at all.

* The year of publication of my initial RAND report, "Alchemy and Artificial Intelligence."

## NOTES

1. Hubert Dreyfus, *What Computers Can't Do,* revised edition, Harper and Row, 1979.
2. For an account of the experiments that show how human beings actually use images, and the unsuccessful attempts to understand this capacity in terms of programs that use features and rules, see *Imagery,* ed. Ned Block, M.I.T. Press, 1981. See also Ned Block, "Mental Pictures and Cognitive Science," *The Philosophical Review,* 1983, pp. 499–541.
3. *Scientific American,* Oct. 1982, p. 133.
4. *What Computers Can't Do.*
5. Hubert Dreyfus and Stuart Dreyfus, *Mind over Machine,* Macmillan, 1986. My brother Stuart has played an essential part in all of the critical study of machine intelligence in which I have been involved. It was Stuart, working then at RAND as a programmer in the new field of operations research, who was responsible for RAND's hiring me in 1964 as a consultant to evaluate their pioneering work in what was then called Cognitive Simulation. And it is Stuart's intuitions about the nature of human skill acquisition, and his working out of those intuitions, that are summarized in the remainder of this essay.
6. See Patricia Benner, *From Novice to Expert: Excellence and Power in Clinical Nursing Practice,* Addison-Wesley, 1984.
7. See Edward Feigenbaum and Pamela McCorduck, *The Fifth Generation, Artificial Intelligence and Japan's Computer Challenge to the World,* Addison-Wesley, 1983, p. 82.

## *John R. Searle (b. 1932)*

John R. Searle is a contemporary philosopher of language and philosopher of mind who has only recently become involved in the artificial intelligence debate, the debate over whether or not a programmed digital computer is capable of having mental states and processes. The essay below, which was published in 1980, probably added more heat to that controversy than any other single publication to date. Among the books that Searle has authored or edited are the following: *Speech Acts* (1969), *The Philosophy of Language* (1971), *Expression and Meaning* (1979), *Speech Act Theory and Pragmatics* (1980), *Intentionality* (1983), and *Minds, Brains and Science* (1984).

In the following, Searle argues that **formal operations** on symbols, the only kind of operation of which the digital computer is capable, are not sufficient to produce any mental state or process. Even if such a process mimicked human mental input and output relations perfectly, the relevant human mental state or process would still be entirely absent in the case of the computer. Thus what makes human mental behavior mental cannot be formally defined operations on symbols or symbolic representations. Searle suggests that what is crucial are the actual causal properties of the brain, that is, the nonformal properties of representations to which the computer has, in principle, no access.

# Minds, Brains, and Programs

## *John R. Searle*

What psychological and philosophical significance should we attach to recent efforts at computer simulations of human cognitive capacities? In answering this question, I find it useful to distinguish what I will call "strong" AI from "weak" or "cautious" AI (Artificial Intelligence). According to weak AI, the principal value of the computer in the study of the mind is that it gives us a very powerful tool. For example, it enables us to formulate and test hypotheses in a more rigorous and precise fashion. But according to strong AI, the computer is not merely a tool in the study of the mind; rather, the appropriately programmed computer really *is* a mind, in the sense that computers given the right programs can be literally said to *understand* and have other cognitive states. In strong AI, because the programmed computer has cognitive states, the programs are not mere tools that enable us to test psychological explanations; rather, the programs are themselves the explanations.

I have no objection to the claims of weak AI, at least as far as this article is concerned. My discussion here will be directed at the claims I have defined as those of strong AI, specifically the claim that the appropriately programmed computer literally has cognitive states and that the programs thereby explain human cognition. When I hereafter refer to AI, I have in mind the strong version, as expressed by these two claims.

I will consider the work of Roger Schank and his colleagues at Yale, because I am more familiar with it than I am with any other similar claims, and because it provides a very clear example of the sort of work I wish to examine. But nothing that follows depends upon the details of Schank's programs. The same arguments would apply to Winograd's SHRDLU, Weizenbaum's ELIZA, and indeed any **Turing machine** simulation of human mental phenomena.

Very briefly, and leaving out the various details, one can describe Schank's program as follows: the aim of the program is to simulate the human ability to understand stories. It is characteristic of human beings' story-understanding capacity that they can answer questions about the story even though the information that they give was never explicitly stated in the story. Thus, for

"Minds, Brains, and Programs," by John R. Searle in *The Behavioral and Brain Sciences* 3, 1980. (New York: Academic Press), pp. 417–24. Reprinted by permission of Cambridge University Press.

example, suppose you are given the following story: "A man went into a restaurant and ordered a hamburger. When the hamburger arrived it was burned to a crisp, and the man stormed out of the restaurant angrily, without paying for the hamburger or leaving a tip." Now, if you are asked "Did the man eat the hamburger?" you will presumably answer, "No, he did not." Similarly, if you are given the following story: "A man went into a restaurant and ordered a hamburger; when the hamburger came he was very pleased with it; and as he left the restaurant he gave the waitress a large tip before paying his bill," and you are asked the question, "Did the man eat the hamburger?," you will presumably answer, "Yes, he ate the hamburger." Now Schank's machines can similarly answer questions about restaurants in this fashion. To do this, they have a "representation" of the sort of information that human beings have about restaurants, which enables them to answer such questions as those above, given these sorts of stories. When the machine is given the story and then asked the question, the machine will print out answers of the sort that we would expect human beings to give if told similar stories. Partisans of strong AI claim that in this question and answer sequence the machine is not only simulating a human ability but also

1. that the machine can literally be said to *understand* the story and provide the answers to questions, and

2. that what the machine and its program do *explains* the human ability to understand the story and answer questions about it.

Both claims seem to me to be totally unsupported by Schank's[1] work, as I will attempt to show in what follows.

One way to test any theory of the mind is to ask oneself what it would be like if my mind actually worked on the principles that the theory says all minds work on. Let us apply this test to the Schank program with the following *Gedankenexperiment*. Suppose that I'm locked in a room and given a large batch of Chinese writing. Suppose furthermore (as is indeed the case) that I know no Chinese, either written or spoken, and that I'm not even confident that I could recognize Chinese writing as Chinese writing distinct from, say, Japanese writing or meaningless squiggles. To me, Chinese writing is just so many meaningless squiggles. Now suppose further that after this first batch of Chinese writing I am given a second batch of Chinese script together with a set of rules for correlating the second batch with the first batch. The rules are in English, and I understand these rules as well as any other native speaker of English. They enable me to correlate one set of formal symbols with another set of formal symbols, and all that "formal" means here is that I can identify the symbols entirely by their shapes. Now suppose also that I am given a third batch of Chinese symbols together with some instructions, again in English, that enable me to correlate elements of this third batch with the first two batches, and these rules instruct me how to give back certain Chinese symbols with certain sorts of shapes in response to certain sorts of shapes given me in the third batch. Unknown to me, the people who are giving me all of these symbols call the first batch "a script," they call the second batch a "story," and they call the third batch "questions." Furthermore, they call the symbols I give them back in response to the third batch "answers to the questions," and the set of rules in English that they gave me, they call "the program." Now just to complicate the story a little, imagine that these people also give me stories in English, which I understand, and they then ask me questions in English about these stories, and I give them back answers in English. Suppose also that after a while I get so good at following the instructions for manipulating the Chinese symbols and the programmers get so good at writing the programs that from the external point of view — that is, from the point of view of somebody outside the room in which I am locked — my answers to the questions are absolutely indistinguishable from those of native Chinese speakers. Nobody just looking at my answers can tell that I don't speak a word of Chinese. Let us also suppose that my answers to the English questions are, as they no doubt would be, indistinguishable from those of other native English speakers, for the simple reason that I am a native English speaker. From the external point of view—from the point of view of someone reading my "answers"—the answers to the Chinese questions and the English questions are equally good. But in the Chinese case, unlike the English case, I produce the answers by manipulating uninterpreted formal symbols. As far as the Chinese is concerned, I simply behave like a computer; I perform computational operations on formally specified elements. For the purposes of the Chinese, I am simply an instantiation of the computer program.

Now the claims made by strong AI are that the programmed computer understands the stories and that the program in some sense explains human understanding. But we are now in a position to examine these claims in light of our thought experiment.

1. As regards the first claim, it seems to me quite obvious in the example that I do not understand a word of the Chinese stories. I have inputs and outputs that are indistinguishable from those of the native Chinese speaker, and I can have any formal program you like, but I still understand nothing. For the same reasons, Schank's computer understands nothing of any stories, whether in Chinese, English, or whatever, since in the Chinese case the computer is me, and in cases where the computer is not me, the computer has nothing more than I have in the case where I understand nothing.

2. As regards the second claim, that the program explains human understanding, we can see that the computer and its program do not provide sufficient conditions of understanding since the computer and the program are functioning, and there is no understanding. But does it even provide a necessary condition or a significant contribution to understanding? One of the claims made by the supporters of strong AI is that when I understand a story in English, what I am doing is exactly the same—or perhaps more of the same—as what I was doing in manipulating the Chinese symbols. It is simply more formal symbol manipulation that distinguishes the case in English, where I do understand, from the case in Chinese, where I don't. I have not demonstrated that this claim is false, but it would certainly appear an incredible claim in the example. Such plausibility as the claim has derives from the supposition that we can construct a program that will have the same inputs and outputs as native speakers, and in addition we assume that speakers have some level of description where they are also instantiations of a program. On the basis of these two assumptions we assume that even if Schank's program isn't the whole story about understanding, it may be part of the story. Well, I suppose that is an empirical possibility, but not the slightest reason has so far been given to believe that it is true, since what is suggested—though certainly not demonstrated—by the example is that the computer program is simply irrelevant to my understanding of the story. In the Chinese case I have everything that artificial intelligence can put into me by way of a program, and I understand nothing; in the English case I understand everything, and there is so far no reason at all to suppose that my understanding has anything to do with computer programs, that is, with computational operations on purely formally specified elements. As long as the program is defined in terms of computational operations on purely formally defined elements, what the example suggests is that these by themselves have no interesting connection with understanding. They are certainly not **sufficient conditions,** and not the slightest reason has been given to suppose that they are **necessary conditions** or even that they make a significant contribution to understanding. Notice that the force of the argument is not simply that different machines can have the same input and output while operating on different formal principles—that is not the point at all. Rather, whatever purely formal principles you put into the computer, they will not be sufficient for understanding, since a human will be able to follow the formal principles without understanding anything. No reason whatever has been offered to suppose that such principles are necessary or even contributory, since no reason has been given to suppose that when I understand English I am operating with any formal program at all.

Well, then, what is it that I have in the case of the English sentences that I do not have in the case of the Chinese sentences? The obvious answer is that I know what the former mean, while I haven't the faintest idea what the latter mean. But in what does this consist and why couldn't we give it to a machine, whatever it is? I will return to this question later, but first I want to continue with the example.

I have had the occasions to present this example to several workers in artificial intelligence, and, interestingly, they do not seem to agree on what the proper reply to it is. I get a surprising variety of replies, and in what follows I will consider the most common of these (specified along with their geographic origins).

But first I want to block some common misunderstandings about "understanding": in many of these discussions one finds a lot of fancy footwork about the word "understanding." My critics point out that there are many different degrees of understanding; that "understanding" is not a simple two-place predicate; that there are even different kinds and levels of understanding, and often the law of excluded middle doesn't even apply in a straightforward way to statements of the form "x understands y"; that in many cases it is a matter for decision and not a simple matter of fact whether x understands y; and so on. To all of these points I want to say: of course, of course. But they have nothing to do with the points at issue. There are clear cases in which "understanding" literally applies and clear cases in which it does not apply; and these two sorts of cases are all I need for this argument.[2] I understand stories in English; to a lesser degree I can understand stories in French; to a still lesser degree, stories in German; and in Chinese, not at all. My car and my adding machine, on the other hand, understand nothing: they are not in that line of business. We often attribute "understanding" and other cognitive predicates by metaphor and analogy to cars, adding machines, and other artifacts, but nothing is proved by such attributions. We say, "The door *knows* when to open because of its photoelectric cell," "The adding machine *knows how* (*understands how,* is *able*) to do addition and subtraction but not division," and "The thermostat *perceives* changes in the temperature." The reason we make these attributions is quite interesting, and it has to do with the fact that in artifacts we extend our own **intentionality;**[3] our tools are extensions of our purposes, and so we find it natural to make metaphorical attributions of intentionality to them; but I take it no philosophical ice is cut by such examples. The sense in which an automatic door "understands instructions" from its photoelectric cell is not at all the sense in which I understand English. If the sense in which Schank's programmed computers understand stories is supposed to be the metaphorical sense in which the door understands, and not the sense in which I understand English, the issue would not be worth discussing. But Newell and Simon write that the kind of cognition they claim for computers is exactly the same as for human beings. I like the straightforwardness of this claim, and it is the sort of claim I will be considering. I will argue that in the literal sense the programmed computer understands what the car and the adding machine understand, namely, exactly nothing. The computer understanding is not just (like my understanding of German) partial or incomplete; it is zero.

Now to the replies:

## I. THE SYSTEMS REPLY (BERKELEY)

"While it is true that the individual person who is locked in the room does not understand the story, the fact is that he is merely part of a whole system, and the system does understand the story. The person has a large ledger in front of him in which are written the rules, he has a lot of scratch paper and pencils for doing calculations, he has 'data banks' of sets of Chinese symbols. Now, understanding is not being ascribed to the mere individual; rather it is being ascribed to this whole system of which he is a part."

My response to the systems theory is quite simple: let the individual internalize all of these elements of the system. He memorizes the rules in the ledger and the data banks of Chinese symbols, and he does all the calculations in his head. The individual then incorporates the entire system. There isn't anything at all to the system that he does not encompass. We can even get rid of the room and suppose he works outdoors. All the same, he understands nothing of the Chinese, and a fortiori neither does the system, because there isn't anything in the system that isn't in him. If he doesn't understand, then there is no way the system could understand because the system is just a part of him.

Actually I feel somewhat embarrassed to give even this answer to the systems theory because the theory seems to me so unplausible to start with. The idea is that while a person doesn't understand Chinese, somehow the *conjuction* of that person and bits of paper might understand Chinese. It is not easy for me to imagine how someone who was not in the grip of an ideology would find the idea at all plausible. Still, I think many people who are committed to the ideology of strong AI will in the end be inclined to say something very much like this; so let us pursue it a bit further. According to one version of this view, while the man in the internalized systems example doesn't understand Chinese in the sense that a native Chinese speaker does (because, for example, he doesn't know that the story refers to restaurants and hamburgers, etc.), still "the man as a formal symbol manipulation system" *really does understand Chinese.* The subsystem of the man that is the formal symbol manipulation system for Chinese should not be confused with the subsystem for English.

So there are really two subsystems in the man; one understands English, the other Chinese, and "it's just that the two systems have little to do with each other." But, I want to reply, not only do they have little to do with each other, they are not even remotely alike. The subsystem that understands English (assuming we allow ourselves to talk in this jargon of "subsystems" for a moment) knows that the stories are about restaurants and eating hamburgers, he knows that he is being asked questions about restaurants and that he is answering questions as best he can by making various inferences from the content of the story, and so on. But the Chinese system knows none of this. Whereas the English subsystem knows that "hamburgers" refers to hamburgers, the Chinese subsystem knows only that "squiggle squiggle" is followed by "squoggle squoggle." All he knows is that various formal symbols are being introduced at one end and manipulated according to rules written in English, and other symbols are going out at the other end. The whole point of the original example was to argue that such symbol manipulation by itself couldn't be sufficient for understanding Chinese in any literal sense because the man could write "squoggle squoggle" after "squiggle squiggle" without understanding anything in Chinese. And it doesn't meet that argument to postulate subsystems within the man, because the subsystems are no better off than the man was in the first place; they still don't have anything even remotely like what the English-speaking man (or subsystem) has. Indeed, in the case as described, the Chinese subsystem is simply a part of the English subsystem, a part that engages in meaningless symbol manipulation according to rules in English.

Let us ask ourselves what is supposed to motivate the systems reply in the first place; that is, what *independent* grounds are there supposed to be for saying that the agent must have a subsystem within him that literally understands stories in Chinese? As far as I can tell the only grounds are that in the example I have the same input and output as native Chinese speakers and a program that goes from one to the other. But the whole point of the examples has been to try to show that that couldn't be sufficient for understanding, in the sense in which I understand stories in English, because a person, and hence the set of systems that go to make up a person, could have the right combination of input, output, and program and still not understand anything in the relevant literal sense in which I understand English. The only motivation for saying there *must* be a subsystem in me that understands Chinese is that I have a program and I can pass the Turing test; I can fool native Chinese speakers. But precisely one of the points at issue is the adequacy of the Turing test. The example shows that there could be two "systems," both of which pass the Turing test, but only one of which understands; and it is no argument against this point to say that since they both pass the Turing test they must both understand, since this claim fails to meet the argument that the system in me that understands English has a great deal more than the system that merely processes Chinese. In short, the systems reply simply begs the question by insisting without argument that the system must understand Chinese.

Furthermore, the systems reply would appear to lead to consequences that are independently absurd. If we are to conclude that there must be cognition in me on the grounds that I have a certain sort of input and output and a program in between, then it looks like all sorts of noncognitive subsystems are going to turn out to be cognitive. For example, there is a level of description at which my stomach does information processing, and it instantiates any number of computer programs, but I take it we do not want to say that it has any understanding. But if we accept the systems reply, then it is hard to see how we avoid saying that stomach, heart, liver, and so on, are all understanding subsystems, since there is no principled way to distinguish the motivation for saying the Chinese subsystem understands from [the motivation for] saying that the stomach understands. It is, by the way, not an answer to this point to say that the Chinese system has information as input and output and the stomach has food and food products as input and output, since from the point of view of the agent, from my point of view, there is no information in either the food or the Chinese — the Chinese is just so many meaningless squiggles. The information in the Chinese case is solely in the eyes of the programmers and the interpreters, and there is nothing to prevent them from treating the input and output of my digestive organs as information if they so desire.

This last point bears on some independent problems in strong AI, and it is worth digressing for a moment to explain it. If strong AI is to be a branch of psychology, then it must be able to distinguish those systems that are genuinely mental from those that are not. It must be able to distinguish the principles on which the mind works from those on which nonmental systems work; otherwise it will offer us no explanations of what is specifically mental about the mental. And the mental-nonmental distinction cannot be just in the eye of the beholder but it must be intrinsic to the systems; otherwise it would be up to any beholder to treat people as nonmental and, for example, hurricanes as mental if he likes. But quite often in the AI literature the distinction is blurred in ways that would in the long run prove disastrous to the claim that AI is a cognitive inquiry. McCarthy, for example, writes, "Machines as simple as thermostats can be said to have beliefs, and having beliefs seems to be a characteristic of most machines capable of problem solving performance." Anyone who thinks strong AI has a chance as a theory of the mind ought to ponder the implications of that remark. We are asked to accept it as a discovery of strong AI that the hunk of metal on the wall that we use to regulate the temperature has beliefs in exactly the same sense that we, our spouses, and our children have beliefs, and furthermore that "most" of the other machines in the room — telephone, tape recorder, adding machine, electric light switch — also have beliefs in this literal sense. It is not the aim of this article to argue against McCarthy's point, so I will simply assert the following without argument. The study of the mind starts with such facts as that humans have beliefs, while thermostats, telephones, and adding machines don't. If you get a theory that denies this point you have produced a counterexample to the theory and the theory is false. One gets the impression that people in AI who write this sort of thing think they can get away with it because they don't really take it seriously, and they don't think anyone else will either. I propose, for a moment at least, to take it seriously. Think hard for one minute about what would be necessary to establish that that hunk of metal on the wall over there had real beliefs, beliefs with direction of fit, propositional content, and conditions of satisfaction; beliefs that had the possibility of being strong beliefs or weak beliefs; nervous, anxious, or secure beliefs; dogmatic, rational, or superstitious beliefs; blind faiths or hesitant cogitations; any kind of beliefs. The thermostat is not a candidate. Neither is stomach, liver, adding machine, or telephone. However, since we are taking the idea seriously, notice that its truth would be fatal to strong AI's claim to be a science of the mind. For now the mind is everywhere. What we wanted to know is what distinguishes the mind from thermostats and livers. And if McCarthy were right, strong AI wouldn't have a hope of telling us that.

## II. THE ROBOT REPLY (YALE)

"Suppose we wrote a different kind of program from Schank's program. Suppose we put a computer inside a robot, and this computer would not just take in formal symbols as input and give out formal symbols as output, but rather would actually operate the robot in such a way that the robot does something very much like perceiving, walking, moving about, hammering nails, eating, drinking—anything you like. The robot would, for example, have a television camera attached to it that enabled it to 'see,' it would have arms and legs that enabled it to 'act,' and all of this would be controlled by its computer 'brain.' Such a robot would, unlike Schank's computer, have genuine understanding and other mental states."

The first thing to notice about the robot reply is that it tacitly concedes that cognition is not solely a matter of formal symbol manipulation, since this reply adds a set of causal relation[s] with the outside world. But the answer to the robot reply is that the addition of such "perceptual" and "motor" capacities adds nothing by way of understanding, in particular, or intentionality, in general, to Schank's original program. To see this, notice that the same thought experiment applies to the robot case. Suppose that instead of the computer inside the robot, you put me inside the room and, as in the original Chinese case, you give me more Chinese symbols with more instructions in English for matching Chinese symbols to Chinese symbols and feeding back Chinese symbols to the outside. Suppose, unknown to me, some of the Chinese symbols that come to me come from a television camera attached to the robot and other Chinese symbols that I am giving out serve to make the motors inside the robot move the robot's legs or arms. It is important to emphasize that all I am doing is manipulating formal symbols: I know none of these other facts. I am receiving "information" from the robot's "perceptual" apparatus, and I am giving out "instructions" to its motor apparatus without knowing either of these facts. I am the robot's **homunculus,** but unlike the traditional homunculus, I don't know what's going on. I don't understand anything except the rules for symbol manipulation. Now in this case I want to say that the robot has no intentional states at all; it is simply moving about as a result of its electrical wiring and its program. And furthermore, by instantiating the program I have no intentional states of the relevant type. All I do is follow formal instructions about manipulating formal symbols.

## III. THE BRAIN SIMULATOR REPLY (BERKELEY AND M.I.T.)

"Suppose we design a program that doesn't represent information that we have about the world, such as the information in Schank's scripts, but simulates the actual sequence of neuron firings at the synapses of the brain of a native Chinese speaker when he understands stories in Chinese and gives answers to them. The machine takes in Chinese stories and questions about them as input, it simulates the formal structure of actual Chinese brains in processing these stories, and it gives out Chinese answers as outputs. We can even imagine that the machine operates, not with a single serial program, but with a whole set of programs operating in parallel, in the manner that actual human brains presumably operate when they process natural language. Now surely in such a case we would have to say that the machine understood the stories; and if we refuse to say that, wouldn't we also have to deny that native Chinese speakers understood the stories? At the level of the synapses, what would or could be different about the program of the computer and the program of the Chinese brain?"

Before countering this reply I want to digress to note that it is an odd reply for any partisan of artificial intelligence (or functionalism, etc.) to make: I thought the whole idea of strong AI is that we don't need to know how the brain works to know how the mind works. The basic hypothesis, or so I had supposed, was that there is a level of mental operations consisting of computational processes over formal elements that constitute the essence of the mental and can be realized in all sorts of different brain processes, in the same way that any computer program can be realized in different computer hardwares: on the assumptions of strong AI, the mind is to the brain as the program is to the hardware, and thus we can understand the mind without doing neurophysiology. If we had to know how the brain worked to do AI, we wouldn't bother with AI. However, even getting this close to the operation of the brain is still not sufficient to produce understanding. To see this, imagine that instead of a monolingual man in a room shuffling symbols we have the man operate an elaborate set of water pipes with valves connecting them. When the man receives the Chinese symbols, he looks up in the program, written in English, which valves he has to turn on and off. Each water connection corresponds to a synapse in the Chinese brain, and the whole system is rigged up so that after doing all the right firings, that is after turning on all the right faucets, the Chinese answers pop out at the output end of the series of pipes.

Now where is the understanding in this system? It takes Chinese as input, it simulates the formal structure of the synapses of the Chinese brain, and it gives Chinese as output. But the man certainly doesn't understand Chinese, and neither do the water pipes, and if we are tempted to adopt what I think is the absurd view that somehow the *conjunction* of man *and* water pipes understands, remember that in principle the man can internalize the formal structure of the water pipes and do all the "neuron firings" in his imagination. The problem with the brain simulator is that it is simulating the wrong things about the brain. As long as it simulates only the formal structure of the sequence of neuron firings at the synapses, it won't have simulated what matters about the brain, namely its causal properties, its ability to produce intentional states. And that the formal properties are not sufficient for the causal properties is shown by the water pipe example: we can have all the formal properties carved off from the relevant neurobiological causal properties.

## IV. THE COMBINATION REPLY (BERKELEY AND STANFORD)

"While each of the previous three replies might not be completely convincing by itself as a refutation of the Chinese room counterexample, if you take all three together they are collectively much more convincing and even decisive. Imagine a robot with a brain-shaped computer lodged in its cranial cavity, imagine the computer programmed with all the synapses of a human brain, imagine the whole behavior of the robot is indistinguishable from human behavior, and now think of the whole thing as a unified system and not just as a computer with inputs and outputs. Surely in such a case we would have to ascribe intentionality to the system."

I entirely agree that in such a case we would find it rational and indeed irresistible to accept the hypothesis that the robot had intentionality, as long as we knew nothing more about it. Indeed, besides appearance and behavior, the other elements of the combination are really irrelevant. If we could build a robot whose behavior was indistinguishable over a large range from human behavior, we would attribute intentionality to it, pending some reason not to. We wouldn't need to know in advance that its computer brain was a formal analogue of the human brain.

But I really don't see that this is any help to the claims of strong AI; and here's why: According to strong AI, instantiating a formal program with the right input and output is a sufficient condition of, indeed is constitutive of, intentionality. As Newell puts it, the essence of the mental is the operation of a physical symbol system. But the attributions of intentionality that we make to the robot in this example have nothing to do with formal programs. They are simply based on the assumption that if the robot looks and behaves sufficiently like us, then we would suppose, until proven otherwise, that it must have mental states like ours that cause and are expressed by its behavior, and it must have an inner mechanism capable of producing such mental states. If we knew independently how to account for its behavior without such assumptions we would not attribute intentionality to it, especially if we knew it had a formal program. And this is precisely the point of my earlier reply to objection II.

Suppose we knew that the robot's behavior was entirely accounted for by the fact that a man inside it was receiving uninterpreted formal symbols from the robot's sensory receptors and sending out uninterpreted formal symbols to its motor mechanisms, and the man was doing this symbol manipulation in accordance with a bunch of rules. Furthermore, suppose the man knows none of these facts about the robot, all he knows is which operations to perform on which meaningless symbols. In such a case we would regard the robot as an ingenious mechanical dummy. The hypothesis that the dummy has a mind would now be unwarranted and unnecessary, for there is now no longer any reason to ascribe intentionality to the robot or to the system of which it is a part (except of course for the man's intentionality in manipulating the symbols). The formal symbol manipulations go on, the input and output are correctly matched, but the only real locus of intentionality is the man, and he doesn't [have] any of the relevant intentional states; he doesn't, for example, *see* what comes into the robot's eyes, he doesn't *intend* to move the robot's arm, and he doesn't *understand* any of the remarks made to or by the robot. Nor, for the reasons stated earlier, does the system of which man and robot are a part.

To see this point, contrast this case with cases in which we find it completely natural to ascribe intentionality to members of certain other primate species such as apes and monkeys and to domestic animals such as dogs. The reasons we find it natural are, roughly, two: we can't make sense of the animal's behavior without the ascription of intentionality, and we can see that the beasts are made of similar stuff to ourselves—that is an eye, that a nose, this is its skin, and so on. Given the coherence of the animal's behavior and the assumption of the same causal stuff underlying it, we assume both that the animal must have mental states underlying its behavior, and that the mental states must be produced by mechanisms made out of the stuff that is like our stuff. We would certainly make similar assumptions about the robot unless we had some reason not to, but as soon as we knew that the behavior was the result of a formal program, and that the actual causal properties of the physical substance were irrelevant we would abandon the assumption of intentionality.

There are two other responses to my example that come up frequently (and so are worth discussing) but really miss the point.

## V. THE OTHER MINDS REPLY (YALE)

"How do you know that other people understand Chinese or anything else? Only by their behavior. Now the computer can pass the behavioral tests as well as they can (in principle), so if you are going to attribute cognition to other people you must in principle also attribute it to computers."

This objection really is only worth a short reply. The problem in this discussion is not about how I know that other people have cognitive states, but rather what it is that I am attributing to them when I attribute cognitive states to them. The thrust of the argument is that it couldn't be just computational processes and their output because the computational processes and their output can exist without the cognitive state. It is no answer to this argument to feign anesthesia. In "cognitive sciences" one presupposes the reality and knowability of the mental in the same way that in physical sciences one has to presuppose the reality and knowability of physical objects.

## VI. THE MANY MANSIONS REPLY (BERKELEY)

"Your whole argument presupposes that AI is only about analogue and digital computers. But that just happens to be the present state of technology. Whatever these causal processes are that you say are essential for intentionality (assuming you are right), eventually we will be able to build devices that have these causal processes, and that will be artificial intelligence. So your arguments are in no way directed at the ability of artificial intelligence to produce and explain cognition."

I really have no objection to this reply save to say that it in effect trivializes the project of strong AI by redefining it as whatever artificially produces and explains cognition. The interest of the original claim made on behalf of artificial intelligence is that it was a precise, well defined thesis: mental processes are computational processes over formally defined elements. I have been concerned to challenge that thesis. If the claim is redefined so that it is no longer that thesis, my objections no longer apply because there is no longer a testable hypothesis for them to apply to.

Let us now return to the question I promised I would try to answer: granted that in my original example I understand the English and I do not understand the Chinese, and granted therefore that the machine doesn't understand either English or Chinese, still there must be something about me that makes it the case that I understand English and a corresponding something lacking in me that makes it the case that I fail to understand Chinese. Now why couldn't we give those somethings, whatever they are, to a machine?

I see no reason in principle why we couldn't give a machine the capacity to understand English or Chinese, since in an important sense our bodies with our brains are precisely such machines. But I do see very strong arguments for saying that we could not give such a thing to a machine where the operation of the machine is defined solely in terms of computational processes over formally defined elements; that is, where the operation of the machine is defined as an instantiation of a computer program. It is not because I am the instantiation of a computer program that I am able to understand English and have other forms of intentionality (I am, I suppose, the instantiation of any number of computer programs), but as far as we know it is because I am a certain sort of organism with a certain biological (i.e. chemical and physical) structure, and this structure, under certain conditions, is causally capable of producing perception, action, understanding, learning, and other intentional phenomena. And part of the point of the present argument is that only something that had those causal powers could have that intentionality. Perhaps other physical and chemical processes could produce exactly these effects; perhaps, for example, Martians also have intentionality but their brains are made of different stuff. That is an empirical question, rather like the question whether photosynthesis can be done by something with a chemistry different from that of chlorophyll.

But the main point of the present argument is that no purely formal model will ever be sufficient by itself for intentionality because the formal properties are not by themselves constitutive of intentionality, and they have by themselves no causal powers except the power, when instantiated, to produce the next stage of the formalism when the machine is running. And any other causal properties that particular realizations of the formal model have are irrelevant to the formal model because we can always put the same formal model in a different realization where those causal properties are obviously absent. Even if, by some miracle, Chinese speakers exactly realize Schank's program, we can put the same program in English speakers, water pipes, or computers, none of which understand Chinese, the program notwithstanding.

What matters about brain operations is not the formal shadow cast by the sequence of synapses but rather the actual properties of the sequences. All the arguments for the strong version of artificial intelligence that I have seen insist on drawing an outline around the shadows cast by cognition and then claiming that the shadows are the real thing.

By way of concluding I want to try to state some of the general philosophical points implicit in the argument. For clarity I will try to do it in a question and answer fashion, and I begin with that old chestnut of a question:

"Could a machine think?"

The answer is, obviously, yes. We are precisely such machines.

"Yes, but could an artifact, a man-made machine, think?"

Assuming it is possible to produce artificially a machine with a nervous system, neurons with axons and dendrites, and all the rest of it, sufficiently like ours, again the answer to the question seems to be obviously, yes. If you can exactly duplicate the causes, you could duplicate the effects. And indeed it might be possible to produce consciousness, intentionality, and all the rest of it using some other sorts of chemical principles than those that human beings use. It is, as I said, an empirical question.

"OK, but could a digital computer think?"

If by "digital computer" we mean anything at all that has a level of description where it can correctly be described as the instantiation of a computer program, then again the answer is, of course, yes, since we are the instantiations of any number of computer programs, and we can think.

"But could something think, understand, and so on *solely* in virtue of being a computer with the right sort of program? Could instantiating a program, the right program of course, by itself be a sufficient condition of understanding?"

This I think is the right question to ask, though it is usually confused with one or more of the earlier questions, and the answer to it is no.

"Why not?"

Because the formal symbol manipulations by themselves don't have any intentionality; they are quite meaningless; they aren't even *symbol* manipulations, since the symbols don't symbolize anything. In the linguistic jargon, they have only a syntax but no semantics. Such intentionality as computers appear to have is solely in the minds of those who program them and those who use them, those who send in the input and those who interpret the output.

The aim of the Chinese room example was to try to show this by showing that as soon as we put something into the system that really does have intentionality (a man), and we program him with the formal program, you can see that the formal program carries no additional intentionality. It adds nothing, for example, to a man's ability to understand Chinese.

Precisely that feature of AI that seemed so appealing—the distinction between the program and the realization—proves fatal to the claim that simulation could be duplication. The distinction between the program and its realization in the hardware seems to be parallel to the distinction between the level of mental operations and the level of brain operations. And if we could describe the level of mental operations as a formal program, then it seems we could describe what was essential about the mind without doing either introspective psychology or neurophysiology of the brain. But the equation, "mind is to brain as program is to hardware" breaks down at several points, among them the following three:

First, the distinction between program and realization has the consequence that the same program could have all sorts of crazy realizations that had no form of intentionality. Weizenbaum, for example, shows in detail how to construct a computer using a roll of toilet paper and a pile of small stones. Similarly, the Chinese story understanding program can be programmed into a sequence of water pipes, a set of wind machines, or a monolingual English speaker, none of which thereby acquires an understanding of Chinese. Stones, toilet paper, wind, and water pipes are the wrong kind of stuff to have intentionality in the first place—only something that has the same causal powers as brains can have intentionality—and though the English speaker has the right kind of stuff for intentionality you can easily see that he doesn't get any extra intentionality by memorizing the program, since memorizing it won't teach him Chinese.

Second, the program is purely formal, but the intentional states are not in that way formal. They are defined in terms of their content, not their form. The belief that it is raining, for example, is not defined as a certain formal shape, but as a certain mental content with conditions of satisfaction, a direction of fit, and the like. Indeed the belief as such hasn't even got a formal shape in this syntactic sense, since one and the same belief can be given an indefinite number of different syntactic expressions in different linguistic systems.

Third, as I mentioned before, mental states and events are literally a product of the operation of the brain, but the program is not in that way a product of the computer.

"Well if programs are in no way constitutive of mental processes, why have so many people believed the converse? That at least needs some explanation."

I don't really know the answer to that one. The idea that computer simulations could be the real thing ought to have seemed suspicious in the first place because the computer isn't confined to simulating mental operations, by any means. No one supposes that computer simulations of a five-alarm fire will burn the neighborhood down or that a computer simulation of a rainstorm will leave us all drenched. Why on earth would anyone suppose that a computer simulation of understanding actually understood anything? It is sometimes said that it would be frightfully hard to get computers to feel pain or fall in love, but love and pain are neither harder nor easier than cognition or anything else. For simulation, all you need is the right input and output and a program in the middle that transforms the former into the latter. That is all the computer has for anything it does. To confuse simulation with duplication is the same mistake, whether it is pain, love, cognition, fires, or rainstorms.

Still, there are several reasons why AI must have seemed — and to many people perhaps still does seem — in some way to reproduce and thereby explain mental phenomena, and I believe we will not succeed in removing these illusions until we have fully exposed the reasons that give rise to them.

First, and perhaps most important, is a confusion about the notion of "information processing": many people in cognitive science believe that the human brain, with its mind, does something called "information processing," and analogously the computer with its program does information processing, but fires and rainstorms, on the other hand, don't do information processing at all. Thus, though the computer can simulate the formal features of any process whatever, it stands in a special relation to the mind and brain because when the computer is properly programmed, ideally with the same program as the brain, the information processing is identical in the two cases, and this information processing is really the essence of the mental. But the trouble with this argument is that it rests on an ambiguity in the notion of "information." In the sense in which people "process information" when they reflect, say, on problems in arithmetic or when they read and answer questions about stories, the programmed computer does not do "information processing." Rather, what it does is manipulate formal symbols. The fact that the programmer and the interpreter of the computer output use the symbols to stand for objects in the world is totally beyond the scope of the computer. The computer, to repeat, has a syntax but no semantics. Thus, if you type into the computer "2 plus 2 equals?" it will type out "4." But it has no idea that "4" means 4 or that it means anything at all. And the point is not that it lacks some second-order information about the interpretation of its first-order symbols, but rather that its first-order symbols don't have any interpretations as far as the computer is concerned. All the computer has is more symbols. The introduction of the notion of "information processing" therefore produces a dilemma: either we construe the notion of "information processing" in such a way that it implies intentionality as part of the process or we don't. If the former, then the programmed computer does not do information processing, it only manipulates formal symbols. If the latter, then, though the computer does information processing, it is only doing so in the sense in which adding machines, typewriters, stomachs, thermostats, rainstorms, and hurricanes do information processing; namely, they have a level of description at which we can describe them as taking information in at one end, transforming it, and producing information as output. But in this case it is up to outside observers to interpret the input and output as information in the ordinary sense. And no similarity is established between the computer and the brain in terms of any similarity of information processing.

Second, in much of AI there is a residual behaviorism or operationalism. Since appropriately programmed computers can have input-output patterns similar to those of human beings, we are tempted to postulate mental states in the computer similar to human mental states. But once we see that it is both conceptually and empirically possible for a system to have human capacities in some realm without having any intentionality at all, we should be able to overcome this impulse. My desk adding machine has calculating capacities, but no intentionality, and in this paper I have tried to show that a system could have input and output capabilities that duplicated those of a native Chinese speaker and still not understand Chinese, regardless of how it was programmed. The Turing test is typical of the tradition in being unashamedly behavioristic and operationalistic, and I believe that if AI workers totally repudiated behaviorism and operationalism much of the confusion between simulation and duplication would be eliminated.

Third, this residual operationalism is joined to a residual form of dualism; indeed strong AI only makes sense given the dualistic assumption that, where the mind is concerned, the brain doesn't matter. In strong AI (and in functionalism, as well) what matters are programs, and programs are independent of their realization in machines; indeed, as far as AI is concerned, the same program could be realized by an electronic machine, a Cartesian mental substance, or a Hegelian world spirit. The single most surprising discovery that I have made in discussing these issues is that many AI workers are quite shocked by my idea that actual human mental phenomena might be dependent on actual physical-chemical properties of actual human brains. But if you think about it a minute you can see that I should not have been surprised; for unless you accept some form of dualism, the strong AI project hasn't got a chance. The project is to reproduce and explain the mental by designing programs, but unless the mind is not only conceptually but empirically independent of the brain you couldn't carry out the project, for the program is completely independent of any realization. Unless you believe that the mind is separable from the brain both conceptually and empirically—dualism in a strong form—you cannot hope to reproduce the mental by writing and running programs since programs must be independent of brains or any other particular forms of instantiation. If mental operations consist in computational operations on formal symbols, then it follows that they have no interesting connection with the brain; the only connection would be that the brain just happens to be one of the indefinitely many types of machines capable of instantiating the program. This form of dualism is not the traditional Cartesian variety that claims there are two sorts of *substances*, but it is Cartesian in the sense that it insists that what is specifically mental about the mind has no intrinsic connection with the actual properties of the brain. This underlying dualism is masked from us by the fact that AI literature contains frequent fulminations against "dualism"; what the authors seem to be unaware of is that their position presupposes a strong version of dualism.

"Could a machine think?" My own view is that *only* a machine could think, and indeed only very special kinds of machines, namely brains and machines that had the same causal powers as brains. And that is the main reason strong AI has had little to tell us about thinking, since it has nothing to tell us about machines. By its own definition, it is about programs, and programs are not machines. Whatever else intentionality is, it is a biological phenomenon, and it is as likely to be as causally dependent on the specific biochemistry of its origins as lactation, photosynthesis, or any other biological phenomena. No one would suppose that we could produce milk and sugar by running a computer simulation of the formal sequences in lactation and photosynthesis, but where the mind is concerned many people are willing to believe in such a miracle because of a deep and abiding dualism: the mind they suppose is a matter of formal processes and is independent of quite specific material causes in the way that milk and sugar are not.

In defense of this dualism the hope is often expressed that the brain is a digital computer (early computers, by the way, were often called "electronic brains"). But that is no help. Of course the brain is a digital computer. Since everything is a digital computer, brains are too. The point is that the brain's causal capacity to produce intentionality cannot consist in its instantiating a computer program, since for any program you like it is possible for something to instantiate that program and still not have any mental states. Whatever it is that the brain does to produce intentionality, it cannot consist in instantiating a program since no program, by itself, is sufficient for intentionality.

## ACKNOWLEDGMENTS

I am indebted to a rather large number of people for discussion of these matters and for their patient attempts to overcome my ignorance of artificial intelligence. I would especially like to thank Ned Block, Hubert Dreyfus, John Haugeland, Roger Schank, Robert Wilensky, and Terry Winograd.

## NOTES

1. I am not, of course, saying that Schank himself is committed to these claims.
2. Also, "understanding" implies both the possession of mental (intentional) states and the truth (validity, success) of these states. For the purposes of this discussion we are concerned only with the possession of the states.
3. Intentionality is by definition that feature of certain mental states by which they are directed at or about objects and states of affairs in the world. Thus, beliefs, desires, and intentions are intentional states; undirected forms of anxiety and depression are not.

# *Part 3—Study Questions*

## *MINDS AND BODIES*

1. Explain how Broad attempts to solve the following problem: Minds and bodies are utterly opposite in nature and causal interaction between them is therefore inconceivable. Does Broad succeed? Why or why not?
2. What is the important difference between Huxley's theory of human behavior and Broad's? Does Huxley's theory avoid the problem of the inconceivability of causal interaction? Explain.
3. What is the difference between reductive and eliminative materialism? Which is preferable and why?
4. Distinguish between scientific and logical behaviorism. What are the advantages of each compared to dualism?
5. What are the important differences between functionalism and behaviorism? between

functionalism and reductive materialism? between functionalism and dualism?

## ARTIFICIAL INTELLIGENCE AND HUMAN MENTALITY

1. Pylyshyn maintains that most human behavior will have to be explained in terms of mental representations and that this rules out behaviorism as a psychological theory. Why does he think representations are essential to psychological explanation and why is this incompatible with behaviorism?
2. Pylyshyn claims that there is reason to think that mental operations are computational. What reasons does he offer and are they good ones?
3. Dennett argues that AI has solved "the problem of the homunculus" in psychological and philosophical theories of the mind that utilize representations. What exactly is the problem and how has AI provided a solution?
4. What exactly are the differences between us and digital computers that will keep the computer from producing truly intelligent behavior according to Dreyfus? Why do these differences make such a difference?
5. If Searle's thought experiment has the consequences he claims, it means at least that AI has not solved the problem of the homunculus that Dennett thought it had. Explain why this is so? What more does Searle's thought experiment claim to show? Is it successful?

# Part 3 — Glossary

**Ad hoc** See Part 2 glossary.

**Algorithm** An algorithm is a rule for solving a particular type of problem. The term is commonly used to describe rules in mathematics, the mechanical application of which is sufficient to achieve the specified result (for example, finding the roots of a quadratic equation).

**Aprioristic** See **a priori** in Part 2 glossary.

**Attribute theory** Armstrong uses the term *attribute theory* to refer to what we have called *double aspect* theories. See the subsection of this part on double aspect theories.

**Computational** An operation or process is computational if it can be performed by a **Turing machine.** Put very roughly, a computational operation is one that consists of discrete and well-defined changes of state of a system.

**Contingent** A proposition is contingent if its denial is logically possible, that is, does not produce a contradiction. A fact can be described as contingent when the proposition expressing it is contingent. See the entry for **logically necessary,** to which **contingent** is opposed, below.

**Epiphenomenalism** Epiphenomenalism is a version of dualism that maintains that bodily events cause mental events, but that mental events have no causal power whatsoever. For a discussion of the theory, see the last part of the introduction to the subsection on dualism (in this part).

**Folk psychology** Folk psychology refers to psychological theories that utilize our ordinary mental concepts such as emotions, hopes, fears, beliefs, and so on. It is to be contrasted with *eliminative materialism,* which holds that such concepts do not (even confusedly) refer to any entities that are scientifically useful in explaining human behavior.

**Formal operations** Formal operations or processes are those defined solely in terms of the nonsemantic (or syntactic) properties of the things they operate on. (See **semantic** and **syntactic** below.)

**Functional analysis** A functional analysis defines a thing by means of its causal role, that is, in terms of the causal relations in which it is involved.

**Functional plasticity** Functional plasticity is used by Ziff in describing the following feature of the human brain: For a number of its functions, the brain is plastic rather than rigid with respect to what specific area can perform the function. If a particular area of tissue is damaged, other areas typically take over the function which used to be performed in that area.

**Heuristic** A heuristic technique provides help in solving a problem for which no **algorithm** (see above) exists. In computer science this term is used to describe programs that utilize the evaluation of feedback to modify and improve their performance.

**Homunculus** A homunculus (plural, homunculi) is a little person inside a person used to explain behavior. In psychology and philosophy of mind, it is a little mental agent inside the person whose performance somehow explains the intelligent behavior of the person. See the essay by Dennett in this part for a discussion of the problem created by postulating homunculi to explain behavior and the suggestion that AI has solved this problem.

**Intentionality** Intentionality is the property of mental representations or symbols that consists of their referring to or being directed toward the real objects or states of affairs they represent or symbolize.

**Interactionism** Interactionism is the form of dualism that maintains that bodily events cause mental events and that mental events cause bodily events—that is, that mind and body interact causally. For a discussion of the theory, see the first part of the introduction to the subsection on dualism (in this part).

**Logically necessary** A proposition is logically necessary if its denial is a contradiction. Logically necessary propositions are sometimes called logical truths. The opposite of logically necessary is **contingent** (see the entry above).

**Mnemonic** A mnemonic is a name given to something designed to aid in remembering it or its function.

**Necessary condition** A necessary condition is a condition without which a particular object wouldn't exist or a particular event wouldn't occur. For example, being a male is a necessary condition for fathering a child. It is not, however, a **sufficient condition** (see entry below).

**Occasionalism** Occasionalism is the obsolete dualistic solution to the mind-body problem that consists of the following: Minds and bodies do not interact causally. Mental events and physical events of a given person coincide because on the occasion of each physical event, God produces the appropriate mental state in the person's mind so that he or she can get around in the world successfully.

**Ontology** Ontology is the branch of philosophy that identifies the basic kinds of things that really exist and of which every real thing is either an instance or a composite of instances.

**Phenomenalist** As used in Armstrong's essay, a phenomenalist is a philosopher who defines dispositions solely in terms of behavioral manifestations or appearances and not in terms of some real property that is present even when the disposition is not manifested in observable behavior.

**Physicalism** Physicalism is just another word for materialism. See the subsection on materialism in this part for a discussion of this philosophical view.

**Preestablished harmony** Preestablished harmony is the obsolete dualistic solution to the mind-body problem that consists of the following: Minds and bodies do not interact causally. A mechanism in place from the beginning and usually divine in origin keeps the careers of the independent mind and body of each person synchronized from birth to death or beyond.

**Prima facie** Prima facie is a Latin phrase that means "at first glance," "initially" or "before considering possible complications or conflicts."

**Psychoneural parallelism** Psychoneural parallelism is used by Broad to refer to any version of dualism that involves no causal relations between minds and bodies. The parallelism between the mental and physical histories of a person is noted by such theories but can be explained in any way that does not require causal relations between the two. **Occasionalism** and **preestablished harmony** (see above) are instances of this general kind of theory, as would be a theory that explained the parallelism as simple coincidence.

**Realist** As used in Armstrong's essay, a realist account of dispositions is one that identifies them with a real and enduring property of persons rather than the appearances that exist only when the disposition is manifested in actual behavior.

**Reduction** Reduction is the process of substituting one theory for another by means of a term-by-term equivalence. The identity theory makes possible a reduction of psychology to physiology. Reduction is contrasted with elimination as a relation between theories. See the introduction to the subsection on materialism in this part for a discussion of the difference between reduction and elimination.

**Representational** A theory of mental states is representational if it holds that such states consist in part of ideas or representations of objects, events, or states of affairs.

**Semantic** The semantic properties of a symbol or representation are the properties of meaning, reference, and truth. *Semantic* is contrasted with **syntactic** (see entry below).

**Sufficient condition** A sufficient condition is a condition which by itself requires the existence of a particular object or the occurrence of a particular event. This is frequently contrasted with **necessary condition** (see entry above).

**Syntactic** The syntactic properties of a symbol or representation are the properties it has merely as an object of a certain size, shape, or constitution, and independent of its symbolizing or representing anything. *Syntactic* is contrasted with **semantic** (see entry above).

**Token** A token is a specific example or instance of a general type. Token physicalism would be the theory that each individual occurrence of a mental state or process is identical to a particular physical state or process of the central nervous system.

**Transitivity of identity** Transitivity of identity refers to the following: If A is identical to B and B is identical to C, then A is identical to C. Many relations are transitive; for example, "is larger than" could be substituted for "is identical to" in the above. Many relations are not transitive; for example "is the father of" could not be substituted for "is identical to" in the formulation above.

**Turing machine** A Turing machine is a particular kind of universal computing machine or computer conceptualized by the mathematician A. M. Turing. A universal computing machine is a machine capable of carrying out any well defined computational operation. Turing machines differ from actual computing machines by virtue of having an unlimited memory and only a few simple mechanical operations. But they differ in no important respects. Within the limits of their memory or storage capacity, modern digital computers are, like Turing machines, universal machines capable of performing any computational operation.

**Type** Type is another term for general kind or class. The relation between general kinds and particular instances or examples is the same as that between types and **tokens** (see entry above). Type physicalism is the theory that types of mental states (for example, the class of all belief states that are states of believing that snow is white) are identical to physical states of the central nervous system. This would be incompatible with AI and would rule out the possibility of anything, living or nonliving, having that belief if it did not have our exact physical constitution.

# Part 3 — Suggestions for Further Reading

Some of these readings may be too difficult for many introductory students. Consult your instructor for assistance in selecting from this list or for further suggestions to make sure that additional material is well suited to your interests and abilities.

## MINDS AND BODIES


1. Armstrong, D. M., *A Materialist Theory of the Mind* (Routledge & Kegan Paul, 1968).
2. Block, Ned, *Philosophy of Psychology* Vols. 1 & 2 (Harvard, 1981).
3. Churchland, Paul, *Matter and Consciousness* (MIT, 1984).
4. Dennett, Daniel, *Brainstorms* (Bradford, 1978).
5. Fodor, Jerry, *Representations* (MIT, 1981).
6. Ryle, Gilbert, *The Concept of Mind* (Barnes & Noble, 1949).
7. Searle, John, *Minds, Brains and Science* (Harvard, 1985).
8. Shaffer, Jerome, *Philosophy of Mind* (Prentice Hall, 1968).
9. Taylor, Richard, *Metaphysics* (Prentice Hall, 1963).
10. Wittgenstein, Ludwig, *Philosophical Investigations* (Macmillan, 1953).


## ARTIFICIAL INTELLIGENCE AND HUMAN MENTALITY


1. Dreyfus, Hubert, *What Computers Can't Do* (Revised Edition, Harper-Row, 1979).
2. Dreyfus, Hubert, and Dreyfus, Stuart, *Mind Over Machine* (Macmillan, 1986).
3. Haugeland, John, *Mind Design* (MIT, 1981).
4. Pylyshyn, Zenon, *Computation and Cognition* (MIT, 1984).

# FREEDOM AND DETERMINISM

In his fascinating novel *Erewhon,* Samuel Butler describes a society where illness is punished and crime is treated. The citizens of Erewhon are brought to trial and punished when they are found guilty of being sick. What we consider criminal conduct, stealing for example, is treated in Erewhon the way we treat the sick. A person who steals is treated. Our reaction to social practice in Erewhon is that it is indeed bizarre. I submit that what makes it bizarre is that we believe people are not responsible for getting cancer or catching the flu but they usually are responsible for stealing. That's why we put sick people in hospitals and thieves in jail. What distinguishes our culture from that of Erewhon is a difference in beliefs concerning responsibility.

But why don't we hold people responsible for getting the flu? Because we believe that whereas people are usually *free* to refrain from stealing, they are not usually free to refrain from getting the flu. Getting the flu is something that happens to people; it's something they can't prevent. And we can't be responsible for something we can't prevent.

The principle underlying this discussion is often expressed by the phrase "Ought implies can." The point of the expression is that if I tell someone she ought to do something, then I presume she has the capability to do it. (I presume she is free to do it.) Another way of explaining the expression is by saying that human freedom is a presupposition of ethical practice. Unless human beings are free, ethical behavior is impossible. The logical sequence works like this: To be a moral being, a person must be an agent who can be held responsible for any of her actions that are subject to praise or blame. To be responsible for those actions, she must have been free in some sense or other either to do or not to do those acts. In the absence of freedom in this sense, it would be bizarre to hold someone morally responsible for them.

In fact the notion that human beings are free agents is a fundamental assumption of both our legal and moral systems. With respect to law, a quotation from Lon Fuller gets us to the heart of the matter.

> . . . In the law of property our familiar standards fail when nature intervenes and takes control, as when a river shifts its course, removing twenty acres from A's land

and adding twenty-five to B's. In cases like these the litigants do not appear as responsible agents, but as the helpless victims of outside forces. We can no longer ask: Who was to blame? What did they intend? Since our usual standards of justice fail us, we are at a loss to know what justice requires. If we were to lose throughout the law the view of man as a responsible center of action, all legal problems would become like those I have just suggested.*

Perhaps it is no accident that our legal and moral systems presuppose that human beings have sufficient freedom to be held responsible for their actions. We feel free; we believe we are free and we act on that belief. If someone told us that none of our actions were free, that we couldn't do otherwise, and that essentially our lives were closed books, we would protest most strenuously. Sometimes we don't feel free. We experience pressures and constraints and hence we admit to being more free on some occasions than on others. But we are free. Aren't we?

It might be instructive to look at human behavior from two points of view —from the perspective of an observer and from the perspective of the actor (the person actually performing the behavior).† Consider a child sitting at a desk making marks on paper. If we ask the child what she is doing, suppose she replies by saying, "I am doing my homework." But suppose we didn't ask the child what she was doing. Suppose a group of us just watched and reported on our observations. Note that our observations could be reported in different ways. A scientist who watched the behavior much as she might watch the behavior of atomic particles in a cloud chamber or the collision of billiard balls could simply report movements of certain parts of the body at certain times. For example at 7:35 the child moved the pencil with her right hand and made the following marks "7," "3," "4" while simultaneously opening the mouth widely. But surely that information is not very helpful in telling us what the

* Lon Fuller, *The Morality of Law*, rev. ed. (New Haven, Conn.: Yale University Press, 1964), p. 76.

† This discussion of the perspectives of the actor and the spectator is taken from Lewis White Beck's *The Actor and the Spectator* (New Haven, Conn.: Yale University Press, 1975).

child is doing. Another observer might avoid mentioning the movements of the child's body. She might say something like at 7:35 the child solved the problem of 968 minus 234, wrote the answer 734, and smiled broadly. Surely the second observation gives more insight into what the child is doing. Indeed many philosophers would argue that the second observation uses concepts of explanation that are fundamentally different from those of the first observation. These concepts include such things as motives, intentions, and purposes. Moreover, the claim is often made that motives, intentions, and purposes cannot be reduced to bodily movements and the corresponding electrical chemical reactions that cause the motion of muscles. Perhaps an illustration will make this point clearer. Consider the following three events:

1. A plant gradually grows toward the sun.
2. A fifth grader correctly computes that $3 \times 3 = 9$.
3. A mother saves a large percentage of her income so that her daughter may get a college education.

In each case there is an explanation for the event. The question why the event happened can be answered with a great deal of certainty. However, which events, if any, occurred voluntarily? For which events, if any, was the agent responsible?

Most of us would agree that the plant's turning to the sun was caused, and involuntary. Given the laws of nature and the composition of the plant, the plant couldn't do anything else but grow toward the sun. It would be a misuse of language to say that the plant was responsible for growing toward the sun. The philosophical question is whether or not *all* events can be explained in just the way we explain the plant's growing toward the sun.

Determinists would argue that all human behavior can ultimately be explained the way we explain the plant's growing toward the sun. Some determinists have been influenced by the methodology of the natural sciences. If the study of human behavior is to be a science in the strict sense, then the "laws" that apply to human behavior must be able to explain and predict human behavior with the same degree of reliability that "laws" that apply to nonhuman behavior do. And you can get that kind of reliability only if human behavior is ultimately reducible to the behavior reported by observer I in our "child doing homework" example. In a world where ultimately *everything* can be explained as you would explain the plant growing toward the sun, there is no place for human freedom.

Indeed in the branch of psychology called behaviorism, human behavior is to be explained and predicted using genuine scientific laws. The founder and chief exponent of behaviorism, B. F. Skinner, has characterized the postulate of human freedom as unscientific. Skinner argues that human behavior responds to negative and positive reinforcement. We repeat behavior that brings pleasure and avoid behavior that brings pain. If we can determine what brings people pleasure and pain and if we sufficiently control the environment, we can explain and predict human behavior. No concept of free will is needed. If we ask why the child is doing her homework, the behaviorist will answer that the child has learned that she will be rewarded if she does and punished if she doesn't. If you give the child enough consistent conditioning, the laws for explaining human behavior will resemble the laws for explaining nonhuman behavior. But suppose on occasion the child does not behave as predicted. Some evenings she refuses to do her homework, and suppose on many of those nights there is no obvious explanation—no competing interest like a favorite TV program or party at her girlfriend's. On these occasions she simply doesn't feel like doing her homework. Even here the discipline of psychology is not without an answer. Psychoanalysts using their laws of unconscious motivation, compulsion, and neurosis would explain why the child didn't feel like doing her homework. Indeed these psychoanalysts would even try to predict future occasions of failing to do homework or would try to manipulate the patient so that the cause of her neurosis could be removed.

But in solving mathematical problems, the child is using reasons for getting the answers she does. Perhaps she is doing the homework in order to receive a reward. But she is not putting the mark "734" on the paper to get a reward. She is doing that because she uses good mathematical reasons. Certainly. But does that show that the chain of reasoning in solving a mathematical puzzle is different in kind from the chain of events that pushes the child to do her homework? In other words, is there something special about reasoning that exempts it from the realm of causal explanation? Philosophers who answer this question in the negative are determinists with respect to mental events.

The attempt to explain and predict human behavior on scientific grounds is not the only threat to the idea that humans have free will. Suppose the course of all future events has already been determined—by God's will, for example. Then wouldn't human freedom be impossible? This doctrine, known as fatalism, begins our discussion of free will.

However, whereas many thinkers argue either that fatalism makes free will impossible or that the concept of free will is unscientific, others are just as insistent that human beings are free and that that is why social science based on the methodology of the natural sciences is such an abysmal failure. Certainly it would be more convenient for science if human beings weren't free. However, the fact that a concept of causality is convenient for the "scientific" study of behavior is not a sufficient reason for adopting it. The right question to ask is whether the scientific view is plausible in terms of helping us understand human behavior. In the section on nondeterminism, a number of philosophers discuss the question of free will from a nonscientific point of view. James argues that a kind of **indeterminism** is the best explanation of some of the human behavior we actually observe. Campbell and Sartre argue that the postulate of freedom is necessary to explain moral behavior and our sense of responsibility.

Despite the apparent irreconcilability of the two perspectives on human behavior, perhaps free will and causal explanation are not inconsistent. Perhaps there is a place for both. Although this view has a long tradition, it became especially prominent during the mid-twentieth century and has been given the name **compatibilism.** One branch of compatibilism tries to give an explanation of praise and blame and other moral concepts in a causal world. Most exponents of free will have rejected this branch of compatibilism on the grounds that the view of morality presented is an impoverished and truncated one. It does not do justice to moral experience. Still others attempt to show that free will requires causality. If you choose to accomplish some act, like losing weight rather than going to the pub, you can only accomplish your goal in a causally ordered world. You depend on a world where exercising has a positive correlation with weight loss and drinking beer doesn't.

But to show that free will requires some causal laws is not the same as showing that we can be free in a world with nothing but causal laws. The most recent trend is to focus on the agent as an actor in the causal world. Rather than think of ourselves as observers of human behavior, think of ourselves as actors, as participants in the causal chain. But are we genuine participants or puppets playing out a role? If we are actors, do we have some control over the script or must we always do what the director requires?

# *Fatalism*

In the popular mind, philosophy is often identified with a particular philosophical theory —the theory of fatalism. A recent television news story carried interviews with refugees from an Atlantic Coast hurricane. While most of the interviewees appeared emotionally distraught about possible major damage to their homes, one man said that you must be philosophical. "Que sera, sera." What will be will be. Persons who show anxiety about dying on their next airplane trip or in the next war are advised not to worry. If your time has come then your time has come. You will only get the bullet with your name on it. These expressions of fatalism and particularly the emotional stance one should take in response to fate are what many people mean when they characterize a person as philosophical. In reality very few philosophers are fatalists—either emotionally or intellectually.

Fatalism is the view that what will happen and what will not happen has already been decided. Since events are predestined, the only thing under human control is our response to events—our emotions. As one of the early Stoics said, "Man should be like a dog tied behind a cart, he should decide that he wants to go where the cart is going to go." In the classic Stoic view, human beings should not "fight fate"; they should be emotionally accepting of what life brings them. The Stoic way of life is the life of acceptance.

But what reasons do we have to think that fatalism is true? One reason is provided by logic and epistemology. The position can be illustrated by considering a problem that bothered Aristotle. Consider any possible present state of affairs. Either that state of affairs is occurring and the statement describing it is true or the state of affairs is not occurring and the statement describing it is false. It is raining or it is not raining. You are studying now or you are not studying now. What is true of the present is true of the past. Either Napoleon lost the Battle of Waterloo or he did not lose the Battle of Waterloo. Either astronauts have walked on the moon or they have not walked on the moon. Now consider statements about the future. Either there will be a major earthquake in California in 1995 or there will not be a major earthquake in California in 1995. Suppose it is true there will be a major earthquake in California in 1995; then it is true now there will be a major earthquake in 1995. Of course, if you make the contradictory supposition, then it is false there will be a major earthquake in California in 1995 and hence it is false now that there will be an earthquake in 1995. We may not know whether the statement, "There will be a major earthquake in California in 1995" is true or false, but the statement is either true or false now.

Some students take the fatalist view too far when they say, "Either I will pass the exam tomorrow or I will not pass the exam tomorrow. If it is true I will pass the exam tomorrow, then I will. If it is false I will pass the exam tomorrow, then I won't pass it. In either case, why study?"

What the student forgets is that fatalism is the view that *all* events are predetermined. If it is fated that you will pass the exam, it is also fated that you will study. The student's question would make sense only if some events were fated and some were not. Only then could the student claim that since the outcome of the exam is fated, studying is irrelevant. Under fatalism both the outcome of the exam and whether or not the student studies for it are equally fated.

One way to avoid fatalism is not to make truth claims about the future. Suppose we can speak truthfully only about events in the present or past. One disadvantage of that view according to many is that such a view restricts the application of logic. Except for the problem created by fatalism, the laws of logic work just fine for statements about the future. Applying the rules of logic to the future does not create invalid arguments. Isn't it arbitrary to restrict logic because the implications of its use create a metaphysical problem? Perhaps the problem should be addressed instead.

But logic isn't the only problem. As we shall see in the religion chapter, many people believe in an all-knowing God—an **omniscient** God. But if God knows everything, God knows the future. Since knowing the future means knowing what will happen in the future, the existence of an omniscient being seems to require fatalism. God now knows all true statements about the future. God knows whether there will be an earthquake in 1995 in California.

Some believe that the problem created by an omniscient God is a special case of the "Book of Life" example. Suppose you went to the library and found a book that described your life. Every statement up to and including the present was true. If you read ahead, wouldn't you believe the statements about your future and become a fatalist? It is only because we have not seen the book of our life that we think we can do differently than we do. Either there is no book of life or everything that happens to us and everything that we do has already been decided. To adopt the latter point of view is to be a fatalist.

## *Aristotle (384–322 B.C.)*

Aristotle was a pupil of Plato. Many consider Aristotle's philosophy to be a reaction to the otherworldly epistemology and metaphysics of his teacher; however, Aristotle, universally recognized as one of the greatest philosophers, did far more than reformulate the theory of his teacher. He made original contributions in all branches of philosophy. He is the founder of traditional logic; his laws of thought are still accepted today, and the details of his class inclusion logic were accepted until the turn of this century. Aristotle's three fundamental laws of thought are the following:

1. A thing is what it is and is not another thing (Law of Identity).
2. Something cannot take on a property and its opposite property in the same way at the same time (Law of Noncontradiction).
3. Either something is the case or it is not the case (Law of Excluded Middle).

These laws are meant to be universal principles of human thought. However, a peculiar problem arises when you apply the Law of Excluded Middle to statements about the future. Either the future event will occur or it won't. But suppose the event will occur. If it will, it is true now that it will. On the other hand, suppose the event will not occur. If it won't, it is true now that it won't. Since these are the only two possibilities, fatalism seems to be the result. In the selection included here, Aristotle illustrates the problem with a sea battle as the example. Should we give up the law of the excluded middle and accept fatalism, or is there some way out?

# The Sea Battle

## *Aristotle*

. . . An affirmation is a positive assertion of something about something, a denial a negative assertion. . . .

We will call such a pair of propositions a pair of contradictories. Those positive and negative propositions are said to be contradictory which have the same subject and predicate. The identity of subject and of predicate must not be **"equivocal."**. . .

In the case of that which is or which has taken place, **propositions,** whether positive or negative, must be true or false. . . . When the subject . . . is individual, and that which is predicated of it relates to the future, the case is altered. For if all propositions whether positive or negative are either true or false, then any given predicate must either belong to the subject or not, so that if one man affirms that an event of a given character will take place and another denies it, it is plain that the statement of the one will correspond with reality and that of the other will not. For the predicate cannot both belong and not belong to the subject at one and the same time with regard to the future.

Thus, if it is true to say that a thing is white, it must necessarily be white; if the reverse proposition is true, it will of necessity not be white. Again, if it is white, the proposition stating that it is white was true; if it is not white, the proposition to the opposite effect was true. And if it is not white, the man who states that it is is making a false statement; and if the man who states that it is white is making a false statement, it follows that it is not white. It may therefore be argued that it is necessary that affirmations or denials must be either true or false.

Now if this be so, nothing is or takes place fortuitously, either in the present or in the future, and there are no real alternatives; everything takes place of necessity and is fixed. For either he that affirms that it will take place or he that denies this is in correspondence with fact, whereas if things did not take place of necessity, an event might just as easily not happen as happen; for the meaning of the word **"fortuitous"** with regard to present or future events is that reality is so constituted that it may issue in either of two opposite directions.

Again, if a thing is white now, it was true before to say that it would be white, so that of anything that has taken place it was always true to say "it is" or "it will be." But if it was always true to say that a thing is or will be, it is not possible that it should not be or not be about to be, and when a thing cannot not come to be, it is impossible that it should not come to be, and when it is impossible that it should not come to be, it must come to be. All, then, that is about to be must of necessity take place. It results from this that nothing is uncertain or fortuitous, for if it were fortuitous it would not be necessary.

Again, to say that neither the affirmation nor the denial is true, maintaining, let us say, that an event neither will take place nor will not take place, is to take up a position impossible to defend. In the first place, though facts should prove the one proposition false, the opposite would still be untrue. Secondly, if it was true to say that a thing was both white and large, both these qualities must necessarily belong to it; and if they will belong to it the next day, they must necessarily belong to it the next day. But if an event is neither to take place nor not to take place the next day, the element of chance will be eliminated. For example, it would be necessary that a sea-fight should neither take place nor fail to take place on the next day.

These awkward results and others of the same kind follow, if it is an irrefragable law that of every pair of contradictory propositions,

Abridged from *The Oxford Translation of Aristotle*. Edited by W. D. Ross, Vol. 1 (1928). Reprinted by permission of Oxford University Press.

whether they have regard to universals and are stated as universally applicable, or whether they have regard to individuals, one must be true and the other false, and that there are no real alternatives, but that all that is or takes place is the outcome of necessity. There would be no need to deliberate or to take trouble, on the supposition that if we should adopt a certain course, a certain result would follow, while, if we did not, the result would not follow. For a man may predict an event ten thousand years beforehand, and another may predict the reverse; that which was truly predicted at the moment in the past will of necessity take place in the fullness of time.

Further, it makes no difference whether people have or have not actually made the contradictory statements. For it is manifest that the circumstances are not influenced by the fact of an affirmation or denial on the part of anyone. For events will not take place or fail to take place because it was stated that they would or would not take place, nor is this any more the case if the prediction dates back ten thousand years or any other space of time. Wherefore, if through all time the nature of things was so constituted that a prediction about an event was true, then through all time it was necessary that that prediction should find fulfilment; and with regard to all events, circumstances have always been such that their occurrence is a matter of necessity. For that of which someone has said truly that it will be, cannot fail to take place; and of that which takes place, it was always true to say that it would be.

Yet this view leads to an impossible conclusion; for we see that both deliberation and action are causative with regard to the future, and that, to speak more generally, in those things which are not continuously actual there is a potentiality in either direction. Such things may either be or not be; events also therefore may either take place or not take place. There are many obvious instances of this. It is possible that this coat may be cut in half, and yet it may not be cut in half, but wear out first. In the same way, it is possible that it should not be cut in half; unless this were so, it would not be possible that it should wear out first. So it is therefore with all other events which possess this kind of potentiality. It is therefore plain that it is not of necessity that everything is or takes place; but in some instances there are real alternatives, in which case the affirmation is no more true and no more false than the denial; while some exhibit a predisposition and general tendency in one direction or the other, and yet can issue in the opposite direction by exception.

Now that which is must needs be when it is, and that which is not must needs not be when it is not. Yet it cannot be said without qualification that all existence and non-existence is the outcome of necessity. For there is a difference between saying that that which is, when it is, must needs be, and simply saying that all that is must needs be, and similarly in the case of that which is not. In the case, also, of two contradictory propositions this holds good. Everything must either be or not be, whether in the present or in the future, but it is not always possible to distinguish and state determinately which of these alternatives must necessarily come about.

Let me illustrate. A sea-fight must either take place tomorrow or not, but it is not necessary that it should take place tomorrow, neither is it necessary that it should not take place, yet it is necessary that it either should or should not take place tomorrow. Since propositions correspond with facts, it is evident that when in future events there is a real alternative, and a potentiality in contrary directions, the corresponding affirmation and denial have the same character.

This is the case with regard to that which is not always existent or not always non-existent. One of the two propositions in such instances must be true and the other false, but we cannot say determinately that this or that is false, but must leave the alternative undecided. One may indeed be more likely to be true than the other, but it cannot be either actually true or actually false. It is therefore plain that it is not necessary that of an affirmation and a denial one should be true and the other false. For in the case of that which exists potentially, but not actually, the rule which applies to that which exists actually does not hold good. . . .

## *Richard Taylor (b. 1919)*

Richard Taylor is a contemporary philosopher who has made significant contributions in metaphysics and ethics. Of special interest to Taylor is the problem of free will. His theory of agency is represented in another section. Taylor's published works include the influential text *Metaphysics* (1963); his original contribution to the free will debate, *Action and Purpose* (1965); and his contributions to ethics and political philosophy, *Good and Evil* (1960), *Freedom, Anarchy and the Law* (1973), and *With Heart and Mind* (1973).

Professor Taylor's entry to the free will debate was through the issue of fatalism. His early articles revived fatalistic arguments. These arguments spawned a flurry of articles designed to meet the challenge of fatalism. The selection from *Metaphysics* included here reviews the various routes to fatalism and possible responses.

# Fate

## *Richard Taylor*

We all, at certain moments of pain, threat, or bereavement, are apt to entertain the idea of fatalism, the thought that what is happening at a particular moment is unavoidable, that we are powerless to prevent it. Sometimes we find ourselves in circumstances not of our own making, in which our very being and destinies are so thoroughly anchored that the thought of fatalism can be quite overwhelming, and sometimes consoling. One feels that whatever then happens, however good or ill, will be what those circumstances yield, and we are helpless. Soldiers, it is said, are sometimes possessed by such thoughts. Perhaps all men would feel more inclined to them if they paused once in a while to think of how little they ever had to do with bringing themselves to wherever they have arrived in life, how much of their fortunes and destinies were decided for them by sheer circumstance, and how the entire course of their lives is often set, once and for all, by the most trivial incidents, which they did not produce and could not even have foreseen. If we are free to work out our destinies at all, which is doubtful, we have a freedom that is at best exercised within exceedingly narrow paths. All the important things—when we are born, of what parents, into what culture, whether we are loved or rejected, whether we are male or female, our temperament, our intelligence or stupidity, indeed everything that makes for the bulk of our happiness and misery—all these are decided for us by the most casual and indifferent circumstances, by sheer coincidences, chance encounters, and seemingly insignificant fortuities. One can see this in retrospect if he searches, but few search. The fate that has given us our very being has given us also our pride and conceit, and has thereby formed us so that, being human, we congratulate ourselves on our blessings, which we call our achievements, blame the world for our blunders, which we call our misfortunes, and scarcely give a thought to that impersonal fate which arbitrarily dispenses both. . . .

A fatalist . . . is someone who believes that whatever happens is and always was unavoidable. He thinks it is not up to him what will hap-

Abridged from *Metaphysics,* 2d ed., by Richard Taylor. (Englewood Cliffs: Prentice-Hall, Inc., © 1974), pp. 58–68. Reprinted by permission of Prentice-Hall, Inc.

pen a thousand years hence, next year, tomorrow, or the very next moment. Of course he does not pretend always to *know* what is going to happen. Hence, he might try sometimes to read signs and portents, as meteorologists and astrologers do, or to contemplate the effects upon him of the various things that might, for all he knows, be fated to occur. But he does not suppose that whatever happens could ever have really been avoidable.

A fatalist thus thinks of the future in the way we all think of the past, for all men are fatalists as they look *back* on things. To a large extent we know what has happened—some of it we can even remember—whereas the future is still obscure to us, and we are therefore tempted to invest it, in our imagination, with all sorts of "possibilities." The fatalist resists this temptation, knowing that mere ignorance can hardly give rise to any genuine possibility in things. He thinks of both past and future "under the aspect of eternity," the way God is supposed to view them. We all think of the past this way, as something settled and fixed, to be taken for what it is. We are never in the least tempted to try to modify it. It is not in the least up to us what happened last year, yesterday, or even a moment ago, any more than are the motions of the heavens or the political developments in Tibet. If we are not fatalists, then we might think that past things once *were* up to us, to bring about or prevent, as long as they were still future—but this expresses our attitude toward the future, not the past.

Such is surely our conception of the whole past, whether near or remote. But the consistent fatalist thinks of the future in the same way. We say of past things that they are no longer within our power. The fatalist says they never were.

A fatalistic way of thinking most often arises from theological ideas, or from what are generally thought to be certain presuppositions of science and logic. Thus, if God is really all-knowing and all-powerful, it is not hard to suppose that He has arranged for everything to happen just as it is going to happen, that He already knows every detail of the whole future course of the world, and there is nothing left for you and me to do except watch things unfold, in the here or hereafter. But without bringing God into the picture, it is not hard to suppose, as we have seen, that everything that happens is wholly determined by what went before it, and hence that whatever happens at any future time is the only thing that can then happen, given what precedes it. Or even disregarding that, it seems natural to suppose that there is a body of truth concerning what the future holds, just as there is such truth concerning what is contained in the past, whether or not it is known to any man or even to God, and hence, that everything asserted in that body of truth will assuredly happen, in the fullness of time, precisely as it is described therein.

No one needs to be convinced that fatalism is the only proper way to view the past. That it is also the proper way to view the future is less obvious, due in part, perhaps, to our vastly greater ignorance of what the future holds. The consequences of holding such fatalism are obviously momentous. To say nothing of the consolation of fatalism, which enables a person to view all things as they arise with the same undisturbed mind with which he contemplates even the most revolting of history's horrors, the fatalist teaching also relieves one of all tendency toward both blame and approbation of others and of both guilt and conceit in himself. It promises that a perfect understanding is possible, and removes the temptation to view things in terms of human wickedness and moral responsibility. This thought alone, once firmly grasped, yields a sublime acceptance of all that life and nature offer, whether to oneself or one's fellows; and although it thereby reduces one's pride, it simultaneously enhances the feelings, opens the heart, and expands the understanding. . . .

Let us suppose that God has revealed a particular set of facts to a chosen scribe who, believing (correctly) that they came from God, wrote them all down. The facts in question then turned out to be all the more or less significant episodes in the life of some perfectly ordinary man named Osmo. Osmo was entirely unknown to the scribe, and in fact to just about everyone, but there was no doubt concerning whom all these facts were about, for the very first thing received by the scribe from God, was: "He of whom I speak is called Osmo." When the revelations reached a fairly voluminous bulk and appeared to be completed, the scribe arranged them in chronological order and assembled them into a book. He at first gave it the title *The Life of Osmo, as Given by God,* but thinking that people would take this to be some sort of joke, he dropped the reference to God.

The book was published, but attracted no attention whatsoever, because it appeared to be nothing more than a record of the dull life of a very plain man named Osmo. The scribe wondered, in fact, why God had chosen to convey such a mass of seemingly pointless trivia.

The book eventually found its way into various libraries, where it gathered dust until one day a high school teacher in Indiana, who rejoiced under the name of Osmo, saw a copy on the shelf. The title caught his eye. Curiously picking it up and blowing the dust off, he was thunderstruck by the opening sentence: "Osmo is born in Mercy Hospital in Auburn, Indiana, on June 6, 1942, of Finnish parentage, and after nearly losing his life from an attack of pneumonia at the age of five, he is enrolled in the St. James school there." Osmo turned pale. The book nearly fell from his hands. He thumbed back in excitement to discover who had written it. Nothing was given of its authorship nor, for that matter, of its publisher. His questions of the librarian produced no further information, he being as ignorant as Osmo of how the book came to be there.

So Osmo, with the book pressed tightly under his arm, dashed across the street for some coffee, thinking to compose himself and then examine this book with care. Meanwhile he glanced at a few more of its opening remarks, at the things said there about his difficulties with his younger sister, how he was slow in learning to read, of the summer on Mackinac Island, and so on. His emotions now somewhat quieted, Osmo began a close reading. He noticed that everything was expressed in the present tense, the way newspaper headlines are written. For example, the text read, "Osmo is born in Mercy Hospital," instead of saying he *was* born there, and it recorded that he quarrels with his sister, is a slow student, is fitted with dental braces at age eight, and so on, all in the journalistic present tense. But the text itself made quite clear approximately when all these various things happened, for everything was in chronological order, and in any case each year of its subject's life constituted a separate chapter, and was so titled—"Osmo's Seventh Year," "Osmo's Eighth Year," and so on through the book.

Osmo became absolutely engrossed, to the extent that he forgot his original astonishment, bordering on panic, and for a while even lost his curiosity concerning authorship. He sat drinking coffee and reliving his childhood, much of which he had all but forgotten until the memories were revived by the book now before him. He had almost forgotten about the kitten, for example, and had entirely forgotten its name, until he read, in the chapter called "Osmo's Seventh Year," this observation: "Sobbing, Osmo takes Fluffy, now quite dead, to the garden, and buries her next to the rose bush." Ah yes! And then there was Louise, who sat next to him in the eighth grade—it was all right there. And how he got caught smoking one day. And how he felt when his father died. On and on. Osmo became so absorbed that he quite forgot the business of the day, until it occurred to him to turn to Chapter 26, to see what might be said there, he having just recently turned twenty-six. He had no sooner done so than his panic returned, for lo! what the book said was *true!* That it rains on his birthday for example, that his wife fails to give him the binoculars he had hinted he would like, that he receives a raise in salary shortly thereafter, and so on. Now how in God's name, Osmo pondered, could anyone know that, apparently before it had happened? For these were quite recent events, and the book had dust on it. Quickly moving on, Osmo came to this: "Sitting and reading in the coffee shop across from the library, Osmo, perspiring copiously, entirely forgets, until it is too late, that he is supposed to collect his wife at the hairdresser's at four." Oh my god! He had forgotten all about that. Yanking out his watch, Osmo discovered that it was nearly five o'clock — too late. She would be on her way home by now, and in a very sour mood.

Osmo's anguish at this discovery was nothing, though, compared to what the rest of the day held for him. He poured more coffee, and it now occurred to him to check the number of chapters in this amazing book. Only twenty-nine! But surely, he thought, that doesn't mean anything. How anyone could have gotten all this stuff down so far was puzzling enough, to be sure, but no one on God's earth could possibly know in advance how long this or that man is going to live. (Only God could know that sort of thing, Osmo reflected.) So he read along; though not without considerable uneasiness and even depression, for the remaining three chapters were on the whole discouraging. He thought he had gotten that ulcer under control, for example. And he didn't see any reason to suppose his job was going to turn out that badly, or that he was really going to break a leg skiing; after all, he could just give up skiing. But then the book ended on a terribly dismal note. It said: "And Osmo, having taken Northwest flight 569 from O'Hare, perishes when the aircraft crashes on the runway at Fort Wayne, with considerable loss of life, a tragedy rendered the more calamitous by the fact that Osmo had neglected to renew his life insurance before the expiration of the grace period." And that was all. That was the end of the book.

So *that's* why it had only twenty-nine chapters. Some idiot thought he was going to get killed in a plane crash. But, Osmo thought, he just wouldn't get on that plane. And this would also remind him to keep his insurance in force.

(About three years later our hero, having boarded a flight for St. Paul, went berserk when the pilot announced they were going to land at Fort Wayne instead. According to one of the stewardesses, he tried to hijack the aircraft and divert it to another airfield. The Civil Aeronautics Board cited the resulting disruptions as contributing to the crash that followed as the plane tried to land).

Osmo's extraordinary circumstances led him to embrace the doctrine of fatalism. Not quite completely, perhaps, for there he was, right up to the end, trying vainly to buck his fate — trying, in effect, to make a fool of God, though he did not know this, because he had no idea of the book's source. Still, he had the overwhelming evidence of his whole past life to make him think that everything was going to work out exactly as described in the book. It always had. It was, in fact, precisely this conviction that terrified him so.

But now let us ask these questions, in order to make Osmo's experiences more relevant to our own. First, why did he become, or nearly become, a fatalist? Second, just what did his fatalism amount to? Third, was his belief justified in terms of the evidence he had? And finally, is that belief justified in terms of the evidence *we* have — or in other words, should we be fatalists too?

This last, of course, is the important metaphysical question, but we have to approach it through the others.

*Why did Osmo become a fatalist?* Osmo became a fatalist because there existed a set of true statements about the details of his life, both past and future, and he came to know what some of these statements were and to believe them, including many concerning his future. That is the whole of it.

No theological ideas entered into his conviction, nor any presuppositions about causal determinism, the coercion of his actions by causes, or anything of this sort. The foundations of Osmo's fatalism were entirely in logic and epistemology, having only to do with truth and knowledge. Ideas about God did not enter in, for he never suspected that God was the ultimate source of those statements. And at no point did he think God was *making* him do what he did. All he was concerned about was that someone seemed somehow to *know* what he had done and was going to do.

*What, then, did Osmo believe?* He did not, it should be noted, believe that certain things were going to happen to him, *no matter what.* That does not express a logically coherent belief. He did not think he was in danger of perishing in an airplane crash even in case he did not get into any airplane, for example, or that he was going to break his leg skiing, whether he went skiing or not. No one believes what he considers to be plainly impossible. If anyone believes that a given event is going to happen, he does not doubt that those things necessary for its occurrence are going to happen too. The expression, "no matter what," by means of which some philosophers have sought an easy and even childish refutation of fatalism, is accordingly highly inappropriate in any description of the fatalist conviction.

Osmo's fatalism was simply the realization that the things described in the book were unavoidable.

Of course we are all fatalists in this sense about some things, and the metaphysical question is whether this familiar attitude should not be extended to everything. We know the sun will rise tomorrow, for example, and there is nothing we can do about it. Each of us knows he is sooner or later going to die, too, and there is nothing to be done about that either. We normally do not know just when, of course, but it is mercifully so! For otherwise we would simply sit checking off the days as they passed, with growing despair, like a man condemned to the gallows and knowing the hour set for his execution. The tides ebb and flow, and heavens revolve, the seasons follow in order, generations arise and pass, and no one speaks of taking preventive measures. With respect to those things each of us recognizes as beyond his control, we are of necessity fatalists.

The question of fatalism is simply: Of all the things that happen in the world, which, if any, are avoidable? And the philosophical fatalist replies: None of them. They never were. Some of them only seemed so.

*Was Osmo's fatalism justified?* Of course it was. When he could sit right there and read a true description of those parts of his life that had not yet been lived, it would be idle to suggest to him that his future might, nonetheless, contain alternative possibilities. The only doubts Osmo had were whether those statements could really be true. But here he had the proof of his own experience, as one by one they were tested. Whenever he tried to prevent what was set forth, he of course failed. Such failure, over and over, of even the most herculean efforts, with never a single success, must surely suggest, sooner or later, that he was *destined* to fail. Even to the end, when Osmo tried so desperately to save himself from the destruction described in the book, his effort was totally in vain—as he should have realized it was going to be had he really known that what was said there was true. No power in heaven or earth can render false a statement that is true. It has never been done, and never will be.

*Is the doctrine of fatalism, then, true?* This amounts to asking whether our circumstances are significantly different from Osmo's. Of course we cannot read our own biographies the way he could. Only men who become famous ever have their lives recorded, and even so, it is always in retrospect. This is unfortunate. It is too bad that someone with sufficient knowledge—God, for example—cannot set down the lives of great men in advance, so that their achievements can be appreciated better by their contemporaries, and indeed, by their predecessors—their parents, for instance. But mortals do not have the requisite knowledge, and if there is any god who does, he seems to keep it to himself.

None of this matters, as far as our own fatalism is concerned. For the important thing to note is that, of the two considerations that explain Osmo's fatalism, only one of them was philosophically relevant, and that one applies to us no less than to him. The two considerations were: (1) there existed a set of true statements about his life, both past and future, and (2) he came to know what those statements were and to believe them. Now the second of these two considerations explains why, as a matter of psychological fact, Osmo became fatalistic, but it has nothing to do with the validity of that point of view. Its validity is assured by (1) alone. It was not the fact that the statements happened to be written down that rendered the things they described unavoidable: that had nothing to do with it at all. Nor was it the fact that, because they had been written, Osmo could read them. His reading them and coming to believe them likewise had nothing to do with the inevitability of what they described.

This was ensured simply by there being such a set of statements, whether written or not, whether read by anyone or not, and whether or not known to be true. All that is required is that they should *be* true.

Each of us has but one possible past, described by that totality of statements about us in the past tense, each of which happens to be true. No one ever thinks of rearranging things there; it is simply accepted as given. But so also, each of us has but one possible future, described by that totality of statements about oneself in the future tense, each of which happens to be true. The sum of these constitutes one's biography. Part of it has been lived. The main outlines of it can still be seen, in retrospect, though most of its details are obscure. The other part has not been lived, though it most assuredly is going to be, in exact accordance with that set of statements just referred to. Some of its outlines can already be seen, in prospect, but it is on the whole more obscure than the part belonging to the past. We have at best only premonitory glimpses of it. It is no doubt for this reason that not all of this part, the part that awaits us, is perceived as given, and men do sometimes speak absurdly of altering it—as though what the future holds, as identified by any true statement in the future tense, might after all *not* hold.

Osmo's biography was all expressed in the present tense because all that mattered was that the things referred to were real events; it did not matter to what part of time they belonged. His past consisted of those things that preceded his reading of the book, and he simply accepted it as given. He was not tempted to revise what was said there, for he was sure it was true. But it took the book to make him realize that his future was also something given. It was equally pointless for him to try to revise what was said there, for it, too, was true. As the past contains what has happened, the future contains what will happen, and neither contains, in addition to these things, various other things that did not and will not happen.

Of course we know relatively little of what the future contains. Some things we know. We know the sun will go on rising and setting, for example, that taxes will be levied and wars rage, that men will continue to be callous and greedy, and that people will be murdered and robbed. It is just the details that remain to be discovered. But the same is true of the past; it is only a matter of degree. When I meet a total stranger I do not know, and will probably never know, what his past has been, beyond certain obvious things—that he had a mother, and things of this sort. I know nothing of the particulars of that vast realm of fact that is unique to his past. And the same for his future, with only this difference—that *all* men are strangers to me as far as their futures are concerned, and here I am even a stranger to myself.

Yet there is one thing I know concerning any stranger's past and the past of everything under the sun; namely, that whatever it might hold, there is nothing anyone can do about it now. What has happened cannot be undone. The mere fact that it has happened guarantees this.

And so it is, by the same token, of the future of everything under the sun. Whatever the future might hold, there is nothing anyone can do about it now. What will happen cannot be altered. The mere fact that it is going to happen guarantees this. . . .

# Determinism

Determinism is the view that all events in the world are caused wholly and only by antecedent (past) events. Under this definition, it looks as if all events could not have been and could not be otherwise. Traditionally the doctrine of determinism has been associated with the rise of science and with the scientific worldview. Thus the first materialist, the atomist Democritus, was also a determinist. He argued that nothing ever happened by chance. Perhaps the most sweeping scientific determinism was stated by the French astronomer Laplace: If a superhuman intelligence knew all the facts at a given point in time as well as all the causal laws governing those facts he or she would be able to deduce all the facts about the past (know all of history) and know everything about the future. Scientific explanation is causal explanation that is complete explanation.

One does not have to be a Laplacean to argue that determinism is the correct perspective for a scientist of human behavior to take. Scientists and philosophers who would like to build a science of human behavior on the model of the natural sciences make two complementary arguments. On the one hand, they argue that a genuine explanation of human behavior is possible only within the determinist framework. On the other hand, they argue that those aspects of human life such as "uniqueness," the capacity for moral choice, and our propensity to hold persons responsible for their actions can be adequately accounted for within a deterministic system.

Determinism is not solely in the preserve of those who wish to model a science of human behavior on the natural sciences. Psychoanalytic theory can be equally deterministic. The Oedipal complex functions as a cause just as other scientific entities do. At least that is the argument of many psychoanalysts and their philosopher allies. The technique of psychoanalytic determinism has been well demonstrated in the courtroom tactics of famous trial lawyers. Perhaps the master here was Clarence Darrow whose articles and defense pleadings have been collected in a book *Attorney for the Damned.* In a famous 1924 trial, Darrow defended two boys from wealthy families, Nathan Leopold and Richard Loeb, in the kidnap murder of Bobby Franks, the son of a prominent Chicago businessperson. Arguing against the perception that this was a senseless, purposeless, useless act, Darrow tried to show how the act had to be determined.

> Why did they kill little Bobby Franks? Not for money, not for spite, not for hate. They killed him as they might kill a spider or a fly, for the experience. They killed him because they were made that way. . . . Intelligent people now know that every human being is the product of the endless heredity back of him and the infinite environment around him. . . . it is just as often a great misfortune to be the child of the rich as it is to be the child of the poor.*

What Darrow did not provide were the details —the specific causes. But contemporary psychoanalytic theory has many potential causes for our conduct—from a senseless murder to a slip of the tongue. These psychoanalytic causes are discussed in great detail in the article by John Hospers.

Although psychoanalytic theory has a range of causes for all our behavior, it has achieved its greatest success and notoriety in explaining unusual or bizarre behavior. Another deterministic school of psychology—behaviorism—is more closely associated with ordinary behavior. Human beings avoid pain and seek pleasure. Through **conditioning,** human beings learn which activities are associated with pleasure and which are associated with pain. Humans will then pursue the former and avoid the latter. Reward and punishment are incorporated into behaviorist theory as positive and negative **reinforcement.** Desirable behavior is rewarded and undesirable behavior is punished. Through this technique,

---

* Clarence Darrow, *Attorney for the Damned* (New York: Simon and Schuster, 1957), pp. 35, 56, 59.

which is called conditioning, human beings are trained to do what is morally appropriate. The most successful method for making people behave morally is to reward morally appropriate behavior. Significantly, most determinists would accept some version of this account of reward, punishment, and moral responsibility.

Nondeterminists and others who reject determinism would find the account unsatisfactory. Consider, for example, standard criticisms of behaviorism. If behaviorism were to prevail, our legal (and moral) institutions would have to be completely redesigned. Rehabilitation and treatment would be emphasized at the expense of due process and findings of fault. Those standards of fault and due process have no real role to play in settings where behavior is controlled by operant conditioning. If the societal practice changes extensively toward the behavioral model, a radical and revolutionary change would have to take place in the practice of law and morals.

Moreover, behaviorism has no way of providing an objective test for what is right and wrong. The type of person we are—including our beliefs about matters of ethics—is a result of environmental forces including the forces of other human conditioners. Hence your views about what is right and wrong depend on the views of others—specifically on the views of those that condition behavior. But what about the ethical views of the conditioners? Either those views were in turn conditioned and we have the start of an infinite regress or the ethical views of the conditioners were not established by conditioning. If the behaviorist opts for the latter alternative, then he or she must admit that not all behavior and beliefs are conditioned. But that contradicts the behaviorist's central postulate. For behaviorism what is good is what those in charge of conditioning say is good. But what reason do we have to think that the conditioners are right?

One final area a determinist must address is the realm of mental processes. Aren't conscious processes immune from causal analysis? In the final selection, Brand Blanshard applies the determinist thesis to mental events including thought processes governed by rational laws. In his multilayered theory of causality, Blanshard distinguishes physical determinism from rational determinism. In the homework example cited in the general introduction, the answer 734 is not physically determined; it is rationally determined. But it is determined none the less.

## *Adolf Grünbaum (b. 1923)*

Adolf Grünbaum is a contemporary American analytic philosopher who has made significant contributions to the philosophy of science and metaphysics. Professor Grünbaum has been a strong defender of applying the scientific method to the study of human behavior. In a piece for *American Scientist* which is reprinted here, Professor Grünbaum challenges many of the traditional arguments that attempt to show that human behavior is unpredictable. In articles published later in his career Professor Grünbaum has tried to show how causal explanations of human behavior leave room for traditional concepts like reward and punishment, praise and blame.

# Causality and the Science of Human Behavior

*Adolf Grünbaum*

It is not uncommon to find that even those who have complete confidence in the continued success of the scientific method when applied to inanimate nature are highly skeptical of its applicability to the study of human behavior. Some go so far as to assert quite categorically that the methods of the natural sciences are in principle incompetent to yield predictions of man's individual or social behavior. . . .

Several important arguments have been offered against the hypothesis that cause-effect relationships exist in human behavior. These arguments are intended to deny the possibility of making the predictions which only the existence of such relationships would render feasible. In this article I shall attempt to show that the arguments in question are invalid and that there are good reasons for accepting the causal hypothesis against which they are directed. . . .

Before analyzing critically some of the reasons which have been given for supposing that human behavior is inherently unpredictable, I wish to point out several important consequences of this widely held belief, and also of its denial. It is essential to state explicitly what these consequences are, since few of the proponents of this doctrine realize all of its implications.

If human behavior, both individual and social, does not exhibit cause-effect sequences, then the scientific method is essentially irrelevant to the elucidation of the nature of man, and both scientific psychology and the social sciences are permanently barred from achieving the status of sciences. This conclusion follows, since it is the essence of a scientific explanation in any field outside of pure mathematics to "explain" a past phenomenon or predict a future event by showing that these are instances of a certain law (or laws) and that their occurrence is attributable to the fact that the conditions for the applicability of the relevant law(s) were satisfied. Therefore, scientific or rational learning from past experience consists in ascertaining causal regularities from which to anticipate the future. Accordingly, to deny the existence of uniformities in human behavior, both individual and social, is to assert that significant lessons cannot be drawn from the past and that man's future is capricious and elusive. Nevertheless, some historians and social scientists tell us that the absence of causal law is the distinguishing feature of their subject as contrasted with the natural sciences. In the same breath, they maintain that the only way in which individuals and nations will become manageable is by a drastic intensification in the cultivation of the social studies. It is plain that this position is untenable. For nothing can be learned from history regarding the wise conduct of international relations, if no such wisdom is to be found in history. The distinction between wisdom and foolishness in practical affairs first becomes meaningful through the existence of cause-effect relationships in human behavior and by reference to the predictions which the existence of these relationships makes possible. Rules for managing individuals and nations can be based only on causal laws which tell us that *if* such and such is done, it is likely that the outcome will be thus and so, either in all cases or in an explicitly stated percentage of cases. It is useless to bemoan the great gap between our mastery of physical nature and our scientific under-

Abridged from "Causality and the Science of Human Behavior," by Adolf Grünbaum in *American Scientist,* Vol. 39, No. 1, Jan. 1951. Published by The Society of the Sigma Xi, The Scientific Research Society. Reprinted by permission of the publishers.

standing of man, if one denies the existence of the conditions which alone would make a scientific analysis of man possible. Only if human behavior does display some kind of causal law is it significant to emphasize the need for closing the dangerous gap between man's control over physical nature and his scientific knowledge of himself lest he destroy himself.

By contrast, the assumption that causal laws are discoverable in human behavior presents enormous possibilities. For in this case we can ask the social scientist to ascertain what means will bring about given ends. Thus it is possible to get a factually true rather than an emotional answer to some of the burning questions of our time. For example, we could hope for an authentic answer to the question, What system of organizing economic relationships will in fact lead to the maximum satisfaction of certain types of human needs? Whatever the answers to such questions, they would merit the assent of all rational men who share the same goals. To be sure, the history of physical science does record the defiance and acrimony evinced by men whose theories failed to be confirmed by the evidence. Nevertheless, we have learned to reject physical theories which fail to pass the test of observable fact, no matter how ingenious the theory or how dear it may be to our hearts when first propounded. For this reason the history of physical science is in a sense the history of discarded theories. What an advance toward sanity it would be, if it were equally generally accepted that theories of human nature, like physical theories, need careful, disciplined checking through observation. In our time, the ordinary person is very much aware of the need for scrupulous care in ascertaining the facts of nature but will hold forth dogmatically and evangelically about the alleged facts of "human nature." Despite the serious divisions among mankind today, most scientific knowledge concerning inanimate nature commands assent among thinking men everywhere. It would seem, therefore, that scientific knowledge of man, specifying the requirements for attaining given ends, would also merit such universal assent. In so far as this assent would actually be forthcoming, it would constitute a partial step toward human brotherhood.

So much for the implications of rival answers to the issue under discussion. Let us now deal directly with the merits of the answers themselves.

## ARGUMENTS AGAINST CAUSALITY IN HUMAN BEHAVIOR, AND THEIR REFUTATION

There are four arguments which I wish to consider against the hypothesis that causality is present in human behavior. These are:

1. Human behavior is not amenable to causal description and therefore not predictable, since each individual is unique and not exactly like anyone else.
2. Even if there is a causal order in the **phenomena** of human behavior, it is so complex as to elude discovery permanently.
3. In the physical sciences, a present fact is always determined by past facts, but in human behavior present behavior is oriented toward future goals and thus "determined" by these future goals.
4. If human behavior were part of the causal order of events and thereby in principle predictable, it would be futile to attempt to make a choice between good and evil, meaningless to hold men responsible for their deeds, unjust to inflict punishment, and naive to take seriously such remorse or guilt as is professed for past misdeeds. In short, the argument is that to assume the principle of causality in human behavior is incompatible with the known fact that people respond meaningfully to moral imperatives.

In the following pages I shall try to show that all four of these arguments are the result of superficial or specious analysis. The fourth has been by far the most influential. . . .

## Argument from the Uniqueness of Human Individuals

This objection to the possibility of constructing a scientific psychology rests on several misunderstandings of the meaning of causality in science. To remove these misunderstandings it must be pointed out that *all* particulars in the world are unique, whether they are physical objects like trees, physical events like light flashes, or human beings. The mere assertion that a thing is a particular, means that it is in one way or another unique, different from all other objects of its own kind or of other kinds. Every insignificant tick of my watch is a unique event, for no two ticks can be simultaneous with a given third event. With respect to uniqueness, each tick is on a par with Lincoln's delivery of the Gettysburg address! It is clear, however, that the uniqueness of physical events does not prevent them from being connected by causal laws, for present causal laws relate only *some* of the features of a given set of events with *some* of the features of another set of events. For example, frictional processes are accompanied by the development of heat in so far as they are frictional, whatever else they may be. A projectile fired under suitable conditions will describe a parabolic orbit regardless of the color of the projectile, its place of manufacture, and so on. Since the cause-effect relation is a relation between *kinds* of events, it is never necessary that all the features of a given cause be duplicated in order to produce the same kind of effect. It follows that when scientific psychologists assume the existence of causal laws for human behavior, this standpoint is not incompatible with the existence of great individual differences among men, nor does it infringe on the uniqueness and dignity of each particular person.

Every individual is unique by virtue of being a distinctive assemblage of characteristics not precisely duplicated in any other individual. Nevertheless, it is quite conceivable that the following psychological law *might* hold: If a male child having specifiable characteristics is subjected to maternal hostility and has a strong paternal attachment at a certain stage of his development, he will develop paranoia during adult life. If this law holds, then children who are subjected to the stipulated conditions would in fact become paranoiacs, however much they may have differed in other respects in childhood and whatever their other differences may be once they are already insane.

A variant of the argument against scientific psychology is that no psychologist can ever feel exactly like each of the diverse people whose feelings and behavior he is trying to understand. This form of the argument contains an additional misconception of the kind of understanding or explanation that is sought by science—the impression that in order to explain aspects of human experience or behavior scientifically, the psychologist must himself directly have the experience in question in all its complexity. One who objects to scientific psychology on these grounds virtually equates scientific understanding with genuinely empathic understanding. To understand a phenomenon scientifically, however, is, in the first place, to know the conditions necessary for its occurrence. A physician interested in understanding cancer (including the psychic consequences of that disease) is not interested in becoming a cancer victim himself but only in knowing the conditions associated with the occurrence and non-occurrence of cancer. Strictly empathic understanding may have great heuristic value and sometimes aesthetic value as well. However, from the standpoint of achieving scientific understanding and making the predictions which such mastery makes possible, the empathic method in psychology and in history . . . is quite insufficient.

## The Argument from the Complexity of Human Behavior

This argument, it will be recalled, is to the effect that human behavior involves so complex a proliferation of factors that it is futile to attempt to unravel them. A glance at the history of science will deprive this point of view of such plausibility as it may possess. Consider what a person advancing such an argument about psychology today would have said about the physics of motion before the time of Galileo. Probably he would have said that it is hopeless to attempt to reduce the vast diversity of terrestrial and celestial motions to a few simple laws of motion. Before the rise of scientific chemistry, this kind of person would have dismissed the possibility of reducing the seemingly unsurveyable variety of substances in nature to some 96 elements. This argument rests its case on what is not known, and therefore, like all such arguments, it has no case.

### The Argument from the "Determination" of the Present by the Future in Goal-seeking Human Behavior

If a person is now taking action toward the realization of a future goal, it is argued that the immediate action is the effect of a future cause —a kind of causation not encountered among physical phenomena. The answer to this contention is that, not the future goal-event, but rather the present expectation of its realization causally controls forward-looking behavior. Indeed, the goal sought may never be attained. Moreover, both the motives for achieving the given goal and the contemplation of action in its behalf function as antecedent conditions in the same way as the causal factors in physical phenomena. Thus in motivational situations causal determination is quite unaffected by the ideational reference of motives to the future.

### The Argument from Moral Choice

The name "determinism" is applied to the thesis that all phenomena, including those of human behavior, fall into causal patterns. This formulation of determinism is logically objectionable in some respects, but it will suffice for this discussion. It is clear that determinism is one of the key (regulative) principles of all scientific research. The denial of determinism is called **"indeterminism,"** and the indeterminist argument from moral choice to be considered here has been summarized by a critic somewhat as follows: If determinism is true, then my will also is always determined by my character and my motives. Hence I do not make free choices and should not be held responsible for my acts, since I can do nothing about my decisions and cannot help doing what I do. If the determinist is right, I have not chosen either my motives or my character; my motives come to me from both external and internal causes and my character is the necessary product of the influences which have been effective during my lifetime. Thus determinism and moral responsibility are incompatible. Moral responsibility presupposes freedom, that is, exemption from causality.

The question before us is whether the argument of the indeterminist is valid. Before arguing that the answer to this question is emphatically in the negative, I wish to distinguish between two types of determinism and attempt to show that they must each be objectionable to the indeterminist, once he has set forth his argument from moral choice.

The first type of determinism is the 100 per cent type, which maintains that under specifiable conditions a specifiable outcome will occur in all cases. For example, whenever a metal is heated (under ordinary conditions) it will expand. The second type of determinism is the statistical type, which maintains (roughly) that under specifiable conditions a certain result will occur but only in an explicitly stated percentage of cases. An instance of this is the statement that of all the people born in slums, 80 per cent will commit a crime at some time during their lifetime. The claim which I wish to make first is that if the moral argument of the indeterminist were valid against the 100 per cent type of determinism, it would also have relevance against the statistical type of determinism. This point is particularly important, since many indeterminists attempt to acknowledge the incontestable existence of an impressive measure of regularity in human behavior by emphasizing that they object on moral grounds only to the 100 per cent type of determinism and not to the statistical type.

To establish my case, let us suppose that, contrary to fact, we knew that all hunters are subject to the following 100 per cent deterministic law: All hunters commit homicide at some time after returning from jungle life. The indeterminist would say that if these hunters were really subject to such a causal law, they could not help becoming murderers and therefore we should have no right to punish them for their crimes. What would the position taken by the indeterminist have to be if we had a statistical type of law stating with near certainty that, of all the people born in slums, in the long run 80 per cent will commit a crime at some time during their lifetime? To be sure, this statistical law would not entitle us to say that any particular individual(s) born in the slums will become criminal; hence, it does not preclude the possibility that some particular person (or persons) be among the 20 per cent whose conduct is legal and that, to this extent, the person in question be regarded as having acted "freely" in the indeterminist sense. In so far as responsibility is an individual matter, it might even seem that our statistical law would permit the indeterminist to employ his own criteria for assigning individual responsibility to as many as 20 per cent of those persons originating in the slums. But if the 80 per cent who actually did commit a crime at some time during a long interval of time were simultaneously brought to trial before a judge holding the indeterminist point of view, the statistical law in question would deny him the logical right of making individual assignments of responsibility; this law would not enable the judge to designate among the culprits any one or any group of whom it could meaningfully be said that they "could" have avoided the crime by being among the 20 per cent who did, in fact, avoid it. For if a procedure for carrying out such a designation were possible—which it is not—the statistical law would remind us that not only all the remaining defendants arraigned before the judge but also some of those actually belonging to the 20 per cent *could then not have helped* violating the statutes. This means that if over a long period of time we select all those having originated in a slum and not guilty of any crime, the remainder having a similar origin will *always* as a matter of fact commit a crime and will constitute 80 per cent of those born in slums. Thus by the indeterminist's own criteria for assigning responsibility, the judge would not be able to carry out such an assignment individually as he must, because sufficent causality is assured by the statistical law to preclude his doing so consistently with indeterminist premises. If the indeterminist denies the justice of punishment, as he does in the case of 100 per cent determinism, he cannot assent to the punishment of individuals belonging to groups concerning which statistical laws make only a statistical prediction of conduct. Accordingly, the indeterminist must have moral objections to 100 per cent determinism and statistical determinism alike. This means that he must be a foe of the belief that any kind of scientific study of man is possible! . . .

## OTHER ARGUMENTS OF THE INDETERMINIST

It is sometimes said that, when applied to man, the deterministic doctrine becomes untenable by virtue of becoming self-contradictory. This contention is often stated as follows: "The determinist, by his own doctrine, must admit that his very acceptance of determinism was causally conditioned or determined. Since he could not help accepting it, he cannot argue that he has chosen a true doctrine." To justify this claim, it is first pointed out rightly that determinism implies a causal determination of its own acceptance by its defenders. Then it is further maintained, however, that since the determinist could not, by his own theory, help accepting determinism, he can have no confidence in its truth. Thus it is asserted that the determinist's acceptance of his own doctrine was forced upon him. I submit that this inference involves a radical fallacy. The proponent of this argument is gratuitously invoking the view that if our beliefs have causes, these causes *force* the beliefs in question upon us, against our better judgment, as it were. Nothing could be further from the truth. My belief that I am now looking at symbols on paper derives from the fact that their presence is causally inducing certain images on the retinas of my eyes, and that these images, in turn, cause me to infer that corresponding symbols are actually present before me. The reason why I do not suppose that I am now addressing a group of students in a classroom is that the images which the students would produce are not now in my visual field. The causal generation of a belief in no way detracts from its reliability. In fact, if a given belief were not produced in us by definite causes, we should have no reason to accept that belief as a correct description of the world, rather than some other belief arbitrarily selected. Far from making knowledge either adventitious or impossible, the deterministic theory about the origin of our beliefs alone provides the basis for thinking that our judgments of the world are or may be true. Knowing and judging are indeed causal processes in which the facts we judge are determining elements along with the cerebral mechanism employed in their interpretation. It follows that although the determinist's assent to his own doctrine is caused or determined, the truth of determinism is not jeopardized by this fact; if anything, it is made credible.

We have yet to consider the bearing of developments in atomic physics on this problem, since a number of writers have argued that these developments provide evidence for the indeterminist position.

It is known that for measurements in the domain of subatomic dimensions, the Heisenberg Uncertainty Relation comes into play. This relation states that for a given uncertainty or vagueness in the value of an observable quantity like position, there is a definite limit, imposed by the laws of nature, on the accuracy with which the simultaneous value of another empirical quantity like velocity can be known, and that this limit is independent of the particular apparatus or method used in the determination. Since the apparatus used in measurement disturbs the system under observation, it would seem that the possibilities for refining measurements are not unlimited and that the dream of classical physics can therefore never come true. No refinement of experimental technique could ascertain the present values of the observables of a physical system accurately enough to enable us to make a *precise* prediction of the future values. Consequently, the new quantum mechanics is content to specify the frequencies or probabilities with which different values will be found in a given set of measurements. These probability predictions are thus based on a statistico-determinism for the micro-processes of subatomic physics rather than upon the 100 per cent type of determinism which prevails in the physics of the macrocosm.

What are the implications of this situation for the controversy between the philosophical indeterminist and the scientific psychologist? In his *Atomic Theory and the Description of Nature,* Bohr gives several reasons for supposing that the most precise experimentally ascertainable knowledge of the momentary state of the constituent particles of the nervous system and of the external stimuli affecting it permits only a statistical prediction and not a completely detailed prediction of the fate of these stimuli in the nervous system. Nevertheless, there are important reasons why the philosophical indeterminist can derive no comfort from this situation. It has already been shown that if the moral argument for indeterminism is to be valid, statistico-determinism is objectionable along with 100 per cent determinism. For genuine free will would prevail only if the quantum theory were to conclude that all human acts (macrophenomena) can occur with the same frequency. But the theory does not make this assertion at all. The microscopic probabilities yielded by the theory are such that the acts which a macroscopic psychology would predict are overwhelmingly likely to occur. From the standpoint of the macrophenomena of human conduct, a 100 per cent type of determinism holds, to all intents and purposes. . . .

## CONCLUSION

In this paper an attempt has been made to show that the arguments advanced against the possibility of a scientific study of man are without foundation. Of course, the truth of either strict determinism or statistico-determinism has not been established conclusively; for this cannot be done by logical analysis alone, but requires actual success in the scientific search for uniformities. Since the important arguments against determinism which we have considered are without foundation, the psychologist need not be deterred in his quest and can confidently use the causal hypothesis as a regulative principle, undaunted by the *caveat* of the philosophical indeterminist.

## *John Hospers (b. 1918)*

John Hospers is a contemporary philosopher who has made contributions in ethics, political philosophy, metaphysics, and the philosophy of psychology. He is also the only philosopher who has ever been a candidate for President of the United States. He was the nominee of the Libertarian Party in the election of 1972. He is the author of several textbooks in philosophy as well as the author of *Libertarianism: A Political Philosophy for Tomorrow* (1971) and *The Prospects of Capitalism* (1982).

Professor Hospers has published a number of articles that show how the concepts of psychoanalytic theory serve as causal explanations of human behavior. His theory, complete with a number of rich examples, is included in the selection reprinted here.

# Psychoanalysis and Free Will

## *John Hospers*

. . . In practice most of us would not call free many persons who behave voluntarily and even with calculation aforethought, and under no compulsion either of any obvious sort. A metropolitan newspaper headlines an article with the words "Boy Killer Is Doomed Long before He Is Born," and then goes on to describe how a twelve-year-old boy has just been sentenced to thirty years in Sing Sing for the murder of a girl; his family background includes records of drunkenness, divorce, social maladjustment, epilepsy, and paresis. He early displays a tendency to sadistic activity to hide an underlying masochism and "prove that he's a man"; being coddled by his mother only worsens this tendency, until, spurned by a girl in his attempt on her, he kills her — not simply in a fit of anger, but calculatingly, deliberately. Is he free in respect of his criminal act, or for that matter in most of the acts of his life? Surely to ask this question is to answer it in the negative. . . . Though not everyone has criminotic tendencies, everyone has been molded by influences which in large measure at least determine his present behavior; he is literally the product of these influences, stemming from periods prior to his "years of discretion,"

Abridged from "Meaning and Free Will," in *Philosophy and Phenomenological Research,* Vol. X, No. 3 (March 1950), pp. 307–27. Reprinted by permission of *Philosophy and Phenomenological Research.* Footnotes renumbered.

giving him a host of character traits that he cannot change now even if he would. So obviously does what a man is depend upon how a man comes to be, that it is small wonder that philosophers and sages have considered man far indeed from being the master of his fate. It is not as if man's will were standing high and serene above the flux of events that have molded him; it is itself caught up in this flux, itself carried along on the current. An act is free when it is determined by the man's character, say moralists; but when there was nothing the man could do to shape his character, and even the degree of will power available to him in shaping his habits and disciplining himself to overcome the influence of his early environment is a factor over which he has no control, what are we to say of this kind of "freedom?" Is it not rather like the freedom of the machine to stamp labels on cans when it has been devised for just that purpose? Some machines can do so more efficiently than others, but only because they have been better constructed.

It is not my purpose here to establish this thesis in general, but only in one specific respect which has received comparatively little attention, namely, the field referred to by psychiatrists as that of unconscious motivation. In what follows I shall restrict my attention to it because it illustrates as clearly as anything the points I wish to make.

Let me try to summarize very briefly the psychoanalytic doctrine on this point. The conscious life of the human being, including the conscious decisions and **volitions,** is merely a mouthpiece for the unconscious — not directly for the enactment of unconscious drives, but of the compromise between unconscious drives and unconscious reproaches. There is a Big Three behind the scenes which the automaton called the conscious personality carries out: the **id**, an "eternal gimme," presents its wish and demands its immediate satisfaction; the **super-ego** says no to the wish immediately upon presentation, and the unconscious **ego,** the mediator between the two, tries to keep peace by means of compromise.[1]

To go into examples of the functioning of these three "bosses" would be endless; psychoanalytic case books supply hundreds of them. The important point for us to see in the present context is that it is the unconscious that determines what the conscious impulse and the conscious action shall be. Hamlet, for example, had a strong Oedipus wish, which was violently counteracted by super-ego reproaches; these early wishes were vividly revived in an unusual adult situation in which his uncle usurped the coveted position from Hamlet's father and won his mother besides. This situation evoked strong strictures on the part of Hamlet's super-ego, and it was this that was responsible for his notorious delay in killing his uncle. A dozen times Hamlet could have killed Claudius easily; but every time Hamlet "decided" not to: a free choice, moralists would say — but no, listen to the super-ego: "What you feel such hatred toward your uncle for, what you are plotting to kill him for, is precisely the crime which you yourself desire to commit: to kill your father and replace him in the affections of your mother. Your fate and your uncle's are bound up together." This paralyzes Hamlet into inaction. Consciously all he knows is that he is unable to act; this conscious inability he rationalizes, giving a different excuse each time.[2]

We have always been conscious of the fact that we are not masters of our fate in every respect — that there are many things which we cannot do, that nature is more powerful than we are, that we cannot disobey laws without danger of reprisals, etc. Lately we have become more conscious, too, though novelists and dramatists have always been fairly conscious of it, that we are not free with respect to the emotions that we feel — whom we love or hate, what types we admire, and the like. More lately still we have been reminded that there are unconscious motivations for our basic attractions and repulsions, our compulsive actions or inabilities to act. But what is not welcome news is that our very acts of volition, and the entire train of deliberations leading up to them, are but facades for the expression of unconscious wishes, or rather, unconscious compromises and defenses.

A man is faced by a choice: shall he kill another person or not? Moralists would say, here is a free choice — the result of deliberation, an action consciously entered into. And yet, though the agent himself does not know it, and has no awareness of the forces that are at work within him, his choice is already determined for him: his conscious will is only an instrument, a slave, in the hands of a deep unconscious motivation which determines his action. If he has a great deal of what the analyst calls "free-floating guilt," he will not; but if the guilt is such as to demand immediate absorption in the form of self-damaging behavior, this accumulated guilt will have to be discharged in some criminal action. The man himself does not know what the inner clockwork is; he is like the hands on the clock, thinking they move freely over the face of the clock.

A woman has married and divorced several husbands. Now she is faced with a choice for the next marriage: shall she marry Mr. A, or Mr. B, or nobody at all? She may take considerable time to "decide" this question, and her decision may appear as a final triumph of her free will. Let us assume that A is a normal, well-adjusted, kind, and generous man, while B is a leech, an impostor, one who will become entangled constantly in quarrels with her. If she belongs to a certain classifiable psychological type, she will inevitably choose B, and she will do so even if her previous husbands have resembled B, so that one would think that she "had learned from experience." Consciously, she will of course "give the matter due consideration," etc., etc. To the psychoanalyst all this is irrelevant chaff in the wind — only a camouflage for the inner workings about which she knows nothing consciously. If she is of a certain kind of masochistic strain, as exhibited in her previous set of symptoms, she *must* choose B: her super-ego, always out to maximize the torment in the situation, seeing what dazzling possibilities for self-damaging behavior are promised by the choice of B, compels her to make the choice she does, and even to conceal the real basis of the choice behind an elaborate facade of rationalizations.

A man is addicted to gambling. In the service of his addiction he loses all his money, spends what belongs to his wife, even sells his property and neglects his children. For a time perhaps he stops; then, inevitably, he takes it up again, although he himself may think he chose to. The man does not know that he is a victim rather than an agent; or, if he sometimes senses that he is in the throes of something-he-knows-not-what, he will have no inkling of its character and will soon relapse into the illusion that he (his conscious self) is freely deciding the course of his own actions. What he does not know, of course, is that he is still taking out on his mother the original lesion to his infantile narcissism, getting back at her for her fancied refusal of his infantile wishes — and this by rejecting everything identified with her, namely education, discipline, logic, common sense, training. At the roulette wheel, almost alone among adult activities, chance — the opposite of all these things — rules supreme; and his addiction represents his continued and emphatic reiteration of his rejection of Mother and all she represents to his unconscious.

This pseudo-aggression of his is of course masochistic in its effects. In the long run he always loses; he can never quit while he is winning. And far from playing in order to win, rather one can say that his losing is a *sine qua non* of his psychic equilibrium (as it was for example with Dostoyevsky): guilt demands punishment, and in the ego's "deal" with the super-ego the super-ego has granted satisfaction of infantile wishes in return for the self-damaging conditions obtaining. Winning would upset the neurotic equilibrium.[3]

A man has wash-compulsion. He must be constantly washing his hands — he uses up perhaps 400 towels a day. Asked why he does this, he says, "I need to, my hands are dirty"; and if it is pointed out to him that they are not really dirty, he says "They feel dirty anyway, I feel better when I wash them." So once again he washes them. He "freely decides" every time; he feels that he must wash them, he deliberates for a moment perhaps, but always ends by washing them. What he does not see, of course, is the invisible wires inside him pulling him inevitably to do the thing he does: the infantile id-wish concerns preoccupation with dirt, the super-ego charges him with this, and the terrified ego must respond, "No, I don't like dirt, see how clean I like to be, look how I wash my hands!"

Let us see what further "free acts" the same patient engages in (this is an actual case history): he is taken to a concentration camp, and given the worst of treatment by the Nazi guards. In the camp he no longer chooses to be clean, does not even try to be—on the contrary, his choice is now to wallow in filth as much as he can. All he is aware of now is a disinclination to be clean, and every time he must choose he chooses not to be. Behind the scenes, however, another drama is being enacted: the super-ego, perceiving that enough torment is being administered from the outside, can afford to cease pressing its charges in this quarter—the outside world is doing the torturing now, so the super-ego is relieved of the responsibility. Thus the ego is relieved of the agony of constantly making terrified replies in the form of washing to prove that the super-ego is wrong. The defense no longer being needed, the person slides back into what is his natural predilection anyway, for filth. This becomes too much even for the Nazi guards: they take hold of him one day, saying "We'll teach you how to be clean!" drag him into the snow, and pour bucket after bucket of icy water over him until he freezes to death. Such is the end-result of an original id-wish, caught in the machinations of a destroying super-ego.

Let us take, finally, a less colorful, more everyday example. A student at a university, possessing wealth, charm, and all that is usually considered essential to popularity, begins to develop the following personality-pattern: although well taught in the graces of social conversation, he always makes a *faux pas* somewhere, and always in the worst possible situation; to his friends he makes cutting remarks which hurt deeply—and always apparently aimed in such a way as to hurt the most: a remark that would not hurt A but would hurt B he invariably makes to B rather than to A, and so on. None of this is conscious. Ordinarily he is considerate of people, but he contrives always (unconsciously) to impose on just those friends who would resent it most, and at just the times when he should know that he should not impose: at 3 o'clock in the morning, without forewarning, he phones a friend in a near-by city demanding to stay at his apartment for the weekend; naturally the friend is offended, but the person himself is not aware that he has provoked the grievance ("common sense" suffers a temporary eclipse when the neurotic pattern sets in, and one's intelligence, far from being of help in such a situation, is used in the interest of the neurosis), and when the friend is cool to him the next time they meet, he wonders why and feels unjustly treated. Aggressive behavior on his part invites resentment and aggression in turn, but all that he consciously sees is other's behavior toward him—and he considers himself the innocent victim of an unjustified "persecution."

Each of these choices is, from the moralist's point of view, free: he chose to phone his friend at 3 a.m.; he chose to make the cutting remark that he did, etc. What he does not know is that an ineradicable masochistic pattern has set in. His unconscious is far more shrewd and clever than is his conscious intellect; it sees with uncanny accuracy just what kind of behavior will damage him most, and unerringly forces him into that behavior. Consciously, the student "doesn't know why he did it"—he gives different "reasons" at different times, but they are all, once again, rationalizations cloaking the unconscious mechanism which propels him willy-nilly into actions that his "common sense" eschews.

The more of this sort of thing you see, the more you can see what the psychoanalyst means when he talks about "the illusion of free-will." And the more of a psychiatrist you become, the more you are overcome with a sense of what an illusion this precious free-will really is. In some kinds of cases most of us can see it already: it takes no psychiatrist to look at the epileptic and sigh with sadness at the thought that soon this person before you will be as one possessed, not the same thoughtful intelligent person you knew. But people are not aware of this in other contexts, for example when they express surprise at how a person whom they have been so good to could treat them so badly. Let us suppose that you help a person financially or morally or in some other way, so that he is in your debt; suppose further that he is one of the many neurotics who unconsciously identify kindness with weakness and aggression with strength, then he will unconsciously take your kindness to him as weakness and use it as the occasion for enacting some aggression against you. He can't help it, he may regret it himself later; still, he will be driven to do it. If we gain a little knowledge of psychiatry, we can look at him with pity, that a person otherwise so worthy should be so unreliable—but we will exercise realism too and be aware that there are some types of people that you cannot be good to; . . . they will use your own goodness against you.

Sometimes the persons themselves will become dimly aware that "something behind the scenes" is determining their behavior. The divorcee will sometimes view herself with detachment, as if she were some machine (and indeed the psychoanalyst does call her a "repeating-machine"): "I know I'm caught in a net, that I'll fall in love with this guy and marry him and the whole ridiculous merry-go-round will start all over again."

We talk about free will, and we say, yes, the person is free to do so-and-so if he can do so *if* he wants to—and we forget that his wanting to is itself caught up in the stream of determinism, that unconscious forces drive him into the wanting or not wanting to do the thing in question. The idea of the puppet whose motions are manipulated from behind by invisible wires, or better still, by springs inside, is no mere figure of speech. The analogy is a telling one at almost every point.

And the pity of it is that it all started so early, before we knew what was happening. The personality-structure is inelastic after the age of five, and comparatively so in most cases after the age of three. Whether one acquires a neurosis or not is determined by that age—and just as involuntarily as if it had been a curse of God. If, for example, a masochistic pattern was set up, under pressure of hyper-narcissism combined with real or fancied infantile deprivation, then the masochistic snowball was on its course downhill long before we or anybody else know what was happening, and long before anyone could do anything about it. To speak of human beings as "puppets" in such a context is no mere metaphor, but a stark rendering of a literal fact: only the psychiatrist knows what puppets people really are; and it is no wonder that the protestations of philosophers that "the act which is the result of a volition, a deliberation, a conscious decision, is free" leave these persons, to speak mildly, somewhat cold.

But, one may object, all the states thus far described have been abnormal, neurotic ones. The well-adjusted (normal) person at least is free.

Leaving aside the question of how clearly and on what grounds one can distinguish the neurotic from the normal, let me use an illustration of a proclivity that everyone would call normal, namely, the decision of a man to support his wife and possibly a family, and consider briefly its genesis.[4]

Every baby comes into the world with a full-fledged case of megalomania—interested only in himself, naively assuming that he is the center of the universe and that others are present only to fulfill his wishes, and furious when his own wants are not satisfied immediately no matter for what reason. Gratitude, even for all the time and worry and care expended on him by the mother, is an emotion entirely foreign to the infant, and as he grows older it is inculcated in him only with the greatest difficulty; his natural tendency is to assume that everything that happens to him is due to himself, except for denials and frustrations, which are due to the "cruel, denying" outer world, in particular the mother; and that he owes nothing to anyone, is dependent on no one. This omnipotence-complex, or illusion of non-dependence, has been called the "autarchic fiction." Such a conception of the world is actually fostered in the child by the conduct of adults, who automatically attempt to fulfill the infant's every wish concerning nourishment, sleep, and attention. The child misconceives causality and sees in these wish-fulfillments not the results of maternal kindness and love, but simply the result of his own omnipotence.

This fiction of omnipotence is gradually destroyed by experience, and its destruction is probably the deepest disappointment of the early years of life. First of all, the infant discovers that he is the victim of organic urges and necessities: hunger, defecation, urination. More important, he discovers that the maternal breast, which he has not previously distinguished from his own body (he has not needed to, since it was available when he wanted it), is not a part of himself after all, but of another creature upon whom he is dependent. He is forced to recognize this, e.g., when he wants nourishment and it is at the moment not present; even a small delay is most damaging to the "autarchic fiction." Most painful of all is the experience of weaning, probably the greatest tragedy in every baby's life, when his dependence is most cruelly emphasized; it is a frustrating experience because what he wants is no longer there at all; and if he has been able to some extent to preserve the illusion of non-dependence heretofore, he is not able to do so now—it is plain that the source of his nourishment is not dependent on him, but he on it. The shattering of the autarchic fiction is a great disillusionment to every child, a tremendous blow to his ego which he will, in one way or another, spend the rest of his life trying to repair. How does he do this?

First of all, his reaction to frustration is anger and fury; and he responds by kicking, biting, etc., the only ways he knows. But he is motorically helpless, and these measures are ineffective, and only serve to emphasize his dependence the more. Moreover, against such responses of the child the parental reaction is one of prohibition, generally accompanied by physical force of some kind. Generally the child soon learns that this form of rebellion is profitless, and brings him more harm than good. He wants to respond to frustration with violent aggression, and at the same time learns that he will be punished for such aggression, and that in any case the latter is ineffectual. What face-saving solution does he find? Since he must "face facts," since he must in any case "conform" if he is to have any peace at all, he tries to make it seem as if he himself is the source of the commands and prohibitions: the *external* prohibitive force is *internalized*—and here we have the origin of conscience. By making the prohibitive agency seem to come from within himself, the child can "save face"—as if saying, "The prohibition comes from within me, not from outside, so I'm not subservient to external rule, I'm only obeying rules I've set up myself," thus to some extent saving the autarchic fiction, and at the same time avoiding unpleasant consequences directed against himself by complying with parental commands.

Moreover, the boy[5] has unconsciously never forgiven the mother for his dependence on her in early life, for nourishment and all other things. It has upset his illusion of non-dependence. These feelings have been repressed and are not remembered; but they are acted out in later life in many ways—e.g., in the constant deprecation man has for woman's duties such as cooking and housework of all sorts ("All she does is stay home and get together a few meals, and she calls that work"), and especially in the man's identification with the mother in his sex experiences with women. By identifying with someone one cancels out in effect the person with whom he identifies—replacing that person, unconsciously denying his existence, and the man, identifying with his early mother, playing the active role in "giving" to his wife as his mother has "given" to him, is in effect the denial of his mother's existence, a fact which is narcissistically embarrassing to his ego because it is chiefly responsible for shattering his autarchic fiction. In supporting his wife, he can unconsciously deny that his mother gave to him, and that he was dependent on her giving. Why is it that the husband plays the provider, and wants his wife to be dependent on no one else, although twenty years before he was nothing but a parasitic baby? This is a face-saving device on his part: he can act out the reasoning "See, I'm not the parasitic baby, on the contrary I'm the provider, the giver." His playing the provider is a constant face-saving device, to deny his early dependence which is so embarrassing to his ego. It is no wonder that men generally dislike to be reminded of their babyhood, when they were dependent on women.

Thus we have here a perfectly normal adult reaction which is unconsciously motivated. The man "chooses" to support a family—and his choice is as unconsciously motivated as anything could be. (I have described here only the "normal" state of affairs, uncomplicated by the well-nigh infinite number of variations that occur in actual practice.)

Now, what of the notion of responsibility? What happens to it on our analysis? . . .

Heretofore it was pretty generally thought that, while we could not rightly blame a person for the color of his eyes or the morality of his parents, or even for what he did at the age of three, or to a large extent what impulses he had and whom he fell in love with, one *could* do so for other of his adult activities, particularly the acts he performed voluntarily and with premeditation. Later this attitude was shaken. Many voluntary acts came to be recognized, at least in some circles, as compelled by the unconscious. Some philosophers recognized this too. . . . The usual examples, such as the kleptomaniac and the schizophrenic, apparently satisfy most philosophers, and with these exceptions removed, the rest of mankind is permitted to wander in the vast and alluring fields of freedom and responsibility. So far, the inroads upon freedom left the vast majority of humanity untouched; they began to hit home when psychiatrists began to realize, though philosophers did not, that the domination of the conscious by the unconscious extended, not merely to a few exceptional individuals, but to all human beings, that the "big three behind the scenes" are not respecters of persons, and dominate us all, even including that *sanctum sanctorum* of freedom, our conscious will. To be sure, the domination in the case of "normal" individuals is somewhat more benevolent than the tyranny and despotism exercised in neurotic cases, and therefore the former have evoked less comment; but the principle remains in all cases the same: the unconscious is the master of every fate and the captain of every soul.

We speak of a machine turning out good products most of the time but every once in a while it turns out a "lemon." We do not, of course, hold the product responsible for this, but the machine, and via the machine, its maker. Is it silly to extend to inanimate objects the idea of responsibility? Of course. But is it any less silly to employ the notion in speaking of human creatures? Are not the two kinds of cases analogous in countless important ways? Occasionally a child turns out badly too, even when his environment and training are the same as that of his brothers and sisters who turn out "all right." He is the "bad penny." His acts of rebellion against parental discipline in adult life (such as the case of the gambler, already cited) are traceable to early experiences of real or fancied denial of infantile wishes. Sometimes the denial has been real, though many denials are absolutely necessary if the child is to grow up to observe the common decencies of civilized life; sometimes, if the child has an unusual quantity of narcissism, every event that occurs is interpreted by him as a denial of his wishes, and nothing a parent could do, even granting every humanly possible wish, would help. In any event, the later neurosis can be attributed to this. Can the person himself be held responsible? Hardly. If he engages in activities which are a menace to society, he must be put into prison, of course, but responsibility is another matter. The time when the events occurred which rendered his neurotic behavior inevitable was a time long before he was capable of thought and decision. As an adult, he is a victim of a world he never made—only this world is inside him.

What about the children who turn out "all right"? All we can say is that "it's just lucky for them" that what happened to their unfortunate brother didn't happen to them; *through no virtue of their own* they are not doomed to the life of unconscious guilt, expiation, conscious depression, terrified ego-gestures for the appeasement of a tyrannical super-ego that he is. The machine turned them out with a minimum of damage. But if the brother cannot be blamed for his evils, neither can they be praised for their good. It will take society a long time to come round to this attitude. We do not blame people for the color of their eyes, but we have not attained the same attitude toward their socially significant activities.

We all agree that machines turn out "lemons," we all agree that nature turns out misfits in the realm of biology—the blind, the crippled, the diseased; but we hesitate to include the realm of the personality, for here, it seems, is the last retreat of our dignity as human beings. Our ego can endure anything but this; this island at least must remain above the encroaching flood. But may not precisely the same analysis be made here also? Nature turns out psychological "lemons" too, in far greater quantities than any other kind; and indeed all of us are "lemons" in some respect or other, the difference being one of degree. Some of us are lucky enough not to have a gambling-neurosis or criminotic tendencies or masochistic mother-attachment or overdimensional repetition-compulsion to make our lives miserable, but most of our actions, those usually considered the most important, are unconsciously dominated just the same. And, if a neurosis may be likened to a curse of God, let those of us, the elect, who are enabled to enjoy a measure of life's happiness without the hell-fire of neurotic guilt, take this, not as our own achievement, but simply for what it is—a gift of God.

Let us, however, quit metaphysics and put the situation schematically in the form of a deductive argument.

1. An occurrence over which we had no control is something we cannot be held responsible for.
2. Events E, occurring during our babyhood, were events over which we had no control.
3. Therefore events E were events which we cannot be held responsible for.
4. But if there is something we cannot be held responsible for, neither can we be held responsible for something that inevitably results from it.
5. Events E have as inevitable consequence Neurosis N, which in turn has as inevitable consequence Behavior B.
6. Since N is the inevitable consequence of E and B is the inevitable consequence of N, B is the inevitable consequence of E.
7. Hence, not being responsible for E, we cannot be responsible for B. . . .

## NOTES

1. This view is very clearly developed in Edmund Bergler, *Divorce Won't Help,* especially Chapter I.
2. See *The Basic Writings of Sigmund Freud,* Modern Library Edition, p. 310. (In *The Interpretation of Dreams.*) Cf. also the essay by Ernest Jones, "A Psycho-analytical Study of Hamlet."
3. See Edmund Bergler's article on the pathological gambler in *Diseases of the Nervous System* (1943). Also "Suppositions about the Mechanism of Criminosis," *Journal of Criminal Psychopathology* (1944) and "Clinical Contributions to the Psychogenesis of Alcohol Addiction," *Quarterly Journal of Studies on Alcohol,* 5:434 (1944).
4. Edmund Bergler, *The Battle of the Conscience,* Chapter I.
5. The girl's development after this point is somewhat different. Society demands more aggressiveness of the adult male, hence there are more super-ego strictures on tendencies toward passivity in the male; accordingly his defenses must be stronger.

## B. F. Skinner (b. 1904)

B. F. Skinner is a contemporary psychologist and one of the founders of the school of psychology known as behaviorism. He received the National Medal of Science in 1968. Among his many books are *Walden Two* (1948), *Science and Human Behavior* (1953), *Contingencies of Reinforcement: A Theoretical Analysis* (1969), *Beyond Freedom and Dignity* (1971), *About Behaviorism* (1976), *The Shaping of a Behaviorist* (1979).

To develop a science that makes the prediction of human behavior possible, Skinner argued that scientists should focus on observable behavior rather than on inner states. The task of the scientist is to formulate laws of human behavior. Skinner developed a technique known as operant conditioning where desirable behavior was reinforced. Operant conditioning works on the principle that human beings avoid painful experiences and repeat pleasurable ones. *Walden Two* describes a society where operant conditioning is used as the method of child rearing and individual development. Skinner's version of behaviorism has been criticized by both philosophers and psychologists, yet behaviorism survives, albeit in a more sophisticated form, as a school of psychology. In the selection included here, Skinner argues that the concept of freedom no longer serves a useful function in the scientific understanding of human behavior and that it can be eliminated from ordinary discourse.

# Beyond Freedom and Dignity

## B. F. Skinner

### I

Almost all living things act to free themselves from harmful contacts. A kind of freedom is achieved by the relatively simple forms of behavior called reflexes. A person sneezes and frees his respiratory passages from irritating substances. He vomits and frees his stomach from indigestible or poisonous food. He pulls back his hand and frees it from a sharp or hot object. More elaborate forms of behavior have similar effects. When confined, people struggle ("in rage") and break free. When in danger they flee from or attack its source. Behavior of this kind presumably evolved because of its survival value; it is as much a part of what we call the human genetic endowment as breathing, sweating, or digesting food. And through conditioning similar behavior may be acquired with respect to novel objects which could have played no role in evolution. These are no doubt minor instances of the struggle to be free, but they are significant. We do not attribute them to any love of freedom; they are simply forms of behavior which have proved useful in reducing various threats to the individual and hence to the species in the course of evolution.

A much more important role is played by behavior which weakens harmful stimuli in another way. It is not acquired in the form of conditioned reflexes, but as the product of a different process called operant **conditioning.** When a bit of behavior is followed by a certain kind of consequence, it is more likely to occur again, and a consequence having this effect is called a reinforcer. Food, for example, is a reinforcer to a

---

hungry organism; anything the organism does that is followed by the receipt of food is more likely to be done again whenever the organism is hungry. Some stimuli are called negative reinforcers; any response which reduces the intensity of such a stimulus—or ends it—is more likely to be emitted when the stimulus recurs. Thus, if a person escapes from a hot sun when he moves under cover, he is more likely to move under cover when the sun is again hot. The reduction in temperature reinforces the behavior it is "contingent upon"—that is, the behavior it follows. Operant conditioning also occurs when a person simply avoids a hot sun—when, roughly speaking, he escapes from the *threat* of a hot sun.

Negative reinforcers are called aversive in the sense that they are the things organisms "turn away from." The term suggests a spatial separation—moving or running away from something—but the essential relation is temporal. In a standard apparatus used to study the process in the laboratory, an arbitrary response simply weakens an aversive stimulus or brings it to an end. A great deal of physical technology is the result of this kind of struggle for freedom. Over the centuries, in erratic ways, men have constructed a world in which they are relatively free of many kinds of threatening or harmful stimuli—extremes of temperature, sources of infection, hard labor, danger, and even those minor aversive stimuli called discomfort.

Escape and avoidance play a much more important role in the struggle for freedom when the aversive conditions are generated by other people. Other people can be aversive without, so to speak, trying: they can be rude, dangerous, contagious, or annoying, and one escapes from them or avoids them accordingly. They may also be "intentionally" aversive—that is, they may treat other people aversively because of what follows. Thus, a slave driver induces a slave to work by whipping him when he stops; by resuming work the slave escapes from the whipping (and incidentally reinforces the slave driver's behavior in using the whip). A parent nags a child until the child performs a task; by performing the task the child escapes nagging (and reinforces the parent's behavior). The blackmailer threatens exposure unless the victim pays; by paying, the victim escapes from the threat (and reinforces the practice). A teacher threatens corporal punishment or failure until his students pay attention; by paying attention the students escape from the threat of punishment (and reinforce the teacher for threatening it). In one form or another intentional aversive control is the pattern of most social coordination—in ethics, religion, government, economics, education, psychotherapy, and family life.

A person escapes from or avoids aversive treatment by behaving in ways which reinforce those who treated him aversively until he did so, but he may escape in other ways. For example, he may simply move out of range. A person may escape from slavery, emigrate or defect from a government, desert from an army, become an apostate from a religion, play truant, leave home, or drop out of a culture as a hobo, hermit, or hippie. Such behavior is as much a product of the aversive conditions as the behavior the conditions were designed to evoke. The latter can be guaranteed only by sharpening the contingencies or by using stronger aversive stimuli.

Another anomalous mode of escape is to attack those who arrange aversive conditions and weaken or destroy their power. We may attack those who crowd us or annoy us, as we attack the weeds in our garden, but again the struggle for freedom is mainly directed toward intentional controllers—toward those who treat others aversively in order to induce them to behave in particular ways. Thus, a child may stand up to his parents, a citizen may overthrow a government, a communicant may reform a religion, a student may attack a teacher or vandalize a school, and a dropout may work to destroy a culture. . . .

The literature of freedom has encouraged escape from or attack upon all controllers. It has done so by making any indication of control aversive. Those who manipulate human behavior are said to be evil men, necessarily bent on exploitation. Control is clearly the opposite of freedom, and if freedom is good, control must be bad. What is overlooked is control which does not have aversive consequences at any time. Many social practices essential to the welfare of the species involve the control of one person by another, and no one can suppress them who has any concern for human achievements. . . .

The problem is to free men, not from control, but from certain kinds of control, and it can be solved only if our analysis takes all consequences into account. How people feel about control, before or after the literature of freedom has worked on their feelings, does not lead to useful distinctions.

Were it not for the unwarranted generalization that all control is wrong, we should deal with the social environment as simply as we deal with the nonsocial. Although technology has freed men from certain aversive features of the environment, it has not freed them from the environment. We accept the fact that we depend upon the world around us, and we simply change the nature of the dependency. In the same way, to make the social environment as free as possible of aversive stimuli we do not need to destroy that environment or escape from it; we need to redesign it. . . .

## II

It is in the nature of an experimental analysis of human behavior that it should strip away the functions previously assigned to autonomous man and transfer them one by one to the controlling environment. The analysis leaves less and less for autonomous man to do. But what about man himself? Is there not something about a person which is more than a living body? Unless something called a self survives, how can we speak of self-knowledge or self-control? To whom is the injunction "Know thyself" addressed? . . .

A self is a repertoire of behavior appropriate to a given set of contingencies. A substantial part of the conditions to which a person is exposed may play a dominant role, and under other conditions a person may report, "I'm not myself today," or, "I couldn't have done what you said I did, because that's not like me." The identity conferred upon a self arises from the contingencies responsible for the behavior. Two or more repertoires generated by different sets of contingencies compose two or more selves. A person possesses one repertoire appropriate to his life with his friends and another appropriate to his life with his family, and a friend may find him a very different person if he sees him with his family or his family if they see him with his friends. The problem of identity arises when situations are intermingled, as when a person finds himself with both his family and his friends at the same time. . . .

The picture which emerges from a scientific analysis is not of a body with a person inside, but of a body which is a person in the sense that it displays a complex repertoire of behavior. The picture is, of course, unfamiliar. The man thus portrayed is a stranger, and from the traditional point of view he may not seem to be a man at all. . . .

What is being abolished is autonomous man—the inner man, the homunculus, the possessing demon, the man defended by the literatures of freedom and dignity. His abolition has long been overdue. Autonomous man is a device used to explain what we cannot explain in any other way. He has been constructed from our ignorance, and as our understanding increases, the very stuff of which he is composed vanishes. Science does not dehumanize man, it de-homunculizes him, and it must do so if it is to prevent the abolition of the human species. To man *qua* man we readily say good riddance. Only by dispossessing him can we turn to the real causes of human behavior. Only then can we turn from the inferred to the observed, from the miraculous to the natural, from the inaccessible to the manipulable. . . .

Science has probably never demanded a more sweeping change in a traditional way of thinking about a subject, nor has there ever been a more important subject. In the traditional picture a person perceives the world around him, selects features to be perceived, discriminates among them, judges them good or bad, changes them to make them better (or, if he is careless, worse), and may be held responsible for his action and justly rewarded or punished for its consequences. In the scientific picture a person is a member of a species shaped by evolutionary contingencies of survival, displaying behavioral processes which bring him under the control of the environment in which he lives, and largely under the control of a social environment which he and millions of others like him have constructed and maintained during the evolution of a culture. The direction of the controlling relation is reversed: a person does not act upon the world, the world acts upon him.

It is difficult to accept such a change simply on intellectual grounds and nearly impossible to accept its implications. The reaction of the traditionalist is usually described in terms of feelings. One of these, to which the Freudians have appealed in explaining the resistance to psychoanalysis, is wounded vanity. Freud himself expounded, as Ernest Jones has said, "the three heavy blows which narcissism or self-love of mankind had suffered at the hands of science. The first was cosmological and was dealt by Copernicus; the second was biological and was dealt by Darwin; the third was psychological and was dealt by Freud." (The blow was suffered by the belief that something at the center of man knows all that goes on within him and that an instrument called will power exercises command and control over the rest of one's personality.) But what are the signs or symptoms of wounded vanity, and how shall we explain them? What people *do* about such a scientific picture of man is call it wrong, demeaning, and dangerous, argue against it, and attack those who propose or defend it. They do so not out of wounded vanity but because the scientific formulation has destroyed accustomed reinforcers. If a person can no longer take credit or be admired for what he does, then he seems to suffer a loss of dignity or worth, and behavior previously reinforced by credit or admiration will undergo extinction. Extinction often leads to aggressive attack. . . .

The traditional conception of man is flattering; it confers reinforcing privileges. It is therefore easily defended and can be changed only with difficulty. It was designed to build up the individual as an instrument of countercontrol, and it did so effectively but in such a way as to limit progress. We have seen how the literatures of freedom and dignity, with their concern for autonomous man, have perpetuated the use of punishment and condoned the use of only weak nonpunitive techniques, and it is not difficult to demonstrate a connection between the unlimited right of the individual to pursue happiness and the catastrophes threatened by unchecked breeding, the unrestrained affluence which exhausts resources and pollutes the environment, and the imminence of nuclear war.

Physical and biological technologies have alleviated pestilence and famine and many painful, dangerous, and exhausting features of daily life, and behavioral technology can begin to alleviate other kinds of ills. In the analysis of human behavior it is just possible that we are slightly beyond Newton's position in the analysis of light, for we are beginning to make technological applications. There are wonderful possibilities—and all the more wonderful because traditional approaches have been so ineffective. It is hard to imagine a world in which people live together without quarreling, maintain themselves by producing the food, shelter, and clothing they need, enjoy themselves and contribute to the enjoyment of others in art, music, literature, and games, consume only a reasonable part of the resources of the world and add as little as possible to its pollution, bear no more children than can be raised decently, continue to explore the world around them and discover better ways of dealing with it, and come to know themselves accurately and, therefore, manage themselves effectively. Yet all this is possible, and even the slightest sign of progress should bring a kind of change which in traditional terms would be said to assuage wounded vanity, offset a sense of hopelessness or nostalgia, correct the impression that "we neither can nor need to do anything for ourselves," and promote a "sense of freedom and dignity" by building "a sense of confidence and worth." In other words, it should abundantly reinforce those who have been induced by their culture to work for its survival.

An experimental analysis shifts the determination of behavior from autonomous man to the environment—an environment responsible both for the evolution of the species and for the repertoire acquired by each member. Early versions of environmentalism were inadequate because they could not explain how the environment worked, and much seemed to be left for autonomous man to do. But environmental contingencies now take over functions once attributed to autonomous man, and certain questions arise. Is man then "abolished"? Certainly not as a species or as an individual achiever. It is the autonomous inner man who is abolished, and that is a step forward. But does man not then become merely a victim or passive observer of what is happening to him? He is indeed controlled by his environment, but we must remember that it is an environment largely of his own making. The evolution of a culture is a gigantic exercise in self-control. It is often said that a scientific view of man leads to wounded vanity, a sense of hopelessness, and nostalgia. But no theory changes what it is a theory about; man remains what he has always been. And a new theory may change what can be done with its subject matter. A scientific view of man offers exciting possibilities. We have not yet seen what man can make of man.

## *Brand Blanshard (b. 1892)*

The reader was introduced to Professor Blanshard's view of philosophy in Part 1. Although Blanshard is in the idealist tradition of philosophy, he parts company with most idealists in accepting determinism. This acceptance of determinism is particularly atypical in light of Blanshard's rational ethics and his rejection of subjectivist or emotivist theories of ethics. One of the standard objections to determinism is that it allows no place for human deliberation and hence no place for reasoned ethical behavior. But Blanshard rejects that view. He believes that mental events are causally governed and hence that rational thought is governed by causal laws. In this respect Blanshard shares something in common with certain contemporary philosophers who argue that reasons are causes and that there is no ultimate incompatibility between causal explanation and logical explanation.

# The Case For Determinism

## *Brand Blanshard*

I am a determinist. None of the arguments offered on the other side seem of much weight except one form of the moral argument, and that itself is far from decisive. Perhaps the most useful thing I can do in this paper is explain why the commoner arguments for **indeterminism** do not, to my mind, carry conviction. In the course of this explanation the brand of determinism to which I am inclined should become gradually apparent. . . .

By determinism, then, I mean the view that every event *A* is so connected with a later event *B* that, given *A, B* must occur. By indeterminism I mean the view that there is some event *B* that is not so connected with any previous event *A* that, given *A*, it must occur. Now, what is meant here by "must"? We cannot in the end evade that question, but I hope you will not take it as an evasion if at this point I am content to let you fill in the blank in any way you wish. Make it a logical "must," if you care to, or a physical or metaphysical "must," or even the watered-down "must" that means "*A* is always in fact followed by *B*." We can discuss the issue usefully though we leave ourselves some latitude on this point.

With these definitions in mind, let us ask what are the most important grounds for indeterminism. This is not the same as asking what commonly moves people to be indeterminists; the answer to that seems to me all too easy. Everyone vaguely knows that to be undetermined is to be free, and everyone wants to be free. My question is rather, When reflective people accept the indeterminist view nowadays, what considerations seem most cogent to them? It seems to me that there are three: first, the stubborn feeling of freedom, which seems to resist all dialectical solvents; second,* the conviction that natural science itself has now gone over to the indeterminist side; and, third, that determinism would make nonsense of moral responsibility. The third of these seems to me the most important, but I must try to explain why none of them seem to me conclusive.

One of the clearest heads that ever devoted itself to this old issue was Henry Sidgwick. Sidgwick noted that, if at any given moment we stop to think about it, we always feel as if more than one course were open to us, that we could speak or be silent, lift our hand or not lift it. If the determinist is right, this must be an illusion, of course, for whatever we might have done, there must have been a cause, given which we had to do what we did. Now, a mere intuitive assurance about ourselves may be a very weak ground for belief; Freud has shown us that we may be profoundly deceived about how we really feel or why we act as we do. But the curious point is that, though a man who hates his father without knowing it can usually be shown that he does and can often be cured of his feeling, no amount of dialectic seems to shake our feeling of being free to perform either of two proposed acts. By this feeling of being free I do not mean merely the freedom to do what we choose. No one on either side questions that we have that sort of freedom, but it is obviously not the sort of freedom that the indeterminist wants, since it is consistent with determinism of the most rigid sort. The real issue, so far as the will is concerned, is not whether we can do what we choose to do, but whether we

* Blanshard's discussion of this point has been omitted. Eds.

Abridged from "The Case for Determinism," by Brand Blanshard in *Determinism and Freedom in the Age of Modern Science.* Edited by Sidney Hook (New York: New York University Press, 1958), pp. 19–30. Reprinted by permission of New York University Press. Footnotes renumbered.

can choose our own choice, whether the choice itself issues in accordance with law from some antecedent. And the feeling of freedom that is relevant as evidence is the feeling of an open future as regards the choice itself. After the noise of argument has died down, a sort of intuition stubbornly remains that we can not only lift our hand if we choose, but that the choice itself is open to us. Is this not an impressive fact?

No, I do not think it is. The first reason is that when we are making a choice our faces are always turned toward the future, toward the consequences that one act or the other will bring us, never toward the past with its possible sources of constraint. Hence these sources are not noticed. Hence we remain unaware that we are under constraint at all. Hence we feel free from such constraint. The case is almost as simple as that. When you consider buying a new typewriter your thought is fixed on the pleasure and advantage you would gain from it, or the drain it would make on your budget. You are not delving into the causes that led to your taking pleasure in the prospect of owning a typewriter or to your having a complex about expenditure. You are too much preoccupied with the ends to which the choice would be a means to give any attention to the causes of which your choice may be an effect. But that is no reason for thinking that if you did preoccupy yourself with these causes you would not find them at work. You may remember that Sir Francis Galton was so much impressed with this possibility that for some time he kept account in a notebook of the occasions on which he made important choices with a full measure of this feeling of freedom; then shortly after each choice he turned his eye backward in search of constraints that might have been acting on him stealthily. He found it so easy to bring such constraining factors to light that he surrendered to the determinist view.

But this, you may say, is not enough. Our preoccupation with the future may show why we are not aware of the constraints acting on us, and hence why we do not feel bound by them; it does not explain why our sense of freedom persists after the constraints are disclosed to us. By disclosing the causes of some fear, for example, psychoanalytic therapy can remove the fear, and when these causes are brought to light, the fear commonly does go. How is it, then, that when the causes of our **volition** are brought to light volition continues to feel as free as before? Does this not show that it is really independent of those causes?

No again. The two cases are not parallel. The man with the panic fear of dogs is investing all dogs with the qualities — remembered, though in disguised form — of the monster that frightened him as a child. When this monster and his relation to it are brought to light, so that they can be dissociated from the Fidos and Towsers around him, the fear goes, because its appropriate object has gone. It is quite different with our feeling of freedom. We feel free, it was suggested, because we are not aware of the forces acting on us. Now, in spite of the determinist's conviction that when a choice is made there are always causal influences at work, he does not pretend to reveal the influences at work in our present choice. The chooser's face is always turned forward; his present choice is always unique; and no matter how much he knows about the will and the laws, his present choice always emerges out of deep shadow. The determinist who buys a typewriter is as little interested at the moment in the strings that may be pulling at him from his physiological or subconscious cellars as his indeterminist colleague, and hence feels just as free. Thus, whereas the new knowledge gained through psychoanalysis does remove the grounds of fear, the knowledge gained by the determinist is not at all of the sort that would remove the grounds for the feeling of freedom. To make the persistence of this feeling in the determinist an argument against his case is therefore a confusion.

We come now to the third of the reasons commonly advanced in support of indeterminism. This is that determinism makes a mess of morality. The charge has taken many forms. We are told that determinism makes praise and blame meaningless, punishment brutal, remorse pointless, amendment hopeless, duty a deceit. All these allegations have been effectively answered except the one about duty, where I admit I am not quite satisfied. But none of them are in the form in which determinism most troubles the plain man. What most affronts him, I think, is the suggestion that he is only a machine, a big foolish clock that seems to itself to be acting freely, but whose movements are controlled completely by the wheels and weights inside, a Punch-and-Judy show whose appearance of doing things because they are right or reasonable is a sham because everything is mechanically regulated by wires from below. He has no objections to determinism as applied by physicists to atoms, by himself to machines, or by his doctor to his body. He has an emphatic objection to determinism as applied by anyone to his reflection and his will, for this seems to make him a gigantic mechanical toy, or worse, a sort of Frankenstein monster.

In this objection I think we must agree with the plain man. If anyone were to show me that determinism involved either materialism or mechanism, I would renounce it at once, for that would be equivalent, in my opinion, to reducing it to absurdity. The **"physicalism"** once proposed by Neurath and Carnap as a basis for the scientific study of behavior I could not accept for a moment, because it is so dogmatically antiempirical. To use empirical methods means, for me, not to approach nature with a preconceived notion as to what facts must be like, but to be ready to consider all kinds of alleged facts on their merits. Among these the introspectively observable fact of reflective choice, and the inference to its existence in others, are particularly plain, however different from anything that occurs in the realm of the material or the publicly observable or the mechanically controlled.

Now, what can be meant by saying that such choice, though not determined mechanically, is still determined? Are you suggesting, it will be asked, that in the realm of reflection and choice there operates a different kind of causality from any we know in the realm of bodies? My answer is: Yes, just that. To put it more particularly, I am suggesting (1) that even within the psychical realm there are different causal levels, (2) that a causality of higher level may supervene on one of lower level, and (3) that when causality of the highest level is at work, we have precisely what the indeterminists, without knowing it, want.

1. First, then, as to causal levels. I am assuming that even the indeterminist would admit that most mental events are causally governed. No one would want to deny that his stepping on a tack had something to do with his feeling pain, or that his touching a flame had something to do with his getting burned, or that his later thought of the flame had something to do with his experience of its hotness. A law of association is a causal law of mental events. In one respect it is like a law of physical events: in neither case have we any light as to *why* the consequent follows on the antecedent. Hume was right about the billiard balls. He was right about the flame and the heat; we do not see why something bright and yellow should also be hot. He was right about association; we do not understand how one idea calls up another; we only know that it does. Causality in all such cases means to us little if anything more than a routine of regular sequence.

Is all mental causation like that? Surely not. Consider a musician composing a piece or a logician making a deduction. Let us make our musician a philosopher also, who after adding a bar pauses to ask himself, "Why did I add just that?" Can we believe he would answer, "Because whenever in the past I have had the preceding bars in mind, they have always been followed by this bar"? What makes this suggestion so inept is partly that he may never have thought of the preceding bars before, partly that, if he had, the repetition of an old sequence would be precisely what he would avoid. No, his answer, I think, would be something like this: "I wrote what I did because it seemed the right thing to do. I developed my theme in the manner demanded to carry it through in an aesthetically satisfactory way." In other words, the constraint that was really at work in him was not that of association; it was something that worked distinctly against association; it was the constraint of an aesthetic ideal. And, if so, there is a causality of a different level. It is idle to say that the musician is wholly in the dark about it. He can see not only *that B* succeeded *A*; as he looks back, he can see in large measure *why* it did.

It is the same with logical inference, only more clearly so. The thinker starts, let us say, with the idea of a regular solid whose faces are squares, and proceeds to develop in thought the further characteristics that such a solid must possess. He constructs it in imagination and then sees that it must have six faces, eight vertices, and twelve edges. Is this association merely? It may be. It is, for example, if he merely does in imagination what a child does when it counts the edges on a lump of sugar. This is not inference and does not feel like it. When a person, starting with the thought of a solid with square faces, deduces that it must have eight vertices, and then asks why he should have thought of that, the natural answer is, Because the first property entails the second. Of course this is not the only condition, but it seems to me contrary to introspectively plain fact to say that it had nothing to do with the movement of thought. It is easy to put this in such a way as to invite attack. If we say that the condition of our thinking of *B* is the observed necessity between *A* and *B*, we are assuming that *B* is already thought of as a means of explaining how it comes to be thought of. But that is not what I am saying. I am saying that in thinking at its best thought comes under the constraint of necessities in its object, so that the objective fact that *A* necessitates *B* partially determines our passing in thought from *A* to *B*. Even when the explanation is put in this form, the objection has been raised that necessity is a timeless link between concepts, while causality is a temporal bond between events, and that the two must be kept sharply apart. To which the answer is: Distinct, yes; but always apart, no. A timeless relation may serve perfectly well as the condition of a temporal passage. I hold that in the course of our thinking we can easily verify this fact, and, because I do, I am not put off by pronouncements about what we should and should not be able to see.

2. My second point about the causal levels is that our mental processes seldom move on one level alone. The higher is always supervening on the lower and taking over partial control. Though brokenly and imperfectly rational, rational creatures we still are. It must be admitted that most of our so-called thinking moves by association, and is hardly thinking at all. But even in the dullest of us "bright shoots of everlastingness," strands of necessity, aesthetic or logical, from time to time appear. "The quarto and folio editions of mankind" can follow the argument with fewer lapses than most of us; in the texts of the greatest of all dramas, we are told, there was seldom a blot or erasure; but Ben Jonson added, and no doubt rightly, that there ought to have been a thousand. The effort of both thought and art is to escape the arbitrary, the merely personal, everything that, causal and capricious, is irrelevant, and to keep to lines appointed by the whole that one is constructing. I do not suggest that logical and aesthetic necessity are the same. I do say that they are both to be distinguished from association or habit as representing a different level of control. That control is never complete; all creation in thought or art is successful in degree only. It is successful in the degree to which it ceases to be an expression of merely personal impulses and becomes the instrument of a necessity lying in its own subject matter.

3. This brings us to our last point. Since moral choice, like thought and art, moves on different causal levels, it achieves freedom, just as they do, only when it is determined by its own appropriate necessity. Most of our so-called choices are so clearly brought about by association, impulse, and feeling that the judicious indeterminist will raise no issue about them. When we decide to get a drink of water, to take another nibble of chocolate, to go to bed at the usual hour, the forces at work are too plain to be denied. It is not acts like these on which the indeterminist takes his stand. It is rather on those where, with habit,

impulse, and association prompting us powerfully to do *X*, we see that we ought to do *Y* and therefore do it. To suppose that in such cases we are still the puppets of habit and impulse seems to the indeterminist palpably false.

So it does to us. Surely about this the indeterminist is right. Action impelled by the sense of duty, as Kant perceived, is action on a different level from anything mechanical or associative. But Kant was mistaken in supposing that when we were determined by reason we were not determined at all. This supposition seems to me wholly unwarranted. The determination is still there, but, since it is a determination by the moral necessities of the case, it is just what the moral man wants and thus is the equivalent of freedom. For the moral man, like the logician and the artist, is really seeking self-surrender. Through him as through the others an impersonal ideal is working, and to the extent that this ideal takes possession of him and molds him according to its pattern, he feels free and is free.

The logician is most fully himself when the wind gets into his sails and carries him effortlessly along the line of his calculations. Many an artist and musician have left it on record that their best work was done when the whole they were creating took the brush or pen away from them and completed the work itself. It determined them, but they were free, because to be determined by this whole was at once the secret of their craft and the end of their desire. This is the condition of the moral man also. He has caught a vision, dimmer perhaps than that of the logician or the artist, but equally objective and compelling. It is a vision of the good. This good necessitates certain things, not as means to ends merely, for that is not usually a necessary link, but as integral parts of itself. It requires that he should put love above hate, that he should regard his neighbor's good as of like value with his own, that he should repair injuries, and express gratitude, and respect promises, and revere truth. Of course it does not guide him infallibly. On the values of a particular case he may easily be mistaken. But that no more shows that there are no values present to be estimated, and no ideal demanding a special mode of action, than the fact that we make a mistake in adding figures shows that there are no figures to be added, or a right way of adding them. In both instances what we want is control by the objective requirements of the case. The saint, like the thinker and the artist, has often said this in so many words. I feel most free, said St. Paul, precisely when I am most a slave. . . .

# *Nondeterminism*

"If every event is wholly and only determined by antecedent events, there is no place for human freedom. But human freedom exists. Hence determinism is false. There are at least some events that are not determined wholly and only by antecedent events." That in a nutshell is the core argument for every nondeterminist position.

But how do you justify the claim that human freedom exists? One of the more effective arguments is to base the claim on human experience. Under that strategy freedom becomes the best hypothesis to explain the facts. In its most simplistic form the argument rests on our experience of feeling free. You are confronted with several alternative courses of action and report that you are under no compulsion to choose one rather than the other. You report that you are capable of choosing freely.

The quick response to this argument is that your sense of felt freedom may be illusory. There are many examples of people feeling free when they aren't. Suppose you are in a room doing a crossword puzzle. A prankster locks the door and then unlocks it two hours later. During the two-hour period when the door was locked, you felt free to leave the room; you felt you could have left when you wanted to. However, you were not free to leave the room during that two-hour period. If you had tried, you could not have succeeded. Hence, it is tempting to argue that feeling free is no argument for the truth of the claim that you are free.

But the argument from our experience of felt freedom need not be so simplistic. Hardly anyone would claim that we really are free every time we think we are. All that need be claimed is that we are often, or perhaps sometimes free, when we think we are. Moreover, with the locked room example, the person's felt sense of freedom is never tested. If the person had tried to leave the room he or she would have seen that the felt sense of freedom was an illusion. But sometimes we test our freedom against constraints and overcome the constraints. Dieting is a very difficult endeavor. We feel pressure to do the very things we know will interfere with dieting and we try to resist those pressures. In resisting them, we exercise our freedom in the form of will power. Felt freedom is not the freedom of the happy slave; felt freedom is the freedom of the triumphant dieter.

But perhaps the felt freedom of the triumphant dieter is equally illusory. Chemical and genetic factors could account for the triumph. However, there is even more to the feeling of freedom argument. Our sense of feeling free is not limited to prudential experiences in overcoming resistance as when we diet or study when we would rather be at the pub. We are also moral agents and we feel free when we overcome the pressures of self-interest so that we might act in behalf of the interests of others. Indeed many nondeterminists argue that our experiences as moral agents are more than a matter of moral will power. The very notion of morality requires the existence of freedom in the nondeterministic sense. To say that one ought to do something is to say that one can do it. To say that one can do it is to say one could do otherwise. But if determinism is true, whether one can do something or not is determined wholly and only by antecedent events. Hence, one can't do otherwise than what one does. Therefore if determinism is true, the demands of morality are futile (except in the way explained by the determinists).

There is also our experience of feeling responsible. To make sense of the experience of feeling responsible, freedom is required. One of the most extreme analyses of human responsibility is provided by Jean-Paul Sartre. Responsibility, according to Sartre, arises in a set of circumstances whose significance is at least in part of our own making. Human beings have an environment, limited powers, a history, and relations with other human beings. But what makes human existence significant is the ability of human beings to choose goals. This ability enables them to represent a future state of affairs that in turn gives the present situation a certain significance in virtue of its relation to that projected future. On the mundane level, you can choose, for example, to quench your thirst by going to the cold drink machine to purchase a Coke. Having made this choice, certain features of your situation take on a particular significance. The presence or absence of the right coins in your pocket becomes a help or hindrance to you. The "Out of Order" sign that you find on the machine when you get close enough to it becomes irritating and frustrating. On a more elevated plane, you can decide to try to bring about a more democratic and peace-loving society. This choice will then give a certain political significance to various features of your world, make certain further actions seem almost necessary, make certain facts about your past or your abilities appear as limitations, make certain others appear as obstacles. Or again that a mother earns a certain income may be a fact. But it is the choice she makes, for example, to educate her daughter in a certain way that gives her financial situation a particular significance, that of being too poor, and which requires certain courses of action on her part such as scrimping and saving or finding additional work. For Sartre we are responsible not just for our decisions and actions but for our situation as well. We are responsible for what we make of our world through our choices and for how we attempt to transform it. This is what Sartre means when he declares that man "is responsible for the world and for himself as a way of being."

As the discussion of the feeling free argument is broadened, a sophisticated version of that argument has developed. The argument isn't limited simply to the fact that persons feel free. People experience themselves resisting temptation both for their own good and for the good of others. They experience themselves being responsible and in these experiences they feel that they are free—that they could have done otherwise. But our feeling free occurs because we experience ourselves as responsible moral agents in the first place. Upon reflection, free will is the best hypothesis for that total experience.

Freedom functions as the best hypothesis for other experiences as well. Some nondeterminists argue that freedom is required to explain chance events. William James takes the simple case of choosing between two alternative routes home as requiring the hypothesis of freedom. Sometimes we choose one route; sometimes the other; yet in most cases we surely could have chosen otherwise. Other philosophers focus on creativity. How is something creative possible in a deterministic world. Creativity implies that something new has occurred. Yet how is that possible if everything that occurs is wholly and only the result of something that has occurred. Again, the nondeterminists argue, freedom is the best explanation.

## *William James (1842–1910)*

William James is one of the foremost figures in the history of American intellectual thought. While William's brother Henry distinguished himself as a novelist, William made lasting contributions in psychology and philosophy. James was one of the trio of great American pragmatists (the others were Charles Peirce and John Dewey) who flourished in the first half of the twentieth century. As a philosopher, James paid more attention to emotions and temperament than most philosophers. Although he was not antirationalistic, he did believe that reason clearly had its limits.

As a metaphysician, James adopted the position that is most commonly known as indeterminism. With respect to persons, he argued that human behavior was, at least on occasion, unpredictable. But James's indeterminism was not limited to individual persons. He denied causal determinism in the natural world as well. In both instances he argued that determinism could not account for creativity. Hence James would deny Laplace's claim that if we knew all the facts and the causal laws that govern the universe, we could accurately know the future. James's theory of science, psychology, truth, and religion were all consistent with his metaphysical worldview.

## The Dilemma of Determinism

### *William James*

. . . The arguments I am about to urge all proceed on two suppositions: first, when we make theories about the world and discuss them with one another, we do so in order to attain a conception of things which shall give us subjective satisfaction; and, second, if there be two conceptions, and the one seems to us, on the whole, more rational than the other, we are entitled to suppose that the more rational one is the truer of the two. I hope that you are all willing to make these suppositions with me; for I am afraid that if there be any of you here who are not, they will find little edification in the rest of what I have to say. I cannot stop to argue the point; but I myself believe that all the magnificent achievements of mathematical and physical science—our doctrines of evolution, of uniformity of law, and the rest—proceed from our indomitable desire to cast the world into a more rational shape in our minds than the shape into which it is thrown there by the crude order of our experience. The world has shown itself, to a great extent, plastic to this demand of ours for rationality. How much farther it will show itself plastic no one can say. Our only means of finding out is to try; and I, for one, feel as free to try conceptions of moral as of mechanical or of logical rationality. If a certain formula for expressing the nature of the world violates my moral demand, I shall feel as free to throw it overboard, or at least to doubt it, as if it disappointed my demand for uniformity of sequence, for example; the one demand being, so far as I can see, quite as subjective and emotional as the other is. The principle of causality, for example—what is it but a postulate, an empty name covering simply a demand that the sequence of events shall some day manifest a deeper kind of belonging of one thing with another than the mere arbitrary juxtaposition which now phenomenally appears? It is as much an altar to an unknown god as the one that Saint Paul found at Athens. All our scientific and philosophic ideals are altars to unknown gods. Uniformity is as much so as is free-will. If this be admitted, we can debate on even terms. But if any one pretends that while freedom and variety are, in the first instance, subjective demands, necessity and uniformity are something altogether different, I do not see how we can debate at all.

To begin, then, I must suppose you acquainted with all the usual arguments on the subject. I cannot stop to take up the old proofs from causation, from statistics, from the certainty with which we can foretell one another's conduct, from the fixity of character, and all the rest. But there are two *words* which usually encumber these classical arguments, and which we must immediately dispose of if we are to make any progress. One is the eulogistic word *freedom,*

---

Abridged from *Essays on Faith and Morals,* by William James. Selected by Ralph Barton Perry. A Meridian Book. (Cleveland: World Publishing, 1962, 1965).

and the other is the opprobrious word *chance*. The word "chance" I wish to keep, but I wish to get rid of the word "freedom." Its eulogistic associations have so far overshadowed all the rest of its meaning that both parties claim the sole right to use it, and determinists today insist that they alone are freedom's champions. Old-fashioned determinism was what we may call ***hard* determinism.** It did not shrink from such words as fatality, bondage of the will, necessitation, and the like. Nowadays, we have a ***soft* determinism** which abhors harsh words, and, repudiating fatality, necessity, and even predetermination, says that its real name is freedom; for freedom is only necessity understood, and bondage to the highest is identical with true freedom. . . .

Now, all this is a quagmire of evasion under which the real issue of fact has been entirely smothered. Freedom in all these senses presents simply no problem at all. No matter what the soft determinist mean by it—whether he mean the acting without external constraint; whether he mean the acting rightly, or whether he mean the acquiescing in the law of the whole—who cannot answer him that sometimes we are free and sometimes we are not? But there *is* a problem, an issue of fact and not of words, an issue of the most momentous importance, which is often decided without discussion in one sentence—nay, in one clause of a sentence—by those very writers who spin out whole chapters in their efforts to show what "true" freedom is; and that is the question of determinism. . . .

Fortunately, no ambiguities hang about this word or about its opposite, **indeterminism.** Both designate an outward way in which things may happen, and their cold and mathematical sound has no sentimental associations that can bribe our partiality either way in advance. Now, evidence of an external kind to decide between determinism and indeterminism is, as I intimated a while back, strictly impossible to find. Let us look at the difference between them and see for ourselves. What does determinism profess?

It professes that those parts of the universe already laid down absolutely appoint and decree what the other parts shall be. The future has no ambiguous possibilities hidden in its womb: the part we call the present is compatible with only one totality. Any other future complement than the one fixed from eternity is impossible. The whole is in each and every part, and welds it with the rest into an absolute unity, an iron block, in which there can be no equivocation or shadow of turning.

With earth's first clay they did the last man knead,
And there of the last harvest sowed the seed.
And the first morning of creation wrote
What the last dawn of reckoning shall read.

Indeterminism, on the contrary, says that the parts have a certain amount of loose play on one another, so that the laying down of one of them does not necessarily determine what the others shall be. It admits that possibilities may be in excess of actualities, and that things not yet revealed to our knowledge may really in themselves be ambiguous. Of two alternative futures which we conceive, both may now be really possible; and the one become impossible only at the very moment when the other excludes it by becoming real itself. Indeterminism thus denies the world to be one unbending unit of fact. It says there is a certain ultimate pluralism in it; and, so saying, it corroborates our ordinary unsophisticated view of things. To that view, actualities seem to float in a wider sea of possibilities from out of which they are chosen; and, *somewhere*, indeterminism says, such possibilities exist, and form a part of truth.

Determinism, on the contrary, says they exist *nowhere*, and that necessity on the one hand and impossibility on the other are the sole categories of the real. Possibilities that fail to get realized are, for determinism, pure illusions: they never were possibilities at all. There is nothing inchoate, it says, about this universe of ours, all that was or is or shall be actual in it having been from eternity virtually there. . . .

The issue, it will be seen, is a perfectly sharp one, which no eulogistic terminology can smear over or wipe out. The truth *must* lie with one side or the other, and its lying with one side makes the other false.

The question relates solely to the existence of possibilities, in the strict sense of the term, as things that may, but need not, be. Both sides admit that a **volition,** for instance, has occurred. The indeterminists say another volition might have occurred in its place: the determinists swear that nothing could possibly have occurred in its place. Now, can science be called in to tell us which of these two point-blank contradicters of each other is right? Science professes to draw no conclusions but such as are based on matters of fact, things that have actually happened; but how can any amount of assurance that something actually happened give us the least grain of information as to whether another thing might or might not have happened in its place? Only facts can be proved by other facts. With things that are possibilities and not facts, facts have no concern. If we have no other evidence than the evidence of existing facts, the possibility-question must remain a mystery never to be cleared up.

And the truth is that facts practically have hardly anything to do with making us either determinists or indeterminists. Sure enough, we make a flourish of quoting facts this way or that; and if we are determinists, we talk about the infallibility with which we can predict one another's conduct; while if we are indeterminists, we lay great stress on the fact that it is just because we cannot foretell one another's conduct, either in war or statecraft or in any of the great and small intrigues and businesses of men, that life is so intensely anxious and hazardous a game. But who does not see the wretched insufficiency of this so-called objective testimony on both sides? What fills up the gaps in our minds is something not objective, not external. What divides us into possibility men and anti-possibility men is different faiths or postulates—postulates of rationality. To this man the world seems more rational with possibilities in it—to that man more rational with possibilities excluded; and talk as we will about having to yield to evidence, what makes us monists or pluralists, determinists or indeterminists, is at bottom always some sentiment like this.

The stronghold of the deterministic sentiment is the antipathy to the idea of chance. As soon as we begin to talk indeterminism to our friends, we find a number of them shaking their heads. This notion of alternative possibility, they say, this admission that any one of several things may come to pass, is, after all, only a roundabout name for chance; and chance is something the notion of which no sane mind can for an instant tolerate in the world. What is it, they ask, but barefaced crazy unreason, the negation of intelligibility and law? And if the slightest particle of it exist anywhere, what is to prevent the whole fabric from falling together, the stars from going out, and chaos from recommencing her topsy-turvy reign?

Remarks of this sort about chance will put an end to discussion as quickly as anything one can find. I have already told you that "chance" was a word I wished to keep and use. Let us then examine exactly what it means, and see whether it ought to be such a terrible bugbear to us. I fancy that squeezing the thistle boldly will rob it of its sting.

The sting of the word "chance" seems to lie in the assumption that it means something positive, and that if anything happens by chance, it must needs be something of an intrinsically irrational and preposterous sort. Now, chance means nothing of the kind. It is a purely negative and relative term, giving us no information about that of which it is predicated, except that it happens to be disconnected with something else—not controlled, secured, or necessitated by other things in advance of its own actual presence. As this point is the most subtile one of the whole lecture, and at the same time the point on which all the rest hinges, I beg you to pay particular attention to it. What I say is that it tells us nothing about what a thing may be in itself to call it "chance." It may be a bad thing, it may be a good thing. It may be lucidity, transparency, fitness incarnate, matching the whole system of other things, when it has once befallen, in an unimaginably perfect way. All you mean by calling it "chance" is that this is not guaranteed, that it may also fall out otherwise. For the system of other things has no positive hold on the chance-thing. Its origin is in a certain fashion negative: it escapes, and says, Hands off! coming, when it comes, as a free gift, or not at all. . . .

Nevertheless, many persons talk as if the minutest dose of disconnectedness of one part with another, the smallest modicum of independence, the faintest tremor of ambiguity about the future, for example, would ruin everything, and turn this goodly universe into a sort of insane sand-heap or nulliverse, no universe at all. Since future human volitions are as a matter of fact the only ambiguous things we are tempted to believe in, let us stop for a moment to make ourselves sure whether their independent and accidental character need be fraught with such direful consequences to the universe as these.

What is meant by saying that my choice of which way to walk home after the lecture is ambiguous and matter of chance as far as the present moment is concerned? It means that both Divinity Avenue and Oxford Street are called; but that only one, and that one *either* one, shall be chosen. Now, I ask you seriously to suppose that this ambiguity of my choice is real; and then to make the impossible hypothesis that the choice is made twice over, and each time falls on a different street. In other words, imagine that I first walk through Divinity Avenue, and then imagine that the powers governing the universe annihilate ten minutes of time with all that it contained, and set me back at the door of this hall just as I was before the choice was made. Imagine then that, everything else being the same, I now make a different choice and traverse Oxford Street. You, as passive spectators, look on and see the two alternative universes—one of them with me walking through Divinity Avenue in it, the other with the same me walking through Oxford Street. Now, if you are determinists you believe one of these universes to have been from eternity impossible: you believe it to have been impossible because of the intrinsic irrationality or accidentality somewhere involved in it. But looking outwardly at these universes, can you say which is the impossible and accidental one, and which the rational and necessary one? I doubt if the most iron-clad determinist among you could have the slightest glimmer of light on this point. In other words, either universe *after the fact* and once there would, to our means of observation and understanding, appear just as rational as the other. There would be absolutely no criterion by which we might judge one necessary and the other matter of chance. Suppose now we relieve the gods of their hypothetical task and assume my choice, once made, to be made forever. I go through Divinity Avenue for good and all. If, as good determinists, you now begin to affirm, what all good determinists punctually do affirm, that in the nature of things I *couldn't* have gone through Oxford Street—had I done so it would have been chance, irrationality, insanity, a horrid gap in nature—I simply call your attention to this, that your affirmation is . . . a mere conception fulminated as a dogma and based on no insight into details. Before my choice, either street seemed as natural to you as to me. Had I happened to take Oxford Street, Divinity Avenue would have figured in your philosophy as the gap in nature; and you would have so proclaimed it with the best deterministic conscience in the world.

But what a hollow outcry, then, is this against a chance which, if it were present to us, we could by no character whatever distinguish from a rational necessity! I have taken the most trivial of examples, but no possible example could lead to any different result. For what are the alternatives which, in point of fact, offer themselves to human volition? What are those futures that now seem matters of chance? Are they not one and all like the Divinity Avenue and Oxford Street of our example? Are they not all of them *kinds* of things already here and based in the existing frame of nature? Is any one ever tempted to produce an *absolute* accident, something utterly irrelevant to the rest of the world? Do not all the motives that assail us, all the futures that offer themselves to our choice, spring equally from the soil of the past; and would not either one of them, whether realized through chance or through necessity, the moment it was realized, seem to us to fit that past, and in the completest and most continuous manner to interdigitate with the phenomena already there? . . .

## *C. A. Campbell (1897–1974)*

C. A. Campbell was a twentieth century British philosopher who made contributions in epistemology, metaphysics, and ethics. His Gifford Lectures were published as *On Selfhood and Godhood* (1956). He also published *Scepticism and Construction* (1931) and *In Defense of Free Will* (1956). His contributions to philosophy were recognized by his election as Fellow of the British Academy.

Campbell criticized the logical positivist philosophy which became fashionable in the 1940s. This antipositivist view is exemplified in Campbell's theory of human freedom. He argued that attempts to find a place for freedom within a causal universe were bound to be failures. He coined a term **contra-causal** freedom to express his own nondeterministic view.

# Contra-causal Freedom

## *C. A. Campbell*

### I

. . . So far as the *meaning,* as distinct from the *conditions,* of moral responsibility is concerned, the common view is very simple. If we ask ourselves whether a certain person is morally responsible for a given act, . . . what we are considering, it would be said, is whether or not that person is a fit subject upon whom to pass moral judgment; whether he can fittingly be deemed morally good or bad, morally praiseworthy or blameworthy. This does not take us any great way: but . . . so far as it goes it does not seem to me seriously disputable. The really interesting and controversial question is about the *conditions* of moral responsibility, and in particular the question whether freedom of a **contra-causal** kind is among these conditions.

The answer of the common man to the latter question is that it most certainly *is* among the conditions. Why does he feel so sure about this? Not . . . because the common man supposes that causal law exercises "compulsion" in the sense that prescriptive laws do, but simply because he does not see how a person can be deemed morally praiseworthy or blameworthy in respect of an act which he could not help performing. From the stand-point of moral praise and blame, he would say—though not necessarily from other stand-points—it is a matter of indifference whether it is by reason of some external constraint or by reason of his own given

Abridged from C. A. Campbell, "Is 'Freewill' A Pseudo-Problem?" Reprinted from *Mind,* Vol. LX, No. 239, July 1951, pp. 450–64. Reprinted by permission of Oxford University Press.

nature that the man could not help doing what he did. It is quite enough to make moral praise and blame futile that in either case there were no genuine alternatives, no open possibilities, before the man when he acted. He could not have acted otherwise than he did. And the common man might not unreasonably go on to stress the fact that we all, even if we are linguistic philosophers, do in our actual practice of moral judgment appear to accept the common view. He might insist upon the point . . . that we do all, in passing moral censure, "make allowances" for influences in a man's hereditary nature or environmental circumstances which we regard as having made it more than ordinarily difficult for him to act otherwise than he did: the implication being that if we supposed that the man's heredity and environment made it not merely very *difficult* but actually *impossible* for him to act otherwise than he did, we could not properly assign moral blame to him at all.

Let us put the argument implicit in the common view a little more sharply. The moral "ought" implies "can." If we say that A morally ought to have done X, we imply that in our opinion, he could have done X. But we assign moral blame to a man only for failing to do what we think he morally ought to have done. Hence if we morally blame A for not having done X, we imply that he could have done X even though in fact he did not. In other words, we imply that A could have acted otherwise than he did. And that means that we imply, as a necessary condition of a man's being morally blameworthy, that he enjoyed a freedom of a kind not compatible with unbroken causal continuity.

## II

Now what is it that is supposed to be wrong with this simple piece of argument? . . . The argument looks as though it were doing little more than reading off necessary implications of the fundamental categories of our moral thinking. One's inclination is to ask "If one is to think morally at all, how else than this *can* we think?"

In point of fact, there is pretty general agreement among the contemporary critics as to what is wrong with the argument. Their answer in general terms is as follows. No doubt A's moral responsibility does imply that he could have acted otherwise. But this expression "could have acted otherwise" stands in dire need of analysis. When we analyze it, we find that it is not, as is so often supposed, simple and unambiguous, and we find that in *some* at least of its possible meanings it implies *no* breach of causal continuity between character and conduct. Having got this clear, we can further discern that only in one of these *latter* meanings is there any compulsion upon our moral thinking to assert that if A is morally blameworthy for an act, A "could have acted otherwise than he did." It follows that, contrary to common belief, our moral thinking does *not* require us to posit a contra-causal freedom as a condition of moral responsibility. . . .

What then *does* one mean in this class of cases by "A could have acted otherwise"? I submit that the expression is taken in its simple, categorical meaning, without any suppressed "if" clause to qualify it. Or perhaps, in order to keep before us the important truth that it is only as expressions of *will* or *choice* that acts are of moral import, it might be better to say that a condition of A's moral responsibility is that he could have *chosen* otherwise. . . . There is a very real question, at least for any person who approaches the question of moral responsibility at a tolerably advanced level of reflection, about whether A could have *chosen* otherwise. Such a person will doubtless be acquainted with the claims advanced in some quarters that causal law operates universally: or/and with the theories of some philosophies that the universe is throughout the expression of a single supreme principle; or/and with the doctrines of some theologians that the world is created, sustained and governed by an **Omniscient** and Omnipotent Being. Very understandably such world-views awaken in him doubts about the validity of his first, easy, instinctive assumption that there are genuinely open possibilities before a man at the moment of moral choice. It thus becomes for him a real question whether a man could have chosen otherwise than he actually did, and, in consequence, whether man's moral responsibility is really defensible. For how can a man be morally responsible, he asks himself, if his choices, like all other events in the universe, could not have been otherwise than they in fact were? It is precisely against the background of world-views such as these that for reflective people the problem of moral responsibility normally arises. . . .

The unreflective or unsophisticated person, the ordinary "man in the street," who does not know or much care what scientists and theologians and philosophers have said about the world, sees well enough that A is morally responsible only if he could have acted otherwise, but in his intellectual innocence he will, very probably, envisage nothing capable of preventing A from having acted otherwise except some material impediment. . . . Accordingly, for the unreflective person, "A could have acted otherwise, as a condition of moral responsibility," *is* apt to mean no more than "A could have acted otherwise *if* he had so chosen."

It would appear, then, that the view now favored by many philosophers, that the freedom required for moral responsibility is merely freedom from external constraint, is a view which they share only with the less reflective type of layman. Yet it should be plain that on a matter of this sort the view of the unreflective person is of little value by comparison with the view of the reflective person. There are some contexts, no doubt, in which lack of sophistication is an asset. But this is not one of them. The question at issue here is as to the kind of impediments which might have prevented a man from acting otherwise than he in fact did: and on this question knowledge and reflection are surely prerequisites of any answer that is worth listening to. It is simply on account of the limitations of his mental vision that the unreflective man interprets the expression "could have acted otherwise," in its context as a condition of moral responsibility, solely in terms of external constraint. He has failed (as yet) to reach the intellectual level at which one takes into account the implications for moral choices of the world-views of science, religion, and philosophy. If on a matter of this complexity the philosopher finds that his analysis accords with the utterances of the uneducated he has, I suggest, better cause for uneasiness than for self-congratulation. . . .

## III

A contra-causal freedom, it is argued, such as is implied in the "categorical" interpretation of the proposition "A could have chosen otherwise than he did," posits a breach of causal continuity between a man's character and his conduct. Now apart from the general presumption in favor of the universality of causal law, there are special reasons for disallowing the breach that is here alleged. It is the common assumption of social intercourse that our acquaintances will act "in character"; that their choices will exhibit the "natural" response of their characters to the given situation. And this assumption seems to be amply substantiated, over a wide range of conduct, by the actual success which attends predictions made on this basis. Where there should be, on the contra-causal hypothesis, chaotic variability, there is found in fact a large measure of intelligible continuity. Moreover, what is the alternative to admitting that a person's choices flow from his character? Surely just that the so-called "choice" is not *that person's* choice at all: that, relatively to the person concerned, it is a mere "accident." Now we cannot really believe this. But if it *were* the case, it would certainly not help to establish *moral* freedom, the freedom required for *moral* responsibility. For clearly a man cannot be morally responsible for an act which does not express his own choice but is, on the contrary, attributable simply to chance. . . .

To begin with the less troublesome of the two main objections indicated — the objection that the break in causal continuity which free will involves is inconsistent with the predictability of conduct on the basis of the agent's known character. All that is necessary to meet this objection, I suggest, is the frank recognition, which is perfectly open to the **Libertarian,** that there is a wide area of human conduct, determinable on clear general principles, within which free will does not effectively operate. The most important of these general principles . . . has often enough been stated by Libertarians. Free will does not operate in these practical situations in which no conflict arises in the agent's mind between what he conceives to be his "duty" and what he feels to be his "strongest desire." It does not operate here because there just is no occasion for it to operate. There is no reason whatever why the agent should here even contemplate choosing any course other than that prescribed by his strongest desire. In all such situations, therefore, he naturally wills in accordance with strongest desire. But his "strongest desire" is simply the specific ***ad hoc*** expression of that system of conative and emotive dispositions which we call his "character." In all such situations, therefore, whatever may be the case elsewhere, his will is in effect determined by his character as so far formed. Now when we bear in mind that there are an almost immeasurably greater number of situations in a man's life that conform to *this* pattern than there are situations in which an agent is aware of a conflict between strongest desire and duty, it is apparent that a Libertarianism which accepts the limitation of free will to the *latter* type of situation is not open to the stock objection on the score of "predictability." For there still remains a vast area of human behavior in which prediction on the basis of known character may be expected to succeed: an area which will accommodate without difficulty, I think, all these empirical facts about successful prediction which the critic is apt to suppose fatal to Free Will.

So far as I can see, such a delimitation of the field of effective free will denies to the Libertarian absolutely nothing which matters to him. For it is precisely that small sector of the field of choices which our principle of delimitation still leaves open to free will—the sector in which strongest desire clashes with duty—that is crucial for moral responsibility. It is, I believe, with respect to such situations, and in the last resort to such situations alone, that the agent himself recognizes that moral praise and blame are appropriate. They are appropriate, according as he does or does not "rise to duty" in the face of opposing desires; always granted, that is, that he is free to choose between these courses as genuinely open possibilities. If the reality of freedom be conceded *here,* everything is conceded that the Libertarian has any real interest in securing.

But, of course, the most vital question is, can the reality of freedom be conceded even here? In particular, can the standard objection be met which we stated, that if the person's choice does not, in these situations as elsewhere, flow from his *character,* then it is not *that person's* choice at all.

This is, perhaps, of all the objections to a contra-causal freedom, the one which is generally felt to be the most conclusive. For the assumption upon which it is based, *viz,* that no intelligible meaning can attach to the claim that an act which is not an expression of the self's *character* may nevertheless be the *self's* act, is apt to be regarded as self-evident. The Libertarian is accordingly charged with being in effect an *In*determinist, whose "free will," in so far as it does not flow from the agent's character, can only be a matter of "chance." Has the Libertarian—who invariably repudiates this charge and claims to be a *Self*-determinist—any way of showing that, contrary to the assumption of his critics, we *can* meaningfully talk of an act as the self's act even though, in an important sense, it is not an expression of the self's "character"?

I think that he has. I want to suggest that what prevents the critics from finding a meaning in this way of talking is that they are looking for it in the wrong way; or better, perhaps, with the wrong orientation. They are looking for it from the stand-point of the *external observer;* the stand-point proper to, because alone possible for, apprehension of the physical world. Now from the external stand-point we may observe processes of change. But one thing which, by common consent, *cannot* be observed from without is *creative activity.* Yet—and here lies the crux of the whole matter—it is precisely creative activity which we are trying to understand when we are trying to understand what is traditionally designated by "free will." For if there should be an act which is genuinely the self's act and is nevertheless not an expression of its character, such an act, in which the self "transcends" its character as so far formed, would seem to be essentially of the nature of creative activity. It follows that to look for a meaning in "free will" from the external stand-point is absurd. It is to look for it in a way that ensures that it will not be found. Granted that a creative activity of any kind is at least *possible* (and I know of no ground for its *a priori* rejection), there is one way, and one way only, in which we can hope to apprehend it, and that is from the *inner* stand-point of direct participation.

It seems to me therefore, that if the Libertarian's claim to find a meaning in a "free" will which is genuinely the self's will, though not an expression of the self's character, is to be subjected to any test that is worth applying, that test must be undertaken from the inner stand-point. We ought to place ourselves imaginatively at the stand-point of the agent engaged in the typical moral situation in which free will is claimed, and ask ourselves whether from *this* stand-point the claim in question does or does not have meaning for us. That the appeal must be to introspection is no doubt unfortunate. But he would be a very doctrinaire critic of introspection who declined to make use of it when in the nature of the case no other means of apprehension is available. Everyone must make the introspective experiment for himself: but I may perhaps venture to report, though at this late stage with extreme brevity, what I at least seem to find when I make the experiment myself.

In the situation of moral conflict, then, I (as agent) have before my mind a course of action X, which I believe to be my duty; and also a course of action Y, incompatible with X, which I feel to be that which I most strongly desire. Y is, as it is sometimes expressed, "in the line of least resistance" for me—the course which I am aware I should take if I let my purely desiring nature operate without hindrance. It is the course towards which I am aware that my *character,* as so far formed, naturally inclines me. Now, as actually engaged in this situation, I find that I cannot help believing that I *can* rise to duty and choose X; the "rising to duty" being effected by what is commonly called "effort of will." And I further find, if I ask myself just what it is I am believing when I believe that I "can" rise to duty, that I cannot help believing that it lies with me here and now, quite absolutely, which of two genuinely open possibilities I adopt; whether, that is, I make the effort of will and choose X, or, on the other hand, let my desiring nature, my character as so far formed, "have its way," and choose Y, the course "in the line of least resistance." These beliefs may, of course, be illusory, but that is not at present in point. For the present argument all that matters is whether beliefs of this sort are in fact discoverable in the moral agent in the situation of "moral temptation." For my own part, I cannot doubt the introspective evidence that they are.

Now here is the vital point. No matter which course, X or Y, I choose in this situation, I cannot doubt, *qua* practical being engaged in it, that my choice is *not* just the expression of my formed character, and yet *is* a choice made by my *self.* For suppose I make the effort and choose X (my "duty"). Since my very purpose in making the "effort" is to enable me to act against the existing "set" of desire, which is the expression of my character as so far formed, I cannot possibly regard the act itself as the expression of my *character.* On the other hand, introspection makes it equally clear that I am certain that it is *I* who choose: that the act is not an "accident," but is genuinely *my* act. Or suppose that I choose Y (the end of "strongest desire"). The course chosen here is, it is true, in conformity with my "character." But since I find myself unable to doubt that I *could* have made the effort and chosen X, I cannot possibly regard the choice of Y as *just* the expression of my character. Yet here again I find that I cannot doubt that the choice is *my* choice, a choice for which *I* am justly to be blamed.

What this amounts to is that I *can* and *do* attach meaning, *qua* moral agent, to an act which is not the self's character and yet is genuinely the self's act. And having no good reason to suppose that other persons have a fundamentally different mental constitution, it seems to me probable that anyone else who undertakes a similar experiment will be obliged to submit a similar report. I conclude, therefore, that the argument against "free will" on the score of its "meaninglessness" must be held to fail. "Free Will" does have meaning; though, because it is of the nature of a creative activity, its meaning is discoverable only in an intuition of the practical consciousness of the participating agent. To the agent making a moral choice in the situation where duty clashes with desire, his "self" is known to him as a creatively active self, a self which declines to be identified with his "character" as so formed. Not, of course, that the self's character—let it be added to obviate misunderstanding—either is, or is supposed by the agent to be, devoid of bearing upon his choices, even in the "sector" in which free will is held to operate. On the contrary, such a bearing is manifest in the empirically verifiable fact that we find it "harder" (as we say) to make the effort of will required to "rise to duty" in proportion to the extent that the "dutiful" course conflicts with the course to which our character as so far formed inclines us. It is only in the polemics of the critics that a "free" will is supposed to be incompatible with recognizing the bearing of "character" upon choice. . . .

## *Jean-Paul Sartre (1905–1980)*

Jean-Paul Sartre was the most prominent member of the school of philosophy known as existentialism. This philosophical view was not limited to philosophers; novelists, literary critics, and even theologians become known as existentialists. The philosophical foundation of French **existentialism** is Sartre's *Being and Nothingness* (1943). However, Sartre also wrote two well-known existentialist plays, *The Flies* and *No Exit.* During World War II, Sartre was active in the French Resistance. In the 1950s Sartre was active in leftist politics and at various times was both supportive and critical of communism. As with any philosophical school that has an impact on popular thought, existentialism has been both oversimplified and misunderstood. Perhaps Sartre's best known philosophical view is his account of freedom—a view often referred to as a radical account of freedom. Sartre's view is that in *all* circumstances, human beings are free. The selection on freedom included here is from *Being and Nothingness.*

# Freedom: An Existential Explanation

## *Jean-Paul Sartre*

### I

It is strange that philosophers have been able to argue endlessly about determinism and free-will, to cite examples in favor of one or the other thesis without ever attempting first to make explicit the structures contained in the very idea of *action*. The concept of an act contains, in fact, numerous subordinate notions which we shall have to organize and arrange in a hierarchy: to act is to modify the shape of the world; it is to arrange means in view of an end; it is to produce an organized instrumental complex such that by a series of concatenations and connections the modification effected on one of the links causes modifications throughout the whole series and finally produces an anticipated result. But this is not what is important for us here. We should observe first that an action is on principle *intentional*. The careless smoker who has through negligence caused the explosion of a powder magazine has not *acted*. On the other hand the worker who is charged with dynamiting a quarry and who obeys the given orders has acted when he has produced the expected explosion; he knew what he was doing or, if you prefer, he intentionally realized a conscious project. . . .

. . . Since freedom is identical with my existence, it is the foundation of ends which I shall attempt to attain either by the will or by passionate efforts. Therefore it can not be limited to voluntary acts. **Volitions,** on the contrary, like passions are certain subjective attitudes by which we attempt to attain the ends posited by original freedom. By original freedom, of course, we should not understand a freedom which would be prior to the voluntary or passionate act but rather a foundation which is strictly contemporary with the will or the passion and which these manifest, each in its own way. . . .

If these ends are already posited, then what remains to be decided at each moment is the way in which I shall conduct myself with respect to them; in other words, the attitude which I shall assume. Shall I act by volition or by passion? Who can decide except me? In fact, if we admit that circumstances decide for me (for example, I can act by volition when faced with a minor danger but if the peril increases, I shall fall into passion), we thereby suppress all freedom. It would indeed be absurd to declare that the will is autonomous when it appears but that external circumstances strictly determine the moment of its appearance. . . .

. . . This does not mean that I am free to get up or to sit down, to enter or to go out, to flee or to face danger — if one means by freedom here a pure capricious, unlawful, gratuitous, and incomprehensible contingency. To be sure, each one of my acts, even the most trivial, is entirely free in the sense which we have just defined; but this does not mean that my act can be anything *whatsoever* or even that it is *unforeseeable*. Someone, nevertheless may object and ask how if my act can be understood *neither* in terms of the state of the world nor in terms of the ensemble of my past taken as an irremediable thing, it could possibly be anything but gratuitous. . . .

### II

The decisive argument which is employed by common sense against freedom consists in reminding us of our impotence. Far from being able to modify our situation at our whim, we seem to

---

Abridged from *Being and Nothingness,* by Jean-Paul Sartre. (New York: Philosophical Library, Inc.,

be unable to change ourselves. I am not "free" either to escape the lot of my class, of my nation, of my family, or even to build up my own power or my fortune or to conquer my most insignificant appetites or habits. I am born a worker, a Frenchman, an hereditary syphilitic, or a tubercular. The history of a life, whatever it may be, is the history of a failure. The **coefficient of adversity** of things is such that years of patience are necessary to obtain the feeblest result. Again it is necessary "to obey nature in order to command it"; that is, to insert my action into the network of determinism. Much more than he appears "to make himself," man seems "to be made" by climate and the earth, race and class, language, the history of the collectivity of which he is a part, heredity, the individual circumstances of his childhood, acquired habits, the great and small events of his life.

This argument has never greatly troubled the partisans of human freedom. . . . Many of the facts set forth by the determinists do not actually deserve to enter into our considerations. In particular the coefficient of adversity in things can not be an argument against our freedom, for it is by *us*—*i.e.*, by the preliminary positing of an end—that this coefficient of adversity arises. A particular crag, which manifests a profound resistance if I wish to displace it, will be on the contrary a valuable aid if I want to climb upon it in order to look over the countryside. In itself—if one can even imagine what the crag can be in itself—it is neutral; that is, it waits to be illuminated by an end in order to manifest itself as adverse or helpful. Again it can manifest itself in one or the other way only within an instrumental-complex which is already established. Without picks and piolets, paths already worn, and a technique of climbing, the crag would be neither easy nor difficult to climb; the question would not be posited, it would not support any relation of any kind with the technique of mountain climbing. Thus although brute things . . . can from the start limit our freedom of action, it is our freedom itself which must first constitute the framework, the technique, and the ends in relation to which they will manifest themselves as limits. Even if the crag is revealed as "too difficult to climb," and if we must give up the ascent, let us note that the crag is revealed as such only because it was originally grasped as "climbable"; it is therefore our freedom which constitutes the limits which it will subsequently encounter. . . .

## III

The essential consequence of our earlier remarks is that man being condemned to be free carries the weight of the whole world on his shoulders; he is responsible for the world and for himself as a way of being. We are taking the word "responsibility" in its ordinary sense as "consciousness (of) being the incontestable author of an event or of an object." . . . He must assume the situation with the proud consciousness of being the author of it, for the very worst disadvantages or the worst threats which can endanger my person have meaning only in and through my project; and it is on the ground of the engagement which I am that they appear. It is therefore senseless to think of complaining since nothing foreign has decided what we feel, what we live, or what we are.

Furthermore this absolute responsibility is not resignation; it is simply the logical requirement of the consequences of our freedom. What happens to me happens through me, and I can neither affect myself with it nor revolt against it nor resign myself to it. Moreover everything which happens to me is *mine*. By this we must understand first of all that I am always equal to what happens to me *qua* man, for what happens to a man through other men and through himself can be only human. The most terrible situations of war, the worst tortures do not create a non-human state of things; there is no non-human situation. It is only through fear, flight, and recourse to magical types of conduct that I shall decide on the non-human, but this decision is human, and I shall carry the entire responsibility for it. But in addition the situation is *mine* because it is the image of my free choice of myself, and everything which it presents to me is *mine* in that this represents me and symbolizes me. Is it not I who decide the coefficient of adversity in things and even their unpredictability by deciding myself?

Thus there are no accidents in a life; a community event which suddenly bursts forth and involves me in it does not come from the outside. If I am mobilized in a war, this war is my war; it is in my image and I deserve it. I deserve it first because I could always get out of it by suicide or by desertion; these ultimate possibles are those which must always be present for us when there is a question of envisaging a situation. For lack of getting out of it, I have chosen it. This can be due to inertia, to cowardice in the face of public opinion, or because I prefer certain other values to the value of the refusal to join in the war (the good opinion of my relatives, the honor of my family, etc.). Anyway you look at it, it is a matter of choice. This choice will be repeated later on again and again without a break until the end of the war. . . .

But in addition the war is *mine* because by the sole fact that it arises in a situation which I cause to be and that I can discover it there only by engaging myself for or against it, I can no longer distinguish at present the choice which I make of myself from the choice which I make of the war. To live this war is to choose myself through it and to choose it through my choice of myself. There can be no question of considering it as "four years of vacation" or as a "reprieve," as a "recess," the essential part of my responsibilities being elsewhere in my married, family, or professional life. In this war which I have chosen I choose myself from day to day, and I make it mine by making myself. If it is going to be four empty years, then it is I who bear the responsibility for this. . . .

Yet this responsibility is of a very particular type. Someone will say, "I did not ask to be born." This is a naive way of throwing greater emphasis on our facticity. I am responsible for everything, in fact, except for my very responsibility, for I am not the foundation of my being. Therefore everything takes place as if I were compelled to be responsible. I am *abandoned* in the world, not in the sense that I might remain abandoned and passive in a hostile universe like a board floating on the water, but rather in the sense that I find myself suddenly alone and without help, engaged in a world for which I bear the whole responsibility without being able, whatever I do, to tear myself away from this responsibility for an instant. For I am responsible for my very desire of fleeing responsibilities. To make myself passive in the world, to refuse to act upon things and upon Others is still to choose myself, and suicide is one mode among others of being-in-the-world. . . . That is why I can not ask, "Why was I born?" or curse the day of my birth or declare that I did not ask to be born, for these various attitudes toward my birth—*i.e.,* toward the *fact* that I realize a presence in the world—are absolutely nothing else but ways of assuming this birth in full responsibility and of making it *mine.* . . . The one who realizes in anguish his condition as *being* thrown into a responsibility which extends to his very abandonment has no longer either remorse or regret or excuse; he is no longer anything but a freedom which perfectly reveals itself and whose being resides in this very revelation. But . . . most of the time we flee anguish in bad faith.

# Compatibilism

Can you have your cake and eat it too? On the one hand most scientists argue that if you are to have a science of human behavior, you must take the perspective of determinism. On the other hand many philosophers argue that if you are to have a place for morals and responsibility in human behavior then you must adopt the free will hypothesis. Is it possible to have freedom in a deterministic universe?

At first it might seem as if the obvious answer to that question is "no." Genuine freedom requires that some events not be determined wholly and only by antecedent events. However, some philosophers have argued that the two positions really aren't inconsistent after all. They only seem that way.

Perhaps the differences are merely verbal. The positions seem inconsistent only because they are stated badly. This represents the line of argument taken by W. T. Stace. To eliminate the inconsistency one could argue that either the determinist view is incorrectly stated or that free will has been improperly defined or that both determinism and free will are improperly characterized. What Stace does is draw a distinction between the actions of individuals that are caused by psychological states and those that are caused by events external to the agent. Thus if you leave your office to get a sandwich because you are hungry you have freely left your office. On the other hand, if you have left your office because the police arrested you, your leaving the office was not free. The difference between free acts and nonfree acts is the difference between inner and outer causation.

However, neither the determinist nor the nondeterminist would be satisfied with Stace's account. The determinists believe that psychological events are determined by the same or similar causes as nonpsychological events. The nondeterminists would reject Stace's analysis of what it means to be a free agent. They would argue that inner psychological states like motives are causes for behavior and hence Stace's account of our inner lives is easily compatible with determinism. Stace's agent looks like a puppet controlled by mental events rather than physical ones.

As for moral responsibility, Stace argues that moral behavior is determined by character and that society doesn't hesitate to reward people whose good acts result from a good character and punish people whose bad acts result from a bad character—even when we usually know beforehand that persons with good character will behave well and those with bad character will behave badly. Indeed, the two justifications for punishment are to correct bad character and to deter people from doing similar acts. This analysis of character, reward, and punishment is perfectly consistent with the deterministic framework.

Stace's suggestions for a compatibilist account of reward and punishment, praise, and blame receive their most comprehensive treatment in the article by J. J. C. Smart. Smart draws the distinction between the boy who does not do his homework because he is stupid and the boy who does not do his work because he is lazy. It makes no sense to punish the former, but it does make sense to punish the latter. Stupidity cannot be changed by punishment but laziness surely can. Causal laws operate in both cases, but in one case punishment would have pragmatic effects; in the other case it wouldn't.

Smart admits that reward and punishment fit more neatly into a causal world than such moral concepts as praise and blame. Smart reminds us, however, that we do praise people for being attractive and we dispraise people for not being as good at something, football or philosophy for example, even though given their natural endowment they are as good at it as they can be. Praise and blame function as grading terms. This captures what is essential in these terms. Any additional residue is just residue and should be treated as such. Grading people is appropriate, judging them is not.

But most ethicists would reject Stace's and

Smart's accounts as impoverished. The grading function of praise and blame is *secondary* to the judging function. The primary function of a moral system is to guide human conduct so that people carry out their moral obligations. Praise is positive judgment for the carrying out of one's duties; blame is negative judgment for failure to carry out one's duties. It is true that the judging function is irrelevant in a completely causal world but that doesn't mean that the judging function is wrong or misguided in a world where obligations are voluntarily assumed and rejected. Whether there is such a world where obligations are voluntarily assumed or rejected is the point at issue. And what are Smart and Stace to do with terms like *duty* and *rights*? How about a causal analysis of them?

Whereas many nondeterminists try to show that moral action requires free will, R. E. Hobart argues that moral action requires determinism. Character is both deterministic in providing an antecedent cause and is required if moral action is to be explained. A bad action from a person of good character is not a testimony to human freedom; it's a mystery to be explained. But the existence of antecedent events that can serve as explanation for human actions does not destroy freedom. Your volitions explain what you do but you produce your volitions. You can do something because you have the power to do it and you have the power to do it because you are the person you are.

However, the determinist critic would respond to Hobart's compatibilist analysis by denying that we are free to be other than we are and hence the determinist would deny that we really have the power to do other than we do. But Hobart rejects that criticism by saying that naturally we didn't have the power to choose an alternative when we were doing what we did, but before we started doing what we did, we might have had the volition to do the other thing.

But doesn't that analysis just postpone the inevitable question? Did we really have the power to do other than what we did before we started doing it? If the question is answered affirmatively, then it seems as if determinism is denied. Yet if answered negatively, it seems as if free will is denied. In other words, doesn't Hobart's compatibilist solution succeed only because we didn't push the set of questions back far enough? Having one's cake and eating it too continues to be a difficult feat.

## *Walter T. Stace (1886–1967)*

W. T. Stace was a twentieth century American philosopher with broad philosophical interests. His views cannot be associated with one philosophical school. Although he is associated with Hegel and idealism, his epistemology was most influenced by such empiricists as David Hume, Bertrand Russell, and G. E. Moore. He spent considerable time abroad, particularly in Ceylon where he was influenced by Hinayana Buddhism. He tried to reconcile empiricism and mysticism in *Mysticism and Philosophy*. Stace believed that ethics was bound up with human desires, wants, and approvals; in other words, what was good or bad was a function of the nature of man. Stace also was an objectivist in ethics because he believed that ethical judgments could be rationally defended. Just as Stace tried to reconcile empiricism and mysticism, Stace tried to reconcile free will and determinism. All human actions were caused, but free actions were caused by inner mental events (psychological states), and nonfree acts were caused by states of affairs external to the agent.

# Resolving a Semantic Problem

## *W. T. Stace*

. . . I shall . . . discuss the problem of free will, for it is certain that if there is no free will there can be no morality. Morality is concerned with what men ought and ought not to do. But if a man has no freedom to choose what he will do, if whatever he does is done under compulsion, then it does not make sense to tell him that he ought not to have done what he did and that he ought to do something different. All moral precepts would in such case be meaningless. Also if he acts always under compulsion, how can he be held morally responsible for his actions? How can he, for example, be punished for what he could not help doing?

It is to be observed that those learned professors of philosophy or psychology who deny the existence of free will do so only in their professional moments and in their studies and lecture rooms. For when it comes to doing anything practical, even of the most trivial kind, they invariably behave as if they and others were free. They inquire from you at dinner whether you will choose this dish or that dish. They will ask a child why he told a lie, and will punish him for not having chosen the way of truthfulness. All of which is inconsistent with a disbelief in free will. This should cause us to suspect that the problem is not a real one; and this, I believe, is the case. The dispute is merely verbal, and is due to nothing but a confusion about the meanings of words. It is what is now fashionably called a semantic problem.

How does a verbal dispute arise? Let us consider a case which, although it is absurd in the sense that no one would ever make the mistake which is involved in it, yet illustrates the principle which we shall have to use in the solution of the problem. Suppose that someone believed that the word "man" means a certain sort of five-legged animal; in short that "five-legged animal" is the correct *definition* of man. He might then look around the world, and rightly observing that there are no five-legged animals in it, he might proceed to deny the existence of men. This preposterous conclusion would have been reached because he was using an incorrect definition of "man." All you would have to do to show him his mistake would be to give him the correct definition; or at least to show him that his definition was wrong. Both the problem and its solution would, of course, be entirely verbal. The problem of free will, and its solution, I shall maintain, is verbal in exactly the same way. The problem has been created by the fact that learned men, especially philosophers, have assumed an incorrect definition of free will, and then finding that there is nothing in the world which answers to their definition, have denied its existence. As far as logic is concerned, their conclusion is just as absurd as that of the man who denies the existence of men. The only difference is that the mistake in the latter case is obvious and crude, while the mistake which the deniers of free will have made is rather subtle and difficult to detect.

Throughout the modern period, until quite recently, it was assumed, both by the philosophers who denied free will and by those who defended it, that *determinism is inconsistent with free will.* If a man's actions were wholly determined by chains of causes stretching back into the remote past, so that they could be predicted beforehand by a mind which knew all the causes, it was assumed that they could not in that case be free. This implies that a certain definition of actions done from free will was assumed, namely that they are actions *not* wholly determined by

---

Abridged from *Religion and the Modern Mind,* by W. T. Stace. (Philadelphia and New York: J. B. Lippincott Co., © 1952 by W. T. Stace). Reprinted by permission of Harper & Row.

causes or predictable beforehand. Let us shorten this by saying that free will was defined as meaning **indeterminism.** This is the incorrect definition which has led to the denial of free will. As soon as we see what the true definition is we shall find that the question whether the world is deterministic, as Newtonian science implied, or in a measure indeterministic, as current physics teaches, is wholly irrelevant to the problem.

Of course there is a sense in which one can define a word arbitrarily in any way one pleases. But a definition may nevertheless be called correct or incorrect. It is correct if it accords with a *common usage* of the word defined. It is incorrect if it does not. And if you give an incorrect definition, absurd and untrue results are likely to follow. For instance, there is nothing to prevent you from arbitrarily defining a man as a five-legged animal, but this is incorrect in the sense that it does not accord with the ordinary meaning of the word. Also it has the absurd result of leading to a denial of the existence of men. This shows that *common usage is the criterion for deciding whether a definition is correct or not.* And this is the principle which I shall apply to free will. I shall show that indeterminism is not what is meant by the phrase "free will" *as it is commonly used.* And I shall attempt to discover the correct definition by inquiring how the phrase is used in ordinary conversation.

Here are a few samples of how the phrase might be used in ordinary conversation. It will be noticed that they include cases in which the question whether a man acted with free will is asked in order to determine whether he was morally and legally responsible for his acts.

*Jones* I once went without food for a week.
*Smith* Did you do that of your own free will?
*Jones* No. I did it because I was lost in a desert and could find no food.

But suppose that the man who had fasted was Mahatma Gandhi. The conversation might then have gone:

*Gandhi* I once fasted for a week.
*Smith* Did you do that of your own free will?
*Gandhi* Yes. I did it because I wanted to compel the British Government to give India its independence.

Take another case. Suppose that I had stolen some bread, but that I was as truthful as George Washington. Then, if I were charged with the crime in court, some exchange of the following sort might take place:

*Judge* Did you steal the bread of your own free will?
*Stace* Yes. I stole it because I was hungry.

Or in different circumstances the conversation might run:

*Judge* Did you steal of your own free will?
*Stace* No. I stole because my employer threatened to beat me if I did not.

At a recent murder trial in Trenton some of the accused had signed confessions, but afterwards asserted that they had done so under police duress. The following exchange might have occurred:

*Judge* Did you sign this confession of your own free will?
*Prisoner* No. I signed it because the police beat me up.

Now suppose that a philosopher had been a member of the jury. We could imagine this conversation taking place in the jury room.

*Foreman of the Jury* The prisoner says he signed the confession because he was beaten, and not of his own free will.
*Philosopher* This is quite irrelevant to the case. There is no such thing as free will.
*Foreman* Do you mean to say that it makes no difference whether he signed because his conscience made him want to tell the truth or because he was beaten?
*Philosopher* None at all. Whether he was caused to sign by a beating or by some desire of his own—the desire to tell the truth, for example—in either case his signing was causally determined, and therefore in neither case did he act of his own free will. Since there is no

such thing as free will, the question whether he signed of his own free will ought not to be discussed by us.

The foreman and the rest of the jury would rightly conclude that the philosopher must be making some mistake. What sort of a mistake could it be? There is only one possible answer. The philosopher must be using the phrase "free will" in some peculiar way of his own which is not the way in which men usually use it when they wish to determine a question of moral responsibility. That is, he must be using an incorrect definition of it as implying action not determined by causes.

Suppose a man left his office at noon, and were questioned about it. Then we might hear this:

*Jones* Did you go out of your own free will?
*Smith* Yes. I went out to get my lunch.

But we might hear:

*Jones* Did you leave your office of your own free will?
*Smith* No. I was forcibly removed by the police.

We have now collected a number of cases of actions which, in the ordinary usage of the English language, would be called cases in which people have acted of their own free will. We should also say in all these cases that they *chose* to act as they did. We should also say that they could have acted otherwise, if they had chosen. For instance, Mahatma Gandhi was not compelled to fast; he chose to do so. He could have eaten if he had wanted to. When Smith went out to get his lunch, he chose to do so. He could have stayed and done some more work, if he had wanted to. We have also collected a number of cases of the opposite kind. They are cases in which men were not able to exercise their free will. They had no choice. They were compelled to do as they did. The man in the desert did not fast of his own free will. He had no choice in the matter. He was compelled to fast because there was nothing for him to eat. And so with the other cases. It ought to be quite easy, by an inspection of these cases, to tell what we ordinarily mean when we say that a man did or did not exercise free will. We ought therefore to be able to extract from them the proper definition of the term. Let us put the cases in a table (see below).

It is obvious that to find the correct definition of free acts we must discover what characteristic is common to all the acts in the left-hand column, and is, at the same time, absent from all the acts in the right-hand column. This characteristic which all free acts have, and which no unfree acts have, will be the defining characteristic of free will.

Is being uncaused, or not being determined by causes, the characteristic of which we are in search? It cannot be, because although it is true that all the acts in the right-hand column have causes, such as the beating by the police or the absence of food in the desert, so also do the acts in the left-hand column. Mr. Gandhi's fasting was caused by his desire to free India, the man leaving his office by his hunger, and so on. Moreover there is no reason to doubt that these causes of the free acts were in turn caused by prior conditions, and that these were again the results of

| *Free Acts* | *Unfree Acts* |
| --- | --- |
| Gandhi fasting because he wanted to free India. | The man fasting in the desert because there was no food. |
| Stealing bread because one is hungry. | Stealing because one's employer threatened to beat one. |
| Signing a confession because one wanted to tell the truth. | Signing because the police beat one. |
| Leaving the office because one wanted one's lunch. | Leaving because forcibly removed. |

causes, and so on back indefinitely into the past. Any physiologist can tell us the causes of hunger. What caused Mr. Gandhi's tremendously powerful desire to free India is no doubt more difficult to discover. But it must have had causes. Some of them may have lain in peculiarities of his glands or brain, others in his past experiences, others in his heredity, others in his education. Defenders of free will have usually tended to deny such facts. But to do so is plainly a case of special pleading, which is unsupported by any scrap of evidence. The only reasonable view is that all human actions, both those which are freely done and those which are not, are either wholly determined by causes, or at least as much determined as other events in nature. It may be true, as the physicists tell us, that nature is not as deterministic as was once thought. But whatever degree of determinism prevails in the world, human actions appear to be as much determined as anything else. And if this is so, it cannot be the case that what distinguishes actions freely chosen from those which are not free is that the latter are determined by causes while the former are not. Therefore, being uncaused or being undetermined by causes, must be an incorrect definition of free will.

What, then, is the difference between acts which are freely done and those which are not? What is the characteristic which is present to all the acts in the left-hand column and absent from all those in the right-hand column? Is it not obvious that, although both sets of actions have causes, the causes of those in the left-hand column are *of a different kind* from the causes of those in the right-hand column? The free acts are all caused by desires, or motives, or by some sort of internal psychological states of the agent's mind. The unfree acts, on the other hand, are all caused by physical forces or physical conditions, outside the agent. Police arrest means physical force exerted from the outside; the absence of food in the desert is a physical condition of the outside world. We may therefore frame the following rough definitions. *Acts freely done are those whose immediate causes are psychological states in the agent. Acts not freely done are those whose immediate causes are states of affairs external to the agent.*

It is plain that if we define free will in this way, then free will certainly exists, and the philosopher's denial of its existence is seen to be what it is — nonsense. For it is obvious that all those actions of men which we should ordinarily attribute to the exercise of their free will, or of which we should say that they freely chose to do them, are in fact actions which have been caused by their own desires, wishes, thoughts, emotions, impulses, or other psychological states.

In applying our definition we shall find that it usually works well, but that there are some puzzling cases which it does not seem exactly to fit. These puzzles can always be solved by paying careful attention to the ways in which words are used, and remembering that they are not always used consistently. I have space for only one example. Suppose that a thug threatens to shoot you unless you give him your wallet, and suppose that you do so. Do you, in giving him your wallet, do so of your own free will or not? If we apply our definition, we find that you acted freely, since the immediate cause of the action was not an actual outside force but the fear of death, which is a psychological cause. Most people, however, would say that you did not act of your own free will but under compulsion. Does this show that our definition is wrong? I do not think so. Aristotle, who gave a solution of the problem of free will substantially the same as ours (though he did not use the term "free will") admitted that there are what he called "mixed" or borderline cases in which it is difficult to know whether we ought to call the acts free or compelled. In the case under discussion, though no actual force was used, the gun at your forehead so nearly approximated to actual force that we tend to say the case was one of compulsion. It is a borderline case.

Here is what may seem like another kind of puzzle. According to our view an action may be free though it could have been predicted beforehand with certainty. But suppose you told a lie, and it was certain beforehand that you would tell it. How could one then say, "You could have told the truth"? The answer is that it is perfectly true that you could have told the truth *if* you had wanted to. In fact you would have done so, for in that case the causes producing your action, namely your desires, would have been different, and would therefore have produced different effects. It is a delusion that predictability and free will are incompatible. This agrees with common sense. For if, knowing your character, I predict that you will act honorably, no one would say when you do act honorably, that this shows you did not do so of your own free will.

Since free will is a condition of moral responsibility, we must be sure that our theory of free will gives a sufficient basis for it. To be held morally responsible for one's actions means that one may be justly punished or rewarded, blamed or praised, for them. But it is not just to punish a man for what he cannot help doing. How can it be just to punish him for an action which it was certain beforehand that he would do? We have not attempted to decide whether, as a matter of fact, all events, including human actions, are completely determined. For that question is irrelevant to the problem of free will. But if we assume for the purposes of argument that complete determinism is true, but that we are nevertheless free, it may then be asked whether such a deterministic free will is compatible with moral responsibility. For it may seem unjust to punish a man for an action which it could have been predicted with certainty beforehand that he would do.

But that determinism is incompatible with moral responsibility is as much a delusion as that it is incompatible with free will. You do not excuse a man for doing a wrong act because, knowing his character, you felt certain beforehand that he would do it. Nor do you deprive a man of a reward or prize because, knowing his goodness or his capabilities, you felt certain beforehand that he would win it.

Volumes have been written on the justification of punishment. But so far as it affects the question of free will, the essential principles involved are quite simple. The punishment of a man for doing a wrong act is justified, either on the ground that it will correct his own character, or that it will deter other people from doing similar acts. The instrument of punishment has been in the past, and no doubt still is, often unwisely used; so that it may often have done more harm than good. But that is not relevant to our present problem. Punishment, if and when it is justified, is justified only on one or both of the grounds just mentioned. The question then is how, if we assume determinism, punishment can correct character or deter people from evil actions.

Suppose that your child develops a habit of telling lies. You give him a mild beating. Why? Because you believe that his personality is such that the usual motives for telling the truth do not cause him to do so. You therefore supply the missing cause, or motive, in the shape of pain and the fear of future pain if he repeats his untruthful behavior. And you hope that a few treatments of this kind will condition him to the habit of truth-telling, so that he will come to tell the truth without the infliction of pain. You assume that his actions are determined by causes, but that the usual causes of truth-telling do not in him produce their usual effects. You therefore supply him with an artificially injected motive, pain and fear, which you think will in the future cause him to speak truthfully.

The principle is exactly the same where you hope, by punishing one man, to deter others from wrong actions. You believe that the fear of punishment will cause those who might otherwise do evil to do well.

We act on the same principle with non-human, and even with inanimate, things, if they do not behave in the way we think they ought to behave. The rose bushes in the garden produce only small and poor blooms, whereas we want large and rich ones. We supply a cause which will produce large blooms, namely fertilizer. Our automobile does not go properly. We supply a cause which will make it go better, namely oil in the works. The punishment for the man, the fertilizer for the plant, and the oil for the car, are all justified by the same principle and in the same way. The only difference is that different kinds of things require different kinds of causes to make them do what they should. Pain may be the appropriate remedy to apply, in certain cases, to human beings, and oil to the machine. It is, of course, of no use to inject motor oil into the boy or to beat the machine.

Thus we see that moral responsibility is not only consistent with determinism, but requires it. The assumption on which punishment is based is that human behavior is causally determined. If pain could not be a cause of truth-telling there would be no justification at all for punishing lies. If human actions and volitions were uncaused, it would be useless either to punish or reward, or indeed to do anything else to correct people's bad behavior. For nothing that you could do would in any way influence them. Thus moral responsibility would entirely disappear. If there were no determinism of human beings at all, their actions would be completely unpredictable and capricious, and therefore irresponsible. And this is in itself a strong argument against the common view of philosophers that free will means being undetermined by causes. . . .

## *R. E. Hobart (1868–1963)*

"R. E. Hobart" is a pseudonym for Dickinson S. Miller, an American ethical philosopher and epistemologist. He traveled widely abroad and became friends with a number of well-known philosophers including William James, George Santayana, and the logical positivists of the Vienna circle. He received a Doctor of Divinity degree as well as a doctorate in philosophy. He served as a Unitarian minister. His best-known article, reprinted here, develops the position known as **compatibilism.** He argued that free will and causal explanation of human behavior were not inconsistent. They only appeared inconsistent because people confused causality with compulsion. All human behavior is caused, but not all human behavior is compelled. Hence, Hobart argued, free will theorists need not adopt a theory like James's.

# Free Will as Involving Determination and Inconceivable Without It

### *R. E. Hobart*

The thesis of this article is that there has never been any ground for the controversy between the doctrine of free will and determinism, that it is based upon a misapprehension, that the two assertions are entirely consistent, that one of them strictly implies the other, that they have been opposed only because of our natural want of the analytical imagination. In so saying I do not

Abridged from "Free Will as Involving Determination and Inconceivable Without It," by R. E. Hobart, *Mind,* Vol. XLIII, No. 169, Jan. 1934. Reprinted by permission of Macmillan, London and Basingstoke.

tamper with the meaning of either phrase. That would be unpardonable. I mean free will in the natural and usual sense, in the fullest, the most absolute sense in which for the purposes of the personal and moral life the term is ever employed. I mean it as implying responsibility, merit and demerit, guilt and desert. I mean it as implying, after an act has been performed, that one "could have done otherwise" than one did. I mean it as conveying these things also, not in any subtly modified sense but in exactly the sense in which we conceive them in life and in law and in ethics. These two doctrines have been opposed because we have not realized that free will can be analyzed without being destroyed, and that determinism is merely a feature of the analysis of it. . . .

The reason for thinking that there is no occasion for the controversy lies exclusively in the analysis of the terms employed in it. But the several analyses must all be taken together, realized jointly, before the position can be fully understood.

## SELF AND CHARACTER

We are not concerned with the total nature of the self, but only with the aspect of it strictly involved in our question. We are not dealing with the problem of knowledge and therefore not with the self as mere knower. It is clear that the self merely as knower in general (irrespective of just what particulars it knows) is similar in all men. The relation of subject to object, whatever it may be, is the same with you and with me. But the self as it interests ethics is not the same in different persons. It is the concrete, active self, existing through time and differing from others. The whole stress of morality arises because moral selves are not alike, because there is need of influencing some moral selves to make them refrain from certain acts or neglects, that is, in order to make them better moral selves. How do we express the difference? We call it a difference of moral qualities, traits, or character. We are having regard to the question what acts will come from these selves. By character we mean, do we not, the sum of a man's tendencies to action, considered in their relative strength; or that sum in so far as it bears upon morals.

Now the position of the indeterminist is that a free act of will is the act of the self. The self becomes through it the author of the physical act that ensues. This **volition** of the self causes the physical act but it is not in its turn caused, it is "spontaneous." To regard it as caused would be determinism. The causing self to which the indeterminist here refers is to be conceived as distinct from character; distinct from temperament, wishes, habits, impulses. He emphasizes two things equally: the physical act springs from the self through its volition, and it does not spring merely from character, it is not simply the result of character and circumstances. If we ask, "Was there anything that induced the self thus to act?" we are answered in effect, "Not definitively. The self feels motives but its act is not determined by them. It can choose between them."

The next thing to notice is that this position of the indeterminist is taken in defense of moral conceptions. There would be no fitness, he says, in our reproaching ourselves, in our feeling remorse, in our holding ourselves or anyone guilty, if the act in question were not the act of the self instead of a product of the machinery of motives.

We have here one of the most remarkable and instructive examples of something in which the history of philosophy abounds—of a persistent, an age-long deadlock due solely to the indisposition of the human mind to look closely into the meaning of its terms.

How do we reproach ourselves? We say to ourselves, "How negligent of me!" "How thoughtless!" "How selfish!" "How hasty and unrestrained!" "That I should have been capable even for a moment of taking such a petty, irritated view!" etc. In other words, we are attributing to ourselves at the time of the act, in some respect and measure, a bad character, and regretting it. And that is the entire point of our self-reproach. We are turning upon ourselves with disapproval and it may be with disgust; we wish we could undo what we did in the past, and, helpless to do that, feel a peculiar thwarted poignant anger and shame at ourselves that we *had it in us* to perpetrate the thing we now condemn. It is self we are reproaching, *i.e.,* self that we are viewing as bad in that it produced bad actions. . . . All self-reproach is self-judging, and all judging is imputing a character. We are blaming ourselves. If spoken, what we are thinking would be dispraise. And what are praise and dispraise? Always, everywhere, they are *descriptions* of a person (more or less explicit) with favorable or unfavorable feeling at what is described. . . . In moral instances they are descriptions of his character. We are morally characterizing him in our minds (as above) with appropriate feelings. We are attributing to him the character that we approve and like and wish to see more of, or the contrary. All the most intimate terms of the moral life imply that the act has proceeded from *me,* the distinctive me, from the manner of man I am or was. And this is the very thing on which the **libertarian** lays stress. What the indeterminist prizes with all his heart, what he stoutly affirms and insists upon, is precisely what he denies, namely, that I, the concrete and specific moral being, am the author, the source of my acts. For, of course, that is determinism. To say that they come from the self is to say that they are determined by the self—the moral self, the self with a moral quality. He gives our preferrings the bad name of the machinery of motives, but they are just what we feel in ourselves when we decide. When he maintains that the self at the moment of decision may act to some extent independently of motives, *and is good or bad according as it acts in this direction or that,* he is simply setting up one character within another, he is separating the self from what he understands by the person's character as at first mentioned, only thereupon to attribute to it a character of its own, *in that he judges it good or bad.*

The whole controversy is maintained by the indeterminist in order to defend the validity of the terms in which we morally judge—for example, ourselves. But the very essence of all judgment, just so far as it extends, asserts determination.

If in conceiving the self you detach it from all motives or tendencies, what you have is not a morally admirable or condemnable, not a morally characterizable self at all. Hence it is not subject to reproach. You cannot call a self good because of its courageous free action, and then deny that its action was determined by its character. In calling it good because of that action you have implied that the action came from its goodness (which means its good character) and was a sign thereof. By their fruits ye shall know them. The indeterminist appears to imagine that he can distinguish the moral "I" from all its propensities, regard its act as arising in the moment undetermined by them, and yet can then (for the first time, in his opinion, with propriety) ascribe to this "I" an admirable quality. At the very root of his doctrine he contradicts himself. How odd that he never catches sight of that contradiction! He fights for his doctrine in order that he may call a man morally good, on account of his acts, with some real meaning; and his doctrine is that a man's acts (precisely so far as "free" or undetermined) do not come from his goodness. So they do not entitle us to call him good. He has taken his position in defense of moral conceptions, and it is fatal to all moral conceptions.

We are told, however, that it is under determinism that we should have no right any more to praise or to blame. At least we could not do so in the old sense of the terms. We might throw words of praise to a man, or throw words of blame at him, because we know from observation that they will affect his action; but the old light of meaning in the terms has gone out. Well, all we have to do is to keep asking what this old meaning was. We praise a man by saying that he is a good friend, or a hard worker, or a competent man of business, or a trusty assistant, or a judicious minister, or a gifted poet, or one of the noblest of men—one of the noblest of characters! In other words, he is a being with such and such qualities. If it is moral praise, he is a being with such and such tendencies to bring forth good acts. If we describe a single act, saying, for instance: "Well done!" we mean to praise the person for the act as being the author of it. It is he who has done well and proved himself capable of doing so. If the happy act is accidental we say that no praise is deserved for it. If a person is gratified by praise it is because of the estimate of him, in some respect or in general, that is conveyed. Praise (once again) means description, with expressed or implied admiration. If any instance of it can be found which does not consist in these elements our analysis fails. . . .

**Indeterminism** maintains that we need not be impelled to action by our wishes, that our active will need not be determined by them. Motives "incline without necessitating." We choose amongst the ideas of action before us, but need not choose solely according to the attraction of desire, in however wide a sense that word is used. Our inmost self may rise up in its autonomy and moral dignity, independently of motives, and register its sovereign decree.

Now, *in so far* as this "interposition of the self" is undetermined, the act is not *its* act, it does not issue from any concrete continuing self; it is born at the moment, of nothing, hence it expresses no quality; it bursts into being from no source. The self does not register *its* decree, for the decree is not the product of just that *"it."* The self does not rise up in *its* moral dignity, for dignity is the quality of an enduring being, influencing its actions, and therefore expressed by them, and that would be determination. *In proportion* as an act of volition starts of itself without cause it is exactly, so far as the freedom of the individual is concerned, as if it had been thrown into his mind from without — "suggested" to him — by a freakish demon. It is exactly like it in this respect, that in neither case does the volition arise from what the man is, cares for or feels allegiance to; it does not come out of him. *In proportion* as it is undetermined, it is just as if his legs should suddenly spring up and carry him off where he did not prefer to go. Far from constituting freedom, that would mean, in the exact measure in which it took place, the loss of freedom. It would be an interference, and an utterly uncontrollable interference, with his power of acting as he prefers. In fine, then, *just so far* as the volition is undetermined, the self can neither be praised nor blamed for it, since it is not the act of the self.

The principle of free will says: "*I* produce my volitions." Determinism says: "My volitions are produced by *me*." Determinism is free will expressed in the passive voice.

After all, it is plain what the indeterminists have done. It has not occurred to them that our free will may be resolved into its component elements. . . . When it is thus resolved they do not recognize it. . . . They solve the problem by forgetting analysis. The solution they offer is merely: "There is a self inside which does the deciding." . . . They take the whole thing to be analyzed, imagine a duplicate of it reduced in size, so to speak, and place this duplicate-self inside as an explanation — making it the elusive source of the "free decisions." They do not see that they are merely pushing the question a little further back, since the process of deciding, with its constituent factors, must have taken place within that inner self. Either it decided in a particular way because, on the whole, it preferred to decide in that way, or the decision was an underived event, a rootless and sourceless event. It is the same story over again. In neither case is there any gain in imagining a second self inside, however wonderful and elusive. Of course, it is the first alternative that the indeterminist is really imagining. If you tacitly and obscurely conceive the self as deciding *its own way, i.e.,* according to its preference, but never admit or recognize this, then you can happily remain a libertarian indeterminist; but upon no other terms. In your theory there is a heart of darkness.

## FREEDOM

In accordance with the genius of language, free will means freedom of persons in willing, just as "free trade" means freedom of persons (in a certain respect) in trading. The freedom of anyone surely always implies his possession of a power, and means the absence of any interference (whether taking the form of restraint or constraint) with his exercise of that power. Let us consider this in relation to freedom in willing.

## "CAN"

We say, "I can will this or I can will that, whichever I choose." Two courses of action present themselves to my mind. I think of their consequences, I look on this picture and on that, one of them commends itself more than the other, and I will an act that brings it about. I knew that I could choose either. That means that I had the power to choose either.

What is the meaning of "power"? A person has a power if it is a fact that when he sets himself in the appropriate manner to produce a certain event that event will actually follow. I have the power to lift the lamp; that is, if I grasp it and exert an upward pressure with my arm, *it will rise.* I have the power to will so and so; that is, if I want, that act of will will take place. That and none other is the meaning of power, is it not? A man's being in the proper active posture of body or of mind is the cause, and the sequel in question will be the effect. . . .

Thus power depends upon, or rather consists in, a law. The law in question takes the familiar form that if something happens a certain something else will ensue. If A happens then B will happen. The law in this case is that if the man definitively so desires then volition will come to pass. There is a series, wish — will — act. The act follows according to the will (that is a law — I do not mean an underived law) and the will follows according to the wish (that is another law). A man has the power (sometimes) to act as he wishes. He has the power (whenever he is not physically bound or held) to act as he wills. He has the power always (except in certain morbid states) to will as he wishes. All this depends upon the laws of his being. Wherever there is a power there is a law. In it the power wholly consists. A man's power to will as he wishes is simply the law that his will follows his wish.

What, again, does freedom mean? It means the absence of any interference with all this. Nothing steps in to prevent my exercising my power.

All turns on the meaning of "can." "I can will either this or that" means, I am so constituted that if I definitively incline to this, the appropriate act of will will take place, and if I definitively incline to that, the appropriate act of will will take place. The law connecting preference and will exists, and there is nothing to interfere with it. My free power, then, is not an exemption from law but in its inmost essence an embodiment of law.

Thus it is true, after the act of will, that I could have willed otherwise. It is most natural to add, "if I had wanted to"; but the addition is not required. The point is the meaning of "could." I could have willed whichever way I pleased. I had the power to will otherwise, there was nothing to prevent my doing so, and I should have done so if I had wanted. If someone says that the wish I actually had prevented my willing otherwise, so that I could not have done it, he is merely making a slip in the use of the word "could." He means, that wish could not have produced anything but this volition. But "could" is asserted not of the wish (a transient fact to which power in this sense is not and should not be ascribed) but of the person. And the person *could* have produced something else than that volition. He could have produced any volition he wanted; he had the power to do so.

But the objector will say, "The person as he was at the moment — the person as animated by that wish — could not have produced any other volition." Oh, yes, he could. "Could" has meaning not as applied to a momentary actual phase of a person's life, but to the person himself of whose life that is but a phase; and it means that (even at that moment) he had the power to will just as he preferred. *The idea of power, because it is the idea of a law, is hypothetical, carries in itself hypothesis as part of its very intent and meaning — "if he should prefer this, if he should prefer that" — and therefore can be truly applied to a person irrespective of what at the moment he does prefer. It remains hypothetical even when applied.* This very peculiarity of its meaning is the whole point of the idea of power. It is just because determinism is true, because a law obtains, that one "could have done otherwise." . . .

But it may be asked, "Can I will in opposition to my strongest desire at the moment when it is strongest?" If the words "at the moment when it is strongest" qualify "can," the answer has already been given. If they qualify "will," the suggestion is a contradiction in terms. Can I turn-on-the-electric-light-at-a-moment-when-I-am-not-trying-to-do-so? This means, if I try to turn on the light at a moment when I am not trying to, will it be turned on? A possible willing as I do not prefer to will is not a power on my part, hence not to be expressed by "I can."

Everybody knows that we often will what we do not want to will, what we do not prefer. But when we say this we are using words in another sense than that in which I have just used them. In *one* sense of the words, whenever we act we are doing what we prefer, on the whole, in view of all the circumstances. We are acting for the greatest good or the least evil or a mixture of these. In the *other* and more usual sense of the words, we are very often doing what we do not wish to do, *i.e.*, doing some particular thing we do not wish because we are afraid of the consequences or disapprove of the moral complexion of the particular thing we do wish. We do the thing that we do not like because the other thing has aspects that we dislike yet more. We are still doing what we like best on the whole. It is again a question of the meaning of words.

If the initiative for volition is not a wish, what is it? Indeterminism says that a moral agent sometimes decides against the more tempting course. He does so, let us say, because it is wrong, the other course is the right one. In other words, the desire to do right is at the critical moment stronger within him than the temptation. No, no, replies indeterminism, it is not that; he sometimes decides against the stronger desire. Very well; "can" meaning what it does, tell us what is the leaning or favorable disposition on the part of the ego, in a case of undetermined willing, toward the volition it adopts; what is that which constitutes the ego's initiative in that direction—since it is not a wish? Shall we say it is an approval or conscientious acceptance? Does this approval or acceptance arise from the agent's distinctive moral being? That is determinism, quite as much as if you called the initiative a wish. But the indeterminist has already answered in effect that there is no such initiative, or no effectual initiative. The act of will causes the physical act but is not itself caused. This is to deny the presence of power, according to its definition. How has it a meaning to say in advance that "I can" will this way or that? The self, considering the alternatives beforehand, is not in a position to say, "If I feel thus about it, this volition will take place, or if I feel otherwise the contrary will take place; I know very well how I shall feel, so I know how I shall will." The self now existing has not control over the future "free" volition, since that may be undetermined, nor will the self's future feelings, whatever they may be, control it. Hence the sense expressed by "I can," the sense of power inhering in one's continuous self to sway the volition as it feels disposed, is denied to it. All it is in a position to mean by "I can" is, "I do not know which will happen," which is not "I can" at all. Nay, even looking backward, it is unable to say: "I could have willed otherwise," for that clearly implies, "Had I been so disposed the other volition would have taken place," which is just what cannot, according to indeterminism, be said. Surely, to paraphrase a historic remark, our "liberty" does not seem to be of very much use to us. The indeterminist is in a peculiarly hapless position. The two things that he is most deeply moved to aver, that the free volition is the act of the self, and that the self can will one way or the other—these two things on his own theory fall utterly to pieces, and can only be maintained on the view that he opposes.

## COMPULSION

The indeterminist conceives that according to determinism the self is carried along by wishes to acts which it is thus necessitated to perform. This mode of speaking distinguishes the self from the wishes and represents it as under their dominion. This is the initial error. This is what leads the indeterminist wrong on all the topics of his problem. And the error persists in the most recent writings. In fact, the moral self is the wishing self. The wishes are its own. It cannot be described as under their dominion, for it has no separate predilections to be overborne by them; they themselves are its predilections. To fancy that because the person acts according to them he is compelled, a slave, the victim of a power from whose clutches he cannot extricate himself, is a confusion of ideas, a mere slip of the mind. The answer that has ordinarily been given is surely correct; all compulsion is causation, but not all causation is compulsion. Seize a man and violently force him to do something, and he is compelled—also caused—to do it. But induce him to do it by giving him reasons and his doing it is caused but not compelled.

## PASSIVITY

We have to be on our guard even against conceiving the inducement as a cause acting like the impact of a billiard ball, by which the self is precipitated into action like a second billiard ball, as an effect. The case is not so simple. Your reasons have shown him that his own preferences require the action. He does it of his own choice; he acts from his own motives in the light of your reasons. The sequence of cause and effect goes on within the self, with contributory information from without.

It is not clarifying to ask, "Is a volition free or determined?" It is the person who is free, and his particular volition that is determined. Freedom is something that we can attribute only to a continuing being, and he can have it only so far as the particular transient volitions within him are determined.

It is fancied that, owing to the "necessity" with which an effect follows upon its cause, if my acts of will are caused I am not free in thus acting. Consider an analogous matter. When I move I use ligaments. "Ligament" means that which binds, and a ligament does bind bones together. But *I* am not bound. I . . . am rendered possible by the fact that my bones are bound one to another; that is part of the secret of my being able to act, to move about and work my will. If my bones ceased to be bound one to another I should be undone indeed. The human organism is detached, but it is distinctly important that its component parts shall not be detached. Just so my free power of willing is built up of tight cause-and-effect connections. The point is that when I employ the power thus constituted nothing determines the particular employment of it but *me*. Each particular act of mine is determined from outside itself, *i.e.*, by a cause, a prior event. But not from outside me. I, the possessor of the power, am not in my acts passively played upon by causes outside me, but am enacting my own wishes in virtue of a chain of causation within me. What is needed is to distinguish broadly between a particular effect, on the one hand, and, on the other, the detached, continuous life of a mental individual and his organism; a life reactive, but reacting according to its own nature. . . .

## SPONTANEITY

The conception of spontaneity in an act or an utterance is the conception of its springing straight from the being himself, from his individuality, with naught to cause it but the freest impulse, the sheerest inclination, of that being. The term implies and requires but one causation, that from within. If we deny all causation behind the volition itself, even that from within his nature, we deny spontaneity on his part. We have emptied our formula of all human meaning.

## SOURCE

The indeterminist declares a man to be "the absolute source" of his acts. Let us scrutinize the term. The source of a stream is not a point where the water constituting the stream comes suddenly into existence, but on the contrary that from which it issues, that which supplies it because it has contained it. The stream—that particular stream—begins there, just as the action begins at its source, though the active energy flows from within it. The word "absolute" must mean true, genuine, complete, without reservation or qualification. Now such a genuine source a man in fact is; he knowingly and deliberately creates an act; the act issues forth from his chosen purpose, from his moral individuality. What the indeterminist, however, must mean by "absolute source" is a source that has in turn no source; a source, he thinks, cannot in the fullest and truest sense be such if it derives what it emits. This, as we see, certainly receives no support from the natural uses of the word, but is flatly incompatible with them. But the final objection is deeper. Will the indeterminist point out anything in the definition of the word "source" which implies that the thing defined is itself sourceless, or is imperfectly realized if it has a source? If he cannot, then the addition of the word "absolute" does not import that sourcelessness into the idea. Obviously "the man," as figuring in the indeterminist's conception here, would have to be the momentary man, not the enduring moral being. The truth clearly is that the indeterminist is confusing the idea of *flowing from this source and previously from another* with the quite distinct idea of *not flowing from this source but from another.* He feels that they cannot both be sources of the same act. And this is part of his confusion between causation and compulsion. If the agent were compelled to act as he does, not he but the compeller would be the intentional, the moral source of the act.

## PREDICTION

If we knew a man's character thoroughly and the circumstances that he would encounter, determinism (which we are not here completely asserting) says that we could foretell his conduct. This is a thought that repels many libertarians. Yet to predict a person's conduct need not be repellent. If you are to be alone in a room with £1000 belonging to another on the table and can pocket it without anyone knowing the fact, and if I predict that you will surely *not* pocket it, that is not an insult. I say, I know you, I know your character; you will not do it. But if I say that you are "a free being" and that I really do not know whether you will pocket it or not, that is rather an insult. On the other hand, there are cases where prediction is really disparaging. If I say when you make a remark, "I knew you were going to say that," the impression is not agreeable. My exclamation seems to say that your mind is so small and simple that one can predict its ideas. That is the real reason why people resent in such cases our predicting their conduct; that if present human knowledge, which is known to be so limited, can foresee their conduct, it must be more naive and stereotyped than they like to think it. It is no reflection upon the human mind or its freedom to say that one who knew it through and through (a human impossibility) could foreknow its preferences and its spontaneous choice. It is of the very best of men that even we human beings say, "I am sure of him." It has perhaps in this controversy hardly been observed how much at this point is involved, how far the question of prediction reaches. The word "reliable" or "trustworthy" is a prediction of behavior. Indeed, all judgment of persons whatever, in the measure of its definitude, is such a prediction. . . .

## *J. J. C. Smart (b. 1920)*

J. J. C. Smart is a distinguished contemporary Australian philosopher who has made significant contributions in metaphysics, the philosophy of science, and ethics. He has written extensively on the mind-body problem and defends a materialist theory of mind-body identity. With respect to the free will problem, Smart defends a compatibilist position — chiefly on the grounds that such ethical concepts as rewards and punishments, praise and blame, do make sense within a causal system. As an ethicist, J. J. C. Smart is one of the relatively few contemporary defenders of act-utilitarianism. His books include *Philosophy and Scientific Realism* (1963), *Between Science and Philosophy* (1969), and *Utilitarianism: For And Against* (1973, with Bernard Williams).

# Free-Will, Praise and Blame

## *J. J. C. Smart*

. . . When, in nineteenth-century England, the rich man brushed aside all consideration for his unsuccessful rivals in the battle for wealth and position, and looking at them as they starved in the gutter said to himself, "Well, they had the same opportunities as I had. If I took more advantage of them than they did, that is not my fault but theirs," he was most probably not only callous but (as I shall try to show) metaphysically confused. A man who said "heredity and environment made me what I am and made them what they are" would be less likely to fall a prey to this sort of callousness and indifference. Metaphysical views about free-will are therefore practically important, and their importance is often in inverse proportion to their clarity.

What is this metaphysical view about free-will that I wish to attack? Its supporters usually characterize it negatively, by contrasting it with what it is not, namely determinism on the one hand and pure chance or caprice on the other. This is a dangerous procedure, because a negative characterization may rule out absolutely every possibility; as if we defined a new sort of natural number, a "free" number, as one which is neither prime nor divisible by a number which is greater than one and smaller than itself. Our negative characterization, that is, may be so comprehensive as to leave room for no possibility whatever. However let us play the metaphysician's game as long as we can, and let us try to see what the metaphysical doctrine of free-will is, at least by investigating what it is not. And what it is not is, first of all, determinism.

"What would become of your laws, your morality, your religion, your gallows, your Paradise, your Gods, your Hell, if it were shown that such and such fluids, such fibers, or a certain acridity in the blood, or in the animal spirits, alone suffice to make a man the object of your punishments or your rewards?" So wrote the notorious Marquis de Sade.[1] According to Nigel Balchin, "The modern endocrinologist sometimes goes far to support de Sade, and draws a rather humiliating picture of a man as a sort of chemico-electric experiment, in which a drop too much of this, or a grain too little of that, is the origin of personality. The psychologist insists that an apparently minor incident or accident in the early stages of our development may affect the whole course of

Abridged from "Free-Will, Praise and Blame," by J. C. C. Smart. Reprinted from *Mind*, Vol. LXX, No. 279, July 1961, pp. 291 – 306. Reprinted by permission of Oxford University Press and J. C. C. Smart. Footnotes renumbered.

our lives. In the face of this comparison of views most of us are inclined to compromise. We believe that heredity, accident, and incident have a bearing on man's character and actions, and may even sometimes have a determinative one. But we do not accept the complete suspension of moral judgment implicit in de Sade's view."[2]

These quotations come from literary, rather than professionally philosophical sources, but there is nothing in them, I think, which would not be endorsed by the ablest philosophical defenders of the metaphysical notion of freedom, for example, C. A. Campbell. Two comments are important at this stage. The first is that not only de Sade, but his biographer Nigel Balchin and the philosopher Campbell, and very many men in the street, hold that to accept the deterministic position is to give up the notion of moral responsibility. The second is that the view outlined by Balchin does not entail the absurdity that we can never predict what people will do. According to Balchin, heredity and environment are important, though they do not exhaust the matter. And, as Campbell holds, free-will need only be supposed to operate in cases of moral conflict, when our nature as determined by heredity and environment pulls us away from the path of duty. Since cases of moral conflict are rare, we can usually predict people's behavior just as confidently as if we believed wholeheartedly in the determinist position. So the common argument against metaphysical freedom, that it makes nonsense of our confidence in predicting human behavior, falls to the ground. . . . So I shall not press this particular objection.

Those who hold that determinism and moral responsibility are incompatible with one another do not, of course, hold that we are responsible for those of our actions which are due to pure chance. Somehow they want our moral choices to be neither determined nor a matter of chance. Campbell has a word for it: he says that our moral choices are instances of **"contra-causal freedom."**[3] There is not "unbroken causal continuity" in the universe but we are sometimes able to choose between "genuinely open possibilities." None of these concepts is at all precisely defined by Campbell, but I propose to give . . . [a definition] of "unbroken causal continuity" . . . that may be acceptable to him, and to like-minded thinkers, and I shall then enquire whether in the light of . . . [this definition] there is any room for "contra-causal freedom" and "genuinely open possibilities."

*D1*. I shall state the view that there is "unbroken causal continuity" in the universe as follows. It is in principle possible to make a sufficiently precise determination of the state of a sufficiently wide region of the universe at time $t_o$, and sufficient laws of nature are in principle ascertainable to enable a super-human calculator to be able to predict any event occurring within that region at an already given time $t_l$.[4] . . .

Campbell (like Balchin and de Sade) holds that if the whole universe is deterministic in the sense of *D1*, then no one is morally responsible, for on this hypothesis if a person does a certain action "he could not have done otherwise," and that he could have done otherwise is a condition of moral responsibility. Now there is perhaps a sense of "could not have done otherwise" in which whether or not a person could or could not have done otherwise depends on whether or not the universe is deterministic in the sense of *D1*. But it does not follow that if a person could not have done otherwise in this special sense then he could not have done otherwise, in any *ordinary* sense. Taken in any ordinary sense, within some concrete context of daily life, "he could have done otherwise" has no metaphysical implications. Does a child have to learn about Laplacian determinism before he can say that his little sister could have eaten her apple instead of his candy? Now it is the ordinary sense which we use when we talk about moral responsibility. How then can it follow that if a person "could not have done otherwise," in the *special* sense, that he was not morally responsible? . . .

Campbell holds that if determinism in the sense of *D1* is true then a man could never correctly be said to have been able to do otherwise than he did. That this is not so can be seen if we consider the following example. Suppose that when washing the dishes you drop a plate, but that fortunately it does not break. You say, however, that it *could* have broken. That is, within the range of possible initial conditions covered by possible cases of "dropping," the known dispositional characteristics of the plate do not allow us to rule out the proposition "it will break." If, however, it had been an aluminum plate, then it would not have broken. That is, whatever the initial conditions had been (within a wide range) it would not have broken. Whether dropped flat or on its edge, with a spinning motion or with no spinning motion, from three feet or four feet or five feet, it still would not have broken. Thus such cases in which we use the words "could have" or "could not have" are cases in which we either cannot or can use a law or a law-like proposition to rule out a certain possibility despite our uncertainty as to the precise initial conditions. Briefly: *E* could not have happened if there are laws or law-like propositions which rule out *E*. Campbell wants to use "could not have happened" in a different way: he will say that *E* could not have happened if *E* is ruled out by certain laws or law-like propositions *together with the initial conditions.*

However it is pretty certain that Campbell would resist the suggestion that "John Smith could have done otherwise" is analogous to "the plate could have broken." He would say[5] that it is an actual particular person in a particular set of circumstances with whom we are concerned when we ask "Could he have done otherwise? Was he morally responsible?" and that we are in no way concerned with hypothetical possibilities. It is difficult to see the force of this sort of criticism. It is but a tautology to say that if we ask whether John Smith could have done otherwise then we are asking a question about John Smith. Clearly we are interested in John Smith as an individual who has to deal with a particular situation, but what follows? That nothing follows can be made evident if we develop our example of the dropped plate. Suppose that I have a very valuable plate, made in China and once the property of some ancient emperor and the only one of its kind. While showing it to a friend I drop it but fortunately it does not break. Gasping with relief I say, "It could have broken but thank goodness it did not." Here we are using the words "could have" and yet our interest is very much in this particular plate in this set of circumstances. There is no suggestion here, however, that a very precise determination of the initial conditions together with an exact knowledge of the physical properties of the plate would not have enabled us to predict that in these (rather fortunate) circumstances it would not break.

On this analysis "could have" implies "would have if certain conditions had been fulfilled." In moral contexts the conditions that are of most importance are "if he had chosen," "if he had tried," and "if he had wanted to." . . .

We can now consider Campbell's phrase "genuinely open possibility." If I drop a china plate it is an open possibility that it will break. It is not an open possibility that an aluminum plate will break. The possibility of an aluminum plate breaking can be ruled out for any likely range of initial conditions from a knowledge of the physical properties of aluminum. Whether the aluminum plate is dropped on its side or on its edge, with a rotary motion or without a rotary motion, in hot weather or cold weather, from a height of two feet or six feet, it still will not break. With the china plate, in some of these cases it will break and in some not. The phrases "an open possibility" and "not an open possibility" are therefore easily understood. What about "genuinely open possibility"? We might suggest that a possibility is "genuinely open" if from the relevant laws and law-like propositions together with a determination, however precise, of the initial conditions, not even Laplace's superhuman calculator could predict what will happen. This is . . . just a case of pure chance. . . .

Campbell tries by introspection to distinguish "contra-causal freedom" from both "causal necessitation" and "pure chance." That is, he hopes by appealing to introspection to give a sense to "could have done otherwise" which is different from both that in *(a)* "the plate could have broken" and that in *(b)* "even if the initial conditions had been precisely the same that atom could have shot out a photon." His appeal to introspection is an appeal to our feeling that in certain situations we can do either of two alternative things. Well, in certain situations I certainly do feel that I can do either of two things. That is, I say to myself, "I can do this and I can do that." *Either* I say this to myself using "can" in an ordinary way (as in "the plate could break, and it could fall without breaking") *or* I say these words to myself using "can" in some new way. In the former case introspection has yielded no new sense of "can," and in the latter case some new use of "can" must already have been established. For unless this new use of "can" can be explained antecedently to such introspection, introspection will only yield the fact of my saying to myself a meaningless sentence. But, as I have already argued, logic leaves no room for such a new sense of "can."

A similar situation arises if any alternative description of the predicament of moral choice is attempted. Thus Campbell says[6] that "I further find, if I ask myself just what it is I am believing when I believe that I 'can' rise to duty, that I cannot help believing that it lies with me here and now quite absolutely, which of two genuinely open possibilities I adopt." Our reply must be that we cannot say whether this is so or not. Perhaps we believe this, perhaps we do not, but we cannot tell until Campbell can explain to us what he means by "lies with me here and now quite absolutely" (as opposed to "lies with me here and now"), and until he can explain what is meant by "genuinely open possibilities" (as opposed to "open possibilities"). The same difficulty crops up[7] when he appeals to "creative activity." "Granted that creative activity is possible . . . ," he says. But in any ordinary sense of these words creative activity is not only possible but actual. There are poets, novelists, mathematicians, architects and inventors. In what sense of "creative activity" is it an open question whether creative activity is possible or not? Some writers again bring in the concept of "spontaneity." But you do not have to reject metaphysical determinism before you can believe that your rubbish heap burst into flames as a result of spontaneous combustion.

Most of our ordinary senses of "could have" and "could not have" are not, in my view, incompatible with determinism. Though some of our ordinary talk about moral responsibility is frequently vitiated by a confused metaphysics of free-will, much of it can be salvaged.

When in a moral context we say that a man could have or could not have done something we are concerned with the ascription of responsibility. What is it to ascribe responsibility? Suppose Tommy at school does not do his homework. If the schoolmaster thinks that this is because Tommy is really very stupid, then it is silly of him to abuse Tommy, to cane him or to threaten him. This would be sensible only if it were the case that this sort of treatment made stupid boys intelligent. With the possible exception of certain nineteenth-century schoolmasters, no one has believed this. The schoolmaster says, then, that Tommy is not to blame, he just *could not* have done his homework. Now suppose that the reason why Tommy did not do his homework is that he was lazy: perhaps he had just settled down to do it when some other boy tempted him to come out and climb a tree. In such a case the schoolmaster will hold Tommy responsible, and he will say that Tommy could have done his homework. By this he will not necessarily mean to deny that Tommy's behavior was the outcome of heredity and environment. The case is similar to that of the plate which could have broken. The lazy boy is analogous to the china plate which could break and also could fall without breaking. The stupid boy is like the aluminum plate: whatever the initial conditions the same thing happens. If Tommy is sufficiently stupid, then it does not matter whether he is exposed to temptation or not exposed to temptation, threatened or not threatened, cajoled or not cajoled. When his negligence is found out, he is not made less likely to repeat it by threats, promises, or punishments. On the other hand, the lazy boy can be influenced in such ways. Whether he does his homework or not is perhaps solely the outcome of environment, but one part of the environment is the threatening schoolmaster.

Threats and promises, punishments and rewards, the ascription of responsibility and the non-ascription of responsibility, have therefore a clear pragmatic justification which is quite consistent with a wholehearted belief in metaphysical determinism. Indeed it implies a belief that our actions are very largely determined: if everything anyone did depended only on pure chance (*i.e.* if it depended on nothing) then threats and punishments would be quite ineffective. But even a **libertarian** of course may admit that *most* of our actions are pretty well determined. (Campbell excepts only those acts which are done from a sense of duty against our inclination.)

It begins to appear that the metaphysical question of determinism is quite irrelevant to the rationality of our ascription of responsibility.

What about praise and blame? These concepts are more difficult. We must at the outset distinguish two ways in which we commonly use the word "praise." In one sense praise is the opposite of blame. We praise Tommy for his industry, blame him for his laziness. But when we praise a girl for her good looks this does not mean that we should have blamed her if her looks had been bad. When we praise one footballer for his brilliant run, we do not blame his unfortunate team mate who fumbled a pass. (Unless, of course, the fumble was due to carelessness.) When we praise Smith for his mathematical talent we do not imply that we blame Jones because, try as hard as he may, he cannot handle *x*'s and *y*'s. Of course we may well say that a girl is ugly, a footballer incompetent, or a man unmathematical, and this is the opposite of praise. But it is not blame. Praise and dispraise, in this sense, is simply grading a person as good or bad in some way. A young philosopher may feel pleasure at being praised by one of his eminent colleagues because he thereby knows that his work is assessed highly by one who is competent to judge, and he may be pained to hear himself dispraised because he thereby knows that his work is being assessed as of poor quality. Praise and dispraise of this sort has an obvious function just as has the grading of apples. A highly graded apple is bought and a highly graded philosopher is appointed to a lecturership, while a low graded apple is not bought and the low graded philosopher is not appointed.

In general to praise or dispraise a man, a woman's nose, or a footballer's style is to grade it, and if the grader is competent we feel sure that there are good reasons for the grading. In practice, of course, reasons are frequently given, and this giving of reasons in itself can constitute what is called praise or dispraise. For example, if a philosopher writes about some candidate for a lecturership that he has some illuminating new ideas about the logic of certain psychological concepts, this is the sort of thing that is meant by "praise," and if he says that the candidate is muddle-headed and incapable of writing clear prose, this is the sort of thing which is meant by "dispraise." It is not the sort of thing we mean when we contrast praise with blame. To say that a man cannot write clear prose is not necessarily to blame him. He may have been brought up among muddle-headed people and always given muddle-headed books to read. The fact that we do not feel like blaming him, however, does not alter the fact that we warn prospective employers about him.

Just as we may praise or dispraise a woman for her figure, a footballer for his fleetness or slowness of foot, a lecturer in philosophy for his intelligence or lack of intelligence, and a writer for clarity or obscurity, so naturally enough, we may praise or dispraise a man for his honesty or dishonesty, truthfulness or untruthfulness, kindness or unkindness and so on. In *this* sense of "praise" we may praise moral qualities and moral actions in exactly the same way as we may praise beauty, intelligence, agility or strength. Either we may do so quite generally, using a grading word like "good," "excellent" or "first-class," or we may simply give a description. (For example: her cheeks are like roses, her eyes are like stars.) Praise has a primary function and a secondary function. In its primary function it is just to tell people what people are like. To say that one candidate for a lecturership writes clear prose whereas another cannot put a decent sentence together is to help the committee to decide who should be given the lecturership. Naturally enough, therefore, we like to be praised, hate to be dispraised. And even if no actual advantage is to come from praise, we like to be praised by a competent judge for work we have done because we take this as evidence that we have been on the right track and done something valuable. Because we come to like being praised and to hate being dispraised, praise and dispraise come to have an important secondary function. To praise a class of actions is to encourage people to do actions of that class. And utility of an action normally, but not always, corresponds to utility of praise of it.

So far I have talked of praise and dispraise, not of praise and blame. This is because I wanted a contrary for "praise" in the sense in which we can praise not only a moral action but a woman's nose. What about the contrast of praise with blame? Here I suggest that a clear headed man will use the word "praise" just as before, and the word "blame" just like the previous "dispraise," with one proviso. This is that to praise (in this sense) or to blame a person for an action is not only to grade it (morally) but to imply that it is something for which the person is responsible, in the perfectly ordinary and non-metaphysical sense of "responsible" which we have analyzed earlier in this article. So we blame Tommy for his bad homework if this is due to laziness, not if it is due to stupidity. Blame in this sense can be just as dispassionate as dispraise of a woman's nose: it is just a grading plus an ascription of responsibility. It is perfectly compatible with a recognition that the lazy Tommy is what he is simply as a result of heredity plus environment (and perhaps pure chance).

Now most men do not, in my opinion, praise and blame people in this dispassionate and clear-headed way. This is brought out, in fact, by the quotations from de Sade and Balchin: most men do *not* feel that blame, in the way they use the word "blame," would be appropriate if a man's action was the result of heredity plus environment. The appropriateness of praise and blame is bound up, in the eyes of the ordinary man, with a notion of free-will which is quite metaphysical. Admittedly this metaphysics is incoherent and unformulated (as indeed it has to be, for when formulated it becomes self-contradictory). Nevertheless we can see that a rather pharisaical attitude to sinners and an almost equally unhealthy attitude to saints is bound up with this metaphysics in the thinking of the ordinary man if we look at the way in which very often his whole outlook and tendency to *judge* (not just to grade) other men changes when he is introduced to, and becomes convinced by, a philosophical analysis of free-will like the one in the present paper. How, again, can we explain the idea, held by so many religious people, that an omnipotent and benevolent God can *justly* condemn people to an eternity of torture? Must we not suppose that they have some confused idea that even with the same heredity and environmental influences, and quite apart from pure chance, the sinner *could* have done otherwise? (Of course, even granting this, the utility of Hell in the eyes of a benevolent God still remains obscure.) Or consider the man who excuses himself for his indifference to his less fortunate neighbor by saying, "Hadn't he the same opportunities as I had? He could have got on if he had acted with my drive, initiative, etc." There is sense in such a remark only in so far as the contempt for laziness and lack of drive to which it gives expression is socially useful in spurring others on to display more drive than they otherwise would.

But a man's drive is determined by his genes and his environment, and such a remark as the one above is after all a rather unimportant part of the environment. So I did not think that the remark can be regarded as just a way of influencing people to display drive and resourcefulness. It does depend on a metaphysics of free-will. After all, if everyone had the genes that make for drive and energy they could not *all* get to the top. Dog would still eat dog.

The upshot of the discussion is that we should be quite as ready to *grade* a person for his moral qualities as for his non-moral qualities, but we should stop *judging* him. (Unless "judge" just means "grade," as in "judging apples.") Moreover, if blame in general is irrational, so must be self-blame or self-reproach, unless this comes simply to resolving to do better next time.

## NOTES

1. Quoted by Nigel Balchin, *The Anatomy of Villainy,* p. 174.
2. *Op. cit.* p. 251.
3. "Is 'Freewill' a Pseudo-Problem?" *Mind* (1951).
4. *Cf.* Laplace: *Théorie Analytique des Probabilités,* 2nd edition (Paris, 1814), p. ii of the Introduction.
5. See *op. cit.* p. 453.
6. *Op. cit.* p. 463.
7. *Op. cit.* p. 462.

# *Agency*

In many discussions of the free will question, the person performing the action is often ignored. Determinists want to establish a scientific study of human behavior—a study that they believe requires the deterministic postulate. Behaviorists reinterpret concepts like punishment, praise, and blame to be consistent with such behavioristic notions as operant conditioning. Even some nondeterminists emphasize the argument that our legal and moral institutions would have to be changed if the deterministic hypothesis were adopted rather than focus on arguments as to whether or not the individual is free.

But what about us—the actors? Shouldn't we be the focus of the discussion? As you recall, one of the more common arguments for free will is our sense of feeling free. Although that argument can be naive, it can be interpreted in fairly sophisticated ways as well—as we have seen. Agency theories of free will often begin with a version of this sense of feeling free argument. As agents we believe we initiate causal sequences; we are not passive links in the causal chain, but rather we initiate changes. Consider the decision to write a book. Once the decision is made, a number of events occur that wouldn't have occurred had the decision not been made. Our decision made a change in the world and it was our decision to make. The view that human beings are not merely links in causal chains but rather are initiators of causal events is called *agency theory.* It represents the most contemporary contribution to the free will debate.

To provide an adequate account of this theory, a good definition of what it means to be an agent who initiates causal sequences must be provided. Often when we speak of someone doing something, such as planting a garden, we want to know why the person is doing it. Frequently the answer has been in terms of desires, motives, or volitions. John is planting the garden because he desires to plant the garden. But where did the desire come from? Once the question is posed in that way, a determinist analysis is set up. That desire was caused by another desire and so on until you reach some desire that was caused by an external source. Agency theorists believe that to answer the question, "Why is John planting the garden?" in terms of desires is a mistake. For some activities the question is best answered in terms of intentions and purposes. John is planting the garden to get exercise, to have fresh vegetables, and to save money. Purposes and intentions do not fit so easily into a determinist analysis. The question, "What is the cause of this desire?" is a natural one. The question, "What is the cause of this purpose?" is less natural and is usually best answered, if it can be answered at all, in terms of higher purposes.

An agent when acting as an agent and not merely as a link in the causal chain is acting purposively or intentionally. For an agent to act, the agent must have the capacity to act. Without the capacity the agent is not free to do the act. But having the capacity to perform an action is not the same as being free to perform it. Suppose you have the capacity to perform an action but you don't have the opportunity. Suppose you have both the capacity and the opportunity, but no genuine alternatives. You are in a locked room that contains only a grand piano. You have the capacity to play the piano and certainly the opportunity. Are you free to play the piano? You do have the alternative of doing nothing. But is that a genuine alternative?

The issue as to what counts as a genuine alternative becomes important in discussions as to whether social, legal, and moral constraints are genuine impediments to free will. A robber says, "Your money or your life." Are you free to keep your money? Most everyone would agree that you aren't free in this case even though you have an alternative. But are you free to be a robber? Assume you have the capacity, but you know there is a severe penalty if you rob and are caught. Are you free to be a robber? Perhaps the relation between coercion and free will is more important or at least as important as the relation between causation and free will. All events might be caused without being coerced.

Another perspective for examining agency theory is to draw out the implications of the fact that only agents look upon the future as fundamentally different from the past. If something is merely a link in a causal chain, then what comes before is no different in principle from what comes after. At any time *T*, for any event *E*, there is no way in which the events that are antecedent to *E* are, with respect to *E*, different from the events that will follow *E*. The only distinction is a temporal one—a distinction between before and after. However, with an agent the situation is very different. There is nothing an agent can do about the past. But our use of words like *prevention* indicates that we do think we can do something about the future. If agents could not initiate causal changes, agents could no more control the future than they could control the past. Agents are different from other objects in the causal nexus. A number of considerations work together to show how our conceptual scheme gives agents a special place.

Although agency theory seems attractive because it fits comfortably with our beliefs about our behavior, most determinists find it very unsatisfactory. It resembles the indeterminism of James in the sense that causal initiation is an unexplained event.

## *Max Hocutt (b. 1936)*

Professor Hocutt is a contemporary American philosopher whose interests are in the philosophy of mind and the problem of free will. He is the author of two books: *The Elements of Logical Analysis and Inference* and *First Philosophy,* and has coauthored several other books. He has also published a number of articles in professional journals.

In the selection reproduced here, Professor Hocutt makes a distinction that is crucial for agency theory. He distinguishes between being free to do something and having the capacity to do it. Failure to make this distinction, Professor Hocutt argues, makes the free will problem even more intractable.

# Freedom and Capacity

## *Max Hocutt*

Smith has the capacity, let us suppose, to shoot his neighbor, or rape his neighbor's wife, or burn his neighbor's house. He is quite capable of any, or all, of these misdeeds. As a citizen of the U.S., however, Smith cannot correctly be said to enjoy the freedom to do any of these things. The law forbids such actions, and prescribes severe punishments for those who do them. This shows that

Abridged from "Freedom and Capacity," by Max Hocutt in *The Review of Metaphysics,* Vol. XXIX, No. 2, Dec. 1975, pp. 256–62. Reprinted by permission of *The Review of Metaphysics.*

there is a difference between the *capacity* to do a thing and the *freedom* to do it. The difference is this: Smith *can* do all these things; he *may not* do any of them. Capacity does not imply permission; ability does not guarantee license.

Nor does the converse relation hold. Freedom does not insure facility, as the following case shows. Jones is free, any time he wishes, to press five hundred pounds. There is no law against it and nobody will object if he makes the attempt. Nevertheless, Jones, who weighs only a hundred pounds himself, is unable to lift fifty pounds, much less five hundred, and must fail if he tries. Again, the distinction is that between "may" and "can." Jones *may* lift five hundred pounds; he *can't*. He has the prerogative but not the power; he has the right but not the strength.

This distinction seems to me to be not only plain but important. Deficiencies in freedom can be cured only by removing restraints, but deficiencies in skill require increase in skill for their correction. It helps to know which is which, but if we confuse liberty with ability, permission with power, restraints with constraints, we shall apply the wrong solution to the wrong problem. If blacks are poor because of discrimination, they need more freedom; if because they lack knowledge, they need more training. To make them prosperous, we and they really must know which.

But if the distinction is that clear and critical, why is it so common to blur it? Why do some social workers feel obliged to say that drunkards lack "freedom" from the desire to drink, when it is plain that the alcoholic's problem is, rather, that he lacks ability to refrain from drinking. Why do some clinical psychologists diagnose the problem of the alcoholic as lack of "psychological" freedom, which suggests that the solution is to give him wider scope, when they know very well that confinement is often necessary to correct dependence on drink? And why do philosophers encourage these usages by formally defining freedom as ability, or vice versa?

Part of the answer, surely, is simple imprecision of speech. It causes imprecision of thought. We have almost lost the word "may" from our vocabularies, and in consequence we have almost lost the concept it stands for from our understandings. Almost everybody now says "can" whether he means to describe capacity or to grant or report permission. "You can't run red lights" does not mean that you are unable to run them, but that you are forbidden to do so. The result of this extension of the word "can" is that we have lost sight of the difference between what you are prohibited from doing and what you are unable to do. But if I can't tell lies because I suffer from inhibitions of conscience, that is a lack of ability, not a lack of liberty. If I "can't" tell lies because my friends will shun me, that is lack of liberty, not lack of capacity. The two cases are importantly different, but the use of the word "can't" in both obscures the difference.

Another cause of confusion is our metaphors. We personify everything. We say that the alcoholic is a "slave to drink," and suppose that is like being slave to a plantation owner; we say that Nature "punishes" those who break her laws, and thus assimilate the painful consequences of foolhardiness to the punitive measures of persons; we say that the "compulsive neurotic" is "compelled" by his feelings of guilt, as though his case were analogous to being compelled by one's boss to do unpleasant work; and so on. There is nothing wrong with these metaphors as metaphors. The mistake is to take them literally. Alcoholics are not slaves; they drink of their own free wills. Nature does not punish, and you cannot break her laws; although if you are foolish, you will suffer. Compulsive neurotics do not act under compulsion; they only act *as though* they were under compulsion. The metaphors may be good poetry; they are bad psychology.

But careless speech and poetic fallacies cannot be the whole explanation of why linguistically sensitive and intelligent people have identified freedom with capacity. There are more substantial reasons. Perhaps the best is that it is not wrong to do it. You can define freedom in terms of capacity: you can define "*x* may do *y*" as "*x* can do *y* with impunity." That will not be wrong because we do say that in societies where there are no effective sanctions for such crimes, people are free to burn, rape, or kill, even when laws forbid it.

You can not only define freedom as capacity. The reverse trick is also possible, and permissible. Capacity may be defined as freedom if you think of it as freedom from constraint or limitation and not merely as freedom from restraint or retribution. We may and do say that an honest man is not free to lie, in the sense that he is not free from pangs of conscience if he does.

In short, the identification of freedom with capacity is not wrong; it violates no convention of proper speech. It is just ill-advised. There are differences between them that it pays to preserve. We should not blur these differences; and still less should we deny that they exist.

Perhaps the main cause of the confusion of freedom with capacity in the minds of philosophers is that they have traditionally approached the question by way of responsibility, noticing along the way that we don't normally hold a man to account for what he does under compulsion, against his own wishes. When they have also noticed that lack of capacity is as good an excuse as lack of freedom, the philosophers have usually concluded that it is indifferent whether one's lack is freedom or capacity, when they should have concluded instead that there are two importantly different grounds on which one can escape punishment. The result is that philosophers tend to call whatever reduces liability "freedom" or "capacity," as they prefer.

A good illustration of this is Campbell's answer to Schlick.[1] Schlick had pointed out that determinism does not rule out freedom because causation does not entail coercion. Then he concluded that determinism does not rule out responsibility. Campbell rightly and astutely observed that the premise was right but the conclusion wrong. Causation is not coercion, but if determinism means that a person could not have done otherwise, then it renders dubious the justice of any punishment for any act. For ability to do better is normally as much a condition of culpability as is liberty to do differently. . . .

In any case, Schlick not Campbell was right about free will. It is perfectly compatible with determinism. That an act is caused does not mean it is coerced. Consider two children, A and B. A eats ice cream because he likes ice cream; B eats spinach because he has been threatened with a spanking. Both actions were caused, one by the liking of ice cream, the other by the disliking of spankings. A's action, however, was, unlike B's, an action of his own free will; A did what he wanted to do, voluntarily, under no threats. It does not matter how strong A's passion for ice cream was. Suppose it was so strong as to be irresistible. That only means that A did the thing he most wanted to do when he ate the ice cream. But as we normally use the expression, to do what one most wants to do is to act voluntarily. It is B, who ate spinach under threat of punishment, who acted against his will.

To argue that acts resulting from strong desires or emotions are not voluntary is to personify desires, to think of them as coercive agents, demons. That is witchcraft, but not psychology. It also confuses *pain* with *punishment*. Consider a drug addict. When he indulges his habit, he is acting of his own free will because he is doing the thing he most wants to do. Nobody holds a gun to his head and says "Do or die." It is true that he will suffer withdrawal symptoms if he does not feed his habit. But pain is punishment only when it is administered by another party, and an action is coerced only when it is done under threat of punishment.

It is true that the addict may be ambivalent towards the drug; he may simultaneously wish to use it and to avoid it. If, finally, his desire to use it wins out, the action will not be in accord with all his wishes. Still, it will be voluntary in the sense that it will be what he most wishes to do, as is proved by the fact that he chooses to do it.

It is also true that, in a sense, he "had no choice"; there was no equally attractive alternative. But this is only because he desired none of the available alternatives as much. It is not because someone else precluded him from choosing them. My capacity can be limited in many ways; my freedom can be limited only by another party, someone who either prohibits me or prevents me from doing what I wish. Nothing like that happens in the case of the drug addict. There is nothing he wishes to do more than take his drug. That is what constitutes his being a drug addict. . . .

In short, all I am urging is that we preserve a distinction. I think we all know what the distinction is, but sometimes we blur it and confuse ourselves about it. Roughly, it is this: A man is *free* to do what he may do, that is, what he is neither prohibited nor prevented by some other person (or quasi-person) from doing. He is *able* to do what he can do, whether he is permitted by other parties to do so or not. The two come together only in the case where the limitation on capacity is effected by prevention. When we restrict a man's movements by shackling him to the wall, we limit both his powers and his freedoms. Such a man is neither able nor free to move. He is not able because he can't; he is not free because he is prevented. We can prohibit a man from doing something without thereby limiting his capacity to do it, but to prevent him from doing something is to limit his capacity to do it. Thus, there is a borderline case, a twilight zone, which is neither exclusively freedom nor capacity, but a mixture of both.

The case of prevention may be one more reason why we tend to confuse freedom with capacity. But instead of confusing us, it ought to instruct us. In its primary and literal uses, freedom is a social concept; it can be lost only to another who deprives us of it. The case of prevention merely reveals that there is another way to deprive us of freedom than by threat of punishment; it can also be done by limiting our capacities. That is an important fact, but it is still no good reason to confuse freedom with capacity.

On the contrary, there is every reason to keep them distinct. For distinctions are useful and this one is particularly so. To repeat, only if we can discriminate between lack of freedom and lack of capacity will we know which measures to take to increase which.

## NOTE

1. The articles I have in mind are Chapter 7 of Moritz Schlick's *Problems of Ethics,* first published in Vienna in 1931, and C. A. Campbell's classic reply in *Mind,* 1951. . . .

## *Richard Taylor (b. 1919)*

Despite his reformulation of fatalist arguments, Taylor is neither a fatalist nor a determinist. Rather he is one of the chief spokespersons for the contemporary agency theorists. Taylor rejected those who tried to save freedom, by arguing that some human acts are free in virtue of being caused by internal mental events like motives. Taylor argued that a cause is a cause and that its source as an internal or external cause is irrelevant. Free action is action that is self-caused. Free action is intentional. In the style of contemporary linguistic analysts, Taylor shows how determinism is inconsistent with some of our central linguistic expressions. For example, if determinism were true we would not need the concept of prevention. We could no more change the future than we could the past.

# Prevention, Postvention and the Will

*Richard Taylor*

When a philosopher approaches a problem as old as that of free will, there may be not much point in his addressing himself to it directly with arguments pro or con. It is not likely that any really new argument of either sort can be invented, and if the old ones have not settled the issue, it seems unlikely that any reformulations of them will.

I propose, then, to get into the problem in an indirect way, which is, I think, fairly novel. In part I of this discussion, I am going to compare the ordinary notion of *prevention* with the extraordinary one of ***postvention,*** in order to call attention to a difference in the way men view future things as opposed to how they view past things, at least in so far as these bear upon their weal or woe. I shall then show that this difference is not to be accounted for in the ways that are most apt to occur to philosophically sophisticated persons. In part II, I am going to suggest that this difference is accounted for by the fact that men conceive of themselves as purposeful beings, and of their actions as, at least ordinarily, means to ends or goals. Then in part III I shall show that, while this purposeful nature of men's actions does not by itself prove that men are free in any metaphysical sense, it renders that claim reasonable and plausible and the denial of it, I think, somewhat arbitrary and implausible. No theory of metaphysical freedom will be thus proved, to be sure — I think in fact that none can be either proved or disproved — but at least certain considerations that have in the past seemed to cast doubt upon human freedom will, I think, be seen to be somewhat irrelevant.

## I PREVENTION AND POSTVENTION

We do not have the term "postvent," even though it would seem to be the exact complement of "prevent." This latter term appears to have a perfectly clear and common meaning, which lends itself to straightforward analysis, and the former can be given a similarly clear meaning. The reason why "postvent" does not occur in our language is, of course, that we have no use for it, but that in itself is not interesting. What is philosophically interesting is to try seeing just *why* we have no use for it. The most usual answers to this question are quite unsatisfactory.

### Prevention

To have *prevented* some event is, precisely, to have done something that was, under the conditions then and thereafter prevailing, both sufficient and necessary for, although logically independent of, the subsequent non-occurrence of that event. We shall see shortly, in terms of the types of inference warranted by prevention statements, why an action that was genuinely preventive must have been both sufficient and necessary for the non-occurrence of what was thereby prevented. Here we need only note that a preventive action and the event that it prevents are always logically independent of each other, or that it is not a logical contradiction, even though it is false, to assert that both of them occurred. . . .

To illustrate this, let us suppose that a physician rightly claims to have prevented another

Abridged from "Prevention, Postvention and the Will," by Richard Taylor in *Freedom and Determinism.* Edited by Keith Lehrer. Reprinted by permission of Humanities Press Inc., Atlantic Highlands, N.J.

man's death by a timely operation. This means that he did something—performed a certain operation with scalpel and other instruments—which was, under the other conditions then and thereafter prevailing, sufficient for the nonoccurrence of that man's death, and also necessary, in the sense that the man would not have lived had he, the physician, not done what he did. . . .

Again, let us suppose that a policeman rightly claims to have prevented another man from murdering someone, by secretly removing the bullets from the man's gun. This amounts to saying that he eliminated a certain condition, which was, under the other conditions then and thereafter prevailing, necessary for that murder and also, under those same conditions, sufficient for that murder, so that, all else then happening just as it did, the man would not have failed in his attempt at murder had the policeman not taken his timely precaution. . . .

### Postvention

If that is what prevention is, it is not at all difficult to say what postvention is. The two are exactly analogous.

Thus, to have *postvented* some event is, precisely, to have done something which was, under the conditions then and theretofore prevailing, both sufficient and necessary for, though logically independent of, the antecedent nonoccurrence of that event. . . .

But *do* men ever postvent things in this sense? Clearly, they often do, though for some reason this is never referred to as postvention. Indeed, whenever a man does anything whatever under conditions which are such that the prior nonoccurrence of some event was both necessary and sufficient for his doing it, he postvents that event. The relationship between what he does and the event thus postvented is exactly the same, save only for the direction of the temporal relation, as the relationship between what any man does and the event that he thereby prevents. Any event that is postvented does not, of course, occur, so that there may seem to be a certain strangeness in speaking of its relationship to someone's subsequent postventive action. But similar remarks can be made about any event that is prevented: it, too, does not occur. And yet the very explanation of its nonoccurrence is to be found in its connection with someone's preventive action. . . .

Suppose, then, that a certain woman breakfasts with her husband as usual on some given morning. Clearly, his not having overslept might well be a necessary condition for her doing that, and we can suppose that all the other conditions are such that his not having overslept is also sufficient for her doing that, or, that nothing else occurs to prevent husband and wife from breakfasting together as usual that day. By breakfasting with him in the usual way and at the usual time the wife guarantees, in the best possible way, that he has not overslept, and his not oversleeping also guarantees, under the conditions we are assuming to prevail, that he breakfasts with her as usual. The wife, accordingly, can properly claim to have postvented his oversleeping by breakfasting with him in the usual way. If she did claim to have done this, and if she meant by "postvented" exactly what we all mean by "prevented," except with the time reversed, she would appear to be right. Of course, by breakfasting with him that morning, she does not postvent his *ever* having overslept, but she does not claim to. She claims only to have postvented it this time.

Again, suppose a woman has breakfasted alone on some given morning. Suppose further that conditions were such that, had her husband not gone on a trip the day before, he would have been there too, having breakfast with her as usual. Clearly, she has managed to put herself in a situation—breakfasting alone—which is sufficient, under the other conditions then and theretofore prevailing, for his not having forgone the trip the day before. His having gone on a trip is also, under the conditions we are assuming, sufficient for her then breakfasting alone, there being no one else for her to have breakfast with, and so on. . . .

Besides being a subsequent necessary condition, however, a postventive action must also be something that was, under the conditions then and theretofore prevailing, *sufficient* for the antecedent nonoccurrence of the event thereby postvented. This scarcely needs argument. Had the first man, for example, somehow managed to oversleep and still have breakfast with his wife as usual, and had the second man somehow managed to stay home and still leave his wife to breakfast alone, then obviously neither event could truly be claimed to have been postvented. . . .

Why, then, if postvention and prevention are such exactly analogous concepts, differing only in the tenses in which examples are described, do we have no use for the concept of postvention? . . .

## II PREVENTION AND PURPOSE

I do not think we should suppose that the absence of the word "postvent" from our vocabulary represents any odd lacuna. I think that the notion is truly useless. However clearly it can be explicated, and however similar it may at first appear to be to the notion of prevention, one can hardly help feeling that there is something highly artificial in my foregoing discussion, something significant that has been left out of account. I want now to show that this is indeed so, and to bring forth the missing element that has thus far been ignored.

### Preventive Actions as Means to Ends

The first thing to note is that the two examples I gave of typically preventive actions are both aptly described as actions performed as the means to achieving some end or, what amounts to the same thing, as means for the avoidance of something. Thus, the physician operated as a means to preserving someone's life, and the policeman removed the bullets as a means to protecting someone. The same cannot be said of the postventive actions I cited. Thus, it is plainly untrue that the first woman breakfasted with her husband as a means of getting him up on time, or that the second breakfasted alone as a means of getting her husband off on a trip. Even if we suppose these two women to have had such goals or purposes, we cannot represent *these* actions as suitable or even intelligible means to their accomplishment. . . .

### Doing Something with Something

Having described preventive actions as means to the realization of ends, we find now another striking disanalogy in our examples. It concerns the senses of the word "with" in those examples. The physician operated upon a man *with* a scalpel, the policeman removed some bullets *with* his fingers, and the housewife ate breakfast *with* her husband. These statements are all grammatically similar, but the third "with" is utterly different in meaning from the first two. The first conveys the idea that the physician operated, using the scalpel as a tool or means to his end. The second, similarly, means that the policeman removed the bullets, using his fingers for this. But the third certainly does not mean that the housewife ate breakfast by means of her husband, that she used him in the way another person might use a fork. This "with" expresses only the idea of accompaniment. The wife merely ate in the presence of her husband.

It is thus misleading to describe the wife's *action* as eating with her husband. Her action consisted solely of eating, and would have been no different had her husband not been there. It is not, however, misleading to describe the policeman's action as removing bullets with his fingers. This is a different action than removing them with one's teeth—though it is still true that he removes them in the presence of, even if not by means of, his teeth.

These observations are meant to reinforce the point already made, that preventive actions, unlike postventive ones, can only be understood as involving the idea of means and ends. The word "with" as it sometimes figures in the description of a preventive action has no other function than to convey this idea of a means. No postventive action, on the other hand, can be so understood, and when the word "with" is introduced into the description of such an action it never conveys the idea of a means-end relation. No philosophical ingenuity can contrive descriptions in which it has, in such descriptions, any meaning remotely analogous to that of a means.

### Preventive States and Events Which Are Not Actions

So far I have labored the point that preventive actions are always, or at least typically, means to ends. This, of course, does not entail that nothing can be described as preventive *unless* it is an action; in fact, many things that are preventive are not actions at all.

Thus, a man can be prevented from leaving a burning building by smoke, even though no one is making the smoke. A man can be prevented from reaching a mountaintop by a landslide, even though no one starts the landslide, and so on. Examples are easy to multiply, and they all show that not all states and events which are preventive of something are preventive actions.

What is still left, however, even in such cases as these, is the notion of an end or purpose, and I want to insist that this notion is still essential to the description of anything whatever as preventive. Thus, the smoke could not be described as *preventing* a man from leaving a burning building except on the supposition that it was his purpose, goal or intention to leave, and the landslide can be considered as preventing a man from reaching a mountain top only on the supposition that he was trying to reach it, that he had that goal. Had the first man, for example, intended to stay in the burning building all the while, had this been his purpose—perhaps in order to test some fireproof suit—then he could not be said to have been prevented by the smoke from leaving. The most one could say is that he would have been prevented, in case he had tried.

One further observation should make this last point perfectly obvious. I have said that the idea of prevention is unintelligible apart from the idea of a purpose or goal, and that this is what distinguishes preventive events and states of affairs from those that are merely necessary and sufficient for the subsequent non-occurrence of something. Now if this were *not* so, then, in the case of every event that does not occur and for which there are antecedent conditions necessary and sufficient for its nonoccurrence, we would have to say that it was *prevented* from occurring. And this would be an absurd thing to say. There are, for example, infinitely many things that are *not* happening in my room now. The carpet is not disintegrating, the ash tray is not changing color, the dust mote that is drifting towards the door is not drifting towards the window, and so on, *ad infinitum.* It can hardly be said that all those things are being *prevented* from happening, even though it can be said, presumably, that there are antecedent conditions necessary and sufficient for their not happening. To say they were being prevented would imply that it was someone's purpose or goal either that they should happen, or that they should not.

Again, however, no such notion of a purpose or goal of any agent is required for the understanding of postvention, nor is there any intelligible way to fit such a notion into the concept of postvention. Everything that does not happen, and for which there are subsequent conditions necessary and sufficient for its not happening—which probably includes, simply, everything that does not happen—*is* thereby postvented from happening. . . .

## III THE WILL

We have now to see what bearing the foregoing might have on the problem of free will. I have already indicated that the thesis of determinism, as I understand it, cannot, in my opinion, be either proved or disproved. It is the thesis to the effect that for every event, and hence every human action, and hence every preventive action, and every action that is purposeful or goal-directed, there are antecedent conditions (causes) sufficient for the performance of just that action and for the avoidance of any and every alternative action. This is a perfectly *general* thesis, and I do not see how anyone could profess to know that it is true, or that it is false. Most purported proofs of its truth amount to maintaining that it is implied by the basic beliefs and conceptions that all men have. It is certainly not implied by the conception of a preventive action; it is, I think, rendered somewhat implausible in the light of that conception.

Not every preventive state of affairs, I have maintained, is itself purposeful or goal-directed, though it cannot be conceived as preventive except in relation to the purpose or goal of some agent. The smoke that obstructs a passageway may not be of purposeful origin, but it cannot be spoken of as preventing anything except on the supposition that it frustrates some agent's purpose. I have also maintained, however, that every preventive *action is* purposeful or goal-directed. This should perhaps be qualified by saying that every action which is *as such* preventive is also purposeful—in order to allow for those actions that prevent, but are not as such preventive. A man might, for instance, incidentally to making a smoke screen, unintentionally prevent another man from leaving a building, in which case his action is preventive, but not as such. It is only preventive *per accidens,* being, in this regard, quite purposeless. Typically preventive actions are, in any case, distinguished from postventive actions in being purposeful, for nothing remotely like the idea of purpose can be fitted into the idea of postvention.

## Goals and Causes

This entails that the idea of a preventive action cannot be analyzed in terms of necessary and sufficient conditions. Postventive actions can be so analyzed—indeed, they are simply defined in those terms. There is an additional element contained in the very idea of a preventive action, and that is the idea of a purpose, goal or end. Nor will it do simply to add this as another necessary causal condition—by saying, for instance, that an action is preventive in case one of the conditions constituting part of the cause of it is an agent's purpose. A purpose, end or goal is no part of the *cause* of a preventive action. It is part of the very *concept* of such an action, just as being a sibling is part of the concept, but no part of the cause, of being a twin.

Besides this, it would seem artificial in the extreme to suppose that preventive actions are causally explained in terms of purposes or goals. A preventive action can, indeed, be *explained* in terms of a goal or purpose—indeed, that is the standard and normal way of explaining them—but there is no reason whatever for thinking that such explanations fit the pattern of *causal* explanation. If the policeman of our earlier example were asked to explain why he removed the bullets from the gun, he would say what his purpose was, what he was trying to accomplish, but this is very far from saying or implying that his behavior was antecedently rendered unavoidable by, among other things, his having or resolving upon such a purpose or goal. There is not the slightest appearance of absurdity in supposing that, while he did act from such a purpose or goal, he might have declined to act upon it, or might have sought to realize it in some other way.

But does the supposition that men sometimes act preventively, and hence purposefully, entail that determinism is false? Some persons have thought so. It seems to some that the very idea of pursuing an end or goal, particularly over a long period of time, implies that the end is freely chosen, as well as the means to its achievement.

I believe this is clearly not true, however. The supposition that men sometimes act preventively, and hence purposefully, does not by itself entail that determinism is false. Perhaps the further supposition that such actions are sometimes the result of deliberation might entail that they are, or at least are believed to be, free, in the sense of being not causally determined, but that is a question I do not choose to go into. All that follows, I think, from the supposition that men sometimes act preventively is that they sometimes act in ways that cannot be *analyzed* in terms of antecedent necessary and sufficient conditions. This by itself does not by any means imply that, when they so act, there do not sometimes *exist* such conditions.

## The Metaphysical Meaning of "Free"

To say that a given preventive act was free means, I take it, that the agent who performed it was free with respect to that act. And this, I take it, means that, under the conditions then and theretofore prevailing, he was able to perform that act *and* he was also able to refrain from performing it. To say, on the other hand, that he was *not* free with respect to that act means, I take it, that he was not able to refrain from performing it, or, that circumstances rendered his action unavoidable.

## Prevention Consistent with Determinism and Indeterminism

Any statement of the form "I prevented X by doing A" is clearly *consistent* with "Something made (or caused) me to do A, thereby preventing X." These must be consistent, since the second entails the first. It is important to note, however, that the first does not in the least entail the second. It may be, as I suspect it is, that in some cases a statement of the first form is *true* and the corresponding statement of the second form is *false.* They are nevertheless consistent with each other. In other words, I suspect that men sometimes prevent certain things by certain of their actions, when nothing makes them perform just those actions to the exclusion of any others. Certainly there is no evidence that this cannot be true. The supposition is not itself inconsistent, nor is it inconsistent with anything else that anyone knows to be true. It is inconsistent with the thesis of determinism, to be sure, but while many philosophers believe in that thesis, no one knows that it is true. It seems to me, in any case, that the thesis just enunciated—that men sometimes prevent certain things by their actions, when nothing makes them perform those actions—is more likely to be true than the metaphysical thesis of determinism, with which it is inconsistent.

The supposition, then, that men sometimes act preventively, is consistent both with the affirmation and the denial of determinism. "I prevented X by doing A" is consistent with "Something made (or caused) me to do A, thereby preventing X," but it is equally consistent with "Nothing made (or caused) me to do A, thereby preventing X." Nor can anyone argue, I think, that in case a statement of the second form were true—i.e., in case someone were free with respect to a preventive act he performed—then that act would be "inexplicable." A preventive act can still be explained, or rendered intelligible, in terms of the very purpose or goal by virtue of which it is a preventive act, even if that act, as distinguished from the bodily behavior associated with it, is uncaused. Such a statement, for example, as "He removed the bullets in order to prevent that man from killing someone" renders the act of removing the bullets quite intelligible and at least partially explained. That explanation is not in the least wiped out if one makes the further supposition that the agent in question was free with respect to that act, or, that nothing made him do it.

## The Doubtful Status of Determinism

Can we, then, draw any conclusion concerning the truth or falsity of determinism from this discussion? We cannot, on the basis of anything I have said, conclude that determinism must be false. If, on the other hand, anyone maintains that determinism is true, and that, accordingly, no preventive act is free, in the sense defined, then I think his position is at least doubtful. He cannot, I feel sure, *analyze* the concept of a preventive act in such a way as to make it even *look* like an act which is, by its very nature, metaphysically unfree, or causally determined. Moreover, he will be in the position of maintaining that in the case of *every* true statement of the form, "O prevented X by doing A," there is a corresponding statement of the form "Something made O do A, thereby preventing X," which is also true. And this, to say the very least, is something I think no one has the slightest reason for believing.

# Part 4 — Glossary

**Ad hoc** See Part 2 Glossary.

**Coefficient of adversity** The term *coefficient of adversity* appears in Sartre's philosophy and refers to an impediment that exists with respect to a specific human goal or purpose.

**Compatibilism** Compatibilism is the view that it is possible to assert both that all events are caused and that with respect to some events human beings have free will.

**Conditioning** In behavioral psychology, conditioning refers to the techniques of positive and negative reinforcement. See **reinforcement** below. This use of reinforcement is often called operant conditioning.

**Contra-causal freedom** Contra-causal freedom is the theory of freedom espoused by C. A. Campbell that holds that a person can make a choice that is counter or opposed to all of the causal factors influencing her or him at the time, and hence that at least some choices are independent of causes entirely and completely within the agent's power. It is the kind of freedom necessary for moral responsibility.

**Ego** In psychoanalytic theory, the ego is that division of the psyche that serves as the organized conscious mediator between the person and reality.

**Equivocal** A word or proposition is equivocal if it is capable of more than one meaning.

**Existentialism** Existentialism is a philosophical school that differs from traditional philosophical schools in both method and content. The method of existential philosophy is to study human existence as it is lived from inside the experience of the active and interested participant, rather than objectively from the outside as would a disinterested (objective) spectator. The method is in this sense subjective or, "first-personal" rather than objective, scientific, or "third-personal." The principal content of existentialist philosophy that separates it from all other views is the claim that human nature is essentially divided and self-contradictory, that it is objectively impossible to be fully human. The religious existentialists like Kierkegaard believe that there is a subjective solution to the problem set us by human nature, a subjective way to do or be the impossible. Atheistic existentialists like Sartre conclude that being human is a "futile passion" with no way to be what we need to be and no way to stop needing to be it.

**Fortuitous** An event is fortuitous if it occurs by chance.

**Hard determinism** Hard determinism is the view that every event is caused by antecedent events over which the agent has no control and hence that there is no room for human freedom. Since a person cannot be responsible for acts determined by events over which the agent has no control, we are not responsible for any of our actions.

**Id** In psychoanalytic theory the id is that division of the psyche which is totally unconscious; it represents the instinctual needs and drives.

**Indeterminism** Indeterminism is a doctrine of free will which has been given a number of meanings. Indeterminism often refers to the doctrine that some events are uncaused. Other times it refers to the view that some events happen by chance. Some persons argue that indeterminism is simply the philosophical position that holds that determinism is false.

**Libertarian** For purposes of Part 4, a libertarian is one who believes that persons have free will, and that people are responsible for their free actions.

**Omniscient** Someone or something is omniscient when they know everything there is to know. An omniscient being is all-knowing.

**Phenomenon** (plural, *phenomena*) As used in the articles in this part, a "phenomenon" refers to an observable fact or event. In the philosophical school known as phenomenology, *phenomenon* has a technical meaning.

**Physicalism** Thesis that the descriptive terms of a scientific language are reducible to terms that refer to spatiotemporal things or events or to their properties. Physicalism is another word for materialism, which was discussed in Part 3.

**Postvention** As used by Richard Taylor, *postvention* is prevention applied to the past. However, since we can't do anything about the past, the term has no practical meaning for human beings. Taylor used the silliness of the notion of postvention in contrast with the practical use of prevention as an argument for his theory of agency.

**Proposition** A proposition is a sentence that must be either true or false. "The earth has one natural satellite" is a proposition. "Ugh!" is not a proposition.

**Reinforcement** In behavioral psychology, reinforcement refers to the structured attempt to affect specific behavior. If an animal or person behaves in an "undesirable" way, some punishment is administered and after sufficient association of the behavior with punishment, the behavior ceases. That behavior was negatively reinforced. Positive reinforcement is represented by the opposite technique. Behavior that is desired is rewarded (positively reinforced) so that it will be repeated. Most behaviorists agree that positive reinforcement is more effective than negative reinforcement.

**Soft determinism** Soft determinism is the view that there is a place for human freedom in a world totally governed by causal laws. Soft determinists differ in their explanation of what that place is. Sometimes this term is used as a synonym for compatibilism.

**Superego** In psychoanalytic theory, the superego is the division of the psyche that represents the internalization of parental conscience and the rules of society; its function is to reward and punish through a system of moral attitudes, conscience, and a sense of guilt.

**Volition** A volition is the act of making a choice. Determinists argue that volitions are caused. Nondeterminists usually argue that volitions are uncaused or that they are self-caused. Some nondeterminists, for example, Richard Taylor, argue that volitions are fictitious entities; they should be abandoned because they encourage determinist analyses of human choice. The determinist always asks what caused the mental event designated as the volition.

# Part 4—Study Questions

## FATALISM

1. Many people believe in an omniscient (all-knowing) God. Shouldn't these people be fatalists? Explain.
2. a. If I am going to die in a traffic accident, then I will.
   b. If I am not going to die in a traffic accident, then I won't.
   c. Therefore it doesn't matter if I take chances on the highway.

   Is this a good argument? Why or why not?
3. Some fatalists have argued that since we can't control events, we should control our reaction to events. Is that contradictory advice for a fatalist to give? Why or why not?

## DETERMINISM

1. Must all fatalists be determinists? Must all determinists be fatalists? Explain your answer.
2. Would the existence of free will make ac-

counts of human behavior unscientific? Explain.

3. Suppose someone shoots another and then is in turn shot by the police. An autopsy on the murderer reveals a large brain tumor. One scientist argues that the pain caused by the brain tumor caused the murderer to shoot the victim. But the murderer's psychoanalyst argues that repressed rage resulting from parental neglect caused the murderer to shoot the victim. What was the cause of the murder? Explain.

4. A child uses the laws of arithmetic to compute $9 + 9 = 18$. Do the laws of arithmetic cause the child to compute 18 as the answer? Explain.

## *NONDETERMINISM*

1. A person who commutes to the same job for twenty years would get pretty bored if he or she took the same route every day. To avoid boredom, the commuter uses four alternative routes. There is no observable pattern of variation. If a scientist asks the commuter why a particular route is taken, the reply is that there is no reason; the choice was based on a whim. Does the existence of that whim establish free will? Do you agree that the choice of a route was uncaused? Explain your answers.

2. What does Campbell mean by "contra-causal" freedom? Is it anything more than James's whim? Explain.

3. a. If determinism is true, there can be nothing new under the sun (there can be no genuine creativity).
   b. But there are things new under the sun.
   c. Therefore determinism is false.

   Evaluate this argument.

4. Jean-Paul Sartre argues that we are always responsible for our condition. This is why Sartre is called an apostle of radical freedom. How would Sartre analyze the following situation so that his theory of freedom plausibly describes it?

   A group of settlers cross the country by wagon train. They approach a river which is wide, swift flowing, and deep (the result of late fall storms). Winter is approaching.

   How can Sartre say these settlers are responsible for their situation and are free with respect to their journey?

## *COMPATIBILISM*

1. Is the following argument a genuine argument or is it simply a debate about words? Explain.

   Proponent: Everything has a cause and hence there is no free will.

   Antagonist: Since we have free will, there can't be a cause for everything.

2. Some compatibilists have reinterpreted the concept of blame so that it seems very close to our concept of treatment. Is this analysis acceptable? Explain.

3. "Every event is caused but not every event occurs under compulsion. Therefore there is a place for freedom in a causally determined world." Evaluate this argument.

4. "An unexplained action is not a testimony on behalf of free will. It's a mystery." Explain. Do you agree or disagree? Why or why not?

## *AGENCY*

1. Agency theorists argue that some events are self-caused. What do they mean? If you had to classify agency theorists on the basis of their explanation of "self-caused," would you classify them as determinists, nondeterminists, or compatibilists?

2. An agency theorist might well answer the question, "What caused the refrigerator door to open?" by replying "Sam did because he wanted to see if there was enough butter to bake a cake." How would an agency theorist answer the following question? "What caused

Sam to want to see if there was enough butter to bake a cake?"

3. A boy with an IQ of 70 doesn't have the capacity to be an atomic physicist. How would an agency theorist reply to a determinist who says that if determinism is true we don't have the capacity to do anything other than what we do and hence we really aren't agents?

# *Part 4 — Suggestions for Further Reading*


*BOOKS*

1. Beck, Lewis White. *The Actor and The Spectator* (New Haven: Yale University Press, 1975).
2. Darrow, Clarence. *Crime, Its Cause and Treatment* (New York: Crowell, 1922). Also see Darrow, "The Crime of Compulsion" in A. Weinberg (ed), *Attorney for the Damned* (New York: Simon & Schuster, 1957).
3. Davis, Lawrence H. *A Theory of Action* (Englewood Cliffs, N.J.: Prentice Hall, 1979).
4. Dennett, Daniel C. *Elbow Room, The Varieties of Free Will Worth Wanting* (Cambridge, MA: The MIT Press, 1984).
5. Hampshire, Stuart. *Freedom of the Individual* (Princeton: Princeton University Press, 1975).
6. Melden, A. I. *Free Action* (London: Routledge and Kegan Paul, 1961).
7. Peters, R. S. *The Concept of Motivation* (New York: Humanities Press, 1958).
8. Skinner, B. F. *Walden Two* (New York: Macmillan Publishing Co., 1948).
9. Taylor, Richard. *Action and Purpose* (Englewood Cliffs, N.J.: Prentice Hall, 1966).
10. Van Inwagen, Peter. *An Essay on Free Will* (Oxford: Clarendon, 1983).

*ANTHOLOGIES*

Most of the best-known contemporary articles as well as selections from the views of historical figures are found in at least one of these anthologies.

11. Berofsky, Bernard (ed). *Free Will and Determinism* (New York: Harper & Row, 1966).
12. Dworkin, Gerald (ed). *Determinism, Free Will and Moral Responsibility* (Englewood Cliffs, N.J.: Prentice Hall, 1970).
13. Hook, Sidney (ed). *Determinism and Freedom in The Age of Modern Science* (New York: New York University Press, 1958).
14. Lehrer, Keith (ed). *Freedom and Determinism* (New York: Random House, 1966).
15. Morgenbesser, Sidney and James Walsh (eds). *Free Will* (Englewood Cliffs, N.J.: Prentice Hall, 1962).
16. Peaks, D. F. (ed). *Freedom and the Will* (New York: St. Martin's Press, 1963).
17. Watson, Gary (ed). *Free Will* (New York: Oxford University Press, 1982).

# RIGHT AND WRONG

# 5

As members of the human community, each of us faces ethical issues. Do I have a moral obligation to report cheating? to come forward as a witness when I have observed an automobile accident? Do I owe my country two years of my life either in the armed services or in something like a domestic peace corps? How much, if any, of my income should I give to the poor? Is it morally wrong to choose a dangerous career such as smoke jumping?

These few examples provide some hint at the richness of issues that call for ethical decisions. On what basis should these decisions be made? People can decide such questions on the basis of feeling: "I just wouldn't feel right if I didn't come forward." People can decide such questions on the basis of authority, either religious or parental: "My religion doesn't permit service in the armed forces." Some people try to avoid making difficult ethical decisions, but that just postpones the decisions; and, besides, postponing a decision is a decision in its own right. Is it right to postpone ethical decisions?

One of the more common suggestions for making ethical decisions is to appeal to conscience. Let your conscience be your guide. Despite our admiration for the "person of conscience," philosophers have generally judged appeals to conscience *alone* as insufficient and untrustworthy. Consciences vary radically from person to person and time to time and are often altered by circumstance and training. For example, views about the right to publish pornography and rights of the press are matters of hot debate and deep conviction, but these convictions alone hardly seem to advance or resolve the issues. Consciences seem subject to impulse and whim. Moreover, many appeals to the rightness of an action on the ground that "my conscience was my guide" seem to external observers to be rationalizations for an immoral act. Political assassins and terrorists, for example, commonly appeal to conscience as a source of justification for their actions.

Most philosophers are not satisfied by such appeals to conscience or religion. Neither would they be satisfied by an appeal to the ethical standards of our culture. The reasons for their dissatisfaction are developed in the section of this part entitled "Relativism." Most philosophers agree that you can't go from the recognition of ethical diversity among cultures to the assertion that what is right or wrong, good or bad, is simply a function of the culture in which one lives. Nonetheless, ethical judgments are bound up in some complicated way with the facts of one's culture. The existence of simple, safe birth control methods has implications for sexual morality. The existence of sophisticated mechanical techniques for prolonging human life has implications for medical ethics. Since our ethical judgments depend in part upon what the facts are, the first step in resolving disputes about ethics should be to determine whether or not the disputants are disagreeing over the facts. If the disagreement is factual, that disagreement will need to be resolved before tackling any ethical disagreement. If the factual disagreement is resolved, the ethical disagreement often dissolves. For example, much of the disagreement about nuclear power plants centers on factual disputes about the existence of risk. Until these factual disputes are resolved, the value judgment about the acceptability of risk cannot be made. It is not the job of the philosopher to settle the factual disputes embedded in ethical disputes.

But what then is the job of the philosopher? One job is to raise questions about the meaning and justification of ethical concepts and principles. Is what our society forbids really wrong? Is what our society values really good? What is the purpose of morality? Do the moral rules of society fit together in a unified whole, or are there conflicts and inconsistencies in society's moral rules? If there are conflicts and inconsistencies, how should they be resolved? What should we do when we face a moral problem for which society has, as yet, provided no instruction?

One who raises such questions and works at answering them is engaged in rudimentary ethical inquiry. Philosophical ethics is the inquiry into theories of what is good and evil and into what is right and wrong, and thus is the inquiry into what we ought and ought not to do. Rather than appeal to authority or culture, the philosopher appeals to ethical concepts and ethical theories—concepts and theories that pass the tests of reason.

However, appeals to ethical concepts and theories do not mean that everyone who uses ethical knowledge will make the same ethical decisions. Persons might use different theories; for example, a charitable act might be justified on duty theories but not on utilitarian ones. They might disagree on what the implications of a given ethical principle are; for example, does the principle of respect for persons forbid abortions under all circumstances? And they might disagree as to how virtues should be weighted; for example, does the virtue of courage or love weigh most in considering whether or not a young man should register for the selective service? However, all these disagreements take place within the framework of ethics. They are very different in kind from a disagreement where one religion forbids abortion and another permits it, or where one father encourages his son to join the armed services and another father discourages his son from joining. Since ethical decisions should be made on the basis of reason rather than authority, the scope of disagreement can be narrowed.

With these thoughts in mind, let us see how far rational inquiry can take us in answering ethical questions. One of the most important questions is about the enterprise of ethics itself and it goes by the name of the "Why be moral?" question. The "Why be moral?" question is often expressed by such questions as "Why shouldn't I put myself first; after all, it's a dog-eat-dog world?" "Why shouldn't I pursue my interest at the expense of the interests of others; after all, that's what others do to me?" "Why should I do what is right?" The selections in the first section raise and provide an answer to this question.

Until recently, most contemporary philosophers supported one of two opposing ethical theories—either utilitarianism or some version of duty theory (deontology). Utilitarians believe that people ought to maximize good consequences. Utilitarians differ as to what counts as good consequences and as to the most desirable means to achieve them. Some utilitarians believe that only pleasure is good; they are called hedonists. Others include a wider array of goods such as beauty, truth, and justice—as well as pleasure. Utilitarians treat ethics as future looking: they believe that to determine what is right or wrong, one should look ahead to what will be achieved (what will result). They analyze certain central notions of ethics such as promise keeping or justice in terms of their contribution to the good.

The most significant contemporary distinction between utilitarians is between act and rule utilitarians. Act utilitarians argue that one ought to do those acts that produce the greatest good for the greatest number. According to the act-utilitarian view, rules are mere shorthand devices that are suitable as rules of thumb but that are to be abandoned when following them would not lead to the greatest good for the greatest number.

According to rule utilitarianism, however, rules have a very different status: The appropriate answer to the question, "What ought I to do?" is, "You ought to follow the appropriate rule for that type of situation." However, the appropriate answer to the question, "What rules should one adopt?" is, "One should adopt those rules that lead to the greatest good for the greatest number." Perhaps the difference between the types of utilitarianism can be illustrated by an example.

Consider the practice of grading college students for course work. Suppose that one of the rules for a grade of A in Mathematics 11 is a 90 average on quizzes and examinations. An act utilitarian would treat the rule of 90 for an A as a rule of thumb. In circumstances where utility would be maximized one could give an A for less than 90. For example, suppose the professor knows that an overachieving student is despondent over the death of a parent. There is some indication that the student might commit suicide if the typical A grades were lost. On the other hand, there is some evidence that the student might bounce back from the loss if the usual high grades were achieved. In such a case utility would be maximized by an A for work of less than 90. What determines each act of grading is the consequences of giving a certain grade in that particular case. The rule of A for 90 is a guide but it is not authoritative. For the rule utilitarian, things are different. A student with an 85 could not argue for an A on the basis of the special circumstances of his or her case alone. Rather, he or she would have to show that the grading rule of A for 90 does not provide the greatest good for the greatest number. The task of the moral philosopher, according to the rule-utilitarian view, is to formulate those rules that pass the utilitarian test.

But many philosophers (duty theorists) find utilitarian theory to be inadequate. In part, they object to utilitarianism because they believe that it would, on occasion, require or permit actions that are morally wrong, such as punishing the innocent or permitting the practice of preventive detention. Nearly all duty theorists agree that achieving the good or bringing about good consequences is often the right thing to do *but not always.* Put more formally, deontological theories maintain that actions are not justified simply by their consequences. The right cannot be defined in terms of the good. Ethics must be "past looking" rather than simply "future looking," or at least it should not look *only* to future consequences. In considering what you ought to do you often must consider what you have done. When making an ethical decision it is not sufficient simply to see what good will result; you must consider your present and past circumstances and treat them as relevant to your ethical decision. Do you stand in a special relationship to anyone your decision will affect? For example, mother/daughter, teacher/student, physician/patient? Do you occupy a job, profession, or role that places special moral obligations upon you? The duty to respect privacy and confidentiality is especially binding on lawyers and priests. The police ought to be especially scrupulous in respecting the law. What are your motives? Are you trying to bring about good results because you genuinely respect your fellow human beings, or are you trying to become Rotarian of the year? Did you make a promise? Most duty theorists think that a promise is morally binding even if it doesn't lead to good consequences. There is something special about promises, contracts, oaths of loyalty, and so on. In general when making ethical decisions, duty theorists treat desert or giving people their due very seriously.

However, one of the disadvantages of the deontological perspective is that we are presented with an embarrassing variety of duties—to follow justified moral rules, to respect rights claims, to develop the virtues, and to carry out our role-related obligations—among others. But how do we order these duties and resolve the inevitable conflicts that arise among them? Most philosophers agree that deontological theorists have not adequately answered this question.

A discussion of ethics cannot ignore the moral agent—the person who actually makes moral decisions. The duty theorist Immanuel Kant argued that one of the marks of personhood was the ability to function as a moral agent. For

Kant the ability to reason consistently and impartially was sufficient to establish a person as a moral agent. However, many philosophers argue that consistency and impartiality are not enough. Consider a college or university where students do not have a right to know the basis for their grade. Students can ask, beg, or cajole. Professors might, out of the goodness of their hearts, out of pity, or out of benevolence give the basis for their grades. However, the students have no right to know the basis for their grades and the professors have no duty to provide it. Isn't such a world morally impoverished? Doesn't a situation where students have no right to know the basis for their grades diminish the students—take away from their self-respect or humanity? In other words, the possession of **human rights** is also necessary if we are to have the self-respect necessary to function as human agents. Rights are essential moral furniture. They enable us to stand up on our own two feet. Of course, if we insist that others recognize our rights claims, we must recognize the rights claims of others.

Other philosophers emphasize the development of individual moral character. One way to assess character is to consider whether or not the individual practices the moral **virtues.** Possessing virtue promotes both the quality of our ethical decisions and our ability to withstand temptation and act morally. One of the chief functions of the virtues is to enable moral agents to overcome the condition known as weakness of will. **Weakness of will** occurs when we know what is morally required but we don't do it. Studying is put off so that you can spend an evening with your friends at the pub. As the exam arrives and an opportunity to cheat occurs, you take it. You know you did wrong and you knew it when you did it. Why did you do it? You had weakness of will. Possessing virtue gives you willpower. Genuinely moral virtues are dispositions that help us overcome weakness of will with respect to our treatment of others.

Yet another function of the virtues is to make life in the human community possible. Some have argued that such cardinal virtues as wisdom, temperance, justice, and courage are necessary if human cooperation is to be possible. Indeed since most philosophers agree that taking the moral point of view requires that we take into account the interests of others, perhaps the greatest task of morality is to provide the basis for living with one another. Although we live in a large country and although many of our interactions with others are transitory and commercial, we do owe *everyone* with whom we come into contact a minimum amount of respect. However, we also have more stable and primary interactions with others. These interactions are determined by the roles we play and the positions we hold. Let us illustrate using a vocational role as an example. One distinguishes between being a bricklayer and being a good bricklayer. Just because someone is a member of the bricklayer's union, there is nothing inconsistent in a disgruntled homeowner saying, "I don't care if Jones does have his union card; he's no bricklayer." This distinction shouldn't prove mysterious to students. All students know professors certified by their college or university as teachers but who, in the opinion of the students, aren't teachers at all. By the way, we professors apply the distinction equally well to students.

But our moral obligations to others can neither be determined nor limited by the obligations associated with our roles. Some roles are immoral on their face, for example, assassin, extortionist, or pimp. There are no professional standards for extortionists. However, more pertinent questions of legitimacy can be raised about well-established institutions. The institutions of a society and the roles associated with those institutions ought to pass the tests of justice. If an individual owes loyalty to institutions, these institutions themselves ought to be morally legitimate. To determine whether a society is just, we need to know the principles that govern its institutions. Would such principles pass the tests of justice? Are the procedures embodied in the social institutions just? Is there an appropriate match between theoretical justice and the realities of the social situation? But what is justice?

One of the earliest analyses of justice was by the Greek philosopher Plato. Justice is a matter of giving each person his or her due. Of course the next question is obvious. What constitutes a person's due? Plato's theory was tied to the Greek idea of function. Everything has its function and when everything is performing its function, the world is in order and everything is receiving its due. Consider a human being. Although we are composed of several faculties such as reason, appetites, and will, reason is the ruler of the human being. When reason is in control, humans behave justly. If reason is not in control, our desires are not properly ordered and we behave unjustly.

For Plato, what is true of a human being is true of the state as well. A state is composed of various classes, with the business class, the military, and the ruling class figuring prominently in Plato's discussion. These three classes are analogous to the three parts of the human soul. So long as each class performs its appropriate function, all the citizens receive their due and justice results. For Plato, justice results when everything is in its proper place and performing its proper function.

You will notice that there is nothing egalitarian or democratic about Plato's account. A slave receives her due when she is treated like a slave. A queen receives her due when she is treated like a queen. The first link between equality and justice occurs in the thought of Plato's student Aristotle. Aristotle identified justice as one of the moral virtues and hence as a mean between two extremes. For Aristotle, unfairness results when departures are made from either distributive justice or remedial justice. Distributive justice occurs when, with respect to merit, equals are treated equally. Distributive justice is justice according to equal proportions. If John shows twice as much courage in battle as Jim, then John deserves twice as much praise. With respect to remedial justice, someone has gained at someone else's expense. If John robs Jim of $100, John has gained $100 at the expense of Jim. Remedial justice requires that the $100 be returned to Jim. Of course with physical or psychological injury, rectifying the unjust gain is a complicated matter, but it should be noted that such rectification is not identical with the philosophy of "an eye for an eye and a tooth for a tooth." Judges need not resort to this kind of reciprocal justice in order to provide remedial justice. The important task is to return to a state of equality by compensating the victim for his or her loss.

Both distributive justice and remedial justice take place against a social background. With distributive justice, there are certain standards of merit that provide the basis of the distribution. With remedial justice we are restoring a status quo; we are taking from the perpetrator of the injustice an amount proportionate to the loss of the victim. The equality involved is to return just that amount that brings the state of affairs back to a specified starting point. But are the criteria for merit just, and was the initial starting point that is being restored just? Aristotle focused on justice between individuals, but what about the justice of the institution the individuals participate in? Our selection from John Rawls focuses on the justice of institutions.

Crucial in any account of institutional justice is the notion of **procedural justice** and the distinction between just procedures and just results. Let us examine the notion of procedural justice by supposing that three friends order a pizza. When the pizza arrives, how should it be divided? Barring special circumstances, the result or outcome that seems most just is that each person receives an equal share. But what procedure should be used to ensure that result? An appropriate procedure for this purpose is to make the person cutting the pizza take the last piece. The pizza example provides an illustration of fairness in both procedures and results. In some cases, however, just procedures alone must be relied upon to determine just results. Consider a lottery as an example. It makes perfect sense to speak of the conditions of a fair lottery. But what makes it fair? Suppose that most entrants are poor, but the winner is an extremely rich man. Can we say that the lottery is unjust? Certainly not. As with horse races, we condemn a lottery that is fixed, but we do not condemn one where the rich are winners. In situations like these, as long as the procedures are just, the results too are just. Many problems of justice that we must handle as a cooperative society are ones of designing a system or set of procedures that provides as much justice as possible. Once we agree on appropriate procedures, then as long as a person is treated according to those procedures, the procedure is just—even if on occasion it turns out to produce inequalities that seem by other standards unjust. Naturally, in situations where procedural justice is the best we can do, we should accept the results of our procedural system with a certain amount of humility, and where possible we should perhaps make allowances for inevitable inequalities.

Perhaps a political system functions as an instrument of procedural justice. After all, the purposes of a state include provision of law and order and the settling of conflicts of rights among citizens. But there are a wide variety of political systems. Which political system is most just? Americans naturally conclude that their own system of a representative democracy conjoined with a free enterprise economic system is most just. However, many philosophers argue that both democratic and free enterprise institutions need to meet certain conditions if they are to be considered just. Other philosophers doubt that free enterprise institutions can ever be just. At this point discussions of ethics intertwine with discussions of political philosophy. Questions of how we ought to treat one another expand into questions of what constitutes just political and economic institutions.

# *Why Be Moral?*

One of the first lessons in ethics parents give their children is that children shouldn't be selfish. The child is told to share her toys, to play ball with her brother, and to pick up her room. It's no accident that the obligation not to be selfish is at the center of a child's training in ethics. The shift from securing our own interests to sacrificing, at least on occasion, our interests on behalf of the interests of others is the essential part of what we mean by "making ethical decisions." The selfish person by definition cannot habitually make moral decisions. Such is the tradition—both in child rearing and in ethical theory.

Well, why should anyone take account of the interests and desires of others? Why shouldn't one just look out for his or her own interests and desires?

Plato raises this challenge to morality in the first selection. In the famous dialogue the *Republic,* Plato has Glaucon relate the myth of Gyges. Essentially this is the story of a shepherd who has discovered a ring that when rubbed makes the wearer invisible. Why should the owner of such a ring take the interests of others into account? Why should such a person take the point of view of morality? After all, the owner of such a ring has the power to fulfill his own interests without worrying about fulfilling the interests of others. Indeed, the ring's owner could fulfill his interests at the expense of the interests of others.

One attempt to answer this question argues that immorality really isn't in our interest. Plato makes this point with respect to the shepherd's magic ring. Plato believed that a human being is essentially composed of appetites, will, and reason and that a happy and productive person is one whose reason controls appetite and will. Plato then tries to prove that the immoral person is a person whose reason has lost control. Such a person would have a disordered soul and would be unhappy. His having a magic ring wouldn't change that fact. Hence Plato tries to argue that immorality is ultimately self-defeating. Whether or not Plato is right depends on psychological fact. Some tyrants certainly give the impression that they are happy and that their happiness is not short lived but rather long lasting. At the very least they would claim to be happier than the purely moral person.

In the second selection, Kurt Baier tries a slightly different approach. He answers this challenge by trying to show why moral reasons that take into account the interests of others are superior to reasons of self-interest. In the real world we can achieve our aims only if we agree to a set of rules that sets limits on the means individuals can use to achieve their aims. Many social scientists, especially economists, argue that rationality is seeking the most efficient means to achieve a given end. Baier argues that morality is the device that rational persons would use to promote their ends. Morality, so conceived, is, as Baier puts it, "in the interests of everyone."

Baier asks us to conduct a thought experiment. Consider two worlds—one where moral reasons are treated as superior and one where they aren't. Anyone would agree that the world where moral reasons are treated as superior is the better world. It is better because it is the world with the better quality of life and because it is a better world it is rational to prefer it to the other.

But suppose someone wants to know why we should be rational about such things. To raise this question is to ask the question, "Why be rational?" Baier then points out that if the questioner is asking for a reason for being rational, she is talking nonsense. In asking for a reason, one is accepting the legitimacy of reason.

Baier also considers other interpretations of the "why be rational" question. It might be interpreted as "Why should I follow reason as opposed to authority," for example. Baier's answer is that you need a reason for accepting this authority rather than some other authority for your own reasoning. It is fair to add that if a choice for authority is not made on reason, it must be made on a whim or such. In any case such a choice couldn't be justified because an appeal to justification is an appeal to reason.

Baier's arguments and similar ones developed by other philosophers may not have persuaded everyone but they have had an important impact on ethical theory. Any discussion of this issue must confront Baier's analysis. Let us consider a common objection to Baier's argument.

A critic could argue that there is a difference between saying that morality is in the best interest of everyone including my best interest and that following morality in this particular case is in my best interest. Just because it is in my interest that society has a rule against lying, it doesn't follow that it is in my interest not to lie in this particular case. In fact, what is really in my best interest is that everyone else not lie but that I lie whenever it is beneficial for me to do so and I can get away with it. Why should I follow morality in such cases and not lie?

Philosophers do not answer that challenge with a unanimous voice. One plausible response goes like this. Either the individual in question agreed not to lie or she didn't. If she did agree to tell the truth in those circumstances where it was not in her interest to do so and now she doesn't, she is acting inconsistently. She both did and did not agree to tell the truth in circumstances where it was not in her interest. On the other hand, if she didn't agree not to lie when it was in her best interest to do so, others would not agree not to lie to her when it was in their best interest to do so. Hence, in this set of circumstances the opportunity to lie when you are assured that no one else would lie would never arise. Since no one would agree not to lie, that world would be chaotic. It would be a world where everyone is at war with everyone else, and that is just the world morality is designed to prevent. Hence, lying in circumstances when you can get away with it is either contradictory or self-defeating. Hence, a person should not be immoral, because to do so would be irrational.

## Plato (427 – 347 B.C.)

As the first systematic Western philosopher, Plato made contributions in all major areas of philosophy. Whereas many persons in the twentieth century believe that scientific knowledge is more firmly grounded and objective than moral knowledge, Plato held just the opposite view. Since scientific knowledge was knowledge based on sense experience and since sense experience is by nature individual and variable, a science like physics could never be more than a "likely story." Moral knowledge on the other hand was based on universal truths.

Although most philosophers think Plato's account of moral knowledge is mistaken, just suppose for a moment that he is correct. He would still have to show why people should behave morally even if they know what they ought to do. Suppose people could get away with behaving immorally? Why shouldn't they? This is the problem presented by the myth of Gyges. Plato's own answer to the question, not included in the selection below, is that ultimately immoral behavior harms the perpetrator. In the long run, it is *always* in the individual's best interest to behave morally. Plato then explains any actual immoral behavior on the grounds of ignorance. People behave immorally because they don't know any better. Baier's answer to Plato's question is in the selection that follows Plato's.

# The Myth of Gyges

## *Plato*

. . . First, I will state what is commonly held about the nature of justice and its origin; secondly, I shall maintain that it is always practised with reluctance, not as good in itself, but as a thing one cannot do without; and thirdly, that this reluctance is reasonable, because the life of injustice is much the better life of the two—so people say. . . . Accordingly, I shall set you an example by glorifying the life of injustice with all the energy that I hope you will show later in denouncing it and exalting justice in its stead. Will that plan suit you?

Nothing could be better, I replied. Of all subjects this is one on which a sensible man must always be glad to exchange ideas.

Good, said Glaucon. Listen then, and I will begin with my first point: the nature and origin of justice.

What people say is that to do wrong is, in itself, a desirable thing; on the other hand, it is not at all desirable to suffer wrong, and the harm to the sufferer outweighs the advantage to the doer. Consequently, when men have had a taste of both, those who have not the power to seize the advantage and escape the harm decide that they would be better off if they made a compact neither to do wrong nor to suffer it. Hence they began to make laws and covenants with one another; and whatever the law prescribed they called lawful and right. That is what right or justice is and how it came into existence; it stands half-way between the best thing of all—to do wrong with impunity—and the worst, which is to suffer wrong without the power to retaliate. So justice is accepted as a compromise, and valued, not as good in itself, but for lack of power to do wrong; no man worthy of the name, who had that power, would ever enter into such a compact with anyone; he would be mad if he did. That, Socrates, is the nature of justice according to this account, and such the circumstances in which it arose.

The next point is that men practise it against the grain, for lack of power to do wrong. How true that is, we shall best see if we imagine two men, one just, the other unjust, given full licence to do whatever they like, and then follow them to observe where each will be led by his desires. We shall catch the just man taking the same road as the unjust; he will be moved by self-interest, the end which it is natural to every creature to pursue as good, until forcibly turned aside by law and custom to respect the principle of equality.

Now, the easiest way to give them that complete liberty of action would be to imagine them possessed of the talisman found by Gyges, the ancestor of the famous Lydian. The story tells how he was a shepherd in the King's service. One day there was a great storm, and the ground where his flock was feeding was rent by an earthquake. Astonished at the sight, he went down into the chasm and saw, among other wonders of which the story tells, a brazen horse, hollow, with windows in its sides. Peering in, he saw a dead body, which seemed to be of more than human size. It was naked save for a gold ring, which he took from the finger and made his way out. When the shepherds met, as they did every month, to send an account to the King of the state of his flocks, Gyges came wearing the ring. As he was sitting with the others, he happened to turn the bezel of the ring inside his hand. At once he became invisible, and his companions, to his surprise, began to speak of him as if he had left them. Then, as he was fingering the ring, he turned the bezel outwards and became visible again. With that, he set about testing the ring to see if it really had this power, and always with the

---

Abridged and reprinted from *The Republic of Plato*. Translated by F. M. Cornford (1941). By permission of Oxford University Press.

same result: according as he turned the bezel inside or out he vanished and reappeared. After this discovery he contrived to be one of the messengers sent to the court. There he seduced the Queen, and with her help murdered the King and seized the throne.

Now suppose there were two such magic rings, and one were given to the just man, the other to the unjust. No one, it is commonly believed, would have such iron strength of mind as to stand fast in doing right or keep his hands off other men's goods, when he could go to the market-place and fearlessly help himself to anything he wanted, enter houses and sleep with any woman he chose, set prisoners free and kill men at his pleasure, and in a word go about among men with the powers of a god. He would behave no better than the other; both would take the same course. Surely this would be strong proof that men do right only under compulsion; no individual thinks of it as good for him personally, since he does wrong whenever he finds he has the power. Every man believes that wrongdoing pays him personally much better, and, according to this theory, that is the truth. Granted full licence to do as he liked, people would think him a miserable fool if they found him refusing to wrong his neighbors or to touch their belongings, though in public they would keep up a pretence of praising his conduct, for fear of being wronged themselves. So much for that. . . .

## *Kurt Baier (b. 1917)*

Kurt Baier is a contemporary American philosopher. His main contribution is in ethical theory. His best-known book is *The Moral Point of View —A Rational Basis of Ethics* (1958). This important book has greatly influenced philosophers and social scientists who apply decision theory to ethics.

In the selection included here, Baier answers the "Why Be Moral?" question by trying to show that moral reasons are superior to reasons of self-interest. They are superior, Baier argues, because they are in the interests of everyone. Baier builds his case by pointing out the links among concepts of morality, rationality, and self-interest.

# The Supremacy of Moral Reasons

### *Kurt Baier*

. . . Are moral reasons really superior to reasons of self-interest as we all believe? Do we really have reason on our side when we follow moral reasons against self-interest? What reasons could there be for being moral? Can we really give an answer to "Why should we be moral?" It is obvious that all these questions come to the same thing. When we ask, "Should we be moral?" or

"Why should we be moral?" or "Are moral reasons superior to all others?" we ask to be given a reason for regarding moral reasons as superior to all others. What is this reason?

Let us begin with a state of affairs in which reasons of self-interest are supreme. In such a state everyone keeps his impulses and inclinations in check when and only when they would lead him into behavior detrimental to his own interest. Everyone who follows reason will discipline himself to rise early, to do his exercises, to refrain from excessive drinking and smoking, to keep good company, to marry the right sort of girl, to work and study hard in order to get on, and so on. However, it will often happen that people's interests conflict. In such a case, they will have to resort to ruses or force to get their own way. As this becomes known, men will become suspicious, for they will regard one another as scheming competitors for the good things in life. The universal supremacy of the rules of self-interest must lead to what Hobbes called the state of nature. At the same time, it will be clear to everyone that universal obedience to certain rules overriding self-interest would produce a state of affairs which serves everyone's interest much better than his unaided pursuit of it in a state where everyone does the same. Moral rules are universal rules designed to override those of self-interest when following the latter is harmful to others. "Thou shalt not kill," "Thou shalt not lie," "Thou shalt not steal" are rules which forbid the inflicting of harm on someone else even when this might be in one's interest.

The very *raison d'être* of a morality is to yield reasons which overrule the reasons of self-interest in those cases when everyone's following self-interest would be harmful to everyone. Hence moral reasons are superior to all others.

"But what does this mean?" it might be objected. "If it merely means that we do so regard them, then you are of course right, but your contention is useless, a mere point of usage. And how could it mean any more? If it means that we not only do so regard them, but *ought* so to regard them, then there must be *reasons* for saying this. But there could not be any reasons for it. If you offer reasons of self-interest, you are arguing in a circle. Moreover, it cannot be true that it is always in my interest to treat moral reasons as superior to reasons of self-interest. If it were, self-interest and morality could never conflict, but they notoriously do. It is equally circular to argue that there are moral reasons for saying that one ought to treat moral reasons as superior to reasons of self-interest. And what other reasons are there?"

The answer is that we are now looking at the world from the point of view of *anyone*. We are not examining particular alternative courses of action before this or that person; we are examining two alternative worlds, one in which moral reasons are always treated by everyone as superior to reasons of self-interest and one in which the reverse is the practice. And we can see that the first world is the better world, because we can see that the second world would be the sort which Hobbes describes as the state of nature.

This shows that I ought to be moral, for when I ask the question "What ought I to do?" I am asking, "Which is the course of action supported by the best reasons?" But since it has just been shown that moral reasons are superior to reasons of self-interest, I have been given a reason for being moral, for following moral reasons rather than any other, namely, they are better reasons than any other. . . .

Moralities are systems of principles whose acceptance by everyone as overruling the dictates of self-interest is in the interest of everyone alike, though following the rules of a morality is not of course identical with following self-interest. If it were, there could be no conflict between a morality and self-interest and no point in having moral rules overriding self-interest. . . .

The answer to our question "Why should we be moral?" is therefore as follows. We should be moral because being moral is following rules designed to overrule reasons of self-interest whenever it is in the interest of everyone alike that such rules should be generally followed. This will be the case when the needs and wants and aspirations of individual agents conflict with one another and when, in the absence of such overriding rules, the pursuit of their ends by all concerned would lead to the attempt to eliminate those who are in the way. Since such rules will always require one of the rivals to abandon his pursuit in favor of the other, they will tend to be broken. Since, ex hypothesi it is in everyone's interest that they should be followed, it will be in everyone's interest that they should not only be taught as "superior to" other reasons but also adequately enforced, in order to reduce the temptation to break them. A person instructed in these rules can acknowledge that such reasons are superior to reasons of self-interest without having to admit that he is always or indeed ever attracted or moved by them.

But is it not self-contradictory to say that it is in a person's interest to do what is contrary to his interest? It certainly would be if the two expressions were used in exactly the same way. But they are not. . . .

. . . Moral rules are not designed to serve the agent's interest directly. Hence it would be quite inappropriate for him to break them whenever he discovers that they do not serve his interest. They are designed to adjudicate primarily in cases where there is a conflict of interests so that from their very nature they are bound to be contrary to the interest of one of the persons affected. However, they are also bound to serve the interest of the other person, hence his interest in the other's observing them. It is on the assumption of the likelihood of a reversal of roles that the universal observation of the rule will serve everyone's interest. The principle of justice and other principles which we employ in improving the moral rules of a given society help to bring existing moralities closer to the ideal which is in the interest of everyone alike. . . . [S]o following the rules of morality *is* in everyone's interest only if the assumptions underlying it are correct, that is, if the moral rules come close to being true and are generally observed. Even then, to say that following them is in the interest of everyone alike means only that it is better for everyone that there should be a morality generally observed than that the principle of self-interest should be acknowledged as supreme. It does not of course mean that a person will not do better for himself by following self-interest than by doing what is morally right, when others are doing what is right. But of course such a person cannot *claim* that he is following a superior reason.

It must be added to this, however, that such a system of rules has the support of reason only where people live in societies, that is, in conditions in which there are established common ways of behavior. Outside society, people have no reason for following such rules, that is, for being moral. In other words, outside society, the very distinction between right and wrong vanishes. . . .

But someone might now ask whether and why he should follow reason itself. He may admit that moral reasons are superior to all others, but doubt whether he ought to follow reason. He may claim that this will have to be proved first, for if it is not true that he ought to follow reason, then it is not true that he ought to follow the strongest reason either. . . .

. . . During the last hundred years or so, reason has had a very bad press. Many thinkers have sneered at it and have recommended other guides, such as the instincts, the unconscious, the voice of the blood, inspiration, charisma, and the like. They have advocated that one should not follow reason but be guided by these other forces.

. . . In the most obvious sense of the question "Should I follow reason?" this is a tautological question like "Is a circle a circle?"; hence the advice "You should not follow reason" is as nonsensical as the claim "A circle is not a circle." Hence the question "Why should I follow reason?" is as silly as "Why is a circle a circle?" We need not, therefore, take much notice of the advocates of unreason. They show by their advocacy that they are not too clear on what they are talking about.

How is it that "Should I follow reason?" is a tautological question like "Is a circle a circle?" Questions of the form "Shall I do this?" or "Should I do this?" or "Ought I to do this?"

are . . . requests to someone (possibly oneself) to deliberate on one's behalf. That is to say, they are requests to survey the facts and weigh the reasons for and against this course of action. These questions could therefore be paraphrased as follows. "I wish to do what is supported by the best reasons. Tell me whether this is so supported." As already mentioned, "following reason" means "doing what is supported by the best reasons." Hence the question "Shall (should, ought) I follow reason?" must be paraphrased as "I wish to do what is supported by the best reasons. Tell me whether doing what is supported by the best reasons is doing what is supported by the best reasons." It is, therefore, not worth asking.

The question "*Why* should I follow reason?" simply does not make sense. Asking it shows complete lack of understanding of the meaning of "why questions." "Why should I do this?" is a request to be given the reason for saying that I should do this. It is normally asked when someone has already said, "You should do this" and answered by giving the reason. But since "Should I follow reason?" means "Tell me whether doing what is supported by the best reasons is doing what is supported by the best reasons," there is simply no possibility of adding "Why?" For the question now comes to this, "Tell me the reason why doing what is supported by the best reasons is doing what is supported by the best reasons." It is exactly like asking, "Why is a circle a circle?"

However, it must be admitted that there is another possible interpretation to our question according to which it makes sense and can even be answered. "Why should I follow reason?" may not be a request for a reason in support of a tautological remark, but a request for a reason why one should enter on the theoretical task of deliberation. . . . Following reason involves the completion of two tasks, the theoretical and the practical. The point of the theoretical is to give guidance in the practical task. We perform the theoretical only because we wish to complete the practical task in accordance with the outcome of the theoretical. On our first interpretation, "Should I follow reason?" mear practical task completed when it is completed in accordance with the outcome of the theoretical task?" And the answer to this is obviously "Yes," for that is what we mean by "completion of the practical task." On our second interpretation, "Should I follow reason?" is not a question about the practical but about the theoretical task. It is not a question about whether, given that one is prepared to perform both these tasks, they are properly completed in the way indicated. It is a question about whether one should enter on the whole performance at all, whether the "game" is worth playing. And this is a meaningful question. It might be better to "follow inspiration" than to "follow reason," in this sense: better to close one's eyes and wait for an answer to flash across the mind.

But while, so interpreted, "Should I follow reason?" makes sense, it seems to me obvious that the answer to it is "Yes, because it pays." Deliberation is the only reliable method. Even if there were other reliable methods, we could only tell whether they were reliable by checking them against this method. Suppose some charismatic leader counsels, "Don't follow reason, follow me. My leadership is better than that of reason"; we would still have to check his claim against the ordinary methods of reason. We would have to ascertain whether in following his advice we were doing the best thing. And this we can do only by examining whether he has advised us to do what is supported by the best reasons. His claim to be better than reason can in turn only be supported by the fact that he tells us precisely the same as reason does.

Is there any sense, then, in his claim that his guidance is preferable to that of reason? There may be, for working out what is supported by the best reasons takes a long time. Frequently, the best thing to do is to do something quickly now rather than the most appropriate thing later. A leader may have the ability to "see," to "intuit," what is the best thing to do more quickly than it is possible to work this out by the laborious methods of deliberation. In evaluating the qualities of leadership of such a person, we are evaluating *his ability to perform correctly the practical task of following reason* without having to go through the lengthy operations of the theoretical. Reason is required to tell us whether anyone has qualities of leadership better than ordinary, in the same way that pencil and paper multiplications are required to tell us whether a mathematical prodigy is genuine or a fraud. . . .

# *Relativism*

Led by anthropology, the social sciences have amassed a large body of empirical evidence that establishes the wide diversity of ethical standards throughout the world. Frequently what is regarded as right in one culture is taken to be wrong in another. But what are the implications of this cultural diversity for ethics? Does it show that what is right and wrong is simply dependent upon one's culture and hence that individuals ought to follow cultural norms? "No," is the response of the vast majority of philosophers.

Philosophers certainly agree that anthropologists and other social scientists have discovered important facts about other cultures. Moreover, these facts should have a bearing both on our attitudes about other cultures and on our collective treatment of them. The facts show that referring to some cultures as primitive is unjustifiably condescending and that often our moral judgments about other cultures have been too harsh. If we properly understood another culture we would be more tolerant when its practices diverge from our own. However, many social scientists have pointed to the *fact* that different individuals and cultures hold different views about what constitutes moral behavior as *evidence* for the truth of moral **relativism**? Philosophers are virtually unanimous in the opinion that this is an invalid argument.

First, many philosophers claim that the "facts" aren't really what they seem. Several writers refer to the fact that in some cultures after a certain age parents are put to death. In our culture such behavior would be murder. We take care of our parents. Does this difference in behavior prove that the two cultures disagree about matters of ethics? No, it does not. Suppose the other culture believes that people exist in the afterlife in the same condition that they leave this life. It would be very cruel to have one's parents exist eternally in an unhealthy state. By killing them when they are relatively active and vigorous you ensure their happiness for all eternity. The underlying ethical principle of this culture is that children have duties to their parents including the duty to be concerned with their parents' happiness as they approach old age. This ethical principle is identical with our own. What looked like a difference in ethics between our culture and another turned out upon close examination to be a difference in beliefs about matters of fact.

Here is a second way that the "facts" really aren't what they seem. Cultures differ in physical setting, in economic development, in the state of their science and technology, in their literacy rate, and in many other ways. Even if there were universal moral principles, these principles would have to be applied in these different cultural contexts. Given the different situations in which cultures exist, it would come as no surprise to find these universal principles applied in different ways. Hence, the differences in so-called ethical behavior among cultures would be surface differences only. The cultures would agree on the fundamental universal moral principles. One selection in this part defends the ethical theory known as utilitarianism. On one formulation, the general principle of utilitarianism argues that social institutions and individual behavior should be so ordered that they lead to the greatest good for the greatest number. Obviously, great variety in social organization and individual behavior is consistent with that principle. The point of these two arguments is that surface diversities among cultures in so-called ethical behavior may not reflect genuine disagreement about ethics. Unless the relativist can establish basic differences about matters of ethics, the case for relativism cannot be made.

Another common strategy for criticizing relativism is to show that taking the perspective of an ethical relativist leads to some rather bizarre results. One of the bizarre results is that if relativism is true, then agreement in morals is impossible in principle. Of course by "agreement" I mean agreement on the basis of reasons. There can be agreement by force, which is equivalent to saying,

"Worship my God or I'll cut off your head." Why there can be no rational agreement is obvious on an examination of the definition of relativism. Cultural relativism is the view that what is right or wrong is determined by culture. So if one culture says that abortion is right and another says it is wrong, that has to be the end of the matter. Abortion *is* morally permissible in one culture and abortion *is* morally wrong in the other.

But suppose a person in one culture moves to another and tries to persuade the other culture to change its view. Suppose someone moves from a culture where slavery is immoral, to one where slavery is morally permitted. Normally if a person were to try to convince the culture where slavery was permitted that slavery was morally wrong, we would refer to such a person as a moral reformer. But if cultural relativism were true, there would be no place for the concept of a moral reformer. Slavery is right in those cultures that say it is right and wrong in those cultures that say it is wrong. If the reformer fails to persuade a slave-holding country to change its mind, the reformer's antislavery position was never right. If the reformer is successful in persuading a country to change its mind, the reformer's antislavery view was wrong until the country did in fact change its view. Then the reformer's antislavery view was right. Now that's a bizarre result.

Underlying these two objections is the broader objection that relativism is inconsistent with our use of moral language. When Russia and the United States argue about the moral rights that human beings have, they seem to be genuinely disagreeing about a matter of ethics. How unfortunate it would be if that dispute had to be resolved by nonrational means, since rational agreement is in principle impossible. People do marshal arguments in behalf of ethical views. If relativism is true, such arguments are doomed to failure or are a mere subterfuge to create agreement. Similarly, we do have a place in our language for the concept of a moral reformer. Is this use of language really deviant as it would have to be if relativism were true?

Finally, there is an argument that tries to show that if relativism is true, then it sometimes really is immoral to hold true beliefs. The argument works like this:

1. In Iran, holding a position of cultural relativism is considered wrong.
2. In the United States, holding a position of cultural relativism is morally permissible (not wrong).

By the definition of cultural relativism both (1) and (2) can be true. (As a matter of fact, they probably are.) If relativism is true, then holding cultural relativism really is wrong in Iran, and we have the bizarre result that in Iran holding a true moral theory is morally wrong.

By the arguments developed so far, we see you can't move from the facts of diversity in so-called ethical behavior and disagreement in ethical beliefs to the theory of moral relativism. The facts really don't establish ethical relativism and the facts about our use of moral language are inconsistent with a relativist theory.

Of course, arguments against the view that the diversity of ethical practices establishes relativism—even if successful—do not establish any universal principles that cut across all cultures. Whether or not there are any adequate universal principles of ethics is quite another matter and depends on independent arguments.

## *Edward Westermarck (1862–1939)*

Westermarck made important contributions in anthropology, sociology, and philosophy. Although many philosophers became interested in the issue of relativism as a result of the empirical research of social scientists, Westermarck became interested in a social scientific study of moral norms as a result of philosophical reflections on the status of moral judgments. Westermarck was a **subjectivist** in ethics because he believed that ethical judgments were incapable of objective proof and that ethical judgments depended in large part on our emotions — albeit on our emotions as shaped by religion and other cultural forces. Since Westermarck found evidence of the ethical beliefs of "civilized" peoples in the practices of "primitive" culture, and of "barbarous" behavior in civilized peoples, he saw no simple path of moral advance through history. Indeed, Westermarck was one of the chief spokespersons for tolerance as the appropriate response to ethical diversity among cultures. Nonetheless, he believed there was a trend in human history toward the expansion of altruistic sentiments beyond our own culture — to the cultures of others and to animals. His chief philosophical works are *The Origin and Development of Moral Ideals,* two volumes (1906 - 1908), and *Ethical Relativity* (1932).

## The Variability of Moral Judgments

### *Edward Westermarck*

. . . The variability of moral valuation depends in a very large measure upon intellectual factors of another kind, namely, different ideas relating to the objective nature of similar modes of conduct and their consequences. Such differences of ideas may arise from different situations and external conditions of life, which consequently influence moral opinion. We find, for instance, among many peoples the custom of killing or abandoning parents worn out with age or disease. It prevails among a large number of savage tribes and occurred formerly among many Asiatic and European nations, including the Vedic people and peoples of Teutonic extraction; there is an old English tradition of "the Holy Mawle, which they fancy hung behind the church door, which when the father was seaventie, the sonne might fetch to knock his father in the head, as effete and of no more use." This custom is particularly common among nomadic hunting tribes, owing to the hardships of life and the inability of decrepit persons to keep up in the march. In times when the food-supply is insufficient to support all the members of a community it also seems more reasonable that the old and useless should have to perish than the young and vigorous. And among peoples who have reached a certain degree of wealth and comfort, the practice of killing the old folks, though no longer justified by necessity, may still go on, partly through survival of a custom inherited from harder times, and partly from the humane intent of putting an end to lingering misery. What appears to most of us as an atrocious practice may really be an act of kindness, and is commonly approved of, or even insisted upon, by the old people themselves. . . .

The variability of moral judgments largely originates in different measures of knowledge, based on experience of the consequences of conduct, and in different beliefs. In almost every branch of conduct we notice the influence which

Abridged from "The Variability of Moral Judgments," by Edward Westermarck in *Ethical Relativity.* (London: Routledge & Kegan Paul P L C, 1932, pp. 184 - 219.) Reprinted by permission of Routledge & Kegan Paul P L C.

the belief in supernatural forces or beings or in a future state has exercised upon the moral ideas of mankind, and the great diversity of this influence. Religion or superstition has on the one hand stigmatized murder and suicide, on the other hand it has commended human sacrifice and certain cases of voluntary self-destruction. It has inculcated humanity and charity, but has also led to cruel persecutions of persons embracing another creed. It has emphasized the duty of truth-speaking, and has itself been a cause of pious fraud. It has promoted cleanly habits and filthiness. It has enjoined labor and abstinence from labor, sobriety and drunkenness, marriage and celibacy, chastity and temple prostitution. It has introduced a great variety of new duties and virtues, quite different from those which are recognized by the moral consciousness when left to itself, but nevertheless in many cases considered more important than any other duties or virtues. . . .

In so far as differences of moral opinion depend on knowledge or ignorance of facts, on specific religious or superstitious beliefs, on different degrees of reflection, or on different conditions of life or other external circumstances, they do not clash with that universality which is implied in the notion of the objective validity of moral judgments. We shall now examine whether the same is the case with other differences that, at least apparently, are not due to purely cognitive causes.

When we study the moral rules laid down by the customs of savage peoples we find that they in a very large measure resemble the rules of civilized nations. In every savage community homicide is prohibited by custom, and so is theft. Savages also regard charity as a duty and praise generosity as a virtue, indeed their customs relating to mutual aid are often much more exacting than our own; and many of them are conspicuous for their avoidance of telling lies. But in spite of the great similarity of moral commandments, there is at the same time a difference between the regard for life, property, truth, and the general well-being of a neighbor which displays itself in savage rules of morality and that which is found among ourselves: it has, broadly speaking, only reference to members of the same community or tribe. Primitive peoples carefully distinguish between an act of homicide committed within their own community and one where the victim is a stranger: while the former is in ordinary circumstances disapproved of, the latter is in most cases allowed and often considered worthy of praise. And the same holds true of theft and lying and the infliction of other injuries. Apart from the privileges granted to guests, which are always of very short duration, a stranger is in early society devoid of all rights. And the same is the case not only among savages but among nations of archaic culture as well.

When we pass from the lower races to peoples more advanced in civilization we find that the social unit has grown larger, that the nation has taken the place of the tribe, and that the circle within which the infliction of injuries is prohibited has been extended accordingly. But the old distinction between injuries committed against compatriots and harm done to foreigners remains. In Greece in early times the "contemptible stranger" had no legal rights, and was protected only if he was the guest of a citizen; and even later on, at Athens, while the intentional killing of a citizen was punished with death and confiscation of the murderer's property, the intentional killing of a non-citizen was punished only with exile. . . . In the thirteenth century there were still several places in France in which a stranger who remained there for a year and a day became the serf of the lord of the manor. In England, till upwards of two centuries after the Conquest, foreign merchants were considered only as sojourners who had come to a fair or market, and were obliged to employ their landlords as brokers to buy and sell their commodities; and one stranger was often arrested for the debt or punished for the misdemeanor of another. . . .

It would be in vain to deny that the old distinction between a tribesman or fellow-countryman and a foreigner is dead among ourselves. . . . But both law and public opinion certainly show a very great advance in humanity with regard to the treatment of foreigners. And if we pass to the rules laid down by moralists and professedly accepted by a large portion of civilized humanity, the change from the savage attitude has been enormous. The doctrine of universal love is not peculiar to Christianity. The Chinese moralists inculcated benevolence to all men, without making any reference to national distinctions. Mih-tsze, who lived in the interval between Confucius and Mencius, even taught that we ought to love all men equally; . . . In Greece and Rome philosophers arose who opposed national narrowness and prejudice. Thus the Cynics attached slight value to the citizenship of any special state, declaring themselves to be citizens of the world. But it was the Stoic philosophy that first gave to the idea of a world-citizenship a definite positive meaning and raised it to historical importance.

It is obvious that the expansion of the moral rules has been a consequence of the expansion of the social unit and of increased intercourse between different societies, and if, as I maintain, the range of the moral emotions varies with the range of the altruistic sentiment, there is every reason to assume that an immediate cause of the greater comprehensiveness of the moral rules has been a corresponding widening of that sentiment. Among gregarious animals it is apt to be felt towards any member of their species that is not an object of their fear or anger. In mankind it has been narrowed by social isolation, by differences in race, language, habits, and customs, by enmity and suspicion. But peaceful intercourse leads to conditions favorable to its expansion, as well as to friendly behavior for prudential reasons in the relations between those who come into contact with each other. People of different nationalities feel that in spite of all dissimilarities there is much that they have in common; and frequent intercourse makes the differences less marked or obliterates many of them altogether. . . .

It will perhaps be argued that the impartiality which is a characteristic of all moral judgments required a universalization of the moral rules, and that this could only be accomplished by a process of reasoning, which gradually extended them to wider and wider circles of men and finally to the whole human race. But let us remember what the impartiality of moral judgments really implies. . . . When a person pronounces an act right or wrong, it implies that *ceteris paribus* it is so whether he, or some friend or enemy of his, does it to another; *or* another does it to him, or to some friend or enemy of his. This impartiality has nothing to do with the question whether the agent and he to whom the act is done belong to the same or different families, tribes, nations, or other social groups. If it is considered wrong of a person to cheat another belonging to his own group but not wrong to cheat a foreigner, the impartiality of the moral emotion of disapproval, which underlies the concept of wrongness, merely leads to a general rule that applies to all similar cases independently of the nationality of him who holds the view. If I maintain that a foreigner, or a member of another class in my own society, has a duty towards me but that I have not the same duty towards him, my opinion can be justified only on condition that there is some difference in the circumstances affecting the morality of the case. People are certainly only too prone to assume that there are such differences. When they attribute different rights to different individuals, or classes of individuals, they are often in reality influenced by the relationship in which they stand to them; and reflection may be needed to decide whether the assumed impartiality of their moral judgment is real or illusory. Indeed, some degree of reasoning, however small, may always be needed in order to know whether a retributive emotion is felt impartially. . . .

But it seems to me to be a sheer illusion to maintain that reason requires of us an impartiality in our conduct which makes no difference between one man and another. . . . I cannot find it unreasonable to endeavor to promote the welfare of my own family or country in preference to that of other families or countries. But my moral emotions tell me that I must allow anybody else to show a similar preference for *his* family or country.

I think that the question, why moral rules should differ because the persons to whom they refer are members of different social groups, would hardly arise unless there were a correspondingly broad altruistic sentiment behind it. Whatever part reflection may have played in the expansion of the moral rules—prudence has also, no doubt, had something to do with the matter—it seems to me obvious that the dominant cause has been the widening of the altruistic sentiment. Beyond its limits the equalization of duties in our moral consciousness cannot go, whatever theorists may have to say on the subject; and the varying strength of this sentiment with regard to its objects will always prevent the rules from being anything like uniform and always make their equalization extremely incomplete. . . .

The variations of the altruistic sentiment in range and strength are also responsible for other differences of moral opinion. Even among ourselves there is no unanimity as to the dictates of duty in cases where a person's own interests collide with those of his fellow-men. . . . In some men the altruistic sentiment is stronger than in others and, consequently, more apt to influence their consciences with regard to their own conduct and their judgments on other people's conduct. And while everybody will no doubt agree that some amount of self-sacrifice is a duty in certain circumstances, the amount and the circumstances can hardly be fixed in general rules, and on the whole, in cases of conflicting interests the judgment must to a large extent remain a matter of private opinion. . . .

To ethical writers who believe in the objective validity of moral judgments moral evolution implies a progressive discovery of values as a matter of reflection or thought, which follows in the wake of experience. They are fond of arguing that the changes of moral opinion are on a par with the discoveries made in mathematics, physics, and other sciences, which have been disputed quite as fiercely as any differences of moral valuation. . . .

But while the **objectivists** cannot be accused of exaggerating the changes in our theoretical knowledge as compared with those in moral opinion, they have failed to see that the causes of these changes are in a large measure fundamentally different. The theoretical differences can be removed by sufficient observation and reflection, owing to the general uniformity of our sense-perceptions and intellect. It has been said that "the moral convictions of thoughtful and well-educated people are the data of ethics just as sense-perceptions are the data of a natural science. Just as some of the latter have to be rejected as illusory, so have some of the former; but as the latter are rejected only when they are in conflict with other more accurate sense-perceptions, the former are rejected only when they are in conflict with other convictions which stand better the test of reflection." But, surely, there is an enormous difference between the possibility of harmonizing conflicting sense-perceptions and that of harmonizing conflicting moral convictions. When the sense-perceptions vary in the presence of the same object, as when the object looks different under different objective conditions or if the beholding eye is normal or colorblind, the variations can be accounted for by reference to the external conditions or the structure of the organ, and they in no way affect our conceptions of things as they really are. So also a hallucination is easily distinguished from a perception when we learn by experience that its object does not exist, whereas the perception has an existing object. On the other hand we all know that there often is a conflict between the moral convictions of "thoughtful and well-educated people," nay, even between the moral "intuitions" of philosophers, which proves irreconcilable. This is just what may be expected if moral opinions are based on emotions. The moral emotions depend upon cognitions, but the same cognitions may give rise to emotions that differ, in quality or intensity, in different persons or in the same person on different occasions, and then there is nothing that could make the emotions uniform. Certain cognitions inspire fear into nearly every breast, but there are brave men and cowards in the world, independently of the accuracy with which they realize impending danger. Some cases of suffering can hardly fail to call forth compassion in the most pitiless heart; but men's disposition to feel pity varies greatly, both in regard to the beings for whom it is felt and as to the intensity of the emotion. The same holds true of the moral emotions. To a large extent, as we have seen, their differences depend upon the presence of different cognitions, but very frequently the emotions also differ though the cognitions are the same. The variations of the former kind do not interfere with the belief in the universality of moral judgments, but when the variations of the moral emotions may be traced to different persons' tendencies to feel differently in similar circumstances on account of the particular nature of their altruistic sentiments, the supposed universality of moral judgments is a delusion.

It will perhaps be argued that, with sufficient insight into facts, there would be no diversity of moral opinion if only the moral consciousness of all men were "sufficiently developed"; . . . But what is meant by a sufficiently developed moral consciousness? Practically, I suppose, nothing else than agreement with the speaker's own moral convictions. The expression is faulty and deceptive, because, if intended to mean anything more, it presupposes a universality of moral judgments which they do not possess, and at the same time may appear to prove what it presupposes. We may speak of an intellect sufficiently developed to grasp a certain truth, because truth is one; but it is not proved to be one by the fact that it is recognized as such by a "sufficiently" developed intellect. The universality of truth lies in the recognition of judgments as true by all who have a *full* knowledge of the facts concerned, and the appeal to a *sufficient* knowledge rightly *assumes* that truth is universal.

That moral judgments could not possibly possess that universality which is characteristic of truth becomes particularly obvious when we consider that their predicates vary not only in quality but in quantity. There are no degrees of truth and falsehood; but there are degrees of goodness and badness, virtues and merits may be greater or smaller, a duty may be more or less stringent, and if there are no degrees of rightness, the reason for it is that right simply means conformity to the rule of duty. . . .

The quantitative differences of moral estimates are plainly due to the emotional origin of all moral concepts. Emotions vary in intensity almost indefinitely, and the moral emotions form no exception to this rule. Indeed, it may be fairly doubted whether the same mode of conduct ever arouses exactly the same degree of approval or disapproval in any two individuals. Many of these differences are of course too slight to manifest themselves in the moral judgment; but very frequently the intensity of the emotion is indicated by some special word, or by the tone in which the judgment is pronounced. It should be noticed, however, that the quantity of the estimate expressed in a moral predicate is not identical with the intensity of the moral emotion which a certain course of conduct arouses on a particular occasion. We are liable to feel more indignant if an injury is committed before our eyes than if we read of it in a newspaper, and yet we admit that the degree of badness is in both cases the same. The comparative quantity of moral estimates is determined by the intensity of the emotions which their objects tend to evoke in exactly similar circumstances.

## Paul W. Taylor (b. 1923)

Paul W. Taylor is a contemporary philosopher whose chief contribution is in ethics. In addition to providing an excellent text (*Principles of Ethics: An Introduction,* 1975) and two anthologies, Taylor has provided an extensive analysis of the process of ethical justification. See *Normative Discourse* (1961). In this selection Taylor distinguishes descriptive relativism and normative relativism, points out that descriptive relativism does not have the implications often attributed to it, and argues that the rejection of relativism entails neither intolerance nor absolutism.

# Ethical Relativism and Ethical Absolutism

## *Paul W. Taylor*

One of the most commonly held opinions in ethics is that all moral norms are *relative* to particular cultures. The rules of conduct that are applicable in one society, it is claimed, do not apply to the actions of people in another society. Each community has its own norms, and morality is entirely a matter of conforming to the standards and rules accepted in one's own culture. To put it simply: What is right is what my society approves of; what is wrong is what my society disapproves of.

This view raises serious doubts about the whole enterprise of normative ethics. For if right and wrong are completely determined by the given moral code of a particular time and place, and if moral codes vary from time to time and place to place, it would seem that there are no unchanging cross-cultural principles that could constitute an ideal ethical system applicable to everyone. Since the purpose of normative ethics is to construct and defend just such a universal system of principles, belief in the relativity of moral norms denies the possibility of normative ethics. It is therefore important at the outset to examine the theory of ethical **relativism.**

The question raised by the ethical relativist may be expressed thus: Are moral values absolute, or are they relative? We may understand this question as asking, Are there any moral standards and rules of conduct that are universal (applicable to all mankind) or are they all culture-bound (applicable only to the members of a particular society or group)? Even when the question is interpreted in this way, however, it still remains unclear. For those who answer the question by claiming that all moral values are relative or culture-bound may be expressing . . . one of [two] different ideas. They may, first, be making an empirical or factual assertion. Or secondly, they may be making a normative claim. . . . The term "ethical relativism" has been used to refer to [either] of these positions. In order to keep clear the differences [between] them, the following terminology will be used. We shall call the first position "descriptive relativism," the second "normative ethical relativism." . . . Let us consider each in turn.

---

## DESCRIPTIVE RELATIVISM

Certain facts about the moral values of different societies and about the way an individual's values are dependent on those of his society have been taken as empirical evidence in support of the claim that all moral values are relative to the particular culture in which they are accepted. These facts are cited by the relativist as reasons for holding a general theory about moral norms, namely, that no such norms are universal. This theory is what we shall designate "descriptive relativism." It is a factual or empirical theory because it holds that, as a matter of historical and sociological fact, no moral standard or rule of conduct has been universally recognized to be the basis of moral obligation. According to the descriptive relativist there are no moral norms common to all cultures. Each society has its own view of what is morally right and wrong and these views vary from society to society because of the differences in their moral codes. Thus it is a mistake to think there are common norms that bind all mankind in one moral community.

Those who accept the position of descriptive relativism point to certain facts as supporting evidence for their theory. These facts may be conveniently summed up under the following headings:

1. The facts of cultural variability.
2. Facts about the origin of moral beliefs and moral codes.
3. The fact of **ethnocentrism.**

1. The facts of cultural variability are now so familiar to everyone that they need hardly be enumerated in detail. We all know from reading anthropologists' studies of primitive cultures how extreme is the variation in the customs and taboos, the religions and moralities, the daily habits and the general outlook on life to be found in the cultures of different peoples. But we need not go beyond our own culture to recognize the facts of variability. Historians of Western civilization have long pointed out the great differences in the beliefs and values of people living in different periods. Great differences have also been discovered among the various socioeconomic classes existing within the social structure at any one time. Finally, our own contemporary world reveals a tremendous variety of ways of living. No one who dwells in a modern city can escape the impact of this spectrum of different views on work and play, on family life and education, on what constitutes personal happiness, and on what is right and wrong.

2. When we add to these facts of cultural and historical variability the recent psychological findings about how the individual's values reflect those of his own social group and his own time, we may begin to question the universal validity of our own values. For it is now a well-established fact that no moral values or beliefs are inborn. All our moral attitudes and judgments are learned from the social environment. Even our deepest convictions about justice and the rights of man are originally nothing but the "introjected" or "internalized" views of our culture, transmitted to us through our parents and teachers. Our very conscience itself is formed by the internalizing of the sanctions used by our society to support its moral norms. When we were told in childhood what we ought and ought not to do, and when our parents expressed their approval and disapproval of us for what we did, we were being taught the standards and rules of conduct accepted in our society. The result of this learning process (sometimes called "acculturation") was to ingrain in us a set of attitudes about our own conduct, so that even when our parents were no longer around to guide us or to blame us, we would guide or blame ourselves by thinking, "This is what I ought to do"; "That would be wrong to do"; and so on. If we then did something we believed was wrong we would feel guilty about it, whether or not anyone caught us at it or punished us for it.

It is this unconscious process of internalizing the norms of one's society through early childhood training that explains the origin of an individual's moral values. If we go beyond this and ask about the origin of society's values, we find a long and gradual development of traditions and customs which have given stability to the society's way of life and whose obscure beginnings lie in ritual magic, taboos, tribal ceremonies, and practices of religious worship. Whether we are dealing with the formation of an individual's conscience or the development of a society's moral code, then, the origin of a set of values seems to have little or nothing to do with rational, controlled thought. Neither individuals nor societies originally acquire their moral beliefs by means of logical reasoning or through the use of an objective method for gaining knowledge.

3. Finally, the descriptive relativist points out another fact about people and their moralities that must be acknowledged. This is the fact that most people are ethnocentric (group centered). They think not only that there is but one true morality for all mankind, but that the one true morality is their own. They are convinced that the moral code under which they grew up and which formed their deepest feelings about right and wrong—namely, the moral code of their own society—is the only code for anyone to live by. Indeed, they often refuse even to entertain the possibility that their own values might be false or that another society's code might be more correct, more enlightened, or more advanced than their own. Thus ethnocentrism often leads to intolerance and dogmatism. It causes people to be extremely narrow-minded in their ethical outlook, afraid to admit any doubt about a moral issue, and unable to take a detached, objective stance regarding their own moral beliefs. Being absolutely certain that their beliefs are true, they can think only that those who disagree with them are in total error and ignorance on moral matters. Their attitude is: We are advanced, they are backward. We are civilized, they are savages.

It is but a short step from dogmatism to intolerance. Intolerance is simply dogmatism in action. Because the moral values of people directly affect their conduct, those who have divergent moral convictions will often come into active conflict with one another in the area of practical life. Each will believe he alone has the true morality and the other is living in the darkness of sin. Each will see the other as practicing moral abominations. Each will then try to force the other to accept the truth, or at least will not allow the other to live by his own values. The self-righteous person will not tolerate the presence of "shocking" acts which he views with outraged indignation. Thus it comes about that no differences of opinion on moral matters will be permitted within a society. The ethnocentric society will tend to be a closed society, as far as moral belief and practice are concerned.

The argument for descriptive relativism, then, may be summarized as follows. Since every culture varies with respect to its moral rules and standards, and since each individual's moral beliefs—including his inner conviction of their absolute truth—have been learned within the framework of his own culture's moral code, it follows that there are no universal moral norms. If a person believes there are such norms, this is to be explained by his ethnocentrism, which leads him to project his own culture's norms upon everyone else and to consider those who disagree with him either as innocent but "morally blind" people or as sinners who do not want to face the truth about their own evil ways.

In order to assess the soundness of this argument it is necessary to make a distinction between (a) specific moral standards and rules, and (b) ultimate moral principles. Both (a) and (b) can be called "norms," and it is because the descriptive relativist often overlooks this distinction that his argument is open to doubt. A specific moral standard (such as personal courage or trustworthiness) functions as a criterion for judging whether and to what degree a person's character is morally good or bad. A specific rule of conduct (such as "Help others in time of need" or "Do not tell lies for one's own advantage") is a prescription of how people ought or ought not to act. It functions as a criterion for judging whether an action is right or wrong. In contrast with specific standards and rules, an ultimate moral principle is a universal proposition or statement about the conditions that must hold if a standard or rule is to be used as a criterion for judging *any* person or action. . . . An example of an ultimate moral principle is that of utility, which we shall be examining [later]. . . . The principle of utility may be expressed thus: A standard or rule applies to a person or action if, and only if, the use of the standard or rule in the actual guidance of people's conduct will result in an increase in everyone's happiness or a decrease in everyone's unhappiness.

Now it is perfectly possible for an ultimate moral principle to be consistent with a variety of specific standards and rules as found in the moral codes of different societies. For if we take into account the traditions of a culture, the beliefs about reality and the attitudes toward life that are part of each culture's world-outlook, and if we also take into account the physical or geographical setting of each culture, we will find that a standard or rule which increases people's happiness in one culture will not increase, but rather decrease, people's happiness in another. In one society, for example, letting elderly people die when they can no longer contribute to economic production will be necessary for the survival of everyone else. But another society may have an abundant economy that can easily support people in their old age. Thus the principle of utility would require that in the first society the rule "Do not keep a person alive when he can no longer produce" be part of its moral code, and in the second society it would require a contrary rule. In this case the very same kind of action that is wrong in one society will be right in another. Yet there is a single principle that makes an action of that kind wrong (in one set of circumstances) and another action of that kind right (in a different set of circumstances). In other words, the reason why one action is wrong and the other right is based on one and the same principle, namely utility.

Having in mind this distinction between specific standards and rules on the one hand and ultimate moral principles on the other, what can we say about the argument for descriptive relativism given above? It will immediately be seen that the facts pointed out by the relativist as evidence in support of his theory do not show that ultimate moral principles are relative or culture-bound. They show only that specific standards and rules are relative or culture-bound. The fact that different societies accept different norms of good and bad, right and wrong, is a fact about the standards and rules that make up the various moral codes of those societies. Such a fact does not provide evidence that there is no single ultimate principle which, explicitly or implicitly, every society appeals to as the final justifying ground for its moral code. For if there were such a common ultimate principle, the actual variation in moral codes could be explained in terms of the different world-outlooks, traditions, and physical circumstances of the different societies.

Similarly, facts about ethnocentrism and the causal dependence of an individual's moral beliefs upon his society's moral code do not count as evidence against the view that there is a universal ultimate principle which everyone would refer to in giving a final justification for his society's standards and rules, if he were challenged to do so. Whether there is such a principle and if there is, what sort of conditions it specifies for the validity of specific standards and rules, are questions still to be explored. . . . But the facts cited by the descriptive relativist leave these questions open. We may accept those facts and still be consistent in affirming a single universal ultimate moral principle.

## NORMATIVE ETHICAL RELATIVISM

The statement, "What is right in one society may be wrong in another," is a popular way of explaining what is meant by the "relativity of morals." It is usually contrasted with "ethical **universalism,**" taken as the view that "right and wrong do not vary from society to society." These statements are ambiguous, however, and it is important for us to be mindful of their ambiguity. For they may be understood either as factual claims or as normative claims, and it makes a great deal of difference which way they are understood. . . .

When it is said that what is right in one society may be wrong in another, this may be understood to mean that what is *believed* to be right in one society is *believed* to be wrong in another. And when it is said that moral right and wrong vary from society to society, this may be understood to mean that different moral norms are adopted by different societies, so that an act which fulfills the norms of one society may violate the norms of another. If this is what is meant, then we are here being told merely of the cultural variability of specific standards and rules, which we have already considered in connection with descriptive relativism.

But the statement, "What is right in one society may be wrong in another," may be interpreted in quite a different way. It may be taken as a normative claim rather than as a factual assertion. Instead of asserting the unsurprising fact that what is believed to be right in one society is believed to be wrong in another, it expresses the far more radical and seemingly paradoxical claim that what *actually is* right in one society may *actually be* wrong in another. According to this view, moral norms are to be considered valid only within the society which has adopted them as part of its way of life. Such norms are not to be considered valid outside that society. The conclusion is then drawn that it is not legitimate to judge people in other societies by applying the norms of one's own society to their conduct. This is the view we shall designate "normative ethical relativism." In order to be perfectly clear about what it claims, we shall examine two ways in which it can be stated, one focusing our attention upon moral judgments, the other on moral norms.

With regard to moral judgments, normative ethical relativism holds that two *apparently* contradictory statements can both be true. The argument runs as follows. Consider the two statements:

1. It is wrong for unmarried women to have their faces unveiled in front of strangers.

2. It is not wrong for . . . (as above).

Here it seems as if there is a flat contradiction between two moral judgments, so that if one is true the other must be false. But the normative ethical relativist holds that they are both true, because the statements as given in (1) and (2) are incomplete. They should read as follows:

3. It is wrong for unmarried women *who are members of society S* to have their faces unveiled in front of strangers.

4. It is not wrong for unmarried women *outside of society S* to have their faces unveiled in front of strangers.

Statements (3) and (4) are not contradictories. To assert one is not to deny the other. The normative ethical relativist simply translates all moral judgments of the form "Doing act X is right" into statements of the form "Doing X is right when the agent is a member of society S." The latter statement can then be seen to be consistent with statements of the form "Doing X is wrong when the agent is not a member of society S."

The normative ethical relativist's view of moral norms accounts for the foregoing theory of moral judgments. A moral norm, we have seen, is either a standard used in a judgment of good and bad character or a rule used in a judgment of right and wrong conduct. Thus a person is judged to be good insofar as he fulfills the standard, and an action is judged to be right or wrong according to whether it conforms to or violates the rule. Now when a normative ethical relativist says that moral norms vary from society to society, he does not intend merely to assert the fact that different societies have adopted different norms. He is going beyond descriptive relativism and is making a normative claim. He is denying any universal validity to moral norms. He is saying that a moral standard or rule is correctly applicable only to the members of the particular society which has adopted the standard or rule as part of its actual moral code. He therefore thinks it is illegitimate to judge the character or conduct of those outside the society by such a standard or rule. Anyone who uses the norms of one society as the basis for judging the character or conduct of persons in another society is consequently in error.

It is not that a normative ethical relativist necessarily believes in *tolerance* of other people's norms. Nor does his position imply that he grants others the *right* to live by their own norms, for he would hold a relativist view even about tolerance itself. A society whose code included a rule of tolerance would be right in tolerating others, while one that denied tolerance would be right (relative to its own norm of intolerance) in prohibiting others from living by different norms. The normative ethical relativist would simply say that *we* should not judge the tolerant society to be any better than the intolerant one, for this would be applying our own norm of tolerance to other societies. Tolerance, like any other norm, is culture-bound. Anyone who claims that every society has a *right* to live by its own norms, provided that it respects a similar right in other societies, is an ethical universalist, since he holds at least one norm valid for all societies, namely, the right to practice a way of life without interference from others. And he deems this universal norm a valid one, whether or not every society does in fact accept it.

If the normative ethical relativist is challenged to prove his position, he may do either of two things. On the one hand, he may try to argue that his position follows from, or is based on, the very same facts that are cited by the descriptive relativist as evidence for *his* position. Or, on the other hand, he may turn for support to metaethical considerations. Putting aside the second move for the moment, let us look more closely at the first.

The most frequent argument given in defense of normative ethical relativism is that, if the facts pointed out by the descriptive relativist are indeed true, then we must accept normative ethical relativism as the only position consistent with those facts. For it seems that if each person's moral judgments are formed within the framework of the norms of his own culture and historical epoch, and if such norms vary among cultures and epochs, it would follow necessarily that it is unwarranted for anyone to apply his own norms to conduct in other societies and times. To do so would be ethnocentrism, which is, as the descriptive relativist shows, a kind of blind, narrow-minded dogmatism. To escape the irrationality of being ethnocentric, we need but realize that the only norms one may legitimately apply to any given group are the ones accepted by that group. Since different peoples accept different norms, there are no universal norms applicable to everyone throughout the world. Now, to say that there are no universal norms applicable worldwide is to commit oneself to normative ethical relativism. Thus, the argument concludes, normative ethical relativism follows from the facts of descriptive relativism.

Is this a valid argument? Suppose one accepts the facts pointed out by the descriptive relativist. Must he then also accept normative ethical relativism? Let us examine some of the objections that have been raised to this argument. In the first place, it is claimed that the facts of cultural variability do not, *by themselves,* entail normative ethical relativism. The reason is that it is perfectly possible for someone to accept those facts and deny normative ethical relativism without contradicting himself. No matter how great may be the differences in the moral beliefs of different cultures and in the moral norms they accept, it is still possible to hold that some of these beliefs are true and others false, or that some of the norms are more correct, justified, or enlightened than others. The fact that societies differ about what is right and wrong does not mean that one society may not have better reasons for holding its views than does another. After all, just because two people (or two groups of people) disagree about whether a disease is caused by bacteria or by evil spirits does not lead to the conclusion that there is no correct or enlightened view about the cause of the disease. So it does not follow from the fact that two societies differ about whether genocide is right that there is no correct or enlightened view about this moral matter.

A similar argument can be used with regard to the second set of facts asserted by the descriptive relativist. No contradiction is involved in affirming that all moral beliefs come from the social environment and denying normative ethical relativism. The fact that a belief is learned from one's society does not mean that it is neither true nor false, or that if it is true, its truth is "relative" to the society in which it was learned. All of our beliefs, empirical ones no less than moral ones, are learned from our society. We are not born with any innate beliefs about chemistry or physics; we learn these only in our schools. Yet this does not make us skeptical about the universal validity of these sciences. So the fact that our moral beliefs come from our society and are learned in our homes and schools has no bearing on their universal validity. The origin or cause of a person's *acquiring* a belief does not determine whether the *content* of the belief is true or false, or even whether there are good grounds for his accepting that content to be true or false.

If it is claimed that our moral beliefs are based on attitudes or feelings culturally conditioned in us from childhood, the same point can still be made. Suppose, for example, that a person who believes slavery is wrong feels disapproval, dislike, or even abhorrence towards the institution of slavery. His negative attitude, which has undoubtedly been influenced by the value system of his culture, may be contrasted with a positive stance (approval, liking, admiring) of someone brought up in an environment where slave owning was accepted. Here are positive and negative attitudes toward slavery, each being causally conditioned by the given cultural environment. It does not follow from this that the two are equally justified, or that neither can be justified. The question of whether a certain attitude toward slavery is justified or unjustified depends on whether good reasons can be given *for* anyone taking the one attitude and *against* anyone taking the other. This question requires the exercise of our reasoning powers. . . . The mere fact that the attitudes which underlie moral beliefs are all learned from the social environment leaves open the question of what attitudes an intelligent, rational, and well-informed person would take toward a given action or social practice.

The same kind of argument also holds with respect to the third fact of descriptive relativism: ethnocentrism. People who are ethnocentric *believe* that the one true moral code is that of their own society. But this leaves open the question, Is their belief true or false? Two people of different cultures, both ethnocentric but with opposite moral beliefs, may each think his particular moral norms are valid for everyone; however, this has no bearing on whether either one—or neither one—is correct. We must inquire independently into the possibility of establishing the universal validity of a set of moral norms, regardless of who might or might not believe them to be universally true.

It should be noted that these various objections to the first argument for normative ethical relativism, even if sound, are not sufficient to show that normative ethical relativism is false. They only provide reasons for rejecting one argument in support of that position. To show that the position is false, it would be necessary to give a sound argument in defense of ethical universalism. It is only if one or more of these arguments proves acceptable that normative ethical relativism is refuted. . . .

## ETHICAL ABSOLUTISM

When someone asks, "Are moral norms relative or absolute?" there is often an ambiguity in his question, not only with respect to the word "relative" but also with respect to the word "absolute." We have seen that "relative" can mean, among other things, "causally dependent on variable factors in different cultures" (descriptive relativism); *or* "validly applicable only within the culture which accepts the norm" (normative ethical relativism). . . . Let us now examine an important ambiguity in the term "absolute" as it is applied to moral norms. For unless this ambiguity is cleared up, we cannot give a straightforward answer to the question of whether moral norms are relative or absolute.

That moral norms (that is, specific moral rules and standards) are "absolute" can mean either of two things. It can mean that at least some moral norms are justifiable on grounds that can be established by a cross-cultural method of reasoning and that, consequently, these norms correctly apply to the conduct of all human beings. This, we have seen, is ethical universalism. It entails the denial of normative ethical relativism. . . .

Hence, in this first sense of the term "absolute," ethical absolutism may simply be equated with ethical universalism.

The second meaning of the term "absolute" is entirely different from the first. According to the second meaning, to say that moral norms are "absolute" is to say that they *have no exceptions.* Thus, if the rule "It is wrong to break a promise" is an absolute moral norm in this second sense, then one must never break a promise no matter what the circumstances. It follows that it is our duty to keep a promise, even if doing so brings suffering to innocent people. It means, for example, that a hired gunman who promises his boss to murder someone should commit the murder. It signifies that, if we have promised a friend to go to a movie with him on Saturday night, we must do so even if our parents are injured in an automobile accident Saturday afternoon and desperately need our help. Extreme cases like these show that, at least in our ordinary unreflective moral judgments, the rule "Do not break promises" has exceptions and that, consequently, ethical **absolutism** in the second sense of the term is not true of that particular moral rule.

Are there *any* rules of conduct that are "absolute" in the second sense? The reader should try to work out his own answer to this question for himself. What is important for present purposes is to notice the *logical independence* of the two meanings of "ethical absolutism."

According to the first meaning, an ethical absolutist holds that there are moral norms that apply to everyone, no matter what norms are actually accepted in a given society. According to the second meaning, an ethical absolutist is one who claims that at least some moral norms allow for no legitimate or justifiable exceptions. It is clear that the first meaning of ethical absolutism does not necessarily entail the second. In other words, it is possible to be an ethical absolutist in the first sense but not in the second. For it may be that all moral norms valid for everyone in any society are norms that allow for legitimate exceptions in special circumstances, *whenever* those circumstances occur. Let us consider an example.

Suppose we think that in almost all situations of life it is wrong for one person to take the life of another. Suppose, further, that we hold the rule "Thou shalt not kill" to be a universal moral norm, believing that it applies to all persons in all societies (even if a certain group of people in a given society do not accept the rule). Thus, with respect to this rule we are ethical universalists. Now suppose that we also think that there are very unusual conditions which, when they occur, make it permissible for one person to kill another. For instance, we might think that if a person's only means of defending his life or the lives of his children against the attack of a madman is to kill him, then it is not wrong to kill him. Or we might think that killing is permissible when such an act is necessary to overthrow a totalitarian government carrying out a policy of systematic genocide. If we hold these cases to be legitimate exceptions to the rule "Thou shalt not kill," are we contradicting our position of ethical universalism with regard to that rule? The answer is no, since we may be willing to consider these exceptions universally legitimate whenever they occur, no matter whether a given society accepts them as legitimate exceptions or not. In this case the *full* statement of our rule against killing would be expressed thus: It is wrong for anyone, in any society, to take the life of another, except when such an act is necessary for self-defense or the prevention of systematic genocide.

When a moral rule is stated in this manner, it encompasses its own exceptions. In other words, the complete rule stipulates all the kinds of situations in which an action of the sort *generally* forbidden by the rule is right. If we then accept the rule in its complete form, *including the list of exceptions,* as validly applicable to all human beings, we are ethical universalists (and hence ethical absolutists in the first sense of the term) with respect to this rule. However, we are not ethical absolutists in the second sense of the term, since we hold that the simple rule "Thou shalt not kill" does have legitimate exceptions.

It is true that in this case we may not be willing to allow for exceptions to the whole rule in its *complete* form, since we may think our statement of the rule includes all the possible exceptions it could have. With regard to the rule in its complete form, we would then be ethical absolutists in both senses of the term. On the other hand, if we are not sure we have included all the exceptions that could possibly be legitimate, then with regard to such an *incomplete* rule we would not be ethical absolutists in the second sense. The rule as we have formulated it may still have legitimate exceptions which we have overlooked, but we can nevertheless be ethical universalists about such an incomplete rule. For we might believe that, even in its incomplete form, it correctly applies to all mankind.

The main point of this discussion may now be indicated. When an ethical universalist says that there are moral norms applicable to everyone everywhere, he does not mean that the application of these norms to particular circumstances must determine that one kind of action is always right (or that it is always wrong). He means only that, whenever the norms do apply, they apply regardless of whether a given society may have accepted them in its actual moral code and another society may have excluded them from *its* moral code. The (normative) ethical relativist, on the other hand, claims that what makes an act right is precisely its conformity to the accepted norms of the society in which it occurs, while its violation of such accepted norms makes it wrong. Consider, then, two acts of the very same kind done in the very same sort of circumstances, but each occurring in a different society. One can be right and the other wrong, according to the relativist, since the moral norms of the two societies may disagree concerning the behavior in question. The ethical universalist (or "absolutist" in the first sense), however, would say that if one act is right the other is too and if one is wrong so is the other. For both are acts of an identical kind performed in identical circumstances. Therefore a rule which required or prohibited the one would also require or prohibit the other, and only one rule validly applies to such actions performed in circumstances of that sort. Thus the universalist holds that the rightness and wrongness of actions do not change according to variations in the norms accepted by different societies, even though (contrary to what the "absolutist" in the second sense says) the rightness and wrongness of actions do vary with differences in the sorts of circumstances in which they are performed.

If we keep this distinction between the two meanings of ethical absolutism clearly in mind, we can then see that it is possible to be an absolutist in one sense and not in the other. Whether either sense of absolutism is a correct view is a matter that cannot be settled without further study of normative and analytic ethics. Perhaps the reader will be able to decide these questions for himself as he pursues his own ethical inquiry.

# *Ultimate Moral Principles*

## *Kantianism*

In the general introduction to this part we indicated that most contemporary philosophers were either duty theorists or utilitarians. The most well-known duty theorist is Immanuel Kant. He accepted most of the popular moral rules of his day but wanted to place them on a secure foundation. But what could provide the basis for such a foundation? It couldn't be human wants, desires, and inclinations because they are notoriously individual; any agreement would be impossible. The only other candidate is human reason. Human reason, unlike human desires, is universal. All cultures agree that $2 + 2 = 4$ and the Russians and Americans both use the same principles to put rockets in space. Suppose you say it is permissible to tell a lie; then you must agree to say it is permissible for all others to lie in similar situations. But what would happen if it were permissible for everyone to lie? The use of language would be undermined. We would never know whether people were telling the truth or not, and, hence, the communication function of language would break down. Therefore, it is impossible to argue that it is permissible to lie, since a universalized practice of lying would undermine language that you need in order to lie in the first place. Note that this argument works in any culture. The argument applies universally.

This example provides the basis for Kant's fundamental moral principle which he calls the **categorical imperative:** "Act only according to that maxim which you can at the same time will that it should become a universal law." The maxim "it is permissible to lie" cannot for the reason shown become a universal law. Therefore, you ought not to lie.

Kant formulated another version of the categorical imperative. "Treat persons as ends and never as merely a means." In defense of his principle Kant asks the question, "How does anything come to be valued?" How do the Grand Canyon or a painting by Picasso get their value? The Grand Canyon, the painting, and everything else come to be valued because human beings bestow value on them. All these things have value with respect to us. However, because we are rational autonomous human beings, Kant argues that human beings have a special kind of value. Our value does not depend on anyone else.

But what gives human beings this special place? Why are human beings the only objects that have this special value? Is it just an accident of nature based on the fact that human beings have more power? That wouldn't be Kant's view. Rather, Kant appeals to reason. It is in our capacity as rational creatures that we bestow value on other creatures and that human beings have special value. Indeed Kant views human beings as a kind of ideal rational community (a **realm of ends**) whose members are both subject and sovereign at the same time. Persons are sovereign because they formulate the rules that apply to all, and they are subject because they should obey the rules made by themselves and others. However, because in the ideal rational community all rule making is rational, the rules are universal and hence we can be both subject and sovereign with respect to them. Again Kant's fundamental principles can be construed as analogous to fundamental principles in mathematics. The same fundamental moral rules hold for all rational moral beings just as the same mathematical principles hold for all mathematicians. It is just this capacity to legislate universal moral rules on the basis of reason that gives human beings their dignity. Human beings are special because we are capable of being moral agents.

It is this analysis of human reason that enables us to show how this version of the respect for persons principle, "Treat persons as ends and never as merely a means," avoids arbitrarily excluding anyone from the realm of persons. Like the ability to use mathematical reason, the ability to use moral reason does not depend on any other feature associated with being human—with height, weight, race, or sex. No subgroup of human beings can be excluded because all types of human beings share the capacity for moral thought.

Of course, Kant needs a theory of potential capacity and diminished capacity to make room for infants and the brain damaged. Moreover, Kant ignored people that today are classified as social psychopaths. According to his definition they wouldn't be persons because they are incapable of subjecting themselves to the moral law—they have no sense of right and wrong. And even here Kant may not be totally wrong: such creatures are considered human beings in a very diminished sense if they are considered human beings at all. A son who murders his mother, cuts her up, and puts her in the garbage can and feels no guilt or shame isn't considered human by a lot of people. A moral sensitivity and a capacity for reason are considered essential human characteristics and are not the sole property of any sex, race, or class. That is Kant's point.

Although most philosophers agree that Kant has something very important to say about moral philosophy, his work on ethics suffers from two distinct problems. First, his account of morality is certainly incomplete. The categorical imperative might provide a necessary test for determining whether an action is moral, but there is more to it than that. Second, there are objections to the categorical imperative itself.

As for the difficulties with the categorical imperative, one of the more vexing is how to handle exceptions. Lying is wrong, and one reason may be that if lying were universalized, lying would be self-defeating. But some lies are not wrong. Lying to save a life is not wrong, and if that stipulation were built into the rule, it would pass the test of the categorical imperative. Kant provided little help in telling us how narrowly or widely the rules governing actions are to be construed. If they are construed too widely, then the categorical imperative seems too flexible. Some individual lies are not immoral, even if the general practice of lying cannot be universalized. On the other hand, if you narrow the rule, by building in hundreds of exceptions, then you allow so many cases of lying that the categorical imperative is undermined.

Kant also expects one fundamental moral rule to do too much work. Consider any moral discussion involving trade-offs. I have a duty of loyalty to my employer and a duty of loyalty to my children. Often both demand more of me than I can give. How do I make that decision? The categorical imperative doesn't have anything to say in these types of cases. After all, any of a number of trade-offs would pass the test of the categorical imperative.

## *Utilitarianism*

Although utilitarian views were espoused throughout the early history of ethical theory, the classical utilitarian writings were those of Jeremy Bentham (1748–1832) and John Stuart Mill (1806–1873). Bentham provides an especially appropriate example because he came to his utilitarian views as a result of his unhappiness with the British legal system and the writings of its chief apologist, William Blackstone. Bentham thought the British system for classifying crimes was outdated, because it was based on an abstract moral theory concerning the gravity of offenses. As an alternative, Bentham suggested that crimes be classified according to the unhappiness and misery a crime caused to the victims and to society. His revisions in the classification scheme were intended to bring about revisions in views on how severely certain crimes should be punished. A utilitarian could argue, for example, that at best capital punishment is justified only for certain types of murder. To punish rape by death—a suggestion that is still heard today—would only encourage the rapist to kill the victim. Hence the death penalty for rape could not be justified on utilitarian grounds even if some deontological considerations might lead to the conclusion that the rapist deserved the death penalty. Similar considerations might lead the utilitarian to reduce the punishment for so-called "crimes of passion." Given the nature of "crimes of passion," extreme punishment for them has little deterrent effect. Whether the person who commits a crime of passion deserves an extreme punishment is an abstract theoretical issue that distorts the criminal justice system. By emphasizing the question of desert, it is easy to lose sight of the public welfare. On utilitarian grounds, the purpose for the criminal justice system is to make sure that crime does not pay; it is not the purpose of the criminal justice system to seek revenge.

With respect to the measurement of pleasure, Bentham developed a hedonic calculus. The quantitative measure of any pleasurable experience is reached by considering its intensity, duration, certainty, nearness, fecundity (its ability to produce additional pleasure), purity, and extent. Bentham's hedonic calculus provided a means for evaluating matters of policy and legislation. In facing a problem of what to do, for example, staying with your sick mother or joining the Resistance to fight the Nazis, make your decision on the basis of the greatest happiness. Use the hedonic calculus to get a quantitative figure for the happiness of all relevant individuals affected by your act. Then, after adding the happiness and subtracting the unhappiness for each alternative act, perform the act that produces the most happiness. However, Bentham's calculus was so imprecise that it never caught on—even among utilitarians.

What caused Bentham the most trouble was his hedonism—his view that pleasure was the sole good. Bentham's view that the only intrinsic good was pleasure received such ridicule that his philosophy was sometimes referred to as "pig philosophy." It received this name because on hedonistic grounds it seemed better to be a satisfied pig than a dissatisfied Socrates. Less pejoratively it seems that under hedonism the pleasures of artistic creation may be no better than, or even inferior to, the pleasures of wine, women, and song, so long as the pleasure of the latter is more than the former.

John Stuart Mill was particularly sensitive to the charge that utilitarianism was a pig philosophy. He believed that utilitarianism was consistent with the commonsense view that the life of a dissatisfied Socrates was better than the life of a satisfied pig. In the selection included in this section, Mill introduces distinctions among pleasures so that some pleasures are higher or better than others.

Having introduced the distinction between higher and lower pleasures, Mill could not appeal to the hedonic calculus even if he had wanted to. The calculus contained no way for determining which pleasures were higher. Mill's device was to consult a panel of experts whose members had had the experiences in question.

To those who might retort that such a panel of experts could not take the perspective of the pig, Mill argued that humans were qualitatively different animals. Humans have a higher capacity that prevents them from desiring a lower grade of existence even if they would be happier. Mill refers to this capacity as man's sense of **dignity.** This sense of dignity provides the ground for qualitative distinctions among pleasures.

## Immanuel Kant (1724–1804)

Immanuel Kant is almost universally recognized as one of the greatest philosophers in the Western tradition. He made major contributions to every branch of philosophy. Throughout his philosophy, Kant starts with human experience and attempts to show how certain principles of reason are necessary to give an account of that experience. For example, it is universally agreed that human beings have the ability to tell time. Suppose the clock strikes twelve o'clock. Because experience provides only the sensation of the strikes of the bell, the human mind must have the ability to hold those strikes together and apply the concept "twelve" to the set of them. Otherwise, human beings couldn't keep time.

Kant uses the same strategy in ethical theory. In this selection Kant tries to show how the practice of making false promises or failing to assist others would be self-defeating. Given this analysis Kant is able to provide a principle he calls "the categorical imperative" which any proposed action would have to pass if it were to be morally permissible. He also tries to show how the principle of consistency makes the moral principle of respect for persons a requirement of reason. Finally, Kant explains how an ethics based on reason would enable us to be a moral community where we can both subject others to the moral rules we make and be subject to the moral rules they make.

# The Rational Foundation of Ethics

### Immanuel Kant

### A. THE FUNDAMENTAL PRINCIPLE OF ETHICS

Everything in nature works according to laws. Only a rational being has the capacity of acting according to the conception of laws, i.e., according to principles. This capacity is will. . . . The conception of an objective principle, so far as it constrains a will, is a command (of reason), and the formula of this command is called an *imperative*.

All imperatives are expressed by an "ought" and thereby indicate the relation of an objective law of reason to a will which is not in its subjective constitution necessarily determined by this law. This relation is that of constraint. Imperatives say that it would be good to do or to refrain from doing something, but they say it to a will which does not always do something simply because it is presented as a good thing to do. Practical good is what determines the will by means of the conception of reason and hence not by subjective causes but, rather, objectively, i.e., on grounds which are valid for every rational being as such. . . .

All imperatives command either hypothetically or categorically. The former present the practical necessity of a possible action as a means to achieving something else which one desires

Abridged from and reprinted with permission of the publisher, ITT Bobbs-Merrill Educational Publishing Company, Inc. Kant, *Foundations of the Metaphysics of Morals and What is Enlightenment.* 

(or which one may possibly desire). The **categorical imperative** would be one which presented an action as of itself objectively necessary, without regard to any other end.

Since every practical law presents a possible action as good and thus as necessary for a subject practically determinable by reason, all imperatives are formulas of the determination of action which is necessary by the principle of a will which is in any way good. If the action is good only as a means to something else, the imperative is **hypothetical;** but if it is thought of as good in itself, and hence as necessary in a will which of itself conforms to reason as the principle of this will, the imperative is categorical. . . . It concerns not the material of the action and its intended result but the form and the principle from which it results. What is essentially good in it consists in the intention, the result being what it may. This imperative may be called the imperative of morality. . . . For instance, when it is said, "Thou shalt not make a false promise," we assume that the necessity of this avoidance is not a mere counsel for the sake of escaping some other evil, so that it would read, "Thou shalt not make a false promise so that, if it comes to light, thou ruinest thy credit"; we assume rather that an action of this kind must be regarded as of itself bad and that the imperative of the prohibition is categorical. . . .

There is . . . only one categorical imperative. It is: Act only according to that maxim by which you can at the same time will that it should become a universal law.

Now if all imperatives of duty can be derived from this one imperative as a principle, we can at least show what we understand by the concept of duty and what it means, even though it remain undecided whether that which is called duty is an empty concept or not.

The universality of law according to which effects are produced constitutes what is properly called nature in the most general sense (as to form), i.e., the existence of things so far as it is determined by universal laws. [By analogy], then, the universal imperative of duty can be expressed as follows: Act as though the maxim of your action were by your will to become a universal law of nature.

We shall now enumerate some duties, adopting the usual division of them into duties to ourselves and to others and into perfect and imperfect duties.

1. A man who is reduced to despair by a series of evils feels a weariness with life but is still in possession of his reason sufficiently to ask whether it would not be contrary to his duty to himself to take his own life. Now he asks whether the maxim of his action could become a universal law of nature. His maxim, however, is: For love of myself, I make it my principle to shorten my life when by a longer duration it threatens more evil than satisfaction. But it is questionable whether this principle of self-love could become a universal law of nature. One immediately sees a contradiction in a system of nature whose law would be to destroy life by the feeling whose special office is to impel the improvement of life. In this case it would not exist as nature; hence that maxim cannot obtain as a law of nature, and thus it wholly contradicts the supreme principle of all duty.

2. Another man finds himself forced by need to borrow money. He well knows that he will not be able to repay it, but he also sees that nothing will be loaned him if he does not firmly promise to repay it at a certain time. He desires to make such a promise, but he has enough conscience to ask himself whether it is not improper and opposed to duty to relieve his distress in such a way. Now, assuming he does decide to do so, the maxim of his action would be as follows: When I believe myself to be in need of money, I will borrow money and promise to repay it, although I know I shall never do so. Now this principle of self-love or of his own benefit may very well be compatible with his whole future welfare, but the question is whether it is right. He changes the pretension of self-love into a universal law and then puts the question: How would it be if my maxim became a universal law? He immediately sees that it could never hold as a universal law of nature and be consistent with itself; rather it must necessarily contradict itself. For the universality of a law which says that anyone who believes

himself to be in need could promise what he pleased with the intention of not fulfilling it would make the promise itself and the end to be accomplished by it impossible; no one would believe what was promised to him but would only laugh at any such assertion as vain pretense.

3. A third finds in himself a talent which could, by means of some cultivation, make him in many respects a useful man. But he finds himself in comfortable circumstances and prefers indulgence in pleasure to troubling himself with broadening and improving his fortunate natural gifts. Now, however, let him ask whether his maxim of neglecting gifts, besides agreeing with his propensity to idle amusement, agrees also with what is called duty. He sees that a system of nature could indeed exist in accordance with such a law, even though man (like the inhabitants of the South Sea Islands) should let his talents rust and resolve to devote his life merely to idleness, indulgence, and propagation—in a word, to pleasure. But he cannot possibly will that this should become a universal law of nature or that it should be implanted in us by a natural instinct. For, as a rational being, he necessarily wills that all his faculties should be developed, inasmuch as they are given to him for all sorts of possible purposes.

4. A fourth man, for whom things are going well, sees that others (whom he could help) have to struggle with great hardships, and he asks, "What concern of mine is it? Let each one be as happy as heaven wills, or as he can make himself; I will not take anything from him or even envy him; but to his welfare or to his assistance in time of need I have no desire to contribute." If such a way of thinking were a universal law of nature, certainly the human race could exist, and without doubt even better than in a state where everyone talks of sympathy and good will, or even exerts himself occasionally to practice them while, on the other hand, he cheats when he can and betrays or otherwise violates the rights of man. Now although it is possible that a universal law of nature according to that maxim could exist, it is nevertheless impossible to will that such a principle should hold everywhere as a law of nature. For a will which resolved this would conflict with itself, since instances can often arise in which he would need the love and sympathy of others, and in which he would have robbed himself, by such a law of nature springing from his own will, of all hope of the aid he desires.

The foregoing are a few of the many actual duties, or at least of duties we hold to be actual, whose derivation from the one stated principle is clear. We must be able to will that a maxim of our action become a universal law; this is the canon of the moral estimation of our action generally. Some actions are of such a nature that their maxim cannot even be *thought* as a universal law of nature without contradiction, far from it being possible that one could will that it should be such. In others this internal impossibility is not found, though it is still impossible to *will* that their maxim should be raised to the universality of a law of nature, because such a will would contradict itself. . . .

When we observe ourselves in any transgression of a duty, we find that we do not actually will that our maxim should become a universal law. That is impossible for us; rather, the contrary of this maxim should remain as a law generally, and we only take the liberty of making an exception to it for ourselves or for the sake of our inclination, and for this one occasion. Consequently, if we weighed everything from one and the same standpoint, namely, reason, we would come upon a contradiction in our own will, viz., that a certain principle is objectively necessary as a universal law and yet subjectively does not hold universally but rather admits exceptions. . . .

## B. PERSONS AS ENDS

. . . Now, I say, man and, in general, every rational being exists as an end in himself and not merely as a means to be arbitrarily used by this or that will. In all his actions, whether they are directed to himself or to other rational beings, he must always be regarded at the same time as an end. All objects of inclinations have only a conditional worth, for if the inclinations and the needs founded on them did not exist, their object would be without worth. The inclinations themselves as the sources of needs, however, are so lacking in absolute worth that the universal wish of every rational being must be indeed to free himself completely from them. Therefore, the worth of any objects to be obtained by our actions is at all times conditional. Beings whose existence does not depend on our will but on nature, if they are not rational beings, have only a relative worth as means and are therefore called "things"; on the other hand, rational beings are designated "persons" because their nature indicates that they are ends in themselves, i.e., things which may not be used merely as means. Such a being is thus an object of respect and, so far, restricts all [arbitrary] choice. Such beings are not merely subjective ends whose existence as a result of our action has a worth for us, but are objective ends, i.e., beings whose existence in itself is an end. Such an end is one for which no other end can be substituted, to which these beings should serve merely as means. For, without them, nothing of absolute worth could be found, and if all worth is conditional and thus contingent, no supreme practical principle for reason could be found anywhere.

Thus if there is to be a supreme practical principle and a categorical imperative for the human will, it must be one that forms an objective principle of the will from the conception of that which is necessarily an end for everyone because it is an end in itself. Hence this objective principle can serve as a universal practical law. The ground of this principle is: rational nature exists as an end in itself. Man necessarily thinks of his own existence in this way; thus far it is a subjective principle of human actions. Also every other rational being thinks of his existence by means of the same rational ground which holds also for myself; thus it is at the same time an objective principle from which, as a supreme practical ground, it must be possible to derive all laws of the will. The practical imperative, therefore, is the following: Act so that you treat humanity, whether in your own person or in that of another, always as an end and never as a means only. Let us now see whether this can be achieved.

To return to our previous examples:

First, according to the concept of necessary duty to one's self, he who contemplates suicide will ask himself whether his action can be consistent with the idea of humanity as an end in itself. If, in order to escape from burdensome circumstances, he destroys himself, he uses a person merely as a means to maintain a tolerable condition up to the end of life. Man, however, is not a thing, and thus not something to be used merely as a means; he must always be regarded in all his actions as an end in himself. Therefore, I cannot dispose of man in my own person so as to mutilate, corrupt, or kill him. (It belongs to ethics proper to define more accurately this basic principle so as to avoid all misunderstanding, e.g., as to the amputation of limbs in order to preserve myself, or to exposing my life to danger in order to save it; I must, therefore, omit them here.)

Second, as concerns necessary or obligatory duties to others, he who intends a deceitful promise to others sees immediately that he intends to use another man merely as a means, without the latter containing the end in himself at the same time. For he whom I want to use for my own purposes by means of such a promise cannot possibly assent to my mode of acting against him and cannot contain the end of this action in himself. This conflict against the principle of other men is even clearer if we cite examples of attacks on their freedom and property. For then it is clear that he who transgresses the rights of men intends to make use of the persons of others merely as a means, without considering that, as rational beings, they must always be esteemed at the same time as ends, i.e., only as beings who must be able to contain in themselves the end of the very same action.

Third, with regard to contingent (meritorious) duty to one's self, it is not sufficient that the action not conflict with humanity in our person as an end in itself; it must also harmonize with it. Now in humanity there are capacities for greater perfection which belong to the end of nature with respect to humanity in our own person; to neglect these might perhaps be consistent with the preservation of humanity as an end in itself but not with the furtherance of that end.

Fourth, with regard to meritorious duty to others, the natural end which all men have is their own happiness. Humanity might indeed exist if no one contributed to the happiness of others, provided he did not intentionally detract from it; but this harmony with humanity as an end in itself is only negative rather than positive if everyone does not also endeavor, so far as he can, to further the ends of others. For the ends of any person, who is an end in himself, must as far as possible also be my end, if that conception of an end in itself is to have its full effect on me.

This principle of humanity and of every rational creature as an end in itself is the supreme limiting condition on freedom of the actions of each man. It is not borrowed from experience, first, because of its universality, since it applies to all rational beings generally and experience does not suffice to determine anything about them; and, secondly, because in experience humanity is not thought of (subjectively) as the end of men, i.e., as an object which we of ourselves really make our end. Rather it is thought of as the objective end which should constitute the supreme limiting condition of all subjective ends, whatever they may be. Thus this principle must arise from pure reason. Objectively the ground of all practical legislation lies (according to the first principle) in the rule and in the form of universality, which makes it capable of being a law (at most a natural law); subjectively, it lies in the end. But the subject of all ends is every rational being as an end in itself (by the second principle); from this there follows the third practical principle of the will as the supreme condition of its harmony with universal practical reason, viz., the idea of the will of every rational being as making universal law.

By this principle all maxims are rejected which are not consistent with the universal lawgiving of will. The will is thus not only subject to the law but subject in such a way that it must be regarded also as self-legislative and only for this reason as being subject to the law (of which it can regard itself as the author). . . .

If we now look back upon all previous attempts which have ever been undertaken to discover the principle of morality, it is not to be wondered at that they all had to fail. Man was seen to be bound to laws by his duty, but it was not seen that he is subject only to his own, yet universal, legislation, and that he is only bound to act in accordance with his own will, which is, however, designed by nature to be a will giving universal laws. For if one thought of him as subject only to a law (whatever it may be), this necessarily implied some interest as a stimulus or compulsion to obedience because the law did not arise from his will. Rather, his will was constrained by something else according to a law to act in a certain way. By this strictly necessary consequence, however, all the labor of finding a supreme ground for duty was irrevocably lost, and one never arrived at duty but only at the necessity of action from a certain interest. This might be his own interest or that of another, but in either case the imperative always had to be conditional and could not at all serve as a moral command. This principle I will call the principle of *autonomy* of the will in contrast to all other principles which I accordingly count under ***heteronomy.***

The concept of each rational being as a being that must regard itself as giving universal law through all the maxims of its will, so that it may judge itself and its actions from this standpoint, leads to a very fruitful concept, namely, that of a ***realm of ends.***

By "realm" I understand the systematic union of different rational beings through common laws. Because laws determine ends with regard to their universal validity, if we abstract from the personal difference of rational beings and thus from all content of their private ends, we can think of a whole of all ends in systematic connection, a whole of rational beings as ends in themselves as well as of the particular ends which each may set for himself. This is a realm of ends, which is possible on the aforesaid principles. For all rational beings stand under the law that each of them should treat himself and all others never merely as means but in every case also as an end in himself. Thus there arises a systematic union of rational beings through common objective laws. This is a realm which may be called a realm of ends (certainly only an ideal), because what these laws have in view is just the relation of these beings to each other as ends and means.

A rational being belongs to the realm of ends as a member when he gives universal laws in it while also himself subject to these laws. He belongs to it as sovereign when he, as legislating, is subject to the will of no other. The rational being must regard himself always as legislative in a realm of ends possible through the freedom of the will, whether he belongs to it as member or as sovereign. He cannot maintain the latter position merely through the maxims of his will but only when he is a completely independent being without need and with power adequate to his will.

Morality, therefore, consists in the relation of every action to that legislation through which alone a realm of ends is possible. This legislation, however, must be found in every rational being. It must be able to arise from his will, whose principle then is to take no action according to any maxim which would be inconsistent with its being a universal law and thus to act only so that the will through its maxims could regard itself at the same time as universally lawgiving. If now the maxims do not by their nature already necessarily conform to this objective principle of rational beings as universally lawgiving, the necessity of acting according to that principle is called practical constraint, i.e., duty. Duty pertains not to the sovereign in the realm of ends, but rather to each member, and to each in the same degree.

The practical necessity of acting according to this principle, i.e., duty, does not rest at all on feelings, impulses, and inclinations; it rests merely on the relation of rational beings to one another, in which the will of a rational being must always be regarded as legislative, for otherwise it could not be thought of as an end in itself. Reason, therefore, relates every maxim of the will as giving universal laws to every other will and also to every action toward itself; it does so not for the sake of any other practical motive or future advantage but rather from the idea of the **dignity** of a rational being who obeys no law except that which he himself also gives.

In the realm of ends everything has either a *price* or a *dignity*. Whatever has a price can be replaced by something else as its equivalent; on the other hand, whatever is above all price, and therefore admits of no equivalent, has a dignity.

That which is related to general human inclinations and needs has a *market price*. That which, without presupposing any need, accords with a certain taste, i.e., with pleasure in the mere purposeless play of our faculties, has an *affective price*. But that which constitutes the condition under which alone something can be an end in itself does not have mere relative worth, i.e., a price, but an intrinsic worth, i.e., *dignity*.

Now morality is the condition under which alone a rational being can be an end in itself, because only through it is it possible to be a legislative member in the realm of ends. Thus morality and humanity, so far as it is capable of morality, alone have dignity. Skill and diligence in work have a market value; wit, lively imagination, and humor have an affective price; but fidelity in promises and benevolence on principle (not from instinct) have intrinsic worth. . . .

And what is it that justifies the morally good disposition or virtue in making such lofty claims? It is nothing less than the participation it affords the rational being in giving universal laws. He is thus fitted to be a member in a possible realm of ends to which his own nature already destined him. For, as an end in himself, he is destined to be legislative in the realm of ends, free from all laws of nature and obedient only to those which he himself gives. Accordingly, his maxims can belong to a universal legislation to which he is at the same time also subject. A thing has no worth other than that determined for it by the law. The legislation which determines all worth must therefore have a dignity, i.e., unconditional and incomparable worth. For the esteem which a rational being must have for it, only the word "respect" is a suitable expression. Autonomy is thus the basis of the dignity of both human nature and every rational nature. . . .

From what has just been said, it can easily be explained how it happens that, although in the concept of duty we think of subjection to law, we do nevertheless ascribe a certain sublimity and dignity to the person who fulfills all his duties. For though there is no sublimity in him in so far as he is subject to the moral law, yet he is sublime in so far as he is legislative with reference to the law and subject to it only for this reason. We have also shown above how neither fear of nor inclination to the law is the incentive which can give a moral worth to action; only respect for it can do so. Our own will, so far as it would act only under the condition of a universal legislation rendered possible by its maxims — this will, ideally possible for us, is the proper object of respect, and the dignity of humanity consists just in its capacity of giving universal laws, although with the condition that it is itself subject to this same legislation. . . .

## *John Stuart Mill (1806–1873)*

John Stuart Mill was another philosopher who made contributions to all areas of philosophy. He was both a child prodigy and the son of a demanding father who supervised a program of rigorous study. Although Mill was trained in law, his early works were in the philosophy of science. Mill formulated principles of inductive logic which he thought more useful than the Aristotelian principles of deductive logic.

In ethics, he attempted to defend the utilitarian theory of Bentham against the chorus of criticism that had arisen. In making that defense, Mill emphasized happiness rather than pleasure as the supreme good to be maximized — an important difference in connotation. He also replaced Bentham's hedonic calculus with a panel of experts. More important, many commentators think Mill shifted the strategy of utilitarianism from considering the consequences of individual actions to considering the consequences of practices. For example, the practice of free speech leads to good consequences even if every individual act of free speech doesn't. If these commentators are right, Mill was an early rule utilitarian. This selection concludes with Mill's discussion of the proof for utilitarianism.

# Utilitarianism

## *John Stuart Mill*

### I

. . . The creed which accepts as the foundation of morals, Utility, or the Greatest Happiness Principle, holds that actions are right in proportion as they tend to promote happiness, wrong as they tend to produce the reverse of happiness. By happiness is intended pleasure, and the absence of pain; by unhappiness, pain, and the privation of pleasure. To give a clear view of the moral

Abridged from *Utilitarianism,* by John Stuart Mill. Reprinted by permission of Longman Group Ltd., London.

standard set up by the theory, much more requires to be said; in particular, what things it includes in the ideas of pain and pleasure; and to what extent this is left an open question. But these supplementary explanations do not affect the theory of life on which this theory of morality is grounded—namely, that pleasure, and freedom from pain, are the only things desirable as ends; and that all desirable things (which are as numerous in the utilitarian as in any other scheme) are desirable either for the pleasure inherent in themselves, or as means to the promotion of pleasure and the prevention of pain.

Now, such a theory of life excites in many minds, and among them in some of the most estimable in feeling and purpose, inveterate dislike. To suppose that life has (as they express it) no higher end than pleasure—no better and nobler object of desire and pursuit—they designate as utterly mean and grovelling; as a doctrine worthy only of swine, to whom the followers of Epicurus were, at a very early period, contemptuously likened; and modern holders of the doctrine are occasionally made the subject of equally polite comparisons by its German, French, and English assailants.

When thus attacked, the Epicureans have always answered, that it is not they, but their accusers, who represent human nature in a degrading light; since the accusation supposes human beings to be capable of no pleasures except those of which swine are capable. If this supposition were true, the charge could not be gainsaid, but would then be no longer an imputation: for if the sources of pleasure were precisely the same to human beings and to swine, the rule of life which is good enough for the one would be good enough for the other. The comparison of the **Epicurean** life to that of beasts is felt as degrading, precisely because a beast's pleasures do not satisfy a human being's conception of happiness. Human beings have faculties more elevated than the animal appetites, and when once made conscious of them, do not regard anything as happiness which does not include their gratification. I do not, indeed, consider the Epicureans to have been by any means faultless in drawing out their scheme of consequences from the utilitarian principle. To do this in any sufficient manner, many Stoic, as well as Christian elements require to be included. But there is no known Epicurean theory of life which does not assign to the pleasures of the intellect, of the feelings and imagination, and of the moral sentiments, a much higher value as pleasures than to those of mere sensation. It must be admitted, however, that utilitarian writers in general have placed the superiority of mental over bodily pleasures chiefly in the greater permanency, safety, uncostliness, etc., of the former—that is, in their circumstantial advantages rather than in their intrinsic nature. And on all these points utilitarians have fully proved their case; but they might have taken the other, and, as it may be called, higher ground, with entire consistency. It is quite compatible with the principle of utility to recognize the fact, that some *kinds* of pleasure are more desirable and more valuable than others. It would be absurd that while, in estimating all other things, quality is considered as well as quantity, the estimation of pleasures should be supposed to depend on quantity alone.

If I am asked, what I mean by difference of quality in pleasures, or what makes one pleasure more valuable than another, merely as a pleasure, except its being greater in amount, there is but one possible answer. Of two pleasures, if there be one to which all or almost all who have experience of both give a decided preference, irrespective of any feeling of moral obligation to prefer it, that is the more desirable pleasure. If one of the two is, by those who are competently acquainted with both, placed so far above the other that they prefer it, even though knowing it to be attended with a greater amount of discontent, and would not resign it for any quantity of the other pleasure which their nature is capable of, we are justified in ascribing to the preferred enjoyment a superiority in quality, so far outweighing quantity as to render it, in comparison, of small account.

Now it is an unquestionable fact that those who are equally acquainted with, and equally capable of appreciating and enjoying both, do give a most marked preference to the manner of existence which employs their higher faculties. Few human creatures would consent to be changed into any of the lower animals, for a promise of the fullest allowance of a beast's pleasures; no intelligent human being would consent to be a fool, no instructed person would be an ignoramus, no person of feeling and conscience would be selfish and base, even though they should be persuaded that the fool, the dunce, or the rascal is better satisfied with his lot than they are with theirs. They would not resign what they possess more than he, for the most complete satisfaction of all the desires which they have in common with him. If they ever fancy they would, it is only in cases of unhappiness so extreme, that to escape from it they would exchange their lot for almost any other, however undesirable in their own eyes. A being of higher faculties requires more to make him happy, is capable probably of more acute suffering, and is certainly accessible to it at more points, than one of an inferior type; but in spite of these liabilities, he can never really wish to sink into what he feels to be a lower grade of existence. . . . Whoever supposes that this preference takes place at a sacrifice of happiness —that the superior being, in anything like equal circumstances, is not happier than the inferior— confounds the two very different ideas, of happiness, and content. It is indisputable that the being whose capacities of enjoyment are low, has the greatest chance of having them fully satisfied; and a highly-endowed being will always feel that any happiness which he can look for, as the world is constituted, is imperfect. But he can learn to bear its imperfections, if they are at all bearable; and they will not make him envy the being who is indeed unconscious of the imperfections, but only because he feels not at all the good which those imperfections qualify. It is better to be a human being dissatisfied than a pig satisfied; better to be Socrates dissatisfied than a fool satisfied. And if the fool, or the pig, is of a different opinion, it is because they only know their own side of the question. The other party to the comparison knows both sides. . . .

From this verdict of the only competent judges, I apprehend there can be no appeal. On a question which is the best worth having of two pleasures, or which of two modes of existence is the most grateful to the feelings, apart from its moral attributes and from its consequences, the judgment of those who are qualified by knowledge of both, or, if they differ, that of the majority among them, must be admitted as final. And there needs be the less hesitation to accept this judgment respecting the quality of pleasures, since there is no other tribunal to be referred to even on the question of quantity. What means are there of determining which is the acutest of two pains, or the intensest of two pleasurable sensations, except the general suffrage of those who are familiar with both? Neither pains nor pleasures are homogeneous, and pain is always heterogeneous with pleasure. What is there to decide whether a particular pleasure is worth purchasing at the cost of a particular pain, except the feelings and judgment of the experienced? . . .

## II

It has already been remarked, that questions of ultimate ends do not admit of proof, in the ordinary acceptation of the term. To be incapable of proof by reasoning is common to all first principles; to the first premises of our knowledge, as well as to those of our conduct. But the former, being matters of fact, may be the subject of a direct appeal to the faculties which judge of fact —namely, our senses, and our internal consciousness. Can an appeal be made to the same faculties on questions of practical ends? Or by what other faculty is cognizance taken of them?

Questions about ends are, in other words, questions [about] what things are desirable. The utilitarian doctrine is, that happiness is desirable, and the only thing desirable, as an end; all other things being only desirable as means to that end. What ought to be required of this doctrine— what conditions is it requisite that the doctrine should fulfil—to make good its claim to be believed?

The only proof capable of being given that an object is visible, is that people actually see it. The only proof that a sound is audible, is that people hear it: and so of the other sources of our experience. In like manner, I apprehend, the sole evidence it is possible to produce that anything is desirable, is that people do actually desire it. If the end which the utilitarian doctrine proposes to itself were not, in theory and in practice, acknowledged to be an end, nothing could ever convince any person that it was so. No reason can be given why the general happiness is desirable, except that each person, so far as he believes it to be attainable, desires his own happiness. This, however, being a fact, we have not only all the proof which the case admits of, but all which it is possible to require, [that] happiness is a good: that each person's happiness is a good to that person, and the general happiness, therefore, a good to the aggregate of all persons. Happiness has made out its title as *one* of the ends of conduct, and consequently one of the criteria of morality.

But it has not, by this alone, proved itself to be the sole criterion. To do that, it would seem, by the same rule, necessary to show, not only that people desire happiness, but that they never desire anything else. Now it is palpable that they do desire things which, in common language, are decidedly distinguished from happiness. They desire, for example, virtue, and the absence of vice, no less really than pleasure and the absence of pain. The desire of virtue is not as universal, but it is as authentic a fact, as the desire of happiness. And hence the opponents of the utilitarian standard deem that they have a right to infer that there are other ends of human action besides happiness, and that happiness is not the standard of approbation and disapprobation.

But does the utilitarian doctrine deny that people desire virtue or maintain that virtue is not a thing to be desired? the very reverse. . . . The ingredients of happiness are very various, and each of them is desirable in itself, and not merely when considered as swelling an aggregate. The principle of utility does not mean that any given pleasure, as music, for instance, or any given exemption from pain, as for example, health, are to be looked upon as means to a collective something termed happiness, and to be desired on that account. They are desired and desirable in and for themselves; besides being means, they are a part of the end. Virtue, according to the utilitarian doctrine, is not naturally and originally part of the end, but it is capable of becoming so; and in those who love it disinterestedly it has become so, and is desired and cherished, not as a means to happiness, but as a part of their happiness.

To illustrate this farther, we may remember that virtue is not the only thing, originally a means, and which if it were not a means to anything else, would be and remain indifferent, but which by association with what it is a means to, comes to be desired for itself, and that too with the utmost intensity. What, for example, shall we say of the love of money? There is nothing originally more desirable about money than about any heap of glittering pebbles. Its worth is solely that of the things which it will buy; the desires for other things than itself, which it is a means of gratifying. Yet the love of money is not only one of the strongest moving forces of human life, but money is, in many cases, desired in and for itself; the desire to possess it is often stronger than the desire to use it, and goes on increasing when all the desires which point to ends beyond it, to be compassed by it, are falling off. It may then be said truly, that money is desired not for the sake of an end, but as part of the end. From being a means to happiness, it has come to be itself a principal ingredient of the individual's conception of happiness. The same may be said of the majority of the great objects of human life—power, for example, or fame; except that to each of these there is a certain amount of immediate pleasure annexed, which has at least the semblance of being naturally inherent in them; a thing which cannot be said of money. Still, however, the strongest natural attraction, both of power and fame, is the immense aid they give to the attainment of our other wishes; and it is the strong association thus generated between them and all our objects of desire, which gives to the direct desire of them the intensity it often assumes, so as in some characters to surpass in strength all other desires. In these cases the means have become a part of the end, and a more important part of it than any of the things which they are means to. What was once desired as an instrument for the attainment of happiness, has come to be desired for its own sake. In being desired for its own sake it is, however, desired as *part* of happiness. The person is made, or thinks he would be made, happy by its mere possession; and is made unhappy by failure to obtain it. The desire of it is not a different thing from the desire of happiness, any more than the love of music, or the desire of health. They are included in happiness. They are some of the elements of which the desire of happiness is made up. Happiness is not an abstract idea, but a concrete whole; and these are some of its parts. And the utilitarian standard sanctions and approves their being so. Life would be a poor thing, very ill provided with sources of happiness, if there were not this provision of nature, by which things originally indifferent, but conducive to, or otherwise associated with, the satisfaction of our primitive desires, become in themselves sources of pleasure more valuable than the primitive pleasures, both in permanency, in the space of human existence that they are capable of covering, and even in intensity.

Virtue, according to the utilitarian conception, is a good of this description. There was no original desire of it, or motive to it, save its conduciveness to pleasure, and especially to protection from pain. But through the association thus formed, it may be felt a good in itself, and desired as such with as great intensity as any other good; and with this difference between it and the love of money, of power, or of fame, that all of these may, and often do, render the individual noxious to the other members of the society to which he belongs, whereas there is nothing which makes him so much a blessing to them as the cultivation of the disinterested love of virtue. And consequently, the utilitarian standard, while it tolerates and approves those other acquired desires, up to the point beyond which they would be more injurious to the general happiness than promotive of it, enjoins and requires the cultivation of the love of virtue up to the greatest strength possible, as being above all things important to the general happiness.

It results from the preceding considerations, that there is in reality nothing desired except happiness. Whatever is desired otherwise than as a means to some end beyond itself, and ultimately to happiness, is desired as itself a part of happiness, and is not desired for itself until it has become so. Those who desire virtue for its own sake, desire it either because the consciousness of it is a pleasure, or because the consciousness of being without it is a pain, or for both reasons united; as in truth the pleasure and pain seldom exist separately, but almost always together, the same person feeling pleasure in the degree of virtue attained, and pain in not having attained more. If one of these gave him no pleasure, and the other no pain, he would not love or desire virtue, or would desire it only for the other benefits which it might produce to himself or to persons whom he cared for.

We have now, then, an answer to the question, of what sort of proof the principle of utility is susceptible. If the opinion, which I have now stated, is psychologically true — if human nature is so constituted as to desire nothing which is not either a part of happiness or a means of happiness, we can have no other proof, and we require no other, that these are the only things desirable. If so, happiness is the sole end of human action, and the promotion of it the test by which to judge of all human conduct; from whence it necessarily follows that it must be the criterion of morality, since a part is included in the whole.

And now to decide whether this is really so; whether mankind do desire nothing for itself but that which is a pleasure to them, or of which the absence is a pain; we have evidently arrived at a question of fact and experience, dependent, like all similar questions, upon evidence. It can only be determined by practised self-consciousness and self-observation, assisted by observation of others. I believe that these sources of evidence, impartially consulted, will declare that desiring a thing and finding it pleasant, aversion to it and thinking of it as painful, are phenomena entirely inseparable, or rather two parts of the same phenomenon; in strictness of language, two different modes of naming the same psychological fact: that to think of an object as desirable (unless for the sake of its consequences), and to think of it as pleasant, are one and the same thing; and that to desire anything, except in proportion as the idea of it is pleasant, is a physical and metaphysical impossibility. . . .

# The Moral Person

No discussion of ethics can ignore the moral agent—the person who makes the moral decisions. The utilitarians argue that *each* person should count in the calculations of good consequences. Kant grounded his categorical imperative in the rational autonomy of individual persons, and he insisted that *every* person was entitled to respect as a person.

Other philosophers have argued that to be treated as a full moral agent, a person must be conceived as having certain human rights. Some make this point by arguing that individuals are treated as full members of the human community only when they are conceived of as possessing rights. Moral agency, self-respect, and possessing rights are conceptually linked; you don't have one without the others. Others would make the weaker claim that a world without rights is a morally impoverished world.

What are rights? They are moral entitlements—moral claims we can make against other persons and against institutions. They usually invoke corresponding duties on the part of others—be they persons or institutions. American democracy was born in a time when ethics was dominated by a philosophy of rights.

> We hold these truths to be self-evident: that all men are endowed by their Creator with certain unalienable rights; that among these are life, liberty, and the pursuit of happiness.

Since Great Britain had allegedly denied these rights, the signers of the Declaration of Independence believed they had moral justification for rebelling. During the transition of the United States from a confederation to a federation, many individual states adopted the constitution on the condition that a series of amendments (now called the Bill of Rights) was enacted to protect individuals from the state. The Bill of Rights is a statement of the moral entitlements that individuals have against the state. In political philosophy the vocabulary of rights has long been in use.

But what kinds of rights are there and more specifically what rights do we have? Basically, rights have been divided into two classes, those created by societal agreement, for example, rights created by a collective bargaining agreement, and rights persons have independently of any societal agreement. These latter are called natural rights. The rights referred to in the Declaration of Independence are natural rights. They are the rights that individual persons have against all social institutions. Rather than being created by society, natural rights are entitlements that morally influence how social institutions ought to develop.

Let us take it as established that the concept of rights has a useful role to play in moral language. What rights do we have? The human rights that have received the most attention are the rights to liberty (freedom) and well-being.

If all persons do have rights to freedom and well-being, it becomes our moral duty to respect them. Traditionally, philosophers believed that respecting a person's right to liberty could simply be accomplished by leaving the person alone. To respect the right to well-being often required positive action, either directly or indirectly through the state. Some contemporary philosophers deny that there is any sharp distinction between these two kinds of rights. Nearly all philosophers agree, however, that a moral agent should respect the legitimate rights claims of other agents.

Whereas a theory of rights may tell us something about things to which a moral person is entitled, virtues are habits that moral persons should develop in order to carry out their obligations. A moral individual should develop the capacity for virtuous behavior. Until recently, talk about virtue was considered out of fashion. Perhaps the connotations of the word that linked it with sexual purity made reference to virtue especially out of place during the sexual revolution of the 1960s and 1970s. However, to abandon talk about the virtues is to ignore a central ingredient in the moral life. To behave morally one needs a set of attitudes and beliefs, a certain personality, and character. The person needs to possess virtues. Possessing virtue promotes both the quality of our ethical decisions and our ability to withstand temptation and act morally. The virtues enable us to overcome the phenomenon of weakness of will; they promote human cooperation, and, according to the contemporary philosopher Alasdair MacIntyre, they support those human practices and traditions that we need to make sense of our lives. A theory of virtue is required if we are to have a complete understanding of ethics.

## *Richard Wasserstrom (b. 1936)*

Richard Wasserstrom is a contemporary philosopher and lawyer who has taught both philosophy and law. He also served in 1963–64 as an attorney in the Civil Rights Division of the Department of Justice. He has written a book on jurisprudence, *The Judicial Decision* (1961), and has contributed numerous articles in contemporary moral problems.

Wasserstrom believes that a world without rights would be a greatly impoverished world. A person can't fully respect another person unless that person treats the other as a bearer of rights. People can't become complete moral persons unless they consider themselves rights' bearers. Wasserstrom also agrees that human beings have the human rights to liberty and well-being and that all human beings are equal with respect to these rights. Wasserstrom argues that freedom and well-being are the things we must have to develop our capabilities as human beings. Those things that are necessary for our development as human beings are the things to which we have human rights. What makes that right equal is the kind of argument used so effectively by Kant. That kind of argument contends there is no rational ground for simply preferring one person's well-being or liberty to another's. Simply preferring is arbitrary.

# Human Rights

## *Richard Wasserstrom*

### I

If there are any such things as human rights, they have certain important characteristics and functions just because rights themselves are valuable and distinctive moral "commodities." This is, I think, a point that is all too often overlooked whenever the concept of a right is treated as a largely uninteresting, derivative notion—one that can be taken into account in wholly satisfactory fashion through an explication of the concepts of duty and obligation.

Now, it is not my intention to argue that there can be rights for which there are no correlative

---

Abridged from "Rights, Human Rights, and Racial Discrimination," by Richard Wasserstrom in *The Journal of Philosophy*, Vol. LXI, No. 20, Oct. 29, 1964, pp. 628–41. Reprinted by permission of *The Journal of Philosophy* and Richard Wasserstrom. Footnotes renumbered.

duties, nor that there can be duties for which there are no correlative rights—although I think that there are, e.g., the duty to be kind to animals or the duty to be charitable. Instead, what I want to show is that there are important differences between rights and duties, and, in particular, that rights fulfill certain functions that neither duties (even correlative duties) nor any other moral or legal concepts can fulfill.

Perhaps the most obvious thing to be said about rights is that they are constitutive of the domain of entitlements. They help to define and serve to protect those things concerning which one can make a very special kind of claim—a claim of right. To claim or to acquire anything as a matter of right is crucially different from seeking or obtaining it as through the grant of a privilege, the receipt of a favor, or the presence of a permission. To have a right to something is, typically, to be entitled to receive or possess or enjoy it now, and to do so without securing the consent of another. As long as one has a right to anything, it is beyond the reach of another properly to withhold or deny it. In addition, to have a right is to be absolved from the obligation to weigh a variety of what would in other contexts be relevant considerations; it is to be entitled to the object of the right—at least *prima facie*—without any more ado. To have a right to anything is, in short, to have a very strong moral or legal claim upon it. It is the strongest kind of claim that there is.

Because this is so, it is apparent, as well, that the things to which one is entitled as a matter of right are not usually trivial or insignificant. The objects of rights are things that matter.

Another way to make what are perhaps some of the same points is to observe that rights provide special kinds of grounds or reasons for making moral judgments of at least two kinds. First, if a person has a right to something, he can properly cite that right as the *justification* for having acted in accordance with or in the exercise of that right. If a person has acted so as to exercise his right, he has, without more ado, acted rightly—at least *prima facie*. To exercise one's right is to act in a way that gives appreciable assurance of immunity from criticism. Such immunity is far less assured when one leaves the areas of rights and goes, say, to the realm of the permitted or the nonprohibited.

And second, just as exercising or standing upon one's rights by itself needs no defense, so invading or interfering with or denying another's rights is by itself appropriate ground for serious censure and rebuke. Here there is a difference in emphasis and import between the breach or neglect of a duty and the invasion of or interference with a right. For to focus upon duties and their breaches is to concentrate necessarily upon the person who has the duty; it is to invoke criteria by which to make moral assessments of his conduct. Rights, on the other hand, call attention to the injury inflicted; to the fact that the possessor of the right was adversely affected by the action. Furthermore, the invasion of a right constitutes, as such, a special and independent injury, whereas this is not the case with less stringent claims.

Finally, just because rights are those moral commodities which delineate the areas of entitlement, they have an additional important function: that of defining the respects in which one can reasonably entertain certain kinds of expectations. To live in a society in which there are rights and in which rights are generally respected is to live in a society in which the social environment has been made appreciably more predictable and secure. It is to be able to count on receiving and enjoying objects of value. Rights have, therefore, an obvious psychological, as well as moral, dimension and significance.

## II

If the above are some of the characteristics and characteristic functions of rights in general, what then can we say about human rights? More specifically, what is it for a right to be a human right, and what special role might human rights play?

Probably the simplest thing that might be said of a human right is that it is a right possessed by human beings. To talk about human rights would be to distinguish those rights which humans have from those which nonhuman entities, e.g., animals or corporations, might have.

It is certain that this is not what is generally meant by human rights. Rather than constituting the genus of all particular rights that humans have, human rights have almost always been deemed to be one species of these rights. If nothing else about the subject is clear, it is evident that one's particular legal rights, as well as some of one's moral rights, are not among one's human rights. If any right is a *human* right, it must, I believe, have at least four very general characteristics. First, it must be possessed by all human beings, as well as only by human beings. Second, because it is the same right that all human beings possess, it must be possessed equally by all human beings. Third, because human rights are possessed by all human beings, we can rule out as possible candidates any of those rights which one might have in virtue of occupying any particular status or relationship, such as that of parent, president, or promisee. And fourth, if there are any human rights, they have the additional characteristic of being assertable, in a manner of speaking, "against the whole world." That is to say, because they are rights that are not possessed in virtue of any contingent status or relationship, they are rights that can be claimed equally against any and every other human being.

Furthermore, to repeat, if there are any human *rights,* they also have certain characteristics as rights. Thus, if there are any human rights, these constitute the strongest of all moral claims that all men can assert. They serve to define and protect those things which all men are entitled to have and enjoy. They indicate those objects toward which and those areas within which every human being is entitled to act without securing further permission or assent. They function so as to put certain matters beyond the power of anyone else to grant or to deny. They provide every human being with a ready justification for acting in certain ways, and they provide each person with ready grounds upon which to condemn any interference or invasion. And they operate, as well, to induce well-founded confidence that the values or objects protected by them will be readily and predictably obtainable. If there are any human rights, they are powerful moral commodities.

Finally, it is, perhaps, desirable to observe that there are certain characteristics I have not ascribed to these rights. In particular, I have not said that human rights need have either of two features: absoluteness and self-evidence. . . . I have not said that human rights are absolute in the sense that there are no conditions under which they can properly be overridden, although I have asserted—what is quite different—that they are absolute in the sense that they are possessed equally without any special, additional qualification by all human beings.

Neither have I said (nor do I want to assert) that human rights are self-evident in any sense. Indeed, I want explicitly to deny that a special manner of knowing or a specific epistemology is needed for the development of a theory of human rights. I want to assert that there is much that can be said in defense or support of the claim that a particular right is a human right. And I want to insist, as well, that to adduce reasons for human rights is consistent with their character as human, or natural, rights. Nothing that I have said about human rights entails a contrary conclusion.

## III

To ask whether there are any human, or natural, rights is to pose a potentially misleading question. Rights of any kind, and particularly natural rights, are not like chairs or trees. One cannot simply look and see whether they are there. There are, though, at least two senses in which rights of all kinds can be said to exist. There is first the sense in which we can ask and answer the empirical question of whether in a given society there is intellectual or conceptual acknowledgment of the fact that persons or other entities have rights at all. We can ask, that is, whether the persons in that society "have" the concept of a right (or a human right), and whether they regard that concept as meaningfully applicable to persons or other entities in that society. And there is, secondly, the sense in which we can ask the question, to what extent, in a society that acknowledges the existence of rights, is there general respect for, protection of, or noninterference with the exercise of those rights.

These are not, though, the only two questions that can be asked. For we can also seek to establish whether any rights, and particularly human rights, ought to be both acknowledged and respected. I want now to begin to do this by considering the way in which an argument for human rights might be developed.

It is evident, I think, that almost any argument for the acknowledgment of any rights as human rights starts with the factual assertion that there are certain respects in which all persons are alike or equal. The argument moves typically from that assertion to the conclusion that there are certain human rights. What often remains unclear, however, is the precise way in which the truth of any proposition about the respects in which persons are alike advances an argument for the acknowledgment of human rights. And what must be supplied, therefore, are the plausible intermediate premises that connect the initial premise with the conclusion.

One of the most careful and complete illustrations of an argument that does indicate some of these intermediate steps is that provided by Gregory Vlastos in an article entitled, "Justice and Equality."[1] Our morality, he says, puts an equal intrinsic value on each person's well-being and freedom. In detail, the argument goes like this:

There is, Vlastos asserts, a wide variety of cases in which all persons are capable of experiencing the same values.

> Thus, to take a perfectly clear case, no matter how A and B might differ in taste and style of life, they would both crave relief from acute physical pain. In that case we would put the same value on giving this to either of them, regardless of the fact that A might be a talented, brilliantly successful person, B "a mere nobody". . . . [I]n all cases where human beings are capable of enjoying the same goods, we feel that the intrinsic value of their enjoyment is the same. In just this sense we hold that (1) *one man's well-being is as valuable as any other's.* . . . [Similarly] we feel that choosing for oneself what one will do, believe, approve, say, read, worship, has its own intrinsic value, the same for all persons, and quite independently of the value of the things they happen to choose. Naturally we hope that all of them will make the best possible use of their freedom of choice. But we value their exercise of the freedom, regardless of the outcome; and we value it equally for all. For us (2) *one man's freedom is as valuable as any other's.* . . . [Thus], since we do believe in equal value as to human well-being and freedom, we should also believe in the *prima facie* equality of men's *right* to well-being and to freedom (51–52).

As it is stated, I am not certain that this argument answers certain kinds of attack. In particular, there are three questions that merit further attention. First, why should anyone have a right to the enjoyment of any goods at all, and, more specifically, well-being and freedom? Second, for what reasons might we be warranted in believing that the intrinsic value of the enjoyment of such goods is the same for all persons? And third, even if someone ought to have a right to well-being and freedom and even if the intrinsic value of each person's enjoyment of these things is equal, why should all men have the equal right—and hence the human right—to secure, obtain, or enjoy these goods?

I think that the third question is the simplest of the three to answer. If anyone has a right to well-being and freedom and if the intrinsic value of any person's enjoyment of these goods is equal to that of any other's, then all men do have an equal right—and hence a human right—to secure, obtain, or enjoy these goods, just because it would be irrational to distinguish among persons as to the possession of these rights. That is to say, the principle that no person should be treated differently from any or all other persons unless there is some general and relevant reason that justifies this difference in treatment is a fundamental principle of morality, if not of rationality itself. Indeed, although I am not certain how one might argue for this, I think it could well be said that all men do have a "second-order" human right — that is, an absolute right — to expect all persons to adhere to this principle.

This principle, or this right, does not by itself establish that there are any specific human rights. But either the principle or the right does seem to establish that well-being and freedom are human rights if they are rights at all and if the intrinsic value of each person's enjoyment is the same. For, given these premises, it does appear to follow that there is no relevant and general reason to differentiate among persons as to the possession of this right.

I say "seem to" and "appear to" because this general principle of morality may not be strong enough. What has been said so far does not in any obvious fashion rule out the possibility that there is some general and relevant principle of differentiation. It only, apparently, rules out possible variations in intrinsic value as a reason for making differentiations.

The requirement of *relevance* does, I think, seem to make the argument secure. For, if *the reason* for acknowledging in a person a right to freedom and well-being is the intrinsic value of his enjoyment of these goods, then the nature of the intrinsic value of any other person's enjoyment is the only relevant reason for making exceptions or for differentiating among persons as to the possession of these rights.

As to the first question, that of whether a person has a right to well-being and freedom, I am not certain what kind of answer is most satisfactory. If Vlastos is correct in asserting that these enjoyments are *values,* then that is, perhaps, answer enough. That is to say, if enjoying well-being is something *valuable* — and especially if it is intrinsically valuable — then it seems to follow that this is the kind of thing to which one ought to have a right. For if anything ought to be given the kind of protection afforded by a right, it ought surely be that which is valuable. Perhaps, too, there is nothing more that need be said other than to point out that we simply do properly value well-being and freedom.

I think that another, more general answer is also possible. Here I would revert more specifically to my earlier discussion of some of the characteristics and functions of rights. There are two points to be made. First, if we are asked, why ought anyone have a right to anything? or why not have a system in which there are not rights at all? the answer is that such a system would be a morally impoverished one. It would prevent persons from asserting those kinds of claims, it would preclude persons from having those types of expectations, and it would prohibit persons from making those kinds of judgments which a system of rights makes possible.

Thus, if we can answer the question of why have rights at all, we can then ask and answer the question of what things — among others — ought to be protected by *rights.* And the answer, I take it, is that one ought to be able to claim as entitlements those minimal things without which it is impossible to develop one's capabilities and to live a life as a human being. Hence, to take one thing that is a precondition of well-being, the relief from acute physical pain, this is the kind of enjoyment that ought to be protected as a right of some kind just because without such relief there is precious little that one can effectively do or become. And similarly for the opportunity to make choices, examine beliefs, and the like.

To recapitulate. The discussion so far has indicated two things: (1) the conditions under which any specific right would be a human right, and (2) some possible grounds for arguing that certain values or enjoyments ought to be regarded as matters of right. The final question that remains is whether there are any specific rights that satisfy the conditions necessary to make them human rights. Or, more specifically, whether it is plausible to believe that there are no general and relevant principles that justify making distinctions among persons in respect to their rights to well-being and freedom.

Vlastos has it that the rights to well-being and freedom do satisfy these conditions, since he asserts that we, at least, do regard each person's well-being and freedom as having equal intrinsic value. If this is correct, if each person's well-being and freedom does have *equal* intrinsic value, then there is no general and relevant principle for differentiating among persons as to these values and, hence, as to their rights to secure these values. But this does not seem wholly satisfactory. It does not give us any reason for supposing that it is plausible to ascribe equal intrinsic value to each person's well-being and freedom.

The crucial question, then, is the plausibility of ascribing equal intrinsic value to each person's well-being and freedom. There are, I think, at least three different answers that might be given.

First, it might be asserted that this ascription simply constitutes another feature of our morality. The only things that can be done are to point out that this is an assumption that we do make and to ask persons whether they would not prefer to live in a society in which such an assumption is made.

While perhaps correct and persuasive, this does not seem to me to be all that can be done. In particular, there are, I think, two further arguments that may be made.

The first is that there are cases in which all human beings *equally* are capable of enjoying the same goods, e.g., relief from acute physical pain, or that they are capable of deriving equal enjoyment from the same goods. If this is true, then if anyone has a right to this enjoyment, that right is a human right just because there is no rational ground for preferring one man's enjoyment to another's. For, if all persons do have equal capacities of these sorts and if the existence of these capacities is the reason for ascribing these rights to anyone, then all persons ought to have the right to claim equality of treatment in respect to the possession and exercise of these rights.

The difficulty inherent in this argument is at the same time the strength of the next one. The difficulty is simply that it does seem extraordinarily difficult to know how one would show that all men are equally capable of enjoying any of the same goods, or even how one might attempt to gather or evaluate relevant evidence in this matter. In a real sense, interpersonal comparisons of such a thing as the ability to bear pain seems to be logically as well as empirically unobtainable. Even more unobtainable, no doubt, is a measure of the comparative enjoyments derivable from choosing for oneself. These are simply enjoyments the comparative worths of which, as different persons, there is no way to assess. If this is so, then this fact gives rise to an alternative argument.

We do know, through inspection of human history as well as of our own lives, that the denial of the opportunity to experience the enjoyment of these goods makes it impossible to live either a full or a satisfying life. In a real sense, the enjoyment of these goods differentiates human from nonhuman entities. And therefore, even if we have no meaningful or reliable criteria for comparing and weighing capabilities for enjoyment or for measuring their quantity or quality, we probably know all we need to know to justify our refusal to attempt to grade the value of the enjoyment of these goods. Hence, the dual grounds for treating their intrinsic values as equal for all persons: either these values are equal for all persons, or, if there are differences, they are not in principle discoverable or measurable. Hence, the argument, or an argument, for the human rights to well-being and freedom. . . .

## NOTE

1. In Richard B. Brandt, ed., *Social Justice* (Englewood Cliffs, N.J.: Prentice-Hall, 1962), pp. 31–72.

## *Aristotle (384–322 B.C.)*

We have already encountered the work of Aristotle. Aristotle's most substantial contributions to ethical theory are his account of happiness as the highest good and his account of virtue. Central to his account is his distinction between intellectual virtues and moral virtues. With respect to intellectual virtue, he identifies five ways that we can know something, and there is a corresponding intellectual virtue for each of these five ways of knowing. One of the chief characteristics distinguishing intellectual virtues from moral ones is the fact that moral virtues represent a mean between excess and deficiency; intellectual virtues do not have this characteristic. Intellectual virtues do not have excesses; you can't have too much wisdom.

More attention has been directed to Aristotle's account of the moral virtues. Some refer to Aristotle's theory of virtue as the theory of the Golden Mean. With respect to moral virtues, Aristotle's theory of virtue is corrective. Virtues are habits that enable us to avoid overdoing and underdoing. How do we correct the tendency to drink too much or to overeat? Develop the virtue of temperance. How do we get the strength to stand up for our rights? Develop the virtue of courage. Temperance is the mean between the excess *profligacy* and the deficiency *insensibility.* (Aristotle admits that you don't find many people with the vice of insensibility.) Courage is the mean between *cowardice* and *recklessness.* Aristotle works out in great detail the means, excesses, and deficiencies for all the moral virtues.

Plato posed the question as to whether virtue could be taught. Aristotle's answer to Plato's question was that whereas the intellectual virtues are taught, the moral virtues are in us potentially as a result of our human nature and are developed by habit. We become morally virtuous by practicing the moral virtues. Aristotle's advice is not empty. If you get used to being honest or courageous, then each subsequent act of honesty or courage is easier. That's why it is important to give children the opportunity to practice virtue. Presumably it is easier to be honest in the situations where honesty is less in danger of being compromised than when it is easy to compromise. Courage on the football field makes it easier to show courage on the battlefield.

In another work, *Politics,* Aristotle argued that we could become virtuous and truly happy only within the state. The isolated individual cannot become a full person.

# Virtue

## *Aristotle*

I

There are, then, two sorts of virtue: intellectual and moral. Intellectual virtue is mostly originated and promoted by teaching, which is why it needs experience and time. Moral virtue is produced by habit, which is why it is called "moral," a word only slightly different from our word for habit.

It is quite plain that none of the moral **virtues** is produced in us by nature, since none of the

Abridged from *The Philosophy of Aristotle.* Edited by Renford Bambrough, translated by J. L. Creed and A. E. Wardman.  Paragraphs renumbered.

things with natural properties can be trained to acquire a different property. For example, the stone, which has a natural downward motion, cannot be trained to move upwards, not even if one "trains" it by countless upward throws. Similarly, fire cannot be trained to move downwards. In general, none of the things with a given natural property can be trained to acquire another.

The virtues, then, are neither innate nor contrary to nature. They come to be because we are fitted by nature to receive them; but we perfect them by training or habit.

Further, in the case of all our natural faculties, we have them first potentially, but it is only later on that we make them fully active. This is clear in the case of the senses: we do not acquire our senses as a result of innumerable acts of seeing or hearing, but the opposite is the case. We have them, and then make use of them; we do not come to get them by making use of them. However, we do acquire the virtues by first making use of them in acts, as is also the case with techniques. Where doing or making is dependent on knowing how, we acquire the know-how by actually doing. For example, people become builders by actually building, and the same applies to lyre players. In the same way, we become just by doing just acts; and similarly with "temperate" and "brave." There is further evidence in contemporary institutions: legislators make citizens good by training them. Indeed, all legislators aim at that, and those who do it incorrectly miss their objective. That is the point of difference between the institutions of a good and of a bad community. . . .

## II

Since the present inquiry is not "theoretical" like the rest—we are not studying in order to know what virtue is, but to become good, for otherwise there would be no profit in it—we must consider the question of how we ought to act. Action is lord and master of the kind of resulting disposition, as we said. Action should be in accordance with right reason; that is true of all actions, and it will serve as our basis. (We shall define right reason later on, and state its relation to the other virtues.) Before going on, it must be agreed that all our statements about action have to be general, not exact. The point is, as we said at the start, that the type of answer turns upon the kind of subject matter, and matters dealing with action and questions of expediency are always changing like the circumstances that promote health. Since this is true in general, it is still truer to say that answers about particular issues cannot be exact. These issues cannot be dealt with by a single technique or a set of rules; those who are engaged in action must study the special circumstances, as in the case of medicine and navigation.

But although the present discussion is of this type, we must try to help. Let us consider this first: it is in the nature of things for the virtues to be destroyed by excess and deficiency, as we see in the case of health and strength—a good example, for we must use clear cases when discussing abstruse matters. Excessive or insufficient training destroys strength, just as too much or too little food and drink ruins health. The right amount, however, brings health and preserves it. So this applies to moderation, bravery, and the other virtues. The man who runs away from everything in fear, and faces up to nothing, becomes a coward; the man who is absolutely fearless, and will walk into anything, becomes rash. It is the same with the man who gets enjoyment from all pleasures, abstaining from none: he is immoderate; whereas he who avoids all pleasures, like a boor, is a man of no sensitivity. Moderation and bravery are destroyed by excess and deficiency, but are kept flourishing by the mean. . . .

## III

Now, we must consider what virtue is. There are three things in the soul: emotions, capacities, and dispositions. Virtue must be one of these.

By emotions I mean appetite, anger, fear, confidence, envy, joy, friendliness, hatred, desire, emulation, pity — in short, everything that is accompanied by pleasure and pain.

By capacities I mean our ability to experience the emotions — for instance, the capacity of feeling anger, pain, and pity.

Disposition describes how we react — well or badly — toward the emotions, e.g., feeling anger. If the reaction is either excessive or insufficient, we are bad; if moderate, good; and so with other feelings.

Neither the virtues nor the vices are emotions. It is not our emotions that decide whether we are called good or bad, but our virtues and vices. We are not praised or blamed for our emotions (men are not praised for feeling fear or anger, nor does feeling anger as such get blamed, but feeling anger in a certain way), whereas we are for our virtues and vices. Another point: we feel anger and fear without choosing to, whereas the virtues are a sort of choice, or at least not possible without choice. In addition, the emotions are said to "move" us whereas in respect to the virtues and vices, we are said not to be moved, but to be in a certain state.

For this reason, the virtues are not capacities either. We are not called good or bad merely because we have a capacity for feeling, nor are we praised or blamed for that reason. Also, we have capacities by nature, but we are not good or bad by nature. . . . If, therefore, virtue is neither emotion nor capacity, it must, by elimination, be disposition. This is a statement as to the generic meaning of virtue.

We must not leave it at that — just "disposition"; we must also say what kind. It should be said that all virtue, whatever it belongs to, renders that thing good and makes it function well. The virtue of the eye makes the eye good and makes it function well, since it is by the virtue of the eye that we have good sight. Similarly, the virtue or excellence of a horse makes the horse good, good at running and at carrying its rider and at facing the enemy. Now, if this is always the case, the virtue of man will be the disposition through which he becomes a good man and through which he will do his job well. How that will come about, we have already said, but it will be still clearer if we examine the nature of this virtue.

Of every continuous — that is, divisible thing — one can take more or less or the equal amount; and these divisions can be made either by reference to the thing itself as standard, or relatively to us. Equal is the mean between excess and deficiency. What is the mean relative to the thing? It is that which is equidistant from each end, which is one and the same for all. The mean relative to us is that which is neither too much nor too little; and this is not one and the same for all. If ten is a lot and two a little, then six is the mean relative to the thing: six exceeds two by the same amount that it is exceeded by ten; it is the mean by proportion. The mean relative to us should not be interpreted like that. If ten pounds are a lot for a man to eat, whereas two are too little, the trainer will not order six. Perhaps that will be too much or too little for the particular man: too little for Milo, but too much for the man who is just starting to train. Similarly with running and wrestling.

In this same way, everyone who knows, in any field, avoids excess and deficiency; he looks for the mean and chooses the mean, not the mean according to the thing, but the mean relative to us. Every art does its job well in this way, by looking to the mean and leading its products toward it — which is why people say of things well done that you cannot add anything or take anything away, since "well done" is ruined by excess and deficiency and achieved by the mean; and good craftsmen, as we were saying, work with their eye on the mean. To resume: if virtue, like nature, requires more accuracy and is better than any art, then it will aim at the mean. I speak here of moral virtue, since that is concerned with emotions and actions; and excess, deficiency, and the mean occur in these. In feeling fear, confidence, desire, anger, pity, and in general pleasure and pain, one can feel too much or too little; and both extremes are wrong. The mean and the good is feeling at the right time, about the right things, in relation to the right people, and for the right reason; and the mean and the good are the task of virtue. Similarly, in regard to actions, there are excess, deficiency, and the mean.

Virtue is concerned with emotions and actions, where excess is wrong, as is deficiency, but the mean is praised and is right. Both being praised and being right belong to virtue. So virtue is a kind of mean, since it does at least aim at the mean. Also, going wrong happens in many ways (for bad belongs to the unlimited . . . and good to the limited), whereas doing right happens in one way only. That is why one is easy, the other difficult: missing the target is easy, but hitting it is hard. For these reasons, excess and deficiency belong to evil, the mean to good:

"There is only one kind of good man, but many kinds of bad."

Virtue, then, is a disposition involving choice. It consists in a mean, relative to us, defined by reason and as the reasonable man would define it. It is a mean between two vices—one of excess, the other of deficiency. Also, virtue discovers and chooses the mean, whereas the vices exceed or fall short of the essential, in the spheres of both emotions and acts. . . .

## IV

We must not only put this in general terms but also apply it to particular cases. In statements concerning acts, general statements cover more ground, but statements on a specified point are more accurate. Acts are concerned with particulars, after all; and theory should agree with particular facts. Let us, then, take these particular virtues from our table. . . .

Now, courage is the mean in matters of fearing and feeling brave. The man who exceeds in fearlessness has no special name (there are many vices and virtues that have no names). He who exceeds in confidence is overconfident, whereas the man who exceeds in feeling fear and falls short in confidence is a coward.

Concerning pleasures and pains (not all are involved, and indeed pains are less so), the mean is temperance, and the excess profligacy. As for falling short in connection with pleasures, there are hardly any such people, and that is why they, too (compare the instances above), do not have a name. But let us call them "insensible."

As regards giving and taking money, the mean is liberality, whereas the excess and the deficiency are, in order, spendthriftness and illiberality. In this case, excess and deficiency work in opposite ways. The spendthrift exceeds in spending and falls short in taking, whereas the illiberal man exceeds in taking and falls short in spending. . . .

As for honor and dishonor, the mean is grandeur of soul, whereas the excess is a sort of vanity, and the deficiency meanness of soul. We said above that liberality differs from magnificence in the minor scale of its operation. Similarly, there is a minor virtue related to grandeur of soul; whereas the latter has great honor as its object, this one is concerned with small honors. It is possible to strive for honor in the right way, and also more or less than one should: he who strives too much is called ambitious, he who falls short unambitious, and the man in the middle has no name. There are no names for the dispositions, except for ambition—which is why the extremes lay claim to the middle territory, so that there are times when we call the mean "ambitious" and other times when we call it "unambitious"; and sometimes we praise the one, at other times the other. Why we do this will be explained later; but now let us speak about the rest of the dispositions in the manner indicated.

In connection with anger also, there are excess, deficiency, and the mean, although they have no established names. But let us call the middle man good-tempered and speak of the mean as good temper. Now for the extremes: he who exceeds is quick tempered, and the corresponding vice is quick temper; but the man who falls short is without temper, and the deficiency is an absence of temper.

There are also three other means. They have a certain resemblance to one another, but they do differ. All are concerned with human relations in word and action. The difference, however, is that one is concerned with truth, the others with pleasure, pleasure being here of two sorts, one in the sphere of amusement, the other in all matters that have to do with life.

We must discuss these, too, to see more clearly that the mean is always praiseworthy, and the extremes neither praiseworthy nor right, but blameworthy. Most of these, too, have no name, but we must try to coin names for them, as we did before, for the sake of clarity and ease of understanding.

Let us take truth. The man who exemplifies the mean is the truthful man, and the mean should be called truthfulness; pretence of this virtue by way of excess in boastfulness, and the corresponding man boastful; but pretence by way of deficiency is false modesty.

Now, for pleasure by way of amusement. The middle man is the wit, and his disposition wittiness; the excess is buffoonery, and the man a buffoon; the deficiency is boorishness, and the man a boor. As for the other sorts of pleasure in life, the man who pleases in the right way is a friend, and the mean is friendship. The man who exceeds this, if he does so for no ulterior motive, is obsequious, but if it is for his own advantage, he is a flatterer. He who falls short and never gives pleasure is quarrelsome and a surly fellow.

There are means, too, in the sphere of the feelings. Shame is not a virtue, but the man who is modest is praised. In this case, too, we speak of the mean (the man mentioned above) and of the excess: the man who feels shame about everything is cowed, whereas the man who falls short, or feels no shame at all, is shameless. The mean, again, is the man who is modest.

Indignation is the mean between envy and malice. These concern the pleasure and pain experienced over what happens to neighbors. The indignant man feels pain when people prosper without deserving to; the envious man, who exceeds the former, feels pain at all good fortune; whereas the malicious man, so far from feeling pain, actually feels pleasure. . . .

V

Now that we have discussed things having to do with the virtues . . . our last task is to give an outline account of happiness, since that is what we make the goal of human activity. If we sum up what we said before, the argument will be shorter.

We said that it was not a disposition: if it were, it could be present in a man who slept out his whole life, living like a vegetable, or who had very great misfortune. If this is unacceptable, we must count it as an activity, as we said before. But some activities are necessary means and to be chosen for the sake of something else, others are chosen for their own sake. Clearly, happiness is one of these activities that are chosen for their own sake, and not for the sake of something else, since happiness is self-sufficient and needs nothing else to complete it. Activities chosen for their own sake are those from which nothing is sought apart from the activity itself. These would appear to be acts in accordance with virtue, since doing fine, good acts is something to be chosen for its own sake. So, too, are those amusements that are pleasant, since people do not choose them for the sake of other things. People are harmed by them rather than helped, since they are led to neglect their persons and their property. . . .

If happiness is activity in accordance with virtue, then it must be the best activity, i.e., that of the best in man. Whether it is mind or something else that seems naturally to rule and to lead, and to take notice of good and divine things—whether it is itself divine, or the most divine thing in man—the activity of this in accordance with its own proper virtue will be complete happiness. We have said that this is contemplation, which appears to agree both with our former arguments and with the truth. This is the best activity (mind is the best in us; and "intelligible" things, which are apprehended by the mind, are the best objects in the known world), and also the most continuous. We are better able to contemplate continuously than to *do* anything.

We think it essential that pleasure should be

mixed in with happiness, and the most pleasant of activities in accordance with virtue is admittedly activity in accordance with wisdom. Philosophy has pleasures that are marvelous for their purity and permanence. Besides, it is likely that those who have knowledge have a more pleasant life than those who are seeking it. Sufficiency, as people call it, will be associated above all with contemplation. The wise man, the just, and all the rest of them need the necessities of life; further, once there is an adequate supply of these, the just man needs people with and towards whom he may perform just acts; and the same applies to the temperate man, the brave man, and so on. But the wise man is able to contemplate, even when he is on his own; and the more so, the wiser he is. It is better, perhaps, when he has people working with him; but still he is the most self-sufficient of all.

Contemplation, alone, seems to be admired for its own sake. Nothing comes from it apart from contemplating; whereas, in matters of action, we hope for something more or less apart from the action. Happiness appears to depend on leisure: we work in order to have leisure; and we make war in order to have peace. Now, the activity of the practical virtues is exercised in war and politics; and actions concerned with these are full of work — in the case of war, absolutely so. No one chooses war for the sake of war, or precipitates war with that end in mind; he would seem to be an utter butcher if he turned his friends into enemies just to produce battles and slaughter. However, the politician's life is also full of work. Apart from just carrying on politics, politicians aim at power and honor or even happiness for themselves and for the citizens — a happiness that is different from political activity. . . .

Now, political and military activity stand high for nobility and grandeur among the activities carried on in accordance with virtue. However, they are laborious; they aim at an end; and they are not chosen for their own sake. But the activity of the mind — contemplation — seems to be outstanding in its seriousness, and it has no goal apart from itself. It has its own pleasure (which increases the activity), and it also has sufficiency; and it is leisurely and unlaborious (so far as these are possible for man). All the attributes of the blessed man seem to be present in this activity; this will be complete human happiness — if a complete lifetime is involved, for there is nothing incomplete in the case of happiness.

Such a life would be more than human. A man will not live like that by virtue of his humanness, but by virtue of some divine thing within him. His activity is as superior to the activity of the other virtues as this divine thing is to his composite character. Now, if mind is divine in comparison with man, the life of the mind is divine in comparison with mere human life. We should not follow popular advice and, being human, have only human ambitions or, being mortal, have only mortal thoughts. As far as is possible, we should become immortal and do everything toward living by the best that is in us. Even if it is small in bulk, in power and value it is far above everything.

It may be thought that each individual is really this, since this is the master-part, the best thing in man. It is absurd to choose not one's own life, but the life proper to something else. What we said before applies now. What is by nature proper to a thing is best and most pleasant for that thing. The life of reason will be best for man, then, if reason is what is truly man. That sort of man, then, will be the happiest. . . .

## VI

If we have given an adequate general outline of this topic . . . , should we consider that our proposed investigation is now complete? Or, as is said, since the end in matters of action is not contemplating and knowing each thing, but rather doing it, is it insufficient just to know about virtue? Should we not try to have and use it or, in whatever other way, to become good? If arguments were in themselves sufficient for making people good, they would have earned many high rewards, . . . and all that would have been necessary would be merely to supply such arguments. But, as things are, although arguments appear to have the power to encourage and stimulate liberal young people and to render a noble character — one that truly loves good — susceptible to virtue, they are nevertheless unable to turn the mass of the people toward goodness. Their nature is to obey by fear, rather than by right shame; and they do not abstain from the bad because it is wrong, but because of the possible punishment. They live by emotion and pursue those pleasures that are related to emotion, and the means to these pleasures. They avoid the opposite pains, and have no idea of the good or the really pleasant, for they have not tasted them.

What argument would change the character of such people? It is not possible, or at least it is not easy, to change by argument practices long since settled by habit. Perhaps we must be content if we get virtue to some extent even when we have at hand *all* the means whereby we are thought to attain goodness.

Some think that men become good by nature; others, through habit; others, by being taught. As for "nature," it is clearly not within our power, but comes to those who are truly fortunate, as the result of certain divine causes. Argument and teaching, it is to be feared, do not always have the same power. The student's soul must have had good prior training and habituation with a view to taking pleasure rightly and hating rightly, like earth that is to nourish the seed. The man who lives by emotion would not listen to a dissuasive argument, nor would he understand it. How can one change someone like that? In general, emotion does not seem to submit to reason, but to force.

Therefore, there must already be character related in some way to virtue, loving the fine and hating the ugly. It is hard to get the right approach to virtue from youth onwards, unless you are brought up under that kind of law. Living temperately, with restraint, is not pleasant to most people, especially for the young. Therefore, their training and their pursuits should be matters arranged by the laws; they will not be painful when they have become matters of habit. But perhaps it is not enough to get the right training and care while young. Since we have to practice these things habitually when grown up, we shall need laws about adult life, too, and in general for the whole of human life; for the majority obey necessity rather than reason, and punishment rather than honor. For this reason, some people think that lawgivers should urge and exhort to virtue for its own sake, since those who have had a good moral training will pay attention; but that they should impose penalties and punishments on the disobedient and those with bad disposition, whereas the incurable should simply be exiled. . . .

Now, the best course is for training to be the subject of state control of the right kind; but when states neglect these matters, it seems to be fitting for each individual himself to contribute toward the virtue of his own children and friends, to have the power to do that or at least to choose to do so. On the basis of what we have said, a man would be better able to do that by becoming a lawgiver. . . .

Next, then, should we not see whence or by what means one may become a lawgiver? As in other cases, is this not to be learned from the politicians? It has been thought that lawgiving is a part of politics. . . .

How . . . can someone become a lawgiver through studying laws, or learn how to pick the best laws? People do not become doctors through treatises; yet they try to determine not only what the various treatments are but also how particular people can be cured and how individuals should be treated, by distinguishing the different states of the body. To those with experience, this seems useful; but it is useless to those without. Perhaps, then, collections of laws and constitutions will be of use to those who can see the whole subject and judge what is good or bad and what suits certain people. Those who study such things without a trained mind will not be able to judge rightly thereby, except by accident, even though they may become sharper-witted at politics.

Previous writers have neglected the subject of lawgiving. It is better perhaps for us to investigate it, and the subject of constitutions in general, so that as far as is possible we may complete our philosophy relating to man. . . .

# The Moral Community

One of the most common problems that any star-studded athletic team can have is that each "star" performs to enhance his or her own reputation rather than performing in the best interest of the team. In basketball, players take too many low percentage shots. In baseball, a slugger goes for the fences when the appropriate play, if your team is behind in the ninth, is to use the surprise bunt to get on base. Hence, the championship team is often not the team with the best individual players. Rather, it's the team that functions best *as a team.* Since the team members are performing for the good of the team, in an important sense the team is greater than the sum of its parts.

A common criticism of traditional ethics in the liberal tradition is the excessive emphasis on the individual. The starting point of most Anglo-American ethical theory is the individual, and the adequacy of an ethical theory depends on its ability to accommodate individual interests and individual rights. But isn't the notion of an individual outside a social context a mere abstraction? F. H. Bradley argues that all individuals exist in a social context. Without that context individuals couldn't survive or, at the very least, they couldn't grow and develop. An individual person is what she is because of the position she holds in society. She is a family member, an employee, a colleague, and a friend. In a very real sense these relations make her the individual she is. An individual apart from all social relations is an abstract entity. For this reason it is easy to see how to defend the view that the good of the individual is bound up with the good of society. The coach who continually points out that a collection of players wins or loses as a team has a valid philosophical point.

In society, the individual plays a number of roles—as student, friend, son, or daughter, and many of the ethical decisions we make take place in that role context. Roles carry norms of appropriate behavior with them. The selection by Bradley develops this notion of role morality.

However, even if our tradition has been excessively individualistic, it may well be correct in its insistence that institutions must benefit individuals if they are to be morally legitimate. To deserve our allegiance, social institutions ought to be just.

Moral problems often occur when individual interests compete. Principles of procedural justice are designed to resolve these clashes of legitimate interest, and these procedures are made effective in political and economic institutions. The civil courts resolve legal disputes among citizens; businesses supply scarce goods and services in response to consumer demand. But what about the justice of these institutions: Do the courts settle these individual disputes justly? Do businesses supply goods and services justly?

For John Rawls, the principles of justice are determined as part of a social contract where everyone affected by social institutions is a contractee. Moreover, to prevent people from adopting a bias, people must pretend to be ignorant of all idiosyncracies such as level of income, the job skills one has, and level of educational attainment. In this type of contract situation, the contractees could reach unanimity on the principles of justice. These principles would be adopted by free and equal moral persons meeting as hypothetical institutional planners. Political, legal, and economic institutions are just if they conform to the principles of justice adopted by the hypothetical contract makers.

In actual practice, democracy could serve as an imperfect social contract. Periodically we pass judgment on our legislators and executives who shape and manage our political institutions. Our legislators represent us as contract makers. More formally put, the paradigm features of democracy are *(a)* the holding of regular elections, the results of which can genuinely alter policy and the people who make it; *(b)* the existence of universal suffrage; and *(c)* the provision of civil liberties essential to the election process itself. According to this view, legal and economic institutions are just if they rest on democratic support. But is democracy just?

The selections by John Dewey argue that democracy is an ethical and just procedure for resolving conflicts and providing for the needs of citizens. However, Dewey and nearly all defenders of democratic procedures insist that democracy is much more than majority vote. Political decisions settled wholly and only by majority vote **(majoritarianism)** have the danger of developing into the tyranny of the majority. The majority itself must be constrained, and a Constitutional Bill of Rights is often the device to accomplish this goal. In a classic essay, reprinted in part here, John Stuart Mill argues for the right of free speech as one of the constraints needed to avoid a tyranny of the majority.

Despite the nearly unanimous agreement that American democracy is not majoritarian and that it is constrained by protection of individual liberties, many critics of our culture have found the conjunction of democracy and capitalism to be in violation of the canons of justice. This section concludes with a selection from Marx's *Communist Manifesto.* In that selection Marx argues that the capitalist owners exploit those who labor in the factories and mines and that mass production alienates the worker from the object of his labor.

Critics of Marx, especially critics in the United States, indicate that workers certainly don't feel exploited or alienated. Neither communism nor socialism has gained a foothold in the United States. There is no hope for a working-class revolution; there is no intellectual–working-class alliance. The American mixture of capitalism and democracy certainly rests on the consent of the American public, and that consent cuts across all social and economic classes. Isn't Marx thus refuted?

Contemporary Marxists are undaunted. They argue that American cultural pressure is so great that the working class has become co-opted into approving the system. The working class has been coerced into accepting the materialistic values of the culture and hence its members compromise themselves as workers so that they may be consumers. Contemporary Marxists are troubled by some of the same problems that troubled Mill. Do the pressures of the culture so coerce individuals that their autonomy and hence their self-respect are lost?

A dilemma confronts us. On the one hand, both the state and social institutions that comprise it seem necessary if people are to develop fully as human beings. On the other hand, those same institutions have the ability to stultify human growth. What procedures and principles will produce just institutions? What principles and attitudes will produce moral citizens? In answering these questions, ethics expands into political philosophy.

## F. H. Bradley (1846–1924)

F. H. Bradley was a well-known English philosopher whose ethical theory had more in common with the German philosopher Hegel than with the utilitarianism that was prominent in England during Bradley's time. Indeed Bradley was a strong critic of John Stuart Mill. He was also a strong critic of Kant. Although utilitarianism and Kantianism are usually treated as opposites, Bradley thought they had a common flaw—namely that both were excessively individualistic. The problem with individualistic moral philosophy is that in the real world you don't know people as individuals. To really know someone you need to know about their family, friends, and business associates. You come to know someone only when you know them in relation with others. Hence moral philosophy ought to focus on the roles people play rather than on the individual *per se*. By focusing on roles, ethical theory focuses on the relationships that exist among people. Bradley did contend that all individuals had a duty to develop their potentialities. (He referred to this ethics as an *ethics of self-realization.*) Nonetheless, an individual could only "realize" himself or herself in a social context.

## My Station and Its Duties

### *F. H. Bradley*

I

. . . The good will (for morality) is meaningless, if, whatever else it be, it be not the will of living human beings. . . . It is an organism and a moral organism; and it is conscious self-realization, because only by the will of its self-conscious members can the moral organism give itself reality. It is the self-realization of the whole body, because it is one and the same will which lives and acts in the life and action of each. It is the self-realization of each member, because each member can not find the function, which makes him himself, apart from the whole to which he belongs; to be himself he must go beyond himself, to live his life he must live a life which is not *merely* his own, but which, none the less, but on the contrary all the more, is intensely and emphatically his own individuality. . . . It is real, and real for me. It is in its affirmation that I affirm myself, for I am but as a "heart-beat in its system." And I am real in it; for, when I give myself to it, it gives me the fruition of my own personal activity, the accomplished ideal of my life which is happiness. In the realized idea which, superior to me, and yet here and now in and by me, affirms itself in a continuous process, we have found the end, we have found self-realization, duty, and happiness in one;—yes, we have found ourselves, when we have found our station and its duties, our function as an organ in the social organism.

"Mere rhetoric," we shall be told, "a bad metaphysical dream, a stale old story once more warmed up," which can not hold its own against the logic of facts. That the state was prior to the individual, that the whole was sometimes more than the sum of the parts, was an illusion which preyed on the thinkers of Greece. But that illusion has been traced to its source and dispelled, and is in plain words exploded. The family, society, the state, and generally every community of men, consists of individuals, and there is nothing in them real except the individuals. Individuals have made them, and make them, by placing themselves and by standing in certain relations. . . . The whole is the mere sum of the parts, and the parts are as real away from the whole as they are within the whole. Do you really suppose that the individual would perish if every form of community were destroyed? . . . To put the matter shortly, the community is the sum of its parts, is made by the addition of parts; and the parts are as real before the addition as after; the relations they stand in do not make them what they are, but are accidental not essential to their being; and, as to the whole, if it is not a name for the individuals that compose it, is a name of nothing actual. . . .

A discussion that would go to the bottom of

Abridged from and reprinted with the permission of the publisher, ITT Bobbs-Merrill Educational Publishing Company, Inc. F. H. Bradley, *Ethical Studies*. 

the question, What is an individual? is certainly wanted. . . . But we are not going to enter on a metaphysical question to which we are not equal; we meet the metaphysical assertion of the "individualist" with a mere denial; and, turning to facts, we will try to show that they lead us in another direction. To the assertion, then, that selves are "individual" in the sense of exclusive of other selves, we oppose the (equally justified) assertion, that this is a mere fancy. We say that, out of theory, no such individual men exist; and we will try to show from fact that, in fact, what we call an individual man is what he is because of and by virtue of community, and that communities are thus not mere names but something real, and can be regarded (if we mean to keep to facts) only as the one in the many.

And to confine the subject, and to keep to what is familiar, we will not call to our aid the life of animals, nor early societies, nor the course of history, but we will take men as they are now; we will take ourselves, and endeavor to keep wholly to the teaching of experience.

Let us take a man, an Englishman as he is now, and try to point out that, apart from what he has in common with others, apart from his sameness with others, he is not an Englishman — nor a man at all; that if you take him as something by himself, he is not what he is. Of course we do not mean to say that he can not go out of England without disappearing, nor, even if all the rest of the nation perished, that he would not survive. What we mean to say is, that he is what he is because he is a born and educated social being, and a member of an individual social organism; that if you make abstraction of all this, which is the same in him and in others, what you have left is not an Englishman, nor a man, but some I know not what residuum, which never has existed by itself, and does not so exist. If we suppose the world of relations, in which he was born and bred, never to have been, then we suppose the very essence of him not to be; if we take that away, we have taken him away; and hence he now is not an individual, in the sense of owing nothing to the sphere of relations in which he finds himself, but does contain those relations within himself as belonging to his very being; he is what he is, in brief, so far as he is what others also are. . . .

The "individual" man, the man into whose essence his community with others does not enter, who does not include relation to others in his very being, is, we say, a fiction, and in the light of facts we have to examine him. Let us take him in the shape of an English child as soon as he is born; for I suppose we ought not to go further back. Let us take him as soon as he is separated from his mother, and occupies a space clear and exclusive of all other human beings. At this time, education and custom will, I imagine, be allowed to have not as yet operated on him or lessened his "individuality." But is he now a mere "individual" in the sense of not implying in his being identity with others? . . . The child is not fallen from heaven. He is born of certain parents who come of certain families, and he has in him the qualities of his parents, and, as breeders would say, of the strains from both sides. Much of it we can see, and more we believe to be latent, and, given certain (possible or impossible) conditions, ready to come to light. On the descent of mental qualities modern investigation and popular experience, as expressed in uneducated vulgar opinion, altogether, I believe, support one another, and we need not linger here. . . .

But the child is not merely the member of a family; he is born into other spheres, and (passing over the subordinate wholes, which nevertheless do in many cases qualify him) he is born a member of the English nation. . . .

Thus the child is at birth; and he is born not into a desert, but into a living world, a whole which has a true individuality of its own, and into a system and order which it is difficult to look at as anything else than an organism, and which, even in England, we are now beginning to call by that name. . . . He learns, or already perhaps has learnt, to speak, and here he appropriates the common heritage of his race, the tongue that he makes his own is his country's language, it is (or it should be) the same that others speak, and it carries into his mind the ideas and sentiments of the race (over this I need not stay); and stamps them in indelibly. He grows up in an atmosphere of example and general custom, his life widens out from one little world to other and higher worlds, and he apprehends through successive stations the whole in which he lives, and in which he has lived. Is he now to try and develop his "individuality," his self which is not the same as other selves? Where is it? What is it? Where can he find it? The soul within him is saturated, is filled, is qualified by, it has assimilated, has got its substance, has built itself up from, it *is* one and the same life with the universal life, and if he turns against this he turns against himself; if he thrusts it from him, he tears his own vitals; if he attacks it, he sets his weapons against his own heart. He has found his life in the life of the whole, he lives that in himself, "he is a pulsebeat of the whole system, and himself the whole system.". . .

So far, I think, without aid from metaphysics, we have seen that the "individual" apart from the community is an abstraction. It is not anything real, and hence not anything that we can realize, however much we may wish to do so. We have seen that I am myself by sharing with others, by including in my essence relations to them, the relations of the social state. If I wish to realize my true being, I must therefore realize something beyond my being as a mere this or that; for my true being has in it a life which is not the life of any mere particular, and so must be called a universal life.

What is it then that I am to realize? We have said it in "my station and its duties." To know what a man is (as we have seen) you must not take him in isolation. He is one of a people, he was born in a family, he lives in a certain society, in a certain state. What he has to do depends on what his place is, what his function is, and that all comes from his station in the organism. Are there then such organisms in which he lives, and if so, what is their nature? Here we come to questions which must be answered in full by any complete system of Ethics, but which we can not enter on. We must content ourselves by pointing out that there are such facts as the family, then in a middle position a man's own profession and society, and, over all, the larger community of the state. Leaving out of sight the question of a society wider than the state, we must say that a man's life with its moral duties is in the main filled up by his station in that system of wholes which the state is, and that this, partly by its laws and institutions, and still more by its spirit, gives him the life which he does live and ought to live. . . .

## John Rawls (b. 1921)

John Rawls' influential book *A Theory of Justice* (1971) turned ethical and political philosophy in a different direction. Rawls did not limit his discussion to the analysis of abstract moral concepts like "right" and "ought." Rather, he drew upon the moral philosophy of Immanuel Kant and the contract theorists in political philosophy to develop a full-blown theory of justice. The focus of this selection is on just institutions. Just institutions must be in conformity with the fundamental principles of justice. These principles of justice are those principles that free and equal moral persons would adopt if they were to meet as hypothetical institutional planners. For Rawls, the principles of justice are determined as part of a social contract where everyone affected by social institutions is a contractee. Moreover, to prevent people from adopting a bias, people must pretend to be ignorant of all idiosyncracies such as level of income, the job skills one has, and level of educational attainment. There are natural inequalities (some live on more fertile land, some enjoy the benefits of a better climate, and so on) and social inequalities (only some people enjoy the benefits of social class, fair governments, good schools, well-paying occupations, and so on). The **veil of ignorance** is meant to make sure that moral legislators don't favor those who happen to enjoy the natural and social advantages not available to everyone in a society. In this way those individual characteristics that provide merit within social institutions are prevented from having any impact on the design of these institutions. The principles of justice that the contractees adopt are the benchmarks against which social institutions are to be judged. This type of social contract represents a *fair procedure* for determining the principles of justice. Indeed, Rawls' theory is often called a theory of justice as fairness.

# Just Institutions

## *John Rawls*

### I

An important assumption of my book *A Theory of Justice*[1] is that the **basic structure** of society is the primary subject of justice. By the basic structure is meant the way in which the major social institutions fit together into one system, and how they assign fundamental rights and duties and shape the division of advantages that arises through social cooperation. Thus the political constitution, the legally recognized forms of property, and the organization of the economy, all belong to the basic structure. I held that the first test of a conception of justice is whether its principles provide reasonable guidelines for the classical questions of social justice in this case.

In my book I did not consider in any detail why the basic structure is to be taken as the primary subject. I left this to be gathered from various remarks made while discussing other matters. Here I shall try to remedy this lack. Of course, it is perfectly legitimate at first to restrict inquiry to the basic structure. We must begin somewhere, and this starting point may turn out to be justified by how everything works out. But certainly we would like to find a more illuminating answer than this; and moreover one that draws upon the special features of the basic structure in contrast with other social arrangements, and connects these features with the particular role and content of the principles of justice themselves. I aim to present an explanation that meets these conditions.

Now a social contract is an agreement (1) between all rather than some members of society, and it is (2) between them as members of society (as citizens) and not as individuals who hold some particular position or role within it. In the Kantian form of this doctrine, of which the conception of justice as fairness is an example, (3) the parties are regarded as, and also regard themselves as, free and equal moral persons; and (4) the content of the agreement is the first principles that are to regulate the basic structure. We take as given a short list of conceptions of justice developed by the tradition of moral philosophy and then ask which of these the parties would acknowledge, when the alternatives are thus restricted. Assuming that we have a clear enough idea of the circumstances necessary to insure that any agreement reached is fair, the content of

Abridged from "The Basic Structure as Subject," by John Rawls in *American Philosophical Quarterly*, Vol. 14, No. 2, April 1977, pp. 159–65. Reprinted by permission of *American Philosophical Quarterly*.

justice for the basic structure can be ascertained, or at least approximated, by the principles that would be agreed to. (Of course, this presupposes the reasonableness of the tradition; but where else can we start?) Thus **pure procedural justice** is invoked at the highest level: the fairness of the circumstances transfers to fairness of the principles adopted.

I wish to suggest the following: first that once we think of the parties to a social contract as free and equal (and rational) persons, then it is natural to take the basic structure as the primary subject. Second, that in view of the distinctive features of this structure, the initial agreement, and the conditions under which it is made, must be understood in a special way that distinguishes this agreement from all others; and doing this allows a Kantian view to take account of the fully social nature of human relationships. And finally, that while a large element of pure procedural justice transfers to the principles of justice, these principles must embody an ideal form for the basic structure in the light of which ongoing institutional processes are to be constrained and the accumulated results of individual transactions continually corrected.

## II

Several lines of reasoning point to the basic structure as the primary subject of justice. One is the following: suppose we begin with the initially attractive idea that society should develop over time in accordance with free agreements fairly arrived at and fully honored. Straightway we need an account of when agreements are free and the social circumstances under which they are reached are fair. In addition, while these conditions may be fair at an earlier time, the accumulated results of many separate ostensibly fair agreements, together with social and historical contingencies, are likely as time passes to alter institutions and opportunities so that the conditions for free and fair agreements no longer hold. The role of the basic structure is to secure just background conditions against which the actions of individuals and associations take place. Unless this structure is appropriately regulated and corrected, the social process will cease to be just, however free and fair particular transactions may look when viewed by themselves.

We recognize this fact when we say, for example, that the distribution resulting from voluntary market transactions (even should all the ideal conditions for competitive efficiency obtain) is not, in general, fair unless the antecedent distribution of income and wealth as well as the structure of the system of markets is fair. The existing wealth must have been properly acquired and all must have had fair opportunities to earn income, to learn wanted skills, and so on. Again, the conditions necessary for background justice can be undermined, even though nobody acts unfairly or is aware of how the conjunction of contingencies affects the opportunities of others. There are no feasible rules that it is practicable to impose on economic agents that can prevent these undesirable consequences. These consequences are often so far in the future, or so indirect, that the attempt to forestall them by restrictive rules that apply to individuals would be an excessive if not impossible burden. Thus we start with the basic structure and try to see how this system itself should make the corrections necessary to preserve background justice.

## III

A second reflection points in the same direction. Consider the situation of individuals engaged in market transactions. We have seen that certain background conditions are necessary for these transactions to be fair. But what about the nature of individuals themselves: how did they get to be what they are? A theory of justice cannot take their final aims and interests, their attitude to themselves and their life, as given. Everyone recognizes that the form of society affects its members and determines in large part the kind of persons they want to be as well as the kind of persons they are. It also limits people's ambitions and hopes in different ways, for they will with reason view themselves in part according to their place in it and take account of the means and opportunities they can realistically expect. Thus an economic regime is not only an institutional scheme for satisfying existing desires and aspirations but a way of fashioning desires and aspirations in the future.

Nor, similarly, can we view the abilities and talents of individuals as fixed natural gifts, even if there is an important genetic component. These abilities and talents cannot come to fruition apart from social conditions and as realized they always take but one of many possible forms. An ability is not, for example, a computer in the head with a definite measurable capacity unaffected by social circumstances. Among the elements affecting the realization of natural capacities are social attitudes of encouragement and support and the institutions concerned with their training and use. Thus even a potential ability at any given time is not something unaffected by existing social forms and particular contingencies over the course of life up to that moment. So not only our final ends and hopes for ourselves but our realized abilities and talents reflect, to a large degree, our personal history, opportunities, and social position. What we might have been had these things been different, we cannot know.

Finally, both of the preceding considerations are strengthened by the fact that the basic structure most likely contains significant social and economic inequalities. These I assume to be necessary, or else highly advantageous, in maintaining effective social cooperation; presumably there are various reasons for this, among which the need for incentives is but one. Even if these inequalities are not very great, they seem bound to have a considerable effect and so to favor some over others depending upon their social origins, their realized natural endowments, and the chance coincidences and opportunities that have come their way. The basic structure includes inequalities between certain starting-places, so to speak, and this feature, together with the earlier observations, prompts us to take this structure as the primary subject.

## IV

In the conception of justice as fairness the institutions of the basic structure are viewed as just provided they (reasonably) satisfy the principles that free and equal moral persons, in a situation that is fair between them, would adopt for the purpose of regulating that structure. The main two principles read as follows: (1) Each person has an equal right to the most extensive scheme of equal basic liberties compatible with a similar scheme of liberties for all. (2) Social and economic inequalities are permissible provided that (a) they are to the greatest expected benefit of the least advantaged; and (b) attached to positions and offices open to all under conditions of fair equality of opportunity.

Let us consider how the special features of the basic structure affect the conditions of the initial agreement and hence the content of these principles. Now by assumption the basic structure is the all-inclusive social system that determines background justice; so any fair situation between individuals conceived as free and equal moral persons must be one that suitably evens out the contingencies within this system. Agreements reached when people know their present place in an ongoing society would be influenced by disparate social and natural contingencies. The principles adopted would then be selected by the historical course of events that took place within that structure. We would not have gotten beyond social happenstance in order to find an independent standard.

It is also clear why, when we interpret the parties as free and equal moral persons, they are to reason as if they know very little about themselves (referring here to the restrictions of the **veil of ignorance**). For to proceed otherwise is still to allow the disparate and deep contingent effects of the social system to influence the principles adopted; and this is true even if the parties have no particular information about themselves but only general facts about their own society (which is perhaps all that a condition of impartiality requires). When we as contemporaries are influenced by a general description of the present state of society in agreeing how we are to treat each other, and those generations that come after us, we have not yet left out of account the accidents of the basic structure. And so one arrives at the thicker rather than the thinner veil of ignorance: the parties are to be understood so far as possible solely as moral persons, that is, in abstraction from all those contingencies that the basic structure over time has shaped and influenced; and to be fair between them, the initial situation must situate them equally for as moral persons they are equal: the same essential properties qualify each.

Finally, the social contract must be regarded as hypothetical. Of course, any actual agreement is liable to the distortions just noted; but in any case, historically valid compacts, were such to exist, would have but limited force and could not serve as the basis of a general theory. Equally decisive is the fact that society is a system of cooperation that extends over time: it is cooperation between generations and not just cooperation among contemporaries. If we are to account for the duties and obligations between generations, there is no clear way to do this in a contract view without interpreting the initial agreement as hypothetical. The correct principles for the basic structure are those that the members of any generation (and hence all generations) would agree to as the ones their generation is to follow and as the principles they would want other generations to have followed and to follow subsequently, no matter how far back or forward in time.

Once we note the distinctive role of the basic structure and abstract from the various contingencies within it to find an appropriate conception of justice to regulate it, something like the notion of the original position seems inevitable. It is a natural extension of the idea of the social contract when the basic structure is taken as the primary subject of justice.

## V

The essential point is the distinctive role of the basic structure: we must distinguish between particular agreements made and associations formed within this structure, and the initial agreement and membership in society as a citizen. Consider first particular agreements: typically these are based on the parties' known (or probable) assets and abilities, opportunities and interests, as these have been realized within background institutions. We may assume that each party, whether an individual or an association, has various alternatives open to them, that they can compare the likely advantages and disadvantages of these alternatives, and act accordingly. Under certain conditions someone's contribution to a joint venture, or to an on-going association, can be estimated: one simply notes how the venture or association would fare without that person's joining, and the difference measures their worth to the venture or association. The attractiveness of joining to the individual is similarly given by a comparison with their opportunities. Thus particular agreements are reached within the context of existing and foreseeable configurations of relationships as these have been and most likely will be realized within the basic structure; and it is these configurations that give meaning to contractual calculations.

The context of a social contract is strikingly different, and must allow for three facts, among others: namely, that membership in our society is given, that we cannot know what we would have been like had we not belonged to it (perhaps the thought itself lacks a sense), and that society as a whole has no ends or ordering of ends in the sense that associations and individuals do. The bearing of these facts is clear once we try to view the social contract as an ordinary agreement and ask how deliberations leading up to it would proceed. Since membership in their society is given, there is no question of the parties comparing the attractions of other societies. Moreover, there is no way to identify potential contribution to society as an individual not yet a member of it; for this potentiality cannot be known and is, in any case, irrelevant to their present situation. Not only this, but from the standpoint of society as a whole *vis-à-vis* any one member, there is no set of agreed ends by reference to which the potential social contributions of an individual could be assessed. Associations and individuals have such ends, but not a well-ordered society; although it has the aim of giving justice to all its citizens, this is not an aim that ranks their expected contributions and on that basis determines their social role. The notion of an individual's contribution to society as itself an association falls away. It is necessary, therefore, to construe the social contract in a special way that distinguishes it from other agreements.

In the conception of justice as fairness this is done by constructing the notion of the original position. This construction must reflect the fundamental contrasts just noted and it must supply the missing elements so that an appropriate agreement may be reached. Consider in turn the points in the preceding paragraph. First, the parties in the original position suppose that their membership in the society is given. This presumption reflects the fact that we are born into our society and within its framework realize but one of many possible forms of our person; the question of entering another society does not arise. The task is to agree on principles for the basic structure of the society of one's birth. Second, the veil of ignorance not only establishes fairness between equal moral persons, but by excluding information about the parties' actual interests and abilities, it represents the fact that apart from our place and history in a society, even our potential abilities cannot be known and our interests and character are still to be formed. Thus, the initial situation suitably recognizes that our nature apart from society is but a potential for a whole range of possibilities. Third and finally, there is no social end except that established by the principles of justice themselves, or else authorized by them; but these principles have yet to be adopted.

Nevertheless, although the calculations that typically influence agreements within society have no place, other aspects of the original position provide the setting for rational deliberation. Thus the alternatives are not opportunities to join other societies, but instead a list of conceptions of justice to regulate the basic structure of one's own society. The parties' interests and preferences are given by their desire for primary goods. Their particular final ends and aims indeed are already formed, although not known to them; and it is these already formed interests that they seek to protect by ranking conceptions on the basis of their preference (in the original position) for primary goods. Finally, the availability of general social theory gives a sufficient basis for estimating the feasibility and consequences of the various conceptions of justice. These aspects of the original position allow us to carry through the idea of the social contract despite the unusual nature of this agreement.

## VI

I now point out three ways in which the social aspect of human relationships is reflected in the content of the principles of justice themselves. First, the difference principle (which governs economic and social inequalities) does not distinguish between what is acquired by individuals as members of society and what would have been acquired by them had they not been members. Indeed, no sense can be made of the notion of that part of an individual's social benefits that exceed what would have been their situation in another society or in a state of nature. We can, if we like, in setting up the argument from the original position, introduce the state of nature in relation to the so-called no-agreement point.[2] This point can be defined as general **egoism** and its consequences, and this can serve as the state of nature. But these conditions do not identify a definite state. All that is known in the original position is that each of the conceptions of justice available to the parties has consequences superior to general egoism. There is no question of determining anyone's contribution to society, or how much better off each is than they would have been had they not belonged to society and then adjusting the social benefits of citizens by reference to these estimates. Although we may draw this kind of distinction for agreements made within society, the requisite calculations for principles holding for the basic structure itself have no foundation. Neither our situation in other societies, nor in a state of nature, has any role in comparing conceptions of justice. And clearly these notions have no relevance at all in the application of the principles of justice.

Second, and related to the preceding, the two principles of justice regulate how entitlements are acquired in return for contributions to associations, or to other forms of cooperation, within the basic structure. As we have seen, these contributions are estimated on the basis of particular configurations of contingencies, which are influenced in part by individual efforts and achievements, in part by social accident and happenstance. Contributions can only be locally defined as contributions to this or that association in this or that situation. Such contributions reflect an individual's worth (marginal usefulness) to some particular group. These contributions are not to be mistaken for contributions to society itself, or for the worth to society of its members as citizens. The sum of an individual's entitlements, or even of their uncompensated contributions to associations within society, is not to be regarded as a contribution to society. To this kind of contribution we can give no meaning; there is no clear or useful notion of an individual's contribution to society that parallels the idea of individual contributions to associations within society. Insofar as we compare the worth of citizens at all, their worth in a well-ordered society is always equal; and this equality is reflected in the system of basic equal liberties and fair opportunities, and in the operations of the difference principle.

Third and last, recall that in a Kantian view the parties are regarded as free and equal moral persons. Now freedom means a certain form of social institutions, namely, a certain pattern of rights and liberties; and equality in turn means, for example, that certain basic liberties and opportunities are equal and that social and economic inequalities are regulated by principles suitably expressive of equality. Moral persons are those with a conception of the good (a system of final ends) and a capacity to understand a conception of justice and to follow it in their life. Of course, we cannot define free and equal moral persons as those whose social relations answer to precisely the principles that are agreed to in the social contract. For then we should have no argument for these principles. But it is no accident that once the parties are described in terms that require some social expression, the first principles of justice are themselves institutional and apply to the public structure of society. The content of the two principles fulfills this expectation. And this is in contrast, for example, with utilitarianism which takes as basic the capacity for pleasure and pain, or for certain valuable experiences. Nevertheless, the social manner in which the parties are described does not mean a lapse into some kind of holism; what results is a conception of a well-ordered society regulated by the two principles of justice.

## VII

Now I come to the last point: namely, why it is that, although society may reasonably rely on a large element of pure procedural justice in determining distributive shares, a conception of justice must incorporate an ideal form for the basic structure in the light of which the accumulated results of on-going social processes are to be limited and corrected.

First a remark about pure procedural justice: the two principles make considerable use of this notion. They apply to the basic structure and its system for acquiring entitlements; within appropriate limits, whatever distributive shares result are just. A fair distribution can be arrived at only by the actual working of a fair social process over time in the course of which, in accordance with publicly announced rules, entitlements are earned and honored. These features define pure procedural justice. Therefore, if it is asked in the abstract whether one distribution of a given stock of things to definite individuals with known desires and preferences is more just than another, then there is simply no answer to this question.[3]

Thus the principles of justice, in particular the difference principle, apply to the main public principles and policies that regulate social and economic inequalities. They are used to adjust the system of entitlements and earnings and to balance the familiar everyday standards and precepts which this system employs. The difference principle holds, for example, for income and property taxation, for fiscal and economic policy. It applies to the announced system of public law and statutes and not to particular transactions or distributions, nor to the decisions of individuals and associations, but rather to the institutional background against which these take place. There are no unannounced and unpredictable interferences with citizens' expectations and acquisitions. Entitlements are earned and honored as the public system of rules declares. Taxes and restrictions are all in principle foreseeable, and holdings are acquired on the known condition that certain corrections will be made. The objection that the difference principle enjoins continuous and capricious interference with private transactions is based on a misunderstanding.

Again, the two principles of justice do not insist that the actual distribution reflect any observable pattern, say equality, nor any measure computed from the distribution, such as a certain Gini coefficient (as a measure of the degree of equality). What is enjoined is that (permissible) inequalities make a certain functional contribution over time to the expectations of the least favored. The aim, however, is not to eliminate the various contingencies from social life, for some such contingencies seem inevitable. Thus even if an equal distribution of natural assets seemed more in keeping with the equality of free persons, the question of redistributing these assets (were this conceivable) does not arise, since it is incompatible with the integrity of the person. Nor need we make any specific assumptions about how great these natural variations are; we only suppose that, as realized in later life, they are influenced by many kinds of contingencies. Institutions must organize social cooperation so that they encourage constructive efforts. We have a right to our natural abilities and a right to whatever we become entitled to by taking part in a fair social process. The two principles of justice define the relevant fair process and so whatever distributive shares result are fair.

At the same time, these principles specify an ideal form for the basic structure in the light of which pure procedural processes are constrained and corrected. Among these constraints are the limits on the accumulation of property (especially if private property in productive assets exists) that derive from the requirements of the fair value of political liberty and fair equality of opportunity, and the limits based on considerations of stability and excusable envy, both of which are connected to the essential primary good of self-respect.[4] We need such an ideal to guide the corrections necessary to preserve background justice. As we have seen, even if everyone acts fairly as defined by rules that it is both reasonable and practicable to impose on individuals, the upshot of many separate transactions will undermine background justice. This is obvious once we view society, as we must, as involving cooperation over generations. Thus even in a well-ordered society, adjustments in the basic structure are always necessary. What we have, in effect, is an institutional division of labor between the basic structure and rules applying directly to particular transactions. Individuals and associations are left free to advance their ends more effectively within the framework of the basic structure secure in the knowledge that elsewhere in the social system the necessary corrections to preserve background justice are being made.

The essential point, then, is that the need for a structural ideal to specify constraints and to guide corrections does not depend upon injustice. Even with strict compliance with all reasonable and practical rules, such adjustments are continually required. The fact that actual political and social life is often pervaded by much injustice merely underlines this necessity. A procedural theory that contains no structural principles for a just social order would be of no use in our world, where the political goal is to eliminate injustice and steer change towards a fair basic structure. The notion of a well-ordered society provides the requisite structural principles and specifies the overall direction of political action. There is no rational basis for preventing or eliminating injustice if such an ideal form for background institutions is rejected. . . .

## NOTES

1. Cambridge, Mass., 1971.
2. See *A Theory of Justice (op. cit.),* pp. 136, 147; see also p. 80.
3. On pure procedural justice, see *ibid.,* pp. 64, 66, 72ff, 79, 84–89, 274–280, 305–315.
4. See *ibid.,* pp. 224–227, 277f; 534–537, 543–546.

## *John Dewey (1859–1952)*

John Dewey was perhaps America's best known philosopher. He was a leading exponent of pragmatism. Although pragmatism is a uniquely American philosophy, *pragmatism* is not simply a synonym for *practical.* Pragmatism is often defined by the slogan "whatever works is true," but pragmatism is much more sophisticated than that. Dewey believed that knowledge began with experience. Since individuals are constantly interacting with a changing environment, obtaining knowledge is a dynamic rather than a static process. Indeed, Dewey's philosophy is a philosophy of doing.

Dewey is best known for his philosophy of education, which was perfectly consistent with his theories of epistemology and metaphysics. Students were not to be passive creatures who passively received information. Although Dewey may have been somewhat naive in his assessment of the student's ability to choose wisely, he is surely right in arguing that education is an active process. Just as education is active, so is democracy. In an effective democracy citizens must participate actively. The selection included here states Dewey's faith in democracy as a means for individual self-realization and his plea for citizen participation. The selection below is a composite of a 1937 speech and a 1940 article.

# Creative Democracy*

*John Dewey*

Democracy is much broader than a special political form, a method of conducting government, of making laws and carrying on governmental administration by means of popular suffrage and elected officers. It is that, of course. But it is something broader and deeper than that. The political and governmental phase of democracy is a means, the best means so far found, for realizing ends that lie in the wide domain of human relationships and the development of human personality. It is, as we often say, though perhaps without appreciating all that is involved in the saying, a way of life, social and individual. The keynote of democracy as a way of life may be expressed, it seems to me, as the necessity for the participation of every mature human being in formation of the values that regulate the living of men together: which is necessary from the standpoint of both the general social welfare and the full development of human beings as individuals.

Universal suffrage, recurring elections, responsibility of those who are in political power to the voters, and the other factors of democratic government are means that have been found expedient for realizing democracy as the truly human way of living. They are not a final end and a final value. They are to be judged on the basis of their contribution to [the] end. It is a form of idolatry to erect means into the end which they serve. Democratic political forms are simply the best means that human wit has devised up to a special time in history. But they rest back upon the idea that no man or limited set of men is wise enough or good enough to rule others without their consent; the positive meaning of this statement is that all those who are affected by social institutions must have a share in producing and managing them. The two facts that each one is influenced in what he does and enjoys and in what he becomes by the institutions under which he lives, and that therefore he shall have, in a democracy, a voice in shaping them, are the passive and active sides of the same fact.

The development of political democracy came about through substitution of the method of mutual consultation and voluntary agreement for the method of subordination of the many to the few enforced from above. Social arrangements which involve fixed subordination are maintained by coercion. The coercion need not be physical. There have existed, for short periods, benevolent despotisms. But coercion of some sort there has been; perhaps economic, certainly psychological and moral. The very fact of exclusion from participation is a subtle form of suppression. It gives individuals no opportunity to reflect and decide upon what is good for them. Others who are supposed to be wiser and who in any case have more power decide the question for them and also decide the methods and means by which subjects may arrive at the enjoyment of what is good for them. This form of coercion and suppression is more subtle and more effective than are overt intimidation and restraint. When it is habitual and embodied in social institutions, it seems the normal and natural state of affairs. The mass usually become unaware that they have a claim to a development of their own powers.

* From *Democracy and Educational Administration,* an address before the National Education Association, Feb. 22, 1937, and published in *School and Society,* April 3, 1937.

Abridged from *Intelligence in the Modern World.* Edited by Joseph Ratner. (New York: The Modern Library, Random House, 1939). Reprinted by permission of The Center for Dewey Studies, Southern Illinois University at Carbondale.

Their experience is so restricted that they are not conscious of restriction. It is part of the democratic conception that they as individuals are not the only sufferers, but that the whole social body is deprived of the potential resources that should be at its service. The individuals of the submerged mass may not be very wise. But there is one thing they are wiser about than anybody else can be, and that is where the shoe pinches, the troubles they suffer from.

The foundation of democracy is faith in the capacities of human nature; faith in human intelligence and in the power of pooled and cooperative experience. It is not belief that these things are complete but that if given a show they will grow and be able to generate progressively the knowledge and wisdom needed to guide collective action. Every autocratic and authoritarian scheme of social action rests on a belief that the needed intelligence is confined to a superior few, who because of inherent natural gifts are endowed with the ability and the right to control the conduct of others; laying down principles and rules and directing the ways in which they are carried out. It would be foolish to deny that much can be said for this point of view. It is that which controlled human relations in social groups for much the greater part of human history. The democratic faith has emerged very, very recently in the history of mankind. Even where democracies now exist, men's minds and feelings are still permeated with ideas about leadership imposed from above, ideas that developed in the long early history of mankind. After democratic political institutions were nominally established, beliefs and ways of looking at life and of acting that originated when men and women were externally controlled and subjected to arbitrary power, persisted in the family, the church, business and the school, and experience shows that as long as they persist there, political democracy is not secure.

Belief in equality is an element of the democratic credo. It is not, however, belief in equality of natural endowments. Those who proclaimed the idea of equality did not suppose they were enunciating a psychological doctrine, but a legal and political one. All individuals are entitled to equality of treatment by law and in its administration. Each one is affected equally in quality if not in quantity by the institutions under which he lives and has an equal right to express his judgment, although the weight of his judgment may not be equal in amount when it enters into the pooled result to that of others. In short, each one is equally an individual and entitled to equal opportunity of development of his own capacities, be they large or small in range. Moreover, each has needs of his own, as significant to him as those of others are to them. The very fact of natural and psychological inequality is all the more reason for establishment by law of equality of opportunity, since otherwise the former becomes a means of oppression of the less gifted.

While what we call intelligence may be distributed in unequal amounts, it is the democratic faith that it is sufficiently general so that each individual has something to contribute, and the value of each contribution can be assessed only as it enters into the final pooled intelligence constituted by the contributions of all. Every authoritarian scheme, on the contrary, assumes that its value may be assessed by some *prior* principle, if not of family and birth or race and color or possession of material wealth, then by the position and rank a person occupies in the existing social scheme. The democratic faith in equality is the faith that each individual shall have the chance and opportunity to contribute whatever he is capable of contributing and that the value of his contribution be decided by its place and function in the organized total of similar contributions, not on the basis of prior status of any kind whatever.

I have emphasized in what precedes the importance of the effective release of intelligence in connection with personal experience in the democratic way of living. I have done so purposely because democracy is so often and so naturally associated in our minds with freedom of *action,* forgetting the importance of freed intelligence which is necessary to direct and warrant freedom of action. Unless freedom of individual action has intelligence and informed conviction back of it, its manifestation is almost sure to result in confusion and disorder. The democratic idea of freedom is not the right of each individual to *do* as he pleases, even if it be qualified by adding "provided he does not interfere with the same freedom on the part of others." While the idea is not always, not often enough, expressed in words, the basic freedom is that of freedom of *mind* and of whatever degree of freedom of action and experience is necessary to produce freedom of intelligence. The modes of freedom guaranteed in the Bill of Rights are all of this nature: Freedom of belief and conscience, of expression of opinion, of assembly for discussion and conference, of the press as an organ of communication. They are guaranteed because without them individuals are not free to develop and society is deprived of what they might contribute.

## The Philosopher of the Common Man . . .

. . . At the present time, the frontier is moral, not physical. The period of free lands that seemed boundless in extent has vanished. Unused resources are now human rather than material. They are found in the waste of grown men and women who are without the chance to work, and in the young men and young women who find doors closed where there was once opportunity. The crisis that one hundred and fifty years ago called out social and political inventiveness is with us in a form which puts a heavier demand on human creativeness.

At all events this is what I mean when I say that we now have to re-create by deliberate and determined endeavor the kind of democracy which in its origin one hundred and fifty years ago was largely the product of a fortunate combination of men and circumstances. We have lived for a long time upon the heritage that came to us from the happy conjunction of men and events in an earlier day. The present state of the world is more than a reminder that we have now to put forth every energy of our own to prove worthy of our heritage. It is a challenge to do for the critical and complex conditions of today what the men of an earlier day did for simpler conditions.

If I emphasize that the task can be accomplished only by inventive effort and creative activity, it is in part because the depth of the present crisis is due in considerable part to the fact that for a long period we acted as if our democracy were something that perpetuated itself automatically; as if our ancestors had succeeded in setting up a machine that solved the problem of perpetual motion in politics. We acted as if democracy were something that took place mainly at Washington and Albany—or some other state capital—under the impetus of what happened when men and women went to the polls once a year or so—which is a somewhat extreme way of saying that we have had the habit of thinking of democracy as a kind of political mechanism that will work as long as citizens were reasonably faithful in performing political duties.

Of late years we have heard more and more frequently that this is not enough; that democracy is a way of life. This saying gets down to hard pan. But I am not sure that something of the ex-

---

Abridged from *The Philosopher of the Common Man: Essays in Honor of John Dewey.* Edited by Horace Kallen. 

ternality of the old idea does not cling to the new and better statement. In any case we can escape from this external way of thinking only as we realize in thought and act that democracy is a *personal* way of individual life; that it signifies the possession and continual use of certain attitudes, forming personal character and determining desire and purpose in all the relations of life. Instead of thinking of our dispositions and habits as accommodated to certain institutions we have to learn to think of the latter as expressions, projections, and extensions of habitually dominant personal attitudes.

Democracy as a personal, an individual, way of life involves nothing fundamentally new. But when applied it puts a new practical meaning in old ideas. Put into effect it signifies that powerful present enemies of democracy can be successfully met only by the creation of personal attitudes in individual human beings; that we must get over our tendency to think that its defense can be found in any external means whatever, whether military or civil, if they are separated from individual attitudes so deep-seated as to constitute personal character.

Democracy is a way of life controlled by a working faith in the possibilities of human nature. Belief in the Common Man is a familiar article in the democratic creed. That belief is without basis and significance save as it means faith in the potentialities of human nature as that nature is exhibited in every human being irrespective of race, color, sex, birth, and family, of material or cultural wealth. This faith may be enacted in statutes, but it is only on paper unless it is put in force in the attitudes which human beings display to one another in all the incidents and relations of daily life. To denounce Naziism for intolerance, cruelty and stimulation of hatred amounts to fostering insincerity if, in our personal relations to other persons, if, in our daily walk and conversation, we are moved by racial, color, or other class prejudice; indeed, by anything save a generous belief in their possibilities as human beings, a belief which brings with it the need for providing conditions which will enable these capacities to reach fulfillment. The democratic faith in human equality is belief that every human being, independent of the quantity or range of his personal endowment, has the right to equal opportunity with every other person for development of whatever gifts he has. The democratic belief in the principle of leadership is a generous one. It is universal. It is belief in the capacity of every person to lead his own life free from coercion and imposition by others provided right conditions are supplied.

Democracy is a way of personal life controlled not merely by faith in human nature in general but by faith in the capacity of human beings for intelligent judgment and action if proper conditions are furnished. I have been accused more than once and from opposed quarters of an undue, a utopian, faith in the possibilities of intelligence and in education as a correlate of intelligence. At all events, I did not invent this faith. I acquired it from my surroundings as far as those surroundings were animated by the democratic spirit. For what is the faith of democracy in the rôle of consultation, of conference, of persuasion, of discussion, in formation of public opinion, which in the long run is self-corrective, except faith in the capacity of the intelligence of the common man to respond with common sense to the free play of facts and ideas which are secured by effective guarantees of free inquiry, free assembly, and free communication? I am willing to leave to upholders of totalitarian states of the right and the left the view that faith in the capacities of intelligence is utopian. For the faith is so deeply embedded in the methods which are intrinsic to democracy that when a professed democrat denies the faith he convicts himself of treachery to his profession.

When I think of the conditions under which men and women are living in many foreign countries today, fear of espionage, with danger hanging over the meeting of friends for friendly conversation in private gatherings, I am inclined to believe that the heart and final guarantee of democracy is in free gatherings of neighbors on the street corner to discuss back and forth what is read in uncensored news of the day, and in gatherings of friends in the living rooms of houses and apartments to converse freely with one another. Intolerance, abuse, calling of names because of differences of opinion about religion or politics or business, as well as because of differences of race, color, wealth, or degree of culture, are treason to the democratic way of life. For everything which bars freedom and fullness of communication sets up barriers that divide human beings into sets and cliques, into antagonistic sects and factions, and thereby undermines the democratic way of life. Merely legal guarantees of the civil liberties of free belief, free expression, free assembly are of little avail if in daily life freedom of communication, the give and take of ideas, facts, experiences, is choked by mutual suspicion, by abuse, by fear and hatred. These things destroy the essential condition of the democratic way of living even more effectually than open coercion, which—as the example of totalitarian states proves—is effective only when it succeeds in breeding hate, suspicion, intolerance in the minds of individual human beings.

Finally, given the two conditions just mentioned, democracy as a way of life is controlled by personal faith in personal day-by-day working together with others. Democracy is the belief that even when needs and ends or consequences are different for each individual, the habit of amicable cooperation—which may include, as in sport, rivalry and competition—is itself a priceless addition to life. To take as far as possible every conflict which arises—and they are bound to arise—out of the atmosphere and medium of force, of violence as a means of settlement, into that of discussion and of intelligence, is to treat those who disagree—even profoundly—with us as those from whom we may learn, and in so far, as friends. A genuinely democratic faith in peace is faith in the possibility of conducting disputes, controversies, and conflicts as cooperative undertakings in which both parties learn by giving the other a chance to express itself, instead of having one party conquer by forceful suppression of the other—a suppression which is none the less one of violence when it takes place by psychological means of ridicule, abuse, intimidation, instead of by overt imprisonment or in concentration camps. To cooperate by giving differences a chance to show themselves because of the belief that the expression of difference is not only a right of the other persons but is a means of enriching one's own life-experience, is inherent in the democratic personal way of life.

If what has been said is charged with being a set of moral commonplaces, my only reply is that that is just the point in saying them. For to get rid of the habit of thinking of democracy as something institutional and external and to acquire the habit of treating it as a way of personal life is to realize that democracy is a moral ideal and so far as it becomes a fact is a moral fact. It is to realize that democracy is a reality only as it is indeed a commonplace of living.

Since my adult years have been given to the pursuit of philosophy, I shall ask your indulgence if in concluding I state briefly the democratic faith in the formal terms of a philosophic position. So stated, democracy is belief in the ability of human experience to generate the aims and methods by which further experience will grow in ordered richness. Every other form of moral and social faith rests upon the idea that experience must be subjected at some point or other to some form of external control; to some "authority" alleged to exist outside the processes of experience. Democracy is the faith that the process of experience is more important than any special result attained, so that special results achieved are of ultimate value only as they are used to enrich and order the ongoing process. Since the process of experience is capable of being educative, faith in democracy is all one with faith in experience and education. All ends and values that are cut off from the ongoing process become arrests, fixations. They strive to fixate what has been gained instead of using it to open the road and point the way to new and better experiences.

If one asks what is meant by experience in this connection, my reply is that it is that free interaction of individual human beings with surrounding conditions, especially the human surroundings, which develops and satisfies need and desire by increasing knowledge of things as they are. Knowledge of conditions as they are is the only solid ground for communication and sharing; all other communication means the subjection of some persons to the personal opinion of other persons. Need and desire—out of which grow purpose and direction of energy—go beyond what exists, and hence beyond knowledge, beyond science. They continually open the way into the unexplored and unattained future.

Democracy as compared with other ways of life is the sole way of living which believes wholeheartedly in the process of experience as end and as means; as that which is capable of generating the science which is the sole dependable authority for the direction of further experience and which releases emotions, needs, and desires so as to call into being the things that have not existed in the past. For every way of life that fails in its democracy limits the contacts, the exchanges, the communications, the interactions by which experience is steadied while it is also enlarged and enriched. The task of this release and enrichment is one that has to be carried on day by day. Since it is one that can have no end till experience itself comes to an end, the task of democracy is forever that of creation of a freer and more humane experience in which all share and to which all contribute.

## *John Stuart Mill (1806–1873)*

The section on utilitarianism has already introduced the reader to the philosophy of John Stuart Mill. In this selection Mill discusses a fundamental problem with democracy—the tendency for democracy to become a tyranny of the majority. As a check on government power Mill enunciates his famous statement against **paternalism:** "the only purpose for which power can be rightfully exercised over any member of a civilized community, against his will, is to prevent harm to others. His own good, either physical or moral, is not a sufficient warrant." Mill then applies his antipaternalistic principle to freedom of thought and discussion. Constraints on freedom of thought to protect an individual are never legitimate. However, Mill's argument extends far beyond his antipaternalism. As a good utilitarian, he points out all the good consequences that follow from a policy of free thought and discussion. Not the least of these good results is the existence of a better-informed citizenry in a democratic society.

# On Liberty

## *John Stuart Mill*

. . . A time . . . came, in the progress of human affairs, when men ceased to think it a necessity of nature that their governors should be an independent power, opposed in interest to themselves. It appeared to them much better that the various magistrates of the State should

Abridged from *The English Philosophers from Bacon to Mill.* Edited by Edwin A. Burtt. 

be their tenants or delegates, revocable at their pleasure. In that way alone, it seemed, could they have complete security that the powers of government would never be abused to their disadvantage. . . . In time . . . a democratic republic came to occupy a large portion of the earth's surface, and made itself felt as one of the most powerful members of the community of nations; and elective and responsible government became subject to the observations and criticisms which wait upon a great existing fact. It was now perceived that such phrases as "self-government," and "the power of the people over themselves," do not express the true state of the case. The "people" who exercise the power are not always the same people with those over whom it is exercised; and the "self-government" spoken of is not the government of each by himself, but of each by all the rest. The will of the people, moreover, practically means the will of the most numerous or the most active *part* of the people; the majority, or those who succeed in making themselves accepted as the majority: the people, consequently *may* desire to oppress a part of their number, and precautions are as much needed against this as against any other abuse of power. The limitation, therefore, of the power of government over individuals loses none of its importance when the holders of power are regularly accountable to the community, that is, to the strongest party therein. . . .

Like other tyrannies, the tyranny of the majority was at first, and is still vulgarly, held in dread chiefly as operating through the acts of the public authorities. But reflecting persons perceived that when society is itself the tyrant—society collectively over the separate individuals who compose it—its means of tyrannizing are not restricted to the acts which it may do by the hands of its political functionaries. . . . Protection, therefore, against the tyranny of the magistrate is not enough: there needs protection also against the tyranny of the prevailing opinion and feeling; against the tendency of society to impose, by other means than civil penalties, its own ideas and practices as rules of conduct on those who dissent from them; to fetter the development, and, if possible, prevent the formation, of any individuality not in harmony with its ways, and compels all characters to fashion themselves upon the model of its own. There is a limit to the legitimate interference of collective opinion with individual independence; and to find that limit, and maintain it against encroachment, is as indispensable to a good condition of human affairs, as protection against political despotism. . . .

The object of this essay is to assert one very simple principle, as entitled to govern absolutely the dealings of society with the individual in the way of compulsion and control, whether the means used be physical force in the form of legal penalties, or the moral coercion of public opinion. That principle is, that the sole end for which mankind are warranted, individually or collectively, in interfering with the liberty of action of any of their number, is self-protection. That the only purpose for which power can be rightfully exercised over any member of a civilized community, against his will, is to prevent harm to others. His own good, either physical or moral, is not a sufficient warrant. He cannot rightfully be compelled to do or forbear because it will be better for him to do so, because it will make him happier, because, in the opinions of others, to do so would be wise, or even right. These are good reasons for remonstrating with him, or reasoning with him, or persuading him, or entreating him, but not for compelling him, or visiting him with any evil in case he do otherwise. To justify that, the conduct from which it is desired to deter him must be calculated to produce evil to someone else. The only part of the conduct of anyone, for which he is amenable to society, is that which concerns others. In the part which merely concerns himself, his independence is, of right, absolute. Over himself, over his own body and mind, the individual is sovereign. . . .

There is . . . in the world at large an increasing inclination to stretch unduly the powers of society over the individual, both by the force of opinion and even by that of legislation; and as the tendency of all the changes taking place in the world is to strengthen society, and diminish the power of the individual, this encroachment is not one of the evils which tend spontaneously to disappear, but, on the contrary, to grow more and more formidable. The disposition of mankind, whether as rulers or as fellow-citizens, to impose their own opinions and inclinations as a rule of conduct on others, is so energetically supported by some of the best and by some of the worst feelings incident to human nature, that it is hardly ever kept under restraint by anything but want of power; and as the power is not declining, but growing, unless a strong barrier of moral conviction can be raised against the mischief, we must expect, in the present circumstances of the world, to see it increase.

It will be convenient for the argument, if, instead of at once entering upon the general thesis, we confine ourselves in the first instance to a single branch of it, on which the principle here stated is, if not fully, yet to a certain point, recognized by the current opinions. This one branch is the *liberty of thought:* from which it is impossible to separate the cognate liberty of speaking and of writing. Although these liberties, to some considerable amount, form part of the political morality of all countries which profess religious toleration and free institutions, the grounds, both philosophical and practical, on which they rest, are perhaps not so familiar to the general mind, nor so thoroughly appreciated by many even of the leaders of opinion, as might have been expected. . . .

## OF THE LIBERTY OF THOUGHT AND DISCUSSION

. . . Were an opinion a personal possession of no value except to the owner; if to be obstructed in the enjoyment of it were simply a private injury, it would make some difference whether the injury was inflicted only on a few persons or on many. But the peculiar evil of silencing the expression of an opinion is, that it is robbing the human race: posterity as well as the existing generation; those who dissent from the opinion, still more than those who hold it. If the opinion is right, they are deprived of the opportunity of exchanging error for truth; if wrong, they lose, what is almost as great a benefit, the clearer perception and livelier impression of truth, produced by its collision with error.

It is necessary to consider separately these two hypotheses, each of which has a distinct branch of the argument corresponding to it. We can never be sure that the opinion we are endeavoring to stifle is a false opinion; and if we were sure, stifling it would be an evil still.

First: the opinion which it is attempted to suppress by authority may possibly be true. Those who desire to suppress it, of course deny its truth; but they are not infallible. They have no authority to decide the question for all mankind, and exclude every other person from the means of judging. To refuse a hearing to an opinion, because they are sure that it is false, is to assume that *their* certainty is the same thing as *absolute* certainty. All silencing of discussion is an assumption of infallibility. Its condemnation may be allowed to rest on this common argument, not the worse for being common. . . .

The objection likely to be made to this argument would probably take some such form as the following. There is no greater assumption of infallibility in forbidding the propagation of error, than in any other thing which is done by public authority on its own judgment and responsibility. Judgment is given to men that they may use it. Because it may be used erroneously, are men to be told that they ought not to use it at all? To prohibit what they think pernicious, is not claiming exemption from error, but fulfilling the duty incumbent on them, although fallible, of acting on their conscientious conviction. If we were never to act on our opinions, because those opinions may be wrong, we should leave all our interests uncared for, and all our duties unperformed. An objection which applies to all conduct can be no valid objection to any conduct in particular. It is the duty of governments, and of individuals, to form the truest opinions they can; to form them carefully, and never impose them upon others unless they are quite sure of being right. But when they are sure (such reasoners may say), it is not conscientiousness but cowardice to shrink from acting on their opinions, and allow doctrines which they honestly think dangerous to the welfare of mankind, either in this life or in another, to be scattered abroad without restraint, because other people, in less enlightened times, have persecuted opinions now believed to be true. Let us take care, it may be said, not to make the same mistake; but governments and nations have made mistakes in other things, which are not denied to be fit subjects for the exercise of authority: they have laid on bad taxes, made unjust wars. Ought we therefore to lay on no taxes, and, under whatever provocation, make no wars? Men, and governments, must act to the best of their ability. There is no such thing as absolute certainty, but there is assurance sufficient for the purposes of human life. We may, and must, assume our opinion to be true for the guidance of our own conduct: and it is assuming no more when we forbid bad men to pervert society by the propagation of opinions which we regard as false and pernicious.

I answer that it is assuming very much more. There is the greatest difference between presuming an opinion to be true because, with every opportunity for contesting it, it has not been refuted, and assuming its truth for the purpose of not permitting its refutation. Complete liberty of contradicting and disproving our opinion is the very condition which justifies us in assuming its truth for purposes of action; and on no other terms can a being with human faculties have any rational assurance of being right.

When we consider either the history of opinion, or the ordinary conduct of human life, to what is it to be ascribed that the one and the other are no worse than they are? Not certainly to the inherent force of the human understanding; for, on any matter not self-evident, there are ninety-nine persons totally incapable of judging of it for one who is capable; and the capacity of the hundredth person is only comparative: for the majority of the eminent men of every past generation held many opinions now known to be erroneous, and did or approved numerous things which no one will now justify. Why is it, then, that there is on the whole a preponderance among mankind of rational opinions and rational conduct? If there really is this preponderance—which there must be unless human affairs are, and have always been, in an almost desperate state—it is owing to a quality of the human mind, the source of everything respectable in man either as an intellectual or as a moral being, namely, that his errors are corrigible. He is capable of rectifying his mistakes, by discussion and experience. Not by experience alone. There must be discussion, to show how experience is to be interpreted. Wrong opinions and practices generally yield to fact and argument; but facts and arguments, to produce any effect on the mind, must be brought before it. Very few facts are able to tell their own story, without comments to bring out their meaning. The whole strength and value, then, of human judgment, depending on the one property, that it can be set right when it is wrong, reliance can be placed on it only when the means of setting it right are kept constantly at hand. In the case of any person whose judgment is really deserving of confidence, how has it become so? Because he has kept his mind open to criticism of his opinions and conduct. Because it has been his practice to listen to all that could be said against him; to profit by as much of it as was just, and expound to himself, and upon occasion to others, the fallacy of what was fallacious. Because he has felt that the only way in which a human being can make some approach to knowing the whole of a subject, is by hearing what can be said about it by persons of every variety of opinion, and studying all modes in which it can be looked at by every character of mind. No wise man ever acquired his wisdom in any mode but this; nor is it in the nature of human intellect to become wise in any other manner. The steady habit of correcting and completing his own opinion by collating it with those of others, so far from causing doubt and hesitation in carrying it into practice, is the only stable foundation for a just reliance on it: for, being cognizant of all that can, at least obviously, be said against him, and having taken up his position against all gainsayers—knowing that he has sought for objections and difficulties, instead of avoiding them, and has shut out no light which can be thrown upon the subject from any quarter —he has a right to think his judgment better than that of any person, or any multitude, who have not gone through a similar process.

It is not too much to require that what the wisest of mankind, those who are best entitled to trust their own judgment, find necessary to warrant their relying on it, should be submitted to by that miscellaneous collection of a few wise and many foolish individuals, called the public. The most intolerant of churches, the Roman Catholic Church, even at the canonization of a saint, admits, and listens patiently to, a "devil's advocate." The holiest of men, it appears, cannot be admitted to posthumous honors, until all that the devil could say against him is known and weighed. If even the Newtonian philosophy were not permitted to be questioned, mankind could not feel as complete assurance of its truth as they now do. The beliefs which we have most warrant for, have no safeguard to rest on but a standing invitation to the whole world to prove them unfounded. If the challenge is not accepted, or is accepted and the attempt fails, we are far enough from certainty still; but we have done the best that the existing state of human reason admits of; we have neglected nothing that could give the truth a chance of reaching us: if the lists are kept open, we may hope that if there be a better truth, it will be found when the human mind is capable of receiving it; and in the meantime we may rely on having attained such approach to truth as is possible in our own day. This is the amount of certainty attainable by a fallible being, and this the sole way of attaining it. . . .

Let us now pass to the second division of the argument, and dismissing the supposition that any of the received opinions may be false, let us assume them to be true, and examine into the worth of the manner in which they are likely to be held, when their truth is not freely and openly canvassed. However unwillingly a person who has a strong opinion may admit the possibility that his opinion may be false, he ought to be moved by the consideration that, however true it may be, if it is not fully, frequently, and fearlessly discussed, it will be held as a dead dogma, not a living truth.

There is a class of persons (happily not quite so numerous as formerly) who think it enough if a person assents undoubtingly to what they think true, though he has no knowledge whatever of the grounds of the opinion, and could not make a tenable defense of it against the most superficial objections. Such persons, if they can once get their creed taught from authority, naturally think that no good, and some harm, comes of its being allowed to be questioned. Where their influence prevails, they make it nearly impossible for the received opinion to be rejected wisely and considerately, though it may still be rejected rashly and ignorantly; for to shut out discussion entirely is seldom possible, and when it once gets in, beliefs not grounded on conviction are apt to give way before the slightest semblance of an argument. Waiving, however, this possibility—assuming that the true opinion abides in the mind, but abides as a prejudice, a belief independent of, and proof against, argument—this is not the way in which truth ought to be held by a rational being. This is not knowing the truth. Truth, thus held, is but one superstition the more, accidentally clinging to the words which enunciate a truth.

If the intellect and judgment of mankind ought to be cultivated, a thing which Protestants at least do not deny, on what can these faculties be more appropriately exercised by anyone, than on the things which concern him so much that it is considered necessary for him to hold opinions on them? If the cultivation of the understanding consists in one thing more than in another, it is surely in learning the grounds of one's own opinions. Whatever people believe, on subjects on which it is of the first importance to believe rightly, they ought to be able to defend against at least the common objections. But, some one may say, "Let them be *taught* the grounds of their opinions. It does not follow that opinions must be merely parroted because they are never heard controverted. Persons who learn geometry do not simply commit the theorems to memory, but understand and learn likewise the demonstrations; and it would be absurd to say that they remain ignorant of the grounds of geometrical truths, because they never hear anyone deny, and attempt to disprove them." Undoubtedly: and such teaching suffices on a subject like mathematics, where there is nothing at all to be said on the wrong side of the question. The peculiarity of the evidence of mathematical truths is that all the argument is on one side. There are no objections, and no answers to objections. But on every subject on which difference of opinion is possible, the truth depends on a balance to be struck between two sets of conflicting reasons. Even in natural philosophy, there is always some other explanation possible of the same facts—some geocentric theory instead of heliocentric, some phlogiston instead of oxygen—and it has to be shown why that other theory cannot be the true one; and until this is shown, and until we know how it is shown, we do not understand the grounds of our opinion. But when we turn to subjects infinitely more complicated, to morals, religion, politics, social relations, and the business of life, three-fourths of the arguments for every disputed opinion consist in dispelling the appearances which favor some opinion different from it. The greatest orator, save one, of antiquity, has left it on record that he always studied his adversary's case with as great, if not still greater, intensity than even his own. What Cicero practiced as the means of forensic success requires to be imitated by all who study any subject in order to arrive at the truth. He who knows only his own side of the case, knows little of that. His reasons may be good, and no one may have been able to refute them. But if he is equally unable to refute the reasons on the opposite side; if he does not so much as know what they are, he has no ground for preferring either opinion. The rational position for him would be suspension of judgment, and unless he contents himself with that, he is either led by authority, or adopts, like the generality of the world, the side to which he feels most inclination. Nor is it enough that he should hear the arguments of adversaries from his own teachers, presented as they state them, and accompanied by what they offer as refutations. That is not the way to do justice to the arguments, or bring them into real contact with his own mind. He must be able to hear them from persons who actually believe them; who defend them in earnest, and do their very utmost for them. He must know them in their most plausible and persuasive form; he must feel the whole force of the difficulty which the true view of the subject has to encounter and dispose of; else he will never really possess himself of the portion of truth which meets and removes that difficulty. Ninety-nine in a hundred of what are called educated men are in this condition; even of those who can argue fluently for their opinions. Their conclusion may be true, but it might be false for anything they know: they have never thrown themselves into the mental position of those who think differently from them, and considered what such persons may have to say; and consequently they do not, in any proper sense of the word, know the doctrine which they themselves profess. They do not know those parts of it which explain and justify the remainder; the considerations which show that a fact which seemingly conflicts with another is reconcilable with it, or that, of two apparently strong reasons, one and not the other ought to be preferred. All that part of the truth which turns the scale, and decides the judgment of a completely informed mind, they are strangers to; nor is it ever really known but to those who have attended equally and impartially to both sides, and endeavored to see the reasons of both in the strongest light. So essential is this discipline to a real understanding of moral and human subjects, that if opponents of all important truths do not exist, it is indispensable to imagine them, and supply them with the strongest arguments which the most skillful devil's advocate can conjure up. . . .

It still remains to speak of one of the principal causes which make diversity of opinion advantageous, and will continue to do so until mankind shall have entered a stage of intellectual advancement which at present seems at an incalculable distance. We have hitherto considered only two possibilities: that the received opinion may be false, and some other opinion consequently true; or that, the received opinion being true, a conflict with the opposite error is essential to a clear apprehension and deep feeling of its truth. But there is a commoner case than either of these: when the conflicting doctrines, instead of being one true and the other false, share the truth between them; and the nonconforming opinion is needed to supply the remainder of the truth, of which the received doctrine embodies only a part. Popular opinions, on subjects not palpable to sense, are often true, but seldom or never the whole truth. They are a part of the truth; sometimes a greater, sometimes a smaller part, but exaggerated, distorted, and disjointed from the truths by which they ought to be accompanied and limited. Heretical opinions, on the other hand, are generally some of these suppressed and neglected truths, bursting the bonds which kept them down, and either seeking reconciliation with the truth contained in the common opinion, or fronting it as enemies, and setting themselves up, with similar exclusiveness, as the whole truth. The latter case is hitherto the most frequent, as, in the human mind, one-sidedness has always been the rule, and many-sidedness the exception. Hence, even in revolutions of opinion, one part of the truth usually sets while another rises. Even progress, which ought to superadd, for the most part only substitutes, one partial and incomplete truth for another: improvement consisting chiefly in this, that the new fragment of truth is more wanted, more adapted to the needs of the time, than that which it displaces. Such being the partial character of prevailing opinions, even when resting on a true foundation, every opinion which embodies somewhat of the portion of truth which the common opinion omits, ought to be considered precious, with whatever amount of error and confusion that truth may be blended. No sober judge of human affairs will feel bound to be indignant because those who force on our notice truths which we should otherwise have overlooked, overlook some of those which we see. Rather, he will think that so long as popular truth is one-sided, it is more desirable than otherwise that unpopular truth should have one-sided assertors too; such being usually the most energetic, and the most likely to compel reluctant attention to the fragment of wisdom which they proclaim as if it were the whole. . . .

In politics, again, it is almost a commonplace, that a party of order or stability, and a party of progress or reform, are both necessary elements of a healthy state of political life; until the one or the other shall have so enlarged its mental grasp as to be a party equally of order and of progress, knowing and distinguishing what is fit to be preserved from what ought to be swept away. Each of these modes of thinking derives its utility from the deficiencies of the other; but it is in a great measure the opposition of the other that keeps each within the limits of reason and sanity. Unless opinions favorable to democracy and to aristocracy, to property and to equality, to cooperation and to competition, to luxury and to abstinence, to sociality and individuality, to liberty and discipline, and all the other standing antagonisms of practical life, are expressed with equal freedom, and enforced and defended with equal talent and energy, there is no chance of both elements obtaining their due: one scale is sure to go up, and the other down. Truth, in the great practical concerns of life, is so much a question of the reconciling and combining of opposites, that very few have minds sufficiently capacious and impartial to make the adjustment with an approach to correctness, and it has to be made by the rough process of a struggle between combatants fighting under hostile banners. On any of the great open questions just enumerated, if either of the two opinions has a better claim than the other, not merely to be tolerated, but to be encouraged and countenanced, it is the one which happens at the particular time and place to be in a minority. That is the opinion which, for the time being, represents the neglected interests, the side of human well-being which is in danger of obtaining less than its share. I am aware that there is not, in this country, any intolerance of differences of opinion on most of these topics.

They are adduced to show, by admitted and multiplied examples, the universality of the fact that only through diversity of opinion is there, in the existing state of human intellect, a chance of fair play to all sides of the truth. When there are persons to be found who form an exception to the apparent unanimity of the world on any subject, even if the world is in the right, it is always probable that dissentients have something worth hearing to say for themselves, and that truth would lose something by their silence. . . .

We have now recognized the necessity to the mental well-being of mankind (on which all their other well-being depends) of freedom of opinion, and freedom of the expression of opinion, on four distinct grounds; which we will now briefly recapitulate.

First, if any opinion is compelled to silence, that opinion may, for aught we can certainly know, be true. To deny this is to assume our own infallibility.

Secondly, though the silenced opinion be an error, it may, and very commonly does, contain a portion of truth; and since the general or prevailing opinion on any subject is rarely or never the whole truth, it is only by the collision of adverse opinions that the remainder of the truth has any chance of being supplied.

Thirdly, even if the received opinion be not only true, but the whole truth; unless it is suffered to be, and actually is, vigorously and earnestly contested, it will, by most of those who receive it, be held in the manner of a prejudice, with little comprehension or feeling of its rational grounds. And not only this, but, fourthly, the meaning of the doctrine itself will be in danger of being lost, or enfeebled, and deprived of its vital effect on the character and conduct: the dogma becoming a mere formal profession, inefficacious for good, but cumbering the ground, and preventing the growth of any real and heartfelt conviction, from reason or personal experience. . . .

## *Karl Marx (1818–1883)*

Although nearly every American has heard of Karl Marx, few have ever read him. Moreover, since Marxism is the official state philosophy of the Soviet Union, Marxism is often confused with the pronouncements and policies of the Soviet Union. Although Marx was born a German, he spent most of his life in England where he was supported by the industrialist Engels. During this period, he spent most of his time in the British Museum where he composed his great work *Das Kapital*. The selection included here is from the earlier and more popular *Communist Manifesto* which he coauthored with Engels. Nonetheless, the *Manifesto* does adequately introduce the main themes of Marxist philosophy. Marx's economic determinism is evident in the proposition that the history of society is the history of class struggle, and in his account of the rise and predicted overthrow of capitalism. Section II of the *Manifesto* presents Marx's communist alternative to capitalism.

# The Communist Manifesto

## *Karl Marx*

I

The history of all hitherto existing society is the history of class struggles.

Freeman and slave, patrician and plebeian, lord and serf, guildmaster and journeyman, in a word, oppressor and oppressed, stood in constant opposition to one another, carried on an uninterrupted, now hidden, now open fight, a fight that each time ended, either in a revolutionary reconstitution of society at large, or in the common ruin of the contending classes.

In the earlier epochs of history, we find almost everywhere a complicated arrangement of society into various orders, a manifold gradation of social rank. In ancient Rome we have patricians, knights, plebeians, slaves; in the Middle Ages, feudal lords, vassals, guild-masters, journeymen, apprentices, serfs; in almost all of these classes, again, subordinate gradations.

The modern bourgeois society that has sprouted from the ruins of feudal society, has not done away with class antagonisms. It has but established new classes, new conditions of oppression, new forms of struggle in place of the old ones. . . .

The **bourgeoisie,** wherever it has got the upper hand, has put an end to all feudal, patriarchal, idyllic relations. It has pitilessly torn asunder the motley feudal ties that bound man to his "natural superiors," and has left no other bond between man and man than naked self-interest, than callous "cash payment." It has drowned the most heavenly ecstasies of religious fervor, of chivalrous enthusiasm, of philistine sentimentalism, in the icy water of egotistical calculation. It has resolved personal worth into exchange value, and in place of the numberless indefeasible chartered freedoms, has set up that single, unconscionable freedom — Free Trade. In one word, for exploitation, veiled by religious and political illusions, it has substituted naked, shameless, direct, brutal exploitation.

The bourgeoisie has stripped of its halo every occupation hitherto honored and looked up to with reverent awe. It has converted the physician, the lawyer, the priest, the poet, the man of science, into its paid wage-laborers.

The bourgeoisie has torn away from the family its sentimental veil, and has reduced the family relation to a mere money relation.

The bourgeoisie has disclosed how it came to pass that the brutal display of vigor in the Middle Ages, which reactionaries so much admire, found its fitting complement in the most slothful indolence. It has been the first to show what man's activity can bring about. It has accomplished wonders far surpassing Egyptian pyramids, Roman aqueducts, and Gothic cathedrals; it has conducted expeditions that put in the shade all former migrations of nations and crusades.

The bourgeoisie cannot exist without constantly revolutionizing the instruments of production, and thereby the relations of production, and with them the whole relations of society. Conservation of the old modes of production in unaltered form, was, on the contrary, the first condition of existence for all earlier industrial classes. Constant revolutionizing of production, uninterrupted disturbance of all social conditions, everlasting uncertainty and agitation distinguish the bourgeois epoch from all earlier ones. All fixed, fast-frozen relations, with their train of ancient and venerable prejudices and opinions, are swept away, all new-formed ones become antiquated before they can ossify. All that is solid melts into air, all that is holy is profaned, and man is at last compelled to face with sober senses his real conditions of life and his relations with his kind.

The need of a constantly expanding market for its products chases the bourgeoisie over the whole surface of the globe. It must nestle everywhere, settle everywhere, establish connections everywhere.

The bourgeoisie has through its exploitation of the world market given a cosmopolitan character to production and consumption in every country. To the great chagrin of reactionaries, it has drawn from under the feet of industry the national ground on which it stood. All old-established national industries have been destroyed or are daily being destroyed. They are dislodged by new industries, whose introduction becomes a life and death question for all civilized nations, by industries that no longer work up indigenous raw material, but raw material drawn from the remotest zones; industries whose products are consumed, not only at home, but in every quarter of the globe. In place of the old wants, satisfied by the production of the country, we find new wants, requiring for their satisfaction the products of distant lands and climes. In place of the old local and national seclusion and self-sufficiency, we have intercourse in every direction, universal interdependence of nations. And as in material, so also in intellectual production. The intellectual creations of individual nations become common property. National one-sidedness and narrow-mindedness become more and more impossible, and from the numerous national and local literatures there arises a world literature.

The bourgeoisie, by the rapid improvement of all instruments of production, by the immensely facilitated means of communication, draws all nations, even the most barbarian, into civilization. The cheap prices of its commodities are the heavy artillery with which it batters down all Chinese walls, with which it forces the barbarians' intensely obstinate hatred of foreigners to capitulate. It compels all nations, on pain of extinction, to adopt the bourgeois mode of production; it compels them to introduce what it calls civilization into their midst, *i.e.*, to become bourgeois themselves. In a word, it creates a world after its own image.

The bourgeoisie has subjected the country to the rule of the towns. It has created enormous cities, has greatly increased the urban population as compared with the rural, and has thus rescued a considerable part of the population from the idiocy of rural life. Just as it has made the country dependent on the towns, so it has made barbarian and semibarbarian countries dependent on the civilized ones, nations of peasants on nations of bourgeois, the East on the West. . . .

Modern industry has converted the little workshop of the patriarchal master into the great factory of the industrial capitalist. Masses of laborers, crowded into the factory, are organized like soldiers. As privates of the industrial army they are placed under the command of a perfect hierarchy of officers and sergeants. Not only are they slaves of the bourgeois class, and of the bourgeois state; they are daily and hourly enslaved by the machine, by the overlooker, and, above all, by the individual bourgeois manufacturer himself. The more openly this despotism proclaims gain to be its end and aim, the more petty, the more hateful and the more embittering it is.

The less the skill and exertion of strength implied in manual labor, in other words, the more modern industry develops, the more is the labor of men superseded by that of women. Differences of age and sex have no longer any distinctive social validity for the working class. All are instruments of labor, more or less expensive to use, according to their age and sex.

No sooner has the laborer received his wages in cash, for the moment escaping exploitation by the manufacturer, than he is set upon by the other portions of the bourgeoisie, the landlord, the shopkeeper, the pawnbroker, etc.

The lower strata of the middle class—the small tradespeople, shopkeepers, and retired tradesmen generally, the handicraftsmen and peasants—all these sink gradually into the **proletariat,** partly because their diminutive capital does not suffice for the scale on which modern industry is carried on, and is swamped in the competition with the large capitalists, partly because their specialized skill is rendered worthless by new methods of production. Thus the proletariat is recruited from all classes of the population.

The proletariat goes through various stages of development. With its birth begins its struggle with the bourgeoisie. At first the contest is carried on by individual laborers, then by the work people of a factory, then by the operatives of one trade, in one locality, against the individual bourgeois who directly exploits them. They direct their attacks not against the bourgeois conditions of production, but against the instruments of production themselves; they destroy imported wares that compete with their labor, they smash machinery to pieces, they set factories ablaze, they seek to restore by force the vanished status of the workman of the Middle Ages.

At this stage the laborers still form an incoherent mass scattered over the whole country, and broken up by their mutual competition. If anywhere they unite to form more compact bodies, this is not yet the consequence of their own active union, but of the union of the bourgeoisie, which class, in order to attain its own political ends, is compelled to set the whole proletariat in motion, and is moreover still able to do so for a time. At this stage, therefore, the proletarians do not fight their enemies, but the enemies of their enemies, the remnants of absolute monarchy, the landowners, the nonindustrial bourgeois, the petty bourgeoisie. Thus the whole historical movement is concentrated in the hands of the bourgeoisie; every victory so obtained is a victory for the bourgeoisie.

But with the development of industry the proletariat not only increases in number; it becomes concentrated in greater masses, its strength grows, and it feels that strength more. The various interests and conditions of life within the ranks of the proletariat are more and more equalized, in proportion as machinery obliterates all distinctions of labor and nearly everywhere reduces wages to the same low level. The growing competition among the bourgeois, and the resulting commercial crises, make the wages of the workers ever more fluctuating. The unceasing improvement of machinery, ever more rapidly developing, makes their livelihood more and more precarious; the collisions between individual workmen and individual bourgeois take more and more the character of collisions between two classes. Thereupon the workers begin to form combinations (trade unions) against the bourgeoisie; they club together in order to keep up the rate of wages; they found permanent associations in order to make provision beforehand for these occasional revolts. Here and there the contest breaks out into riots.

Now and then the workers are victorious, but only for a time. The real fruit of their battles lies, not in the immediate results, but in the ever expanding union of the workers. This union is furthered by the improved means of communication which are created by modern industry, and which place the workers of different localities in contact with one another. It was just this contact that was needed to centralize the numerous local struggles, all of the same character, into one national struggle between classes. But every class struggle is a political struggle. And that union, to attain which the burghers of the Middle Ages, with their miserable highways, required centuries, the modern proletarians, thanks to railways, achieve in a few years.

This organization of the proletarians into a class, and consequently into a political party, is continually being upset again by the competition between the workers themselves. But it ever rises up again, stronger, firmer, mightier. It compels legislative recognition of particular interests of the workers, by taking advantage of the divisions among the bourgeoisie itself. . . .

Altogether, collisions between the classes of the old society further the course of development of the proletariat in many ways. The bourgeoisie finds itself involved in a constant battle. At first with the aristocracy; later on, with those portions of the bourgeoisie itself whose interests have become antagonistic to the progress of industry; at all times with the bourgeoisie of foreign countries. In all these battles it sees itself compelled to appeal to the proletariat, to ask for its help, and thus, to drag it into the political arena. The bourgeoisie itself, therefore, supplies the proletariat with its own elements of political and general education, in other words, it furnishes the proletariat with weapons for fighting the bourgeoisie.

Further, as we have already seen, entire sections of the ruling classes are, by the advance of industry, precipitated into the proletariat, or are at least threatened in their conditions of existence. These also supply the proletariat with fresh elements of enlightenment and progress.

Finally, in times when the class struggle nears the decisive hour, the process of dissolution going on within the ruling class, in fact within the whole range of old society, assumes such a violent, glaring character, that a small section of the ruling class cuts itself adrift, and joins the revolutionary class, the class that holds the future in its hands. Just as, therefore, at an earlier period, a section of the nobility went over to the bourgeoisie, so now a portion of the bourgeoisie goes over to the proletariat, and in particular, a portion of the bourgeois ideologists, who have raised themselves to the level of comprehending theoretically the historical movement as a whole.

Of all the classes that stand face to face with the bourgeoisie today, the proletariat alone is a really revolutionary class. The other classes decay and finally disappear in the face of modern industry; the proletariat is its special and essential product.

The lower middle class, the small manufacturer, the shopkeeper, the artisan, the peasant, all these fight against the bourgeoisie, to save from extinction their existence as fractions of the middle class. They are therefore not revolutionary, but conservative. Nay more, they are reactionary, for they try to roll back the wheel of history. If by chance they are revolutionary, they are so only in view of their impending transfer into the proletariat; they thus defend not their present, but their future interests; they desert their own standpoint to adopt that of the proletariat.

The "dangerous class," the social scum *(Lumpenproletariat),* that passively rotting mass thrown off by the lowest layers of old society, may, here and there, be swept into the movement by a proletarian revolution; its conditions of life, however, prepare it far more for the part of a bribed tool of reactionary intrigue.

The social conditions of the old society no longer exist for the proletariat. The proletarian is without property; his relation to his wife and children has no longer anything in common with bourgeois family relations; modern industrial labor, modern subjection to capital, the same in England as in France, in America as in Germany, has stripped him of every trace of national character. Law, morality, religion, are to him so many bourgeois prejudices, behind which lurk in ambush just as many bourgeois interests.

All the preceding classes that got the upper hand, sought to fortify their already acquired status by subjecting society at large to their conditions of appropriation. The proletarians cannot become masters of the productive forces of society, except by abolishing their own previous mode of appropriation, and thereby also every other previous mode of appropriation. They have nothing of their own to secure and to fortify; their mission is to destroy all previous securities for, and insurances of, individual property.

All previous historical movements were movements of minorities, or in the interest of minorities. The proletarian movement is the self-conscious, independent movement of the immense majority, in the interest of the immense majority. The proletariat, the lowest stratum of our present society, cannot stir, cannot raise itself up, without the whole superincumbent strata of official society being sprung into the air.

Though not in substance, yet in form, the struggle of the proletariat with the bourgeoisie is at first a national struggle. The proletariat of each country must, of course, first of all settle matters with its own bourgeoisie.

In depicting the most general phases of the

development of the proletariat, we traced the more or less veiled civil war, raging within existing society, up to the point where that war breaks out into open revolution, and where the violent overthrow of the bourgeoisie lays the foundation for the sway of the proletariat.

Hitherto, every form of society has been based, as we have already seen, on the antagonism of oppressing and oppressed classes. But in order to oppress a class, certain conditions must be assured to it under which it can, at least, continue its slavish existence. The serf, in the period of serfdom, raised himself to membership in the commune, just as the petty bourgeois, under the yoke of feudal absolutism, managed to develop into a bourgeois. The modern laborer, on the contrary, instead of rising with the progress of industry, sinks deeper and deeper below the conditions of existence of his own class. He becomes a pauper, and pauperism develops more rapidly than population and wealth. And here it becomes evident, that the bourgeoisie is unfit any longer to be the ruling class in society, and to impose its conditions of existence upon society as an overriding law. It is unfit to rule because it is incompetent to assure an existence to its slave within his slavery, because it cannot help letting him sink into such a state, that is has to feed him, instead of being fed by him. Society can no longer live under this bourgeoisie, in other words, its existence is no longer compatible with society.

The essential condition for the existence and sway of the bourgeois class, is the formation and augmentation of capital; the condition for capital is wage-labor. Wage-labor rests exclusively on competition between the laborers. The advance of industry, whose involuntary promoter is the bourgeoisie, replaces the isolation of the laborers, due to competition, by their revolutionary combination, due to association. The development of modern industry, therefore, cuts from under its feet the very foundation on which the bourgeoisie produces and appropriates products. What the bourgeoisie therefore produces, above all, are its own gravediggers. Its fall and the victory of the proletariat are equally inevitable.

## II

In what relation do the Communists stand to the proletarians as a whole?

The Communists do not form a separate party opposed to other working-class parties.

They have no interests separate and apart from those of the proletariat as a whole.

They do not set up any sectarian principles of their own, by which to shape and mold the proletarian movement.

The Communists are distinguished from the other working-class parties by this only: 1. In the national struggles of the proletarians of the different countries, they point out and bring to the front the common interests of the entire proletariat, independently of all nationality. 2. In the various stages of development which the struggle of the working class against the bourgeoisie has to pass through, they always and everywhere represent the interests of the movement as a whole.

The Communists, therefore, are on the one hand, practically, the most advanced and resolute section of the working-class parties of every country, that section which pushes forward all others; on the other hand, theoretically, they have over the great mass of the proletariat the advantage of clearly understanding the line of march, the conditions, and the ultimate general results of the proletarian movement.

The immediate aim of the Communists is the same as that of all the other proletarian parties: Formation of the proletariat into a class, overthrow of bourgeois supremacy, conquest of political power by the proletariat.

The theoretical conclusions of the Communists are in no way based on ideas or principles that have been invented, or discovered, by this or that would-be universal reformer.

They merely express, in general terms, actual relations springing from an existing class struggle, from a historical movement going on under our very eyes. The abolition of existing property relations is not at all a distinctive feature of communism.

All property relations in the past have continually been subject to historical change consequent upon the change in historical conditions.

The French Revolution, for example, abolished feudal property in favor of bourgeois property.

The distinguishing feature of **communism** is not the abolition of property generally, but the abolition of bourgeois property. But modern bourgeois private property is the final and most complete expression of the system of producing and appropriating products that is based on class antagonisms, on the exploitation of the many by the few.

In this sense, the theory of the Communists may be summed up in the single sentence: Abolition of private property.

We Communists have been reproached with the desire of abolishing the right of personally acquiring property as the fruit of a man's own labor, which property is alleged to be the groundwork of all personal freedom, activity and independence.

Hard-won, self-acquired, self-earned property! Do you mean the property of the petty artisan and of the small peasant, a form of property that preceded the bourgeois form? There is no need to abolish that; the development of industry has to a great extent already destroyed it, and is still destroying it daily.

Or do you mean modern bourgeois private property?

But does wage-labor create any property for the laborer? Not a bit. It creates capital, *i.e.*, that kind of property which exploits wage-labor, and which cannot increase except upon condition of begetting a new supply of wage-labor for fresh exploitation. Property, in its present form, is based on the antagonism of capital and wage-labor. Let us examine both sides of this antagonism.

To be a capitalist, is to have not only a purely personal, but a social *status* in production. Capital is a collective product, and only by the united action of many members, nay, in the last resort, only by the united action of all members in society, can it be set in motion.

Capital is therefore not a personal, it is a social, power.

When, therefore, capital is converted into common property, into the property of all members of society, personal property is not thereby transformed into social property. It is only the social character of the property that is changed. It loses its class character.

Let us now take wage-labor.

The average price of wage-labor is the minimum wage, *i.e.*, that quantum of the means of subsistence which is absolutely requisite to keep the laborer in bare existence as a laborer. What, therefore, the wage-laborer appropriates by means of his labor, merely suffices to prolong and reproduce a bare existence. We by no means intend to abolish this personal appropriation of the products of labor, an appropriation that is made for the maintenance and reproduction of human life, and that leaves no surplus wherewith to command the labor of others. All that we want to do away with is the miserable character of this appropriation, under which the laborer lives merely to increase capital, and is allowed to live only insofar as the interest of the ruling class requires it.

In bourgeois society, living labor is but a means to increase accumulated labor. In Communist society, accumulated labor is but a means to widen, to enrich, to promote the existence of the laborer.

In bourgeois society, therefore, the past dominates the present; in Communist society, the present dominates the past. In bourgeois society capital is independent and has individuality, while the living person is dependent and has no individuality.

And the abolition of this state of things is called by the bourgeois, abolition of individuality and freedom! And rightly so. The abolition of bourgeois individuality, bourgeois independence, and bourgeois freedom is undoubtedly aimed at.

By freedom is meant, under the present bourgeois conditions of production, free trade, free selling and buying.

But if selling and buying disappears, free selling and buying disappears also. This talk about free selling and buying, and all the other "brave words" of our bourgeoisie about freedom in general, have a meaning, if any, only in contrast with restricted selling and buying, with the fettered traders of the Middle Ages, but have no meaning when opposed to the Communist abolition of buying and selling, of the bourgeois conditions of production, and of the bourgeoisie itself.

You are horrified at our intending to do away with private property. But in your existing society, private property is already done away with for nine-tenths of the population; its existence for the few is solely due to its nonexistence in the hands of those nine-tenths. You reproach us, therefore, with intending to do away with a form of property, the necessary condition for whose existence is the nonexistence of any property for the immense majority of society.

In a word, you reproach us with intending to do away with your property. Precisely so; that is just what we intend.

From the moment when labor can no longer be converted into capital, money, or rent, into a social power capable of being monopolized, *i.e.*, from the moment when individual property can no longer be transformed into bourgeois property, into capital, from that moment, you say, individuality vanishes.

You must, therefore, confess that by "individual" you mean no other person than the bourgeois, than the middle-class owner of property. This person must, indeed, be swept out of the way, and made impossible.

Communism deprives no man of the power to appropriate the products of society; all that it does is to deprive him of the power to subjugate the labor of others by means of such appropriation.

It has been objected, that upon the abolition of private property all work will cease, and universal laziness will overtake us.

According to this, bourgeois society ought long ago to have gone to the dogs through sheer idleness; for those of its members who work, acquire nothing, and those who acquire anything, do not work. The whole of this objection is but another expression of the tautology: There can no longer be any wage-labor when there is no longer any capital.

All objections urged against the Communist mode of producing and appropriating material products, have, in the same way, been urged against the Communist modes of producing and appropriating intellectual products. Just as, to the bourgeois, the disappearance of class property is the disappearance of production itself, so the disappearance of class culture is to him identical with the disappearance of all culture.

That culture, the loss of which he laments, is, for the enormous majority, a mere training to act as a machine.

But don't wrangle with us so long as you apply, to our intended abolition of bourgeois property, the standard of your bourgeois notions of freedom, culture, law, etc. Your very ideas are but the outgrowth of the conditions of your bourgeois production and bourgeois property, just as your jurisprudence is but the will of your class made into a law for all, a will whose essential character and direction are determined by the economic conditions of existence of your class.

The selfish misconception that induces you to transform into eternal laws of nature and of reason, the social forms springing from your present mode of production and form of property — historical relations that rise and disappear in the progress of production — this misconception you share with every ruling class that has preceded you. What you see clearly in the case of ancient property, what you admit in the case of feudal property, you are of course forbidden to admit in the case of your own bourgeois form of property.

Abolition of the family! Even the most radical flare up at this infamous proposal of the Communists.

On what foundation is the present family, the bourgeois family, based? On capital, on private gain. In its completely developed form this family exists only among the bourgeoisie. But this state of things finds its complement in the practical absence of the family among the proletarians, and in public prostitution.

The bourgeois family will vanish as a matter of course when its complement vanishes, and both will vanish with the vanishing of capital.

Do you charge us with wanting to stop the exploitation of children by their parents? To this crime we plead guilty.

But, you will say, we destroy the most hallowed of relations, when we replace home education by social.

And your education! Is not that also social, and determined by the social conditions under which you educate, by the intervention of society, direct or indirect, by means of schools, etc.? The Communists have not invented the intervention of society in education; they do but seek to alter the character of that intervention, and to rescue education from the influence of the ruling class.

The bourgeois claptrap about the family and education, about the hallowed co-relation of parent and child, becomes all the more disgusting, the more, by the action of modern industry, all family ties among the proletarians are torn asunder, and their children transformed into simple articles of commerce and instruments of labor.

But you Communists would introduce community of women, screams the whole bourgeoisie in chorus.

The bourgeois sees in his wife a mere instrument of production. He hears that the instruments of production are to be exploited in common, and, naturally, can come to no other conclusion than that the lot of being common to all will likewise fall to the women.

He has not even a suspicion that the real point aimed at is to do away with the status of women as mere instruments of production.

For the rest, nothing is more ridiculous than the virtuous indignation of our bourgeois at the community of women which, they pretend, is to be openly and officially established by the Communists. The Communists have no need to introduce community of women; it has existed almost from time immemorial.

Our bourgeois, not content with having the wives and daughters of their proletarians at their disposal, not to speak of common prostitutes, take the greatest pleasure in seducing each other's wives.

Bourgeois marriage is in reality a system of wives in common and thus, at the most, what the Communists might possibly be reproached with is that they desire to introduce, in substitution for a hypocritically concealed, an openly legalized community of women. For the rest, it is self-evident, that the abolition of the present system of production must bring with it the abolition of the community of women springing from that system, *i.e.*, of prostitution both public and private.

The Communists are further reproached with desiring to abolish countries and nationality.

The workingmen have no country. We cannot take from them what they have not got. Since the proletariat must first of all acquire political supremacy, must rise to be the leading class of the nation, must constitute itself *the* nation, it is, so far, itself national, though not in the bourgeois sense of the word.

National differences and antagonisms between peoples are vanishing gradually from day to day, owing to the development of the bourgeoisie, to freedom of commerce, to the world market, to uniformity in the mode of production and in the conditions of life corresponding thereto.

The supremacy of the proletariat will cause them to vanish still faster. United action, of the leading civilized countries at least, is one of the first conditions for the emancipation of the proletariat.

In proportion as the exploitation of one individual by another is put an end to, the exploitation of one nation by another will also be put an end to. In proportion as the antagonism between classes within the nation vanishes, the hostility of one nation to another will come to an end.

The charges against communism made from a religious, a philosophical, and, generally, from an ideological standpoint, are not deserving of serious examination.

Does it require deep intuition to comprehend that man's ideas, views, and conceptions, in one word, man's consciousness, changes with every change in the conditions of his material existence, in his social relations and in his social life?

What else does the history of ideas prove, than that intellectual production changes its character in proportion as material production is changed? The ruling ideas of each age have ever been the ideas of its ruling class.

When people speak of ideas that revolutionize society, they do but express the fact that within the old society the elements of a new one have been created, and that the dissolution of the old ideas keeps even pace with the dissolution of the old conditions of existence.

When the ancient world was in its last throes, the ancient religions were overcome by Christianity. When Christian ideas succumbed in the eighteenth century to rationalist ideas, feudal society fought its death-battle with the then revolutionary bourgeoisie. The ideas of religious liberty and freedom of conscience, merely gave expression to the sway of free competition within the domain of knowledge.

"Undoubtedly," it will be said, "[religious], moral, philosophical and juridical ideas have been modified in the course of historical development. But religion, morality, philosophy, political science, and law, constantly survived this change."

"There are, besides, eternal truths, such as Freedom, Justice, etc., that are common to all states of society. But communism abolishes eternal truths, it abolishes all religion, and all morality, instead of constituting them on a new basis; it therefore acts in contradiction to all past historical experience."

What does this accusation reduce itself to? The history of all past society has consisted in the development of class antagonisms, antagonisms that assumed different forms at different epochs.

But whatever form they may have taken, one fact is common to all past ages, *viz.*, the exploitation of one part of society by the other. No wonder, then, that the social consciousness of past ages, despite all the multiplicity and variety it displays, moves within certain common forms, or general ideas, which cannot completely vanish except with the total disappearance of class antagonisms.

The Communist revolution is the most radical rupture with traditional property relations; no wonder that its development involves the most radical rupture with traditional ideas.

But let us have done with the bourgeois objections to communism.

We have seen above, that the first step in the revolution by the working class, is to raise the proletariat to the position of ruling class, to establish democracy.

The proletariat will use its political supremacy to wrest, by degrees, all capital from the bourgeoisie, to centralize all instruments of production in the hands of the state, *i.e.*, of the proletariat organized as the ruling class; and to increase the total of productive forces as rapidly as possible.

Of course, in the beginning, this cannot be effected except by means of despotic inroads on the rights of property, and on the conditions of bourgeois production; by means of measures, therefore, which appear economically insufficient and untenable, but which, in the course of the movement, outstrip themselves, necessitate further inroads upon the old social order, and are unavoidable as a means of entirely revolutionizing the mode of production.

These measures will of course be different in different countries.

Nevertheless in the most advanced countries, the following will be pretty generally applicable.

1. Abolition of property in land and application of all rents of land to public purposes.
2. A heavy progressive or graduated income tax.
3. Abolition of all right of inheritance.

4. Confiscation of the property of all emigrants and rebels.
5. Centralization of credit in the hands of the state, by means of a national bank with state capital and an exclusive monopoly.
6. Centralization of the means of communication and transport in the hands of the state.
7. Extension of factories and instruments of production owned by the state; the bringing into cultivation of waste lands, and the improvement of the soil generally in accordance with a common plan.
8. Equal obligation of all to work. Establishment of industrial armies, especially for agriculture.
9. Combination of agriculture with manufacturing industries; gradual abolition of the distinction between town and country, by a more equable distribution of the population over the country.
10. Free education for all children in public schools. Abolition of child factory labor in its present form. Combination of education with industrial production, etc.

When, in the course of development, class distinctions have disappeared, and all production has been concentrated in the hands of a vast association of the whole nation, the public power will lose its political character. Political power, properly so called, is merely the organized power of one class for oppressing another. If the proletariat during its contest with the bourgeoisie is compelled, by the force of circumstances, to organize itself as a class; if, by means of a revolution, it makes itself the ruling class, and, as such sweeps away by force the old conditions of production, then it will, along with these conditions, have swept away the conditions for the existence of class antagonisms, and of classes generally, and will thereby have abolished its own supremacy as a class.

In place of the old bourgeois society, with its classes and class antagonisms, we shall have an association, in which the free development of each is the condition for the free development of all.

# Part 5 — Glossary

**Absolutism** Ethical absolutism is the view that there is one and only one correct answer to every ethical problem. Another version of ethical absolutism asserts that there are no exceptions to ethical rules or principles.

**Basic structure** *Basic structure* is Rawls' term for the institutions that make a society what it is.

**Bourgeoisie** In Marxian philosophy the bourgeoisie are the capitalists who own the machines and factories and hence control the means of production.

**Categorical imperative** A categorical imperative holds no matter what; it holds with no "ifs," "ands," or "buts" and hence holds independently of your goals and purposes. "Respect the rights of others" is an example of a categorical imperative. See also **hypothetical imperative,** below.

**Communism** Communism is the political philosophy that originated with Karl Marx and Friedrich Engels in the nineteenth century. Essential features of communist theory include *(a)* economic determinism and *(b)* a history of revolutionary changes in economic and political institutions that will result in the overthrow of capitalism and culminate in the withering away of the state and an era of economic abundance where distribution can be made on the basis of need.

**Dignity** *Dignity* has a special meaning in Kant's philosophy. It refers to the special intrinsic quality human beings have as a result of their capacity to formulate and be bound by moral law.

**Egoism** There are two types of egoism that are frequently confused. Psychological egoism is a factual theory about human motivation. It says that people always act in their perceived best interest. Ethical egoism is a normative theory about how people *ought* to act. It says that people always should act in their perceived best interest. The chief difficulty with psychological egoism is that it has a hard time explaining away altruistic acts. The chief difficulty with ethical egoism is the existence of numerous paradoxes. For example, if John and Sally ask an ethical egoist what ought to be done when the interests of John and Sally conflict, the ethical egoist must say that John ought to advance his interests at the expense of Sally and that Sally ought to advance her interests at the expense of John. What kind of advice is that? Finally, note that if psychological egoism were true, ethical egoism (and any other ethical theory for that matter) would be futile. If people do as a matter of fact always pursue their own perceived best interest, exhortations to pursue either their own interest or the interests of others are futile.

**Epicurean** A follower of *Epicureanism,* the philosophy of Epicurus that maintains that pleasure is the greatest good. This philosophy is popularly known as the philosophy of "wine, women, and song." However, the historical Epicurus was an ascetic. He once wrote, "Send me a cheese so that I might dine sumptuously."

**Ethnocentrism** Ethnocentrism is the view that one's own culture is intellectually and morally superior to other cultures.

**Heteronomy of the will** *Heteronomy of the will* is a term in Kant's philosophy that refers to the determination of the will on nonrational grounds. Heteronomy of the will refers to cases where one's will is dominated or controlled by some power foreign to one's own rational nature. In contrast, an autonomous will is one that wills in accordance with that individual's rational nature.

**Human rights** The term *human rights* has replaced the older term *natural rights.* Human rights or natural rights are rights that all persons have just because they are persons. Persons have these rights independently of their society and social institutions. Rather than being created by society, human rights are entitlements that morally influence how social institutions ought to develop.

**Hypothetical imperative** A hypothetical imperative is instrumental in the sense that it tells you what you should do if you want to achieve a certain goal. For example, "You ought to study" holds only if your goal is to get a good grade.

**Intrinsic good** An intrinsic good is a good that is valuable in and of itself. Happiness is the perfect example. Intrinsic goods are distinguished from extrinsic goods. Extrinsic goods are simply useful as a means to an end, e.g., money.

**Majoritarianism** Majoritarianism is a form of democracy where all decisions are made either by the majority vote of the citizens or by the majority vote of the citizens' representatives or by some combination of the two. This view is often criticized because it may lead to a tyranny of the majority.

**Objectivist** One who holds the theory of objectivism. As an epistemological theory, objectivism in the strong sense is the view that ethical judgments are true or false. A weaker form of objectivism claims that moral judgments are capable of rational defense. As a metaphysical theory, objectivism is the view that ethical judgments refer to real properties in the world. One can be an epistemological objectivist without being a metaphysical objectivist.

**Paternalism** Paternalism occurs whenever an individual or the state restricts the freedom of the individual against that person's will on the grounds that it is in the interest of the person whose freedom is restricted.

**Procedural justice** Procedural justice is distinguished from just results. In grading students, the justice of the grade can be distinguished from the justice of the method of arriving at the grade. A student might receive a just grade of an A but nonetheless receive the grade for the wrong reasons—unjustly. Suppose a student's average was 93, but the professor never did the arithmetic calculation. The teacher gave the student an A simply because the student had elected philosophy as a major.

**Proletariat** In Marxian philosophy the proletariat are the laborers who are exploited by the bourgeoisie.

**Pure procedural justice** In Rawls' philosophy pure procedural justice refers to that special case where just procedures are sufficient for justice. So long as the procedures are just, any outcome that results from those procedures is also just. A fair lottery is an example. The type of social contract that Rawls propounds also serves as an example.

**Realm of ends** *Realm of ends* is a term in Kant's moral philosophy that refers to that ideal community of moral persons. *Ends* is a term that Kant uses to refer to people. In the ideal realm of ends, persons test proposed courses of action against the categorical imperative. Because the categorical imperative is a principle of reason, the obligations required by the imperative are required of all human beings. Hence all members of the realm of ends are subject to them. On the other hand, because we are rational beings the obligations required by the imperatives are autonomously chosen by us. Hence all members of the realm of ends are sovereign over the obligations that bind us all.

**Relativism** Relativism is the view that what is right or wrong, good or bad depends either on the culture or on the feelings of the individual. Hence, adherents are called either *cultural relativists* or *individual relativists.* Actually there are many different types of relativists. Some relativists make the very weak claim that as a matter of fact there is a great diversity among cultures as to what is considered right or wrong, good or bad. These persons are called *descriptive relativists* since they simply describe the world. Other relativists make the stronger claim that there are no universal principles in ethics and hence that what is right or wrong depends on one's culture. Note that cultural relativism is often confused with another position—ethical scepticism. Ethical scepticism holds that there is no way to establish one ethical view or theory as rationally superior to any other. These positions are distinct because a consistent ethical sceptic would argue that relativism cannot be shown to be rationally superior to any universalist theory.

**Subjectivist** One who holds the theory of subjectivism. As an epistemological theory, subjectivism is the view that ethical judgments are neither true or false nor can they be rationally justified. As a metaphysical theory, subjectivism is the view that ethical judgments do not refer to any properties in the external world; rather they express the emotional or attitudinal state of the speaker.

**Universalism** Universalism is the view that there is at least one ethical principle that holds true across all cultures. The principle of utility and the principle of respect for persons are two of the most commonly proposed universal principles. If univeralism is true, ethical relativism must be false. If ethical relativism is true, universalism must be false. However, a person holding the universalist view should not be confused with a person who argues that there is one and only one right answer to every ethical problem. A person can be an ethical universalist and still argue that universal ethical principles can be applied differently in different cultures and hence that universalism is consistent with a rich variety of subsidiary ethical principles and practices.

**Veil of ignorance** In Rawls' philosophy, *veil of ignorance* is the term used to describe the technique used to avoid bias in deriving the principles of justice. The technique involves ignoring people's specific characteristics, such as race, sex, class, and education, that might bias the result.

**Virtues** Virtues are commendable traits of character. When those traits of character are peculiarly ethical, the character traits are moral virtues. Virtues are not limited to moral virtues. It is common to speak of intellectual virtues or aesthetic virtues.

**Weakness of will** A person shows weakness of will whenever he or she knows what ought to be done but doesn't do it. "Weakness of will" is often synonymous with "yielding to temptation."

# *Part 5 — Study Questions*

## *WHY BE MORAL*

1. Although Gyges is a mythical person, can you think of any real life situations where individuals or institutions have powers almost as strong as Gyges? If you do, what arguments could you construct to urge them to behave morally?
2. Plato thinks that ultimately immorality does not pay. Do you agree or disagree? Why or why not?
3. Baier argues that morality is in the interest of society and hence that morality "pays off." Do you agree that morality is in the interest of society? Why or why not?
4. If morality is in the interest of society, does that reduce morality to prudence or self-interest? Explain your answer.
5. Suppose an individual agrees that morality is in society's interest but argues that an individual, nonetheless, should not follow morality when he or she can get away with it. After all, what is in society's interest is not always in an individual's interest. What response would you make to such an argument?

## *RELATIVISM*

1. What arguments does Westermarck bring against the theory that ethical judgments have objective validity? Are these arguments good ones? Defend your answer.
2. Explain why the fact that different cultures have different ethical practices does not establish relativism. Does this failure to move from the fact of diversity to the correctness of an ethical theory show that ethical theories have no relation to the facts? Explain.

3. "If relativism is rejected, ethnocentrism and intolerance inevitably follow." Evaluate this statement.
4. If relativism is true, is there any place in the culture for a moral reformer? Explain.
5. Show how the statement of relativism can lead to logical paradoxes similar in kind to those created by the first sentence in a book that reads "Every statement in this book is false."

## *ULTIMATE MORAL PRINCIPLES*

1. Use a Kantian argument to convince a fellow student that his or her planned cheating is either self-contradictory or self-defeating.
2. Since the maxim "It is OK to lie" could not pass the test of the categorical imperative, does that mean that a Kantian must hold that telling a lie is *always* wrong? Explain.
3. Both Kant and Mill discuss the proof that can be given for the categorical imperative and the principle of utility. Which philosopher gives the best proof for his theory? Explain your answer.
4. Critics of Bentham's utilitarianism said that utilitarianism is committed to the view that the life of a satisfied pig is better than the life of a dissatisfied Socrates. How could the critics make that argument? How did Mill try to counter the argument? How could Mill answer the criticism, "But your solution doesn't take account of the perspective of the pig"?
5. "Utilitarianism ignores the individual." Explain what is correct and what is incorrect in that assertion. (You may try to argue that the statement is wholly correct or wholly incorrect.)

## *THE MORAL PERSON*

1. The utilitarian philosopher Jeremy Bentham referred to human rights philosophy as "nonsense on stilts," and many contemporary philosophers have argued that the ever-expanding claim of moral rights threaten to make ethics chaotic. Do you agree or disagree? Explain.
2. How does Wasserstrom argue for the existence of the human rights of freedom and well-being? Is his argument a good one? Explain. Would any other rights pass Wasserstrom's test for a human right—for example, the right to life, the right to privacy, or the right to a vacation with pay?
3. Do you agree with Aristotle that all moral virtues represent a mean between excess and deficiency? In giving your answer, indicate what account should be given of the virtues of truth telling and love.
4. Aristotle seems to argue that the development of virtue can take place only in a community. Does this mean that in Aristotle's view a hermit could not be virtuous? Explain.
5. Aristotle seems to say that only the virtuous person can be happy. Explain what Aristotle meant. Do you agree or disagree with him? Explain.

## *THE MORAL COMMUNITY*

1. Some charge that a morality of "my station and its duties" is subject to abuse. Whenever a person commits an immoral act, he or she can always say, "I was only following orders." Do you agree or disagree with these critics? Explain.
2. What are Rawls' two principles for just institutions, and how did he arrive at them? Do you think they are adequate principles? Defend your answer.
3. How do you think American democracy can be improved as a system of imperfect procedural justice?
4. John Stuart Mill argues that the state should never engage in paternalism. Therefore, he

would be against the recent New York law requiring persons to wear seat belts. Do you think Mill would be right? Explain.

5. State Marx's argument against private property. Which system is more just—the kind of capitalism you experience or the alternative system presented in *The Communist Manifesto?* Explain.

# *Part 5—Suggestions for Further Reading*

*BOOKS*

1. Ackerman, Bruce A. *Social Justice In the Liberal State* (New Haven: Yale University Press, 1980).
2. Bentham, Jeremy. *An Introduction to the Principles of Morals and Legislation,* New Edition (Oxford: Oxford University Press, 1832).
3. Dworkin, Ronald. *Taking Rights Seriously* (Cambridge, MA: Cambridge University Press, 1977).
4. Gert, Bernard. *The Moral Rules* (New York: Harper & Row, 1966).
5. Gewirth, Alan. *Reason and Morality* (Chicago: The University of Chicago Press, 1978).
6. Hare, R. M. *Freedom and Reason* (Oxford: Oxford University Press, 1963).
7. ———. *Moral Thinking: Its Levels, Method, and Point* (New York: Oxford University Press, 1981).
8. Hohfeld, Wesley. *Fundamental Legal Conceptions* (New Haven: Yale University Press, 1923).
9. MacIntyre, Alasdair. *After Virtue: A Study in Moral Theory* (Notre Dame, IN: University of Notre Dame Press, 1981).
10. Ross, W. D. *The Right and the Good* (Oxford: Clarendon Press, 1930).
11. Sidgwick, Henry. *Methods of Ethics* (London: Macmillan, 1962).
12. Smart, J. J. C. and Bernard Williams. *Utilitarianism, For and Against* (Cambridge: Cambridge University Press, 1973).

*TEXTS*

13. Bluhm, William T. *Theories of the Political System* (Englewood Cliffs, N.J.: Prentice-Hall, Inc., 1978).
14. Bowie, Norman and Robert L. Simon. *The Individual and the Political Order,* Second Edition (Englewood Cliffs, N.J.: Prentice-Hall, Inc., 1986).
15. Feinberg, Joel. *Social Philosophy* (Englewood Cliffs, N.J.: Prentice-Hall, Inc., 1973).
16. Frankena, William. *Ethics,* Second Edition (Englewood Cliffs, N.J.: Prentice-Hall, Inc., 1973).
17. Hospers, John. *Human Conduct: Problems of Ethics* (New York: Harcourt Brace Jovanovich, Inc., 1982).
18. Taylor, Paul W. *Principles of Ethics: An Introduction* (Encino, CA: Dickenson Publishing Co., 1975).

# FAITH AND REASON

Religious experience can be among the most intense of all human experiences. On the one hand it can enrich human lives by bestowing on them a dignity and purpose that transcends human suffering and death. On the other hand where religious differences erupt into disputes, violent disagreement, warfare, and even acts of atrocity can result. Religion has certainly been a force for good but, in the name of religion, religious zealots have committed unspeakable evil.

Many academic disciplines, including theology, philosophy, anthropology, sociology, and psychology, have examined religious experience. Not surprisingly, each academic discipline has its own perspective on religious phenomena. For purposes of our discussion, the first task is to narrow the scope of religion so that it does not encompass all experience that human beings find to be of intrinsic value. We will use the concept of religion common in the Western tradition. Within that tradition, a set of beliefs is properly called religious if the set contains: *(a)* a belief in a supernatural being, *(b)* an account of the relation of individuals and our world to the supernatural being and its world, and *(c)* a distinction between the sacred and the profane and a belief in sacred objects. A group of persons belong to a religion when they share a set of similar or identical religious beliefs and, given these beliefs, act in a religious manner. Acting in a religious manner usually includes such things as engaging in ritual acts and prayer and in sharing religious feelings such as awe, a sense of mystery, and adoration, either in houses of worship or in the presence of sacred objects.

This definition eliminates certain "secular religions" from consideration. According to this definition, humanist beliefs are not religious because the set contains no belief in a supernatural being. For similar reasons, a belief system that tries to substitute the state for supernatural beings as the focus of worship does not qualify as a religion on this account. In a significant sense, a religion is otherworldly in its orientation. A religious world view stands in contrast to a secular world view.

Religion is a group phenomenon; adherence to religious beliefs or experiences on the part of one person can't constitute a religion. From about the 1960s some people, while under the influence of mind-altering drugs, claimed to have had supernatural experiences that they call religious. Rather than saying the experience was simply the result of drugs and hence not supernatural, let us say that such experiences lack the developed ritual and communal sharing characteristic of a genuine religion. Undoubtedly there will be borderline cases, but the definition provided here does encompass all of the great Western religious traditions.

Some of the academic studies of religion have tried to explain religious experience away—usually by giving psychological or sociological explanations of the experience. For example, one branch of the sociology of religion with roots in the work of the French sociologist Emile Durkheim argued that the supernatural beings that figure in religious beliefs are simply unconsciously fabricated imaginary beings that society uses to exercise control over individuals. The sense of being in touch with a supernatural or transcendent reality is nothing more than the awe inspired by being part of something greater than ourselves—specifically the larger social order. But why do human beings mythologize society in this way? Philosophers like Aristotle and F. H. Bradley argue that the individual requires society for growth and sustenance. Why aren't these insights sufficient? Durkheim's answer is that human beings universally exercise their capacity to express deep-seated needs and emotions in mental images and symbols.

There are a number of difficulties with Durkheim's account. First, many religions make universal claims that transcend the society in which they spring up. Moreover, some religious leaders actively condemn the society in which they live. Prophets stand in judgment on society. If religion is simply a device for control by particular societies, how can we account for these phenomena of universal religions and religious prophets? If Durkheim's theory were true, how would a religious prophet be possible?

Moreover, what evidence do Durkheim and his followers bring forth to show that supernatural beings are imaginary creations formed unconsciously. Showing that something occurred as a result of unconscious motivation is very tricky. After all, the unconscious is neither directly observed by others nor experienced by anyone. As you might expect after studying the scientific method in Part 2, whether or not the "unconscious" can function as a genuine scientific explanation is a matter of some controversy. In any case, as we have shown in the previous paragraph, it isn't evident that Durkheim's theory can explain all the religious data.

Yet another well known attempt to reduce the religious to the secular is that of Sigmund Freud. Freud's theory of religious belief is tied to his theory of the Oedipus complex. Rather than explain all the complexities of the Oedipus complex (the interested reader should consult Freud's *Totem and Taboo*), suffice it to say that according to Freud, religious belief is a throwback to an infantile state of mind where we were dependent on our parents. Supernatural beings are projections of childhood father images. In more popular Freudian theory, religion is nothing more than a psychological crutch.

The details of Freud's theory are rejected by most psychologists, and Freud's overall thesis has come under the criticism of both theologians and philosophers. Chief among the difficulties is the problem Freud would have in verifying his theory. As we saw in the discussion of Durkheim, it is very difficult to establish hypotheses based on unconscious thoughts and desires. But the problem is deeper than that. Freud and people like him are apt to fall into the trap of committing the genetic fallacy. The genetic fallacy occurs when someone confuses the issue of whether a belief is true or false with the way a belief came about (with the cause of a person's holding the belief he or she does). During the Vietnam war, persons who protested the war on moral and even prudential grounds were called cowards. They protested, it was said, only because they were afraid to fight. Now suppose that fear was the proper explanation of the cause of the protesters' belief that the war was morally wrong. That cowardice does not subtract one bit from the possibility that the Vietnam war was immoral. The issue of immorality has to be settled on independent grounds. Similarly, even if the image of God is based on a child's relation to its father, whether or not such a supernatural being exists must be argued for on independent grounds. The psychological basis or cause of a belief must not be confused with the issue of whether or not the belief is true.

We hope the reader can now see why Durkheim's and Freud's criticisms do not prove that religious experience is illusory or mistaken. At most, they provide hypotheses about the cause of religious beliefs; but the philosopher focuses on whether or not religious beliefs are true or well justified.

For example, our first section focuses on the question of whether revelation can be a legitimate source of religious belief. In the history of the topic this debate is known as the "faith-reason" controversy. The first difficulty with accepting revelation as a source of religious truth is that revelation provides no mechanism for settling disputes between competing revelations. If the God of Moses reveals something to the Jews that conflicts with what the God of Mohammad reveals to the Muslims, how is this dispute to be resolved? Where revelations conflict some method is needed to resolve the conflict. Traditionally one would call in reason. But are religious beliefs capable of rational justification? On this question there is a tremendous diversity of opinion. Some have argued that religious beliefs are contrary to reason, others that religious beliefs are simply nonrational but are not in conflict with reason. Still others have argued that some, but not all, religious beliefs can be rationally justified, and finally still others argue that no religious beliefs can be rationally justified and hence that religious beliefs should be rejected.

The belief that a supernatural being exists is a fundamental religious tenet that many philosophers and theologians regard as a rationally justifiable belief. The selections in the section "Proofs for the Existence of God," consider three traditional arguments for God's existence. In reading these selections, it should be noted that some truly religious persons believe they have all the proof they need for the existence of God without such arguments. They feel God's presence as they live their religion. Hence even if the proofs fail, some religious persons are unswayed. But the proofs are important for nonbelievers or agnostics or for genuine believers who need rational arguments to maintain the leap of faith. They provide arguments against Freud's theory that belief in a supernatural being is simply juvenile projection of a complex father figure. The arguments take many forms. The **ontological** argument is based solely on the concept of God and the logical analysis of that concept. Others begin with experiences of the world. The cosmological argument argues that God is necessary to explain the origin of the cosmos or alternatively of contingent things like ourselves that obviously did not bring themselves into existence. The teleological argument proceeds by analogy to argue that God is necessary to explain the high degree of order and adaptation in the universe. Still another argument is based on the integrity of the moral life. Suffice it to say that several sorts of argument have been used to try to establish the existence of God.

Although the alleged inadequacies of the traditional proofs of God's existence may not shake the religious person's faith, the acute experience of suffering that afflicts so many often has. How can a loving God permit such suffering? This question, asked in anguish by the faithful, is what philosophers call the problem of evil. Succinctly put, does the amount and intensity of evil in the world provide conclusive or probable evidence against the existence of the sort of God theists believe in? Every religion with an omnipotent, loving God must try to provide some answer to this question. In the section "The Problem of Evil," some of the best-known answers to the problem of evil are presented.

Virtually all believers admit that the existence of evil is not something to be fully explained. Some of it will remain a mystery. Believers often claim that we can't be certain there is no justification for the existence of evil, and even though we may not be able to understand the evils that beset us or others, we take them as a trial of faith. Indeed in our attempt to overcome evil we most resemble a loving God and in that sense can be truly called the children of God.

How the religious person actually responds to evil is a measure of how the religious person sees human destiny. The inevitability of death is one of the most difficult brute facts of human existence to accept. Whereas secular philosophers argue that the fact of death must be accepted and hence that the full meaning of a human life is what we make of our lives here and now, most religious persons see human life in this world as only one step in the journey of life. Our individual stories do not end with our deaths. Some faithful believe that at some point in history the dead will be resurrected. Others believe that even if the body dies, individual souls are immortal. In the final section, "Immortality," various accounts of life after death are considered and criticized. As with other topics in the philosophy of religion,the status of so-called empirical evidence for survival is considered. However, even in the absence of conclusive proof, the faithful believe that they will survive to come face to face with a loving God and be accepted into God's eternal kingdom.

# Religious Commitment and the Nature Of Faith

Two topics to avoid at a dinner party are religion and politics. The reason for that rule of etiquette seems to be that convictions about both topics are so deeply held that there seems little in the way of argument that will convince one party to change allegiance. Arguments about religion are heated but usually unconvincing.

Nonetheless the philosophical investigation of religion requires an examination of the epistemology of religious claims. Your study of Part 2 will be of great help here. In this section the concern is both with the source of religious claims and with their justification.

In Part 2 you saw that the two sources of knowledge about the world were sense experience and reason. Philosophers heatedly debated the importance of each as a source of knowledge. Traditionally there are two main sources of religious knowledge—reason and revelation.* As in traditional epistemology, the role and importance of each is heatedly debated.

Revelation is a source of religious knowledge that comes from God. God reveals religious truth to human beings either directly or indirectly—directly through visions or other supernatural communication, or indirectly through a sacred text, human emissaries (priests and churches, for example), or through miracles. Revelation is purportedly an otherworldly source of knowledge.

What are the similarities and dissimilarities between otherworldly revelation and worldly reason? A somewhat surprising similarity is that both are tested by how successfully they explain human experience. A scientific theory that doesn't explain the phenomena of human experience wouldn't be a good scientific theory. A set of religious claims that do not enable a group of human beings to successfully address those questions we have designated as distinctively religious questions would not be experientially validated. Those religious claims would not be justified.

However, consider the contrast between the experiential justification of science and religion. Scientific hypotheses should make sense of our experience of this world of physical objects and events. Religious claims should make sense of this world and of the world that is purportedly beyond the physical world (the supernatural). It should also attempt to address concerns about the meaning or point of human life. However, there seems to be an important difference between scientific theories and religious outlooks. Since *all* human beings live in the physical world, tests of scientific hypotheses are repeatable and hence verifiable by all human beings. Scientific knowledge is universally valid for all cultures. The principles of mathematics or physics hold everywhere. But the same cannot be said for religious outlooks.

It seems that in theory religious knowledge gained through revelation might be universal in just the same way that scientific knowledge is. Religious hypotheses could be tested against religious experience and sooner or later one set of hypotheses about the truths of religion would emerge. Obviously it hasn't worked that way, but could it? One reason for doubting that it could is the fact that many religions are exclusive in their claims. Calvinistically inclined believers sometimes claim that revealed truths can be accepted only by a select few—the elect. A portion of humanity is to be saved; the rest are to be damned and there is nothing a human being can do to be among the saved. Election is by grace (will of God) rather than by works. For such religions, there can be no analogy between religious truth and scientific truth. There is no possible method for adjudicating disputes between the revealed "truths" of two or more religions of this type.

---

* Sense experience does make a contribution to religious knowledge, although in the philosophy of religion reason and sense experience are usually considered together as the rational faculty together with its worldly source of "raw materials."

But not all religions are restricted in this way. Some claim that the revealed truths of their religion apply to all humans and hence that they can be tested against religious experience in general. Hence, perhaps ultimately the "truths" of revelation are universal after all. If so, a further question is whether or not these "truths" of revelation are capable of rational justification.

A few philosophers and theologians have argued that the revealed truths are not only unique, but that revealed truths and the truths of reason are in contradiction. If a belief in something contrary to reason is absurd, you can understand the defiance of Tertullian when he proclaimed, "I believe because it is absurd." For Tertullian the very depth of a religious person's faith is captured by the willingness of that person to believe something contrary to reason. If Tertullian were right there would be no means for settling religious disputes. Since each disputant would claim that truth is on its side and since reason would have to be irrelevant, universal agreement would be impossible—at least up to the time that one group changed its mind.

A more moderate position is the one that argues that revealed truths are nonrational but not irrational. In other words, revealed truths can't be established by reason but they don't fly in the face of reason either. Indeed some philosophers including Pascal and William James argue that human lives can't be lived by the truths of reason alone. Leaps of faith are a necessary part of human life. James's classic statement of that position is reproduced here and the reader will have the opportunity to assess it. However, let us suppose that James is right; the living of a human life requires a leap of faith. That knowledge will not tell us which leap of faith is correct. Since the claims of revelation on this view are nonrational, there is no way to settle disputes among revelations. Hence little advice can be offered to those who must take the leap of faith as to which way they should jump.

In response to this state of affairs, some have argued for the primacy of making the leap. This view is captured by Augustine's remark, "I believe in order that I may understand." Consider a circle that contains the revealed truths of Christianity. So long as you are outside the circle, the revealed truths of Christianity won't make any sense. They seem nonrational. However, once the leap of faith is made, they will make sense. The believer will understand. Augustine's remarks are based on some rather acute observations of human nature. Many practices of a group or culture make no sense to us so long as we aren't participants. However, once one becomes a participant, everything becomes clear. Some anthropologists adopt a similar position when they argue that to fully understand a culture, they must be active participants in it.

However, there is one significant difference between the anthropologist and the person who makes the leap of faith. Once the anthropologist has made the leap, the various claims the alien culture makes about this world can be assessed by reason. If the culture believes that the earth rests in a large bowl of water, that belief can be shown to be false. Usually such falsification by reason can take place when someone makes the leap of faith. However, the revealed claims of religious faith are often nonrational and hence disputes between them cannot be settled by reason.

Kierkegaard's view, which begins this section, shares elements of Tertullian's, James's, and Augustine's positions. With respect to religious doctrines (objective truth), Kierkegaard agrees with Tertullian that the central Christian truth that the Eternal God became Man in Christ at a point in time is contrary to reason. He also believes that to accept Christianity (to accept it as subjective truth), you must make a leap of faith. Only in living Christianity can you accept its truth; however, it is the truth of a lived faith (subjective truth) rather than doctrinal (objective) truth. As subjective truth the truth of Christianity is nonrational. As you can see, Kierkegaard's position is very complicated and may be easily misinterpreted. When someone says that religious claims are contrary to reason, some conceptual analysis is called for. A person holding such a view could mean:

1. that religious doctrines are contradictory,
2. that religious doctrines are consistent but that convincing evidence is lacking for them,
3. that religious commitment is not a matter of accepting doctrines, but is simply a matter of living a religiously committed life, or
4. that one must accept some religious doctrines on faith before the religious outlook makes rational sense.

We now turn to another approach that claims that at least some of the claims of revelation are in conformity with reason and hence can be assessed by the canons of rational thought. Saint Thomas Aquinas held that there are truths of revelation that cannot be established rationally, although these claims do not contradict reason. This approach is taken in the selection included here. Hence some religious truths that have been revealed are nonetheless universal truths because they are capable of justification by human reason.

A final position rejects the claim of revelation to be a legitimate source of knowledge. If the claims of revelation are absurd they should not be believed. If they are nonrational they should not be accepted. If they are alleged to be in conformity with reason, rational analysis will show they should be rejected. On this basis, Thomas Huxley argues for the rejection of religion. Huxley coined the term **agnosticism** to describe his own position. To be an agnostic means that we are not able to answer the ultimate questions that religion asks about the meaning of human existence.

## *Søren Kierkegaard (1813–1855)*

Kierkegaard was a nineteenth century philosopher and religious thinker who is often viewed as one of the forerunners of existentialism. Although there are many dangers in trying to understand a thinker's philosophy by looking at crises in his or her life, Kierkegaard's philosophy is bound up with his life experience. Throughout his life, he was subject to bouts of melancholy. Although he studied to be a Lutheran minister, his studies were interrupted by a period of hedonistic living, and even after completing his studies he soon refused to practice his vocation. Indeed, he bitterly criticized the Danish Lutheran Church. Finally he broke his engagement to Regine, the only love in his life because, in part at least, he believed he could not devote himself sufficiently to her. For Kierkegaard, the pursuit of truth was not simply an objective of study; it was a way of life.

This emphasis on a lived philosophy has led many to characterize Kierkegaard as a subjectivist. However, one must be careful not to think that Kierkegaard believed that any view or that any way of life was as good as any other. Kierkegaard was neither an epistemological nor an ethical relativist. Because philosophy was a matter of human action, he emphasized human will and commitment rather than reason and disinterested (that is, unbiased) inquiry, and hence anticipated William James. In exercising the will to achieve an authentic life, Kierkegaard argued that human beings must be willing to live in ways that seem absurd or paradoxical from the standpoint of conventional wisdom, and this absurdity or paradox becomes the defining feature of authentic religiousness. In *Fear and Trembling,* Kierkegaard repeats the famous Bible story of Abraham and his son Isaac. Abraham loves his only son, Isaac, but is willing to slay him if God commands it. Here the religious person transcends the ethical. Ethics prohibits the murder of one's son. One of Kierkegaard's tasks is to enable us to distinguish the madman from the religious person who lives subjective truth. Whether Kierkegaard ever succeeded in making that distinction is a matter of great debate.

# Faith and Subjectivity

## *Søren Kierkegaard*

. . . When one man investigates objectively the problem of immortality, and another embraces an uncertainty with the passion of the infinite: where is there most truth, and who has the greater certainty? The one has entered upon a never-ending approximation, for the certainty of immortality lies precisely in the subjectivity of the individual; the other is immortal and fights for his immortality by struggling with the uncertainty. . . .

*The objective accent falls on WHAT is said, the subjective accent on HOW it is said.* This distinction holds even in the aesthetic realm, and receives definite expression in the principle that what is in itself true may in the mouth of such and such a person become untrue. In these times this distinction is particularly worthy of notice, for if we wish to express in a single sentence the difference between ancient times and our own, we should doubtless have to say: "In ancient times only an individual here and there knew the truth; now all know it, except that the inwardness of its appropriation stands in an inverse relationship to the extent of its dissemination. Aesthetically the contradiction that truth becomes untruth in this or that person's mouth, is best construed comically: In the ethico-religious sphere, accent is again on the "how." But this is not to be understood as referring to demeanor, expression, or the like; rather it refers to the relationship sustained by the existing individual, in his own existence, to the content of his utterance. Objectively the interest is focussed merely on the thought-content, subjectively on the inwardness. At its maximum this inward "how" is the passion of the infinite, and the passion of the infinite is the truth. But the passion of the infinite is precisely subjectivity, and thus subjectivity becomes the truth. Objectively there is no infinite decisiveness, and hence it is objectively in order to annul the difference between good and evil, together with the principle of contradiction, and therewith also the infinite difference between the true and the false. Only in subjectivity is there decisiveness, to seek objectivity is to be in error. It is the passion of the infinite that is the decisive factor and not its content, for its content is precisely itself. In this manner subjectivity and the subjective "how" constitute the truth.

But the "how" which is thus subjectively accentuated precisely because the subject is an existing individual, is also subject to a dialectic with respect to time. In the passionate moment of decision, where the road swings away from objective knowledge, it seems as if the infinite decision were thereby realized. But in the same moment the existing individual finds himself in the temporal order, and the subjective "how" is transformed into a striving, a striving which receives indeed its impulse and a repeated renewal from the decisive passion of the infinite, but is nevertheless a striving.

When subjectivity is the truth, the conceptual determination of the truth must include an expression for the antithesis to objectivity, a memento of the fork in the road where the way swings off; this expression will at the same time serve as an indication of the tension of the subjective inwardness. Here is such a definition of truth: *An objective uncertainty held fast in an* ***appropriation-process*** *of the most passionate inwardness is the truth,* the highest truth attainable for an *existing* individual. At the point where the way swings off (and where this is cannot be specified objectively, since it is a matter of subjectivity), there objective knowledge is placed in

---

Abridged from *Concluding Unscientific Postscript,* by Søren Kierkegaard. Translated by David Swenson and Walter Lowrie.  Excerpt pp. 180–99, 290–91, 371. Reprinted by permission of Princeton University Press.

abeyance. Thus the subject merely has, objectively, the uncertainty; but it is this which precisely increases the tension of that infinite passion which constitutes his inwardness. The truth is precisely the venture which chooses an objective uncertainty with the passion of the infinite. I contemplate the order of nature in the hope of finding God, and I see omnipotence and wisdom; but I also see much else that disturbs my mind and excites anxiety. The sum of all this is an objective uncertainty. But it is for this very reason that the inwardness becomes as intense as it is, for it embraces this objective uncertainty with the entire passion of the infinite. In the case of a mathematical proposition the objectivity is given, but for this reason the truth of such a proposition is also an indifferent truth.

But the above definition of truth is an equivalent expression for faith. Without risk there is no faith. Faith is precisely the contradiction between the infinite passion of the individual's inwardness and the objective uncertainty. If I am capable of grasping God objectively, I do not believe, but precisely because I cannot do this I must believe. If I wish to preserve myself in faith I must constantly be intent upon holding fast the objective uncertainty, so as to remain out upon the deep, over seventy thousand fathoms of water, still preserving my faith. . . .

Subjectivity is the truth. By virtue of the relationship subsisting between the eternal truth and the existing individual, the paradox came into being. Let us now go further, let us suppose that the eternal essential truth is itself a **paradox.** How does the paradox come into being? By putting the eternal essential truth into juxtaposition with existence. Hence when we posit such a conjunction within the truth itself, the truth becomes a paradox. The eternal truth has come into being in time: this is the paradox. If in accordance with the determinations just posited, the subject is prevented by sin from taking himself back into the eternal, now he need not trouble himself about this; for now the eternal essential truth is not behind him but in front of him, through its being in existence or having existed, so that if the individual does not existentially and in existence lay hold of the truth, he will never lay hold of it. . . .

When the eternal truth is related to an existing individual it becomes a paradox. The paradox repels in the inwardness of the existing individual, through the objective uncertainty and the corresponding Socratic ignorance. But since the paradox is not in the first instance itself paradoxical (but only in its relationship to the existing individual), it does not repel with a sufficient intensive inwardness. For without risk there is no faith, and the greater the risk the greater the faith; the more objective security the less inwardness (for inwardness is precisely subjectivity), and the less objective security the more profound the possible inwardness. When the paradox is paradoxical in itself, it repels the individual by virtue of its absurdity, and the corresponding passion of inwardness is faith. But subjectivity, inwardness, is the truth; for otherwise we have forgotten what the merit of the Socratic position is. But there can be no stronger expression for inwardness than when the retreat out of existence into the eternal by way of recollection is impossible; and when, with truth confronting the individual as a paradox, gripped in the anguish and pain of sin, facing the tremendous risk of the objective insecurity, the individual believes. But without risk no faith, not even the Socratic form of faith, much less the form of which we here speak.

When Socrates believed that there was a God, he held fast to the objective uncertainty with the whole passion of his inwardness, and it is precisely in this contradiction and in this risk, that faith is rooted. Now it is otherwise. Instead of the objective uncertainty, there is here a certainty, namely, that objectively it is absurd; and this absurdity, held fast in the passion of inwardness, is faith. The Socratic ignorance is as a witty jest in comparison with the earnestness of facing the absurd; and the Socratic existential inwardness is as Greek light-mindedness in comparison with the grave strenuosity of faith.

What now is the absurd? The absurd is — that the eternal truth has come into being in time, that God has come into being, has been born, has grown up, and so forth, precisely like any other individual human being, quite indistinguishable from other individuals. . . .

Christianity has declared itself to be the eternal essential truth which has come into being in time. It has proclaimed itself as the *Paradox*, and it has required of the individual the inwardness of faith in relation to that which stamps itself as an offense to the Jews and a folly to the Greeks—and an absurdity to the understanding. It is impossible more strongly to express the fact that subjectivity is truth, and that the objectivity is repellent, repellent even by virtue of its absurdity. And indeed it would seem very strange that Christianity should have come into the world merely to receive an explanation; as if it had been somewhat bewildered about itself, and hence entered the world to consult that wise man, the speculative philosopher, who can come to its assistance by furnishing the explanation. It is impossible to express with more intensive inwardness the principle that subjectivity is truth, than when subjectivity is in the first instance untruth, and yet subjectivity is the truth. . . .

That God has existed in human form, has been born, grown up, and so forth, is surely . . . the absolute paradox. As such it cannot relate itself to a relative difference between men. A relative paradox relates itself to the relative difference between more or less cleverness and brains; but the absolute paradox, just because it is absolute, can be relevant only to the absolute difference that distinguishes man from God, and has nothing to do with the relative wrangling between man and man with respect to the fact that one man has a little more brains than another. But the absolute difference between God and man consists precisely in this, that man is a particular existing being (which is just as much true of the most gifted human being as it is of the most stupid), whose essential task cannot be to think *sub specie aeterni,* since as long as he exists he is, though eternal, essentially an existing individual, whose essential task it is to concentrate upon inwardness in existing; while God is infinite and eternal. As soon as I make the understanding of the paradox commensurable for the difference between more or less of intellectual talent (a difference which cannot take us beyond being human, unless a man were to become so gifted that he was not merely a man but also God), my words show . . . that what I have understood is not the absolute paradox but a relative one, for in connection with the absolute paradox the only understanding possible is that it cannot be understood. "But if such is the case, speculative philosophy cannot get hold of it at all." "Quite right, this is precisely what the paradox says; it merely thrusts the understanding away in the interests of inwardness in existing." This may possibly have its ground in the circumstance that there is objectively no truth for existing beings, but only approximations; while subjectively the truth exists for them in inwardness, because the decisiveness of the truth is rooted in the subjectivity of the individual. . . .

The object of faith is the reality of another, and the relationship is one of infinite interest. The object of faith is not a doctrine, for then the relationship would be intellectual, and it would be of importance not to botch it, but to realize the maximum intellectual relationship. The object of faith is not a teacher with a doctrine; for when a teacher has a doctrine, the doctrine is . . . more important than the teacher, and the relationship is again intellectual, and it again becomes important not to botch it, but to realize the maximum intellectual relationship. The object of faith is the reality of the teacher, that the teacher really exists. The answer of faith is therefore unconditionally yes or no. For it does not concern a doctrine, as to whether the doctrine is true or not; it is the answer to a question concerning a fact: "Do you or do you not suppose that he has really existed?" And the answer, it must be noted, is with infinite passion. In the case of a human being, it is thoughtlessness to lay so great and infinite a stress on the question whether he has existed or not. If the object of faith is a human being, therefore, the whole proposal is the vagary of a stupid person, who has not even understood the spirit of the intellectual and the aesthetic. The object of faith is hence the reality of the God-man in the sense of his existence. But existence involves first and foremost particularity, and this is why thought must abstract from existence, because the particular cannot be thought, but only the universal. The object of faith is thus God's reality in existence as a particular individual, the fact that God has existed as an individual human being.

Christianity is no doctrine concerning the unity of the divine and the human, or concerning the identity of subject and object; nor is it any other of the logical transcriptions of Christianity. If Christianity were a doctrine, the relationship to it would not be one of faith, for only an intellectual type of relationship can correspond to a doctrine. Christianity is therefore not a doctrine, but the fact that God has existed.

The realm of faith is thus not a class for numskulls in the sphere of the intellectual, or an asylum for the feeble-minded. Faith constitutes a sphere all by itself, and every misunderstanding of Christianity may at once be recognized by its transforming it into a doctrine, transferring it to the sphere of the intellectual. The maximum of attainment within the sphere of the intellectual, namely, to realize an entire indifference as to the reality of the teacher, is in the sphere of faith at the opposite end of the scale. The maximum of attainment within the sphere of faith is to become infinitely interested in the reality of the teacher. . . .

The fact is that the individual becomes infinite only by virtue of making the absolute venture. Hence it is not the same individual who makes this venture among others, yielding as a consequence one more predicate attaching to one and the same individual. No, but in making the absolute venture he becomes another individual. Before he has made the venture he cannot understand it as anything else than madness; and this is far better than the thoughtless galimatias which imagines that it understands the venture as wisdom—and yet omits to venture, whereby the individual directly accuses himself of being mad, while one who regards the venture as madness at any rate consistently asserts his own sanity by refusing to commit himself. And after the individual has made the venture he is no longer the same individual. Thus there is made room for the transition and its decisiveness, an intervening yawning chasm, a suitable scene for the infinite passion of the individual, a gulf which the understanding cannot bridge either forward or backward. . . .

## *Saint Thomas Aquinas (1225?–1274)*

Since 1879, Thomas Aquinas has been the official philosopher of the Roman Catholic Church. This position did not come quickly. Many of Aquinas's ideas were based on the philosophy of Aristotle. Within the Church of the fourteenth century, Aquinas's ideas were revolutionary and struggled for acceptance against the Augustinian ideas that were influenced by Plato and his followers, the Neoplatonists. It would be wrong, however, to view Aquinas simply as a follower of Aristotle. Aquinas used Aristotle as a vehicle for making some aspects of the Christian faith more understandable, but he had no difficulty in departing from Aristotle when his Christian faith required it.

Aquinas made many original contributions to philosophy—especially in the philosophy of history and in that branch of metaphysics concerned with universal properties—like yellow—that appear in different objects while retaining their own identity. In the very non-Aristotelian selection that follows, Aquinas resolves the so-called faith-reason controversy by arguing that whereas certain truths of Christian revelation can also be obtained through the use of human reason, others cannot. He also argues that we can supplement the knowledge we obtain by making rational inferences from sense experience with revealed truths of faith that are not susceptible of rational demonstration.

# On the Way in Which Divine Truth Is to Be Made Known

## *Saint Thomas Aquinas*

The way of making truth known is not always the same, and, as the Philosopher has very well said, "it belongs to an educated man to seek such certitude in each thing as the nature of that thing allows."[1] . . . But, since such is the case, we must first show what way is open to us in order that we may make known the truth which is our object.

There is a twofold mode of truth in what we profess about God. Some truths about God exceed all the ability of the human reason. Such is the truth that God is triune. But there are some truths which the natural reason also is able to reach. Such are that God exists, that He is one, and the like. In fact, such truths about God have been proved demonstratively by the philosophers, guided by the light of the natural reason.

That there are certain truths about God that totally surpass man's ability appears with the greatest evidence. . . . For the human intellect is not able to reach a comprehension of the divine substance through its natural power. For, according to its manner of knowing in the present life, the intellect depends on the sense[s] for the origin of knowledge; and so those things that do not fall under the senses cannot be grasped by the human intellect except in so far as the knowledge of them is gathered from sensible things. Now, sensible things cannot lead the human intellect to the point of seeing in them the nature of the divine substance; for sensible things are effects that fall short of the power of their cause. Yet, beginning with sensible things, our intellect is led to the point of knowing about God that He exists, and other such characteristics that must be attributed to the First Principle. There are, consequently, some intelligible truths about God that are open to the human reason; but there are others that absolutely surpass its power.

We may easily see the same point from the gradation of intellects. Consider the case of two persons of whom one has a more penetrating grasp of a thing by his intellect than does the other. He who has the superior intellect understands many things that the other cannot grasp at all. Such is the case with a very simple person who cannot at all grasp the subtle speculations of philosophy. But the intellect of an angel surpasses the human intellect much more than the intellect of the greatest philosopher surpasses the intellect of the most uncultivated simple person; for the distance between the best philosopher and a simple person is contained within the limits of the human species, which the angelic intellect surpasses. For the angel knows God on the basis of a more noble effect than does man; and this by as much as the substance of an angel, through which the angel in his natural knowledge is led to the knowledge of God, is nobler than sensible things and even than the soul itself, through which the human intellect mounts to the knowledge of God. The divine intellect surpasses the angelic intellect much more than the angelic surpasses the human. For the divine intellect is in its capacity equal to its substance, and therefore it understands fully what it is, including all its intelligible attributes. But by his natural knowledge the angel does not know what God is, since the substance itself of the angel, through which he is led to the knowledge of God, is an effect that is not equal to the power of its cause. Hence, the angel is not able, by means of his natural knowledge, to grasp all the things that God understands in Himself; nor is the human reason sufficient to grasp all the things that the angel understands through his own natural power. Just as, therefore, it would be the height of folly for a simple person to assert that what a philosopher proposes is false on the ground that he himself cannot understand it, so (and even more so) it is the acme of stupidity for a man to suspect as false what is divinely revealed through the ministry of the angels simply because it cannot be investigated by reason. . . .

Now, although the truth of the Christian faith which we have discussed surpasses the capacity of the reason, nevertheless that truth that the human reason is naturally endowed to know cannot be opposed to the truth of the Christian faith. For that with which the human reason is naturally endowed is clearly most true; so much so, that it is impossible for us to think of such truths as false. Nor is it permissible to believe as false that which we hold by faith, since this is confirmed in a way that is so clearly divine. Since, therefore, only the false is opposed to the true, as is clearly evident from an examination of their definitions, it is impossible that the truth of faith should be opposed to those principles that the human reason knows naturally.

Furthermore, that which is introduced into the soul of the student by the teacher is contained in the knowledge of the teacher—unless his teaching is fictitious, which it is improper to say of God. Now, the knowledge of the principles that are known to us naturally has been implanted in us by God; for God is the Author of our nature. These principles, therefore, are also contained by the divine Wisdom. Hence, whatever is opposed to them is opposed to the divine Wisdom, and, therefore, cannot come from God. That which we hold by faith as divinely revealed, therefore, cannot be contrary to our natural knowledge. . . .

There is also a further consideration. Sensible things, from which the human reason takes the origin of its knowledge, retain within themselves some sort of trace of a likeness to God. This is so imperfect, however, that it is absolutely inadequate to manifest the substance of God. For effects bear within themselves, in their own way, the likeness of their causes, since an agent produces its like; yet an effect does not always reach to the full likeness of its cause. Now, the human reason is related to the knowledge of the truth of faith (a truth which can be most evident only to those who see the divine substance) in such a way that it can gather certain likenesses of it, which are yet not sufficient so that the truth of faith may be comprehended as being understood demonstratively or through itself. Yet it is useful for the human reason to exercise itself in such arguments, however weak they may be, provided only that there be present no presumption to comprehend or to demonstrate. For to be able to see something of the loftiest realities, however thin and weak the sight may be, is, as our previous remarks indicate, a cause of the greatest joy. . . .

It is clearly apparent, from what has been said, that the intention of the wise man ought to be directed toward the twofold truth of divine things, and toward the destruction of the errors that are contrary to this truth. One kind of divine truth the investigation of the reason is competent to reach, whereas the other surpasses every effort of the reason. . . .

Now, to make the first kind of divine truth known, we must proceed through demonstrative arguments, by which our adversary may become convinced. However,since such arguments are not available for the second kind of divine truth, our intention should not be to convince our adversary by arguments: it should be to answer his arguments against the truth; for, as we have shown, the natural reason cannot be contrary to the truth of faith. The sole way to overcome an adversary of divine truth is from the authority of Scripture—an authority divinely confirmed by miracles. For that which is above the human reason we believe only because God has revealed it. Nevertheless, there are certain likely arguments that should be brought forth in order to make divine truth known. This should be done for the training and consolation of the faithful, and not with any idea of refuting those who are adversaries. For the very inadequacy of the arguments would rather strengthen them in their error, since they would imagine that our acceptance of the truth of faith was based on such weak arguments. . . .

## NOTE

1. Aristotle, *Nicomachean Ethics,* I, 3 (1094b 24).

## *William James (1842–1910)*

The reader is already acquainted with James's indeterminist philosophy. Just as James's defense of free will ran counter to the scientific determinism of his day, his defense of religious faith ran counter to the sceptical religious climate that had developed in intellectual circles. In his classic essay, "The Will to Believe," he argued that on occasion one has to accept or reject a proposition in the absence of sufficient evidence. In such cases, the propositions available for us to accept or reject (which James calls options) may be living or dead, forced or avoidable, momentous or trivial. Though everyone finds some religious outlooks incredible, whether or not one should accept some other religious outlook may be a live, forced, momentous option. For example, Christianity is such an option for many of us whereas Zoroastrianism is not! The acceptance or rejection of a religious faith is one of the most important choices we make. James admits that the evidence for the canons of religious faith is incomplete, but a person must choose one way or another before one dies, even though sufficient evidence will probably never be in—at least in one's lifetime. In such cases it is passion that determines our belief; in particular, whether we are more afraid of falling into error, or of missing out on some supremely significant truth.

Sometimes our beliefs can create facts. If we believe we can jump a creek, that confidence may enable us to jump the creek—make it true that we can jump the creek. But we should not be so naive as to suppose that James defended the silly view that believing something makes it true. People who hold that view are out of touch with reality. Sometimes, when some facts are known and when we have some control over other facts, our beliefs may influence how things turn out, but simply *believing* something religious, no matter how sincerely or passionately, will not make that religious proposition come true.

But what if we fall into error when we embrace a religious outlook because we don't want to miss out on something of supreme significance? Shouldn't we seek to avoid error? James shuns this timid approach. Indeed he thinks worse things can happen to a person than to be duped. In love if you wait until the evidence is all in, you might lose out—you might lose the love. Accepting religious faith is like committing yourself to someone unreservedly with the assurance that you are loved in return, even though you can't prove that yours is a true love. But how much better it is to have loved and been mistaken, than never to have loved at all.

# The Will to Believe

## *William James*

I

Let us give the name of *hypothesis* to anything that may be proposed to our belief; and just as the electricians speak of live and dead wires, let us speak of any hypothesis as either *live* or *dead.* A live hypothesis is one which appeals as a real possibility to him to whom it is proposed. If I ask you to believe in the **Mahdi,** the notion makes no electric connection with your nature — it refuses to scintillate with any credibility at all. As an hypothesis it is completely dead. To an Arab, however (even if he be not one of the Mahdi's followers), the hypothesis is among the mind's possibilities: it is alive. This shows that deadness and liveness in an hypothesis are not intrinsic properties, but relations to the individual thinker. They are measured by his willingness to act. The maximum of liveness in an hypothesis means willingness to act irrevocably. Practically, that means belief; but there is some believing tendency wherever there is willingness to act at all.

Next, let us call the decision between two hypotheses an *option.* Options may be of several kinds. They may be — 1, *living* or *dead;* 2, *forced* or *avoidable;* 3, *momentous* or *trivial;* and for our purposes we may call an option a *genuine* option when it is of the forced, living, and momentous kind.

1. A living option is one in which both hypotheses are live ones. If I say to you: "Be a **theosophist** or be a Mohammedan," it is probably a dead option, because for you neither hypothesis is likely to be alive. But if I say: "Be an agnostic or be a Christian," it is otherwise: trained as you are, each hypothesis makes some appeal, however small, to your belief.

2. Next, if I say to you: "Choose between going out with your umbrella or without it," I do not offer you a genuine option, for it is not forced. You can easily avoid it by not going out at all. Similarly, if I say, "Either love me or hate me," "Either call my theory true or call it false," your option is avoidable. You may remain indifferent to me, neither loving nor hating, and you may decline to offer any judgment as to my theory. But if I say, "Either accept this truth or go without it," I put on you a forced option, for there is no standing place outside of the alternative. Every dilemma based on a complete logical disjunction, with no possibility of not choosing, is an option of this forced kind.

3. Finally, if I were Dr. Nansen and proposed to you to join my North Pole expedition, your option would be momentous; for this would probably be your only similar opportunity, and your choice now would either exclude you from the North Pole sort of immortality altogether or put at least the chance of it into your hands. He who refuses to embrace a unique opportunity loses the prize as surely as if he tried and failed. *Per contra,* the option is trivial when the opportunity is not unique, when the stake is insignificant, or when the decision is reversible if it later prove unwise. Such trivial options abound in the scientific life. A chemist finds an hypothesis live enough to spend a year in its verification: he believes in it to that extent. But if his experiments prove inconclusive either way, he is quit for his loss of time, no vital harm being done.

It will facilitate our discussion if we keep all these distinctions well in mind.

---

Abridged from *Essays on Faith and Morals,* by William James. (Cleveland, Ohio: Meridian Books, The World Publishing Co.) Sections renumbered.

II

. . . In Pascal's Thoughts there is a celebrated passage known in literature as Pascal's wager. In it he tries to force us into Christianity by reasoning as if our concern with truth resembled our concern with the stakes in a game of chance. Translated freely his words are these: You must either believe or not believe that God is—which will you do? Your human reason cannot say. A game is going on between you and the nature of things which at the day of judgment will bring out either heads or tails. Weigh what your gains and your losses would be if you should stake all you have on heads, or God's existence: if you win in such case, you gain eternal beatitude; if you lose, you lose nothing at all. If there were an infinity of chances, and only one for God in this wager, still you ought to stake your all on God; for though you surely risk a finite loss by this procedure, any finite loss is reasonable, even a certain one is reasonable, if there is but the possibility of infinite gain. Go, then, and take holy water, and have masses said; belief will come and stupefy your scruples. . . . Why should you not? At bottom, what have you to lose?

You probably feel that when religious faith expresses itself thus, in the language of the gaming-table, it is put to its last trumps. . . . We feel that a faith in masses and holy water adopted willfully after such a mechanical calculation would lack the inner soul of faith's reality; and if we were ourselves in the place of the Deity, we should probably take particular pleasure in cutting off believers of this pattern from their infinite reward. It is evident that unless there be some pre-existing tendency to believe in masses and holy water, the option offered to the will by Pascal is not a living option. Certainly no Turk ever took to masses and holy water on its account; and even to us Protestants these means of salvation seem such foregone impossibilities that Pascal's logic invoked for them specifically, leaves us unmoved. . . .

The talk of believing by our volition seems, then, from one point of view, simply silly. From another point of view it is worse than silly, it is vile. When one turns to the magnificent edifice of the physical sciences, and sees how it was reared; what thousands of disinterested moral lives of men lie buried in its mere foundations; what patience and postponement, what choking down of preference, what submission to the icy laws of outer fact are wrought into its very stones and mortar; how absolutely impersonal it stands in its vast augustness—then how besotted and contemptible seems every little sentimentalist who comes blowing his voluntary smoke-wreaths, and pretending to decide things from out of his private dream! Can we wonder if those bred in the rugged and manly school of science should feel like spewing such subjectivism out of their mouths? . . .

III

All this strikes one as healthy. . . . Free-will and simple wishing do seem, in the matter of our credences, to be only fifth wheels to the coach. Yet if any one should thereupon assume that intellectual insight is what remains after wish and will and sentimental preference have taken wing, or that pure reason is what then settles our opinions, he would fly quite as directly in the teeth of the facts.

It is only our already dead hypotheses that our willing nature is unable to bring to life again. But what has made them dead for us is for the most part a previous action of our willing nature of an antagonistic kind. When I say "willing nature," I do not mean only such deliberate volitions as may have set up habits of belief that we cannot now escape from—I mean all such factors of belief as fear and hope, prejudice and passion, imitation and partisanship, the circumpressure of our caste and set. As a matter of fact we find ourselves believing, we hardly know how or why. . . . Our reason is quite satisfied, in nine hundred and ninety-nine cases out of every thousand of us, if it can find a few arguments that will do to recite in case our credulity is criticized by someone else. Our faith is faith in someone else's faith, and in the greatest matters this is most the case. Our belief in truth itself, for instance, that there is a truth, and that our minds and it are made for each other—what is it but a passionate affirmation of desire, in which our social system backs us up? We want to have a truth; we want to believe that our experiments and studies and discussions must put us in a continually better and better position towards it; and on this line we agree to fight out our thinking lives. But if a **pyrrhonistic** sceptic asks us *how we know* all this, can our logic find a reply? No! Certainly it cannot. It is just one volition against another—we willing to go in for life upon a trust or assumption which he, for his part, does not care to make. . . .

Evidently, then, our non-intellectual nature does influence our convictions. There are passional tendencies and volitions which run before and others which come after belief, and it is only the latter that are too late for the fair; and they are not too late when the previous passional work has been already in their own direction. Pascal's argument, instead of being powerless, then seems a regular clincher, and is the last stroke needed to make our faith in masses and holy water complete. The state of things is evidently far from simple; and pure insight and logic, whatever they might do ideally, are not the only things that really do produce our creeds.

## IV

Our next duty, having recognized this mixed-up state of affairs, is to ask whether it be simply reprehensible and pathological, or whether, on the contrary, we must treat it as a normal element in making up our minds. The thesis I defend is, briefly stated, this: *Our passional nature not only lawfully may, but must, decide an option between propositions, whenever it is a genuine option that cannot by its nature be decided on intellectual grounds; for to say, under such circumstances, "Do not decide, but leave the question open," is itself a passional decision—just like deciding yes or no—and is attended with the same risk of losing the truth.* The thesis thus abstractly expressed will, I trust, soon become quite clear. . . .

## V

One more point, small but important, and our preliminaries are done. There are two ways of looking at our duty in the matter of opinion—ways entirely different, and yet ways about whose difference the theory of knowledge seems hitherto to have shown very little concern. *We must know the truth;* and *we must avoid error*—these are our first and great commandments as would-be knowers; but they are not two ways of stating an identical commandment, they are two separable laws. Although it may indeed happen that when we believe the truth *A*, we escape as an incidental consequence from believing the falsehood *B*, it hardly ever happens that by merely disbelieving *B* we necessarily believe *A*. We may in escaping *B* fall into believing other falsehoods, *C* or *D*, just as bad as *B*; or we may escape *B* by not believing anything at all, not even *A*.

Believe truth! Shun error!—these, we see, are two materially different laws; and by choosing between them we may end by coloring differently our whole intellectual life. We may regard the chase for truth as paramount, and the avoidance of error as secondary; or we may, on the other hand, treat the avoidance of error as more imperative, and let truth take its chance. . . . For my own part, I have also a horror of being duped; but I can believe that worse things than being duped may happen to a man in this world. . . . Our errors are surely not such awfully solemn things. In a world where we are so certain to incur them in spite of all our caution, a certain lightness of heart seems healthier than this excessive nervousness on their behalf. At any rate, it seems the fittest thing for the empiricist philosopher. . . .

## VI

*Moral questions* immediately present themselves as questions whose solution cannot wait for sensible proof. A moral question is a question not of what sensibly exists, but of what is good, or would be good if it did exist. Science can tell us what exists; but to compare the *worths,* both of what exists and of what does not exist, we must consult not science, but what Pascal calls our heart. Science herself consults her heart when she lays it down that the infinite ascertainment of fact and correction of false belief are the supreme goods for man. Challenge the statement, and science can only repeat it oracularly, or else prove it by showing that such ascertainment and correction bring man all sorts of other goods which man's heart in turn declares. The question of having moral beliefs at all or not having them is decided by our will. Are our moral preferences true or false, or are they only odd biological phenomena, making things good or bad for *us*, but in themselves indifferent? How can your pure intellect decide? If your heart does not *want* a world of moral reality, your head will assuredly never make you believe in one. Mephistophelian scepticism, indeed, will satisfy the head's play-instincts much better than any rigorous idealism can. Some men (even at the student age) are so naturally cool-hearted that the moralistic hypothesis never has for them any pungent life, and in their supercilious presence the hot young moralist always feels strangely ill at ease. The appearance of knowingness is on their side, of *naivete* and gullibility on his. Yet, in the inarticulate heart of him, he clings to it that he is not a dupe, and that there is a realm in which (as Emerson says) all their wit and intellectual superiority is no better than the cunning of a fox. Moral scepticism can no more be refuted or proved by logic than intellectual scepticism can. When we stick to it that there *is* truth (be it of either kind), we do so with our whole nature, and resolve to stand or fall by the results. The sceptic with his whole nature adopts the doubting attitude; but which of us is the wiser, Omniscience only knows.

Turn now from these wide questions of good to a certain class of questions of fact, questions concerning personal relations, states of mind between one man and another. *Do you like me or not?*—for example. Whether you do or not depends, in countless instances, on whether I meet you half-way, am willing to assume that you must like me, and show you trust and expectation. The previous faith on my part in your liking's existence is in such cases what makes your liking come. But if I stand aloof, and refuse to budge an inch until I have objective evidence, until you shall have done something apt, . . . ten to one your liking never comes. How many women's hearts are vanquished by the mere sanguine insistence of some man that they *must* love him! he will not consent to the hypothesis that they cannot. The desire for a certain kind of truth here brings about that special truth's existence; and so it is in innumerable cases of other sorts. Who gains promotions, boons, appointments, but the man in whose life they are seen to play the part of live hypotheses, who discounts them, sacrifices other things for their sake before they have come, and takes risks for them in advance? His faith acts on the powers above him as a claim, and creates its own verification.

A social organism of any sort whatever, large or small, is what it is because each member proceeds to his own duty with a trust that the other members will simultaneously do theirs. Wherever a desired result is achieved by the cooperation of many independent persons, its existence as a fact is a pure consequence of the precursive faith in one another of those immediately concerned. A government, an army, a commercial system, a ship, a college, an athletic team, all exist on this condition, without which not only is nothing achieved, but nothing is even attempted. A whole train of passengers (individually brave enough) will be looted by a few highwaymen, simply because the latter can count on one another, while each passenger fears that if he makes a movement of resistance, he will be shot before any one else backs him up. If we believed that the whole car-full would rise at once with us, we should each severally rise, and train-robbing would never even be attempted. There are, then, cases where a fact cannot come at all unless a preliminary faith exists in its coming. *And where faith in a fact can help create the fact,* that would be an insane logic which should say that faith running ahead of scientific evidence is the "lowest kind of immorality" into which a thinking being can fall. Yet such is the logic by which our scientific absolutists pretend to regulate our lives!

## VII

In truths dependent on our personal action, then, faith based on desire is certainly a lawful and possibly an indispensable thing.

But now, it will be said, these are all childish human cases, and have nothing to do with great cosmical matters, like the question of religious faith. Let us then pass on to that. Religions differ so much in their accidents that in discussing the religious question we must make it very generic and broad. What then do we now mean by the religious hypothesis? Science says things are; morality says some things are better than other things; and religion says essentially two things.

First, she says that the best things are the more eternal things, the overlapping things, the things in the universe that throw the last stone, so to speak, and say the final word. . . .

The second affirmation of religion is that we are better off even now if we believe her first affirmation to be true.

Now, let us consider what the logical elements of this situation are *in case the religious hypothesis in both its branches be really true.* . . .

So proceeding, we see, first that religion offers itself as a *momentous* option. We are supposed to gain, even now, by our belief, and to lose by our nonbelief, a certain vital good. Secondly, religion is a *forced* option, so far as that good goes. We cannot escape the issue by remaining sceptical and waiting for more light, because, although we do avoid error in that way *if religion be untrue,* we lose the good, *if it be true,* just as certainly as if we positively chose to disbelieve. It is as if a man should hesitate indefinitely to ask a certain woman to marry him because he was not perfectly sure that she would prove an angel after he brought her home. Would he not cut himself off from that particular angel-possibility as decisively as if he went and married someone else? Scepticism, then, is not avoidance of option; it is option of a certain particular kind of risk. *Better risk loss of truth than chance of error*—that is your faith-vetoer's exact position. He is actively playing his stake as much as the believer is; he is backing the field against the religious hypothesis, just as the believer is backing the religious hypothesis against the field. To preach scepticism to us as a duty until "sufficient evidence" for religion be found, is tantamount therefore to telling us, when in presence of the religious hypothesis, that to yield to our fear of its being error is wiser and better than to yield to our hope that it may be true. . . .

## *Thomas Huxley (1825–1895)*

Thomas Huxley is best known as a biologist who was an early convert to Darwin's theory of evolution. He treated Darwinism as a set of hypotheses rather than the final truth and he did disagree with some of the details of Darwin's account; for example, he rejected the postulate "nature makes no leap."

Huxley was also interested in a number of philosophical questions that arose from his perspective as a scientist. Huxley believed that science was based on certain assumptions: *(a)* that nature is rationally ordered, *(b)* that causation is universal, and *(c)* that scientific explanation is based on causal laws. However, we can never claim that scientific knowledge describes reality as it really is. Our knowledge of the empirical world is based on inferences made by the human mind. Moreover, these inferences do not extend beyond the material world.

These views of science are the basis for

Huxley's **agnosticism**—a term coined by Huxley himself. Huxley's view is directly opposed to that of William James. Whereas James argued that you should in certain circumstances accept statements that aren't backed by conclusive evidence, Huxley argued that you shouldn't. Huxley believed that the adoption of his viewpoint increased the chances of success in science. He further buttressed his religious agnosticism by pointing out inconsistencies in the Bible and the unconvincing nature of reports of miracles. During his lifetime, Huxley debated prominent religious figures on matters of theology.

## Agnosticism and Christianity

### *Thomas Huxley*

It was inevitable that a conflict should arise between **Agnosticism** and Theology; or rather, I ought to say, between Agnosticism and **Ecclesiasticism.** For Theology, the science, is one thing; and Ecclesiasticism, the championship of a foregone conclusion as to the truth of a particular form of Theology, is another. With scientific Theology, Agnosticism has no quarrel. On the contrary, the Agnostic, knowing too well the influence of prejudice and idiosyncrasy, even on those who desire most earnestly to be impartial, can wish for nothing more urgently than that the scientific theologian should not only be at perfect liberty to thresh out the matter in his own fashion; but that he should, if he can, find flaws in the Agnostic position; and, even if demonstration is not to be had, that he should put, in their full force, the grounds of the conclusions he thinks probable. The scientific theologian admits the Agnostic principle, however widely his results may differ from those reached by the majority of Agnostics.

But, as between Agnosticism and Ecclesiasticism, or, as our neighbors across the Channel call it, Clericalism, there can be neither peace nor truce. The Cleric asserts that it is morally wrong not to believe certain propositions, whatever the results of a strict scientific investigation of the evidence of these propositions. He tells us "that religious error is, in itself, of an immoral nature."[1] He declares that he has prejudged certain conclusions, and looks upon those who show cause for arrest of judgment as emissaries of Satan. It necessarily follows that, for him, the attainment of faith, not the ascertainment of truth, is the highest aim of mental life. And, on careful analysis of the nature of this faith, it will too often be found to be, not the mystic process of unity with the Divine, understood by the religious enthusiast; but that which the candid simplicity of a Sunday scholar once defined it to be. "Faith," said this unconscious **plagiarist** of Tertullian, "is the power of saying you believe things which are incredible."

Now I, and many other Agnostics, believe that faith, in this sense, is an abomination; and though we do not indulge in the luxury of self-righteousness so far as to call those who are not of our way of thinking hard names, we do not feel that the disagreement between ourselves and those who hold this doctrine is even more moral than intellectual. It is desirable there should be an end of any mistakes on this topic. If our clerical opponents were clearly aware of the real state of the case, there would be an end of the curious delusion, which often appears between the lines

Abridged from *Selected Works of Thomas H. Huxley,* Vol. 5, *Science and Christian Tradition,* by Thomas H. Huxley. (New York: D. Appleton and Co., 1900).

of their writings, that those whom they are so fond of calling **"Infidels"** are people who not only ought to be, but in their hearts are, ashamed of themselves. It would be discourteous to do more than hint the **antipodal** opposition of this pleasant dream of theirs to facts.

The clerics and their lay allies commonly tell us, that if we refuse to admit that there is good ground for expressing definite convictions about certain topics, the bonds of human society will dissolve and mankind lapse into savagery. There are several answers to this assertion. One is that the bonds of human society were formed without the aid of their theology; and, in the opinion of not a few competent judges, have been weakened rather than strengthened by a good deal of it. Greek science, Greek art, the ethics of old Israel, the social organization of old Rome, contrived to come into being, without the help of any one who believed in a single distinctive article of the simplest of the Christian creeds. The science, the art, the jurisprudence, the chief political and social theories, of the modern world have grown out of those of Greece and Rome — not by favor of, but in the teeth of, the fundamental teachings of early Christianity, to which science, art, and any serious occupation with the things of this world, were alike despicable.

Again, all that is best in the ethics of the modern world, in so far as it has not grown out of Greek thought, or Barbarian manhood, is the direct development of the ethics of old Israel. There is no code of legislation, ancient or modern, at once so just and so merciful, so tender to the weak and poor, as the Jewish law; and, if the Gospels are to be trusted, Jesus of Nazareth himself declared that he taught nothing but that which lay implicitly, or explicitly, in the religious and ethical system of his people.

> And the scribe said unto him, Of a truth, Teacher, thou hast well said that he is one; and there is none other but he, and to love him with all the heart, and with all the understanding, and with all the strength, and to love his neighbour as himself, is much more than all whole burnt offerings and sacrifices. (Mark xii. 32, 33.)

Here is the briefest of summaries of the teaching of the prophets of Israel of the eighth century; does the Teacher, whose doctrine is thus set forth in his presence, repudiate the exposition? Nay; we are told, on the contrary, that Jesus saw that he "answered discreetly," and replied, "Thou art not far from the kingdom of God."

So that I think that even if the creeds, from the so-called "Apostles," to the so-called **"Athanasian,"** were swept into oblivion; and even if the human race should arrive at the conclusion that, whether a bishop washes a cup or leaves it unwashed, is not a matter of the least consequence, it will get on very well. The causes which have led to the development of morality in mankind, which have guided or impelled us all the way from the savage to the civilized state, will not cease to operate because a number of ecclesiastical hypotheses turn out to be baseless. . . .

I trust that I have now made amends for any ambiguity, or want of fullness, in my previous exposition of that which I hold to be the essence of the Agnostic doctrine. Henceforward, I might hope to hear no more of the assertion that we are necessarily Materialists, **Idealists, Atheists, Theists,** or any other **ists,** if experience had led me to think that the proved falsity of a statement was any guarantee against its repetition. And those who appreciate the nature of our position will see, at once, that when Ecclesiasticism declares that we ought to believe this, that, and the other, and are very wicked if we don't, it is impossible for us to give any answer but this: We have not the slightest objection to believe anything you like, if you will give us good grounds for belief; but, if you cannot, we must respectfully refuse, even if that refusal should wreck morality and insure our own damnation several times over. We are quite content to leave that to the decision of the future. The course of the past has impressed us with the firm conviction that no good ever comes of falsehood, and we feel warranted in refusing even to experiment in that direction. . . .

Ecclesiasticism says: The **demonology** of the Gospels is an essential part of that account of that spiritual world, the truth of which it declares to be certified by Jesus.

Agnosticism says: There is no good evidence of the existence of a demoniac spiritual world, and much reason for doubting it.

Hereupon the ecclesiastic may observe: Your doubt means that you disbelieve Jesus; therefore you are an "Infidel" instead of an "Agnostic." To which the agnostic may reply: No, for two reasons: first, because your evidence that Jesus said what you say he said is worth very little; and secondly, because a man may be an agnostic, in the sense of admitting he has no positive knowledge, and yet consider that he has more or less probable ground for accepting any given hypothesis about the spiritual world. Just as a man may frankly declare that he has no means of knowing whether the planets generally are inhabited or not, and yet may think one of the two possible hypotheses more likely that the other, so he may admit that he has no means of knowing anything about the spiritual world, and yet may think one or other of the current views on the subject, to some extent, probable. . . .

## NOTE

1. Dr. Newman, *Essay on Development,* p. 357.

# *Proofs for the Existence of God*

Certainly the central tenet of any religious faith is the proposition that God exists. In the mid-twentieth century, some theologians contended that God was dead. No new religion flourished as a result, although persons who read the works of these theologians had to rethink the nature of the God whose existence was being denied. Those of the Jewish faith—and indeed all humankind—had to face a similar task after the holocaust. Yet even in the face of mankind's cruelest treatment of fellow human beings, religion needed God. The death of God is the death of religion.

For many religious persons no proof of God's existence is needed; the existence of God is evidenced through the living of the religious faith. Some religious persons purportedly feel the presence of God as they practice the faith, and take this as a revelation of the existence of God. But most theologians and many philosophers believe that the existence of God can be proved independently of a person's experience of God. The existence of God, many believe, is a truth of natural theology as well as revealed theology.

In the Western tradition, three proofs have been central: ontological, cosmological, and teleological arguments respectively. Classic statements of these proofs as well as some of the objections to them are included in the selections in this section.

As you approach these proofs, two distinct questions must be kept in mind. The first is whether or not the proof succeeds. Although the proofs have failed to convince many, they have survived hundreds of years of philosophical criticism and have been reformulated or revised in an effort to make them more convincing. Many people are still unconvinced by them. Of course, even if the proofs fail, that failure need not shake the faith of those who claim that they experience God working in their lives. Second, even if the proofs succeed in establishing the existence of a divine being, one must ask whether this divine being is the divine being of their own faith. Some Christians might be tempted to embrace these arguments while forgetting that only the first tries to establish the existence of a divine being anything like the Christian God. To prove the existence of a divine being is one thing; but to prove that the divine being has certain properties like omniscience, omnipotence, personality, or perfect goodness is quite another matter.

The first of the traditional proofs, the **ontological** argument, is based on our conception of God as the Supreme Being. By definition the Supreme Being is that Being greater than any other that can be conceived. The strategy of the ontological argument is to show why the existence of that concept of God enables us to claim that God exists. The existence of God is necessarily contained in the concept of "that being greater than any other that can be conceived." If the existence of God were not contained in that concept, there would be a being greater than any other that can be conceived, namely the greatest being that also exists. But this latter being is just the being of our original concept—the being greater than any other that can be conceived. Therefore the existence of the greatest possible being is contained in our concept of the greatest possible being. Those who criticize the ontological argument generally claim that all the argument proves is that if we think of the greatest possible being, we must also think of that being as existing.

Perhaps the most familiar argument is the cosmological argument. It is a sophisticated version of the idea that the world had to have a cause. One of the first questions children ask is where did the world come from. The classic statement of the cosmological argument is by Saint Thomas, who perfected an earlier argument of Aristotle's. Aquinas actually presents five arguments that collectively are often referred to as Aquinas's cosmological argument. Scholars disagree on whether each of the five arguments can properly be called a cosmological argument. Each argument begins with facts of our experience and asks what must be true to account for these facts. The first argument notes that things that are in motion are put in motion by the motion of something else. Aquinas agrees with Aristotle that motion occurs when a thing's potential for motion is transformed into actual motion by some cause. But there has to be a first mover—a self-mover; otherwise the sequence of motions would have to go back through infinity and that is impossible. The second argument notes that we see one thing causing another but the sequence of causes cannot go back infinitely. Therefore, there must be a first cause.

Many criticize Aquinas's first two formulations of the cosmological argument by arguing that there is nothing contradictory or irrational about an infinite regress. Why can't the string of causes go back to infinity? Some scholars have responded that Aquinas's argument does not depend on the claim that infinite regress is impossible, but rather on the claim that motion and efficient causation need a ground in a final cause. But the necessity of a final cause is as controversial as the denial of an infinite regress, so these two arguments are not convincing.

But that does not dispose of Aquinas's third cosmological argument—the argument from contingency. Not only are things in motion now as a result of one thing causally impacting on another, but everything that is in nature is contingent—that is, there is a time when it won't be and there was a time when it wasn't. But if for each individual thing there is a time when it didn't exist, there was a time when nothing was in existence. And if there was a time when there was nothing in existence, nothing would have come into existence and hence nothing would exist now. But that's absurd. Therefore there must be a necessary being upon which all contingent things depend for their existence. The critics of this argument focus on the statement, "If there is a time when everything wasn't, there was a time when nothing was in existence." They argue that just because each individual thing didn't exist at one time, that doesn't mean that there is a single time when everything doesn't exist. It may be that the world consists of an indefinitely large number of contingent things with overlapping life spans so that although no one thing exists forever, at any and every moment there is at least one thing in existence. Defenders of Aquinas are unconvinced by this objection. They argue that unless there is an imperishable being to prevent a perishable world from perishing, there is a time when it would have perished. Most scholars do not find this reply convincing.

Aquinas's fourth argument calls our attention to the fact that things exist by degrees. They are hotter or taller or whiter and we make these comparisons by using a standard of perfection—tallest, hottest, or whitest. Indeed, perfect whiteness is the cause of something being white. The cause of all these perfections is God. The difficulty with this version is that it assumes the notion of a perfect standard and leaves unexplained the sense in which a standard like perfect whiteness acts as a cause of white in white things. A standard of tallness is not the cause of a giraffe's being tall the way subfreezing temperatures are the cause of the pond becoming frozen. However, the term *cause* had a much broader meaning in medieval times than it does today. Consider *explanation* as a medieval synonym for *cause.* However, why is a standard of perfect tallness needed to explain a giraffe's being tall? Contemporary biological science does have a causal explanation based on evolution and genes. But even in Saint Thomas's time one could have argued that you could use the language of comparison, of something being taller, or whiter, without presupposing the existence of a perfect standard. At the crudest level you could say that the snow is whiter than the chalk, by saying the snow has more whiteness in it. Although such an explanation isn't correct, it seems more plausible or at least as plausible as postulating an ideal standard.*

The final traditional argument is the teleological argument or the argument from design. This is an argument from analogy. One of the more famous formulations, reprinted here, considers what we would have to say if we found a watch

* We treat Aquinas's "fifth way" as a teleological argument and do not discuss it here. [Eds.]

and fully inspected it. Given the intricacy of the design, wouldn't we have to say that the watch exhibits such a high degree of order and adaptation, that it seems inconceivable that the watch could have been produced by chance? What is true of the watch must also be true of the world in which we live. Our world shows such a high degree of order and adaptation that it seems inconceivable that it could have been produced by chance. However, isn't there an obvious competing explanation for adaptation in nature — natural selection. So the question really is whether natural selection or an intelligent designer is the more plausible explanation for such order and adaptation as we find in the universe.

But even if we grant the point that the world must have been purposively designed, what can we say about the designer? This question is discussed at length in Hume's *Dialogues Concerning Natural Religion,* which is partially reprinted here. Hume argues that we certainly can't infer that the God of Christianity is the designer. In more contemporary discussion, the issue is raised as to whether or not the designer might have designed the world and then left it unattended. Just as an unattended garden develops weeds, so this world has developed all manner of evil that might by analogy indicate that the designer of this world has left it unattended.

This reference to evil provides an opportunity both to discuss one other proof for the existence of God and to mark a transition to the next section. Although Immanuel Kant rejected all three of the traditional proofs for God's existence, he found the evil in the world, especially the suffering of innocent moral people, to be such an affront to morality that he claimed we must postulate a God and an afterlife in which the evils of this world are overcome and set right with everyone receiving his or her just rewards or punishments. Otherwise Kant believed the moral order would be undermined. Ultimately a God must stand behind and support humanity — a sentiment expressed by many who attempt proofs for the existence of God.

## *Saint Anselm (1033–1109)*

Anselm is the originator of one of the best-known arguments for the existence of God. His theology followed in the tradition of Augustine. With respect to the faith-reason controversy, Anselm accepted the fideist position: "I believe in order that I may understand." However, once one accepts the faith, many articles of faith can be supported by reason.

The existence of God is one such article of faith. Basically Anselm tries to argue for the existence of God on the basis of the idea of God. Normally such an argument is silly. We can't go from the idea of a unicorn to the existence of one. But our concept of God is a very special concept. It is the one concept that contains as part of its meaning the idea of existence. In the exchange with the monk Gaunilon (of whom little is known) Anselm, in the tradition of much twentieth century philosophy, analyzes the concept of God and tries to explain why in this one case we are permitted to go from the idea to the existence of the object of the idea (from the idea of God to the existence of God). Although Thomas Aquinas and Immanuel Kant both rejected Anselm's argument for the existence of God in favor of ones they thought more convincing, Anselm's argument remains convincing to some. It was revived by the twentieth century American philosopher Norman Malcolm and has more recently been defended by Alvin Plantinga.

# A Dialogue on the Ontological Proof for the Existence of God

## *Saint Anselm and Gaunilon*

### I

*Saint Anselm*

O Lord, who grants understanding to faith, make me, so far as is good for me, to understand that you exist, as we believe, and that you are what we believe you to be. Now we believe you to be something greater than which we can conceive of nothing. Could it be then that there is no such nature, since "the fool says in his heart, 'There is no God' " [Ps. 13:1]? But surely this same fool, when he hears me say this, "something than which we can conceive of nothing greater," understands what he hears and what he understands is in his understanding even if he does not understand it to exist. For it is one thing for something to be in the understanding and quite another to understand that the thing in question exists. When a painter thinks of the work he will make beforehand, he has it in his understanding, but he does not think that what he has yet to make exists. But once he has painted it, he not only has it in his understanding but he understands that what he has made exists. Even the fool then must be convinced that in his understanding at least there is something than which nothing greater can be conceived, for when he hears this, he understands it and whatever is understood is in the understanding. But surely if the thing be such that we cannot conceive of something greater, it does not exist solely in the understanding. For if it were there only, one could also think of it as existing in reality and this is something greater. If the thing than which none greater can be thought were in the mind alone, then this same thing would both be and not be something than which nothing greater can be conceived. But surely this cannot be. Without doubt then there exists both in the understanding and in reality a being greater than which nothing can be conceived.

So truly does such a thing exist that it cannot be thought of as not existing. For we can think of something as existing which cannot be thought of as not existing, and such a thing is greater than what can be thought not to be. Wherefore, if the thing than which none greater can be thought could be conceived of as not existing, then this very thing than which none greater can be thought is not a thing than which none greater can be thought. But this is not possible. Hence, something greater than which nothing can be conceived so truly exists that it cannot be conceived not to be.

O Lord, our God, you are this being. So truly do you exist that you cannot even be thought of as nonexistent. And rightly so, for if some mind could think of something better than you, then the creature would rise above the Creator and would judge him, which is absurd. It is possible indeed to think of anything other than you as nonexistent. Of all beings then you alone have existence in the truest and highest sense, for nothing else so truly is or has existence in so great a measure. Why then does the fool "say in his heart, 'There is no God,' " when it is so evident to a reasoning mind that of all things you exist in a supreme degree? Why indeed save that he is stupid and a fool! . . .

Abridged from *Medieval Philosophy from St. Augustine to Nicholas of Gusa*. Edited by John F. Nippal and Allen B. Walter, O.F.M. (copyright © 1969 by The Free Press). Reprinted by permission of The Free Press, a division of Macmillan, Inc. Sections renumbered.

## II

*Gaunilon*

If one doubts or denies there is some such nature that nothing greater than it can be conceived, he is told that the existence of this being is proved, first, from the fact that in doubting or denying such he already has such a being in his understanding, for in hearing about it, he understands what is said. Next he is told that what he understands must needs exist not only in the intellect but in reality as well. And the proof of this is that a thing is greater if it also exists in reality than if it were in the understanding alone. Were it only in the intellect, even something that once existed would be greater than it. And so what is greater than all is less than something and thus not really greater than everything, which is clearly contradictory. It is necessary then that something greater than all, already proved to exist in the understanding, exists in reality as well, for otherwise it could not be greater than all. To this he might reply: . . .

. . . They say that somewhere in the ocean there is an island, which because of the difficulty, or better, the impossibility of finding what does not exist, some call the lost island. And they say this island is inestimably wealthy, having all kinds of delights and riches in greater abundance even than the fabled "Fortunate Islands." And since it has no possessor or inhabitant, it excels all other inhabited countries in its possessions. Now should someone tell me that there is such an island, I could readily understand what he says, since there is no problem there. But suppose he adds, as though it were already implied: "You can't doubt any more that this island, which is more excellent than any land, really exists somewhere, since you don't doubt that it is in your understanding and that it is more excellent not to be in the understanding only. Hence it is necessary that it really exists, for if it did not, any land which does would excel it and consequently the island which you already understand to be more excellent would not be such." If one were to try to prove to me that this island in truth exists and its existence should no longer be questioned, either I would think he was joking or I would not know whether to consider him or me the greater fool, me for conceding his argument or him for supposing he had established with any certainty such an island's existence without first showing such excellence to be real and its existence indubitable rather than just a figment of my understanding, whose existence is uncertain.

This then is an answer the fool could make to your arguments against him. When he is first assured that this being is so great that its nonexistence is inconceivable, and that this in turn is established for no other reason than that otherwise it would not excel all things, he could counter the same way and say: "When have I admitted there really is any such thing, i.e. something so much greater than everything else that one could prove to me it is so real, it could not even be conceived as unreal?" What we need at the outset is a very firm argument to show there is some superior being, bigger and better than all else that exists, so that we can go on from this to prove all the other attributes such a bigger and better being has to have. As for the statement that it is inconceivable that the highest thing of all should not exist, it might be better to say its nonexistence or even its possibility of nonexistence is unintelligible. For according to the true meaning of the word, unreal things are not intelligible, but their existence is conceivable in the way that the fool thinks that God does not exist. I most certainly know I exist, but for all that, I know my nonexistence is possible. As for that supreme being which God is, I understand without doubt both his existence and the impossibility of his nonexistence. But whether I can conceive of my nonexistence as long as I most certainly know I exist, I don't know. But if I am able to, why can I not conceive of the nonexistence of whatever else I know with the same certainty? But if I cannot, then such an inability will not be something peculiar to God. . . .

## III

*Saint Anselm*

It was a fool against whom I argued in my little work. But since my critic is far from a fool, and is a Catholic speaking in the fool's behalf, it is enough for me if I can answer the Catholic. . . .

But you claim our argument is on a par with the following. Someone imagines an island in the ocean which surpasses all lands in its fertility. Because of the difficulty, or rather impossibility, of finding what does not exist, he calls it "Lost Island." He might then say you cannot doubt that it really exists, because anyone can readily understand it from its verbal description. I assert confidently that if anyone finds something for me, besides that "than which none greater is conceivable," which exists either in reality or concept alone to which the logic of my argument can be applied, I will find and give him his "Lost Island," never to be lost again. But it now seems obvious that a thing such that none greater can be conceived cannot be thought of as nonexistent since it exists on such firm grounds of truth. For otherwise it would not exist at all. If anyone says he thinks it does not exist, then I declare that when he thinks this he either thinks of something than which a greater is inconceivable, or else he does not think at all. If he does not think, then neither does he think that what he is not thinking of is nonexistent. But if he does think, then he thinks of something which cannot be thought of as not existing. For if it could be conceived as nonexistent, it could be conceived as having a beginning and an end. Now this is impossible. Hence if anyone thinks of it, he thinks of something that cannot even be conceived to be nonexistent. Now whoever conceives it thus doesn't think of it as nonexistent, for if he did he would conceive what can't be conceived. Nonexistence is inconceivable, then, of something greater than which nothing can be conceived.

You claim moreover that when we say this supreme reality cannot be conceived of as nonexistent, it would be perhaps better to say that its nonexistence or even the possibility of its nonexistence is not understandable. But it is better to say it cannot be conceived. For had I said that the reality itself could not be understood not to exist, perhaps you, who insist that according to proper usage what is false cannot be understood, would object that nothing existing could be understood not to exist. For it is false to claim that what exists does not exist. Hence it would not be peculiar to God to be unable to be understood as nonexistent. If any one of the things that most certainly exist can be understood to be nonexistent, however, then other certain things can also be understood to be nonexistent. But this objection cannot be applied to "conceiving," if this is correctly understood. For though none of the things that exist can be understood not to exist, still they can all be conceived as nonexistent, except the greatest. For all — and only — those things can be conceived as nonexistent which have a beginning or end or consist of parts or do not exist in their entirety in any time or place, as I have said. Only that being which cannot be conceived to be nonexistent must be conceived as having no beginning or end or composition of parts but is whole and entire always and everywhere.

Consequently you must realize that you can conceive of yourself as nonexistent, though you most certainly know that you exist. You surprise me when you say you are not sure of this. For we conceive of many things as nonexistent which we know to exist and of many things as existent which we know do not exist. And we conceive them thus not by judging but by imagining them so. We can indeed conceive of something as existent even while we know it does not exist, because we are able to conceive the one at the same time that we know the other. But we cannot conceive nonexistence while knowing existence, because we cannot conceive existence and nonexistence at the same time. If anyone distinguishes between the two senses of the statement in this fashion, then, he will understand that nothing, as long as it is known to be, can be conceived not to be, and that whatever exists, with the exception of a thing such that no greater is conceivable, can be conceived of as nonexistent even when it is known to exist. This inability to be conceived of as nonexistent, then, is peculiar to God, even though there are many objects which cannot be conceived not to be while they are. . . .

## *Saint Thomas Aquinas (1225?–1274)*

Saint Thomas agrees with Saint Anselm that the existence of God can be established by reason. However, he rejects Saint Anselm's ontological proof based on the concept of God alone. Saint Thomas believed that all Saint Anselm had shown was that if you conceived of God you must conceive of God as existing. That you must conceive of God as existing does not prove, however, that God exists.

In the tradition of Aristotle, Saint Thomas's argument starts with our experience of the physical world. Although Saint Thomas's argument is often referred to as the cosmological proof, Saint Thomas actually has five arguments (called the "five ways" because they represent five proofs for the existence of God). A fairly detailed discussion of the "five ways" is provided in the introduction to this section.

In summary, all of Aquinas's arguments make God the only reasonable hypothesis to account for some of what we experience in the world. A weakness of this form of argument is that the argument is always open to newer and better hypotheses.

# The Existence of God

## *Saint Thomas Aquinas*

. . . The existence of God can be proved in five ways.

The first and more manifest way is the argument from motion. It is certain, and evident to our senses, that in the world some things are in motion. Now whatever is moved is moved by another, for nothing can be moved except it is in potentiality to that towards which it is moved; whereas a thing moves inasmuch as it is in act. For motion is nothing else than the reduction of something from potentiality to actuality. But nothing can be reduced from potentiality to actuality, except by something in a state of actuality. Thus that which is actually hot, as fire, makes wood, which is potentially hot, to be actually hot, and thereby moves and changes it. Now it is not possible that the same thing should be at once in actuality and potentiality in the same respect, but only in different respects. For what is actually hot cannot simultaneously be potentially hot; but it is simultaneously potentially cold. It is therefore impossible that in the same respect and in the same way a thing should be both mover and moved, *i.e.*, that it should move itself. Therefore, whatever is moved must be moved by another. If that by which it is moved be itself moved, then

Abridged from *Introduction to Saint Thomas Aquinas.* Edited and Introduction by Anton C. Pegis.

this also must needs be moved by another, and that by another again. But this cannot go on to infinity, because then there would be no first mover, and, consequently, no other mover, seeing that subsequent movers move only inasmuch as they are moved by the first mover; as the staff moves only because it is moved by the hand. Therefore it is necessary to arrive at a first mover, moved by no other; and this everyone understands to be God.

The second way is from the nature of efficient cause. In the world of sensible things we find there is an order of efficient causes. There is no case known (neither is it, indeed, possible) in which a thing is found to be the efficient cause of itself; for so it would be prior to itself, which is impossible. Now in efficient causes it is not possible to go on to infinity, because in all efficient causes following in order, the first is the cause of the intermediate cause, and the intermediate is the cause of the ultimate cause, whether the intermediate cause be several, or one only. Now to take away the cause is to take away the effect. Therefore, if there be no first cause among efficient causes, there will be no ultimate, nor any intermediate, cause. But if in efficient causes it is possible to go on to infinity, there will be no first efficient cause, neither will there be an ultimate effect, nor any intermediate efficient causes; all of which is plainly false. Therefore it is necessary to admit a first efficient cause, to which everyone gives the name of God.

The third way is taken from **possibility** and **necessity,** and runs thus. We find in nature things that are possible to be and not to be, since they are found to be generated, and to be corrupted, and consequently, it is possible for them to be and not to be. But it is impossible for these always to exist, for that which can not-be at some time is not. Therefore, if everything can not-be, then at one time there was nothing in existence. Now if this were true, even now there would be nothing in existence, because that which does not exist begins to exist only through something already existing. Therefore, if at one time nothing was in existence, it would have been impossible for anything to have begun to exist; and thus even now nothing would be in existence—which is absurd. Therefore, not all beings are merely possible, but there must exist something the existence of which is necessary. But every necessary thing either has its necessity caused by another, or not. Now it is impossible to go on to infinity in necessary things which have their necessity caused by another, as has been already proved in regard to efficient causes. Therefore we cannot but admit the existence of some being having of itself its own necessity, and not receiving it from another, but rather causing in others their necessity. This all men speak of as God.

The fourth way is taken from the gradation to be found in things. Among beings there are some more and some less good, true, noble, and the like. But *more* and *less* are predicted of different things according as they resemble in their different ways something which is the maximum, as a thing is said to be hotter according as it more nearly resembles that which is hottest; so that there is something which is truest, something best, something noblest, and, consequently, something which is most being, for those things that are greatest in truth are greatest in being. . . . Now the maximum in any genus is the cause of all in that genus, as fire, which is the maximum of heat, is the cause of all hot things, as is said in the same book. Therefore there must also be something which is to all beings the cause of their being, goodness, and every other perfection; and this we call God.

The fifth way is taken from the governance of the world. We see that things which lack knowledge, such as natural bodies, act for an end, and this is evident from their acting always, or nearly always, in the same way, so as to obtain the best result. Hence it is plain that they achieve their end, not fortuitously, but designedly. Now whatever lacks knowledge cannot move towards an end, unless it be directed by some being endowed with knowledge and intelligence; as the arrow is directed by the archer. Therefore some intelligent being exists by whom all natural things are directed to their end; and this being we call God.

## *William Paley (1743–1805)*

William Paley was an English theologian who is best known as an exponent of the third major kind of argument for the existence of God — the teleological argument or argument from design. That argument, like Saint Thomas's five ways, starts from human experience and then argues that God is the best hypothesis to account for the experiences we have. The teleological argument makes extensive use of analogy. Paley's most famous analogy is the watch. Just as the discovery and examination of the intricate design of a watch would lead one to argue that there must have been a watchmaker, so an examination of our world exhibits the kind of planning and design that requires us to see there must have been a creator that we call God. In the selection included here, the intricate order of the human eye serves as the kind of example Paley needs. Although arguments based on analogy have their legitimate uses, they do suffer from various weaknesses. On the one hand, critics can argue that the analogy does not lead to the kind of conclusion wanted. For example, the evidence of design and planning in the world of our experience may require a creator, but not creation by an omnipotent, omniscient, or perfectly good being. On the other hand, critics may attack the analogy itself — for example, by saying that the world we know is not really like a watch. Paley's watch metaphor has been attacked on both these grounds.

# The Argument from Design

## *William Paley*

I

In crossing a heath, suppose I pitched my foot against a *stone* and were asked how the stone came to be there, I might possibly answer that for anything I knew to the contrary it had lain there forever; nor would it, perhaps, be very easy to show the absurdity of this answer. But suppose I had found a *watch* upon the ground, and it should be inquired how the watch happened to be in that place, I should hardly think of the answer which I had before given, that for anything I knew the watch might have always been there. Yet why should not this answer serve for the watch as well as for the stone; why is it not as admissible in the second case as in the first? For this reason, and for no other, namely, that when we come to inspect the watch, we perceive — what we could not discover in the stone — that its several parts are framed and put together for a purpose, e.g., that they are so formed and adjusted as to produce motion, and that motion so regulated as to point out the hour of the day; that if the different parts had been differently shaped from what they are, or placed after any other manner or in any other order than that in which they are placed, either no motion at all would have been carried on in the machine, or none which would have answered the use that is now served by it. To reckon up a few of the plainest of

Abridged from "The Argument from Design" in *Natural Theology,* by William Paley (1802).

these parts and of their offices, all tending to one result: we see a cylindrical box containing a coiled elastic spring, which, by its endeavor to relax itself, turns round the box. We next observe a flexible chain—artificially wrought for the sake of flexure—communicating the action of the spring from the box to the fusee. We then find a series of wheels, the teeth of which catch in and apply to each other, conducting the motion from the fusee to the balance and from the balance to the pointer, and at the same time, by the size and shape of those wheels, so regulating that motion as to terminate in causing an index, by an equable and measured progression, to pass over a given space in a given time. We take notice that the wheels are made of brass, in order to keep them from rust; the springs of steel, no other metal being so elastic; that over the face of the watch there is placed a glass, a material employed in no other part of the work, but in the room of which, if there had been any other than a transparent substance, the hour could not be seen without opening the case. This mechanism being observed—it requires indeed an examination of the instrument, and perhaps some previous knowledge of the subject, to perceive and understand it; but being once, as we have said, observed and understood—the inference we think is inevitable, that the watch must have had a maker—that there must have existed, at some time and at some place or other, an artificer or artificers who formed it for the purpose which we find it actually to answer, who completely comprehended its construction and designed its use.

1. Nor would it, I apprehend, weaken the conclusion, that we had never seen a watch made—that we had never known an artist capable of making one—that we were altogether incapable of executing such a piece of workmanship ourselves, or of understanding in what manner it was performed; all this being no more than what is true of some exquisite remains of ancient art, of some lost arts, and, to the generality of mankind, of the more curious productions of modern manufacture. Does one man in a million know how oval frames are turned? Ignorance of this kind exalts our opinion of the unseen and unknown artist's skill, if he be unseen and unknown, but raises no doubt in our minds of the existence and agency of such an artist, at some former time and in some place or other. Nor can I perceive that it varies at all the inference, whether the question arise concerning a human agent or concerning an agent of a different species, or an agent possessing in some respects a different nature.

2. Neither, secondly, would it invalidate our conclusion, that the watch sometimes went wrong or that it seldom went exactly right. The purpose of the machinery, the design, and the designer might be evident, and in the case supposed, would be evident, in whatever way we accounted for the irregularity of the movement, or whether we could account for it or not. It is not necessary that a machine be perfect in order to show with what design it was made: still less necessary, where the only question is whether it were made with any design at all.

3. Nor, thirdly, would it bring any uncertainty into the argument, if there were a few parts of the watch, concerning which we could not discover or had not yet discovered in what manner they conduced to the general effect; or even some parts, concerning which we could not ascertain whether they conduced to that effect in any manner whatever. For, as to the first branch of the case, if by the loss, or disorder, or decay of the parts in question, the movement of the watch were found in fact to be stopped, or disturbed, or retarded, no doubt would remain in our minds as to the utility or intention of these parts, although we should be unable to investigate the manner according to which, or the connection by which, the ultimate effect depended upon their action or assistance; and the more complex the machine, the more likely is this obscurity to arise. Then, as to the second thing supposed, namely, that there were parts which might be spared without prejudice to the movement of the watch, and that we had proved this by experiment, these superfluous parts, even if we were completely assured that they were such, would not vacate the reasoning which we had instituted concerning other parts. The indication of contriv-

ance remained, with respect to them, nearly as it was before. . . .

Every observation which was made . . . concerning the watch may be repeated with strict propriety concerning the eye, concerning animals, concerning plants, concerning, indeed, all the organized parts of the works of nature. As, when we are inquiring simply after the *existence* of an intelligent Creator, imperfection, inaccuracy, liability to disorder, occasional irregularities may subsist in a considerable degree without inducing any doubt into the question; just as a watch may frequently go wrong, seldom perhaps exactly right, may be faulty in some parts, defective in some, without the smallest ground of suspicion from thence arising that it was not a watch, not made, or not made for the purpose ascribed to it. When faults are pointed out, and when a question is started concerning the skill of the artist or the dexterity with which the work is executed, then, indeed, in order to defend these qualities from accusation, we must be able either to expose some intractableness and imperfection in the materials or point out some invincible difficulty in the execution, into which imperfection and difficulty the matter of complaint may be resolved; or, if we cannot do this, we must adduce such specimens of consummate art and contrivance proceeding from the same hand as may convince the inquirer of the existence, in the case before him, of impediments like those which we have mentioned, although, what from the nature of the case is very likely to happen, they be unknown and unperceived by him. This we must do in order to vindicate the artist's skill, or at least the perfection of it; as we must also judge of his intention and of the provisions employed in fulfilling that intention, not from an instance in which they fail but from the great plurality of instances in which they succeed. But, after all, these are different questions from the question of the artist's existence; or, which is the same, whether the thing before us be a work of art or not; and the questions ought always to be kept separate in the mind. So likewise it is in the works of nature. Irregularities and imperfections are of little or no weight in the consideration when that consideration relates simply to the existence of a Creator. When the argument respects his attributes, they are of weight; but are then to be taken in conjunction — the attention is not to rest upon them, but they are to be taken in conjunction with the unexceptional evidences which we possess of skill, power, and benevolence displayed in other instances; which evidences may, in strength, number, and variety, be such and may so overpower apparent blemishes as to induce us, upon the most reasonable ground, to believe that these last ought to be referred to some cause, though we be ignorant of it, other than defect of knowledge or of benevolence in the author. . . .

## David Hume (1711–1776)

The reader has already been introduced to the work of David Hume — one of the giants in the field. As one of the classic empiricists, his rigorous consistent application of empiricism ended in scepticism. Nowhere is his scepticism more evident than in his philosophy of religion. For example, Hume argued that one should never accept a miracle because having sufficient evidence to accept a miracle would require a miracle greater than the one for which evidence was being offered. Perhaps his best known work in the philosophy of religion is his methodical criticism of the teleological argument. Since the argument is based on analogy, Hume attacked the analogy. He argued that the machine (watch) metaphor was a bad analogy. The world resembled an animal or a vegetable as much as it did a machine like a watch. Moreover, even if the analogy with a machine were accepted, you could not infer the existence of the kind of creator most religious persons worshipped. You might infer a watchmaker from the existence of a watch, but you couldn't infer much about the watchmaker.

Hume also raised the problem of evil (discussed in the next section) and criticized anthropological arguments that belief in religion was a natural human belief. Whether or not Hume actually believed in God is still a matter of intellectual controversy. If he did, it could not be because he found theism acceptable on rational grounds.

Hume's ideas on religion are presented in the form of a dialogue. In the selection that follows there are three characters, Demea, Cleanthes, and Philo. Although there is some controversy as to whether Hume's position is best represented by Cleanthes or Philo, the position of the three characters can be roughly characterized as follows. Demea is a fideist who argues that religious claims cannot be established by arguments from experience, while Cleanthes tries to show how empirical evidence can be adduced to support religious claims. Philo is the sceptic who points out the errors in Cleanthes' reasoning.

# Dialogues Concerning Natural Religion

## *David Hume*

Not to lose any time in circumlocutions, said Cleanthes, . . . I shall briefly explain how I conceive this matter. Look round the world: Contemplate the whole and every part of it: You will find it to be nothing but one great machine, subdivided into an infinite number of lesser machines, which again admit of subdivisions to a degree beyond what human senses and faculties can trace and explain. All these various machines, and even their most minute parts, are adjusted to each other with an accuracy which ravishes into admiration all men who have ever contemplated them. The curious adapting of means to ends, throughout all nature, resembles exactly, though it much exceeds, the productions of human contrivance—of human design, thought, wisdom, and intelligence. Since therefore the effects resemble each other, we are led to infer, by all the rules of analogy, that the causes also resemble, and that the Author of Nature is somewhat similar to the mind of man, though possessed of much larger faculties, proportioned to the grandeur of the work which he has executed. By this argument ***a posteriori,*** and by this argument alone, do we prove at once the existence of a Deity and his similarity to human mind and intelligence.

I shall be so free, Cleanthes, said Demea, as to tell you that from the beginning I could not approve of your conclusion concerning the similarity of the Deity to men, still less can I approve of the mediums by which you endeavor to establish it. What! No demonstration of the Being of God! No abstract arguments! No proofs ***a priori!*** Are these which have hitherto been so much insisted on by philosophers all fallacy, all sophism? Can we reach no farther in this subject than experience and probability? I will say not that this is betraying the cause of a Deity; but surely, by this affected candor, you give advantages to atheists which they never could obtain by the mere dint of argument and reasoning.

What I chiefly scruple in this subject, said Philo, is not so much that all religious arguments are by Cleanthes reduced to experience, as that they appear not to be even the most certain and irrefragable of that inferior kind. That a stone will fall, that fire will burn, that the earth has solidity, we have observed a thousand and a thousand times; and when any new instance of this nature is presented, we draw without hesitation the accustomed inference. The exact similarity of the cases gives us a perfect assurance of a similar event, and a stronger evidence is never desired nor sought after. But wherever you depart, in the least, from the similarity of the cases, you diminish proportionably the evidence; and may at last bring it to a very weak *analogy,* which is confessedly liable to error and uncertainty. . . .

If we see a house, Cleanthes, we conclude, with the greatest certainty, that it had an architect or builder because this is precisely that species of effect which we have experienced to proceed from that species of cause. But surely you will not affirm that the universe bears such a resemblance to a house that we can with the same certainty infer a similar cause, or that the analogy is here entire and perfect. The dissimilitude is so striking that the utmost you can here pretend to is a guess, a conjecture, a presumption concerning a similar cause; and how that pretension will be received in the world, I leave you to consider.

It would surely be very ill received, replied Cleanthes; and I should be deservedly blamed and detested did I allow that the proofs of a Deity amounted to no more than a guess or conjecture. But is the whole adjustment of means to ends in a house and in the universe so slight a resemblance? the economy of final causes? the order, proportion, and arrangement of every part? Steps of a stair are plainly contrived that human legs may use them in mounting; and this inference is certain and infallible. Human legs are also contrived for walking and mounting; and this inference, I allow, is not altogether so certain because of the dissimilarity which you remark; but does it, therefore, deserve the name only of presumption or conjecture? . . .

[Philo:] That all inferences, Cleanthes, concerning fact are founded on experience, and that all experimental reasonings are founded on the supposition that similar causes prove similar effects, and similar effects similar causes, I shall not at present much dispute with you. But observe, I entreat you, with what extreme caution all just reasoners proceed in the transferring of experiments to similar cases. Unless the cases be exactly similar, they repose no perfect confidence in applying their past observation to any particular phenomenon. Every alteration of circumstances occasions a doubt concerning the event; and it requires new experiments to prove certainly that the new circumstances are of no moment or importance. A change in bulk, situation, arrangement, age, disposition of the air, or surrounding bodies — any of these particulars may be attended with the most unexpected consequences. And unless the objects be quite familiar to us, it is the highest temerity to expect with assurance, after any of these changes, an event similar to that which before fell under our observation. The slow and deliberate steps of philosophers here, if anywhere, are distinguished from the precipitate march of the vulgar, who, hurried on by the smallest similitude, are incapable of all discernment or consideration.

But can you think, Cleanthes, that your usual phlegm and philosophy have been preserved in so wide a step as you have taken when you compared to the universe houses, ships, furniture, machines; and, from their similarity in some circumstances, inferred a similarity in their causes? Thought, design, intelligence, such as we discover in men and other animals, is no more than one of the springs and principles of the universe, as well as heat or cold, attraction or repulsion, and a hundred others which fall under daily observation. It is an active cause by which some particular parts of nature, we find, produce alterations on other parts. But can a conclusion, with any propriety, be transferred from parts to the whole? Does not the great disproportion bar all comparison and inference? From observing the growth of a hair, can we learn anything concerning the generation of a man? Would the manner of a leaf's blowing, even though perfectly known, afford us any instruction concerning the vegetation of a tree?

But allowing that we were to take the *operations* of one part of nature upon another for the foundation of our judgment concerning the *origin* of the whole (which never can be admitted), yet why select so minute, so weak, so bounded a principle as the reason and design of animals is found to be upon this planet? What peculiar privilege has this little agitation of the brain which we call *thought,* that we must thus make it the model of the whole universe? Our partiality in our own favor does indeed present it on all occasions, but sound philosophy ought carefully to guard against so natural an illusion.

So far from admitting, continued Philo, that the operations of a part can afford us any just conclusion concerning the origin of the whole, I will not allow any one part to form a rule for another part if the latter be very remote from the former. Is there any reasonable ground to conclude that the inhabitants of other planets possess thought, intelligence, reason, or anything similar to these faculties in men? When nature has so extremely diversified her manner of operation in this small globe, can we imagine that she incessantly copies herself throughout so immense a universe? And if thought, as we may well suppose, be confined merely to this narrow corner and has even there so limited a sphere of action, with what propriety can we assign it for the original cause of all things? The narrow views of a peasant who makes his domestic economy the rule for the government of kingdoms is in comparison a pardonable sophism.

But were we ever so much assured that a thought and reason resembling the human were to be found throughout the whole universe, and were its activity elsewhere vastly greater and more commanding than it appears in this globe; yet I cannot see why the operations of a world constituted, arranged, adjusted, can with any propriety be extended to a world which is in its embryo-state, and is advancing towards that constitution and arrangement. By observation we know somewhat of the economy, action, and nourishment of a finished animal; but we must transfer with great caution that observation to the growth of a fetus in the womb, and still more to the formation of an animalcule in the loins of its male parent. Nature, we find, even from our limited experience, possesses an infinite number of springs and principles which incessantly discover themselves on every change of her position and situation. And what new and unknown principles would actuate her in so new and unknown a situation as that of the formation of a universe, we cannot, without the utmost temerity, pretend to determine.

A very small part of this great system, during a very short time, is very imperfectly discovered to us; and do we thence pronounce decisively concerning the origin of the whole?

Admirable conclusion! Stone, wood, brick, iron, brass, have not, at this time, in this minute globe of earth, an order or arrangement without human art and contrivance; therefore, the universe could not originally attain its order and arrangement without something similar to human art. But is a part of nature a rule for another part very wide of the former? Is it a rule for the whole? Is a very small part a rule for the universe? Is nature in one situation a certain rule for nature in another situation vastly different from the former? . . .

But to show you still more inconveniences, continued Philo, in your **anthropomorphism,** please to take a new survey of your principles. *Like effects prove like causes.* This is the experimental argument; and this, you say too, is the sole theological argument. Now it is certain that the liker the effects are which are seen and the liker the causes which are inferred, the stronger is the argument. Every departure on either side diminishes the probability and renders the experiment less conclusive. You cannot doubt of the principle; neither ought you to reject its consequences. . . .

Now, Cleanthes, said Philo, with an air of alacrity and triumph, mark the consequences. *First,* by this method of reasoning you renounce all claim to infinity in any of the attributes of the Deity. For, as the cause ought only to be proportioned to the effect, and the effect, so far as it falls under our cognizance, is not infinite, what pretensions have we, upon your suppositions, to ascribe that attribute to the divine Being? You will still insist that, by removing him so much from all similarity to human creatures, we give in to the most arbitrary hypothesis, and at the same time weaken all proofs of his existence.

*Secondly,* you have no reason, on your theory, for ascribing perfection to the Deity, even in his finite capacity; or for supposing him free from every error, mistake, or incoherence, in his undertakings. There are many inexplicable difficulties in the works of nature which, if we allow a perfect author to be proved *a priori,* are easily solved, and become only seeming difficulties from the narrow capacity of man, who cannot trace infinite relations. But according to your method of reasoning, these difficulties become all real; and, perhaps, will be insisted on as new instances of likeness to human art and contrivance. At least, you must acknowledge that it is impossible for us to tell, from our limited views, whether this system contains any great faults or deserves any considerable praise if compared to other possible and even real systems. Could a peasant, if the *Aeneid* were read to him, pronounce that poem to be absolutely faultless, or even assign to it its proper rank among the productions of human wit, he who had never seen any other production?

But were this world ever so perfect a production, it must still remain uncertain whether all the excellences of the work can justly be ascribed to the workman. If we survey a ship, what an exalted idea must we form of the ingenuity of the carpenter who framed so complicated, useful, and beautiful a machine? And what surprise must we feel when we find him a stupid mechanic who imitated others, and copied an art which, through a long succession of ages, after multiplied trials, mistakes, corrections, deliberations, and controversies, had been gradually improving? Many worlds might have been botched and bungled, throughout an eternity, ere this system was struck out; much labor lost; many fruitless trials made; and a slow but continued improvement carried on during infinite ages in the art of world-making. In such subjects, who can determine where the truth, nay, who can conjecture where the probability lies, amidst a great number of hypotheses which may be proposed, and a still greater which may be imagined?

And what shadow of an argument, continued Philo, can you produce from your hypothesis to prove the unity of the Deity? A great number of men join in building a house or ship, in rearing a city, in framing a commonwealth; why may not several deities combine in contriving and framing a world? This is only so much greater similarity to human affairs. By sharing the work among several, we may so much further limit the attributes of each, and get rid of that extensive power and knowledge which must be supposed in one deity, and which, according to you, can only serve to weaken the proof of his existence. And if such foolish, such vicious creatures as man can yet often unite in framing and executing one plan, how much more those deities or demons, whom we may suppose several degrees more perfect?

To multiply causes without necessity is indeed contrary to true philosophy, but this principle applies not to the present case. Were one deity antecedently proved by your theory who were possessed of every attribute requisite to the production of the universe, it would be needless, I own (though not absurd), to suppose any other deity existent. But while it is still a question whether all these attributes are united in one subject or dispersed among several independent beings; by what phenomena in nature can we pretend to decide the controversy? Where we see a body raised in a scale, we are sure that there is in the opposite scale, however concealed from sight, some counterpoising weight equal to it; but it is still allowed to doubt whether that weight be an aggregate of several distinct bodies or one uniform united mass. And if the weight requisite very much exceeds anything which we have ever seen conjoined in any single body, the former supposition becomes still more probable and natural. An intelligent being of such vast power and capacity as is necessary to produce the universe—or, to speak in the language of ancient philosophy, so prodigious an animal—exceeds all analogy and even comprehension.

But further, Cleanthes, men are mortal, and renew their species by generation; and this is common to all living creatures. The two great sexes of male and female, says Milton, animate the world. Why must this circumstance, so universal, so essential, be excluded from those numerous and limited deities? Behold, then, the theogeny of ancient times brought back upon us.

And why not become a perfect anthropomorphite? Why not assert the deity or deities to be corporeal, and to have eyes, a nose, mouth, ears, etc.? Epicurus maintained that no man had ever seen reason but in a human figure; therefore, the gods must have a human figure. And this argument, which is deservedly so much ridiculed by Cicero, becomes, according to you, solid and philosophical.

In a word, Cleanthes, a man who follows your hypothesis is able, perhaps, to assert or conjecture that the universe sometime arose from something like design; but beyond that position he cannot ascertain one single circumstance, and is left afterwards to fix every point of his theology by the utmost license of fancy and hypothesis. This world, for aught he knows, is very faulty and imperfect, compared to a superior standard; and was only the first rude essay of some infant deity who afterwards abandoned it, ashamed of his lame performance; it is the work only of some dependent, inferior deity, and is the object of derision to his superiors; it is the production of old age and dotage in some superannuated deity; and ever since his death has run on at adventures, from the first impulse and active force which it received from him. You justly give signs of horror, Demea, at these strange suppositions; but these, and a thousand more of the same kind, are Cleanthes' suppositions, not mine. From the moment the attributes of the Deity are supposed finite, all these have place. And I cannot, for my part, think that so wild and unsettled a system of theology is, in any respect, preferable to none at all.

These suppositions I absolutely disown, cried Cleanthes; they strike me, however, with no horror, especially when proposed in that rambling way in which they drop from you. On the contrary, they give me pleasure when I see that, by the utmost indulgence of your imagination, you never get rid of the hypothesis of design in the universe, but are obliged at every turn to have recourse to it. To this concession I adhere steadily; and this I regard as a sufficient foundation for religion.

It must be a slight fabric, indeed, said Demea, which can be erected on so tottering a foundation. While we are uncertain whether there is one deity or many, whether the deity or deities, to whom we owe our existence, be perfect or imperfect, subordinate or supreme, dead or alive, what trust or confidence can we repose in them? What devotion or worship address to them? What veneration or obedience pay them? To all the purposes of life the theory of religion becomes altogether useless; and even with regard to speculative consequences its uncertainty, according to you, must render it totally precarious and unsatisfactory. . . .

But here, continued Philo, in examining the ancient system of the soul of the world there strikes me, all on a sudden, a new idea which, if just, must go near to subvert all your reasoning, and destroy even your first inferences on which you repose such confidence. If the universe bears a greater likeness to animal bodies and to vegetables than to the works of human art, it is more probable that its cause resembles the cause of the former than that of the latter, and its origin ought rather to be abscribed to generation or vegetation than to reason or design. Your conclusion, even according to your own principles, is therefore lame and defective.

Pray open up this argument a little further, said Demea, for I do not rightly apprehend it in that concise manner in which you have expressed it.

Our friend Cleanthes, replied Philo, as you have heard, asserts that since no question of fact can be proved otherwise than by experience, the existence of a Deity admits not of proof from any other medium. The world, says he, resembles the works of human contrivance; therefore its cause must also resemble that of the other. Here we may remark that the operation of one very small part of nature, to wit, man, upon another very small part, to wit, that inanimate matter lying within his reach, is the rule by which Cleanthes judges of the origin of the whole; and he measures objects, so widely disproportioned, by the same individual standard. But to waive all objections drawn from this topic, I affirm that there are other parts of the universe (besides the machines of human invention) which bear still a greater resemblance to the fabric of the world, and which, therefore, afford a better conjecture concerning the universal origin of this system. These parts are animals and vegetables. The world plainly resembles more an animal or a vegetable than it does a watch or a knitting-loom. Its cause, therefore, it is more probable, resembles the cause of the former. The cause of the former is generation or vegetation. The cause, therefore, of the world we may infer to be something similar or analogous to generation or vegetation.

But how is it conceivable, said Demea, that the world can arise from anything similar to vegetation or generation?

Very easily, replied Philo. In like manner as a tree sheds its seed into the neighboring fields and produces other trees; so the great vegetable, the world, or this planetary system, produces within itself certain seeds which, being scattered into the surrounding chaos, vegetate into new worlds. A comet, for instance, is the seed of a world; and after it has been fully ripened, by passing from sun to sun, and star to star, it is at last tossed into the unformed elements which everywhere surround this universe, and immediately sprouts up into a new system.

Or if, for the sake of variety (for I see no other advantage) we should suppose this world to be an animal; a comet is the egg of this animal; and in like manner as an ostrich lays its egg in the sand, which, without any further care, hatches the egg and produces a new animal, so. . . . I understand you, says Demea: But what wild, arbitrary suppositions are these? What *data* have you for such extraordinary conclusions? And is the slight, imaginary resemblance of the world to a vegetable or an animal sufficient to establish the same inference with regard to both? Objects which are in general so widely different; ought they to be a standard for each other?

Right, cries Philo: This is the topic on which I have all along insisted. I have still asserted that we have no *data* to establish any system of **cosmogony.** Our experience, so imperfect in itself and so limited both in extent and duration, can afford us no probable conjecture concerning the whole of things. But if we must needs fix on some hypothesis, by what rule, pray, ought we to determine our choice? Is there any other rule than the great similarity of the objects compared? And does not a plant or an animal, which springs from vegetation or generation, bear a stronger resemblance to the world than does any artificial machine, which arises from reason and design? . . .

I must confess, Philo, replied Cleanthes, that, of all men living, the task which you have undertaken, of raising doubts and objections, suits you best and seems, in a manner, natural and unavoidable to you. So great is your fertility of invention that I am not ashamed to acknowledge myself unable, on a sudden, to solve regularly such out-of-the-way difficulties as you incessantly start upon me; though I clearly see, in general, their fallacy and error. And I question not, but you are yourself, at present, in the same case, and have not the solution so ready as the objection; while you must be sensible that common sense and reason are entirely against you, and that such whimsies as you have delivered may puzzle but never can convince us.

It is my opinion, I own, replied Demea, that each man feels, in a manner, the truth of religion within his own breast; and, from a consciousness of his imbecility and misery rather than from any reasoning, is led to seek protection from that Being on whom he and all nature are dependent.

So anxious or so tedious are even the best scenes of life that futurity is still the object of all our hopes and fears. We incessantly look forward and endeavor, by prayers, adoration, and sacrifice, to appease those unknown powers whom we find, by experience, so able to afflict and oppress us. Wretched creatures that we are! What resource for us amidst the innumerable ills of life did not religion suggest some methods of atonement, and appease those terrors with which we are incessantly agitated and tormented?

I am indeed persuaded, said Philo, that the best and indeed the only method of bringing everyone to a due sense of religion is by just representations of the misery and wickedness of men. And for that purpose a talent of eloquence and strong imagery is more requisite than that of reasoning and argument. For is it necessary to prove what everyone feels within himself? It is only necessary to make us feel it, if possible, more intimately and sensibly. . . .

Observe, too, says Philo, the curious artifices of nature in order to embitter the life of every living being. The stronger prey upon the weaker and keep them in perpetual terror and anxiety. The weaker, too, in their turn, often prey upon the stronger, and vex and molest them without relaxation. Consider that innumerable race of insects, which either are bred on the body of each animal or, flying about, infix their stings in him. These insects have others still less than themselves which torment them. And thus on each hand, before and behind, above and below, every animal is surrounded with enemies which incessantly seek his misery and destruction. . . .

[Demea:] Were a stranger to drop on a sudden into this world, I would show him, as a specimen of its ills, a hospital full of diseases, a prison crowded with malefactors and debtors, a field of battle strewed with carcases, a fleet foundering in the ocean, a nation languishing under tyranny, famine, or pestilence. To turn the gay side of life to him and give him a notion of its pleasures—whither should I conduct him? To a ball, to an opera, to court? He might justly think that I was only showing him a diversity of distress and sorrow. . . .

And is it possible, Cleanthes, said Philo, that after all these reflections, and infinitely more which might be suggested, you can still persevere in your anthropomorphism, and assert the moral attributes of the Deity, his justice, benevolence, mercy, and rectitude, to be of the same nature with these virtues in human creatures? His power, we allow, is infinite; whatever he wills is executed; but neither man nor any other animal is happy; therefore, he does not will their happiness. His wisdom is infinite; he is never mistaken in choosing the means to any end; but the course of nature tends not to human or animal felicity; therefore, it is not established for that purpose. Through the whole compass of human knowledge there are no inferences more certain and infallible than these. In what respect, then, do his benevolence and mercy resemble the benevolence and mercy of men?

Epicurus' old questions are yet unanswered.

Is he willing to prevent evil, but not able? then is he impotent. Is he able, but not willing? then is he malevolent. Is he both able and willing? whence then is evil?

You ascribe, Cleanthes (and I believe justly), a purpose and intention to nature. But what, I beseech you, is the object of that curious artifice and machinery which she has displayed in all animals—the preservation alone of individuals, and propagation of the species? It seems enough for her purpose, if such a rank be barely upheld in the universe, without any care or concern for the happiness of the members that compose it. No resource for this purpose: no machinery in order merely to give pleasure or ease: no fund of pure joy and contentment: no indulgence without some want or necessity accompanying it. At least, the few phenomena of this nature are overbalanced by opposite phenomena of still greater importance.

Our sense of music, harmony, and indeed beauty of all kinds, gives satisfaction, without being absolutely necessary to the preservation and propagation of the species. But what racking pains, on the other hand, arise from gouts, gravels, megrims, toothaches, rheumatisms, where the injury to the animal machinery is either small or incurable? Mirth, laughter, play, frolic seem gratuitous satisfactions which have no further tendency; spleen, melancholy, discontent, superstition are pains of the same nature. How then does the divine benevolence display itself, in the sense of you anthropomorphites? None but we mystics, as you were pleased to call us, can account for this strange mixture of phenomena, by deriving it from attributes infinitely perfect but incomprehensible. . . .

Here, Cleanthes, I find myself at ease in my argument. Here I triumph. Formerly, when we argued concerning the natural attributes of intelligence and design, I needed all my sceptical and metaphysical subtilty to elude your grasp. In many views of the universe and of its parts, particularly the latter, the beauty and fitness of final causes strike us with such irresistible force that all objections appear (what I believe they really are) mere cavils and sophisms; nor can we then imagine how it was ever possible for us to repose any weight on them. But there is no view of human life or of the condition of mankind from which, without the greatest violence, we can infer the moral attributes or learn that infinite benevolence, conjoined with infinite power and infinite wisdom, which we must discover by the eyes of faith alone. It is your turn now to tug the laboring oar, and to support your philosophical subtilties against the dictates of plain reason and experience.

I scruple not to allow, said Cleanthes, that I have been apt to suspect the frequent repetition of the word *infinite,* which we meet with in all theological writers, to savor more of panegyric than of philosophy, and that any purposes of reasoning, and even of religion, would be better served were we to rest contented with more accurate and more moderate expressions. The terms *admirable, excellent, superlatively great, wise,* and *holy*—these sufficiently fill the imaginations of men, and anything beyond, besides that it leads into absurdities, has no influence on the affections or sentiments. Thus, in the present subject, if we abandon all human analogy, as seems your intention, Demea, I am afraid we abandon all religion and retain no conception of the great object of our adoration. If we preserve human analogy, we must forever find it impossible to reconcile any mixture of evil in the universe with infinite attributes; much less can we ever prove the latter from the former. But supposing the Author of Nature to be finitely perfect, though far exceeding mankind, a satisfactory account may then be given of natural and moral evil, and every untoward phenomenon be explained and adjusted. A less evil may then be chosen in order to avoid a greater; inconveniences be submitted to in order to reach a desirable end; and, in a word, benevolence, regulated by wisdom and limited by necessity, may produce just such a world as the present. You, Philo, who are so prompt at starting views and reflections and analogies, I would gladly hear, at length, without interruption, your opinion of this new theory; and if it deserve our attention, we may afterwards, at more leisure, reduce it into form.

My sentiments, replied Philo, are not worth being made a mystery of; and, therefore, without any ceremony, I shall deliver what occurs to me with regard to the present subject. It must, I think, be allowed that, if a very limited intelligence whom we shall suppose utterly unacquainted with the universe were assured that it were the production of a very good, wise, and powerful being, however finite, he would, from his conjectures, form *beforehand* a different notion of it from what we find it to be by experience; nor would he ever imagine, merely from these attributes of the cause of which he is informed, that the effect could be so full of vice and misery and disorder, as it appears in this life. Supposing now that this person were brought into the world, still assured that it was the workmanship of such a sublime and benevolent being, he might, perhaps, be surprised at the disappointment, but would never retract his former belief if founded on any very solid argument, since such a limited intelligence must be sensible of his own blindness and ignorance, and must allow that there may be many solutions of those phenomena which will forever escape his comprehension. But supposing, which is the real case with regard to man, that this creature is not antecedently convinced of a supreme intelligence, benevolent, and powerful, but is left to gather such a belief from the appearances of things — this entirely alters the case, nor will he ever find any reason for such a conclusion. He may be fully convinced of the narrow limits of his understanding, but this will not help him in forming an inference concerning the goodness of superior powers, since he must form that inference from what he knows, not from what he is ignorant of. The more you exaggerate his weakness and ignorance, the more diffident you render him, and give him the greater suspicion that such subjects are beyond the reach of his faculties. You are obliged, therefore, to reason with him merely from the known phenomena, and to drop every arbitrary supposition or conjecture.

Did I show you a house or palace where there was not one apartment convenient or agreeable; where the windows, doors, fires, passages, stairs, and the whole economy of the building were the source of noise, confusion, fatigue, darkness, and the extremes of heat and cold, you would certainly blame the contrivance, without any further examination. The architect would in vain display his subtilty, and prove to you that, if this door or that window were altered, greater ills would ensue. What he says may be strictly true: The alteration of one particular, while the other parts of the building remain, may only augment the inconveniences. But still you would assert in general that, if the architect had had skill and good intentions, he might have formed such a plan of the whole, and might have adjusted the parts in such a manner as would have remedied all or most of these inconveniences. His ignorance, or even your own ignorance of such a plan, will never convince you of the impossibility of it. If you find any inconveniences and deformities in the building, you will always, without entering into any detail, condemn the architect. . . .

Thus Philo continued to the last his spirit of opposition, and his censure of established opinions. But I could observe that Demea did not at all relish the latter part of the discourse; and he took occasion soon after, on some pretence or other, to leave the company.

After Demea's departure, Cleanthes and Philo continued the conversation in the following manner. . . .

[Philo:]* Could I meet with one of this species [a philosopher who doubts the existence of a Supreme Intelligence] (who, I thank God, are very rare), I would ask him: Supposing there were a God who did not discover himself immediately to our senses, were it possible for him to give stronger proofs of his existence than what appear on the whole face of nature? What indeed could such a Divine Being do but copy the present economy of things, render many of his artifices so plain that no stupidity could mistake them, afford glimpses of still greater artifices which demonstrate his prodigious superiority above our narrow apprehensions, and conceal altogether a great many from such imperfect creatures? Now, according to all rules of just reasoning, every fact must pass for undisputed when it is supported by all the arguments which its nature admits of, even though these arguments be not, in themselves, very numerous or forcible: How much more in the present case where no human imagination can compute their number, and no understanding estimate their cogency.

I shall further add, said Cleanthes, to what you have so well urged, that one great advantage of the principle of theism is that it is the only system of cosmogony which can be rendered intelligible and complete, and yet can throughout preserve a strong analogy to what we every day see and experience in the world. The comparison of the universe to a machine of human contrivance is so obvious and natural, and is justified by so many instances of order and design in nature, that it must immediately strike all unprejudiced apprehensions and procure universal approbation. Whoever attempts to weaken this

* Some students may notice, as have some scholars, that Philo's position may have changed after Demea's departure. [Eds.]

theory cannot pretend to succeed by establishing in its place any other that is precise and determinate: It is sufficient for him if he start doubts and difficulties; and, by remote and abstract views of things, reach that suspense of judgment which is here the utmost boundary of his wishes. But, besides that this state of mind is in itself unsatisfactory, it can never be steadily maintained against such striking appearances as continually engage us into the religious hypothesis. A false, absurd system, human nature, from the force of prejudice, is capable of adhering to with obstinacy and perseverance; but no system at all, in opposition to a theory supported by strong and obvious reason, by natural propensity, and by early education, I think it absolutely impossible to maintain or defend.

So little, replied Philo, do I esteem this suspense of judgment in the present case to be possible that I am apt to suspect there enters somewhat of a dispute of words into this controversy, more than is usually imagined. That the works of nature bear a great analogy to the productions of art is evident; and, according to all the rules of good reasoning, we ought to infer, if we argue at all concerning them, that their causes have a proportional analogy. But as there are also considerable differences, we have reason to suppose a proportional difference in the causes, and, in particular, ought to attribute a much higher degree of power and energy to the supreme cause than any we have ever observed in mankind. Here, then, the existence of a *Deity* is plainly ascertained by reason; and if we make it a question whether, on account of these analogies, we can properly call him a *mind* or *intelligence,* notwithstanding the vast difference which may reasonably be supposed between him and human minds; what is this but a mere verbal controversy? No man can deny the analogies between the effects: to restrain ourselves from inquiring concerning the causes is scarcely possible. From this inquiry the legitimate conclusion is that the causes have also an analogy; and if we are not contented with calling the first and supreme cause a *God* or *Deity,* but desire to vary the expression, what can we call him but *Mind* or *Thought,* to which he is justly supposed to bear a considerable resemblance? . . .

And here I must also acknowledge, Cleanthes, that, as the works of nature have a much greater analogy to the effects of *our* art and contrivance than to those of *our* benevolence and justice, we have reason to infer that the natural attributes of the Deity have a greater resemblance to those of men than his moral have to human virtues. But what is the consequence? Nothing but this, that the moral qualities of man are more defective in their kind than his natural abilities. For, as the Supreme Being is allowed to be absolutely and entirely perfect, whatever differs most from him departs the farthest from the supreme standard of rectitude and perfection.

These, Cleanthes, are my unfeigned sentiments on this subject; and these sentiments, you know, I have ever cherished and maintained. But in proportion to my veneration for true religion is my abhorrence of vulgar superstitions; and I indulge a peculiar pleasure, I confess, in pushing such principles sometimes into absurdity, sometimes into impiety. And you are sensible that all bigots, notwithstanding their great aversion to the latter above the former, are commonly equally guilty of both.

My inclination, replied Cleanthes, lies, I own, a contrary way. Religion, however corrupted, is still better than no religion at all. The doctrine of a future state is so strong and necessary a security to morals that we never ought to abandon or neglect it. For if finite and temporary rewards and punishments have so great an effect, as we daily find, how much greater must be expected from such as are infinite and eternal?

How happens it then, said Philo, if vulgar superstition be so salutary to society, that all history abounds so much with accounts of its pernicious consequences on public affairs? Factions, civil wars, persecutions, subversions of government, oppression, slavery—these are the dismal consequences which always attend its prevalence over the minds of men. If the religious spirit be ever mentioned in any historical narration, we are sure to meet afterwards with a detail of the miseries which attend it. And no period of time can be happier or more prosperous than those in which it is never regarded or heard of.

The reason of this observation, replied Cleanthes, is obvious. The proper office of religion is to regulate the hearts of men, humanize their conduct, infuse the spirit of temperance, order, and obedience; and, as its operation is silent and only enforces the motives of morality and justice, it is in danger of being overlooked and confounded with these other motives. When it distinguishes itself, and acts as a separate principle over men, it has departed from its proper sphere and has become only a cover to faction and ambition. . . .

# The Problem of Evil

Few, if any, human beings live their lives without some degree of unhappiness and suffering. Some of that unhappiness and suffering we bring on ourselves. Some of that unhappiness and suffering is a result of the intentional actions of other human beings. But surely some of that unhappiness and suffering is caused neither by ourselves nor by others. Bad luck and the nature of the world are the culprits. This is a world filled with illness, natural disasters, and ultimately death. Indeed the existence of evil in all its manifestations may well give rise to many of the religious questions that people ask. What is the purpose of individual human life in a world where there is so much evil? How can an individual life take on meaning when it is so short and accompanied by so much pain?

To make matters worse, that evil is unevenly distributed. Some have much more suffering and unhappiness than others. This inequality might be justified if those who were the perpetrators of evil were those who suffered the most. Most people agree, however, that frequently it is the innocent who suffer the most. That view is captured in the refrain, "Only the good die young." More seriously it is captured in the sorrow of devoted parents who stand helplessly by while a young child painfully struggles and then succumbs to a disease like cancer. Unhappiness, suffering, and death are facts of human existence and most people believe that misfortune afflicts the innocent as much as or even more than the guilty.

Hence, the existence of evil calls into question the meaning of individual human lives and assaults morality by inflicting so much suffering on the individual. But some theologians think they can maintain both the meaning of individual lives and the integrity of morality in the face of evil. God gives meaning and purpose to human lives and ultimately he will make everything come out right. At least many religions would seek to solve the problem of evil in that or some similar way. Whether or not that claim is true takes us back to the selections in the first section in this part, "Religious Commitment and the Nature of Faith."

When addressed by philosophers, the problem of evil focuses on the question, "Why does God permit evil?" For some religions the answer to that question is fairly simple. God is not sufficiently powerful to prevent it. For example, **Manicheanism** postulates the existence of two gods—a good one and an evil one who are locked in permanent struggle. Human beings then effectively choose sides and either work for good or evil. Indeed the meaning of an individual human life is bound up with that choice. With that world view, evil is neither a problem nor a surprise. (Of course, one might wonder why ultimate reality is such a battleground.) The Manichean religion has few contemporary adherents but its influence has been felt in the major religions—consider the Satan of Christianity.

However, most major religions do not believe in a god with limited powers. In most, God is all-powerful **(omnipotent).** Similarly, most religions have a God who is all-knowing (omniscient) and all-good (omnibeneficent). Such a being is worthy of worship and emulation. The early Greek gods had none of these qualities and do not seem to be objects worthy of worship. These Greek gods had most human foibles but were more powerful and hence capable of greater mischief. Hence, it is no surprise that the gods that have captured the human spirit and imagination are those that are all-powerful, all-good, and all-knowing. But it is with these gods that the problem of evil becomes most acute. How could such a god permit evil?

Not surprisingly, there have been many attempts to answer that question. Some have argued that our world must contain some evil, which is just another way of saying that the world must be less than perfectly good. Otherwise this world would equal God in goodness and that is blasphemous. Human beings and their world are not the moral equal of God and his world. This evil as the absence of good solution is represented in the selection by Saint Augustine. There are many criticisms of this solution. One of the more obvious is to concede the point but deny the amount. Our world could contain much less evil and still be far inferior to the moral perfection of God's world. Moreover, there are dangers in emphasizing the imperfections of this world with respect to God. The more imperfect the world is, the less it is like God, and hence it becomes more difficult to understand why the world is so unlike and opposed to the sorts of things that God supposedly stands for and to the things he is purportedly trying to bring about.

A second attempt is to argue that God's respect for human free will, including the possibility of its abuse, requires evil. If God eliminated evil it could be done only by making human beings puppets. And a world of human puppets is an evil world in its own right. However, this defense has the danger of giving human beings so much power that they can thwart the will of God. Of course, if human beings had this much power, God's omnipotence would be denied. Moreover, the defense usually does not address the question of natural evil—illness, natural disasters, and death. One of the strengths of Davis's free will defense, which is included here, is that Davis does attempt to bring natural evils within the context of the free will defense.

A third attempt looks at evil as providing a period of human testing which, if passed, will ensure eternal happiness in the afterlife. In this way, views about individual immortality become central to religion. Those who have suffered and prevailed in this life will go on to eternal happiness. And on many accounts those who have perpetrated evil will go on to an eternity of misery.

Even if we put aside the question of whether or not human beings are in some sense immortal, many moral problems remain. Suffering from natural disasters is distributed unequally. How can that inequality be made up? Either there is an inequality of happiness in eternity and those who have less happiness there can protest that the inequality in this world was not their fault, or everyone is equally happy in eternity and then those who suffered most here can protest. As for the evildoers, is there any crime so heinous that it requires eternal damnation?

Finally, some dismiss these discussions as futile attempts of finite minds to understand the inscrutable purposes of a divine being. Since the motives of the divine being are unavailable to reason, it is futile to try to ascertain them. But this move brings us back to the discussions in the first section in this part and to the costs involved by making faith a matter of accepting revelation alone.

## *Saint Augustine (354–430)*

Augustine was perhaps the first Christian philosopher. During his early years, he was no saint. His account of his conversion to Christianity is documented in the *Confessions.* For a period of time he did embrace Manicheism, and he was strongly influenced by the philosophy of **Neoplatonism.** His conversion to Christianity occurred in 386.

The influence of Neoplatonism is apparent in Augustine's attempt to explain the existence of evil. In giving his account, Augustine had to walk a fine line. If he insisted on the reality of evil, evil would become as ultimately real as God, which would lead back into the heresy of Manicheism which said that evil is as ultimately real as good. On the other hand, he wanted to avoid making God the cause of evil. His rather ingenious solution was to deny evil any positive reality. To the extent that things are real they are good and evil is simply the absence of good. As creatures created by God, we must be less than God; that's what it means to be a creature. Since we are part of God's creation, we are good, but as creatures we are finite as well. Finiteness itself is not an evil; God created everything good after its own kind. We become evil when we use our God-given freedom against God in opposition to God's wise and holy purposes for us and against our own best interests. Unfortunately, the fall of Adam and Eve corrupted not only Adam and Eve but all their descendants — that is the basis for the doctrine of original sin. Even a little baby is sinful in Augustine's sense, since it somehow inherits Adam's guilt and corruption as well as the image of God in man which is tainted at every point but not by any means extinguished.

# The Problem of Evil

## *Saint Augustine*

All of nature, therefore, is good, since the Creator of all nature is supremely good. But nature is not supremely and immutably good as is the Creator of it. Thus the good in created things can be diminished and augmented. For good to be diminished is evil; still, however much it is diminished, something must remain of its original nature as long as it exists at all. For no matter what kind or however insignificant a thing may be, the good which is its "nature" cannot be destroyed without the thing itself being destroyed. There is good reason, therefore, to praise an uncorrupted thing, and if it were indeed an incorruptible thing which could not be destroyed, it would doubtless be all the more worthy of praise. When, however, a thing is corrupted, its corruption is an evil because it is, by just so much, a privation of the good. Where there is no privation of the good, there is no evil. Where there is evil, there is a corresponding diminution of the good. As long, then, as a thing is being corrupted, there is good in it of which it is being deprived; and in this process, if something of its being remains that cannot be further corrupted, this will then be an incorruptible entity, . . . and to this great good it will have come through the process of corruption. But even if the corruption is not arrested, it still does not cease having some good of which it cannot be further deprived. If, however, the corruption comes to be total and entire, there is no good left either, because it is no longer an entity at all. Wherefore corruption cannot consume the good without also consuming the thing itself. Every actual entity . . . is therefore good; a greater good if it cannot be corrupted, a lesser good if it can be. Yet only the foolish and unknowing can deny that it is still good even when corrupted. Whenever a thing is consumed by corruption, not even the corruption remains, for it is nothing in itself, having no subsistent being in which to exist.

From this it follows that there is nothing to be called evil if there is nothing good. A good that wholly lacks an evil aspect is entirely good. Where there is some evil in a thing, its good is defective or defectible. Thus there can be no evil where there is no good. This leads us to a surprising conclusion: that, since every being, in so far as it is a being, is good, if we then say that a defective thing is bad, it would seem to mean that we are saying that what is evil is good, that only what is good is ever evil and that there is no

Abridged from *Augustine: Confessions and Enchiridion.* Translated and edited by Albert C. Outler (Volume VII: The Library of Christian Classics). First published MCMLV. (Great Britain: SCM Press, Ltd., London and USA: The Westminster Press, Philadelphia.) Reprinted by permission of Westminster Press. Footnotes renumbered.

evil apart from something good. This is because every actual entity is good. . . . Nothing evil exists *in itself,* but only as an evil aspect of some actual entity. Therefore, there can be nothing evil except something good. Absurd as this sounds, nevertheless the logical connections of the argument compel us to it as inevitable. At the same time, we must take warning lest we incur the prophetic judgment which reads: "Woe to those who call evil good and good evil: who call darkness light and light darkness; who call the bitter sweet and the sweet bitter."[1] Moreover the Lord himself saith: "An evil man brings forth evil out of the evil treasure of his heart."[2] What, then, is an evil man but an evil entity . . . , since man is an entity? Now, if a man is something good because he is an entity, what, then, is a bad man except an evil good? When, however, we distinguish between these two concepts, we find that the bad man is not bad because he is a man, nor is he good because he is wicked. Rather, he is a good entity in so far as he is a man, evil in so far as he is wicked. Therefore, if anyone says that simply to be a man is evil, or that to be a wicked man is good, he rightly falls under the prophetic judgment: "Woe to him who calls evil good and good evil." For this amounts to finding fault with God's work, because man is an entity of God's creation. It also means that we are praising the defects in this particular man *because* he is a wicked person. Thus, every entity, even if it is a defective one, in so far as it is an entity, is good. In so far as it is defective, it is evil.

Actually, then, in these two contraries we call evil and good, the rule of the logicians fails to apply.[3] No weather is both dark and bright at the same time; no food or drink is both sweet and sour at the same time; no body is, at the same time and place, both white and black, nor deformed and well-formed at the same time. This principle is found to apply in almost all disjunctions: two contraries cannot coexist in a single thing. Nevertheless, while no one maintains that good and evil are not contraries, they can not only coexist, but the evil cannot exist at all without the good, or in a thing that is not a good. On the other hand, the good can exist without evil. For a man or an angel could exist and yet not be wicked, whereas there cannot be wickedness except in a man or an angel. It is good to be a man, good to be an angel; but evil to be wicked. These two contraries are thus coexistent, so that if there were no good in what is evil, then the evil simply could not be, since it can have no mode in which to exist, nor any source from which corruption springs, unless it be something corruptible. Unless this something is good, it cannot be corrupted, because corruption is nothing more than the deprivation of the good. Evils, therefore, have their source in the good, and unless they are parasitic on something good, they are not anything at all. There is no other source whence an evil thing can come to be. If this is the case, then, in so far as a thing is an entity, it is unquestionably good. If it is an incorruptible entity, it is a great good. But even if it is a corruptible entity, it still has no mode of existence except as an aspect of something that is good. Only by corrupting something good can corruption inflict injury.

But when we say that evil has its source in the good, do not suppose that this denies our Lord's judgment: "A good tree cannot bear evil fruit."[4] This cannot be, even as the Truth himself declareth: "Men do not gather grapes from thorns," since thorns cannot bear grapes. Nevertheless, from good soil we can see both vines and thorns spring up. Likewise, just as a bad tree does not grow good fruit, so also an evil will does not produce good deeds. From a human nature, which is good in itself, there can spring forth either a good or an evil will. There was no other place from whence evil could have arisen in the first place except from the nature—good in itself—of an angel or a man. This is what our Lord himself most clearly shows in the passage about the trees and the fruits, for he said: "Make the tree good and the fruits will be good, or make the tree bad and its fruits will be bad."[5] This is warning enough that bad fruit cannot grow on a good tree nor good fruit on a bad one. Yet from that same earth to which he was referring, both sorts of trees can grow.

## NOTES

1. Isa. 5:20.
2. Matt. 12:35.
3. This refers to Aristotle's well-known principle of "the excluded middle."
4. Matt. 7:18.
5. Cf. Matt. 12:33.

## *Stephen T. Davis (b. 1940)*

Stephen T. Davis has made a number of contributions to the philosophy of religion. He is, on his own account, both an analytic philosopher and an evangelical Christian. In this article, he tries to show that the existence of free will enables the adherent of faith the possibility of escaping from the problem of evil. He accepts the traditional formulation of the problem and then argues that an all-knowing, all-powerful God would consistently create a world where human beings are free to commit evil. In this respect Davis has much in common with the traditional adherents of the free will defense. But what about natural evil, disease, earthquakes, tornadoes, and the like? Davis argues that these "natural" evils could be explained by the free will of the devil. Davis admits that it might be hard for nonbelievers to accept the devil as the cause of natural evil. But, the difficulty of acceptance is not the point, although Davis does give arguments to mitigate the difficulty. What Davis argues is that he has shown that the following three statements are consistent: God is all-powerful; God is all-good; evil exists.

# Free Will and Evil

## *Stephen T. Davis*

Let me begin by exposing the main assumptions that control what I will say. . . . I approach the problem of evil—as I approach all philosophical and theological problems—wearing, as it were, two hats. I am both an analytic philosopher and an evangelical Christian. As an analytic philosopher, trained in logic and twentieth century linguistic philosophy, I am interested in the rigor and soundness of the arguments I encounter. My controlling presuppositions are that people ought to believe what it is rational for them to believe and that human reason is a normative guide to all belief and action.

As an evangelical Christian, I accept orthodox Christian claims about God, Christ, human beings, and human history. I believe that all truth is from God and is consistent with the existence, goodness, and omnipotence of God. Evangelicals are not the theological obscurantists they are sometimes made out to be, but it is quite correct

Abridged from "Free Will and Evil," by Stephen T. Davis in *Encountering Evil*. Edited by Stephen T. Davis, (Atlanta: John Knox Press, 1981), pp. 69–79. Reprinted by permission of John Knox Press. Footnotes renumbered.

that they are loath to give up crucial Christian claims. This includes the following claims:

1. *Evil exists;*

2. *God is omnipotent;*

and

3. *God is perfectly good.*

So as I approach the problem of evil my aim is to find a solution that is both philosophically defensible and consistent with these (and other) central Christian affirmations.

Thus I will not be interested in any "solution" which denies that evil exists—e.g., which claims that evil is "an illusion of the material sense," or some other sort of metaphysically unreal thing. Nor will I be interested in any "solution" which denies God's omnipotence—e.g., which says that God is very powerful but is simply not able to prevent evil. Nor will I be interested in any "solution" which denies that God is wholly good—e.g., which says that he has an evil or demonic side which sometimes expresses itself in malevolent acts.

Let me distinguish between two aspects of the problem of evil, what I will call the logical problem of evil (LPE) and the emotive problem of evil (EPE). I will introduce the EPE later, but let us call the LPE the problem of reconciling (1), (2), and (3), i.e., the problem of showing that these three statements are logically consistent. That this is one serious aspect of the problem of evil is clear. Many critics of theism state the problem of evil in such a way as to suggest that (1), (2), and (3) form an inconsistent set of statements. That is, they claim that it cannot be the case that (1), (2), and (3) are all true; the truth of any two of these statements, they say, implies the falsity of the third. Thus the rational theist must give up (1), (2), or (3). If God is omnipotent it seems he is *able* to prevent evil; if God is perfectly good it seems he is *willing* to prevent evil; why then (they ask) does evil exist?

What I want to argue, then, is that (1), (2), and (3) are quite consistent and can all be accepted by a rational person. Many theists have tried to argue to this conclusion, but the reasoning of most seems (to me, at least) weak and quite unable to solve the problem of evil. The one line of argument I have always found promising is the so-called free will defense (or FWD, as I will call it). It was first presented with great vigor by St. Augustine (354–430 A.D.) and has recently been skillfully defended by Alvin Plantinga (among others). Let me now sketch out the FWD as a solution to the LPE.

What were God's aims in creating the universe? According to the FWD, he wanted two things. First, he wanted to create the best universe he could, i.e., the best possible balance of moral and natural good over moral and natural evil. And second, he wanted to create a world in which created rational agents (e.g., human beings) would decide *freely* to love and obey him. Accordingly he created a world in which there originally existed no moral or natural evil, and he created human beings with the facility of free moral choice.

Let us say that people are *free moral agents* if and only if in the case of the decisions they make

4. *their choice is not coerced or causally determined.*

and

5. *they have genuine alternatives, i.e., it is actually in their power, under the same antecedent conditions, to do one thing or another.*

Obviously, in making humans free God ran the risk that they would choose evil rather than good. The possibility of freely doing evil is the inevitable companion of the possibility of freely doing good. Unfortunately this is just what human beings did: they chose to go wrong; they fell into sin. So God is not to be blamed for the existence of evil in the world—we are. Of course God is *indirectly* responsible for evil in the sense that he created the conditions given which evil would come into existence (i.e., he gave us free choice), and he foreknew the evil choices we would make. But even given these conditions, it was not inevitable that evil exist. The non-existence of evil was quite possible; humans could have chosen to obey God. Sadly, they didn't.

Why then did God create free moral agents in the first place? Does it not look as if his plan went wrong, as if his righteous desires were thwarted? Not so, says the FWD. God's policy decision to make us free was wise, for it will turn out better in the long run that we act freely, even if we sometimes err, than it would have turned out had we been created innocent automata, programmed always to do the good. God's decision will turn out to be wise because the good that will in the end result from his decision will outweigh the evil that will in the end result from it.[1] In the eschaton it will be seen that God chose the best course and that the favorable balance of good over evil that will then exist was obtainable by God in no other way.

In response to the problem of evil, some theists have argued that this is "the best of all possible worlds." Must the FWD make this claim? I believe not. In the first place, it is not clear that the notion *the best of all possible worlds* is coherent. Take the notion *tallest conceivable man.* This notion is incoherent because no matter how tall we conceive a tall man to be we can always conceptually add another inch and thus prove that he was not, after all, the tallest conceivable man. Just so, it may be argued, the notion *the best of all possible worlds* is incoherent. For any possible world, no matter how much pleasure and happiness it contains, we can think of a better one, i.e., one with slightly more pleasure and happiness. Accordingly, there logically *cannot* exist such a world, and the FWD need not claim that this world is the best of all possible worlds.

But even if this argument is incorrect, even if the notion is coherent, the FWD still need not claim that this is the best of all possible worlds. Better worlds than this world are quite conceivable, in my opinion. For example, so far as I am able to tell, this world would have been morally better (would have contained less moral evil) had Hitler not hated Jews. The death of six million Jews in the Holocaust, I believe, was based on decisions made by free and morally responsible human agents, Hitler and others. So the FWD must in a sense say that the amount of good and evil that exists in the world is partially up to us and not entirely up to God. If so, it then becomes easy to imagine worlds better than this one — e.g., a world otherwise as much as possible like this one except that no Jews are ever murdered. Thus this is not the best of all possible worlds.

What the FWD must insist on is, first, that the amount of evil that in the end will exist will be outweighed by the good that will then exist; and second, that this favorable balance of good over evil was obtainable by God in no other way. (The free will defender need not claim, incidentally, to be able to explain how or why each evil event that occurs in history helps lead to a greater good. As regards the Holocaust, for example, I confess I am quite unable to do so.)

But let us return to propositions (1), (2), and (3), which the LPE critic says form an inconsistent set. Is this true? How does the FWD answer this charge? Let me restructure the problem slightly. It will be less cumbersome to work with two rather than three propositions, so let us now ask whether

3. *Evil exists*

is consistent with the conjunction of (1) and (2), which we can call

6. *God is omnipotent and God is good.*

Those who push the LPE will claim that (3) and (6) are inconsistent — if one is true the other must be false. Is this true?

Well, Alvin Plantinga has used in this connection a recognized procedure for proving that two propositions are logically consistent. Let us see if it is usable here. We can prove that (3) and (6) are consistent if the FWD can provide us with a third proposition (I will call it [7]), which has three properties. First, it must be possibly true. Second, it must be consistent with (6). And third, in conjunction with (6) it must entail (3).

Now what is the proposition that the free will defender can use to show that (3) and (6) are consistent? Let me suggest the following:

7. *All the evil that exists in the world is due to the choices of free moral agents whom God created, and no other world which God could*

*have created would have had a better balance of good over evil than the actual world will have.*

What this says is that God's policy decision to create free moral agents will turn out to be wise and that it was not within God's power to have created a better world. Now (7) certainly seems *possibly true* (the question of its truth will come up later); I can detect no contradiction or incoherence in (7). And (7) seems consistent with (6) — I see no reason to call them inconsistent, at any rate. And the conjunction of (6) and (7) does indeed entail (3). Thus (3) and (6) are consistent and the LPE is apparently solved. A rational person can believe that God is omnipotent, that God is good, and that evil exists. It is apparently false to claim that the LPE shows that Christianity and other forms of theism are contradictory. . . .

. . . If the FWD works at all it is perhaps a solution only to *part* of the LPE, viz., that part that concerns moral evil. But how can such natural evils as earthquakes, disease, and famine be attributed to moral agents? This seems absurd, which is precisely why we call such evils *natural* rather than moral in the first place. Thus (7) is clearly false, and the FWD fails.

For years I would have been inclined to agree with the substance of this objection. I was of the opinion that the FWD solved the problem of moral evil but not the problem of natural evil. I felt that other arguments beside the FWD had to be appealed to when dealing with natural evil, although I confess none of these arguments seemed particularly convincing to me. But in recent years Alvin Plantinga has suggested that the FWD can indeed solve the problem of natural evil. He appeals to an often neglected aspect of Christian tradition, which was also used by Augustine in his writings on the problem of evil, viz., the notion of Satan or Lucifer as the cause of natural evil. Augustine, Plantinga says,

> attributes much of the evil we find to Satan or to Satan and his cohorts. Satan, so the traditional doctrine goes, is a mighty nonhuman spirit who, along with many other angels, was created long before God created man. Unlike most of his colleagues, Satan rebelled against God and has been wreaking whatever havoc he can. The result is natural evil. So the natural evil we find is due to the free actions of nonhuman spirits.[2]

What is to be said about this? Plantinga admits many people find belief in the devil preposterous, let alone Augustine's idea that the devil is responsible for whatever natural evil we find. But this does not amount to much of an argument against Augustine's thesis, Plantinga insists. Truth is not decided by majority vote. However, Plantinga's main point against those who object to his luciferous defense is to insist that to do the job of solving what I am calling the LPE, proposition (7) (which, as we have seen, claims that *all* evil is due to the choices of created free moral agents) need only be *possibly true*. And this seems quite correct. As we saw, in order to solve the LPE, (7) need only be consistent with (6), capable of entailing (3) when conjoined with (6), and possibly true. As far as the LPE is concerned, Plantinga seems to be quite correct, and I confess he has convinced me. It certainly does seem *possible* that natural evil is due to the choices of Satan. Thus the luciferous defense can solve the LPE as concerns natural evil. . . .

But even if it is true that theism is logically consistent, there is another difficulty that remains, viz., what I call the EPE. This difficulty too concerns this proposition that is believed by theists:

8. *God is omnipotent and God is good and evil exists.*

Now against (8), someone might say something like this:[3]

> I admit there is no logical inconsistency in (8), but the problem of evil, when grasped in its full depth, is deeper than a mere logical exercise. A cold logical approach that merely shows the consistency of (8) fails to touch the problem at its deepest nerve. To show, as a sheer logical exercise, that (8) is consistent does nothing to convince people to believe (8). To show that (8) is *possibly true* does not show that it is *true* or even *probably true*, i.e., it does nothing to show that people should believe in God's omnipotence and goodness.

There is much that must be sorted out in these words. What exactly does the EPE come to? This is not altogether clear in the above lines, and perhaps it might help to suggest some possible interpretations.

Words such as those above are sometimes expressed with deep emotion. Perhaps the EPE means something like this: the existence of evil in the world somehow *makes us deeply feel* that

6. *God is omnipotent and God is good*

is false. That is, the existence of evil in the world makes us deeply feel that (2) and/or (3) must be rejected or modified. Because of evil, we find (6) *hard to believe.* Now there are obviously people about whom this could truly be said. Albert Camus comes to mind. So does Elie Wiesel. But despite this, it is hard to detect any real difficulty for theism here. By itself, this seems no more serious an objection to theism than, say, the following comment: "You theists believe in God but somehow I can't."

But perhaps the EPE means something more than this. Perhaps the claim is that the existence of evil makes (6) *improbable* or *implausible,* that the existence of evil constitutes *strong evidence against* (6). But the problem with this is that it is difficult to see how any probabilistic judgments can be made here. And this is for the obvious reason that we do not seem to be in a position to make a probability judgment about the truth of the FWD. As I have claimed, the FWD claims that (8) is consistent because the following proposition is possibly true:

7. *All the evil that exists in the world is due to the choices of free moral agents whom God created, and no other world which God could have created would have had a better balance of good over evil than the actual world will have.*

If we knew that (7) was false or improbable we might have good reason to deny (6). But in fact we do not know that (7) is false or improbable (at least I am aware of no good argument or evidence that falsifies [7]), and so we do not seem to be in a position to say that (6) is false or improbable. . . .

But perhaps there is another way of stating the "probability" interpretation of the EPE. "If you were the Christian God—the omnipotent and good creator of the world—what sort of world would you create? One thing is certain: you wouldn't create this sort of world. You wouldn't create a world containing cancer, atomic bombs, child abuse, and famine. You would create a world without these evils. Thus it appears highly improbable that the world was created by the Christian God."[4]

I will say some things later that are relevant to this objection, but for now I wish simply to insist that I have not the vaguest idea what sort of world I would create given the stated conditions, nor do I believe anyone else does. Of course, my general aim would be to create a world with the best possible balance of good over evil. Would eliminating cancer or free moral agents achieve this end? I just don't know, and I do not believe anyone else does either. Of course it is *possible* that if I knew all relevant facts I would create a world much different than this one. But it is also *possible* that I would create a world as much like this one as I could. I just don't know enough to say, and neither does anyone else, in my opinion. And I fail to see any argument here that renders the first more probable than the second. Perhaps, somehow, the existence of evil in the world (or the existence of a large amount of evil in the world) does render (6) improbable. But I am unable to see how it does or even can. At best, we must await the skeptic's explanation precisely how the existence of evil renders (6) improbable. It is not clear at this point that it does.

Possibly there are other interpretations of the EPE that are more threatening to theism than these. I cannot think of any, however, and so I conclude that the EPE poses no philosophical difficulty for theism. If the theist's problem when confronted with the LPE is the apologetic task of responding to the critic's charge that theism is inconsistent, then if the LPE can be solved (by the FWD or any other argument) I see no added philosophical problem for theism in the EPE. I believe I have shown that (8) is consistent, and so believe that this defensive apologetic task has been accomplished.

But perhaps there is still a residual feeling that the problem of evil has not been completely disposed of. *I* confess to having such a feeling, and perhaps other theists will too. But I believe this residual feeling that somehow still not all is well is based on no philosophical difficulty but rather on what might be called the *evangelistic difficulty* that the problem of evil poses for theists. This difficulty is not the negative apologetic task of responding to a philosophical criticism, but rather the positive evangelistic task of *convincing people to believe* (6). . . .

One obvious weakness of many **theodicies** is that they cannot account for the huge *amount* of evil that apparently exists in the world. For example, some theodicists claim that pain and adversity are really good because they help people rise to new moral and spiritual heights in overcoming them. No doubt this is true in some cases — the athlete who improves performance because of a rigorous and painful training regime, the novelist whose works are more deeply insightful into human nature because of early struggles, say, with poverty and rejection notices from unappreciative publishers. But this theodicy simply cannot account for the amount of suffering that we see in the world. How can the murder of six million Jews in World War II lead people to new and otherwise unobtainable heights? The very thought seems absurd, almost obscene.

At first glance, the FWD seems less embarrassed than other theodicies by the amount of evil that exists in the world; the free will defender will simply say of all evil events that they are due not to God (or at least not directly to God) but rather to created free moral agents who choose to do evil. But at a deeper level, the FWD still seems open to this objection. For when we consider people like Hitler and events like the Holocaust we are bound to wonder whether the facility of free moral choice, which the FWD says God gave human beings, has turned out to be worth the price. Even if we grant that it is a *prima facie* good that God created us free moral agents rather than causally determined automata, we can still wonder, to put it in economic terms, whether this freedom has turned out to be cost-effective. Surely some will say (perhaps one of the millions of surviving Jews who lost family and friends in the Holocaust), "I wish God had created a world of more determinism and less murder."

The notion of our being *less free* than the FWD claims that we are seems to make perfectly good sense. For example, I am not now free to destroy the planet Saturn: apparently God has not given me that ability. But then why couldn't God have created me with an analogous inability to commit murder? Why didn't God, for example, place us in an environment that provided fewer opportunities or temptations to go wrong than he in fact did? Or why didn't he create us with a stronger psychological endowment — say, a stronger desire to do good or a weaker desire to do evil?

There are two points I wish to make about this. First, we do not know whether freedom is cost-effective. Let us be clear what it is we are evaluating: it is the policy decision God made (according to the FWD) to allow human beings moral freedom, i.e., freedom to do right or wrong without interference. Obviously, a correct decision on whether or not a given policy is cost-effective cannot be made till the results of the policy are in and can be evaluated. But how can we now correctly decide whether freedom will turn out to be cost-effective when we have no idea how human history will turn out? Perhaps it is true, as Christians believe, that the eschaton holds in store for us such great goods that all preeschaton evils will be outweighed. We do not know whether this claim is true, and so we do not know whether God's policy will turn out to be cost-effective.

Of course decisions often have to be made on the basis of inconclusive evidence. Perhaps it is true that each person, here and now, must decide whether to believe that freedom is cost-effective, just in the sense that each person must decide, here and now, whether to believe in a good, omnipotent God despite the presence of evil in the world. And such a decision can obviously be made only on the basis of evidence that is presently available (although some people believe there is evidence that the Christian eschaton is coming). But even if, for pragmatic reasons, such a decision must be made here and now, it can still be seen that it is ultimately unfair to try to make (at this time and with the evidence we now have) a correct judgment about the cost-effectiveness of God's policy. If there turns out to be no Christian eschaton, or if history ends in a violent bang or a desperate whimper, then perhaps we will see that freedom is not cost-effective. But we cannot see that now.

The second point is that only God knows whether freedom will turn out to be cost-effective. Only he knows how human history turns out, what our destiny is. Furthermore, only God is in a position to weigh huge goods and evils against each other in order to make correct judgments whether, say, World War II was, on balance, a morally good or morally evil event. Thus only God is in a position to judge whether moral freedom will turn out to be worth the price.

Of course it may be difficult for Christians and other theists to *convince people* that freedom is cost-effective. But this reduces to the evangelistic difficulty, which, as I said, is not a philosophical difficulty. Questions about the cost-effectiveness of freedom do not succeed in showing that theism is inconsistent, nor do they give the theist any good reason to doubt that freedom is cost-effective. Thus, so far as I can see, they raise no philosophical difficulties for theism. . . .

## NOTES

1. Alvin Plantinga, *God, Freedom, and Evil* (New York: Harper and Row, 1974), p. 25.
2. *Ibid.*, p. 58.
3. I am indebted to my friend and colleague John Roth for making remarks that led me to see that the EPE is distinct from the LPE.
4. Hume has Philo make this sort of statement. See *Dialogues Concerning Natural Religion* (New York: Hafner Publishing Company, 1959), p. 73.

## *J. L. Mackie (b. 1917)*

John Mackie is a well known contemporary philosopher who has made contributions to epistemology, ethics, and the philosophy of religion. The selection reprinted here is one of the most reprinted articles in the philosophy of religion. In the crisp logical form of an analytic philosopher, Mackie describes the problem of evil as an attempt to hold a set of inconsistent beliefs, namely, God is **omnipotent,** God is wholly good, and yet evil exists. Put in this form it is clear that the problem of evil is not a problem for all religions. It is only a problem for those that accept an omnipotent, omnibenevolent God. Mackie then examines the best-known solutions to the problem of evil—including many familiar to many readers, and finds them all wanting. Not surprisingly, Mackie's analysis is not universally accepted.

# Evil and Omnipotence

*J. L. Mackie*

. . . The problem of evil, in the sense in which I shall be using the phrase, is a problem only for someone who believes that there is a God who is both omnipotent and wholly good. And it is a logical problem, the problem of clarifying and reconciling a number of beliefs: it is not a scientific problem that might be solved by further observations, or a practical problem that might be solved by a decision or an action. These points are obvious; I mention them only because they are sometimes ignored by theologians, who sometimes parry a statement of the problem with such remarks as "Well, can you solve the problem yourself?" or "This is a mystery which may be revealed to us later" or "Evil is something to be faced and overcome, not to be merely discussed."

In its simplest form the problem is this: God is omnipotent; God is wholly good; and yet evil exists. There seems to be some contradiction between these three propositions, so that if any two of them were true the third would be false. But at the same time all three are essential parts of most theological positions: the theologian, it seems, at once *must* adhere and *cannot consistently* adhere to all three. (The problem does not arise only for theists, but I shall discuss it in the form in which it presents itself for ordinary theism.)

However, the contradiction does not arise immediately; to show it we need some additional premises, or perhaps some quasi-logical rules connecting the terms "good," "evil," and "omnipotent." These additional principles are that good is opposed to evil, in such a way that a good thing always eliminates evil as far as it can, and that there are no limits to what an omnipotent thing can do. From these it follows that a good omnipotent thing eliminates evil completely, and then the propositions that a good omnipotent thing exists, and that evil exists, are incompatible.

## A. ADEQUATE SOLUTIONS

Now once the problem is fully stated it is clear that it can be solved, in the sense that the problem will not arise if one gives up at least one of the propositions that constitute it. If you are prepared to say that God is not wholly good, or not quite omnipotent, or that evil does not exist, or that good is not opposed to the kind of evil that exists, or that there are limits to what an omnipotent thing can do, then the problem of evil will not arise for you.

There are, then, quite a number of adequate solutions of the problem of evil, and some of these have been adopted, or almost adopted, by various thinkers. For example, a few have been prepared to deny God's omnipotence, and rather more have been prepared to keep the term "omnipotence" but severely to restrict its meaning, recording quite a number of things that an omnipotent being cannot do. Some have said that evil is an illusion, perhaps because they held that the whole world of temporal, changing things is an illusion, and that what we call evil belongs only to this world, or perhaps because they held that although temporal things *are* much as we see them, those that we call evil are not really evil. Some have said that what we call evil is merely the privation of good, that evil in a positive sense, evil that would really be opposed to good, does not exist. Many have agreed with Pope that disorder is harmony not understood, and that partial evil is universal good. Whether any of these views is *true* is, of course, another

From "Evil and Impotence," by J. L. Mackie. Reprinted from *Mind,* Vol. LXIV (1955) by permission of Oxford University Press and Mrs. Joan Mackie.

question. But each of them gives an adequate solution of the problem of evil in the sense that if you accept it this problem does not arise for you, though you may, of course, have *other* problems to face.

But often enough these adequate solutions are only *almost* adopted. The thinkers who restrict God's power, but keep the term "omnipotence," may reasonably be suspected of thinking, in other contexts, that his power is really unlimited. Those who say that evil is an illusion may also be thinking, inconsistently, that this illusion is itself an evil. Those who say that "evil" is merely privation of good may also be thinking, inconsistently, that privation of good is an evil. . . .

In addition, therefore, to adequate solutions, we must recognize unsatisfactory inconsistent solutions, in which there is only a half-hearted or temporary rejection of one of the propositions which together constitute the problem. In these, one of the constituent propositions is explicitly rejected, but it is covertly re-asserted or assumed elsewhere in the system.

## B. FALLACIOUS SOLUTIONS

Besides these half-hearted solutions, which explicitly reject but implicitly assert one of the constituent propositions, there are definitely fallacious solutions which explicitly maintain all the constituent propositions, but implicitly reject at least one of them in the course of the argument that explains away the problem of evil.

There are, in fact, many so-called solutions which purport to remove the contradiction without abandoning any of its constituent propositions. These must be fallacious, as we can see from the very statement of the problem, but it is not so easy to see in each case precisely where the fallacy lies. I suggest that in all cases the fallacy has the general form suggested above: in order to solve the problem one (or perhaps more) of its constituent propositions is given up, but in such a way that it appears to have been retained, and can therefore be asserted without qualification in other contexts. Sometimes there is a further complication: the supposed solution moves to and fro between, say, two of the constituent propositions, at one point asserting the first of these but covertly abandoning the second, at another point asserting the second but covertly abandoning the first. These fallacious solutions often turn upon some equivocation with the words "good" and "evil," or upon some vagueness about the way in which good and evil are opposed to one another, or about how much is meant by "omnipotence." I propose to examine some of these so-called solutions, and to exhibit their fallacies in detail. Incidentally, I shall also be considering whether an adequate solution could be reached by a minor modification of one or more of the constituent propositions, which would, however, still satisfy all the essential requirements of ordinary theism.

1. "Good cannot exist without evil" or "Evil is necessary as a counterpart to good."

It is sometimes suggested that evil is necessary as a counterpart to good, that if there were no evil there could be no good either, and that this solves the problem of evil. It is true that it points to an answer to the question "Why should there be evil?" But it does so only by qualifying some of the propositions that constitute the problem.

First, it sets a limit to what God can do, saying that God *cannot* create good without simultaneously creating evil, and this means either that God is not omnipotent or that there are *some* limits to what an omnipotent thing can do. It may be replied that these limits are always presupposed, that omnipotence has never meant the power to do what is logically impossible, and on the present view the existence of good without evil would be a logical impossibility. This interpretation of omnipotence may, indeed, be accepted as a modification of our original account which does not reject anything that is essential to theism, and I shall in general assume it in the subsequent discussion. It is, perhaps, the most common theistic view, but I think that some theists at least have maintained that God can do what is logically impossible. Many theists, at any rate, have held that logic itself is created or laid down by God, that logic is the way in which God arbitrarily chooses to think. . . . And *this* account of logic is clearly inconsistent with the view that God is bound by logical necessities — unless it is possible for an omnipotent being to bind himself. . . . This solution of the problem of evil cannot, therefore, be consistently adopted along with the view that logic is itself created by God.

But, secondly, this solution denies that evil is opposed to good in our original sense. If good and evil are counterparts, a good thing will not "eliminate evil as far as it can." Indeed, this view suggests that good and evil are not strictly qualities of things at all. Perhaps the suggestion is that good and evil are related in much the same way as great and small. Certainly, when the term "great" is used relatively as a condensation of "greater than so-and-so," and "small" is used correspondingly, greatness and smallness are counterparts and cannot exist without each other. But in this sense greatness is not a quality, not an intrinsic feature of anything; and it would be absurd to think of a movement in favor of greatness and against smallness in this sense. Such a movement would be self-defeating, since relative greatness can be promoted only by a simultaneous promotion of relative smallness. I feel sure that no theists would be content to regard God's goodness as analogous to this — as if what he supports were not the *good* but the *better,* and as if he had the paradoxical aim that all things should be better than other things.

This point is obscured by the fact that "great" and "small" seem to have an absolute as well as a relative sense. I cannot discuss here whether there is absolute magnitude or not, but if there is, there could be an absolute sense for "great," it could mean of at least a certain size, and it would make sense to speak of all things getting bigger, of a universe that was expanding all over, and therefore it would make sense to speak of promoting greatness. But in *this* sense great and small are not logically necessary counterparts: either quality could exist without the other. There would be no logical impossibility in everything's being small or in everything's being great.

Neither in the absolute nor in the relative sense, then, of "great" and "small" do these terms provide an analogy of the sort that would be needed to support this solution of the problem of evil. In neither case are greatness and smallness *both* necessary counterparts *and* mutually opposed forces or possible objects for support and attack.

It may be replied that good and evil are necessary counterparts in the same way as any quality and its logical opposite: redness can occur, it is suggested, only if non-redness also occurs. But unless evil is merely the privation of good, they are not logical opposites, and some further argument would be needed to show that they are counterparts in the same way as genuine logical opposites. Let us assume that this could be given. There is still doubt of the correctness of the metaphysical principle that a quality must have a real opposite: I suggest that it is not really impossible that everything should be, say, red, that the truth is merely that if everything were red we should not notice redness, and so we should have no word "red"; we observe and give names to qualities only if they have real opposites. If so, the principle that a term must have an opposite would belong only to our language or to our thought, and would not be an **ontological** principle, and, correspondingly, the rule that good cannot exist without evil would not state a logical necessity of a sort that God would just have to put up with. God might have made everything good, though *we* should not have noticed it if he had.

But, finally, even if we concede that this *is* an ontological principle, it will provide a solution for the problem of evil only if one is prepared to say, "Evil exists, but only just enough evil to serve as the counterpart of good." I doubt whether any theist will accept this. After all, the *ontological* requirement that non-redness should occur would be satisfied even if all the universe, except for a minute speck, were red, and, if there were a corresponding requirement for evil as a counterpart to good, a minute dose of evil would presumably do. But theists are not usually willing to say, in all contexts, that all the evil that occurs is a minute and necessary dose.

2. "Evil is necessary as a means to good."

It is sometimes suggested that evil is necessary for good not as a counterpart but as a means. In its simple form this has little plausibility as a solution of the problem of evil, since it obviously implies a severe restriction of God's power. It would be a *causal* law that you cannot have a certain end without a certain means, so that if God has to introduce evil as a means to good, he must be subject to at least some causal laws. This certainly conflicts with what a theist normally means by omnipotence. This view of God as limited by causal laws also conflicts with the view that causal laws are themselves made by God, which is more widely held than the corresponding view about the laws of logic. This conflict would, indeed, be resolved if it were possible for an omnipotent being to bind himself, and this possibility has still to be considered. Unless a favorable answer can be given to this question, the suggestion that evil is necessary as a means to good solves the problem of evil only by denying one of its constituent propositions, either that God is omnipotent or that "omnipotent" means what it says.

3. "The universe is better with some evil in it than it could be if there were no evil."

Much more important is a solution which at first seems to be a mere variant of the previous one, that evil may contribute to the goodness of a whole in which it is found, so that the universe as a whole is better as it is, with some evil in it, than it would be if there were no evil. This solution may be developed in either of two ways. It may be supported by an aesthetic analogy, by the fact that contrasts heighten beauty, that in a musical work, for example, there may occur discords which somehow add to the beauty of the work as a whole. Alternatively, it may be worked out in connection with the notion of progress, that the best possible organization of the universe will not be static, but progressive, that the gradual overcoming of evil by good is really a finer thing than would be the eternal unchallenged supremacy of good.

In either case, this solution usually starts from the assumption that the evil whose existence gives rise to the problem of evil is primarily what is called physical evil, that is to say, pain. In Hume's rather half-hearted presentation of the problem of evil, the evils that he stresses are pain and disease, and those who reply to him argue that the existence of pain and disease makes possible the existence of sympathy, benevolence, heroism, and the gradually successful struggle of doctors and reformers to overcome these evils. In fact, theists often seize the opportunity to accuse those who stress the problem of evil of taking a low, materialistic view of good and evil, equating these with pleasure and pain, and of ignoring the more spiritual goods which can arise in the struggle against evils.

But let us see exactly what is being done here. Let us call pain and misery "first order evil" or "evil (1)." What contrasts with this, namely, pleasure and happiness, will be called "first order good" or "good (1)." Distinct from this is "second order good" or "good (2)" which somehow emerges in a complex situation in which evil (1) is a necessary component—logically, not merely causally, necessary. (Exactly *how* it emerges does not matter: in the crudest version of this solution good (2) is simply the heightening of happiness by the contrast with misery, in other versions it includes sympathy with suffering, heroism in facing danger, and the gradual decrease of first order evil and increase of first order good.) It is also being assumed that second order good is more important than first order good or evil, in particular that it more than outweighs the first order evil it involves.

Now this is a particularly subtle attempt to solve the problem of evil. It defends God's goodness and omnipotence on the ground that (on a sufficiently long view) this is the best of all logically possible worlds, because it includes the important second order goods, and yet it admits that real evils, namely first order evils, exist. But does it still hold that good and evil are opposed? Not, clearly, in the sense that we set out originally: good does not tend to eliminate evil in general. Instead, we have a modified, a more complex pattern. First order good (e.g., happiness) *contrasts with* first order evil (e.g., misery): these two are opposed in a fairly mechanical way; some second order goods (e.g., benevolence) try to maximize first order good and minimize first order evil; but God's goodness is not this, it is rather the will to maximize *second* order good. We might, therefore, call God's goodness an example of a third order goodness, or good (3). While this account is different from our original one, it might well be held to be an improvement on it, to give a more accurate description of the way in which good is opposed to evil, and to be consistent with the essential theist position.

There might, however, be several objections to this solution.

First, some might argue that such qualities as benevolence—and *a fortiori* the third order goodness which promotes benevolence—have a merely derivative value, that they are not higher sorts of good, but merely means to good (1), that is, to happiness, so that it would be absurd for God to keep misery in existence in order to make possible the virtues of benevolence, heroism, etc. The theist who adopts the present solution must, of course, deny this, but he can do so with some plausibility, so I should not press this objection.

Secondly, it follows from this solution that God is not in our sense benevolent or sympathetic: he is not concerned to minimize evil (1), but only to promote good (2); and this might be a disturbing conclusion for some theists.

But, thirdly, the fatal objection is this. Our analysis shows clearly the possibility of the existence of a *second* order evil, an evil (2) contrasting with good (2) as evil (1) contrasts with good (1). This would include malevolence, cruelty, callousness, cowardice, and states in which good (1) is decreasing and evil (1) increasing. And just as good (2) is held to be the important kind of good, the kind that God is concerned to promote, so evil (2) will, by analogy, be the important kind of evil, the kind which God, if he were wholly good and omnipotent, would eliminate. And yet evil (2) plainly exists, and indeed most theists (in other contexts) stress its existence more than that of evil (1). We should, therefore, state the problem of evil in terms of second order evil, and against this form of the problem the present solution is useless.

An attempt might be made to use this solution again, at a higher level, to explain the occurrence of evil (2): indeed the next main solution that we shall examine does just this, with the help of some new notions. Without any fresh notions, such a solution would have little plausibility: for example, we could hardly say that the really important good was a good (3), such as the increase of benevolence in proportion to cruelty, which logically required for its occurrence the occurrence of some second order evil. But even if evil (2) could be explained in this way, it is fairly clear that there would be third order evils contrasting with this third order good: and we should be well on the way to an infinite regress, where the solution of a problem of evil, stated in terms of evil *(n)*, indicated the existence of an evil $(n + 1)$, and a further problem to be solved.

4. "Evil is due to human freewill."

Perhaps the most important proposed solution of the problem of evil is that evil is not to be ascribed to God at all, but to the independent actions of human beings, supposed to have been endowed by God with freedom of the will. This solution may be combined with the preceding one: first order evil (e.g. pain) may be justified as a logically necessary component in second order good (e.g. sympathy) while second order evil (e.g. cruelty) is not *justified,* but is so ascribed to human beings that God cannot be held responsible for it. This combination evades my third criticism of the preceding solution.

The freewill solution also involves the preceding solution at a higher level. To explain why a wholly good God gave men freewill although it would lead to some important evils, it must be argued that it is better on the whole that men should act freely, and sometimes err, than that they should be innocent automata, acting rightly in a wholly determined way. Freedom, that is to say, is now treated as a third order good, and as being more valuable than second order goods (such as sympathy and heroism) would be if they were deterministically produced, and it is being assumed that second order evils, such as cruelty, are logically necessary accompaniments of freedom, just as pain is a logically necessary pre-condition of sympathy.

I think that this solution is unsatisfactory primarily because of the incoherence of the notion of freedom of the will: but I cannot discuss this topic adequately here, although some of my criticisms will touch upon it.

First I should query the assumption that second order evils are logically necessary accompaniments of freedom. I should ask this: if God has made men such that in their free choices they sometimes prefer what is good and sometimes what is evil, why could he not have made men such that they always freely choose the good? If there is no logical impossibility in a man's freely choosing the good on one, or on several, occasions, there cannot be a logical impossibility in his freely choosing the good on every occasion. God was not, then, faced with a choice between making innocent automata and making beings who, in acting freely, would sometimes go wrong: there was open to him the obviously better possibility of making beings who would act freely but always go right. Clearly, his failure to avail himself of this possibility is inconsistent with his being both omnipotent and wholly good.

If it is replied that this objection is absurd, that the making of some wrong choices is logically necessary for freedom, it would seem that "freedom" must here mean complete randomness or indeterminacy, including randomness with regard to the alternatives good and evil, in other words that men's choices and consequent actions can be "free" only if they are not determined by their characters. Only on this assumption can God escape the responsibility for men's actions; for if he made them as they are, but did not determine their wrong choices, this can only be because the wrong choices are not determined by men as they are. But then if freedom is randomness, how can it be a characteristic of *will*? And, still more, how can it be the most important good? What value or merit would there be in free choices if these were random actions which were not determined by the nature of the agent?

I conclude that to make this solution plausible two different senses of "freedom" must be confused, one sense which will justify the view that freedom is a third order good, more valuable than other goods would be without it, and another sense, sheer randomness, to prevent us from ascribing to God a decision to make men such that they sometimes go wrong when he might have made them such that they would always freely go right.

This criticism is sufficient to dispose of this solution. But besides this there is a fundamental difficulty in the notion of an omnipotent God creating men with free will, for if men's wills are really free this must mean that even God cannot control them, that is, that God is no longer omnipotent. It may be objected that God's gift of freedom to men does not mean that he *cannot* control their wills, but that he always *refrains* from controlling their wills. But why, we may ask, should God refrain from controlling evil wills? Why should he not leave men free to will rightly, but intervene when he sees them beginning to will wrongly? If God could do this, but does not, and if he is wholly good, the only explanation could be that even a wrong free act of will is not really evil, that its freedom is a value which outweighs its wrongness, so that there would be a loss of value if God took away the wrongness and the freedom together. But this is utterly opposed to what theists say about sin in other contexts. The present solution of the problem of evil, then, can be maintained only in the form that God has made men so free that he *cannot* control their wills. . . .

## CONCLUSION

Of the proposed solutions of the problem of evil which we have examined, none has stood up to criticism. There may be other solutions which require examination, but this study strongly suggests that there is no valid solution of the problem which does not modify at least one of the constituent propositions in a way which would seriously affect the essential core of the theistic position. . . .

## *John Hick (b. 1922)*

John Hick is one of the best known contemporary philosophers of religion. His *Philosophy of Religion* now in its third edition is a classic text, and his *Death and Eternal Life* (1976) is considered a major contribution to the field. The selection in this section on the problem of evil has ties to the previous section on the existence of God and looks ahead to the final section on immortality. Hick is no Augustinian regarding the existence of evil. The Nazi death camps are not simply the absence of good. If human suffering is to be justified, there must be both a God and an afterlife that allows human suffering to be overcome by good. Otherwise human suffering is a rebuke to the moral life. These sentiments Hick shares with Immanuel Kant.

But what does it mean to overcome human suffering—especially that suffering caused by the cruel malicious acts of another. Hick rejects the somewhat traditional notion that the evildoers go to Hell and the virtuous go to Heaven. Evil is really overcome only when the evildoers become transformed into complete and perfected persons. Such transformation is, according to Hick, what ultimate forgiveness is all about.

# Humanism and the Problem of Evil

## *John Hick*

How does the christian view of our human situation differ from the humanist view, if not by the former's emphatic denial that man's existence is in the end irredeemably tragic? Christian faith asserts that our life has its meaning within the great *Divina Commedia* of the creation of perfected finite spiritual life, and that it is good not only because of the present elements of happiness and joy within it but also because it is in process towards a universal fulfillment of limitless value. Thus whilst in the humanist vision man's existence as a whole is seen as largely tragic, in the christian vision it is seen as ultimately good; in the words of Mother Julian of Norwich, "all shall be well and all shall be well, and all manner thing shall be well."[1] Christian faith is a final optimism

Abridged from *Death and Eternal Life,* by John Hick (New York: Harper & Row). Reprinted by permission of Harper & Row, Publishers, Inc. Footnotes renumbered.

because it sees the human story in its relation to God—God who, as we read in the New Testament, is *agape,* love.

Thus the issue between religion and humanism hinges upon the agony endured by men and women in generation after generation, whether through human cruelty or indifference or through the frailty of the human organism and its liability to pain in an environment which includes famine, drought, violent storms and earthquakes, animal predators and the other hazards of nature. The issue is whether the incalculable weight of suffering which has been borne during the hundred or so millennia of man's prehistory and history down to the present time, and as it seems likely to continue in the future, is or is not sheer meaningless, unredeemed and unredeemable suffering.

Now since a final bringing of good out of evil in the triumphant climax of the *Divina Commedia* does not belong to this earthly life, it can only happen—if it happens at all—beyond it. And so I conclude that the question of immortality forms a vital crux between Humanism and Christianity. For the idea of immortality (still in the minimal sense of our life not being terminated by bodily death) is an essential basis for any view which could count towards a solution of the theological problem of human suffering. Such a "solution" must consist, not in denying the reality of suffering, but in showing how it is to be justified or redeemed. But what would it mean to justify, or redeem, the world's suffering? Presumably it would mean showing it to be rationally and morally acceptable either in itself or in relation to a future which will render it worthwhile. But the notions of the "acceptability" and "worthwhileness" of someone's suffering are highly ambiguous: acceptable or worthwhile from whose point of view? There seem to be three possibilities, two of which do not and one of which does require man's immortality. The first is a religious justification, but one which is compatible (as in ancient hebrew religion) with man's being a mortal creature, briefly endowed with conscience and the awareness of his Maker but, like the other animals, destined to return to the dust of the earth. It might be said that the experiences of such a fleeting creature, including his pains, travails and agonies as well as his joys, are justified in the eyes of his Creator. For if God wishes to create such beings, to observe their lives, and graciously to enter into personal communication with them during their brief careers, his omnipotent wish might be said to be its own justification. As St Paul asked, "Will what is molded say to its molder, 'Why have you made me thus?' Has the potter no right over the clay?"[2] This, then, is the first kind of justification that is possible for human suffering, namely that it should be part of a situation which is willed by an all-powerful creator; this is a justification which need not involve human immortality.

The second possibility is more humanistic. There might be a justification of human suffering through the ages from the point of view of a more ideal humanity or super-humanity in the future which will have evolved out of the painful process of human life as we know it. Individuals perish forever in generation after generation; but the species goes on and from it there may develop a higher humanity which will justify the lower forms out of which it has come. Such a justification would function in a way analogous to that in which we ourselves regard the harsh struggle for survival through which the human species has evolved as being justified by its human end-product. This, too, would not involve individual immortality.

Whether these first two kinds of justification are morally acceptable depends upon a fundamental judgment concerning the worth of the individual human person. Kant focused the attention of the modern world upon this value judgment when he presented it as a basic moral principle, a form of the categorical imperative, that humanity is always to be treated, whether in one's own person or in the person of any other, never simply as a means but always at the same time as an end.[3] And the acceptability of these two putative justifications of human suffering depends upon whether individual persons are to be valued as ends in themselves or may properly be treated purely as means to some further end.

Although it took Christianity a long time to clarify and is taking even longer for it to implement its valuation of individual personality, perhaps its chief contribution to the life of the world has been its insistence that each human being is equally a child of God, made for eternal fellowship with his Maker and endowed with unlimited value by the divine love which has created him, which sustains him in being, and which purposes his eternal blessedness. Thus, in spite of so many failures in christian practice, Christianity teaches that the human individual is never a mere means, expendable in the interests of some further goal, but is always an end in himself as the object of God's love. A humanist would not of course use this religious language in expressing his own valuation of individual human life; but nevertheless humanists oppose acts of genocide, injustice and racial discrimination on the ground that these deny to other human beings the intrinsic worth and dignity which we each claim for ourselves. There can of course be no proof of any such fundamental valuation. But for all who adopt this christian-humanist attitude to mankind the two possible justifications of human suffering which I have thus far outlined must be entirely unacceptable. For they imply a view of the individual human personality not only as expendable in the sense that he can be allowed to pass out of existence but, more importantly, as exploitable in the sense that he can be subjected to any extent and degree of physical pain and mental suffering for a future end in which he cannot participate and of which he knows nothing. This is a dangerous doctrine because, as B. H. Streeter pointed out, "if the Divine righteousness may lightly 'scrap' the individual, human righteousness may do the same."[4] The individual's lack of any significant personal moral status or value is a corollary of the suggestion that his involuntary sufferings, however extreme they may be, are justified if they form part of a process which produces a good end, even though that end is entirely separate from the individual's own brief existence. Dostoyevsky voices the inadequacy of this approach when he makes one of his characters say, "Surely I haven't suffered simply that I, my crimes and my sufferings, may manure the soil of the future harmony for somebody else. I want to see with my own eyes the hind lie down with the lion and the victim rise up and embrace his murderer. I want to be there when every one suddenly understands what it has all been for."[5] Thus the only morally acceptable justification of the agonies and heartaches of human life must be of a third kind in which the individuals who have suffered *themselves* participate in the justifying good and are themselves able to see their own past sufferings as having been worthwhile. And this is the third kind of justification, to which the argument now leads us.

At this point, if we are to avoid being led off immediately along a major false trail, we must distinguish between, on the one hand, the idea of compensation in the form of future happiness enjoyed to balance past misery endured, and on the other hand the very different idea of the eventual all-justifying fulfillment of the human potential in a perfected life. There has always been something morally unattractive about the idea of the compensatory joys of heaven. It suggests a comparatively low level of ethical insight centered upon the notion of justice as exact reciprocity, "an eye for an eye and a tooth for a tooth," a certain quantum of pleasure cancelling out a certain quantum of pain. The individual is treated as though he were a creditor in a hedonic bank, whose needs are adequately met by ensuring a mathematical balance. He is not seen as a free personal will capable of growth and of the exercise of positive acceptance, understanding and forgiveness. But surely the individual would be much more truly valued for his own sake as a living end in himself by a justification of the pains and sorrows through which he has passed in terms of a fulfillment which is a state of his own self and of the human community of selves of which he is a part. The good that comes about, and that justifies all that has occurred on the way to it, is then the personal growth and perfecting, the spiritual maturation to a state of full humanity, the free awareness and acceptance of the divine love which has brought men and women through so many sorrows to their Father's house.

Such a justification treats each individual as an end in himself within a kingdom of ends, both because it functions as a justification in his own estimation and because the good on which it depends is a state of which the individual himself is to be a part.

Now it is clear that this third kind of justification of human suffering presupposes the individual's survival of bodily death under conditions in which it is possible for him to undergo further personal growth and development. What these conditions might be will be considered later. The point of the present argument is that any morally acceptable justification of the sufferings of humanity is bound to postulate a life after death. Attempted justifications which refuse to take this step fail under the criterion of universal love: only a fortunate few are regarded as ends in themselves, the less fortunate mass being treated as involuntary means to an end of which they are not aware and in which they do not participate. And the issue between a humanistic and a religious view of our human situation crystallizes at this point in their disagreement as to whether or not the universe is such that human suffering is to be finally justified. Humanism says that it will never be justified (in the only morally acceptable sense of this word), and thus presents man's situation as a whole as a tragic scene involving an immensity of unredeemed and unredeemable suffering and of unfulfilled and unfulfillable potentiality. The religions, on the other hand, say that our human situation is not ultimately tragic because it is leading to a universal fulfillment of such worth that in relation to it all human suffering will be rendered manifestly worthwhile.

We are now at the heart of the **theodicy** problem, where it meets the problem of man's destiny. The crucial question is whether any human fulfillment could provide a morally acceptable justification for the creation of a world containing all the suffering and all the wickedness which our world contains. I have been arguing that it *is* possible for a history including great evils to be rendered worthwhile by bringing about a sufficiently great good. But the issue is so important that this answer must be tested by confronting it with its direct denial. For it can be questioned whether *any* fulfillment, however good, in which men might eventually participate could ever render worthwhile the worst of human sufferings. Dostoyevsky has put the negative case in an unforgettable chapter of *The Brothers Karamazov*. The whole chapter (and indeed the entire novel) should be read; but the point comes through with great force in the following:

> It was in the darkest days of serfdom at the beginning of the century, and long live the Liberator of the People! There was in those days a general of aristocratic connections, the owner of great estates, one of those men — somewhat exceptional, I believe, even then — who, retiring from the service into a life of leisure, are convinced that they've earned absolute power over the lives of their subjects. There were such men then. So our general, settled on his property of two thousand souls, lives in pomp, and domineers over his poor neighbors as though they were dependants and buffoons. He has kennels of hundreds of hounds and nearly a hundred dog-boys — all mounted, and in uniform. One day a serf boy, a little child of eight, threw a stone in play and hurt the paw of the general's favorite hound. "Why is my favorite dog lame?" He is told that the boy threw a stone that hurt the dog's paw. "So you did it." The general looked the child up and down. "Take him." He was taken — taken from his mother and kept shut up all night. Early that morning the general comes out on horseback, with the hounds, his dependents, dog-boys, and huntsmen, all mounted around him in full hunting parade. The servants are summoned for their edification, and in front of them all stands the mother of the child. The child is brought from the lock-up. It's a gloomy cold, foggy autumn day, a capital day for hunting. The general orders the child to be undressed; the child is stripped naked. He shivers, numb with terror, not daring to cry . . . "Make him run," commands the general . . . and he sets the whole pack of hounds on the child. The hounds catch him, and tear him to pieces before his mother's eyes! . . . I believe the general was afterwards declared incapable of administering his estates. Well — what did he deserve? To be shot? To be shot for the satisfaction of our moral feelings? Speak, Alyosha!"
>
> "To be shot," murmured Alyosha, lifting his eyes to Ivan with a pale, twisted smile . . .
>
> "Listen! If all must suffer to pay for the eternal harmony, what have children to do with it, tell me, please? It's beyond all comprehension why they should suffer, and why they should pay for the harmony. Why should they, too, furnish material to

enrich the soil for the harmony of the future? I understand solidarity in sin among men. I understand solidarity in retribution, too; but there can be no such solidarity with children. And if it is really true that they must share responsibility for all their fathers' crimes, such a truth is not of this world and is beyond my comprehension . . . I understand, of course, what an upheaval of the universe it will be, when everything in heaven and earth blends in one hymn of praise and everything that lives and has lived cries aloud: "Thou art just, O Lord, for Thy ways are revealed." When the mother embraces the fiend who threw her child to the dogs, and all three cry aloud with tears, "Thou art just, O Lord!" then, of course, the crown of knowledge will be reached and all will be made clear. But what pulls me up here is that I can't accept that harmony. And while I am on earth, I make haste to take my own measure. You see, Alyosha, perhaps it really may happen that if I live to that moment, or rise again to see it, I, too, perhaps, may cry aloud with the rest, looking at the mother embracing the child's torturer, "Thou art just, O Lord!" but I don't want to cry aloud then. While there is still time, I hasten to protect myself and so I renounce the higher harmony altogether. It's not worth the tears of that one tortured child who beat itself on the breast with its little fist and prayed in its stinking outhouse, with its unexpiated tears to "dear, kind God"! It's not worth it, because those tears are unatoned for. They must be atoned for, or there can be no harmony. But how? How are you going to atone for them? Is it possible? By their being avenged? But what do I care for avenging them? What do I care for a hell for oppressors? What good can hell do, since those children have already been tortured? And what becomes of a harmony, if there is hell? I want to forgive. I want to embrace. I don't want more suffering. And if the sufferings of children go to swell the sum of suffering which was necessary to pay for truth, then I protest that the truth is not worth such a price . . . I would rather be left with my unavenged suffering and unsatisfied indignation, *even if I were wrong*. Besides, too high a price is asked for harmony; it's beyond our means to pay so much to enter on it. And so I hasten to give back my entrance ticket, and if I am an honest man I am bound to give it back as soon as possible. And that I am doing. It's not God that I don't accept, Alyosha, only I most respectfully return Him the ticket."

"That's rebellion," murmured Alyosha, looking down.

"Rebellion? I am sorry you call it that," said Ivan earnestly. "One can hardly live in rebellion, and I want to live. Tell me yourself, I challenge you—answer. Imagine that you are creating a fabric of human destiny with the object of making men happy in the end, giving them peace and rest at last, but that it was essential and inevitable to torture to death only one tiny creature—that baby beating its breast with its fist, for instance—and to found that edifice on its unavenged tears, would you consent to be the architect on those conditions? Tell me, and tell the truth."

"No, I wouldn't consent," said Alyosha softly.[6]

Dostoyevsky is surely right in seeing deliberate human cruelty—rather than any of the pain-producing aspects of nature—as the worst form of evil. But there is more to be said and pondered than even he considers. Two immensely important facts have to be brought into relation with the fact of wickedness—the experience of freedom and the achievement of forgiveness. The acts of savage and sadistic inhumanity which Dostoyevsky describes—which can certainly be matched outside the pages of a novel—can be taken as showing the cruel character of the power which has created a universe in which such things happen. But they can also be taken as showing the tremendous importance which that power attaches to our own character as free and responsible moral agents. If human beings were not free to be cruel, they would never *be* cruel, but they would also not be free or, therefore, moral beings. Thus the question is whether a good human fulfillment, the realization of which requires man's freedom, can render worthwhile the whole process of freely interacting human lives which ultimately leads to this fulfillment but which includes on the way the fearful misuse of freedom in acts of wickedness and cruelty. Such a state of human fulfillment would necessarily involve an ultimate universal forgiveness for the cruelties, injustices, and inhumanities which men have inflicted upon one another in their earthly lives. Dostoyevsky imagines such a final heavenly reconciliation and rejects it:

"I don't want the mother to embrace the oppressor who threw her son to the dogs! She dare not forgive him! Let her forgive him for herself, if she will, let her forgive the torturer for the immeasurable suffering of her mother's heart. But the sufferings of her tortured child she has no right to forgive; she dare not forgive the torturer, even if the child were to forgive him!"[7]

Dostoyevsky is evidently thinking of this

meeting taking place when the general is still the same cruel (or perhaps insane) person who committed the appalling brutality; and he is thinking of forgiveness as a condoning of the general's behavior. But forgiveness does not mean condoning, still less approving, the unspeakably brutal act that was committed. Pascal was right when he said, "Time heals griefs and quarrels, for we change and are no longer the same persons. Neither the offender nor the offended are any more themselves. It is like a nation which we have provoked, but meet again after two generations. They are still Frenchmen, but not the same."[8] In Dostoyevsky's case this means forgiving and accepting the perfect person whom the perpetrator of the terrible act has ultimately become. In the doubtless long course of this perfecting he may well have suffered fearful purgatorial consequences of his own cruelty—not divine punishments, but the effect of his actions encountered in his own conscience. His perfecting will have involved his utter revulsion against his own cruelty and a deep shame and sorrow at the memory of it. At the end of this hard creative process he will be the same person in the sense that he will remember how he treated the serf boy, and will feel ashamed and sorry and in desperate need of forgiveness. But in another sense he will no longer be the same person; for he will have changed in character into someone who is now morally incapable of behaving in such a way and who is, in comparison with his former self, "a new creature." In these circumstances, is forgiveness impossible or wrong? Would unforgiveness really be admirable at the termination of such a process of soul-making? Surely not; and certainly the idea of an ultimate universal mutual forgiveness, which even includes those who have committed history's most brutal and inhuman crimes, is in harmony with the deepest insights of the christian faith.

Could such ultimate forgiveness be part of an acceptance of the creative process as a whole, including the almost limitless pain and suffering that it has involved? Can we conceive of completed and perfected persons, having arrived at the state of full intensity of existence, full consciousness of reality, and fullness of joy in being, looking back upon the long, checkered story of human freedom in all its grandeur and all its misery, its agony and tragedy and failure as well as its moments of happiness and glory, and seeing it as worthwhile as the road by which they have at last come to this fulfillment? I believe so. I am not suggesting that it will be seen *sub specie aeternitatis* that each particular evil experienced by human beings was specifically necessary to the bringing about of this fulfillment. What was necessary was human freedom; and the particular detailed course that man's history has taken, as the expression of human freedom, is not necessary but contingent. The specific misuses of freedom which have so largely constituted human history were not necessary in order that mankind should move through the exercise of freedom to an eventual full humanization and perfection. But it was necessary that there should be genuine human freedom, carrying with it the possibility of appalling misuses; and all these inhumanities of man to man are part of the contingent form which the story of human freedom has in fact taken.

The conclusion to which all this points is that to say that human existence taken in its totality is a *Divina Commedia,* rather than an almost limitless tragedy, is to say that it leads to a good fulfillment which presupposes man's continued individual existence beyond death. This is the basic religious argument for "immortality."

## NOTES

1. Mother Julian of Norwich, *The Revelations of Divine Love,* ch. 27, p. 92.
2. Romans 9:20–1.
3. Immanuel Kant, *Grundlegung zur Metaphysik der Sitten,* pp. 66–7 (*The Moral Law,* p. 96).
4. B. H. Streeter, *Immortality,* p. 85.
5. Fyodor Dostoyevsky, *The Brothers Karamazov,* part II, book V, ch. 4, p. 289.
6. *The Brothers Karamazov,* from part II, book V, ch. 4.
7. ibid., p. 291.
8. *Pensées,* p. 37 (Brunschvicg's ed., no. 122).

# *Immortality*

Perhaps the greatest challenge to each individual's attempt to give meaning to life is the inevitability of death. Our existence in terms of the totality of time is infinitesimally brief. But perhaps our individual life does not end with our death in this world. Perhaps we survive our death. Moreover, according to one scenario, perhaps our bodies are resurrected at some later time after our death.

Although some form of survival is a central tenet of many religions, there is little agreement on what survival beyond death means. The religious person is not content with the survival of our good works and deeds through their continuing effects or with the notion that we live on through our children and our children's children. That is not what is meant by the individual's survival of death.

In the West most religious persons also reject as inadequate the theory of the transmigration of souls. Suppose a person, John, lives from 1920 to 2000. Under a transmigration theory, when John dies, John's body decays but John's soul enters another body. Suppose when John's soul enters the new body, all memories of John's association with the previous body end. Has John survived? Most religious persons would say, "no." Since John has no memory of the life lived between 1920 to 2000, the individual John who lived during that time has not survived. To survive his death, John would have to remember his previous life and recognize that he survived his death in 2000. For purposes of this discussion, individual survival means that the individual survives death and knows that death is survived because the life before death is remembered.

Having, for purposes of this discussion, defined individual survival, we now need to determine what survives — the total person (the body and soul) or just a part of a person such as the soul. Those who argue for the survival of the total person often argue for a theory of bodily resurrection. At death, the body dies but the soul survives. At some later time, the body is resurrected and the individual's soul is joined with the resurrected body.

One of the difficulties with resurrection is that it seems to violate physical laws. The resurrection of the body involves a miracle. Suppose the date of the final judgment is 3000. John of our previous example has been dead since 2000. There's not much left of his body. Nor is there much left of the bodies of those who were cremated in 2999 and had their ashes scattered over the ocean. How does the resurrection of the body occur except through a miracle? The resurrection of the body is a hypothesis that has little or no empirical foundation, and thus it cannot be a truth of natural theology. The claim for the resurrection of the body must have its source in revelation.

An alternative account of survival is to have a person be composed of two parts — a mortal body that does not survive death and an immortal soul that does. This account of the person goes back to Plato and has remained a significant theory of personal identity and survival. Although this theory avoids a miraculous resurrection of the body, it has serious problems of its own. If you think about your life, most everything significant has a bodily aspect. Playing baseball, being in love, pursuing your career all involve the body. Indeed even thinking is manifested in bodily behavior. For each thought there is an electrical discharge and a chemical reaction. Of course it might be possible for thinking, and hence remembering, to take place in the absence of the electrical discharge and the chemical reaction.

But what would life be like as a disembodied soul? Adherents of the disembodied soul view, such as Plato, argue that such a life would be better. For example, on the assumption that pain is a physical phenomenon, life as a disembodied soul would be a life without pain. However, it would also be a life without bodily pleasures and hence it would certainly not be life as we know it.

Proponents of the survival of the soul, unlike

proponents of resurrection, can appeal to alleged empirical evidence in support of their view. That area of psychic research called **parapsychology** provides the empirical data. Since parapsychological experiences violate the most generally accepted laws of nature, it is no surprise that most of the scientific community looks at parapsychology with great suspicion. The empirical evidence for survival is assessed in the article by Ducasse.

Of course the data of science are not the only data we have on human experience. Human beings are not merely physical beings; they are moral beings as well. In his article, John Hick follows in the tradition of Kant by arguing that the survival of the person is required by morality. He then argues for the creation of a replica in the spiritual world of persons who have died in the physical world. In this way Hick hopes to avoid the objections to both the resurrection hypothesis and the disembodied immortal soul hypothesis, while at the same time avoiding objections specific to his own theory.

As with the proofs for the existence of God, the failure of proofs for individual survival will not deter the steadfastly religious person. A leap of faith has taken place. If reason supports revelation, so much the better; however, the religious person finds the revealed faith sufficient. For religious persons, philosophy does have its limits.

## *Plato (427–347 B.C.)*

The first selection in this text was from the first great systematic philosopher, Plato. As you will learn from the following dialogue, Plato believed that the knowledge we gained of this world could not be derived from sense experience but rather had to be derived through rational apprehension of another world of forms. Thus our knowledge of equality, or whiteness, or justice depended on the forms Equality, Whiteness, and Justice. Plato thought that a world of perfect forms was the only explanation that could be provided for the knowledge which we in fact have. After all our sense experiences are individualistic and brief. How can a body of knowledge that is universal and eternal ever be built up from sense experience? Well, it can't.

Since experience comes through the body, if knowledge doesn't come from sense experience, it must come from the mind. Plato thought a person was composed of a body and mind (soul). Thus Plato held the metaphysical theory of **dualism,** that a person is composed of two distinctly different substances. Since knowledge is of the universal and eternal (namely of the perfect and eternal forms), what does the knowing must also be universal and eternal. Therefore human minds are immortal. At death they escape from the body. The wise man does not fear death because in death the mind escapes from the body and is no longer dragged down by sense experience.

A doctrine of the immortality of the soul has always been attractive to those who are not committed to the resurrection of the body. Dualism continues to have many adherents, although not all dualists are committed to the immortality of the soul. The chief objection to those who believe in the immortality of the soul is that such persons cannot provide a coherent account of personal identity in the absence of a body. A disembodied soul or mind is not like an individual person.

# The Immortality of the Soul

## *Plato*

[SOCRATES:] . . . When I was young, Cebes, I had an extraordinary passion for that branch of learning which is called natural science. I thought it would be marvelous to know the causes for which each thing comes and ceases and continues to be. I was constantly veering to and fro, puzzling primarily over this sort of question. Is it when heat and cold produce fermentation, as some have said, that living creatures are bred? Is it with the blood that we think, or with the air or the fire that is in us? Or is it none of these, but the brain that supplies our senses of hearing and sight and smell, and from these that memory and opinion arise, and from memory and opinion, when established, that knowledge comes? Then again I would consider how these faculties are lost, and study celestial and terrestrial phenomena, until at last I came to the conclusion that I was uniquely unfitted for this form of inquiry. I will give you a sufficient indication of what I mean. I had understood some things plainly before, in my own and other people's estimation, but now I was so befogged by these speculations that I unlearned even what I had thought I knew, especially about the cause of growth in human beings. Previously I had thought that it was quite obviously due to eating and drinking—that when, from the food which we consume, flesh is added to flesh and bone to bone, and when in the same way the other parts of the body are augmented by their appropriate particles, the bulk which was small is now large, and in this way the small man becomes a big one. That is what I used to believe—reasonably, don't you think?

Yes, I do, said Cebes. . . .

However, I once heard someone reading from a book, as he said, by Anaxagoras, and asserting that it is mind that produces order and is the cause of everything. This explanation pleased me. Somehow it seemed right that mind should be the cause of everything, and I reflected that if this is so, mind in producing order sets everything in order and arranges each individual thing in the way that is best for it. Therefore if anyone wished to discover the reason why any given thing came or ceased or continued to be, he must find out how it was best for that thing to be, or to act or be acted upon in any other way. On this view there was only one thing for a man to consider, with regard both to himself and to anything else, namely the best and highest good, although this would necessarily imply knowing what is less good, since both were covered by the same knowledge. . . .

Well, after this, said Socrates, when I was worn out with my physical investigations, it occurred to me that I must guard against the same sort of risk which people run when they watch and study an eclipse of the sun; they really do sometimes injure their eyes, unless they study its reflection in water or some other medium. I conceived of something like this happening to myself, and I was afraid that by observing objects with my eyes and trying to comprehend them with each of my other senses I might blind my soul altogether. So I decided that I must have recourse to theories, and use them in trying to discover the truth about things. Perhaps my illustration is not quite apt, because I do not at all admit that an inquiry by means of theory employs "images" any more than one which confines itself to facts. But however that may be, I started off in this way, and in every case I first lay down the theory which I judge to be soundest, and then whatever seems to agree with it—with regard either to causes or to anything else—I

Abridged from *Phaedo* from Plato: *The Last Days of Socrates.* Translated by Hugh Tredennick. (Penguin Classics, Revised ed. 1969), pp. 97–183. 

assume to be true, and whatever does not I assume not to be true. But I should like to express my meaning more clearly, because at present I don't think that you understand.

No, indeed I don't, said Cebes, not a bit.

Well, said Socrates, what I mean is this, and there is nothing new about it. I have always said it; in fact I have never stopped saying it, especially in the earlier part of this discussion. As I am going to try to explain to you the theory of causation which I have worked out myself, I propose to make a fresh start from those principles of mine which you know so well — that is, I am assuming the existence of absolute beauty and goodness and magnitude and all the rest of them. If you grant my assumption and admit that they exist, I hope with their help to explain causation to you, and to find a proof that soul is immortal.

Certainly I grant it, said Cebes. You need lose no time in drawing your conclusion.

Then consider the next step, and see whether you share my opinion. It seems to me that whatever else is beautiful apart from absolute beauty is beautiful because it partakes of that absolute beauty, and for no other reason. Do you accept this kind of causality?

Yes, I do.

Well, now, that is as far as my mind goes; I cannot understand these other ingenious theories of causation. If someone tells me that the reason why a given object is beautiful is that it has a gorgeous color or shape or any other such attribute, I disregard all these other explanations — I find them all confusing — and I cling simply and straightforwardly and no doubt foolishly to the explanation that the one thing that makes that object beautiful is the presence in it or association with it, in whatever way the relation comes about, of absolute beauty. I do not go so far as to insist upon the precise details — only upon the fact that it is by beauty that beautiful things are beautiful. This, I feel, is the safest answer for me or for anyone else to give, and I believe that while I hold fast to this I cannot fall; it is safe for me or for anyone else to answer that it is by beauty that beautiful things are beautiful. Don't you agree?

Yes, I do.

Then is it also by largeness that large things are large and larger things larger, and by smallness that smaller things are smaller?

Yes.

So you too, like myself, would refuse to accept the statement that one man is taller than another "by a head," and that the shorter man is shorter by the same. You would protest that the only view which you yourself can hold is that whatever is taller than something else is so simply by tallness — that is, because of tallness — and that what is shorter is so simply by shortness, that is, because of shortness. You would be afraid, I suppose, that if you said that one man is taller than another by a head, you would be faced by a logical objection — first that the taller should be taller and the shorter shorter by the same thing, and secondly that the taller person should be taller by a head, which is a short thing, and that it is unnatural that a man should be made tall by something short. Isn't that so?

Cebes laughed and said, Yes, it is.

Then you would be afraid to say that ten is more than eight "by two," or that two is the cause of its excess over eight, instead of saying that it is more than eight by, or because of, being a larger number, and you would be afraid to say that a length of two feet is greater than one foot by a half, instead of saying that it is greater by its larger size — because there is the same danger here too?

Quite so.

Suppose next that we add one to one. You would surely avoid saying that the cause of our getting two is the addition, or in the case of a divided unit, the division. You would loudly proclaim that you know of no other way in which any given object can come into being except by participation in the reality peculiar to its appropriate universal, and that in the cases which I have mentioned you recognize no other cause for the coming into being of two than participation in duality, and that whatever is to become two must participate in this, and whatever is to become one must participate in unity. You would dismiss these divisions and additions and other such niceties, leaving them for persons wiser than yourself to use in their explanations, while you, being nervous of your own shadow, as the saying is, and of your inexperience, would hold fast to the security of your hypothesis and make your answers accordingly. If anyone should fasten upon the hypothesis itself, you would disregard him and refuse to answer until you could consider whether its consequences were mutually consistent or not. And when you had to substantiate the hypothesis itself, you would proceed in the same way, assuming whatever more ultimate hypothesis commended itself most to you, until you reached one which was satisfactory. You would not mix the two things together by discussing both the principle and its consequences, like one of these destructive critics—that is, if you wanted to discover any part of the truth. They presumably have no concern or care whatever for such an object, because their cleverness enables them to muddle everything up without disturbing their own self-complacence, but you, I imagine, if you are a philosopher, will follow the course which I describe.

You are perfectly right, said Simmias and Cebes together.

*Echecrates:* I can assure you, Phaedo, I am not surprised. It seems to me that Socrates made his meaning extraordinarily clear to even a limited intelligence.

*Phaedo:* That was certainly the feeling of all of us who were present, Echecrates.

*Echecrates:* No doubt, because it is just the same with us who were not present and are hearing it now for the first time. But how did the discussion go on?

*Phaedo:* I think that when Socrates had got this accepted, and it was agreed that the various forms exist, and that the reason why other things are called after the forms is that they participate in the forms, he next went on to ask, If you hold this view, I suppose that when you say that Simmias is taller than Socrates but shorter than Phaedo, you mean that at that moment there are in Simmias both tallness and shortness?

Yes, I do.

But do you agree that the statement "Simmias is bigger than Socrates" is not true in the form in which it is expressed? Surely the real reason why Simmias is bigger is not because he is Simmias but because of the height which he incidentally possesses, and conversely the reason why he is bigger than Socrates is not because Socrates is Socrates, but because Socrates has the attribute of shortness in comparison with Simmias' height.

True.

And again Simmias' being smaller than Phaedo is due not to the fact that Phaedo is Phaedo, but to the fact that Phaedo has the attribute of tallness in comparison with Simmias' shortness.

Quite so.

So that is how Simmias comes to be described as both short and tall, because he is intermediate between the two of them, and allows his shortness to be surpassed by the tallness of the one while he asserts his superior tallness over the shortness of the other.

He added with a smile, I seem to be developing an artificial style, but the facts are surely as I say.

Simmias agreed.

I am saying all this because I want you to share my point of view. It seems to me not only that the form of tallness itself absolutely declines to be short as well as tall, but also that the tallness which is in us never admits smallness and declines to be surpassed. It does one of two things. Either it gives way and withdraws as its opposite shortness approaches, or it has already ceased to exist by the time that the other arrives. It cannot stand its ground and receive the quality of shortness in the same way as I myself have done. If it did, it would become different from what it was before, whereas I have not lost my identity by acquiring the quality of shortness—I am the same man, only short—but my tallness could not endure to be short instead of tall. In the same way the shortness that is in us declines ever to become or be tall, nor will any other quality, while still remaining what it was, at the same time become or be the opposite quality; in such a situation it either withdraws or ceases to exist.

I agree with you entirely, said Cebes. . . .

So we are agreed upon this as a general principle, that an opposite can never be opposite to itself.

Absolutely.

Then consider this point too, and see whether you agree about it too. Do you admit that there are such things as heat and cold?

Yes, I do.

Do you think they are the same as snow and fire?

Certainly not.

Heat is quite distinct from fire, and cold from snow?

Yes.

But I suppose you agree, in the light of what we said before, that snow, being what it is, can never admit heat and still remain snow, just as it was before, only with the addition of heat. It must either withdraw at the approach of heat, or cease to exist.

Quite so.

Again, fire must either retire or cease to exist at the approach of cold. It will never have the courage to admit cold and still remain fire, just as it was, only with the addition of cold.

That is true.

So we find, in certain cases like these, that the name of the form is eternally applicable not only to the form itself, but also to something else, which is not the form but invariably possesses its distinguishing characteristic. But perhaps another example will make my meaning clearer. Oddness must always be entitled to this name by which I am now calling it, isn't that so?

Certainly.

This is the question. Is it unique in this respect, or is there something else, not identical with oddness, to which we are bound always to apply not only its own name but that of odd as well, because by its very nature it never loses its oddness? What I mean is illustrated by the case of the number three; there are plenty of other examples, but take the case of three. Don't you think that it must always be described not only by its own name but by that of odd, although odd and three are not the same thing? It is the very nature of three and five and all the alternate integers that every one of them is invariably odd, although it is not identical with oddness. Similarly two and four and all the rest of the other series are not identical with even, but each one of them always *is* even. Do you admit this, or not?

Of course I do.

Well, then, pay careful attention to the point which I want to make, which is this. It seems clear that the opposites themselves do not admit one another, but it also looks as though any things which, though not themselves opposites, always have opposites in them, similarly do not admit the opposite form to that which is in them, but on its approach either cease to exist or retire before it. Surely we must assert that three will sooner cease to exist or suffer any other fate than submit to become even while it is still three?

Certainly, said Cebes.

And yet two and three are not opposites.

No, they are not.

So it is not only the opposite forms that cannot face one another's approach; there are other things too which cannot face the approach of opposites.

That is quite true.

Shall we try, if we can, to define what sort of things these are?

By all means.

Well, then, Cebes, would this describe them —that they are things which are compelled by some form which takes possession of them to assume not only its own form but invariably also that of some other form which is an opposite?

What do you mean?

Just what we were saying a minute ago. You realize, I suppose, that when the form of three takes possession of any group of objects, it compels them to be odd as well as three.

Certainly.

Then I maintain that into such a group the opposite form to the one which has this effect can never enter.

No, it cannot.

And it was the form of odd that had this effect?

Yes.

And the opposite of this is the form of even?

Yes.

So the form of even will never enter into three.

No, never.

In other words, three is incompatible with evenness.

Quite.

So the number three is uneven.

Yes.

I proposed just now to define what sort of things they are which, although they are not themselves directly opposed to a given opposite, nevertheless do not admit it, as in the present example, three, although not the opposite of even, nevertheless does not admit it, because three is always accompanied by the opposite of even—and similarly with two and odd, or fire and cold, and hosts of others. Well, see whether you accept this definition. Not only does an opposite not admit its opposite, but if anything is accompanied by a form which has an opposite, and meets that opposite, then the thing which is accompanied never admits the opposite of the form by which it is accompanied. Let me refresh your memory; there is no harm in hearing a thing several times. Five will not admit the form of even, nor will ten, which is double five, admit the form of odd. Double has an opposite of its own, but at the same time it will not admit the form of odd. Nor will one and a half, or other fractions such as one half or three quarters and so on, admit the form of whole. I assume that you follow me and agree.

I follow and agree perfectly, said Cebes.

Then run over the same ground with me from the beginning, and don't answer in the exact terms of the question, but follow my example. I say this because besides the "safe answer" that I described at first, as the result of this discussion I now see another means of safety. Suppose, for instance, that you ask me what must be present in body to make it hot. I shall not return the safe but ingenuous answer that it is heat, but a more sophisticated one, based on the results of our discussion—namely that it is fire. And if you ask what must be present in a body to make it diseased, I shall say not disease but fever. Similarly if you ask what must be present in a number to make it odd, I shall say not oddness but unity, and so on. See whether you have a sufficient grasp now of what I want from you.

Quite sufficient.

Then tell me, what must be present in a body to make it alive?

Soul.

Is this always so?

Of course.

So whenever soul takes possession of a body, it always brings life with it?

Yes, it does.

Is there an opposite to life, or not?

Yes, there is.

What?

Death.

Does it follow, then, from our earlier agreement, that soul will never admit the opposite of that which accompanies it?

Most definitely, said Cebes.

Well, now, what name did we apply just now to that which does not admit the form of even?

Uneven.

And what do we call that which does not admit justice, or culture?

Uncultured, and the other unjust.

Very good. And what do we call that which does not admit death?

Immortal.

And soul does not admit death?

No.

So soul is immortal.

Yes, it is immortal.

Well, said Socrates, can we say that that has been proved? What do you think?

Most completely, Socrates.

Here is another question for you, Cebes. If the uneven were necessarily imperishable, would not three be imperishable?

Of course.

Then again, if what is not hot were necessarily imperishable, when you applied heat to snow, would not the snow withdraw still intact and unmelted? It could not cease to exist, nor on the other hand could it remain where it was and admit the heat.

That is true.

In the same way I assume that if what is not cold were imperishable, when anything cold approached fire, it could never go out or cease to exist; it would depart and be gone unharmed.

That must be so.

Are we not bound to say the same of the immortal? If what is immortal is also imperishable, it is impossible that at the approach of death soul should cease to be. It follows from what we have already said that it cannot admit death, or be dead — just as we said that three cannot be even, nor can odd; nor can fire be cold, nor can the heat which is in the fire. But, it may be objected, granting, as has been agreed, that odd does not become even at the approach of even, why should it not cease to exist, and something even take its place? In reply to this we could not insist that the odd does not cease to exist — because what is not even is not imperishable — but if this were conceded, we could easily insist that, at the approach of even, odd and three retire and depart. And we could be equally insistent about fire and heat and all the rest of them, could we not?

Certainly.

So now in the case of the immortal, if it is conceded that this is also imperishable, soul will be imperishable as well as immortal. Otherwise we shall need another argument.

There is no need on that account, said Cebes. If what is immortal and eternal cannot avoid destruction, it is hard to see how anything else can.

And I imagine that it would be admitted by everyone, said Socrates, that God at any rate, and the form of life, and anything else that is immortal, can never cease to exist.

Yes indeed, by all men certainly, and even more, I suppose, by the gods.

Then since what is immortal is also indestructible, if soul is really immortal, surely it must be imperishable too.

Quite inevitably.

So it appears that when death comes to a man, the mortal part of him dies, but the immortal part retires at the approach of death and escapes unharmed and indestructible.

Evidently.

Then it is as certain as anything can be, Cebes, that soul is immortal and imperishable, and that our souls will really exist in the next world.

Well, Socrates, said Cebes, for my part I have no criticisms, and no doubt about the truth of your argument. But if Simmias here or anyone else has any criticism to make, he had better not keep it to himself, because if anyone wants to say or hear any more about this subject, I don't see to what other occasion he is to defer it.

As a matter of fact, said Simmias, I have no doubts myself either now, in view of what you have just been saying. All the same, the subject is so vast, and I have such a poor opinion of our weak human nature, that I can't help still feeling some misgivings.

Quite right, Simmias, said Socrates, and what is more, even if you find our original assumptions convincing, they still need more accurate consideration. If you and your friends examine them closely enough, I believe that you will arrive at the truth of the matter, in so far as it is possible for the human mind to attain it, and if you are sure that you have done this, you will not need to inquire further.

That is true, said Simmias.

But there is a further point, gentlemen, said Socrates, which deserves your attention. If the soul is immortal, it demands our care not only for that part of time which we call life, but for all time. And indeed it would seem now that it will be extremely dangerous to neglect it. If death were a release from everything, it would be a boon for the wicked, because by dying they would be released not only from the body but also from their own wickedness together with the soul, but as it is, since the soul is clearly immortal, it can have no escape or security from evil except by becoming as good and wise as it possibly can. For it takes nothing with it to the next world except its education and training, and these, we are told, are of supreme importance in helping or harming the newly dead at the very beginning of his journey there. . . .

## *C. J. Ducasse (1881–1969)*

Although born and educated in France, C. J. Ducasse spent most of his philosophical career in the United States. He contributed to all branches of philosophy from symbolic logic to the philosophy of religion. Indeed he helped found the Association for Symbolic Logic and served as its president from 1936 to 1938. His best known book is *Nature, Mind, and Death* (1951).

Ducasse is one of the best known twentieth-century dualists. He argued that the human mind is not a part of the material world and that the mind and body affect each other by causal interaction (a doctrine that has come to be known as interactionism).

Although many mind-body dualists are theists, Ducasse was not. The problem of evil stood as a stumbling block. Nonetheless Ducasse maintained a lifelong interest in parapsychological phenomena. The existence of such phenomena would require extensive revisions in scientific theory, in our conceptual notions of time, causality, and perception, and would force us to rethink the question of survival after death. A selection from Ducasse's balanced consideration of parapsychological phenomena follows.

# The Case for the Possibility of Survival

## *C. J. Ducasse*

. . . A positive case has to establish that survival is both theoretically and empirically possible.

The *theoretical* possibility can be established only on the basis of an analysis of what it is to be a mind: if no incompatibility appears between what the analysis reveals and the supposition of a mind's existing without a body, then the contention that survival is theoretically possible is in so far vindicated. . . .

As regards the *empirical* possibility of survival, on the other hand, the only sort of evidence ultimately capable of establishing it would

Abridged from "The Case for the Possibility of Survival" in *Nature, Mind, and Death,* by C. J. Ducasse. (LaSalle, Ill.: Open Court Publishing Co., 1951), pp. 464–502. Reprinted by permission of Open Court Publishing Company. Footnotes renumbered.

be empirical evidence that, in some instances at least, survival *actually* occurs. Accordingly, what we must consider in this chapter is the empirical evidence there may be that survival has actually occurred. But as soon as one undertakes this task, three questions thrust themselves forward. One of them is whether the alleged facts, which are adduced as evidence of survival, really are facts. Then, if they really are facts, the second question is whether survival is the only possible or at least the most probable explanation of them. And if this appears to be so, the third question is: What then exactly is it, the survival of which those facts prove or make probable. A complete mind? or only certain parts or certain capacities of it? or only certain of its memories? or perhaps something else altogether? . . .

## 1. THE EMPIRICAL EVIDENCE FOR THE POSSIBILITY OF SURVIVAL

. . . This evidence, which is of a variety of kinds, was reviewed and discussed by Professor Gardner Murphy in two articles, published in the *Journal of the American Society for Psychical Research*,[1] on which the present exposition is largely based.

The first category of evidence he mentions consists of apparitions of a person dying or having just died but not known to have been ill or in danger. . . .

Sometimes the apparition brings, either automatically or by exercise of initiative, knowledge of facts until then unknown to the percipient. An example is that of the apparition of a girl to her brother nine years after her death, with a conspicuous scratch on her cheek. Their mother then revealed to him that she herself had made that scratch accidentally while preparing her daughter's body for burial, but that she had then at once covered it with powder and never mentioned it to anyone. Another famous case is that of a father whose apparition some time after death revealed to one of his sons the existence and location of an unsuspected second will, benefiting him, which was then found as indicated. Still another case would be the report by General Barter, then a subaltern in the British Army in India, of the apparition to him of a lieutenant he had not seen for two or three years. The lieutenant's apparition was riding a brown pony with black mane and tail. He was much stouter than at their last meeting, and, whereas formerly clean shaven, he now wore a peculiar beard in the form of a fringe encircling his face. On inquiry the next day from a person who had known the lieutenant at the time he died, it turned out that he had indeed become very bloated before his death; that he had grown just such a beard while on the sick list; and that he had some time before bought and eventually ridden to death a pony of that very description.

Other striking instances are those of an apparition seen simultaneously by several persons. It is on record that an apparition of a child was perceived first by a dog, that the animal's rushing at it, loudly barking, interrupted the conversation of the seven persons present in the room, thus drawing their attention to the apparition, and that the latter then moved through the room for some fifteen seconds, followed by the barking dog.[2]

Another type of empirical evidence of survival consists of communications purporting to come from the dead, made through the persons commonly called sensitives, mediums, or automatists. Some of the most remarkable of these communications have been given by Mrs. Leonard in London, and by the celebrated American medium, Mrs. Piper, who for many years was studied by the Society for Psychical Research with the most elaborate precautions against all possibility of fraud. In several instances, the evidences of identity supplied by the dead persons who purportedly were thus communicating with the living were of the very kinds, and of the same precision and detail, which would ordinarily satisfy a living person of the identity of another living person with whom he was not able to communicate directly, but only through an intermediary, or by letter or telephone.[3] In communications through a medium, the only ones having any evidential value are of course those where the facts communicated were not known to the medium. That this was the case in many instances is certain. Sometimes the facts communicated and later verified were unknown to the sitter as well as to the medium, and sometimes were not all known by any one living person. In a few cases, indeed, they were not known by any living person or persons at all. Sometimes the purportedly communicating deceased had never during life been known either to the medium or to the sitter, but was later found to have existed and to have recently died, and the communicated facts to be true.

There are cases on record also where the same purporting communicator manifests through several mediums independently, identifying himself by using the same symbol, phrase, or message in each case. The most impressive, however, are those which have come to be known as "cross-correspondences," for they seem to indicate on the part of the communicator not only survival of memories, but also of the actively working intelligence needed for the devising of some ingenious proof of identity. In them, for example, two mediums sometimes thousands of miles apart give each a different communication, neither of which is intelligible by itself, but when put together they are found to constitute an unmistakable allusion to an obscure passage in some work of classical literature. Or again, one communication mentions that a specific and uncommon question which is being asked had been asked before through another medium, and mentions the name of the person who had asked it.

In some cases, the person who seeks to obtain communication does not himself have a sitting with the medium but is represented at the sitting by a proxy, who was not acquainted with the deceased from whom a communication is sought and also sometimes is unacquainted with the person seeking the communication, or indeed does not even know for whom he is acting as proxy. Under such conditions, communications *prima facie* strongly evidential of the identity of the purported communicator are nevertheless obtained.

Of course, when facts of these kinds are recounted, as I have just done, only in summary or in the abstract, they make little if any impression upon us. And the very word "medium" at once brings to our minds the innumerable instances of demonstrated fraud perpetrated by charlatans to extract money from the credulous bereaved. But the modes of trickery and sources of error which immediately suggest themselves to us as easy natural explanations of the seemingly extraordinary facts suggest themselves just as quickly to the members of the research committees of the Society for Psychical Research. Usually, these men have had a good deal more experience than the rest of us with the tricks of conjurers and fraudulent mediums and take against them precautions far more strict and ingenious than would occur to the average skeptic.

But when, instead of stopping at summaries, one takes the trouble to study the detailed original reports, it then becomes evident that they cannot all be just laughed off; for to accept the hypothesis of fraud or malobservation would often require more credulity than to accept the facts reported. . . .

From this outline account of the empirical evidence for survival, let us now turn to the difficulties which confront it.

## 2. CRITIQUE OF THE EMPIRICAL EVIDENCE FOR SURVIVAL

One difficulty is that . . . survival is not the only hypothesis capable of accounting for the empirical facts, since telepathy, even if it too involves difficulties, provides an alternative explanation for most even if perhaps not quite all of the facts. But there are other difficulties in the survival explanation. For one, as emphasized by Professor E. R. Dodds,[4] the purported nature of the communicators seems to depend on what, according to the beliefs prevalent in the medium's milieu, that nature is expected to be: among spiritualists, the spirits of the dead; in medieval times, demons or the devil; in classical antiquity, sometimes gods or goddesses, etc. And he points out that facts of the same kinds as those in communications purportedly from spirits have been obtained from psychics who have no "controls" or "communicators," and who do not regard themselves as media of communication with spirits. There are instances where persons purporting to have survived death and to be communicating were in fact still living; and instances where they had been invented out of whole cloth by the sitter. Again, although the communicators often strikingly reproduce characteristic traits of the deceased, they also at times manifest traits sharply at variance with some of those known to have been possessed by the deceased.

As regards the evidence constituted by apparitions, a difficulty arises from the fact that the apparitions are not only of persons, but also of animals (*e.g.*, the lieutenant's horse), and of inanimate objects, such, in particular, as the clothing the apparitions wear. Furthermore, what, if anything, is proved to survive by the apparitions is not directly, if at all, the *mind* of the deceased, but some sort of appearance of his *body*. In some cases the apparition may be accounted for as a subjective hallucination in the percipient. This explanation, however, is not equally plausible in cases where several persons see the apparition. But some of the facts recorded by V. Schrenck-Notzing in connection with the medium Eva Carriere suggest that, strange as it seems, *images* in a medium's mind can sometimes become objectified in some manner sufficient to make them visible to others; so that such "ideomorphs," and not the deceased himself, may be what the apparitions really are. Moreover, as Gardner Murphy points out, when in day or night dreams one forms an image of a person, one's image is of the person as *doing something;* and as likely as not, something we subconsciously wish or fear he would do. This could account for the fact that sometimes the apparition behaves as if motivated by definite purpose. It would equally account for evidences of purpose and initiative in the personalities manifesting through mediums.

The empirical evidence for survival, when it is not merely mentioned more or less in the abstract as mostly was done in what precedes, but is considered in the full concreteness of the original reports, is sometimes very impressive. On the other hand, the difficulties which we have similarly mentioned, that stand in the way of the survival explanation of the facts, are, as Professor Dodds's article makes very clear, hard indeed to dispose of. In either case, it is virtually impossible in the present state of our knowledge to define the issues sharply, for the attempt to do so is complicated by the necessity of taking into consideration the strange Psi capacities—clairvoyance, precognition, retrocognition, besides telepathy—which in ordinary life do not function or do so to but a negligible extent, but which both the record of well attested spontaneous occurrences and the experimental demonstrations in recent years by J. B. Rhine, Whately Carington, and others, have shown to be parts of the latent equipment of at least some human minds.

When these three sets of considerations are taken fully into account, it seems to me that not only the empirical evidence, but the question itself as to whether it shows survival to be a fact more probably than not, is so ambiguous as to preclude answering the question "yes" or "no." We need to deal first with the question: What exactly is it, about which we ask whether "it" does or does not survive the death of the body? . . . That what we might call a man's "noon-day personality," *i.e.*, the whole set of capacities ready to function in him as occasion calls for when he is at his best, survives intact the death of his body seems very unlikely indeed. The Psi evidence does not show that *that* survives; and ordinary observation shows that that noon-day personality is a precarious thing, easily robbed of some of its component capacities by physiological and psychological accidents of various kinds; so that the times when a man is "really" himself—meaning the times at which he is at his best—are perhaps the exception rather than the rule even during life.

According to our analysis . . . , a mind is a composite of parts more or less well integrated, the parts, which we have denominated role-selves, being sets of systematically interrelated capacities or properties. These various parts too—down to what we have called molecular minds—are genuinely minds, though simpler, more specialized, less versatile than the whole of which they are parts. No reason has appeared not to regard as possible that any one of such parts should become more or less completely detached from the whole. And, with such parts as with the whole, no contradiction has appeared in the supposition that some of them may exist independently of connection with a material body, although without one the possibility of exercise of other than psycho-psychical capacities would be lacking. . . .

The conclusion I now wish to submit is that no contradiction appears to be involved in the supposition that some parts or capacities of man's mind survive the death of his body, and therefore that such survival is theoretically quite possible. As to whether it is actually as well as theoretically possible, there is strong *prima facie* evidence that in some instances *something* survives, which appears to be some part or some set of capacities of the mind whose body has died. But the demonstrated reality and occasional functioning of the paranormal capacities mentioned above—in particular, telepathy, clairvoyance, and retrocognition—so complicate the interpretation of the facts ordinarily adduced as empirical evidence of survival that, with our present very meager knowledge of the latent paranormal capacities of the human mind, and with the rather drastic revision of the ordinary ideas of our relation to *time* which the fact of precognition would appear to require, nothing both definite and well evidenced can yet be concluded concerning the actual, as distinguished from the theoretical, possibility of partial survival.

## 3. THE SIMPLEST THEORETICALLY POSSIBLE FORM OF SURVIVAL

The simplest form which survival, if it should be a fact, could take would consist in the continuation of a single state of consciousness after death. This state conceivably might be the last state of a person's consciousness immediately before death; or it might be one which, when bodily concerns are cut off, psychologically emerges out of the attitudes and feelings that have been prevalent in the person's life. It might be a state of blissful ecstasy similar to that of the mystic trance; or on the contrary one of anguish, or pain, or fear; or indeed any other single state of consciousness.

If some one state thus absorbed the whole consciousness and no change in it occurred, then no passage of time would be experienced and the given state would therefore be eternal in the sense of timeless, whether or not it were eternal also in the sense of enduring forever in the time of a possible external observer.

It is obvious that survival such as just described would not be *personal* survival. If, however, the persisting state of consciousness were of the kind the mystics have called union with God, the peace that passeth understanding, Samadhi, Nirvana, and by yet other names, it might well be better than anything which the activities and experiences of life in personal terms can yield. At least, so testify the mystics, who have tested both. . . . But it goes without saying that even if survival in the form of continuation of a single unchanging state of consciousness should be a fact, no reason whatever appears for believing that it would be a state of the blissful kind just referred to rather than one of anguish, or some other particular sort of state. . . .

## 4. SURVIVAL AS TRANSMIGRATION

The hypothesis of survival as rebirth (whether immediate or delayed) in a material world (whether the earth or some other planet) is of course not novel. It has been variously called reincarnation, transmigration, metempsychosis, or palingenesis. . . .

The hypothesis of survival as rebirth—let us say, on this earth—at once raises the question whether one's present life is not itself a rebirth; for logically, even if not in point of practical interest, the hypothesis of earlier lives is exactly on a par with that of later lives. Hence, assuming transmigration, to suppose that one's present life is the first of one's series of lives would be as arbitrary as to suppose that it is going to be the last, *i.e.*, that one will not survive the death of it although it is a survival of earlier deaths.

Now, the supposition that one's present life not only will have successors but also has had predecessors, immediately brings up the objection that we have no recollection of having lived before. But, . . . if absence of memory of having existed at a certain time proved that we did not exist at that time, it would then prove far too much; for it would prove that we did not exist during the first few years of the life of our present body, nor on most of the days since then, for we have no memories whatever of the great majority of them, nor of those first few years. Lack of memory of lives earlier than our present one is therefore no evidence at all that we did not live before.

Moreover, there is occasional testimony of recollection of a previous life, where the recollection is quite circumstantial and even alleged to have been verified. One such case may be cited here without any claim that it establishes preexistence, but only to substantiate the assertion that specific testimony of this kind exists. Evidently, testimony cannot be dismissed here any more than elsewhere merely because it happens to clash with an antecedent belief the empirical basis of which is only that we have not met before with such testimony. So to proceed would be to become guilty of *argumentum ad ignorantiam*. If preexistence should happen to be a fact, it is obvious that the only possible empirical evidence of it would consist of verifiable recollections such as testified to in the case about to be described.

It is that of "The Rebirth of Katsugoro," recorded in detail and with many affidavits respecting the facts, in an old Japanese document translated by Lafcadio Hearn.[5] The story is, in brief, that a young boy called Katsugoro, son of a man called Genzo in the village of Nakanomura, declared that in his preceding life a few years before he had been called Tozo; that he was then the son of a farmer called Kyubei and his wife Shidzu in a village called Hodokubo; that his father had died and had been replaced in the household by a man called Hanshiro; and that he himself, Tozo, had died of smallpox at the age of six, a year after his father. He described his burial, the appearance of his former parents, and their house. He eventually was taken to their village, where such persons were found. He himself led the way to their house and recognized them; and they confirmed the facts he had related. Further, he pointed to a shop and a tree, saying that they had not been there before; and this was true.

Testimony of this kind is directly relevant to the question of rebirth. The recollections related in this case are much too circumstantial to be dismissed as instances of the familiar and psychologically well-understood illusion of ***déja vu,*** and although the testimony that they were verified is not proof that they were, it cannot be rejected *a priori*. Its reliability has to be evaluated in terms of the same standards by which the validity of testimonial evidence concerning anything else is appraised.

A second objection to the transmigration hypothesis is that the native peculiarities of a person's mind as well as the characteristics of his body appear to be derived from his forebears in accordance with the laws of heredity. McTaggart . . . considers that objection and makes clear that "there is no impossibility in supposing that the characteristics in which we resemble the ancestors of our bodies may be to some degree characteristics due to our previous lives." He points out that "hats in general fit their wearers with far greater accuracy than they would if each man's hat were assigned to him by lot. And yet there is very seldom any causal connection between the shape of the head and the shape of the hat. A man's head is never made to fit his hat, and, in the great majority of cases, his hat is not made to fit his head. The adaptation comes about by each man selecting, from hats made without any special reference to his particular head, the hat which will suit his particular head best." And, McTaggart goes on to say: "This may help us to see that it would be possible to hold that a man whose nature had certain characteristics when he was about to be reborn, would be reborn in a body descended from ancestors of a similar character. His character when reborn would, in this case, be decided, as far as the points in question went, by his character in his previous life, and not by the character of the ancestors of his new body. But it would be the character of the ancestors of the new body, and its similarity to his character, which determined the fact that he was reborn in that body rather than another."[6]

McTaggart's use of the analogy of the head and the hats if taken literally would mean, as a correspondent of mine suggests, that, like a man looking for a hat to wear, a temporarily bodiless soul would shop around, trying on one human fetus after another until it finds one which in some unexplained manner it discovers will develop into an appropriate body. McTaggart, however, has in mind nothing so far fetched, but rather an entirely automatic process. He refers to the analogy of chemical affinities in answer to the question how each person might be brought into connection with the new body most appropriate to him.

But although McTaggart's supposition is adequate to dispose of the difficulty which the facts of heredity otherwise constitute, the rebirth his supposition allows is nevertheless not personal rebirth if, by a man's personality, one means what we have meant in what precedes, namely, the habits, the skills, the knowledge, character, and memories, which he gradually acquires during life on earth. These, we have said, may conceivably persist for a longer or shorter time after death, but, if our present birth is indeed a rebirth, they certainly are not brought to a new earth life; for we know very well that we are not born with the knowledge, habits, and memories we now have, but gained them little by little as a result of the experiences and efforts of our present lifetime.

But this brings up another difficulty, namely, what then is there left which could be supposed to be reborn? A possible solution of it . . . is definable in terms of the difference familiar in psychology between, on the one hand, *acquired* skills, habits, and memories, and on the other *native* aptitudes, instincts, and proclivities; that is, in what a human being is at a given time we may distinguish two parts, one deeper and more permanent, and another more superficial and transient. The latter consists of everything he has acquired since birth: habits, skills, memories, and so on. This is his personality. The other part, which, somewhat arbitrarily for lack of a better name we may here agree to call his individuality, comprises the aptitudes and dispositions which are native in him. These include not only the simple ones, such as aptitude for tweezer dexterity, which have been studied in laboratories because they so readily lend themselves to it, but also others more elusive: intellectual, social, and esthetic aptitudes, dispositions, and types of interest or of taste. Here the task of discriminating what is innate from what is acquired is much more difficult, for it is complicated by the fact that some existent aptitudes may only become manifest after years have passed, or perhaps never, simply because not until then, or never, did the external occasion present itself for them to be exercised—just as aptitude for tweezer dexterity, for instance, in those who have it, must remain latent so long as they are not called upon to employ tweezers.

There can be no doubt that each of us, on the basis of his same individuality—that is, of his same stock of innate latent capacities and incapacities—would have developed a more or less different empirical mind and personality if, for instance, he had been put at birth in a different family, or had later been thrust by some external accident into a radically different sort of environment, or had had a different kind of education, or had met and married a very different type of person, and so on. Reflection on this fact should cause one to take his present personality with a large grain of salt, viewing it no longer humorlessly as his absolute self, but rather, in imaginative perspective, as but one of the various personalities which his individuality was equally capable of generating had it happened to enter phenomenal history through birth in a different environment. Thus, to the question: What is it that could be supposed to be reborn? an intelligible answer may be returned by saying that it might be the core of positive and negative aptitudes and tendencies which we have called a man's individuality, as distinguished from his personality. And the fact might further be that, perhaps as a result of persistent striving to acquire a skill or trait he desires, but for which he now has but little gift, aptitude for it in future births would be generated and incorporated into his individuality.

A man's individuality, as we have here defined it, would . . . be what remains of a man after not only the death of his body but also after the disintegration of his lifetime-acquired "personal" mind, whether at bodily death or at some longer or shorter time thereafter. On the other hand, although his "individuality" would not itself be a personal mind, it would be an intrinsic and indeed the basic constituent of what his *total* mind is at any time. Out of the union of this basic or seminal constituent with a living body there would gradually develop a personal mind, whose particular nature would be the resultant on the one hand of the experiences due to the circumstances of that body, and on the other, of the core of aptitudes and tendencies therein embodied. Such parts or activities of a personal mind as we described in earlier sections of this chapter can, without theoretical difficulty, be supposed to survive the body's death at least for sometime; and *these* could . . . be what, in the mediumistic trance, becomes temporarily united with the medium's "bodily factor," which then furnishes it the possibility of expression vocally or by writing. Thus, what would be so expressing itself in the trance communications would not be the whole personal mind of the deceased, but only so much of it as still persisted; and even this, more or less colored or distorted by the necessity for it of making use of the particular set of acquired neural connections . . . in the medium's brain, which are certain to be more or less different from those that had been built up in the brain of the deceased. . . .

Another objection which has been advanced against the transmigration hypothesis is that without the awareness of identity which memory provides, rebirth would not be discernibly different from the death of one person followed by the birth of another. In this connection, Lamont quotes Leibniz's question: "Of what use would it be to you, sir, to become king of China, on condition that you forgot what you have been? Would it not be the same as if God, at the same time he destroyed you, created a king in China?"[7]

But continuousness of memory, rather than preservation of a comprehensive span of memories, is what is significant for consciousness of one's identity. Thus, for example, none of us finds his sense of identity impaired by the fact that he has no memories of the earliest years of his present life. And if, on each day, he had a stock of memories relating to, let us say, only the then preceding ten years, or some other perhaps even shorter period, this would provide all that would be needed for a continuous sense of identity. The knowledge he would have of his personal history would, it is true, comprise a shorter span than it now does, but the span in either case would have an earliest term, and in either case the personality known would have a substantial amount of historical dimension. That the sense of identity depends on *gradualness of change* in ourselves, rather than on preservation unchanged of any specific part of ourselves, strikes one forcibly when he chances to find letters, perhaps, which he wrote thirty or forty years before. Many of them may awaken no recollections whatever, even of the existence of the persons to whom they were addressed or whom they mentioned, and it sometimes seems incredible also that the person who wrote the things they contain should be the same as his present self. In truth, it is not the same in any strict sense, but only continuous with the former person. The fact, as the Buddha insisted, is that one's personality, like everything else that exists in time, changes as time passes — some constituents of it remaining for shorter or longer periods, the while others are being lost and others acquired. Yet, because of the gradualness and diverse speeds of the changes between one's earlier and one's present personality, the sense of identity is at no time lacking.

One more difficulty in the conception of survival as transmigration remains to be examined. It concerns not so much the theoretical possibility of transmigration as its capacity to satisfy certain demands which death appears to thwart—such capacity being what alone gives to a conception of survival practical importance and interest for us in this life.

One of these demands, as we have seen, is that the injustices of this life should somehow be eventually redressed; hence, conceptions of survival have generally included the idea of such redress as effected in the life after death. And, when survival has been thought of as later lives on earth, the redress has been conceived to consist in this—that the good and evil deeds, the strivings, the experiences, and the merits and faults of one life, all would have their just fruits in subsequent lives; in short, that as a man soweth, so shall he also reap.

Now, however, it may be objected that, without memory of what one is being rewarded or punished for, one learns nothing from the retribution, which is then ethically useless. This, in fact, was the essential point of the passage from Leibniz quoted earlier. Leibniz was considering Descartes's conception of the soul as an immortal substance, and contending that "like matter, so the soul will change in shape, and as with matter . . . it will indeed be possible for this soul to be immortal, but it will go through a thousand changes and will not remember what it has been. But this immortality without memory is wholly useless to ethics; for it subverts all reward and all punishment." And then comes the passage quoted earlier: "Of what use would it be to you, sir, to become king of China, on condition that you forgot what you have been?"

But all this is obviously based on a tacit and gratuitous ascription to the universe of the twin human impulses, vindictiveness and gratitude. It is these only which lead one to conceive a just future life as one of punishment and reward. For punishment and reward, although they satisfy vindictiveness and gratitude, are morally defensible only in so far as they contribute to the moral education of the recipient. But the eye-for-eye-and-tooth-for-tooth mode of moral education is not the only one there is, nor necessarily always the most effective. If, for example, impatience caused Tom to do Dick an injury, the morally important thing as regards Tom is that he should acquire the patience he lacks; but the undergoing by him of a similar injury at the hand of Dick is not the only possible way in which he could come to do so. Indeed, it would contribute to this only in proportion as Dick's retaliation were prompt and were known to be retaliation for the injury resulting from Tom's impatience. Other ways in which Tom might learn patience are conceivable. He might, for example, eventually find himself in a situation psychologically conducive to the development of patience—one, for example, where his love for someone would cause him to endure year after year without resentment the vagaries or follies of the loved person—or, more generally, some situation which for one reason or another he would be powerless to alter or to escape and in which only patient resignation would avail to bring him any peace.

As regards Dick, on the other hand, compensation for his unmerited injury at the hand of Tom need not consist in the immoral pleasure of retaliation upon Tom. The injury, which as such robs him of certain powers or opportunities, might lead him to develop other and more significant capacities latent in him, or might awaken him to other and better opportunities of which he would otherwise have remained unaware. Compensation for injury can be paid in various kinds of coin, and can truly compensate no matter at whose hands the payment comes; and, on the side of the doer of injury, the ends of justice are truly served if the wages of vice turn out to be eventual virtue.

It is further conceivable that Tom's eventual landing into a situation forcing him to practice patience should be a perfectly natural consequence of his vice of impatience. Each of us that is old and mature enough to view the course of his life in perspective can see that again and again his aptitudes, his habits, his tastes or interests, his virtues or his vices — in short, what he was at a given time — brought about, not by plan but automatically, changes in his material or social circumstances, in his associates, in his opportunities and so on; and that these changes in turn, quite as much as those due to purely external causes, contributed to shape for the better or the worse what he then became. This, which is observable within one life, could occur equally naturally as between the present and the subsequent bodied lives of a continuous though gradually changing self.

These suppositions have been introduced here only to make clear that the ***lex talionis*** conception of the justice for which later lives would provide the opportunity is crude and limited, and is far from being the only imaginable form justice could take, or necessarily the most effective. Those suppositions have also made clear that, for the moral education and the compensation which are the ends of justice, memory of the injury done and knowledge that an eventual educative consequence or piece of good fortune is a consequence of the injury done or sustained, is not in the least necessary, as on the contrary it is, where the *lex talionis* is the instrument of justice employed.

We have now considered the chief of the difficulties in the way of the transmigration form of the survival hypothesis. In attempting to meet them and to take into account the survival possibilities described in earlier sections of this chapter, we have gradually defined a form of survival which appears possible and which, if it should be a fact, would have significance for the living. The main features of that conception may now be summarily recited. They would be:

*(a)* That in the mind of man two comprehensive constituents are to be discerned — one, acquired during his lifetime and most obvious, which we have called his *personality* or the personal part of his mind; and another, less obvious but more basic, which exists in him from birth, and which for lack of a better name we have called his *individuality* or the individual part of his mind;

*(b)* That this part, consisting of aptitudes, instincts, and other innate dispositions or tendencies, is the product gradually distilled from the actions, experiences, and strivings of the diverse personalities which developed by union of it with the bodies of a succession of earlier lives on earth (or possibly elsewhere);

*(c)* That, between any two such successive lives, there is an interval during which some parts of the personality of the preceding life persist — consciousness then being more or less dreamlike, but perhaps gradually learning to discriminate between images of subjective origin and memory images, and between either of these and images of objective, *i.e.,* of telepathic or clairvoyant, origin, if any;

*(d)* That some time during the interval is occupied by more or less complete recollection of the acts and events of the preceding life, and of their discernible consequences; and that dispositions of various apposite sorts are generated thereby, in some such automatic way as that in which, during life, deep changes of attitude are sometimes generated in us by our reading or seeing and hearing performed a tragedy or other impressive drama, or indeed by witnessing highly dramatic real events;

*(e)* That, partly because the specific nature of a man's individuality automatically shapes to some extent the external circumstances as well as the nature of the personality he develops from a given birth, and perhaps partly also because what his individuality has become may determine automatically . . . where and when and from whom he will be reborn, justice is immanent in the entire process, though not necessarily in the primitive form of *lex talionis.*

In conclusion, however, let it be emphasized again that no claim is made that this conception of survival is known to be true, or even known to be more probably true than not; but only (1) that it is possible in the threefold sense stated earlier; (2) that belief or disbelief of it has implications for conduct; (3) that, if true, it would satisfy pretty well most of the demands which make the desire for survival so widespread; and (4) that, notwithstanding some gaps in that conception due to our ignorance of mechanisms such as certain of those it postulates, it is yet clear and definite enough to refute the allegation it was designed to refute, namely, that no life after death both possible and significant can be imagined.

## NOTES

1. G. Murphy, "An Outline of Survival Evidence," *Jour. of Amer. Soc. for Psychical Research,* Vol. XXXIX, No. 1, Jan. 1945; and "Difficulties Confronting the Survival Hypothesis," *loc. cit.,* No. 2, April 1945.
2. The documents obtained by the Society for Psychical Research concerning this case, that of the lieutenant's apparition, and that of the girl with the scratch, are reproduced in Sir Ernest Bennett's *Apparitions and Haunted Houses* (London: Faber and Faber, 1945), pp. 334–337, 28–35, and 145–150, respectively.
3. A summary of some of the most evidential facts may be found in the book by M. Sage, entitled *Mrs. Piper and the Society for Psychical Research* (New York: Scott-Thaw Co., 1904); and others of them are related in some detail in Sir Oliver Lodge's *The Survival of Man,* Sec. IV (New York: Moffat, Yard, and Co. 1909), and in A. M. Robbins's *Both Sides of the Veil,* Part II (Boston: Sherman, French, and Co., 1909). The fullest account is in the *Proceedings of the Society for Psychical Research.*
4. Dodds, "Why I Do Not Believe in Survival," *Proc. Soc. for Psych. Research,* Vol. XLII, 1934, pp. 147–172. The paper also contains a critique of Broad's "psychic factor" hypothesis and an impressive defense of the telepathy explanation.
5. L. Hearn, *Gleanings in Buddha Fields,* Chap. X.
6. McTaggart, *Some Dogmas of Religion,* p. 125.
7. Corliss Lamont, *The Illusion of Immortality,* p. 22; Leibniz, *Philosophische Schriften,* ed. Gerhardt, IV, 300.

## *John Hick (b. 1922)*

In the previous section, John Hick argued that immortality was necessary if the problem of evil was to be satisfactorily addressed. To argue that immortality is morally necessary is one thing. To describe how immortality is possible is quite another. The two most common descriptions of survival, the resurrection of the body and the immortality of a soul that survives the body, both have serious difficulties. In the selection included here, John Hick presents an alternative account which he describes as the replica theory: When a person dies in this world, an exact psychophysical replica of the deceased person is created in another world.

# The Resurrection of the Person

## *John Hick*

### 1. THE BASIC RELIGIOUS ARGUMENT FOR IMMORTALITY

. . . If we are to transcend our own personal and atypically fortunate standpoint in order to survey the human situation as a whole we can perhaps best think of the satisfactoriness of man's life in terms of the fulfilling of its potential. The human potential includes love and friendship, cooperation between people in common causes, enjoyment of the natural world and appreciation of all the innumerable aspects of human thought and art. Given a state of society functioning at a technological level at which men's attention is not excessively absorbed in the struggle to survive, and given a human environment which is both adequately stable and adequately stimulating, men and women are capable of creating and enjoying all that has in fact been produced and enjoyed in the realms of philosophy and religion, science and technology, music, painting, poetry, prose, drama, dance, architecture, and all the other dimensions of human culture.

But we have to remember that this potentiality has in fact been realized to any appreciable extent only in a very small minority of human lives. Most of the earth's inhabitants, in every generation including the present one, have had to live in a condition of chronic malnutrition and under threat of starvation, and very many have always had to dwell in the insecurity of oppression, exploitation and slavery, constantly menaced by the possibility of disasters of both human and natural origin. . . .

What however of the more intimate goods of personal relationship and family life—are not these independent both of poverty and of affluence? The answer, I think, must be both affirmative and negative. The family is indeed the main focus of the deepest personal satisfactions. And it is true that mutual love within a family does not directly depend upon economic welfare. But at the same time it does make a great difference to the happiness of the family if it is starving and without hope; and to the satisfaction involved in bringing up children if it is known that they must live on the starvation line and must lack both education and decent work. We in our minority western situation expect our children to be able to receive more or less as full an education as they are capable of assimilating, to find decent jobs, and to live in a society in which a predominantly satisfying life is possible. But this "we" includes only a small minority of the human beings now alive, and an even smaller proportion of all the human beings who have lived during the hundred thousand or so years of the period over which it is possible to speak of man.

And when we take account of these sombre facts it is hard to deny what the Buddha formulated as the first of his Four Noble Truths, namely that all life is permeated by *dukkha,* ill or suffering. As he said in his sermon at Sarnath, "Birth is ill, decay is ill, sickness is ill, death is ill. To be conjoined with what one dislikes means suffering. To be disjoined from what one likes means suffering. Not to get what one wants, also that means suffering."[1]

At this point we may profitably continue to listen to the witness of Buddhism and the concurring witness of the other faiths of indian origin. We shall have to attend at a later stage to the conceptions which these religions present of the

Abridged from *Death and Eternal Life,* by John Hick. (New York: Harper & Row, © 1976 by John Hick.) Reprinted by permission of Harper & Row, Publishers, Inc. Sections and footnotes renumbered.

nature of human fulfillment either as nirvana or as realization of oneness with the Absolute Mind. The insight I want to heed at the moment is that such fulfillment is not to be attained in a single earthly life. Gautama, for example, when he attained to enlightenment at Bodh Gaya and became a Buddha had, so he believed, already lived hundreds of thousands of previous lives, which he remembered in that period of final spiritual attainment. One earthly life is not enough. Likewise in the hindu understanding of the process of human completion, when a man attains to *moksha,* enlightenment, and becomes *jivanmukti,* a vast—perhaps infinite—number of lives lies behind him. Once again, it is believed that a single life is not enough. And this, surely, is realistic. In western and christian terms, if we understand the divine purpose for human beings as their realization of the human potential, their full humanization, it is clear that this does not usually occur within the space of a single earthly life. Within this one life some men advance a long way towards the fulfillment of the human potential, most advance a little, but many hardly advance at all and some on the contrary regress. The general picture is certainly not one in which the human potential is normally or even often fulfilled in the course of this present life. Erich Fromm has well said that "living is a process of continuous birth. The tragedy in the life of most of us is that we die before we are fully born."[2] . . .

## 2. THE IDEA OF RESURRECTION

"I believe," says the Apostles' Creed, "in the resurrection of the body and the life everlasting." The resurrection of the body, or of the flesh, has been given a variety of meanings in different ages and different theological circles; but we are not at present concerned with the history of the concept. We are concerned with the meaning that can be given to it today in terms of our contemporary scientific and philosophical understanding. . . .

## 3. THE "REPLICA" THEORY

I wish to suggest that we can think of it as the divine creation in another space of an exact psycho-physical "replica" of the deceased person.

The first point requiring clarification is the idea of spaces in the plural.[3] In this context the possibility of two spaces is the possibility of two sets of extended objects such that each member of each set is spatially related to each other member of the same set but not spatially related to any member of the other set. Thus everything in the space in which I am is at a certain distance and in a certain direction from me, and vice versa; but if there is a second space, nothing in it is at any distance or in any direction from where I now am. In other words, from my point of view the other space is nowhere and therefore does not exist. But if there *is* a second space, unobservable by me, the objects in it are entirely real to an observer within that space, and our own world is to him nowhere—not at any distance nor in any direction—so that from his point of view it does not exist. Now it is logically possible for there to be any number of worlds, each in its own space, these worlds being all observed by the universal consciousness of God but only one of them being observed by an embodied being who is part of one of these worlds. And the idea of bodily resurrection requires (or probably requires) that there be at least two such worlds, and that when an individual dies in our present world in space number one he is either immediately or after a lapse of time re-created in a world in space number two.

In order to develop this idea more fully I shall present a series of three cases, which I claim to be logically possible of fulfillment.

We begin with the idea of someone suddenly ceasing to exist at a certain place in this world and the next instant coming into existence at another place which is not contiguous with the first. He has not moved from A to B by making a path through the intervening space but has disappeared at A and reappeared at B. For example, at some learned gathering in London one of the company suddenly and inexplicably disappears and the next moment an exact "replica" of him suddenly and inexplicably appears at some comparable meeting in New York. The person who appears in New York is exactly similar, as to both bodily and mental characteristics, to the person who disappears in London. There is continuity of memory, complete similarity of bodily features, including fingerprints, hair and eye coloration and stomach contents, and also of beliefs, habits, and mental propensities. In fact there is everything that would lead us to identify the one who appeared with the one who disappeared, except continuous occupancy of space.

It is I think clear that this is a logically possible sequence of events. It is of course factually impossible: that is to say, so long as matter functions in accordance with the "laws" which it has exhibited hitherto, such things will not happen. But nevertheless we can imagine changes in the behavior of matter which would allow it to happen, and we can ask what effect this would have upon our concept of personal identity. Would we say that the one who appears in New York is the same person as the one who disappeared in London? This would presumably be a matter for decision, and perhaps indeed for a legal decision affecting such matters as marriage, property, debts, and other social rights and obligations. I believe that the only reasonable and generally acceptable decision would be to acknowledge identity. The man himself would be conscious of being the same person, and I suggest that his fellow human beings would feel obliged to recognize him as being the one whom he claims to be. We may suppose, for example, that a deputation of the colleagues of the man who disappeared fly to New York to interview the "replica" of him which is reported there, and find that he is in all respects but one exactly as though he had travelled from London to New York by conventional means. The only difference is that he describes how, as he was listening to Dr Z reading a paper, on blinking his eyes he suddenly found himself sitting in a different room listening to a different paper by an american scholar. He asks his colleagues how the meeting had gone after he had ceased to be there, and what they had made of his disappearance, and so on. He clearly thinks of himself as the one who was present with them at their meeting in London. He is presently reunited with his wife, who is quite certain that he is her husband; and with his children, who are quite certain that he is their father. And so on. I suggest that faced with all these circumstances those who know him would soon, if not immediately, find themselves thinking of him and treating him as the individual who had so inexplicably disappeared from the meeting in London; and that society would accord legal recognition of his identity. We should be extending our normal use of "same person" in a way which the postulated facts would both demand and justify if we said that the person who appears in New York is the same person as the one who disappeared in London. The factors inclining us to identify them would, I suggest, far outweigh the factors disinclining us to do so. The personal, social, and conceptual cost of refusing to make this extension would so greatly exceed the cost of making it that we should have no reasonable alternative but to extend our concept of "the same person" to cover this strange new case.

This imaginary case, bizarre though it is, establishes an important conceptual bridgehead for the further claim that a post-mortem "replica" of Mr X in another space would likewise count as the same person as the this-world Mr X before his death. However, let me strengthen this bridgehead at two points before venturing upon it.

The **cyberneticist,** Norbert Wiener, has graphically emphasized the non-dependence of human bodily identity through time upon the identity of the physical matter momentarily composing the body. He points out that the living human body is not a static entity but a pattern of change: "The individuality of the body is that of a flame rather than that of a stone, of a form rather than of a bit of substance."[4] The pattern of the body can be regarded as a message that is in principle capable of being coded, transmitted, and then translated back into its original form, as sight and sound patterns may be transmitted by radio and translated back into sound and picture. Hence "there is no absolute distinction between the types of transmission which we can use for sending a telegram from country to country and the types of transmission which at least are theoretically possible for transmitting a living organism such as a human being."[5] Strictly, one should not speak, as Wiener does here, of a living organism or body being transmitted; for it would not be the body itself but its coded form that is transmitted. At other times, however, Wiener is more precise. It is, he says, possible to contemplate transmitting "the whole pattern of the human body, of the human brain with its memories and cross connections, so that a hypothetical receiving instrument could re-embody these messages in appropriate matter, capable of continuing the processes already in the body and the mind, and of maintaining the integrity needed for this continuation by a process of homeostasis."[6] Accordingly Wiener concludes that the telegraphing of the pattern of a man from one place to another is theoretically possible even though it remains at the present time technically impossible.[7] And it does indeed seem natural in discussing this theoretical possibility to speak of the bodily individual who is constituted at the end of the process as being the same person as the one who was "encoded" at the beginning. He is not composed of numerically the same parcel of matter; and yet it is more appropriate to describe him as the same person than as a different person because the matter of which he is composed embodies exactly the same "information." Similarly, the rendering of Beethoven's ninth symphony which reaches my ears from the radio loudspeaker does not consist of numerically the same vibrations that reached the microphone in the concert hall; those vibrations have not travelled on through another three hundred miles to me. And yet it is more appropriate to say that I am hearing this rendering of the ninth symphony than that I am hearing something else.

The kind of transmission which Wiener envisages differs of course from my case number one in that I have postulated no machinery for coding and decoding, and no procession of radio impulses proceeding from London to New York and requiring a certain elapse of time for their journey. It differs even more radically from the notion of resurrection as "replication" in another space, since *ex hypothesi* in this case no physical connection between the two spaces, as by radio impulses, is possible. But if we abstract from all questions of practical logistics, Wiener's contribution to the present argument is his insistence that psycho-physical individuality does not depend upon the numerical identity of the ultimate physical constituents of the body but upon the pattern or "code" which is exemplified. So long as the same "code" operates, different parcels of matter can be used, and those parcels can be in different places.[8]

The second strengthening of the bridgehead concerns the term "replica" which, it will be observed, I have used in quotes. The quotes are intended to mark a difference between the normal concept of a replica and the more specialized concept in use here. The paradigm sense of "replica" is that in which there is an original object, such as a statue, of which a more or less exact copy is then made. It is logically possible (though not of course necessary) for the original and the replica to exist simultaneously; and also for there to be any number of replicas of the same original. In contrast to this, in the case of the disappearance in London and re-appearance in New York it is not logically possible for the original and the "replica" to exist simultaneously or for there to be more than one "replica" of the same original. . . . For "replica" is the name that I am proposing for the second entity in the following case. A living person ceases to exist at a certain location, and a being exactly similar to him in all respects subsequently comes into existence at another location. And I have argued so far that it would be a correct decision, causing far less linguistic and conceptual disruption than the contrary one, to regard the "replica" as the same person as the original.

Let us now move on to a second imaginary case, a step nearer to the idea of resurrection. Let us suppose that the event in London is not a sudden and inexplicable disappearance, and indeed not a disappearance at all, but a sudden death. Only, at the moment when the individual dies a "replica" of him as he was at the moment before his death, and complete with memory up to that instant, comes into existence in New York. Even with the corpse on our hands it would still, I suggest, be an extension of "same person" required and warranted by the postulated facts to say that the one who died has been miraculously re-created in New York. The case would, to be sure, be even odder than the previous one because of the existence of the dead body in London contemporaneously with the living person in New York. And yet, striking though the oddness undoubtedly is, it does not amount to a logical impossibility. Once again we must imagine some of the deceased's colleagues going to New York to interview the person who has suddenly appeared there. He would perfectly remember them and their meeting, be interested in what had happened, and be as amazed and dumbfounded about it as anyone else; and he would perhaps be worried about the possible legal complications if he should return to London to claim his property; and so on. Once again, I believe, they would soon find themselves thinking of him and treating him as the same person as the dead Londoner. Once again the factors inclining us to say that the one who died and the one who appeared are the same person would far outweigh the factors inclining us to say that they are different people. Once again we should have to extend our usage of "same person" to cover the new case.

However, rather than pause longer over this second picture let us proceed to the idea of "replication" in another space, which I suggest can give content to the notion of resurrection. For at this point the problem of personal identity shifts its focus from second- and third-person criteria to first-person criteria. It is no longer a question of how we in this world could know that the "replica" Mr X is the same person as the now deceased Mr X, but of how the "replica" Mr X himself could know this. And since this raises new problems it will be well to move directly to this case and the issues which it involves.

The picture that we have to consider is one in which Mr X dies and his "replica," complete with memory, etc., appears, not in America, but as a resurrection "replica" in a different world altogether, a resurrection world inhabited by resurrected "replicas" — this world occupying its own space distinct from the space with which we are familiar. It is, I think, manifestly an intelligible hypothesis that after my death I shall continue to exist as a consciousness and shall remember both having died and some at least of my states of consciousness both before and after death. Suppose then that I exist, not as a disembodied consciousness but as a psycho-physical being, a psycho-physical being exactly like the being that I was before death, though existing now in a different space. I have the experience of waking up from unconsciousness, as I have on other occasions woken up from sleep; and I am no more inclined in the one case than in the others to doubt my own identity as an individual persisting through time. I realize, either immediately or presently, that I have died, both because I can remember being on my death-bed and because my environment is now different and is populated by people some of whom I know to have died. Evidences of this kind could mount up to the point at which they are quite as strong as the evidence which, in the previous two pictures, convinces the individual in question that he has been miraculously translated to New York. Resurrected persons would be individually no more in doubt about their own identity than we are now, and would presumably be able to identify one another in the same kinds of ways and with a like degree of assurance as we do now.

## 4. IDENTITY FROM WORLD TO WORLD

But if it be granted that resurrected persons might be able to arrive at a rationally founded conviction that their existence is *post-mortem,* how could they know that the world in which they find themselves is in a different space from that of their pre-mortem life? How could such a person know that he is not in a number-two type situation in which he has died and has been re-created somewhere else in the same physical universe—except that the "replica" is situated, not in New York, but on a planet of some other star?

It is no doubt conceivable that the space of the resurrection world should have properties which are manifestly incompatible with its being a region of physical space as we know it. But on the other hand, it is not of the essence of the notion of a resurrection world that its space should have different properties from those of physical space. And supposing it not to have different properties it is not evident that a resurrected individual could learn from any direct observations that he was not on a planet of some sun at so great a distance from our own sun that the stellar scenery visible from it does not correlate with that which we now see. And indeed, it is not essential to the conception of resurrection which I am presenting that God's re-creation of us should in fact take place in another space rather than elsewhere in this space. There are however probable arguments in favor of the plural space hypothesis. The main ground that a resurrected person would have for believing that he is in another space would be his belief that case-one and case-two type events would be incompatible with the "laws" of the space in which he was before death. Thus although such "replication" is logically conceivable within our space we have good reason to believe that it does not in fact occur. But on the other hand we have no experience to indicate that "replication" does not (or does) occur as between different spaces; and we should I think therefore be strongly, and reasonably, inclined to opt for the latter hypothesis. . . .

## NOTES

1. Buddhist Scriptures, trans. Edward Conze (New York: Penguin, 1959), p. 186.
2. Erich Fromm, "Values, Psychology and Human Existence" in New Knowledge in Human Values, ed., A. H. Maslow, p. 156.
3. The conceivability of plural spaces is argued by Anthony Quinton in an important article to which I should like to draw the reader's attention: "Spaces and Times," in *Philosophy,* April 1962.
4. Norbert Wiener, *The Human Use of Human Beings,* 1950 (Avon Books, New York, 1967, and Sphere Books, London, 1968), p. 91.
5. ibid.
6. ibid., p. 86.
7. ibid., p. 92.
8. For a discussion of Norbert Wiener's ideas in this connection, see David L. Mouton, "Physicalism and Immortality," in *Religious Studies,* March 1972.

## *Peter Geach (b. 1916)*

Peter Geach is a contemporary British philosopher whose father was also a philosopher. Geach attended Wittgenstein's lectures and engaged in logical research with G. H. Von Wright. He has made significant contributions to logic and the philosophy of mind. In addition to *God and the Soul* (1969), he published *Mental Acts: Their Content and Their Objects* (1957).

In this selection on immortality, Geach argues that the only basis for hope in survival beyond death is God's promise. Interestingly enough, in the course of his argument he explains why reincarnation seems untenable and why the sort of parapsychological evidence that Ducasse discusses is utterly unconvincing. Furthermore, he gives us a careful discussion of the conditions which, he thinks, must be satisfied if a resurrected person is to be the same person as a previously existing mortal. He frankly admits that he does not know how these conditions can be satisfied. In other words, survival must be accepted on faith. Attempts to provide rational accounts of survival all fail. The survival Geach accepts on faith is the survival promised by the Christian God—the resurrection of the body.

# Immortality

## *Peter Geach*

Everybody knows that men die, and though most of us have read the advertisement "Millions now living will never die," it is commonly believed that every man born will some day die; yet historically many men have believed that there is a life after death, and indeed that this after-life will never end. That is: there has been a common belief both in *survival* of bodily death and in *immortality*. . . .

When *philosophers* talk of life after death, what they mostly have in mind is a doctrine that may be called Platonic—it is found in its essentials in the *Phaedo.* It may be briefly stated thus: Each man's make-up includes a wholly immaterial thing, his mind and soul. It is the mind that sees and hears and feels and thinks and chooses—in a word, is conscious. The mind is the person; the body is extrinsic to the person, like a suit of clothes. Though body and mind affect one another, the mind's existence is quite independent of the body's; and there is thus no reason why the mind should not go on being conscious indefinitely after the death of the body, and even if it never again has with any body that sort of connection which it now has.

This Platonic doctrine has a strong appeal, and there are plausible arguments in its favor. It appears a clearly intelligible supposition that I should go on after death having the same sorts of experience as I now have, even if I then have no body at all. For although these experiences are connected with processes in the body—sight, for example, with processes in the eyes, optic nerves, and brain—nevertheless there is no necessity of thought about the connection—it is easy to conceive of someone who has no eyes having the experience called sight. He would be having the same experience as I who have eyes do, and I know what sort of experience that is because I have the experience.

Let us now examine these arguments. When a word can be used to stand for a private experience, like the words "seeing" or "pain," it is certainly tempting to suppose that the giving these words a meaning is itself a private experience—indeed that they get their meaning just from the experiences they stand for. But this is really nonsense: if a sentence I hear or utter contains the word "pain," do I help myself to grasp its sense by giving myself a pain? Might not this be, on the contrary, rather distracting? . . . Our concepts of seeing, hearing, pain, anger, etc., apply in the first instance to human beings; we willingly extend them (say) to cats, dogs, and horses, but we rightly feel uncomfortable about extending them to very alien creatures and speaking of a slug's hearing or an angry ant. Do we know at all what it would be to apply such concepts to an immaterial being? I think not.

One may indeed be tempted to evade difficulties by saying: "An immaterial spirit is angry or in pain if it feels *the same way* as I do when I am

Abridged from "Immortality" in *God and the Soul,* by Peter Geach. (London: Routledge & Kegan Paul, Ltd., 1969), pp. 17–29. Reprinted by permission of Peter Geach.

angry or in pain." But, . . . if there is a difficulty in passing from "I am in pain" or "Smith is in pain" to "an immaterial spirit is in pain," there is equally a difficulty in passing from "Smith feels the same way as I do" to "an immaterial spirit feels the same way as I do."

In fact, the question is, whether a private experience does suffice, as is here supposed, to give a meaning to a psychological verb like "to see." I am not trying to throw doubt on there being private experiences; of course men have thoughts they do not utter and pains they do not show; of course I may see something without any behavior to show I see it; nor do I mean to emasculate these propositions with neo-behaviorist dialectics. But it is not a question of whether seeing is (sometimes) a private experience, but whether one can attach meaning to the verb "to see" by a private uncheckable performance; and this is what I maintain one cannot do to any word at all.

One way to show that a word's being given a meaning cannot be a private uncheckable performance is the following: We can take a man's word for it that a linguistic expression has given him some private experience — e.g. has revived a painful memory, evoked a visual image, or given him a thrill in the pit of the stomach. But we cannot take his word for it that he attached a sense to the expression, even if we accept his *bona fides;* for later events may convince us that in fact he attached no sense to the expression. Attaching sense to an expression is thus not to be identified with any private experience that accompanies the expression; and I have argued this, not by attacking the idea of private experiences, but by contrasting the attaching of sense to an expression with some typical private experiences that may be connected with the expression.

We give words a sense — whether they are psychological words like "seeing" and "pain," or other words — by getting into a way of using them; and though a man can invent for himself a way of using a word, it must be a way that other people *could* follow — otherwise we are back to the idea of conferring meaning by a private uncheckable performance. Well, how do we eventually use such words as "see," "hear," "feel," when we have got into the way of using them? We do not exercise these concepts only so as to pick our cases of seeing and the rest in our separate worlds of sense-experience; on the contrary, these concepts are used in association with a host of other concepts relating, e.g., to the physical characteristics of what is seen and the behavior of those who do see. In saying this I am not putting forward a theory, but just reminding you of very familiar features in the everyday use of the verb "to see" and related expressions; our ordinary talk about seeing would cease to be intelligible if there were cut out of it such expressions as "I can't see, it's too far off," "I caught his eye," "Don't look round," etc. Do not let the bogy of behaviorism scare you off observing these features; I am not asking you to believe that "to see" is itself a word for a kind of behavior. But the concept of seeing can be maintained only because it has threads of connection with these other non-psychological concepts; break enough threads, and the concept of seeing collapses.

We can now see the sort of difficulties that arise if we try to apply concepts like *seeing* and *feeling* to disembodied spirits. Let me give an actual case of a psychological concept's collapsing when its connections were broken. Certain **hysterics** claimed to have a magnetic sense; it was discovered, however, that their claim to be having magnetic sensations did not go with the actual presence of a magnet in their environment, but only with their belief that a magnet was present. Psychologists did not now take the line: We may take the patients' word for it that they have peculiar sensations — only the term "magnetic sensations" has proved inappropriate, as having been based on a wrong causal hypothesis. On the contrary, patients' reports of magnetic sensations were thenceforward written off as being among the odd things that hysterical patients sometimes say. Now far fewer of the ordinary connections of a sensation-concept were broken here than would be broken if we tried to apply a sensation-concept like seeing to a disembodied spirit.

If we conclude that the ascription of sensations and feelings to a disembodied spirit does not make sense, it does not obviously follow, as you might think, that we must deny the possibility of disembodied spirits altogether. Aquinas for example was convinced that there are disembodied spirits but ones that cannot see or hear or feel pain or fear or anger; he allowed them no mental operations except those of thought and will. Damned spirits would suffer from frustration of their evil will, but not from aches and pains or foul odors or the like. It would take me too far to discuss whether his reasons for thinking this were good; I want to show what follows from this view. In our human life thinking and choosing are intricately bound up with a play of sensations and mental images and emotions; if after a lifetime of thinking and choosing in this human way there is left only a disembodied mind whose thought is wholly nonsensuous and whose rational choices are unaccompanied by any human feelings—can we still say there remains the same person? Surely not: such a soul is not the person who died but a mere remnant of him. And this is just what Aquinas says (in his commentary on I Corinthians 15): *anima mea non est ego,* my soul is not I; and if only souls are saved, *I* am not saved, nor is any man. If some time after Peter Geach's death there is again a man identifiable as Peter Geach, then Peter Geach again, or still, lives: otherwise not.

Though a surviving mental remnant of a person, preserving some sort of physical continuity with the man you knew, would not be Peter Geach, this does not show that such a measure of survival is not possible; but its possibility does raise serious difficulties, even if such dehumanized thinking and willing is really conceivable at all. For *whose* thinking would this be? Could we tell whether *one* or *many* disembodied spirits thought the thoughts in question? We touch here on the old problem: what constitutes there being two disembodied minds (at the same time, that is)? Well, what constitutes there being two pennies? It may happen that one penny is bent and corroded while another is in mint condition; but such differences cannot be what make the two pennies to be two—the two pennies could not have these varied fortunes if they were not already distinct. In the same way, differences of memories or of aims could not constitute the difference between two disembodied minds, but could only supervene upon a difference already existing. What does constitute the difference between two disembodied human minds? If we could find no ground of differentiation, then not only would that which survived be a mere remnant of a person—there would not even be a surviving individuality.

Could we say that souls are different because in the first instance they were souls of different bodies, and then remain different on that account when they are no longer embodied? I do not think this solution would do at all if differentiation by reference to different bodies were merely retrospective. It might be otherwise if we held, with Aquinas, that the relation to a body was not merely retrospective—that each disembodied human soul permanently retained a capacity for reunion to such a body as would reconstitute a man identifiable with the man who died. This might satisfactorily account for the individuation of disembodied human souls; they would differ by being fitted for reunion to different bodies; but it would entail that the possibility of disembodied human souls stood or fell with the *possibility* of a dead man's living again *as a man.*

Some Scholastics held that just as two pennies or two cats differ by being different bits of matter, so human souls differ by containing different "spiritual matter." Aquinas regarded this idea as self-contradictory; it is at any rate much too obscure to count as establishing a possibility of distinct disembodied souls. Now this recourse to "spiritual matter" might well strike us merely as the filling of a conceptual lacuna with a nonsensical piece of jargon. But it is not only Scholastic philosophers who assimilate mental processes to physical ones, only thinking of mental processes as taking place in an *immaterial* medium; and many people think it easy to conceive of distinct disembodied souls because they are illegitimately ascribing to souls a sort of differentiation — say, by existing *side by side* — that can be significantly ascribed only to bodies. The same goes for people who talk about souls as being "fused" or "merged" in a Great Soul; they are imagining some such change in the world of souls as occurs to a drop of water falling into a pool or to a small lump of wax that is rubbed into a big one. Now if only people *talked* about "spiritual matter," instead of just thinking in terms of it unawares, their muddle could be more easily detected and treated.

To sum up what I have said so far: The possibility of life after death for Peter Geach appears to stand or fall with the possibility of there being once again a man identifiable as Peter Geach. The existence of a disembodied soul would not be a survival of the person Peter Geach; and even in such a truncated form, individual existence seems to require at least a persistent possibility of the soul's again entering into the make-up of a man who is identifiably Peter Geach.

This suggests a form of belief in survival that seems to have become quite popular of late in the West — at any rate as a half-belief — namely, the belief in reincarnation. Could it in fact have a clear sense to say that a baby born in Oxford this year is Hitler living again?

How could it be shown that the Oxford baby was Hitler? Presumably by memories and similarities of character. I maintain that no amount of such evidence would make it reasonable to identify the baby as Hitler. Similarities of character are of themselves obviously insufficient. As regards memories: If on growing up the Oxford baby reveals knowledge of what we should ordinarily say only Hitler can have known, does this establish a presumption that the child is Hitler? Not at all. In normal circumstances we know when to say "only he can have known that"; when queer things start happening, we have no right to stick to our ordinary assumptions as to what can be known. And suppose that for some time the child "is" Hitler by our criteria, and later on "is" Goering? or might not several children simultaneously satisfy the criteria for "being" Hitler?

These are not merely captious theoretical objections. Spirit-mediums, we are told, will in trance convincingly enact the part of various people: sometimes of fictitious characters, like Martians, or Red Indians ignorant of Red Indian languages, or the departed "spirits" of Johnny Walker and John Jamieson; there are even stories of mediums' giving convincing "messages" from people who were alive and normally conscious at the time of the "message." Now a medium giving messages from the dead is not said to be the dead man, but rather to be controlled by his spirit. What then can show whether the Oxford child "is" Hitler or is merely "controlled" by Hitler's spirit? For all these reasons the appearance that there might be good evidence for reincarnation dissolves on a closer view.

Nor do I see, for that matter, how the mental phenomena of mediumship could ever make it reasonable to believe that a human soul survived and communicated. For someone to carry on in a dramatic way quite out of his normal character is a common hysterical symptom; so if a medium does this in a trance, it is no evidence of anything except an abnormal condition of the medium's own mind. As for the medium's telling us things that "only the dead can have known," I repeat that in these queer cases we have no right to stick to our ordinary assumptions about what can be known. Moreover, as I said, there are cases, as well-authenticated as any, in which the medium convincingly enacted the part of X and told things that "Only X could have known" when X was in fact alive and normally conscious, so that his soul was certainly not trying to communicate by way of the medium! Even if we accept all the queer stories of spirit-messages, the result is only to open up a vast field of queer possibilities — not in the least to force us to say that mediums were possessed by such-and-such souls. This was argued by Bradley long ago in his essay "The Evidences of Spiritualism," and he has never been answered.

How could a living man be rightly identifiable

with a man who previously died? Let us first consider our normal criteria of personal identity. When we say an old man is the same person as the baby born seventy years before, we believe that the old man has material continuity with the baby. Of course this is not a criterion in the sense of being what we judge identity by; for the old man will not have been watched for seventy years continuously, even by rota! But something we regarded as disproving the material continuity (e.g. absence of a birthmark, different fingerprints) would disprove personal identity. Further, we believe that material continuity establishes a one–one relation: one baby grows up into one old man, and one old man has grown out of one baby. (Otherwise there would have to be at some stage a drastic change, a fusion or fission, which we should regard as destroying personal identity.) Moreover, the baby-body never coexists with the aged body, but develops into it.

Now it seems to me that we cannot rightly identify a man living "again" with a man who died unless *material* conditions of identity are fulfilled. There must be some one–one relation of material continuity between the old body and the new. I am not saying that the new body need be even in part materially *identical* with the old; this, unlike material continuity, is not required for personal identity, for the old man need not have kept even a grain of matter from the baby of seventy years ago.

We must here notice an important fallacy. I was indicating just now that I favor Aquinas's doctrine that two coexisting souls differ by being related to two different bodies and that two coexisting human bodies, like two pennies or two cats, differ by being different bits of matter. Well, if it is difference of matter that makes two bodies different, it may seem to follow that a body can maintain its identity only if at least some identifiable matter remains in it all the time; otherwise it is no more the same body than the wine in a cask that is continuously emptied and refilled is the same wine. But just this is the fallacy: it does not follow, if difference in a certain respect at a certain time suffices to show non-identity, that sameness in that respect over a period of time is necessary to identity. Thus, Sir John Cutler's famous pair of stockings were the same pair all the time, although they started as silk and by much mending ended as worsted; people have found it hard to see this, because if at a given time there is a silk pair and also a worsted pair then there are two pairs. Again, it is clear that the same man may be in Birmingham at noon and in Oxford at 7 p.m., even though a man in Birmingham and a man in Oxford at a given time must be two different men. Once formulated, the fallacy is obvious, but it might be deceptive if not formulated.

"Why worry even about material continuity? Would not mental continuity be both necessary and sufficient?" Necessary, but not sufficient. Imagine a new "Tichborne" trial. The claimant knows all the things he ought to know, and talks convincingly to the long-lost heir's friends. But medical evidence about scars and old fractures and so on indicates that he cannot be the man; moreover, the long-lost heir's corpse is decisively identified at an exhumation. Such a case would bewilder us, particularly if the claimant's *bona fides* were manifest. (He might, for example, voluntarily take a lie-detecting test.) But we should certainly not allow the evidence of mental connections with the long-lost heir to settle the matter in the claimant's favor: the claimant cannot be the long-lost heir, whose body we know lies buried in Australia, and if he honestly thinks he is then we must try to cure him of a delusion.

"But if I went on being conscious, why should I worry which body I have?" To use the repeated "I" prejudges the issue; a fairer way of putting the point would be: If there is going to be a consciousness that includes ostensible memories of my life, why should I worry about which body this consciousness goes with? When we put it that way, it is quite easy to imagine circumstances in which one would worry — particularly if the ostensible memories of my life were to be produced by processes that can produce entirely spurious memories.

If, however, memory is not enough for personal identity; if a man's living again does involve some bodily as well as mental continuity with the man who lived formerly; then we might fairly call his new bodily life a resurrection. So the upshot of our whole argument is that unless a man comes to life again by resurrection, he does not live again after death. At best some mental remnant of him would survive death; and I should hold that the possibility even of such survival involves at least a permanent *capacity* for renewed human life; if reincarnation is excluded, this means: a capacity for resurrection. It may be hard to believe in the resurrection of the body: but Aquinas argued in his commentary on I Corinthians 15, which I have already cited, that it is much harder to believe in an immortal but permanently disembodied human soul; for that would mean believing that a soul, whose very identity depends on the capacity for reunion with one human body rather than another, will continue to exist for ever with this capacity unrealized.

Speaking of the resurrection, St. Paul used the simile of a seed that is planted and grows into an ear of corn, to show the relation between the corpse and the body that rises again from the dead. This simile fits in well enough with our discussion. In this life, the bodily aspect of personal identity requires a one–one relationship and material continuity; one baby body grows into one old man's body by a continuous process. Now similarly there is a one–one relationship between the buried seed and the ear that grows out of it; one seed grows into one ear, one ear comes from one seed; and the ear of corn is materially continuous with the seed but need not have any material identity with it.

There is of course no philosophical reason to expect that from a human corpse there will arise at some future date a new human body, continuous in some way with the corpse; and in some particular cases there appear strong empirical objections. But apart from the *possibility* of resurrection, it seems to me a mere illusion to have any hope for life after death. I am of the mind of Judas Maccabeus: if there is no resurrection, it is superfluous and vain to pray for the dead.

The traditional faith of Christianity, inherited from Judaism, is that at the end of this age Messiah will come and men rise from their graves to die no more. That faith is not going to be shaken by inquiries about bodies burned to ashes or eaten by beasts; those who might well suffer just such death in martyrdom were those who were most confident of a glorious reward in the resurrection. One who shares that hope will hardly wish to take out an occultistic or philosophical insurance policy, to guarantee some sort of survival as an annuity, in case God's promise of resurrection should fail.

# Part 6 — Glossary

**Agnosticism** Agnosticism is the view that we don't know whether God exists.

**Anthropomorphism** Anthropomorphism is the ascription of human characteristics to nonhumans, for example, to God.

**Antipodal** Antipodal means "opposite."

**A posteriori** A posteriori reasoning is reasoning from observed facts or sense experience.

**Appropriation process** In Kierkegaard's philosophy an appropriation process is committing one's life to a belief.

**A priori** A priori reasoning is reasoning from self-evident propositions. It is reasoning without benefit of experience.

**Argumentum ad ignorantiam** Argumentum ad ignorantiam (argument from ignorance) is a name given to a fallacy in reasoning that is committed whenever someone argues that something is true because it hasn't been proved false. Example: "It's true that ghosts exist because no one has proved they don't."

**Athanasian** An Athanasian is a follower of the early Christian thinker Athanasius who held that God and Christ are one identical substance yet two distinct persons. Athanasius's view about Christ won out over the competing view of Arius that Christ was not divine (not God).

**Atheist** An atheist is one who believes there is no God.

**Cosmogony** A cosmogony is a theory of the origin of the universe.

**Cyberneticist** A cyberneticist is a specialist in or one who studies automatic control systems (both human and nonhuman). Automatic control systems are self-regulating and respond automatically to changes in the environment. A common thermostat in your house is an excellent example.

**Déjà vu** Déjà vu is a French word meaning "already seen." In parapsychology it refers to sensing that one has already seen or experienced something in another life that one is seeing or experiencing now.

**Demonology** Demonology is the study of or belief in demons or evil spirits.

**Dualism** Dualism is the metaphysical theory that contends that the world is composed of at least two different kinds of ultimate reality. Some traditional dualists argue that everything is mind or matter.

**Ecclesiasticism** (clericalism) Ecclesiasticism is excessive deference to or support of a religious hierarchy.

**Hysterics** A hysteric is one who shows a marked emotional excitability and disturbance of the psyche.

**Idealists** Idealists are philosophers who hold that ultimate reality is basically mental.

**Infidel** An infidel is a nonbeliever in religion, especially a nonbeliever in Christianity.

**Lex talionis** Lex talionis is roughly translated in English as the law of the jungle.

**Mahdi** Mahdi is the expected messiah of the Muslim tradition.

**Manicheanism** Manicheanism is the belief that the universe is governed by two roughly equal competing forces of good and evil.

**Natural theology** Natural theology is that part of theology based on our experience with this world. The claims of natural theology are known through reason; revelation is not required. An excellent example of a set of claims based on natural theology is the argument from design — a proof for the existence of God.

**Necessity** Necessity can be understood in two ways. Something is causally necessary if it must occur as a result of the laws that govern this world. Logical necessity is much stronger. Logical necessity occurs as a result of a logical truth. The opposite of a logical truth is self-contradictory. "Humans necessarily have two eyes" is an example of causal necessity but not logical necessity. It's rationally conceivable that humans have three eyes. It's logically necessary, however, that humans cannot both have two eyes and not have two eyes.

**Neoplatonism** Neoplatonism is a school of philosophy strongly indebted to Plato. Neoplatonism is less dualistic because all reality emanates from the Absolute (One). As a result, evil is simply the absence of good because emanated being is just less real than the absolute.

**Omnipotent** A being is omnipotent when it is all-powerful. The Judeo-Christian God is an example of such a being.

**Ontological** Related to or based upon being or essence. The ontological argument claims that God's existence follows necessarily from God's *essence.*

**Paradox** A paradox is something that seems contradictory or opposed to common sense. In Kierkegaard's philosophy the notion that God became human in time through the person of Christ is a paradox.

**Parapsychology** Parapsychology is an unorthodox branch of psychology concerned with the investigation of evidence for telepathy, clairvoyance, and psychokinesis.

**Plagiarist** A plagiarist is one who steals or passes off the words or ideas of another as his or her own.

**Possibility** There is a distinction between causal possibility and logical possibility. See **Necessity,** above. An event is logically possible if it doesn't violate a truth of reason and physically possible if it doesn't violate a law of nature.

**Pyrrhonistic** Pyrrhonistic is synonymous with sceptical. This doctrine was enunciated by the fourth century B.C. Greek philosopher Pyrrho. Pyrrho and his disciples suspended judgment on every proposition.

**Theist** A theist is a believer in God—specifically in a personal God, usually one who is omnipotent, omniscient, and perfectly good, and who is the creator and sustainer of the universe. The theist God is one who is both outside the world and yet who is active in the world.

**Theodicy** A theodicy is a rational defense of God's goodness and omnipotence in view of the existence of evil.

**Theogony** A theogony is an account of the origin and descent of the gods.

**Theosophist** A theosophist is one whose religious beliefs are eclectically drawn from many religious traditions, with emphasis upon spiritualism, the occult, and the mystical.

# Part 6—Study Questions

## *RELIGIOUS COMMITMENT AND THE NATURE OF FAITH*

1. Explain Kierkegaard's distinction between objective and subjective truth. Do you think there is such a thing as subjective truth? If not, explain why not. If you think there is such a thing as subjective truth, give an example and explain how your example constitutes a subjective truth.
2. What arguments does Aquinas give for his claim that not all religious truths could be known through human reason and hence that human reason must be supplemented? Are these arguments convincing? Explain.
3. Explain what James means by a live hypothesis. In addition to the acceptance of faith, can you think of any similar live hypotheses in your own life? James opts for faith. Could there have been equally good reasons for con-

fronting the live hypothesis by rejecting faith? Explain.

4. What are the grounds for Huxley's agnosticism? Are Huxley's arguments against Christianity sufficient to establish agnosticism?

5. Do you believe that revelation provides an adequate source of religious knowledge or should all claims to religious truth through revelation be rejected? Explain.

## *PROOFS FOR THE EXISTENCE OF GOD*

1. If an ontological proof works for the greatest being that can be conceived, why can't it work for the greatest pizza that can be conceived? Explain.

2. Is an infinite regress repugnant to reason? If it is, explain why. If it isn't, why do you think Aquinas was committed to the view that an infinite regress is repugnant to reason? Indicate the nature of Aquinas's mistake.

3. "If everything has a cause, what caused God?" Is this a legitimate question or not? Explain.

4. Suppose you find a watch and after examining it, you argue that there must have been a watchmaker. After further examination of the watch, what could you say about the nature of the watchmaker?

5. How would you evaluate the following argument?
    1. The world resembles the planning and order characteristic of a garden.
    2. The world has sufficient disorder to resemble a garden with weeds.
    3. There must have been a gardener who has left the garden unattended.

## *THE PROBLEM OF EVIL*

1. Evaluate the following argument: If there is to be a *created* world, there must be some bad in it. Otherwise it would not have been created.

2. Is the hypothesis of a devil with free will a good explanation of natural evil? Explain your answer.

3. Evaluate the following argument:
    1. If human beings have free will, God is not all-powerful.
    2. If human beings don't have free will, God is the cause of evil and hence God is not all-good.
    3. Therefore, either God is not all-powerful or God is not all-good.

4. Evaluate the following position: Suffering is a test for human beings to see whether they are worthy of entering the Kingdom of Heaven.

5. Suppose there is no afterlife. If many wicked people prosper and many good people suffer, does that mean you shouldn't behave morally? Explain.

## *IMMORTALITY*

1. Plato argues that the subject of knowledge (the person or part of the person who has knowledge) must be like the object of knowledge (what is known). After all, how could the knower actually know something different from himself or herself? Plato uses these premises to argue for the immortality of the soul. Could you refute Plato's argument by showing that to cut a hacksaw you need something different from a hacksaw? Explain.

2. Suppose, through a medium, you were able to communicate with a dead relative. Would that prove human survival of death? If yes, explain. If not, explain what additional evidence you would need for proof.

3. Suppose personal survival were limited to a person's disembodied soul. Describe an afterlife in which only your disembodied soul survives.

4. Explain Hick's replica theory. Is it superior to the survival of the soul theory? Explain.

5. Is the resurrection of the body irrational, nonrational, or rationally defensible? Explain.

# Part 6 — Suggestions for Further Reading


*BOOKS*

1. Flew, Anthony and Alasdair MacIntyre (eds). *New Essays in Philosophical Theology* (London: S.C.M. Press LTD, 1955).
2. Freud, Sigmund. *Moses and Monotheism* (New York : A. A. Knopf, 1939).
3. Hartshorne, Charles. *The Logic of Perfection* (Lasalle, IL: Open Court Publishing Co., 1962).
4. Hick, John. *Evil and the God of Love,* Revised Edition (Harper & Row, 1978).
5. Lewis, Hywel D. *The Self and Immortality* (New York: The Seabury Press, 1973).
6. Martin, Charles B. *Religious Belief* (Ithaca, NY: Cornell University Press, 1959).
7. Matson, Wallace I. *The Existence of God* (Ithaca, NY: Cornell University Press, 1965).
8. Mitchell, Basil (ed.) *Faith and Logic* (Atlantic Highlands, N.J.: Humanities Press, 1958).
9. Penelhum, Terence. *Religion and Rationality* (New York: Random House, 1971).
10. ——— (ed.). *Immortality* (Belmont, CA: Wadsworth Publishing Company, 1973).
11. Plantinga, Alvin. *God and Other Minds: A Study of the Rational Justification of Belief in God* (Ithaca, NY: Cornell University Press, 1967).
12. Ross, James F. *Philosophical Theology* (Indianapolis: Hackett Publishing Company, Inc., 1980).
13. Swinburne, Richard. *The Coherence of Theism* (Oxford: Clarendon Press, 1977).

*TEXTS*

14. Brody, Baruch. *Readings in the Philosophy of Religion* (Englewood Cliffs, NJ: Prentice Hall, 1974).
15. Cahn, Steven M. and David Shatz (eds). *Contemporary Philosophy of Religion* (New York: Oxford University Press, 1982).
16. Hick, John. *Philosophy of Religion,* Third Edition (Englewood Cliffs, NJ: Prentice Hall, Inc., 1983).
17. Rowe, William. *Philosophy of Religion: An Introduction* (Belmont, CA: Wadsworth Publishing Company, 1978).
18. Rowe, William I. and William J. Wainwright. *Philosophy of Religion: Selected Readings* (New York: Harcourt Brace Jovanovich, Inc., 1973).

# Appendix: Criticizing and Creating Philosophical Arguments

One of the more difficult tasks facing the introductory philosophy student is writing a philosophy paper. This usually involves both understanding and criticizing the arguments of others and creating arguments of one's own. Even if you don't have to write a philosophy paper, you will want to critically evaluate the arguments in the reading assignments. The material in this appendix is designed to make these tasks easier. Note that we did not say we would make them easy. Criticizing arguments is hard work; creating them is even harder. Indeed we think writing a philosophy paper has some important things in common with creating a work of art.

## I. Identifying and Appreciating Arguments

Each philosopher in this text has made at least one philosophical claim and has argued for it. In your reading, your main task should be to identify the argument or arguments made on behalf of these claims. Our first task in this appendix, then, is to help you identify arguments.

Normally arguments are supported by an appeal to the facts. Indeed most people think that constructing an argument is simply a matter of establishing the facts. They think the person with the most facts should be declared the winner in any argument. Although it can be easily proven that this is not the case, facts *are important* in arguments. Facts are often less important in typical philosophical arguments (and it is important to see why), but even here facts are usually important and sometimes decisive.

As you may recall from many arguments you have had, establishing the facts is often grounds for an argument in its own right. What are the facts concerning the existence of other planets, the relation of cigarette smoking to cancer, the effects of nuclear war? One reason many philosophers don't argue about the facts is because many philosophical arguments are arguments about arguments about the facts. Such arguments occur before we get down to the facts, at a level or two of abstraction above the facts. Their premises are frequently about the meanings of concepts or the relations among concepts rather than about facts of the ordinary sort.

Another reason why arguments aren't simply about facts is because facts by themselves don't prove anything. Facts just are. What really count are relations among the facts. It's a fact that all mammals have backbones. It's also a fact that a dog is a mammal. It's also a fact that a dog has a backbone. By themselves these are just three facts. You make an argument when you can use some facts to establish or give good evidence for other facts. For example, if it is a fact both that all mammals have backbones and that a dog is a mammal, then we know another fact without any independent evidence for it—namely, that a dog has a backbone. Sometimes we can get information from information we already have. That's the way most arguments are built.

But many of the philosophers in this text use few if any facts to establish their claims. Sometimes we can use the laws of reason to draw conclusions on the basis of the information we have or the information we are willing to accept. Even if we can't get to the facts, we may be able to get to some agreement, or at least we may be able to show that some arguments are better than others. Let us give some examples.

One of the major debates in the history of philosophy has been about whether knowledge comes only from sense experience or from other sources as well. Suppose you think that those who believe all knowledge comes from sense experience are wrong and you wish to try to argue to that effect in a philosophy paper. How would you go about it? Notice that you can't settle this argument by appealing to the facts. We can't know what the facts are until we decide how to decide what is a fact and what isn't. Arguments about how we came to know what we know take place at a higher level of abstraction. In an important sense we are arguing about how we can establish whether or not something is a fact.

Consider an argument of Immanuel Kant. Suppose you start with the fact that people are able to tell time. They can hear the clock strike "bong," "bong," "bong" and can hold those sounds together in the mind so that they are able to say, "It is three o'clock." All that sense experience provides is the three separate bongs. These separate bongs must be held together by the mind over time so that we can apply the concept of three o'clock to them. Hence we can't get all the information we need to tell time from sense experience alone. Knowledge cannot come only from sense experience.

Yet another example could be taken from our discussion of free will. A defender of free will points out that both our legal and moral talk distinguish intentional actions from things that merely happen to us. We hold people responsible for intentional actions and treat them in ways that are different from the way we treat undesirable events that merely happen to people. Now if there is no free will, then the way we talk and the way we treat people will have to be changed. Notice that such a strategy does not show that free will exists. It merely shows that the belief that we don't have free will is inconsistent with our moral and legal practice. For anyone who believes that our moral and legal practices rest on an adequate understanding of human nature, a belief in the nonexistence of free will is especially troublesome. Such a person will either have to change his or her mind about our understanding of human nature or accept the doctrine of free will, or try to show that our legal and moral practices and the denial of free will are not inconsistent despite appearances to the contrary. Again the strategy is to look at beliefs and to try to build an argument by showing that certain beliefs a person has are incompatible with other beliefs the person has.

Up to this point we have been giving some examples of philosophical arguments without really providing a general definition. An argument seeks to justify a belief by showing that it is warranted by already justified or uncontroversial beliefs and appropriate rules of reasoning. We call the belief we are trying to establish the conclusion of an argument; the statements used to justify the conclusion are called *premises.* There are different types of arguments. What distinguishes arguments, among other things, is the degree of certainty the premises would provide, if true, for the belief that is the argument's conclusion.

Let's take our previous example.

1. All mammals have backbones.
2. A dog is a mammal.
3. Therefore a dog has a backbone.

The strongest justification an argument can provide for accepting its conclusion is the sort illustrated above, where it is impossible for the premises to be true and the conclusion to be false. By "impossible" we mean "inconceivable." There is no conceivable world in which the premises of this argument could be true and yet the conclusion be false.

*Note:* We are not saying that the premises are true. Whether or not the premises are true has to be established independently. For example, the conclusion of the following argument is as justified by its premises as the one above.

1. All mammals have four legs.
2. A human being is a mammal.
3. Therefore a human being has four legs.

Obviously premise 1 is false, and this allows the conclusion to be false as well. But *if* the premises had been true, it would have been impossible for the conclusion to be false.

In other words, one aspect of making an argument is to arrange your beliefs so that if your beliefs are true, they will establish the truth of the conclusion. A second aspect, of course, is to make sure that the beliefs (premises) on which your conclusion is based are themselves true—and this may require further argument.

An argument of the sort above is *valid* if its conclusion can be legitimately deduced from its premises (if the premises are true, the conclusion could not be false). A valid argument is *sound* if all the premises are true. In other words, the first argument above is both valid and sound whereas the second argument is only valid. It is not sound. The strongest or most warranted belief one can have is one that is the conclusion of an argument like the first one above that is both valid and sound. Unfortunately, such arguments are usually found in logic courses and almost nowhere else.

Consider some of the arguments we normally make. Usually we cannot claim that if the premises of our arguments were true, it would be impossible for the conclusion to be false. Consider the claim that all crows are black. Suppose as premises you have

1. All the crows that have been observed in Boston are black.
2. All the crows that have been observed in London are black.
3. All the crows that have been observed in Moscow are black.

   Therefore,

4. All crows are black.

Although premises 1 through 3 provide good reasons for believing that all crows are black, it is certainly not the case that if those premises are true, it is impossible for the conclusion to be false. An albino crow in China or even an unobserved albino crow in Boston would make the conclusion false even though all three premises were true.

Science involves arguments somewhat like the one above. Suppose you want to argue that January is always the coldest month in New York. What you would do is check weather bureau records to see whether the average monthly temperature in New York has been lowest in January. Suppose the weather bureau has been keeping records for 100 years and in fact the lowest average monthly temperature in New York has always been in January. Surely that is good evidence for your belief. But note that the truth of the conclusion is not absolutely certain. Before the weather bureau began keeping records, it might have been colder in February, or perhaps at some future date it will be colder in December. Since the premises are based upon a limited sample, they cannot provide absolute certainty that such a conclusion is true. The conclusions of arguments of this sort go beyond the evidence provided in the premises. The argument will be stronger as the evidence in the premises makes it more and more likely that the conclusion is true, but such arguments, unlike those examined earlier, are never able to guarantee the truth of their conclusions. Hence science deals, for the most part, with probable truth and rational grounds for belief rather than absolute certainty. This issue is more fully explored in Part 2 of this text, where methods are provided for distinguishing the more likely claims of science from the less likely ones and from wholly unscientific beliefs.

So there are at least two tasks involved in identifying and understanding arguments. First, we must distinguish the claim being argued for — the conclusion — from the claims offered in support of it — the premises. Second, we must decide which sort of argument is being given. Is it the kind in which the truth of the premises would guarantee, make absolutely certain, the truth of the conclusion? This sort is commonly called *deductive* and the argument we considered about mammals, dogs, and backbones is a good example. Or are we being given the kind of argument in which the truth of the premises would make it very likely, but not absolutely certain, that the conclusion is true? This sort is commonly called *inductive* and the argument about the color of crows that we examined earlier provides an example of this kind of argument.

There are two corresponding tasks involved in critically evaluating arguments as well. The first is to ask whether or not the premises are in fact true. If one or more of the premises is false or probably false, the argument will guarantee neither the truth nor the likelihood of its conclusion. The second task is to ask whether the structure of the argument really does what the arguer claims. If it is deductive, would the premises, even if true, guarantee the truth of the conclusion? That is, is it valid? If it is inductive, how strong is the support that the premises, if true, would provide for the conclusion? Deductive arguments that are not valid give us no good reason to accept their conclusions, even if all of their premises are true. And inductive arguments that are weak, even if they have all true premises, give us very little reason to accept their conclusions.

Of course, knowing this much about arguments will not give you an assurance of the truth or probable truth of their conclusions in very many cases. Without much more substantial training in logic you will not be certain of the deductive validity or inductive strength of most of the arguments that confront you in this text. And you would have to be a complete and accurate living encyclopedia of knowledge to be absolutely assured of the truth of all of their premises. But even this minimum introduction gives you some very powerful tools for criticizing arguments. If you can produce reasonable doubt as to the truth of any of the premises, you will have taken much of the force out of any argument. For deductive arguments, if you can even imagine a situation in which all of the claims in the premises would be true and yet the conclusion false, you will have shown the argument to be invalid and disarmed it completely. For inductive arguments, if you can imagine scenarios in which the conclusion comes out false in spite of the truth of the premises, you will have shown the argument to be at least as weak as the likelihood that any of those scenarios are true.

There are a large number of specific ways in which arguments can go wrong. All of them involve unwarranted claims in the premises, deductive invalidity or inductive weakness, or some combination of these faults. But it may help to focus on a few of the more specific flaws.

The articles in this text do not contain obvious examples of any of the mistakes described below. But even some of these have been alleged to involve arguments that embody sophisticated and disguised versions of faults such as circular reasoning or a commitment to contradictory or incompatible claims. And as you move from identifying and analyzing the arguments in the readings to constructing arguments of your own in papers or exams, it will be very useful to keep in mind a number of errors that professional philosophers seldom make but to which students seem especially prone.

**Authority** Generally it will never do to defend a belief on the basis of authority. For example, suppose we believe there are no ghosts. It won't do to argue that there are no ghosts because my professor told me there aren't. That isn't to say that we should never accept authority. At one level such advice would surely be bad and unwarranted. We have to make so many decisions in our lives that we must rely on authority to make some of them. We rely on the authority of our physicians and our accountants. But we shouldn't rely on them blindly. We should assess our physicians and accountants both in the beginning when we initially choose them and continually as they interact with us in their professional practice. So in a significant sense we should never accept authority. We should accept authority only when we have good independent reason to believe that the alleged authority is both more able to correctly assess the situation than we are and is likely to be a source of reliable advice. Hence in writing your philosophy papers, don't simply appeal to authorities.

A word of explanation is in order here. If you are writing a paper on free will and consult scholarly works by philosophers or psychologists, then a standard footnote reference will do. On the other hand, if you appeal to the opinion of your mother, a rock singer, or even a French professor on the subject of free will, you will need to give some argument as to why these people or similar people can be considered authorities. Some philosophy professors may insist that your paper be solely your own work and will not allow you to consult any authorities. Other professors will allow you to cite other philosophers or relevant experts in defense of your ideas. In this latter case you must ultimately be prepared to defend the authorities you cite; make sure you could provide good arguments for your choices.

*Note:* If you do borrow someone else's idea and put his or her idea in your own words, you must indicate your indebtedness to the person whose idea you have borrowed. You do this by using footnotes. On occasion, you may not only borrow someone's idea, but even repeat their words. In these instances you must indicate that you are *quoting* someone. Failure to do so is plagiarism. Plagiarism is a form of dishonesty and is a serious academic offense.

Finally, treat "everybody" in the same way you would treat authority. Often students try to defend their beliefs or practices by saying that everyone believes it or everybody does it. By itself an appeal to "everybody" is not an acceptable way to argue. Just as with other appeals to authority you must be prepared to defend your decision to appeal to the fact that everyone believes or does such and such—that is, you must have good reason in the specific area in question to think that everyone can't be wrong.

**Circular Reasoning (or Question Begging)** One reasons in a circular manner or begs the issue that is in question whenever the conclusion of an argument is smuggled into the premises and simply asserted there without justification. Of course the conclusion follows from such premises (because it's already there), but if the conclusion is in need of rational support or justification, such premises miss the point entirely by assuming the claim whose truth needs to be established by the argument. Usually the conclusion is in the premises in slightly disguised form. For example:

Nixon didn't do anything wrong.
So he wasn't really a criminal.

But not doing anything (legally) wrong and not being a criminal are exactly the same thing. So a claim is being asserted twice, but argued for not at all. Or, consider the slightly longer and, perhaps, less obvious example below.

1. The Bible provides ample evidence of the existence of God.
2. And this evidence, being divinely inspired, is absolutely trustworthy.
3. Therefore, we can be certain that God exists.

The problem here is in the second premise. The Bible can be a product of divine inspiration only if God actually exists and inspired it. So the conclusion is implicit in this premise and, once again, simply asserted rather than argued for.

**Contradictory or Incompatible Claims** Sometimes in the course of a lengthy discussion we make claims that are incompatible or contradictory—that is, which lead to two conclusions that cannot (logically) both be true. These claims may not be parts of any single argument, but putting them into argument form and drawing such conclusions from them demonstrates that they cannot all be true and weakens any argument being made that depends on one or more of them. Consider the following claims on the topics of freedom, determinism, and moral responsibility that might seem independently plausible.

1. Human behavior is the inevitable product of causes.
2. If human behavior is the inevitable product of causes, then human beings don't have free will.
3. If human beings don't have free will, then they can't be held responsible.
4. All human beings are capable of behaving morally.
5. Anyone capable of behaving morally can be held responsible for his or her behavior.

We may not know just which claim/claims is/are wrong here, but we know that something isn't right. From the first three claims as premises this conclusion follows:

3′. Therefore, human beings can't be held responsible.

And from the last two claims we can legitimately conclude:

5′. Therefore, human beings can be held responsible.

And these claims are clearly contradictory or incompatible. It is (logically) impossible that human beings both can and cannot be held responsible for their behavior.

**Playing Fair** Just as there are rules of fair play in sports, there are rules of fair play in arguments. Sometimes you can "win" an argument with a person by threatening bodily harm if he or she doesn't agree with you. But that isn't arguing at all; that's using naked power. The basic rule of fair play in arguing is to limit the argument to rational considerations—to facts and principles—and to abide by the rules of good reasoning. Other nonrational appeals—no matter how effective these nonrational appeals might be in other contexts—are not acceptable in philosophical argument. A commitment to philosophical argument is a commitment to the rules of rational discourse.

A few moments of thought will provide you with numerous examples of unfair moves in arguments. You can't call your opponents names. To call someone a commie or a facist, or an atheist, or a wimp is unfair. Name calling is unfair in part because it is immoral; the person being called a name is not being treated with the respect a person deserves. It is also unfair because the truth or adequacy of a person's beliefs are not determined by the kind of person he or she is. Suppose a person is a wimp; a wimp can still have adequate or true beliefs. Suppose a person is a communist. We might be able to argue that a communist's political beliefs are unjustified or inadequate but note (1) if they are inadequate they are inadequate on grounds independent of the person's being a communist and (2) other beliefs held by communists may be perfectly adequate. A communist can have perfectly adequate beliefs about physics or any number of other topics for example. As a general rule, classifying someone as a certain type of person says nothing about the adequacy or the inadequacy of his or her beliefs. Even where classifying someone as a person of a certain type enables you to directly predict what his or her beliefs are, you cannot show that this person's beliefs are wrong simply by showing that this person is the kind of person who has those beliefs. To show that beliefs are wrong or unjustified, you must be able to get at the beliefs themselves.

Yet another unfair ploy is to use ignorance as evidence. Suppose your friend believes that there are no ghosts. You can't argue from the fact that we have not disproved the existence of ghosts to the conclusion that they exist. The most such a fact could establish is that we don't know whether ghosts exist or not. The fact that your opponent has not proven his or her position is not proof that you have established yours. This seems obvious when you think about it, but it might be fun to observe how many people make this very major mistake.

Another common but more subtle error is to think that when we know something about someone's history, we know whether their beliefs about things are true or false. For example, the largest class of people criticizing the Vietnam War in its early stages were young people. Since young people were the ones being drafted to fight the war, it was fashionable for many to dismiss the young people's beliefs about the war on the grounds that these young people were cowards who were afraid to fight. But the adequacy or inadequacy of a person's beliefs about the war is not a function of whether a person is a coward or not. To repeat a remark made earlier: To show that beliefs are inadequate you must get at the beliefs themselves. Similarly, you can't show that a person's beliefs are wrong because they were brought up in the slums, or were raised in Tokyo, or had alcoholic parents. Sometimes philosophers make this point by saying that the origin or cause of a belief has nothing to do with the truth or falsity of that belief.

## II. Writing a Paper

In writing a philosophy paper you will want to have a position that you wish to argue for. You will then need one or more arguments to establish that position. Sometimes it is useful in an introductory paragraph to give the overall conclusion of the paper and the reasons you will use to support that conclusion. All paragraphs that follow could then be arguments in support of those reasons.

In writing the paper remember both the rules for good paragraph construction and the rules for good reasoning. Every paragraph should have a topic sentence and the other sentences in the paragraph should relate to the topic sentence. In other words, you should be able to rewrite your paragraph as an argument with premises and conclusion. We have found that students often either create two-sentence paragraphs or else put several different topics into one paragraph. Adopt the following motto: one idea, one paragraph. If you keep that motto in mind, and avoid two-sentence paragraphs, you will force yourself to develop your arguments. In other words, you won't end up making a bunch of assertions that you group into a paragraph and repeat over and over. You won't be tempted into thinking that you have made an argument when in fact you haven't.

Students often violate the one idea – one paragraph rule because they really don't know what it is to use arguments to develop a thesis that they want to defend. This is because although we have many opinions and beliefs—for example, that people are free but selfish, that God exists, that science is superior to magic in treating disease—we have never really thought about those opinions or beliefs. We have just had them; we have neither developed nor defended them. This failure to critically reflect on our opinions and beliefs is reflected in our language about them. How often have you heard others or caught yourself saying, "I *feel* this way or I feel that." Our beliefs or opinions rest on mere feelings. To appreciate how hard it is to discuss your beliefs philosophically, try taking a belief or opinion you feel strongly about and arguing for it. Just as an artist tries to shape a medium, for example marble or paint, to express an idea, so you might try to give shape to your beliefs by seeing what can be said on behalf of them. However, if after examination, a belief turns out to be unwarranted, you should have the courage to abandon it. Sometimes an artist discovers that an idea he or she had could not be expressed in the medium chosen. Sometimes we discover that beliefs that feel right can't be supported by argument. And like the artist, we must have the courage to abandon them.

Students sometimes become frustrated with philosophical arguments because the arguments seem to be no more than verbal quibbling. Although it is perfectly correct to say that philosophers frequently argue about words, it is usually wrong to say that such arguments are mere verbal quibbles. In the part on free will, there is considerable debate as to what "free will" means. However that debate is no mere verbal quibble. How free will gets defined may well affect our legal institutions and our moral practices. In analyzing a piece of philosophical reasoning or in creating one yourself, great attention should be paid to definitional matters. Whenever possible, use plain English rather than more technical philosophical vocabulary. Then there will be no question about your understanding of what you are talking about. If you are forced to use technical terms, make it very clear in plain English what you understand and what your readers are expected to understand by them. If you are critically evaluating the work of another, you are entitled to similar expectations of clarity and simplicity. Unclear and confusing use of language provides good grounds for legitimate criticism of anyone's writing.

You should try, for the most part, to avoid emotional or colorful language. Your aim is to rationally convince, not to emotionally arouse or impress. What you want to communicate clearly is why you are, and why your reader should be, rationally convinced of the truth of the claim that is the conclusion of your paper. Language that interferes with that purpose, although very useful in other contexts, is out of place in a typical philosophy paper.

Keep track of where you are and where you are going throughout the course of the paper. A good introductory paragraph will outline the rest of the paper by giving the main steps in the argumentation that is to follow. Make sure that you stick to that outline. This ensures that your readers will have no trouble following the development of your thoughts. At each point they will know what claim is being argued for and why, and what the next step in the reasoning will be.

As far as the content and structure of the individual arguments, or the overall argument, of your paper are concerned, all we can say at this point is to remember the discussion in the first part of this appendix. Keep in mind what kind of argument you are producing and don't try to get more mileage out of your reasoning than is possible—for example, deductive validity from an inductive argument. Make very clear which claims you regard as not requiring argumentation, and just what the argumentation consists of for the rest. Finally, check your arguments and your paper as a whole for any of the faults we described. The first and most important step in producing a good argument is to make sure you haven't produced a very bad one by falling prey to any of the most common errors.

As with any skill, writing a philosophy paper is something to be learned primarily by practice and not by reading a brief appendix to a textbook. Your instructor's criticism of your first attempts and your efforts to improve by taking such criticism seriously and following the suggestions offered will probably pay the greatest dividends.